Leach's Tax Dictionary

by Robert Leach FCA FCCA

First published March 2021
by Spiramus Press Ltd
102 Blandford Street
London W1U 8AG
Telephone +44 20 7224 0080
www.spiramus.com

ISBN
9781913507190 Paperback
9781913507206 Digital

British Library Cataloguing-in-Publication Data.

A catalogue record for this book is available from the British Library.

Printed and bound in Great Britain by Grosvenor Group (Print Services) Ltd

Preface

This dictionary is intended as a single volume aid to accountants, lawyers and others who deal with tax. This book is not a tax manual, nor teaching material. It is intended to complement other books for use by those who already have some knowledge of tax.

The book has three sections.

The first section is the main part of the dictionary. It lists terms that are used in tax and gives a definition, sometimes supplemented with further comment such as the implications of the item being defined. These definitions should not be regarded as an exhaustive or comprehensive discussion of the subject.

Verbatim quotes from legislation or other authoritative sources are sometimes given when this is thought to be useful.

This section also includes terms that are not tax terms but relate to matters where there are tax implications. Examples include *cars* and *water*. These entries are restricted to items where there are specific tax provisions contained in legislation or official guidance, or where the matter has gone to a court or tribunal. So the book does not list every item of food just to state that it is zero-rated for VAT, but does list those items of food referred to in law or VAT notices, or where the issue has gone to a tribunal or court.

Statutory and other references are generally included. For statute laws, these refer to the laws as they currently are, including those which have been amended by subsequent legislation.

The section includes terms that, while not strictly tax, are often dealt with by tax accountants. These include national minimum wage, money laundering regulations, payroll and social security.

Tax does not happen in isolation. The accounts from which tax computations are prepared must comply with accounting standards. Tax appeals are conducted in accordance with general law. For this reason, section 1 includes many terms from adjacent disciplines, and some remoter disciplines, where this may be useful to a tax practitioner. Law terms are generally confined to those branches of law likely to be encountered in tax. So there are many terms relating to procedure and few relating to motoring offences.

This dictionary is not a directory and so, with a few exceptions, it does not generally list individuals, companies or other bodies, however eminent. Similarly, the dictionary does not list all tax cases by name other than those few whose names which may be regarded as part of tax vocabulary.

With about 500 tax cases a year, it is not possible to include every judicial comment on a word or phrase. The dictionary includes those comments that help to define the term.

Terms are not included when they are too general in nature, such as "appointed day" or "relevant amount".

For very specialist areas, such as banking and the oil industry, section 1 may simply refer the reader to where details may be found.

The convention has been used of listing terms in alphabetical order regardless of the length of the words. So "taxable" appears before "tax year". A surprisingly large number of terms can be given as one or two words.

Section 2 of the dictionary lists abbreviations which appear to have gained some currency.

This means that almost all the definitions have appeared in an official publication, such as a government press release. New abbreviations seem to be coined almost every week.

Abbreviations do not include terms used only in algebraic formulae in tax law.

Section 3 is a series of tables of tax rates and other data that may be useful. Like section 1, it includes both tax rates and other data from adjacent disciplines. Some effort has been made to devise layouts of data that make it as easily readable as possible.

The whole dictionary relates to all taxes charged in the UK. It also includes details on charges that are not tax but similar to it. A few details are given about non-UK taxes and some principles of international taxation, but this dictionary is not international.

Details are given of some repealed provisions. An experience tax accountant may not always know whether a provision is still in force, particularly if it relates to an area of tax where he or she is not normally involved.

There are also some provisions that are more easily understood if a little history is provided. In addition to some comments in section 1 of the dictionary, section 3 includes some notes on the history of tax and of developments in recent years.

The book reflects the law and general position as at 1 January 2021. At this time, we still do not how Brexit and Covid will fully play out. The dictionary gives such details as were known on that date.

This dictionary generally cannot give tax or other rates for the 2021/22 tax year as these were not known as the book went to press. There are few instances where these rates were announced, such as for national insurance and the national minimum wage, and these are given.

This dictionary is in effect an edited version of a more comprehensive and wider ranging dictionary that can be accessed on the author's company's website:
www.taxtrainingltd.co.

The author is happy to hear from users of the book about any errors or ambiguities, or in any other way that you believe this book could be made more useful. Neither the author nor the publisher can accept any liability for any loss suffered in connection with the book.

I have enjoyed compiling this dictionary. I hope you enjoy using it.

Robert Leach FCA FCCA FCIPP

Epsom

January 2021

The author can be contacted at robert.leach04@googlemail.com or 020 8224 5695.

Biographical details

Robert Leach FCA FCCA FCIPP is a qualified accountant who first qualified in 1983. For 14 years, he worked in industry, including being accountant and company secretary for groups of companies engaged in finance, property, employment and retail.

For two years he was assistant editor of the magazine *The Accountant*.

Since 1986, he has been self-employed. He has had more than 40 books published. He also writes for national newspapers and magazines. He has appeared on national radio and television several times, and has been in demand as a lecturer. He lectured to HMRC itself four times.

Robert is also a qualified musician.

Abbreviations used for definitions

ACCA	Association of Chartered Certified Accountants
AIM	Alternative Investment Market
ALDA 1979	Alcoholic Liquor Duties Act 1979
APD	air passenger duty
ATED	annual tax on enveloped dwellings
CA 2006	Companies Act 2006
CAA 2001	Capital Allowances Act 2001
CCL	climate change levy
CEMA 1979	Customs and Excise Management Act 1979
CGT	capital gains tax
Ch	Chapter (of a statute)
CIMA	Chartered Institute of Management Accountants
CIOT	Chartered Institute of Taxation
CIPFA	Chartered Institute of Public Finance and Accountancy
COP	code of practice
CRCA 2005	Commissioners of Revenue and Customs Act 2005
CTA 2009	Corporation Tax 2009
CTA 2010	Corporation Tax 2010
DPT	diverted profits tax
DWP	Department of Work and Pensions
EIS	enterprise investment scheme
ERA 1996	Employment Rights Act 1996
ESC	extra-statutory concession
EU	European Union
FA	Finance Act
FA (2)	Finance (No 2) Act
FCA	Financial Conduct Authority
FRC	Financial Reporting Council
FRS	Financial Reporting Standard
HMRC	HM Revenue and Customs
HODA	Hydrocarbon Oil Duty Act 1979
ICAEW	Institute of Chartered Accountants in England and Wales
ICAI	Institute of Chartered Accountants of Ireland
ICAS	Institute of Chartered Accountants of Scotland
IFRS	International Financial Reporting Standard
IHT	inheritance tax
IHTA 1984	Inheritance Tax Act 1984
IPT	insurance premium tax
ITA 2007	Income Tax Act 2007
ITEPA 2003	Income Tax (Earnings and Pensions) Act 2003
ITTOIA 2005	Income Tax (Trading and Other Income) Act 2005
LBTTA 2013	Land and Buildings Transaction Tax (Scotland) Act 2013
LLP	limited liability partnership

NI	national insurance
NMWA 1998	National Minimum Wage Act 1998
OECD	Organization for Economic Co-operation and Development
p	page
PACE 1994	Police and Criminal Evidence Act 1984
para	paragraph
PAYE	Pay As You Earn
PRT	petroleum revenue tax
QCB	qualifying corporate bond
regs	regulations
RPI	retail prices index
RSTPA 2014	Revenue Scotland and Tax Powers Act 2014
s	section
S2P	state second pension
SAP	statutory adoption pay
SC	Supreme Court
SDLT	stamp duty land tax
SDMA	Stamp Duty Management Act 1891
SDRT	stamp duty reserve tax
Sch	Schedule
SEIS	seed enterprise investment scheme
SERPS	state earnings-related pension scheme
SI	statutory instrument
SMP	statutory maternity pay
SSCBA 1992	Social Security Contributions and Benefits Act 1992
SSAP	statement of standard accounting practice
SSI	Scottish statutory instrument
SSP	statutory sick pay
SP	statement of practice
TCGA 1992	Taxation of Chargeable Gains Act 1992
TIOPA 2010	Taxation (International and Other Provisions) Act 2010
TMA 1970	Taxes Management Act 1970
UK	United Kingdom
VAT	value added tax
VATA	Value Added Tax Act 1994
VCT	venture capital trust
VED	vehicle excise duty
WDV	written down value
WRA 2012	Welfare Reform Act 2012

Tax law

Authority

In the UK, tax may only be levied by Parliament; there is no such thing as common law taxation. There is also no taxation by custom. A tax may only be imposed by statute.

The monarch may not levy taxation without the approval of Parliament. King Henry I explicitly stated this in his coronation oath in 1100. One of the grounds for executing King Charles I in 1649 was that he attempted to levy tax without Parliamentary approval. The requirement for Parliamentary approval was a provision of Magna Carta in 1215 and is now enshrined in Bill of Rights 1689.

Act of Parliament

An Act of Parliament must generally be passed by the House of Commons and the House of Lords. Since 1911, the House of Lords debates tax legislation but cannot amend it. In theory, any MP may initiate tax legislation. In practice, it is introduced by the government, usually by the Chancellor of the Exchequer in a Budget speech. Draft legislation is called a Bill.

A Bill becomes an Act when it receives Royal Assent. This means that the monarch has formally agreed the Bill. This is now a formality as a monarch has not declined assent since 1707. Royal Assent to Bills is formally announced in the House of Commons by the Speaker, and in the House of Lords by the Lord Speaker.

An Act may not take effect immediately. It may have a date when it is to take effect. Often the Act will say that provisions will come into effect by order of the secretary of state. The secretary of state is a Cabinet minister. This is known as a commencement order. In some cases, it may be years before such an order is issued. Easter Act 1928 has still not been brought into force more than 90 years later.

An Act of Parliament has a title which includes the year it was enacted, such as Income Tax Act 2007 or Finance Act 2020. This is the short title. Underneath it is the long title consisting of a sentence or a paragraph of a few sentences. This states the purpose of the Act in general terms. There is also the date of Royal Assent.

An Act is divided into sections and may also have one or more Schedules. The sections are usually indicated in the form "s27" or "ss27-34". For convenience these sections are given titles which are not part of the law.

Sections may be divided into subsections indicated by numbers in brackets, as in the form s47(3). This means the third subsection of section 47. Subsections may be further divided by lower case letters in brackets such as (a), (b) etc, and may be further divided by lower case Roman numerals. The definition of a cheque voucher for an employee to buy goods is found in Income Tax (Earnings and Pensions) Act 2003 s84(4)(b)(ii).

Detailed provisions are often put in Schedules which can therefore often be the longer and more complex part of an Act. Schedules have the same legal effect as the sections of an Act. There will be a section of the Act that says that a particular Schedule shall have effect.

Schedules are said to be divided into paras (paragraphs) rather than sections. The conventions for subsection numbering is the same as for sections.

Many taxes have their own Act. VAT, for example, is governed by the Value Added Tax Act 1994; inheritance tax by Inheritance Tax Act 1984.

Some of the main taxes may have more than Act. Corporation tax, for example, is governed by Corporation Tax 2009 and Corporation Tax 2010. Income tax is governed by Income Tax Act 2007, Income Tax (Earnings and Pensions) Act 2003 and Income Tax (Trading and Other Income) Act 2005.

There also Acts that deal with matters that affect more than one tax. Capital gains, which may be subject to capital gains tax or corporation tax, are covered in Taxation of Chargeable Gains Act 1992. Some of the administrative matters for income tax, capital gains tax and corporation tax are covered in Taxes Management Act 1970.

Tax Acts are among the longest Acts passed. Corporation Tax 2009, for example, has 1,330 sections. Long Acts are grouped into Parts which are grouped in Chapters.

Finance Acts

Each year, a Finance Act is passed. Some minor taxes are enacted in a Finance Act rather than in a separate Act. For example, climate change levy does not have its own Act, but is enacted by Finance Act 2000 s30 and Sch 6.

Many main taxes started life as parts of a Finance Act. VAT was originally enacted as part of Finance Act 1973. Corporation tax and capital gains tax were both originally enacted in Finance Act 1965.

Sometimes two Finance Acts are passed in the same year. This usually happens in a year where there is a general election. The first Finance Act enacts the less contentious parts of the Budget. These are usually agreed by the government and the main opposition party. After the election, the new government (which may be of the same political party) enacts a Finance (No 2) Act which contains their other provisions. So there have been Finance (No 2) Acts for 1975, 1979, 1983, 1997, 2005, 2010 and 2015. In 2010, uniquely, there was a Finance (No 3) Act.

Much of a Finance Act amends existing Acts. In 2020, the limit for entrepreneur's relief (renamed business asset disposal relief) was reduced from £10 million to £1 million. This was given effect by Finance Act 2020 s23 authorising Schedule 3 of which para 1(a) says "in section 169N of TCGA 1992 (entrepreneur's relief: amount of relief) in subsection (4), for "£10 million" substitute "£1 million". This means that Finance Act 2020 has amended a provision of Taxation of Chargeable Gains Act 1992.

Many times amendments are made by adding new sections. In Taxation of Chargeable Gains Act 1992, new provisions needed to be added between sections 164 and 165. For these sections or Schedules, capital letters are used. So there are sections 164A, 164B etc. When a section is needed to be added between these sections, a second capital letter is used. So there is a section 164MA, for example. Sometimes a section needs to be added before one ending A, so Z is used. This can get complicated. There is a section 444AECB in Income and Corporation Taxes Act 1988. Museum and galleries exhibition tax relief is given in Corporation Tax 2009 s1218ZCB.

Sometimes these additional sections use numbers. Some provisions on disguised remuneration are given in Income Tax (Earnings and Pensions) Act 2003 in sections 554Z1 to 554Z21. Some of these sections have been further amended, so we have, for example, section 554Z2A.

Consolidating Acts

After some years, the text of tax law can become complex. So occasionally a consolidating Act is passed which sweeps up the previous law and all the amendments and presents them as a new tidied up Act. This new Act then gets amended and the process is repeated. Income tax law has gone through six incarnations since it was adopted (for a third time) in 1842:

Property Tax Act 1842
Income Tax Act 1918
Income Tax Act 1952
Income and Corporation Taxes Act 1970
Income and Corporation Taxes Act 1988
Income Tax Act 2007 (and other Acts).

Other taxes need consolidation less frequently. Stamp duty is still governed by Stamp Act 1891.

In 1996, the government launched the Tax Law Rewrite Project. This was designed to make tax law much clearer. Here is part of Income Tax Act 2007 s4:

4 Income tax an annual tax

4 (1) Income tax is charged for a year only if an Act so provides.

4 (2) A year for which income tax is charged is called a "tax year".

4 (3) A tax year begins on 6 April and ends on the following 5 April.

In contrast, here is some impenetrable prose (now mercifully repealed) on termination payments from Finance Act 1982 s43:

(1) Subject to sub-paragraph (2) below, in the case of a payment which exceeds £50,000 and in respect of which tax is chargeable under section 187 of the Act, the following relief shall be allowed by way of deduction from the tax chargeable by virtue of that section, that is to say, there shall be ascertained —

(a) the amount of tax which would be chargeable apart from this paragraph and paragraph 7 above in respect of the income of the holder or past holder of the office or employment for the chargeable period of which the payment is treated as income, and

(b) the amount of tax which would be so chargeable if the amount of the payment had been £50,000 exactly,

and the amount to be deducted shall be one quarter of the difference between the amount ascertained at (a) and the amount ascertained at (b).

In 1986, four years later, someone bothered to read this verbiage and discovered that tax law did not mean what everyone thought it meant. Large amounts of tax had to be refunded.

The Project also re-expressed the law in contemporary English. Taxes Management Act 1970 s118(1) originally referred to lunatics and idiots. These were originally acceptable legal terms. An idiot was incapable of rational behaviour whereas a lunatic had lucid periods. These terms were removed by Finance Act 2012 s222(4)(a) by which time they had long become pejorative.

The Project did not change tax law other than to remove spent provisions and remove contradictions and anomalies.

Finding the law

Acts of Parliament can be bought from the Stationery Office and some specialist bookshops, but they are expensive. Finance Act 2020, for example, costs £31.60. And the Acts soon become out of date as they are amended.

Acts are available for free download from: http://www.legislation.gov.uk/ukpga. This gives every Act passed from 1988 (even if now repealed), and Acts before then that are still in force, including Finance Acts back to 1895 (of which s12 remains in force). Other extant Acts go back to 1295.

The website lists Acts as originally passed, and as amended. Unfortunately tax Acts are not kept up to date very promptly, if at all. So you can see the original Act, and possibly some amendments, but not all of them.

In practice, tax accountants and lawyers usually buy one of two sets of tax laws produced annually by two commercial publishers:

- Lexis Nexis, who produce yellow and orange books, and
- Croner-i: who produce red and green books.

The orange and green books deal mainly with value added tax.

The pages are printed on thin paper, but a set will take up at least three feet of shelf space.

The length of tax law is not easy to ascertain. In 2010, it was believed to be 11,520 pages. Soon after, the UK overtook India in having the longest tax code in the world. By 2015, it was believed to be 21,000 pages. Current estimates are as high as 36,000 pages.

This is a comparison of the length of the five main Acts of Parliament about income tax as originally passed compared to other works of literature:

Work	**Number of words**
Hound of the Baskervilles, by Conan Doyle	59,046
Pride and Prejudice, by Jane Austen	123,880
Great Expectations, by Charles Dickens	185,258
War and Peace, 5 volumes by Tolstoy	587,287
The Bible, Authorised Version	774,746
Complete Works of Shakespeare	884,429
Harry Potter, 7 volumes by J K Rowling	1,082,170
Five income tax Acts	1,450,566

(This dictionary contains 438,202 words.)

Devolution

All four parts of the UK now have their own legislatures with some ability to amend tax law to some extent. Most tax law remains the same for the whole of the UK. There are no significant differences for VAT, for example. Scotland and Wales have introduced alternative taxes to stamp duty land tax which contain significant differences. Scotland has also used its powers to introduce higher rates of income tax and several new social security benefits. Wales may also vary income tax rules from England but has not yet done so.

Northern Ireland law is largely the same as in England, though this is often enacted by separate legislation largely using the same words. Northern Ireland does not have council tax. It also has an unused provision from 2015 allowing it to set a lower rate of corporation tax so that it is not disadvantaged to the Republic of Ireland.

Europe

The UK was a member of the European Union and its predecessor bodies from 1973 to 2020.

European law contains many tax provisions. Much law on VAT and Customs duties was set by the EU rather than the UK parliament. The European Union wished to go further. Attempts to have uniform rates of VAT and common definitions for corporation tax have failed.

There have been several instances where UK tax law has been found not to comply with EU law. Examples include allowance of dividends and losses from foreign subsidiaries, and the three-year cap (now four years) for VAT reclaims. In both cases, European law trumped UK law which had to be amended.

The UK left the European Union on 31 January 2020 and ceased to be part of the single market and EU customs union on 31 December 2020 at the end of a transitional period. The current position is that all EU laws and court decisions have been transferred as UK law, subject to minor amendments. The difference is that the UK can now amend those laws without reference to the EU.

Statutory instruments

Many detailed provisions are not contained in Acts of Parliament but in statutory instruments (SIs). An Act will say that a minister or other body may make further provisions.

For example, Income Tax (Earnings and Pensions) Act 2003 s684 says that the Commissioners of Inland Revenue (now of HM Revenue and Customs) must make regulations to administer PAYE to collect income tax from employees' wages. The Commissioners made these detailed regulations as Income Tax (Pay As You Earn) Regulations SI 2003 No 2682, which remain in force, though with many amendments. The 2003 Act is the enabling act that allows an SI to be issued.

An SI is broken down into regulations, rules or clauses depending on its nature. The provisions on employees' tax codes, for example, is found in SI 2003 No 2682 reg 7(1).

An SI may also be used to bring in a statutory provision. The SI is then called a commencement order.

A statutory instrument can be annulled by Parliament. The last time this happened was in 2000 when the House of Lords annulled the Greater London Authority Election rules. The High Court last annulled an SI in 1979 which related to the price of paraffin.

An even rarer event is an SI being struck down by the courts as not within the scope of the enabling Act. In 1987, the court struck down regulation 11 in SI 1986 No 482 on building society dividends. In 2014, the Court of Appeal struck down SI 2014 No 2604 on asylum appeals.

Scotland now issues its own Scottish Statutory instruments (SSIs). Wales also issues statutory instruments which are printed in both English and Welsh.

Extra-statutory concessions

HMRC and its predecessor bodies have seen fit to use their general powers of administration to relax some provisions of tax law, particularly where the strict rule would lead to a harsh outcome. It should be noted that many unintended harsh outcomes have still been enforced by HMRC and upheld by the courts and tribunals.

These relaxations are known as extra-statutory concessions. Their legality has often been questioned, but as their effect is usually to relieve a taxpayer of tax, they have not often been challenged.

In 2005, the House of Lords ruled (in *re Wilkinson)* that the tax authorities had exceeded their authority in many extra-statutory concessions. As a consequence, many have now been put into Acts of Parliament.

A further curiosity of ESCs is that HMRC have discretion whether to allow them, which departs from the fundamental principle that all taxpayers must be treated with equal fairness. The tax authorities have disallowed an ESC when it is being used for tax avoidance, so there is little evidence of abuse by HMRC, however unsatisfactory their existence is.

ESCs are listed in **categories,** so A lists all concessions applicable to individuals. A 4 relates to travel expenses of directors, A 10 to lump sums from overseas pensions, and so on. Other ESCs have been repealed or put into an Act. For example, the 15p a day concession for luncheon vouchers that was given by ESC A 2 was enacted as Income Tax (Earnings and Pensions) Act 2003 s89, and has now been repealed.

A current list of concessions can be found at

https://www.gov.uk/government/collections/extra-statutory-concessions.

There is also a similar Working Rule Agreement first established in 1981 that provides some tax relief for travelling and subsistence allowances for site-based employees in the construction industry.

Statements of practice

HMRC and its predecessor bodies produced statement of practices (SPs) on various technical matters. This gives the tax authority's opinion on the tax treatment. Only a few are issued each year.

Before 17 July 1978, statement of practices were numbered in the same way as extra-statutory concessions. A few of these old SPs are still in force. The oldest is A6 issued in 1973 about VAT on earnings.

Since 1978, Statement of practices are indicated as SP followed by a number and two-digit year indicator. So SP 1/10 means the first (and only) SP of 2010. It relates to HMRC contact centres.

It should be remembered that an SP is just HMRC's opinion, which may not be upheld by a judge. HMRC will always accept a tax return compiled in accordance with an SP, but you may challenge an SP as not being in accordance with tax law. If you do, make sure of your grounds, and explicitly tell HMRC that you are not following the SP.

There have been successful challenges. In relation to capital gains tax on a disposal by trustees, SP 7/78 was overruled in the case *Roome v Edwards [1981].* So SP 9/81 was issued as a replacement, only to be overruled in *Bond v Pickford [1983].* This has now been further replaced by SP 7/84, which may be correct.

Guidance is also given in many other types of publication from HMRC and its predecessor bodies. From 1983, it has published Revenue Interpretations (RIs), and a few Revenue Decisions (RDs) of which just two remain effective.

RIs are now published in *Tax Bulletin* issued six times a year. An RI has a lower status than an SP. In particular, HMRC may not follow an interpretation because of the facts of a case. There are now hundreds of RIs.

Since 2007, HMRC has published HMRC Briefs. These are intended to clarify the tax consequence in a particular area, particularly after a significant court case. They are issued promptly and intended to be of effect for a year or so.

HMRC also publish:

- Codes of Practice (COPs) on how it will behave;
- Factsheets which seek simply to explain tax law;
- Toolkits and Helpsheets to assist taxpayers in completing returns; and
- Spotlights dealing with tax avoidance.

There is a significant body of miscellaneous material in the form of press releases and statements.

Between 1990 and 1996, Inland Revenue published its Inspectors' Manuals. Since 2015, these have been called Tax Manuals as they are now written for taxpayers as well as tax staff. For the sake of consistency, they are all referred to as HMRC Manuals in this dictionary.

This was originally guidance to its own staff that was regarded as confidential. Although now published, some parts are redacted, usually because they relate to specific taxpayers. However these large volumes do contain much useful information. A problem is that they are not always up to date, though HMRC is now much better at updating them.

Until 1997, Inland Revenue published Business Economic Notes (BENs) on specific trades, such as fish and chip shops. From 2006, it has published Tactical and Information Packages (TIPs) that serve a similar purpose.

HMRC also publishes hundreds of leaflets and other forms of guidance. For VAT, some provisions in notices have the force of law. This is clearly indicated in the leaflet.

Some guidance may be given in Parliamentary answers, and quoted in Hansard. Other material may be agreed with a professional body or a representative body.

All HMRC material is available for free download from the website www.hmrc.gov.uk. The quantity and quality of material is very good. It is clearly written, kept to up to date, and is nicely laid out. Although it has its own website search engine, it is often more convenient to use a general one like Google.

HMRC provides briefings on matters of tax policy, mainly to politicians. These often contain useful background information on significant developments. They can be downloaded from https://www.gov.uk/government/collections/briefings.

HMRC has moved a long way in the right direction from seeing itself as purely a tax enforcement body. It now rightly sees itself as having the duty to help taxpayers comply with their tax obligations. A tax authority is unlikely ever to win the popular affection of the National Health Service, but it should be acknowledged that HMRC is generally a well-run, efficient and polite organisation of high integrity. The occasional lapse is only newsworthy because it is untypical. And this has been achieved while the government has passed more and more responsibility to HMRC while not giving it adequate resources.

Court and tribunal decisions

Another source of law comes from tribunals and courts when they deal with specific disputes that cannot be resolved by the taxpayer and HMRC.

English law comprises not just Acts and statutory instruments, but also the unwritten law of common law, equity and custom. No new common law can now be made, but existing common law remains in force. For example, there is no Act of Parliament which makes murder illegal; it is illegal under the common law historically made by judges over many centuries.

There is no common law or unwritten law for tax, but courts and tribunals have provided interpretations. These decisions are part of tax law.

A court case may set a precedent, of which there are two types. A binding precedent is a decision that must be followed in a subsequent case heard in the same court or a lower court. A persuasive precedent is one that is not binding but suggests a position that other courts and tribunals should consider. A decision of a tribunal is usually seen as a persuasive precedent.

For binding precedents, a distinction is made between the ratio decidendi and obiter dicta. The ratio decidendi is the reason for the decision. This is the part that creates the binding precedent. For someone to argue that a binding precedent does not apply if the case under consideration can be distinguished from the ratio decidendi. The obiter dicta comprises other remarks which can be viewed as a persuasive precedent,

The principles of English law have been incorporated into many other countries' legal systems. These include the Republic of Ireland, USA, Canada, Australia and many Commonwealth countries. Although these countries pass their own laws, they still contain large chunks of English law and follow many of the same principles. Decisions from these countries may also be regarded as persuasive precedents.

Case citations

Court decisions have been published from the earliest days. These are reported in various series of law reports, as indicated by a citation. This is the convention by which a case may be identified in the reports.

The name of a court case usually states:

- the names of the parties;
- the year the decision was given;
- the court where it was heard; and
- the citation where the report may be found.

For example, the issue of whether an employee should be taxed on the direct cost or marginal cost of a benefit in kind was finally resolved by the House of Lords in the case:

Pepper v Hart. [1992] HL. 65 TC 421.

Mr Pepper is the tax inspector who brought the case for Inland Revenue. Sometimes Inland Revenue is identified as IRC or CIR for Commissioners of Inland Revenue.

Mr Hart was the taxpayer. To be precise, he was the first name of nine taxpayers with an identical issue. The case could be cited as *Pepper v Hart and others.*

The decision was given in 1992 by the House of Lords, indicated as HL. The Supreme Court is indicated as SC. The Court of Appeal is indicated as CA. The Queen's Bench Division, Chancery Division and Family Division of the High Court are indicated as QBD, Ch D and Fam respectively. Other courts usually have their names written in full.

The last part indicates that the decision can be found in volume 65 of *Tax Cases* starting at page 421.

Tax Cases is the official publication produced by Inland Revenue and HMRC. Volume 1 starts at 1875. These are published as booklets about six times a year. These can be then be rebound as volumes.

However *Tax Cases* is just one series of law reports. The case *Pepper v Hart* can also be cited as any one of:

[1992] STC 898

[1992] 3 WLR 1032

[1993] 1 All ER 42.

STC means Simon's Tax Cases. These are volumes produced from 1973 in distinctive blue covers by Lexis Nexis, previously Butterworths, with one or two volumes for each year. The citation above means that you can read the case from page 898 of the 1982 volume.

WLR and All ER are respectively the Weekly Law Reports and All England Law Reports. These cover all court cases and not just those that relate to tax. For this reason, there are several volumes each year. This case can be found in volume 3 of WLR for 1992 and volume 1 of All ER for 1993 on the pages indicated.

There are other series of law reports, including BTR for *British Tax Reports* published by CCH Editions. *The Times* newspaper also publishes brief law reports. There are many other series of law reports relating to other branches of the law.

There is now a free website called British and Irish Legal Information Institute or BAILII at www.bailii.org. This gives summaries of cases from courts and tribunals completely free under a neutral citation. So *Pepper v Hart* can be found under neutral citation UKHL 3. The case reports are excellent, the search engine much less so, so it can be easier to use Google first.

Tribunal decisions

Many tax decisions are heard by tribunals rather than courts.

Before 1 April 2009, most direct taxes were heard by Special Commissioners or general commissioners. Since 1995, Special Commissioners' decisions have been made public, usually with the citation SpC and a number and year. The last was number 742 in 2009.

VAT cases were heard by a VAT tribunal from 1973 (when the tax was introduced) until 1 April 2009. They heard 20,983 cases.

There were various other tribunals that heard appeals against taxes or specific provisions. From 1 April 2009, all these tribunals are replaced by First Tier Tax Tribunals and Upper Tier Tax Tribunals, known as FTT and UKUT.

FTT cases are indicated as TC followed by a number. While UKUT cases are indicated as UKUT followed by a number, sometimes with a letter.

All FTT and predecessor tribunal decisions from April 2003 can be downloaded free from the website www.financeandtaxtribunals.gov.uk. UKUT decisions can be downloaded free from the website www.tribunals.gov.uk/financeandtax.

Tribunal decisions are also widely reported in tax publications and on website, including this one.

Other sources

There are many other sources of tax information. These include many other excellent books published by Spiramus Ltd, and a news database on the author's company's website www.taxtrainingltd.co.

Section 1: Definitions

a Indefinite article. In tax law, it means "one". For example, in the case *Bell's College [2015] TC 4369,* a college did not meet the requirement of providing services to "a university" when it provided those services to several universities.

A1 form Document issued from 1 May 2010 to UK workers travelling to another EU or EEA country. It broadly states that the holder is paying UK national insurance and is therefore exempt from other EU social security contributions. This provision continues from 2021 under the social security co-ordination of the EU Withdrawal Agreement where the worker is within the scope of the agreement.

A1P1 Article 1 of the First Protocol to the European Convention on Human Rights. It allows tax to be levied as an exception to the general rule on not being deprived of possessions. It reads:

"Every natural or legal person is entitled to the peaceful enjoyment of his possessions. No one shall be deprived of his possessions except in the public interest and subject to the conditions provided for by law and by the general principles of international law.

"The preceding provisions shall not, however, in any way impair the right of a State to enforce such laws as it deems necessary to control the use of property in accordance with the general interest or to secure the payment of taxes or other contributions or penalties."

abandoned premises Dwelling that appears no longer to have a tenant (Housing and Planning Act 2016 from s57).

abandoned project VAT input tax that can be claimed for a taxable project remains claimable if the project is abandoned. The Court of Justice of the European Union so ruled in the Romanian case *ITH Comercial Timişoara SRL [2019] CJEU Case C-734/19.*

abandonment Process of disowning property, either explicitly or implicitly. In relation to Customs, the term means forfeiture of property to avoid paying duty (Customs notice 34).

abandonment expenditure Costs of abandoning plant, particularly oil installations. This includes rectifying environmental damage. The accounting treatment is to reflect such expenditure in the accounts from the period when such liability is first incurred. This can often be at construction, when such costs can be capitalised as a long-term liability and charged as an expense during the plant's useful life.

abandonment guarantee In relation to petroleum revenue tax, a contract where someone guarantees the default of a participator in an oil field in relation to a field agreement relating to abandonment costs (FA 1991 s104(1)).

abatable loan A loan which may be reduced if an eventuality occurs. The term is used in relation to exclusivity agreements between oil companies and petrol stations which restrict whose petrol and diesel may be sold. The loan is abated if the agreement ends early.

For income tax and corporation tax purposes, a loan is treated as a grant. That means it is taxed as revenue income unless the taxpayer can show the grant was for capital expenditure.

abatement Reduction from a full amount. This can apply in such tax situations as penalties and inheritance tax exemptions. The term is used in some tax contexts. Under IHTA 1984 s29A, an exemption from inheritance tax is abated to the extent that it is settled from the beneficiary's own resources.

abattoir Place for slaughtering animals for food. Abattoir services are standard-rated for VAT but meat carcasses for human consumption are zero-rated as food. The difference was shown in the case *Darlington Borough Council [1980] VTD 961.*

abbreviated accounts Less detailed accounts that a small company may file at Companies House (CA 2006 s445 and supporting regulations).

ABC Islands Aruba, Bonaire and Curaçao. These are three islands off the north coast of Venezuela. Before 2010, they were part of Netherlands Antilles, widely used in international tax planning.

ABCP internal assessment Method of calculating the risk weighted exposure amount for a securitisation position in relation to an asset-backed commercial paper programme (FCA glossary).

abettor Person who did aid, abet, counsel or procure the commission of an offence (Accessories and Abettors Act 1861 s8; Magistrates' Courts Act 1980 s44).

ability to pay Principle first espoused by economist Adam Smith that contributions to public expenditure should be paid by citizens according to their means, and not on a flat rate basis or according to the benefits received. In the UK, this applied mainly to income tax on net income after deductions for life assurance, mortgage interest, pensions and family responsibilities. In the last 40 years, most of these have been removed so ability to pay now largely relates to gross income.

ab initio Latin for "from the beginning".

abnormal dividend Dividend of abnormally large size. Its payment can trigger a provision that cancels any corporation tax advantage (CTA 2010 from s731).

abnormal rent increase Provision that applied before 2013 (FA 2003 Sch 17A). It broadly triggered a further stamp duty land tax charge if rent doubled after five years.

abode Old term for a place of residence. Having a UK abode and occasionally visiting it was once sufficient to establish that a turnover was UK resident. The matter is now determined by the statutory residence test as set out in section 3 of this dictionary,

abolition date Date from which an occupational pension scheme ceases to qualify for the contracting rebate for national insurance (Pensions Act 2007 s15(2) and Sch 13). The dates are 6 April 2012 for a defined contribution scheme, and 6 April 2016 for a defined benefit scheme (Pensions Act 2014 Sch 13).

abortion Deliberate termination of pregnancy (Abortion Act 1967 s1). An employee with a conscientious objection to abortion may refuse to participate (Abortion Act 1967 s4). A woman who has an abortion is regarded as having never been pregnant and is therefore not entitled to maternity leave or statutory maternity pay. As pregnancy is not a sickness, she is not entitled to statutory sick pay unless she needs medical attention. In medical parlance, the word also means a pregnancy that ends naturally.

abortive acquisition expenses Cost incurred by an employee in trying to find new accommodation in relocating (ITEPA 2003 s278). Such expenses may be allowed as part of relocation expenditure.

abortive cost Expenditure that does not lead to a return. For all taxes, such expenditure is generally allowed if the expenditure would be allowable had it been successful.

abortive expenditure Expenditure in the unsuccessful acquisition of an asset. In general, the tax treatment is the same as if the acquisition had succeeded. The matter is discussed in HMRC's tax manual at BIM35325. Tax provisions for loan relationship are in CTA 2009 s329; and for derivative contracts in CTA 2009 s607.

above par Description of share whose market value is above its nominal value.

above the line In accounting, description of an item that determines how profit is calculated rather than how the profit is applied.

above the line tax credit Deduction from profits rather than from taxation for research and development. The change was made in 2013 to make the tax credit more obvious in the accounts.

ab ovo Usual form of the expression "ab ovo usque ad mala" which is Latin for "from the egg to the apple". It means from beginning to end. It is an allusion to a Roman feast.

abridged accounts Accounts that a small company could file at Companies House before 1 January 2016. They were less detailed than full accounts prepared for its members. A small company may now file abbreviated accounts instead. There is nothing to stop a company producing abridged accounts, or any other version of its accounts, for whatever purpose it wishes.

absence condition In relation to a missing person, the general requirement that the person must have been missing for 90 days for a guardianship order to be made (Guardianship (Missing Persons) Act 2017 s3(3)).

absence from work Periods when an employee is not at work for any reason. If the reason is one that justifies payment, such as sickness or holiday, the period is regarded as employment for tax (ITEPA 2003 s38).

absence of records For national insurance, lack of records relating to earnings from 1987/88 (SSCBA 1992 s24).

absence reliefs Periods of absence that allow a taxpayer still to claim main residence relief from capital gains tax (TCGA 1992 s223). The main reliefs are:

- delay in taking up occupation,
- overlap relief when two properties are owned,
- sandwich reliefs for periods of work elsewhere,
- living-in job-related accommodation, and
- a period of final absence.

The period of final absence is 36 months if the taxpayer moves into care. Otherwise, it is reduced to 18 months from 6 April 2015, and to 9 months from 6 April 2020.

absent parent Term used until 18 January 2001 for the parent who does not live with a child and who may pay maintenance to the other parent. The term now used is "non-resident parent".

absolute entitlement When a person acquires rights to settled property (TCGA 1992 s71).

absolute interest Full and complete ownership of property, where no-one has a better title.

absolute poverty Inadequacy of funds such that a person cannot pay for the basics of life. It is an alternative concept to the more widely used relative poverty where a person is financially disadvantaged relative to his or her peer group. In Scotland, the term has been given the specific meaning of having less than 60% of median income for the year from 1 April 2010 as adjusted for inflation (Child Poverty (Scotland) Act 2017 s4(1)).

absolute rate Rate expressed as a figure rather than a reference rate which relates to another rate. So 5% is an absolute rate; base rate plus 2% is a reference rate.

absolute ratings In human resources, measure of performance or behaviour that is determined according to predetermined standards, rather than by comparison with others.

absolute title Evidence of ownership of land for which no-one has a better right (Land Registration Act 1925 s5).

Absolvitor In Scots law, the judgment pronounced when a court decides in favour of a party against whom an action has been raised.

absolute value In mathematics, a number regardless of whether it is positive or number. So 7 and -7 have the same absolute value. The symbol is a vertical line used as a bracket thus: |7|.

absorption In management accounting, the process by which overheads are attributed to units of production or supply. If a business has overheads of £1 million and produces 20 million items, each item can be said to absorb 5p of overheads.

absque dubio Latin for "without a doubt". The term may be used in court to mean a statement whose validity is so obvious, it needs no proof.

abstract In law, summary of a financial, factual or legal statement.

abstracting electricity Crime of dishonestly causing electricity to be diverted or wasted (Theft Act 1968 s13).

abstraction of water Taking water from a natural source. This may require a licence, though there are exceptions for small quantities and for collecting rain (Water Resources Act 1991 s24A). Charges for abstraction are generally zero-rated for VAT under VATA 1994 Sch 8 Group 2, as explained in VAT Notice 701/16.

absurdity State of ridiculousness. In interpreting tax law, an absurd conclusion is not necessarily wrong, but a sensible interpretation is usually preferred to an absurd one.

abus de droit French for "abuse of right". It is a principle of French and some other European law that allows the tax authorities to restate an agreement in terms that reflect its reality and to tax it accordingly. This does not apply under UK law, though there are some anti-avoidance provisions that have a similar effect.

abuse of dominant position Using a dominant position in a market to impose unfair trading conditions (Competition Act 1998 s18).

abuse of position Form of fraud set out in Fraud Act 2006 s2(2). It involves a person in a position of responsibility abusing that trust.

abusive practice For VAT only, a transaction that is contrary to the purpose of law even if it complies with the letter. The term was particularly applied in the *Halifax* case of 2006.

abusive relationship Marriage or other domestic relationship where one party seeks to intimidate the other by violence or abuse. Being in an abusive relationship was a factor in excusing a wife from a tax liability as a company director in the case *R v Vowles [2017] TC 6123.*

academic year This is generally 1 September to 31 August, even though many educational establishments use an accounting period starting on 1 April.

academy Educational establishment, particularly established under Academies Act 2010. Their VAT provisions are set out in VATA s33B.

ACAS Advisory, Conciliation and Arbitration Service. Arbitration body founded in 1975 and now regulated by Trade Union and Labour Relations (Consolidation) Act 1992 s247. It seeks to resolve workplace problems.

accelerated depreciation Writing down a fixed asset at a rate greater than that for normal accounting purposes. Capital allowances are an example.

accelerated payment notice (APN) Notice that HMRC may issue to a person engaged in tax avoidance, requiring prompt payment and denying the taxpayer the cashflow advantage of not paying during appeals (FA 2014 from s219). The main points of such a notice are:

- HMRC sends a letter warning of an APN
- the tax must ordinarily be paid within 90 days. Failure to pay tax from an APN is itself an offence, attracting penalties additional to any other penalties. APNs are issued on a scheme basis, so a taxpayer may not receive all APNs at once
- an APN only applies to one tax year, so several APNs may be issued in respect of the same issue. Paying an APN does not discharge the tax liability, nor does it extinguish any penalties
- there is no appeal against an APN, but the taxpayer may make representations to HMRC
- the amount of an APN may be different from the amount of a settlement opportunity.

acceptable distribution policy Provision that a controlled foreign company (CFC) could use before 1 July 2009. It broadly excused a company from CFC provisions if it distributed 90% of its profits as dividends within 18 months of the end of the accounting period.

acceptance In contract law, acceptance of an offer creates a contract which is binding on both parties. A contract may be made with HMRC to settle a tax liability, so if HMRC accepts a taxpayer offer, or a taxpayer accepts an HMRC offer, a contract is created and both HMRC and the taxpayer are bound by it.

acceptance in lieu Provision whereby a liability for inheritance tax may be settled by disposing of a work of art or historically significant item to HMRC (IHTA 1984 from s230).

acceptilation In Scots law, extinguishment of rights under a verbal contract by one party declaring that the other party has paid or otherwise satisfied the contract. There is no equivalent provision in English law.

access Right to enter land, such as Custom's right to board a vessel under CEMA 1979 s28.

access and copying Right of an individual whose property has been seized by police to have access to such material and to make copies (Police and Criminal Evidence Act 1984 s21). HMRC adopts a similar policy.

access controls Systems to ensure that computer systems are only accessed by those authorised. This includes access to online tax facilities. Typically this involves two stages: authentication and authorisation. Authentication means that the person is established as a user. For tax, this involves a 12-digit Gateway number. Authorisation means that only the authenticated person may access their files. This is done by use of user names, passwords and authorisation codes. Financial Reporting Council provides guidance on access controls for financial records.

accessories Additional products that typically provide additional functionality to equipment. Spare parts are sometimes regarded as accessories. Generally, the VAT treatment of accessories follows that of the main product. An accessory added to a company car may increase its list price for the purpose of calculating the taxable value as a benefit in kind (ITEPA 2003 s 125).

access road Road built to provide access to a property or area. For VAT, road building is standard-rated and cannot be zero-rated as part of a new construction. The matter was considered by a tribunal in the case *M, G & N Smith [2001] VTD 17035.*

accident This term is used for some social security benefits. It has its ordinary meaning of an untoward event that was neither expected nor designed.

accidental death benefit Addition to a life insurance or assurance policy whereby a higher amount is paid for a death arising from an accident. Company insurance against accidental death is tax-deductible as a business expense (CTA 2009 s1296).

accommodation Provision of a dwelling. Where this is provided by an employer, this can be a taxable benefit in kind under ITEPA 2003 from s97. There is not taxable benefit in kind if the accommodation

- is necessary for the job (such as a caretaker or care home warden),

- is traditional for the better performance of the duties (such as a vicar)
- is needed for the personal security of the employee.

Certain accommodation expenses may be tax-free under ITEPA 2003 s313.

Where accommodation is taxed, the benefit in kind value has up to three elements:

- the property's rateable value
- the amount by which the property's cost exceeded £75,000 (unchanged from 1984) multiplied by the official rate of interest (the same rate as used for employees' beneficial loans)
- the amount of bills paid by the employer, such as council tax, utilities and insurance.

Before 1983, there was a tax allowance when an employee was required to move to a higher cost housing area. This is no longer available. An employee who is required to relocate may be able to claim some expenses as relocation. A business may provide accommodation to a non-employee such as a contractor doing building work. This is generally regarded as part of the contract price, so expenses are tax-deductible. This is discussed in HMRC Manual at BIM45046. General tax deductibility is discussed at BIM37928.

The special provision for MPs is given in ITEPA 2003 s292. Where a business provides domestic accommodation for employees, the business may claim VAT input tax on such expenses (VAT Notice 700).

accommodation agency Body that provides details of available accommodation to prospective tenants. It is generally illegal to charge tenants for this service (Accommodation Agencies Act 1953).

accommodation offset Amount that may be regarded as part of the national minimum wage when an employer provides accommodation to an employee (SI 1999 No 584 para 9(a)). From 1 October 2003, this is quoted annually as a daily rate. The figure is given under National Minimum Wage in section 3 of this dictionary.

accommodation outgoings Expenses of heating, lighting, cleaning and gardening that may be paid tax-free to a minister of religion who otherwise earns no more than £8,500 a year (ITEPA ss290A-290B).

accommodation tie One of the ties that may help establish residence under the statutory residence test.

accompanying administrative document Document that accompanies goods subject to excise duty that move within the EU.

account In bookkeeping, a category of income, expenditure, asset, liability or similar to which debits and credits are posted to reflect accounting transactions and accounting adjustments. The word has several specific meanings in other contexts.

accountancy The work of an accountant. The practice is more commonly called accounting. Accountancy is not a single profession. There are six accounting bodies that have royal charters:

a. Institute of Chartered Accountants in England and Wales;
b. Institute of Chartered Accountants of Scotland;

c. Institute of Chartered Accountants of Ireland;
d. Association of Chartered Certified Accountants;
e. Chartered Institute of Management Accountants; and
f. Chartered Institute of Public Finance and Administration.

These are commonly known by their abbreviations:
ICAEW, ICAS, ICAI, ACCA, CIMA and CIPFA.

There is also the Association of Accounting Technicians (AAT). There are some specialist bodies Association of Tax Technicians (ATT), Chartered Institute of Taxation (CIOT), Chartered Institute of Payroll Professionals (CIPP), Institute of Company Secretaries and Administrators (ICSA) and Society of Trust and Estate Planners (STEP).

The bodies co-operate in many areas, such as in setting accounting standards.

The term is not protected, so anyone may say there are an accountant.

Accountancy Europe Body that represents 51 accounting organisations in 35 countries (in 2020), with a view to sharing experience in areas where accountants work. These include tax. Before December 2016, it was called the Federation of European Accountants.

accountancy fees The extent to which accountancy fees are tax-deductible depends on what the fees are for. For routine work, such as auditing and preparing accounts and tax returns, they are deductible as revenue expenditure. For work in relation to capital projects, they are treated as part of the capital expenditure. The matter is discussed in HMRC Manual at BIM37850.

accountancy rental earnings/excess These terms are used in connection with an anti-avoidance provision when there is a finance lease with a return in capital form. The provision is set out in ITA 2007 ss614B-614BY.

accountancy service provider Person or business who provides the services of auditing, accounting or tax advice but who is not a member of a professional body or otherwise regulated. From 1 April 2008, such a provider must register with HMRC under money laundering regulations.

accountant Person who is qualified or experienced in accountancy. There is no legal bar on anyone calling themselves an accountant or practising as one. There are certain areas where, in practice, a qualified accountant is required, such as in auditing and insolvency. This usually means a member of one of the recognised accountancy bodies.

The rights of audience at a tax tribunal are governed by SI 1994 No 1812. In the case *Cassell v Crutchfield (No 1) Ch D [1995] 69 TC 253*, it was held that an accountant meant someone qualified by one of the accounting bodies. In that case, the tribunal refused to hear a man who had been struck off from two accounting bodies.

Accountant in Bankruptcy Official who oversees bankruptcies in Scotland.

accountants' papers Documents created by an accountant in preparing accounts and tax computations. Although they do not enjoy legal privilege, HMRC will not require production of such papers relating to audit, tax advice or a tax appeal (SP 5/90). Every document produced in accounting must have three headings:

- name or client or entity to which it relates
- accounting period or date to which it relates
- nature of the document, such as trial balance, tax computation, bank reconciliation etc.

Such papers should be filed. The papers should be so clear that another accountant can readily understand them.

account for lifetime transfer Statement to HMRC in connection with inheritance tax when there is a taxable transfer (IHTA 1984 s52).

account forfeiture notice Notice that may be issued while an account freezing order is in effect (Proceeds of Crime Act 2002 s303Z9).

account freezing order Order that a magistrates' court may make to freeze an account under Proceeds of Crime Act 2002 from s303Z1.

accounting The practice of an accountant. Accounting includes financial accounting and management accounting. Financial accounting is recording transactions and producing financial statement. Management accounting analyses where profits or losses are made, such as which product lines are profitable. The requirement of accounting is that one person must answer to another, such as directors to shareholders, or a treasurer to members.

accounting basis Way in which an accounting concept is applied to a transaction. For example, depreciation is an accounting concept; how many years a particular asset is depreciated is an accounting basis. Implication for a company changing its basis are given in CTA 2009 s180.

accounting body In relation to accounts used for tax, this means the International Accounting Standards Board or the Accounting Standards Board or the successor body to either of these (CTA 2009 s465A(8) and s701A(8)).

accounting concept Basic principle of accounting. It is assumed that all accounts follow these concepts unless the contrary is expressly stated. The number and scope of these concepts has varied but has always been at least four. CA 2006 lists five:

- going concern, the entity will continue in existence for the foreseeable future
- accruals: income and expenditure are matched in the same accounting period
- consistency: transactions are accounted in the same way in succeeding accounting periods
- prudence: accounts are prepared on a conservative basis
- separate entity: accounts refer only to the named entity.

The first four of these were contained in the old accounting standard SSAP 2 (now repealed) and in the EU Fourth Directive on Company Law. Accounting standard FRS 102 section 3 has replaced concepts with a more detailed list of provisions.

There are many other concepts that are not listed. For example, substance over form is a concept on which accounting for leases is based. Materiality is another concept.

accounting date Date to which a set of accounts are produced. It is sometimes called the balance sheet date (ITTOIA 2005 s197). For corporation tax, it is the date at which an accounting period ends (CTA 2009 s10). There are special tax provisions for a change of date (ITTOIA 2005 from s214).

accounting entity Body or similar for whom accounts are prepared. The entity need not have separate legal form, so accounts may be prepared for a group of companies or a division of company, for example.

accounting equation Fundamental principle that lies behind double entry bookkeeping. It is usually expressed as:

assets + expenses = liabilities + capital + revenue.

accounting information Factual information as presented in financial statements. Statements of Principles imposes four requirements: relevance, reliability, comparability and understandability.

accounting period Period for which a company is assessed to corporation tax. FRS 102 calls an accounting period, a "reporting period". An accounting period does not start when a company is formed. Instead an accounting period starts when:

- a company first has taxable income
- a company starts to trade
- a company goes into administration or liquidation, or
- 12 months after the end of the last accounting period.

If a company deposits its initial capital and earns some interest, that starts an accounting period. If a month later, it starts trading, that starts another accounting period. An accounting period can only be a whole number of days and must be at least one day. An accounting period may not be more than 12 months. If a company prepares accounts for more than 12 months, the first 12 months are regarded as one accounting period, and the balance as another. The term is also used in some specific contexts, such as for pool betting duty (Customs notice 147) and for a non-corporate licensed deposit taker (ITA 2007 s948(1).

accounting policy Specific principles, bases and similar that a business regards as appropriate for its accounts (FRS 102 s10). The policies must be disclosed in the accounts (FRS 102 s8.5). Similar provisions apply to international accounting standards (IAS 8 para 5).

accounting records Written and equivalent records of financial transactions and adjustments that a taxpayer is regarded to prepare and keep. The OECD defines this as "all documents and books used in the preparation of the tax return and all financial statements, including general ledger, subsidiary ledgers, sales slips and invoices". The general requirement is TMA 1970 s12B. Companies have a further obligation under CA 2006 s386.

accounting reference date For a company incorporated in Great Britain from 1 April 1996 or in Northern Ireland from 22 August 1997, this is the last day of the month in which the company was incorporated (CA 2006 s391). This date is also called the balance sheet date. It is the end of an accounting period. A company may change its date to any day it wants. It simply serves a notice to Companies House to that effect (CA 2006 s392). The date does not have to be the end of a month, though this is normal. A company may have a date that varies by up to three days, such as the last Friday in December, which is within three days of 28 December.

accounting reference period Period determined by reference to a company's accounting reference date (CA 2006 s391(1)). The first period is between 6 and 18 months. An accounting period for corporation tax may not exceed 12 months.

accounting standards Requirements as set out by a UK or international standards body. All accounts used for determining tax must comply with either of these sets of standards (ITTOIA 2005 from s25; CTA 2009 s46). The notes to the accounts must say which standards have been used. If the entity has departed from an accounting standard, it must say where it has departed and why (SI 2008 No 410 reg 10).Compliance with accounting standards has been a key element in cases such as *Odeon Associated Theatres v Jones [1971] 1 WLR 442* and *Balloon Promotions Ltd v Wilson [2006]*. The matter is discussed in HMRC Manual at BIM31003.

A list of current and prospective accounting standards is given in section 3 of this dictionary.

Accounting Standards Board Body that issued accounting standards between 1990 and 2012, when it was replaced by the Financial Reporting Council.

accounting technician Person who holds a proper accounting qualification while not being a member of one of the main bodies listed under accountancy. The main body for such technicians is the Association of Accounting Technicians. There is a separate body for Tax Technicians.

accounting value For asset values for corporation tax, this is the net book value of the asset (CTA 2009 s719).

account monitoring order Order made under Proceeds of Crime Act 2002 s370 to investigate bank and similar accounts held by a suspect.

account of estate Account that a personal representative is generally required to provide to HMRC within 12 months of death, for inheritance tax purposes (IHTA 1984 s216). An account need not be delivered for a small estate, whose limits are given under Inheritance tax in section 3 of this dictionary.

account of profits Equitable remedy for breach of contract. It requires one party to surrender profits earned to a party who suffered loss from wrongdoing.

accounts Financial records. There are some tax provisions that give the term a specific meaning. Accounts used for computing tax must comply with accounting standards. A specific is meaning is given in relation to decommissioning expenditure (CTA 2010 s331(9)).

accounts meeting In company law, the general meeting of the company before which the company's accounts are to be laid (CA 2006 s439(6)).

accounts payable Amounts owed by an entity; its creditors.

accounts receivable Amounts owed to an entity; its debtors.

account stated An amount agreed by both debtor and creditor, particularly for an IOU. The existence of an IOU is not conclusive but is evidence.

accredited training rate One of the original rates for national minimum wage. It is now the reduced rate.

accretion Means of natural growth. In property law, it means land gradually reclaimed from a river or sea. A gradual accretion generally belongs to the owner of adjacent land, whereas a sudden accretion may belong to the Crown. In finance, it can mean gradual increases caused by interest earned.

accrual Amount paid in one accounting period in relation to an earlier period, such as payment for telephone calls or energy used. Unless the accounts are produced on the cash basis, this requires a journal entry. The amount is credited to accruals and debited to the relevant expense, such as telephone charges. The opposite, when a payment is made in one period for a liability in a future period, such as rent or insurance, requires a journal entry the other way round. The amount is debited to prepayments and credited to the relevant expense. These journal entries are reversed at the start of the next accounting period. The UK accounting standard is FRS 102 section 2.36.

accrual rate The rate at which entitlement increases under a final salary pension scheme. A common rate is 1/60 of final salary for each year of work. This means that someone who has 40 years' service would receive 40/60, or two-thirds, of final salary as a pension.

accruals basis Usual form of accounting where transactions are recorded when the underlying liabilities arise. It is generally required by FRS 102 s2.36. The main alternative is cash accounting.

accruals concept Basic principle of accountancy that income and expenditure must be matched for the accounting period to which they relate.

accrued benefits The pension entitlement earned by a scheme member so far.

accrued income scheme Tax provision that requires income from an interest-bearing security to be treated as belonging to the transferor up to the date of transfer (ITA 2007 from s615). Capital gains tax implications are given in TCGA 1992 s119. HMRC also provides helpsheet HS343.

accumulated dividend Dividend that has not been paid to a holder of a cumulative preference share, or other cumulative security, and which is carried forward for payment in a future period.

accumulation Process by which an amount increases, such as by adding interest. There can be legal restrictions on the period of accumulation for trusts and estates. For estates and non-charitable trusts created from 6 April 2010, these restrictions are generally removed by Properties and Accumulations Act 2009. Older trusts and estates are governed by Law of Property Act 1925 s164 which restricts the accumulation period to the life of the settlor plus 21 years. There are separate provisions for perpetuities.

accumulation and maintenance trust A trust that could once be set up for children under 25. It was widely used to avoid inheritance tax (IHTA 1984 s71). No such trusts can be formed from 22 March 2006 and existing trusts ended on 6 April 2008. There is transitional provisions, such as the age 18-25 trust which can still be used.

accumulation share In relation to open-ended investment company, this is a share in respect of which income is added periodically to the capital part of the company's scheme property (ITTOIA 2005 s375(2)).

accumulation unit Additional unit added to a unit trust or other collective investment. Their capital gains tax treatment is set out in TCGA 1992 s99A.

accumulator In gambling, a series of bets where the winnings of one bet becomes the stake for the next bet.

accuracy State of being correct with sufficient precision. It is one of the basic requirements of accounting.

accused In Scots law, person charged with a crime. The word "defendant" is not used. The term "the accused" is sometimes used in English law.

ace of spades Card in a pack of playing cards that was stamped on its face to show that excise duty had been paid. Excise duty was charged on playing cards from 1711 to 1920. From 1765, the ace did not have to be hand stamped. From 1862, the duty could be shown on the wrapper, but the tradition of an ornate card for the ace of spades continues to this day.

acescence Loss of value from souring, such as from a stock of milk.

acid test In accounting, another name for the liquidity ratio or quick ratio. It is the current assets divided by current liabilities. A ratio of 1 is considered healthy but lower ratios can be adequate for some businesses such as supermarkets. It is an indication of solvency. The term comes from the Californian gold rush of around 1845. Prospectors had difficulty distinguishing valuable gold ore from worthless iron pyrites. A simple test was to pour readily available nitric acid which fizzed on the pyrites.

acknowledge Confirm. An order from a customer may be acknowledged before being supplied. A debt may be acknowledged before being paid. Where a debtor is struggling to pay, a debt may be acknowledged by making regular payments of a nominal sum, such as £1 a month. This prevents the debt becoming statute-barred. In litigation, a defendant may acknowledge receipt of documents served on him or her.

a coelo usque ad centrum Latin for "from heaven to the centre [of the earth]". This is the legal term for the rights of an owner of freehold land.

a/c payee only Words that may be written on a cheque. It means that the cheque may only be paid into an account with the name on the cheque. This provision was introduced on 16 June 1992 by Cheques Act 1992 which inserted Bills of Exchange Act 1882 s81A.

acquired gender New sex acquired by a person under Gender Recognition Act 2004. It is effective for tax, social security and other purposes.

acquired goodwill Amount paid for a business above the value of its net assets. Such goodwill may be shown on the balance sheet. The taxation of goodwill changed in 2002.

acquired rights Rights an employee has acquired during employment. These rights are transferred to a new employer if the business is taken over under Transfer of Undertakings (Protection of Employment) Regulations 1981.

acquiree Business that is acquired.

acquirer Person or business that acquires a business.

acquis communitaire Body of EU law that is binding on all member states. From 2021, the UK is no longer bound by EU law, but law passed up to 31 December 2020 is transferred to English law, subject to minor changes, where it may become amended.

acquisition Term used for goods brought in from another EU state (while the UK remains in the EU). Such goods are not said to be imported because of the single market. The law is VATA 1994 s10 and is explained in VAT Notice 725. [The word has other meanings.]

acquisition accounting One of the two methods by which a business may account for a newly acquired subsidiary. The other method is merger accounting. Under acquisition accounting, the assets and liabilities of the two businesses are added, debts between them are cancelled, and acquired goodwill is written off.

acquisition benefit Benefit provided by an employer in respect of a new residence acquired by an employee who has relocated (ITEPA 2003 s277).

acquittance Written acknowledgment of the payment of money or of a due debt. It has more legal authority than a receipt.

acre Unit of land measure equal to 4,840 square yards (Weights and Measures Act 1878) or 43,560 square feet. There are 640 acres to a square mile. An acre is about 0.405 hectares or 4,046 square metres.

Acrobat Software developed by Adobe Systems from 15 June 1993 and revised many time since. It produces an image of a document, known as PDF, which can be sent as a document.

Act Law as passed by Parliament (Interpretation Act 1978 Sch 1).

act and warrant In Scots law, the interlocutor in sequestration proceedings which confirms the appointment of the trustee.

acting nearest relative Person who is most closely related to a person for whom an application is made under Mental Health Acts 1983 or 2007, and who is willing to act for that person.

acting partner Person who habitually acts in the partnership business (Partnership Act 1890 s16). A notice to an acting partner is a notice to the whole partnership.

action In law, civil proceedings commenced by a writ.

Action Fraud Body to which suspected frauds may be reported, either online or at any time on 0300 123 2040.

activation In computing, procedure by which access rights are created. These typically involve providing identity check and security questions, and setting up a user name and password.

active listening Counselling skill of listening constructively to someone. Typically this involves not interrupting beyond interjections to indicate that the counsellor is still listening.

actively seeking work Condition for continued receiving of jobseeker's allowance or universal credit. It means that the person is honouring a commitment to find work. This can include writing a CV, applying for jobs, registering with an employment agency and visiting potential employers. A claimant who fails to do these things could lose benefits.

active member Employee or other person accruing benefits in an occupational pension scheme, as against deferred members and pensioner members.

active membership period Period for which a person is regarded as an active member of a pension scheme. It is the later of when the benefits start to accrue and 6 April 2006.

active ownership Concept developed for the patent box, so that those involved in the early stages of development can still claim the corporation tax relief.

active service Service in the military that involves fighting as against preparation, training and similar. The estate of someone killed on active service is exempt from inheritance tax (IHTA 1984 s154).

active trust Trust that requires the trustees to do something, such as to maintain a property.

active window In computing, a window on the screen identifying what program or data are in use.

activity chart Plan showing how much work has been done, such as on a project, compared with how much should have been done.

act of bankruptcy Obsolete provision of Bankruptcy Act 1914 which defines such acts as justifying bankruptcy. Current law is Insolvency Act 1986.

act of God Accident or event which happens without human cause, such as a storm, and where human prudence is not required to recognise the probability. So normal weather is not included. There is no liability in tort for an act of God, but it is possible to obtain insurance. Acts of God should be considered as part of a risk assessment in determining whether a business is a going concern.

Act of Parliament Law as made by Parliament to which Royal Assent has been given. A Court cannot declare an Act of Parliament illegal. A tax case *Cheney v Conn [1968]* attempted to do this when a taxpayer appealed against a tax assessment on the grounds that the government was illegally spending money on nuclear weapons contrary to the Geneva Conventions Act 1957. The Court held that, even if there was such a conflict of laws, Finance Act 1964 was the later law and so would prevail. The House of Lords did once suspend the *provisions* of an Act, namely Merchant Shipping Act 1988 which the European Court of Justice held did not comply with EU law *(Factortame Ltd v Secretary of state for Transport (No 2) [1991]).* An Act of Parliament does not expire by the mere passing of time. In the case *Prince of Hanover v Attorney General [1957],* it was held that an Act passed in 1705 and not repealed was still in force. It naturalised Princess Sophie of Hanover and thus her descendants.

Act of Settlement Law of 1701 to settle the succession to the throne. It made king James VI of Scotland king James I of England.

acts of sederunt rules In Scots law, rules passed relating to civil procedures.

actual basis Method for determining the basis period for income tax. Usually the actual basis is used for the first year and last year of a business, while other years used the current year basis.

actual birth Date a baby is born, as against expected birth. Actual birth automatically triggers compulsory maternity leave and (unless already commenced) the statutory maternity pay period.

actuals Commodities on hand, ready for shipment, storage or manufacture. Commodities not on hand are futures.

actual tax point Date when VAT is charged on a supply. This is when an invoice is issued up to 14 days after the supply or where payment is made before the supply. It is distinguished from basic tax point, which is when the supply was made.

actuarial assumption In accounting, an unbiased best estimate of the demographic and financial variables that determine the cost of providing pensions.

actuarial gain/loss Changes in a pension fund's surplus or deficit because either events have not coincided with actuarial assumptions, or the actuary has changed those assumptions.

actuarial method Method of calculating depreciation of a fixed asset, particularly when it was acquired by a finance lease. Broadly, depreciation is linked to the finance charge.

actuary Person who is professionally qualified in the mathematics and statistical methods used in pensions and insurance. The two main professional bodies are the Institute of Actuaries, and the Faculty of Actuaries.

actus reus Latin for "guilty act". For most crimes, there needs to be *mens rea* and *actus reus*. In other words, the person must both intend to do wrong and must do so.

A-day The date of 6 April 2006 when the tax provisions for pensions radically changed.

add back Part of a tax computation. A business may prepare accounts with many items properly deducted in the profit and loss account, but which are not tax-deductible. These include depreciation, personal expenditure and fines. A tax computation starts with net profits per the accounts. Items disallowed for tax are added back to this figure, increasing profits (or decreasing the loss). Further adjustments are made to give the taxable figure.

added sugar ingredients Term used for soft drinks industry levy. The levy is charged when sugar is added to a soft drink. The levy is not charged on the sugar that is naturally there such as in fruit or milk. Sugar is defined as calorific mono-saccharides or di-saccharides (FA 2017 s29(2)).

added to loan In banking, fees and charges that are added to the amount of loan and repaid as if it were part of the loan.

added years In defined benefit pensions, amount of additional service added to a member's pension entitlement, expressed in years. This often happens when a member transfers from another pension scheme. In relation to the annual allowance for pension schemes, the term is defined in FA 2009 Sch 35 para 13(5).

adding machine Mechanical or (now, more likely) electronic machine for addition and other simple arithmetical functions. The machine usually has the facility to print the calculation on a roll of paper. The total is usually indicated by an asterisk * while a sub-total is indicated by a diamond ◊. The print-out on the till roll should be checked that it starts with an asterisk. that the numbers have been entered correctly, and the answer is credible.

addition Process of combining two values to give a total or sum. The first number is the augend, and the second the addend. In the addition:

$2 + 3 = 5$

2 is the augend, 3 is the addend, and 5 is the total.

additional calculation rule Rule that applies for certain receipts from leases (ITTOIA 2005 s288; CTA 2009 s228).

additional class 3 contributions Payments of class 3 national insurance to increase the number of years of national insurance contributions that count towards the state pension and some other benefits (SSCBA 1992 s13A). From 2016, a person needs 35 complete years of contributions for a full state pension. Gaps may be plugged by buying class 3 national insurance contributions for the current year and up to six years previously. These gaps may be plugged once someone has passed state pension age but only if within the six-year time limit.

additional class 4 percentage Class 4 national insurance payable on the amount that profits from self-employment exceed the class 4 upper limit. This was introduced by National Insurance Contributions Act 2002, initially at 1%. This was increased to 2% from 6 April 2011.

additional disagreement factor (ADF) Amount by which the risk of disagreement is increased by adding people to a group. The formula is ADF = n/(n-2) where n is the number of people already in the group. So if there are 5 people in a group and a sixth person is added, the ADF is 6/4 or 1½. The chances of disagreement have increased by 50%. The formula is based on the number of combinations of two people in a group.

additional duties Additional work done by an employee for additional pay. Almost always this is simply added to gross pay and subject to PAYE and class 1 national insurance in the normal way. This was tested in the case *Mudd v Collins [1925] 9 TC 297* where a director was paid a commission for selling a branch. The matter is discussed in HMRC Manual at EIM00730. This needs to be contrasted with the case *Donnelly v Williamson [1981] 54 TC 636.* A teacher was not taxed on a refund of expenses to attend a parents' evening as that was not part of her duties.

additional dwelling supplement Additional charge to land and buildings transaction tax in Scotland for a second home from 1 April 2016 (LBTTA 2013 s26A and Sch 2A). The supplement is 3% from 1 April 2016, and 4% from 25 January 2019. There are similar provisions for the rest of the UK.

additional expenses Term used for expenses paid by an employer for an employee sent overseas (ITEPA 2003 s205(4)).

additional land transaction Term used in relation to stamp duty land tax on notional land transactions in relation to pre-completion transactions (FA 2013 Sch 39 para 5). Broadly, any payment for an additional land transaction is added to the notional land transaction in determining the amount of SDLT payable.

additional maternity leave Period of up to 13 weeks that a woman may take off work after 39 weeks of maternity leave (Employment Rights Act 1996 s73). She has no entitlement to pay or statutory maternity pay for this additional leave.

additional pay Amount that is added to gross pay on a payslip for a tax code of K to determine the amount of taxable pay (PAYE Regulations 2003 reg 2(1)).

additional payment This term is given two specific meanings in tax law. First, it is an additional payment to an employee made redundant when a trade ceases (ITTOIA 2005 s79; CTA 2009 s79). Second, it is part of the alternative finance arrangement of an investment bond arrangement (TCGA 1992 ss151N and 151S).

additional pension Government-run scheme allowing a person to make additional payments for additional state pension. There have been three such schemes for years of work:

- graduated pension: 1961-75
- SERPS: 1978-2002
- state second pension: 2002-2016.

For retirements from 6 April 2012, a person is entitled to the greater of a single tier pension or the entitlement built up under previous schemes.

additional personal allowance Addition to the personal allowance that could be claimed between 1973 and 2000. It could be claimed by a single parent. From 1975, it was the difference between the higher and lower personal allowances. From 1995, it ceased to be an allowance and became a deduction from tax capped at 20% from 1994, 15% from 1995 and 10% from 1999, before abolition in 2000.

additional primary percentage Rate of class 1 national insurance payable by an employee on earnings above the upper earnings limit. It was introduced at 1% in 2002, and increased to 2% from 2011. The rates and thresholds are set by regulations issued under SSCBA 1992 s5. More details are given under National Insurance in section 3 of this dictionary.

additional rate For income tax, a rate above the higher rate. This was 50% from 6 April 2010, and reduced to 45% from 2013. In Scotland, it is known as the top rate, and has been 46% since 6 April 2018.

additional rate code PAYE code which means that all income is taxed at the additional rate (PAYE Regs 2003 reg 7(3)(ba)). The code is D1.

additional rate income In determining entitlement to the savings nil rate for income tax, this term is defined in ITA 2007 s12B(8)(a).

additional room For VAT, an additional room is usually regarded as an extension which means it is standard-rated. If the room was part of the original plan, it may be taxed according to the original construction. The matter was considered in the case *Castle Caereinion Recreation Associates [2002] VTD 18303.*

additional secondary percentage Rate of class 1 national insurance payable by an employer on earnings above the upper earnings limit. It was introduced at 1% in 2002, and increased to 2% from 2011. The rates and thresholds are set by regs issued under SSCBA 1992 s5.

additional statutory paternity pay Provision between 6 April 2011 and 5 April 2015 whereby a woman could transfer some of her entitlement to statutory maternity pay to her partner (SSCBA 1992 s171ZEB). The take-up rate was just 0.6%, so it is now replaced by shared parental leave, whose take-up is a little higher.

additional tax Further tax charged on income, gain, transaction or similar which has already been taxed or was exempt from tax. An example is an unauthorised payment from a pension fund (ITA 2007 s30).

additional voluntary contributions Additional payments a member of a pension scheme could make before 6 April 2006 to get a bigger pension.

add-lister Adding machine with a print-out facility.

address book Item of stationery for recording addresses. It was held to be standard-rated for VAT and not zero-rated as a book in the case *Customs and Excise Commissioners v Colour Offset Ltd [1995] QB. STC 85.*

ademption Failure of a legacy, such as when a bequeathed item no longer exists.

adequacy Condition required for most contracts. In *Chappell v Nestlé Co Ltd [1959],* it was held that a used chocolate wrapper, which was thrown away, was adequate consideration.

adhesive label Item of stationery that is standard-rated for VAT. In the case *HP Lansdown (Linguistickers) Ltd [1996] VTD 14714,* it was held that it did not come within the scope of zero-rating for leaflets.

adhesive picture Picture designed to be stuck in a book to make an album. The picture was held not to be within the zero-rating for books in the case *Panini Publishing Ltd [1988] VTD 3876.* The sale of a book with pictures already stuck in would be zero-rated.

adjudication stamp Stamp representing the value as adjudicated for stamp duty (Stamp Act 1891 s12).

ad hoc trust for sale Rare form of trust for sale of land where the trustees are two individuals approved by a court, their successors or a trust corporation. Under Law of Property Act 1925, a sale of land for this type of trust overreaches other equitable interests that would not overreached for other types of trust.

ad idem Latin for "to the same". It is a condition for a contract. If a contract is made to buy one car when the seller has two and the buyer thought it was the other one, the parties are not ad idem and the contract is void.

adjacent premises For beer duty, premises within five kilometres of a brewery that may be registered on the same licence (Customs notice 226).

adjourned meeting Unfinished meeting which is to be completed at a later time. A company resolution passed at an adjourned meeting is passed on that date and not that of the original meeting (CA 2006 s332).

adjudication Process where a third party decides a matter where the two parties cannot agree. This differs from mediation in that the adjudicator makes the decision rather than trying to bring the parties together. For stamp duty, it refers to the procedure whereby HMRC determines the amount payable (Stamp Act 1891 s12). In relation to the commercial relationships between a small business and a large business, adjudication includes arbitration (Enterprise Act 2016 s13).

adjudication stamp For stamp duty, a stamp representing the value as adjudicated (Stamp Act 1891 s12).

Adjudicator Independent officer who investigates complaints of poor service from the tax authorities, such as slowness, rudeness, non-co-operation, and improper use of discretion. Application should only be made after an attempt to resolve the matter with HMRC. The office was created in 1993. The Adjudicator cannot require the tax authorities to take any action, but publication of a report often prompts action. The address is The Adjudicator's Office, Haymarket House, 28 Haymarket, London SW1Y 4SP. Tel: 020 7930 2292. Fax 020 7930 2298. E-mail Adjudicators@gtnet.gov.uk. Website www.adjudicatorsoffice.gov.uk.

adjusted age For pensions and insurance, the age of a person increased or decreased to reflect their medical condition. So a person of 60 in poor health may be given an adjusted age of 70. This can be relevant for inheritance tax, if the person has taken out a bond under the discounted gift scheme.

adjusted allowance For residence nil rate band for inheritance tax, this figure is calculated as the default allowance less (E – TT)/2 where E is the value of the person's estate immediately before death, and TT is the taper threshold at death (IHTA 1984 s8D(5)(g)).

adjusted earnings Earnings of a business which exclude extraordinary items.

adjusted income Figure of income used to determine the tapered reduction in annual allowance for pension contributions (FA 2004 s228ZA(4)).

adjusted net gain Total amount of gain subject to CGT less deductions for reliefs and losses (TCGA 1992 s3).

adjusted net income Amount of income used to determine restrictions on some income tax allowances, such as on personal allowance or age allowance. It is broadly taxable income minus pension contributions and Gift Aid donations. (ITA 2007 s58).

adjusted profit Figure on which corporation tax is charged. It is the profit per the accounts subject to adjustments required by tax law, mainly by adding back amounts disallowed for tax purposes, such as depreciation and customer entertainment.

adjuster clause Clause in a contract that adjusts a figure if an eventuality happens. An example is a clause that reduces the amount paid for a business if HMRC agrees a lower figure for goodwill. A practical problem is that the existence of such a clause could in itself lead HMRC to challenge the figure for goodwill.

adjustment income Amount that may be added to taxable income when there has been a change of accounting date (ITTOIA 2005 from s226).

administration

(1) Process of dealing with the estate of someone who died without a will.
(2) Insolvency arrangement where the management of a business is replaced but the business may continue.
(3) General running of a business, as opposed to its functions.

administration action Proceedings in court started by a personal representative to get letters of administration to deal with the estate of someone who died without leaving a will.

Administrative Burden Advisory Board (ABAB) Government-supported independent board established in 2006. It comprises members from different business backgrounds to advise HMRC on issues relating to regulation and administration of tax for small businesses.

administration levy Charge that the Pension Protection Fund may levy on pension funds under Pensions Act 2004 s117. The rates are given in section 3 of this dictionary.

administration order Court-overseen debt management plan when indebtedness does not exceed £5,000. Payment is usually made in instalments.

administration period For income tax from estates in administration, the term is defined in CTA 2009 s938. For inheritance tax, the term is defined in Inheritance Tax Act 1984 s91.

administrative agreement Agreement between HMRC and a trade body with regard to VAT issues. A list of such agreements is given in VAT Notice 700/57.

administrative receiver Formerly, a receiver appointed under a debenture. This was abolished from 15 September 2003 and replaced by an administrator.

administrative removal Power of Companies House to remove a company from the register under CA 2006 from s1000.

administrative restoration Procedure whereby a company may be restored to the register at Companies House (CA 2006 from s1024).

administrator

(1) A person who deals with the estate of someone who died without a will.
(2) A person who takes over the management of a company in insolvency.

administratrix Term, now rarely used, for a female administrator of an estate where the deceased did not leave a will.

admissibility Extent to which evidence may be used in legal proceedings. Many of these rules are now found in Civil Evidence Act 1968 and SI 1998 No 132.

Admission

(1) Entry to premises, or the charge for doing so. Admission to some cultural establishments are exempt from VAT.

(2) Statement where a person acknowledges facts, often of wrongdoing.

(3) Process by which someone becomes a partner in a partnership (Partnership Act 1890 s15).

admonition

(1) Formal rebuke.

(2) In Scots law, a rebuke with an instruction not to offend again, but which otherwise attracts no penalty.

adoption Process by which a person assumes parental rights for someone else's child. It has been legal since 1926. It is now regulated by Adoption Act 2002, or in Scotland: Adoption and Children (Scotland) Act 2007. The UK recognises overseas adoptions which are in accordance with the Hague Convention. The baby must be at least six weeks old, though a younger baby may be placed before then. An adopter may claim statutory adoption pay (SSCBA 1992 from s171ZL) and take adoption leave. This does not affect the rights of the birth mother to claim maternity leave and statutory maternity pay. A woman does not have to disclose to her employer that she has given up her baby for adoption. From 1950, an adopted child has the same rights as other children with regard to such matters as inheritance, except that an adopted child cannot inherit a title. An adopted child is treated the same as a natural child for inheritance purposes, including being entitled to benefit from the residence nil rate band for inheritance tax. The case *Gregg v Piggott [2012] EWHC 732* held that an adopted child could inherit from a trust established in 1948.

adoption allowance Sum occasionally paid by an adoption agency to adopters. Such payments are not taxable (ITTOIA 2005 ss744-747) and extra-statutory concession A40.

adoption leave The right to take time off in respect of an adoption. From 1 April 2015, this right applies from the first day of employment.

adoption pay period Period for which statutory adoption pay is payable (SSCBA 1992 s171ZN(2)).

adult Person of full age. From 1 January 1971, this is from 18 (Family Law Reform Act 1969 s1). Previously it was 21.

adult at risk Term used in Scotland for an adult who is unable to safeguard his or her wellbeing (Adult Support and Protection (Scotland) Act 2007 s3(1)).

adultery Sexual relationship by a married person outside their marriage. Since 1970, adultery is no longer a tort, but it can be grounds for divorce. Divorce, Dissolution and Separation Act 2020 introduces no-fault divorces which ends this provision.

adults' barred list List kept by the Independent Barring Board of people not allowed to work with vulnerable adults (Safeguarding Vulnerable Groups Act 2006 s2(1)).

ad valorem Basis of stamp duty that is related to value as against a fixed duty (Stamp Act 1890 s6). Almost all stamp duty is now ad valorem.

advance Sum lent to an employee from their next payslip. It is ignored for tax purposes.

advance assurance Limited provision that allows a company to check the tax position with HMRC for a future transaction. Its scope is very limited, such as for seed enterprise investment scheme, transfer pricing and research and development credit.

advance corporation tax Prepayment of corporation tax made between 1973 and 1999 when a dividend was paid. The amount was deducted from the mainstream corporation tax up to a limit. This was also a tax credit in the hands of the shareholder. If a company paid large dividends, it could find it is limited in the amount it could deduct from its mainstream corporation tax. If a company still has unrelieved advance corporation tax, it may offset it against corporation tax as if the old regulations still applied. These are set out in FA 1998 s32.

advance funding When HMRC provided advance funds to meet a liability that would otherwise be deducted from PAYE payments. It applied to working family tax credits between 2000 and 2003, and can still apply in exceptional cases for statutory maternity pay.

advancement of capital Arrangement whereby trustees may advance capital to a beneficiary before the normal entitlement date. Trustee Act 2000 provides a general right allowing trustees to advance up to half the eventual entitlement of a beneficiary. The sum advanced is deducted from the eventual payment of the entitlement. If there is a life tenant whose income is reduced by such advancement, his or her consent is required. A trust deed may give trustees the power to advance more than half.

advance payment Payment for goods or services before they are received. In VAT, an advance payment creates a tax point which triggers the liability to VAT. The payment need not be for the whole amount, so a deposit can trigger a liability for the whole work. This needs to be particularly considered in relation to construction contracts. If an advance payment comprises a returnable deposit, such as when goods are hired, the payment does not trigger a tax point.

advance pricing agreement Agreement reached between a taxpayer and HMRC in relation to transfer pricing, under the provisions of FA 1999 s85 and SP 3/99.

advance thin capitalisation agreement Agreement between a taxpayer and HMRC regarding thin capitalisation, made under provisions of FA 1999 s85 and SP 4/07.

Adventure In finance, an activity in the nature of a trade. The incidence of an adventure usually triggers a liability to income tax or corporation tax. The matter was considered in the case *Edwards v Bairstow and Harrison [1955].*

adversarial system System used for most forms of court cases under English and Scots law. Each side either represents themselves or are represented by an advocate.

The main alternative is the inquisitorial system, used in coroner's courts in the UK and more widely in many European jurisdictions.

adverse opinion Audit report which states that the records are not true or fair, or that they do not comply with the Companies Act. A change in 1989 led to tougher auditing reports. At the time, Inland Revenue (now HMRC) and the Institute of Chartered Accountants in England and Wales agreed a statement that a qualified audit report does not automatically mean that HMRC will investigate the company but makes it more likely (ICAEW Technical Release 800).

advertising Advertising one's products or services, advertising for staff, and most other forms of advertising are standard-rated for VAT, and tax-deductible for income tax or corporation tax. Some advertising is banned, such as for cigarettes, or for return on stolen property with no questions asked (Theft Act 1968 s23). Giving away free samples is generally tax-deductible (HMRC Manual at BIM45032). This was also noted in the case *Fleming v Associated Newspapers Ltd [1972] 48 TC 382*. Advertising leaflets generally come within the scope of VAT zero-rating. In the case *Cronsvale Ltd [1983] VTD 1552*, zero-rating was refused for advertising material printed on sheets measuring 20 inches by 15. This was considered too big to be a leaflet. A television advertisement is specifically excluded from the scope of television production relief (CTA 2009 s1216AD(1)(a)). The erection of an advertisement hoarding is not in itself a material development of land (TCGA 1992 Sch 2 para 13(1)(d)).

advice note Document sent to confirm that goods have been shipped. Sometimes the note is sent with the goods. An advice note is not an accounting document and should not be treated as an invoice, even if it has prices indicated.

Advisory, Conciliation and Arbitration Service Government sponsored body charged with improving industrial relations. It is generally known by its initials as ACAS.

advisory fuel rates Rates produced by HMRC in relation to company cars. They are given as so many pence per mile according to the car's fuel and engine size. The rate may be used in two circumstances:

- when the employer pays for fuel, the employee may pay it to the employer for private mileage and thus avoid the car fuel benefit charge for tax, or
- when the employer does not pay for fuel, the employer may pay it to the employee for business mileage.

This is different from the approved mileage rate when an employee uses his or her own car for business. The advisory rate is less than a third of the mileage rate as the employer has already borne the cost of providing the car.

The rates were introduced from 28 January 2002. From September 2011, rates are given every three months on 1 March, 1 June, 1 September and 1 December. The employer may use the rates from those dates or from one month later. From 1 June 2011, rates are given for petrol cars according to whether their engine size is up to 1400cc, 1401-2000cc, or over 2000cc. The same sizes are used for liquid petroleum gas. For diesel cars, the sizes are up to 1600cc; 1601-2000cc, and over 2000cc. Electricity is not regarded as road fuel, but a figure of 4p a mile is now allowed for electric vehicles. These figures are not a legal entitlement; the employer and employee may agree any figure. If the amount is greater than the advisory rate, the employer must be able to justify it.

advocacy Skill in arguing a case before a court or tribunal. The qualification for advocates in court is given by Courts and Legal Services Act 1990.

advocate One who argues the case for another, such as a barrister. A qualified accountant may represent a client at a tax tribunal. In Scotland, the term advocate means a barrister. They are appointed by the Faculty of Advocates.

Advocate General Member of the Court of Justice of the European Union whose function is to present opinions on cases brought before the Court. In practice, the Court usually follows the Advocate General's view.

Advowson The right to appoint an incumbent in the Church of England. It is now a property right that can be inherited or given away, but not sold.

aerial photograph This is not regarded as a map and therefore does not qualify for VAT zero-rating for maps and other printed material.

aerodrome Any area of land or water designed, equipped, set apart or commonly used for landing and departure of aircraft (CEMA 1979 s1(1)). Aerodrome fees are charges for using such facilities (Civil Aviation Act 1982 s38).

aerosol (1) Spray, such as in a deodorant or air freshener. If an aerosol contains an environmentally damaging gas, it may require a licence to be imported.

(2) Small particulates from breath or sneezing that travel further than normal breath. Their consideration was a factor in social distancing regulations for coronavirus.

affidavit Statement of fact written, signed and sworn by a person called the deponent, where the facts are derived from the deponent's own knowledge. An affidavit carries more weight in legal proceedings than a simple statement.

affiliate In auditing, this term means a body that has control or influence over another. In other contexts, this is an imprecise term indicating a more general relationship.

affinity card Credit card or other card that is branded with the name of an organisation that usually receives a small commission on the card's use. The VAT position is explained in VAT notice 701/1.

affluent society Term that gained currency from the 1960s. It refers to a society that can buy what it wants without being constrained by poverty, restricted supply or wartime regulation.

Affordable Homes Programme Government-backed programme launched in 2016 to provide more affordable housing by 2021. The programme also runs from 2021 to 2026. The government provides funding to local authorities to provide affordable homes.

affordable housing Provision of homes arranged by a local authority for key workers to live in an area where market price is unaffordable. Typically such property has a price or rent at least 20% below market rate. This includes starter homes under

Housing and Planning Act 2016 ss2-3. A planning application for a residential development may include a requirement that a percentage is affordable housing.

afghani Currency of Afghanistan.

Afghanistan Eastern country. Its currency is the afghani. The UK has no tax treaty. The country is subject to UK sanctions.

African Caribbean and Pacific States Collective term for many states in the areas indicated. They are often treated the same way for trade preference under Customs procedures.

African Development Bank Body set up in 1964 to promote development in Africa. It is exempt from UK tax under SI 1997 No 168.

Aga cooker In a VAT case this was held not to be a space heater and therefore it was not zero-rated as material for a new construction *(R Cusdin [2005] VTD 19739).*

age Time which has passed since a person was born. For this purpose, parts of a day are ignored. So someone born at 12 noon on 1 January 2000 is 21 years old from the first moments of 1 January 2021. There are many laws that impose age limits. For example, national insurance is only payable by someone aged between 16 and state pension age.

age 18-25 trust Type of trust that may be set up for a beneficiary under 25 at least one of whose parents has died. They were introduced on 22 March 2006 to replace accumulation and maintenance trusts which enjoyed greater exemption from inheritance tax (IHTA 1984 s71D). The restrictions were imposed by FA 2006 Sch 20.

age allowance Additional income tax allowance for older taxpayers. The only extant age allowance is for taxpayers born before 6 April 1938. Other age allowances were frozen in cash terms in 2013, and became otiose by 2016.

aged debt analysis Analysis of an entity's debtors according to the age of the date.

age discrimination Treating a person less favourably because of their age. This is generally outlawed from 1 October 2006, though there are exceptions.

age exemption Additional income tax allowance for older taxpayers. In 1973, it was replaced by age allowance which has itself been generally abolished.

agency When one person acts for someone else, known as the principal. For VAT, provisions are given in VATA 1994 s47. A definition was given in the case *C & E Commrs v E Johnson [1980] QBD. STD 624.* There have been other VAT cases on agency. FRS 102 has a definition in its glossary. The OECD has provided a definition for international tax. The main elements of agency law are:

- the agent binds his principal;
- someone who purports to act as agent without authority is regarded as the principal and becomes personally liable;
- the agent may only act within such authority as granted by the principal;
- the agent must perform those duties himself (except that incidental duties, such as typing, may be delegated);

- the agent may not make a secret profit.

Once an agent has performed the duties of the agency, the principal resumes his position and may sue or be sued on whatever has been concluded by the agent.

agency worker Worker provided via an employment agency rather than being directly employed (ITEPA 2003 s47(1)). From 1975, they are taxed as employees of the agency and are not treated as self-employed (PAYE regs reg 2(1)). An agency is obliged to provide details of workers to HMRC under TMA 1970 s16A. There is a special provision in relation to research and development expenditure (CTA 2009 s1129). From 27 October 2008, an agency worker is entitled to statutory sick pay after three months. From 1 October 2011, an agency worker acquires many employment rights after 12 weeks. An agency worker is entitled to the national minimum wage, Working Time Directive protection, no unlawful deductions from pay, and protection from unlawful discrimination.

agent Person who works for someone else, called the principal, as explained under agency. The term can be specifically used to mean a tax agent. Someone may act as such if authorised by the taxpayer in a letter or on form 64-8.

Agent Dedicated Line Telephone line provided by HMRC for tax agents.

aggregates levy Tax introduced on 1 April 2002 on the commercial exploitation of rock, sand and gravel (FA 2001 ss16-49). It is charged at a flat rate per tonne extracted. The rate is given in section 3 of this dictionary.

aggregation Adding together, particularly when HMRC rules that two businesses have been artificially split to avoid VAT registration and should be regarded as one. It is also used in PAYE when two payments are made in the same payment period and tax is calculated on a non-cumulative basis (PAYE Regs 2003 reg 29).

aggressive tax avoidance Informal term for a tax avoidance scheme that goes against what Parliament intended. The government made clear in a Treasury statement in January 2014 that aggressive avoidance is unacceptable, and has taken many steps to counter it.

agreement Concurrence of two people with regard to a fact or position. Tax disputes may be settled by agreement under TMA 1970 s54.

agricultural activity For accounting standards, this is the management of the transformation of biological assets for sale (FRS 102 glossary). There are many special tax provisions for agriculture.

agricultural buildings allowance Capital allowance available for agricultural buildings before 6 April 2011. Such buildings now qualify for structures and buildings allowance.

agricultural co-operative Organisation established by farmers, market gardeners and fishermen for a common purpose, such as storage, selling or bulk-buying. There are particular provisions in CTA 2009 from 499. In particular, distributions are not taxed as dividends. The co-operative is usually regarded as mutual trading and not taxed. This is discussed in HMRC Manual at BIM24705.

agricultural engine Generic term for farm machinery. If it is restricted to such purposes, it may use rebated oil (HODA 1979 Sch 1 para 4).

Agricultural Flat Rate Scheme VAT scheme for farmers and others engaged in agricultural activities. VAT is accounted as a percentage of turnover. Guidance is given in VAT Notice 700/46.

agricultural land Land used for agriculture (Agricultural Holdings Act 1986 s1(4)). It includes meadows, pasture, cottage gardens, orchards, allotments, livestock buildings and apiaries. It excludes parks, racecourses and pleasure grounds. Agricultural land may qualify for agricultural property relief from inheritance tax. (IHTA 1984 s117). Capital gains tax provisions are given in TCGA 1992 from s249.

agricultural property relief Relief from inheritance tax on farming property (IHTA 1984 s16). From 10 March 1992, relief is 100%. It is similar to business property relief except that a farmhouse qualifies.

agricultural society Society established to promote agriculture, and similar. Its profits are not subject to corporation tax (CTA 2010 s989(2)).

Ahmedabad principle Principle that a prior year adjustment must make the same adjustment to the prior year and subsequent year. The name comes from the case *Ahmedabad Bombay Commissioners of Income Tax v Ahmedabad New Cotton Milles Company Ltd [1929] 8ATC574.* The matter is discussed in HMRC Manual at BIM34030.

air ambulance charity Charity that provides an air ambulance service at the request of an NHS body (VATA 1994 s33D(3)). From 1 April 2015, such a charity may reclaim VAT input tax.

air consignment note Equivalent to a bill of lading for goods sent by air. The note is broadly a copy of the consignment contract.

air cooling This is a features integral to a building and so qualifies for capital allowance at the lower rate for plant and machinery (CAA 2001 s33A).

air corridor Link between the UK and another country where passengers could travel without having to quarantine under coronavirus regulations in 2020.

aircraft Vehicle that transports people or good by air. There is a definition in Armed Forces Act 2006 s374. Goods may only be imported by air to a Customs-approved airport. The Customs control of aircraft is given in CEMA 1979 s21. For VAT, an aircraft is zero-rated if it weighs at least 8,000 kilograms and is not primarily for recreation or pleasure (VATA 1994 Sch 8 Group 8). Aircraft are plant and qualify for capital allowance. Some special provisions have been agreed with airlines. Aircraft qualify for rollover relief (TCGA 1992 ss155-156). There are special tax provisions for derivative contracts relating to aircraft (SI 2004 No 3256 reg 4(3)).

air departure tax Tax charged in Scotland as a replacement for air passenger duty. It is imposed by Air Departure Tax (Scotland) Act 2017. Its introduction has been put back to an unspecified date.

air fares if these are between the UK and another country, they are usually zero-rated under VATA 1994 Sch 8 Group 8.

airline pilot A pilot operating from the UK is generally regarded as performing those duties in the UK (ITEPA 2003 s40).

air passenger duty Tax introduced from 1 November 1994 on inland and international flights (FA 1994 ss28-44). Its regulations are SI 1994 No 1738.) From April 2018, Scotland has the power to replace this with air departure tax.

air purification This is a feature integral to a building and so qualifies for the lower rate of capital allowance for plant and machinery.

air source heat pump From 7 April 2005, this may qualify for the reduced rate of VAT when fitted to a residential or charitable building (VATA 1994 Sch 7A Group 2).

airspace Right to use air above the land. Under English law, this right belongs to the freeholders, subject to exceptions such as for aircraft. An unsuccessful attempt to split this right from the land was made in the case *Rolfe v Wimpey Waste Management Ltd [1989] 62 TC 399.* This is discussed in HMRC Manual at BIM35605.

Albania East European country. Its currency is the lek. The UK has no tax treaty.

alcohol Organic compound that occurs in liquor. For liquor it means ethanol (ALDA 19789 s2(2)). Such drinks are usually subject to alcoholic liquor duty and VAT.

alcohol by volume Method for determining alcoholic liquor duty. It replaced proof spirit in 1993. A drink with an alcoholic content of less 1.2% by volume is not regarded as alcoholic.

alcoholic beverage For duty purposes, a drink with an alcoholic strength of 1.2% by volume or more.

alcoholic liquor duty Excise duty charged on alcoholic drinks according to their nature and strength. The duty has been charged since 1660.

alcoholic wholesaler registration scheme Scheme introduced in October 2015 and administered by HMRC. It requires wholesalers to prove they are fit and proper persons to be registered.

alco-pops Popular name for spirits flavoured and sweetened by fruit juices. For duty purposes, they are regarded as spirits from 27 April 2002.

algae For VAT, algae is not zero-rated as food. Cases include *Nature's Balance Ltd [1993] VTD 12295* and *Hunter Ridgeley Ltd [1994] VTD 13662.*

Algeria African country. The currency is the Algerian dinar. UK has no comprehensive tax treaty but has an agreement of 1981 for air transport.

Algerian dinar Currency of Algeria.

alienation of income In international taxation, the transfer of the right to receive income while not necessarily transferring the ownership of the source.

aliment Payment for food and nourishment, or the food and nourishment itself. In Scots law, it means the legally required financial support of a spouse or child.

alimony Old term for payment to support a former spouse. It is now called maintenance.

all employee share ownership plan Former name of the share incentive plan.

All England Law Reports One of two official series of law reports for the whole of England. (The other is Weekly Law Reports.) All England reports have been produced since 1936. The reports use the citation *All ER*.

allocation of cases Process to determine how a tax appeal will be heard. The decision is made by the tribunal between default paper case, basic case, standard case or complex case (SI 2009 No 273 rule 23).

allocation rate Amount of payment, such as to a pension fund or investment, that is actually applied to the purpose. So an allocation rate of 70% means that 70% of the payments are so applied, while the other 30% pays overheads and profit.

all one transaction Principle for stamp duty and stamp duty land tax that two transactions may be regarded as one if sufficiently close in time and nature. A leading case is *Cohen and Moore v IRC [1933]*.

allotment (1) Process of allocating new shares to those who subscribe for them. If demand exceeds supply, a subscriber receives a lower pro rata number of shares. The shareholder is notified by an allotment letter (CA 2006 s560(2)).

(2) Piece of land of between 250 and 1000 square metres that a local authority hires to residents for growing vegetables, fruit and flowers, and sometimes for keeping certain animals.

allowance Sum that may be deducted in determining the amount subject to tax. A common example is the personal allowance for income tax.

allowance buying Acquiring an asset or a business for its capital allowances. This is generally disallowed by CAA 2001 Part 2 Chapter 16A.

alloy Mixture of two or more metals. Examples include brass and pewter. The gold, silver, bronze and cupro-nickel used in coins are all alloys.

all-paper deal One way by which a listed company pays for an acquired company. In this deal, the shareholders of the acquired company are given shares in the acquiring company. No cash changes hands. There can be a capital gains tax advantage as a swap of shares is generally not regarded as a disposal.

all-up Description of total weight of a loaded aircraft.

alluvion Land that is gradually gained from a river or sea by washing up of sand, stones and similar.

almond VAT Notice 701/38 lists this as zero-rated food both as the nut and plant from which it is grown. A flowering almond is standard-rated as a flower.

almond oil This is generally VAT zero-rated as food except when sold for medical purposes, when it is standard-rated.

almoner Person who collects money for the poor.

alms Gifts for the poor. Church of England canon F 10 requires each of its churches to have a box to collect money for such purposes. The minister and church council determine how it is used.

aloe vera Products from this plant were held not to be VAT zero-rated as food as they have no nutritional value *(Forever Living Products Ltd [1997] VTD 16263.*

alpha Investment term used to describe the risk-adjusted outperformance of an investment, as against the beta which indicates factors that affect the whole market. It is sometimes called the alpha coefficient.

alphabet shares Ordinary shares designed as A, B etc. They are often used to allow different amounts to be paid to shareholders. They can also be used to give different voting rights.

alpha stocks Term used between October 1986 and January 1991 to describe the most actively traded securities on the London Stock Exchange. The term is now replaced by the normal market size measure.

alteration (1) Amendment of a text. In a legal document this can have the effect of invalidating the document. For such documents as cheques and wills, an alteration is valid if the signatory notes the alteration and, for wills, the witnesses attest it.

(2) In bookkeeping, changing a figure. This must always be done so that the original figure remains visible or known. The reason for the alteration must be stated. Alteration is best made by making a further entry.

(3) For inheritance tax and alteration of capital in a close company, alteration includes extinguishment (IHTA 1984 s98(2)).

altered duty Customs duty whose rate has changed between making the contract and delivering the goods. The supplier may charge the new rate of duty (FA 1901 s10).

alternative accounting rules Form of accounting that allows for inflation. Its provisions are set out in SI 2008 No 410. Little use is made of this provision.

alternative banking platform (ABP) Financial institution that is not a bank but provides the functions of one. The use of an ABP can raise suspicions with HMRC about the validity of transactions. An example is the case *Field Opportunities Ltd [2019] TC 7326.*

alternative compliance Term used in CA 2006 s410 when directors believe that normal disclosure would lead to notes of excessive length. The directors may include only those undertakings whose results principally affect the reported figures.

alternative dispute resolution (ADR) A method of resolving a dispute without going to court. Subject to conditions, it can be used to resolve a tax dispute with HMRC. A tribunal may draw the attention of parties to ADR (SI 2009 No 273 rule 3(1)).

alternative finance arrangements Financial provisions designed to get round the ban on interest under Islamic law. From 7 April 2005, there are tax provisions to ensure that the alternative is generally taxed on the same basis as the arrangement it copies. Use of these arrangements is available to all taxpayers, including non-Muslims. A list of such arrangements is given in TCGA from s151H and ITA 2007 s564A. These list five categories of such arrangement:

- purchase and resale arrangements
- diminishing shared ownership arrangements
- deposit arrangements

- profit share agency arrangements, and
- investment bond arrangements.

  Guidance is provided in helpsheet HS340 and the HMRC manual at BIM45780.

alternative financing This term usually means borrowing from non-traditional sources. Recent examples include crowdfunding and peer-to-peer lending.

Alternative Investment Fund A collective investment undertaking that is not subject to the UCITS regime. It includes hedge funds, private equity funds, retail investment funds, investment companies, and real estate funds, among others (FCA website).

Alternative Investment Market (AIM) Stock market for smaller companies opened by London Stock Exchange on 19 June 1995. There are tax advantages in investing in such a company. There can be various tax advantages in investing in AIM companies:

- from 2014, AIM shares may be held in an ISA, meaning that no capital gains tax is paid on disposal and no income tax on dividend income
- AIM shares may qualify for business property relief from inheritance tax
- AIM shares may be held in an enterprise investment scheme or venture capital trust.

alternatively secured pension Misnomer for a scheme operated like a money purchase pension but operated for some who is at least 75 years old. The conditions are laid down in FA 2004 Sch 28.

alternative penalty For VAT, a stricter penalty that can apply when there has been an intention to deceive HMRC (VATA s72).

alternative receipt Benefit offered to a shareholder as an alternative to a cash dividend. From 6 April 2015, this is taxed as income of the amount of dividend it replaced (ITTOIA s396A).

alum Class of chemical compounds found as a mineral. Profits from an alum mine are specifically listed as a trade (ITTOIA 2005 s12; CTA 2009 s39(4)(b)). Rent received is taxed under CTA 2009 s270.

ambassador Diplomatic agent resident in another country. An ambassador has diplomatic immunity which means he or she is not liable to pay tax in the host country.

ambience Those aspects of premises that create an atmosphere designed to attract custom. Such expenditure may qualify for capital allowance as plant, as in the case *IRC v Scottish & Newcastle Breweries Ltd [1982] 55 TC 262.*

ambulance Vehicle that is designed for the transport of the sick or injured. Such a vehicle is exempt from VAT. VAT Notice 701/1 states that the ambulance must have a lift or ramp to raise a person on a stretcher, and have clamps to secure a person in transport. An ambulance does not have to be a road vehicle, so a helicopter or boat can qualify. An ambulance that can carry ten or more people may alternatively be zero-rated under VATA 1994 Sch 8 Group 8 Item 4. In the case *Jigsaw Medical Services Ltd [2017] TC 5985,* it was held that an ambulance still qualified if such had a vehicle had equipment for the disabled which reduced its capacity below ten people. An ambulance comes within the scope of charity funded equipment (VAT Notice 701/6). From 6 April 2004, the use of an emergency car as an ambulance is not a taxable benefit in kind (ITEPA 2003 s248A).

ambulatory Capable of change during a person's lifetime. A will is ambulatory.

amelioration Gradual reduction of something.

American depositary receipt (ADR) Document issued by an American bank to its citizens making them unregistered shareholders in foreign companies. ADRs can be within the scope of stamp duty reserve tax.

American option Option that may be exercised at any time *up to* the expiry date, whereas most other options may only be exercised *at* or after the expiry date.

ammonium nitrate Substance used as an explosive and fertiliser. Customs clearance for either use requires an Exemption Certificate or Detonation Resistance Test Certificate. On 4 August 2020, 2,750 tons of ammonium nitrate that had sat in a warehouse with Customs clearance exploded in Beirut, killing 220 people, injuring more than 5,000, and destroying the main port.

ammunition Items within the scope of explosives (Explosives Act 1875 s3(1)) which Customs may seize. Another definition is given in Firearms Act 1968 s57(2).

amnesty Period for which an offence may be admitted without incurring a penalty. The UK has never offered a tax amnesty but has allowed voluntary disclosures for a reduced penalty.

amortisation Process of writing off an intangible asset, such as goodwill. It is the exact equivalent to depreciation.

amortised cost basis Term used in connection with loan relationship (CTA 2009 s313).

amount foregone Basis on which an optional remuneration arrangement is taxed (ITEPA 2003 s69B).

amusement machine Machine such as fruit machine, video game, pinball or quiz machine, but which does not involve betting. They are subject to gaming machine duty from 1 November 1995. (FA 1995 s14). For VAT, this is a machine where either there is no prize, or any prize is dependent on the person's knowledge or skill, such as a quiz machine (Vat Notice 701/13).

analytic income tax In international taxation, any system of income tax that taxes income according to its nature. UK has analytic income tax.

ancient document Document of sufficient age, properly produced and free from suspicion. In UK law, the age is 20 years from 1938, before which it was 30 years. Such a document may be admitted as evidence.

ancient monument Monument that is listed on a similar basis to listed buildings. Certain work on an ancient monument may be zero-rated for VAT.

ancillary trade Second trade that may be regarded as a separate trade for tax purposes, even though it supports the main trade. A leading case is *Reid's Brewery Co Ltd* *v Male [1891] 3 TC 279* where a brewery had an ancillary business of lending money to its tenants.

and This common conjunction has been considered in different tax contexts. In a sentence construction of [adjective] [noun] and [noun], it has been held that the adjective applied to both nouns. So "fixed plant and machinery" meant fixed plant and fixed machinery, and not fixed plant and any machinery. This parsing was followed when VAT was charged on "hot takeaway food and drink". VAT is charged under this heading on hot takeaway drink, not any drink. In the case *Ross Young Holdings Ltd [1996] VTD 13972,* the company produced a product that was similar to ice cream but was not similar to a water ice. The issue was whether this was standard-rated under VATA 1994 Sch 8 Group 1 Excepted Item 1 as "ice cream, ice lollies, frozen yogurt, water ices and similar products". It was held that "and similar products" referred to all the listed items and not just the last one. It was also held that a comma before the word "and" (known as the Oxford comma) would not have made any difference.

and his/her heirs Term sometimes used in a will to indicate that the rights of a beneficiary pass to the beneficiary's heirs if the beneficiary has died before the testator.

Andorra Principality between Spain and France. It is not a member of the EU but has some special agreements, such as being part of the mutual assistance recovery directive (FA 2004 s322). Its currency is the euro. The UK has no tax treaty.

angel In investment, a private investor who backs a business that is too small for the usual sources of finance. Many shows are funded by angels. If the show is successful, the angel receives his or her funding back and then a percentage of the show's profits. If the show fails, the angel loses his or her investment. Before 6 April 2017, an angel could claim their profit or loss as trading income or loss under extra-statutory concession A94, now withdrawn. From 6 April 2017, an angel's profits are subject to income tax under ITTOIA 2005 s683. There is no income tax relief for any losses, but this may count as a loss for capital gains tax.

angel's share For liquor duty, the amount of liquor lost from evaporation.

Anglo-Brewing Case that established that a payment for winding up a business is not tax-deductible as a business expense. The full citation is *Anglo Brewing Co Ltd [1925] 12 TC 803*. It is discussed in HMRC Manual at BIM42955.

Angola African country. Its currency is the kwanza. The UK has no tax treaty.

Anguilla British colony. Its currency is the East Caribbean dollar.

animal Any creatures that breathes and is not human. A tax definition is "any animal or other living creature". This is used in ITTOIA 2005 s112(1)(a) and CTA 2009 s110(1)(a) in relation to the herd basis for farmers. It is also used in ITTOIA 2005 s225ZG in relation to expenses for compulsory slaughter. For VAT, live animals are zero-rated if they:

- are used as food for human consumption
- yield food for human consumption, or
- produce food for human consumption

(VATA 1994 Sch 8 Group 1 Note 2). These categories respectively zero rate pigs, cows and bees, for example. Foodstuff for such animals is zero-rated under the same provision. Animals and feed for other animals are standard-rated. This includes pets, racing pigeons and work horses. Details are given in VAT Notice 701/15. There are Customs restrictions on importing animals or animal products. An imported live animal usually needs to be quarantined unless they have an appropriate health certificate. Pet birds must be licensed by Animal Health. Endangered species are banned or need licensing under Convention on International Trade in Endangered Species (CITES). Animals kept for a trade are treated as stock (ITTOIA 2005 s30; CTA 2009 s50). This does not apply if the farmer uses the herd basis. It does not apply if the animal is kept for working, such as a carthorse, racehorse or public exhibition animal. Use of a performing animal invalidates a claim for theatrical productions relief (CTA 2009 s1217FB(1)(c). From 20 January 2020, it is anyway illegal to use a wild animal in a travelling circus (Wild Animals in Circuses Act 2019 s1). No capital allowance may be claimed for an animal (CAA 2001 s38), even though the first legal definition of plant was for a horse.

Animals are always wasting assets, which means they are not subject to capital gains tax on their disposal.

Boarding and caring for animals on a commercial basis is a trade.

animal fat Triglyceride of animal origin (HODA 1979 s23C(5)(c)).

animal health certificate Document required to take an animal between Great Britain and the EU from 1 January 2021 when pet passports cease to be valid. Pet passports allowed a pet cat, dog or ferret to move between UK and other EU states without the need for quarantine.

A certificate is also needed to move an animal between Northern Ireland and Great Britain. A new certificate is needed each time the pet travels. It must be obtained up to 10 days before travel and is valid for four months.

animal rearing For VAT, this is regarded as a single standard-rated supply. It is not possible to strip out feedstuffs for zero rating. Cases include *D D Scott [1977] QB. STC 191* and *A R M Smith [1987] VTD 2954.*

Animation Such a film can attract television production relief under CTA 2009 s1215AC(3).

animo et facto Latin for "by mind and deed". The term may be when deciding whether a taxpayer has established a domicile of choice.

animus testandi Latin for "the intention to make a will".

Ankara agreement Agreement reached in 1995 which ensures that taxes are not charged on goods passing between Turkey and the EU.

annexe An extension to an existing purpose, particularly when intended for a particular purpose. There have been many cases on whether building work is new work or an annexe, often with huge amounts at stake. It cannot be stressed too strongly that careful consideration is needed before such construction work is started. For council tax, an annexe, such as a granny annexe, is usually regarded as a separate unit (SI 2013 No 2977).

anniversary rate Term sometimes used to mean the ten-yearly charge for inheritance tax for relevant property trusts.

annual accounting VAT scheme where one return is made each year with nine monthly payments on account. It is a voluntary alternative to the usual arrangement of making quarterly returns and payments. It may be used by businesses up to a certain size. There is a separate lower limit scheme. Details are given in value added tax in section 3 of this dictionary.

annual accounts Financial statements that a company or group is required to produce each year (CA 2006 s471(1)).

annual allowance Limit on the amount of pension contributions that qualify for tax relief in a tax year.

annual equivalent rate (AER) Common method for evaluating and comparing interest rates for financial products. It is the equivalent to the APR for loans.

annual exempt amount Amount that may be subtracted from capital gains for capital gains tax (TCGA 1992 s3). The rates are given under Capital Gains Tax in section 3 of this dictionary.

annual exemption Amount that may be given to an individual outside the scope of inheritance tax (IHTA 1984 s19(1)). The amount has been £3,000 since 1986.

annual general meeting (AGM)

Meeting a public company must have once a year within six months of its accounting reference date (CA 2006 s336(1)). Most other companies and organisations have annual meetings in accordance with their own constitutions. For a company, the AGM is when, among other business, the accounts are approved, the auditors are appointed, any new directors are appointed, and the final dividend is declared. Shareholders may reduce the amount of the final dividend but cannot increase it, nor require one to be paid when the directors have decided otherwise.

annual information notice In relation to serial tax avoidance regulations, a notice from HMRC that the taxpayer must submit each year during a five-year warning period details of any defeated avoidance scheme used. There are penalties for using a further defeated scheme during the period, in addition to other penalties that may be imposed.

annual investment allowance (AIA) Capital allowance for plant and machinery which allows the whole cost to be tax-deductible up to a limit. That limit has varied considerably since AIA was introduced in April 2008 (CAA s38A). The rates are given in section 3 of this dictionary.

It may be offset against any plant except cars. Where there is a choice, it is usually better to use it against plant written down at 6% rather than at 18%.

The annual investment allowance may be claimed in addition to the writing down allowance for the same plant. So, if the annual investment allowance is £100,000 and the writing down allowance is 18%, and the taxpayer buys £300,000 of plant, the taxpayer may claim £100,000 plus 18% of the other £200,000, giving a total capital allowance of £136,000.

annual limit The amount of pension contributions for which a taxpayer may claim income tax relief in a year. The limit is the greater of £3,600 and 100% of earnings. Contributions are also subject to an annual limit and a lifetime limit. Details are given under Pensions in section 3 of this dictionary.

annual party Party or other social event provided by an employer to employees which others may attend. This is generally tax free up to a value of £150 per attendee per year (ITEPA s264). If the annual limit is breached, the event that breached the limit and any other events in the same tax year are not tax-free, For example, if an employer organises four social events where the cost is £60 per attendee, only the first two will be tax-free. The third breaches the limit, so its whole cost is a taxable benefit in kind, as is the fourth.

annual payment Payment of interest, royalties and similar. Such payments are usually allowable for income tax purposes. (ITA 2007 s448; CTA 2009 s1301).

annual percentage rate (APR) Rate that makes all forms of loan comparable. APR takes into account all costs, interest charges, arrangement fees and similar, and expresses them as a single percentage.

annual report Report produced annually by a company or other organisation. A company is generally required to produce, as appropriate, accounts (CA 2006 s394), group accounts (s 399), a strategic report (s414A), and a directors' report (s415). Quoted companies must also include a directors' remuneration report (s420). Where the accounts have been audited, the auditor's report should be included (s495). Other information may be added. This report must be sent to shareholders. Charities must produce an annual report under Charities Act 2011 from s162.

annual subscription An annual subscription to a professional body is tax-deductible if:

- it relates to the work done by the taxpayer, and
- the body is on HMRC's List 3, available from its website (ITEPA 2003 s344).

If the employer pays such subscription, that is not a taxable benefit in kind.

annual tax Description of income tax given in ITA 2007 s4. Unlike other taxes, income tax may only be charged for a year if a specific Act allows it. So, for example, FA 2020 s1 simply says "income tax is charged for the tax year 2020-21". Income tax has been "temporarily" collected every year since 1842. The only year the authority briefly lapsed was in 1909.

annual tax on enveloped dwellings (ATED) Tax on residential properties owned by companies, subject to some exceptions. It was introduced on 1 April 2013. It is a fixed annual charge on properties worth more than £500,000. (FA 2013 s94(1).

annual tax summary Statement that HMRC has issued to taxpayers since 2014 setting out how their tax and national insurance is being spent.

annual value A nominal figure used in the calculation of the income tax charge payable by an employee whose employer provides accommodation. It is the amount of rent that would be reasonably expected for such a property. (ITEPA 2003 s110).

annual voluntary settlement An informal arrangement that an employer could make with Inland Revenue (now HMRC) to pay tax on certain benefits provided to employees. These were all revoked from 6 April 1996 and replaced by PAYE settlement agreements.

annuitant Person who receives an annuity.

annuity Conversion of a lump sum into regular payments, such as when a pension pot provides a regular pension. HMRC defines an annuity as "a series of fixed payments paid over a fixed number of years or during the lifetime of an individual, or both. An annuity is often used to provide a pension. It can also be an annual payment provided for in a will". There are many types of annuity, and many options. A flat rate annuity pays the same amount each month (or other period) with no allowance for inflation to the annuitant. An indexed annuity pays an amount which increases in line with a published index, but starts at a lower figure than a flat rate annuity. The indexation is often capped, so it is, perhaps, the lower of retail prices index inflation and 5%. Another alternative is for the pension to be increased by a fixed percentage, often around 3%, each year. A pension is most often paid for the rest of the person's life. This means that those who die young subsidise those who die old. It is possible to have a pension guarantee. This guarantees that the pension will be paid for a minimum period, often five years, even if the annuitant dies before then. Another alternative is that a pension is taken for a fixed number of years. At the end of this period, a further annuity may be taken according to what the existing funds will provide. An annuity may provide for dependants, such as a spouse or young children. More details are given under pensions. Rates of annuity are given in section 3 of this dictionary.

annulment Formal declaration that something is invalid, particularly a marriage. In law, an annulled marriage is one that is deemed never to have happened. In tax, an annulment is treated in the same way as a divorce. In other words, a taxpayer is treated as having been married until the annulment *(Dodworth v Dale [1936] 20 TC 285).*

Annunciation Day Another name for Lady Day, 25 March.

anova Abbreviation of analysis of variance.

Anstalt Form of entity that has no shareholders or other members. It has no duty to earn a profit or provide funds to a beneficiary. It can be commercial or non-commercial. Ownership is by owning a document. They are most commonly found in Liechtenstein where they were introduced from 1926 to attract foreign capital. As non-residents may use them, they have been used for tax avoidance, such as a place to park assets off a balance sheet. Jurisdictions have usually treated a commercial Anstalt as a company, and a non-commercial Anstalt as a trust.

antenatal care Period of preparation for a woman about to give birth. An employee is entitled to paid leave from work to attend antenatal care if so advised by a doctor, midwife or health visitor (Employment Rights Act 1996 s55).

anti-avoidance Legislation or other provision designed to counter tax avoidance.

Anti-Avoidance Board Board comprising HMRC staff. According to HMRC Notice of 20 December 2013, "it approves and monitors strategy to handle tax avoidance issues, and makes strategic decisions about HMRC's anti-avoidance work".

anticipation of loss Principal of tax law that a loss may not be taken to the profit and loss account before it has been incurred. There are some limited exceptions when anticipation is permitted by tax law. The matter is discussed in HMRC's tax manual at BIM31100.

anticipation of profit Taking profit before it has been earned. Recognition of revenue, and thus of profit, has often proved problematic. It has been addressed to some extent by accounting standard IFRS 15 and supporting documentation. For tax, the general rule is that profit should not be anticipated. There is a limited exception for long-term contracts, particularly in construction where accounting standards can require an element of profit to be included in the accounts before completion. There was also an exception regarding discounted bills of exchange in the case *Wllingale v International Commercial Bank Ltd [1978] 52 TC 242*. HMRC regards this as exceptional and particular to the facts. The matter is discussed in HMRC Manual at BIM40090.

antidilution Provision designed to prevent dilution, that is a reduction in the relative worth of a shareholding when options are exercised. A definition is given in international accounting standard IAS 33 para 5.

anti-diversion Rules to prevent a controlled foreign company escaping a UK tax charge (FA 2011 s48 and Sch 13).

anti-dumping duty Customs duty that may be imposed on goods from another country that are otherwise sold at such a low price as to kill off the domestic market. The law is contained in EU Council Regulation 384/96 which has been transposed into UK law

anti-embarrassment clause Provision in a contract for the sale of a business which requires an additional payment if the business is sold for a much higher price soon after acquisition. Such a clause may be used when the price is proving difficult to agree or where the seller suspects that the buyer already has a sale in mind. The clause has many euphemisms. In the case *Starbev GP Ltd v Interbrew Central European Holdings BV [2016] EWCA Civ 449*, it was called a contingent value right agreement.

anti-forestalling Any temporary tax provision designed to stop an announced future tax change being used for avoidance.

Antigua and Barbuda Caribbean state. Its currency is the East Caribbean dollar. The UK has a double taxation treaty of 1947, amended in 1968.

antique An item that is at least 100 years old. There is a special VAT scheme for antiques which is broadly the same as for second-hand goods and works of art. VAT is charged on the difference between the purchase price and selling price. VAT is one sixth (20/120) of the difference. Details are given in VAT Notice 701/12. The import of an antique may be relieved from import duties under Customs and Excise Duties (General Reliefs) Act 1979 s9.

Anti Tax Avoidance Directive EU directive 2016/1164 effective from 1 January 2020 to deal with corporation tax avoidance. The UK has undertaken to follow the directive after Brexit.

APB pronouncements Pronouncements from the Auditing Practices Board on standards for auditing.

apparently insolvent In Scots law, description of a person in the sequestration procedure.

appeal commissioners Lay people, similar to magistrates, who heard tax appeals until they were replaced in 2009 by tax tribunals.

appearance fee Sum paid to a person, often a celebrity, for appearing at a function. It is normally taxed as income. VAT Notice 701/5 gives guidance on the treatment of such payments in relation to competitions run by clubs.

appellant Person who brings an appeal before a court or tribunal. The term is defined in SI 2009 No 273 rule 1(3).

appendix 6 arrangement Procedure that allows an employer to make an agreement with HMRC to pay a foreign worker's tax. Details are given in HMRC's tax manual at PAYE82003. There are also appendix 7A and 7B arrangements.

applicable law The national laws which apply to a particular transaction or arrangement. Under the International Rome Convention, the courts usually respect any agreement made by the parties. Failing this, the courts regard the country with the closest connection as determining applicable law.

appointed day Day on which a provision acquires legal effect. A taxing Act may have a provision with the effective day to be announced later, usually by statutory instrument.

appointee Person who has been appointed.

apportionment Any procedure whereby a sum is allocated according to different criteria. For VAT, an apportionment may be needed for a mixed supply, or where one supply has both business and personal use. An apportionment may be used by a retailer who would otherwise have difficulty in determining how much of his supplies are VAT zero-rated or exempt. For income tax and corporation tax, expenses are not usually apportioned as they must be "wholly" for the business to be deductible. The word is also used in allocating profits to particular tax years under ITTOIA 2005 from s203.

appraisal work Term used for exploratory work in the oil industry in relation to capital allowances (CAA 2001 s553(6)).

appreciation For bookkeeping, this is when an asset gains value. It is the opposite to depreciation.

apprentice System under which a (usually) young person worked beside an experienced worker to learn a trade or craft. This is an ancient arrangement dating back to the Statute of Artifices 1563. The system started to die out in the 1970s, but efforts are now being made to revive it. A definition is given in Apprenticeships, Skills, Children and Learning Act 2009 sA8(4). Only a scheme that meets this definition may legally be called an apprenticeship (Apprenticeships, Skills, Children and Learning Act 2009 sA11). From 6 April 2016, employer's national insurance is 0% for apprentices under 25 provided they do not earn more than the upper earnings limit (SSCBA 1992 s9B). From April 2017, apprentices are organised under Enterprise Act 2016 with payments of the apprenticeship levy. A further incentive under coronavirus provisions is that from 1 September 2020, the government pays £2,000 to an employer who engages an apprentice up to the age of 24, and £1,500 from the age of 25.

apprenticeship levy Charge imposed on employers in England from April 2017 to fund apprenticeships. It is charged at a rate of 0.5% on payrolls of more than £3 million. The charge is imposed under FA 2016 from s98. Devolved areas have similar schemes. The levy is collected through the PAYE system. The payments go into an account which the employer may use to fund apprenticeships from 1 May 2017. This fund may only be used for training, and not for expenditure such as travel, licences and workplace expenses.

apprentice upper secondary threshold Legally this is a separate threshold from the upper earnings limit in relation to employer's national insurance for apprentices. The two thresholds have been the same figure.

appropriate percentage The percentage taken from tables and used to calculate the taxable benefit in kind of a company car (ITEPA 200 (ITEPA 200 s121). These tables are given under Company Cars in section 3 of this dictionary.

appropriate personal pension scheme (APPS) Private pension scheme that, before April 2012, some of an employee's national insurance was paid into. The employee received less state pension as a consequence.

appropriation

(1) Where the property of one person passes to another.

(2) In bookkeeping, where the profits of an entity are apportioned between various provisions, reserves and retained profit.

In partnerships, dividing the profits between the partners.

approved mileage allowance payment System used before April 2002 to reimburse an employee who used his or her own car for business. This may now be reimbursed as a similar allowance. The rates are given in Travel expenses in section 3 of this dictionary.

approved profit-sharing Tax-advantaged scheme that ran from 1979 to 2002.

approximation Best guess. A tax return should never be delayed beyond its due date because a figure is not available. Instead an approximation should be used for missing figures. An approximation is usually acceptable if:

- it is sufficiently close to the likely answer as still to be a useful figure;
- the real answer is not readily available at that time;
- the number is identified as an approximation;
- an indication is given on how accurate the approximation is considered to be.

When the correct figure is known, the tax return should be adjusted.

arbitrage Process of buying something with a view to selling it. It is particularly used for securities and commodities where the activity exploits small differences in prices in different markets. Arbitrage has been used in tax avoidance. There are provisions in TIOPA 2010 from s231 that allow HMRC to require companies to calculate their tax less advantageously in avoidance schemes.

arbitrageur Someone who engages in arbitrage activities.

arbitration Means of settling a dispute by asking a third party, the arbitrator, to determine the matter. Law is given in Arbitration Act 1969. Arbitration differs from mediation in that the latter seeks to get the parties to resolve their difference. HMRC may offer arbitration. Otherwise arbitration has little role in tax as there are separate appeals procedures. Many tax treaties have arbitration clauses.

archive Repository of old records. The maintenance of a business archive is accepted as a business expense (HMRC Manual at BIM42501). There are various legal requirements to keep business records for at least six years. This includes not only accounts, but price lists, correspondence and other records. They may be kept in computer format or microfiche, provided the company keeps equipment to access them.

archive paper Specially produced durable paper. It has an official life of 250 years and an expected life of 500 years. Since 1956, it has been used as an alternative to vellum for recording private Acts of Parliament. On 2 November 2015, Parliament voted that, instead of making two copies of every Act of Parliament (including long Finance Acts) on vellum, one could be made on archive paper.

Arctic Systems Notorious case which was the converse of tax avoidance in that Inland Revenue (now HMRC) used tax law in a way not intended by Parliament to create a tax liability. A couple set up a husband and wife company where they each held one share. The husband did most of the work. They drew their income as dividends rather than salary. HMRC claimed that the husband had created a trust for his wife in a novel interpretation of law that had existed since 1922. The consequence would be that the wife's income was held to be that of her husband. The case was finally won in the House of Lords as *Jones v Garrett [2007]* which upheld the decision of the Court of Appeal though for different reasons. The widely differing decisions as this case slowly wended its way through the legal system was not tax litigation's finest hour. The government said this was income splitting and promised to legislate, though this has not happened.

Argentina South American country. Its currency is the peso. The UK has a double taxation convention of 1996.

ariary Currency of Madagascar.

arising basis When income tax is charged on foreign income regardless of whether it is remitted to the UK. It is paid by UK residents, and by non-residents who wish to avoid the non-dom charge.

Arithmetic Branch of mathematics that deals with calculations. Accounts and tax computations must be free of arithmetical errors as this could lead to penalties.

In practice, the widespread use of computers has eliminated most arithmetical errors.

arithmetic mean Average determined by adding up *n* numbers and dividing by n. More details are given under Mean.

Arithmos Forologikou Mitroou (FPA) Greek for value added tax. In Greek letters this is Φόρος Προστιθέμενης Αξίας (ΦΠΑ).

armchair principle Rule for interpreting wills. It imagines the testator sitting in an armchair, dictating its provisions. It allows wide discretion in what words mean and in identifying beneficiaries.

armed forces Royal Navy, Royal Marines, regular army, regular air force, and reserve or auxiliary force of any of these services which has been called out on service (CEMA 1979 s1(1)). UK forces are subject to UK tax and national insurance wherever they are engaged (SSCBA 1992 s116). The allowability of expenses are given in ITEPA 2003 from s296. UK armed forces based in Scotland receive an additional allowance to compensate for the higher rates of Scottish income tax. Accommodation for armed forces is specifically exempt from council tax.

Armed Forces Early Departure Scheme Scheme that makes payments to members of the armed forces who leave early, under the provisions of SI 2014 No 2328. Such payments are exempt from income tax under ITEPA 2003 s640.

Armenia Eastern republic. Its currency is the dram. The UK has a double taxation convention of 2011.

armour From 6 April 2011 this may be added to a company car when needed to provide personal security to an employee, without the cost being taxed as a benefit in kind (ITEPA 2003 s125A).

arm's length price Price that would be agreed for a transaction between two unconnected persons in full knowledge of the facts. In transfer pricing, the arm's length price may be substituted for the actual price.

Army Cadet Corps Officers, adult instructors and adult warrant officers of this corps are taxed as reservists (PAYE Regulations 2003 reg 122(2)).

Army Reserve Name given to the Territorial Army under Defence Reform Act 2014 s44(2). The previous Army Reserve is renamed Regular Reserve (s44(1)).

arrangement In tax planning, any pre-ordained transaction or series of transactions designed for tax avoidance. There are various laws to counter such arrangements. In company law, this means a provision of a company reorganisation (CA 2006 s895(2)). In pensions, this means a contractual or trust-based arrangement by or for a scheme member (FA 2004 s152(1)).

arrestable (1) Description of a criminal offence for which a person may legally be arrested, with or without a warrant. Offences that need no warrant include theft and fraud (Police and Criminal Evidence Act 1984 s24).

(2) Earnings that can be subject to arrestment in Scotland under Debtors (Scotland) Act 1987.

arrestment Legal provision in Scotland similar to attachment of earnings (Debtors (Scotland) Act 1987). It requires an employer to make deductions from a payslip to pay to a third party. There are three types of arrestment:

- earnings arrestment
- current maintenance arrestment
- conjoined arrestment.

For the first, the court states how much needs to be collected. This is determined by payroll using tables. For the second, the court provides a daily figure which payroll must multiply by the number of days in the pay period. The third is a combination of the other two. Each element is administered under its own rules. The employer may deduct a further £1 from wages to cover the expenses of operating the scheme.

The rates are given in section 3 of this dictionary.

arson Criminal offence of setting fire to premises (Criminal Justice Act 1972 s47).

art See works of art.

Article 50 Provision of the Lisbon Treaty that allows a member state to leave the EU on two years' notice. The UK invoked the article on 27 March 2017.

articled clerk Clerk engaged under written articles of clerkship with a view to joining a profession such as accountant or solicitor.

article 184 reliefs Various reliefs from customs duty, such as for the personal effects of someone moving to the UK.

articles of association Document that a company must file with Companies House (CA 2006 s18). It is in effect a contract between the shareholders or other members of a company. Its significance has reduced in recent years, as most operative clauses are more likely to be contained in a shareholders' agreement.

artificial Not what it seems. The term is widely used to refer to contrived tax avoidance schemes. In Scots law, this is defined in Revenue Scotland and Tax Powers Act 2014 s64.

artificial arrangement For VAT, this means an arrangement that has no commercial purpose other than avoiding tax. Artificial arrangements are a hallmark of a tax avoidance scheme.

artificial price Price that differs from normal for no obvious commercial reason. This is often for tax avoidance. HMRC has powers to negate such a price.

artificial tax avoidance Term used for tax avoidance that goes beyond tax planning.

artificial trade Activity that appears to be a trade but is not. Examples include hobby activities, capital gains and investments. This is discussed in HMRC Manual at BIM38400.

artistic work An artist, sculptor, composer or other creator of art may be eligible to average profits over three years for income tax. ITTOIA 2005 s221(3).

Aruba One of the islands in what was known as Netherlands Antilles.

asbestos Mineral that was widely used for fire protection before its harmful properties were recognised. It is generally banned from import under Asbestos

Regulations SI 1969 No 690. Otherwise it is subject to prior informed consent procedures as a condition of getting Customs clearance.

asbestos compensation settlement Settlement made before 24 March 2010 to someone who had an asbestos-related health condition (ITA 2007 s838A(2)). The settlement is not subject to income tax (ITA 2007 s838A(1)) or inheritance tax (IHTA 1984 s5894)).

Ascension Island UK overseas territory of an island in the South Atlantic Ocean. Its currency is the Saint Helena pound.

A-shares Shares that have different voting rights from ordinary shares. They can be used to allow a small number of shareholders to keep control, particularly in media companies. They can also be used in small companies to pay shareholders different amounts by declaring a different rate of dividend. Care is needed if the company has received funds under enterprise investment scheme as the existence of A-shares can have the effect of denying relief.

Asian Development Bank Bank founded in 1966 to help development in Asia. It is exempt from income tax under SI 1997 No 168. It is separate from the Asian Infrastructure Investment Bank, formed in 2014, and of which the UK is a member.

Asian option Option that has an exercise price calculated on the *average* price of the underlying security over the period.

ask/asked price Price at which a security or commodity is offered for sale, or at which a loan will be granted.

assault Criminal offence of putting someone in fear of harm. In addition to the general criminal law, there is a specific offence of assaulting an officer of HMRC under Commissioners for Revenue and Customs Act 2005 s32.

assessing procedure Means by which HMRC determines the amount of tax payable, as set out in TMA 1970 s30A.

assessment Determination of any tax due by HMRC, usually when the taxpayer has not submitted a return. The provisions are largely set out in TMA 1970 from s28A. An assessment must be made to the officer's best judgment. What this means was set out in the case *Johnson v Scott [1978] 52 TC 373.*

assessment phase First weeks of entitlement to employment and support allowance, which usually lasts for 13 weeks. During this phase, the claimant receives just the basic allowance. The assessment phase is followed by the main phase where either the support component or work-related activity component may be added.

asset Money, property, debts, prepayments and similar. In accounting standard FRS 102, it is defined as "a resource controlled by the entity as a result of past events and from which future economic benefits are expected to flow to the entity". An asset expected to last for more than one year is a fixed asset. Examples include land, buildings, furniture, vehicles, machinery and computers. Assets expected to be used in the next year are current assets. These include cash, debtors and prepayments. A business will often have a capitalisation threshold below which an asset is not regarded as a fixed asset. This is designed to exclude low value items like coffee mugs and staplers. It should be noted that for tax purposes, many fixed assets will be treated as plant. They must have an expected life of at last *two years,* and there is no capitalisation threshold.

asset backed Description of a business whose value is largely represented by assets.

asset cover Accounting ratio that provides a measure of a company's solvency. It is calculated as net assets divided by debt. The higher the figure, the more solvent is the company.

asset derived from another asset Asset which has been merged or divided, or which has otherwise changed its nature. The capital gains tax treatment is given in TCGA 1992 s43.

asset held on 6 April 1982 There are specific provisions for such an asset in relation to CGT. Broadly gains that accrued before this date are exempt from tax under TCGA 1992 Sch 3.

asset management plan Method of maintaining a large fixed asset by routine replacement of parts. This was often reflected by renewals accounting, permitted by former accounting standard FRS 15 and acceptable to HMRC. Current UK and international accounting standards do not allow for renewals accounting. Instead the replacement parts must be accounted for at their cost or fair value. Where an entity had used renewals accounting, it must establish the cost or fair value of assets and useful life and depreciate accordingly. The matter is discussed in HMRC Manual at BIM31065.

Asset Protection Scheme Scheme introduced on 26 February 2009 to protect banks in the banking crisis. Its provisions are contained in Financial Services Act 2010 s19.

asset rich, cash poor Description of a person or business with valuable assets but little assets.

Assets Recovery Agency Agency established under Proceeds of Crime Act 2002 s1(1).

asset transfer In relation to tax avoidance, this is a scheme where ownership of shares in a person with significant control is transferred. HMRC explains in Spotlight 50 why it believes the scheme does not work.

asset used by an employee Benefit in kind when an employer provides an asset for the personal use of an employee. Unless another specific provision applies, this triggers a taxable charge of 20% of the asset's value under ITEPA 2003 s205.

assignation In Scots law, the transfer of a right from one party to another.

assignment Transaction where the rights of ownership are transferred to another person. It is widely used for insurance policies. For VAT, the word means assignation in Scotland.

assistance dog Guide dog or other dog that assist a disabled person. The term is used in Private Hire Vehicles (Carriage of Guide Dogs etc) Act 2002 s1.

Assizes Former sessions of the criminal court, now replaced by the Crown Court under Courts Act 1971 s4. In Scotland, the term is sometimes used to mean a trial by jury.

associated benefit Benefit a donor receives from a charity when making a donation, such as a badge or a book. The donation may be regarded as charitable for tax purposes if, from April 2019, the value of the benefit does not exceed 25% up to £100, plus 5% above £100. These provisions are in ITA 2007 s418(2).

associate In accounting, an entity over which an investor has significant influence (FRS 102 glossary; IAS 28 para 3). Accounting standard once defined this as meaning ownership of between 20% and 50% of the entity. Less than 20% was an investment, more than 50% was a subsidiary. Modern standards are less prescriptive as it is recognised that a holding of less than 20% can represent significant influence. In relation to a close company, the term means an associated person such as a relative or trustee of a participator (ICTA 1988 s417(3)). For community investment tax relief, the term is defined in CTA 2010 s268. For members of a company, the term is defined in CA 2006 s1152. In relation to a takeover, a definition is given in CA 2006 s988.

associated benefit Benefit received by a charitable donor from the charity. The law is designed to achieve a balance between allowing a charity to provide a small gift as a thank you, such as a book, badge or free admission, while not allowing tax relief for charities to be used for tax avoidance (ITA 2007 s418(2); CTA 2010 ss195-198). The rates of associated benefit are given under Charities Associated Benefit in section 3 of this dictionary.

associated company Company where either one owns the other or both are owned by the same person (ICTA 1988 s416(1)). There are some corporation tax implications (e.g. CTA 2010 s25). Note that this differs from the meaning used in accounting standards. The term associated company was used in old accounting standard SSAP 14. It was replaced by participating interest in 1992 by FRS 2, which is now also repealed. Stamp duty is not payable on property transferred between associated companies (FA 1930 s42).

associated employment Where a person has two or more employments with the same employer or associated employers. They may each pay the employer without any need to aggregate income, provided the proper tax codes are used. The incomes must be aggregated where such an arrangement generates chargeable overseas earnings (ITEPA 2003 s24(4)(b)).

associated operations In inheritance tax, when two or more transactions are so closely related that they are treated as one. An example is when a person transfers assets to their spouse who transfers them to a discretionary trust.

associated properties Properties that are connected, such as an outbuilding to a main residence. The term is relevant for inheritance tax under IHTA 1984 s32A in relation to conditionally exempt transfers.

associated transaction For stamp duty, a transaction that is regarded as being part of a single transaction.

association Informal group of people who meet for a common purpose. In so far as they are subject to tax, they are liable to corporation tax as they come within the definition of a company as given in CTA 2010 s1121(1). Their VAT liability is explained in VAT leaflet 701/5.

Association for Payment Clearing Services (APACS) Association formed by clearing banks in 1985 to manage clearing systems for cheques, CHAPS and BACS.

Association of Accounting Technicians (AAT) Professional body for accounting technicians. It was formed in 1980 from a merger of technician bodies. It is sponsored by the main accounting bodies (except ACCA from 2017). Its qualifications provide exemption from some of those bodies' examinations. ACCA sponsors its own certified accounting technician (CAT) qualification.

Association of Chartered Certified Accountants (ACCA) Professional body formed in 1904 as an alternative to the Institutes of Chartered Accountants. It gained its royal charter in 1974. Members used the designatory letters ACCA for associates and FCCA for fellows.

Association of Corporate Treasurers (ACT) Professional body formed in 1979 for corporate treasurers.

Association of Financial Advisers Trade association for independent financial advisers.

Association of Taxation Technicians (ATT) Professional body for tax technicians. Its qualified members use the designatory letters ATT or ATT (Fellow).

assumed mean Method of calculating an arithmetic mean. This is useful when the numbers being averaged are particularly large or where the unit of measure is not decimal. Instead of adding up the numbers themselves, a number is chosen as one that appears to be close to the mean. The differences between the number and assumed mean are then averaged. For example, suppose we want the arithmetic mean of: 24678, 24645, 24662 and 24617. We can see that the arithmetic mean is probably around 24650. The differences are +28, -5, +12 and -31. These add up to -4, of which the average is -1, so we know that the arithmetic mean is 24649. Suppose we want the arithmetic mean of four people whose ages are 44 years 3 months; 44 years 6 months; 46 years 1 month and 47 years 2 months. We could adopt an assumed mean of 45 years. From this the differences are -9, -6, +13 and +26. These add up to +24, of which the average is +6, so we know that the arithmetic mean is 45 years 6 month. Note that this method gives the exact answer, and it does not matter what the assumed mean is.

assumed notional council tax The level of council tax for a band D property used in local government finance. Tax for properties in other bands are calculated as multiples of this figure. Details are given under Council Tax in section 3 of this dictionary.

assumption Something which is regarded as so obvious that it does not need proving. They are widely used in cost accounting and other areas of business management. In most cases, the assumptions should be stated.

assurance commissioner Senior officer of HMRC who, from 2012, is required to agree any arrangements between HMRC and a taxpayer that involve more than £100 million in tax.

astatki Fuel made from the residue of petroleum distillation.

asterisk The sign * used for many purposes. On adding machines, it denotes a total.

asymmetry condition Condition for anti-avoidance rule for group mismatch schemes (CTA 2010 s938C).

ATA carnet Admission Temporaire Carnet, a pack of documents that can be used temporarily to take goods out of the UK. They may be used in about 70 countries. The exporter is asked to call 0300 322 9434 to check that a Customs officer will be able to stamp the carnet at a port or airport. If the goods are to be taken to a country that does not recognise the carnet or if the exporter does not wish to pay the fee for a carnet, goods may be temporarily taken out using a duplicate list which is provided to Customs with a completed from C&E 1246. If neither a carnet or duplicate list procedure is followed, the goods must be declared and duty paid.

atebolrwydd Welsh for "liability".

attachment of earnings Legal notice that requires an employer to make deductions from an employee's pay and pass them to a third party, such as a court. Most of such notices are now made under Courts Act 2003. Orders can also be made for child maintenance and council tax. The employer may make a charge of £1 from wages for each attachment. The Scottish equivalent is called arrestment. Rates of attachment are given in section 3 of this dictionary.

attendance allowance Social security benefit payable to someone who looks after a disabled person who is over 65, who may be a husband, wife or other relation. It is not means-tested, does not depend on having paid national insurance contributions, and is tax-free. It is paid under SSCBA 1992 s64. The main points are:

- the benefit is not means-tested, so it may be claimed regardless of income or capital
- the benefit does not depend on anyone's national insurance record, nor on whether the carer has other work
- it may be paid regardless of whatever other benefits are being claimed
- the income is disregarded in calculating other benefits such as universal credit or tax credits
- the level of disability must be the same as for the middle or highest rates of disability living allowance
- the allowance is paid at either a higher or lower rate
- the lower rate is payable if the claimant meets one of the daytime or night time conditions. These are broadly that the claimant needs help either with bodily functions or to protect them from harm. It may also be claimed by someone having renal dialysis
- the higher rate is payable if the claimant meets one condition for both daytime and night time conditions, or is terminally ill

- unless the claimant is terminally ill, the claimant must have had the condition for at least six months before claiming.

The rates for this allowance are given under Social Security in section 3 of this dictionary.

attestation clause Statement in a will signed by two witnesses under Wills Act 1837 s8.

at the money Description of an option whose exercise price is equal to or very close to the current price of the underlying instrument.

attention For some disability benefits, a distinction is made between attention and supervision. Attention means that a person must do something for the disabled person, whereas supervision means that a person must be present while the disabled person does it.

attenuation charge Addition to spirits duty for a further period of distillation (ALDA 1979 s14).

attestation clause Clause that a will has been witnessed by two people (Wills Act 1837 s8). A will is not valid unless it has such a clause.

If the testator is in poor health or there may otherwise be questions about his or her capacity, it can be advisable for a doctor or medical professional to be a witness. Failing that, a doctor may be asked for a letter confirming that the testator had sufficient mental capacity. This is not a legal requirement but can help if the will is challenged. A witness simply witnesses the testator signature. They need not know that it is a will. The witnesses must have a clear line of sight to the testator, which can include looking through a window or a Perspex screen, witnessing from a corridor through an open door into a room, or outdoors from a short distance such as in a garden. The witnesses may not be beneficiaries of the will, but may otherwise be an executor. In the case *Payne v Payne [2018] EWCA Civ 985,* the Court of Appeal held that the witnesses need not sign with their usual signature. A will was held to be valid when a witness wrote his name in block capitals. As a coronavirus provision, a will be attested by video conference between 31 January 2020 and 31 January 2022, the government announced on 25 July 2020. The attestation clause must reflect this, such as by saying "I [name], wish to make a will of my own free will and sign it here before these witnesses, who are witnessing me doing this remotely". The witnesses must watch the will being signed live. They cannot witness from a video recording. If possible, the signing and witnessing should be recorded, though this is not a legal requirement. The witnesses must be able to see each other and the testator. The witnesses must be able to see the signature of the testator. If the witnesses do not already know the testator they should see evidence of identity, such as a driving licence or passport. The witnesses should still sign the document, ideally within 24 hours of the testator signing it. The testator should see the witnesses sign. A will cannot be witnessed using an electronic signature.

attested copy Document that is confirmed as being a true copy, and signed by an accountant, lawyer or person of similar standing.

attorney This word is often used in its original meaning as someone who acts for another, such as under a power of attorney. Such a person may sign a tax return on behalf of the taxpayer. The term also has the more specific meaning of a lawyer. It is the Scottish equivalent to barrister.

Attorney-General Principal law officer of the Crown and head of the Bar. The office dates from 1315. Traditionally, the office is held by an MP of the ruling party, but is not a Cabinet minister. There are many offences for which the Attorney-General is the only person who may bring charges or where his or her consent is needed. The Attorney-General is the person who brings proceedings against the state under Crown Proceedings Act 1947.

auction Sale made by potential buyers making competitive bids. A seller may set a reserve price, below which there is no sale. Otherwise, the sale is a legally binding contract between seller and highest bidder. The sale is made when the auctioneer bangs a gavel *(Bristol Car Auctions v Wright [1972]).* It is a criminal offence to rig an auction (Mock Auctions Act 1961) or to pay someone not to bid (Auctions (Bidding Agreements) Act 1927 s1). An auctioneer may be required to submit a record of transactions to HMRC under TMA 1970 s25(7).

auction credit Right to bid in an auction sold in units. This scheme is used by Madbid and others. The Court of Justice of the European Union held that, for VAT, these units were a supply of services and not goods *(Marcandi Ltd [2018] CJEU. Case 5-44.16).*

auctioneer's scheme VAT scheme that allows an auctioneer to pay VAT on the profit margin.

AUDDIS Automated direct debit instruction service. This is the direct debit scheme operated by BACS.

audit Any form of check on accounts. A company's accounts must be audited unless the company is small, a subsidiary, non-profit-making or dormant (CA 2006 s475). A small company may still be required to be audited if its articles of association require it, or the members vote for it. A company may choose to be audited, even if this is not required. This may happen if the company believes it will become large, or if it wants to be taken over. A company that is not audited must include in its balance sheet a statement to that effect, citing the grounds for exception.

Auditing is a passive activity; it comes from the Latin for "he hears". The auditor generally reproduces a statement from an auditing standard saying that, in his or her opinion, the accounts are true and fair, and comply with the Companies Act 2006. It does not guarantee that the accounts are correct, nor that the company is free of fraud.

The auditors are, in theory at least, appointed by the shareholders to check on the directors. In practice, the auditors usually report their main concerns to the directors in a letter of weakness.

Auditing is governed by auditing standards produced by the Financial Reporting Council. There are also International Standards on Auditing. An audit for a local authority has a different purpose, such as checking value for money. Audits may be for any other financial purpose as agreed between the client and auditor. At the time of writing, there are plans to reform the auditing profession, particularly with regard to separating auditing functions from other functions in accounting firms.

Audit Commission Body established under Audit Commission Act 1998 and previous legislation to audit local authorities from 1 April 1983 to 31 March 2016. It was replaced from 1 April 2016 by Public Sector Audit Appointments Ltd under Local Audit and Accountability Act 2014.

Auditing Practices Board Body which issues UK auditing standards, formed in 1991.

Auditing, Reporting and Governance Authority (ARGA) Body that the government announced on 11 March 2019 will replace the Financial Reporting Council with tougher powers.

Audit Inspection Unit Part of the Financial Reporting Council that monitors the published accounts of listed companies.

audit liability limitation agreement (ALLA) Agreement between a company and its auditors that restricts the latter's liability under a negligence claim. An ALLA became legal from 6 April 2008 under CA 2006 ss532-538. An ALLA is only effective to the extent that it is "fair and reasonable". The Financial Reporting Council has produced guidance.

auditor Accountant who reviews the accounts. Auditors have a measure of protection from HMRC in that it cannot require the auditor to reveal audit information (FA 2008 Sch 36 para 24; in Scotland Revenue Scotland and Tax Powers Act 2014 s139). HMRC has set out its policy in SP 5/90 of 11 April 1990.

auditor of court Under Scots law, a person who examines legal accounts.

Auditor's Code Statement issued by the Auditing Practices Board as Appendix 2 to its statement on Scope and Authority of Pronouncements. The Code provides a framework of fundamental principles. It requires the auditor to show accountability, integrity, objectivity and independence, competence, rigour, judgment, clear complete and effective communication, association and providing value.

audit report Statement from an auditor giving his or her opinion about accounts. Such a report is either qualified or unqualified. A qualified report indicates that there is a matter of concern. In extreme cases, an auditor may refuse to give an opinion.

Audit Scotland Body in Scotland that checks the spending of public money.

audit trail In accounting, a system of folios and other references that allow a transaction to be easily traced through the accounts system to and from the final accounts.

augend Number to which another number is added.

augmented profits For corporation tax, the taxable profits plus franked investment income (CA 2010 s32). For oil companies, the definition is in CTA 2010 s279G.

au pair Person who comes from abroad to perform domestic duties in return for accommodation and a small payment. The immigration category for au pairs was closed in November 2008.

Australia Southern country. Its currency is the Australian dollar. The UK has a double taxation convention of 2003.

Australian dollar Currency of Australia.

Austria European country. It joined the EU in 1995. Its currency from 2002 is the euro; previously it was the schilling. The UK has a double taxation convention of 1969, amended by two protocols of 1977 and 1993, and a further protocol of 2009.

Austrian Reconciliation Fund Fund that pays compensation to those engaged in forced law during the second world war. On 16 December 2015, the UK government said such payments are exempt from inheritance tax.

author An artist, sculptor, composer or other creator of art may average profits over three years under certain conditions (Income Tax (Trading And Other Income) Act 2005 s221). For VAT, royalties to authors may be paid by the publisher using self-billing.

authorised capital The maximum amount of capital that may be issued by a company. This must be stated in its memorandum of association. The amount of issued share capital is an amount up to this maximum. It is, for example, common for a small company to have authorised capital of perhaps £100 but issued share capital of £2.

authorised contractual scheme Scheme for reorganising a collective investment (Financial Services and Markets Act 2000 s237(3). Such a scheme is exempt from stamp duty reserve tax (FA 1999 Sch 13 para 25A as amended by SI 2013 No 1401).

authorised disclosure Disclosure of crime that is properly made to a police officer, tax official or similar person under Proceeds of Crime Act 2002 s338.

authorised economic operator Customs scheme whereby someone who meets certain standards may benefit from faster clearance times (Taxation (Cross-border Trade) Act 2018 s22).

authorised investment funds (AIFs) Financial products including unit trusts, OEICs and others within the scope of SI 2006 No 964. They are regulated by Financial Conduct Authority under Financial Services and Markets Act 2000.

authorised minimum Minimum amount of allotted share capital required for a public company (CA 2006 s763(1)). The minimum is £50,000, though most public companies have a much higher figure.

AutoclenzLeading case from Supreme Court on whether someone is employed or self-employed. The citation is *Autoclenz Ltd v Belcher [2011] UKSC 41*. The case concerned people who washed cars. A significant element was that the court considered the relative bargaining power of the parties.

auto-enrolment Requirement that an employer must automatically enrol certain employees into a workplace pension, unless the employee opts out. Provisions are contained in Pensions Act 2008 from s2. The provisions were phased in from 2012 (SI 2010 No 4).

autogratuity Gratuity or tip that is automatically charged to customers, particularly on cruises.

automated teller machine (ATM) Cash dispenser provided at banks and other locations. They allow bank customers to check account balances, and draw fund using a card and four-digit PIN number.

automatically unfair dismissal Dismissal for a reason which the law considers is unfair. These reasons are:

- belonging or not belonging to a trade union
- claiming the national minimum wage
- childbirth or pregnancy
- asserting a statutory right
- whistle-blowing
- seeking to be represented when disciplined
- acting as a safety representative or employee representative of a pension fund.

There is no qualifying period of employment for these reasons.

automatic overseas tests Series of tests to determine statutory residence where the automatic UK tests are not conclusive. If these tests are also inconclusive, the sufficient ties tests are considered. These are set out under Statutory residence test in section 3 of this dictionary.

automatic UK tests Series of tests that are considered first under the statutory residence test. One of the tests is that anyone who was in the UK for at least 183 days in the tax year is UK resident. If these tests are inconclusive, the automatic overseas tests are considered. These are set out under Statutory residence test in section 3 of this dictionary.

automatic write-off Provision of HMRC's computer system that automatically writes off small amounts of tax.

automation Process of replacing human workers with machines, sometimes called robots. For management accounting, the process typically results in much higher upfront costs and much lower marginal costs.

autrefois acquit Defence to a criminal charge that a person has already been tried and acquitted. It protects a person from the double jeopardy of being repeatedly tried for the same offence. From 2005, there is a limited exception in Criminal Justice Act 2003 which allows for a second trial if there is new and compelling evidence for a serious offence.

autrefois convict Defence to a criminal charge that a person has already been tried and convicted for the offence.

autumn statement Statement given by the Chancellor of the Exchequer in autumn when the Budget has been given in spring.

available for work Requirement for claimants of jobseeker's allowance or universal credit. It means that the claimant is able and willing immediately to take up paid work, more paid work, or better paid work (WRA 2012 s18(2)).

available total profits Amount of profit which may be used in group relief, as explained in CTA 2010 s140.

average Number used to represent a series of numbers. There are four measures of average:

- arithmetic mean: *n* numbers are added and divided by *n*. This is the most common method.
- geometric mean: *n* numbers are multiplied and the *nth* root is taken. This is used in calculating the FT-SE 100 index and the consumer prices index
- median: the midpoint in a range of numbers. This is commonly used for wages as it avoids distortion by a few people with very high incomes
- mode: the commonest number in a series.

average capital balance Term used in relation to community investment tax relief (ITA 2007 s362(2); CTA 2010 s246(6)).

average rate of income tax Average rate of income tax paid as a percentage of a person's income. For example, someone earning £100,000 may, in 2020/21, pay £27,496 income tax. The average rate is 27.496%.

average turnover amount Term defined for enterprise investment scheme under ITA 2007 s175A(7) and for venture capital trusts under ITA 2007 s280C(8).

average weekly earnings Figure used to determine an entitlement. For example, statutory maternity pay depends on average earnings over eight weeks.

averaging In insurance, a provision to deal with under-insurance. For example, someone with four shops worth £500,000 may consider that the chances of more than one burning down is unlikely and so insure them all for £500,000. The insurance policy will have a clause reducing the claim to one quarter of the sum assured. For marine insurance, it can mean a provision in Marine Insurance Act 1906 where the owner must share some of the loss.

averaging profits Provisions whereby a profit received in one tax year may be spread over more than one year. Such schemes exist for income tax for farmers and creators of artistic works.

averment Legal argument on a specific point. In tax, a person may admit receiving income but aver that it is not taxable.

aviation gasoline A light oil produced as aircraft fuel, as defined for hydrocarbon oil duty in HODA s1(3D).

avizandum In Scots law, a term meaning "to be considered" when judgment is to be given later.

avo One hundredth of a pataca, currency of Macao.

avoidance In tax, a legal method of not paying tax as against illegal evasion. There are many provisions to counter avoidance. There are many provisions in tax law to counter artificial avoidance where the law is used in a way not intended.

avoidance arrangements Arrangements to avoid tax. The term is given a specific meaning for manufactured payments in ITA 2007 s572A(1) and for apprenticeship levy in FA 2016 s103.

Avon Cosmetics Leading European VAT case. It held that goods sold by an agent are treated as sold by the company. In this case, the agents were often self-employed women who held parties to demonstrate the company's cosmetic products. The company unsuccessfully claimed these sales were not made by them but by the agents who were below the VAT threshold. The case is *Avon Cosmetics Ltd v HMRC [2017] CJEU Case 305/16. The Times 11 January 2018.*

avulsion Process of cutting off land, such as when a river changes course. The ownership rights of land are usually unaffected.

award Something given in recognition of an achievement. Some awards by employers to employees may be exempt from income tax.

award date The date on which deferred remuneration has been awarded (ITEPA 2003 s554H(1)(a).

award for bravery Award such as Victoria Cross that carry a right to a pension or annuity that is tax free under ITEPA 2003 s638.

Azerbaijan Eastern republic. Its currency is the new manat. The UK has a double taxation agreement of 1994.

baby bond Bond offered by a friendly society where up to £25 a month may be invested for up to ten years.

baby credit Additional amount of child tax credit that could be claimed for the first year of a child's life.

backdated interest Interest charged for a past period. These were common in "buy now pay later" deals where there was an interest-free period of perhaps six months. If that period expired without payment, interest was charged, often at a high rate, from the beginning of the period. From 12 November 2019, this practice has largely been outlawed.

back duty Any arrears of tax.

back-ended Description of a tax relief given at a later point, such as for personal equity plans.

background plant Another name for features integral to a building.

back pay Salary or wages paid in arrears such as a retrospective pay rise. These are taxed when received, and not when earned. Back pay may require statutory maternity pay to be recalculated.

back-to-back credit Letter of credit used in international trade when a trader buys goods from one country for immediate resale to another. Under back-to-back credit, one letter of credit is raised on the security of another.

back-to-back plan Inheritance tax avoidance scheme that involves a life assurance policy and an annuity on the same life. The idea is to move funds out of the taxable estate.

back to work bonus Bonus introduced in 1996 and revised in 2004 payable to social security claimants who start employment (SSCBA 1992 s36). The bonus is exempt from tax (ITEPA 2003 s677). This has now been replaced by allowing some benefits to continue after starting work. The term was also used for a coronavirus scheme announced in 2020 for workers who had been furloughed. This scheme did not proceed as the furlough scheme was extended.

bacon-slicing Advocacy method of reducing an argument into a series of narrow propositions each of which is then considered separately.

bad character Evidence or disposition about an accused person in relation to criminal charges (Criminal Justice Act 2003 s98).

bad debt Sum owed which reasonably is not expected to be paid. A bad debt is said to be written off which means it is shown as an expense in the profit and loss account. This does not extinguish the debt nor prevent action to recover it. If a bad debt is paid, it is taken to profit in the period when paid or when it is realised that payment will be made. Provided there are reasonable grounds for such expectation, bad debts may be deducted from profits subject to income tax (ITTOIA s35) or corporation tax (CTA 2009 s55). For VAT, bad debt relief must be specifically claimed (VATA 1994 s36 and VAT Regulations regs 165-172J) unless the business uses cash accounting. Guidance is given in VAT Notice 700/18.

badge For VAT, this is not regarded as an item of clothing and so is not zero-rated when provided for children. The case *BG Supplies (Birmingham) Ltd [1993] VTD 11663* concerned badges, sashes and woggles for Brownies and Guides, which were not zero-rated. Children's clothing with badges already attached may be zero-rated.

bad leaver Employee who was dismissed. The term is used in relation to disguised remuneration.

badges of trade Six principles established in 1954 by a Royal Commission to determine whether an activity is treated as a trade.

- the subject matter of the realisation
- the length of the period of ownership
- the frequency or number of similar transactions by the same person
- supplementary work on or in connection with the property realised
- the circumstances that were responsible for the realisation
- motive.

bagel For VAT, a toasted bagel was held to be a zero-rated supply of food and not a standard-rated supply of hot takeaway food in the case *Great American Bagel Factory Ltd [2000] VTD 17018*. The heating was held to be to create a crunchy interior and to promote freshness rather than to allow it to be consumed above room temperature.

baggage Luggage and other items carried by a traveller. Customs requirements for baggage are given in Customs notice 6.

baguette For VAT, a toasted baguette was held to be a zero-rated supply of food and not a standard-rated supply of hot takeaway food in the case *Tuscan Food Ltd [2003].* The toasting was to release the flavour; the baguette could be eaten hot or cold.

Bahamanian dollar Currency of the Bahamas.

Bahamas Atlantic state. Its currency is the Bahamanian dollar. The UK has no tax treaty.

Bahrain Kingdom in Persian Gulf. Its currency is the Bahraini dinar. The UK has a double taxation agreement signed in 2010.

baht Currency of Thailand.

bailee Person who is entrusted with possession of goods.

bailiff Office of the court who is entrusted with functions such as serving a writ or seizing goods.

bailii Website that provides free summaries of court decisions from High Court and higher courts, including tax cases. The website is www.baillii.org. It reports decisions from the Court of Appeal, House of Lords and Supreme Court from 2001, and from the High Court from 2002.

baillie Scottish civic officer.

baisa One hundredth of a rial Omani, currency of Oman.

bait For VAT, fish bait was held to be standard-rated and not zero-rated when used to catch edible fish, in the case *Fluff Ltd (t/a Mag-It) [2001] STC 674.* Although the fish ate the bait, its purpose was not to feed the fish but to catch them.

bait and switch Unethical practice of advertising items that are either not for sale, or for sale in very small quantities, as a means of attracting customers to higher priced items.

baked potato For VAT, the sale of a baked potato with a filling is a single standard-rated supply of hot takeaway food. An unsuccessful attempt to zero-rate a cold filling was made in the case *M Rourke (t/a The Market Pantry) [1999] VTD 16671.*

bakery products Bread, biscuits, cakes and other products usually made in a bakery. Most such items, other than biscuits, are VAT zero-rated as food. More details are given in VAT Notice 701/14.

baksheesh Persian word for a gratuity. It is a practice in Near Eastern countries of making a payment to facilitate everyday business. To the extent that it is a payment in appreciation, it is a tax-deductible business expense. To the extent that it has the nature of a bribe, it is disallowed as a criminal payment.

balance Amount of money after all transactions have been completed. The word has some specific meanings in particular tax provisions.

balance of probabilities Basis of civil court cases that the person bringing the case must show that one outcome is more likely than another. This is the standard for tax cases, other than the few conducted under criminal law.

balance sheet Summary of an entity's financial position at a moment in time. A balance sheet is a "financial photograph" for a specific moment, usually the end of the last day of the accounting period, and does not relate to a period of time like the profit and loss account. It shows the assets and liabilities of an entity, and how this is represented by its capital. Thus there are two columns of figures which have the same total.

Traditionally one side lists assets as fixed assets and current assets. The latter are listed in order of liquidity. From this are subtracted current liabilities and long-term liabilities. The other column shows capital in the form of share capital (or equivalent), other capital and retained profit.

A balance sheet must be signed by a director of a company, or equivalent officer, to indicate that they are final. The balance sheet sent to HMRC does not have to be signed.

balance sheet date Date on which a balance sheet is prepared.

balance sheet value In relation to allowance buying, this is the balance sheet value of relevant plant and machinery (CAA 2001 s212L).

balancing allowance Capital allowance equal to the excess of written down value over disposal proceeds (CAA 2001 s65).

balancing charge Negative equivalent to the balancing allowance. It arises when disposal proceeds exceed the asset's written down value. Such an amount is subject to income tax or corporation tax.

balancing event Event that triggers a balancing allowance or a balancing charge. For qualifying buildings, these are defined in CAA 2001 s360N.

balancing payment This usually refers to the balance of tax owed by IR 35 taxpayers due by 31 January following the end of the tax year to which the payment relates (HMRC Notice of 10 January 2014).

ballet This may qualify for theatrical productions tax relief (CTA 2009 s1217FA(1)).

balloon In banking and finance, a large payment to clear a loan rather than by regular payments.

balloon mortgage Mortgage in which the last payment is much larger than others. Typically such a mortgage is for a period of up to seven years.

ball park General imprecise assessment of the size or amount of something. The term comes from guessing how many people are likely to attend a ball game.

ballpoint Writing implement containing a special gelatinous ink applied by a small ball at the end. The first patent for such a pen was issued in 1888, but the modern form was invented by László Biró (1899-1985) in 1938. Note that the word "Biro" is a trade name. Ballpoint pens were originally banned for use in banking and accounting as they were considered to be prone to smudging.

Baltic Exchange Place in London where, traditionally, shippers and ship brokers plied for cargo.

BAME Black, Asian and minority ethnic. The term is often used in relation to discrimination against such people.

banc Judge's bench.

Banca Rìoghail na h-Alba Gaelic name for Royal Bank of Scotland, now called NatWest Group.

Band Aid Musical ensemble of leading pop musicians who recorded the song *Do They Know It's Christmas?*, written by Bob Geldoff and Midge Ure, in 1984. It was re-recorded in 1989, 2004 and 2014. The proceeds were applied to famine relief. The Treasury agreed to make a donation equal to the VAT collected to the charity. This practice has been followed for some other charity records.

Band D equivalent The weighted value of dwellings subject to council tax, where band D has a weight of 1. So if an area has 1000 dwellings in band D and 900 dwellings in band B (where the weight is 7/9), the band D equivalent is 1700 dwellings.

band earnings Amount of salary earned between lower earnings limit and either upper accruals point or upper earnings limit for national insurance. This is the basis for determining entitlement to state second pension or SERPS.

Bangladesh Eastern country. It was created as East Pakistan when India was partitioned in 1947, and became independent in 1971. It is one of the poorest countries in the world. Its currency is the taka, comprising 100 paisa. The UK has a double taxation treaty of 1979.

bani One hundredth of a new leu, currency of Romania.

bank Body that holds money for clients, lends money, and engages in other financial activities. A tax definition appears in Income and Corporation Taxes Act 1988 s840A. There are several specific tax provisions for banks, including the bank levy, and paying corporation tax at an extra 8 percentage points from 1 January 2016 (CTA 2010 s269D).

bank certificate Document from a bank confirming the balances held by a customer. Such certificates are often requested during an audit. If the bank is advised to confirm figures, the certificate is sometimes called a bank confirmation.

bank charges Charges made by a bank for providing its services to customers. If an employer pays an employee's bank charges, that is a taxable benefit in kind as explained in HMRC Manual at EIM01010.

Bank Charter Act Law passed in 1844 after a series of banking crises, and which is still law. It gives greater power to the Bank of England in issuing notes and regulating banks.

Bankers' Automated Clearing Service (BACS) Company that oversees the system of direct debits, standing orders, salaries and computer-generated payments for most banks.

banker's payroll tax Tax charged in the one year of 2010 on banks in respect of staff bonuses above £25,000 (FA 2010 Sch 1).

bank giro Method used by clearing banks to transfer funds between them. It allows anyone to pay money into any account if they know the six-digit sort code and eight-digit account number. HMRC accepts that giro payments are electronic payments. HMRC asks that taxpayers use the payments slips that they provide.

bank holiday Day on which a bank is allowed to close. There are eight bank holidays in England and Wales, eight different bank holidays in Scotland, and ten in Northern Ireland. Additional holidays may be declared by the monarch. The law is Financial Dealings Act 1971. An employee has no right not to work on a bank holiday, unless this is given in law or contract of employment. Dates are given in section 3 of this dictionary.

banking company This term is variously but similarly defined for bank levy (CTA 2010 s269B), corporation tax (CTA 2010 s269B), and company law (CA 2006 s1164(2).

banking surcharge The additional 8 percentage points of corporation tax for which banks are liable from 2016 (CTA 2010 s269D).

bank levy Tax on banks according to figures on their balance sheet, in accordance with FA 2011 Sch 19.

bank note Legal tender issued by the Bank of England under Bank Charter Act 1844. They are currently issued for £5, £10, £20 and £50. Bank notes were originally receipts for gold held by trusted traders who owned a safe. They were originally regarded as promissory notes. Their status as currency largely derives from court cases such as *Miller v Race [1791]* and *Suffell v Bank of England [1882].* The 1844 Act allowed banks already issuing notes to continue to do so. Currently three Scottish banks and four Irish banks are still allowed to issue notes under arrangements with the Bank of England. These are not legal tender anywhere in the UK, but as the Bank accepts them, they may be accepted as such.

Bank of England Central bank of the UK. It was founded in 1694. Its duties include issuing bank notes, setting interest rates, and other administrative and economic functions (Interpretation Act 1978 Sch 1). The Bank has responsibility for setting interest rates from 1870 and sole responsibility from 1997, except in a national emergency. The Bank also issues the only bank notes that are legal tender in the UK.

Bank of England rate The rate announced by the monetary policy committee of the Bank of England or, in a national emergency, by the Treasury (Inheritance and Trustees' Powers Act 2014 s1(4)).

Bank of Scotland Scottish bank formed on 17 July 1695. It is the oldest bank in the UK and the only surviving company from the pre-1707 Scottish Parliament. It had a monopoly in Scotland until the rival Royal Bank of Scotland was formed in 1724. It was the first bank to use a computer, in 1959. It still issues its own bank notes. The Bank merged with Halifax in 2001 to become HBOS.

bank rate Rate of interest periodically set by the Bank of England. It was known as the base rate before 1972. This rate is used to determine the interest rate on late paid tax. Bank rates are given in section 3 of this dictionary.

bank reconciliation Process of checking accounting records against a bank statement. The steps usually involve:

- adjusting accounting records in respect of items not otherwise recorded, such as dishonoured cheques or bank charges
- adjusting the balance shown on the statement by adding items such as cheques paid in but not shown on the statement and subtracting payments made but not shown on the statement.

It should be remembered that it is the bank statement that is reconciled to the accounting records.

bankruptcy Legal status of an insolvent individual. It should be noted that this is a legal status and not a financial one. Bankruptcy aims to strike a balance between being fair to creditors owed money and giving the individual, known as a bankrupt, a second chance. An individual should consider alternatives before accepting bankruptcy. These include:

- a debt management plan
- an administration order for debts under £5,000
- individual voluntary agreement (IVA),
- from 2021, a moratorium under Breathing Space
- a debt relief order
- in Scotland, a debt arrangement scheme.

Bankruptcy proceedings may be started by:

- the individual in respect of himself or herself
- creditor or creditors owed £5,000 or more, or
- an intellectual property if the debtor has broken the terms of an individual voluntary agreement.

If the debts are less than £20,000 a debt relief order is probably the better option. The fee for bankruptcy is £680.

A person who chooses to make himself or herself bankrupt can now start the process online. If someone else starts it, the person gets a copy of the petition.

The bankruptcy is started by the official receiver, an employee of the Insolvency Service answerable to the court. The official receiver acts as trustee until an insolvency practitioner is appointed. This is an accountant or solicitor who specialises in insolvency. The official receiver or insolvency practitioner is the trustee of the bankrupt.

The bankrupt must co-operate and be honest with the trustee. Any non-co-operation is likely to lead to a longer bankruptcy.

The trustee takes control of the bankrupt's assets and income, but cannot take essentials for life (such as clothing and furniture) or tools of trade. Even those items may be seized and replaced with less expensive alternatives. Other assets are sold.

A person's home may be sold, with the balance after repaying any mortgage passing to the trustee. If the property is jointly owned, the bankrupt's share is passed to the trustee. This is noted at the Land Registry under a Form J restriction. A trustee is prevented from selling a home for a year without the bankrupt's agreement if he or she has a partner or children living with them. There is a limit of three years for selling a home.

A vehicle will be sold unless needed for work. The bankrupt remains responsible for the MOT and road tax.

These are first used to pay the trustees' fees, which often run into tens of thousands of pounds. The Official Receiver fees are given in section 3 of this dictionary. After that, funds are paid according to Insolvency rankings, given in section 3 of this dictionary.

Any business run by a bankrupt is closed.

An undischarged bankrupt is subject to these restrictions:

- cannot borrow more than £500 without declaring they are bankrupt
- cannot act as a director or company promoter without the court's permission
- works as an insolvency practitioner.

These restrictions end when the bankruptcy ends unless they are extended for dishonesty or non-co-operation. Non-compliance with a restriction is a criminal offence.

The person's bankruptcy is recorded on their credit file for six years. Income is assigned to the trustee after allowing sufficient for living expenses. State benefits are not usually assigned. This assignment lasts for three years which can mean they continue after the bankruptcy has ended.

A bankruptcy is discharged (i.e. ended) after 12 months unless the bankrupt has failed to co-operate or has committed an offence. The bankrupt is given a certificate of discharge and is free to engage in normal domestic and commercial activities, albeit with an impaired credit record.

All debts outstanding at discharge are extinguished, except for:

- debts obtained by fraud
- money owed under family proceedings
- damages for personal injuries
- student loans
- court fines
- debts created after the bankruptcy order.

These debts remain owed after discharge.

There are some procedural differences for bankruptcy in Scotland. A bankrupt is not able to claim income tax personal allowance for income taken during a bankruptcy *(CIR v Fleming [1928] CS. 14 TC 78).*

bank statement Document provided by a bank showing transactions on the account for a period, usually a month. The statements should be kept and reconciled to the accounting records.

banned and restricted goods Goods that either may not be imported at all or need a licence to be imported.

Barbados Country of the West Indies. Its currency is the Barbados dollar from 1935. The UK has a double tax treaty of 2012. The Barbados stock exchange was recognised for tax purposes from 2 April 2017.

Barbados dollar Currency of Barbados.

Barclays Bank Major bank formed in 1690.

Bar Council Senate of the Inns of Court which regulates conduct of barristers.

bare trust The simplest form of trust where a person simply asks someone else to look after their property. For tax purposes, a bare trust is disregarded and the beneficiary is taxed as if the trust did not exist. Capital gains tax provisions are given in TCGA 1992 s60. Provisions in relation to a partnership are given in CTA 2009 s1258A.

barge Large flat-bottomed boat designed to carry loads by river or canal. VAT leaflet 701/20 notes that it is unlikely to qualify for zero-rating as a houseboat.

Barnett consequential Treasury mechanism under which the UK government provides funds to devolved assemblies for national provisions. It is named after Treasury secretary Joel Barnett MP (1933-2014).

barrel Unit of measure of oil equal to 42 US gallons. This equates to 35 UK gallons or about 159 litres.

barrier option In finance, an option whose value depends on the underlying security reaching a particular price or value.

barrister Lawyer who represents clients in court. A statutory definition is given in Legal Services Act 2007 s207(1). They are traditionally instructed by a solicitor though from 2004 there are public access barristers who may be instructed directly. There are barristers who specialise in tax law. Before 2013/14, barristers in independent practice could account for their fee income for the first seven years on the basis of either cash received or fee income billed (ITTOIA 2005 s160). Subject to a transitional provision, this basis is no longer available, as a barrister may use the cash basis for small businesses. VAT guidance for barristers is given in VAT Notice 700/44.

barter Transaction involving exchange of goods rather than money. For income tax and corporation tax, this may be regarded as trading by both parties. For VAT, each party is regarded as making a supply.

base cost In capital gains tax, the cost of an asset to the user. This includes the costs of the asset plus such charges as delivery and installation.

base erosion Loss of a nation's tax revenue because businesses or profits are moved to another country (OECD Action Plan of 19 July 2013). The OECD is co-ordinating action to deal with Base Erosion and Profit Shifting (BEPS).

Basel Series of documents produced by the Basel Committee on Banking Supervision on standard of bank regulation. It is named after a city in Switzerland. Basel I of 1988 required banks to have capital of at least 8% of risk-weighted assets. This was followed by Basel II in 2004, and Basel III in the wake of the banking crisis. Each of these sought to strengthen bank supervision.

base pay Rate of pay for a job before any additions for overtime or unsocial hours. The national minimum wage relates to base pay.

base rate Rate set by the Bank of England as the minimum rate at which banks lend money to each other. These rates are given in section 3 of this dictionary.

base stock Method of valuing stock where a number of units are valued at a fixed amount and a different method is used for additional units. This was held not to be an acceptable method in the case *Patrick v Broadstone Mills Ltd [1953] 35 TC 44* and other cases. The matter is discussed in HMRC Manual at BIM33125.

basic allowance For employment and support allowance, a set rate paid for the assessment phase, usually of 13 weeks. This is followed by the main phase when additional components may also be paid.

basic case Tax tribunal case that can be disposed of after a hearing with minimal exchange of documents before the hearing (SI 2009 No 273 rule 23(2)(b)).

basic earnings assessment Assessment that an employer may have to make regarding an employee's likely earnings for a future tax year to determine the maximum value of tax-free childcare vouchers that may be provided. Provided the assessment was reasonable when made, no additional tax is payable if the assessment proves to be wrong.

basic financial instrument Accounting term defined in FRS 102 from section 11.8 as including cash, debt instruments, loan instruments and preference shares.

basic pay Amount a person receives for his or her normal work. It may be supplemented by bonuses, commission, overtime etc. For termination payments, this is defined in ITEPA 2003 s452D(7). National minimum wage relates to basic pay.

basic payment scheme Rural grant to help farmers with at least 5 hectares of land and 5 entitlements. It was introduced in 2015 as a successor to the single payment scheme.

basic rate A rate of tax, particularly income tax, that applies to the main slice of income. In England and Wales and Northern Ireland, this is followed by the higher rate and additional rate. Historically there have also been lower starter rates for a slice of income before the basic rate applies. The basic rate of income tax has been 20% since 2008. In Scotland, the basic rate is replaced by three rates from 2018: starter rate, basic rate and intermediate rate.

basic rate code For PAYE, the code BR which requires all earnings to be taxed at the basic rate (PAYE Regulations 2003 ref 7(3)(a)).

basic rate taxpayer Taxpayer who pays income tax at the basic rate only. Some provisions apply only to such taxpayers such as transferable marriage allowance and childcare vouchers.

basic tax point Date when a supply is made for VAT purposes. There are some circumstances when a different tax point may be used. The law is VATA 1994 s6.

basis period Period of time for which a trader's income tax is determined. A trader may choose a date to which his or her accounts are made up. The basis period is usually the year to that date, with special provisions for the first and last years. The main law is ITTOIA 2005 from s196. Where an early period is taxed twice, that creates overlap relief which may be claimed in the last year of the business.

battery Device for providing electricity. For VAT, this is standard-rated. It does not come within the scope of reduced-rated domestic energy (VAT Notice 701/19).

bear Someone who expects the financial markets to fall.

bearer security Security where ownership is determined by who owns the document. These are outlawed in the UK from 26 May 2015. Previously, they were subject to a higher rate of stamp duty.

Beatles clause Tax provision introduced in 1969 to stop someone selling their income from personal activities to avoid tax. These provisions are now in Income Tax Act 2007 from section 773.

bed and breakfast Capital gains tax avoidance scheme that involves selling an asset at the end of the tax year and buying it the next day, so as to utilise the annual exemption. The law was changed in 1998 to counter this, though similar avoidance schemes have subsequently appeared. The tax provisions are TCGA 1992 from s105. They are also addressed in IR interpretations 218 and 224.

bedroom tax Popular name for a reduction in social security payments if a claimant has unused bedrooms. It was introduced in 2013. It is not a tax.

beer Brewed drink using hops. It is subject to beer duty (ALDA 1979 s1(3)) and VAT. Beer brewed for private consumption is exempt (ALDA 1979 s41).

beer duty Alcoholic liquor duty charged on beer. This is defined as a drink with an alcoholic strength of at least 1.2%, which is made by brewing and which is not cider or perry. Details are given in Customs leaflet 226.

beer regulations Regulations relating to beer duty. They are SI 1993 No 1228 as amended by SI 1995 No 3059.

behavioural effect Consequence of a tax change. It is one of two effects of a tax change. The first is the mechanistic effect, which is simply mathematical. It assumes that if a tax rate is doubled, the yield is doubled. The behavioural effect considers how the mechanistic effect is changed by behaviour, such as people spending less.

Belarus Eastern republic. Its currency is the Belarusian rouble of 100 kopeks. The UK has a double taxation convention signed in 1985 with the USSR which still applies for Belarus. The country is subject to UK sanctions.

Belarusian rouble Currency of Belarus.

Belasting over de Toegevoegde Waarde (BTW) Dutch: value added tax. The term may be seen on invoices from Belgium or Netherlands.

Belgium European country, founder member of the EU. Its currency from 2002 is the euro, prior to which it was the Belgian franc from 1945. The UK has a double taxation protocol of 2012. Some provisions remain from a double taxation convention of 1987.

Belize South American state. Its currency is the Belize dollar. The UK has a double taxation agreement of 1947, amended by supplementary agreements of 1968 and 1973.

bell ringing For VAT, this is exempt when provided as part of a funeral service. Further details are given in VAT Notice 701/32.

Bellwin scheme Arrangement whereby central government reimburses local authorities for costs incurred in dealing with emergencies. It is named after Lord Bellwin who introduced it in 1983.

belong A condition for a capital allowance is that the asset must belong to the taxpayer (CAA 2001 ss167-170). This has been amended so that a lessee or tenant may claim capital allowance for an asset they provide.

belongings For Customs purposes, goods kept for personal use, such as clothing, camera, bicycle, furniture and pets (Customs notice 3).

below the line Items in a profit and loss account that appear below "net profit after tax". These items indicate how the profit is applied rather than how it is earned.

benchmark scale rate Amount which HMRC allows to be paid to an employee when on business overseas under ITEPA 2003 from s289A with effect from April 2016. From April 2019, an employers need only show that the employee was on business; there is no requirement to show expenditure.

benefaction Altruistic motive, such as donating to charity. An element of benefaction does not necessarily disqualify expenditure as business expenditure, provided there is a trade connection. The matter is discussed in HMRC's Tax Manual at BIM37400.

beneficial loan Sum lent by an employer to an employee either interest free or at a low rate of interest. The amount by which any interest is less than the official rate is a taxable benefit in kind. There is no tax for loans of less than £10,000 (£5,000 before April 2014). The rates of interest are given under Beneficial Loans in section 3 of this dictionary.

beneficiary Person who receives property from a trust, will or intestacy. For social security, it means a person entitled to a benefit (SSCBA 1992 s122(1)).

beneficiary's own resources Term used in connection with an anti-avoidance law for inheritance tax. Suppose a man in his will leaves £100,000 to his wife and £200,000 to his brother. The brother's inheritance is taxable. Under the avoidance scheme, the wife would pay the brother £200,000 from her own resources and claim £300,000 from the estate which would avoid inheritance tax using spousal exemption. From 26 July 1989, this is prevented by IHTA 1984 s29A.

benefit associated with gifts Benefit received by a company or individual from a charity in respect of a donation. If it exceeds a limit, the benefit is subject to tax under CGTA 2009 s108 or ITA 2007 s418. The limits are given in section 3 of this dictionary.

benefit cap The maximum amount of some social security benefits that may be received by a claimant in a year (WRA 2012 from s96). The cap was introduced in April 2013 at £500 a week (£26,000 a year) for a couple and £350 a week (£18,200 a year) for a single claimant. In 2017, the cap was reduced to £23,000 in London, or £20,000 elsewhere for a claimant couple, and £15,400 in London or £13,400 elsewhere for a single claimant. The benefit cap applies to universal credit, income support, jobseeker's allowance, housing benefit, child benefit, carer's allowance and industrial injuries benefit. It does not apply for disability benefits, and is disapplied in some circumstances.

benefit cost In relation to income tax on trivial benefits provided in employment, this means the cost of providing the benefit. If the benefit is provided to more than one employee, it is the total cost divided by the number of employees (ITEPA 2003 s323A(5)).

benefit in kind Benefit provided to an employee in a form other than cash. Common examples are a company car, mobile phone, and private medical insurance. Such a benefit is generally taxable on the employee under ITEPA 2003 ss62-226E on the value. Some benefits are exempt from tax, such as a mobile phone. Other benefits are valued according to a formula, such as company cars. Otherwise a benefit is taxed on the marginal cost of providing it. Benefits are reported annually on form P11D, except that from 2016 some benefits may be taxed at source under a procedure known as payrolling. Provision of a benefit in kind is not subject to employees' national insurance, but the employer may be liable to pay class 1A national insurance.

benefit offence Criminal offence in relation to social security (SSCBA 1992 s121DA(5)). In relation to tax credits, the term is defined in Social Security Fraud Act 2001 s36A(10).

benefits code Provisions of ITEPA 2003 Chapters 3 to 7, and 10 and 11. They explain how benefits in kind are taxed.

benefit year Year in which a contributory social security benefit is paid in respect of the contribution year or years (SSCBA 1992 s21(6)). It runs from the first Sunday in January to the day before the first Sunday in the following year.

Benelux Belgium, Netherlands and Luxembourg, particularly the Customs union they formed from 1944 until it was subsumed into the EU.

benign test One of three tests a person must pass not to be regarded as a promoter of a tax avoidance scheme. The test is that the designer did not contribute to the avoidance elements.

Benjamin order Order made by a court for distribution of assets when it is not known whether a beneficiary is alive. The name comes from the case *re Benjamin [1902]*.

bequeath Leave money or assets in a will. Strictly speaking, land is not bequeathed but devised.

bereaved minor Person under the age of 18, at least one of whose parents or step-parents has died. There is a specific trust that may be set up for a bereaved minor that avoids inheritance tax (IHTA 1984 s71C).

bereaved parent Parent who has lost a child under the age of 18 or a baby after 24 weeks of pregnancy. If employed, the parent may, from 6 April 2020, be entitled to statutory parental bereavement leave and statutory parental bereavement pay (SSCBA 1992 s171ZZ6(3)).

bereavement allowance Social security benefit that was paid for 52 weeks to a young widow, widower or surviving civil partner. From 6 April 2017, it is replaced by bereavement support payment.

bereavement payment Lump sum social security benefit paid in respect of death. From 6 April 2017, it is replaced by bereavement support payment.

bereavement support payment Social security payment to a claimant whose spouse or partner died on or after 6 April 2017 (Pensions Act 2014 s30). It comprises a lump sum followed by monthly payments up to 18 months. It is not taxable (ITEPA 2003 s671(1) Table B).

Bermuda Group of Caribbean islands that are a British Overseas Territory. The currency is the Bermudan dollar. The UK has no double taxation treaty, but has a tax information exchange agreement of 2017.

Bermudan dollar Currency of Bermuda.

bespoke retail scheme VAT scheme under which a large business may agree with HMRC how to account for VAT on retail sales.

best judgment Term used to describe the requirement exercised by a tax officer when making an assessment. The law is TMA 1970 s28C(1A) and elsewhere; for VAT it is VATA 1994 s73(1). The scope of what constitutes best judgment has been much litigated. The case *Shah Aziz [2018] TC 6405* set out these principles:

- HMRC must have some basis for making their assessment
- the duty to disclose tax due rests with the taxpayer. HMRC cannot be expected to do the taxpayer's work
- a tribunal should not set aside an assessment just because it disagrees as to how HMRC should exercise its judgment
- a tribunal needs "a much stronger finding" to set aside an assessment, such as evidence of dishonesty, vindictiveness or capriciousness, or by being guesswork, or wholly unreasonable
- where an assessment is based on sampling, such as test purchases, there must be sufficient samples
- the fact that cash has been removed from a till does not necessarily mean that the owner removed it.

best start grant Social security benefit payable from 2019 only in Scotland to a mother in respect of childbirth and who is receiving a means-tested benefit or who is under 18. The grant is not taxable. It comprises three single payments for each child:

- pregnancy and baby payment: £600
- early learning payment: £250
- school age payment: £250.

The law is Social Security (Scotland) Act 2018.

Best Start Foods Benefit that replaces Healthy Start in Scotland from 12 August 2019. It provides a tax-free weekly benefit of £4.25 until the child is born, £8.50 a week in respect of each child up to 1, and £4.25 for a child of 2. A mother may claim if she is either under 18 or receiving a means-tested benefit. The benefit is provided by a card that can be used to buy certain basic foods.

bet A wager on the outcome of an uncertain event. The Australian case of *Evans v FCT [1989]* held that placing bets is not a trade unless it is organised as one. The matter is discussed in HMRC Manual at BIM22016. A bet can be tax-deductible if it has the nature of hedging or insurance. For example, a business is vulnerable to changes in exchange rates. It could place a bet on future exchange rates so that if they moved against the business, it would "win" a sum to compensate.

beta phase Stage of a website which is made available to the public but has not been fully tested.

betterment levy Charge made on the improvement of land between 1967 and 1970 (Land Commission Act 1967). Its provisions for capital gains tax are in TCGA 1992 s38 and Sch 11. The matter is discussed in HMRC Manual at CG72651.

betting The placing of a bet (see separate entry). Betting is subject to Betting and Gaming Duties. The VAT position is explained in VAT Notice 701/29.

betting duties Excise duties imposed on various forms of gambling under Betting and Gaming Duties Act 1981. For Northern Ireland, they are given in FA 1986 s6.

betting odds How the winnings are calculated for betting. Odds are usually quoted as two numbers such as 4-1 (four to one). This means that if a punter stakes £1 and wins, he or she receives £4 plus a refund of their £1 stake. Odds of 7-2 mean that a stake of £2 can win £7 plus a refund of the £2 stake. An "odds on" bet means that the win is less than the stake. So a 1-4 bet means that a £4 stake will win £1 plus a refund of the £4 stake. These odds apply on a bet "to win". A bet may be placed "each way". This is in effect two bets equally split. So a £10 bet is £5 wagered to win, and £5 for the horse (or whatever) to come second or lower. Typically this pays out for second place for 5 to 7 runners at a quarter of the winning odds; and second or third for 8 or more runners at one fifth of the winning odds.

beverage For VAT, this comprises milk, tea, coffee, cocoa and malted drinks. These are zero-rated under VATA 1994 Sch 8 Group 1 Excepted Item 3. Other manufactured drinks are standard-rated. This is explained in VAT Notice 701/14.

Beveridge Report Plan presented by economist Sir William Beveridge in 1942 which led to all-party consensus on welfare reform, introduced in 1948.

beyond reasonable doubt Standard of proof required to prove a criminal charge, as against balance of probabilities for a civil charge.

Bhutan Eastern country. Its currency is the ngultrum of 100 chetrum, though Indian currency is also used. The UK has no tax treaty.

bias Improper influence. The Statement of Principles for accounting sets out four principles. One of these is reliability which requires an absence of bias.

bicarbonate of soda Common name for sodium bicarbonate. For VAT, it is zero-rated as food when sold for culinary use (*Phoenix Foods Ltd [2018] TC 6296).* It is standard-rated when sold as a cleaning agent.

bicycle There are many tax provisions for bicycles. As a bicycle is not mechanically propelled, it is not subject to vehicle excise duty. An employer may provide a bicycle and related equipment tax free to an employee to cycle to work (ITEPA

2003 s244). The employee may then buy this bicycle after a year or more for a small percentage of its cost. These are listed in section 3 of this dictionary. In July 2020, the government announced the introduction of £50 cycling vouchers to pay for a bicycle to be repaired or refurbished. Bicycle facilities, such as showers, are not a taxable benefit in kind. An employee may be reimbursed at up to 20p a mile for cycling in the course of work.

bicycle helmet This is zero-rated for VAT if it complies with the European Community directive on personal protective equipment. The European standard is EN 1078:1997. The British Standard is BS EN 1078:1997. Further details are given in VAT Notice 701/23.

Big Bang Name given to two radical changes to how the London Stock Exchange worked on 27 October 1986 and 20 October 1997.

Big Four The four largest accounting firms from 2001, namely Deloitte, EY, KPMG and PWC. [The term has other meanings.]

Big Mac index Simple index produced by *The Economist* magazine on how much a Big Mac burger costs round the world. It was first published in 1986 as a joke, but has been produced each year since as an indication of how currencies and countries are performing.

big six Game that is specifically listed in Betting and Gaming Duties Act 1981 s13(3) as subject to duty.

bid price Price at which a market maker or other person offers shares or other securities or other items for sale.

bi-fuel For capital allowances, description of a car that can run on road fuel gas and either petrol or diesel (CAA 2001 s268C(4)).

bill (1) Invoice or other document seeking payment. The term originally meant a document served under seal.
(2) Draft of an Act of Parliament.

billet Temporary accommodation to members of the armed forces or people displaced by war. Tax relief was granted to workers for the additional cost of travel to work by billeted employees.

billing authority Local authority that collects council tax for itself and, sometimes, for other bodies who serve a precept on the billing authority.

billion Now taken to mean a thousand million, or 1 followed by 9 zeros. Historically in UK it meant a million times a million, or 1 followed by 12 zeros. The UK Treasury adopted the change in 1975.

bill of advocation In Scots law, a document that requires a higher court to review a decision by a lower court.

bill of discharge For Customs duties from 1 May 2016, a document that a trader must submit for the discharge of inward processing or end use relief.

bill of exchange Written and signed instruction from one person to another requiring them to pay a fixed sum to a third person or bearer from funds held for such purpose (Bills of Exchange Act 1882 s3). A cheque is a form of a bill of exchange.

bill of lading List of goods carried by a ship on a single journey. It is widely used for Customs purposes.

Bill of Rights In the UK, an Act of Parliament of 1689 which asserts the rights of Parliament against the monarch. This includes the right to levy taxation.

bill of sale Document that a seller gives to the buyer to show that a sale has occurred. Bills of Sale Act 1878 extends the scope to other documents. A bill of sale attracts stamp duty (Stamp Act 1891 s41).

bill of suspension In Scots law, an application to have a warrant set aside.

BillPay Method of making Internet payments using a debit card or credit card. It may be used to make payments to HMRC.

bimetallic Made from two metals, particularly the £2 coin and (from 2017) the £1 coin.

binder Folder designed to hold documents. For VAT, this is generally standard-rated. If it is sold with documents already in, it may be zero-rated as a book.

binding information Statement from HMRC on the rate of customs duty. Provided the request was made honestly and properly, HMRC is bound by its answer for four years.

binding precedent Decision of a court which is binding in subsequent cases in lower courts where the facts are the same.

bingo duty Excise duty charged on operators of bingo games. The main law is Betting and Gaming Duties Act 1981 from s17, Finance Act 2003 s9 and Bingo Regulations SI 1988 No 333, all of which have been amended.

bioblend Mixture of biodiesel and heavy oil (HODA 1979 s6AB(2)).

biodiesel Equivalent to diesel produced from either biomass or waste cooking oil (HODA 1979 s2AA).

bioethanol Liquid fuel produced from either biomass or waste cooking oil (HODA 1979 s21B(1)). Further details are given in Customs notice 179E.

bioethanol blend Mixture of bioethanol and hydrocarbon oil, typically in the ratio 5:95 (HODA 1979 s6AE(2)(b)).

biofuel Oil made from plants that may be used as a road fuel. There are some special provisions for hydrocarbon oil duty (SI 1996 No 2536 reg 2).

biological asset Living animal or plant (FRS 102 glossary; IAS 41 para 5).

biometric data Personal data derived from the physical or behavioural characteristics of the person, including fingerprints, retinal images and voiceprints (Data Protection Act 2018 s205(1)).

biometric immigration document Document used by someone entering the UK which includes biometric data (UK Borders Act 2007 s5).

bird For VAT, birds are standard-rated unless sold as food, such as certain species of fowl. Bird food is standard-rated unless sold for poultry or game birds (VAT Notice 701/15).

bird of prey This is likely to be an endangered species protected by the Convention on International Trade in Endangered Species.

birth Date on which a person is born. A birth must be registered within 42 days in England, though an extension is allowed when prevented by coronavirus. Under the Tell Us Once scheme, a birth only needs to be registered once for all official purposes. For statutory maternity pay, the expected birth is when a doctor or midwife believes the baby is due. This determines when the maternity pay period may start. The actual birth triggers a maternity pay period that has not already started.

biscuit Biscuits are generally zero-rated for VAT under VATA 1994 Sch 8 Group 1 Excepted Item 2. Exceptions are chocolate biscuits, and biscuits for cats or dogs, which are standard-rated (VAT Notice 701/14). Guidance on what constitutes a biscuit was given in *Marcantonia Food Ltd [1997] VTD 15486.*

biscuit tin For VAT, this is almost always regarded as part of the supply of biscuits, even in the case *United Biscuits [1992] STC 325* where the tin represented 55% of the cost of the product. It was held not to be relevant that the customer would probably keep the tin. This decision was followed in the case *Paterson Arran Ltd [1996] VTD 15041* where a ceramic jar was held to be held incidental to the biscuits, even though it represented 70% of the cost.

bit In computing, a binary digit, i.e. either 1 or 0. Eight bits comprises a byte.

bitcoin Cryptocurrency which exists solely as computer code. It was created in 2009. In UK, cryptocurrency is regarded as an asset, not as currency. Its place is that of its owner. Conversion of cryptocurrency to sterling or another currency is a disposal for capital gains tax purposes.

black box In tax, an arrangement that is legal but has no commercial function other than tax avoidance. The term was used by the CBI in 2012 but appears not to have gained currency.

black economy Part of a nation's economy that is unofficial. It is usually illegal as it is not declared for tax, and often ignores other laws such as national minimum wage and safety regulations.

blackjack Card game that is specifically listed as dutiable under Betting and Gaming Duties Act 1981 s13(3).

blackmail Criminal offence of making a demand for money with menaces (Theft Act 1968 s21). From 30 November 1993, payment of blackmail is a criminal payment and therefore not tax-deductible (CTA 2009 s1304). The matter is discussed in HMRC Manual at BIM43160.

Black-Scholes Mathematical method of valuing an financial option.

black web Secret part of the worldwide web for illegal activities.

Black Wednesday When the UK was forced out of the European exchange rate mechanism on 16 September 1992. Although intended as a temporary suspension, the UK never rejoined.

blasting powder Substance included in the list of explosives in Explosives Act 1875 s3(1) for which there are special Customs provisions.

blended rate Single rate of tax used when different rates would otherwise apply. The term is used for VAT on vouchers.

blending Process of mixing two or more alcoholic drinks. There are special provisions for alcoholic liquor duty in ALDA 1979 s54(3A).

bless Act of declaring that an asset is for religious use or wishing well for users of the asset. A blessed asset is included as a fixed account in the entity's accounts where as a consecrated asset usually is not.

blight In relation to property, loss of value because of a proposed development nearby.

blind person's allowance Addition to personal allowance for income tax that may be claimed under ITA 2007 s38 by a person who is registered as blind.

blind trust Trust administered so that the settlor does not know what assets it holds. Such a trust is often established when the settlor is elected to public or political office as a means of avoiding any risk or perception of bias.

blockchain In computing, the software and protocols for a distributed ledger system, as originally developed for bitcoin and other cryptocurrencies. A purchase by one business is a sale by another. Blockchain would adjust both sets of records, turning double entry bookkeeping into quadruple entry bookkeeping. At the present, blockchain is not used in accounting, but papers and research are in hand to develop its potential and to consider the implications.

blocked earnings Earnings from overseas that are blocked by a foreign government. An election may be made not to be taxed on such earnings under ITEPA 2003 s36.

block transfer In pensions, the single transfer of all sums and rights from one scheme to another.

blood relation Person to whom one is related through birth rather than marriage.

blue badge Indicator that a person is registered as disabled. The badge attaches to the person, not to a vehicle. A vehicle carrying a blue badge holder has particular rights, particularly with regard to parking. A vehicle adapted or a blue badge holder may attract VAT relief. From 30 August 2019, the scope is extended to less visible disabilities such as dementia, anxiety and reduced mobility.

blue chip Term denoting a large, safe and respected company for investment.

blue pencil Legal provision that a legal document remains valid if unenforceable clauses may be deleted and the remaining document still makes sense.

board and lodging Provision of meals and sleeping accommodation. If provided by an employer, it may be taxable under ITEPA 2003 s97. The matter is discussed in HMRC's Tax Manual at EIM01020.

boarding powers Rights of Customs officer to board an aeroplane or vessel in connection with their duties (CEMA 1979 s27).

Board of HMRC Body that controls HM Revenue and Customs. It was formed in 2005 when Inland Revenue merged with HM Customs and Excise.

bodily functions Washing, dressing and using a toilet. A person who has difficulties in performing such functions may qualify for disability benefits.

body corporate Any formally constituted single group of people with a common purpose (Companies Act 2006 s1173(1)). Such a body is generally subject to corporation tax, except for partnerships and trusts.

body of persons Term used in TMA 1970 s71 to mean two or more people who are taxed on a similar basis to a single person. The term is defined for this purpose in TMA 1970 s118(1).

Bolam standard Legal principle that a professional person is not negligent if he or she acts in accordance with a practice considered proper by their professional body. The name comes from the case *Bolam v Friern [1957] 2 All ER 118.* That case concerned a doctor, but the standard can be applied to other professions.

bold type Type that is a little wider than ordinary type and therefore is blacker and stands out. This sometimes means that characters are made wider by 1/144 of an inch. Bold type is widely used in published accounts to highlight the current year's figures.

bolivar soberano Currency of Venezuela which replaced the bolivar fuerto on 19 August 2018.

Bolivia South American state. its currency from 2018 is the bolivar soberano. The UK has a double taxation convention of 1994.

bolsa Spanish, Portuguese or South American stock exchange.

bona vacantia Goods that have no owner. They belong to the Crown (except in Lancaster and Cornwall, where, for historic reasons, they pass to the respective Duchies). Assets of a company that has been struck off are bona vacantia (Companies Act 2006 s1012), though, since 2011, the Treasury solicitor has said he will not seek to recover assets so distributed. The tax rules for distributions on winding up were amended at the same time.

bond A security that has the nature of a debt. The government issues bonds commonly known as gilts.

bonded warehouse Place where dutiable goods may be stored until the duties are paid (CEMA 1979 s46 and Excise Warehousing (Etc) Regulations 1988 No 809).

Bond House decision Ruling of the Court of Justice of the European Union in 2006 that an innocent party to the missing trade fraud may claim back VAT input tax.

bonus shares Shares issued at no charge to the shareholder in the ratio of existing holdings (ITA 2007 s151(1); CTA 2010 s90(1)).

Different provisions apply for a bonus issue of *redeemable* shares, or any other security where the distribution confers a future benefit rather than a current benefit. When the shares are redeemed, the redemption is treated as a distribution. Any tax paid by the shareholder on the initial distribution may be set against tax due on the later distribution (ITTOIA 2005 ss399-401; CTA 2010 ss1100-1101).

bookkeeping Process of recording financial transactions and keeping records from which financial accounts are prepared.

bookmaker levy Levy on British bookmakers on the amount by which horseracing bets exceed £500,000 a year. It is charged under Betting Gaming and Lotteries Act 1963 from s27A and other provisions.

bond of caution In Scots law, where the court appoints a person to find caution (a sum of money or a bond) as security for a person. In this context, the word "caution" rhymes with "station".

bondwashing The practice of selling a bond cum div so that the dividend is treated as part of the capital gain and not as income. Tax law changed on 27 February 1986 to make this ineffective.

bond yield Income from a bond expressed as a percentage of the price paid for the bond.

bonus Additional sum, particularly paid to staff or under an investment or insurance policy. A bonus to staff is taxed as gross income. It is disregarded for the purposes of national minimum wage.

bonus issue Issue of shares to shareholders for no payment in proportion to their existing holding. This is usually done either because the company wishes to capitalise its profit, or as a means of splitting shares into smaller amounts.

bonus share Share issued otherwise than for payment (ITA 2007 s151(1); CTA 2010 s90(1)). For community investment tax relief, the term has the same definition in CTA 2010 s209(1).

book Bound collection of pages. For VAT, text books are zero-rated, while exercise books are standard-rated. Further details are given in VAT Notice 701/10. In the case *Colour Offset Ltd [1995] STC 85*, a book was defined as "an object whose necessary minimum characteristics are that it has a significant number of leaves, now usually of paper, held together front and back by covers usually more substantial than the leaves". The word "book" has been applied to bound copies of an insurance policy, and to a bound volume of photographs taken by a customer.

booking fee Fee paid in advance to secure a service, such as to reserve a hotel room. For VAT, this is a service in its own right. If the customer does not take up the hotel room or theatre seat, they have still been provided with the service of having had one reserved. Accordingly, the booking fee is (usually) standard-rated and is not treated as a cancellation fee (VAT Notice 700).

bookkeeping Keeping financial records.

booklet For VAT, a booklet is generally zero-rated under VATA 1994 Sch 8 Group 3. Guidance is given in VAT Notice 701/10. In the case *Paragon Customer Communications Ltd [2018] TC 6415*, the tribunal held that a booklet that included stapled in pages about an insurance policy comprised a booklet, contrary to the VAT Notice.

bookmaker levy Levy on bookmakers charged by Horserace Betting Levy Board under Betting Gaming and Lotteries Act 1963 from s27A.

book of prime entry Book or equivalent computer file where similar transactions are recorded. Examples include cash books, invoices issued, invoices received, petty cash book and wages book. The totals for each day or other period are entered into the nominal ledger as part of the bookkeeping procedure.

books Accounting records.

book value Value of an asset as shown in an entity's financial records. For fixed assets this is usually cost minus depreciation. For animals compulsorily slaughtered, the term is given a specific meaning in ITTOIA 2005 s225ZC.

Boolean logic Means of expressing functions mathematically. For example, entering "pigs +legs" in a search engine will find all references that contain both words. Entering "pigs -guinea" will find references to pigs but exclude guinea pigs.

booster cushion/seat For a child safety seat in a car, a cushion is reduced rated for VAT under VATA 1994 Sch 7A Group 5 para 5. A seat is reduced rated under para 4. Further details are given in VAT Notice 701/23.

bootleg Illegal manufacture of an item, such as one that is banned or subject to duty. The term originally referred to liquor in flat and slightly rounded bottles that could be kept in the leg of a boot. The term also applies to copies of literary, artistic and musical works produced without payment of copyright royalties. The UK privy council held that bootlegging is a taxable trade even though it is illegal *(Canadian Minister of Finance v Smith [1927] PC. ATC 621).*

boot money Informal fee paid to a footballer who makes a guest appearance for a club. The fee was traditionally left in his boots. The fee is taxed as income.

boot strap Cash offer for a controlling interest in a company, followed by a lower offer for the remaining shares.

booty Strictly, this term applies to military arms and stores captured on land. Colloquially, the term is applied to anything acquired other than as expected.

borrowing cost Cost of borrowing funds (FRS 102 glossary; IAS 23 para 5).

Börse German stock exchange.

Bosnia Usual name for the East European country of Bosnia and Herzegovina which became independent from Yugoslavia on 1 March 1992. Its currency is the convertible mark of 100 fenings. The UK double taxation convention of 1981 with Yugoslavia remains in effect.

Botswana African republic. Its currency is the pula of 100 thebe. The UK has a double taxation convention of 2005.

bottle conditioned beer Beer that continues fermenting after bottling. Alcoholic liquor duty is calculated on the expected strength at consumption (Customs notice 226).

bottle deposit scheme Old scheme where a customer was refunded a small amount for returning a bottle which had contained drink. In 21st century, consideration is given to a scheme to recycle plastic bottles, such as by a reverse vending machine.

bottled water For VAT, this is standard-rated. It does not come within the scope of either zero-rated food nor zero-rated water.

bottle sizes The imperial measure for wine, comprising 26⅔ ounces. Multiples of this size are given these names:

magnum	=	2 bottles
Jeroboam	=	4 bottles
Rehoboam	=	6 bottles
Methuselah	=	8 bottles
Salmanazar	=	12 bottles
Balthazar	=	16 bottles
Nebuchadnezzar	=	20 bottles

A nip is a quarter of a bottle, and a baby is half a bottle.

bottom line In accounts, the figure of net profit after tax in the profit and loss account.

bottom fishing Investment strategy of buying shares that have become cheap in the hope that some will recover.

bottomry Secured loan to repair a ship.

bought ledger Financial record of purchases made by an organisation. It is also called a purchase ledger.

boule Gambling game similar to roulette but with just 18 pockets and using a small rubber ball. The game is specifically listed in Betting and Gaming Duties Act 1981 s13(3) as subject to betting duties.

Bounce Back loan Government funded loan scheme to help small and medium-sized businesses during the coronavirus outbreak. It was launched on 27 April 2020. It allows a business to borrow between £2,000 and £50,000 for six years. The loan may not exceed 25% of its annual turnover. The government pays the interest and charges for the first 12 months, and provides a 100% guarantee to the lender. From the second year, interest is pegged at 2.5%. Some businesses are ineligible. A legal definition is given in Consumer Credit Act 1974 s140A(7) as inserted by Business and Planning Act 2020 s12.

boundary fare Fare charged for travelling further than allowed by the ticket, card or similar. A legal challenge has been made against the practice by some rail companies of requiring the traveller to pay for the whole cost of the journey and not just the part from where the ticket ends.

bound books Companies Act 1948 s436 required accounts to be kept in bound books or otherwise protected against falsification. The current requirement is simply a general duty to keep "adequate accounting records" (CA 2006 s386(1)).

bourse French term for a stock exchange.

boutique French word for a shop. In the UK it has acquired several specific meanings, such as a small shop selling clothes, then small shops selling other goods, and to businesses offering financial services from shop premises.

Boxing Day Public holiday celebrated in all parts of UK on 26 December, or 27 December if 26th is a Sunday (Banking and Financial Dealings Act 1971 Sch 1). It became a public holiday in Scotland in 1974, and in the rest of the UK from 1871.

box ticking Pejorative term for auditing or other compliance work which consists of ticking boxes rather than taking a more considered look.

bracket creep US term for fiscal drag.

bracketed duty Any form of tax or duty that is levied at rates according to a range of values. Council tax is a bracketed duty. The term was once applied to stamp duty.

brackets (1) The convention that numbers in brackets in accounts are treated as the opposite to unbracketed numbers. So (40) appearing in a list of expenses represents income of 40.
(2) In algebra, calculation that must be done first.
(3) In Boolean logic, a range of terms, any one of which may be selected.

Braille System of raised dots by which a blind person may read text. A book printed in Braille may be zero-rated as a book (VAT Notice 701/10).

brand name Name given to a product. This has a value which can be quantified. This is treated as an intangible asset, separate from goodwill.

branch rule In international tax, a rule in some non-UK jurisdictions that treats a foreign branch as if it were a separate company.

Brazil South American republic. Its currency is the real of 100 centavos. The UK has no comprehensive double taxation treaty, but has agreements of 1967 relating to shipping and air transport of 1967 and 2005.

BR code PAYE code that requires all gross pay to be subject to the basic rate of income tax.

breach of contract When a party to a contract fails to honour its side of the bargain. The other party may sue for damages or, in some cases, for specific performance. Civil damages are generally tax-deductible as a business expense while fines for breaking the law are not. Where expenditure serves a dual purpose, it is usually disallowed (HMRC Manual at BIM37960). A leading case is *Knight v Parry [1972] 48 TC 580.*

break charge Charge paid by a borrower to be released early from a loan. The tax implications are given in ITTOIA 2005 s58 and are discussed in HMRC's Tax Manual at BIM45820.

breakfast duties Name given to excise duties on sugar, tea, cocoa and coffee. They were abolished in 1962.

Breathing Space Provision due to be introduced in England and Wales in 2021. It provides a degree of protection to someone in debt. For 60 days, interest charges are frozen and enforcement action is suspended, provided the debtor meets conditions and co-operates with a debt adviser.

Brent crude Price of a barrel of crude oil from the Brent and Ninian areas of the North Sea. The price is widely used as an economic indicator.

Bretton Woods International money agreement reached in 1944 which lasted until 1971. Its main provision was fixed exchange rates between currencies.

Brexit Term coined in 2014 to mean Britain leaving the EU following a referendum on 23 June 2016. The UK finally left on 31 January 2020 with a transitional period to 31 December 2020. Brexit has implications for VAT and Customs duties, and some relevance to other taxes.

bribery Offence of offering money to someone to make them do what they should not, or not to do what they should. The offences have now been consolidated in Bribery Act 2010. A bribe is not tax-deductible as it is a criminal payment. There are separate offences of bribing, or attempting to bribe, a tax officer, and for an officer to accept a bribe.

bridge (1) A structure that may qualify for structures and buildings allowance. (2) Card game, that was held to be not a sport (see **contract bridge**).

bridging loan Loan to meet a short-term need, such as to pay a mortgage on a new home before the old one has been sold.

brigading Practice of putting laws and other provisions into one place for convenience. An example if VATA 1994 Sch 7A which puts the categories of reduced-rated supplies in one place.

bring forward In bookkeeping, to start a period or page with the figure carried forward from the previous period or page.

Britannia Gold bullion coin first introduced in 1987. The coins are exempt from capital gains tax and are zero-rated for VAT. These tax provisions do not apply to silver Britannia coins, introduced from 1997, nor to the definitive Britannia introduced in 2015. The name also refers to the female personification of Britain as shown on many notes and coins.

British Bankers Association Body formed in 1919 to represent the interests of British bankers.

British Business Bank Body whose function is to make British banks work more efficiently.

British Chamber of Commerce Organisation comprising a network of local chambers.

British compounded spirits Spirits which have been mixed with other ingredients (ALDA 1979 s4(1); Customs leaflet 41).

British dependent territory One of the territories so designated. The current list comprises: Anguilla; Bermuda; British Antarctic Territory; British Indian Ocean Territory; Cayman Islands; Falkland Islands and dependencies; Gibraltar; Montserrat; Pitcairn, Henderson, Ducie and Oeno Islands; St Helena and dependencies; the sovereign base areas of Akrotiri and Dhekelia; Turks and Caicos Islands; and Virgin Islands. Hong Kong ceased to be a British dependent territory on 30 June 1997 when its sovereignty returned to China. St Christopher and Nevis ceased to be a territory on 18 September 1983 when it became an independent Commonwealth country.

British film Film which meets criteria for special tax relief using a points system. A British film is defined by Films Act 1965 s1. The tax relief is given by CTA 2009 from s1197. The points system is set out in SI 2007 No 1050.

British islands The United Kingdom, Channel Islands and Isle of Man (Interpretation Act 1978 Sch 1).

British Museum This body is specifically exempt from capital gains tax (TCGA 1992 s271).

British national Person who has a form of British status of which there are six:

- British citizenship
- British overseas citizenship
- British overseas territories citizenship
- British protected person
- British subject
- British national (overseas).

British Tax Cases Publication of tax cases produced by CCH Editions from 1982. They are indicated by the citation BTC.

British Virgin Islands British territory in the Atlantic Ocean. It uses the US dollar as currency.

broadband Wide bandwidth data transmission system, particularly for the Internet, which is permanently connected. It is fast expanding in the UK with government support.

broiler house Place where chickens are bred. Such a property may qualify for agricultural property relief from inheritance tax if its activities are a subsidiary part of the overall agricultural purpose of the land *(Williams v CIR [2005] STC 783).*

broker Person who deals on someone else's behalf, particularly in buying shares and other securities. In relation to controlled foreign companies, the term is defined in ICTA 1988 Sch 25 para 9(2)).

bronze Alloy of copper and tin. It was used to make "copper" coins from 1860 to 1992.

brought forward An amount that is brought into one accounting period from a previous one. There are some tax allowances that may be brought forward, such as unused capital allowances. There are also restrictions on the amount of bought forward loss relief that can be claimed in a year by larger companies.

brought into account Description of an event that is reflected in the accounts. In relation to insurance companies, it is given a specific meaning in FA 1989 s83A. In relation to allowability of expenses in an investment company, it is given a specific meaning in CTA 2009 s1255(2)).

brown envelope barrier Psychological barrier when someone cannot bring themselves to open an envelope from HMRC. The term was used by the Office of Tax Simplification in a Notice of 2015.

brownfield Area of land that has already been developed and which now houses unused building. Housing and Planning Act 2016 requires local authorities to register such land for future residential development.

browser Program that allows a computer user to connect to the Internet and view pages. Popular browsers include Microsoft Internet Explorer, Firefox and Google Chrome.

Brunei African state. Its currency is the Brunei dollar of 100 sen, though Singaporean currency is also widely used. The UK has a double taxation agreement of 1950, amended by supplementary agreements of 1968 and 1973.

Brunei dollar Currency of Brunei.

Brussels Capital of Belgium where the European Commission meets. It is often used to mean the European Union.

Brydon Review Review into the purpose, scope and quality of audit in the UK, chaired by Sir Donald Brydon. It reported in December 2019, suggesting radical reforms, many of which are in the process of being implemented.

B-shares Shares in a company that have different voting rights, and possibly different dividend rates, from ordinary shares and A-shares.

bubble (1) In company law, an entity that has size but little substance. Typically it is represented by overprice shares which lose most of their value when the bubble bursts. The most famous was the South Sea Company in 1720. More recent examples include housing companies in the early 1980s, and dot.com companies in the late 1990s. An attempt to prevent this was made in Bubble Act 1719, which proved ineffective and was repealed in 1825.
(2) A support group allowed to meet during the coronavirus lockdown of 2020.

bucket shop Place where something may be bought less expensively than from its usual source. The term is now generally applied to places that unofficially sell shares, often in non-existent or overvalued companies.

buckshee Free. This is an Anglicised form of backsheesh.

Budget Statement made by the Chancellor of the Exchequer on proposals for taxation and public spending.

budget Statement of projected incomes and expenditure in an organisation. Unlike a forecast, this is not just a prediction but a management direction (though such distinction is not always made in practice).
The main types of budget are:
- fixed budget: where amounts are stated
- flexible budget: where some items depend on others, such as marketing being a percentage of turnover
- zero-based budget: where amounts start from zero each year.

Budget deficit Term used in relation to government spending, where expenditure exceeds tax revenue.
The Treasury usually splits this into two elements:
- cyclical deficit: when there is a downturn in economic activity leading to lower taxation and increased social security. This can be eliminated by economic growth
- structural deficit: when spending exceeds income, even though the economy may be strong. This is eliminated by reduced public spending or higher taxes.

budgeting loan Social fund payment available in England, Wales and Scotland. These are interest-free loans to meet need, which must be repaid. The main elements are:

- the claimant must be receiving a qualifying benefit, namely income support, income-based jobseeker's allowance, income-based employment and support allowance, or pension credit
- the qualifying benefit must have been received for at least 26 weeks before claiming the loan
- the claimant must have no more than £1,000 capital (£2,000 if 63 or over)
- the claimant must not be subject to immigration control, nor taking part in an industrial dispute
- the claimant must be able to show that he or she can repay the loan.

The loan must be for one or more of:

- furniture and household equipment
- clothing, including footwear
- maternity expenses
- funeral expenses
- advances on rent
- removal expenses
- improvement, maintenance and security of home
- travelling expenses
- expenses in seeking work
- hire purchase or similar for any of the above.

The minimum loan is £100. The maximum (2020/21) is:

- £348 for a single person
- £464 for a couple
- £612 if claiming child benefit.

The amount may be reduced if the claimant has other loans outstanding. The maximum amount of total loans is £1,500. Loans are repaid by deduction from benefits, but cannot exceed 20% of those benefits.

Budget Payment Plan Arrangement where a taxpayer makes regular payments to HMRC for his or her tax liability. Payments must usually be made by direct debit. A taxpayer may only participate if less than £10,000 tax is owed.

buffer Provision designed to provide a measure of protection, such as an overdraft facility to protect against accidentally withdrawing.

building A structure on land. There are many tax provisions for buildings. The acquisition can attract stamp duty land tax or a devolved equivalent. Acquisition on work on buildings can be subject to VAT. A building may qualify for structures and buildings allowance against taxable profits. Profit from the sale of a building can be subject to capital gains tax.

building materials Materials within the scope of a VAT zero-rated construction. They are set out in VATA 1994 Sch 8 Group 5 Item 4 Note 22.

building society Body that receives investments and provides fund for buying property. They started in the 17th century. They are now regulated by Building Societies

Act 1986, the year that several demutualised and became banks. The taxation of building society dividends is given in CTA 2009 s498. The treatment of dividends by investors is given in ITTOIA 2005 s372.

Bulgaria East European republic that joined the EU in 2007. Its currency is the lev of 100 stotinki. The UK has a double taxation convention of 1987.

bulk buying Buying in large quantities to obtain a lower price. An organisation set up to do this for its members is regarded as mutual trading, as discussed in HMRC Manual at BIM24784.

bulk licence Amusement machine licence duty that may be obtained when an operator has machines at more than one location.

bulk transfer For pensions, the transfer of a group pension scheme members and their assets from one occupational pension scheme to another.

bull Investor who believes that financial markets will rise. The opposite is a bear.

bullet-resistant glass From 6 April 2011, this may be added to a company car to protect its driver from a threat to his or her physical safety, without that being a taxable benefit in kind (ITEPA 2003 s125A).

bullion Precious metal in readily recognisable form as a store of wealth. The metal is usually gold, and sometimes silver or platinum. The forms are usually bars, ingots or coins.

bull note Bond whose redemption value is linked to an index such as the FT-SE 100 index. The name comes from the fact that such notes tend to be worth more in a bull market.

Bullock order Legal procedure when there are two defendants. The judge may join the defendants. The costs of a successful defendant are added to the claimant's costs which may be claimed from an unsuccessful defendant. The name comes from the case *Bullock v LGO Co [1907]*.

bumping Its various meanings include:

- in airlines, booking more passenger than there are seats to maximise revenue on the assumption that some passengers will not turn up
- in gambling, raising the stake
- in human resources, laying off one member of staff to avoid laying off another. The employment appeal tribunal said in the case *Mirab Mentor Graphics (UK) Ltd [2018]* that an employer should consider whether bumping is appropriate in a redundancy.

bunce Colloquialism for unexpected money.

bunched gains Accumulated gains that have arisen over several years but where those gains are taxed once together at disposal. Capital gains tax can be saved by avoiding bunching.

Bundesbank Central bank of Germany.

bundling Practice of only selling a product with one or more other products, so a customer who wants the product must buy other products also.

bung Slang term for a payment, particularly an improper one like a bribe.

bunny bond Bond that gives its holder a choice of receiving interest or further bonds.

buoyancy vest For VAT, this is not regarded as clothing. It therefore does not qualify for zero rating when sold for children *(British Vita Co Ltd]1976] VTD 332).*

burden of proof In law, the duty to satisfy the court on the truth of a matter. The two main standards are:

- balance of probabilities for civil cases
- beyond reasonable doubt for criminal cases.

The lower standard for civil cases is a factor when HMRC brings proceedings for a tax offence. The difference was illustrated by the notorious O J Simpson murder case (where US law is the same as UK law). In 1995, Simpson was acquitted of murdering his wife, but in 1997 had to pay civil damages for doing so. In both civil and criminal cases, the onus on proving the case rests with the person or body bringing it. In a case involving a tax penalty, HMRC must prove the offence; the taxpayer does not have to disprove it.

burden of tax Identifying the person responsible for paying a tax, particularly inheritance tax.

bureau de change Place where money is changed from one currency to another. Such a bureau must comply with money laundering requirements.

burglary Crime of improperly entering premises to commit an offence under Theft Act 1968 s9. Stock and cash taken in a burglary is tax-deductible to the extent that is not covered by insurance, as explained in HMRC Tax Manual at BIM45851.

burial The disposal of human remains on death, often stated as the first duty of an executor. This is subject to any requirement for a post mortem examination or donation of organs. For VAT, burial is an exempt supply, as explained in VAT Notice 701/32.

Burkina Faso Landlocked African state known as Upper Volta until 1983. Its currency is the Central French African franc. The UK has no tax treaty.

Burma Country now known as Myanmar.

burn rate How fast a new business spends its initial funding before earning enough to support itself.

Burundi African republic. Its currency is the Burundi franc. The UK has no tax treaty. The country is subject to UK sanctions.

bus For the purposes of vehicle excise duty, a vehicle with more than eight passenger seats (VERA 1994 Sch 1 from para 3). Up to 16 seats, it is a minibus. Further provisions on seating capacity are given in SI 2002 No 2742 para 44. For the purpose of a tax-relieved works transport service, a bus must have seating capacity for 12 or more people (ITEPA 2003 s242(3)).

bus fares Charge for travelling on a bus. These are zero-rated by VATA 1994 Sch 8 Group 8.

business Any commercial activity. For VAT, it is a condition of registering that the person runs a business, as partly defined in VATA s94(1). Guidance is given in VAT

Notice 701/1. For tax reporting, a limited definition is given in TMA 1970 Sch A1 para 6. For accounting, there are definitions in FRS 102 glossary and IFRS 3.A.

business asset An asset used in a business or a small holding in a company. Until 2010, the disposal of such an asset attracted a lower rate of capital gains tax.

business asset disposal relief This is the name given to entrepreneur's relief from 6 April 2020. The relief reduces capital gains tax to 10% on the disposal of a business or businesses (TCGA 1992 ss169H-169V). The relief was introduced in 2008 subject to a lifetime given under Capital Gains Tax in section 3 of this dictionary. Guidance is given in HMRC Manual at CG63950-CG64171. The ICAEW Tax Faculty has also published practical guidance as TAXGUIDE 01/12. The main points to note are:

- the relief may be claimed by individuals only, not by companies. It may be made by a trustee of an interest in possession trust for gains made by a beneficiary
- it is a cumulative lifetime relief, whose value has changed many times
- it is separate from investors' relief. It is possible to claim both reliefs for different shares held in the same company
- the relief must be claimed; it is not given automatically. A taxpayer may wish not to claim the relief so that it is available for a later claim
- it may be claimed for the disposal of a sole trader business; an interest in a partnership or limited liability partnership; shares or securities in the taxpayer's personal company; and associated disposals
- a personal company is broadly one in which the taxpayer held a 5% stake. The definition of this is tightened from 29 October 2018. There have been several cases where relief was lost because, for example, the taxpayer did not have 5% of the voting rights
- the taxpayer must be either an officer or employee of the company, or another company in the same group, at the time of disposal
- for company shares, the company must have been a trading company. Non-trading activities may be ignored if they are not substantial, which HMRC accepts means less than 20% of turnover
- for disposals from 6 April 2019, the taxpayer must have met the conditions for 24 months. Before 6 April 2019, it was 12 months
- from 6 April 2008 to 22 June 2010, relief was given by reducing the gain by four-ninths. The other five-ninths gave an effective rate of 10% when capital gains tax was a single rate of 18%. From 23 June 2020, the relief allows the disposal to be taxed separately at 10%
- any gain not covered by the relief is subject to capital gains tax at 18% or (more likely) 28%
- the relief may be claimed when the disposal is effected in stages
- where there are both gains and losses on assets, they must be netted off
- care needs to be exercised as to whether sale of assets are part of a disposal
- from 3 December 2014, the relief is not available for goodwill when a sole trader incorporates his or her sole trade.

There are many other provisions.

Business Bounce Bank loan scheme Full name for the **Bounce Bank scheme**.

business by telephone Term used by HMRC in relation to those tax matters that may be dealt with by telephone. Their policy is set out in SP1/2010, as amended in 2012.

business combination For accounting, when two or more businesses are brought together into one reporting entity (FRS 102 glossary; IFRS 3 Appendix A).

business day Day on which banks are open for business (Bills of Exchange Act 1882 s92).

business documents Documents that relate to the carrying on of a business or form part of its statutory records. HMRC's inspection powers are set out in Finance Act 2008 Sch 36 para 10. Similar powers for Scotland are set out in Revenue Scotland and Tax Powers Act 2014 s141(4).

business entertainment Hospitality or entertainment provided in the course of a business. Entertainment of customers and potential customers is not tax-deductible (ITTOIA s45). Entertainment of staff is tax-deductible (ITEPA 2003 s356). The term is defined in ITTOIA 2005 s45(4) and CTA 2009 s1298(5), and discussed in HMRC Tax Manual at BIM45010. VAT input tax may be claimed for entertaining staff and overseas customers. The term is define for VAT in SI 1992 No 3222 and explained in VAT Notice 700/65.

Business Expansion Scheme Tax-advantaged business investment scheme that ran from 1983 to 1993, when it was replaced by enterprise investment scheme.

business gift Gift given to promote a business. It is tax-deductible if the value does not exceed £50 per recipient per tax year, provided conditions are met (ITTOIA 2005 s57). For VAT, a gift up to £50 is not regarded as a supply (VATA 1994 Sch 4 para 5(2)).

Business Payment Support Service HMRC body set up in 2008 to help taxpayers in difficulties. Its schemes include Time To Pay and payment plans. It can be contacted by telephone on 0300 200 3835 during office hours.

business premises renovation allowance Capital allowance available between 2007 and 2017 for conversion or renovation of a business premises that been empty for at least one year in a disadvantaged area of UK.

business property relief Relief from inheritance tax on business property. The relief has generally been 100% since 1995. Details are given in IHTA 1984 ss103-114.

business rates Sum paid to local authority in respect of commercial premises. This tax originates from Poor Law Act 1572. Current law is Local Government Finance Act 2012.

The calculation is the rateable value as at 1 April 2015. This is multiplied by either:

- the standard multiplier for a rateable value above £51,000 or
- the small business multiplier below £51,000.

These multipliers are given under Business Rates in section 3 of this dictionary. From 1 April 2013, a local authority may keep half the business rates, subject to adjustments, and sends the rest to central government which makes grants to local authorities. Many premises are exempt from business rates.

There are also reductions for empty properties, charity properties and enterprise zones. There are also generous relief for smaller businesses and rural premises.

business sample Sample of a business's product given to promote the product. It is tax-deductible if its cost per recipient does not exceed £50 a year and other conditions are met (ITTOIA s47). For VAT, the supply of a business gift up to £50 is not regarded as a supply under Value Added Tax Act 1994 Sch 4 para 5(2). From 1 January 2011, the £50 limit applies per gift. Previously it applied to total of gifts per year.

business start-up scheme Government scheme that ran from 1991 to 1995 when it was replaced.

Business Support Government-backed website at ww.businesssupport.gov.uk. launched on 20 February 2020 to give advice on business matters.

business test For VAT, test as to whether a business activity is being carried on. The questions are set out in VAT Notice 701/1:

- is the activity a serious activity earnestly pursued?
- is the activity an occupation or function which is actively pursued with reasonable or recognisable continuity?
- does the activity have a certain measure of substance in terms of the quarterly or annual value of taxable supplies made?
- is the activity conducted in a regular manner and on sound and recognised business principles?
- is the activity predominately concerned with the making of taxable supplies for a consideration?
- are the taxable supplies that are being made of a kind which, subject to differences in detail, are commonly made by those who seek to profit from them?

business travel Travelling in the course of work such as to see a customer (ITEPA 2003 s171(1)).

butut One hundredth of a dalasi, currency of Gambia.

buy to let Property acquired with a view to letting it, usually where the rent covers the mortgage payment. The government has introduced various tax measures intended to kill this activity as it believes it distorts the housing market. Such measures include restrictions on income tax relief for interest payments (see Landlord's Interest Payments in section 3 of this dictionary), additional 3% SDLT and denial of other reliefs.

by When a tax provision requires something to be done "by" a date, that includes doing it on that date. This applies to all tax provisions. It is made explicit in a few places like VATA 1994 s59A(14).

byte Unit of computer data equal to eight bits or binary digits. One byte represents a character or number.

1000 bytes = 1 kilobyte
1000 kilobytes = 1 megabyte
1000 megabytes = 1 gigabyte

1000 gigabytes = 1 terabyte
1000 terabytes = 1 petabyte.

cab rank principle Exception to the general rule that a party has freedom to contract. A taxi, barrister or inn keeper must provide services if able to do so to a customer willing to pay.

cactus Endangered plant whose import may be prohibited under Convention on International Trade in Endangered Species.

cafeteria benefits When an employee may choose which benefits to have from a menu. Such an arrangement can fall foul of the salary sacrifice rules.

Caillebotte Case that established that a business proportion of an expense cannot be claimed as it is not wholly expended for a business purpose. The citation is *Caillebotte v Quinn [1975] 50 TC 222.*

A carpenter's lunch cost 10p at home but 40p on site. He was not able to claim the extra 30p as a business expense. It is discussed in HMRC Manual at BIM37660.

cake decorations For VAT, these are standard-rated when inedible and sold separately, but zero-rated when edible or supplied with the cake. The exact scope is explained in VAT leaflet 701/14.

cakes These are generally zero-rated as food, even if covered with chocolate or other sweet material, under VATA 1994 Sch 8 Group 1 Excepted Item 2. They are standard-rated when provided as part of a supply of catering. More details are given in VAT leaflet 701/14.

Calderbank letter Letter sent by one party to another (which can include HMRC) offering to settle a case "without prejudice". Such a letter may not be used in a trial or shown to the judge until the issue has been determined. It may then be shown to the judge when seeking costs. The name comes from the case *Calderbank v Calderbank [1976].* The use of such letters has declined as litigants may make a Part 36 offer based on Civil Procedure Rules where the costs issue is more defined.

calendar Table of dates. The UK uses the Gregorian calendar under provisions of Calendar (New Style) Act 1750 and Calendar Act 1751, both of which are still law. Under this, the year starts on 1 January. Previously the UK used the Julian calendar where the year started on 25 March. The change meant 2 September 1752 was immediately followed by 14 September 1752. This partly explains why the tax year starts on 6 April.

calendar month One of the 12 months of the calendar, as distinguished from tax months which run from 6th of one month to 5th of the next.

call The many meanings of this word include a part payment of a share. If the call is not paid, the share is forfeited.

Callcredit One of the country's three credit reference agencies, established in 2000. The other two are Experian and Equifax.

call date Date on which a bond may be redeemed by the issuer before maturity. This is usually either at par or at a premium.

called up share capital Share capital where the shareholder has paid all the calls on the share (CA 2006 s547).

calling Religious vocation. For tax, it was held to be a vocation in the case *Partridge v Mallandaine [1896] 2 TC 179.*

call-off stock Stock that a customer has adopted but not taken delivery of. Such stock is often stored at the customer's premises. From 1 January 2020, EU law regards the stock as supplied between businesses in different EU states when supplied, not when later adopted. In the UK this is given effect by VATA 1994 s14A as inserted by FA 2020 s80(2). Details are given in VATA 1994 Sch 4B as inserted by FA 2020 s80(5).

call option The right to buy shares (of other securities) at a specified price at a specified future date. The duty to sell the securities is a put option. A call option is usually sold for a small fraction of the share price and premium. If the shares rise above the option price, the shares may be bought immediately at a premium. If the shares fall below the option price, the option becomes worthless.

calorific gas Gas that can be burned for heating and power. This includes hydrogen, carbon monoxide, methane and various hydrocarbons.

CambodiaIndo-Chinese kingdom, briefly called Kampuchea. Its currency is the riel of 100 sen, though the US dollar is widely used. The UK has no tax treaty.

CameroonAfrican republic. Its currency is the Central French African franc. The UK has no comprehensive tax treaty, but has an air transport agreement of 1981.

camper van The case *Oak Tree Motor Homes Ltd v HMRC [2017]* established that this does not come within the scope of VAT zero-rating for a residential caravan.

Canada North American country. Its currency is the Canadian dollar. The UK has a double taxation protocol of 2003. Also in effect are part of a double taxation convention of 1978 as amended by two protocols of 1980 and 1985.

Canadian dollar Currency of Canada.

canal Man-made inland waterway, widely used for moving goods between 1757 and 1840, and now mainly used for pleasure boating. When run as a trade, profits of a canal are taxed (ITTOIA s005 s12; CTA 2009 s39). A canal is specifically excluded from capital allowance for plant and machinery (CAA 2001 s22(1) List B).

cancellation Act that has the intention of negating a document or act. For a cheque or other bill, cancellation may be effected just by drawing a line across it. For a document, drawing a line is generally insufficient. For a will, there should be a specific declaration from the testator that the will has been cancelled (Wills Act 1837 s20).

cancellation fee Charge made to cover the administrative cost of cancelling something. VAT is not charged on a cancellation fee as there has been no supply. However,

VAT may be charged if a service has been provided, such as reserving a hotel room for someone who later cancels.

Candlemas Christian festival on 2 February which was a Scottish quarter day until 1991 when replaced by 28 February.

Canolfan byd Gwaith Welsh: Jobcentre Plus.

canons of taxation Four principles for a "good" tax as developed by Adam Smith. They are:

- cost of collection is low
- timing and amount must be certain
- timing and means of payment must be convenient
- tax should be related to ability to pay.

canteen Dining facilities at a workplace.

There is generally no tax charge for subsidised or free meals in a canteen (ITEPA 2003 s317). This includes free tea and coffee at work. For VAT, a supply from a canteen is standard-rated when eaten in the canteen, but may be zero-rated as food if eaten elsewhere *(Bishop & P Elcocks [2001] VTD 17620).*

capacity of company Ability of a company to make transaction. This may be restricted by the company's own articles of association, particularly for older companies. CA 2006 s39 makes clear that such restriction does not affect the rights of the other party.

capacity rule Tax rule that the allowability of expenditure can depend on the capacity in which it was incurred. The test was established in the case *Strong & Co of Ramsey Ltd v Woodfield [1906] STC 215.* This held that a brewery incurred expenses as a landlord and not as a trader. The matter is discussed in HMRC Manual at BIM37300.

capacity to contract The extent to which certain persons may make a contract. The law generally assumes that every person has such capacity unless they come within the scope below:

- those under 18 are restricted to buying necessaries at a reasonable price
- people of limited mental capacity are restricted to contracts they are capable of understanding
- people who are drunk or under the influence of drugs are restricted to what they can understand in such state
- bankrupts have some restrictions imposed on them under insolvency law
- enemy aliens, with whom no legal contract may be made
- companies, who may be restricted by their own articles of association.

cap and collar mortgage Mortgage with a variable interest which cannot exceed a figure nor fall below one.

Caparo Industries Court case on auditor's liability. Its full citation is *Caparo Industries plc v Dickman [1990].* Caparo acquired a controlling interest in a company called Fidelity. They reported a profit of £1.3 million, which should have been a loss of £400,000. Caparo sued the auditors for professional liability. The House of Lords held that there was no liability as the auditors owed no duty of care to individual shareholders or to the investing public in general. This needs to be considered in conjunction with cases such as *Hedley Byrne & Co Ltd v Heller & Partners Ltd [1964] AC 465*, where a third party liability was held to exist when the relationship between the parties was "sufficiently proximate".

Cape Verde Island republic in Atlantic Ocean. Its currency is the escudo Caborverdiano. The UK has no tax treaty.

capital This term has many meanings in accounting and tax. In all of them it represents a sum that, to some extent, is fixed. For savings, it is the sum put on deposit to which interest is added. These distinctions are not always clear. For tax, capital expenditure is excluded as a tax deduction from profits (ITTOIA 2005 s33; CTA 2009 s53). This broadly means that items such as property, computers, machinery, vehicles and furniture, which have an expected life of at least two years. Such expenditure and depreciation is added back to taxable profits in the tax computation. This expenditure may instead qualify for a capital allowance. In a partnership, capital refers to the sum that each partner contributed to the partnership when joining. It is distinguished from loans and profits and payments, which are accounted for in a separate current account. Unless the partners decide otherwise, interest accrues on a capital account at 5% a year (Partnership Act 1890 s24(3)). A sole trader or company director may set up a capital account for convenience, though this has no significance for tax. An overdrawn capital account is treated as a loan. The implications are discussed in HMRC Manual at BIM45705. The gain from disposing of a capital asset is subject to capital gains tax rather than income tax. For companies, a capital gain is called a chargeable gain. It is subject to corporation tax but under rules similar to capital gains tax.

For a mortgage, the loan is the sum borrowed.

capital acquisition tax Tax charged in Irish Republic on gifts and inheritances.

capital allowance Deduction made from income tax or corporation tax in respect of some types of capital expenditure. The main law is CAA 2001. Plant and machinery can generally attract a 100% deduction under the annual investment allowance, to a limit. Otherwise they are written down at either 18% or 6% a year. Structures and buildings now attract the structures and buildings allowance at 3% a year. The main types of capital allowance are:

- first year allowance: 100% allowance on a limited range of assets, principally those that are environmentally friendly
- annual investment allowance: allows the whole cost of plant and machinery (except cars) to be claimed in the year of acquisition
- writing down allowance: either reduces the original cost or the written down value by a percentage each year
- balancing allowance: whatever value remains when a business ceases (or a balancing charge if the value is negative).

Historically there have also been initial allowances and investment allowances. The figure for capital allowances soon becomes divorced from financial reality and is just a number used in a tax computation. A written down value of, say,

£100,000 does not mean that the business has £100,000 worth of fixed assets as capital allowances may continue to be claimed for assets disposed of many years before.

Rates of capital allowance are given in section 3 of this dictionary.

capital allowance excess Term used in CTA 2010 s101 in relation to restrictions on loss relief.

capital and interest mortgage Most common form of mortgage where the borrower makes a payment, usually monthly, which pays interest and some capital. Most of the early payments are interest charges. Examples of mortgage repayments are given in section 3 of this dictionary.

capital asset pricing model (CAPM) Method of valuing an investment using discounted cashflow factors to expected future returns.

capital base Capital structure of a business. For a company, this is represented by initial capital plus retained profit.

capital beneficiary Person who is entitled to receive capital but not income from a discretionary trust.

capital contributed Sum a soled trader or partner has provided to a business that is already trading.

capital distribution Distribution of capital from a company to its shareholders other than as a bonus issue of shares. The capital gains tax implications are given in TCGA 1992 from s122.

capital duty Stamp duty charged on the issue of new shares between 1973 and 1987.

capital gain Amount by which a fixed asset has appreciated in value between acquisition and disposal. For an individual, this may be subject to capital gains tax. For a company, a capital gain is called a chargeable gain and is subject to corporation tax.

capital gains tax (CGT) Tax introduced in 1965 to tax gains on the disposal of certain assets, such as shares or works of art. The main legislation is TCGA 1992. Capital Gains Tax Regulations are SI 1969 No 149, as amended. Capital gains tax is paid by individuals, trustees and personal representatives. Companies and other bodies subject to corporation tax pay corporation tax on what are called chargeable gains. Both capital gains tax and chargeable gain corporation tax are regulated by TCGA 1992, with many rules common to both taxes. Main points to note are:

- a gain is only taxed when it is crystallised by a disposal
- the capital gain is broadly disposal proceeds minus acquisition cost
- there is an annual exemption and a further separate exemption for chattels
- indexation allowance was provided for capital gains tax from 1982 to April 1998. Indexation allowance was replaced by introducing a lower rate
- the current rate of CGT is 10% for an individual taxpayer whose income plus capital gains do not exceed the threshold for higher rate tax, and 20% for a higher rate taxpayer. For property gains, the rates are 18% and 28%

- Scottish taxpayers are regarded as higher rate taxpayers if their earnings are above the UK threshold for higher rate tax, rather than the lower threshold for Scottish income tax
- indexation allowance is provided for corporation tax for periods from April 1983 to December 2017. For disposals from January 2018, indexation may be claimed up to December 2017. Indexation is applied by increasing the acquisition cost
- for assets acquired before 6 April 1982, the value on that date is usually substituted for acquisition cost (TCGA 1992 s39).

Further details are given in section 3 of this dictionary.

capital goods scheme Scheme introduced from April 1990 that requires adjustment of VAT input tax when a capital asset changes its nature after acquisition. It particularly applies to a change in the use of property within ten years. The law is VATA 1994 s34. The main points are:

- the scheme applies to a net spend of £250,000 on land or building including construction services or (much less frequently) to a net spend of £50,000 on a single item of computer hardware
- from 1 January 2011, the scheme also applies to boats and aircraft costing more than £50,000
- there is an adjustment period which is ten years for land and buildings, and five years for other assets
- the scheme only applies when there is a change of use or circumstances such that the business could not claim input tax if the supply were made after the change
- the scheme requires an annual calculation to reflect the usage of the asset during that year. This can require consideration of partial exemption. For the year of change it may require a pro rata adjustment according to the number of days from the change
- the scheme can catch a business that lets out surplus space in premises constructed within the adjustment period
- the scheme also applies if a zero-rated construction as a residence or charity building changes to commercial use within the adjustment period.

capital instrument Any instrument issued by an entity as a means of raising funds. Capital instruments include shares, debentures, loans, debt instruments, and options and warrants.

capital interest In the context of a controlled foreign company, this term has particular provisions in ICTA 1988 Sch 25 para 11(4)).

capitalisation

(1) Process of turning a revenue or income item into a fixed asset, such as may apply to development expenditure if conditions are met.

(2) Process of turning profit into shares or a capital redemption reserve (CA 2006 s853(3)).

capitalisation issue A bonus issue of shares that is intended to capitalise retained profit.

capitalisation threshold Amount above which an entity treats an item as a fixed asset. This means that low value items with a life of more than one year are not shown as fixed assets. Examples include hammers, mugs and staplers. Note that there is no equivalent threshold for capital allowances for plant and machinery.

capitalism Political system that favours private property and a free market economy with government regulation but not control. The opposite is often seen as socialism. In reality, most systems have a mixed economy of free market provision and state provision. Where that balance should lie is a matter of political opinion.

capital loss When a fixed asset is disposed of for less than its acquisition cost. Such a loss may, subject to rules, be offset against capital gains. From 1 April 2020, a company is restricted in the amount of loss it may bring forward to a later year. The restriction is basically £5 million plus half the balance of the later year's capital gains. So if the capital gains in a later year is £9 million, the loss brought forward is restricted to £7 million. The other £2 million may be carried forward to the next year.

capital payment Either a sum provided as capital or a payment to acquire a fixed asset.

In relation to non-resident trusts, the term is given a specific meaning in TCGA 1992 s97.

In relation to anti-avoidance for plant and machinery leasing, it has a specific meaning in CTA 2009 s893(2).

capital receipt conditions Term used for anti-avoidance provisions when assets are transferred abroad (ITA 2007 s729).

capital redemption reserve Account where funds are held to redeem capital instruments (CA 2006 s 723).

Capital Requirements Directive EU directive 2013/36/EU on access to the activity of credit institutions and their supervision. This is given effect in UK law by SI 2012 No 3118 from 1 January 2014.

capital reserves The undistributed reserves of a company.

capital resources condition Condition that the bank levy is payable by an entity with capital resources of at least £100 million (FA 2011 Sch 19 para 72).

capital share Share in a unit trust which increases in line with the capital value of its underlying assets but is unaffected by income from dividends.

capital sum

(1) Amount of capital expenditure (CAA 2001 s4).

(2) in relation to a disposal for capital gains tax, means disposal proceeds which is not excluded from the consideration taken into account in the computation of the gain (TCGA 1992 s22(3)).

capital transfer tax Tax charged between 1974 and 1986 on lifetime gifts and inheritances. In 1982, the cumulation period was reduced from life to ten years. It was replaced by inheritance tax.

capital withdrawn Sum drawn by a sole trader from his business. There are usually no tax implications of doing so. This is discussed in HMRC Manual at BIM45700.

cap on care costs The maximum amount that may be charged to a person in respect of their care (Care Act 2014 s15). This is an area currently being reviewed by the government.

capped amount An amount up to a limit. The term is used in ITEPA 2003 s132A(5) to mean the £5,000 cap on the amount an employee may contribute to a company car and have the list price reduced for the purposes of calculating the tax charge.

capping Imposing a financial limit. An example is the power of the government to cap a local authority to restrain increases in council tax.

captain Master of a ship or commander of an aircraft (Immigration Act 1971 s33).

captcha In computing, a security procedure to identify that a website is being used by a human and not a machine. Typically, it provides a short text in distorted form and asks the user to type in the word.

caption Formal heading to a legal document.

car Vehicle of less than 3.5 tonnes designed primarily to carry passengers. There ~~are~~ many specific tax provisions for cars include:

- the purchase of a car is subject to VAT
- a business cannot recover VAT input tax on a car, with a few exceptions
- a car is subject to vehicle excise duty
- a car qualifies for capital allowance as plant and machinery at a rate dependent on its emissions
- annual investment allowance may not be claimed for a car
- an employee provided with a car that may be used for personal mileage may be taxed on the benefit
- if the employee is also provided with petrol, diesel or other fuel, the employee incurs a further benefit charge
- only 85% of a car hire charge is tax-deductible unless the car has low emissions
- cars are not subject to capital gains tax
- petrol and diesel are subject to hydrocarbon oil duty and VAT
- there are fixed rates that may be paid to an employee who uses his or her car for business
- there are advisory rates that may be used to avoid a car fuel benefit charge
- where a car or car fuel (or both) are provided to an employee, the employer is liable to pay class 1A national insurance
- cars imported from outside EU are subject to car duty while the UK is in the transitional period.

Section 3 of this dictionary includes many details about cars.

caravan Vehicle designed with some facilities for everyday living. There are some specific tax provisions for caravans. A caravan may be zero-rated for VAT under VATA 1994 Sch 8 Group 9. Guidance is given in VAT Notice 701/20. Income from a commercially run caravan site is taxed as a trade (ITTOIA 2005 s30; CTA 2009 s43). Otherwise income is taxed as property income. Caravans were subject to car tax until 13 November 1992.

car benefit Taxable benefit of an employee provided with a car.

carbon Naturally occurring element which takes various forms including charcoal, graphite and diamonds. For tax, it often refers to carbon dioxide in terms of emissions. There are various tax provisions designed to reduce emissions.

carbon dioxide Common gas produced by burning. It is a greenhouse gas. Because of its harmful nature, cars are subject to car benefit and vehicle excise duty according to their emissions of this gas. The rates are given in section 3 of this dictionary. Carbon dioxide can be added to drinks to make them fizzy. This was held to be insufficient for carbon dioxide to be VAT zero-rated as a food *(Gas & Chemicals Ltd [2002] VTD 18160).*

carbon price Figure used to calculation climate change levy.

carer's allowance Social security benefit introduced in 2003 paid to someone who looks after a disabled person (SSCBA 1992 s70). The allowance is taxable (ITEPA 2003 s660(1)). The Scottish government plans to introduce different arrangements between 2021 and 2024.

car fuel Petrol, diesel or other road fuel. If an employer pays for an employee's private use of fuel, the employee will generally be subject to a car fuel benefit charge under ITEPA 2003 s149. If the employer claims back VAT input tax on such fuel, an adjustment is required under VATA 1994 s57.

car hire Unless the car has a low emission, only 85% of this expense is tax deductible (CTA 2009 s1251).

cards
(1) To give someone their cards means to sack them. The cards refer to the national insurance card which was discontinued in 1973, and the P45 tax form which has never been produced on card.
(2) Pack of playing cards which were once subject to excise duty.
(3) For VAT, various tribunal decisions have held that packs of cards containing textual information do not qualify for zero-rating as a book. An early case consisted of cards with questions about roadsigns and the Highway Code for learner drivers *(Flipcards Ltd [1995] VTD 13916).* The tribunal has ruled that a leaflet must be limp and has therefore refused zero-rating for tax cards *(Tax Briefs Ltd [1991] VTD 9258),* prayer cards *(Christian Art Ltd [1990] VTD 5940),* recipe cards *(International Master Publishers Ltd [1991] VTD 8807)* and cards that reproduced paintings *(Philip Green Education Ltd [1997] VTD 15669).*

care and support Provision to meet an adult's needs, a carer's needs, or for services or facilities for such purposes (Care Act 2014 s25).

care and support employer An individual who employs someone to provide personal or domestic services (PAYE Regulations 2003 reg 67D(10) and reg 206(4)). Such an employer may be excused the requirement to file PAYE returns under real time information.

care component An element of disability living allowance payable at one of three rates depending on the severity of the disability.

careless Description when a taxpayer makes a wrong declaration as a result of a failure to take reasonable care (FA 2007 Sch 24 para 3(1)).

carer's allowance Social security benefit to someone who looks after a severely disabled person. It replaced invalid care allowance in 2003.

car fuel benefit Taxable benefit of an employee provided with fuel for a car. It is additional to car benefit.

carousel fraud Form of missing trader fraud for VAT where goods are repeatedly sold within the EU.

car parking Provision of a car parking space for an employee is not a taxable benefit in kind (ITEPA 2003 s237). Car parking is generally subject to VAT unless provided by a local authority as a statutory duty.

carried forward Amount in one accounting period that is transferred to the next period. Some tax provisions may be carried forward.

carrier bag A retailer must generally charge for a single use carrier bag. The regulations were introduced under provisions of Climate Change Act 2008 in England by SI 2015 No 776; in Scotland by SI 2014 No 161; in Wales by SI 2011 No 2184; and in Northern Ireland by SI 2013 No 4. The charge of 5p was introduced in:

- Wales on 1 October 2011,
- Northern Ireland on 8 April 2013,
- Scotland on 20 October 2014 and
- England (for stores with 250 employees) on 1 October 2015.
  HMRC provided guidance in HMRC Brief 14/2015.

In England, the charge doubles to 10p and applies to all retailers of any size from April 2021. The charge was waived for online deliveries during the coronavirus outbreak. A single use carrier bag is defined as a new plastic bag with handles and an opening of a thickness of no more than 70 microns. There are many exceptions. This is not a tax as the store can keep the proceeds though most donate the sum to charity. If the store is VAT registered, the 5p charge is 4.17p plus 0.83p VAT. Income from the charge must be accounted for as income and is subject to income tax or corporation tax. More details are given in section 3 of this dictionary.

carrot and stick Reward and punishment for doing something desired. It is an allusion as to how to make a donkey walk. An example of this in tax was the introduction of online filing for PAYE. The carrot was a cash bonus. The stick was a penalty for non-compliance.

carry back Tax provision whereby a relief may be given in an earlier period, usually resulting in a rebate of tax already paid. Examples include terminal loss relief and some payments under Gift Aid.

carry forward When an amount at the end of an accounting period or at the bottom of a page is carried to the start of the next accounting period or page. Loss relief may be carried forward indefinitely until fully utilised by later profits. Before 6 April 2006, this term was curiously used for the right to allow tax relief for pension contributions on the basis of earnings for the previous six years.

carrying amount Value at which an asset is recorded in the financial records. This is often its net book value (FRS 102 glossary; IAS 16 para 6; IAS 36 par 6; IAS 38 para 8). A slightly different definition with the same meaning is given in IAS 40 para 5 and IAS 41 para 8).

carrying on a business In Scotland, this is specifically defined as including the letting of property, the activities of a charity, and the activities of a local authority or other public authority (Revenue Scotland and Tax Powers Act 2014 s121(1)).

carrying value Value at which an asset is shown in the accounting records, such as on the balance sheet. It is specifically defined for some tax purposes. For loan relationship, it is defined in CTA 2009 s317. For contracts that relate to embedded derivatives, it is defined in CTA 2009 s702.

carry trade International financing by borrowing a currency heavily to buy other assets.

car seats Safety seats for children may be reduced-rated for VAT under VATA 1994 Sch 7A Group 5, if they meet the specification.

car sharing When two or more employees arrange transport to work between them. If the arrangement breaks down, the employer may provide alternative transport without this being regarded as a taxable benefit in kind (ITEPA 2003 s248).

car tax Tax charged on cars and caravans from 1973 in addition to VAT introduced at the same time. The tax was abolished in 1992. Note that is not the same as vehicle excise duty or road tax.

cartel Arrangement when a group of people work together to fix a market, such as keeping prices high or not competing. Such arrangements are illegal under competition law. A business can be fined up to 10% of annual worldwide turnover. Individuals can also be fined or even imprisoned. Directors can be disqualified for up to 15 years.

cartridges Item in a list of explosives (Explosives Act 1875 s3(1) for which a special Customs procedure is needed to import.

case (1) A legal dispute brought before a court or tribunal.
(2) A crate for liquor (ALDA 1979 s4(1)).
(3) One of between six and eight divisions of the old Schedule D, or three divisions of Schedule E.

case law Decisions of courts and tribunals which can bind or influence subsequent cases.

case law trust "Employee share ownership trust or general purpose [employee benefit trust] which relies on tax case law rather than specific legislation as authority for allowing tax deductions on employers' contributions" (HMRC Manual at BIM44001). Further details are given at BIM 44140. The main cases are *Heather v PE Consulting Group Ltd 48 TC 293; Rutter v Charles Sharpe Ltd 53 TC 153; Jeffs v Ringtons Ltd 58 TC 680; E Bott Ltd v Price 59 TC 437; Mawsley Machinery Ltd v Robinson [1998] SpC170.*

case management Right of a judge to determine how a case should be managed. For first tier tax tribunals, these are set out in The Tribunal Procedure (First-tier) (Tax Chamber) Rules SI 2009 No 273 rule 5.

case-specific Decision of a court or tribunal that is regarded as decided on the particular facts of the case, and which is not regarded as setting much of a precedent. Examples include *North of England Zoological Society [1999] STC 1027* on VAT partial exemption, and *Pook v Owen [1969] HL. 45 TC 571* on tax relief for travelling expenses.

case stated Summary of the facts by a court or tribunal to be considered by a higher court or tribunal.

cash Money in readily spendable form. It is the most liquid current asset. The exact scope of what constitutes cash is not consistent. Accounting standards FRS 102 and IAS 7 para 6 define it as "cash on hand and demand deposits". In accounting this usually comprises notes and coins held by the entity (such as petty cash and vending machines) and balances held at a bank. Businesses that handle large amounts of cash may need to register under money laundering regulations.

cash accounting Accounting on the basis of money received and spent rather than incurred under the accruals basis. Small businesses may use cash accounting for income tax and VAT. Details are given in the appropriate sections in section 3 of this dictionary.

cash basis The use of cash accounting, particularly for a small business subject to income tax. The provisions are set out in Finance Act 2013 s17 and Sch 4. A trader may use this scheme for turnover up to a limit of £150,000 a year.

cash back Arrangement whereby a supermarket or other retailer allows a customer to add an amount to their payment which it pays out as cash. So someone buying £100 worth of goods may pay £120 by card and be given £20 in cash. A trial is considering whether retailers should be allowed to provide cash against a card without the need for a purchase.

cash basis Description of accounts based on income and expenditure rather than the more usual basis of accruals. A small business may use the cash basis under FA 2013 s17 and Sch 4. Details are given in in section 3 of this dictionary.

cash book A prime book of account (or computer equivalent) which records cash payments and receipts.

cash card Plastic card that may be used to withdraw funds from a cash dispenser. The card may be a credit card, debit card or prepayment card.

cash collateral For a stock lending arrangement, this is an amount of money payable to the lender to transfer the securities back to the borrower (ITA 2007 s597(1)(b)).

cash consideration For the purchase of shares, this is defined in CA 2006 s583(3).

cash control rules Part of money laundering rules. They broadly require a person to declare large sums of cash brought into the UK. Many other countries have equivalent rules for cash brought from the UK. From 1 January 2021 for Great Britain (not Northern Ireland), a declaration is required if more than £10,000 is brought into Great Britain whether or not from an EU state. Before 1 January 2021, a declaration was required for more than €10,000 (not pounds) brought in from outside the EU. That continues to apply in Northern Ireland from 2021.

cash cow Product or service which a business can rely on to provide income for other purposes, such as developing new products and services.

cash declaration Duty of anyone entering the UK from an EU country, or entering a EU country from the UK, to declare any cash of €10,000 or more, or equivalent. Cash does not just mean notes and coins. It includes travellers' cheques and bank drafts. The limit is not per person but per family. A cash declaration can be made up to 72 hours before the journey. The declaration needs to state:

- the currencies used
- the form of cash
- where the cash came from
- how the cash will be used
- who owns the cash
- who is getting the cash
- the person's passport number.

Customs may seize any cash they believe is connected to a crime. They can hold it for 48 hours, or longer with a court order.

cash dispenser Machine that provides cash, usually in the form of banknotes when a card is entered with a code. Some dispensers make a charge for dispensing cash. In 2018, the Court of Appeal overturned a decision that a cash dispenser is subject to business rates separate from the premises where it is installed.

cash equivalent Asset that is so liquid that it may be regarded as cash. Examples include gold coins and National Savings certificates.

cashflow Recording transactions in terms of inflows and outflows of cash, rather than in terms of profit or loss. [This term is sometimes spelled as two words.]

cashflow statement Additional financial statement generally required for a business entity. It is outside the traditional statements of balance sheet, and profit and loss account. Unlike them, a cashflow statement is of fact, without opinion.

cash positive Business where the customer pays for the goods before the seller has to pay for them.

cash register Till that records cash transactions, particularly in shops.

cash shortage A deficit arising in relation to amounts received in connection with retail transactions, such as money going missing from a shop's till during a worker's shift. If it can be shown that the worker took the money, the worker can be prosecuted for theft. In other cases, the employer pay recover it from the employee up to 10% of wages under Employment Rights Act 1996 s17(1).

cash voucher Coupon or similar document that can be exchanged for cash. For payroll purposes, such a voucher is regarded as cash under ITEPA 2003 s75.

casino Place for a person to gamble. Also defined as an arrangement whereby people may participate in casino games (Gambling Act 2005 s7(1)). A casino may be classified as a regional casino, large casino, or small casino, or may be below the limit for licensing (Gambling Act 2005 s7(2)). A casino needs an operating licence provided by the Gambling Commission (Gambling Act 2005 s65(2)(a) and may need a premises licence from the local authority (Gambling Act 2005 s172(3)).

cask General term for a large container for alcoholic drink. A barrel is a cask of predetermined size.

cask conditioned beer Beer whose production continues after being put in a cask. This produces a sediment for which beer duty may be relieved. Details are given in Customs notice 226.

Cassa di Compensazione Garanzia (CC&G) Part of the Italian central bank. It is a recognised clearing house for the purposes of stamp duty and stamp duty reserve tax from 3 October 2011 (SI 2011 No 2205).

casting vote Second vote given to a chairman to settle a tied vote. This is only permitted if the organisation's rules specifically allow it. A company formed before 1 October 2007 may have adopted Table A for its articles of association. Regulation 50 of this Table allows for a casting vote. For other companies, CA s282 does not allow for casting votes. A tied vote is therefore lost.

casual labour People engaged for a short period for a particular task, such as harvesting. Such people are still treated as workers or employees and are entitled to such rights as attach to such status.

cat (1) Domestic animal that may be imported on a pet passport.
(2) Form of goodwill, as explained under cat, dog and rat.
(3) Colloquial name for a zero coupon bond.

Catapult centre Government-backed organisation established in 2011 to promote research and development. They are funded by a mixture of government grant and commercial backing.

CATCH Acronym suggested by HMRC to outline the duties of a registered high value dealer. These are to:

- Control the body by anti-laundering procedures
- Appoint a nominated officer
- Train your staff
- Confirm the identity of all customers
- Hold all records for at least five years.

Catch certificate Certificate issued by the Fish Export Service that allows fish and shellfish caught by a UK flagged vessel to be exported. Each export requires its own certificate. The certificate allows exports to the EU, Iceland, Ivory Coast, Kuwait, Madagascar, Norway. Thailand, Tunisia and Ukraine. It allows exports to other countries if the catch will return to UK or EU.

catching-up charge Term used by HMRC in 2001 when certain professional taxpayers were no longer allowed to use cash accounting. The catching-up charge was the additional tax they became liable to pay. They could spread it over ten years.

cat, dog and rat Names given to three types of goodwill in the property case *Whiteman Smith Motor Co Ltd v Chaplin [1934]*. Cat relates to the premises; dog to the owner; and rat to the customer. This distinction can be relevant in valuation for capital gains tax and stamp duty land tax (and devolved equivalents).

categorisation Determining what class of national insurance should be paid by someone (SSCBA 1992 s2(1) and SI 1978 No 1689).

category A pension Main state pension payable from state pension age on the basis of the person's national insurance record. From April 2016, this requires 35 years of national insurance contributions. Previously from April 2012, this was 30 years. Before that, it was 9 out of 10 years of working life.

category B pension State pension to a widow or widower who does not qualify for a category A pension. It is paid at a maximum of about two-thirds of category A.

category C pension State pension to someone who had retired by 1948, or the spouse of someone who had. This category became extinct in 2003.

category D pension State pension paid to someone aged 80 or older who does not qualify for a category A or B pension. It is paid at the same rate as category B.

category 1 territory Territory that exchanges tax information with the UK (FA 2007 Sch 24 para 21A(1). For international tax evasion, the maximum penalty is 100% of the tax.

category 2 territory Territory that exchanges tax information with the UK on request but not automatically (FA 2007 Sch 24 para 21A(2)). The maximum penalty for evasion involving that territory is 200% of the tax.

category 3 territory Territory that not agreed to exchange tax information with the UK (FA 2007 Sch 24 para 21A(3)). The maximum penalty for evasion involving that territory is 300% of the tax.

catering The provision of food with facilities for eating it. This is standard-rated for VAT unlike provision of food alone which (with some exceptions) is zero-rated (VATA 1994 Sch 8 Group 1 Note 3). From 1 October 2012, the scope is extended to include provision of food to be eaten in any area set aside for such purpose, whether or not other suppliers also use that area. Guidance on when a supply of food becomes a supply of catering was given in the case *Value Catering Ltd [2011] TC 1189.*

catering adaptation Informal term, for a provision that allows a caterer to distinguish supplies of zero-rated food from standard-rated catering. The provision is set out in VAT Notice 727.

cause Term sometimes used to mean proceedings before a court.

cause list List of cases to be heard by a court.

caution (1) Its legal meanings include a document lodged with the Land Registry by someone having an interest in the land. This prevents the land being sold or registered until the cautioner has been notified.

(2) In Scots law (where the word is pronounced to rhyme with station), a sum of money to be lodged by an offender as security for good behaviour.

caveat In insurance, it relates to conditions, breach of which can invalidate the policy. In Scots law, it is a legal document lodged in court so that no order can be made in a person's absence without first notifying them and allowing them to be heard by the court.

caveat emptor Latin for "let the buyer beware". It is the general rule of contract law that it is the buyer's responsibility to be satisfied on the quality of the goods. This is modified for consumer sales under consumer law.

Cayman Islands UK overseas territory in the Caribbean Sea. The currency is the Cayman Islands dollar. The UK has a double taxation agreement of 2010. The EU designated it as a tax haven in February 2020.

Cayman Islands dollar Currency of Cayman Islands.

CDF denial letter Letter that a taxpayer may send to HMRC under the contractual disclosure facility (CDF). If HMRC suspects a person of tax fraud, it may write to the taxpayer. The taxpayer may either send this denial letter to deny the charge or may agree and usually accept a civil penalty. If HMRC accepts the denial letter, the matter ends. If not, the matter is investigated under a criminal procedure.

ceiling Term sometimes used to mean an upper limit.

ceiniog Welsh for "penny".

cellarage Charge for storing wine.

cell bund Divider within a landfill site to separate areas of waste. Material used for bunds is not subject to landfill tax.

cell engineering Using clay and other materials to protect the sides and bottom of a pit for dumping waste. Such material is not subject to landfill tax.

cemetery Place for buying the dead. There is an allowance in respect of burial plots similar to a capital allowance (ITTOIA 2005 s169; CTA 2009 s146). For VAT, cemetery services are usually exempt as a supply of burial (VATA 1994 Sch 9 Group 8). Details are given in VAT Notice 701/32.

Cenlon Leading case that restricts the rights of a tax inspector to re-open an old case. The citation is *Cenlon Finance Co Ltd v Ellwood [1962] 40 TC 176*. It is discussed in HMRC Manual at BIM34035.

cent One hundredth of a dollar, euro or some other currencies.

centavo One hundredth of a peso or other currency.

centésimo One hundredth of a balboa, currency of Panama.

centime One hundredth of a franc.

céntimo One hundredth of a guarani, currency of Paraguay.

Central African Pension Fund Fund established in 1963 to pay pensions from Rhodesia and Nyasaland (now Zimbabwe). These were taxed under FA 1967 s38 as if paid in UK. This was repealed by FA 1975. The current provision is ITEPA 2003 s648, under which payments are tax free if the foreign residence exemption applies.

Central African Republic African republic. Its currency is the Central French African franc. The UK has no tax treaty. The country is subject to UK sanctions.

Central American Common Market Political and economic group formed in the 1960s, and currently comprising Costa Rica, El Salvador, Guatemala and Nicaragua. Panama has observer status.

central bank The main bank of each country. The UK's central bank is the Bank of England. The main functions of a central bank are to:

- accept deposits and grant loans to commercial banks;
- print and control the issue of banknotes;
- control the money supply;
- manage the country's national debt;
- influence or set interest rates;
- influence exchange rates, and intervene when necessary;
- hold the country's reserves of gold and foreign currencies;
- deal with central banks of other countries; and
- act as lender of last resort to the country's banks.

Central Community Transit Office Office of HMRC that deals with transit of goods across national boundaries.

central control and management Determinant of whether a company registered outside the UK may be regarded as a UK-resident company. The lead case is *de Beers Consolidated Mines Ltd v Howe [1906] 5 TC 198.* HMRC's view is given in statement of practice SP1/90.

central government The national government of the UK, as against devolved assemblies and local authorities.

Central Government Borrowing Requirement The public sector borrowing requirement minus borrowings by local authorities and public corporations.

central heating When fitted to a residential or charitable building, this may qualify for the reduced rate of VAT under VATA 1994 Sch 7A Group 2.

central register

(1) Register held by Financial Conduct Authority of persons and firms authorised to conduct investment business.

(2) Register kept at Companies House. Instead of keeping its own registers, a company may elect to keep its registers this way under CA 2006 s128A and s167A.

Central Warrants Trading Service Automatic execution order book system of the London Stock Exchange.

CEO fraud Fraud in which someone impersonates a director to order funds to be transferred or take over a company. This is done by getting information from Companies House, the company's website and possibly contacting the company under some excuse. Companies House offers an alerting system whereby any changes to the company's entry is automatically notified to named officers by email.

For transfers of funds, someone should not follow such an instruction until satisfied that the direction really did come from a director. This fraud is often perpetrated on regional offices where staff are less likely to know the directors. Someone instructed to transfer funds should call the director's office on a number already known to them.

CEO pay ratio Requirement that a listed company with at least 250 employees must publish the ratio of its chief executive officer to other workers. This requirement is introduced from 1 January 2019 under SI 2018 No 860, with the first ratios published in 2020.

The figure for CEO pay is the single total figure of remuneration (STFR). The company is required to report the ratio to:

- the median (i.e. 50th percentile) full-time equivalent (FTE) remuneration of the company's UK employees;
- the 25th percentile FTE remuneration of the company's UK employees;
- the 75th percentile FTE remuneration of the company's UK employees.

The company must also provide as supporting information:

- the methodology for calculating the ratios
- reasons for changes from the previous year
- why the company believes that the median ratio is appropriate.

cereal Plant products used for food. It is traded as a commodity under the main categories of breadgrains, foddergrains, corn and rice. For VAT, cereals are usually zero-rated as food (VAT Notice 701/14).

cereal year Period from 1 July to 30 June used for the Whisky Export Refund Scheme.

certain annuity Annuity that is paid for a fixed number of years rather than for a person's remaining life.

certainty In law, a lack of ambiguity and confusion. Uncertainty can void a contract. Certainty can be adduced for a will. For a trust, there must be the three certainties of intention, subject matter and beneficiaries.

certificate Document issued by a person or organisation of authority confirming some detail about the named person, such as that they have completed a course or passed an examination.

certificate of age exemption Official document that a person has reach state pension age and so no longer pays national insurance. An employer must accept such a certificate but may accept other evidence of age, such as a passport or driving licence.

certificate of debt Certificate issued by HMRC that a sum is owed (Commissioners of Revenue and Customs Act 2005 s25A).

certificate of discharge Document issued by HMRC confirming that no further inheritance tax is payable for an estate, unless there has been fraud or misrepresentation.

certificate of entitlement Document issued by an embassy, high commission, consulate, visiting force, international organisation or equivalent. This is conclusive evidence that supplies to such a body are zero-rated for VAT. Details are given in VAT Notice 725.

certificate of full disclosure Document issued by a taxpayer to HMRC under the contractual disclosure facility where the taxpayer states that he or she has made full disclosure of all tax irregularities to the best of their knowledge.

certificate of incorporation Document issued by Companies House to confirm that a company has been formed and to give its registration number (Companies Act 2006 ss14-16). Companies House automatically notifies HMRC which writes to the company to advise of its tax liabilities. A company is not subject to corporation tax on formation but when it starts trading or earns any income.

certificate of origin Document indicating from which country goods are imported.

certificate of shipment Document issued by packers or consolidators who despatch goods by road, rail or sea (but not air) as evidence of export. The certificate must comply with conditions set out in VAT Notice 725.

certificate of tax deposit Document issued by HMRC or Inland Revenue in respect of funds deposited to pay future tax liability. The payment earns interest. No new certificates are issued from 23 November 2017. Existing certificates may be used until 23 November 2023. Rates are given in section 3 of this dictionary.

certificate of tax paid Document issued by HMRC confirming how much tax has paid, and the income to which it relates, in a transaction in land (CTA 2009 s830).

certificate of value Certificate in relation to a property transaction to confirm that no stamp duty land tax is payable, usually because of its low value.

certificate relating to protected leasing Certificate issued under CAA 2001 s118 in relation to protected leasing. It allows a capital allowance to be claimed for plant and machinery subject to an overseas lease. The matter is explained in HMRC Manual at CA24100.

certificate to commence business Certificate issued to a public company that it has met legal requirements and may start trading.

Certification Officer Public servant who keeps a register of trade unions (Trade Union and Labour Relations (Consolidation) Act 1992 s254).

certified accountant Term widely used for a member of the Association of Chartered Certified Accountants.

certified photocopy Photocopy of a document which a person of standing, such as an accountant or solicitor, has signed to confirm that this is a fair copy of the original which they have seen.

certified public accountant Accountant who qualified in the USA.

certitude In philosophy, belief in a fact because the source is trusted as against certainty which can be proved. In tax, as in most walks of life, truth is almost always based on certitude.

certiorari Injunction granted by a court to overturn a decision of a lower court or tribunal.

cess Word, now almost obsolete, for a tax, particularly a local tax charged on plantation products such as tobacco and jute.

cessation End of a continuous process, such as when a body ceases trading. Provision for companies are given in CTA 2010 s50. Cessation expenditure is not always tax-deductible, as explained in HMRC Manual at BIM38310.

cessation expenditure Expenses of ceasing to trade. A case in 1925 held that such expenses are not tax-deductible.

cesser clause Clause in a charterparty where the charterer intends to transfer his or her right to have the goods carried to a shipper. It gives the shipper a lien over the goods for the freight payable.

cesspool For VAT, the emptying of a residential cesspool is generally zero-rated as a sewerage supply under VATA 1994 Sch 8 Group 2. Details are given in VAT Notice 701/16.

cestui qui vie Term used where the state holds the land in trust until the rightful owner can be established. The law is Cestui Qui Vie Act 1666, parts of which remain in force.

Ceylon Name of Sri Lanka before 1972.

CFI code Single letter used to identify different types of financial instrument.

chain In computing and for cryptocurrency, a record of previous transactions to which a block of current transactions is added in a blockchain.

chain of executorship Principle whereby if an executor named in a will has already died, that executor's executor acts. So A can appoint B who can appoint C and so on (Administration of Estates Act 1925). This can be avoided by naming alternative executors in the will.

chain of leases Series of leases, such as A leases to B who leases to C, and so on. From 19 April 1999, if any link in the chain is overseas, the whole chain is regarded as an overseas lease.

chain payment Payment to a worker through a series of bodies (ITEPA 2003 s61S).

chairman Person who conducts a meeting. Such a person may have a measure of oversight between meetings. The chairman (who may be female) is appointed according to the organisation's own rules. If no-one is present who may act, the meeting itself appoints a chairman. Provisions for appointing a company chairman are given in CA 2006 s319.

chairman's statement Statement made by a chairman of a company or other body. For companies, it is not a compulsory report. It is usually made voluntarily and included as part of the annual report. It often reads like a marketing document for the company. Topics typically covered include:

- strategy and business plans
- general trading performance
- prospects for the next year
- performance of different parts of the company
- acquisitions, disposals and any other significant events.

chair rental Arrangement where a hair salon or similar business allows hairdressers to offer their services on the premises. The hairdresser attracts his or her own clients. There have been several VAT cases as to whether such hairdressers are running a separate business. This is relevant as to whether the business needs to register for VAT.

Chamber of Commerce Representative body for trads in an area. It is treated for tax as a mutual trading body, as explained in HMRC Manual at BIM24750.

chambers (1) Private offices of barristers.
(2) Categories of tribunal, depending on what issues they hear. Each chamber has a first tier tribunal and an upper tier tribunal.

Champagne French sparkling wine, subject to alcoholic liquor duty and VAT.

chancel Part of an Anglican church between the nave and altar. A local land owner (called the lay rector) could be liable to pay for repairs to the chancel under laws going back to the 13th century and now contained in Chancel Repairs Act 1932. A legal challenge to this ancient charge was unsuccessful in the case *Aston Cantlow Wallbanks [2003]*. Under Land Registration Act 2002, existing chancel repair obligations cease on 13 October 2013 unless the church has noted the interest with the Land Registry before this date.

Chancellor of the Exchequer The chief finance minister in the British government. He (there has yet to be a she) usually announces the government's tax and spending plans in a Budget.

Chancery Division of the High Court where tax cases are often heard (Judicature Acts 1873-75).

change of accounting date When a business decides to make up its accounts to a different date. For income tax, the provisions are given in ITTOIA 2005 from s214.

change of name In general, a person is free to use any name they wish, provided it is not done for a fraudulent purpose. HMRC are prepared to accept stage names for performers, for example. For a permanent change of name, a person can simply decide that they wish to have a different name and that is effective, provided it is used for all purposes and is not fraudulent. It is up to different agents, such as the bank, as to whether accept a name change. They are unlikely to accept repeated changes, and may ask for a reason.

Women sometimes adopt their husbands surname on marriage, but this is just a tradition. There is a formal procedure known as deed poll for those aged 16. This can be enrolled or unenrolled.

An unenrolled deed poll is a document that the person drafts and has signed by two witnesses. There is no cost. An enrolled deed poll may be made by someone who is at least 18. It is registered at the court, and costs £36.

A completed form can be downloaded, completed, and sent with payment to Queen's Bench Division of the High Court.

An adult who is baptised in the Church of England may change his or her first name at baptism under Canon B27(6).

A company may change its name under the procedures of CA 2006 ss77-81.

channel For Customs, an exit through which a traveller walks with any luggage and goods. There are three channels:

- red: if the traveller as any goods to declare
- blue: if coming from EU with no goods to declare
- green: if coming from outside EU with no goods to declare.

Channel Tunnel Fixed link between England and France that opened on 1 December 1990. Goods must be declared for travel between the countries. Under a bilateral agreement, British and France Customs officers may operate in each other's territories.

Export clearance facilities are at Ashford in Kent. Incoming freight trains can be cleared at Willesden by arrangement.

chapel For VAT, admission to a chapel was held not to come within the exemption for cultural admission as the dean and canons were paid *(Dean and Canons of Westminster [1997] VTD 15703).*

chapel of rest The use of such chapel can be VAT exempt if provided as part of a funeral service. Details are given in VAT Notice 701/32.

CHAPS Acronym for Clearing House Automatic Payment System.

chapter 2 overlap charge Term used in relation to disguised remuneration (ITEPA 2003 s554Z11C).

chapter 11 In the USA, section of the Bankruptcy Reform Act 1978 which allows a company in financial trouble to be protected while it reorganises itself.

chapter 13 In the USA, section of the Bankruptcy Reform Act 1978 that allows a company to continue trading while paying its creditors by regular monthly instalments.

charcoal For VAT, charcoal used as domestic fuel may be reduced-rated under VATA 1994 Sch 7A Group 1. Details are given in VAT Notice 701/19.

charge (1) In law, the meanings include a legal interest in the assets of a company. These must be reported to Companies House under CA 2006 from s860.

(2) In Scots law, a demand made to a person to pay a sum of money as required by the court.

(3) A general term for any sum of money that a person is expected to pay.

chargeable asset Item that may trigger a capital gains tax liability on disposal.

chargeable disposal Disposal of a fixed asset that may trigger a liability for capital gains tax (TCGA 1992 s34(1)-(3)).

chargeable dwelling Residential property for which council tax is payable.

chargeable gain Capital gain made by a company (TCGA 1992 s15(1)). It is subject to corporation tax rather than capital gains tax, though many provisions are the same. The company is charged on the whole gain, possibly subject to indexation relief to January 2019.

chargeable goods Goods which are liable to VAT on importation.

chargeable income Total income on which an individual is liable to pay income tax.

chargeable lifetime transfer Transfer of funds during a person's lifetime, usually to a trust, on which inheritance tax may be payable.

chargeable period Accounting period for which a corporation tax return is required (TMA 1970 s118(1)).

chargeable soft drink Drink that is liable to soft drinks industry levy.

chargeable transfer Gift made during a person's lifetime that is potentially chargeable to inheritance tax. Usually a gift is chargeable if sufficiently large, not normal expenditure (such as a birthday present) and the donor dies within seven years.

chargeable value For inheritance tax, the value of an estate comprising its assets from which liabilities, exempt gifts and reliefs are subtracted.

charge card Payment card that allows the holder to spend money provided the whole amount is repaid within a defined period. American Express and Diners Club are charge cards.

charge point Device to charge electric vehicles (Automated and Electric Vehicles Act 2018 s9(1)(a)). From 25 November 2016, a 100% first year allowance may be claimed for an electric charge point (CAA 2001 s45EA). The end date of April 2019 has been extended to 31 March 2023 for corporation tax and 5 April 2023 for income tax by FA 2019 s34. From 6 April 2018, an employee is not liable to income tax on the benefit in kind for charging his or her car at their workplace under ITEPA 2003 s237A.

charging clause Clause in a trust that allows a trustee to charge for their services.

charging notice Document issued by HMRC after a preliminary notice stating the amount of diverted profits tax payable (FA 2015 from s95).

charitable company Charity which is a company (Charities Act 2011 s193). Its requirements are given from s194. Such a company may now convert to a Charitable Incorporated Organisation under s228.

charitable donations relief Tax relief that a company may claim for donations to charity under CTA 2010 ss189-217. It replaces what was previously called a charge on income. The present provision is sometimes called Corporate Gift Aid. If the donation to the charity is for the purpose of the business, the expense is allowed under the normal rules for business expenditure. The main points of charitable donations relief are:

- the donation must be of cash or (subject to conditions) of investments
- from 1 April 2014, it also applies to donations to a community amateur sports club, subject to an anti-avoidance rule (FA 2014 s35)
- the donation must not be repayable by the charity
- the donation may reduce the company's taxable profits to zero but cannot turn a profit into a loss, nor increase a loss
- the charity does not provide any benefit to the donor company above a limit (given in section 3 of this dictionary)

If a charity owns a trading company, that company may donate all its profits to the charity. The rules about the charity not providing benefit to its donor are disapplied.

charitable giving This attracts many tax reliefs as set out in HMRC helpsheet HS342.

charitable incorporated organisation (CIO) Legal form for charities. It was created in 2016 under Charities Act 2011 from s205 as an alternative to being a limited company or trust. A CIO only needs to make one return a year.

charitable purpose Purpose for which a body qualifies as a charity. Under Charities Act s3(1) it must be for the public benefit and within the scope of listed categories.

charitable relief Relief from business rates where a premises is used wholly or mainly for a charitable purpose or for a community amateur sports club. The relief must be at least 80%. The local authority has discretion to increase this to 100%.

charity A body that exists for a purpose now set out in Charities Act 2011. Donations to charities may qualify for tax relief under Gift Aid. Bequests to charities are exempt from inheritance tax (IHTA 1984 s23). There are other tax provisions for charities.

Charity Commission Body responsible for overseeing charities in England and Wales. There are equivalent bodies for Scotland and Northern Ireland (Charities Act 2011 s13).

charity exemption Sum left to charity which is exempt from inheritance tax (IHTA 1984 s23).

charity funded equipment Equipment used for medical, veterinary and similar. This may qualify for zero-rating under VATA 1984 Sch 8 Group 15. Details are given in VAT Leaflet 701/6.

charity land Land owned by a charity. Provisions regarding its disposal are given in Charities Act 2011 s123.

charity law The law relating to charities in England and Wales (Charities Act 2006 s2(8); Charities Act 2011 s331(1)).

charity merger When two or more charities become one under Charities Act 2011 from s305.

charity shop Retail unit selling goods to raise funds for charity. Such a ship usually benefits from reduced business rates. Donated goods may be zero-rated for VAT.

charity tribunal Body formed by Charities Act 1993 s2A to hear appeals from the Charity Commission, such as for non-registration of charity.

chartered accountant Member of Institute of Chartered Accountants in England and Wales, Institute of Chartered Accountants of Scotland or Institute of Chartered Accountants of Ireland.

chartered company Company that has been formed by royal charter. Such companies are now usually restricted to professional bodies and similar.

Chartered Institute for Securities and Investment (CISI) Professional body for those who deal with securities and investments. It was formed in 1992 and was given a royal charter on 9 October 2009, prior to which it was called the Securities Institute. It absorbed the Institute for Financial Planning on 1 November 2015.

Chartered Institute of Payroll Professionals (CIPP) Professional body for those who work in payroll. It was formed in 1998 as the Institute of British Payroll Managers. It was given its Royal Charter in November 2010.

Chartered Institute of Public Finance and Accountancy (CIPFA) Professional body for accountants who work in the public sector. It is usually known by its initials, pronounced as "sip-far". It was formed in 1885 and given its Royal Charter in 1959.

Chartered Institute of Taxation (CIOT) Professional tax body, formed in 1930 and given a royal charter in 1994, that deals exclusively with tax.

Chartered Insurance Institute Body maintaining professional standards in the insurance industry.

chartered tax adviser Qualified member of the Chartered Institute of Taxation.

Charter for Budget Responsibility Policy statement produced by HM Treasury in accordance with Budget Responsibility and National Audit Act 2011 s1.

Charter of Fundamental Rights Document of the European Union proclaimed on 7 December 2000 and formally adopted by Lisbon Treaty of 1 December 2009. The Charter has six titles covering dignity, freedoms, equality, solidarity, citizen's rights, justice and general principles. The UK ceases to be bound by it from 1 January 2021 under the European Union (Withdrawal) Act 2018 s5(4)).

charterparty Agreement by which a master lets an entire ship or part of a ship to the charterer and agrees to deliver the cargo for an agreed sum.

charting In investment, plotting a graph of the price of a share of security. From the shape, there may be an indication of future movement.

chart of accounts Listing of accounts, occasionally used. The accounts have six categories: assets, liabilities, capitals. sales, cost of sales, and expenses.

charts In the sense of maps and similar, these may be zero-rated under VATA 1994 Sch 8 Group 3 Item 5 as explained in VAT Notice 701/10. Charts intended as posters, plans or design drawings are not within the scope of this zero-rating. A chart must be geographical in nature. In the case *Brooks Histograph Ltd [1994] VTS 1570*, the tribunal did not allow zero-rating for a historical chart giving genealogies.

chase (1) In commerce, pursue action such as delivery or payment.
(2) In gambling, a further bet in a (usually vain) attempt to recover losses.
(3) In property law, a small unenclosed deer forest protected under common law for a limited number of people.

chattels Tangible moveable property. Bills of Sale Act 1878 s4 defines as "goods, furniture, and other articles capable of complete transfer by delivery". Section 5 adds machinery. It includes fixtures and fittings if either free standing or easily removed. Crops that have been harvested are chattels; crops still attached to the ground are not. Shares, securities and similar are not chattels. HMRC defines chattels as including household and personal goods, furniture, jewellery, antiques and works of art, stamp and coin collections, cars, caravans and boats, electrical equipment, clothes, books and garden equipment.

chattels exemption Relief from capital gains tax for the first £6,000 (unchanged since 1989) of capital gain of chattels, which are tangible moveable property (TCGA 1992 s262). This relief is additional to the annual exemption.

Ch D Chancery Division of the High Court. It is used as part of the citation of cases, including many tax cases, heard there.

cheat Common law offence of fraudulently obtaining the property of another. It has been replaced by statute law except for cheating the Revenue, which remains a criminal offence. It is not necessary for the act to be deceitful. The Supreme Court held on 25 October 2017 in the case *Ivey v Genting Casinos (UK) Ltd [2017]* that there was cheating by a person who gained an advantage by noticing slight variances in the edges of playing cards.

cheating the Revenue Criminal offence of tax evasion.

check digit A number or letter that serves to verify the rest of a code. The final letter of a national insurance number and the last two digits of a VAT number are check digits.

check-off Deducting a sum from wages to pay trade union dues. Before 23 June 1998, this required a detailed procedure. It now requires authorisation from the employee as for any other wages deduction. In 2016, the government announced plans to stop check-off in the public sector, but abandoned the plans.

cheesecake In marketing, an attractive woman used for marketing. The male equivalent is beefcake.

Chemical Weapons Authority Government body whose functions include regulating the import of chemical weapons.

Chelsea tractor Colloquial name for a larger passenger vehicle.

chemin de fer This game is specifically listed in Betting and Gaming Duties Act 1981 s13(3) as being subject to duty.

cheque ***Definition***

Bill of exchange drawn on a banker payable on demands (Bills of Exchange Act 1882 s73). An unindorsed cheque that appears to have been paid is legally a receipt (Cheques Act 1957 s3). Document issued by an individual instructing their bank to make a payment.

Payment of tax

It remains possible to pay tax by cheque, though HMRC promotes online payments. When sending a cheque, time should be allowed for delivery and clearance of the cheque, otherwise the taxpayer risks a penalty for late payment. A postdated cheque may be sent to HMRC, but this should be accompanied by a covering letter explaining why this has been done. Provisions for paying PAYE by cheque are given in PAYE Regs 2003 reg 219. Tax paid by a cheque is generally regarded as having been paid when the cheque was issued (TMA 1970 s70A(1)), provided it is cleared on first presentation. For VAT from 1 April 2010, the tax is regarded as paid when the cheque has been cleared (VATA 1994 s58B).

Cheque forms

A cheque is usually written on forms provided in books by the bank. This has pre-printed the name of the bank, the name of the account holder, a six-digit sort code, and an eight-digit account number. The cheque is completed by hand or may be produced by printer. This requires the name of the payee, and the amount expressed in words (except for amounts of pence) and in figures. The cheque must be signed and dated. It is still legal to write a cheque on plain paper or indeed any other surface, provided all the details are given. Historically cheques have been written on many odd things, either as a protest or publicity stunt. These have included on a cow and on a bikini-clad girl. These are now likely to be rejected by the bank under its terms and conditions.

Stale cheques

A cheque, under strict law, remains legally valid for six years. In practice, most banks regard a cheque as stale after six months.

Other matters

Cheques were subject to 2d stamp duty (that is 2 old pence, less then 1p), but this was abolished when the UK switched to decimal currency in 1971. The Payments Council said that cheques would be abolished in 2018, but that proposal has now been abandoned.

cheque card Plastic card that guaranteed payment of a cheque up to a stated amount. They were introduced in October 1995, became a national scheme in July 1969, and ended on 1 July 2011. At that time, the limit was usually £50, though 12% of cards had a limit up to £250. Some banks still offer cheque cards, though their function has now been replaced by debit cards.

cheque requisition Internal document within an organisation requiring a cheque to be issued.

cheque voucher Document provided by an employer for an employee to acquired goods or services (ITEPA 2003 s84(4)). It is treated as part of gross pay.

cherries Fruit, ordinary zero-rated as food. Drained cherries are specifically zero-rated by VATA 1994 Sch 8 Group 1 Items Overriding the Exceptions 2. Standard-rated rating applies to some other forms of cherry, as explained in VAT Notice 701/14.

cherry-picking Any arrangement whereby someone selects the best parts of a package instead of the whole package. In the USA, the term is particularly used for research and development funding, and for transfer pricing.

chetrum One hundredth of a ngultrum, currency of Bhutan.

Chevening House A government residence, usually provided to the foreign secretary. It is governed by Chevening Estate Act 1959. Accommodation is specifically exempt from income tax under ITEPA 2003 s101. Capital gains tax is also disapplied under TCGA s270.

chiao Chinese coin worth one tenth of a yuan.

chicory Plant whose roots may be baked and used to make a drink similar to coffee. In drink form, the product is specifically VAT zero-rated under VATA 1994 Sch 8 Group 1 Excepted Item 3 Item Overriding the Exception 4. Further guidance is provided in VAT Notice 701/14. If chicory is sold in other forms, such as wood, it is standard-rated.

CHIEF Customs Handing of Import and Export Freight. This is Customs' computerised system for freight handling.

chief Most senior. The term is used in job titles such as chief executive and chief accountant.

Chief Secretary to the Treasury Government minister, usually in the Cabinet, who is second in command to the Chancellor of the Exchequer at The Treasury.

child *Definition*

The word is used in the context of either relationship or age. For age, the term means a person under the age of 14 (Children and Young Person's Act 1933). This definition is used for VAT zero-rating on children's clothing (VATA 1995 Sch 8 Group 16). Someone between the ages of 14 and 17 is legally a young person, and anyone under 18 is legally a minor. Different ages are used for other purposes. A child can be someone up to the age of 24 in relation to welfare for troubled families (Welfare Reform and Work Act 2016 s3(10). There is a general ban on children working under the age of 13 (Children and Young Persons Act 1933 s18). There are limited exceptions for working in a parent's shop or farm, entertaining, and singing in a church choir (Children Act 1972 s1).

Taxes

Children are liable to pay all taxes except national insurance while under 16. While under 18, the responsibility for filing a tax return rests with the parents. The income of a child from a parent is capped at £100. This does not apply to income from another relation. The term means under 18 in relation to child plans (ITTOIA s695A(5)). Child relief against income tax was abolished in 1980, or 1982 for children overseas. Instead child benefit may be claimed for a child who is either under 16, or under 20 and in full-time education (SSCBA 1992 s141). If the parent earns more than £50,000 a year, they may be liable to the high income child benefit charge.

Death of child

From 23 July 2019, the cost of a funeral for a child under 18 is paid by the state from the Children's Funeral Fund. From April 2020, an employee may claim statutory parental bereavement leave, and possibly statutory parental bereavement pay if their child under 18 dies, or if a baby is stillborn after 24 weeks of pregnancy.

Relationship

The word can alternatively be used to describe a relationship. So children means sons and daughters of any age. For wills, "children" from 1969 includes adopted and illegitimate children. Such children may now inherit on the same basis as natural children except they cannot inherit a title.

child bearing age For the purposes of perpetuities, a woman is considered to be of child bearing age between 12 and 55 (Perpetuities and Accumulations Act 1964 a2), though women have given birth when outside this range. There are no age limits for claiming statutory maternity pay.

child benefit Social security benefit, usually paid to the mother, for a child either 16 or under 18 and in full-time education. The benefit does not depend on having paid national insurance. It was introduced by Child Benefit Act 1975 and is now paid under SSCBA 1992 s141. Child benefit is not itself taxed, but if the parent or guardian earns more than £50,000, the high income child benefit charge may, from 7 January 2013, claw back all or some of it.

child benefits records scandal On 20 November 2007, Chancellor of the Exchequer Alistair Darling announced that HMRC had lost two discs containing details of 25 million individuals in connection with child benefit. The discs have not been found, but there is no indication that the data were used improperly.

childcare Any form of provision to look after a child. A workplace nursery is a tax-free benefit from 1990 (ITEPA 2003 s318). The government provides various forms of assistance. This includes up to 30 hours a week tax-free childcare from September 2017 (Children Act 2016 from s1) and childcare accounts (Childcare Payments Act 2014 s2).

childcare account Scheme under which a parent may receive up to £500 every three months (£2,000 a year) per child. This doubles to £4,000 a year for a disabled child. The government pays £2 for every £8 contributed by the parent. The parent must be earning at least an amount equal to the national minimum wage for 16 hours a week but not more than £100,000 a year. If the parent has a partner, they must also meet these conditions. The child must be under 12 (17 if disabled). The scheme was fully introduced from 14 February 2018, having been available for children under 9 from 15 January 2018, and children under 6 from 24 November 2017. The law is Childcare Payments Act 2014.

childcare voucher Voucher that an employer may provide tax-free to an employee to pay towards childcare. The scheme was closed to new entrants on 4 October 2018 but existing recipients may continue to receive them. The maximum amount of voucher ranges from £22 to £55 depending on the employee's marginal rate of income tax. Vouchers up to these limits are free of tax (ITEPA 2003 s84(2A)). Childcare vouchers may continue to be provided during the coronavirus lockdown, even though the employee is furloughed or working from home. If the employer and employee both agree to accept a lower amount, that may be increased again later within the limits. HMRC's employment bulletin of December 2020 notes that some workers may be better off giving up vouchers and moving to tax-free childcare. More details are given in section 3 of this dictionary.

child maintenance bonus Additional that may to jobseeker's allowance under Child Support Act 1995 s10. This is tax-free (ITEPA 2003 s670).

child of the family Child who is regarded as the equivalent to a son or daughter under Matrimonial Causes Act 1973 or Children Act 1989.In relation to capital gains tax on an interest in possession settlement, the term is defined in TCGA 1992 s169F(6).

Child Poverty Action Group Charity formed in 1965 to campaign for an end to child poverty in Britain. It also produces extensive literature on social security and other welfare issues.

child relief Allowance once given against income tax for a child. It was introduced in 1910 and abolished in 1980 for British children and 1982 for overseas children. It was replaced by increased child benefit.

children's barred list List kept by the Independent Barring Board of people not allowed to work with children (Safeguarding Vulnerable Groups Act 2006 s2(1)).

children's books These are specifically VAT zero-rated under VATA 1994 Sch 8 Group 3. This specifically exempts "children's picture books and painting books". The book does not have to be printed on paper. It includes books printed on card, plastic or cloth. Further details are given in VAT Notice 701/10. This has been litigated a few times. The case *W F Graham (Northampton) Ltd [1979] VTD 908* found that it zero-rated a book mainly comprising cut-out characters. *The Book People Ltd [2002] VTD 18240* allowed zero-rating for a book printed on card that could be taken apart and turned into a model house.

children's car seats These may be reduced-rated for VAT under VATA 1995 Sch 7A Group 5.

Children's Funeral Fund Body established to pay for the funerals of children under 18 from 23 July 2019.

children's programme Television programme primarily intended for children under 15. Such programmes attract a specific corporation tax relief (CTA 2009 s1216AC).

child's special allowance Social security benefit paid under SSCBA 1992 s56. It is not taxed (ITEPA 2003 s677).

child support order Form of attachment of earnings order requiring a deduction from an employee's wages to support a child.

Child Survivor Fund Scheme established in September 2015 by the German government to pay €2,500 to each survivor of the Holocaust. On 16 December 2015, the UK government said such payments are not subject to inheritance tax.

child's tax credit Means-tested social security benefit to help low income families pay for children. It is not taxable. It is being replaced by universal credit from 2013. The law is Tax Credits Act 2002 from s8.

child trust fund Government sponsored savings scheme for children introduced in 2005 (Child Trust Funds Act 2004) and discontinued for new claimants in 2011 (Savings Accounts and Health in Pregnancy Grant Act 2010 s1). It is replaced by the junior ISA. The scheme was open to children born between 31 August 2002 and 2 January 2011. A trust fund was created for each child into which the government paid £250. Parents and others may add up to £1,200. In September 2020, the first such trusts funds matured.

child winter heating assistance Scottish benefit introduced on 31 August 2020 whereby a family with children receives an extra £200 each winter towards their heating costs.

Chile South American republic. Its currency is the Chilean peso of 100 centavos. The UK has a double taxation convention of 2003.

Chiltern Hundreds Area of Stoke, Desborough and Burnham in the Chilterns. In medieval times a steward was appointed to suppress robbery. Since 1701, this has remained as a nominal office of profit to which the Chancellor of the Exchequer may appoint someone. This is the curious British means by which an MP resigns.

China Large Eastern republic. Its currency is the yuan or renminbi of 10 jiao or 100 fen. The UK has a double taxation convention of 1984 and an air transport agreement of 1981.

Chinese walls Term used to describe a barrier within an organisation, so that confidential or sensitive material known to one person is not known to others where this could lead to a conflict of interest.

chip (1) Small piece of computer hardware usually on a piece of silicon. There is a VAT scheme of reverse charge for importing such chips.
(2) Token used for gaming, particularly in casinos.

chip and pin Scheme widely adopted for using debit and credit cards from 14 February 2006. The card has a microchip containing basic information. The card holder either enters a four-digit number for payment by any amount, or may tap the card against a reader for payments up to a limit, which has been £45 from April 2020.

chip butties Sandwich or bread roll containing chips. For VAT, this is a single supply of standard-rated hot takeaway food. The bun cannot be separately zero-rated *(P A Marshall [1995] VTD 13766).*

chocolate Confectionery item. For VAT, this is generally standard-rated as confectionery as an exception to the zero-rating of food. However cakes remain as food items, even though they are decorated with chocolate. Further details are given in VAT Notice 701/14.

chocolate biscuit A biscuit wholly or partly covered with chocolate, or something similar in taste and appearance, is standard-rated for VAT under VATA 1994 Sch 8 Group 1 Excepted Item 2. Further details are given in VAT Notice 701/14.

Chocolate Dundee These were held to be VAT standard-rated as chocolate biscuits in the case *Adams Foods Ltd [1983] VTD 1514.*

chocolate marzipan walnut Product comprising a meringue base on which was marzipan, walnuts, buttercream and a chocolate coating. This was held to be zero-rated food in the case *Goodfellow & Steven Ltd [1987] VTD 2453.*

choice-based letting Scheme that allows individuals to bid for council and housing association properties. It is only open to those on a council house waiting list or those who are already a council or housing association tenant and wish to move. Not all councils offer choice-based letting. The council or association gives details of what property is available and invites bids. Some councils restricts the number of properties for which a person may bid. The property often comes with criteria as to who may bid. The property is usually awarded to the bidder who has the highest priority. If they turn it down, it is offered to the next person, and so on. The charity Shelter provides guidance on this letting.

chon Currency of North Korea.

choose option Option where the caller may decide whether to treat it as a call or put option.

chose As a noun, the words means a chattel under the control of the owner.

Christian Adherent of Christianity. Many laws and dates are based on Christian principles.

Christian name A person's first name or forename.

Christmas Festival on 25 December that commemorates the birth of Christ. It is a public holiday, and a quarter day in England and Wales. A large shop may not open on Christmas Day (Christmas Day (Trading) Act 2004 s1(1)).

Christmas bonus

(1) In social security, an additional £10 (unchanged since 1971) paid to claimants at Christmas time.

(2) In employment, a present given by an employer to an employee. This is usually a taxable benefit in kind though the tax may be paid by the employer under a PAYE settlement agreement, or it may come within the scope of a trivial benefit.

A payment in cash is treated as gross pay (ITEPA 2003 s62). A voucher that can be readily exchanged for cash is treated as cash as in the case *Ladler v Perry [1965]*. This matter is discussed in HMRC Manual at EIM01040.

Christmas party Party for employees organised to celebrate Christmas. This is a tax-free benefit up to £150 per attendee, who need not be employees (ITEPA 2003 s264). The tax relief applies to staff parties and social events at any time of the year. The limit is cumulative throughout the tax year. The amount includes VAT even when the employer is able to claim it back as input tax. The limit may not be used to buy Christmas presents. HMRC confirmed in the December 2020 Employers Bulletin that this relief applies to virtual parties held during the coronavirus lockdown.

chuck-a-luck Game that is specifically listed in Betting and Gaming Duties Act 1981 a13(3) as subject to duty.

chugger Informal term for a person who is paid to raise funds for charity.

churning Repeating a financial transaction for an ulterior purpose such as earning more commission. There are anti-avoidance provisions against pension churning, that is withdrawing a sum from a pension fund tax-free and then reinvesting it back into a pension fund.

church Place where Christians meet for worship, or the people who meet. The duty to maintain a Church of England building is given in Canon F13. The duty to keep a record of property is in Canon F17. There is no general relief from VAT for church expenditure, though grants for listed buildings are available under the Listed Places of Worship Scheme.

Church Commissioners Body that manages the historic property assets of the Church of England. It was formed in 1948 from a merger of Queen Anne's Bounty founded in 1704 and Ecclesiastical Commissioners of 1836. The Commissioners provides funds for church and cathedral maintenance, and is responsible for clergy pensions that accrued before 1998.

churning In finance, the recycling of funds. There are often rules against it. Examples include:

- stockbrokers and insurers who repeatedly trade for the primary purpose of earning commission
- moving sums between two bank accounts to create an illusion of trading
- taking sums from a pension fund and reinvesting them in another pension scheme to get extra tax relief.

ciabatta Form of Italian white bread. In the case *Ainsleys of Leeds Ltd [2005] VTD 19694,* it was held that heating it was to provide tasty food. Accordingly it was zero-rated and not standard-rated as hot takeaway food.

cider Alcoholic drink made from the fermentation of apple juice. If it has a strength of more than 1.2% it is subject to its own rate of alcoholic liquor duty and VAT (ALDA 1979 s1(6)). From 1 January 1997, cider with a strength above 5.5% is taxed as wine.

cigar Product made from rolled tobacco leaves. It is subject to tobacco duty under TBDA 1979, and to VAT. A definition of cigars is given in EU Directive 2011/64 Article 4.

cigarette Product made from shredded tobacco in a paper sleeve. It is subject to tobacco duty under TBDA 1979 and to VAT. A definition of cigarettes is given in EU Directive 2011/64 Article 3.

Cinderella rule Provision for main residence relief and statutory residence test that a person is UK resident on a day if he or she was in the UK at midnight.

cinema Place where films are shown to the public. Admission to a cinema is not VAT exempt under cultural services of VATA 1994 Sch 9 Group 13 as it does not involve a live performance *(Chichester Cinema at New Park Ltd [2004] VTD 19344).*

circle of mutuality Scope of tax-free mutual trading. This is discussed in HMRC Manual at BIM24480.

circuit breaker

(1) In financial markets, a measure put in place by an exchange to present large movements in securities or to stop financial speculation. This usually works by suspending trading for a short while.

(2) For coronavirus, a lockdown for long enough to inhibit the spread of the virus.

circular transaction Series of transactions that end up where they started. Such a transaction may be used for tax avoidance or to create an illusion of greater trading. This is a hallmark of a tax avoidance scheme.

circulating capital Capital in the form of cash, debtors, raw material and stock. The tax implications are discussed in HMRC Manual at BIM33015.

circus Travelling company of entertainers who often perform in a large tent. Their performances are specifically brought within the scope of theatrical productions relief from corporation tax under CTA 2009 s1217FA(3).

CIS return Tax return by a building contractor of tax deducted under the construction industry scheme (FA 2004 s70(1)(a)); FA 2007 Sch 24 para 13(1ZD).

citation Name of a court or tribunal case. The citation usually gives the names of the parties, the year the case was heard, the court where it was heard, and the name of the body reporting the case. Each set of law reports has its own conventions for the citation.

Citizens Advice Bureau Charitable organisation that provides free assistance on legal and administrative matters. It was formed in 1939, and became independent of the government (though still receiving some government funding) in 1972.

City Term used for the area of London associated with finance, a role it has had since medieval times. It is an area of about one square meal between Waterloo Bridge and Tower Bridge. The term is often used to mean the financial sector generally.

civil damages Penalty for a minor or technical breach of law, such as for motoring and tax offences. The extent to which they are tax-deductible is discussed in HMRC Manual at BIM38540.

civilian clothing Normal clothing which is generally not tax-deductible. The matter is discussed in HMRC Manual at BIM37910 where the term is used.

civil investigation of fraud Scheme used by HMRC to give a taxpayer a final chance to confess to tax irregularities and avoid criminal proceedings.

civil law Field of law that relates to disputes between parties, as against criminal law.

civil partnership Legal relationship that became possible in England between same sex couples from 5 December 2005 under Civil Partnership Act 2004, and for opposite sex couples from 2 December 2019. As the parties must give 28 days' notice, the first civil partnerships were 28 days after these dates. Civil partnerships were introduced in Northern Ireland from 13 January 2020. Opposite sex civil partnerships were introduced in Scotland from 23 June 2020. A couple in a same sex civil partnership may convert it to marriage under Marriage (Same Sex Couples) Act 2013. For tax purposes, a civil partnership is treated the same as a marriage.

civil penalty Penalty for a minor breach of the law which is dealt with outside the criminal law. Most tax penalties are civil. This means that the matter must be proved on the balance of probabilities rather than beyond doubt. It also means that someone penalised does not get a criminal record.

civil proceedings Legal action brought in the civil courts to settle a dispute between parties. HMRC's right to bring such action is derived from Commissioners of Revenue and Customs Act 2005 s25.

Civil Service Body that provides public administration regardless of which party forms the government. Civil servants work to a code under Constitutional Reform and Governance Act 2010 s5). The four characteristics required by the code are integrity, honesty, objectivity and impartiality. HMRC staff are treated as civil servants.

Civil Society Forum Body that the European Union and UK may each form under Article INST 8 of the EU/UK withdrawal agreement of 24 December 2020. Its function is "to conduct a dialogue on the implementation of Part Two of the agreement".

claimant Person who claims something, including someone entitled to social security benefits.

claimant commitment Requirement for a recipient of universal credit to undertake agreed actions to find work (WRA 2012 s14(1)). The provision was introduced from 1 May 2012. A similar provision applies to jobseeker's allowance under Jobseekers Allowance Act 1995 s9.

claimant company Company that receives the benefit of group relief.

claimant's total tax In relation to jobseeker's allowance, this is given a specific meaning in PAYE Regulations 2003 reg 161(5). A similar meaning is given for employment and support allowance in PAYE Regulations 2003 reg 184N(5).

claim period Period in which a claim must be made. For group relief from, corporation tax, this is explained in CTA 2010 s142.

clandestine entrant Official name for a stowaway. Under Immigration and Asylum Act 1996 s32, a driver of a vehicle is liable for a penalty unless the driver can show that he or she did not know they had stowaways, had an effective system for checking, and had followed that system.

class Term representing a group of people or things defined by one or more criteria. It is used in connection with social status, national insurance contributions, and categories of investment.

class 1 national insurance National insurance paid by employees aged between 16 and state pension age, and by employers for employees above 16 (SSCBA 1992 ss5-9B). There are some exemptions. It is paid on earnings between the earnings threshold and upper earnings limit, and at a lower rate above the upper earnings limit. It is collected by the employer as a payroll function.

class 1A national insurance National insurance paid by the employer alone (not the employee) on the value of benefits in kind provided to employees under SSCBA 1992 ss10-10ZC. It was introduced in 1991 for cars and extended to other benefits in 2000. It is payable as a single annual payment by 6 July after the tax year. From 6 April 2020, class 1A is also assessed on termination payments above £30,000 and sporting testimonials above £100,000.

class 1B national insurance National insurance payable by an employer in respect of any PAYE settlement agreement under SSCBA 1992 s10A. It is payable by 22 July after the tax year.

class 2 national insurance National insurance of a small fixed amount payable by the self-employed unless their earnings are below a threshold (SSCBA 1992 ss11-12). From 6 April 2015, it is collected as part of the annual tax return.

class 3 national insurance Voluntary payment of national insurance by someone who wishes to maintain their contributions record, usually to ensure their right to receive the state pension (SSCBA 1992 ss13-14).

class 3A national insurance Voluntary payment of national insurance that may have been made between 6 October 2015 and 5 April 2017 by someone who received state pension age before 6 April 2016 (SSCBA 1992 ss14A-14C). It gave them the right to make a single payment to receive a higher state pension.

class 4 national insurance National insurance introduced in 1973 as an addition to class 2 payable by the self-employed. The law is SSCBA 1992 ss15-18A. It is collected with income tax according to the annual tax return.

class-closing Provision that allows a personal representative to close a class of beneficiary (Perpetuities and Accumulations Act 1964). For example, a trust created by a will leaving assets to be shared among "my grandchildren" may be closed when the last daughter or daughter-in-law is considered to be past child-bearing age. The closure is effective even if a subsequent grandchild is born.

class gift Gift in a will where the beneficiaries are described rather than defined, such as "to my grandchildren".

classes of shares Shares whose rights are the same (CA 2006 s629(1)).

classes of spirits Eight classes of spirits for reporting alcoholic liquor duty.

class gift Provision in a will that defines the beneficiaries rather than naming them such as "to be shared between my grandchildren".

classical taxation Traditional method of taxation whereby the taxpayer completes a return and is assessed on the tax payable. In the UK this has largely been replaced by self-assessment.

classic car For the purposes of taxing employee benefits, this is defined as a car that is at least 15 years old and has a market value of at least £15,000 (ITEPA 2003 s147). An employee provided with such a car has the taxable benefit assessed on market value rather than list price. The matter is discussed in HMRC Manual at EIM14400.

class meeting Meeting of shareholders only of a particular class (CA 2006 ss334-335).

class of beneficiaries When beneficiaries of a trust or estate are described rather than named, such as "my grandchildren".

class pool Group of assets that are considered as one item for the purposes of calculating capital allowances (CAA 2001 s54(4)).

Claudia's law Guardianship (Missing Persons) Act 2017, effective from 31 July 2019. It allows a guardian to be appointed to look after the property of someone who has been missing for 90 days where it is not known whether they are still alive. It is named after Claudia Lawrence who disappeared in 2009.

clause Section of a document or statutory instrument.

clawback Any provision that allows a payment, allowance or relief to be retrospectively claimed back. Tax examples include the VAT capital goods scheme and the high income child benefit charge.

clean chain Series of legitimate transactions that are run to hide a dirty chain of transactions in the missing trader VAT fraud.

clean cough informal term when HMRC gives a taxpayer a final chance to come clean on possible tax evasion. A taxpayer who makes a full confession, without knowing what information HMRC has, will usually avoid a criminal penalty. The taxpayer will still have to pay the tax, interest and probably also a penalty.

clean price For valuing bonds, the actual price minus accrued interest. It is used to compare bonds.

clearance Procedure whereby HMRC confirms the correctness of a tax position in advance. There are very few instances where this is possible. The term is also used for Customs clearing imported goods.

clearance certificate

(1) Document from HMRC confirming that goods have been cleared by Customs.

(2) For inheritance tax, a certificate from HMRC, requested on from IHT30, confirming that all returns have been made and all inheritance tax has been paid.

Clearing Houses Automated Payment System (CHAPS) Bank procedure for making electronic payments from a bank account.

clearing lock Facility in the HMRC **SAFE** computer system "to prevent payments from being automatically allocated against the next charge" (Inspectors' Manual at DMBM121045).

clergy Ministers of the Christian religion, however called. They are taxed as employees of their church, regardless of their legal status. The vicarage or equivalent is not taxed as a benefit in kind. There is still an exemption for clergy whose basic pay is below £8,500 a year. They are exempt from heating and some other charges (ITEPA 2003 ss290A-290B).

client account Funds held by a solicitor or other professional on behalf of clients. They must be protected from other funds of the solicitor. If the solicitor keeps the interest earned, that is taxed as investment income.

climate change Belief that the climate is changing because of man-made activity, such as the burning of fossil fuels. Many tax provisions have been designed to encourage environmentally friendly behaviour.

climate change agreement Agreement that may be made by a large user of energy. They reduce the amount of climate change levy payable if other environmentally friendly steps are taken.

climate change levy Tax introduced on 1 April 2001 as a charge on electricity production, to encourage greener forms of energy production. The main law is Finance Act 2000 from s30 and Sch 6.

clinical commissioning groups Bodies established under National Health Service Act 2006 s1L. This definition is followed in CTA 2010 s986.

close company Company under the control of five or fewer persons, or where all the shareholders are directors (CTA 2010 s439). Such companies are subject to special corporation tax provisions, particularly with regards to loans to and expenses of participators. Special provisions have existed since 1965. Inheritance tax provisions are given in IHTA 1984 from s94.

closed material Material that may be withheld from an individual at an employment tribunal or other hearing when the material relates to national security. Arrangements must be made to ensure that a party's rights are not compromised by such exclusion. These provisions are contained in SI 2004 No 1861. Their legality was upheld by the Supreme Court in the case *Tariq v Home Office [2011] SC.*

closed period Period of two months before a company announces its results during which directors are not allowed to sell their shares in the company.

closed scheme Pension scheme that is closed to new members but has sufficient assets to meet its existing liabilities (Pensions Act 2004 s153).

closed shop Arrangement that was common in the 1970s whereby a person could only be employed if they belonged to a particular trade union. This is now illegal under Trade Union and Labour Relations (Consolidation) Act 1992.

closed tax year For PAYE, any previous tax year (PAYE Regulations SI 2003 No 2682 reg 2(1)).

close investment holding company Close company that does not trade. It is subject to specific corporation tax provisions. Tax provisions are given in CTA 2010 s34. Income tax provisions for buying an interest in such a company are given in ITA 2007 from s392.

closely inherited Inherited by a close relation for the purpose of inheritance tax residence nil rate band (IHTA 1984 s8K).

closing balance In bookkeeping, the amount of an account, expressed as a debit or credit, at the end of a period.

closing stock Value of stock (or inventory) at the end of the accounting period. This is determined by stocktaking to determine the quantity of each stock item, and then valuing each item. A figure may have to be added to closing stock for work in progress. The total is then entered into the accounting records as a journal entry.

closing the books Process when an accountant or bookkeeper accepts no further transactions for an accounting period.

closure notice Document from HMRC stating that it has finished an enquiry, particularly under TMA 1970 s28B(1).

clothing Clothing is generally not a tax-deductible expense for employment or self-employment as clothing must be worn anyway for warmth and decency. Exceptions are protective clothing, uniforms and performance clothing. A leading case is *Mallalieu v Drummond [1985] 57 TC 330.* For VAT, clothing is standard-rated with exceptions for children's clothing and a few items of protective clothing.

coal Mineral burned to produce energy. Coal is defined and classified according to EC Regulation 1407/2002 which in turn is based on a United Nations definition of 1988. This defines high-grade coal as having a gross calorific value of at least 24 megajoules per kilogram. Producing coal is excluded from some tax-advantaged schemes, such as venture capital trusts (ITA 2007 s307B). Coal for domestic use may be reduced rated for VAT under VATA 1994 Sch 7A Group 1. In practice, a quantity of 1 tonne is usually accepted as for domestic use. There is a tax-free allowance of coal for a miner or former miner (ITEPA s306, which replaces extra-statutory concession A6). The allowances is four tons a year. They may receive a smaller cash allowance instead. The government may buy out this right under Small Business, Enterprise and Employment Act 2015 s158.

coalition When two bodies, usually political ones, agree to work together. It particularly applies to the Conservative and Liberal Democrat coalition government from 2010 to 2015.

coastal erosion Erosion of the coast of any part of England and Wales (Flood and Water Management Act 2010 s1(4)). From 1 January 2015, expenditure on prevention of erosion may be tax-deductible under ITTOIA 2005 s68A.

coasting trade Moving goods from one place in the UK or Isle of Man to another (CEMA 1979 s69).

coastwise Sea traffic between places within the UK and Isle of Man area. It is an offence for coastwise ships to bring in goods from outside the area.

cocoa Beverage that is zero-rated for VAT under VATA 1994 Sch 8 Group 1 Excepted Item 3 Items Overriding the Exception 5. Further guidance is given in VAT Notice 701/14. Cocoa was subject to excise duty until 1962.

code In tax, this usually means the tax code used for PAYE (PAYE Regulations 2003 reg 7(1)).

code of practice Set of rules that govern a body's ethical standards and procedures. HMRC has codes of practice known as COP 1 etc.

codicil Document that is executed in a similar manner to a will but which amends provisions in a will while leaving other provisions unchanged (Wills Act 1837 ss1, 9).

codifying statute Act of Parliament, or part of one, that sets out the existing law rather than creating or amending law. Theft Act 1968 is an example. For tax, CAA 2001 ss21-23, on what assets qualify for capital allowance, are codifying provisions.

coding out Method of recovering tax from an employee by adjusting their tax code (ITEPA s684). From 6 April 2015, coding out may recover between £3,000 and £17,000 depending on how much an employee earns. Someone who wishes arrears of tax to be coded out must submit their tax return online by 31 December.

CO_2 emission figure Amount of carbon dioxide in the exhaust of a vehicle. The figure can be used for determining the taxable benefit of a company car, the capital allowance for a car, vehicle excise duty and some VAT purposes. For VAT, the term is defined in VATA 1994 s57(9).

cod liver oil Dietary supplement. It was held not to be VAT zero-rated as a food in the case *Marfleet Refining Co Ltd [1974] VTS 129.*

coffee Beverage. It is zero-rated as a product used to make the beverage under VATA Sch 8 Group 1 Excepted Item 3 Items Overriding the Exception 4. When served as a drink, it is standard-rated as catering. Further guidance is given in VAT Notice 701/14. Coffee provided to employees at a workplace is not a taxable benefit in kind (ITEPA 2003 s317). Coffee was subject to excise duty until 1962.

coffin Container for burial or cremation of a body. For VAT, this is part of the exemption for burial when provided as part of a funeral. If sold separately, it is standard-rated. Further details are given in VAT Notice 701/32.

cohabitation Two people living together as if they were a married couple or in a civil partnership. In general, such a couple are generally treated as if they were two single people for most tax purposes, with an exception under Scots law. A definition is given for Scots law in Family Law (Scotland) Act 2006 s25(1). There is no spousal exemption under inheritance tax, for example. For social security, they are generally treated on a similar basis to a married couple or civil partnership.

coin *Definition*

Token, usually of metal, that is used as currency or bullion. Legal tender coins are governed by legislation, particularly Coinage Act 1971, as amended. Details of legal tender are given in section 3 of this dictionary. The two functions of money are a store of wealth and a means of exchange. Coins for storing wealth are usually gold coins which are a convenient form of bullion. The commonest such coins are the sovereign and Britannia, still minted in various values. The means of exchange is provided by everyday currency. Since 1914, the value of a coin is as stated by law rather than on the value of the metal from which it is made. This is called fiat money. The difference between the face value of the coin and the value of its metal is called seignorage, which is sometimes regarded as a tax.

VAT

Gold coins come within the exemption for gold under VATA 1994 Sch 9 Group 15 and SI 1999 No 3116, provided the coin:

- was minted after 1800
- is of a purity of at least 900 thousandths
- is of a type normally sold for no more than 180% of the value of the gold alone.

Further guidance is given in VAT Notice 701/21A, parts of which have the force of law.

Coins of any metal may be supplied under the schemes for antiques or second-hand goods.

Accounting and tax

Coins that are legal tender are treated as cash for accounting and tax purposes. A coin not in everyday use may be valued at its value even if legal tender for a lower amount *(Jenkins v Horn [1979] Ch D. 52 TC 591).* That case concerned an employer who paid wages of between £1 and £4 a week but paid in gold sovereigns which are still legal tender for £1.

Chattels

For inheritance tax, coins that are part of a collection or which have been demonetised are chattels and qualify for the chattels exemption.

co-investment Share of an investment. In tax the term is given two specific meanings. For apprenticeship levy, it refers to the 10% contribution a non-levy payer must pay towards the cost of an apprentice. For carried interest on investment management services, the term is defined in TCGA 1992 s103KA(8).

coke The several meanings of this word include the residue from the distillation of coal. This may be used as a fuel. When provided for domestic use, this may be VAT reduced rate under VATA 1994 Sch 7A Group 1. A supply of up to one ton is usually accepted. Further guidance is given in VAT Notice 701/19.

cold calling Approach by a telesales person to someone with whom there is no existing relationship. There are various codes of practice for such activity. From 9 January 2019, it is a specific offence to cold call members of the public with regard to their pensions (SI 2018 No 1396).

cold spell heating assistance Social security benefit that may be provided in Scotland under Social Security (Scotland) Act 2018 s29. It is intended to provide it from winter 2021. It will replace cold weather payments in Scotland.

cold water system This is a feature integral to a building and so many qualify for a capital allowance (CAA 2001 s33A).

cold weather payment Social Fund payment that may be made in England, Scotland or Wales. It is paid to recipients of certain means-tested benefits for periods of seven days when the temperature where the claimant lives falls below zero degrees Centigrade (32 degrees Fahrenheit) for at least seven days. The sum of £25 is paid for each week of sub-zero temperature. The sum should be paid automatically. From winter 2021, it is the intention to replace this payment in Scotland with the cold spell heating assistance.

collar In finance, this means a lower limit, such as an interest rate below which a loan or investment cannot fall.

collector of taxes Tax officer traditionally responsible for collecting tax, rather than an inspector who assesses it.

combined bingo Bingo promoted in one place and combined with a game at another place. The bingo duty provision is in Betting and Gaming Duties Act 1981 s20A.

Comisiwn Elusennau Cymru a Lloegr Welsh name for HM Revenue and Customs.

commercial trade In relation to the remittance basis for income tax, this means a trade conducted on a commercial basis with a view to the realisation of profits (ITA 2007 s809VE(3)).

commercial transaction Loan to an employee on commercial terms which is therefore not within the scope of disguised remuneration. The term is defined for disguised remuneration in ITEPA 2003 s554F, and for assets transferred overseas in ITA 2007 s738.

commercial woodlands Woodlands managed on a commercial basis with a view to realising a profit (ITA 2007 s411(5)). Such an activity is not taxable.

Commerzbank principles Statement of the principle used by the courts in interpreting an international treaty. The principles were set out in the case *Commerzbank AG [1990] STC 285.*

Commissioners for Revenue and Customs Commissioners appointed to run HMRC. They are appointed by the Queen under Letters Patent (Commissioners of Revenue and Customs Act 2005 s1).

commitment fee Fee by a bank for providing a line of credit, or a similar charge. Under normal tax allowability rules, this is not tax-deductible if part of the cost of obtaining capital but may be for securing temporary borrowings. A leading case is *Ascot Gas Water Heaters Ltd v Duff [1942] 24 TC 171.* The matter is discussed in HMRC Manual at BIM45825.

commodities Basic items viewed in large quantities. They comprise hard commodities which are mainly metals, and soft commodities which are mainly foodstuffs. The VAT position on commodities and terminal markets is given in VAT Notice 701/9.

The capital gains tax position on commodity or financial futures is given in TCGA 1992 s143(2). There is a restriction on tax relief for losses from dealing in commodity futures (CTA 2010 s52).

Common Agricultural Policy (CAP) Policy of European Union to provide protection for farmers in a free market (European Communities Act 1972 s6). This has tax implications. The UK ceases to be bound by this Policy from 1 January 2021 when support for farmers is provided under Agriculture Act 2020.

common bond Statement defining who may join a credit union.

common court investment fund Fund established under Administration of Justice Act 1982 s42(1) to provide benefits to a limited range of beneficiaries, such as child victims of road accidents. From 6 April 1999, the fund is taxed as an authorised unit trust.

Common Financial Statement Standard form of debt statement that is widely used by banks and other bodies. Its use can speed up and simplify debt recovery.

Common Fisheries Policy Fishing policy of the European Union established in 1983, replacing an agreement of 1971. The UK ceases to be bound by this from 1 January 2021 when Fisheries Act 2020 applies.

commonhold Form of leasehold where the leaseholders collectively own the communal parts such as staircases and corridors (Commonhold and Leasehold Reform Act 2002).

common law Body of decisions historically made by judges which are part of English law. Tax is outside the scope of common law though judges can still set precedents in interpreting tax law.

common law wife This term means a real wife but where the marriage cannot be proved. This may arise because the marriage took place overseas or (unlikely now), the marriage records cannot be found. A declaration may be made by a court that a couple is married. Note that the term does *not* mean a live-in girlfriend, even if the couple have been together for many years, co-own property or have children. For most tax purposes, a wife means someone to whom a person is legally married *(Rignell v Andrews [1990] Ch D 63 TC 312).*

commorientes Legal principle that where two people die in circumstances where it is not clear who died first, it is assumed that the older died first (Law of Property Act 1925 s184). This provision does not apply in Scotland and is different in Northern Ireland. Commorientes is generally not followed for inheritance tax which assumes they died at the same time (IHTA 1984 s4(2)). In practice, a will may often include a survivorship clause whereby someone may only inherit if they survive the deceased by 28 days (or some other time). For deaths from 1 January 1996, Law Reform (Succession) Act 1995 s1 inserts Administration of Estates Acts 1925 s46(2A) which requires 28 days survivorship where a husband or wife dies intestate.

Common Market Original name given in 1957 to the body that became the European Union.

common ownership When an asset is owned by more than one person. In relation to annual tax on enveloped dwellings on linked dwellings, the term is defined in FA 2013 s117(2).

common parts In relation to leasehold property which is not owned by an individual tenant, this refers to those areas generally used by tenants, such as entrance lobby, corridors, landings, staircases, halls and gardens. For commonhold property, this is defined in Commonhold and Leasehold Reform Act 2002 s25(1).

common premises One of the factors that can indicate commercial interdependence between two companies which can have implications for corporation tax.

common seal Device that a company may use to seal documents. This usually takes the form of a device similar to pliers with a die. When squeezed, this makes an impression on the paper or on a red wafer attached to the paper. Provisions regarding the use of a company seal are contained in CA 2006 from s45. The requirement for every company to have a seal was abolished by Companies Act 1985 s36.

common stock Storage and mixture of goods that have been imported under a Customs relief. They may be regarded as the same goods if they have the same commodity code and have the same and technical and physical characteristics.

common tragedy clause Clause in a will that determines where an estate passes if all the beneficiaries die with the testator.

Commonwealth Term used to describe a political union. The word "wealth" comes from the old word "weal" which means well-meaning. In the UK this usually means a federation of over 50 countries that represent one third of the world's population. The Queen is the head of the Commonwealth. It has been agreed that Prince Charles will succeed her. A pension paid by the government of a Commonwealth country may be free of income tax under ITEPA 2003 s649.

communion Christian commemoration of the death of Christ.
This involves giving the congregation bread (sometimes as wafers) and wine. For VAT purposes, communion wafers are by concession zero-rated as food. Ordinary bread is zero-rated anyway. Fermented communion wine is standard-rated for VAT and subject to alcoholic liquor duty. Unfermented wine is zero-rated. Zero-rating also applies to unfermented grape juice used for the Jewish seder or kaddish, provided it is marked for sacramental use only.

community amateur sports club (CASC) A sporting body open to the whole community, organised on an amateur basis and which provides facilities for more than one sport. Such a body is not a charity but has similar tax treatment (FA 2002 s59 and Sch 18). The matter is discussed in HMRC Manual at BIM24325.

community association Organisation that provides recreational, welfare or similar facilities to a local area. The taxation of their profits is explained in HMRC Manual at BIM24320 and for charities at BIM24790.

community charge Local authority tax imposed in Scotland from 1989, and in England and Wales from 1990 under Local Government Finance Act 1988. It was never imposed in Northern Ireland. It was widely known as the poll tax. It was replaced by council tax in 1993.

community infrastructure levy (CIL) Levy a local authority may make from 6 April 2010 on developments in its area from April 2010 to fund infrastructure (Planning Act 2008 s221).

community interest company (CIC) Company limited by guarantee to provide benefits to the community, created under Companies (Audit, Investigations and Community Enterprise) Act 2004 s26.

community investment tax relief (CITR) Income tax relief of 5% for five years for investment in enterprises for disadvantaged areas. Income tax relief is given by ITA 2007 ss333-382. Corporation tax relief is given by CTA 2010 ss218-269. Capital gains tax relief is provided by TCGA ss151BA-151BC.

Community law Another term for EU law.

Community relief Any relief provided by an EU instrument of a Customs nature (Customs and Excise (General Reliefs) Act 1979 s13(4)).

community society For pool betting duty, a society established for a charitable purpose or to support athletic sports and which is not for private gain (Customs Notice 147).

Community status document Document used in EU to prove that goods originated in the EU.

Community trade mark Trade mark that applies for whole of European Union. It is regulated by EU Regulation 40/94 and given effect in UK by Trade Marks Act 1994.

Community transit goods For Customs purposes, goods that pass through the UK (CEMA 1979 s1(1)).

commutation Giving up a pension for a lump sum. This is often done for small pensions. Provisions are given in FA 2004 Sch 29. The limit was increased from £18,000 to £30,000 from 27 March 2014 by FA 2014 s42. This provision became redundant from 6 April 2015 when members were allowed access to all their funds in a defined contribution scheme.

commuting Normal travel between home and work. This is generally not tax-deductible as it is not "in the performance of" the duties of the employment. The matter is discussed in HMRC Manual at BIM37935.

Comoran franc Currency of The Comoros.

Comoros, The Island state off the African coast in Indian Ocean. Its currency is the Comoran franc. The UK has no tax treaty.

compact disc Thin silvery polycarbonate disc of 160 mm diameter and 1.2 mm thickness, used for music from 1981 and for computer data from 1985. For VAT, compact discs are standard-rated both in blank form and with pre-recorded music or other data. A company did succeed in having a disc zero-rated when it contained worksheets that students would print out *(Fisher Educational Ltd [2002] VTD 17902).* Where a CD is sold with a book or magazine, this is usually regarded as a single supply and taxed accordingly. This usually means that the supply is standard-rated as a CD with an ancillary book. The Court of Appeal so ruled in *International Masters Publishing Ltd v HMRC (No 2) [2007.* This related to a CD of classical music with an accompanying magazine.

Companies Act Act of Parliament that regulates companies. Many such Acts have been issued since 1844, including major consolidations in 1948 and 1985. The latest Act is of 2006. CA 2006(1) defined "Companies Acts" as the 2006 Act and some unrepealed provisions of previous laws.

Companies Act group accounts Group accounts prepared under CA 2006 s404 rather than under international accounting standards.

Companies House Body based in Cardiff where companies file accounts and other documents. Most of these are now publicly available online.

company Corporate body that has a separate legal personality from its owners (CA 2006 s1(1)). A company pays corporation tax on its profits and gains. Further comment can be found in HMRC Manual ay BIM38210.

company car Car provided to an employee. It is generally taxable as a benefit in kind under ITEPA 2003 ss114-172. The value is the list price multiplied by a percentage taken from tables according to its carbon dioxide emissions. If the employee is provided with fuel, there is a further tax charge. The employer will usually be liable to pay class 1A national insurance (SSCBA 1992 s10). A company may not claim VAT input tax on a car. A company may claim a capital allowance for a car but may not claim the annual investment allowance.

company charge Charge created by a company over is assets. Such a charge must be registered with Companies House under CA 2006 from s860.

company in difficulty Broadly, this is a company that has been in existence for at least three years and has lost at least half of its subscribed share capital, or a company that is subject to insolvency proceedings. A full definition is given in EU Commission Regulation 651/2014 article 2(18). Such a company is restricted from receiving state aid. These restrictions includes some tax relief, such as for research and development, and some of the coronavirus provisions. Directors need to consider whether continuing such a company constitutes wrongful trading (Insolvency Act 1986 s214), which provisions were temporarily suspended from 28 March 2020 as a coronavirus provision.

company law Branch of law that deals with companies. The main law is Companies Act 2006.

company limited by guarantee Company whose members have (usually) not subscribed to buy shares but who undertake to pay a sum if the company is wound up (CA 2006 s1(3)). Such companies are usually non-trading companies and the amount is usually a nominal figure such as £1. Such a company may not issue shares from 22 December 1980 in Great Britain or from 1 July 1983 in Northern Ireland (CA 2006 s5).

company limited by shares Company whose members have their liability limited to the amount they have paid or have agreed to pay for their shares (CA 2006 s1(2)).

company migration When a company changes its country of residence. This was generally a criminal offence before 15 March 1988. From 15 March 1988, a company may migrate provided it tells HMRC and pays all outstanding tax, as explained in SP 2/90. From 3 September 1990, a company does not need permission to move capital to another EU country or, from 1994, to an EEA country.

company name Name by which a company is known (CA 2006 s1200). This must not be the same or similar to an existing company. There are some restrictions on certain words, such as one that implies a connection with the state or monarchy.

company records Includes any register, index, accounting records, agreements, memoranda and other documents that a company must keep under CA 2006 s1134.

company residence A company is UK resident if it is either registered in the UK or any part of it (CA 2006 s13), or if its central control and management is in the UK (*De Beers Consolidated Mines Ltd v Howe [1906] HL 5 TC 198*). HMRC practice is stated in SP 1/90.

company seal Another name for a common seal.

company secretary Person who is responsible for a company's legal and financial functions. A public company must have a company secretary (CA 2006 s371), but a private company no longer needs to have one (CA 2006 s270(1)).

company share option plan (CSOP) Tax-advantaged share scheme under which an employee may be granted up to £30,000 in share options free of tax, subject to conditions. They were introduced on 17 July 1995.

The income tax provisions are in ITEPA from s521 and Sch 4.

The capital gains tax provisions are in TCGA 1992 Sch 7D.

HMRC guidance is given in HMRC Manual at EATSSUM40100. The main conditions are:

- up to £30,000 worth of options may be granted to each employee, unless that employee has a material interest in the company. This is, broadly, owning at least 30%
- option must be exercised at a price "not manifestly less" than the market value when the option was granted
- each option must be exercised between three and ten years after it was granted
- the option must be to acquire ordinary shares in the company.

company's purpose Reason for a company's existence. HMRC Manual at BIM38210 says that inspectors must establish the purpose of a company to see if expenditure is tax-deductible.

company voluntary agreement (CVA) Arrangement whereby a company is protected from debts while a scheme is worked out with creditors.

company website A quoted company must have a website. Details of what must be posted on it are given in CA 2006 ss527-531.

comparability Qualitative characteristic required in financial statements. This requires that figures may be sensibly compared within the entity and with other entities. The requirement is given in FRS 102 para 2.11.

comparative figures Figures in financial statements that show the equivalent figures for the previous accounting period. This is required by FRS 102 para 3.14.

compensating goods Goods that are exported having been imported for inward processing. For such goods, the Customs duty is refunded.

compensation Payment in respect of a loss suffered by someone, particularly when it is the fault of another. In general, compensation is not taxed as income. Where the compensation relates to a loss of earnings, the amount may be reduced by a figure equivalent to the amount of income tax they would have paid on those earnings under the Gourley principle. The whole issue of compensation is discussed in HMRC Manual at BIM42951. Compensation payments are not subject to capital gains tax (TCGA 1992 s51, s268B).

compensation for missold pensions Payments made for giving band pension advice between 29 April 1988 and 30 June 1994. The compensation itself is tax-free but interest payments are taxed.

compensatory interest Charge made by HMRC when goods imported under inward processing relief from Customs duty are diverted to free circulation.

Competition and Markets Authority Body that seeks to promote competition for the benefit of consumers. It was formed on 1 April 2014 by a merger of the Competition Commission and the Office of Fair Trading.

completeness Qualitative characteristic required in accounts. It means that the accounts are complete within the bounds of materiality and cost, and are not misleading, false or otherwise unreliable (FRS 102 section 2.10).

completion period Term used in relation to various creative industry reliefs from corporation tax. It is defined for

- films in CTA 2009 s1208(2)
- film loss relief in CTA 2009 s1212(1)
- programme losses in CTA 2009 s1216D(2)
- video games in CTA 2009 s1217D(2)
- orchestras in CTA 2009 s1217S(2)
- museums and galleries in CTA 2009 s1218ZD(2).

complex case Tax case that is expected to be complex, require a long hearing or involves a large sum. Such a case may go straight to the upper tier tribunal rather than to the first tier tribunal (Tribunal Procedure (First-tier Tribunal) (Tax Chamber) Rules SI 2009 No 273 rule 23).

complex lottery Lottery that has two or more stages. The first stage selects a winner at random. There are then further stages that do not rely on chance (Gambling Act 2005 s14(3)).

compliance certificate Document issued by HMRC to a company to confirm that its share issue meets the conditions for enterprise investment scheme (ITA 2007 s20491)).

compliance condition Condition that must be complied with, such as for a claimant of universal credit (WRA 2012 s27(6)) or jobseeker's allowance (Jobseekers Act 1995 s19C).

compliance statement Certificate issued by a company to HMRC under ITA 2007 s205 confirming that an issue of shares meets the conditions for enterprise investment scheme relief.

component of total income Element of a person's income that may be subject to a specific tax provision (ITA 2007 s23).

composite hereditament Premises that are used both for business and as living accommodation. The two elements are separated for the purposes of business rates and council tax.

composite holding Holding of more than one class of share or debenture of a quoted company following a reorganisation. The capital gains tax implications are given in TCGA 1992 s130.

composite rate Rate which is an average of other rates. It particularly refers to the rate used to deduct tax from bank interest between 1986 and 1991.

composition In finance, an arrangement whereby a debtor and creditor agree to settle a sum by part payment. It is also known as compounding.

compound

(1) For excise duty, mixing drinks subject to spirits duty with any other substance other than water, so as to change the character or flavour of the original drink (Customs leaflet 41).

(2) To make a composition with creditors.

compounder Person who holds a licence as such (Alcoholic Liquor Duties Act 1979 s4(1)).

compounder's licence Authorisation to use spirits in the manufacture of food products. Details are given in Customs notice 41.

compound interest Interest that is applied to both the principal sum and previous interest payments. This contrasts with simple interest where interest is charged only on the principal.

Suppose the principal is £1,000 and the interest rate is 10%. For the first year, the interest is £100 under both simple interest and compound interest. In year 2, compound interest is charged on £1,100 giving £110. Under simple interest, the interest is only £100 as it is in all future years.

Interest paid by HMRC on refunded tax earns simple interest *(Littlewoods Ltd v HMRC [2017] SC. The Times 22 November 2017).*

Compound interest factors are given in section 3 of this dictionary.

compound settlement When land is settled by more than one deed, will or other document (Settled Land Act 1925).

Comptroller and Auditor General Head of the National Audit Office, now governed by Budget Responsibility and National Audit Act 2011 s11.

compulsory maternity leave A period of two weeks after birth of a child when a woman is not allowed to return to work (Employment Rights Act 1996 s72). The period is extended to four weeks for a factory worker.

compulsory purchase When land is acquired by the government or local authority under statutory powers. This may be subject to rollover relief under TCGA 1992 s246. A part disposal is covered by TCGA 1992 s243.

The landowner is entitled to:

- compensation for the land and property
- home loss payment for the inconvenience, stress and upset of losing one's home
- disturbance payment to cover the cost or relocation.

computation Method of determining amount of tax payable. It involves calculations and the application of tax rules.

computer Machine capable of calculation and processing data. HMRC extensively uses computers to file and check data. The latter function uses software known as Connect and robots. Finance Act 2020 s103 puts beyond doubt that a notice or penalty issued by a computer is valid except that tribunal decisions made before 11 March 2020 are not disturbed.

computer documents Document produced from a computer. Such documents may be used as evidence in Civil Evidence Act 1968 and under Police and Criminal Evidence Act 1984.

concealment Deliberate hiding. For tax, this can lead to maximum penalties. It is also a serious offence for money laundering and liquidation. It is a specific offence for money laundering (Proceeds of Crime Act 2002 s327).

concert series An election that applies to orchestra tax relief under CTA 2009 s1217QA.

condemnation proceedings Proceedings that a person may bring in a magistrates' court against HMRC that seizure of goods by Customs is not lawful.

conditionally exempt transfer Transfer of property that appears to be pre-eminent for its national, scientific, historic or artistic interest (IHTA 1983 from s78). Such a transaction is exempt from inheritance tax. This is different from a potentially exempt transfer, and from the scheme of using works of art to *pay* for inheritance tax.

conduit company Company set up to avoid tax, typically in a tax haven.

confectionery Sweets and similar. These are generally standard-rated for VAT as they are excepted from the zero-rating for food. VATA 1994 Sch 8 Group 1 Note (5) says that confectionery includes chocolates, sweets, biscuits, drained or glacé or crystallised fruits, and any item of sweetened prepared food which is normally eaten with the fingers. It was held that confectionery must be sweet but need not have any sugar or other sweetening material added *(Premier Foods (Holdings) Ltd. [2008] Ch D. STC 176)*. So barley sugars and fruit bars are confectionery. The distinction between food and confectionery has been litigated many times. HMRC gives its view in VAT Notice 701/14.

Confédération Fiscale Européene (CFE) Body of tax institutes in Europe. In September 2017, it changed its name to CFE Tax Advisers Europe.

Confederation of British Industry (CBI) Body formed in 1965 from an amalgamation of other bodies. It represents the views of employers.

confession Admission of guilt. Confessions of tax law must meet the same standards as for criminal confessions in being admissible. Generally only evidence made freely and voluntarily is admissible.

confidentiality Duty to keep matters private. HMRC is generally bound by such duty under Commissioners for Revenue and Customs Act 2005 s3. In Scotland, this provision is Revenue Scotland and Tax Powers Act 2014 s14. Exceptions are in legal proceedings, sharing tax information with other tax authorities to counter evasion, and publishing names of serious tax defaulters. The duty of confidentiality for tax accountants and advisers is given in Professional Conduct in Relation to Taxation paras 2.14 to 2.18.

Confidentiality can be a hallmark of a tax avoidance scheme.

confidentiality hallmark Condition agreed between a promoter of tax avoidance schemes and clients that details will not be disclosed to a third party. The existence of this hallmark is itself a factor indicating that the scheme requires disclosure under disclosure of tax avoidance schemes (DOTAS).

confinement Old term for labour involved in childbirth. It is used in some regulations regarding statutory maternity pay, such as SSCBA 1992 s171(1).

confirmation of payee Provision introduced by banks in 2019 to counter frauds in which people were tricked into sending money to a wrong account. To counter this, the receiving bank checks the name against the account number. If they do not match, the payer is advised. The payer then has the choice of proceeding to make payment at his or her own risk.

confirmation statement Statement that must be sent by a company to Companies House at least once a year, confirming that existing details remain correct or making amendments. It replaced the annual return in 2016. The law is Companies Act 2006 s853A as added by Small Business, Enterprise and Employment Act 2015 s92.

confiscatory taxation Taxation at an extremely high rate, such as the 98% rate that applied to investment income between 1975 and 1979. It is also known as fiscal theft.

congestion charge Charge imposed on road users for a defined area as a means of reducing traffic. Such a scheme was introduced in central London on 17 February 2003. Details are given in section 3 of this dictionary.

Congo Name of two African states. The Democratic Republic of The Congo is on the Eastern border of the Republic of the Congo. Their currencies are respectively the Congolese franc of 100 centimes and Central French African franc of 100 centimes.

The UK has no tax treaty with either state, but has a shipping and air transport profits agreement of 1976 with the Democratic Republic. This is still in the name Zaire, which was used by the country between 1970 and 1997.

conjoined arrestment In Scotland, an order requiring an employer to make both an earnings arrestment and current maintenance from an employee's pay.

conjunction ticket Condition that allows a connecting flight not to be taxed separately for air passenger duty. Provisions are given in Air Passenger Duty (Connected Flights) Order SI 1994 No 1821.

Connect Powerful software introduced by HMRC in 2009 that allows vast amounts of information from many sources to be collected, cross-referenced and stored for future use.

connected brewery Brewery that has a trade connection with another. Such connection can disqualify it from the lower rate of beer duty, as explained in Customs notice 226.

connected flight Flight that is not taxed separately for air passenger duty, provided the flights were booked together and the gap is short. Details are given in SI 1994 No 1821.

connected person Person who is related to a taxpayer or has a close business relationship. Examples include spouses and trustees. Tax law has many specific provisions. The exact scope for who is a connected person varies.

consensus Broad agreement. For blockchain, the word has the specific meaning of the process where all nodes are able to the identity the longest and most up-to-date ledger and to agree what is on it.

consent order Order given by a court or tribunal in tax and other cases which gives legal effect to whatever the parties agreed between themselves. Provisions are contained in Tribunal Procedure (First-tier Tribunal) (Tax Chamber) Rules SI 2009 No 273 rule 34.

consideration Benefit provided or detriment suffered as an element to a legally binding contract.

consignee Person to whom goods are sent. For Customs duty, it is the person who is responsible for payment.

consignor Person who sends goods.

consistency concept Accounting principle that the same accounting policies are used each year unless there is a good reason to change, and that change is noted in the accounts. Current requirements are expressed in financial reporting standard FRS 102 section 3.11 and international accounting standard IAS 27 para 4 and IAS 28 para 3.

consolidated accounts Accounts for a group of companies prepared as if they were one company. Accounting provisions are given in FRS 102 section 9. Corporation tax is levied on individual companies, not on groups.

consolidation

(1) Process of combining accounts of two or more companies in a group to present them as if they were one entity. This broadly involves two steps:

- removing figures that relate to transactions between the companies
- adding the other figures.

It should be noted that corporation tax is assessed on the accounts of individual companies and not on consolidated accounts.

(2) For shares, reducing the number by increasing their nominal value. This often happens when the value of shares has become low, so 25 shares of 1p may be consolidated as 1 share of 25p.

(3) In law, combining different cases which relate to the same issue.

consolidation act Act of Parliament that brings together old Acts of Parliament into one new and tidier Act, rather than introducing new law (Consolidation of Enactments (Procedure) Act 1949). Most Acts for established taxes are consolidation acts.

consortium Where a company is owned by other companies but is not a subsidiary of any of them. If the consortium company makes a loss, the owners may broadly claim relief in the same ratio as their holding under CTA 2010 ss143-149.

Conspicuous Gallantry Medal Award for bravery. Payments of pension or annuity in respect of the award are free of income tax (Income Tax (Earnings And Pensions) Act 2003 s638).

constituent wines Two or more wines which are blended to make a saleable alcoholic drink. Alcoholic liquor duty is charged in accordance with Alcoholic Liquor Duties Act 1979 s54(3A).

constitution Formal document by which a country or other body is organised and administered. The collection of documents by which a company is administered.

construction (buildings) How something is built, or the process of building it.

For VAT, some construction work is zero-rated under VATA 1994 Sch 8 Group 5. However, this is an area beset with problems and where large sums are often involved, so great care is needed.

A VAT reverse charge is to be introduced from 1 March 2021, postponed from 1 October 2020. The main elements are:

- it applies to both standard-rated and reduced rate supplies
- the contractor is responsible for paying the output VAT but may still claim it back as input tax. The subcontractor no longer pays the VAT
- the scope of supplies is closely related to those for the construction industry scheme, except that supplies of staff or workers are not included
- the legislation introduces the concept of end users and intermediary suppliers. This is so that suppliers are excluded if they do not supply third parties. Examples include landlords, tenants and property developers.

construction (cars) For company cars and vans, the construction can determine an employee's income tax liability under ITEPA 2003 s115. An example is the case *Timothy Jones [2012] TC 1958.* This held that a vehicle was still a car as it had been constructed as one, even though it had been adapted so that it could no longer be used as one.

construction industry scheme (CIS) Scheme for collecting tax on account from self-employed workers (known as subcontractors) in the construction industry. Unless the subcontractor holds a certificate from HMRC saying otherwise, the contractor must deduct a sum from his labour payments and pass it to HMRC. The main regulations are SI 2005 No 2045. The main points are:

- the scheme must be operated by a contractor which is defined as a construction firm and any other business involved in construction work, but excludes businesses where such work costs less than £1 million and excludes all householders (FA 2004 s59)
- the scheme is now operated online. Cards, certificates and vouchers are no longer used
- it is operated by the contractor in respect of self-employed subcontractors. Note that employed staff of the contractor are paid under the normal PAYE arrangements
- unlike PAYE, CIS does not collect the correct amount of tax. It collects an amount on account. The subcontractor must submit a tax return

- a subcontractor is paid net or gross, depending on the status as advised by HMRC. Details are given in section 3 of this dictionary
- there are no CIS annual returns
- payments are made monthly, including nil returns when no payments have been made
- only certain subcontractors are within the scheme. So a bricklayer is included, but an architect is not
- only certain building works are included
- tax is deducted only on the labour element of the subcontractor's charge; not on materials or expenses
- penalties are imposed for being late with CIS returns.

constructive dismissal When an employee resigns because it is unreasonable for him or her to continue working. This is treated as a dismissal rather than a resignation.

constructive obligation In accounting, an obligation that arises from an established pattern that creates an expectation, rather than from a legal obligation. The accounting provisions are given in FRS 102 section 2.20 and IAS 37 para 10.

constructive removal Early payment of excise duty so that goods can be moved from duty suspended to duty paid.

consul Foreign diplomat so recognised by UK government. They are exempt from UK income tax (ITEPA 2003 s300).

consular transaction "Means the procedure of obtaining from a consul of the importing Party in the territory of the exporting Party, or in the territory of a third party, a consular invoice or a consular visa for a commercial invoice, certificate of origin, manifest, shipper's export declaration or any other customs documentation in connection with the importation of the goods" (EU/UK withdrawal agreement of 24 December 2020. Article GOODS 3: definitions (a)).

Consumer Credit Act Major change in consumer protection law introduced in 1974 and amended in 2006.

consumer prices index (CPI) Official measure of inflation, replacing the retail prices index (RPI), though the latter is still published and used for such things as indexed securities and indexation of chargeable gains.

For indexation of some tax figures, the index is defined in ITA 2007 s57(7).

The CPI tends to provide a lower measure of inflation than the retail prices index.

consumption tax Tax charged on an item as a means of reducing demand. Many excise duties may be so regarded.

contained in Words that appear in TMA 1970 s9A(4). Their meaning was considered by the Court of Appeal in the case *HMRC v Cotter [2012] EWCA Civ 81*. It held that the words did not mean "required to be contained in". The consequence was that HMRC was found to have used the wrong enquiry procedure.

container For Customs purposes, this is defined as any bundle, package, box, cash or other receptacle whatsoever under CEMA 1979 s1(1).

contaminated land relief Generous corporation tax relief set out in CTA 2009 from s1143. The provisions also apply to derelict land. The main elements are:

- the relief is 150% of all capital and revenue expenditure within its scope
- if the company cannot utilise the relief, it may instead receive a tax credit of 16%
- the scope includes labour and materials for remediation which has only been incurred because of the contamination or dereliction. It may not be claimed for landfill tax
- employee costs may be included only to the extent that the employees were directly and actively engaged in remediation
- contamination means death or injury to living organisms, pollution of water, adverse effect on ecosystem, or significant damage to other buildings. In practice, land is only regarded as contaminated when this arises from commercial activity
- dereliction means that the buildings are not in a productive state and need removal before the site can be used productively
- the company must have acquired a major interest in the land, which in practice means either the freehold or a lease of at least seven years
- the land must be in a contaminated or derelict state at the time of acquisition. There is an exception if Japanese knotweed is present (SI 2009 No 2037)
- the land must be in the UK
- for dereliction, the land must have been derelict since 1 April 1998, or the date of acquisition if earlier
- a company may not claim if the dereliction or contamination arose from action by the company.

contempt of court Criminal offence of not complying with an order of the court, conduct that resists or insults the authority of the court, and publishing material that will prejudice a fair trial.

Contentious Issues Panel Panel of HMRC staff that "decide the departmental strategy for handling major contentious issues. This ensures that cases are handled in a co-ordinated and consistent manner across HMRC" (HMRC Notice of 20 December 2013). There are separate panels for business tax and personal tax.

contiguity condition Requirement that two hereditaments or business premises must be contiguous to count as one. This condition led to the so-called staircase tax. It was abolished in 2018, allowing the law to return to what it was previously understood to be. The law is Rating (Property in Common Occupation) and Council Tax (Empty Dwelling) Act 2018 s1.

Continental Shelf Sea area beyond territorial waters which have been divided up between the UK and other countries by agreement. The UK law is Continental Shelf Act 1964. National insurance provisions are given in SSCBA 1992 s120.

contingency Asset or liability whose value is not known when accounts are produced, such as an outstanding court case. For tax purposes, this must be accounted for in accordance with accounting standards unless a specific tax provision requires otherwise. These broadly require for the contingency to be recorded at worst likely outcome with a narrative note, and for subsequent accounts to be adjusted when the real value is known.

contingency principle For stamp duty, the rule that if the consideration cannot be established at stamping, the maximum figure should be used (Stamp Act 1891 s56).

contingent discount When goods are sold at a price subject to a condition, such as the customer buys a minimum amount over a period. VAT is charged on the price paid by the customer. If a subsequent discount is given, VAT may be shown on a credit note.

contingent liability Liability whose existence or amount is unsure. For capital gains tax, such a liability is ignored. If the liability is subsequently enforced, the taxpayer may claim a tax refund within four years of 31 January after the end of the tax year of disposal.

continuing operations Term used in a profit and loss account to distinguish current trading from discontinued operations.

continuing professional development Requirement that a professional person must spend part of each year keeping up to date on developments.

Continuity of Education Allowance Payment by Ministry of Defence to service personnel so that children do not have their education interrupted on a change of posting. The payment is specifically exempt from income tax (ITEPA 2003 s297C(2)).

continuous supply Supply that has no discrete times, such as rent, insurance and electricity. It does not apply to a retainer. For VAT, invoices are issued when payments are required or received.

contraband Good which are prohibited by law.

contract Legally enforceable agreement between two or more parties. A contract often indicates a supply for VAT. In general terms, the elements of a contract are:

- all parties must have capacity to contract;
- the parties must agree to the contract voluntarily;
- there must be an intention to create legal relations between the parties;
- the contract must be legal, moral and possible;
- each party must provide a consideration.

Guidance on the interpretation of clauses has been given by the House of Lords in *Investors Compensation Scheme Ltd v West Bromwich Building Society [1997]*. An agreement made between a taxpayer and HMRC to settle a tax dispute can be a contract which is binding on both parties.

contract bridge Card game. It was held not to be a sport in the European case *The English Bridge Union [2017] CJEU*. Case C-90/16. As a consequence, entrance fees to tournaments could not be zero-rated under VATA 1994 Sch 9 Group 10.

contracting out Provision whereby an employee who was in an approved occupational pension scheme could pay a lower rate of national insurance, as could their employer. This provision ended in 2012 for money purchase schemes, and in 2016 for salary-related schemes.

contract for difference (CFD) A contract to pay a sum for the amount by which a stated security or index moves, such as paying £1 for each 1 point added to the FT-SE 100 index. A CFD is similar in purpose and form to a futures contract except that it has no tangible form. For corporation tax, a definition is given in Corporation Tax Act 2009 s582. [The term is sometimes given as contract for *differences.*]

contract for land Contract that relates to land but is not to buy land, which is a contract *of* land. An example of the former is a contract to resolve a boundary dispute. A practical difference is that a contract for land does not have to be in writing as the Court of Appeal ruled in the case *Rollerteam Ltd v Riley [2017].*

contract for service Agreement whereby a person agrees to provide a service rather than to work set hours. It is a factor which can indicate that the person is self-employed for tax, rather than employed.

contract note Document that shows that shares or other securities have been bought or sold but that payment may not yet have been made.

contract of employment Document setting out the rights and duties of employer and employee in an employment. The employer is required to produce the document within two months of the employment starting (Employment Rights Act 1996 s1(2)).

contract of service Legal agreement between an employer and employee. A distinction must be made between such a contract and a **contract for services,** where the latter indicates that the person is self-employed.

For social security, the term specifically includes a contract of apprenticeship (Social Security Contributions and Benefits Act 1992 s122(1)).

contractor loan scheme Tax avoidance scheme whereby a contractor made loans to a subcontractor as a means of avoiding liability under the construction industry scheme. The scheme is ineffective. Those who used it were required to settle their tax by 30 June 2015. Any balance outstanding on 6 April 2019 is subject to the loan charge.

contract profit rate Figure used to calculate price in defence contracts (Defence Reform Act 2014 s15(4)).

contractual disclosure facility (CIF) Scheme introduced in 2011 as an alternative to the COP 9 procedure. These replace the Hansard procedure. Under CDF, a taxpayer suspected of fraud will escape criminal charges (such as imprisonment) if they co-operate with HMRC and accept any civil penalties. Such penalties are likely to be lower. Details were set out in a revised form of COP 9 issued on 19 January 2012. The main steps in CDF are:

- HMRC suspects tax fraud
- the taxpayer is invited to settle under CDF. If the taxpayer declines, HMRC may continue with a criminal investigation
- the taxpayer has 60 days in which to decide whether to use CDF
- provided the taxpayer co-operates honestly, HMRC undertakes not to institute any criminal proceedings

- within 60 days, the taxpayer must provide an outline disclosure of all tax frauds
- this is followed by a formal disclosure which quantifies the amount of tax owed, with the interest and penalties.

CDF is not appropriate for mistakes, careless errors or avoidance schemes.

CDF may be used when a taxpayer is accused of fraud which he or she denies. They may sign a CDF denial letter within the same 60-day time limit.

If someone agrees a CDF and is found still to have concealed tax fraud, a criminal investigation may be started.

contractual remuneration Amounts an employee is entitled to receive under a contract of employment (Employment Rights Act 1996 s32). It includes wages and holiday pay, as against the operation of the law, such as statutory maternity pay and redundancy pay.

contra entry In accounting, an entry made to reduce another figure to zero, such as to correct a mistake.

contra proferentem Rule of law that any ambiguity in a rule is resolved against the person who seeks to rely on it.

contribution Payment or credit of national insurance (among other meanings).

contribution conditions Rules governing what national insurance contributions count towards social security benefits (SSCBA 1992 s21).

contribution to the firm Amount which a partner (including a non-active partner) has contributed to the partnership plus his or her share of retained profits. This figure is used to determine the partner's maximum tax-allowable loss relief from the partnership.

Contributions Agency Body that administered national insurance between 1991 and 1999, when responsibility passed to Inland Revenue.

contributions avoidance arrangement Scheme to avoid paying national insurance. Such a scheme must be disclosed to HMRC under Social Security Administration Act 1992 s132A from 30 March 2006.

contribution to the firm In relation to a limited partner or non-active partner, this represents the amount the partner has contributed to the partnership plus his or her share of profits (ITA 2007 s105; CTA 2010 s57). This figure is used to determine the partner's maximum amount of loss relief.

contribution year Tax year for which national insurance contributions are recorded, though they may be paid in a later year.

contributory benefit Social security benefit where entitlement depends on having paid national insurance. Examples include jobseeker's allowance, and employment and support allowance.

contrived arrangement Arrangement which seems artificial for what it is trying to do. It is a hallmark of a reportable tax avoidance scheme.

contrived employment liability Tax avoidance scheme that sought to generate liabilities and losses to reduced taxable income. They were explicitly outlawed from 12 January 2009. Details are given in Spotlight 4.

control The ability of a person to direct the actions of another. For corporation tax, one company is generally regarded as controlling another if it owns more than 50% of the ordinary shares, controls more than 50% of the voting rights, or is entitled to more than 50% of the assets in a winding up (CTA 2009 s472). Control is also a factor in determining whether a worker is an employee.

controlled activity For alcoholic liquor duty, selling liquor, offering it for sale, or arranging for its sale.

controlled company Company where one person owns 50% of the relevant shareholding. Note that a company can be controlled on a lower holding if it is a sub-subsidiary. For example if A owns 60% of B, and B owns 60% of C, A controls C even though A only owns 36% of it. A controls B, and B controls C.

controlled foreign company (CFC) Company that operates overseas but is controlled by UK residents. There are special tax provisions to ensure a CFC is not used for tax avoidance.

controlled liquor Liquor that is subject to duty before the point of retail sale (ALDA 1979 s88A). Wholesalers of liquor have been required to register with HMRC from 2015.

controlled oil For hydrocarbon oil duty, any oil on which a rebate has been allowed (HODA 1979 s27(1)).

controlled waters Tidal water and parts of the sea in or adjacent to Great Britain up to the seaward limits of territorial waters; and any area designated by order under section 1(7) of the Continental Shelf Act 1964 s1(7) (Mineral Workings (Offshore Installations) Act 1971 s12). For the purposes of land remediation, the term is defined in Corporation Tax Act 2009 s1179.

controlling equity stake fund In relation to taxation of derivatives, this has a specific meaning in Income Tax Act 2007 s809FZM(3) as inserted by Finance Act 2016 s37.

convalescence Period after surgery, illness or injury when it is necessary to rest. Statutory sick pay is payable. Expenditure on convalescence is not tax-deductible. A leading case is *Murgatroyd v Evans-Jackson [1966] 43 TC 581*. The matter is discussed in HMRC Manual at BIM37950.

conventional basis Method of determining taxable income from trading income, as explained in ITCA 1988 s103.

Convention on International Trade in Endangered Species (CITES) Regulation that restricts trading in endangered species of animals or plants, or in products derived from them. It is an important element of Customs control. Some items are banned completely, while others require a licence. Goods that breach the convention are liable to seizure.

convergence criteria The five conditions that EU countries had to meet to take full part in economic and monetary union, such as using the euro. The criteria are:

- inflation no more than 1.5% above the average of the lowest three EU states
- interest rates no more than 2% above lowest three states
- budget deficit no more than 3% of GDP
- national debt no more than 60% of GDP
- exchange rates within the normal bands of the exchange rate mechanism with no re-alignments within two years.

conversion Replacement of one currency with another. Note that if there is no exchange but one currency is simply expressed as its value in another currency, that is a translation.

conversion Changing one thing to another. An example is a preference share becoming an ordinary share. The capital gains tax implications are given in TCGA 1992 s132. The term is also used when one currency is exchanged for another. Note that if one currency is simply expressed as an amount of another currency, that is a translation and not a conversion.

convertible Description of securities that may be exchanged for shares.

conveyance Legal document that transfers ownership of property (Land Charges Act 1972 s17(1)). Stamp duty land tax, or a devolved equivalent, may be payable at this point.

cooking test Ability of someone to cook an ordinary meal on a standard cooker on at least some days. The test can be a factor in determining whether a claimant is entitled to the care component of the disability living allowance.

cooling off period Period in which a person is legally allowed to change his or her mind. Consumer law has many such provisions. There is a six-month cooling off period for VAT option to tax.

co-operative Arrangement whereby people work together for mutual benefit (Industrial Common Ownership Act 1976 s2). Tax provisions for investment in a co-operative are given in ITA 2007 s401.

co-ownership authorised contractual scheme In relation to capital allowance on plant and machinery, "means a co-ownership scheme which is authorised for the purposes of the Financial Services and Markets Act 2000 by an authorisation order in force under section 261D(1) of that Act" (F(2)) Act 2017 s41). The same definition appears in F(2)A 2017 s42 for offshore funds.

COP Code of Practice followed by HMRC. COP 9 deals with suspected tax fraud.

copper Metallic element used in making the lowest value coins. From 1992, British coins are made from copper-plated steel. From 1860 to 1991 they are made from bronze.

copper-bottomed Description of anything that is protected from failure. The term comes from the old practice of plating the bottom of a boat with copper to prevent leakage.

copy A definition for VAT is given in VATA 1994 s96(1).

copyright Right to take copies of an original literary, artistic or musical work. It is a form of intellectual property. The main law is Copyright, Designs and Patents Act 1988, as amended. Copyright now generally lasts for the creator's life plus 70 years from the end of the year of death. Customs may seize imports that breach copyright law. For tax purposes, a definition appears in ITA 2007 s907(2).

core expenditure For the various creative industries relief for corporation tax (such as film production) this is given a specific meaning.

core section Part of a tax return that applies to all taxpayers. This is supplemented with additional pages as required. Examples include form SA100 for self-assessment, and CT601 for corporation tax.

Cornish pasty Traditional baked product designed to be held in the hand when eaten, such as by a miner. In the case *Lutron Ltd [1988] VTD 3686,* it was held that it was zero-rated as food. It was only hot when sold because it had not cooled down from baking. The company did not reheat cold pasties. In 2012, the government abandoned Budget plans to impose VAT on food sold before having cooled down.

Corn Laws Series of enactments from 1360 that regulated the import and export of grain. A law passed in 1815 proved particularly controversial.

coronavirus Family of viral diseases that include the common cold. In practice, the term is widely used to mean the COVID-19 strain, first identified in China in December 2019 which quickly spread round the planet. The World Health Organisation declared it a pandemic on 11 March 2020.

In the UK, it led to a national lockdown from 23 March 2020 under SI 2020 No 350 issued under Public Health (Control of Disease) Act 1984. There is also a separate Coronavirus Act 2020 which gives a legal definition in s1(1). There was a second national lockdown in England 5 November 2020 to 2 December 2020, with similar lockdowns in other parts of the UK. Coronavirus affected almost every aspect of daily life for businesses and individuals, leading to more than 250 regulations. Many tax provisions and deadlines were relaxed, specific help in the form of new tax reliefs and grants were introduced, and new forms of business loan were made available. Some of the announced relaxations were further amended. For tax, the main provisions include:

- deferring payment of income tax due on 31 July 2020
- deferring VAT due between March and June 2020
- introduction of 5% VAT hospitality rate
- threshold increases for stamp duty land tax and devolved equivalents
- generous reliefs from business rates.

HMRC also operated several schemes to provide assistance to businesses adversely affected. A summary of the main coronavirus provisions is given in section 3 of this dictionary.

Coronavirus Act 2020 Emergency legislation to give effect to provisions to deal with the coronavirus outbreak in 2020. It received Royal Assent on 25 March 2020. Its main provisions concern:

- changes to registration of health professionals

- emergency volunteers
- registration of deaths and stillbirths
- changes to certain legal procedures and inquests
- provisions regarding food supply
- school closures
- changes to statutory sick pay
- changes to NHS pension scheme
- provisions to protect public health
- postponement of elections and by-elections
- financial assistance to industry
- uprating of working tax credit and universal credit
- protection of tenants.

Coronavirus Business Interruption Loan Scheme Government-backed scheme to help most businesses with an annual turnover of up to £45 million to secure bank loans of up to £5 million. The first year is free of interest. The government guarantees 80% of the loan. It was announced on 11 March 2020, and made more generous on 23 March 2020. From 30 July 2020 the scheme was extended to some businesses in financial difficulty.

coronavirus job retention bonus Payment of £1,000 made by the government to an employer for each worker who had been furloughed under Coronavirus Job Retention Scheme and who is kept on the payroll between 1 November 2020 and 31 January 2021, and paid at least £520 a month. The bonus is taxable as trading income.

This scheme was abandoned, at least temporarily, when the Coronavirus Job Retention Scheme was re-introduced from 1 November 2020.

Coronavirus Job Retention Scheme Government scheme announced on 23 March 2020 whereby employees would be paid up to 80% of their wages by the state from 1 March 2020 to 31 July 2020. This also initially paid employer's national insurance and workplace pension contributions. The scheme was introduced by a Treasury direction issued under Coronavirus Act 2020 s76. The scheme was extended to 31 October 2020, though on less generous terms:

- August 2020, the employer had to pay employer's national insurance and workplace pension contributions
- September 2020, the government paid 70% of wages and required employers to pay at least 10%
- October 2020, the government paid 60% of wages and required employers to pay at least 20%
- the scheme was planned to end on 31 October 2020, but it was re-introduced for the period from 1 November 2020 to 30 April 2021, initially at 80% of wages.

coronavirus period In relation to protected pensions, this is the period from 1 March 2020 to 1 November 2020 (FA 2004 Sch 36 para (7K)).

coronavirus support payments Various payments made to help businesses during the coronavirus outbreak. The taxation of such payments is given in FA 2020 s106 and Sch 15.

coronavirus test Test to see if an individual either:

- has coronavirus, or
- has had coronavirus.

On 9 July 2020, HMRC confirmed that such a test was not a taxable benefit in kind when provided by an employer or by a third party. There is also no class 1A national insurance liability. All tests provided by the government are free of charge and do not incur a tax liability.

corporate bond Debt instrument issued by a company.

Companies issue bonds to raise money and pay interest on the bonds. Usually bonds expire on a fixed date, when the company repays the borrower. Such bonds can be bought and sold easily (like shares).

Bond prices tend to change when interest rates change and are usually not as risky as shares because a company will pay off all its debts (including bonds) before the shareholders get anything.

corporate governance code Code of conduct for companies issued by the Financial Reporting Council. The latest code was issued in July 2018, effective for accounting periods starting on or after 1 January 2019.

corporate interest restriction Anti-avoidance provision introduced on 1 April 2017 by Finance (No 2) Act 2017 and TIOPA 2010 Part 10. It prevents a company exporting profits by making large interest payments overseas.

corporate manslaughter Criminal offence that may be committed by a company or other corporate body where a death has resulted from the company's "gross breach of a relevant duty of care". The law is Corporate Manslaughter and Corporate Homicide Act 2007. The offence is called corporate homicide in Scotland.

corporate rescue exception Provision in Finance Act 2010 s44 and Sch 15 that disapplies the tax treatment for impaired debt between connected parties for arms' length transactions. Similar provisions are given for deemed debt releases on impaired debts becoming held by a connected company (Corporation Tax Act 2009 s361).

corporate veil Protection that company law gives to shareholders by making a company a separate legal person. The veil is said to be lifted or pierced, making shareholders liable for the company, in a few circumstances such as when the company is a sham or being used for fraud.

corporation (1) Company registered in the USA.

(2) Large company in the UK.

"In the Companies Acts—"body corporate" and "corporation" include a body incorporated outside the United Kingdom, but do not include —

(a) a corporation sole, or

(b) a partnership that, whether or not a legal person, is not regarded as a body corporate under the law by which it is governed"

(Companies Act 2006 s1173(1)).

corporation sole The legal person represented by the office rather than the office-holder. So "the Bishop of Durham" means whoever is the Bishop at that time.

corporation tax Tax introduced in 1965 and paid by companies on profits and gains (CTA 2009 s2). The main Acts are now CTA 2009 and CTA 2010. The main points are:

- corporation tax is charged on profits and gains of companies and unincorporated bodies such as members' clubs. It is not paid by trusts or partnerships
- corporation tax is payable on UK and foreign dividends received, though many in practice will not be taxed
- if a company owns a residential property, it may also be liable to pay annual tax on enveloped dwellings
- liability to corporation tax does not start when the company is formed. It begins when the company starts trading or when it earns income, perhaps interest from a bank account
- a company must notify HMRC when it comes within the scope of corporation tax
- corporation tax is paid for accounting periods of between one day and one year. An accounting period starts when a previous accounting period ends, a company starts trading, or when it goes into insolvency procedures
- an accounting period cannot exceed 12 months. If a company prepares accounts for a longer period, the first 12 months is regarded as one accounting period, and the balance as another
- tax is payable on the adjusted profits. These are the net profit of the business as shown in accounts that must comply with accounting standard, and which are then adjusted in accordance with tax law
- the different sources of income must be identified. These sources can include trading, property, investment, derivative contracts and others
- tax is charged on individual companies not on groups of companies. If one company makes a loss, it may be able to pass that loss to another group company as group relief
- payment of dividends do not affect the amount of corporation tax payable
- an annual return is required for which the company is responsible, though HMRC sends reminders in practice. This is usually filed online. The company is responsible for calculating and paying the tax
- corporation tax is paid for each accounting period in financial years which are named after the calendar year in which they start. So 2021 financial year runs from 1 April 2021 to 31 March 2022. As an accounting period can last for less than one year, a company may be required to make more than one return in a year.
- there is now just one rate of corporation tax, regardless of the size of the company or its profits. There are special rates for banks and the oil industry. A merchant shipping company may pay tonnage tax instead of corporation tax. A company exploiting an invention may reduce its corporation tax using the patent box

- there are many special reliefs that may be claimed, such as for research and development, and land remediation
- corporation tax is generally payable 9 months and 1 day after the end of the accounting period. Large companies may be required to pay in instalments.

There are many other corporation tax provisions. Rates are given in section 3 of this dictionary.

corpus Term sometimes used to mean the capital of a fund, as against its income.

corpus dilecti Latin: body of the offence. The facts which comprise a legal offence.

correcting entry Entry which is designed to correct a mistake previously made in the financial records. It has the same meaning as an adjusting entry, where the bookkeeping requirements are set out.

corrective action Action needed to correct an irregularity in a tax return or equivalent. The professional considerations in such matters are set out in Professional Conduct in Relation to Taxation from para 5.43.

corresponding adjustment Provision in the OECD model treaty article 9 para 2, which broadly requires that tax relief given in one country on an international transaction should be matched by an equivalent tax charge in the other country.

corresponding bonus shares In relation to any shares, means bonus shares which:

(a) are issued in respect of those shares, and
(b) are in the same company, are of the same class, and carry the same rights, as those shares (ITA 2007 s151(1); CTA 2010 s90(1)).

corresponding day rule Rule of legal interpretation that a time limit of (say) one month means by one day less than in the current month. In the case *re O'Connor Utilities Ltd [2009] EWHC 3704,* it was held that a time limit of one month from 4 November 2008 meant by 3 December 2008.

corresponding deficiency relief (CDR) Tax relief that may arise at the end of an insurance policy. The tax implications were considered by the Court of Appeal in *Andrew Scott v HMRC [2020] EWCA Civ 21.*

corresponding partnership case In relation to an LLP run not for profit, this term is defined in Taxes Management Act 1970 s12ABZAA (5) as inserted by Finance Act 2020 s104(1).

corresponding proportion of the weekly PAYE threshold For PAYE, this "is established by dividing the number of days in the payment interval by 7, and multiplying the result by the weekly PAYE threshold" (PAYE regulations SI 2003 No 2682 reg 9(9)).

corresponding retrospective tax provision Term used in Social Security Contributions and Benefits Act 1992 s176 in relation to Parliamentary control of regulations regulating to statutory payments.

corresponding shares Shares that correspond to original shares in a profit-sharing **scheme** (Income and Corporation Taxes Act 1988 Sch 10 para 5).

corresponding UK claim In relation to mutual assistance in recovering taxes between EU states, this "means a claim in the United Kingdom of a kind that appears to the relevant UK authority to correspond most closely to the kind of foreign claim to which a foreign claim belongs" (Finance Act 2011 Sch 25 para 8(1)).

cost Amount paid, directly or indirectly, for something. This term usually needs qualifying, such as between direct cost, marginal cost and opportunity cost.

Suppose a company makes widgets for which the materials and labour cost 50p an item. It makes 1 million a year which it sells for £2 each. It has overheads of £1 million. If it did not sell widgets, it could sell thingummies for a total profit of £400,000.

The direct cost is £1.50 comprising 50p direct cost and £1 overhead cost. The company will make £500,000 profit.

The marginal cost is 50p. That is the cost of making one *extra* widget once the overheads have been absorbed.

The opportunity cost if £400,000. That is the next best alternative.

This was an issue in the landmark case *Pepper v Hart [1992] HL 65 TC 421.* Teachers were allowed to send their own children to a fee-paying school to take up otherwise unused places. The House of Lords decided that the cost on which the teachers were taxed was the marginal cost of providing for one extra pupil, rather than the direct cost which would also include a share of the school's overheads.

corrody Arrangement where a monastery or similar establishment provides someone with lifetime lodging.

corruption Improper conduct to show favour or disfavour to someone. It is a common law criminal offence and is also outlawed in various statutes. Such payments are not tax-deductible (CTA 2009 s1304). The matter is discussed in HMRC Manual at BIM43125.

cosmetic surgery Surgery designed to correct a physical defect. HMRC Manual at BIM37945 states that this is not usually tax-deductible.

Costa Rica South American republic. Its currency is the Costa Rican colon of 100 céntimos.

cost benefit ratio The amount expected to be earned or saved by an item of expenditure. So if £100 expenditure saves £500, the ratio is 5.0.

cost centre Person, group, department or other defined unit to which an entity's costs can be allocated for management accounting purposes.

cost justification Situation where expenditure can be justified in terms of extra earnings or a reduction in other expenditure.

cost of capital Equivalent interest rate for how much the company's capital costs it.

cost of carry

(1) Extent to which the cost of holding funds exceeds the return they earn.

(2) In a futures contract, the cost of holding the underlying security.

cost of funds

(1) In banking, cost of borrowing in the principal money markets. This cost determines the interest rates charged to customers.

(2) In commerce, cost of raising additional finance for a business.

cost of generating funds Figure in a statement of fixed assets of a non-commercial body for the expenses of generating income, such as the cost of a church stewardship campaign or a charity's fund-raising expenses.

cost of goods sold Materials, labour and other costs directly related to the goods or services provided. Turnover minus cost of goods sold gives gross profit. Gross profit minus overheads gives net profit.

cost-plus Pricing method comprising the cost of the item to the seller plus an agreed profit margin. Such provisions are encountered in the public sector and in some specialised areas.

costs Sum awarded to a litigant against the other. In tax tribunals, costs are not awarded unless one party has behaved unreasonably. An explanation was given in the case *Ad Hoc Property Management [2019] TC 7143* at paras 12 and 13. Costs may be awarded on a standard basis or indemnity basis. For the standard basis the court disallows any costs which are unreasonably incurred, unreasonable in amount, are disproportionately incurred or are disproportionate in amount. Any doubt on this point is resolved by the court in favour of the paying party. For the indemnity basis it is only costs which are unreasonably incurred or unreasonable in amount that are disallowed. The indemnity basis requires unreasonableness which is unreasonable to a high degree and takes the case out of the norm.

cost-sharing arrangement In relation to patent box, "is an arrangement under which:

(a) each of the parties to the arrangement is required to contribute to the cost of, or undertake activities for the purpose of, creating or developing an item or process,

(b) each of those parties —

(i) is entitled to a share of any income attributable to the item or process, or

(ii) has one or more rights in respect of the item or process, and

(c) the amount of any income received by each of those parties is proportionate to its participation in the arrangement as described in paragraph (a)"

(CTA 2010 s357GC(2) as inserted by Finance (No 2) Act 2017 s23). In relation to taxation of other intellectual property, an identical definition is given in CTA 2010 s357GC as inserted by Finance Act 2012 s19 and Sch 2.

Cote d'Ivoire Alternative name for Ivory Coast, an African republic. Its currency is the Central French African republic. The UK has a double taxation convention of 1985 in the name of Ivory Coast.

council tax Local authority tax on residential properties according to price bands. It was introduced on 1 April 1993 by Local Government Finance Act 1992, replacing community charge or poll tax. Properties are put into one of eight bands (nine in Wales) according to their value. Band D is regarded as the average. Other bands are taxed at a multiple of the Band D property. There are many types of excepted property and some reliefs. There is a support scheme administered by the local authority for residents on low incomes. There is an attachment of earnings order if the tax is not paid.

Coumarin Colouring agent that identifies road fuel on which duty has not been paid. From 1 April 2015, it is known as 1:2 benzopyrone (Hydrocarbon Oil (Designated Markers) Regulations SI 1996 No 1251 para 2(2).

council house Property owned, and often built, by a local authority and offered to people who cannot afford market housing. The rent is controlled by the council. Housing benefit exists to meet the cost for those who cannot afford this rent.

In 1980, council house tenants were given the right to buy their homes at a significant discount, depending on how long they lived there. The discount was up to 60% on houses and 70% on flats. In the same decade, many councils transferred their houses to housing associations.

councillor Elected member of a local authority. Such a member typically receives a basic allowance, special responsibilities allowances (such as for chairing a committee) plus expenses. For tax purposes, the member is regarded as an office holder. As such, the authority must operate PAYE and class 1 national insurance. The allowances and expenses are taxable as gross income, except to the extent that expenses are deductible. Details are given in PAYE regulations SI 2003 No 2682 from reg 118. Guidance on the allowance of expenses is provided in HMRC Manual at EIM65955. Further guidance is provided in the case *Lorber [2011] TC 986*

From 1 April 2016, there is a specific tax relief for travel expenses incurred in duties within the area and within 20 miles of the boundary. This provision is given in ITEPA 2003 s235A.

council tax Local authority tax introduced on 1 April 1993 to replace the unpopular community charge (commonly called poll tax). The law is Local Government Finance Act 1992. The tax is charged on a mix of people and property. Council tax is paid in respect of a dwelling, which includes land and outbuildings. Properties are categorised into eight bands designated A to H (or nine bands designated A to I in Wales). If the house has been adapted for a disabled person, it is reduced by one band. The band is related to the historic value of the property. These values are given in section 3 of this dictionary. A band D property is regarded as the average value. Other properties have weights varying from two-thirds for band A to double for band H. So if a council had 3,000 properties in each of bands A, D and H, its weight would be 2,000 for band A; 3,000 for band B; and 6,000 for band H, giving a total weight of 11,000. The local authority uses this to set the council tax rate. The amounts (and weights) can be further adjusted by reductions for single occupancy and empty properties. Some residential properties are excluded, such as halls of residence, barracks and diplomatic premises.

A householder is not liable to pay until the local authority has sent a bill. Householders may pay by instalments. Direct debit is widely used.

If an employer pays an employee's council tax, that is a taxable benefit in kind, as explained in HMRC Manual at EIM00585.

council tax benefit Social security benefit that could be claimed between April 1993 and 31 March 1993. It was a payment for means-tested claimants to help pay their council tax. It is now replaced by council tax reduction. Members of the armed forces may receive a special relief towards their council tax. This is exempt from income tax under ITEPA 2003 s297B.

council tax reduction Scheme administered by local authorities where they may, at their discretion, grant a measure of relief from council tax for low income household. The scheme does not apply in Northern Ireland as council tax is not charged there. The legal provisions are contained in Local Government Finance Act 1992 s13A as inserted by Local Government Act 2003 s76. This scheme replaces council tax benefit from April 2013.

counsel Term sometimes used to mean a barrister, particularly one who has been engaged to advise or act for a client.

counselling (practice) Process of assisting someone to deal with problems. It is a specialist skill far removed from preparing tax computations. However, tax does not happen in isolation from other aspects of life. Tax problems are often part of wider tax problems. These may have non-financial causes and will often have non-financial effects. For this reason, some counselling skills are needed by tax agents, tax staff, accountants and others involved. The British Association for Counselling and Psychotherapy defines four needs that may need to be addressed by counselling:

- difficulty — a particular problem or problems
- distress — emotional response to problems
- dissatisfaction with life in general
- loss of direction or purpose.

About 30% of people never need counselling whatever life throws at them, though ordinary conversation, "tea and sympathy", can be seen as a form of counselling. It should not be assumed that someone needs counselling just because they have suffered a misfortune. Counselling must always be requested by the person counselled. The three steps are:

- recognition — acknowledging the problem
- diagnosis — identifying the underlying issues
- prognosis — addressing the problem.

Sometimes prognosis is not needed, as simply recognising and identifying a problem is sufficient to address it. In general, it is advisable to separate the financial provisions from the other aspects. There are clearly defined procedures for dealing with tax issues. HMRC is generally sympathetic when people find themselves in difficulty, though they may need to demonstrate the difficulty by providing evidence. Tribunals and courts are also sympathetic. The steps in therapeutic counselling may be summarised as:

- active listening
- re-expression
- summarising
- questioning
- clarifying answers
- reflection
- clarifying thoughts

- encouraging focus
- challenging the client.

The first is the most important. The client should be allowed to talk without constant interruption. Active listening means making the occasional comment such as "yes", "I see" or "quite" so that the client knows the counsellor is still engaged. Counselling must be non-judgmental, respectful, objective, confidential, client-centred, unpressured and problem-focused. Being non-judgmental does not mean that the client is treated as innocent; if tax is owed, it must be paid. Being non-judgmental means that counselling does not deal with the rightness or wrongness of the client; that is addressed in the separate financial dealings. HMRC has specific services to help taxpayers who have disabilities such as dyslexia, autism or cognitive difficulties, or any kind of mental health issues. HMRC has specific policies to help taxpayers who cannot afford food, energy or rent. No-one is expected to go without essentials of life to pay tax. A friend, relative or adviser may be authorised to speak to HMRC on the taxpayer's behalf. In all such cases, the taxpayer or adviser should tell HMRC of such issues.

counselling (tax) Provision of assistance to help a person deal with a problem. Some forms of counselling employees are outside the scope of a taxable benefit in kind. Outplacement counselling, to help an employee find or train for new work, is exempt from income tax and tax-deductible by the employer (ITTOIA 2005 s 73(2); CTA 2009 s73(2).

counteraction notice Notice that may be served by HMRC under ITA 2007 s698 in limited circumstances to counter a tax advantage.

counterfeit Forgery of currency or branded goods. It is a criminal offence under Forgery and Counterfeiting Act 1981. Customs may seize imported counterfeit goods.

counter-offer In contract law, an offer that is an alternative to a previous offer, and which cancels all previous offers *(Hyde v Wench [1840]).*

counterparty The other party in a contract.

countervailing charge Charge that may be imposed on certain goods under the European Common Agricultural Policy under European regulation EC 815/94 of 12 April 1994. Note that is not the same as countervailing duty.

countervailing duty Additional Customs duty that may be imposed to negate the benefit of a subsidy provided by the government of the exporter. The legal authority is EU regulation 2016/1037, which has been incorporated into UK law so it continues to apply after Brexit. This duty is often imposed with anti-dumping duty. Details are given in Customs notice 376.

country-by-country reporting Requirement for businesses to report how much of their turnover came from each country of operation. It is a measure to help countenance tax avoidance. Its provisions come from OECD Guidance produced in 2014. Provisions became compulsory in the UK for accounting periods that start from 1 January 2016 under Finance Act 2014 s122.

country prefix code Two letters that precede a VAT number to identify the country. The UK's code is GB.

county Administrative district of local government, as defined by Local Government Act 1972 s1(1).

county court Court which hears civil disputes, including some tax disputes. For England and Wales, it is defined in County Courts Act 1984. In Northern Ireland, it is defined by County Courts (Northern Ireland) Order 1980.

couple For most social security purposes, this is defined of two people (whether of the same or different sexes) who are married or in a civil partnership. Some social security rules extend the scope to two people who are living together. Definitions can be found in SSCBA 1992 s137(1) and elsewhere. For tax purposes, such as spousal exemption for inheritance tax and marriage allowance for income tax, a couple means a married couple or a civil partnership.

couple penalty Loss of social security benefits commonly experienced when two single people marry or otherwise become a single household.

coupon Document that states an entitlement, such as for a discount to goods or services, or to receive a payment from a bearer bond. The issue of free coupons for goods and services is generally not regarded as a supply for VAT. VAT is charged on the net price when the coupon is used. In other words, the coupon is seen simply as a discount. Further details are given in VAT Notice 701/7.

courier fraud Fraud first identified in 2015 when someone pretending to be from a bank tells a person that their accounts have been improperly accessed, and that they must hand over all their bank documents to a courier and open a new account.

course manuals Books and other written material provided as part of a supply of education or training. The issue of whether such material can be regarded as a separate supply of zero-rated books has been the subject of litigation. An early case *J Rendle [1982] VTD 1389* held that the books could be zero-rated. The House of Lords reached the opposite conclusion in *HMRC v The College of Estate Management [2005] HL. STC 1597.* HMRC set out its view in Business Brief 20/2005.

court case Formal hearing of a dispute before a judge. Such cases can establish precedents to determine or influence subsequent cases.

Court Martial Court that may be held anywhere in UK or overseas to try an offence committed by military personnel (Armed Forces Act 2006 s154).

Court of Appeal Body that hears appeals against decisions of the High Court or upper tier tribunal. Its own decisions may be appealed to the Supreme Court. It is defined in Interpretation Act 1978 Sch 1.

Court of Protection Court that deals with the affairs of those who lack mental capacity. It is constituted under Mental Capacity Act 2005 s45.

Court of Session Highest supreme court of Scotland, established in 1532.

covenant Term for various forms of one-sided agreement, where someone gives something for nothing in return. There are some special provisions relating to land dating back to 16th century laws and The Law of Property Act 1925 s79. In tax, the term usually means a deed of covenant.

cover The many meanings of this word include dividend cover, the number of times a dividend could be paid from profits.

covered bond vehicle Form of limited liability partnership. For the bank levy, it is defined in FA 2011, Sch 19 para 53(7).

COVID-19 Strain of coronavirus that was declared a pandemic in March 2020, leading to a lockdown and many government schemes and variations in law. It is widely known as coronavirus, where more details are given.

COVID-19 Corporate Financing Facility Scheme instituted by the government from 23 March 2020 where the Bank of England provides liquidity to large companies by buying their commercial paper with a maturity up to one year.

cracking Process of breaking down molecules to make oil, or to make potable spirits. Details of the latter are given in Customs notice 39.

crane grab machine Amusement machine where the user operates a grabber to select a toy or other item. This is specifically excluded from the scope of machine licence duty.

CRC Energy Efficiency Scheme Mandatory scheme previously known as Carbon Reduction Commitment (CRC). It was introduced in April 2010. It requires large public and private sector organisations to reduce carbon dioxide emissions. This excludes reductions already coved by Climate Change Agreements and the EU Emissions Trading Scheme. The scheme covers all organisations that use more than 6,000 megawatts of electricity a year. The scheme works by requiring organisations to buy allowances to cover emissions in the previous year. The scheme has five consecutive phases, each of five years, which run from 1 April 2014 to 31 March 2039, and a final phase of four years from 1 April 2039. The relevant law is CRC Energy Efficiency Scheme Order SI 2013 No 1119, issued under Climate Change Act 2008.

creatine Organic substance. Its products are generally not zero-rated as food.

creative works Literary, dramatic, musical or artistic works, or designs. These can benefit from averaging of taxable profits under ITTOIA s221.

credit In bookkeeping, an entry that reduces an asset or increases a liability. A credit balance on an account denotes a liability, income, profit or value reduction. In ordinary parlance, an account is often said to be credited when money is paid into it. That is the opposite to double entry bookkeeping. If money is paid into a bank account, that is shown as a debit.

credit card Card issued by a bank or similar body, allowing the holder to spend up to a credit limit. From 13 January 2018, it was not possible to pay tax by private card, though tax may be paid by corporate credit card or by any debit card. From 1 November 2020, it is again possible to pay tax by credit card but HMRC makes a charge, even for corporate cards, based on costs imposed by card companies. This last change is imposed by SI 2020 No 657.

credit control Functions in a business which are designed to ensure that a company's invoices are paid. In general, credit control has two parts. The first part is vetting new customers and monitoring existing customers to ensure that they are creditworthy. The second part is chasing up debts by letters and telephone calls. The received wisdom is that telephone calls are particularly effective if you follow the three Ps of being persistent, polite and patient.

credit institution For Companies Acts, "means a credit institution as defined in Article 4.1(1) of Directive 2006/48/EC of the European Parliament and of the Council relating to the taking up and pursuit of the business of credit institutions" (CA 2006 s1173(1)).

credit note Document issued by a supplier to reduce the value of a previously issued invoice. Provided the reason is genuine, output VAT may be reduced by the issue of a credit note with VAT on. The legal provision is VATA 1994 Sch 11 para 2(10). Details are given in VAT Regulations SI 1995 No 2518 para 15.

creditor Person to whom money is owed.

creditor relationship Term used for loan relationship rules for companies. The term is defined in Corporation Tax Act 2009 s302.

creditor repo Corporation tax provisions are given in Corporation Tax Act 2009 s543. Income tax provisions are given in Income Tax Act 2007 s925A.

creditors' voluntary liquidation Winding-up of a company by a special resolution of members with the agreement of any creditors.

credit-token Credit card, debit card, other type of card, token, document or similar whereby the recipient may acquires goods or money. Tax provisions of providing a credit-token to an employee are given in ITEPA 2003 s92(1).

credit union Mutual body that provides financial services to its members under provisions of Credit Unions Act 1979. They were established in the UK in 1960, though based on bodies that had existed since 18th century. A credit union has a common bond that defines who may be a member. A credit union is regarded as not trading (CTA 2009 s40) and its payments are not regarded as annual charges (CTA 2009 s133).

cremation One of the legal methods for disposing of a human body. It has been legal in the UK since 1885. For VAT, cremation is an exempt supply under VATA 1994 Sch 9 Group 8. Further details are given in VAT notice 701/32.

crematorium Place for disposing of bodies by cremation, i.e. burning. It has been legal in the UK since 1885. A crematorium qualifies for a form of tax relief similar to a capital allowance under ITTOIA s169. Cremation is exempt from VAT under VATA 1994 Sch 9 Group 8, as explained in VAT Notice 701/32.

CREST Electronic share dealing system established in 1996 whereby holdings in shares and other securities are recorded electronically without a share certificate or other document.

cricket club The extent to which this is regarded as a trade is discussed in HMRC Manual at BIM24345.

crime-related payment Payment in connection with a crime, such as blackmail or extortion. Such payment is not allowed as a taxable deduction from 11 June 1993. The law is ITTOIA 2005 s55 and CTA 2009 s1304. Making such a payment may itself be a criminal offence.

Criminal Finances Act Law effective from 30 September 2017 to extend the scope of financial crimes. In particular it created the offences of failure to prevent tax evasion. An employer cannot escape prosecution on the grounds that tax evasion was the work of a maverick employee.

Criminal Injuries Compensation Scheme In relation to inheritance tax provisions for a trust for a bereaved minor. the term "means –

(a) the schemes established by arrangements made under the Criminal Injuries Compensation Act 1995;

(b) arrangements made by the Secretary of State for compensation for criminal injuries in operation before the commencement of those schemes, and

(c) the scheme established under the Criminal Injuries Compensation (Northern Ireland) Order 2002"

(Inheritance Tax Act 1984 s81D(8)).

Criminal Investigation Group (CIG) Department of HMRC that deals with serious tax evasion that contravenes the criminal law.

criminal law Law relating to crimes such as theft and fraud. Tax evasion is a crime, though the criminal law is usually reserved for the more serious cases. A criminal case must be proved beyond reasonable doubt whereas a civil case need be proved only on the balance of probabilities.

criminal lifestyle Lifestyle which appears to be funded from the proceeds of crime. An order may made to confiscate property belonging to a person enjoying such a lifestyle under Proceeds of Crime Act 2002 s10. A more detailed definition appears in s75.

criminal payments Payments involving crime such as bribery and extortion. From 11 June 1993, such payments are disallowed for tax purposes even if they otherwise meet the conditions of a business expense. The object is "to stop indirect subsidies to criminal activities" and to encourage people not to submit to extortion. The legislation is now contained in Corporation Tax Act 2009 s1304. This gives three categories of disallowed expenditure:

- where the payment itself is an offence (such as to buy illicit drugs or arms) under s1304(4)(a)
- where a payment is made outside the UK but would be illegal if made in the UK (even if legal where made) under s1304(4)(b)
- (from 30 November 1993) for blackmail or extortion, under s1304(5).

The matter is discussed in the Inspectors' Manual at BIM43101 and following sections.

Criminal Procedure Rules Rules introduced from 3 April 2006 under Courts Act 2003 s69.

crisps These are specifically standard-rated for VAT under VATA 1994 Sch 8 Group 1 Excepted Item 5.

Croatia Eastern European country, a member of the European Union from 1 July 2013. Its currency is the kuna of 100 lipa. It was part of Yugoslavia and remains subject to the UK-Yugoslavia double taxation convention of 1981.

crocodile Large reptile. It is an endangered animal. Imports of the animal and products made from it are generally banned under Convention on International Trade in Endangered Species.

Crofters Commission Body established to regulate and develop crofting in rural communities in the Highlands and Islands of Scotland. It is regulated by the Crofters (Scotland) Act 1993 amended in 2007.

croissant Pastry product. They are generally standard-rated for VAT as they are regarded as being intended to be eaten hot *(Pret A Manger (Europe) Ltd. VTD 16246).*

cross-casting Process of adding up rows and columns in a handwritten accounts book as a means of checking the totals.

crossed cheque Cheque that has two parallel diagonal lines drawn across it to prevent the cheque being exchanged for cash. A crossed cheque may only be paid into a bank account. An uncrossed cheque is called an open cheque and may be paid to bearer. The law on cheque crossings is Bills of Exchange Act 1882 s76.

cross-examination Part of court proceedings where a witness is questioned by the other party or their representative. Points to note are:

- a cross-examination takes place when the examination-in-chief has closed or been waived
- the cross-examination is not confined to matters in the examination-in-chief
- the witness may be asked leading questions. These are questions which suggest an answer
- if a party declines to cross-examine a witness, that may be taken as meaning that the witness's evidence is accepted.

Crown Its many meanings include the state or government as personified by the monarch. It also means a coin for five shillings (25p or a quarter of a pound) issued between 1526 and 1970.

Crown Court Criminal court that hears cases too serious for the magistrates' court. It is defined in Courts Act 1974 s4.

Crown dependency Overseas territories that owe allegiance to the British Crown but are not administered by the UK government. Many of them are seen as tax havens.

Crown disclaimer The right of the Treasury solicitor, or (in Scotland) the Lord Treasurer's Remembrancer, to disclaim property of a struck off company as bona vacantia. This right is set out in Companies Act 2006 s1013. The Treasury solicitor has said that he will not seek to recover any assets of a struck off company, so all assets may be distributed to members.

Crown employment Working for the government. Generally such workers have the same rights as other workers though some of these are contained in separate legal provisions. The trade union rights are contained in Trade Union and Labour Relations (Consolidation) Act 1992 s273. For tax, this is "Employment under the Crown:

(a) which is of a public nature, and

(b) the earnings from which are payable out of the public revenue of the United Kingdom or of Northern Ireland" (ITEPA 2003 s28(2)).

Provisions for national insurance are contained in SSCBA 1992 s115.

Crown preference The right of the state to be treated as a preferential creditor in an insolvency. Until 2003, the state enjoyed a degree of preference in respect of unpaid taxes. From 1 December 2020, a measure of Crown preference is reinstated in respect of taxes collected by a business from others, such as VAT and employees' PAYE and national insurance. It does not apply to taxes imposed on the business, such as corporation tax or employer's national insurance. The change is effected by Finance Act 2020 s98 which amends insolvency law, particularly introducing a new para 15D to Insolvency Act 1986 Sch 6.

Crown Prosecution Service (CPS) Body that is independent of the police and HMRC and deals with prosecutions of criminal offences. From 2010 it deals with tax prosecutions.

Crown set-off The right of the state to set off debts owed by the government in relation to debts owed to it, such as tax. There is no set-off under a Time To Pay arrangement.

crude oil Petroleum oil in the state as it comes out of the ground as a mixture of organic compounds. This is refined into different oil products subject to various rates of hydrocarbon oil duty.

cruise Holiday travel on a liner. For VAT, goods supplied during the cruise are regarded as supplied from the country where the cruise started. However, in the case *Kholer [2004] C-58/104,* it was held that goods sold while in a non-EU port were to be regarded as supplied from the port.

cryptocurrency Form of money that exists as computer code. There are many cryptocurrencies of which bitcoin is probably the most popular. HMRC issued guidance in December 2018. It treats cryptocurrency as an asset and not as currency, which means that gains may be subject to capital gains tax unless the person comes within the scope of trading. A disposal occurs when cryptocurrency is spent, exchanged for currency, or otherwise used.

crystallisation Process by which a charge to tax is created. No tax is payable on the increase in value of an asset owned by a taxpayer. On disposal, that increase crystallises and capital gains tax may be payable.

crystallised fruit Fruit that has been put into heated sugar syrup. These are treated as VAT standard-rated confectionery under VATA 1994 Sch 8 Group 1 Note (5).

Cuba Caribbean republic. Its currency is the Cuban peso. The UK has no tax treaty.

Cuban peso Currency of Cuba.

cui bono? Latin for "for whose benefit?"

cuideachta phoibli' theoranta (CPT) Irish Gaelic: public limited company. These letters may follow the company name if registered in the Irish Republic.

culottes Split skirt. These are zero-rated for VAT if provided for young children. The matter was considered in the case *Dauntgate Ltd [1993] VTD 11663*. Guidance is given in VAT Notice 714.

culpability Extent to which someone is held to blame. Although not used as a tax term, it is a clear principle behind the penalties in FA 2007 Sch 24.

cultural services These may be exempt from VAT. The exact scope has been litigated.

cultural test Test that must be met to qualify for television tax relief (CTA 2009 s1216CB(2) or video games relief (CTA 2009 s1217CB (2) from corporation tax.

cum Latin for "with". It is widely used in abbreviations such as cum div (with dividend).

cumulation period For inheritance tax, period during which lifetime gifts are cumulated to see if the nil rate band has been exceeded. The period has been seven years since 1986.

cumulative basis Means of applying PAYE tax codes for income tax on payslips. It considers earnings and tax paid since the previous 6 April. PAYE is administered on this basis unless either HMRC states or otherwise regulations so require (PAYE Regulations SI 2003 No 2682 reg 22).'

cumulative preference share Form of financial instrument under which a company borrows money on which a payment accrues each year. If the payment is not made one year, it rolls over to future years. Cumulative preference shares were held to be ordinary share capital for entrepreneur's relief (now called business asset disposal relief) by the upper tribunal in the case *Stephen Warshaw [2020] UKUT 0366*. The issue was determined on what the company's articles of association allowed, not on what dividends were actually paid.

cupro-nickel Alloy of copper and nickel to make UK silver coins from 1947 to 2002.

curator Under Scots law, the equivalent of a trustee or guardian of a child or person who lacks mental capacity.

currency Means of exchange for a territory. UK currency is the pound. Where accounts are prepared in another currency, values must be translated into UK currency for tax purposes. HMRC publishes exchange rates for this purpose. There are tax rules when accounts are kept in a non-UK currency.

currency clause Provision in a contract or other document that seeks to avoid issues relating to exchange differences by either stating the currency in which the contract is to be conducted or by stating a method by which currency is to be fixed.

currency contract Form of agreement to hedge a risk from foreign exchange. The three main types of contract are forward currency contracts, currency options, and currency swaps. The tax implications are discussed in HMRC Manual at BIM39523.

currency conversion When an amount of one currency is exchanged for another. Note that if an amount of one currency is simply stated at a value of another currency, it is said to be translated, not converted.

currency option Contract to buy or sell a specified currency at fixed exchange rate within a fixed period. The tax implications are discussed in HMRC Manual at BIM39523.

currency restriction When an overseas debt is not paid because of restrictions or a shortage of currency. In itself, this does not make the debt a bad debt. To the extent that the debt is not covered by ECGD, tax relief may be claimed under extra-statutory concession B38. The matter is discussed in HMRC Manual ay BIM42750.

currency swap Agreement to use a certain currency in exchange for another under a contract. The tax implications are discussed in HMRC Manual at BIM39523.

current asset Cash, debtors, prepayments, stock and other assets expected to be consumed within the next 12 months.

current assets ratio Ratio from dividing current assets by current liabilities. Traditionally a figure of 2 was considered safe. This must be considered in the context of the business. A building company probably needs a higher figure; a supermarket can manage with a much lower one.

current cost accounting Attempt to adjust accounts to reflect the effects of inflation. A previous attempt, known as current purchasing power, was abandoned. Current cost accounting was introduced by the old accounting standard SSAP 16 in 1975. It was widely ignored and scrapped in 1985.

current liability Debt that an entity expects to pay in the next 12 months. Outstanding tax is a current liability.

current maintenance arrestment Provision in Scotland that requires an employer to deduct amounts from a payslip for child maintenance.

current ratio Another name for the current assets ratio.

current tax For accounting, this is the amount of income tax or corporation tax payable or recoverable in respect of the profit or loss for a defined period (FRS 102 glossary; IAS 12 para 5).

current year basis Method of determining the profits of a taxable business in a particular tax year. It broadly requires profits to be taxed on the accounting period that ends in the tax year. Half the estimated tax is payable on 31 January in the tax year. The other half is payable six months later on 31 July after the tax year (which ended on 5 April) with any adjustment on the following 31 January. This system was introduced in 1994, replacing the previous year basis. There are separate provisions for the opening and closing years. Small businesses make just one payment on 31 January after the tax year.

For the first year, the taxable profits are those from the beginning of the accounting period to the next 5 April. This will usually mean that some of the period is taxed twice. That amount attracts overlap relief. In the final period, the profit is taxed on the amount earned from the end of the previous period to cessation minus overlap relief.

current year income Figure used for the income test in determining eligibility for tax credit (Tax Credits Act 2002 s7(4)).

curriculum vitae (CV) Details of a person, particularly a job applicant. It includes personal details, qualifications, work history and other information. The plural is curricula vitae.

cursor A point on a computer screen identifying which part of the data displayed is being used.

curtilage Boundary of land on which a building stands. All land within the curtilage is regarded as part of the property for the purposes of council tax and capital gains tax.

cushion gas Volume of gas remaining in a storage container to maintain pressure (CAA 2001 s70J(7)). For tax purposes, this is treated as plant (FA 2010 s28).

custodian Person who looks after property for another. In finance, it means someone similar to a trustee but who has no other trustee responsibilities.

custom Practice that has become established and which therefore tends to be followed on future occasions. Custom is the original form of English law. It is still possible, at least in theory, for a custom to have the force of law if it can be shown to have had a continuous history from 1189 and to meet other conditions.

customary payment Payment that is usually made though there may be no legal requirement to do so. In employment, such a payment is treated as gross income. The matter is discussed in HMRC Manual at EIM00640.

customer Person who chooses to buy goods or services from a supplier. HMRC uses the word to described taxpayers and others who use its services. The word is given a specific definition in tax law in relation to corporation tax for banks (CTA 2009 s133J) and in Dormant Bank and Building Society Accounts Act 2008 s1(1)(a).

customer accounting record (CAR) Record of a taxpayer held by HMRC in its SAFE accounting system.

customer lottery Lottery where a free ticket is given to a retail customer one of whom periodically wins a prize (Gambling Act 2005 Sch 11). Such a lottery is exempt from lottery duty and other provisions of lottery law.

customer relationship manager (CRM) HMRC official who is assigned to a large taxpayer.

Customs Functions of HMRC that relate to the import and export of goods. They include control of banned or restricted items, and ensuring that Customs duties and import VAT are paid.

Customs agent Person appointed to deal with Customs matters for another person (Taxation (Cross-border Trade) Act 2018 s21(1)).

Customs and Excise Body that dealt with indirect taxes and related matters until merged with Inland Revenue in 2005 to form HM Revenue and Customs (HMRC).

Customs declaration Statement of what goods have passed Customs and what duty is payable on them.

Customs duties Duties charged on imports. In theory, they could also be charged on exports, but are not. It is Britain's oldest tax dating from 1055 and operated on a national basis from 1220. While the UK was a member of the European Union, it is charged only on imports from outside the UK. The EU sets the rates for other countries, many of which are zero. From 2021, it is charged at UK-determined rates. Some examples are given in section 3 of this dictionary.

Customs Hotline Number that may be called to report suspected smuggling or tax fraud. The number is 0800 595 000. It is open for 24 hours on every day of the year. It may also be contacted on website www.hmrc.gov.uk/customs-hotline, or by writing to Customs Hotline, Freepost SEA 939, PO Box 100, Gravesend, Kent DA12 2BR, or by faxing to 0800 528 0506, or e-mailing to customs.hotline@hmrc.gsi.gov.uk.

Customs information Customs information may be shared between the EU and UK under the European Union/UK agreement of 24 December 2020. This is given effect in UK law by European Union (Future Relationship) Act 2020 s20 which adds section 8A into Customs and Excise Management Act 1979.

Customs procedure An outcome for imported goods. The most common is release for free circulation, which means that any duties have been paid and the goods may be sold or used in the UK. Other procedures include Customs warehousing, inward processing, outward processing and temporary importation, among others.

Customs seal Seal attached by a Customs officer to a box or other container to indicate that it has passed Customs.

Customs Tariff Schedule of Customs duties of goods imported into UK from outside the EU, while the UK is a member of the EU. A UK tariff for after Brexit under provisions of Taxation (Cross-Border Trade) Act 2018 s8.

Customs union Group of countries which has agreed not to impose Customs duties on each other's exports. The European Union became a Customs union in 1992.

Customs valuation agreement This means the agreement on the implementation of Article VII of GATT 1994" (EU/UK withdrawal agreement of 24 December 2020. Article GOOD 3 definition (b)).

Customs warehouse Place approved by HMRC where goods may be stored pending payment of Customs duty and import VAT.

cut off with a shilling Old term that means disinherited. It meant that a person inherited one shilling (5p) to show that they had not been forgotten in the will, reducing their scope to challenge the will. The expression is now more commonly rendered in the negative as to be cut off *without* a shilling, meaning not even to be acknowledged.

cutting Where land has been cut away, such as to accommodate a railway. The cutting itself is explicitly excluded from the scope of capital allowances (CAA 2002 s22(1) List B) but what is put in the cutting may qualify.

cwmni Welsh for "company".

cwmni cyfyngedg Cyhoeddus (ccc) Welsh for "public limited company". A company registered in Wales may put these words or the abbreviation ccc after its name.

cycles Word often used to mean bicycles, as in ITEPA 2003 s244.

cycle to work Generic name for a range of tax measures to encourage workers to cycle. These include tax exemptions for use of a bicycle, showers and changing rooms. Before 2013, it included the cyclist's breakfast.

cyclical deficit One of the two elements of a Budget deficit. The other is the structural deficit. HM Treasury glossary says that cyclical deficit "occurs as a result of a downturn in economic activity when tax receipts fall and spending on social security increases. It can be subsequently eliminated by a period of economic growth".

cycling voucher Government scheme announced in July 2020 offering £50 bicycle repair vouchers to the first 50,000 people to apply.

cyclist's breakfast Provision between 2002 and 2013 that allowed an employer to provide a tax-free breakfast to an employee who cycled to work (SI 2002 No 205; SI 2003 No 1434; SI 2004 No 3087).

cylinder In the sense of a gas container, its supply does not come within the scope of the VAT reduced rate for domestic heating. The gas itself may come within the scope. Further details are given in VAT Notice 701/19.

cyf Abbreviation of "cyfyngedig" which is Welsh for "limited". A Welsh limited company may put these letters after its name as an alternative to "ltd".

Cyllid a Thollau Ei Mawrhydi Welsh name for Her Majesty's Revenue and Customs.

Cymru Welsh for "Welsh". Welsh employees have their tax codes prefixed C.

cy-près French for "so near". In English this is used in charity law. If a donation cannot be used for a stated charitable purpose, it may be used for one as near as possible.

Cyprus European state, member of the European Union. It excludes Northern Cyprus where the government has no control. Its currency is the euro. The UK has a double taxation convention of 2018.

Czech republic Eastern European country, also known as Czechia. It was formed in 1992 when Czechoslovakia split. Its currency is the koruna of 100 haleru. The UK has a double taxation convention of 1990. It was modified by a multilateral convention in 2020 to refer to the Czech Republic.

D0 PAYE tax code indicating that all earnings are subject to the 40% tax rate. D1 indicates that they are all subject to the additional rate of 45% (or 46% in Scotland).

daily average agreement Agreement between an employer and a worker engaged in unmeasured work on how to determine compliance with national minimum wage.

daily living component One of the elements of the personal independence payment (WRA 2012 s78).

dalasi Currency of Gambia.

damages Money paid in compensation for a legal claim, such as breach of contract. Generally, damages are regarded as compensation rather than as income, and so are not taxable. Where damages are calculated by reference to lost earnings, the amount may be reduced by an amount to reflect the tax that would have been paid on those earnings. That is known as the Gourley principle. Interest on damages is taxable *(Westminster Bank Ltd v Riches [1947] 28 TC 159).* The tax treatment of damages paid by a business is generally tax-deductible. This is discussed in HMRC Manual at BIM42951.

Daň z přidané hodnoty (DPH) Czech for "value added tax".

data gathering powers Power of a body to gather data. Such powers are given to HMRC in various Acts and statutory instruments such as Finance Act 2011 Sch 23 and SI 2012 No 847.

data holder Person who holds data that HMRC may require producing under Finance Act 2011 Sch 23 para 1(5).

data protection Legal controls on the collection, retention and use of information about living individuals. HMRC is bound by these laws but has some statutory exceptions. The main laws are Data Protection Act 1998 and 2018, and Regulation of Investigatory Powers Act 2000.

data protection principles These are set out in Data Protection Act 2018 ss35-40. The six principles are:

(1) processing of personal data must be lawful and fair (s35)
(2) the purpose of collection must be specified, explicit and legitimate (s26)
(3) data must be adequate and relevant, and not excessive (s37)
(4) law enforcement data must be accurate and kept up to date (s39)
(5) law enforcement data must not be kept for longer than necessary (s40)
(6) law enforcement data must be processed securely (s40).

These principles are repeated at ss86-91.

date Identification of date. It is traditionally expressed as day, month, year, such as 15 January 2021. It can be expressed in numbers, such as 1.15.21. The USA, uniquely, puts the month before the day. In law, parts of a day are usually considered indivisible, so someone born on 19 November 1949 reaches the age of 50 in the first seconds of 19 November 1999, regardless of the time of their birth. Tax provisions said to apply, or cease to apply, from a date also apply from the first second of that date. Exceptions are sometimes made. Changes in excise duty are often made at 6pm. For tax tribunal hearings, a duty to do something by a particular date means by 5pm on that day (The Tribunal Procedure (First-tier Tribunal) (Tax Chamber) Rules SI 2009 No 273 rule 12(1)).

dawn raid In law, a raid of premises early in the morning before people have either arrived for work or got out of bed. The purpose is usually to seize material without giving anyone the chance to destroy it. Chartered Institute of Taxation has produced guidance on how tax advisers should handle a dawn raid on a client. It recommends that tax advisers have plans in place. These include:

- having contact details for 24-hour specialists
- ensuring receptionists and security personnel know who to contact
- telling staff to provide documents
- telling staff not to obstruct a lawful search
- making available a room for the investigators.

Once the search has started, a responsible person should be appointed to act for the taxpayer being investigated. That person should:

- check the authority of the investigators
- get the name of the person leading the search
- check the personal details of tax inspectors present
- check that the search is being conducted in accordance with the warrant or other authority. Is the date, place and time correct? Is there a limit on the number of people present?
- note what documents have been examined
- if possible, take copies of any documents that are removed
- make notes of questions asked and answers given.

day book In accounting, a book where transactions and other financial details are recorded. Their totals are transferred to the nominal ledger.

day X For annual tax on enveloped dwellings, the date that a property becomes unoccupied (FA 2013 s134).

D-day The day that the UK adopted decimal currency, namely 15 February 1971. (It also refers to the allied invasion of Europe on 6 June 1944.)

deaf From 29 June 2015, a deaf taxpayer may communicate with HMRC by a video relay using British Sign Language. The signer will communicate with a tax officer in a three-way conversation. For more complex matters, the taxpayer can use the Advocacy and Advice service provided by the Royal Association for Deaf people. A call can be booked from the Tax Help Centre at https://royaldeaftax.org.uk/.

dealer deposit contribution Payment made by a dealer (usually of cars) to the finance company that funds the purchase. For VAT purposes, this is treated as a discount on the selling price (HMRC Brief 7 of 17 July 2018).

death Point at which a life becomes extinct. It has many tax implications. A person is legally dead when so declared by a doctor. A court may make a presumption of death under Presumption of Death Act 2013 from 1 October 2014 if someone has been missing for seven years and there is no other evidence to suggest they are still alive. This applies for all purposes, unlike previous provisions.

A taxpayer is entitled to a whole year's personal allowance for the year of death, which will often trigger a tax rebate.

Tax penalties are generally extinguished though the tax itself generally remains payable. In 1992, the case *AP, MP and TP v Switzerland. ECHR Case 19958/9* held that the Swiss authorities breached human rights law by trying to make the widow and heirs liable for penalties for tax fraud committed by the deceased.
No national insurance is payable in the pay period in which the death occurred.
PAYE is payable. The position for PAYE on death is given in PAYE regulations 2003 at:

- reg 38 for an employee
- reg 39 for a pensioner
- reg 101 for an employer
- reg 163 for a jobseeker's allowance claimant
- reg 180 for an incapacity benefit claimant
- reg 184M for an employment and support allowance claimant.

On death, a person's property passes to a personal representative. This is an executor if they left a will or an administrator if not. Inheritance tax may be payable in respect of the estate of the deceased.
Property that passes on death does not trigger a liability to capital gains tax.
It may be possible to claim bereavement support payment.

death duties Various taxes that applied to the estate of someone who died between 1694 and 1975. By 1894, there were six different duties. From 1949, the only remaining duty was estate duty. They are now all replaced by inheritance tax.

death on active service Death caused by a wound, accident or disease while on active military service (IHTA 1984 s154). Such a death avoids inheritance tax. The death does not have to be immediate, nor does the injury have to be the sole cause. The fourth Duke of Westminster was exempted from a wound incurred 23 years earlier. The death must be certified by the Defence Council or Secretary of State as being on active service. There are now similar provisions for emergency workers killed in the course of their duties.

death rate The full rate of 40% inheritance tax, as against the 20% lifetime rate.

debenture Written acknowledgment of debt by a company, The legal provisions are set out in CA 2006 from s738.

debenture to bearer Form of debenture in Scotland which is legal under a law made by the old Scottish Parliament in 1696. For the avoidance of doubt, it is also declared legal by Companies Act 2006 s742.

debit Bookkeeping entry that indicates that an asset has increased, such as when money is paid into account. It is one side of a double entry; the other is a credit.

debit card Card issued by a bank or other financial institution which allows money to be taken directly from a bank account. Tax may be paid by debit card though a charge may be made.

debit note Document that states that a customer owes money. It is sometimes used as an alternative to an invoice when the supplier does not wish to incur a VAT liability.

de bonis non Latin for "of goods not..." [administered]. The term is used when one administrator of an estate completes the administration of another.

debt (1) Amount of money owed
(2) Form of financing a company, that is not equity (shares).

Debt Arrangement Scheme Scheme used in Scotland to help debtors pay their creditors under Debt Arrangement and Attachment (Scotland) Act 2002 s1.

debt collection Business of collecting debts. As a business, it is exempt from VAT as a financial service. The exact scope of the exemption was clarified in the case *AXA-UK plc [2009] ECJ. Case C-175/09.*

debt factoring Commercial arrangement where a bank or finance company advances money on the basis of a business's invoices.

debt-for-debt exception Provision in CTA 2009 s361B with regard to loan relationship.

debt management plan Informal agreement between a debtor and his or her creditors.

debtor Person who owes you money. The term has more specific meaning under Scots law of someone whose property may be sequestered (Bankruptcy (Scotland) Act 1985 s73(1)).

debtor quasi-repo Arrangement that is designed to copy a debtor repo. For corporation tax, this is defined in CTA 2009 s548. The tax provisions are given in s549. The matter is discussed in HMRC Manual at CFM46340.

debtor repo Financial arrangement where a borrower sells securities on the basis that it will later buy them back. The strict definition for corporation tax is given in CTA 2009 s547. The matter is discussed in HMRC Manual at CFM46350.

debtors due after more than one year An item that requires separate disclosure in the accounts under FRS 102 section 4.4A.

debt released The discharge of a debt by the creditor. This is taxed as trading income of the debtor.

debt written back When a bad debt is considered not to be bad. This usually happens when the debt is paid or it becomes apparent that it will be. This usually means that the whole debt is added to taxable profits for the accounting period in which it is written back. In the old case *British Mexican Petroleum Co Ltd v Jackson [1932]*, a company was able to avoid a charge by writing the debt back to reserves. Inland Revenue made clear on 14 December 2001 that this practice is not acceptable.

decarbonisation Policy or procedures to reduce or remove emissions of carbon dioxide (Energy Act 2010 s5). There are many tax provisions designed to promote such practices.

decern In Scots law, a formal term meaning to give a final decree or judgment. It authorises an extract of such decree or order.

decile A tenth part of a range. So the top decile of incomes will be the highest paid tenth.

decimal currency System where the pound is divided into 100 pence (Decimal Currency Act 1969). The UK adopted this on 15 February 1971, before which the pound was divided into 20 shillings, each of which was divided into 12 pence.

decimate Damage but not destroy. The term comes from an old military practice of executing one in ten men of a conquered army.

deck-cargo Cargo stored on the deck of a ship rather than in the hold.

declaration Part of a tax form where the taxpayer confirms that the information is true to the best of their knowledge and belief.

declaration date Date on which directors state how much dividend will be paid to shareholders.

declaration of solvency Declaration by directors of a company going into voluntary liquidation that they expect to pay all creditors within 12 months (Insolvency Act 1986 s89(1)).

declared strength Alcoholic strength of beer as declared by the brewer. The provisions are given in Customs notice 226.

decommissioning Process of removing equipment from use. There are tax provisions in relation to capital allowances (CAA 2001 s163(4A)) and oil taxation (CTA 2010 from s298A).

decommissioning relief agreement Payment made by the government to a company to decommission an oilwell (FA 2012 s80).

decoration Medal or similar award for gallantry or valour. Any payment that comes with it is tax free (ITEPA 2003 s638). Medals awarded to the original recipient are exempt from capital gains tax (TCGA 1992 s268).

deductibility provisions Sections of Income Tax (Earnings and Pensions) Act 2003 that relate to the deduction of expenses from earnings (ITEPA 2003 s332).

deduction at source Method of collecting tax from funds before the payee receives them. The UK tax system operates this method in PAYE, construction industry scheme and some deductions from interest or rent payments.

deduction notice Document served by HMRC on a bank, requiring it to make payment from a taxpayer's bank account (Finance (No 2) Act 2015 Sch 8 para 13). It can also mean a notice from HMRC requiring tax to be recalculated in an arbitrage arrangement (TIOPA 2010 ss236-242).

deductions working sheet For PAYE, this meant the P11 card that recorded details of an employee's wages and tax, or its computer equivalent. The definition was amended in 2015 to exclude reference to the card and to mean any computer or manual record of pay and tax. The term is defined in PAYE Regulations 2003 reg 2(1). The duties are given in reg 66.

deed Legal document that gives effect to a transaction. Under Law of Property (Miscellaneous Provisions) Act 1989, a deed must be signed and attested by two witnesses, but no longer needs to be sealed. For inheritance tax, the term is defined in IHTA 1982 s43(4).

deed of covenant Legal arrangement that assigned income to a person who became liable for any income tax. This was widely used to make payments to children at university (where the income would be covered by their personal allowance) or gifts to charity (which are not liable to income tax). The former ended in 1988. Donations to charity are now made under Gift Aid.

deed of variation Agreement made under IHTA 1984 s142 by all the beneficiaries of an estate within two years of death. It changes the terms of the will or intestacy provision for all purposes, including liability to inheritance tax.

deemed acquisition Date that an asset may be regarded as having been acquired for capital gains tax (TCGA 1992 Sch 2). An asset acquired before 6 April 1982 is deemed to have been acquired on 6 April 1982.

deemed contractor A person who does not carry on a construction business but may be regarded as one for the purposes of construction industry scheme (Finance Act 2004 s59(1)). This is broadly someone whose expenditure on construction work averages £1 million a year over three years.

deemed direct payment Term used in connection with tax on payment to worker who provides his or her services to a public body through a personal service company. The calculation is given in ITEPA 2003 s61Q.

deemed domicile Regarding a person as UK domiciled for inheritance tax when they have lived in the UK for at least 17 of the previous 20 years. The law is IHTA 1984 s267.

deemed election For a married woman's election to pay the reduced rate of class 1 national insurance, such an election made between 6 April 1948 and 5 April 1975. Unlike an actual election made between 6 April 1975 and 11 May 1977, a deemed election is not cancelled if a woman has no earnings for two tax years.

deemed employer Person who may be regarded as a temporary worker's employer for the purpose of an anti-avoidance provision in ITA 2007 s46A.

deemed employment payment Additional sum of tax payable when a worker provides his services through an intermediary on terms which would otherwise be regarded as employment. Tax rules, commonly known as IR 35, require an additional payment of tax to be calculated in accordance with ITEPA 2003 s54 or 61E. The employer itself may claim tax relief under CTA2009 s139 or ITTOIA 2005 s163.

deemed realisation Amount that may become taxable in respect of an intra-group transferred asset when a company ceases to be a member of a group (CTA 2009 s780).

deemed surrender End of a life assurance policy if a loan is made against it. There are tax implications.

deeming Legal provision which regards something as having happened regardless of whether it actually has. There are many deeming provisions in tax law.

de-enveloping For annual tax on enveloped dwellings (ATED), this usually means transferring ownership of a residential property from a company to an individual. The consequence is that ATED no longer applies. HMRC issued a notice on 20 December 2013 explaining that de-enveloping will usually not trigger a liability to stamp duty land tax.

deepfake Form of fraud in which modern technology is used to make realistic copies of voices of directors to order transfer of funds. The Institute of Chartered Accountants in England and Wales recommended in 2020 that all verbal instructions to transfer funds are verified before implementation.

deep in the money option (DITMO) Option where the call price or strike price is so far below the current value of the underlying security that exercising the option is almost a certainty. From 25 November 2015, a transfer of a DITMO attracts stamp duty of 1.5% on the higher of the option price and market price.

deep poverty Extreme relative poverty where someone is living on less than 40% of median earnings.

deep sea bed Area of the sea bed outside the limits of the UK or other state (Deep Sea Mining Act 2014 Sch para 3).

de-equitisation Replacing debt capital with share capital, or other equity capital. This has the effect of reducing the cost of capital but gearing up the balance sheet.

defamation Making an untrue statement that lowers the reputation of a living person or of a commercial product. If in writing or other permanent recorded form, this is libel. If spoken, it is slander. Payment of compensation, such as by a newspaper, is usually tax-deductible, as are premiums for libel insurance.

default additional rate Additional rate of income tax that applies if a devolved part of the UK has not set its own additional rate (ITA 2006 s6C).

default basic rate Basic rate of income tax that applies unless within the scope of a devolved rate (ITA 2007 s6C).

default beneficiary Person who receives the whole of a trust fund when the trust period ends. The trust period may not exceed 80 years.

default higher rate Higher rate of income tax that applies unless within the scope of a devolved rate (ITA 2007 s6C).

default interest This term usually refers to the interest charges on VAT that has been overdeclared or underdeclared from when the amount has been paid. Guidance is given in VAT Notice 700/43.

default paper case Simplest form of tax tribunal case where the taxpayer and HMRC provide evidence on paper without a hearing (SI 2009 No 273 rule 23(2)).

default retirement age Age at which a person was obliged to retire in the absence of a contractual provision to the contrary. Such retirement ages are generally outlawed from 2011.

default surcharge Civil penalty imposed for late payment of VAT (VATA 1994 s59). A surcharge starts a surcharge period of 12 months. Provided that there are no further defaults, the period then expires. A further default will start a new surcharge period. If there is a further default, the surcharge period is extended.

Usually no penalty is imposed for a first default in a surcharge period. The taxpayer is notified. A surcharge is imposed for a second or subsequent default in a surcharge periods at successively increasing amounts of 2%, 5%, 10% and the maximum 15%. No surcharge is issued for the 2% or 5% rate if the amount is less than £400. For the 10% and 15% penalties, there is a minimum surcharge of £30.

If a business has a turnover of less than £150,000, it will be offered help to ensure future compliance.

An appeal may be made against any surcharge on grounds of reasonable excuse. Interest may also be charged where VAT is paid late. There is no appeal against the interest charge. There is no appeal against the start of a surcharge period when no surcharge has been imposed. However, if a surcharge is imposed in that period, the taxpayer may then appeal on the grounds of the first default. Guidance is given in VAT Notice 700/50.

defeasance In finance, when a bond issuer places the underlying assets with a trustee who uses them to pay interest on the bond and, eventually, to repay the capital.

defeated tax avoidance Tax avoidance scheme that has been held by a court or tribunal to be ineffective. Participation in such a scheme can attract a penalty (Finance (No 2) Act 2017 s65 and Sch 16). Other participants may be subject to an advance payment notice. A taxpayer may also be issued with a warning notice under the serial tax avoidance regulations.

defective accounts Accounts that do not comply with company law or are required by the court for revised accounts to be prepared.

defendantPerson who is sued in civil proceedings. In Scots law, the person is called a defender.

deferment account Account underwritten by a bank or insurance co into which import duties are posted. This avoids the need to pay duty on every importation.

deferred annuity Annuity that is paid from a later date at a higher figure. They have been available since 30 June 1995. From 6 April 2006, an annuity may be paid equal to between 0% and 120% of the pension that would have been paid. For previous periods, the limit was between 35% and 100%.

deferred asset In accounting, an asset whose benefit is beyond the current accounting period but which is not a fixed asset.

deferred award terms Term used in relation to disguised remuneration (ITPA 2003 s554J(1)(c)).

deferred consideration When payment is not made immediately, such as payment in instalments or where payment depends on future performance. For capital gains tax, the charge is made on the whole consideration if it is paid within 18 months of the disposal. For longer periods, the tax may be paid in instalments. If a deferred consideration cannot be quantified, an estimated value must be used which is adjusted when the real value becomes known. This was established in the court case *Marren v Ingles [1980]* which related to an earn-out provision.

deferred credit Item of income which has not been received but must be reported on the balance sheet. A common example is a government grant.

deferred debit Item of expenditure incurred in an accounting period but where the matching income relates to a later period. Under the accruals concept, it is treated as an asset under prepayments.

deferred expenditure Expenditure incurred in the current accounting period but which relates to a later period, such as a prepayment. The matter is discussed in HMRC Manual at BIM44210.

deferred grant terms Term used in relation to disguised remuneration (ITEPA 2003 s554L(1)(c)).

deferred member Person who has an entitlement under an occupational pension scheme but who is not an active member. The commonest example is a former employee. The member is entitled to the benefit accrued. From 1 July 1988 such benefits must be uplifted by the lower of inflation and 5%.

deferred prosecution agreement (DPA) Agreement reached between a prosecuting authority and an organisation which could be prosecuted. This allows the prosecution to be suspended while the organisation meets conditions.

A DPA is usually used for financial crimes such as tax evasion, fraud, market-rigging and bribery. It is issued at the discretion of the prosecuting authority; an organisation cannot require a matter to be dealt with by a DPA. An organisation offered a DPA does not have to accept it. Such negotiations are confidential. A DPA may be agreed only with organisations, and not with individuals. A DPA requires the approval and supervision of a judge. The judge must be satisfied that a DPA is in the interest of justice. The organisation must make full reparation for the offence and demonstrate procedures to ensure no further offending.

DPAs became available from 24 February 2014 under Crime and Courts Act 2013 Sch 17. They are also governed by a code of practice for prosecutors produced on 14 February 2014 by the Serious Fraud Office and Crown Prosecution Service. This handbook was updated in October 2020.

The handbook does not specifically cover tax. DPAs seem to have been used little for tax offences.

deferred remuneration Term used in connection with disguised remuneration (ITEPA 2003 s554H(1)(b)).

deferred sentence Scots law equivalent to a suspended sentence. The sentence is usually deferred for between 3 and 12 months.

deferred share Share that ranks after all other shares. Such shares are rare in practice, though they were more common historically. A founder would agree that his holding would be in deferred shares so that other shareholders were paid before him in a liquidation. This encouraged those shareholders to invest.

deferred state pension Provision whereby a person may defer their state pension when they have reached state pension age. They receive a higher pension from a later date. A person may not defer if they are receiving certain social security benefits.

For those who reach state pension age from 6 April 2016, the deferment is 1% for every 9 weeks of deferral. This increases the pension by 5.8% for every year of deferral. The minimum deferral period is 9 weeks.

A person who reached state pension age before 6 April 2016 may take the extra pension as either a lump sum or higher payments. Additional income is paid at 1% for every five weeks of deferment, which is 10.4% for a year. The minimum deferment is five weeks. A lump sum may be claimed for a deferral of at least 12 months. It is paid at a year's rate plus 2%. This lump sum is taxable.

Weekly additions are increased each year at the same rate that applies to the basic state pension.

deferred tax Item on a balance sheet representing corporation tax payable in more than 12 months' time. Note that this is purely an *accounting* adjustment. It has no effect whatsoever on the amount of tax paid.

Deferred tax represents the extra tax that would have been payable if tax law followed accounting conventions. The main element is the difference between depreciation and capital allowances.

Deferred tax is usually a credit figure and is shown on the balance sheet under creditors. It is possible for deferred tax to be a debit figure.

Capital allowances are usually for higher amounts than depreciation. For example, plant may qualify for 100% annual investment allowance or 18% writing down allowance, while its depreciation may be, say, 10%. Deferred tax is the tax on the difference of 90% or 8% between capital allowance and depreciation. In the second or a subsequent year, this process can start to be reversed as depreciation can be more than the capital allowance. Eventually both capital allowances and depreciation will write off the whole value of the asset. The differences in amount are purely timing differences that arise from using different figures. Deferred tax reflects those differences from year to year.

The accounting requirements and procedures for deferred tax are given in accounting standard FRS 102 section 29.

Deficiency Shortfall, particularly in an account.

deficiency notice Notice issued by HMRC to say that a person has insufficient class 1 contributions for a year. The person may be able to make up the deficiency by making class 3 contributions, usually for the current year and the previous six years.

deficit Excess of expenditure over income in a non-commercial organisation. It is the equivalent to a loss in a commercial organisation.

defined benefit Term now used for occupational pension schemes based on final salary or other salary-related rules, as against money purchase.

defined contribution Term now used for pension schemes where the pension depends on the amount of contributions and not salary. All private pensions are defined contribution.

deflation Reduction in prices of consumer goods. It is the opposite to inflation.

degrouping Process of removing a company from a group. If a company leaves holding an asset acquired from another group company within the previous six years, any gain or loss is reinstated. This is known as the degrouping charge (TCGA 1992 s171; CTA 2009 s785).

Delaware corporation American corporation established in the state of Delaware. Since 1899, this state has followed a policy of lenient laws and generous tax provisions, making it popular. For UK purposes, a Delaware corporation is not fiscally transparent *(HMRC v George Anson [2011] UKUT B21).*

delayed completion scheme Scheme that sought to avoid or defer stamp duty land tax by delaying the completion of a property. This scheme has been explicitly ended by FA 2013.

delayed remittance Income remitted from overseas which is delayed for reasons beyond the taxpayer's control. The taxpayer may be able to claim relief under ITEPA 2003 s35.

delayed tax Tax that is paid after the due date. This may attract a penalty under FA 2007 Sch 24 part 8 or, in Scotland, Revenue Scotland and Tax Powers Act 2014 s190.

del credere Amount added to a charge to allow for the possibility of non-payment.

delegation Assigning tasks, projects, duties and rights to more junior staff. The right of HMRC Commissioners to delegate to officers is contained in Commissioners of Revenue and Customs Act 2005 s14.

deliberate and concealed Description of a tax inaccuracy which attracts the maximum penalty (FA 2007 Sch 24 para 3(1)(c)).

deliberate but not concealed Description of a tax inaccuracy that is deliberate but where the taxpayer did not attempt to conceal it. It attracts a higher penalty but not as much as if it had been concealed (FA 2007 Sch 24 para 3(1)(b)).

delict In Scots law, a civil wrong.

delivery note Document that accompanies delivered goods. It is not an accounting document and should not be treated as an invoice.

dementia tax Term coined for the proposal in the Conservative manifesto of 2017 that would require a person to sell their home until their capital wealth is no more than £100,000. The proposal has not been implemented.

demerger Separation of a business into two or more businesses. There are capital gains implications.

demesne Manor house with adjacent land not let to tenants.

Demibourne Decision in the case *Demibourne v HMRC [20005] SpC 486* when a worker was retrospectively held to have been an employee and not self-employed. The worker had paid his tax as a self-employed worker but the employer was required to pay the tax again with no relief for the worker's payments. This harsh decision was relaxed by SI 2008 No 782 regs 72E-72G which allows the worker's tax to be offset against the PAYE income tax. The employer is still likely to be liable for additional national insurance.

de minimis Description of a provision that does not apply below a threshold. There are many such provisions in tax law, such as not needing a VAT invoice for amounts below £25.

demolition Removal of a building or other structure. Such costs may qualify as part of the capital allowance for plant and machinery (CAA 2001 s26).

Demolition is also a disposal for capital gains tax. There may also be implications for annual tax on enveloped dwellings (FA 2013 s126).

demonetisation Process by which a coin or banknote ceases to be legal tender.

demurrage Charge for holding goods at a port or airport.

demutualisation When a building society or other mutual body becomes a commercial organisation. The tax implications are discussed in HMRC Manual at BIM35645.

denar Currency of Macedonia.

denatured alcohol Ethyl alcohol that is made into an undrinkable form and so is not subject to alcoholic liquor duty (Finance Act 1995 s5). Examples include methylated spirits and industrial alcohol.

denial route When a taxpayer denies tax evasion or fraud when this is suggested to them under a Contractual Disclosure Facility. The taxpayer has 60 days in which to issue a denial letter. HMRC then either accepts the denial or proceeds under the criminal law. Details of the denial route are given in Code of Practice 9 para 2.7.

denied advantage Attempted benefit of a failed tax avoidance scheme (Finance Act 2014 s208(3) and Sch 31 para 4(3)).

Denmark European country and member of the EU, for which purpose the Faroe Islands and Greenland are excluded. It is the only EU country other than UK that is not required to join the euro. Its currency is the krone of 100 ore. The UK has a double taxation convention of 1980 and a protocol of 1996.

denoting stamp A stamp that indicates the amount of stamp duty paid (Stamp Act 1891 s11).

density The weight of a defined amount of substance. This can be measured for spirits to measure the alcoholic strength as alcohol is lighter than water. Details are given in the Spirits Regulations 1991 and Customs and Excise Notice 39.

departmental registration When a department of part of a business is separately registered for VAT. This is rarely used in practice as it means the department must charge VAT on supplies made to other parties of the same business.

Department for Business, Energy and Industrial Strategy (BEIS) Government department formed on 6 June 2009 as the successor body to Department for Business Enterprise and Regulatory Reform and the Department for Trade and Industry.

Department of Work and Pensions (DWP) Government department formed in 2001 from a reorganisation. It deals with employment benefits, state pensions, disability and child maintenance.

dependant Individual who depends on another for financial support. A pension fund may provide for payments to dependants. Some social security benefits and pension plans provide payments to dependants.

dependent child For capital gains tax on an interest in a settlement, this is a child (including stepchild) who is under 18 and neither married nor in a civil partnership (TCGA 1992 s169F(4A)).

dependent relative relief Addition to the personal allowance for income tax given between 1920 and 6 April 1988 for looking after a dependent relative.

de plano In Scots law, a decree de plano is one which the court issues in the terms as sought.

depletion The using up of a resource as in material extracted from a mine or quarry. The accounting treatment is that the mine or quarry is regarded as a fixed asset and the depletion is accounted as depreciation.

deposit Money placed in a bank or similar for safekeeping, where it may earn interest. For income tax, it is defined in ITA 2007 s983. For income tax deducted at source, it is defined in ITA 2007 s855(2).

deposit arrangements One of the five forms of alternative finance arrangement that comply with Islamic law. The income tax provisions are given in ITA 2007 s564E; the capital gains tax provisions in TCGA 1992 s151L.

depositary receipt Financial instrument issued by a bank to represent shares in a non-resident company. From 1986, such instruments may be subject to stamp duty reserve tax (FA 1986 s93(1)).

deposit interest retention tax Tax charged in the Irish Republic on bank account interest.

deposit-taker Form of minor bank. It may accept deposits from members of the public but is restricted on other banking services (ITA 2007 s 853).

depreciating asset An asset for which holdover relief from capital gains tax may be claimed under TCGA 1992 from s154.

depreciation Charge shown in a profit and loss account to represent the use of a fixed asset. Depreciation is disallowed for tax purposes. In some cases, a capital allowance may be claimable instead.

depreciatory transaction Transaction between a trust and a beneficiary that has a gratuitous element. This usually creates a tax liability.

depression In economics, a sustained recession. It is sometimes defined as a recession that has lasted for at least two years in which at least 10% of GDP has been lost.

deprival value The value of an asset to a business expressed as the business would lose if deprived of the asset.

deprivation of liberty Provision under which a person who does not have full mental capacity is subject to restrictions to prevent him or her coming to harm, such as by wandering into traffic. The law is Mental Capacity (Amendment) Act 2019 which amends Mental Capacity Act 2005.

deregistration Removal from a register, particularly from VAT registration if turnover has fallen below a deregistration threshold. Guidance is given in VAT Notice 700/11.

dereliction State of a property that is uninhabitable. Such a property is exempt from council tax. A business may be able to obtain generous corporation tax relief for contaminated and derelict land.

derecognition When an asset or liability is no longer recognised as such, as may happen on a change of accounting standard. The matter is addressed in accounting standards FRS 102 and IFRS 1 para BC20.

derivative Financial instrument whose value is based on that of another instrument, such as an option related to a share price.

derivative claim Claim brought by a member of a company on behalf of the company under the provisions of CA 2006 ss260-269.

DERV Diesel Engine Road Vehicle. The acronym was widely used to mean diesel oil. This has now generally been replaced by ultra-low sulphur diesel.

descendant Son, daughter, or their descendant. A descendant is usually regarded as a close relative or connected person. A descendant may be eligible for residence nil rate band for inheritance tax.

design and build Simple building contract where the same person both designs and builds the property. If the property is zero-rated, the design element may also be zero-rated.

designated export place (DEP) Customs approved inland location where simplified export procedures may be used.

designated fund Fund which a church or charity has set aside for a specific purpose, such as replacing a roof. The fund is not restricted, so it may be used for another purpose.

designer rate tax System adopted by some territories that allowed a taxpayer to set his or her tax rates so as to avoid higher tax in another territory, such as defeating the old controlled foreign company rules of UK taxation. These rates were effectively outlawed in 1999 by Income and Corporation Taxes Act 1988 s750A and later by Finance Act 2012.

design weight A factor to be taken into account in determining whether a vehicle is a company car or company van (ITEPA 2003 s115(2) and s235(6)). it is the weight that the vehicle is designed or adapted not to exceed when fully laden in normal use.

despatch Movement of goods from one EU state to another. There are no imports or exports in the single market.

destination

(1) Intended place where goods are to be delivered or where a journey ends. This can be relevant in determining what rate of air passenger duty is payable, and whether goods are zero-rated as exports.

(2) In tax law, where provision provisions can be found in newly consolidated tax law such as ITA 2007. The Act is usually accompanied by tables of derivations and destinations.

destination principle Principle that some cross-border supplies are subject to VAT in the country of destination and not the country of supply.

destruction Process of making something useless other than as scrap. Destruction avoids Customs duty. It also counts as a disposal for capital gains tax.

detention Right of Customs officers to detain a ship, aircraft or other vehicle under CEMA 1979 s29.

determination Process by which a tax amount becomes known (TMA 1970 s28c-28E; in Scotland RESTPA 2014 from s91).

determination of code Process by which HMRC allocates a tax code to an employee (PAYE Regs SI 2013 No 2682 from reg 13).

detonation resistance test certificate Document required by Customs for imports of some materials such as fertiliser to certify that it could not detonate.

detonator Item regarded as an explosive (Explosives Act 1875 s3(1)) for which there are special Customs provisions.

Deutschmark Currency of Germany until it adopted the euro in 2002.

devaluation Reduction in the value of an asset or currency, particularly the formal reductions in sterling on 18 September 1949 and 19 November 1967. Devaluation can have a similar economic effect to a tax increase.

devastavit Writ that may be moved for neglect of duty by a personal representative in administering the estate of the deceased (Administration of Estates Act 1925 s29). The word is Latin for "he has wasted".

development In financial accounting, the process of turning research into a saleable product. Subject to conditions, this may be capitalised and not treated as revenue expenditure. Company law provisions are given in Companies Act 2006 s844. The term has a specific meaning in relation to oil taxation (CTA 2010 s356J(4)).

development condition One of the conditions that must be met to claim tax relief under the patent box (CTA 2010 s357BC).

development gains tax Tax charged between 1973 and 1976 on the gain from selling land.

development land tax Tax charged between 1976 and 1985 on the development value of land.

development rate Rate of national minimum wage originally paid to workers aged 22 and above undergoing training. It is now replaced by the reduced rate.

devise Gift of land and buildings in a will. The beneficiary is a devisee.

devolved tax Tax that a devolved assembly may set for part of the UK. Scotland, Wales and Northern Ireland have devolved taxes.

For Scotland, the devolution is contained in various acts. Scotland Act 1998 gave the newly reconstituted Scottish Parliament the power to vary the rate of income tax, which it never used. Scotland Act 2016 gave it powers it has used to set its own income tax rates, devolve aggregate tax and air passenger duty, and to assign VAT. The consequential provisions are set out in SI 2019 No 201. Scotland has also introduced land and buildings transaction tax as a replacement for stamp duty land tax.

For Wales, the devolved taxes are listed in Government of Wales Act 2006 s116A as added by Wales Act 2014 s6(2). Wales has power to introduce an alternative to stamp duty land tax, which it has used, and to set its own income tax rates, which it has not used.

Northern Ireland has not exercised any rights of devolved taxation though it has the unused right to set a different rate of corporation tax.

diabetic food For VAT, this is taxed on the same basis as the non-diabetic equivalent (VAT Notice 701/14).

diary A diary is regarded as stationery. Even though it typically includes some printed text, this is not sufficient for it to be zero-rated as a book. A completed diary, as may be bought by a collector, may be zero-rated as a book. Guidance was given in the case *Colour Offset Ltd [1995] QB. STC 85.*

diastatic seed Seed that contains an enzyme for turning starch into sugar. Diastatic barley is within the scope of inward processing relief from Customs duty under the Whisky Export Refund Scheme. There are similar reliefs when used to make gin or vodka. Guidance is given in Customs and Excise Notice 39.

die In the sense of a stamp, this includes any means of printing or impressing to indicate that stamp duty has been paid (Stamp Act 1891 s27).

diesel Road fuel named after the German engineer Rudolph Diesel (1858-1913) who invented the engine. it is subject to hydrocarbon oil duty and VAT. Between 1992 and 2000, diesel company cars were taxed at a lower rate than petrol cars as they have lower carbon dioxide emissions. From 2001, this policy was reversed to reflect other harmful diesel emissions such as nitrous oxides and carbon particulates.

diesel car Car that uses diesel as road fuel (ITEPA 2003 s141(3)). From 2001/02 an employee is taxed on a diesel company car at 3 percentage points (4 points from 6 April 2018) more than its petrol equivalent unless, from 6 April 2018, it meets the Euro 6d standard.

diet In Scots law, the date fixed for a court hearing.

dietary supplement Generally, a dietary supplement is not zero-rated as food. Further details are given in VAT Notice 701/14. A VAT tribunal did zero-rate a dietary supplement in the case *Arthro Vite Ltd [1996] VTD 14836.* It was described as a borderline case.

diet bar Product designed to replace more fattening food. A product comprising peanuts, beans and with a small amount of sweetening, but generally otherwise not palatable, was held to be food and not confectionary *(Texas Touch Dallas Diets Ltd [1984] VTD 1664).*

differential tariff When Customs duty is imposed at a higher rate for one country than for the same goods from another country.

digging machine This is defined in HODA 1979 Sch 1 para 10(2). Such a machine may use unmarked road fuel.

Digital by Default Government scheme announced in 2010 to move all interaction between government and businesses or individuals to computer-based systems. Making Tax Digital is an example.

digital disclosure service (DDS) Service provided by HMRC from 5 September 2016. It allows a taxpayer to disclose online undeclared income or gains, or overpaid tax credits. A small penalty is usually payable. HMRC usually accepts such disclosures.

digitally excluded Person who cannot use a computer for medical, practical or religious reasons, and who is allowed to submit paper tax returns (TMA 1970 Sch A1 para 14(2)). Only individuals qualify, not companies.

digital signature Electronic signature based on encryption for which the sender holds the key, as opposed to a wet ink signature.

digital services tax Tax introduced in April 2020 at 2% of UK revenues of a digital platform which has annual turnover above £500 million (Finance Act 2020 ss39-72).

Dilnot Report Government report of 2011 dealing with funding the costs of caring for the elderly.

dilution For beer duty, this means adding water to beer to reduce its alcoholic strength. This requires Customs approval, as explained in Customs notice 226. For shares, this means reducing the earnings per share to the figure that would apply if everyone who could exercise an option to acquire shares (such as holders of convertible debentures) did so.

dilution ratio The amount of water that must be added to a liquid such as a concentrate to make a drink. This is used to calculate the amount of soft drinks industry levy (Finance Act 2017 s27(2)).

diminution of value Reduction in value, particularly of an estate for inheritance tax purposes. A reduction of a shareholding of 60% to 40% represents more than a one third diminution as the shareholder has lost control.

dinar Currency if Iraq and some other Arabic nations.

diplomatic immunity Rights of ambassadors and other diplomatic staff as set out in the Vienna Convention 1961. One of the rights is not to pay tax in the host country (Diplomatic Privileges Act 1964 Sch 1 Article 23).

direct collection Collection of tax on earnings directly from a worker where HMRC believes that PAYE is impractical (PAYE Regulations SI 2003 No 2682 from regulation 141).

direct costing Method of costing a product. It is the sum of labour and materials plus a share of overheads.

direct debit Banking procedure allowing someone to draw funds as required from a bank account. It may be used to pay some tax liabilities and is now generally required for Time To Pay.

direct earnings attachment (DEA) Order from the Department of Work and Pensions that it may make from 8 April 2013 requiring an employer to make deductions from an employee's pay to recover overpaid benefits. The amount is calculated at a higher or lower rate. DEAs are administered under Welfare Reform Act 2012. It does not apply in Northern Ireland. DEAs were temporarily suspended from April 2020.

direct EU legislation EU legislation that is binding on the UK while it was a member of the EU. Under European Union (Withdrawal) Act 2018 s3, all such law is transferred as UK law subject to minor amendments, where it may be amended on the same basis as other UK law.

directive Document issued by the European Union setting out a law that is binding on all member states.

director Person who controls a company regardless of title used (Companies Act 2006 s250). A director is always taxed as an employee, regardless of whether he or she has a contract of employment (ITEPA 2003 s67(1)). A director has an earnings period for national insurance of the whole tax year. A negligent director can, in some circumstances, be made personally liable for unpaid PAYE or national insurance.

direct payment scheme Arrangement that allows inheritance tax to be paid from a bank account of the deceased before probate has been granted. Guidance is given in the notes to form IHT400.

direct recovery of debts (DRD) Scheme whereby HMRC may take money directly from a taxpayer's bank account without needing the authority of the taxpayer or a court (Finance (No 2) Act 2015 Sch 8). It came into force in November 2015 but was not fully integrated into HMRC procedures until March 2016. It is subject to safeguards such as requiring at least £5,000 to be left in the bank account, requiring a face-to-face meeting before using DRD, and an appeal to the country court. At least £1,000 tax must be owed, and other methods of recovery must have failed. A review after three years showed that it had a deterrent effect as 22,667 taxpayers paid £178 million on the threat as against just £361,678 collected under DRD in 19 cases.

directrix Rarely used word that means a female director.

direct tax Tax that is paid directly to HMRC. Examples include income tax, corporation tax, capital gains tax and petroleum revenue tax. These are the four taxes described as direct taxes in FA 2007 Sch 24 para 28(c).

dirham Currency of Morocco.

dirty chain Series of fraudulent transactions under VAT missing trader fraud. A parallel clean chain may be used to conceal the dirty chain.

dirty money Money that has been illegally obtained, such as from extortion or drug-dealing. There are strict anti-money laundering regulations to identify such money.

disability Physical or mental impairment of an individual that has a substantial long-term effect in preventing a person carrying out normal day-to-day activities (Disability Discrimination Act 1995 s1(1). There are many tax and trust provisions designed to assist those affected, in addition to social security benefits.

disability assistance Social security benefit planned to replace attendance allowance in Scotland in 2021 under Social Security (Scotland) Act 2018 s31.

Disability Discrimination Act 1995 Law designed to remove discrimination based on disability. HMRC published guidance in 2004 on whether adaptations for the disabled should be considered as capital or revenue.

disability living allowance (DLA) Social security benefit for disabled claimants under 65 made under SSCBA s71. New claims may only be made for children under 16. From 8 April 2013, new claims for those over 16 are for personal independence payment (PIP). Those already receiving DLA are being migrated to PIP under Welfare Reform Act 2012 s90. DLA is not taxed (ITEPA 2003 s677).

disability pension Pension received for a disability sustained in military service or war. Such a pension may be exempt from income tax (ITEPA 2003 s641).

disability reduction Procedure by which the property of a disabled person is put into the next lowest class for council tax.

disabled employee An employee who is entitled to a Blue badge (ITEPA 2003 s172(2)). Transport assistance may be provided by an employer without triggering a tax charge for benefit in kind (ITEPA ss246-247).

disabled person's tax credit Social security benefit provided between 5 October 1999 and 7 April 2003 when it was replaced by working tax credit.

disabled trust Discretionary trust established for a disabled person and which is subject to inheritance tax as an interest in possession trust.

disaggregation Splitting a business into artificially smaller parts, particularly to avoid VAT registration. HMRC has the power to order such parts to register as one business (VATA 1994 Sch 1 and Sch 1A(2)).

disbursement Recharge of an expense, such as when a solicitor recharges telephone calls. A disbursement is not subject to VAT, but the scope of disbursements, as stated in Notice 700, is very narrowly defined. In the case *Ellon Care Hire Ltd [2017] TC 5813*, the tribunal ruled that HMRC could not rely on this Notice as it is not law, and took a more relaxed view of what is a disbursement.

disclaimer Process of not pursuing a claim or entitlement, such as a person not accepting an inheritance. For inheritance tax, a disclaimed inheritance is treated as not having been made. It is no longer necessary to notify HMRC of such disclaimer. The law is IHTA 1984 s93.

disclosure Making known information, particularly with regards to accounts and tax. Generally, disclosure is only required where the law demands it, though a person is free to make greater disclosure. HMRC is generally restricted from disclosing details of a taxpayer, with some closely defined exceptions (CRCA 2005 s18). Disclosure of an underpayment of tax will usually reduce the amount of penalty payable (FA 2007 Sch 24 para 9 and elsewhere).

Disclosure and Barring Service Body established from a merger in 2013 to regulate who may work with children and vulnerable adults. From 18 January 2018, anyone may apply for a basic check from the Service. Payment of fees by an employer are not a taxable benefit in kind under ITEPA 2003 s326A and secondary legislation. Nor are they subject to national insurance (SI 2013 No 1142).

disclosure of tax avoidance schemes (DOTAS) Legal requirement introduced in 2004 (FA 2004 s290 and FA 2007) requiring tax avoidance schemes to be reported to HMRC and registered. Users of the scheme must quote the registration number on their tax returns. DOTAS was introduced for taxes thus:

- 1 August 2004: specific schemes and VAT
- 1 July 2005: stamp duty land tax
- 1 May 2007: national insurance
- 1 August 2008: income tax, corporation tax and capital gains tax
- 1 August 2010: most dealings in residential property
- 6 April 2011: inheritance tax on lifetime transfers
- 1 April 2013: annual tax on enveloped dwellings
- 6 April 2018: all inheritance tax.

From 1 August 2008, hallmarks have been published to identify when a scheme comes within disclosure. A scheme is given a Scheme Registration Number which must be quoted by all users.

disclosure report Report submitted by a taxpayer of underpaid tax under the Contractual Disclosure Facility as set out in code of practice COP 9. It broadly gives a taxpayer one last chance to come clean and avoid criminal proceedings.

Disclosure Scotland Scottish equivalent to Disclosure and Barring Service.

discontinued operations Commercial activities in which an entity is no longer engaged. These must be separately stated under accounting standard FRS 102 section 5.7D.

discount Reduction in price. From 2015, VAT is charged on the price paid by the customer, regardless of the reason for the discount. Where a discount is given retrospectively, the credit note may be issued. Further guidance on VAT and discounts is given in VAT Notice 700.

discount factor Figure between 0 and 1 which represents an interest rate. It is calculated as $1/(1 + r)$ where r is the interest rate expressed as a decimal. The discount factor of 5%, for example, is 0.950119.

discounted cashflow Cashflow that is adjusted to allow for inflation. This is done by multiplying cashflows from the second year by discount factors between 0 and

1. This method is used in calculating stamp duty land tax on leases. Rates are given in section 3 of this dictionary.

Discounted Gift Scheme Acceptable inheritance tax avoidance scheme. It involves the donor buying a single premium investment bond which is given to the desired beneficiary and from which the donor receives an income. The tax advantages are:

- the bond ceases to be part of the donor's estate, so the normal seven-year rule applies for lifetime gifts;
- if the donor dies within the seven years, the value of the bond is likely to be less than the sum paid, creating a potential inheritance tax saving immediately;
- the withdrawals from the bond are tax-free income under the normal rules for bonds.

discounted option Share option that allows the holder to buy the shares or other securities at an exercise price lower than the market value of those shares or other securities when the option was granted. The matter is discussed in HMRC Manual at BIM44180.

discovery assessment Assessment to tax that HMRC may make when it discovers that tax has been underpaid (TMA 1970 s29). The discovery must be something HMRC did not already know, so it cannot discover something disclosed on a tax return, and must be evidence-based. In practice the bar is set very low; a discovery can arise just from a tax officer changing his or her mind. The time limit is 4 years where the underpayment was neither deliberate nor carless; 6 years if careless; and 20 years if deliberate.

discretionary support award Assistance that may be provided to claimants in Northern Ireland under Discretionary Support Regulations (Northern Ireland) SI 2016 No 270. The award is be for "an extreme, exceptional or crisis situation which places you or your immediate family's health, safety or wellbeing at significant risk". The payments are exempt from income tax under ITEPA 2003 s677(1).

discretionary housing payment Benefit provided by a local authority to someone it considers needs extra help to meet housing costs. Each local authority makes its own rules. In Scotland, there is a national scheme under Social Security (Scotland) Act 2018. The payment is exempt from income tax under ITEPA s671(1).

discretionary trust Trust where the trustees exercise judgment on how much to pay the beneficiaries. It is the most flexible form of trust and the most highly taxed. It may be subject to inheritance tax when set up, every ten years thereafter, and when it is closed. From 2006, discretionary trusts are treated as a form of relevant property trust.

discrimination In employment law, exclusion or restriction because of a person's characteristic. Discrimination is generally illegal if it is based on an employee's:

- age
- disability
- gender reassignment

- marital status
- pregnancy or maternity
- race
- religion or belief
- sex
- sexual orientation.

There are exceptions to these categories. The law is largely found in Equality Act 2010. This Act consolidates many existing provision, such as race (illegal from 1968), sex and marriage (1975), disability (1995), religion and sexual orientation (2003) and age (2006).

disease control order Order requiring animals to be slaughtered to control foot and mouth, and other diseases. Such orders in England are issued under SI 2003 No 1729. The tax implications are given in CTA 2009 s115 and s124, and ITTOIA 2005 s126.

disguised remuneration Attempt to avoid PAYE and national insurance on remuneration by disguising it as a loan, investment or similar. Various anti-avoidance measures have been introduced, including exhaustive provisions effective from 6 April 2011 (ITEPA 2003 from s554A). Despite this, attempts are still routinely made.

dishonesty Lack of honesty which can lead to higher tax penalties. It is dishonest to pay assessments, knowing that the tax owed is greater.

In litigation, proving dishonesty is a two-stage test:

- whether the conduct fell below that of a reasonable and honest person, and
- whether the person realised that what they did was dishonest.

This was set out in the case *Mr Terence and Mrs Dawn Walker. TC 2774 [2013].* They paid VAT assessments from HMRC knowing that they understated the tax owed, but had the intention of paying the shortfall later. That conduct was dishonest.

disincorporation relief Tax relief allowed when a limited company disincorporates between 1 April 2013 and 31 March 2018 (FA 2013 ss58-61).

dismissal When an employment is ended by the employer. Unfair dismissal is where the dismissal is for an unfair reason. Wrongful dismissal is for dismissal in an improper manner. Constructive dismissal is when an employee resigns because the employee cannot reasonably continue working.

dispensation Provision whereby HMRC has confirmed that no additional tax is paid, such as where a benefit is provided to an employee for which that employee could claim tax relief (ITEPA 2003 s65(4)). From April 2016, dispensations are replaced by exemptions.

disposal Loss of possession of an asset by any means, including sale, gift, theft, destruction or abandonment. This generally triggers a liability to capital gains tax (TCGA 1992 s21).

disposition for maintenance of family Financial provision for members of a family member, such as housekeeping or pocket money. Such provisions are excluded from the scope of inheritance tax (IHTA 1984 s11).

dispute In tax, this means any area of disagreement between HMRC and the taxpayer. Efforts should be made to resolve the matter with HMRC, failing which there are various remedies, including proceedings before a tax tribunal or court. HMRC published a Notice on the subject on 20 December 2013.

disqualified advice Advice that HMRC ignores when considering whether a taxpayer took reasonable care to avoid inaccuracy (FA 2007 Sch 24 para 3A(3)).

disqualifying event Something that has the effect of removing a tax advantage.

disregard In social security, an amount that may be disregarded in determining income for a means-tested benefit.

dissolution Cessation of an institution such as of a partnership, or where a company has been removed from the register at Companies House by the company itself under Companies Act 2006 s1003 or by the Registrar of Companies under s1000. For a company, the main tax implication is that (from 1 March 2012) the first £25,000 of any distribution on dissolution is treated as capital in the hands of shareholders, and the balance as income. If the company has any share capital remaining, that is bona vacantia, which usually means it belongs to the Crown. From 14 October 2011, the Treasury solicitor said he would not claim any sum below £4,000.

distillation Process for increasing alcoholic strength of drink by boiling off the water. This usually means that the drink is classified as a spirit and subject to a higher rate of alcoholic liquor duty.

distiller's licence Licence that must be held legally to distil liquor (ALDA 1979 s12(1)).

distraint Seizure of goods to pay a debt.

distress warrant Order by a court authorising bailiffs to seize goods for non-payment of a debt.

distribution Share of a company's profits passed to its members. The most common form is the dividend (ITA 2007 s606(3)).

district Local authority administrative area in a county (Local Government Act 1972 s1(1)).

diver The taxation of divers working on the Continental Shelf is given in ITTOIA s15.

diverted profits tax (DPT) Tax introduced on 1 April 2015 by FA 2015 ss77-116, payable by a company that has avoided corporation tax by not having a taxable presence in the UK or uses transactions that lack economic substance to transfer profits overseas. The tax does not apply to smaller companies. The rate is 25%, except for ring-fenced profits taxed at 55%.

dividend Cash distribution by a company to its members. It is the most common form of distribution. A dividend may only be paid from profits. A company may not claim corporation tax relief for dividend payments (CTA 2009 s1305).

From 2016, the shareholder may receive dividends up to a low limit (£2,000 from 6 April 2018) without payment of further tax, and is then subject to a special rate of income tax, starting at 7.5%, on the balance (ITA 2007 s13A). The limit was £5,000 from 6 April 2016 to 5 April 2018. Rates are given in section 3 of this dictionary. This limit means that dividends can result in a higher rate of total tax when an owner-managed business extracts profits that way.
Between 6 April 1999 and 5 April 2016, dividends were taxed at ten ninths of the amount paid. For a basic rate taxpayer, the dividend rate was 10% which meant that no extra tax was paid.

dividend allowance Amount a shareholder may receive as dividends in a tax year before paying tax. This was introduced in 2016 at £5,000 a year, and reduced to £2,000 from April 2018.

dividend cover Accounting ratio of net profit divided by dividend.

dividend income Income from dividends and other company distributions (ITA 2007 s19).

dividend stripping Arrangement where the value of an investee company is materially reduced by the payment of a dividend. The capital gains tax provisions are given in TCGA 1992 s177.

dividend tax credit Notional tax credit on dividends between 1999 and 2016. If a taxpayer received £9 dividend, he or she was regarded as having received £10 and paid tax of £1. As the basic rate of tax for a dividend was then 10%, no further tax was payable. Higher rate taxpayers had an additional tax liability.

dividend trust rate Rate of income tax paid by a relevant property trust on its dividend income. The rate has been 37.5% from 6 April 2013.

diving supervisor The taxation of a diving supervisor working on the Continental Shelf is given in ITTOIA 2005 s15.

division Mathematical process of determining how many times one number needs to be multiplied to equal another. So 12 divides by 4 to give 3. In this example. 12 is the dividend, 4 is the divisor and 3 is the quotient.

Divisional Court Court comprising at least two judges from one of the three divisions of the High Court. The Divisional Court hears appeals in various specific matters and also exercises a supervisory jurisdiction over the High Court.

divisional registration VAT provision that allows part of an entity to be separately registered for VAT. Guidance is given in VAT Notice 700/2. This provision is very rarely used.

divorce Legal ending of a marriage. The law is revised by Divorce, Dissolution and Separation Act 2020 which introduces no-fault divorce. A divorced couple may live in the same home and co-operate on certain matters *(Holmes v Mitchell [1991])*. The issue is whether the martial relationship has ceased to exist. Divorce has several tax consequences. It can affect main residence relief for capital gains tax (TCGA 1992 s225B). The rule about transfers between spouses being on a no gain/no loss basis applies to the end of the tax year in which a couple divorce (TCGA 1992 s58).

The income tax consequences are given in ITA 2007 s1011.

There is generally no stamp duty land tax payable on transfers of property on divorce (Finance Act 2003 Sch 3 paras 3-3A).

Divorce excludes an ex-partner from a will, unless a new will is drawn up naming the ex-partner as a beneficiary.

DIY builders' scheme VAT arrangement whereby someone who builds his or her house may reclaim VAT on building materials (VATA 1994 s35 and Sch8 Group 5). It also applies if a charity building is constructed by volunteers. The aim is to put a DIY builder on the same basis as a commercial builder. This is only partly achieved, as a DIY builder may only make one claim (and within a strict time limit) whereas a commercial builder may claim input tax as materials are acquired. There are strict conditions. The DIY builder is not registered for VAT. Guidance is given on form 431C.

Djibouti Arabic state. Its currency is the Djibouti franc of 100 centimes. The UK has not double taxation treaty.

Djibouti franc Currency of Djibouti.

dock Place where ships berth for loading and unloading of goods or passengers. Profits from running a dock are taxed as a trade (ITTOIA 2005 s12; CTA 2009 s39).

doctor's co-operative Mutual trading organisation that started in 1995 to provide out-of-hours medical cover for GPs' patients. The tax consequences are explained in HMRC Manual at BIM24655.

document Any record in any form, including computer discs and hard drives. HMRC has some defined powers to seize documents. Company law provisions are given in CA 2006 s1168.

dog biscuit This is specifically standard-rated for VAT under VATA 1994 Sch 8 Group 1 Excepted Item 6.

dog licence Licence once issued by a local authority to dog owners. Legally it is a tax. It was introduced in 1878 and abolished in 1988 except in Northern Ireland.

dole Colloquial name for jobseeker's allowance or unemployment benefit.

dollar Unit of currency used in Australia, Bermuda, Canada and USA.

domestic Pertaining to the home. Domestic energy is generally subject to the reduced rate of VAT whereas non-domestic energy is standard-rated. The meaning of the word "domestic" in relation to tax was considered in the purchase tax case *Attorney-General v Milliwatt [1948] 1 All ER 331.* This gave the word a wide scope. It held that an electric blanket was a domestic appliance even though it was then considered a luxury item and was more commonly used in hospitals.

domestic fuel Energy for a residential dwelling. This is subject to the reduced rate of VAT from 1 September 1997 (VATA 1994 Sch 7A Group 1).

domestic goods

(1) Goods produced by a country for its own use.

(2) Goods used in a home.

The extent to which an employee may claim for such goods as relocation expenses is given in ITEPA 2003 s285. For import duties, the term is defined in Taxation (Cross-border Trade) Act 2018 s33.

domestic rates Local tax charged on residential property. It was introduced in 1601 until replaced by community charge in 1990 (1989 in Scotland), which was itself replaced by council tax in 1993. Domestic rates are still charged in Northern Ireland.

domicile Country a person regards as his or her natural home. A person may have only one domicile. There are three types. The most common is domicile of origin: where someone is born. A domicile of choice is when a person chooses to adopt another country. In practice, a UK domicile is difficult to lose. There is the now rare domicile by operation of the law which applied to married women before 1973. For inheritance tax there is also a deemed domicile. Domicile is particularly relevant for inheritance tax.

Dominica Island state in the Caribbean Sea. Its currency is the East Caribbean dollar. The UK has no tax treaty.

Dominican Republic State that shares an island with Haiti in the Caribbean Sea. Note that it is a separate country from Dominica. Its currency is the Dominican Republic peso. The UK has no tax treaty.

donatio mortis causa Death bed gift. To be valid:

- the gift must be made by the donor in contemplation of impending death
- the gift must be contingent on the donor dying
- the donor must part with or deliver the gift in some way
- the subject matter must be capable of being given away. The position regarding land is resolved by the case *Sen v Headley [1945].*

Provided the conditions are met, the gift is valid and thus falls outside the estate of the donor on death.

donation Voluntary gift of money, goods or services. A gift to charity may be tax-advantaged by Gift Aid.

dong Currency of Vietnam.

dormant account Bank account or similar which has not been used for 15 years. Where the owner cannot be established, the funds may be used for charities from 2011 (Dormant Bank and Building Society Accounts Act 2008 s10). Interest on such accounts is not taxed. This provision was extended to assets from 19 December 2015 and to dormant trusts in 2018. Interest on a dormant account is not taxed until a claim has been made (FA 2008 s39; SI 2011 No 22).

dormant asset Shares, securities or similar held by a bank which have not been touched for 15 years. From 2015, they may be sold and applied to charities.

dormant company Company that exists but is not engaging in any activity. Such a company is generally exempt from the need to be audited (CA 2006 s480). A dormant subsidiary is exempt from the requirement to file accounts (CA 2006 s1169(1)).

dormant trust Trust that appears to be inactive. This means that it has had no income or expenditure for five years, or where it has spent less than 30% of its income over the last five years. From 2018, funds of such trusts may be applied for charitable purposes.

douane Custom house.

DOTAS Disclosure of tax avoidance schemes.

double allowance Claiming two capital allowances for the same asset. It is generally prohibited by CAA 2001 s7, though the annual investment allowance and writing down allowance may be claimed for the same asset in the same year.

double entry bookkeeping System of financial recording used from 1496. It works on the principle that every transaction or accounting adjustment is recorded by a debit or debits and by a credit or credits. The debits and credits always add up to the same figure, thus providing a measure of control. There is no legal requirement to use it, though not doing so would be unusual.

double grossing up Situation that can arise under inheritance tax when the residue of an estate is shared between exempt and non-exempt beneficiaries (such as a charity and a relation). The law is IHTA 1984 s38, as explained in HMRC Manual at IHTM26152. The matter was considered in the cases *re Benham Will Trust [1995] STC 210*, and *re Ratcliffe [1999] STC 262*. The practical consequence often is that the non-exempt beneficiary receives little.

double jeopardy Legal principle that a person should not be punished twice for one offence. In tax, there is a rule that a taxpayer cannot have a penalty imposed for an offence if already convicted for it (FA 2008 Sch 36 para 52).

double reasonable test Under the General Anti-Abuse Rule, HMRC must show that a course of action cannot reasonably be regarded as a reasonable course of action. This test, set out in 2016, sets a high bar for ruling a tax avoidance scheme ineffective under GAAR rules.

double taxation When one income, profit or gain falls to be taxed in two countries (TIOPA s2(1)). The UK has tax treaties with more than 100 countries to address this, usually by charging tax at the higher rate of the two countries and then sharing the amount of tax. If the UK has no tax treaty, it will grant unilateral relief by allowing the whole foreign tax to be deducted from UK tax.

doubling clause Trick clause in a lease. It says something like "each year, the rent shall increase by a sum equal to the rent plus the rate of inflation".

At first sight this seems to say that the rent is simply indexed to inflation. In fact, it more than doubles the rent each year, quickly leading to ludicrously high figures. If inflation is 2% and the rent is £100, the doubling clause will increase it not to £102, but *by* £102 to £202. In year 3, it will increase to £408. By year 10, the rent will be £55,996. A notorious example was Blythe Court flats in Birmingham where the £250 ground rent of 1961 doubles every 10 years. By 2019, this was £8,000. In 30 years, it will be £64,000 making the leasehold properties worthless. On 28 March 2019, the government announced that 40 of the country's largest property developers had signed a pledge to free existing leaseholders from onerous deals. Such sharp practices are outlawed from 1 June 2019 under Tenant Fees Act 2019.

doubtful debt Sum owed which a taxpayer believes may not be paid but has not written off. Tax relief is allowed for bad debts but not for doubtful debts. The matter is discussed in HMRC Manual at BIM42701.

Dow Jones index Main stock market index of the USA.

downsizing Moving to a smaller home. For inheritance tax, the proceeds from downsizing may qualify for residence nil rate band.

drachma Currency of Greece until it adopted the euro in 2002.

drained cherries These are specifically zero-rated as food under VATA 1994 Sch 8 Group 1 Items Overriding the Exceptions 2.

drained fruits Apart from cherries, these are standard-rated as they are excluded from zero-rating as food by VATA 1994 Sch 8 Group 1 Note (5).

dram Currency of Armenia.

drama Depiction of fictitious events by actors. This is a condition for television production relief from corporation tax (CTA 2009 s1217FA(3)).

dramatic production Live performance of drama. This is a condition for theatrical production relief from corporation tax (CTA 2009 s1217FA(2)).

drawback Repayment of duty, such as when excise duty is repaid on goods subsequently removed from the UK.

drawdown Taking funds against an entitlement, most commonly from a pension fund.

drawings Sum taken by a sole trader or partner from profits. This does not trigger a tax liability as the drawings are taxed when the profit has been earned. Any drawings shown in the accounts must be added back to determine taxable profit.

dredging Removing silt and similar to make harbours and waterways navigable. It attracts its own capital allowance, a writing down allowance of 4% since 1986 (CAA 2001 s4).

drink For VAT, drink is defined as "a liquid commonly consumed to increase bodily liquid levels, to slake thirst, to fortify or to give pleasure" (VAT Notice 701/14). Many drinks are zero-rated as food. Exceptions are alcoholic drink, purgative and laxative teas, carbonated and sparkling drinks, barley water and similar, fruit cordials and squashed. The exact scope is given in VAT Notice 701/14. Alcoholic drinks are subject to alcoholic liquor duty.

droplock bond Floating rate bond which converts to a fixed rate of interest if interest rates fall to a predetermined rate.

drugs There are strict Customs controls on bringing drugs into the country. Non-prescription drugs and up to 15 days' worth of prescription drugs may generally be brought in freely. Guidance is given in Customs notice 4.

Drugs Free Hotline Telephone number that may be contacted to give confidential information about drug smuggling. The number is 0800 595000.

dual entitlement When a person becomes entitled to two social security benefits under different provisions (WRA 2007 s1(6A)).

duality Where expenditure has more than one purpose, particularly when once is tax-deductible and the other is not. The matter is discussed in HMRC Manual at BIM37007.

dual motive transaction Transaction undertaken for more than one motive. This can determine whether the transaction is part of trading. The matter is discussed in HMRC Manual at BIM24010.

due date Date by which tax should be paid.

dumping Practice of a country of exporting goods very cheaply to kill of the country's domestic market. The UK or EU may impose anti-dumping duty, a form of Customs duty, to prevent this.

Dutch Maror Fund Fund established in Netherlands to pay compensation to those forced to work as slaves of forced labour during second world war. In 2015, such payments were declared free of inheritance tax.

Dutch sandwich Tax avoidance arrangement that exploits EU rules. Typically profits are sent to the Netherlands before being sent on again to somewhere like Bermuda.

dutiable Subject to a duty, usually excise duty.

duty Tax levied on specific goods, such as tobacco products, hydrocarbon oil and alcoholic liquor.

duty-free In practice, this means free of UK duties. It is a personal import allowance. The rates are given in section 3 of this dictionary.

duty point Time and place where excise duty is payable.

duty stamp Adhesive label or equivalent mark to shows that duty has been paid. These had largely disappeared until reintroduced for spirits from 1 April 2006.

DVLA Driving and Vehicle Standards Agency, the body responsible for records on cars and driving licences.

dwelling Building occupied for residential purposes. Such a building is generally liable for council tax (Local Government Finance Act 1992 s3(1)). The construction of a new dwelling may be zero-rated for VAT. A dwelling owned by a company may be subject to annual tax on enveloped dwellings. A dwelling that passes to descendants may qualify for residence nil rate band for inheritance tax.

DWP Department of Work and Pensions.

each way (1) Bet, usually on a horse race, which is really two bets. One is that the horse will win. The other is that the horse will come second or in another high place depending on how many runners there are.
(2) In investing, when a broker earns commission on both the sale and purchase.

Eady levy Charge on box office receipts for showing films between 1957 and 1985. It funded British film making. There are now separate tax reliefs for British films.

earlier hold notice Notice from HMRC issued before a current notice when it is seizing funds from a taxpayer's account under Finance (No 2) Act Sch 8 para 4(7).

earlier year update (EYU) A submission made under real time information for PAYE in respect of data provided for a previous tax year. The EYU is discontinued from April 2020. Such submissions are instead made on the full payment submission.

early leaver Someone who leaves an employment before retirement. If the employee was a member of an occupational pension scheme, he or she generally has the choice of remaining as a deferred member, or transferring their pension to a new fund. If an employee leaves within two years of starting the employment, the employee has a further choice of receiving a refund of their contributions (not the employer's) minus income tax.

early tax year In relation to an individual carrying on a trade, means the tax year in which the trade commenced and the following three tax years (ITA 2007 s112(6)).

early years assistance Money or other assistance that may be provided in Scotland under Social Security (Scotland) Act 2018 s32.

earmarked deferred remuneration Term used in relation to disguised remuneration (ITEPA 2003 s554H(5)).

earned income Income that derives from employment or self-employment as against investment income. The distinction between earned and unearned income reduced after investment income surcharge was abolished in 1984.

earner For national insurance purposes, this is defined as someone who has earnings (SSCBA 1992 s3(1)(b)).

earnings arrestment Provision in Scotland where an employer must make deductions from an employee's pay and pass it in accordance with a court order.

earnings before interest, taxes, depreciation and amortisation (EBITDA) Measure of a business's profitability. It is a halfway house between gross profit and net profit. In practice, this figure is often used by new companies as a milestone where the company is starting to generate sufficient profits to cover its operating costs.

earnings cap Any form of limit on earnings, such as for entitlement to social security or tax relief on pensions.

earnings factor Figure used to calculate contributory social security benefits under national insurance rules. It is broadly the amount of class 1, 2 or 3 contributions, with a cap on class 1 (SSCBA 1992 s22).

earnings limits For national insurance, the lower earnings limit, primary threshold, upper earnings limit and secondary threshold (SSCBA 1992 s5(1)).

earnings per share (eps) Amount of net profit after tax divided by the number of shares in issue. So a net profit of £100,000 when there are 200,000 shares gives an eps of 50p. It is a figure reported in the accounts and also used in the widely reported P/E ratio.

earnings-related Term particularly used for certain social security benefits where additional payments were payable to those who had had higher earnings. This was abolished in 1982.

earnings threshold Level of income at which an employee and employer become liable to pay class 1 national insurance. The former is called the primary earnings threshold (PET) and the latter the secondary earnings threshold (SET).

earn-out Financial arrangement that allows a business founder to use the profits of the business to buy out an outside investor.

earn-out right Right of an individual, usually a director, to acquire shares if conditions are met. These often relate to future profits. The capital gains tax position is given in TCGA 1992 s138A.

ear protectors These may be zero-rated for VAT as protective clothing, either separately or as part of a safety helmet. VAT Notice 701/23 gives details.

easement Right enjoyed by a landowner over the land belonging to another person (Law of Property Act 1925 s1). Easements include rights of way, pipes, cables and similar.

Easter Sunday between 22 March and 25 April that commemorates the resurrection of Christ. The date is defined in Calendar (New Style) Act 1750 s3. The previous Friday and following Monday (Good Friday and Easter Monday) are public holidays.

Eat Out to Help Out A scheme to support the hospitality sector during the coronavirus lockdown. The government paid for half the price of meals to a maximum of £10 each, eaten on Monday to Wednesday during August 2020.

e-book Book or similar text designed to be read from a computer or other electronic device. It is zero-rated for VAT from 1 May 2020.

ecclesiastical corporation Any corporation in the Church of England established for a spiritual purpose (Charities Act 2011 s10(3)).

economic employer Person who funds salaries or wages as against the person who arranges payment.

economic operator Person who is registered with UK Customs or equivalent EU body in relation to savings income (SI 2003 No 3297 reg 2(2)).

Economic Operator Registration Identification (EORI) Number assigned by UK Customs or equivalent body in another EU country for Customs purposes. In the UK, this comprises the letters GB followed by the VAT number and three digits, usually 000. An EORI is valid throughout the EU, including after Brexit.

education In law, this is considered as separate from training which is related to specific work. The distinction was demonstrated in the tax case *Barry v Hughes [1972] Ch D. 48 TC 586*. For VAT, education is defined as a course, class or lesson of instruction in any subject, regardless of when and where it takes place (VAT Notice 701/30). Some supplies of education are VAT exempt.

educational establishment School or other body that provides education. For secondment of employees, the term is defined in ITTOIA 2005 s71(1), or s71(2) for Scotland. The same definition is used for corporation tax in CTA 2009 s71. For national insurance, a definition is given in SI 1978 No 1689 reg 1(2).

Education and Skills Funding Agency Government body that promotes government provisions for further education and apprenticeships. A business may claim tax relief for a donation to the Agency and similar bodies (ITTOIA 2005 ss82-86; CTA 2009 ss82-86).

Edward Medal Award for bravery. Payments of pension or annuity in respect of the award are free of income tax (Income Tax (Earnings And Pensions) Act 2003 s638).

Edwards v Bairstow Leading House of Lords case from 1955 which is an exception to the general rule that a tribunal decision is final on a point of fact. An appeal lies if the tribunal decision is so perverse that a tribunal could not reasonably have reached such a decision.

EEA European Economic Area. It comprises the EU plus Iceland, Liechtenstein and Norway.

effective rate Rate of tax that is actually charged after making allowances for reliefs and other provisions. For example, the combination of the higher rate of income tax and the reduction in the personal allowance means there is an effective rate of 60% income tax on earnings between £100,000 and £125,000 at 2020/21 rates.

Egypt Arabic country. Its currency is the Egyptian pound of 100 piastres. The UK has a double taxation convention of 1977.

Egyptian pound Currency of Egypt.

Eileen Trust Trust established to provide ex gratia help to those infected with HIV from contaminated blood or blood products used in the NHS. Such payments are now made by MFET Ltd. The payments are disregarded for the purposes of social security benefits, and are not taxed.

elective office Office held by winning an election, such as an MP or councillor. Such a person's income is taxed under PAYE and subject to class 1 national insurance as if they were an employee (SSCBA 1992 s2(1)(a)).

electrically propelled Description of an electric car given in CAA 2001 s268B.

electric car Car powered by rechargeable batteries rather than petrol, diesel or LPG. A new car qualifies for a government subsidy, reduced to £3,500 in 2018. Such a car qualifies for 100% first year allowance as a company car. An employee who uses his or her own electric car on business may receive a tax-free payment of 4p a mile from 1 September 2018. An employee may recharge an electric car at the employer's premises tax-free. The installation of such a charging point qualifies for a 100% first year allowance if installed between 23 November 2016 and (currently) 5 April 2023.

electricity For VAT, this is treated as a supply of goods rather than service (VATA 1994 Sch 4 para 3). A supply of up to 33 kilowatts per day or 1,000 per month is accepted as a domestic supply subject to reduced rate of VAT. Guidance is given in VAT Notice 701/19.

electric vehicle Road vehicle that can be propelled by electrical power, whether or not it can also be propelled by another form of power (CAA 2001 s45EA(5)).

electric vehicle charging point A facility for charging an electric vehicle (CAA 2001 s45E). This attracts a 100% first year allowance if installed between 23 November 2016 and 31 March 2023. An employee does not incur a taxable benefit when using a workplace point to charge his or her vehicle (ITEPA 2003 s237A).

electronic communication Provision to send documents by email and similar. It may be used by a company to send details to its members (CA 2006 s333).

Electronic Communications Code This is found in Communications Act 2003 Sch 3A as inserted by Digital Economy Act 2017 Sch 1.

electronic conveyancing Conveyancing of land using electronic filing, as allowed by Land Registration Act 2002 ss91-95.

electronic invoicing Issue and receipts of invoices in electronic form. This does not include invoices produced in a word-processed form such as Microsoft Word and which is sent as an email. That is regarded as a paper invoice, even if no-one prints it out. An electronic invoice is valid, provided it contains all the information required for a paper invoice. Using electronic invoices does not require permission from or notification to HMRC.

electronic point of sale (EPOS) Till-based system now used in most retail stores. They must comply with special provisions to ensure compliance with VAT rules.

electronic presentment Method of paying in a cheque by sending an electronic image of both sides of the cheque without physically sending in the cheque. It is permitted by the Bills of Exchange 1882 s89A as added by the Small Business, Enterprise and Employment Act 2015 s13(2).

electronic signature

(1) Data in electronic form which identifies the sender. It can have the same legal status as a handwritten signature, sometimes called a wet ink signature.

(2) Electronic reading in a coin which allows a machine to identify that the coin is genuine.

electronic suppression of sales (ESS) Form of tax evasion that involves tills which can reduce recorded sales. HMRC is collecting evidence on how widespread this practice is. Using such a till is a criminal offence.

elements of financial statements Term used in the Statement of Principles to mean the seven categories of financial information that must be reported, namely assets, liabilities, ownership interest, gains, losses, contribution from owners, and distribution to owners.

elephant Largest land mammal. Its tusks comprise the valuable material ivory which is covered by the Convention on International Trade in Endangered Species. In the UK, it is also generally banned under Ivory Act 2018, subject to exceptions for some existing items.

elephant test Ability to recognise something without being able to define it. The term has been used in tax cases such as *Golding [2011] TC 1211.*

Elida table Table agreed between HMRC and motor manufacturers to assist in dealing with VAT repayment claims relating to bonuses on car sales.

eligibility declaration Statement that a charity must make confirming that its services are eligible for VAT relief, as set out in VAT notice 701/1.

eligible mixed lease Lease that relates to both plant and machinery, and to other assets. The capital allowances provisions are given in CAA 2001 s701.

email Means of communication via the Internet. HMRC currently makes little use of email. Any email apparently from HMRC should be treated with suspicion as there are many fraudulent sites impersonating HMRC. When an appeal is made by email, the relevant date is when HMRC receives it not when the taxpayer sends it. This was an issue in the case *Edgbaston Golf Club [2018] TC 6430.*

embedded derivative When a financial derivative is part of a contract, often one for another financial derivative. The tax provisions for loan relationship is CTA 2009 from s415, for hybrid derivatives from s584, and for fair value accounting from CTA 2009 from s616.

embezzlement Dishonest misappropriation of property by a person to whom it was entrusted. This is often an employee. Such loss is usually tax-deductible.

emergency Circumstances that are present or imminent and pose a threat of serious harm to a person, animal or property. From 19 March 2014 the estate of someone who dies while dealing with an emergency may be exempt from inheritance tax (IHTA 1984 s153A(3)). In terms of a national emergency, a definition is provided by Civil Contingencies Act 2004 s1(1) and 19(1). A national emergency, such as flooding, is often accepted as reasonable excuse for late filing or late payment of tax.

emergency Budget Name given to Budget of 22 June 2010 six weeks after the coalition government came to power.

emergency code Tax code used under the PAYE system when no other code has been provided by HMRC or the employee. The code is the equivalent to the personal allowance but applied on a week 1 or month 1 basis (SI 2003 No 2682 reg 7(3)(d)).

emergency period In relation to coronavirus, the period in England from 1pm on 26 March 2020 to a day to be advised by regulations (SI 2020 No 350 para 3(1)).

emergency power Authority granted by the monarch in council to Parliament to take emergency steps to deal with the supply and distribution of food, water, fuel, light and other essentials of light (Emergency Powers Act 1920 s1 as amended by Emergency Powers Act 1964). Such an order lasts for no more than one month. The powers have been used 12 times. The last time was during the miners' strike in 1973.

emergency responder Member of police, ambulance service, fire service, or providing a search or humanitarian function. If a person dies with employed providing such response, from 19 March 2014, their estate is exempt from inheritance tax (IHTA 1984 s153A(6)).

emergency tax PAYE where the emergency code is used. For 2020/21, this is 1250L on a week 1 or month 1 basis.

emergency vehicle Vehicle used to respond to emergencies and which either has a flashing light or facility for one.

From 6 April 2004, such a vehicle provided to a worker is not taxed as a company car (ITEPA 2003 s248A).

From 6 April 2017, the condition is relaxed to exclude vehicles *mainly* used for emergency work. There is no fuel benefit charge to an employee if any private fuel is reimbursed by 6 July after the end of the tax year in which the fuel was used (ITEPA 2003 s248A).

emergency volunteer Employee who could agree to volunteer to assist with coronavirus under the provisions of Coronavirus Act 2020 s9. Such volunteers were not needed.

emission reduction unit (ERU) The successful reduction of emissions equivalent to one tonne of carbon dioxide (Kyoto Protocol Article 6).

emissions allowance Allowance allowed under the European Union Emissions Trading Scheme. From 1 November 2010, trading in such allowances is subject to the VAT reverse charge.

emissions trading Trading in emission standards. Various tax and other implications are set out in Finance Act 2007 s16.

emoluments Term for all pay, wages, benefits and fees received by someone, particularly a director.

employee Someone who is under the control of an employer. For tax purposes, an employee includes an office holder (TMA 1970 s15(13). For pensions, an employee is defined as someone gainfully employed under a contract of service or in an elective office (ITEPA 2003 s181(1)). In practice, this definition applies to all purposes. A subtle distinction is made between an employee who has a contract *of service* and a self-employed person who has a contract *of services.* HMRC provides a similar definition in its Further Guide to PAYE. The issue has been litigated many times. Generally, a taxpayer wishes to be regarded as self-employed. Although income tax rates are the same, self-employment has the advantages of:

- being able to claim more expenses
- paying the tax later
- paying less national insurance.

Against this, a self-employed person loses employment rights, such as the right to holiday pay and sick pay, and protection against unfair dismissal. It must be stressed that whether a worker is an employee or not, is a matter of fact and not a matter of agreement. An employee who agrees to be treated as self-employed could lose protection under employment law. HMRC website provides a test to see whether someone is an employee.

employee assistance programme (EAP) Benefit of providing employees, and often their families also, with a free on-line telephone welfare counselling service provided by a specialist company. The employee can discuss matters such as stress, ill health, debt problems, alcohol or drug problems, bereavement, discrimination, abuse, personal relationships and similar. It is claimed that £1 spent on EAP can save up to £14 in improved productivity, and reduced absenteeism and staff turnover. Generally this benefit is exempt as a benefit in kind under ITEPA 2003 s210 which exempts minor benefits, provided that the benefit is made available to all staff. It is not necessary that the EAP covers all types of problem. Welfare counselling is specifically exempted from tax under SI 2000 No 2080. From 6 April 2020, EAP may include some forms of medical treatment such as cognitive behavioural therapy. The tax exemption does not include financial or legal advice, nor advice on leisure or recreation. Where an employer includes this within an EAP package, HMRC suggests it should be provided separately. Where such advice is incidental to welfare counselling, HMRC will not seek to tax it if it is a not significant proportion of the services provided. The matter is discussed in HMRC Manual at EIM21845.

employee benefit trust (EBT) Body that provides benefits to employees from funds provided by the employer (ITEPA 2003 s550). The law was amended in 2011 so that these cannot be used for tax avoidance. The matter is discussed in HMRC Manual at BIM4401.

employee indemnity insurance Insurance policy arranged by an employer to indemnify claims against an employee. This may be tax deductible under ITEPA 2003 s346. The matter is discussed in the Inspector's Manual at BIM45520.

employee numbers Number of employees who work for an organisation. A part-time worker is counted as a fraction. This number must be disclosed by a company (CA 2006 s411). The number of employees can affect other statutory provisions. The definitions of a micro, small and medium-sized company depends in part on having no more than 10, 50 or 250 employees. Entities with 250 or more employees must disclose gender pay gap and CEO pay gap.

employee's code Tax code of an employee (PAYE Regulations 2003 reg 8).

employee shareholder Category of worker that could be created between 1 September 2013 and 1 December 2016 (Growth and Infrastructure Act 2013 s31). The worker lost some employment rights but benefited from some tax provisions. Such a worker must hold at least £2,000 of shares in the employer for whose disposal there is no capital gains tax, among other tax provisions. No new employee shareholders may be created from 2 December 2016 (FA 2017 s12(7)).

employee shareholder plan This is now called a share incentive plan.

employee trusts A tax-advantaged trust where an employer can provide shares in itself for the benefit of employees. A donation to such a trust is exempt from inheritance tax (Inheritance Tax Act 1984 s28).

The capital gains tax provisions are given in Taxation of Chargeable Gains Act 1992 from s239.

Employer Compliance System Part of HMRC SAFE computer system (HMRC Manual at DMBM115040).

employer-finance retirement benefits scheme (EFRBS) Scheme for benefits for employees or former employees (ITEPA 2003 s393A). These have been used for tax avoidance. They are discussed in HMRC Spotlight 6.

employer reference Code of letters and numbers that identifies an employer's PAYE scheme (SI 2003 No 2682 reg 2(1)).

employers' association An organisation "which consists wholly or mainly of employers or individual owners of undertakings of one or more descriptions and whose principal purposes include the regulations of relations between employers of that description or those descriptions and workers or trade unions" or of a body comprising such organisations (Trade Union and Labour Relations (Consolidation) Act 1992 s122).

employer's housing scheme An arrangement whereby an employer compensates an employee in respect of a house transaction, such as when the employee is relocated. A payment under such an arrangement may not be taxable as it has the nature of compensation rather than earnings. Such a case is *Hochstrasser v Mayes [1959] 38TC673*. The matter is discussed in HMRC Manual at EIM00750.

employer's national insurance (ENI) Secondary class 1 national insurance payable by an employer on wages and salaries. There are exemptions for some young workers and apprentices, and an employment allowance.

employer supported childcare (ESC) Arrangement whereby an employer provides assistance to employees for childcare. Details are given in section 3 of this dictionary.

employment Working relationship with a limited definition for tax law (ITEPA s2003 s4(1)) and national insurance (SSCBA 1992 s122(1)). Whether an arrangement is employment is not a matter of choice but a matter of fact depending on the circumstances. HMRC has a tool on its website to indicate whether an arrangement is employment.

employment agency Organisation which finds work for workers, either as a temporary employee or as a permanent placement. An agency must be licensed by the local authority. The agency charges a fee to the client where the worker is engaged. The agency may generally not charge a fee to the worker. There are some exceptions for agencies in entertainment and modelling. Some agencies need to register with other bodies. From 1975, the agency must treat a temporary worker as if they were an employee, and operate PAYE and class 1 national insurance. The tax and national insurance must be paid to HMRC by the due date, even if the agency has not been paid by its client.

employment alignment submission (EAS) A one-off return that an employer may have made, usually in 2013, with the full payment submission under real time information.

employment and support allowance Social security benefit which replaced income support and incapacity benefit from 2008 (Welfare Reform Act 2007 s1). It is being replaced by universal credit.

employment income Income from employment, formerly known as Schedule E. There is a form of definition in ITEPA 2003 s7(2). Employment income includes all salaries, wages, bonuses, commissions, fees, gratuities, profits, benefits in kind, holiday pay, statutory sick pay, statutory maternity pay and similar.

Employment income may be categorised as either general earnings or specific employment income. Some expenses may only be deducted from the latter.

employment-injury assistance Money or other assistance that may be provided in Scotland under Social Security (Scotland) Act 2018 s33.

employment intermediary For the purposes of keeping tax records, "is a person who makes arrangements under or in consequence of which –

(a) an individual works, or is to work, for a third person, or

(b) an individual is, or is to be, remunerated for work done for a third person" (Income Tax (Earnings and Pensions) Act 2003 s716B(2) as inserted by Finance Act 2014 s18(1)).

An intermediary is responsible for ensuring that the correct tax and national insurance are deducted. The intermediary must, from 6 April 2016, make a quarterly return to HMRC. In relation to travelling expenses, the term is defined as "a person, other than the worker or the client, who carries on a business (whether or not with a view to profit and whether or not in conjunction with any other business) of supplying labour" (Income Tax (Earnings and Pensions) Act 2003 s339A(11) as inserted by Finance Act 2016 s14).

employment protection entitlement Sum paid to an employee who has been reinstated after a procedure under employment law. Social Security Contributions and Benefits Act 1992 s112 treats such entitlement as earnings for class 1 national insurance.

employment reference information In relation to electronic disclosure by HMRC "means any of the following information relating to an employer –

(a) the employer's name and address;

(b) any combination of numbers, letters or characters that is uniquely associated with the employer and used by the Revenue and Customs to identify or refer to that employer, whether generally or for particular purposes".

(Digital Economy Act 2017 s77(4) and other sections).

employment share ownership plan (ESOP) The former name for a share incentive plan.

employment status service (ESS) Program on the HMRC website that replaced the employment status indicator from 6 April 2017. It serves the same function but asks some additional questions to allow for changed rules when IR35 workers are engaged in the public sector. The ESS indicates whether a worker is employed or self-employed.

employment tribunal Body that hears appeals on employment matters. They were first set up in 1964 under Industrial Training Act 1964. They became largely concerned with unfair dismissal from 1971, and changed their name to employment tribunals in 1988. They changed their name to employment tribunals in 1988 under Employment Rights (Dispute Resolution) Act 1988. Fees were introduced for their services from 29 July 2013 and abolished on 29 July 2017.

enabler of defeated tax avoidance Such a person can be subject to a tax penalty under Finance (No 2) Act 2017 s65 and Sch 16.

enabling letter Informal term for a letter sent by HMRC to a particular group of taxpayers pointing out their responsibilities. The letter is not an enquiry into the taxpayer's affairs and does not mean that there is any issue with those affairs.

enactment Process by which a rule is made part of the law. The term "does not include an enactment comprised in, or in an instrument made under, an Act of the Scottish Parliament" (Interpretation Act 1978 Sch 1).

encouragement award Sum of up to £25 that may be paid to an employee tax-free for a suggestion that the employer does not follow (ITEPA s322(1)).

endangered species Plants and animals that are considered to be at risk of extinction. The exact scope is determined by **CITES.** Customs may seize any such plants or animals that are imported into the UK. This includes goods made from such plants or animals, even if legally acquired overseas. This includes caviar, ivory, coral, shells and skins of crocodiles, alligators and snakes.

end of period statement Statement that HMRC may require from a business on how it has calculated its income, profits and losses. The authority is TMA 1970 Sch A1 para 8.

end of the employee's strike action Point when an employee may receive tax refunds during a trade dispute (PAYE Regs 2013 reg 64(11)). This is when the employee is no longer absence from work, when the employment ends, when the employee has changed occupation; or when the employee dies.

endowment A life assurance policy related to a mortgage designed to pay off the amount originally borrowed at the end of the mortgage term. An endowment policy will pay you a fixed amount on a set date or if the borrower die before that date. It is both a way of saving and life insurance. People often use endowments to repay interest only mortgages. The drawback is that it is often unclear how much the borrower is paying in charges. The plans are often rigid, so if a borrowers starts an endowment and then decides to cancel it, the borrower might not get back what was paid in.

endowment assurance Insurance policy where the proceeds are invested in shares and similar. The proceeds are paid to the insured if he or she survives to a particular date, or to his estate if he dies before then.

endowment fund Fund where, generally, only the interest may be spent.

enduring Term used in relation to the benefit to be derived from an asset for its acquisition to be taxed as capital rather than revenue. The Inspectors' Manual at BIM35901 explains that there is no formal time limit as the matter must be determined by other criteria. It should be noted that the life of the benefit is distinct from the life of the asset itself, which must be at least two years.

enduring power of attorney (EPA) Power of attorney that may continue after a person has lost the mental capacity to act for himself or herself. From 1 October 2007 this is replaced by a lasting power of attorney (Mental Capacity Act 2005), though existing EPAs may continue.

end-use relief Form of relief from Customs duties for certain imported goods provided they are put to the stated use by an agreed date.

enemy Country which is at war with the monarch, including pirates, armed mutineers, armed rebels and armed rioters (Armed Forces Act 2006 s374). Many restrictions were imposed in wartime laws, some of which remain in force.

energy bar Food product designed to provide energy to the eater. For VAT, such a bar largely made from fruit was held to be zero-rated as food in the case *SIS (Science in Sport) Ltd (No 2) [2000] VTD 17116*. But in another case, where sweetening had been added, it was held to be standard-rated confectionery *(EJ Huczek [1992] VTD 8850)*.

energy drinks For VAT, these are generally zero-rated as food, though there are some exceptions as set out in VAT notice 701/14.

energy generation This activity is, from 6 April 2016, excluded from the scope of activities for which tax-advantaged investments may be made. The scope is set out in Income Tax Act 2007 s192(1) as amended by Finance Act 2016 s28.

energy products For the purposes of oil duty, "means a substance which –

(a) is an energy product for the purposes of Council Directive 2033/96/EC restructuring the Community framework for the taxation of energy products and electricity, and
(b) is not (apart from as a result of this section) hydrocarbon oil or road fuel gas within the meaning of the [Hydrocarbon Oil Duties] 1979 Act" (Finance Act 1993 s10).

energy-saving item Expenditure that qualifies for a special allowance against corporation tax under CTA 2009 s251, and may qualify for a first year allowance under CAA 2001 s45A.

energy-saving materials These may qualify for the reduced rate of VAT under VATA 1994 Sch 7A Note 1. Income tax relief may be claimable under ITTOIA 2005 s312.

energy services agreement Arrangement between an energy services provider and a client. Tax provisions for leases are given in CAA 2001 s175A.

energy services provider For the purposes of long funding leases, "means a person carrying on a qualifying activity consisting wholly or mainly in the provision of energy management services" (Capital Allowances Act 2001 s175A(2)).

Enforcement and Compliance Dispute Resolution Board (ECDRB) Board of HMRC that comprises various senior staff. Its constitution and functions are set out in an HMRC Notice of 20 December 2013.

enforcement receiver Person appointed to recover property which is the subject of a confiscation order (Proceeds of Crime Act 2002 s50).

engagement letter Letter sent by an accountant to a client setting out what work the accountant will do and the basis for charging. This is a professional requirement.

English statutory apprenticeships "Means –

(a) approved English apprenticeships within the meaning given in section A1;
(b) apprenticeships undertaken under apprenticeship agreements within the meaning given in section 32 that were entered into in connection with recognised English frameworks,

(c) apprenticeships in relation to which alternative English completion arrangements apply under section 1(5);

(d) apprenticeships undertaken under arrangements made in relation to England under section 2 of the Employment and Training Act 1973 that are identified by the person them as arrangements for the provision of apprenticeships"

(Apprenticeships, Skills, Children and Learning Act 2009 s40A(3) as inserted by Enterprise Act 2016 s26).

enhanced capital allowance Higher rate of capital allowance for an environmentally friendly asset.

enhanced remote transit shed Place were goods may be held pending payment of Customs duties. They were introduced in 1993.

enjoyment conditions Term used in relation to countering avoidance from transfer of assets abroad. The term is defined in Income Tax Act 2007 s723. There are four conditions. The term is also used in Taxation of Chargeable Gains Act 1992 s103KG.

enquiry window Period in which the tax authorities may enquire into a tax return for any reason. This is a period of 12 months. A later enquiry may be made if fraud is suspected or insufficient information has been disclosed on the tax return, allowing for a discovery assessment.

enterprise allowance Government scheme that provided financial support for those who started a business between 1983 and 1991.

enterprise area Area for which community investment tax relief may be claimed (ITA 2007 ss333-382; CTA 2010 ss218-269).

enterprise investment scheme (EIS) Tax-advantage scheme introduced in 1994 (TCGA 1992 s150A and Sch 5B-5BA). It allows an individual to invest in a qualifying company and deduct 30% of the amount from his or her income tax liability. The shares may also benefit from exemption from capital gains tax. EIS is subject to strict rules and limits. Guidance is given on HMRC helpsheet HS341.

enterprise management incentive (EMI) Scheme under which a director or senior manager of a trading company (with some exceptions) may be given up to £250,000 in options tax-free (ITEPA 2003 from s527). Capital gains tax provisions are given in TCGA 1992 s1691 and Sch 7D. It is subject to strict rules and limits. Guidance is given in HMRC Manual at ETASSUM50000.

enterprise zone Area of the country where businesses are given special tax and other incentives. The first zones were established between 1981 and 1996. They provided a 100% initial allowance for industrial buildings for 20 years and other tax benefits for 10 years. A second tranche of zones was established between 2012 and 2020. They are listed in section 3 of this dictionary.

entertainer For categorisation of earners for national insurance, "means a person who is employed as an actor, singer or musician, or in any similar performing capacity" (Social Security (Categorisation of Earners) Regulations SI 1978 No 1689 reg 1(2)). The position for various types of entertainer was examined in the case *ITV*

Services Ltd. TC 836. As a result of this, HMRC issued Brief 10/11. For income tax, agency fees paid by entertainers are allowable (ITEPA 2003 s352). The provision for an overseas entertainer is set out in ITTOIA 2005s13.

entertainment Provision of hospitality of any kind. Entertainment of customers and potential customers is not tax-deductible (ITTOIA 2005 s45 and CTA 2009 s1298(2)). Entertainment of staff, such as at a Christmas party, is tax-deductible (ITEPA 2003 s264).

entire agreement clause Provision in a contract which states that a written contract extinguishes and supersedes all other agreements between the parties on the subject matter. Under contract law, such a clause is effective if explicitly expressed in clear wording. The case *Al-Hawai v Nottingham Forest Football Club [2018] EWHC 2884 (Ch)* held that the clause did not indemnify a seller against misrepresentation. In that case, the liabilities were said to be £6 million when they were nearer to £10 million.

entirety doctrine Method used to distinguish between revenue repairs and capital expenditure. A leading case is *Bullcroft Man Collieries Ltd v O'Grady [1932] 17 TC 93.* The matter is discussed in HMRC Manual at BIM35330.

entrenched provisions Provisions in a company's articles of association which may only be amended if certain conditions are met (CA 2006 s22). The existence of such provisions must be specifically notified to Companies House. Provisions may only become entrenched when the company is formed, by unanimous agreement of all members. Entrenched provisions do not prevent an alteration to the articles if agreed by all members or ordered by a court.

entrepreneurs' relief This relief is known as business asset disposal relief from 6 April 2020, under which heading its details are noted.

entry Detail of a transaction as recorded in the accounts.

enveloping Practice of acquiring an asset by its being acquired by a company that owns it. In particular, this involves a company acquiring a property as a means of saving stamp duty land tax. This arrangement is now subject to annual tax on enveloped dwellings.

environmentally beneficial plant or machinery The capital allowance provisions are given in Capital Allowances Act 2001 s45H.

ePassport Gates at UK airports that allow quicker checking. They were introduced in 2008 for UK and EU nationals. From 20 May 2019, they may also be used by travellers from Australia, Canada, Japan, New Zealand, Singapore, South Korea and USA. It has been confirmed that EU citizens may continue to use the gates after the UK has left the EU.

equalisation reserve Funds held by an entity for the purpose of reducing large fluctuations between accounting periods. This is now much less common under modern accounting standards. There are some special tax provisions for mutual life assurance businesses (ICTA 1988 s444BA) and corporate members of Lloyd's (FA 2012 s26(7)(a)).

equal pay Right of women to be paid the same rate as men doing the same or similar work. The right was introduced in 1970 with effect from 1975. This law is now contained in Equality Act 2010 s39(1). Equal work conditions are in s65. These provision has now been strengthened by gender pay gap reporting.

equal treatment rule A requirement which every occupational pension must follow, which requires women to be treated equally to men (Pensions Act 1995 s62).

Equatorial Guinea African country. Its currency is the CFA franc. The UK has no tax treaty.

Equifax One of the UK's three credit reference agencies, founded in 1899. (The other two are Experian and Callcredit.)

equipment lessee In relation to long funding leases, "means the person to whom the equipment provides for the plant or machinery to be leased" (CAA 2001 s174(3)).

equipment lessor In relation to long funding leases, "means the person from whom (directly or indirectly) the equipment lease provides for the plant or machinery to be leased" (CAA 2001 s174(3)).

equipment to enable a disabled person to use a car In relation to the taxation of company cars, "means equipment —

(a) which is designed solely for use by a chronically sick or disabled person, or
(b) which is made available for use with the car because it enables a disabled employee to use the car in spite of the disability"

(ITEPA 2003 s172(1)).

equitable construction Legal principle for judicial interpretation of the law. For tax, the principle is that if someone comes within the scope of the letter of tax law, they must be taxed. If they do not, they are not taxed *[Partington v Attorney-General [1869]]*.This is regardless of how unfair or absurd the result appears. In 2016, this principle was amended by general anti-abuse rule guidance which provides an element of discretion against tax avoidance.

equitable liability Provision that allowed HMRC to waive its right not to pursue tax where it arose solely because a deadline had passed. From 1 April 2011, this is replaced by special relief.

Equitable Life Mutual insurance company that became insolvent. The government may make payments to policy-holders under Equitable Life (Payments) Act 2010. Under s3, such a payment is disregarded for tax and social security purposes.

equity (1) Capital of a company as represented by shares rather than loans. The word has other meanings.

(2) Branch of law which complements common law.

equity capital Funding of a company by ordinary shares rather than borrowing.

equity holder Tax term which means someone who is either a shareholder or loan creditor of a company. The term is defined in CTA 2010 s158 in terms of defining who may be part of a group.

equity release Provision whereby a home owner may release funds from the value of their home. There are two types of scheme: home income plans and home reversion schemes.

equity share capital Company's share capital as represented by ordinary shares of any class. The statutory definition in relation to a company is "its issued share capital excluding any part of that capital that, neither as respects dividends nor as respects capital, carries any right to participate beyond a specific amount in a distribution" (Companies Act 2006 s548).

equivalent goods For purposes of Customs inward processing relief, goods of the same description as those imported which are exported.

Eritrea East African state which became independent from Ethiopia in 1993. Its currency is the nakfa of 100 cents. The UK has no tax treaty.

error Something that is incorrect.
For accounting, an error is an omission or misstatement that arises from failure to use information that was available or reasonably obtainable (FRS 102 glossary). Note that a figure is not an error just because it is later established that the figure was wrong. Where a figure is subsequently found to require adjusting, the amount of the adjustment is made in the accounting period when discovered. The historic accounts are not restated unless there is a fundamental error. Income tax and corporation tax generally follows the accounting treatment.
Guidance on correcting VAT errors is given in VAT Notice 700/45.

ESA 220 Linking letter provided to someone who has recently received employment and support allowance. A new employee should be asked if he or she has received such a letter as it can affect the period of incapacity for work for statutory sick pay.

escalation In finance, when a figure increases by a predetermined amount or rate, such as an indexed pension or investment.

escalator A feature integral to a building that qualifies for plant and machinery capital allowance (CAA 2001 s33A).

eskimo If an eskimo (Inuit) kills a seal in a traditional hunt for sustenance, the state authority may issue a seal attestation. This document allows the seal or its products to clear UK Customs.

escrow Third party entrusted with funds to enable a transaction to proceed between two parties who do not trust each other. When the third party sees that the transaction has been completed, he or she passes the funds to the other party.

essence In relation to food essence. This is exempt from excise duty even it contains alcohol. Further guidance is given in Customs Notice 41. For VAT, food essence is standard-rated. It is specifically excluded from the scope of zero-rated food by VATA 1994 Sch 8 Group 1 Note 4.

essence of the contract Provisions of a contract that are essential to its performance.

essential oils Concentrated extracts of plants used for cooking and other uses. These are standard-rated as HMRC considers them not to come within the scope of zero-rated food (VAT Notice 701/14).

established practice Normal procedures of commerce and finance. A departure from such a practice indicates that there may be tax avoidance under the general anti-abuse rule (FA 2013 s207(5)).

estate Term which has acquired different meanings, of which the broadest is simply everything that a person owns. For inheritance tax, a person's estate is defined as "the aggregate of all the property to which he [the person] is beneficially entitled" excluding interest in possession trusts, excluded property or foreign works of art being exhibited in the UK (IHTA 1984 s5(1)). From 22 March 2006, a person's estate comprises:

- assets in the sole name of the deceased
- their share of any jointly owned assets
- assets held in a trust in which the deceased had an immediate post-death interest, or a disabled person's interest or a transitional serial interest
- any nominated assets
- assets given away but where an interest has been retained (as in a gift with reservation)
- value of an alternatively secured pension from which the deceased benefited as an original scheme member, or as a dependant who received benefits from the left over ASP fund of the original scheme member.

Before 22 March 2006, a person's estate comprised:

- assets in the sole name of the deceased
- their share of any jointly owned assets
- assets held in a trust in which the deceased had a right to benefit
- any nominated assets
- assets given away but where an interest has been retained.

In trusteeship and executorship, the term is more usually limited to what a person owns at the time of their death. It is thus distinguished from a trust which is created during a person's life.

Strictly, an estate is only an interest in land, but the term is now generally used to mean the total assets (land, chattels, investments, etc) owned by an individual.

estate administration Process of looking after an estate, particularly of a person who has recently died. In practice this involves obtaining probate or letters of administration, disposing of the body, paying legacies, ascertaining and distributing the residue, and paying inheritance tax.

estate agency work Work undertaken by an estate agent. Its exact scope is set out in Estate Agents Act 1979 s1.

estate duty A death duty introduced in 1894. It was replaced by capital transfer tax in 1975 which was itself replaced by inheritance tax. At its abolition, estate duty was charged at rates from 25% to 75%.

estimate Approximate figure where the exact figure is not known. An estimate may be used in a tax return which should not be delayed while waiting for the exact figure. The return should indicate that a figure is estimated. An adjustment should be made once the exact figure is known.

Estonia Baltic state which is a member of the European Union. Its currency is the euro. The UK has a double taxation convention of 1994.

estoppel Legal rule that stops a person denying what he or she has already admitted. It has sometimes been applied to a tax authority when a taxpayer has relied on their advice which proved to be wrong.

estrangement Term used to describe two people who are no longer living together as a couple in the same household as the previous relationship between them has ended *(Bristol City Council v SJP (HB) [2019] UKUT 360 (AAC)*. A couple may be estranged even though they live together, remain on friendly terms, and co-operate in such areas as finance and childcare.

Eswatini African country known as Swaziland before 19 April 2018. Its currency is the lilangeni (plural emalageni) of 100 cents. This is kept at par with the South African rand. The UK has a double taxation treaty of 1968.

ethanol Alternative name for ethyl alcohol. It has the chemical formula CH_3CH_2OH. It is the active ingredient in liquor, and creates a liability to excise duty and VAT.

ethical investment When investment policy is partly determined by approval or disapproval of what the investee company does or how it does it. Examples include not investing in companies that make arms or are involved in betting or environmentally damaging activities. The investor determines the criteria. Typically this excludes between 10% and 20% of companies.

Ethical Standards for Reporting Accountants (ERSA) Document issued by the Auditing Practices Board. The current edition is from October 2006. It can be downloaded from:
https://www.frc.org.uk/getattachment/077cab08-1728-499f-9eb8-bed37ed7908a/Ethical-Standard-for-Reporting-Accountants-(ESRA)-Oct-2006.pdf.

Ethiopia East African state. Its currency is the birr of 100 cents. The UK has a double taxation convention of 2011.

ethyl alcohol The alcohol in alcoholic liquor, also known as ethanol. Such liquor is subject to alcoholic liquor duty and VAT.

EU-adopted IFRS An International Financial Reporting Standard that has been adopted by the European Union under EU Regulation 1606/2002. Listed companies in the UK must produce accounts that comply with international accounting standards. These must be adopted by the EU.

The EU has adopted all international accounting standards, though IAS 39 was only adopted after it had been amended.

From 1 January 2021, listed companies must comply with international accounting standards that are UK adopted.

Euratom European Atomic Energy Committee formed by a treaty on 25 March 1957. It is one of the bodies that led to the formation of the European Union.

Euribor Euro-denominated inter-bank offering rates. It is the equivalent to LIBOR.

euro Unit of value introduced on 1 January 1999. It was adopted by 19 of the 28 members of the European Union by 2019. Other member states, except Denmark and UK, are required to adopt the euro later, as must any new members. The adoption of the currency occurred thus:

- 1 January 1999: Austria, Belgium, Finland, France, Germany, Irish Republic, Italy, Luxembourg, Netherlands, Portugal, Spain
- 1 January 2001: Greece
- 1 January 2007: Slovenia
- 1 January 2008: Cyprus, Malta
- 1 January 2009: Slovakia
- 1 January 2011: Estonia
- 1 January 2014: Latvia
- 1 January 2015: Lithuania

Another 22 countries either use the euro or have their currency pegged to it. The currency was introduced in 2002. Its symbol is €.

Although the euro is not a currency of the UK, there is no legal bar on UK individuals and businesses trading in euros, or any other currency.

A UK company may publish its accounts in euros but must give equivalents in pounds (CA 2006 s469).

Many UK laws have values that are determined by the value of the euro. These include:

- the size of small and medium-sized entities.
- protection limit for banking deposits
- limits on currency that can be personally imported.

eurobond Long-term bearer bond denominated in euros, usually issued by an international corporation or by a government.

Europa website Website that allows a registered VAT agent to check the VAT number from another EU state. From 1 January 2010, it also allows the name and address to be checked.

Europe Geographical area to the west of Asia, often taken to extend from Russia to Ireland.

European Central Bank Central bank for those countries that have adopted the euro as their currency.

European Commission (EC) One of the three main governing bodies of the European Union. The Commission drafts proposals and is responsible for implementing policy. It is also responsible for ensuring that EU legislation is carried out. European Community – European Community and European Economic Community (EEC) are now referred to as the EU.

European Community Association of European states, originally known as the Common Market. Since 1991, it has been known as the European Union.

European co-operative society (SCE) Body formed under EU Council Regulation 1435/2003 article 7. It is UK-resident for corporation tax if registered in the UK (CTA 2009 s17).

European Council A body of the European Union that makes it strategic decisions. Its members are the European Council president, the European Commission president, and the leader of each member state.

European Economic Area (EEA) All countries of the European Union plus Iceland, Liechtenstein and Norway.

European Free Trade Association (EFTA) Body formed in 1960 between seven countries, including the UK, none of whom were then in the European Community (later European Union). Its current member are Iceland, Liechtenstein, Norway and Switzerland.

European Union (EU) Political union formed in 1992. It is the successor body to the European Community (EC) formed in 1967 which was itself formed from the European Economic Community (EEC) in 1957. The UK joined in 1973, voted to leave in 2016 and did leave on 31 January 2020 followed by a transition period to 31 December 2020. VAT and Customs duties were set by the EU while the UK was a member. Relations between the UK and EU are subject to an agreement reached on 24 December 2020. Its full title is "Trade and Cooperation Agreement Between the European Union and the European Atomic Energy Authority, of the One Part, and the United Kingdom of Great Britain and Northern Ireland, of the Other Part". It was published on 25 December 2020 as an Annex to the Recommendation for a Council Directive under ref COM(2020)857. It has 1,256 pages in the English version. The agreement has been given effect in UK law as European Union (Future Relationship) Act 2020.

Eurozone European countries that have adopted the euro as their currency, seen collectively.

Eversden inheritance tax avoidance scheme of 2003 that used the spousal exemption to override the gift with reservation rules. It has now been stopped by legislation.

evaporation Natural process by which liquid turns to vapour. This can require an adjustment when valuing liquids, particularly for alcoholic liquor duty. By extension, the term is sometimes used to mean losses of assets for other reasons.

evasion Deliberate attempt to avoid liability. In tax, evasion is illegal whereas tax avoidance is generally legal.

evening primrose Plant that HMRC regards as standard-rated. It is listed in VAT Notice 701/38 as not coming within the scope of zero-rating for food as it is primarily grown for oil.

event day Day where a charity holds an event to which the public is admitted (Income Tax Act 2007 s421(4)). Such a day may be excluded from considering whether a right of admission to a charitable donor restricts the tax relief for the donation.

event fee High charge that may be imposed by a landlord when an event happens such as the tenant becoming ill or dying. It is outlawed from 1 June 2019 under Tenant Fees Act 2019.

Eversden Case that allowed an inheritance tax avoidance scheme which used the spouse exemption to override the gift with reservation rules by using a trust. The case was *IR Commissioners v Eversden (as executors for Greenstock deceased) [2003]*. This scheme has now been closed by legislation.

everyday wardrobe Term used in the Inspectors' Manual at BIM37910 to identify clothing that is not tax-deductible. Such clothing is not deductible even where it can be shown that it is worn only for work, that it is a legal or contractual requirement to wear such clothing, that the cost is greater than for normal clothing, or that the nature of the work means that the clothing gets extra wear or requires additional cleaning.

evidence Documents, testimony and other means by which facts are adduced. The courts have developed strict rules about what evidence is admissible. These apply to tax cases as to other branches of law. For tribunal cases, rules of evidence are given in SI 2009 No 273. HMRC documents are admissible in proceedings under Commissioners for Revenue and Customs Act 2005 s24.

The general principle has been clarified in these words: "the presumption must be that all relevant evidence should be admitted unless there is a compelling reason to the contrary" (per *Mobile Export 365 Ltd v HMRC [2007]*).

In the case *Megantic Services Ltd v HMRC [2009]*, it was ruled that late evidence could be accepted even after a date when a direction had been given that no further evidence was to be admitted.

evidence in chief Evidence first provided by a witness. This may be followed by cross-examination in answering questions. There are different rules for the two types of evidence.

evidence of removal Evidence that goods have left the UK and therefore may qualify for EU zero-rating. Details are given in VAT Notice 725.

evidence to correct a false impression Term used in Criminal Justice Act 2003 s105 in relation to evidence in criminal proceedings.

evidential stage The former of two stages of the full code test of the CPS in deciding whether to prosecute. The latter stage is the public interest stage.

For the evidential stage, "prosecutors must be satisfied that there is sufficient evidence to provide a realistic prospect of conviction against each suspect on each charge" (website of the Crown Prosecution Service).

In turn this requires positive answers to three questions:

- can the evidence be used in court?
- is the evidence reliable?
- is the evidence credible?

examination In court, the interrogation of a witness. Examination by the witness's own counsel is examination-in-chief. Examination by opposing counsel is cross-examination. Further examination by the witness's own counsel is re-examination.

examination-in-chief Examination by one's own counsel at the start of evidence by a witness.

examination station Place at an airport where Customs officers may examine imported goods. They must be approved under Customs and Excise Management Act 1979 s22.

excepted estate An estate that does not have to be reported to HMRC as no inheritance tax is due (IHTA 1984 s256). An estate may be excepted because it is of low value, specifically excepted by law, or foreign. Details are given in section 3 of this dictionary under Inheritance tax.

excepted loan relationship outcome Term used for diverted profits tax in FA 2015 s109.

excepted settlement Settlement where there is no qualifying interest in possession for a small amount of cash. From 6 April 2007, no account need be made for inheritance tax, provided no further property has been added to the original settlement.

excepted termination In relation to inheritance tax on an interest in possession in settled property, a termination where:

- the transferor has given notice to the trustees of available exemptions under Inheritance Tax Act 1984 s57(3), and
- the amount of the transfer does not exceed the amount of the exemption specified in the notice.

excepted transfer Transfer of assets that need not be reported to HMRC. From 6 April 2007, these are transfers below the **nil rate band** for inheritance tax.

excepted vehicle Vehicle that is allowed to use road fuel on which hydrocarbon oil duty has not been paid. Such vehicles include construction vehicles, farm vehicles and road maintenance vehicles.

exceptional item In accounting, an item that is within the normal scope of trading but is unusually large. It is included in the normal accounts with a narrative note. It must be distinguished from an extraordinary item.

excess allowance Capital Allowances Act 2001 s111 gives this a specific meaning in relation to capital allowances for plant and machinery subject to overseas leasing. Capital Allowances Act 2001 s260 gives it a specific meaning for special leasing. The section contains a mechanism for recovery of the allowance.

excess expenditure for section 148E In relation to losses under long-funding operating leases, this term is defined in Income Tax (Trading and Other Income) Act 2005 s148F(7).

excess finance and IP income In relation to controlled foreign companies, a term that is used in Income and Corporation Taxes Act 1988 s751AB(7).

excessive remuneration Remuneration that is paid for a non-trade purpose, often when a family member is employed. The case *Stott & Ingham v Trehearne [1924] 9 TC 69* established that the excessive remuneration is not tax-deductible. The matter is considered in HMRC Manual at BIM37707.

excess profits duty Tax charged between 1915 and 1921.

excess profits tax Tax charged between 1940 and 1945.

exchange gains and losses Gains and losses that arise from changes in the relative values of currencies. The corporation tax provisions are given in CTA 2009 from s328.

Exchequer Fund of money received by the government, established in 1100.

excise duties Sales tax charged on items, particularly luxury items. They were first introduced in 1643. The first duties were imposed on ale, then beer, and then food and clothing. The scope was progressively extended, leading to civil unrest in 1647. In 1683, the scheme was recast. The collection of excise duties was no longer farmed out but collected by excise men who established a reputation for ruthlessness. The main duties were imposed on soap, candles, leather, salt and brewing malt. In 1723 bonded warehouses were created, and initially used for tea, coffee and cocoa. Salt was removed from excise in 1730 after popular protest, though it was subsequently re-excised until 1822. Part of their function is to reduce consumption on products seen as harmful, where excise acts as a sumptuary tax. By the 19th century, many items were excised. This included licences for solicitors, hawkers and railway operators. Excise was charged on employment of servants, armorial bearings and any other obvious sign of status or luxury. Many 19th century excises were short-lived.

During the 20th century, the scope of excise duties was progressively rolled back in preference to sales taxes such as purchase tax and value added tax. Excise duty is now limited to hydrocarbon oil duty, alcoholic liquor duty, betting and gaming duty and tobacco duty. There is a separate vehicle excise duty.

Excise Helpline A number that can be called for issues relating to excess duties, such as to extend a distillation period in manufacturing spirits. The number is 0300 200 3700.

excise label Label indicating that **excise duty** has been paid. For forgery, improper use and similar offences, such a label is treated as if it were a stamp for stamp duty (Stamp Duties Management Act 1891 s23).

Excise Payment Security System (EPSS) Procedure that may be used by producers of excised goods (such as liquor) as an alternative to providing a guarantee to secure payment of excise duty. This broadly requires a satisfactory compliance record for excise duty and VAT.

excise warehouse Place authorised by HMRC where goods may be stored pending payment of excise duty (CEMA 1979 s1(1)).

excluded benefit Benefit provided to an employee that is not taxable (Income Tax (Earnings And Pensions) Act 2003 s202).

excluded business expenses For PAYE, payments that an employer may legally make to an employee without having to deduct income tax. A full definition is given in PAYE Regulations SI 2003 No 2682 reg 5.

excluded debits In relation to patent box, this is given a specific meaning in CTA 2010 s357BI.

excluded decision Decision of the Upper Tribunal for which there is no right of appeal to the Court of Appeal (Tribunals, Courts and Enforcement Act 2007 s13(8)).

excluded entity In relation to corporation tax on banking companies, the term refers to non-banking activities that are excluded. A full definition is given in CTA 2010 s269BA.

excluded exemption Category of exclusions from the provisions of optional remuneration arrangements (ITEPA 2003 s228A as inserted by Finance Act 2017 Sch 2).

excluded financial services contract This "is a contract which –

(a) is for financial services (see section 2) or is a regulated agreement within the meaning of the Consumer Credit Act 1974 (see section 189 of that Act); and

(b) is of a prescribed description."

(Small Business, Enterprise and Employment Act 2015 s1(4)).

Such a contract is excluded from the general ban of a non-assignment of receivables term.

excluded notional payments For PAYE, certain payments made by using credit-tokens or vouchers. The term is fully defined in PAYE Regulations SI 2003 No 2682 reg 4(2).

excluded pecuniary liabilities For PAYE, "means payments made to a person other than an employee to meet the employees liability to that other person, but which are not made –

(a) in fulfilment (in whole or in part) of the employee's right to a sum of money, nor

(b) as, or as part of, any scheme or arrangement the purpose, or one of the main purposes of which is to avoid the making of a **relevant payment"**

(PAYE Regulations SI 2003 No 2682 reg 4(2)).

excluded plant and machinery Term used and defined in Capital Allowances Act 2001 s212J(4) in relation to an anti-avoidance provision.

excluded property Property whose transfer cannot give rise to a liability under inheritance tax (Inheritance Tax Act 1984 s3(2) and s6). The main categories of excluded property are:

- non-UK property of someone who is not UK-domiciled;
- holdings in UK authorised unit trusts or open-ended investment companies;
- decorations for bravery or gallantry; and
- a reversionary interest in a settlement, unless it was acquired for money or money's worth.

excluded provision Benefits in kind that are exempt from tax and are therefore exempt from class 1A national insurance unless specifically stated otherwise. The term is used in Social Security Contributions and Benefits Act 1992 s10.

excluded relocation expenses For PAYE, "means payments in respect of removal expenses as defined by section 272 of [Income Tax (Earnings And Pensions) Act 2003] ... if, and to the extent that they are payments of net PAYE income" (PAYE Regulations SI 2003 No 2682 reg 4(2)).

exclusive licence In relation to capital allowance for patents, "means a licence to exercise those [patent] rights to the exclusion of the grantor and of other persons for the period remaining until the rights come to an end" (Capital Allowances Act 2001 s466(4)). For patent box, the term is defined in Corporation Tax 2010 from s357B.

exclusively One of the conditions that must be met for trade expenditure to be tax-deductible. The word relates to the purpose of the payment. It appears with the word "wholly" which relates to the amount.

exclusivity agreement Agreement between a supplier and a seller whereby the latter receives a payment from the former for only selling his product. Such arrangements are common for petrol stations and pubs. In other businesses, such arrangements may fall foul of competition laws. For tax purposes, any payment made in connection with such an agreement is taxed either as income or capital, depending on the nature of the payment. It is usually taxed as income unless the seller can show that the sum was to be spent on capital items.

exclusivity tie Payment by a supplier to restrict a retailer's choice of products. This has been common in the oil industry. Leading cases on this are *Bolam v Regent Oil Co Ltd [1956] 37TC56* and *Strick v Regent Oil Co Ltd [1965] 43TC1.* These are discussed in HMRC Manual at BIM35555 and BIM35560 respectively.

executive share option scheme Tax-advantaged scheme for directors to acquire shares at a future date at a fixed price. It was introduced in 1984 and replaced by company share option plans in 1995.

ex div Without dividend. The term is used to denote a share where the next dividend will be paid to the present owner and not to the purchaser. The opposite is cum div. The price paid usually reflects the lack of the next dividend.

executor Person who deals with the estate of someone who left a will.

executor-dative Person appointed by a Scottish court to administer an estate when there is no will or no executor has been named.

executrix Term, now rarely used, for a female executor.

exempt gift Gift that is exempt from inheritance tax, such as one made more than seven years before death. A full list is given under inheritance tax in section 3 of this dictionary.

exemption Exclusion such as from a tax. It includes an exempt supply for VAT.

exemption from registration The waiver of the requirement to register on request if all, or most, of the applicant's taxable supplies are zero-rated. The law is given in VATA 1994 Sch 1 para 14.

exempt supply Supply on which VAT is not charged but for which no input tax may be claimed (VATA 1994 s31). A list of such supplies is given in VATA 1994 Sch 9.

exes Colloquial abbreviation for expenses.

ex facie absolute disposition Form of charge that may be registered by a company in Scotland (CA 2006 s881).

ex gratia Payment made without any admission of liability to make it.

exhibition Curated public display of items for which museums and galleries exhibition tax relief from corporation tax may be claimed (CTA 2009 s1218ZAA(1)).

exhibition guarantee payment Payment made to underwrite an exhibition. A trader may be able to claim it as a tax deduction under the normal "wholly and exclusively" rules. The matter was litigated in *Morley v Lawford and Co [1928] 14TC229*, and is discussed in HMRC Manual at BIM45305.

exhumation For VAT, this is a standard-rated supply. It is not with the scope of the exemption for burial and cremation. Further details are given in VAT notice 701/32.

existence, ownership and valuation (EOV) The three traditional tests for an auditor checking assets on a balance sheet.

exit charge Amount of inheritance tax payable for a relevant property trust for the period from the last ten-yearly charge to the end of the trust.

exit day The day the UK leaves the European Union. This was to be 19 March 2019 but was repeatedly postponed to 31 January 2020 (European Union (Withdrawal) Act 2018 s1 as amended).

exit tax Charge made on a company when it ceases to be UK-resident (TCGA 1992 s185).

exotic meat Term used in VAT notice 701/14 for the less common sources of meat for human consumption. These include the meat of horses, crocodiles and kangaroos. If prepared for human consumption, the meat may be zero-rated even though a supply of the living animal is not.

expanded job support scheme (EJSS) Coronavirus scheme that was announced in October 2020, but was replaced by a second Coronavirus Job Retention Scheme from November 2020.

expectation of life In insurance and pensions, the period of time which a person is expected to remain living. Life expectancy tables are given in section 3 of this dictionary.

expected birth Date a baby is expected to be born, as stated by a doctor or midwife, usually on form MAT B1. The maternity pay period for statutory maternity pay may start from six weeks before this date.

expected strength Expected alcoholic strength of beer that continues to ferment past the duty point. Alcoholic liquor duty is calculated according to expected strength. Details are given in HMRC notice 226.

expected week of childbirth (EWC) Week starting on a Sunday in which a baby is expected to be born. This determines when the maternity pay period starts for statutory maternity pay and whether the employee qualifies.

expense Cost of a business rather than to the products or services it provides. Expenses are deducted from gross profit to give net profit. For tax purposes, an expense is an item that is properly brought into the profit and loss account and does not necessarily mean that any money has been paid. For a business, the expense must be wholly and exclusively incurred. Unlike employment expenses, it does not also have to be necessary. ITTOIA 2005 s27 states that an expense refers to a tax-deductible item that has properly been brought into account. It does not necessarily mean that any money was paid.

expensive accommodation Accommodation which cost more than £75,000 (unchanged from 1984 when it might have been expensive). If an employee is provided with such accommodation, he or she is liable to pay tax at the excess multiplied by the official rate of interest. This is in addition to paying tax according to the property's rateable value.

expert witness Skilled witness called to assist the court in a specialist area. The use of expert witnesses is governed by the Civil Rules Procedure 1998, Part 35. The issue of expert witnesses in tax matters has been considered in the excise duty case *M W Plant (Contracts) Ltd EDN/05/8007* and the income tax case *Liverpool Roman Catholics Archdiocesan Trustees Incorporated v Goldberg (No 2) Ch D [2001] 4 All ER 950.*

exploration or exploitation activities For tax "means activities carried on in connection with the exploration or exploitation of so much of the seabed and subsoil and their natural resources as is situated in the United Kingdom or a designated area" (ITEPA 2003 s41(2) and FA 1973 s38(2)(a) and CTA 2010 s356L(4)).

exploration or exploitation asset For capital gains tax, means "an asset used in connection with exploration or exploitation activities carried on in the United Kingdom or a designated area" (TCGA 1992 s25(6)).

exploration or exploitation rights For tax, "means rights to assets to be produced by exploration or exploitation activities in or to the benefits of such assets" (FA 1973 s38(2)(b)).

exploration work For chargeable gains in oil industry, "means work carried out for the purpose of searching for oil anywhere in that area" (TCGA 1992 s196(6)). In relation to capital allowances for oil licences relating to undeveloped areas, "means work carried out for the purpose of searching for oil anywhere in that area" (CAA 2001 s553(6)).

explosive A definition of explosives is given in Explosives Act 1875 s3. They are generally banned from importation under CEMA 1979 s75.

export Sending of goods to another country. While Britain was in the EU single market, it meant sending goods to a country outside the EU. Exported goods are zero-rated, but evidence of export must be kept. Exported goods are generally zero-rated for VAT (VATA 1994 s30). Guidance is given in VAT Notice 703.

export controls "In relation to any goods, the prohibition or regulation of their exportation from the United Kingdom or their shipment as stores" (Export Control Act 2002 s1(2)).

Export Credit Guarantee Department (ECGD) British government department which provides insurance to businesses exporting goods against the risk of non-payment. A company may be able to claim tax relief for payments to this body (CTA 2009 s91 and ITTOIA 2005 s91).

export declaration Declaration made in connection with the export of goods. Either a full or a simplified export declaration may be made.

exporter For Customs purposes, this is the person on whose behalf the export declaration is made (CEMA 1979 s1(1)).

Export Health Certificate (EHC) Document needed by British exporters from 1 January 2021 to export animals and plants.

export licensing procedure This is "an administrative procedure, whether or not referred to as licensing, used by a party for the operation of the export licensing regimes. requiring the submission of an application or other documentation, other than that generally required for customs clearance purposes, to the relevant administrative body as a prior condition for exportation from that party" (EU/UK withdrawal agreement of 24 December 2020. Article GOODS 3: Definitions (c)).

exposure draft Draft of an accounting standard.

express trust Trust that is specifically created by a settlor, as against constructive trusts, resulting trusts and implied trusts.

ex rights When a share is offered for sale without the rights that belong to that share.

external audit Audit undertaken by accountants who are not employed by the entity being audited.

externally provided worker (EPW) In relation to research and development tax credits, means staff who are not employees. The term is defined in CTA 2009 s1128.

extraordinary item In accounting a transaction which is abnormal and falls outside the ordinary activities of the entity and which are not expected to recur (FRS 102 section 5.10A). Such an item is reported separately in the profit and loss account. In practice, an extraordinary item is expected to be very rare.

extra pay day For PAYE, "means the last day in a tax year on which a main relevant payment is due to be made to the employee if —

(a) the employee's main relevant payments are made weekly or at greater intervals which results in the number of pay days varying from tax year to tax year (solely because of the number of days in a calendar year), and

(b) the day falls in a short payment period

(PAYE Regulations SI 2003 No 2682 reg 31(4)).

extra-statutory concession (ESC) A relaxation from the strict interpretation of a tax law. An ESC is issued by HMRC under their general authority to manage taxes. HMRC will allow an ESC unless it is being used for tax avoidance. An example of this was the case *ex parte Fulford Dobson [1987]*. Concern as to their legality was expressed by judge Walton J in the case *Vestey v IRC [1979]*. He asked why, for example, free coal for miners was governed by extra-statutory concession A6. He did not question this tax relief itself but the fact that it was granted by the Commissioners of Inland Revenue and not by Parliament. (It does now have statutory authority as Income Tax (Earnings and Pensions) Act 2003 s306).

The House of Lords held in *Wilkinson [2005]* that HMRC did not have authority for many extra-statutory concessions. This decision did not outlaw concessions but narrowed the discretion for issuing them. As a consequence many extra-statutory concessions have been enacted in statute.

For VAT, HMRC publishes VAT Notice 48 which lists concessions for VAT. Extra-statutory concessions for other taxes can be found on HMRC's website.

extreme pornographic material For the purposes of Internet access, this is defined in Digital Economy Act 2017 s22. Under separate powers, Customs may seize imported pornographic material that cannot legally be sold in the UK.

extrinsic evidence Evidence taken from outside sources to clarify a document. This may be done to establish a testator's intentions in a will.

eye test An employer may be liable to pay for eye tests and corrective glasses for an employee who routinely uses a computer screen (Health and Safety (Display Screen Equipment) Regulations SI 1992 No 2792). From April 2006, this is not a taxable benefit in kind (ITEPA 2003 s320A).

FABs Flavoured alcoholic beverages, another name for alco-pops for the purposes of alcoholic liquor duty.

face-value vouchers There are special VAT provisions set out in Value Added Tax Act 1994 Sch 10A and explained in VAT Notice 700/7. Face value vouchers are defined for VAT as one of:

- single purpose vouchers
- credit vouchers
- retail vouchers
- other vouchers.

factor A business that takes on the administrative functions of other businesses. It is regulated by Factors Act 1889.

failure to make a return This is a specific tax offence.

failure to prevent tax evasion This is a specific criminal offence introduced from 30 September 2017 (Criminal Finances Act 2017 s45). An employer can be guilty of this offence, even if the employer had no knowledge of it.

fair market value Price at which a transaction would be completed by a willing buyer and a willing seller in an arm's length transaction where each has reasonable knowledge of the fact. In accounting and tax, this is only used when there is good reason not to use the transaction value, such as in transfer pricing, or calculating the capital gains tax on a disposal to a close relative.

fairness Acting in an honest, reasonable and even-handed manner. Fairness is not often incurred in tax which usually follows the letter of the law. In can be relevant in tax administration. Some judicial guidance was given by Lord Mustill in *R v Secretary of State for the Home Office ex parte Doody [1994] IAC 531 at 560D.*

Fair Tax Mark Scheme launched in February 2014 to recognise organisations that pay the correct amount of corporation tax on time and in the right place.

fair value An alternative to historic cost in recognising an item in the accounts. It is based on the value that would arise in an arm's length transaction. For tax, the value can be required for insurance, loan relationships and some financial instruments such as derivatives.

faithful representation In accounting, one of the five qualities required for accounts to have reliability. This in turn is one of the four requirements for accounting information required by Statement of Principles. Faithful representation broadly requires financial statements to portray transactions in a way that reflects the commercial effect. This underpins such principles as substance over form.

Falkland Islands British dependency comprising islands in the South Atlantic. Britain fought a war against Argentina in 1992 over its sovereignty. The Falklands use British currency. The UK has a double taxation arrangement of 1997.

fall away In relation to married woman's election for class 1 national insurance, the provision that an actual election to pay reduced rate ceases to apply (i.e. falls away) if she has no assessable earnings for two tax years. An actual election is one made between 6 April 1975 and 11 May 1977. The fall away does not apply to a deemed election made between 6 April 1948 and 5 April 1975.

fallback position Tax provision that applies when the usual tax provision cannot be used. An example relates to paying VAT on acquisitions from another EU member state. The normal provision is that the UK acquirer pays the tax. Should that not be possible, there is a fallback position that allows VAT to be charged in the state of supply.

fall in value relief Relief from inheritance tax if an asset loses value within four years for land, and one year for securities and other assets (IHTA 1984 ss179 and 191).

fallopia japonica Latin name for Japanese knotweed for which there is a special landfill tax provision.

fallow land Land that is not currently being used for an agricultural purpose as a means of allowing the soil to recover for future agricultural use. Such land will usually qualify for agricultural property relief from inheritance tax under Inheritance Tax Act 1984 s117.

false accounting Criminal offence (under Theft Act 1968 ss17-20) of deliberately keeping wrong financial records.

false representation This is an element of one of three types of fraud. A person commits this offence if he "dishonestly makes a false representation to make a gain for himself or another, or to cause a loss to another or to expose another to a risk of loss" (Fraud Act 2006 s2(1)).

A representation is false if "it is untrue or misleading, and the person making it knows that it is, or might be, untrue or misleading" (ibid s2(2)).Representation means "any representation as to fact or law, including a representation as to the state of mind of:

(a) the person making the representation, or

(b) any other person". (ibid s2(3)).

The representation may be express or implied (ibid s2(4)).

false statement Statement where someone states something as being true when he knows, or should know, that it is untrue. It is a criminal offence for a director to make a false statement in the directors' report, directors' remuneration report or summary financial statement (CA 2006 s463(1)).

families and friends Term used by HMRC for informal tax agents, such as where an individual is assisted by someone more knowledgeable in tax affairs than the taxpayer but who is not a tax professional.

family For national insurance and social security purposes, this is broadly defined as a couple, their dependent children and other dependent children (SSCBA 1992 s137(1)).

family investment company (FIC) A company (limited or unlimited) that makes investments for a family or other group of individuals. The shareholders' agreement reflects the wishes of its members. Typically each family member is given his or her own category of share. It is an alternative to a discretionary trust. It avoids lifetime inheritance tax when funds are placed in the company, and allows retained profits to be taxed at corporation tax rates (which are often lower than income tax). Its main disadvantage is that the profits attract corporation tax when earned and capital gains tax when realised by the family member. The aggregate of these taxes can exceed the income tax otherwise payable. The FIC can be effective depending on the nature of investments.

family maintenance Usual terms for the arrangements set out in IHTA 1984 s11. Payments of maintenance are excluded from the scope of taxable dispositions. Family maintenance broadly comprises payments to maintain a former spouse or civil partner, payments to maintain or educate a child, or payments to look after a dependent relative.

family tie One of the sufficient ties test considered for statutory residence test. Details are given under statutory residence test in section 3 of this dictionary.

Far Eastern Prisoners of War Ex Gratia Scheme Scheme established by the UK government to pay compensation to certain victims of the second world war. On 16 December 2015, it was announced that payments are exempt from inheritance tax.

farmer Person who carried on the trade of farming either as a sole trader or in partnership (ITTOIA 2005 s225ZG).

farmhouse A working farmhouse may be exempt from annual tax on enveloped dwellings (FA 2013 s148). A farmhouse usually qualifies for agricultural property relief from inheritance tax. Details are given in HMRC Manual at IHTM24051. The house must be ancillary to the farm to qualify. In the case *Higginson's Executors v CIR [2002] SpC 337,* it was held on the facts of the case that the farm was ancillary to the house and so did not qualify.

farming Production of animals or crops for food. For tax, this is construed widely to include forestry and fishing. This is a trade if run commercially (ITTOIA 2005 s225ZG), but not otherwise (ITTOIA 2005 s9; CTA 2009 s36). All farming activities of a person are considered as a single trade, regardless of how many farms they operate and where they are (ITTOIA 2005 s9; CTA 2009 s36). Up to 31 December 2020, UK farms were subject to provisions of the Common

Agricultural Policy. From 1 January 2021, subsidies and other provisions are governed by Agriculture Act 2020.

A farmer may average profits over two or five years.

An animal farmer may elect to use the herd basis.

From 1803 to 1940, farming was subject to income tax under Schedule B.

Farms and farm assets may qualify for agricultural property relief from inheritance tax (IHTA 1984 s122).

VAT provisions are given in VATA 1994 s54.

There are restrictions on investing in farms under tax-advantaged schemes like enterprise investment scheme and venture capital trusts. There are many special tax provisions for farming.

faro This game is specifically listed in Betting and Gaming Duties Act 1981 s13(3) as being subject to duty. The variation faro bank is also listed.

farrier Person who fits horseshoes to horses. It is taxed as a trade. They are regulated by Farriers (Registration) Act 1975 as amended by Farriers (Registration) Act 2017.

farrowing crate Metal cage in which a sow gives birth. This qualifies for capital allowance as plant and machinery in the pig industry when used in connection with the slurry system (HMRC Brief 03/2010 of 23 February 2010).

farthing Old coin equal to a quarter of an old penny, so there were 960 to the pound. The coin was demonetised on 31 December 1960.

Faster Payments Service (FPS) Facility provided by banks from 2011 to allow for almost instant transfer of funds between bank accounts, though some payments may take up to 2 hours. The legal requirement is that payment must have been made by the end of the next working day. FPS may be used to pay HMRC from 16 December 2012. In 2015, it was held that a taxpayer has met the due date for paying tax if funds have been transferred by FPS by the date even if that is a weekend or public holiday *(Fifields Mechanical and Electrical Services Ltd [2015] TC 4567).*

fat finger Colloquial term for a typing or similar mistake that has serious consequences. An extreme example was when the Japanese bank Mizuho mistakenly sold 610,000 shares in J-Com for 1 yen, instead of selling 1 share for 610,000 yen.

fathom Old unit of length equal to 6 feet (1.83 metres), originally the span of a man's arms. In timber, it represents 216 cubic feet (a cube where each side is 6 feet).

fat tax (1) Colloquialism for a sumptuary tax, proposed several times, on foods with a high fat content, such as burgers and chips.

(2) Colloquialism coined in 2018 for the practice of some retailers to charge more for larger sizes of clothes.

fax machine Device that allows documents and images to be transmitted down a telephone line to a similar machine. The machines became standard office equipment from around 1980 to 2000 when they were largely replaced by email.

FCA Handbook Handbook produced by the Financial Conduct Authority under Financial Services and Markets Act 2000. It is referred to in CTA 2009 s133H(7).

FCO advice Advice from the Foreign Office that a country is to be avoided for such reasons as civil unrest. If a taxpayer in the UK cannot return to a country for such reason, those days are not counted as days in the UK for the statutory residence test. This applies for a maximum of 60 days.

Fédération des Experts Comptables Européens (FEE) International body that represents national accounting bodies. In December 2016, it changed its name to Accountancy Europe.

feed-in tariff Payment made for small amounts of excess electricity from microgeneration such as from homes and businesses. The scheme buys electricity produced by solar panels, wind, combined heat and power, hydro-electricity and anaerobic digestion. The maximum amount bought is 5 megawatts (2 megawatts for anaerobic digestion). The scheme opened on 1 April 2010 and closed to new participants from 1 April 2019, with some exceptions. There is a cap on many people and businesses may participate. Payment has two elements: a generation tariff in relation to the amount of electricity generated, and an export tariff which is the amount supplied to the electricity company. Where a payment is received by a business, it is treated as income and is subject to income tax or corporation tax. Where a payment is received by an individual, the generation tariff is not taxed. The export tariff is subject to income tax as miscellaneous income. Further guidance is given in HMRC Manual at BIM40510.

fee simple Legal term for a freehold interest without conditions or limitation. For VAT, a limited definition is given in VATA 1994 s96(1).

feints Impure spirits that arise at the start and end of distillation. The tax implications are set out in Customs notice 39.

felony Serious crime. It was abolished in UK by Criminal Law Act 1967 s1.

feme sole Legal term for a single woman, particularly one who carries on a trade.

feminine gender In interpreting laws, unless the context otherwise requires, the masculine gender includes the feminine gender, and the feminine gender includes the masculine gender (Interpretation Act 1978 s6).

fencing Dealing in stolen goods. Although illegal, a case in 1886 held that it was still trading and taxable.

fermentation Biochemical process of turning carbohydrates into alcohol in the production of liquor which is subject to alcoholic liquor duty.

ferret Animal used to catch rabbits. In 2010, it was held that a ferret is not a working animal, so its food is not zero-rated *(Supreme Petfoods Ltd [2010] TC 896).* A ferret is covered by the Pets Passport scheme.

ferry Passenger boat service. Profits are specifically taxed as a trade (ITTOIA 2005 s12).

fertiliser Because fertiliser contains chemicals that may explode, imports of large quantities may require either an Exemption Certificate or a Detonation Resistance Test Certificate to clear Customs.

festival A festival held for educational reasons may qualify as a charity *(CIR v Glasgow Musical Festival Association [1926] 11 TC 154).* For VAT, admission to a festival may be exempt from VAT (as explained in VAT Notice 701/47).

fiancée Woman who is engaged to be married. The male equivalent is fiancé. Breaking off an engagement was a common law offence until repealed by Law Reform (Miscellaneous Provisions) Act 1970 s1. Under present law, an engagement ring may be kept by the person to whom it was given (ibid s3). Other gifts between the parties are returnable (ibid s2). English law does not recognise engagement as a marital status for such purposes as the transferable allowance for Inland Revenue or spousal exemption for inheritance tax.

fiat money Banknotes and coins which have an intrinsic value below their face value. All UK notes and coins in daily use from 1914 are fiat money. The difference between the two values is seignorage, which is sometimes seen as a tax.

FICO score Most widely used form of credit scoring used in the USA, and used by the main credit reference agencies. It was created by the Fair Isaac Corporation in the USA. It typically considers a person creditworthiness under these elements:

- 35%: payment history
- 30%: use of credit
- 15%: length of credit history
- 10%: types of credit used
- 10%: recent searches for credit.

The method was updated on 23 January 2020. The score is given out of 1000, usually in the range of 300 to 850. The median score is 723. About 60% are in the range 650 to 799. A sub-prime mortgage is one given to someone with a FICO score below 620.

fictitious asset Debit balance that arises from a double entry but where the debit balance does not represent the value of an asset. Examples include deferred expenditure on fixed assets. The term is now little used, as accounting standards generally require such debits to be posted to the profit and loss account as expenses. If such an asset is capitalised, it is classed as an intangible asset.

fictious trading Activity that represents no substantive transactions and is usually undertaken to create an impression of busy trading.

fiddle Colloquial term meaning to falsify. The word connotes something improper, rather than just correcting a figure.

fidelity Faithfulness and loyalty. This is a legal term implied into every contract of employment.

fiduciary Relationship based on trust, such as between a bank and customer.

fiduciary estate Estate or a similar interest in land or other assets, as against the beneficial interest.

field allowance

(1) In oil industry, an amount that reduces the adjusted ring fence profits for supplementary petroleum tax (CTA 2009 from s333; HMRC Manual at OT21405).

(2) Additional sum once paid to military officers engaged in battle.

fi fa Abbreviation of fieri facias.

fieri facias Latin for "cause to be made". A writ directing a sheriff to seize goods to pay a debt.

fieri feci Statement by a sheriff that he or she has been unable to seize goods to pay a debt.

fifty pence coin Coin first introduced on 14 October 1969 to replace the ten-shilling note. The coin has seven curved sides. Its size was reduced in 1997. The older larger coin was demonetised on 28 February 1998.

fifty pound note Highest value bank note from the Bank of England for everyday use. During 2021, the paper note is to be replaced by a polymer plastic note featuring the computer scientist Alan Turing.

FII group litigation Long-running case that started in 2004 on whether a UK company could claim tax relief on dividends from non-resident subsidiaries. Affected companies were part of a group litigation order. The case went to the Supreme Court twice, and the European Court three times. On the substantive issue of allowability, the taxpayers won. The government passed FA 2004 s320 and FA 2007 s107 retrospectively to frustrate the claim by seeking to disapply Limitation Act 1980 s32(1)(c). On 20 November 2020, the Supreme Court ruled [2020 UKSC 19] by 4-3 that the limitation period applies to mistakes of law and runs from when a claimant knows, or with reasonable diligence could have known, that there was a worthwhile claim. It upheld the Court of Appeal's decision, although for a different reason, and overturned a House of Lords decision.

Fiji Nation of islands in the Pacific Ocean. Its currency is the Fijian dollar. The UK has a double taxation convention of 1975.

Fijian dollar Currency of Fiji.

filing date Date by which a document or return must be filed. Tax law has many such provisions though they are usually called due date. In Scotland, the term filing date is used, and defined in Revenue Scotland and Tax Powers Act 2014 s82. For company law, the filing obligations are set out in CA 2006 s1113.

film Any record comprising a series of moving images (Films Act 1985 Sch 1 para 1(1)). For tax relief for film production, a definition is given in CTA 2009 s1181(2). There are some special tax reliefs for British films, including film tax relief. introduced in 2005. These are noted in creative industry tax reliefs in section 3 of this dictionary. The scope of this relief has changed several times, mainly to avoid it being exploited for artificial tax avoidance. Some form of tax relief has been available since 1982.

Expenditure on films is excluded from some provisions relating to the degrouping charge (CTA 2009 s808).

Between 1957 and 1982, films were subject to the Eady levy, which was similar to a tax.

film series For the purposes of corporation tax relief for film production, each film in a series is treated as a separate film "unless —

(a) the films form a series with not more than 26 parts,
(b) the combined playing time is not more than 26 hours, and
(c) the series constitutes a self-contained work or is a series of documentaries with a common theme, in which case the films are treated as a single film" (CTA 2009 s1181(3)).

fils One hundredth of a riyal, currency of Yemen.

final accounting period In relation to beneficiaries' income from an estate in administration, "means the accounting period in which the administration period ends" (CTA 2009 s938(3)).

final accounts The accounts produced at the end of an accounting period and which are no longer in draft form.

final chargeable period The period in which a trade is permanently discontinued. The provisions for **capital allowances** are given in Capital Allowances Act 2001 s65.

final dividend Dividend paid on the basis of the profits of an accounting period per the accounts, as against an interim dividend.

final earnings Amount a person is earning at the end of the career and which is used for a final salary scheme for pensions. There are rules for calculating this figure, which may give a figure different from a person's final salary figure.

final exercise date Term used in relation to disguised remuneration (ITEPA 2003 s554L1(14)).

final gravity For beer duty, another name for present gravity.

final instalment of wages The last pay day of an employee. The term is used in Employment Rights Act 1996 s22 with regards to retail workers. Such workers may have deductions made from their pay for a cash shortage or stock deficiency incurred while they were working. This is limited to 10% of gross earnings except for the last pay day.

finally determined In relation to Scottish tax appeals, this term is specifically defined in Revenue Scotland and Tax Powers Act 2014 s90(3).

final period relief Period of absence at the end of ownership of a main residence that may be ignored for claiming main residence relief from capital gains tax.

final place of destination For air passenger duty, this is as indicated on the ticket (FA 1994 s43(2)).

final salary scheme Salary-related occupational pension scheme where the amount of pension depends on final salary (as defined) and length of service. It is now more commonly called a defined benefit scheme.

final tax year Tax year in which a trade permanently ceases (ITA 2007 s89(1)). There are special provisions for determining the basis period. Overlap relief may be offset against the final profits. A claim for terminal loss relief may be made, allowing any final loss to be offset against profits of the three previous years.

final withholding tax From 2013, an amount deducted by Swiss banks on payments to UK taxpayers under an agreement between the UK and Swiss authorities made in 2011. The rates are 40% for dividend income, 48% for other income, and 27%

from capital gains. These are marginally below the UK rates to reflect the fact that the tax is paid in advance. A UK taxpayer who wishes to avoid this tax may authorise the Swiss banks to disclose details to HRMC.

Finance Act Act of Parliament usually produced each year setting out changes in tax law.

financial benefit share Sum that may be paid by an employer tax-free to an employee for a suggestion that is taken up. The benefit is the greater of half the first year's benefit or 10% of the first five years' benefit.

Finance Bill Draft of a Finance Act that may be amended by Parliament.

finance lease Lease which has the nature of funding the acquisition of an asset rather than an arrangement which simply lends the asset, known as an operating lease. The main difference is that assets acquired under a finance lease are shown as fixed assets on the lessee's balance sheet. FRS 102 glossary defined a finance lease as "a lease that transfers substantially all the risks and rewards incidental to ownership of an asset. Title may or may not eventually be transferred. A lease that is not a finance lease is an operating lease".

International accounting standard IFRS 16 introduces radical changes to accounting for leases. It broadly requires all but the smallest leases to be treated as finance leases, and for leased assets to be shown on the balance sheet. The smallest leases are those that either last for less than 12 months or where the value of the leased item is less than a suggested $5,000.

IFRS 16 applies to accounting periods that begin on or after 1 January 2019.

For tax purposes, a distinction is made between a short lease and a long funded lease. A finance lease "means any arrangements –

(a) which provide for plant or machinery to be leased or otherwise made available by a person (the lessor) to another person (the lessee), and

(b) which under generally accepted accounting practice –

 (i) fall (or would fall) to be treated in the accounts of the lessor or a person connected with the lessor, as a finance lease or a loan, or

 (ii) are comprised in arrangements which fall (or would fall) to be so treated" (CAA 2001 s219(1)).

An effectively identical definition appears in relation to decommissioning expenditure in CTA 2010 s331(6).

For an anti-avoidance provision the term "means a lease which, in accordance with generally accepted accounting principles, falls (or would fall) to be treated as a finance lease or loan in the accounts of C [company] or P [purchaser]" (CAA 2001 s212L(7)).

finance lease test Test set out in Capital Allowances Act 2001 s70N.

finance lessor In relation to finance leases, "means a person who for accounting purposes is treated, in accordance with generally accepted accounting practice, as the person with –

(a) the grantor's interest in relation to a finance lease, or

(b) the lender's interest in relation to a loan"

(ITA 2007 s614DG).

The same definition is used in relation to anti-avoidance provisions for leases in CTA 2009 s937.

financial accounting That branch of accounting concerned with producing statements of values and profits, rather than analysing where those profits were earned.

Financial Action Task Force (FATF) Body that compiled a list of Non-Cooperative Countries or Territories which were seen as being havens for money laundering and terrorism funding. The first list of 15 states and territories was compiled in June 2000. The list includes territories that were unable to deal with the issues in addition to those unwilling to do so. The list was Bahamas, Cayman Islands, Cook Islands, Dominica, Israel, Lebanon, Liechtenstein, Marshall Islands, Nauru, Niue, Panama, Philippines, Russia, Saint Kitts and Nevis, Saint Vincent and the Grenadines. The list was updated until November 2009 when no countries were still listed.

financial adviser Person who offers personal advice on financial matters, such as pensions and investments. Such a person must be regulated by the Financial Conduct Authority. Financial advisers are of three types:

- S: single tier advisers;
- M: multi-tier advisers; and
- WOM: whole of market advisers.

A single-tier adviser only advises on the financial products of one company, and is usually an employee of that company.

A multi-tier adviser advises on the products of a few companies.

A whole of market adviser gives advice on all financial products on the market.

There is also a category D adviser where a person can deal directly with the company, though this is not really advice at all.

A financial adviser must tell clients what type of adviser he or she is.

financial asset Financial instrument which is a security. For accounting standards, a financial asset is defined as "any asset that is:

(a) cash;

(b) an equity instrument of another entity;

(c) a contractual right:

(i) to receive cash or another financial asset from another entity, or

(ii) to exchange financial assets or financial liabilities with another entity under conditions that are potentially favourable for the entity; or

(d) a contract that will or may be settled in the entity's own equity instruments and:

(i) under which the entity is or may be challenged to receive a variable number of the entity's own equity instruments; or

(ii) that will or may be settled other than by the exchange of a fixed amount of cash or another financial asset for a fixed number of the entity's own equity instruments. For this purpose the entity's own equity instruments do not include instruments that are themselves contracts for the future receipt or delivery of the entity's own equity instruments" (FRS 102 glossary).

In accounts, financial assets are shown at "amortised cost less impairment" except for publicly traded securities and those which are valued at fair value (FRS 102 section 2.47).

financial assistance

(1) Help in the form of money. The term has a specific meaning in Companies Act 2006 s677 in relation to a company providing assistance to buy its own shares. This is generally prohibited.

(2) In the context of international aid, includes assistance:

"(a) by way of grant or loan,

(b) in the form of a guarantee, or

(c) by the Secretary of State acquiring securities of a company"

(International Development Act 2002 s6).

Financial Assistance Scheme Scheme for pensions provided by Pensions Act 2004 s286. The Treasury may make regulations in relation to its tax under FA 2009 s73. It made SI 2010 No 1187.

financial benefit share Amount that may be paid tax-free to an employee in respect of a suggestion adopted by the employer. The tax-free limit is the greater of half the first year's benefit, and 10% of the first five years' benefit (ITEPA 2003 s322(5)).

Financial Conduct Authority (FCA) Body formed on 1 April 2013 to replace the Financial Services Authority. It is a company limited by guarantee accountable to Treasury and Parliament. It is regulated by Financial Services Act 2012. It is responsible for regulating the financial services industry. It defines its three objectives as:

- protecting consumers
- enhancing market integrity
- promoting competition.

In March 2020, the FCA introduced stricter customer authentication rules.

financial derivative Financial instrument whose value depends on another instrument. such as an option on a share price.

financial future Contract for the delivery of gilts at a future date. It is subject to specific capital gains tax provisions. For a provision of corporation tax, the term "means financial futures which are for the time being dealt in on a recognised futures exchange" (CTA 2009 s981(3)).

financial health check Requirement of EU law that certain tax provisions do not apply to a company in difficulties. EU law generally bars state aid, which can include some tax reliefs, to businesses in difficulty.

financial institution

Company law

Any company or other body which provides financial services to businesses. Financial institutions include banks, loan companies and similar. For CA, the term "means a financial institution within the meaning of Article 1.1 of the Council Directive on the obligations of branches established in a Member State of credit and financial institutions having their head office outside that Member

State regarding the publication of annual accounting documents (the Bank Branches Directive, 89/117/EC)" (CA 2006 s1173 (1)).

CA 2006 s778 contains special provisions about transfer of shares to such an institution. For this purpose the term is restricted to clearing houses, investment exchanges and equivalent bodies.

Taxation for alternative finance arrangements

In relation to alternative finance arrangements, a definition appears in Taxation of Chargeable Gains Act 1992 s151I and CTA 2009 s502.

Accounting standards

"Any of the following:

(a) a bank which is:

(i) a firm with a Part IV permission [as defined in Financial Services and Markets Act 2000 s40(4)] which includes accepting deposits and:

(a) which is a credit institution; or

(b) whose Part IV permission includes a requirement that it complies with the rules in the General Prudential sourcebook and the Prudential Sourcebook for Banks, Building Societies and Investment Firms, relating to banks, but which is not a bank, building society, a friendly society or a credit union;

(ii) an EEA bank which is a full credit institution;

(b) a building society which is defined in section 119(1) of the Building Societies Act 1986 as a building society incorporated (or deemed to be incorporated) under that act;

(c) a credit union, being a body corporate registered under the Industrial and Provident Societies Act 1965 as a credit union in accordance with the Credit Unions Act 1979, which is an authorised person;

(d) custodian bank, broker-dealer or stockbroker;

(e) an entity that undertakes the business of effecting or carrying out insurance contracts, including general and life assurance activities;

(f) an incorporated friendly society incorporated under the Friendly Societies Act 1992 or a registered friendly society registered under section 7(1)(a) of the Friendly Societies Act 1974 or any enactment which it replaced, including any registered branches;

(g) an investment trust, Irish investment company, venture capital trust, mutual fund, exchange traded fund, unit trust, open-ended investment company (OEIC);

(h) a retirement benefit plan; or

(i) any other entity whose principal activity is to generate wealth or manage risk through financial instruments. This is intended to cover entities that have business activities similar to those listed above but are not specifically included in the list above.

A parent entity whose sole activity is to hold investments in other group entities is not a financial institution" (FRS 102 glossary).

financial institution notice (FIN) Notice that HMRC may issue from Royal Assent to FA 2021. It allows HMRC to get financial information from third parties more quickly than under previous provisions.

financial instrument A contract that gives rise to a financial asset in one entity and a financial liability or equity share in another (FRS s11.3 and glossary).

financial liability "Any liability that is:

(a) a contractual obligation:
  (i) to deliver cash or another financial asset to another entity; or
  (ii) to exchange financial assets or financial liabilities with another entity under conditions that are potentially unfavourable to the entity; or
(b) a contract that will or may be settled in the entity's own equity instruments and
  (i) under which the entity is or may be obliged to deliver a variable number of the entity's own equity instruments; or
  (ii) will or may be settled other than by the exchange of a fixed amount of cash or another financial asset for a fixed number of the entity's own equity instruments. For this purpose the entity's own equity instruments do not include instruments that are themselves contracts for the future receipt or delivery of the entity's own equity instruments" (FRS 102 glossary).

Such an item is shown in the accounts at "amortised cost less impairment" unless it is publicly traded or valued at fair value (FRS 102 section 2.47).

Financial List Court list created on 1 October 2015. It draws judges from the Commercial Court and from the Chancery Division of the High Court to hear claims for more than £50 million. Guidance on transferring a case to the List was given by Sir Terence Etherton, Chancellor, in the case *Property Alliance Group Ltd v Royal Bank of Scotland [2016] QBD.*

financial loss allowance Allowance that may be payable to a member of a parish or community council under Local Government Finance Act 1972 s173(4).

financial management Management of the financial functions, particularly in relation to the use of long-term and short-term capital in a business.

financial option Option which is not a traded option, but which related to currency, interest rate, a share index or similar. An exhaustive list is given in Taxation of Chargeable Gains Act 1992 s144(8).

financial position State of a person's or business's finances. This usually involves looking at current assets and liabilities, and current income and expenditure. "The financial position of an entity is the relationship of its assets, liabilities and equity as of a specific date as presented in the statement of financial position [balance sheet]" (FRS 102 glossary and section 2.15).

financial reinsurance arrangement Term used in determining the tax liability of insurance companies. The term is explained in FA 1989 ss83YE and 83YF.

Financial Reporting Council (FRC) Body established in 1990 when it replaced the Accounting Standards Board. FRC issues UK accounting standards and provides other oversight of published accounts. In 2019, it was announced that it is to be replaced by the Audit, Reporting and Governance Authority.

Financial Reporting Exposure Draft (FRED) Draft of a financial reporting standard.

Financial Reporting Standard (FRS) Accounting standard issued by the Financial Reporting Council or predecessor body. For accounting periods from 1 January 2015, the main standard is FRS 102.

Financial Services Act Law passed in 1986 to regulate the provision of financial services to the public. The Act's provisions have now been largely subsumed into the Financial Services and Markets Act 2000.

Financial Services Authority Regulatory authority created for financial services in 2001. It was replaced by the Financial Conduct Authority from 1 April 2013.

Financial Services Compensation Scheme (FSCS) Body established under Financial Services and Markets Act 2000 Part 15. It was established in 2001 from previous schemes, when it was known as the Investors Compensation Scheme. In its first five years to 2006, it paid out just under £1 billion in compensation. Between 2006 and 2011 it paid out more than £26 billion as a consequence of the banking crisis. The scheme is funded by a levy on banks, building societies and some other financial institutions.

The tax consequences for its interventions are addressed in FA 2009 s74. The income tax treatment of interest paid under FSCS is explained in ITA 2007 s979A.

financial statements Documents presenting accounting information which are expected to have a useful purpose.

"Structured representation of the financial position, financial performance and cash flows of an entity" (FRS 102 glossary). The main financial statements are balance sheet, profit and loss account, and cashflows statement.

Financial Times Daily newspaper printed on pink paper and founded in 1888. It concentrates on financial matters. It produces various indices, such as the FT-SE 100 index.

financial transaction tax Tax proposed by the European Union in 2010 which has yet to be introduced. The UK introduced the bank levy.

financial year For corporation tax, the period from 1 April to the following 31 March (ICTA 1988 s834(1)). Financial years are named from the year in which they start, so Financial Year 2021 means the 12 months from 1 April 2021 to 31 March 2022. The term has other meanings in different contexts.

financing activities For statements of cash flow, "financing activities are activities that result in changes in the size and composition of the contributed equity and borrowings of an entity" (FRS 102 glossary and section 7.6). The section continues with examples.

Find a Job Name given to Universal Jobmatch website from 14 May 2018. It matches job seekers with vacancies.

finders keepers Old saying. It means whoever finds something may keep it. If the property is still owned and has not been abandoned, keeping it may amount to theft (Theft Act 1968 s1). The adage dates from Roman law which gave ownership rights to the first person to find an abandoned item. This principle has been reflected in other legal systems, with provisions to establish when something is abandoned. There are elements of this principle with regard to claiming shipwrecks under maritime law.

The English case *Parker v British Airways Board [1982] 1 QB 1004* established that a finder has a stronger claim than a subsequent possessor. Alan Parker found a gold bracelet on the floor at Heathrow Airport. He handed it to British Airways (who owned the land) to be reunited with its owner and asked that it be returned to him if that owner could not be found. When the company sold the bracelet for £850, Parker successfully challenged their claim to the bracelet.

fine Penalty for breaking a law. Fines are not tax-deductible, though compensation payments are. In general, a fine that is a punishment is not tax deductible whereas a fine that is compensatory is deductible. A leading case is *McKnight v Sheppard [1999] 71TC419.* The matter is discussed in HMRC Manual at BIM42515.

finger buffet For VAT, an issue arises as to whether a supply is zero-rated food or standard-rated catering. A leading case for catering is *P J and L J Lawson (t/a Country Fayre) [1996] VATTR 14903.* A finger buffet was held to be catering even when the customer collected it in *Wendy's Kitchen [1995] VATTR 15531.*

finings Substances that may be added to brewed liquor near the end of the production process to remove organic matter and thus improve the drink's clarity or improve its taste or aroma.

Customs notice 226 explains that the addition of finings does not affect the calculation of the duty unless (exceptionally) the finings contain alcohol.

Finland European state which is a member of the European Union, for which purpose the Åland Islands are excluded. Its currency is the euro of 100 cents. The UK has a double taxation convention of 1969 amended by a protocol of 1996.

fiqh al-Muamalat Arabic: Islamic rules on [financial] transactions.

fire Under the normal rules of tax allowability, stock lost by fire is a tax-deductible expense to the extent that the loss is not compensated by insurance. The matter is briefly discussed in HMRC Manual at BIM45851.

firearms Customs may seize any firearms brought into the country. This includes blank firing and replica guns, self-defence sprays, electric shock devices and stun guns. Realistic copies may only be imported for an authorised purpose such as participating in a historical re-enactment. Customs record-keeping for firearms is explained in Customs and Excise Management Act 1979 s75B.

For criminal law, the term "means a lethal barrelled weapon of any description from which any short, bullet or other missile can be discharged and includes —

(a) any prohibited weapon, whether it such a lethal weapon as aforesaid or not; and

(b) any component part of such a lethal or prohibited weapon; or

(c) any accessory to any such weapon designed or adapted to diminish the noise or flash caused by firing the weapon"

(Firearms Act 1968 s57(1)).

firewood For VAT, firewood may be reduced rated under VATA 1994 Sch 7A Group 1 when supplied for domestic use. Further details are given in VAT notice 701/19. The wood must be specifically held out for sale as domestic firewood.

fireworks Items that may be included in the list of explosives for which there are special Customs provisions (Explosives Act 1875 s3(1)).

firkin Barrel-shaped container used for beer and other liquors. It is equal in capacity to one quarter of a barrel, that is about nine gallons.

firm Any business, particularly a partnership (CA 2006 s1173(2); Partnership Act 1890 s4(1)).

first abolition date The date of 6 April 2012 when employees in a defined contribution occupational pension scheme lost the right to pay a lower rate of class 1 national insurance.

first commercial sale In relation to enterprise investment scheme, "has the same meaning as in the European Commission's Guidelines on State aid to promote risk finance investment (as those guidelines may be amended or replaced from time to time" (ITA 2007 s275A(8) as inserted by Finance (No 2) Act Sch 5). The same definition is used for venture capital trusts in ITA 2007 s280C(9) as inserted by Finance (No 2) Act 2015 Sch 6.

first deliverance In Scots law, "this is the first order in petition proceedings such as petitions for liquidation of a company and sequestrations (personal bankruptcy)" (Judiciary of Scotland website glossary).

first diet In Scots law, "a date on which an indictment calls in the sheriff court in solemn proceedings to determine whether the prosecutor and defence are ready to do trial" (Judiciary of Scotland website glossary).

first division In Scots law, "the Division of the Inner House of the Court of Session presided over by the Lord President" (Judiciary of Scotland website glossary).

First Home Fund Provision of Scottish government to assist first time buyers by providing £25,000 for their first home.

First Homes Proposed government scheme announced on 7 February 2020 to help people buy their first home in their local area. The idea is that certain properties should attract a discount of at least 30%. This discount would be locked in to benefit subsequent purchasers.

first in first out (FIFO) Usual method of stock valuation that assumes that the oldest stock is sold first.

first relevant period of account In relation to reverse premiums, "means the period of account in which the property transaction is first entered into" (Income Tax (Trading and Other Income) Act 2005 s102(4). In relation to such a premium for a trade, the term "means the first period of account in which the recipient carries on the trade" (ibid s102(5)(b)).

first sale period In relation to cemeteries, this term is given a specific meaning in Income Tax (Trading and Other Income) Act 2005 s171(4).

first tax year The part of a tax year in which a person starts to trade. Profits for that tax year are taxed on the amount actually earned in the year. Subsequent years are taxed on earlier periods. This means that some periods are taxed twice. This amount may be deducted as overlap relief (without any allowance for inflation) when the business ceases.

first tier tribunal Tribunal established in 2009 where a first attempt is made to resolve a tax dispute (Tribunals, Courts and Enforcement Act 2007 s3). Its decision is generally final on a point of fact but further appeals may be made on a point of law.

first-tier tax tribunal for Scotland Tribunal established to hear tax cases in Scotland (Revenue Scotland and Tax Powers Act 2014 s21(1)).

first time buyer Person who buys his or her first property either on their own or with another person. There have been tax concessions for such buyers, such as reduced stamp duty land tax from 22 November 2017 under Finance Act 2003 s57B and Sch 6ZA. There are other forms of help such for first-time buyers such as Help-to-Buy ISAs and Lifetime ISAs. Some lenders offer attractive terms to first-time buyers.

first trustee in bankruptcy Position that may be held by the official receiver until the court appoints another trustee (Insolvency Act 1986 s291A).

first unpenalised default Term used by HMRC in relation to the first late payment of PAYE in a tax year under the Real Time Information (RTI) system. HMRC does not charge a penalty for the first late payment. Penalties are imposed for the second and subsequent penalties. An employer may appeal against the first default even though no penalty has been imposed, as that will prevent a penalty being imposed for what would otherwise be the second default.

first use market value In relation to long funding operating leases, "means the market value of the plant or machinery at the time when it is first brought into use for the purpose of the qualifying activity" (Income Tax (Trading and Other Income) Act 2005 s148DB(4)). A similar definition also appears in ITTOIA 2005 s148I(5).

first year allowance Capital allowance available to a small range of assets in the tax year that they are first used (CAA 2001 from s52). More details are given under capital allowances in section 3 of this dictionary.

fiscal Relating to tax policy or government revenue.

fiscal drag Effect inflation has on increasing tax revenues. Many tax allowances have not increased in line with inflation, meaning that more taxpayer comes within the scope of a tax charge.

fiscal mark Sign that a tax or duty has been paid, such as the mark on cigarette packets from 1 April 2001.

fiscal intervention Financial intervention by the government, such as happened in the package of measures introduced in 2020 to deal with coronavirus.

fiscal policy Fiscal policy is "the use of government expenditure and taxation to try to influence the level of economic activity" (HM Treasury glossary). While the main reason for tax is to fund government expenditure, other reasons are redistribution of wealth and influencing behaviour.

fiscal warehouse Place where goods may be stored under special tax arrangements, such as pending payment of duty and VAT (VATA 1994 s18A(3)).

fiscal year Term sometimes used to mean the tax year.

fish For VAT, fish for human consumption is zero-rated as food, whereas fish for other purposes, such as tropical fish, is standard-rated. The fact that a fish is edible is not enough to zero rate it. Further details are given in VAT Notices 701/14 and 701/15.

fishing This activity is now regulated by Fisheries Act 2020. Profits from commercial fishing are taxed as a trade (ITTOIA 2005 s12; CTA 2009 s39).

fishing expedition Exercise that is looking for mistakes rather than following a specific enquiry. Once the normal enquiry period has expired, HMRC may not conduct a fishing expedition but may investigate a particular matter.

fit and proper test Test conducted to see if a person may hold a particular licence, such as to run a money service business.

Fit for Work Government scheme of advice and assessment on fitness for work. It was introduced on 1 January 2015 but has been just a website and helpline since 1 April 2018.

five-minute clause Clause that can be inserted in a deed of separation which declares the deed void if the husband and wife are still together five minutes after the separation is enjoined.

fivepence coin Coin introduced on 23 April 1968 as a replacement for one shilling, of the same size and worth the same amount, namely 5p or one twentieth of a pound. From 2012, it is made from nickel-plated steel, before which it was made of cupro-nickel. From 2013, the cupro-nickel coins are being removed from circulation. The size of the coin was reduced in June 1990 and the old larger coins demonetised in December 1990.

five pound note Bank of England note, first issued in 1793. Some Scottish and Irish banks also issue notes for this value. The current note is a polymer plastic note, depicting Sir Winston Churchill, first issued in 2016.

five-year gap For the herd basis for farmers' tax, a period of five years in which a farmer does not keep a production herd of a particular class.

fixed allowance Set amount that employees in certain occupations may claim as a deduction from their taxable income without having to prove expenditure (ITEPA 2003 from s366). The matter is discussed in HMRC Manual at EIM31623. The list of allowances is given at EP2260 and in section 3 of this dictionary.

fixed annuity Annuity, such as pension payments, which are fixed at the start of a period and do not increase.

fixed asset In bookkeeping, an asset that has an expected life of more than 12 months, such as premises, plant, furniture, computers and vehicles. An entity may also have a capitalisation threshold, perhaps £100, so it does not regard as a fixed asset low value items such as hammers, coffee mugs and staplers. Note that for plant and machinery, there is no capitalisation threshold, and the asset must have a minimum life of *two* years.

fixed capital Finance provided to support the acquisition of fixed assets. In *John Smith and Son v Moore [1921] 12TC266.* fixed capital was defined as "what the owner turns to profit by keeping it in his own possession". This is discussed in HMRC Manual at BIM33015.

fixed cost Cost which is not dependent on quantity of items produced or sold. As opposed to a direct cost. Fixed costs include overheads such as rent, rates, office staff, marketing, inspection, storage etc.

The distinction between fixed costs and direct costs is a matter of management accounting convenience rather than an accurate representation of reality, as few costs are either wholly direct or fixed. The cost of making a metal component can involve a labour cost of setting up a autolathe which is fixed regardless of how many components are made. Conversely fixed costs such as inspection and storage will eventually assume some of the nature of the direct cost, in that the more items made, the greater will be the need to inspect and store them.

fixed deduction Deduction agreed between HMRC and a group of employees which covers general expenditure borne by the employees which they may deduct without having to produce supporting evidence. The deduction is usually in respect of uniforms and tools. A list of these deductions is given in section 3 of this dictionary.

fixed duty Stamp duty that is charged at a fixed amount, as against an ad valorem duty which relates to the value of a transaction.

fixed mortgage Mortgage where the rate of interest is fixed and does not vary with the bank base rate. Such a mortgage is usually offered:

- for a short term only,
- at a higher rate than the current variable rate, or
- as a short-term marketing ploy.

fixed odds betting terminal (FOBT) Machine in betting shops that allow a person to stake a sum every 20 seconds. From 1 April 2019, the maximum stake is reduced from £100 to £2.

fixed protection Provision that allows a pension to continue to attract tax relief when it has exceeded the lifetime allowance only because that allowance has been reduced. The scheme applied in 2012 and some subsequent years.

fixed rate loan Loan on which the rate of interest does not change. Such a loan to an employee is generally not a taxable benefit in kind, provided similar terms were offered to the employer's customers at the time. A full definition is given in ITEPA 2003 s177.

fixed-rate preference shares In determining eligibility to claim tax relief for a venture capital trust, a person's holding or entitlement to acquire such shares is ignored under ITA 2007 s313(6)(a).For this purpose, such shares are defined as "shares which

(a) were issued wholly for **new consideration**,
(b) do not carry any right either to conversion into shares or securities of any other description or to the acquisition of any additional shares or securities, and
(c) do not carry any right to dividends other than dividends which:
  (i) are of a fixed amount or at a fixed rate per cent of the nominal value of the shares, and
  (ii) together with any sum paid on redemption, represent no more than a reasonable commercial return on the consideration for which the shares were issued".

fixture Something attached to the land and which cannot easily be removed. This is usually regarded as part of the land and so may become subject to stamp duty land tax. Some fixtures may qualify for capital allowances as a features integral to a building.

fizzy Description of a drink that is carbonated and has many bubbles. For wine, the term "sparkling" is more commonly used. Sparkling wine attracts a higher rate of alcoholic liquor duty.

Flag It Up Campaign launched by the government to help professional people identify money laundering activities. It involved solicitors from 2014 and accountants from 2015. In 2018, it was extended to estate agents to help identify property bought with dirty money. Under the scheme, a professional person can file a suspicious activity report (SAR) to the National Crime Agency. It is an offence not to report suspicious activity. The scheme is administered by HMRC.

flag of convenience Arrangement whereby a merchant ship is registered in a country other than that of the ship's owners. Such arrangements are often used to avoid taxes and to avoid stricter regulations. The UK introduced tonnage tax to encourage British shipping companies to register in the UK.

flag state State where a ship is registered (or "flagged"). International mariners are generally liable to national insurance and social security according to the laws of the flag state. Most of the exceptions to this general rule were removed from 1 May 2010, from when the only exception is where the mariner is remunerated from a country where he or she also is resident.

flapjack Food item traditionally made with grain, butter and syrup. For VAT, ordinary flapjacks are zero-rated as food. However the VAT tribunal ruled that flapjacks were standard-rated when honey was used *(Asda Stores Ltd [2009] TC 211).*

flat conversion allowance Capital allowance that was abolished from April 2013.

flat rate annuity Arrangement where a pension is paid at the same amount each year with no allowance for inflation.

flat rate scheme Optional VAT arrangement that may be used by small traders whereby the VAT they paid to HMRC is calculated as a percentage of the VAT-inclusive turnover (VATA 1994 s26B).

Fleming claim Claim for VAT relief outside the four-year cap (three years before 2005). The name comes from the case *M Fleming (t/a Bodycraft) v C & E Commissioners*

[2006]. The case concerned a claim for VAT paid on cars acquired in 1989 and 1990. It was held that the three-year cap was ineffective under European law as the British government had not allowed a transitional period.

flavourings For VAT, these are generally zero-rated as food, whether natural or synthetic (VAT notice 701/14). They are also generally exempt from excise duty even if they contain alcohol. Further guidance is given in Customs notice 41.

flax Plant grown for fibre. VAT Notice 701/38 specifically lists this as standard-rated, except that the small yield of seeds may be zero-rated when used as animal feed.

flexi-access Term used to describe funds held by a pension fund member that may be drawn down under the provisions of FA 2004 Sch 28 para 8A as inserted by Taxation of Pensions Act 2014 s3(1) from 6 April 2015.

flexi-access pension Pension from which flexible drawdowns may be made. It extends the pre-April 2015 scope of **flexible drawdown,** and introduces that facility for other defined benefit pension schemes. It allows the scheme member to drawdown as much pension as he or she wishes, either as a lump sum or as regular payments or annuity. Unlike the pre-2015 scheme, there is no requirement to have £12,000 (or £20,000 before 2014) other income.

flexible drawdown Ability to withdraw funds from April 2011 to a limit. From April 2015, limits were removed for defined contribution pension schemes.

flexible furlough Term used for the Coronavirus Job Retention Scheme from 1 July 2020 when furloughed workers were allowed to work part-time.

flexible mortgage A feature of some mortgages that gives the mortgagor freedom to change the amount and frequency of their mortgage payments.

Flexible New Deal Welfare programme introduced in 2008 to replace New Deal 18-24, New Deal 25+ and employment zones. Flexible New Deal was itself replaced in 2010 by the Work Programme.

flexible power of appointment trust An interest in possession trust where the beneficiaries can be varied. Such a trust is often used to hold a single premium bond.

flexible tenancy Secure tenancy for up to 2½ years which has been so designated under the provisions of Housing Act 1985 s107A. There also provisions under Localism Act 2011 s158 as amended by Housing and Planning Act 2016 s121.

flexible working A change in an employee's working conditions to suit the employee. From 6 April 2003, an employee has the statutory right to *request* flexible working to look after a child or dependant relative. An employer is obliged to have a meeting with the employee and give the request serious consideration. An employer that fails to do so can be fined. There is no obligation on an employer to allow flexible working, although about 80% of such requests are agreed in practice. There is a separate right for a person facing retirement to request flexible working.

flight Journey by aircraft (FA 1994 s24(5)). It may attract air passenger duty or a devolved equivalent.

flip-flop scheme Tax avoidance scheme involving offshore trusts. The essence is to manipulate the arrangements to avoid a liability for capital gains tax. The matter was examined in the case *Burton [2009] TC00156.*

float copy In publishing, a catalogue or similar with a blank cover that can be printed on to produce a finished catalogue with the desired cover. For VAT, it was held that they were zero-rated as books even though they were not finished *(GUS Catalogue Order Ltd. [1987] VTD 2958).*

floating charge Security taken by lender which floats over all the assets and crystallises over particular assets if the security is required. In Scotland, these charges must be registered under Bankruptcy and Diligence etc (Scotland) Act 2007 ss37-45.

flood defences Expenditure on flood defences may be allowable as a tax deduction from 1 January 2015 under ITTOIA 2005 s86A as inserted by FA 2015 Sch 5. The position for a company with an investment business is set out in CTA 2009 s1244A.

floppy disc/disk External data storage. They were made in various sizes until the 3½-inch (90 mm) size became standard from 1984, holding 1.4 MB of data. The disc was now usually supplied in a case which meant that it was no longer floppy. From 2003, computer manufacturers started to discontinue them in favour of CDs and hard drives.

florin Two-shilling coin worth one tenth of a pound, introduced in 1847 as an early first step towards decimal currency. It was redenominated as 10p on decimalisation in 1971, and was demonetised in 1993. The name is given to some other coins, such as gold florins issued by Edward III in 1337, and a gold coin from Aruba which qualifies as a gold investment coin according to VAT Notice 701/12A.

flotation Process of **floating** a company, usually by allowing investors to buy its shares. The extent to which flotation costs are tax-deductible is discussed in HMRC Manual at BIM38240.

flotsam Items accidentally lost at sea, such as in an accident or shipwreck, and washed up by the tide. If unclaimed, they belong to the Crown.

flowers For VAT, flowers are generally standard-rated. An exception is made for flowers that are edible. VAT Notice 701/38 gives a list that HMRC considers is exhaustive. An unsuccessful attempt to add further flowers was made in the case *Branded Garden Products [2017] TC 5604.*

fluid ounce Imperial unit of liquid capacity. It is equal to 1/20 of a pint, 1.7339 cubic inches or 28.413 millilitres.

fluorinated greenhouse gas Gas containing fluorine. The main ones are hydrofluorocarbons, perfluorocarbons and sulphur hexafluoride. As strong greenhouse gases, their use is strictly regulated by SI 2015 No 310. Paras 6 and 7 set out strict import regulations.

fly money Term sometimes used by police for funds used to catch criminals such as in an undercover purchase of drugs or stolen goods. The name is also that of a company that provides foreign currency.

folder Stationery item that is standard-rated when sold alone. It may be zero-rated as a book if the folder itself conveys information or if it is part of a bound file of text (VAT Notice 701/10).

folio Reference number used in accounting records, allowing transaction to be traced from voucher to final accounts and vice versa.

follower notice Notice issued by HMRC to a taxpayer who has used a tax avoidance scheme which has been held to be ineffective in litigation between HMRC and another taxpayer. A follower notice requires the taxpayer (the follower) to pay the tax being avoided. The taxpayer may choose not to do so and continue to litigate the matter. In doing so, the taxpayer risks a penalty under FA 2014 Part 4 which may be imposed in addition to any other penalties. The tax advantage being sought is called the asserted advantage. The arrangements are called the chosen arrangements. There are four conditions that must all be met before HMRC may issue a follower notice:

- Condition A: a tax enquiry must be in progress
- Condition B: the return is made on the basis of an asserted advantage from chosen arrangements where it is clear that those arrangements were made primarily for tax avoidance
- Condition C: HMRC believes there has been a judicial ruling that is relevant to the chosen arrangements
- Condition D: no previous follower notice has been given to the same taxpayer in respect of the same arrangements (FA 2014 s197).

food *Value added tax*

This is generally zero-rated for VAT under VATA 1994 Sch 8 Group 1. However there are many exceptions, such as catering, confectionery, ice cream and crisps. Further details are given in VAT Notice 701/14. The zero-rating can extend to animals bred or used for food, and food for such animals. These details are given in VAT Notice 701/15.

Income tax and corporation tax

For income tax and corporation tax, food consumed while away on business or in entertaining staff is generally tax-deductible for the business and not taxed as a benefit in kind on the recipient. Other costs may not be allowable. The law is set out in ITTOIA 2005s57A. A leading case on this is *Edwards v Warmsley Henshall [1967] 44 TC 431* which is discussed in HMRC Manual at BIM 37925. Food provided for customers comprises entertainment and is usually not tax-deductible.

food additive Something added to food. VAT notice 701/14 states that a food additive may be zero-rated as food if it:

- has some measurable nutritional content
- is used solely or predominantly, in the particular form in which it is supplied, in the manufacture of food
- is not one of the excepted items, as set out in the notice.

food bank Store of food for those not able to afford to buy it commercially. Such banks are often run by churches and charities.

From April 2013, local authorities are required to consider the use of food banks in determining locally administered assistance.

football creditor rule Rule imposed by the Football League that a football team becoming insolvent must give priority to paying its players and managers before other creditors. HMRC failed in the High Court to have this rule declared to be contrary to insolvency law *(HMRC v Football League Ltd. Ch D. The Times 28 June 2012).*

football ground improvements A football pools company that pays for such improvements may deduct that expenditure from trading profits (FA 1990 s126). This was part of a package of pool betting duty reforms that included reducing the duty from 42½% to 40% (FA 1990 s4).

Footsie The popular name for the FT-SE 100 Share Index, the UK stock market's main benchmark index, which measures the daily share price performance of Britain's top 100 public limited companies, ranked by their size.

for [a tax year] ITEPA 2003 s16 and s29 defines the word "for" in the expression "earnings for a tax year" as being any earnings which arose in the whole or part of the year.

forced realisation When a business has to sell assets in the hope of avoiding insolvency. Such a business should not use the going concern concept for its accounts.

for consideration In relation to capital gains tax on a disposal of an interest in settled property, the term "a disposal is for consideration if consideration is given or received by any person for, or otherwise in connection with, any transaction by virtue of which the disposal is effected" (TCGA1992 Sch 4ZA para 3(1)).

forecast Estimate of future income and expenditure. Note that this term differs from a budget which is an executive statement.

Foreign Account Tax Compliant Act (FATCA) American law passed in 2010 to combat tax evasion. It became effective on 1 July 2014. It requires the financial institutions of other countries to reach agreement with the US government to report certain information, failing which the US government imposes a 30% withholding tax. The UK complies under provisions of Finance Act 2013.

Foreign and Commonwealth Office (FCO) Government department formed in 1968 by merging the Foreign Office and Commonwealth Office, though the term Foreign Office was and is still widely used. The department's main purpose is to protect British interests worldwide. The department was renamed the Foreign Commonwealth and Development Office on 2 September 2020 when it took over responsibility for the Department for International Development.

foreign assets For capital gains tax, assets held by a UK taxpayer in a foreign country. A taxpayer who is deprived of such assets may be able to claim relief under TCGA1992 s268B.

foreign benefits Social security benefit, or equivalent, paid from outside the UK. The general rule is that it is taxed according to the provisions of its UK equivalent (ITEPA 2003 from s678).

foreign currency Currency of another country. No foreign currency is legal tender in the UK, but there is no law preventing contracting parties agreeing to accept any currency they wish. Capital gains tax is not payable when an individual dispose of foreign currency acquired for personal use (TCGA1992 s269).

foreign currency bank account (FCBA) Bank account in currency other than UK currency. There are special capital gains tax provisions when a non-domiciled individual makes a remittance to the UK into such an account. The capital gains tax provisions are given in TCGA1992 s252A.

foreign dividend "Any annual payment, interest or dividend payable out of, or in respect of the stocks, funds, shares or securities of:

(a) a body not resident in the United Kingdom, or

(b) a government or public or local authority in a country outside the United Kingdom." (TMA 1970 s18(3G)).

foreign estate In relation to beneficiaries' income from estates in administration, this term is defined in CTA 2009 s936.

foreign exchange Business of exchanging one currency for another. If the money is physically changed to another currency, it is said to be **converted.** If an amount which remains in one currency is simply stated as a value of another currency without being changed, the amount is said to be translated. The tax implications are discussed in HMRC Manual from BIM39500.

foreign holdings In relation to sale of foreign dividend coupons, "means shares outside the United Kingdom that are issued by or on behalf of a non-UK resident body of persons" (CTA 2009 s975(1)).

foreign law Any legal system other than English law which is recognised in that territory. Scots law is regarded as foreign law in English courts. An English court may require evidence as to what the foreign law is. English courts may refuse to uphold foreign law that is against English public policy, penal or revenue laws.

foreign seafaring service Such service can be excluded from the charge to tax and national insurance on termination payments. The main condition is that the employee worked in such service for either three quarters of the whole period of service or for 10 of the last 20 years. The law is found in ITEPA 2003 s414B as inserted by FA 2018 s10(4).

foreign sector of the continental shelf Term defined in CAA 2001 s161A(2) in relation to capital allowances for offshore installations. It is similarly defined for decommissioning relief in CAA 2001 s416ZA(11) as inserted by FA 2013 s95(11).

foreign service In relation to pensions on termination of employment, the term is defined in ITEPA 2003 ss413-414. In relation to lump sums for UK residents from foreign pension schemes, the term is defined in ITEPA 2003 s395C.

foreign service allowance Payment to a government employee to meet additional costs of working overseas. It is specifically exempt from income tax.

foreign spouse Non-UK-domiciled husband or wife or civil partner. A transfer to such a spouse is not wholly exempt from inheritance tax. It is subject to a limit. From 6

April 2013, the amount is the same as the nil rate band (IHTA 1984 s18(2)). Previously, from 9 March 1982, it was £55,000.

foreign war disablement pension "Means any retired pay, pension, allowance or similar payment granted by a country outside the United Kingdom –

(a) in respect of disablement arising from forces' service or war injury; or

(b) corresponding in nature to any retired pay or pension to which section 641 of the ITEPA 2003 applies"

(State Pension Credit Act 2002 s17(1)).

foreign war widow's or widower's pension "Means any pension, allowance or similar payment granted to a widow or widower by the government of a country outside the United Kingdom –

(a) in respect of a death due to forces' service or war injury; or

(b) corresponding in nature to a pension or allowance for a widow or widower under any scheme mentioned in section 641(1)(e) or (f) of the ITEPA 2003"

(State Pension Credit Act 2002 s17(1)).

Forestry Commission Inspection Document Document issued by the Forestry Commission in relation to certain timber and forestry products. Such a certificate may be needed to obtain Customs clearance for importation.

forex Foreign exchange.

forex matching Matching of foreign exchange such as in Midland Marine. The tax implications are discussed in HMRC Manual at BIM 39522.

forfeited deposit Part payment made by a customer in respect of goods and services which the customer then cancels, and where the agreement is that the payment is not refunded to the customer. For VAT purposes, this is treated as a cancellation charge. There is no VAT charged on the deposit as there is no supply. If, exceptionally, VAT has already been charged, this may be reclaimed (VAT notice 700).

forfeiture Loss of property without compensation, such as when illegal goods are seized by Customs or when a final call is not paid on shares.

forfeiture order Order that freezes a bank account or similar under Proceeds of Crime Act 2002 s303Z14.

forfeiture rule Rule that a person can benefit from his or her crime, particularly that a person cannot inherit from someone they have murdered. From 1 February 2012, the law is amended so that their innocent child may inherit.

forgery Any document or item which is not what it seems and is intended to deceive. The nature of forgery is the falseness of the document or item. Currency is said not to be forged but counterfeit. Forgery and counterfeiting are crimes under Forgery and Counterfeiting Act 1981. Forging a die used for stamp duties is a specific offence under Stamp Duties Management Act 1891 s13.

forint Currency of Hungary.

formal disclosure Disclosure made by a taxpayer who is suspected of fraud where HMRC deals with the matter under the Contractual Disclosure Facility. The formal disclosure requires:

- a certified statement of worldwide assets and liabilities
- a certificate of bank accounts operated
- a certificate of credit cards operated
- a certificate of full disclosure.

former approved superannuation fund Any fund which immediately before 6 April 1980 was an approved superannuation fund for the purposes Income and Corporation Taxes Act 1970 s208, that has not been approved for the purposes of Chapter 1 Part 14 Income and Corporation Taxes Act 1988 since 5 April 1980, and has not received any contributions since 5 April 1980.

former civil partner Person with whom someone was in a civil partnership which has subsequently been dissolved or annulled. Such a person may make an application to the court in relation to property and financial matters under Civil Partnership Act 2004 s68.

formerly domiciled resident In relation to deemed domicile "in relation to a tax year, means a person –

(a) who was born in the United Kingdom,
(b) whose domicile of origin was in the United Kingdom,
(c) who was resident in the United Kingdom for that tax year, and
(d) who was resident in the United Kingdom for at least one of the two years immediately preceding that tax year"
(Inheritance Tax Act 1984 s272(b) as inserted by Finance (No 2) Act 2017 s30(8)).

former miner Such a person may receive free coal, free smokeless fuel or an allowance in respect of such coal or fuel. Under ITEPA 2003 s646 such provision is free of income tax on the same basis as a miner.

forward currency contract Agreement to buy or sell currency at a predetermined price on a specified future date. This is the commonest form of hedging the risk from foreign exchange. The tax implications are discussed in HMRC Manual at BIM39523.

fossil fuels Oil, coal and natural gas and similar. They are burned to provide energy. This produces carbon dioxide and other harmful emissions. Various tax provisions have been introduced to encourage moves away from fossil fuels to cleaner forms of energy.

foster parent Person who looks after a child without acquiring legal rights of guardianship. Such a person may have class 3 national insurance national insurance credited (SSCBA 1992 s23A). Some payments to a foster carer are exempt from income tax under ITTOIA 2005 from s803.

FOTRA Free of tax to residents abroad. This is a category of gilts that is exempt from capital gains tax if beneficially held by a non-resident.

four freedoms Under European Union provisions: free movement of goods, capital, services in people within the Single Market.

four Rs Political theory that tax has four functions: revenue, redistribution, repricing and representation.

Fourth Directive This expression usually refers to the European directive on company law that requires all company accounts to be true and fair. This directive was introduced into English law by CA 1981 and has subsequently been consolidated, although the concept of true and fair was introduced into English company law in 1947.

fracking Process of extracting shale gas from rock. The government withdrew its support on 2 November 2019, in effect banning it.

fragmented activities Activities in relation to transactions in land for which there are special provisions in CTA 2010 from s356OH.

fragmented undertaking When the activities of an entity are transferred to more than one entity. For employment law, the Court of Justice of the European Union ruled on 30 March 2020 in a Belgian case that Transfer of Undertakings (Protection of Employment) (TUPE) provisions apply when an employee is transferred to more than one new employer (*ISS Facility Services NV v Sonia Govaerts & Atalian NV. CJEU. [2020] Case C-344/18).*

Framework Convention on Tobacco Control (FCTC) Convention produced by the World Health Organisation in 2003 to control the supply of tobacco. It entered force on 27 February 2005. By 2020, 168 countries had signed, including the UK. Clause 6-14 requires countries to raise tax on tobacco products to reduce demand.

franc Currency for France and different currency for Belgium before they adopted the euro in 2002. Switzerland has the Swiss franc as its currency.

franchise Arrangement whereby an established business (franchisor) grants rights to another business (franchisee) usually including the right to use the franchisor's name. An amount paid to become a franchisee is capital expenditure. An annual fee paid to the franchisor is revenue expenditure.

franked income Income on which tax has been paid, such as for a dividend.

franked investment income (FII) Dividends a company receives from other companies. From 1 July 2009, this includes foreign dividends.

fraud Crime of obtaining money by deception. From 15 January 2007, this is a statutory offence under Fraud Act 2006. Section 2(2) identifies three types of fraud:

- fraud by false representation;
- fraud by failing to disclose information; and
- fraud by abuse of position.

The Act also creates the offences of possession of articles for use in frauds (ibid s6) and making or supplying articles for use in frauds (ibid s7). The Act also creates the offence of participating in fraudulent business carried on by sole trader (ibid s9). The Act increases the penalty for participating in a fraud carried on by a company from seven to ten years imprisonment (ibid s10). The latter offence is contained in CA 1985 Sch 24. The Act creates an offence of obtaining services dishonestly (Fraud Act 2006 s11). An auditor is rarely engaged to report on fraud. If discovered, the auditor's position is as set out in International Standard on Auditing ISA 240.

Fraud Compensation Fund Fund established under Pensions Act 2004 s188 to compensate victims of pension fraud.

fraud compensation payments Payment which may be made from Pension Protection Fund when fraud or similar offence has been committed (Pensions Act 2004 s182).

fraud on a power Old offence of using a power to one's own advantage. Under modern fraud law, this is now abuse of power.

fraud on the minority Improper action of majority of shareholders to the disadvantage of minority holders.

fraudulent misrepresentation Misrepresentation which a person makes knowingly, or without believing it to be true, or who is reckless or careless as to whether the representation is true *(Derry v Peek [1889])*. Fraudulent misrepresentation allows the other party to void the contract and to claim damages. Such misrepresentation is also actionable as the tort of deceit, and may also be the crime of fraud.

fraudulent trading Criminal offence of setting up a company for fraud (Insolvency Act 1986 s213). It is also an offence under company law (CA 2006 from s993).

fraud unravels all Legal expression meaning that a fraud generally has the effect of undoing whatever arrangement for which it was used. There are a few exceptions. For example, a certificate of incorporation of a limited company remains valid even if obtained by fraud.

FRED Financial Reporting Exposure Draft, a draft of a proposed accounting standard.

free assets In relation to non-resident insurance companies, "means the amount by which –

(a) the value of assets of the permanent establishment, exceeds

(b) the aggregate of the permanent establishment's loan capital and technical provisions; and for this purpose, the reinsurer's share of technical provisions is not to be included in determining the assets of the permanent establishment"

(Non-Resident Insurance Companies Regulations SI 2003 No 2715 reg 3(2)).

free assets amount Term used in taxation of insurance companies. It means "the excess of the value of the company's long-term business" over its liabilities of that business plus relevant money debts and shareholders' excess assets (Income and Corporation Taxes Act 1988 s431(2)).

free circulation Description of goods from overseas that may be freely traded after payment of any duties and completion of any other import formalities.

freedom of information Right of an individual to know information held by a public authority. The right is contained in Freedom of Information Act 2000.

HMRC's responsibilities under this Act are set out in Commissioners for Revenue and Customs Act 2005 s23.

freedom of testation Right of a person to write what he or she wants in a will.

freehold Ownership of land and all that is on it, under it and over it.

free of tax Expression describing an amount on which any tax has been paid.

free pay Term once used for amount of wages or salary on which no tax was paid because it was covered by part of the personal allowance as indicated by the employee's tax code (PAYE Regs 2003 reg 2(1)). This term is now called pay adjustment, as K codes *add* an amount to gross pay to give taxable pay.

free play Term used in relation to amusement machines. In general, a free play is not in itself regarded as a prize. This means that pinball machines and similar machines are not within the scope of amusement machine duty. For remote gaming duty on a machine with prizes, a free play is treated as if the player had paid the amount that is waived. This provision applies from 1 August 2017 under FA 2014 s159(4) as amended.

free-standing transfer Term used in relation to sub-sale relief from stamp duty land tax, It applies when A agrees to transfer property to B who makes a pre-completion contract to transfer all or some of it to C.

free trade area Group of countries who have agreed not to charge Customs duties on each other's products.

freezing order Order made by a court that imposes a restriction on accounts or other assets, often to stop them being depleted or sent overseas.

free zone Designated area where imported goods may be stored without payment of Customs duty (CEMA 1979 s100A) or import VAT (VATA 1994 s17).

French roulette This game is specifically listed in Betting and Gaming Duties Act 1981 s13(3) as coming within the scope of gaming licence duty.

frequency of reporting How often an entity produces accounts. FRS 102 section 3.10 requires accounts "at least annually". If accounts are prepared for a period other than a year, the same para requires the accounts to disclose:

- that fact
- the reason for using a different period
- the fact that comparative figures are not directly comparable.

frequent absences For statutory sick pay, frequent short absences for sickness. An employer may seek advice from Medical Services as explained in HMRC booklet E14. While the matter is being investigated, statutory sick pay must continue to be paid to an eligible employee.

freshwater fish For VAT purposes, fish for eating are zero-rated but ornamental and coarse fish are standard-rated. VAT notice 701/15 zero-rates eels, salmon, trout and "other fish recognised as food for human consumption". It standard-rates bream, perch, pike, carp and tench. A definition is provided for a different purpose: "freshwater fish does not include fish of the salmon family, or any kinds of fish which migrate to and from tidal waters, but save as aforesaid includes any fish living in fresh water" (Diseases of Fish Act 1937 s10).

frictionless trade Ability of two countries to trade with a minimum of Customs checks and Customs duties.

friendly society Body that is similar to a mutual insurance company which is run for the benefits of its members (Friendly Society Act 1974 or 1992). Some payments to such a society are subject to a specific tax exemption (ICTA 1988 ss459-466). Life assurance provisions are given in SI 1977 No 1143.

fringe benefit Incidental benefit provided to an employee. This may be taxable as a benefit in kind.

from Imprecise preposition. In accounting, "from 1 January 2021" includes 1 January 2021, whereas In the case *Cartwright v Cormack [1963]*, the first day was held to be excluded. To avoid ambiguity, the expression "on or after" is widely used in tax law.

front end loaded Description of an insurance or investment product where most of the charges are incurred at the start.

frozen In relation to VAT on food, frozen means below 0 degrees Centigrade (32 degrees Fahrenheit). The product does not have to be solid. This decision was made in *Meschia's Frozen Foods. [2000] Ch D. STC 1.* The product (frozen yogurt) was supplied at between -1C and -5C but did not solidify because of its high viscosity.

frozen pension Old term for a pension whose amount does not increase and therefore whose value is eroded by inflation. From 1 July 1988, the pension of an early leaver (a deferred member) must be increased each year by the lower of inflation and 5%.

frozen yogurt This is standard-rated when sold to be eaten while frozen. It is excluded from the zero-rating of food by Value Added Tax 1994 Sch 8 Group 1 Excepted Item 1. If sold frozen but with the intention of being thawed out to eat at room temperature, it may come within the scope of zero-rated food. The exact scope is set out in VAT notice 701/14.

FRS Financial reporting standard of the UK. For accounting periods from 1 January 2015, the series is numbered from FRS 100. This replaces FRS 1 to 30 previously issued.

FRSSE Financial Reporting Standard for Smaller Enterprises. A simpler alternative to financial reporting standards. For accounting periods from 1 January 2016, it is replaced by FRS 102 section 1A.

fructus industriales Latin: fruits of industry. Crops which are the result of human effort, such as cereals and potatoes. The tax implication is discussed in HMRC Manual at BIM35410.

fructus naturales Latin: fruits of nature. A description of crops which grow naturally such as grass and timber. The tax implication is discussed in HMRC Manual at BIM35410.

fruit and nut mixtures Raisins, peanuts and coconut chips are zero-rated; banana chips and pineapple pieces are standard-rated. Where they are supplied together, the VAT should be apportioned (*Smiths Foods Ltd [1983] VTD 1346).* HMRC now accepts that the whole packet may be zero-rated if the standard-rated items comprise less than 25% of the mixture's weight. Further guidance is given in VAT notice 701/14.

fruit bar Edible bar whose main ingredient is pulped fruit. The issue was litigated as to whether they were confectionery, which in turn depended on whether confectionery needs additional sweetening. Eventually the High Court ruled that it does not. So fruit bars were confectionery and standard-rated for VAT *(HMRC v Premier Foods (Holdings) Ltd. Ch D [2008] STC 176.*

fruit juices For VAT, these are standard-rated. They are specifically exempted from the scope of zero-rating for food by Value Added Tax 1994 Sch 8 Group 1 Note 3. The addition of fruit juice to a soft drink is not taken to add sugar for the purposes of soft drinks industry levy (FA 2017 s27(3)).

fruit machine Gambling machine where a lever is pulled to set wheels spinning. If they stop with the same picture of fruit appearing across the wheels, the player wins a multiple of his stake. Some other symbols were used, including a bell on machines made by the Bell Fruit company. The early machines not only used fruit pictures but dispensed small pieces of fruit as prizes.

frustration of contract Where a contract cannot be completed for reasons beyond the control of a contracting party. The legal consequence is to void the contract and put the parties in the position as if they had not made the contract. This is a principle of common law and Law Reform (Frustration of Contracts) Act 1943. The tax provisions follow the legal position.

FT 30 Index The ordinary share index produced by the Financial Times based on a representative sample of 30 leading UK companies, not necessarily the largest. The index was started in 1935, making it the oldest continuous share index in the UK, and one of the oldest in the world. It was the main index until the FTSE all share index was produced in 1962 and FT-SE 100 index in 1984.

FTE group skilled employee number For the definition of a **knowledge-intensive company** for enterprise investment scheme and other schemes, this term is defined in ITA 2007 s252A as inserted by Finance (No 2) Act 2015 Sch 5. For venture capital trusts, the same definition is used in ITA 2007 s331A as inserted by Finance (No 2) Act 2015 Sch 6.

FT-SE 100 Leading index of share prices of 100 leading companies. It is calculated by the Financial Times. It started in 1984 at 1000.

FT-SE 250 Index of the stock market for companies from 101 to 350 on the list of largest. Note that it is *not* the 250 largest companies.

FT-SE 350 Combined index of FT-SE 100 and FT-SE 250, giving an index of the largest 350 companies.

FTSE Fledgling Index produced by the Financial Times of companies listed on the London Stock Exchange that are too small to qualify for the All Share index.

FTSE Small Cap Index produced by the Financial Times of companies included in the FTSE Actuaries All Share Index but which are not in the FT-SE 350 list.

fuel benefit Taxable benefit of an employer providing free fuel for private use by an employee. There may also be VAT implications.

fuel oil Heavy oil which contains in solution an amount of asphaltenes of not less than 0.5%, or which contains less than 0.5% but not less than 0.1% of asphaltenes and has a closed flash point not exceeding 150°C (Hydrocarbon Oil Regulations SI 1973 No 1311 reg 2).

fuel poverty Inability of a person to afford sufficient fuel or energy. The government may make schemes to address fuel poverty under Energy Act 2010 s9. Provisions include winter fuel allowance and cold weather payments.

fuel substitute Anything used as a replacement for petrol or diesel for vehicles. It is subject to hydrocarbon oil duty on the same basis as the fuel it replaces (HODA 1979 s6A).

full age When someone is legally regarded as an adult. From 1 January 2010 this is reduced from 21 to 18 (Family Law Reform Act 1969 s1).

full container load (FCL) Quantity of imported goods that fills at least one whole shipping container. This is a factor in calculating the VAT adjust element of the delivery element of the cost of importing goods.

full indexation When a figure, particularly a pension, is fully linked to increases in the rate of inflation, as against limited price indexation.

full payment submission Monthly, or sometimes quarterly, submission made to HMRC under the PAYE system giving a full analysis of how much each employee has earned, and how much tax and national insurance has been deducted.

full-time employee For the purposes of loans for employee-controlled companies, the term means "an individual the greater part of whose time is spent working as an employee or director of the company or of a 51% subsidiary of the company" (ITA 2007 s396(5)).

full time equivalent (fte) Measure of the size of a workforce where a part-time worker is counted as a fraction. Fte is used for many tax-advantaged schemes for smaller businesses.

full-time minister In relation to accommodation expenses, means "a person in full-time employment as a minister of a religious denomination" (ITEPA 2003 s290(5)).

full-time working director For the purpose of calculating the tax on benefits in kind, "a director who is required to devote substantially the whole of his time to the service of the company in a managerial or technical capacity" (ITEPA 2003 s67(3)).

full-time working farmer Condition that allows land to qualify for 100% agricultural property relief from inheritance tax where land has been continuously let from before 10 March 1981, under the provisions of Inheritance Tax Act 1984 s116(2)(b).

fully paid Description of a share which has been fully paid for. Sometimes new issues are paid in instalments known as calls.

fulminate of mercury Substance included in the list of explosives for which there are special Customs provisions (Explosives Act 1875 s3(1)). This description extends to fulminates of other metals.

functional currency Currency in which the accounts are prepared. Currency of the primary economic environment in which the entity operates (FRS 102 glossary).

functions (of HMRC) In relation to HMRC, FA 1989 s182 apportions these between:

- tax functions
- tax credit functions
- child trust fund functions
- social security functions.

This category applies in relation to the disclosure of information to HMRC and the penalties for non-disclosure. HMRC has other functions (e.g. national minimum wage, rateable values and Customs controls) that are covered by separate legislation.

fundamental principles For tax professionals, these are stated to be integrity, objectivity, professional competence and due care, confidentiality and professional behaviour.

funded company Company which is funded by another (ICTA 1988 s209(11)).

funding bond A bond, stock, share or similar security or other certificate of indebtedness. Businesses which pay interest on loans may using a funding bond rather than pay cash. The use of a funding bond has tax consequences. The main one is that the bond is treated as a payment of interest in cash to the value of the bond when issued. This usually means that 20% tax must be deducted. The tax provisions for a funding bond are found in ITTOIA 2005 s380 as amended. This basically requires the bond to be treated as a cash payment with the usual tax deducted at source. The income tax treatment is set out in ITA 2007 from s939.

funding lease Term used to mean what is generally treated as a finance lease, as defined in tax law. The main consequence is that any capital allowance is claimed by the lessee, not the lessor.

fund in medio In Scots law," the property or money in the hands of the holder of the fund (money or property) in an action of multiplepoinding" (Judiciary of Scotland website glossary).

fund of funds (FOF) A collective fund, such as a unit trust, which invests in other funds. They have the advantage of very wide risk-spreading but can have the disadvantage of two sets of charges. In relation to the taxation of derivatives, the term is given a specific meaning in ITA 2007 sFZO(5) as inserted by FA 2016 s37.

fund raising Any activity primarily conducted to generate income such as for a charity or voluntary body. A business that does this commercially is regulated by Charities Act 1992 ss59-64. A fund-raising event by a charity is exempt from

VAT under VATA 1994 Sch 9 Group 12. The same definition exempts such proceeds from income tax under ITA 2007 s529.

funds Imprecise term that means the liquid resources available to a person or business either generally or in a specific context. A statutory definition is given for terrorist assets, where the term is defined to mean "financial assets and benefits of every kind, including (but not limited to) —

(a) cash, cheques, claims on money, drafts, money orders and other payment instructions;

(b) deposits with relevant institutions or other persons, balances on accounts, debts and debt obligations;

(c) publicly and privately traded securities and debt instruments, including stocks and shares, certificates representing securities, bonds, notes, warrants, debentures and derivative products;

(d) interest, dividends and other income on or value accruing from or generated by assets;

(e) credit, rights of set-off, guarantees, performance bonds and other financial commitments;

(f) letters of credit, bills of lading and bills of sale;

(g) documents providing evidence of an interest in funds or financial resources;

(h) any other instrument of export financing"

(Terrorist Asset-Freezing etc Act 2010 s39(1)).

funds in court Money held by a court for the benefit of someone, usually while beneficial ownership is being litigated. For capital gains tax purposes, the court is regarded as a nominee (TCGA1992 s61).

funeral ***Definition***

Arrangement in connection with the death of someone, including any ceremony considered appropriate. Typically this comprises a religious or secular ceremony followed by a reception or wake. The first duty of the executor or administrator is to dispose of the body in accordance with the law. This includes allowing for removal of bodily organs.

Deduction from estate

The reasonable cost of a funeral is deductible from the taxable value of the estate (IHTA 1984 s172), as is the cost of a tombstone or gravestone (SP 7/87) and reasonable expenditure on flowers (HMRC Manual at IHTM10372). The reasonable cost of refreshments for mourners is also allowed (IHTM10377). A reasonable amount for mourning by the family was allowed by extra-statutory concession F1. This was withdrawn from 9 December 2010, but HMRC now takes the view that is part of the cost of a funeral expenses allowed by IHTA 1984 s172. Traditionally this meant mourning clothes and mourning draperies for the house, both of which HMRC considers "should now be rare" (IHTM10375) unless it can be shown that it was a custom. Travelling and accommodation expenses of mourners are not tax-deductible.

The word "reasonable" depends on the standard of living of the deceased. In practice, this appears to be largely uncontested by HMRC. It is known that expenses of lavish funerals have been allowed.

In Scotland, before 1 November 2016, a widow (but not a widower) and children could claim for mourning clothes and an aliment to cover bills until the estate was distributed. This was a common law right that is abolished under Succession (Scotland Act) 2016.

Benefits

A person responsible for a funeral who is receiving universal credit or other means-tested benefit may claim a funeral expenses payment in England or Wales and Northern Ireland, or a funeral support payment in Scotland.

The amount of the benefit is the cost of the funeral with some items capped in amount.

Funeral support payment in Scotland is payable under Social Security (Scotland) Act 2018 s34 from 2019. It is a single payment. The payments are exempt from income tax under ITEPA 2003 s677(1).

Children

The funeral of a child under 18 or a stillborn baby after 24 weeks of pregnancy is paid by the state from the children's funeral fund. If the parent is an employee, he or she may be eligible for statutory parental bereavement leave and statutory parental bereavement pay.

funeral expense assistance Money or other assistance that may be provided in Scotland from 2019 in additional to other UK benefits (Social Security (Scotland) Act 2018 s34. It is exempt from income tax (ITEPA 2003 s677(1)).

funeral expenses payment Social security benefit that may be claimable by someone in receipt of a means-tested benefit.

funeral plan Savings and insurance scheme which a person takes out to fund their own funeral. In 2019, the Competition and Markets Authority investigated these schemes.

For VAT, the sale of the plan is usually exempt as a supply of burial. Commission paid to an agent is standard-rated. If the plan takes the form of insurance, that is exempt as a supply of a financial service. More details are given in VAT Notice 701/32.

fungible assets Assets that are indistinguishable from each other, such as a quantity of oil or gas, or loose items such as screws and washers.

furlong Measure of length, still used in horse racing. It is equal to 220 yards, 660 feet, 201.168 metres or one eighth of a mile.

furlough Leave of absence from duty. The term was widely used in 2020 for the Coronavirus Job Retention Scheme.

furnace fuel Hydrocarbon oil used in a furnace. **Light oil** that is so used may attract a rebate of excise duty under Hydrocarbon Oil Duties Act 1979 s14.

furnished holiday lettings (FHL) Activity that has special tax provisions reflecting its nature as both a trade and investment. It is generally taxed as a trade (CTA 2010 s65; ITTOIA 2005 s323). This means that many expenses may be deducted from taxable profits. Other tax provisions are given in FA 2011 Sch 14 and CAA 2001 s17(1). From 6 April 2012, The two main conditions are that the property is available for commercial letting for at least 210 days a year, and is actually let for 105 days.

Furniss v Dawson Leading tax case heard in House of Lords in 1984. It broadly ignores intervening steps in a series of steps that have no commercial purpose other than tax avoidance.

fusel oil Oil produced in the distillation of spirits. A distiller must measure the quantity and strength of fusel oil. If below 8.7%, it is exempt from alcoholic liquor duty. HMRC must be notified if the distiller wishes to use fusel oil as fuel.

future economic benefits Part of a definition of an asset in accounting. An item must be capable of producing a future economic benefit, directly or indirectly, to be an asset.

Future Fund Scheme established on 20 May 2020 by British Business Bank to provide coronavirus-based loans under FA 2020 s110(5).

Future Revenue Benefit (FRB) From 2013, a factor that must be considered by HMRC in dealing with a tax dispute. It is a calculation that is sensibly based on likely behaviour of the amount of revenue that may be realised in the next five years if the disputed matter is resolved in HMRC's favour.

futures Obligation to buy or sell a specified amount of a commodity, currency or financial instrument at a specified price on a stipulated future date. There are special tax provisions.

GAAP Generally accepted accounting principles. Accounts used to prepare tax computations must either be GAAP-compliant, or the computation must contain adjustments that have the same effect.

GAAP-compliant accounts For corporation tax, means "accounts drawn up in accordance with generally accepted accounting principles" (CTA 2009 s716(4)). CTA 2009 s717 says that provisions of the Act apply even if the accounts are not GAAP-compliant; s718 deals with compliance for group accounts. This term is also used in relation to restitution interest in CTA 2009 s357YF(4).

GAAR From March 2012, general anti-abuse rule (before which it meant general anti-avoidance rule). In 2013, a GAAR panel is established to rule on whether an avoidance scheme is legally effective.

Gabon West African state. Its currency is the CFA franc. The UK has no double taxation treaty.

GAD tables The Government Actuary's Department Tables on a single life expectancy basis. Mortality tables are given in section 3 of this dictionary.

gain Increase in economic benefits that meet the definition of income but is not revenue (FRS 102 section 2,25(b)). The distinction is that income or profit is subject to income tax whereas a gain is subject to capital gains tax.

gain buying Practice whereby a company with chargeable gains bought companies with allowable losses to offset them. It was made ineffective in 1998.

gains In accounting, any increase in economic benefits that is not revenue.

gallery Place for displaying art. A gallery may be able to have VAT refunded under VATA s33A. A gallery may also be eligible for museums and galleries relief. Details are given in section 3 of this dictionary.

Gambia West African state. Its currency is the dalasi of 100 butut. The UK has a double taxation convention of 1980.

gambling Activity of staking a sum on an uncertain outcome in the hope of winning a larger sum (Gambling Act 2005 s3). Such an activity may be subject to betting and gaming duties. Gambling is not a trade *(Graham v Green [1925] 9 TC 309),* but being a bookmaker is *(Partridge v Mallandaine [1886] 18QBD276).* Gambling activities may be subject to betting and gaming duties. A definition for VAT is given in VATA 1994 s23(6).

gambling levy Sum voluntarily paid by betting companies to charities that deal with gambling addiction. In 2019, companies said they would increase the levy from 0.1% to 1.0% of profits.

gaming Form of gambling in which all participants have an equal chance of winning. Bingo is an example. Such activities above a limit are subject to gaming duty from 2009. The VAT position is explained in VAT Notice 701/29.

gaming duty Tax on gaming activities which replaced gaming licence duty in 2009. It is subject to betting and gaming duties.

gaming machine "A machine which is designed or adapted for use by individuals to gamble (whether or not it can also be used for other purposes)" (Gambling Act 2005 s235(1)). S235(2) excludes from the scope ordinary computers, telephones and other communication equipment, machines for placing bets, lottery ticket dispensers, bingo machines and machines for games of chance. For VAT purposes, it is defined as a machine where these conditions are satisfied:

(a) it is constructed or adapted for playing a game of chance by means of it; and

(b) a player pays to play the machine (except where he has the opportunity to play payment-free as a result of having previously played successfully), either by inserting a coin or token into the machine or in some other way; and

(c) the element of chance in the game is provided by means of the machine (VATA 1994 Sch 9 Group 4 Note 3).

Provisions on how much VAT is payable are given in VATA 1994 s23.

gangmaster Person who looks after a team of workers formed for a particular purpose, such as harvesting or cockle picking. From 2004, gangmasters must be registered with the Gangmasters Licensing Authority (Gangmasters (Licensing) Act 2004 s4(2)).

garage Building designed to store a car, regardless of whether it is used for that purpose. For council tax, a garage is taxable if part of a dwelling or if free-standing with a floor area of at least 25 square metres.

garden Land attached to or near a dwelling for its enjoyment. A garden is regarded as part of a dwelling for main residence relief from capital gains tax for up to half a hectare (about 1.2 acres) or a larger size if consistent with the size of the residence (TCGA 1992 s222(2)).

Garden House Court case of 1970 that addressed the "why me?" issue. It was not a tax case. The Court of Appeal held that there was no unfairness when only some offenders were prosecuted.

garnishee order Order requiring a third party to pay money to settle a court debt. Such orders are now more commonly known as third party debt orders.

gas For purposes of hydrocarbon oil duty, a substance is a gas if that is its state of matter at 15°C and 1013.25 millibars pressure (SI 1972 No 846 and other sources). For VAT, gas is reduced rated if supplied as domestic fuel (VATA 1984 Sch 7A Group 1) and zero-rated if oxygen or an anaesthetic gas.

gas oil For hydrocarbon oil duty, a heavy oil as defined by the temperatures at which it distils (HODA 1979 s1(5)).

Gateway A 12-digit number allocated by HMRC to a taxpayer to allow him or her to access their tax records and other government facilities.

gateway test Test that compares UK net debt with worldwide gross debt for the purposes of imposing the worldwide debt cap on tax relief.

GATT General Agreement on Tariffs and Trades. International forum that seeks to reduce Customs duties and other export restrictions between countries. It was formed in 1948.

GAYE Give As You Earn.

gazumping Practice of offering a higher price to a seller (particularly of houses) to force the seller to break an agreement with another person.

gearing Ratio of debt to equity in funding a company. A highly-geared company tends to reward shareholders when profits are high and penalise them when profits are low.

gelatine For VAT, gelatine is zero-rated when supplied for use in food but standard-rated for purposes such as photography (VAT notice 701/14).

gender pay gap information Information legally required by an employer on the difference between rates of pay for men and women. It was introduced in April 2017. It applies to employers of more than 250 employees.

gender reassignment When a person changes sex under Gender Recognition Act 2004. This change is effective from the date of the gender recognition certificate for all purposes, including tax and social security. It is illegal to discriminate against someone because they have had gender reassignment (Equality Act 2010 s7).

gender recognition certificate Certificate that states a person is now legally of a different sex for all purposes, including tax and social security (Gender Recognition Act 2004).

general anti-avoidance rule Tax provision that would generally disallow tax avoidance schemes without the need for separate legislation for each scheme. A GAAR has frequently been proposed but not yet introduced, with some exceptions during wartime. Provisions for the rule in Scotland are set out in Revenue Scotland and Tax Powers Act 2014 from s62.

general beer duty Alcoholic liquor duty charged on beer with a strength between 2.8% and 7.5% (ALDA 1979 s36).

general client account deposits This term is defined for income tax purposes in ITA 2007 s863.

General Commissioners Lay people, independent from Inland Revenue, similar to magistrates who heard tax appeals. In 2009, they were replaced by tax tribunals.

general data processing requirements (GDPR) Stricter data requirements that took effect in the UK from 25 May 2018. It replaces previous data protection regulations from 1995. The basis of the law is EU directive 2016/680 of 27 April 2016 and regulation 2016/679 of the same date. It applies the same rules to all members of the EU and EEA. In the UK, the main law is Data Protection Act 2018. Non-compliance can lead to a fine of up to €20 million or 4% of global turnover.

general ledger Ledger which records an organisation's income and expenditure which is not recorded in any other ledger. The term sometimes is used to mean the nominal ledger.

general legacy Legacy of identifiable but not specified property.

general lien Legal right to hold someone else's goods until they have paid a debt. For example, a repairer may hold goods until the repair bill is paid.

generally accepted accounting principles (GAAP) Either UK accounting standards or international accounting standards. All accounts used for tax computations must comply with GAAP (ITTOIA 2005 s25; CTA 2009 s56).

general partner Member of a partnership whose liability is not limited.

general power "A power or authority enabling the person by whom it is exercisable to appoint or dispose of property as he thinks fit" (Inheritance Tax Act 1984 s5(2)).

general purpose EBT "Trust set up to provide employee with benefits other than

- share-related benefits under employee share schemes set up to give employees a stake in the company or group by which they are employed
- pension and other benefits under retirement benefit schemes
- accident benefits
- healthcare benefits."

(Inspector's Manual at BIM44535).

The manual notes that such EBTs may be established for commercial reasons but that many are established for tax avoidance.

general purpose financial statement "Financial statements directed to the general financial information needs of a wide range of users who are not in a position to demand reports tailored to meet their particular information needs" (FRS 102 glossary). One of two types of general purpose financial report identified by Statement of Principles for Financial Reporting.

A general purpose financial statement is prepared by the entity for general use. It includes the annual accounts, interim statements and the suchlike. Most statements produced by an entity are general purpose financial statements.

For a limited liability company such statements would be: a balance sheet, a profit and loss account, a statement of recognised gains and losses and a cash flow statement.

general reserve Money set aside to be used in the future to meet unforeseen eventualities of any kind. Money side aside for a particular purpose is called a special reserve.

general undertaking Undertaking signed by directors of a company which is applying for listing on the Stock Exchange. The directors undertake to comply with the Exchange's listing requirements.

generating income from land "Means exploiting an estate, interest or right in or over land as a source of income or other receipts" (CTA 2009 s207(1); ITTOIA 2005 s266(1)).

generation skipping Legal method of reducing inheritance tax by leaving assets to grandchildren rather than to children.

gensaki Japanese bond market where there are agreements for the sellers to repurchase the bonds at less than 12 months' notice.

gentleman's agreement Agreement that is not a legal contract but is binding in honour only.

genuine commercial reasons Provision that excuses a taxpayer from anti-avoidance legislation if he or she can show there was a good reason for an action.

genuine triable issue Real dispute that must be resolved before a bankruptcy can proceed.

geometric mean Average calculated by multiplying numbers together and taking the root equal to how many numbers have been multiplied.

The geometric mean of 2, 3 and 7 is thus the cube root of 2 x 3 x 7, or $\sqrt[3]{42}$, which equals 3.476 (rounded). Note that the arithmetic mean would simply add them and divide by 3, giving 4. The FT-SE 100 index and consumer prices index both use a geometric mean. It is regarded as a better indication of trends than arithmetic mean.

George Cross Award for bravery. Payments of pension or annuity in respect of the award are free of income tax (ITEPA 2003 s638).

Georgia Republic that became independent from Russia in 1995. Its currency is the lari of 100 tetri. The UK has a double taxation agreement of 2004, amended by a protocol of 2010. There is also a US state called Georgia.

geothermal energy Heat derived from the sub-surface of the planet. For capital allowance purposes, it is treated as a mineral deposit (CAA 2001 394(3)).

Germany European country and member of the European Union, for which purpose the island of Heligoland and Büsingen are excluded. Since 1990, Germany includes the territory previously known as East Germany. The country was an enemy state of the UK during the world wars of 1914-18 and 1939-45. There are still provisions relating to enemy territory from the second war. There are also special tax provisions relating to payments of Nazi compensation. The currency is the euro of 100 cents from 2002, before which it was the Deutschmark. The UK has a double taxation convention of 2010. The UK also has a memorandum of understanding on termination payments of 2010, a memorandum of understanding on Article 26 mutual agreement procedure, and a bank levy double taxation agreement of 2011. There is also an amending protocol of 2010 that has not come into force.

Ghana West African state. Its currency is the cedi of 100 pesewas. The UK has a double taxation convention of 1993. The previous double taxation treaty of 1977 was regarded as having come into force on 6 June 1978. In 1991 it was discovered that Ghana had not ratified the treaty which had the effect of rendering it ineffective as a putative treaty in the UK and in effect reinstating the treaty of 1947. For the period between 1977 and 1991, Inland Revenue allowed UK taxpayers the choice of the more favourable provisions.

ghost In tax, a person not known to the tax authorities.

Gibraltar British Overseas Territory at the southern tip of the Iberian peninsula. It has been British territory since 1713. Gibraltar left the European Union on 31 December 2020 with the UK, but on the same day it was agreed that Gibraltar would become part of the EU Schengen area. The currency is the Gibraltar pound of 100 pence which is kept at par with UK currency. UK currency is also used as legal tender. Many commemorative coins are minted which are legal tender in Gibraltar. Rates of tax are low, with particularly low rates for companies under a law enacted in 1967. In the early 2000s, many UK bookmakers and online gaming companies relocated to Gibraltar to avoid UK betting taxes.

The UK has a tax treaty signed on 15 October 2019, which came into force on 24 March 2020.

Gibraltar Order Common name for Financial Services and Markets Act 2000 (Gibraltar) Order SI 2001 No 3084.

Gibraltar pound Currency of Gibraltar.

gift Something gratuitously given to another person. A business gift is generally tax deductible if (from 2001) it is worth no more than £50, contains a conspicuous advertisement and is not food, drink or tobacco (ITTOIA 2005 s47; CTA 2009 s1300).

A gift from a third party to an employee is not taxable up to (from 2003) £250. A gift of an asset can be a disposal for capital gains tax.

VAT can be charged on supplied gifts if they exceed (from 2012) £50 per gift (VATA 1994 Sch 4 para 5). Gifts of large amounts during a person's lifetime can trigger a liability to inheritance tax unless the donor lives for another seven years (IHTA 1984 s165).

Gift Aid Scheme that allows a charity to reclaim basic rate income tax paid from a donation from a taxpayer (ITA 2007 ss413-430). This generally increases the gift by 25% (which is 20% grossed up), even in Scotland where a different tax rate may apply. A higher rate taxpayer may claim tax relief at the higher rates. From 6 April 2000, there is no maximum or minimum amount for a donation.

gift and loan trust Discretionary trust where a small sum is settled but a large sum is lent. It is used to shelter significant capital growth from inheritance tax.

gift inter vivos Gift made during a person's lifetime.

gift token Voucher which may be exchanged for goods in a shop or range of shops. Under PAYE, if the token can be exchanged for cash or for something which is readily exchangeable for cash, provision by an employer is treated as payment in cash and is subject to income tax under PAYE and class 1 national insurance. If the token can only be exchanged for goods, the employee may be liable to pay income tax on its cost (unless covered by a PAYE settlement agreement or under the Taxes Award Scheme), and the employer is liable to pay class 1B national insurance.

gill Imperial unit of liquid capacity, equal to one quarter of a pint, 34.677 cubic inches or 568.26 millilitres. Until 1971, certain alcoholic drinks were dispensed as submultiples of a gill. The word has other meanings.

Gill and Gill Court case of 2003 that led to a significant reduction in the use of civil CIF procedures for investigating suspected tax fraud, and led to changes in practice. Its citation is *R v Gill and Gill [2003] STC 1229, [2003] EWCA Crim 2256, [2003] 4 All ER 681.* Gill and Gill was a clothing partnership run by two brothers. In 1995, Inland Revenue interviewed them under the Hansard procedure then in operation. The brothers denied omissions from their trading figure. They were charged with cheating the public revenue. At their trial, Inland Revenue used material from these interviews. The brothers were convicted and imprisoned. They appealed on the grounds that the Hansard evidence was inadmissible. The Court of Appeal held that the brothers should have been cautioned and the interviews recorded. However, the failure to do so did not provide grounds for overturning the convictions as there was still procedural fairness.

Gillespie ruling Court decision that an employee on maternity leave is entitled to the benefit of a general pay rise awarded during her leave. This was given statutory effect by SI 1996 No 1335.

gilt An abbreviation for gilt-edged securities. These are bonds, loans etc issued by the UK government or UK local authorities and are generally considered to be one of the safer forms of investment.

Although the interest rate on the underlying value and the price at maturity are guaranteed, the price will vary during the lifetime of a gilt; so there is some element of risk.

gilt strips The separation of a government-issued security into its individual cash flows. The word STRIPS is an acronym for Separate Trading of Registered Interest and Principal Securities. The tax provisions are set out in CTA 2009 s401. It is discussed in HMRC Manual at CFM37150.

ginger For VAT, the zero-rating for food applies to "ginger preserved in syrup, drained ginger or dusted ginger... as long as it is not held out for sale as confectionery".

Standard-rating applies to "crystallised, sugared or chocolate covered ginger" (VAT notice 701/14).

Gini coefficient Statistical measure of wage inequality. It is expressed as a number between 0 and 1 where 0 means everyone earns the same, and 1 means one person earns the whole nation's wealth. Most developed nations have a coefficient between 0.3 and 0.6.

Girobank Bank established in 1968 by the Post Office. In 2003, it was taken over by Alliance and Leicester. Some of its original functions are now provided by National Savings and Investments.

Give As You Earn Another name for payroll giving.

glacé fruits These are brought within the definition of confectionery by Value Added Tax 1994 Sch 8 Group 1 Note (5). This means they are standard-rated for VAT.

glasses Glasses provided by an employer for someone who works with a computer screen may be exempt as a benefit under ITEPA 2003 s320A.

global accounting Method of accounting for many items of small value such as sweets or nails. There is a special VAT procedure for dealers in stamps or coins.

globe Spherical representation of the planet and the countries on it. For VAT purposes, a globe is not regarded as a map and therefore is not zero-rated under VATA 1994 Sch 8 Group 3, according to VAT notice 701/10.

Gloucester Railway Carriage Leading case whose full name is *Gloucester Railway Carriage and Waggon Company Ltd v CIR [1925] 12TC720* on whether an activity comprises one or two trading activities. The company unsuccessfully argued that hiring railway wagons was a separate trade from making them. The matter is discussed in HMRC Manual at BIM33030.

gm/km Grams per kilometre. This is used to measure carbon dioxide emissions from cars for the purpose of vehicle excise duty and income tax on company cars.

going concern Fundamental accounting basis that an entity will continue in being for the foreseeable future. This is assumed unless the contrary is explicitly stated. The UK standard is FRS 102 section 3.9.

gold Naturally occurring precious metal. Its uses include bullion for storing wealth. Gold coins held for investment are exempt from VAT (VATA 1994 Sch 8 Group 10). Further guidance is provided in VAT Leaflets 701/21 and 701/21A.

gold coin Coin made from gold, and now used solely as a store of value. Gold has been a medium of exchange from earliest times. In Britain gold coins ceased to be used for general circulation during the first world war (1914-18) when replaced by banknotes. Gold coins are still produced for bullion purposes. At least eleven gold coins remain legal tender: the sovereign, half sovereign and gold £2 and £5 coins, plus the seven Britannia coins. Royal Mint has also produced ordinary coins in gold for collectors. For VAT, a gold coin is exempt as an investment gold coin if its purity is at least 900 parts per 1000 and it is one of a long list of bullion coins produced on EU list C291/23. British coins on this list include sovereigns and half sovereigns, Britannia coins, gold £2 and £5 coins and specially minted gold 50p pieces. Before 1 April 1982, gold coins were exempt simply if they were legal tender in the country of issue. Details are provided in VAT notice 701/12A. Gold coins more than 100 years old may benefit from a VAT scheme for antiques.

golden brick Informal term for the VAT rule that a new residential development must have at least one course of bricks laid for a sale to be zero-rated as a residence rather than exempt as a supply of land. The position is explained in the Tax Manual at VCONST03540.

golden handshake Payment to an employee on leaving. This can be free of income tax and national insurance up to £30,000 under certain conditions. It is properly called a termination payment.

golden hello Payment to an individual to persuade a person to become an employee. HMRC Manual at EIM00700 states that this is taxable as employment income under ITEPA 2003 s62. Cases on this include *Glantre Engineering Ltd v Goodhand [1982] 56TC165* concerning an accountant, and *Shilton v Wilmshurst [1991] 64TC78* concerning a footballer.

At EIM00710, this position is qualified when the golden hello is a payment to give up a right, which is not taxable as employment income. In *Jarrold v Boustead [1964] 41TC70*, a signing-on fee paid by a Rugby League club to a Rugby Union player was held to be compensation for losing amateur status. (The rules of Rugby have since changed.) HMRC state that golden hellos are also subject to class 1 national insurance, though some commentators question the correctness of this interpretation.

golden rule One of the rules for interpreting an Act of Parliament. It basically states that words are to be given their ordinary dictionary meaning *(River Wear Commissioners v Adamson [1877})* unless it leads to absurdity *(Hallamshire Estates Ltd v Walford [2004] SpC 412).*

gold grain Pebble-like pieces of gold, about 3mm in diameter and supplied in various purities. It is used to make jewellery. From 29 November 1995, this is included within the scope of gold for VAT purposes.

gold standard International monetary system where the value of currency and other assets is based on the value of gold. Great Britain adopted the standard between 1821 and 1914, and between 1925 and 1931. The UK permanently left the gold standard in 1931. Most countries were on the gold standard between 1894 and 1914. In the USA, the gold standard was the basis of coinage under their Coinage Act 1873. The USA abandoned the gold standard in 1933.

golf club Whether one is a mutual trade is discussed in HMRC Manual at BIM24350. There have also been several VAT cases about golf clubs.

GOMC Gas oil marker concentrate, a composite marking solution that turns oil red. Such oil is subject to a lower rate of hydrocarbon oil duty and must not be used as ordinary road fuel.

Gomez case The European Court of Justice decision in *Maria Paz Merino Gómez v Continental Industrias del Caucho SA [2004]*. This established that a woman is entitled to take her annual leave after any period of maternity leave.

Good Friday Friday immediately before Easter which commemorates the crucifixion of Christ. It is a bank holiday (Banking and Financial Dealings Act 1971 Sch 1).

goods Tangible items. It is usually distinguished from services. Under general law, goods are chattels except for money, legal actions and items attached to the ground (such as unharvested crops). Statutes provide limited definitions for particular purposes. Factors Act 1889 s1(3) defines goods as including "wares and merchandise". CEMA 1979 s1(1) defined goods as including "stores and baggage".

For VAT, a distinction is made between goods and services, for which purpose goods need not tangible. So electricity is regarded as goods. In practice, the distinction is of little practical relevance as the rates and most of the rules are the same. The main areas of difference relate to claiming input tax on pre-registration acquisitions, and the place of supply for some international services.

goods vehicle "Vehicle of a construction primarily suited for the conveyance of goods or burden of any description" (ITEPA 2003 s115(2) and s235(6)). For reimbursement of business journeys by car, "means a mechanically propelled road vehicle which –

(a) is of a construction primarily suited for the conveyance of goods or burden of any description, and

(b) is not a motor cycle" (ITTOIA 2005 s94G(3).

goodwill ***Accounting***

Value of a business in excess of its net assets. Generally, accounts only allow goodwill to be shown on a balance sheet when acquired, such as when paid to take over a business.

"Future economic benefits arising from assets that are not capable of being individually identified and separately recognised" (FRS 102 glossary).

Goodwill is an area where UK and international accounting standards tend to diverge. UK standards generally want goodwill removed from the balance sheet, whereas international accounting standards tend to want it shown.

Tax

The tax treatment follows the accounting treatment: "in this Part "goodwill" has the meaning it has for accounting purposes (and includes internally-generated goodwill" (CTA 2009 s715(3)).

Goodwill includes internally generated goodwill, but this must accord with accounting standards. Goodwill is not recognised for tax purposes just because it appears in the accounts *(Greenbank Holidays Ltd v HMRC [2011] UKUT B11).*

For tax purposes, a leading authority in goodwill was given in the case *IRC v Muller & Co Margarine Ltd [1901]:* "it is a thing very easy to describe, very difficult to define. It is the benefit and advantage of a good name, reputation and connection of a business. It is the attractive force which brings in custom. It is the one thing which distinguishes an old-established business from a new business at its first stage".

HMRC's guidance on goodwill changed in September 2008. Previously goodwill was classified as personal, inherent or free. Under a Practice Note issued on 30 January 2009, HMRC now considers that goodwill should be separated from other intangible assets. The Note sets out how this should be done. This is particularly significant when an existing business is incorporated by its current owner.

The change follows the decision in the case *Balloon Promotions Ltd v Wilson [2006] SSCD 167* which abolished the zoological classification of cat, dog and rabbit. There is also guidance in Tax Bulletin 76.

Writing down

From 2002, goodwill may generally be written down at 4% a year against tax. From 3 December 2014, tax relief was not allowed for internally generated goodwill, such as when a sole trader converted to a limited company.

From 8 July 2015, tax relief was denied on goodwill from any source. From 1 April 2019, the 4% is replaced by 6.5% when goodwill is acquired with intellectual property assets. (This is a very brief summary of complicated provisions.)

Good Work Plan Document produced by the government in December 2018 in response to the **Taylor Report** on working patterns. It notes that there are three status of worker for employment law (employee, worker, self-employed) but only two for tax (employee, self-employed). It looks at how these statuses could be simplified.

Google Widely used **search engine.** The company also offers other services such as e-mail and social networking. It is widely used to find material on HMRC's website in preference to HMRC's own search facility.

goose For VAT, geese for food are zero-rated, but ornamental geese are standard-rated. VAT notice 701/15 states that the former includes Brecon Buff, Chinese Commercial, Embdem, Roman, Toulouse and derivatives and crossbreeds of these.

go public Process by which a company lists its shares on a stock exchange. There are many legal formalities which must be followed.

gourde Currency of Haiti.

Gourley Legal principle that tax-free compensation payments could be adjusted to reflect tax, such as in compensation for lost earnings. This comes from a 1955 court case.

government System of social control that includes the right to make laws and to enforce them. The UK is a constitutional monarchy. The Treasury and HMRC operate in her name. In practice, decisions are made by ministers and endorsed by the Queen. Otherwise, the government is widely seen as having an executive and parliament. Unusually, the UK has no written constitution (though it has many Acts and documents that deal with constitutional matters), nor does it directly elect its leader.

Government Gateway An Internet portal operated by the UK Government that provides UK citizens and businesses with a convenient way to link up their usage of various online services provided by a range of Government departments.

graduated pension Government-backed additional pension scheme that operated for employees between 1961 and 1975. Those who paid contributions under this scheme receive an addition to their state pension. The rates are given under State Pension in section 3 of this dictionary.

graduated tax Tax which increases in rate on larger amounts. Income tax has been a graduated tax since 1907.

grain Old unit of weight based on a grain of barley which varies little. It is equal to 64.8 milligrams. There are 7000 grains to the pound or 437.5 to the ounce.

gram Unit of weight, originally defined as the weight of a cubic centimetre of water. There are 28.3 grams to the ounce.

grandchild A child of a child (TCGA 1992 Sch 5 para 2(7), 2(10) and 9(11)).

granny annex Part of a dwelling built or adapted as living accommodation for a dependent relative, not necessarily a grandmother. This is regarded as a separate dwelling for council tax if someone can live independently in the annex.

grant funding Provision of funds by central or local government, such as to a charity. Such provision is not regarded as a supply for VAT (VAT Notice 701/1).

grant of representation Proof of legal authority required by a person dealing with the estate of a deceased person.

grant pendent lite An interim grant of representation which is effective for a limited sum, such as while a will is being contested.

graphic design For VAT, the services of a graphic designer in designing brochures could not come within the scope of zero-rated brochures *(A P Carpenter [1996] VTD 15253).*

grassroots sports Sport played at a local and amateur level. From 1 April 2017 such company expenditure may qualify for corporation tax relief (CTA 2010 s217A).

gratuitous intent Condition that must be met for a gift to come within the scope of inheritance tax.

gratuity Money given to someone in appreciation for their services but which is not legally required, such as a tip. Such payments are usually subject to income tax in the hands of the recipient. Whether they are also subject to class 1 national insurance depends on how it was provided. If paid other by the employer, such as when a customer leaves cash on a table for the waiter, there is no class 1 national insurance payable. The waiter is obliged to declare the gratuity to HMRC, but the employer is not obliged to deduct PAYE.

grave digging For VAT, this is an exempt supply if provided as part of a funeral service. Further details are given in VAT notice 701/32.

gravel pit Profits from a quarry run as a trade are subject to income tax (ITTOIA 2005s12) or corporation tax (CTA 2009 s39).

gravestone For VAT, this is a standard-rated supply even when provided as part of an exempt funeral service. Further details are given in VAT notice 701/32.

gravity For beer duty, the ratio of the weight of beer compared with the same quantity of distilled water.

grazing licence Licence granted for a period of less than 12 months which allows the licensee to graze animals or take grass from land for a season. The existing of such a licence does not affect the ownership of the land, so agricultural relief at the higher rate may still be claimed for such land.

grazing rights For VAT, such rights are usually zero-rated unless part of a wider supply. The exact scope is explained in VAT notice 701/15.

Great Britain England, Scotland and Wales.

Greece European state that is a member of the European Union. Its currency is the euro of 100 cents. In 2015 it was bailed out for a third time by the EU under a tough austerity programme. The UK has a double taxation convention of 1953 and a road transport agreement of 1978.

Green Budget Term once used for a government publication of what it intended to include in the next Budget.

green channel Customs term for the exit at a port or airport to be used by a traveller from outside the European Union, who is carrying no banned or restricted goods, and no goods in excess of the personal allowance.

green diesel Rebated road fuel in the Irish Republic. Such fuel may legally be used in the UK where red diesel is legal.

Green Homes Grant Scheme Government scheme launched in 2020 whereby the government will pay two-thirds of the cost of improving the energy efficiency of a home up to £5,000, or, in some cases, £10,000.

Green Investment Bank (GIB) Bank established by the government to provide funding for environmental projects. It is set up under Enterprise and Regulatory Reform Act 2013, which received Royal Assent on 25 April 2013. The Bank was officially launched on 28 November 2012. It has offices in London and Edinburgh. It was provided with initial funding of £1 billion from public funds. It is allowed to borrow from 2015. The government disposed of its interests under Enterprise Act 2016 from s37.

Green Paper Report from the government on intended legislation. Proposed legislation is in a white paper.

Gregorian calendar Calendar devised by Pope Gregory XIII to correct some of the anomalies in the previous Julian calendar. In 1752 this was adopted in the UK under the Calendar (New Style) Act 1750 which is still in force.

greenhouse gas Any of carbon dioxide, methane, nitrous oxide, hydrofluorocarbons, perfluorocarbons and sulphur hexafluoride (Climate Change and Sustainable Energy Act 2006 s26(1)). There are tax provisions to discourage their emissions.

Grenada Island state in the Atlantic Ocean. Its currency is the East Caribbean dollar of 100 cents. The UK has a double taxation convention of 1949 amended by an arrangement of 1968.

grey market For shares, unofficial market, particularly in new shares which are traded before the official market opens. For goods, products that infringe trademarks and copyright. This term is used in Customs notice 34). During the war, the term was used for an unofficial market in rationed goods that was considered less serious than the black market.

greywater Lightly contaminated water from a bath, shower, washing machine or similar, but which does not contain faecal matter. Equipment to re-use such water which is approved by the Department for Environment, Food and Rural Affairs (DEFRA) qualifies for a 100% first year allowance (CAA 2001 s45A).

gritter "A vehicle is an excepted vehicle if it is constructed or adapted and used, solely for the conveyance of machinery for spreading material on roads to deal with frost, ice or snow (with or without articles or materials used for the purposes of the machinery)" (HODA 1979 Sch 1 para 8).

grizzly screen Machine for crushing boulders into useable aggregate. The extent to which such a machine is used can be relevant for determining liability to aggregates tax.

groat Small silver coin worth 4p, which is still minted for Maundy money and which is still legal tender, though it has not been used as everyday currency since 1887.

grogging Extracting spirits from the wood of casks. It is illegal under ALDA 1979 s34.

gross An inclusive figure from which an element may be removed to produce a net figure. For example, gross pay minus tax and national insurance is net pay; gross profit minus expenses is net profit.

gross assets requirement Requirement that the tax relief under Enterprise Investment Scheme depends on the company having gross assets no greater than £7 million before investment and £8 million after investment (ITA 2007 s142 and s186). There are similar provisions for VCT relief (ITA 2007 s297).

gross division approach Method of apportioning an estate where the residue of the estate is shared between exempt and non-exempt beneficiaries (such as a charity) so that they each receive the same gross figure before deducting inheritance tax. This may avoid the need for double grossing up. The matter was considered in the case *re Ratcliffe [1999] STC 262.*

gross domestic product (GDP) Measure of economic activity. It is the sum of values of all the goods and services produced by a country during a year. Tax revenues may be expressed as a percentage of GDP.

grossed-up equivalent In relation to occupational pension schemes, "the grossed-up equivalent of the employee's share of the minimum contributions is the sum which, after deduction of income tax at the basic rate in force for the tax year for which the minimum contributions are paid, is equal to that amount" (FA 2004 s202(4)).

gross estate Value of the estate of a deceased person before deductions for debts and taxes.

gross pay Amount an employee earns before deductions such as income tax, national insurance, pension contributions and attachments of earnings.

gross profit Broadly, turnover minus cost of sales, before expenses are deducted.

gross sales Income from sales (or turnover) before deductions are made for discounts, commissions and returned goods.

gross tonnage Official weight of a ship as defined under Merchant Shipping Acts. For VAT purposes, this may be calculated by a special formula given in VAT Notice 744C where there is not otherwise known. A ship is generally zero-rated if its gross tonnage exceeds 15 tonnes.

gross up Increase in number so that when a percentage is deducted, the original number is calculated. For example 20% grosses up to 25%. So if £100 is increased by 25% to £125, the 20% deduction reduces this to the original £100. Grossing up is used in many tax situations, such as Gift Aid, inheritance tax and payment of net wages. The formula is G = 100N/(100-N) where G is the gross rate and N is the original rate.

gross yield Profit or gain from investments before tax is deducted.

groundwater "All water which is below the surface of the ground and in direct contact with the ground or subsoil" (Flood and Water Management Act 2010 s6(4).

group Holding company and its subsidiaries viewed as a single entity (CA 2006 s474). For accounting, a group is simply a parent company and its subsidiaries (FRS 102 glossary). A subsidiary is, broadly, a company where more than 50% of the shares are held or more than 50% of the control is exercised.

For group relief for corporation tax, a group is a parent company and 75% subsidiaries (CTA 2009 from s764).

For VAT, a group is such companies as the holding company may wish to include (VATA 1994 from s43).

group litigation order (GLO) "An order of a court providing for the case management of actions which give rise to common or related issues of fact or law" (FA 2007 s107(6)). Several such orders have been issued for tax disputes.

group registration For VAT, when companies in a group elect to be registered as if they were a single entity.

group relief When a revenue loss suffered by one company may be offset against the profit of another company in the same group. For these purposes, there must be a 75% relationship. The relief is given by CTA 2010 Part 5. For a sub-subsidiary, there must be an effective 75% control. So if A owns 80% of B which owns 80% of C, A and C are not a group as A only has 64% effective control of C. Capital losses may not be offset by group relief, but the asset itself may be transferred between group companies on a no gain/no loss basis. For this purpose, group companies mean where there is 75% effective control or more than 50% indirect control. So in the example above, A and C *would* be group companies.

There are some restrictions on group relief from 1 April 2017. If a company makes a profit of more than £5 million, relief is restricted to £5 million plus half the balance (CTA 2010 from s269ZH).

Provisions for group relief for oil companies is given in CTA 2010 from s305.

Stamp duty land tax relief may be claimed for property transactions under FA 2003 Sch 7 para 1.

group scheme In relation to employee share schemes, " an employee share scheme set up by the parent company of a group under which share-related benefits are provided to employees of nominated companies in the group" (Inspectors' Manual at BIM 44001).

guaranteed minimum pension (GMP) Minimum pension that an occupational pension scheme had to provide in respect of service between 1978 and 1997. Since 1997, it is replaced by the reference scheme test.

guarantee period Minimum period for which a pension will be paid. It is often five years. So a pension will be paid for this period even if the pensioner dies during it.

guardian Person who has responsibility for a child but who is not the child's parent. Such an arrangement is made under Children Act 1989 either privately by a parent or by a court. The guardian automatically assumes parental responsibility for the child. For child trust funds, the term "means a guardian of a child within the meaning of section 5 of the Children Act 1989, section 7 of the Children (Scotland) Act 1995 or Article 2(2) of the Children (Northern Ireland) Order 1995 as the case may be" (Child Trust Funds Regulations SI 2004 No 1450 reg 2(1)(b)). In Scots law, "a person appointed by a parent or a court to act as the legal representative of a child in the event of the parent's death, or a person appointed by a court to act as guardian in relation to the property, financial affairs or personal welfare of a person with incapacity" (Judiciary of Scotland website glossary).

guardian ad litem Person appointed to represent minors in legal action.

guardian's allowance Social security payment to a guardian as an addition to child benefit (SSCBA 1992 s77). It is not taxed (ITEPA 2003 s677). The main points of the allowance are:

- it is not means-tested nor dependent on a national insurance contributions record
- the claimant must be receiving child benefit for the child, or is entitled to the benefit but has disclaimed it to avoid the high income child benefit charge
- the claimant is not the child's parent. The benefit may not be claimed for an adopted child or stepchild
- both parents (or adopters) have died, or one has died and the other one did not have custody, or the mother has died and the father is unknown. It can also be claimed if one parent has died and the other is in prison or detained by court in hospital
- the claimant is contributing at least £17.90 a week towards the child's maintenance

- the allowance is per child. The rate is given in Social Security Rates in section 3 of this dictionary.

guardianship order Order allowing a person to deal with the financial and administrative affairs of someone who has been missing for 90 days (Guardianship (Missing Persons) Act 2017 s2).

Guatemala South American state. Its currency is the quetzal of 100 centavos. The UK has no double taxation treaty.

Guernsey One of the Channel Islands. It is a possession of the British Crown but is not part of the UK. It is not a member of the European Union but is part of its Customs union. Its currency is the Guernsey pound of 100 pence. It has the same value as UK currency but Guernsey currency is not legal tender in the UK. The island has low tax rates. Much of its economy is in the financial sector. The UK has a double taxation arrangement of 2009 and a tax information exchange agreement of 2009.

guilder (1) Currency of Aruba.
(2) Currency of Netherlands before it adopted the euro in 2002.

Guinea East African state. Its currency is the Guinea franc of 100 centimes. The UK has no double taxation treaty. The country is subject to UK sanctions.

guinea Coin minted between 1663 and 1813. It remained an amount of 21 shillings (£1.05) but soon fell from use when decimal currency was adopted in 1971.

Guinea-Bissau East African state. Its currency is the West African CFA franc of 100 centimes. The UK has no double taxation treaty. The country is subject to UK sanctions.

gunpowder Explosive material. It may only be manufactured at licensed premises (Explosives Act 1875 s4). There are special Customs provisions regarding its export (CEMA 1979 s75) and import.

Guyana South American state. Its currency is the Guyana dollar of 100 cents. The UK has a double taxation convention of 1992.

habitat land Land that is set aside to protect the environment. A government scheme requires the land to be set aside for 20 years. From 1 September 1995 such land usually qualifies for 50% agricultural property relief. The relief is given in Statutory Instruments SI 1994 No 1291-1293 and SI 1995 No 134. Details were provided in an Inland Revenue press release of 27 January 1995. This does not include any farmhouse on habitat land unless it also relates to commercial farming on other land. Farmland that is farmed in an environmentally friendly way is not habitat land. Similarly land used for commercial purposes, such as growing reeds for thatching or breeding pheasants for shooting, exclude the land even though it otherwise meets the definition of habitat land.

Haiti State in Caribbean sea on an island shared with the Dominican Republic. Its currency is the gourde of 100 centimes. The UK has no double taxation treaty.

halala One hundredth of a Saudi riyal, currency of Saudi Arabia.

haléru One hundredth of a koruna, currency of Hungary.

half-crown Old coin worth 2 shillings and 6 pence (12½p), or one eighth of a pound. It was introduced as a gold coin in 1526. It became a silver coin in 1551. It was demonetised on 31 December 1969, before decimalisation.

half pay Wages or salaries at half their normal rate. This is often period during a long period of sickness after a period on full pay. Details are given in the contract of employment.

halfpenny Coin worth half a penny. Before 1100, they were made by cutting silver pennies in half. Separate coins were minted from 1135, though they did not enter general use until 1272. A copper coin was minted from 1672. The last mintage for circulation was in 1967. The coin was demonetised on 1 August 1969. There were 480 halfpennies to the pound. In 1971, a decimal halfpenny was issued with a value equal to 2.4 times the old halfpenny. This was demonetised in 1984.

half-test Old social security rule, abolished in December 1984, that a woman only qualified for a state pension on the basis of her contributions if she had paid them for at least half the weeks between her marriage and reaching state pension age.

hallmark (1) For tax avoidance, one of a list of factors to be considered in deciding whether a scheme is one of tax avoidance. They are listed in section 3 of this dictionary.
(2) Assay marks on items of gold or silver.

hall of residence Place in a university or similar establishment where students or others live. This is treated as residential property for most financial, tax and rating purposes. For the purposes of claiming a capital allowance for plant and machinery in a hall of residence, *HMRC Brief 66/2008* explains that no such claim may be made for plant in residential parts of halls, but may be claimed for communal parts, such as stairs and corridors, and parts to which residents do not have access, such as the roof and attic.

Hallstrom's Australian tax case on whether expenditure was capital or revenue. The case related to opposing an extension of another company's patent. The full name of the case is *Hallstrom's Proprietary Ltd v The Federal Commissioner of Taxation 72CLR634*. The case is discussed in HMRC Manual at BIM35045.

Hamada equation In investment, a formula of fundamental analysis. It analyses a company's costs of capital as it uses financial leverage (or gearing), and how that relates to the overall risks within the company. It also reflects the company's tax rate. The equation is:
Hamada = $B_1[1 + (1 - T)(D/E)]$
where B_1 is the firms' beta with zero debt
T = tax rate
D/E = debt to equity ratio.

hamper Basket with a lid, often containing food and drink. It is a traditional present. It is most unlikely that a hamper will ever qualify for tax relief as a business gift, as food is specifically exempted from tax-free business gifts. If given to staff, it is likely to be of too great a value to qualify as a trivial benefit.

handicapped Term now replaced by the word "disabled" from 2017.

handling agent For air passenger duty, a person who allocates seats to passengers and supervises their boarding of aircraft (FA 1994 s37(3)).

Hang Seng Index of the Hong Kong stock market.

Hansard Official written record of what is said in Parliament. Since 1992, a court may consult Hansard to assist in interpreting an Act. (*Pepper v Hart [1992]*). It was also the name of the procedure for investigating tax fraud, until replaced by COP 9 in 2005.

haraam Forbidden or sinful under Islamic law. This includes the payment of interest. Alternative financial products have been designed to copy financial products to be compliant. These are taxed on a similar basis to the products they copy. [The word can be spelled haram.]

Harberger's triangle Representation of deadweight loss that can arise from the imposition of tax on goods and services. The idea was devised by American economist Arnold C Harberger (1924-). The representation is a roughly triangular shape on a supply and demand graph where the curves are cut short so that consumer surplus and producer surplus are also cut short.

hard border Physical infrastructure at a Customs border, such as walls and manned Customs posts.

hard copy "A document or information is sent or supplied in hard copy form if it is sent or supplied in a paper copy or similar form capable of being read. References to hard copy have a corresponding meaning." (CA 2006 s1168(2)). While documents may be stored electronically, it is generally a requirement that a hard copy can be produced. For company law, this is specifically required by CA 2006 s1145.

hard currency Stable currency which is widely recognised, such as pound, euro or US dollar. Where a local currency is weak, traders often revert to a hard currency.

hardship application For tax hearings, an application to a tribunal that a person would suffer undue hardship in meeting the requirement to pay a disputed sum as a condition of starting proceedings on the substantive issue. For example, an appeal against disputed VAT usually requires the sum to be paid first, to prevent appeals being used merely to postpone payment. If the taxpayer cannot afford to pay the sum, a hardship application may be brought first to dispense with the requirement to make payment. The rules for this are set out in The Tribunal Procedure (First-tier Tribunal) (Tax Chamber) Rules SI 2009 No 273 rule 22. A VAT tribunal ruled that "a company may need to borrow in order to pay VAT in dispute if the business had existing unused borrowing facilities" but that a business should not "be expected to pursue other sources of finance purely for the purpose of paying the tax in dispute" *(Buyco Ltd; Sellco Ltd [2006] VTD 19752).*

hardship payment Social security payment that may be paid to a universal credit or jobseeker's allowance claimant whose benefit has been reduced for non-compliance and who suffers hardship as a consequence (WRA 2012 s28). The main points are:

- a payment must be claimed; it is not given automatically
- it is claimed when someone qualifies for a means-tested benefit but does not receive it because they have been sanctioned or committed a benefit offence
- it may be claimed only if the claimant has complied with conditions, such as attending a work-focused interview
- the Department of Work and Pensions must be satisfied that the claimant is suffering hardship
- hardship payments are calculated at a daily rate at 60% of the amount of benefit that would be claimed
- the payment is recoverable once the claimant's income has exceeded a monthly limit.

Harmonised System International system of describing and classifying goods for tax and economic purposes, administered by the World Trade Organisation. It is used for determining Customs duty.

hash For the purposes of blockchain, "a sort of digital signature or summary of a block that is used to authenticate it and its place in the chain" (ICAEW guidance 2017).

hash key The key with the symbol #. It is used (particularly in USA) to mean "number".

hash total A total of an irrelevant field taken from documents as a means of checking that all documents have been dealt with. Early computer systems used hash totals to check that, for example, all invoices had been entered on the system. The batch would come with a hash total of, perhaps, adding up all the invoice numbers. The data entry clerk would then add up these numbers when entering the invoices to check that they had all been entered.

Hastings-Bass Tax case relating to when mistakes by trustees can be reversed. The full citation is *re Hastings Bass deceased [1974] STC 211.* The case was brought by Inland Revenue who argued that an advancement of capital was ineffective. Hastings-Bass was first used by a taxpayer in *Mettoy Pension Trustees Ltd v Evans [1990]* to provide relief when trustees failed to take into account all consequences of their decisions. The first non-pension case was *Green v Cobham [2002].* This started a series of cases where trustees' decisions were declared void when they led to unexpected tax consequences. The rule has been restrained by the Court of Appeal decisions in *Futter v Futter [2013]* and *Pitt v Holt [2013].*

haver In Scots law, a document that another party may wish to obtain in legal proceedings.

hawala Arrangement whereby someone who needs currency in another country pays UK currency to a UK resident who notifies a partner in the other country to pay the sum there. It is commonly organised by family members, particularly from Asian countries. It is legal.

haybote The right of a tenant to take wood for repairing hedges and fences.

hazardous waste For landfill tax, "means any hazardous waste within the meaning of European Parliament and Council Directive 2008/98/EC" (SI 2015 No 1385 para 2).

headband For VAT, this is not regarded as clothing and therefore cannot be zero-rated when supplied to children. It does not come within the definition of a hat as it provides no covering or protection to the head *(Mrs V Cassidy (t/a Balou [1990] VTD 5760).*

headings The first four digits of the commodity code for Customs duties.

health Term usually used to mean the prevention, treatment and convalescence from illnesses and injuries. Health treatment usually involves diagnosis, medicine, surgery, therapy and similar. Such treatment can be exempt, zero-rated or standard-rated for VAT depending on how it is supplied. The VAT implications are set out in VAT Notice 701/31.

health and employment insurance Premiums paid by an employer may be exempt from tax under ITEPA 2003 s325A and s644A.

health and misfortune insurance From 6 April 1996, payments from such policies are generally tax-free provided:

- they do no more than compensate the policy holder for lost income;
- the benefits have not been taken into account in computing trading profits;
- the premiums have not attracted tax relief; and
- the payments only continue during a period of misfortune (such as while sick or unemployed).

health authority association For tax purposes, a definition is given in ITA 2007 s1000. The same definition is used in respect of tax relief for capital gains under TCGA1992 s271.

health benefits Health provisions that are provided free to those receiving certain social security benefits. Examples include prescriptions, eye tests and dentistry.

health care professional In the context of a work-focused health-related assessment for universal credit, means a registered medical practitioner, a registered nurse, an occupational therapist or physiotherapist, or member of certain other health professions (Welfare Reform Act 2012 s16(5)). A definition of health professional is given in Data Protection Act 2018 s204(1).

health certificate Certificate that may be required for certain imported foods and food products. Customs clearance cannot be obtained without the certificate.

health service body Such a body is exempt from capital gains tax on certain disposals as set out in TCGA1992 s271. The definition of such a body is given in CTA 2010 s986.

Healthy Start Welfare provision of providing food and vitamins to mothers on low incomes. The scheme is open to women who are at least 10 weeks pregnant, and to those with children under four. They receive free vouchers each week to buy milk (including infant formula milk), fruit and vegetables (fresh, tinned or frozen), and tinned pulses. The vouchers are worth £3.10 a week in 2020, rising to £4.25 in 2021. If a child is under 1 year old, the mother receives 2 vouchers a week. Those who receive vouchers are also entitled to free vitamins. In Scotland, the equivalent scheme is called Best Start Foods.

hearing Formal judicial proceedings to determine a matter. For tax appeals, means "an oral hearing and includes a hearing conducted in whole or in part by video link, telephone or other means of instantaneous two-way electronic communication" (The Tribunal Procedure (First-tier Tribunal) (Tax Chamber) Rules SI 2009 No 273 rule 1(3)).

heat Provision to warm a building. For VAT, a supply of heat is treated as a supply of goods (VATA 1994 Sch 4 para 3). As such, supplies for residential use are generally reduced-rated under VATA 1994 Sch 7A Group 1, but standard-rated for other supplies. Details are given in VAT notice 701/19. Grant-funded installation of heating appliances may qualify for the reduced rate of VAT under VATA 1994 Sch 7A Group 3. Heating oil for domestic or charitable use qualifies for reduced rating under VATA 1994 Sch 7A Group 1.A heating system is a feature integral to a building and so qualifies for a capital allowance as plant and machinery. There are social security benefits to assist with heating bills in winter.

heavy crude oil Naturally occurring oil before processing which contains a low concentration (down to 50%) of the more valuable hydrocarbons.

heavy goods vehicle (HGV) Vehicle which weighs more than 7.5 tonnes. The proper name is now large goods vehicle (LGV), though the old name and abbreviation remain in popular use. For the purposes of employees' taxable benefits, an HGV "means a mechanically propelled road vehicle which –

(a) is of a construction primarily suited for the conveyance of goods or burden of any kind, and

(b) is designed or adapted to have a maximum weight exceeding 3,500 kilograms when in normal use and travelling on a road laden" (ITEPA 2003 s238(4)).

An employee is not taxed on the "modest" use of such a vehicle.

heavy oil Hydrocarbon oil that is not regarded as light oil for hydrocarbon oil duty. Examples of heavy oil include diesel, kerosene and aviation fuel (HODA 1979 s1(4)).

hectare Unit of land measurement equal to 10,000 square metres. It is about 2.471 acres. For capital gains tax, main residence relief may be claimed for half a hectare of associated land, or larger if consistent with the size of the property.

hectolitre Unit of capacity equal to 100 litres, about 22 gallons. From 1980, alcoholic liquor duty is charged per hectolitre rather than per gallon.

hedge Financial arrangement designed to mitigate adverse effects, such as buying a futures contract if an exchange rate moves adversely.

hedging instrument In relation to corporation tax on loan relationships and the restrictions on debts resulting from revaluation, this term is given a specific meaning in CTA 2009 s324(3A) as inserted by Finance (No 2) Act 2015 Sch 7.

hedging relationship In relation to open-ended investment companies, the term is defined in CTA 2009 s496. For derivative contracts, the term is defined in CTA 2009 s707. For corporation tax and loan relationships, the term is given a specific meaning in CTA 2009 s475A as inserted by Finance (No 2) Act 2015 Sch 7.

held amount Sum in a bank account which HMRC may seize under direct debt recovery without consent of the account holder or a court. The provision was introduced in 2015 with several safeguards.

held out for sale How a product is offered, particularly with regard to it use. This can determine the rate of VAT. For example, gelatine for photographic use is standard-rated while gelatine for food use is zero-rated.

helpsheet One of a series of documents produced by HMRC to assist taxpayers. Their use is optional. They are listed in section 3 of this dictionary.

Help to Buy Government scheme to assist people to buy a home. It provides a five-year interest free loan of up 20% of the property's value, or 40% in London. The scheme was introduced in 2013 and is due to end in 2023.

help to buy ISA A government-supported savings product launched on 1 December 2015. It is an account intended to help first-time home buyers to save for a deposit. The main elements are:

- up to £200 a month may be saved. There is no minimum
- the government adds a 25% bonus to savings
- up to £1,200 may be deposited when the account is opened
- the account is available for four years, but may then continue to be held indefinitely. Accounts are offered by banks and building societies
- the limit is per person, not per home, so a couple can save £400 a month
- the saver must be at least 16 years old
- the saver must be under 40 when taking out the help-to-buy ISA. Payments may be made until the saver is 50. The account may stay open after that, earning interest, but no further payments may be made into it
- the saver must be UK resident or a Crown servant
- the bonus is paid to UK residents buying a property in the UK. This must not be a property that the savers intend to let
- the property must be the only property of the saver
- the minimum bonus payable is £400; the maximum is £3,000
- the bonus is paid for properties up to £450,000 in London, or £250,000 outside London
- the bonus is paid when the home is bought
- the property must be bought with a mortgage
- the property must be bought through a solicitor or conveyancer to whom the bonus is paid
- the bonus may be claimed when savings have reached £1,600
- it is not permitted to hold a cash ISA in the same tax year as a help-to-buy ISA
- the help-to-buy ISA may be used with other government schemes

- funds may be withdrawn to buy a first home or on reaching the age of 60. There is a 25% charge for otherwise withdrawing funds
- the 25% charge also applies if funds from a help-to-buy ISA are transferred to an ordinary ISA.

The ISA may be used for the deposit at exchange of contracts, and for related expenses such as solicitor's and estate agent's fees. The maximum that can be saved per person is £12,000 to which £3,000 may be added. This means a couple could save £30,000.

help to save Government scheme to encourage saving by universal credit or tax credit claimants. It allows a person to save £50 a month for two years to which the government adds 50%. The maximum saving is £1,200 to which the government would add £600. It was introduced on 6 April 2018.

hemline theory Fanciful but popular economic theory that shorter skirts indicate a prosperous economy, as in 1920s, 1960s and 1980s. It has been suggested that both the economy and fashion reflect a feel-good factor.

Henry VIII powers Powers given by an Act of Parliament to a minister allowing for changes in the law without requiring further Parliamentary approval. The EU (Withdrawal) Act 2018 gives ministers such powers to make minor variations to EU law when incorporating it into UK law.

hepatitis C Disease of the blood. In January 2011, payments to people who contracted the disease from contaminated blood were entitled to a compensation payment. From 18 May 2011, such payments are exempt from income tax under SI 2011 No 1157.

herb For VAT, a herb used for culinary purposes is zero-rated but a herb used for medicinal purposes is standard-rated. Herbs used in food supplements, such as ginseng and evening primrose, are standard-rated. Further details are given in VAT Notice 701/38.

herbal products For VAT, there have been several cases to determine whether such a product qualifies for zero-rating as food. The case *Ayurveda Ltd [1988] VTD 3860* held that a herbal fruit concentrate was zero-rated but tablets were not.

herbal tea This is zero-rated for VAT. Under Value Added Tax 1994 Sch 8 Group 1, food is generally zero-rated. Excepted Item 3 standard-rates beverages. Items Overriding The Exception 4 reverses the exception, thus reinstating the zero-rating. Further guidance is given in VAT Notice 701/14.

herd basis Election that may be made by a farmer. Originally It allowed the animals of any species not to be regarded as trading stock. The sale of animals was not taxed, and their cost was not tax-deductible. The current position is that animals are treated as trading stock unless the farmer elects to use the herd basis. An election treats the animals more like a capital asset. This is appropriate when the animals themselves are not traded but their products are, such as milk, eggs, lambs or piglets. The cost of maintaining the herd (or other collective term) is tax-deductible as a revenue expense, and any gain on the ultimate disposal of the animals is tax free. The law is ITTOIA 2005 from s111; CTA 2009 from s109.

An explanation is given in HMRC Manual at BIM55505. In accounting, such animals are called biological assets, which term also applies to crops.

hereditament Property including land and buildings. The term means "a property which is or may become liable to a rate, being a unit of such property which is, or would fall to be, shown as a separate rate item in the valuation list" (General Rates Act 1967 s115(1)). This definition is relevant in determining what is a chargeable dwelling for council tax, and what is chargeable to business rates.

heritable estate Scottish term for land and buildings as against moveable items and animals.

heritage asset Fixed asset that needs special permission for disposal. Such assets are usually excluded from published accounts.

heritage body A body or charity that maintains historic buildings. A definition for income tax is given in ITA 2007 s507(2).

heritage direction Direction given under Inheritance Tax Act 1984 Sch 4 para 1.

Her Majesty's Revenue and Customs (HMRC) The term that collectively refers to the Commissioners and officers of Revenue and Customs (Commissioners for Revenue and Customs Act 2005 s4).

It is a non-ministerial department of the government formed on 18 April 2005 from the merger of Inland Revenue and HM Customs and Excise. It employs 66,000 staff in 2020. The department is responsible for collecting most taxes, paying some benefits such as tax credits and child benefit, valuing property, administering national minimum wage, issuing national insurance numbers, administering money laundering laws, and compilation of some statistics. Responsibility for protecting UK borders passed to UK Border Agency on 1 April 2008, who passed it to UK Border Force in 2013. HMRC's responsibilities in Scotland passed to the newly formed Revenue Scotland, and in Wales to the newly formed Welsh Revenue Authority, both from 1 April 2015. HMRC is headed by a chief executive, who is also HMRC's permanent secretary and accounting officer. In 2019, Jim Harra was appointed to that role. The Board comprises an executive committee and non-executive directors.

hidden economy Economic activity that is hidden from the tax authorities.

High Court Part of the UK legal system that deals with civil and criminal matters. It is above county and crown courts, but below the Court of Appeal. A legal definition is given in Interpretation Act 1978 Sch 1. The High Court has three divisions: Queen's Bench Division; Chancery Division; and Family Division. Tax cases are heard in the Chancery Division.

high income excess relief charge Complex tax provisions introduced in Finance Act 2010 to restrict tax relief for taxpayers with annual earnings above £130,000. It was repealed before introduction and replaced with annual and lifetime allowances for pension contributions.

higher personal allowance Increase in personal allowance that could be claimed by a married man until 1990.

higher rate Rate of income tax greater than the basic rate, payable when a threshold is reached. The higher rate has been 40% since 6 April 1988, except in Scotland where it has been 41% since 6 April 2018. From 6 April 2010, there is an additional rate of 45% (50% before 6 April 2013, and 46% in Scotland from 6 April 2018).

higher rate code Tax code that requires an employer to deduct tax at the higher or additional rate of income tax (PAYE Regulations SI 2003 No 2682 reg 32). It is defined as a special code "which effects the deduction of tax wholly at the higher rate" (ibid reg 7(3)(b)). The commonest higher rate code is D0.

higher rate contribution Special rate of class 2 national insurance payable by share fishermen and volunteer workers (SSCBA 1992 s11(3)).

higher sugar threshold Rate of soft drinks industry levy payable for a soft drink that contains at least 8 grams of added sugar per 100 millilitres (FA 2017 s36(2)).

high income child benefit charge (HICBC) Income tax charge introduced on 7 January 2013 (ITEPA 2003 s681B). The charge claws back some child benefit received by a taxpayer earning £50,000 a year, and all child benefit if earning £60,000. HICBC may be recovered from an employee by adjusting the PAYE code (PAYE Regulations 2003 reg 14B).

high-income individual For the purposes of the tapered reduction of annual allowance for pension contributions, this is someone with earnings above £240,000 (FA 2004 s228ZA(3) as inserted by Finance (No 2) Act 2015 Sch 4 para 10(3). The allowance is also reduced if the earnings net of pension contributions is above £200,000. The reduction is £1 for every £2 of adjusted income above £240,000 to a minimum of £4,000. This minimum is reached at an income of £312,000. For periods between 6 April 2016 and 5 April 2020, the limits of £240,000 and £200,000 were £150,000 and £110,000 respectively.

high likely need In relation to social security, a description of a person for whom alternative payment arrangements should be considered. Categories of such claimants may include those:

- with addiction problems
- who are living in temporary accommodation
- who have serious debt problems
- who are homeless
- suffering from violence
- who are being threatened with eviction
- who have serious mental health problems
- who are aged 16 or 17
- in a family with multiple and complex needs.

highly probable For accounting, this is defined as "significantly more likely than not" (FRS 102 glossary).

high net worth individual Person who has significant personal wealth. Such people have particular accounting and tax requirements, which are usually addressed either by specialist firms or an employed accountant. For HMRC purposes, such a person was one worth more than £20 million. Such taxpayers are subject to a higher level of scrutiny by a customer relationship manager in HMRC's High Net Worth Unit. From 6 April 2016, the threshold is reduced to £10 million. There were 6,500 such individuals in 2015/16, and about 8,500 when the threshold was reduced. The Unit reports increased tax yields from their work. Compliant taxpayers generally report that the Unit is an advantage to them as their affairs are dealt with by a named and contactable specialist. For investment purposes, the definition is broadly someone with an annual income above £100,000 or who has net assets (excluding their home) of £250,000. Such an investor is usually offered tailor-made investment products.

high value dealer Person who deals with large amounts of ready cash, taken to be more than £9,000. Such a dealer must register with HMRC under money laundering rules.

high value dealer (HVD) Person who deal with large amounts of money in the form of cash (i.e. banknotes and coins) in the course of business and who is not otherwise regulated. A car dealer or amusement arcade could be an HVD. The regulations are designed to prevent money laundering. The large amount is €10,000 or sterling equivalent. In practice this is translated as £9,000. A trader is not an HVD if he or she receives payments of large amounts by other means (such as cheque or card) and refuses to accept cash above the limit.

From 1 April 2004, HVDs must register as such with HMRC under laws on money laundering. The registration requirements were tightened on 15 December 2007. A definition of HVD is given in Proceeds of Crime Act 2002 Sch 9 para 1(1)(q) and 2(2).

high value disposal Disposal made by a company subject to ATED. Such a disposal is subject to capital gains tax rather than corporation tax.

hire purchase

Definition

Means of acquiring goods in two stages. The first stage is when the possessor pays a hire charge. The second is when a single payment, often of a nominal amount, is paid to acquire legal title. Some agreements do the opposite and have a "balloon payment" of a larger amount at the end. These arrangements are subject to consumer protection laws.

The supplier of the goods may repossess the goods if the hirer has paid less than one third of the total amount. Above that figure, the hirer needs a court order. Repossessed goods are sold at auction. The net proceeds (after deducting seizure, auction and collections costs) are offset against the debt. If that is insufficient, the hirer remains liable for the balance even though they no longer have the goods. The hirer has the right to use the goods but not to sell them until the last payment has been made.

Law

Hire purchase agreements are now regulated by Consumer Credit Act 1974 and Consumer Rights Act 2015 s7. They were first regulated by Hire Purchase Act 1965. Its strict controls were relaxed in 1982.

Tax

For VAT, hire purchase is treated as if the item had been bought from the start of the hire period (VAT Notice 700).

For income tax and corporation tax, the hire element of the agreement is revenue expenditure and is tax-deductible if it meets the usual "wholly and exclusively" test. HMRC Manual explains when the hire charges should be taken to account at BIM45355.

The payment to acquire the goods (usually a nominal amount) is capital expenditure for which a capital allowance may be claimable. This accounting treatment was confirmed in the case *Darngavil Coal Co Ltd v Francis [1913] 7TC1.* Corporation tax provisions are given in CTA 2009 s875.

Provisions relating to capital allowances for goods acquired by hire purchase or similar contracts are given in CAA 2001 from s67.

In relation to an anti-avoidance provision in relation to leased trading assets, there are provisions in ITA 2007 s681DE.

A hire purchase agreement is not subject to stamp duty under the provisions of FA 1907 s7, which is still law.

historic buildings A donation to a maintenance fund for such buildings does not attract inheritance tax (Inheritance Tax Act 1984 s27).

A historic house open to the public may be exempt from annual tax on enveloped dwellings.

The sale of items from a historic building may be subject to special VAT provisions as explained in VAT Notice 701/12.

historic cost convention Accounting convention that assets, liabilities and other amounts are stated in the accounts at original values with no allowance for inflation. This is the usual accounting treatment. Its current statutory authority is SI 2008 No 409 and SI 2008 No 410 Part B.

HMIT Her Majesty's Inspector of Taxes.

HM Customs and Excise Her Majesty's Customs and Excise. This body was formed in 1909 from the merger of the Board of Excise founded in 1671 and the Board of Custom founded in 1683. HM Customs and Excise merged with Inland Revenue in 2005 to form HM Revenue and Customs.

HM Revenue and Customs Body formed in 2005 from the merger of Inland Revenue and HM Customs and Excise. More details are given under Her Majesty's Revenue and Customs.

HM Treasury United Kingdom government department responsible for managing the public finances. Its origins date back to 1126 when it merged from the Royal Household under Henry I.

Since the 17th century, the Treasury is run by a commission, comprising Lords of the Treasury. The first Lord became recognised as the country's leader, now known as the prime minister and first Lord of the Treasury. Since 1827, the Chancellor of the Exchequer has been the second Lord of the Treasury. The other Lords of the Treasury are now usually government whips.

HM Revenue and Customs is one of the agencies of HM Treasury. Other agencies are Asset Protection Agency, National Savings and Investments, Royal Mint, and UK Debt Management Office.

hobby farming Agricultural activity that is not pursued commercially. For the first five years, any losses may not be offset against other profits (ITA 2007 ss67-68).

hogshead Barrel for alcoholic liquor. Its size varies from 46 to 65 gallons depending on the drink.

hold harmless Letter indemnifying an auditor or other professional adviser from legal action.

holding company In accounting, a company that holds more than 50% of the shares or otherwise controls other companies. In the context of employee-controlled companies means "a company whose business (ignoring any trade carried on by it) consists wholly or mainly of the holding of shares or securities of one or more companies which are its 75% subsidiaries" (ITA 2007 s397(6)). A similar requirement applies for group relief. For corporation tax and distributions, the term is defined more narrowly to mean a company which has a 90% or greater holding in trading companies (CTA 2010 s185(2)).

holding out When a person acts as if he or she holds a position. In some cases, such conduct can make a person liable as if he did hold the position. For example Partnership Act 1890 s14 imposes a liability on someone who holds himself out as a partner.

hold-mail Address of someone else who agrees to hold mail on behalf of another person. Such addresses are often of banks, solicitors or accountants. For savings accounts opened from 6 April 2001, HMRC will not accept a hold-mail address from paying agents of savings funds when making their payment returns.

hold notice Document issued by HMRC which allows it to take funds from a taxpayer's bank account.

holdover relief *General*

Relief from capital gains tax when an asset is given to another party. The two periods of ownership are treated as one. This relief does not in itself reduce the amount of tax payable but usually has the effect of postponing payment of the tax. There are two forms: business assets (TCGA 1992 s165) and gifts subject to inheritance tax (TCGA 1992 s260).

Business assets relief

For business assets, the main points are:

- the asset must be disposed of other than in an arm's length transaction. Usually this is a gift or sale at undervalue
- the transferor and transferee must make a joint claim for the relief
- the transferee must be UK resident
- the relief may not be claimed for a transfer to a foreign company, dual-resident trust or settlor-interested trust
- the relief may not be used to transfer shares or other securities to a company

- the asset must have been used in a business, or be shares or securities in a trading company, or be farmland and buildings eligible for agricultural property relief, or certain settled property disposed of by the trustees of a settlement
- the relief is given by deducting the held over gain from both the chargeable gain and the consideration that the transferee would otherwise be regarded as having given
- if an asset is partly used for business, the relief is restricted to the business element
- if the asset was not used wholly for business during the transferor's ownership, the relief is restricted pro rata
- a restriction may apply if the asset is the transferor's company or a company where the transferor could exercise at least 25% of the voting rights in the previous 12 months.

Inheritance tax relief

Where the transfer of an asset is subject to both inheritance tax and a claim for rollover relief, the transferee may receive relief for the inheritance tax paid when calculating the gain on later disposal of the asset. The deduction cannot exceed the amount of the chargeable gain before the deduction. Where relief qualifies under both sections 165 and 260, relief is given under s260.

holiday When an employee is allowed to be absent for rest. The law requires at least 5.6 weeks' paid holiday. This is 28 days for someone working a five-day week. This right applies to all workers, including employees, agency workers, workers with irregular hours, and workers on zero hours contracts. The 28 days includes any bank holidays the worker is allowed.

Holiday entitlement accrues during the time at work, including periods of sick leave, holiday leave, maternity, paternity and adoption leave.

The contract of employment may provide for further holiday but may not provide less, even if the worker agrees. The 20 days leave derives from Working Time Regulations SI 1998 No 1833 para 13. The further 8 days applies from 1 April 2009 (ibid para 13A). For workers who started from 1 October 1998, the holiday year starts from the first day at work. Previously it ran from 1 October. The right to carry over unused leave is as follows:

- 20 days (4 weeks) of leave must be taken in the holiday year. It is lost without compensation if not taken
- 8 days (1.6 weeks) may be carried one year only
- further days allowed by the contract of employment may be carried forward in accordance with the contract.

A worker who could not take leave because their work was affected by coronavirus may carry unused leave forward two years. For Customs purpose, holiday "in relation to any part of the United Kingdom, means any day that is a bank holiday in that part of the United Kingdom under the Banking and Financial Dealings Act 1971, Christmas Day, Good Friday, and the day appointed for the purposes of customs and excise for the celebration of Her Majesty's birthday" (CEMAs1(1)).

holiday club Arrangement whereby an employee authorises the employer to make a deduction from wages to be put in a separate fund for the employee to spend later, not necessarily on a holiday. In February 2020, HMRC dropped its claim that this breached national minimum wage regulations if the deduction reduced wages below the national minimum wage.

holiday pay Wages or salary paid while an employee is on holiday. This is subject to tax and national insurance under PAYE as if the employee was at work. This applies even when holiday pay is provided from a separate fund (PAYE Regulations 2003 reg 134).

holiday site Place where holiday caravans may be parked. The supply of a caravan on such a site is generally standard-rated for VAT (VAT Notice 701/20).

Holocaust Period of human rights abuses by the Nazi government of Germany between 1933 and 1945, particularly against Jews, gypsies, homosexuals, freemasons and the disabled. Various compensation schemes have since been set up as explained under Nazi compensation.

Holocaust Victim Assets Litigation Arrangements made by Swiss banks in 2015 to compensate those used as slaves or forced labourers in the second world war. Such payments are exempt from inheritance tax.

home income plan Home income plans allow homeowners to use the equity tied up in their home to purchase an income and thus increase their standard of living. Homeowners can release this capital without having to sell their home. With a reversion plan, the home is sold to an insurance company that then pays a regular income to the owner. On the death of the owner, the house becomes the property of the insurance company.

home loss compensation Sum paid to a householder whose home is the subject of a compulsory purchase order. It is a payment in addition to payment for the property as compensation for inconvenience, stress and upset. It is calculated as a percentage of the property's market price subject to a statutory minimum and maximum, set by statutory instrument.

home office Tax-free allowance for an employee who does some work at home. Rates are given in section 3 of this dictionary.

home purchasing agreement In relation to capital gains tax and private residence relief, "means an agreement –

(a) made with the employer or a person operating under an agreement with the employer ("the purchaser"),

(b) which includes a term entitling the individual to receive a share of any such profit as is mentioned in subsection (2)(a)"

(TCGA1992 s225C(3)).

homosexuality Sexual preference for people of the same sex. This was a crime before 1967 and a capital offence before 1861. It is now legal. From 30 April 2007, it is an offence to discriminate on grounds of sexuality. From 5 December 2005, two people of the same sex may form a civil partnership. From 13 March 2014 they may marry. In 2009, HMRC produced leaflet Pride 1 giving tax information for lesbian, gay, bisexual and transgender individuals. A same-sex marriage or civil partnership is treated in the same way as an opposite-sex marriage.

honorarium Sum paid to a person when a salary, wage or fee has not been agreed. It is taxable as wages.

Honduras South American state. Its currency is the lempira of 100 centavos. The UK has nor double taxation treaty.

Hong Kong Territory in China. It was a British dependent territory until 30 June 1997 when sovereignty returned to China. Its currency is the Hong Kong dollar of 100 cents. The UK has a double taxation agreement of 2010.

Hong Kong dollar Currency of Hong Kong, comprising 100 cents.

hook-up charge Charge for connecting a caravan to a supply of electricity or gas. In general, if the caravan user has the option of whether to connect, the charge is subject to VAT at the reduced rate (as an integral supply of domestic energy). Otherwise, it is usually taxed at the standard rate. Further details are provided in VAT leaflet 701/20.

hope value Additional value attached to land in respect of something the buyer hopes will happen, such as land being allowed for development.

horizontal equity Economic term for the principle that taxpayers with equal income should pay the same amount of tax.

Horlicks tablets The VAT tribunal held that these were zero-rated as food. The deciding factor was that they had not been sweetened as confectionery. *(Smith Kline Beecham plc. [1993] VTD 10222).*

horse A horse is plant for the purposes of capital allowance. Indeed the court case widely concerning the nature of plant refers to a horse *(Yarmouth v France [1887] CA. 19 QBD 647).* For VAT, horses are standard-rated though horse meat prepared for human consumption is zero-rated (VAT Notice 701/14). Breeding and rearing horses is considered an agricultural activity for which agricultural property relief may be claimed against inheritance tax. HMRC confirmed this in Tax Bulletin of June 2005. Horse-drawn vehicles are exempt from vehicle excise duty as they are not mechanically propelled.

horsepower Unit of power originally measured as that of a horse. It was introduced in 18th century. It is now defined as the power needed to lift 33,000 pound by one foot in one minute. One horsepower equals 745.7 watts. A horse is actually capable of producing 14.9 horsepower for a short period and 1 horsepower for a sustained period.

hospitality Provision of basic human necessities, particularly light refreshments such as tea, coffee, biscuits and sandwiches. Although there is an element of human sustenance, this is not usually considered sufficient to disallow expenditure as being not exclusively for a trade. The matter is discussed in HMRC Manual at BIM37400. The manual says at BIM45010 that there is no real difference between hospitality and business entertainment. HMRC has confirmed that normal hospitality to its officers during a visit will not be regarded as bribery.

hospitality rate Temporary 5% reduced rate of VAT applied between 15 July 2020 and 31 March 2021 to supplies made by the hospitality industry. The original end date of 12 January 2021 was extended in the winter economy statement of 24 September 2020. The hospitality rate particularly applies to:

- food and non-alcoholic drinks sold for consumption on the premises, such as in restaurants, cafes and pubs
- hot takeaway food and hot takeaway non-alcoholic drinks
- sleeping accommodation in hotels and similar, holiday accommodation, pitch fees for caravans and tents, and associated facilities
- admissions to attractions (to the extent that they are not VAT exempt) such as theatres, circuses, fairs, concerts, museums, zoos, cinemas and exhibitions, and similar.

The change is given legal effect by SI 2020 No 340 which adds these groups to VATA 1994 Sch 7A:

- Group 14: course of catering
- Group 15: holiday accommodation etc
- Group 16: shows and certain other attractions.

This change also affects the VAT flat rates for the period as given effect by SI 2020 No 728 (para 6):

- catering services including restaurants and takeaways: from 12.5% to 4.5%
- hotel or accommodation: from 10.5% to 0%
- pubs: from 6.5% to 1%.

hospital parking Charge made for parking at a hospital. From April 2020, a charge may not be made:

- for Blue Badge holders
- to frequent outpatients who must attend regular appointments to manage a long-term condition
- parents who stay overnight with their sick children
- staff working night shifts.

hospital patient For care purposes, a definition is provided in Care Act 2014 Sch 3 para 7(1).

host contract In relation to index-linked gilt-edged securities with embedded contracts for difference, the term is defined in CTA 2009 s623(7).

host rock Indigenous, and generally worthless rock, to which ore and other useable minerals may be attached. The amount of host rock can be relevant in determining aggregates tax.

hot Above room temperature. Hot food is standard-rated for VAT whereas cold food may be zero-rated (VATA 1994 Group 8 Note (3C)). Food is not hot if it has simply not cooled down from cooking, such as fresh bread.

hotchpot An accumulation of benefits. The word originally meant a pudding from many ingredients. For inheritance and trusts, the term means a commixture of funds and other property for the equitable division among children. If one child took funds early, those funds were added to the total and subtracted from that child's share. For example, a man leaves £1 million to his three children, one of whom had previously been given £200,000. Under hotchpot, the estate is valued at £1.2 million which is split three ways. The child who had received £200,000 has that subtracted from their share of £400,000. So the estate is divided as £400,000; £400,000 and £200,000. In the UK, this rule was abolished from 1 January 1996 under Law Reform (Succession) Act 1995 s1(2). Such provisions now only apply if there is a specific clause in the will or trust deed to that effect. In the case, *re Crosier [1897]*, the judge said "What is the object of every hotchpot clause? It is simply to prevent a person to whom a testator has left a share of his estate, and who has been advanced in the testator's lifetime, from obtaining, by the combined effect of the bequest and the advance, more of the testator's property than he intended the legatee should have."

hotel Building that provides temporary accommodation. It is taxed as a trade and not as property income. A hotel is not subject to annual tax on enveloped dwellings. When an employee stays in a hotel on business, the employer may deduct the VAT charged by the hotel as input tax. Hotels may be able to charge the reduced VAT hospitality rate during the coronavirus outbreak. Hotels are excluded from the scope of investment via enterprise investment scheme (ITA 2007 s197) and venture capital trusts (ITA 2007 s308).

hot food For VAT, food that is sold while hot with the intention of being eaten while hot (such as burgers and chips) is standard-rated. Food that is hot solely because it has not yet cooled down (such as fresh bread) is generally zero-rated. Food that is sold cold to be heated by the customer (such as fresh meat) is generally zero-rated.

"Hot food means any food which (or any part of which) is hot at the time it is provided to the customer and –

(a) has been heated for the purposes of enabling it to be consumed hot,

(b) has been heated to order,

(c) has been kept hot after heating, or

(d) is provided to a customer in packaging that retains heat (whether or not the packaging was primarily designed for that purpose) or in any other packaging that is specifically designed for hot food, or

(e) is advertised or marketed in a way that indicates that it is supplied hot" (Value Added Tax 1994 Group 8 Note (3B)).

Further details are given in VAT notices 701/14 (food) and 709/1 (catering).

hot pie A hot pie can be zero-rated if it is hot only because it has yet to cool down from baking, or to create a pleasant aroma to attract customers. It is only standard-rated if the pie is intended to be eaten hot. The Court of Appeal so ruled in *John Pimblett & Sons Ltd. [1987]. CA STC 358.*

hot springs For VAT, water taken from such a spring and not further heated or treated is zero-rated as water under VATA 1994 Sch 8 Group 2 when supplied for non-industrial use. Details are given in VAT notice 701/16.

hot water For VAT, this is usually regarded as standard-rated supply of heat rather than a zero-rated supply of water. Further details are given in VAT notice 701/16.

hour Unit of time comprising 60 minutes or 3,600 seconds. There are 24 hours in a day, 168 in a week, and 8,760 in a 365-day year. The hour is a common unit for determining wage rates.

houseboat "A floating decked structure:

- which is designed or adapted for use solely as a place of permanent habitation, and
- which does not have the means of, and which is not capable of being readily adapted for, self-propulsion" (VAT leaflet 701/20).

The supply of a houseboat is zero-rated under VATA 1994 Sch 8 Group 8. This includes the non-commercial letting of houseboats. Guidance is given in VAT notice 701/20.

household goods Essentials to everyday living which cannot be seized from a bankrupt. They are also known as chattels. For Customs purposes, "furnishing and fittings for the home, and also personal items such as cameras, linen, jewellery and clothing" (Customs notice 3).

housekeeper allowance An addition to the personal allowance that could be claimed for a housekeeper between 1920 and 1988.

House of Commons Lower house of Parliament where elected MPs sit. The Budget is presented in this House and Finance Acts and other tax law is passed in this house.

House of Commons Members' Fund Fund established under House of Commons Member's Fund Act 1939 s1 to provide for widows, widowers and orphans of past or previous members. The tax treatment of payments from the fund is set out in ITEPA 2003 ss619-622.

House of Lords Upper House of Parliament of appointed members which has limited powers compared to the House of Commons. It debates the Finance Bills and other money bills but cannot reject them (Parliament Act 1911 s1). It was also the highest court in the land, until this function was taken over by the Supreme Court from 1 October 2009.

housing "Means a building, or part of a building, occupied or intended to be occupied as a dwelling or as more than one dwelling" (Housing and Planning Act 2016 s56).

housing administration order Order that may be made in respect of an insolvent provider of social housing under the provisions of Housing and Planning Act 2016 from s95.

housing administrator Officer of the court appointed when a provider of social housing has become insolvent (Housing and Planning Act 2016 s101).

housing assistance Money and other assistance that may be provided in Scotland to assist with housing costs under Social Security (Scotland) Act 2018 s35.

housing association Provider of social housing, also known as social landlords. Tax provisions for tax relief grants in Housing Act 1988 s54. Gifts to housing associations are generally exempt from inheritance tax (Inheritance Tax Act 1984 s24A) and capital gains tax (TCGA1992 s259).

housing benefit (HB) Means-tested social security benefit to help pay rent for people on low incomes. It is paid under Social Security Contributions and Benefits Act 1992 s130. This benefit is not subject to income tax (ITEPA 2003 s677). Housing benefit is being gradually abolished and replaced by universal credit under WRA 2012 s33(1)(d).

housing costs For universal credit, one of the additions that may be made to the standard allowance. The relevant law is WRA 2012 s11.

housing grant Grant provided by a local authority to assist a disabled person. Such grants are usually made under provisions of the Housing Grants, Construction and Regeneration Act 1996. It may also be provided under devolved legislation. Such grants are explicitly excluded from corporation tax by CTA 2009 s1284.

hovercraft Vessel which travels across land and sea on a cushion of air. A hovercraft first crossed the English Channel in 1959. A legal definition is given in Hovercraft Act 1968. This definition is used in tax statutes, such as for hold-over relief from capital gains tax (TCGA1992 s155 class 2). For VAT, "ship includes hovercraft" (Value Added Tax 1994 s96(1)). For VAT, it is generally zero-rated under VATA 1994 Sch 8 Group 8. For customs duties purposes, the control of hovercraft is governed by CEMA 1979 s23. For all other tax purposes, a hovercraft is regarded as a ship.

HS2 High Speed railway line to be built in two phases: phase 1 from London to Birmingham by 2026 and phase 2 to Manchester and Leeds by 2033. Trains would travel at speeds up to 225 mph. Authorisation is the High Speed Rail (London – West Midlands) Act 2017. The government confirmed on 14 February 2020 that HS2 would continue. Construction began later that year.

Huggins formula Method for calculating the tax liability of maintenance payments in Scotland between 1981 and 1988.

human capital accounting Attempt to value the combined knowledge and skill of a workforce. It is not a recognised intangible asset and cannot therefore appear on a balance sheet.

human consumption One of the conditions which must be met for food to be zero-rated for VAT. This means that the item must have both nutrition and palatability. So food does not include appetite suppressants, dietary supplements, food additives and medicines (though some medicines may be zero-rated under other provisions).

humanitarian assistance Provision of such basic supplies as accommodation, food, water and medicine, and also advice and manpower, to alleviate a natural or man-made disaster. The Secretary of State may provide any person or body with such assistance under International Development Act 2002 s3.

human resources (HR) General term for the management functions relating to the staff of an organisation. It includes such areas as personnel, pay, recruitment, working relations, and grievance and discipline.

human rights Fundamental rights of the individual which should be upheld by law. Although the scope varies from context to context, most lists include freedom of:

- speech;
- religion;
- movement;
- association;

and privacy, and the right to a fair trial. Some tax cases have been brought alleging that a tax or penalty contravenes the fundamental right to enjoy personal property. These have almost always failed. Under Equality Act 2006 s9(2) this includes rights under Human Rights Act 1998 and "other human rights".

Human Tissue Authority (HTA) Body corporate established under Human Tissue Act 2004 s13 to deal with human organs of deceased persons, including the issue of licences.

hundredweight Imperial unit of weight equal to 112 pounds. There are 20 hundredweight to a ton. It is equivalent to 50.8 kilograms.

Hungary East European country which is a member of the European Union. Its currency is the forint of 100 filler. The UK has a double taxation convention of 2011.

hunting Generally from 18 February 2005, hunting is illegal if it involves hunting a wild mammal (such as a fox) with a dog, unless exempt (Hunting Act 2004 s1). Hunt point to point meetings are taxed as mutual trading organisations, as is discussed in HMRC Manual at BIM24765. From 1934 to 1998, profits from point-to-point meetings were not taxed.

hurdle rate Term sometimes used to mean discount rate.

hyacinth Flower that is standard-rated for VAT. In VAT Notice 701/38, it is specifically excluded from zero-rating, as it is grown for ornamental purposes and not as food.

hybrid arrangement A pension arrangement where only one type of benefit will ultimately be provided, but the type of benefit that will be provided is not known in advance because it will depend on certain given circumstances at the point benefits are drawn. For example, a hybrid arrangement may provide the member with other money purchase benefits based on a pot derived from the contributions that have accrued over time, but subject to a defined benefit minimum or underpin. If the benefits provided by the money purchase pot at the point benefits are drawn fall below a certain defined level, for example 1/60ths of final remuneration for every year worked, that higher defined benefit will be provided. So the benefits will be either other money purchase benefits, or defined benefits. When benefits are drawn, if the benefits actually provided are other money purchase or cash balance benefits then the arrangement will become a money purchase arrangement. And if the benefits provided are defined benefits then the arrangement will become a defined benefits arrangement. The term is defined in FA 2004 s152(8).

hybrid derivative Financial instrument that contains more than one derivative.

hybrid mismatch Situation where tax laws differ between countries in ways that allow a multinational organisation to take advantage. Since 2011, OECD has been producing guidance on dealing with this.

hybrid rate Rate which is an average of two or more rates. This sometimes occurs in tax, such as when an accounting period spans a change in rate of capital allowance.

hybrid structure Trading arrangement that involves two types of business entity.

hydrocarbon Compound of the two elements of carbon and hydrogen, such as most oils. Such compounds may be subject to hydrocarbon oil duty and VAT.

hydrocarbon oil Liquid form of various compounds of carbon and hydrogen which are used as road fuel. Such oil is liable to hydrocarbon oil duty. For this purpose, oil is divided into five categories:

- light oil;
- heavy oil;
- fuel oil;
- gas oil; and
- biobutanol.

The legal definition is "petroleum oil, coal tar and oil produced from coal, shale, peat or any other bituminous substance, and all liquid hydrocarbons, but does not include such hydrocarbons or bituminous or asphaltic substances as are:

(a) solid or semi-solid at a temperature of 15°C, or
(b) gaseous at a temperature of 15°C and under a pressure of 1013.25 millibars" (HODA1979 s1(2)).

hydrogen Colourless gas, the lightest of all elements, denoted by the letter H. It can be used in a hydrogen cell to propel a vehicle. The advantage is that its exhaust consists solely of water.

hydrogen cell Electrochemical device which stores hydrogen. This is burned in oxygen, usually from the air, to provide energy and produce water. The first hydrogen cell was invented in 1838. There are many different types, some of which can be used to propel vehicles.

hydrogen refuelling point In relation to vehicles, "means a device intended for refuelling a vehicle that is capable of being propelled by electrical power derived from hydrogen" (Automated and Electric Vehicles Act 2018 s9(1)(b)).

hyperinflation Rate where prices increase so fast that the currency becomes worthless. The most extreme example of hyperinflation occurred in Hungary just after the second world war when prices doubled every 15 hours. The most famous example is probably Germany in 1923 when inflation hit 3,250,000%, and prices doubled every 49 hours. Inflation in Zimbabwe in 2008 ran into billions of percent before becoming unmeasurable. Other examples include Argentina 1989; Bolivia 1985; Brazil 1980-1995; Greece 1941-1944; Mexico 1982-1988; Peru 1988-1990; Venezuela 1989 and 2018; Yugoslavia 1993-1994; and Zimbabwe from 2006. An accounting standard defined hyperinflation as 100% or more over three years. The accounting treatment is to restate figures in a stable currency.

hypothecation Process whereby tax revenue is applied to a particular purpose. Climate change levy was applied to reducing employer's national insurance. Generally, the government tends not to favour hypothecation.

hypothetical net income Calculation used when non-residents wish to claim the transferable tax allowance between married couples. The calculation of hypothetical net income is set out in ITA 2007 s55C(3)

iaimbilanja One fifth of an ariary, currency of Madagascar.

IAS accounts "Accounts prepared in accordance with **international accounting** standards" (ICTA 1988 Sch 19ABA para 4(2)). For insurance companies, this is an alternative to IAD accounts.

IB **PAYE** tax code to an employee entitled to blind person's allowance (PAYE regs 2003 reg 7(3)). This code appears not to be in use.

ibid Latin: in the same place, such as from the same Act or other document.

ice Ordinary water that has been frozen is usually zero-rated as water under VATA 1994 Sch 8 Group 2. This does not apply to dry ice (frozen carbon dioxide) nor when sweetening or flavouring has been added. Details are given in VAT notice 701/16.

ICE Clear Europe "The clearing house for ICE's global energy markets, as well as the provider of clearing services for the European credit default swaps (CDS) markets." (company website). Provisions relating to stamp duty and SDRT are given in SI 2013 No 1382.

ice cream For VAT, this is standard-rated as it is specifically excluded from the scope of zero-rated food under VATA 1994 Sch 8 Group 1 Excepted Item 1. There are separate provisions for marshmallow cones and waffle cones.

Iceland European country that is a member of EFTA and EEA, but not of the European Union. Its currency is the Iceland kronur of 100 aurar. The UK has a double taxation convention of 2013.

ice lolly This is standard-rated for VAT. It is specifically excluded from the scope of zero-rated food by Value Added Tax 1994 Sch 8 Group 1 Excepted Item 1.

icon In computing, a small picture symbol to indicate a program or file. This can usually be accessed by double-clicking it.

identifiable asset test Test in determining whether expenditure is capital or revenue. It requires a first step of identifying the asset acquired by the expenditure. This test is established in such cases as *Tucker v Granada Motorway Services Ltd [1979] 53 TC 92* and is discussed in HMRC Manual at BIM35320.

identifiable part Part of expenditure that can clearly be related to a business activity. In general, such a part may be deducted from taxable profits. This is discussed in HMRC Manual at BIM42130.

identification of securities Procedure in capital gains tax to identify the **acquisition cost** when a taxpayer sells some of a holding in a particular security. The identification rules are given in TCGA1992 ss104-109.

identification of the financial statements Requirement that "an entity shall clearly identify each of the financial statements and the notes and distinguish them from other information in the same document" (FRS 102 section 3.23). FRS 102 provides further details in subsequent paragraphs.

identity document Document that evidences the identity of a person. The scope depends on the purpose. Common examples include passport, driving licence, immigration document, debit card, bank statement and utility bill. A list was given in Identity Documents Act 2010 s7(1) which is now repealed.

identity of HMRC staff Fraudsters have been known to impersonate HMRC staff, purportedly collecting debt. This may or may not be genuine. HMRC says the following procedure should be followed. Genuine HMRC staff do not mind being checked. Ask to see the collector's identity card. It has a photograph of the person and an ID number. Make a note of the number. Call 0300 200 3862 and give HMRC the number. Do not call a number provided by the collector. HMRC will confirm whether the collector is genuine.

identity theft When someone takes over the identity of another person for fraudulent purposes.

idle time Time for which an employee is paid though not able to work, usually for factors beyond their control such as a machine breakdown.

IFRIC International Financial Reporting Interpretations Committee. This is used as a prefix for interpretations of international accounting standards. For example, IFRIC 1 deals with "changes in existing decommissioning, restoration and similar liabilities". Before May 2004, such interpretations were prefixed SIC.

IFRS International financial reporting standard.

ignorance of the law The aphorism that ignorance of the law is no excuse is an ancient rule, first set out more than 2,000 years ago by Aristotle (384 BC – 322 BC). Its Latin name is *ignorantia juris non excusat.* The principle is also found in the Bible in Leviticus 5:17. This aphorism does not necessarily apply for tax law. In the case *Christine Perrin [2018] UKUT 156,* the judge said, "it is a much-cited aphorism that 'ignorance of the law is no excuse', and on occasion this has been given as a reason why the defence of reasonable excuse cannot be available in such circumstances. We see no basis for this argument. Some requirements of the law are well-known, simple and straightforward but others are much less so. It will be a matter of judgment for the [first tier tribunal] in each case whether it was objectively reasonable for the particular taxpayer, in the circumstances of the case, to have been ignorant of the requirement in question, and for how long" (para 82).

This has been followed by other cases such as *Bachir Mohamed Belloul [2020] TC 7794* where a taxpayer was excused for ignorance of the high income child benefit charge.

ignorance test For tax avoidance schemes, one of three tests a scheme designer must pass not to be regarded as a promoter. "The ignorance test applies when a person could not reasonably be expected to have either:

- sufficient information to enable them to know whether or not the arrangements are disclosable schemes
- sufficient information so as to enable that person to comply.

" This test might apply where, for example, a person has insufficient knowledge of the overall arrangements to know whether the 'benign' or 'non-adviser' tests are failed; or has only a partial understanding of the scheme so that they would be unable to comply with the disclosure requirements." (HMRC leaflet DOTAS, January 2016).

illegal trade Trade which contravenes the law, such as prostitution, drug dealing and illegal sales of firearms and alcohol. Such activities are subject to income tax, corporation tax and VAT under the normal tax rules for legal trade. Other illegal activities, such as burglary and protection rackets, are not taxable as trade.

illegitimate Not legitimate, particularly in the context of a child born to unmarried parents, including parents who were divorced. An illegitimate child was called a bastard, but this meaning has now generally been abandoned as pejorative. Historically, illegitimate children were often denied many rights. These have been gradually withdrawn. Today the only restriction is that an illegitimate child cannot inherit a title. For tax purposes, an illegitimate child is now treated the same as a legitimate child. The right to inherit was established by Family Law Reform Act 1969.

ill health The tax consequences of ill health are:

- an employee may be entitled to statutory sick pay and sick leave;
- a person may receive their pension before the age of 55;
- the amount of pension may be increased
- the person may benefit from provisions relating to disability.

ill health condition In relation to tax relief for pensions advice, "the ill health condition is met by an employee if the employer is satisfied, on the basis of evidence provided by a registered general medical practitioner, that the employee is (and will continue to be) incapable of carrying on his or her occupation because of physical or mental impairment" (ITEPA 2003 s308C(10) inserted by Finance (No 2) Act 2017 s3).

illicit Not permitted. The term is usually distinguished from illegal in that it refers to an act which is not against the law as such but which is done in a way which is not permitted, such as selling alcoholic drink without a licence. The illegality derives from the lack of licence not from selling alcohol.

illiquid Not easily converted to cash.

illiquidityInability or difficulty to convert an asset to cash. The term is particularly used for current assets. Traditionally these are listed in the balance sheet with the most liquid at the top, the order runs:

- cash;
- prepayments;
- debtors;
- stock.

I minus E basis In relation to taxation of insurance companies, "means the basis under which a company carrying on life insurance business is charged to tax on the relevant profits (within the meaning of section 88(3) of the FA 1989) of that business under Case I of Schedule D" (ICTA 1988 s431(2)). For corporation tax, the provisions are CTA 2009 from s1080.

immaterial Description of an amount so small that it does not matter. Accounts may ignore immaterial figures.

immediate annuity An annuity under which payments commence straight away, in contrast to a deferred annuity, under which the payments do not commence until later (possibly many years later).

immediate care fees annuity plan Annuity taken out when a person needs care. It is funded by a single premium, often built up in a fund established for that purpose but not restricted to that purpose, so the policy holder may use the proceeds for other purposes (or leave them as part of their estate) if care is not needed.

immediately chargeable transfer From 22 March 2006, a transfer of money or assets to a relevant property trust which can trigger a liability to inheritance tax.

immediate payment arrangements Accounting arrangement between two entities whereby a sponsoring entity makes payment to an intermediary. The commonest form is a trust for paying employees. The accounting details are set out in FRS 102 from section 9.33.

immediate post-death interest (IPDI) Form of trust that is advantaged for inheritance tax. It arises when a person has an interest in possession in settled property and:

- the settlement is effected by a will or intestacy, and
- the beneficiary became beneficially entitled to the interest in possession on the death of the deceased.

The law is Inheritance Tax Act 1984 s49A.

Immigration When a person who is not resident in the UK seeks to live or work in the UK. This is strictly regulated by law, particularly Immigration Act 2014. The person may be liable to pay the immigration health surcharge and the employer may be liable to pay the immigration skills charge. Generally a worker from overseas (which includes EU countries from 1 January 2021) needs a visa. This is determined on a points-based system to determine eligibility. There are various special schemes for particular classes of worker and students.

Citizens of the EU, EEA or Switzerland do not need a visa to visit the UK for up to six months. Those who were UK resident on 31 December 2020 can apply for settled status.

UK employers must check that a job applicant is allowed to work in the UK. There are penalties for failure to comply. Employers may accept EU passports and identity cards at least until 30 June 2021. Identity cards containing a chip are accepted at least until 2026.

immigration health surcharge Sum that an immigrant to the UK must pay for the right to use the National Health Service. The rates are given in section 3 of this dictionary. On 1 October 2020, this was refunded for many NHS and care workers.

immigration skills charge Charge imposed from 6 April 2017 on a UK sponsor of a foreign worker from outside the EU or EEA. Some workers are excepted. The rates are given in section 3 of this dictionary. The charge is imposed under Immigration Skills Charge Regulations 2017. The charge is for a minimum period of 12 months plus additions for further periods of six months up to five years. The payment must be made in one go. It is refunded if the application for the worker is unsuccessful or if the application is successful but the worker does not take up the position. No refunds are given for parts of a period.

impact day Day on which a flotation of a company is announced and the prospectus is advertised.

impaired life State when a person is not expected to live as long as normal, usually because of a medical condition. Such a person may receive an enhanced pension.

impairment A reduction in the carrying value of an asset, beyond the expected depreciation, which must be reflected by reducing the amount recorded in the balance sheet.

impairment loss "Means a debit in respect of the impairment of a financial asset" (CTA 2009 s476(1)). "The amount by which the carrying amount of an asset exceeds:
(a) in the case of inventories, its selling price less costs to complete and sell; or
(b) in the cases of other assets, its recoverable amount" (FRS 102 glossary).

imperial system System of historic measurements that predate metric units. Examples include the mile, gallon and ton. There are ancient laws which go back at least to the 11th century. In modern times, measures were first prescribed by Weights and Measures Act 1824 and subsequently amended, most recently in 1959. From 1990, imperial units have generally been replaced by metric units for most legal purposes (Weights and Measures Act 1985). This includes tax provision, for example alcoholic liquor duty is charged by the hectolitre rather than the gallon, and the garden size for main residence relief is half a hectare instead of an acre. The law is now that metric units must be used when selling packaged or loose goods, except for draft beer or cider, milk in returnable containers, and precious metals sold by Troy ounce. An imperial measure may be displayed for comparison.

impersonation of officers A criminal offence of impersonating a police officer or person of similar standing. For social security, the offence is set out in Social Security Administration Act 1992 s181. Impersonation of a Commissioner or officer of HMRC is an offence under Commissioners for Revenue and Customs Act 2005 s30.

import Bring into UK from another country. Goods are not imported within the EU single market, they were said to be acquired.

import duties Customs duties on goods imported from another country. Before 1 January 2021, the duties applied to goods imported from outside the EU.

importer Person who is responsible for bringing goods into the UK. The importer must be identified for Customs purposes, but most of the duties rest with the declarant. A statutory definition is "in relation to any goods at any time between their importation and the time when they are delivered out of charge, includes any owner or other person for the time being possessed of or beneficially interested in the goods and, in relation to goods imported by means of a pipe-line, includes the owner of the pipe-line" (CEMAs1(1)).

import licensing procedure This "means an administrative procedure, whether or not referred to as licensing, used by a Party for the operation of import licensing regimes, requiring the submission of an application or other documentation, other than that generally required for customs clearance purposes, to the relevant administrative body or bodies as a prior condition for importation into the territory of the importing Party" (EU/UK withdrawal agreement of 24 December 2020. Article GOODS 3 Definitions (d)).

import value Value of goods for the purposes of determining the amount of Customs duty payable. The value is the CIF value, that is including carriage, insurance and freight. To this is added certain other costs of purchase, such as commission, royalties and licence fees. This is known as the transaction value. If this method is not possible, such as when the goods are imported on loan, the value is determined by a hierarchy of methods, as set out in Customs notice 252.

import VAT VAT payable in respect of imported goods.

impracticable In accounting, description of a condition that cannot be applied despite every reasonable attempt to do so (FRS 102 glossary).

imprest system Financial arrangement sometimes used for petty cash, where funds are topped up to the value of vouchers, so that the total of cash and vouchers is always the same.

improvement In accounting, a change in a fixed asset that extends its useful life or increases its expected future benefit. Such expenditure is generally treated for tax as capital rather than revenue.

impuesto sobre el Valor Anadidio (IVA) Spanish: value added tax.

imputation System of taxation where liability arises on the assumption of rights over property. Advance corporation tax was such a system.

inaccuracy An inaccuracy may give rise to a penalty if it is a relevant inaccuracy as defined in FA 2007 Sch 24 para 1A(1).

incapacitated person For tax management, this was originally defined as "any infant, person of unsound mind, lunatic, idiot or insane person" (TMA 1970 s118(1)). This definition was repealed by FA 2012 s222(4)(a) with effect from 6 April 2012 to avoid the pejorative meanings, though it did not change tax law. If such a person is unable to submit a tax return, one must be submitted on their behalf by an attorney registered at the Court of Protection. This is stated in statement of practice SP A13 of 1993, which HMRC has confirmed continues to apply despite many tax changes to the tax system since then.

incapacity benefit Social security benefit paid until October 2008 when replaced by employment and support allowance.

inception Start or birth of something. In accounting and tax, it is used to mean the start of a lease, as in CAA 2001 s70YI(1)).

inch Imperial unit of length equal to one twelfth of a foot or 25.4 millimetres.

incidence of tax Indication of where the burden of a tax charge lies. While VAT is paid to HMRC by the trader, the incidence of the tax is usually borne by the customer.

incidental This term is used in various places in tax law, usually to allow expenditure when a small part is for a non-deductible reason, such as incidental personal benefit of a business expense. The term is not further defined, though for business expenditure HMRC Manuals says that it means "any expenditure that is incurred directly or indirectly in connection with the provision of entertainment" (BIM 45020).

incidental benefit Unavoidable personal benefit of business expenditure, such as a uniform avoiding the need for personal clothing. Such incidental benefit does not in itself disqualify expenditure from being tax-deductible.

incidental costs of obtaining finance Incidental costs incurred in obtaining a loan or from issuing loan stock. Such costs may be tax deductible under ITTOIA 2005s58. These rules were originally introduced by FA 1980. It should be noted that the relief applies only to income tax, not to corporation tax. The matter is discussed in HMRC Manual at BIM45801.

incidental overnight expenses An allowance of up to £5 a day in the UK or £10 a day overseas for personal expenditure of an employee on a business trip (ITEPA 2003 s179(6) and s240(1)). The allowance is per trip not per day. So if an employee was overseas for five days, the allowance was £50. It does not matter how much was spent in a particular day. This covers such items as newspapers, laundry and bar drinks. The limits are unchanged from 1995. These expenses allow an employer to disregard expenditure to these amounts on a hotel bill or similar. They cannot otherwise be claimed by an employee. The provision is intended to simplify life for the employer, not to give a tax break to the employee.

inclusive price Term which defines the value used in determining the tax payable by an employee for having a company car. It comprises the **list price** of the car plus any taxes paid and any delivery charge (ITEPA 2003 s123(2)).

income In accounting, money and benefits a person receives from all sources. "Increases in economic benefits during the reporting period in the form of inflows or enhancements of assets or decreases of liabilities that result in increases in equity, other than those relating to contributions from equity investors" (FRS 102 glossary).

"The definition of income encompasses both revenue and gains" (FRS 102 section 2.25).

income and expenditure "The total of income less expenses, excluding the components of other comprehensive income. In the for-profit sector this is known as profit or loss" (FRS 102 glossary).

income bond Bond whose original principal is returned at maturity. The interest is paid as it is earned. The term is sometimes used to mean a specific product offered by National Savings and Investments. This product may be held in amounts from £500 to £1 million. Interest is paid into a bank account and is subject to income tax. Rates are given in section 3 of this dictionary.

income contingent repayment scheme Part of the Repayment of Teachers' Loan scheme that operated between 2002 and 2005. Broadly, the loan was provided to enable qualified teachers to retrain in shortage subjects. Provided the teacher took such a post by 30 June 2005 and remained in post for ten years, the loan is written off. Otherwise any balance is collected under the student loan deduction scheme.

income deduction In relation to deemed manufactured payments, this term has a specific meaning in ITA 2007 s596(5).

income disregard In social security, an amount of increase income that is ignored in determining entitlement to tax credit and to some other benefits. Provided a person's income does not increase by more than figure during the year, a person's tax credit or benefit if not altered. For tax credits, the disregard is £10,000 from 6 April 2011. It was previously £25,000 from 2006.

income from patents In relation to capital allowances for patents, this term is defined in CAA 2001 s483.

income gearing Ratio of interest a company pays on its borrowings as a percentage of its pre-tax pre-interest profits.

income policy Life Insurance contract that provides income on a monthly or other periodic basis, as opposed to a policy which pays proceeds in a lump sum.

income-related Term applied to some social security benefits that are paid on a means-tested basis, although they are more usually paid on the basis of national insurance contributions. Employment and support allowance and jobseeker's allowance are examples.

income-related ESA Employment support allowance that is paid as a result of a means test, as against contributory ESA. This benefit is not subject to income tax (ITEPA 2003 s677).

income replacement benefits Social security benefits that are designed to replace income, such as statutory maternity pay and jobseeker's allowance.

income retention condition One of the conditions for tax relief for a venture capital trust (ITA 2007 s274). It is basically that the company may not keep more than 15% of its profits for its own use.

income shares Shares in a unit trust that are designed to provide income rather than capital growth.

income spreading Practice of sharing income, such as with a spouse, to reduce the overall amount of tax payable. Where this is done in a trade, the amount paid may be disallowed as not wholly and exclusively for the purposes of the trade (ITTOIA 2005; CTA 2009 s54).

income statement Term used in modern accounting standards to mean profit and loss account.

income stream The tax implications of transferring an income stream are given in ITA 2007 from s809ZA.

income support Means-tested social security benefit (SSCBA 1992 s124) that is generally tax free (ITEPA 2003 s660(1)).

From 27 October 2008, it was largely replaced by employment and support allowance and is now being replaced by universal credit (WRA 2012 s33(1)(c)).

Income support tops up a claimant's net income to a level that reflects a person's needs, as viewed by the government. The steps are:

- add up the income support personal allowance and any premiums for special needs plus housing costs. This is the applicable amount
- determine the income of the claimant and any partner. This includes net earnings, other benefits and maintenance payments, but not interest on any capital. Instead include a tariff income on savings at a rate of £1 per £250 of savings
- subtract the income as determined above from the applicable amount. This is the amount of income support.

Rates are given under Social Security in section 3 of this dictionary.

Other provisions of income support are:

- the claimant must be aged 16 or over but below state pension age
- the claimant has less than £6,000 capital (£10,000 if resident in a care home)
- it may not be claimed by a new claimant able to claim universal credit instead
- there is no premium or addition for children, but a claimant may be able to claim child tax credit
- a claim may be made by calling 0800 169 0350 which is the preferred method. A claim may also be made by completing a DWP form. Payment is made for periods from the date of claim
- generally a claim cannot be backdated, subject to a few exceptions where it can be backdated up to three months
- a claimant is required to provide supporting information and may be required to attend an interview
- the benefit is determined weekly, normally paid fortnightly in arrears. The minimum weekly payment is 10p (£5 if in a trade dispute). If entitlement is less than £1 a week, it is paid every three months in arrears.

income support deduction notice (ISDN) Document that could be issued by the Department of Work and Pensions or Benefits Agency to recover overpaid income support. From 6 April 2013, it is replaced by a deduction of earnings order.

income tax

Definition

Tax imposed on the earnings of individuals (including partnerships). It was first introduced from 1799 to 1802, reintroduced from 1803 to 1812, and finally reintroduced in 1842, though it is still, strictly, an annual tax which requires a new Act of Parliament each year to continue levying it.

"Income tax, if I may be pardoned for saying so, is a tax on income. It is not meant to be a tax on anything else. It is one tax, not a collection of taxes essentially distinct."

Lord Macnaghten in Attorney-General v LCC [1900] 4 TC 265.

Scope of income

It is a tax on income and cannot be extended to other sources of wealth generation (*Attorney General v London County Council [1900] 4TC 265).*

The exact scope of what constitutes income has often proved difficult. For example, benefits in kind for employees are brought into the scope of income tax, even though the employee's benefit is that of reducing expenditure rather than generating income. Many sources of income are tax free. This is usually because it is either subject to another tax, or because it is part of a government incentive. Income tax is also used to recover child benefit under high income child benefit charge and to tax the use of pre-owned assets which would otherwise be subject to inheritance tax. Income tax is distinguished from corporation tax which is imposed on companies and other corporate bodies, as well as from capital gains tax which is imposed on capital gains of individuals. Income tax, corporation tax and capital gains tax are mutually exclusive; if an income, profit or gain falls to be taxed under one of these taxes, it is not taxed under either of the other two.

Overview

In general, all individuals of any age are liable to pay income tax. At its simplest, it is calculated by a minimum of three stages:

- adding up all income;
- subtracting allowances and deductions;
- multiplying by various rates.

Most taxpayers are entitled to a personal allowance, which reduces on incomes above £100,000 a year. There are further allowances for a taxpayer who is blind, or who was born (or is married to someone who was born) before 6 April 1935.

A taxpayer may transfer up to 10% of his or her personal allowance to a spouse or civil partner, provided the transferor is not liable to pay tax at the higher or additional rate.

There are some allowance that are specific to particular income, such as rent-a-room, and the trading and investment allowances.

There are also many reliefs that may be claimed, such as for losses brought forward, charitable donations and pension contributions.

Rates

From 6 April 2011, there are only three rates of income tax, a basic rate of 20%, a higher rate of 40%, and an additional rate of 45% (50% before 2013). Historically there have often been three or more rates.

Wales and Scotland are allowed to set their own rates. Wales has so far kept its rates the same as for England and Northern Ireland. Scotland has increased its rates by adding 1 percentage points to the three rates and having a lower threshold for the higher rate. The basic rate has been replaced by three rates: a starting rate of 19%, a basic rate of 20% and an intermediate rate of 21%. The Scottish rates only apply to earned income.

There are special rates of income tax for dividends.

Details of rates and allowances are given under Income tax in section 3 of his dictionary.

Collection

Income tax is collected in various ways.

By far the largest amount is collected from employees' pay packets under Pay As You Earn (PAYE).

In the construction industry, subcontractors may have some tax collected under Construction Industry Scheme.

Some other payments have income tax deducted at source.

Other taxpayers complete a self-assessment return.

Accounting

In accounting, income tax is shown in the statement of cash flows. The accounting treatment is set out in FRS 102 section 7.17. It should be noted that accounting standards often use the term "income tax" to include corporation tax.

income tax advantage Term used in CTA 2010 s687 to denote a gain that may arise from a transaction in securities. The term is also used in ITA 2007 s572A(3) in relation to manufactured dividends.

income tax lock Provision in Finance (No 2) Act 2015 s1 not to increase the basic, higher or additional rates of income tax before the next general election. This provision was not maintained in respect of the 2017 and 2019 general elections.

income tax relief limit The limit on the amount of certain income tax reliefs that may be claimed from 6 April 2013. The relief is the higher of 25% of the taxpayer's adjusted income and £50,000. The main reliefs subject to this limit are

- trade loss relief against general income and early trade losses relief – claimed on the self-employment, Lloyd's underwriters or partnership pages
- property loss relief (relating to capital allowances or agricultural expenses) – claimed on the UK property or foreign pages
- post-cessation trade relief, post-cessation property relief, employment loss relief, former employees deduction for liabilities, losses on deeply discounted securities and strips of government securities
- share loss relief, unless claimed on Enterprise Investment scheme (EIS) or Seed Enterprise Investment Scheme (SEIS) shares – claimed on the capital gains summary pages
- qualifying loan interest – claimed on the additional information pages.

  Guidance is provided by HMRC on helpsheet 204.

income threshold figure Amount of income below which a household may claim the social security benefit called tax credit.

incoming partner Person who joins a partnership. Such a partner is not liable for any partnership debts that arose before he or she joined (Partnership Act 1890 s17). A new partner means that the old partnership is dissolved and a new partnership formed. The old and new partners may make a joint election that the two partnerships should be treated as one.

incomplete records Accounting records which fall short of full double entry bookkeeping. Such records can be incomplete in many ways. The two commonest reasons are:

- keeping single entry records, or
- loss of records, such as in a fire.

For the former, double entries can usually be created from the single entries. For the latter, external evidence must be sought, such as from bank statements and from the records of customers and suppliers. In an extreme case, records can be created using a statement of affairs.

inconsistency notice Notice that the Registrar of Companies may send to a company when a document is received containing information that is inconsistent with information already on file (CA 2006 s1093).

incontinence pad For VAT, these are generally standard-rated unless zero-rated as a product for the handicapped, or reduced-rated or zero-rated as sanitary protection. Details are given in VAT notice 701/18.

incorporate Bring a company into existence.

incorporated society Friendly society that has become incorporated (TCGA 1992 s217A).

incorporation Process of bringing a company into existence.

incorporation relief Relief from capital gains tax when business assets are transferred to a company formed to continue the same business (TCGA 1992 s142).

incorporeal chattels Personal rights and interests that are not tangible assets, such as shares, patents and annuities.

incorporeal hereditament Intangible rights or interest in land, such as a right of way or a right of pasture.

increase Moving to a higher number, or greater quantity or amount. FA 2004 s228ZA(7) says that an increase may be from nil. Although this is in the context of restricted annual allowance for pension contributions, it must apply to any other increase.

incurred basis Old tax rule that income is taxed when incurred. This basis has in effect been scrapped since 1999. Tax generally follows when income and expenditure is recognised under accounting standards, unless a cash basis is used. The matter is discussed in HMRC Manual at BIM42220.

indecent material Customs may seize any indecent material that a traveller attempts to bring into the UK. Indecent material includes improper material featuring children, material containing extreme violence, and any pornography that cannot be legally bought in the UK.

in default For company law, an officer of a company is in default "if he authorises or permits, participates in, or fails to take all reasonable steps to prevent, the contravention" (CA 2006 s1121(3)).

indemnity insurance Insurance against the costs of indemnifying someone. The premium paid by an employer to indemnify an employee is not generally a taxable benefit (ITEPA 2003 s346). The rights of charity trustees to take out such insurance is given in Charities Act 2011 from s189.

independence Requirement in some situations for a person to have no connection with another party. An example is CA 2006 s936 in relation to experts and valuers. For auditors, the Auditing Practices Board defines independence as "freedom from situations and relationships which make it probable that a reasonable and informed third party would conclude that objectivity either is impaired or could be impaired. Independence is related to and underpins objectivity. However, whereas objectivity is a personal behavioural characteristic concerning the auditor's state of mind, independence relates to the circumstances surrounding the audit, including the financial, employment, business and personal relationships between the auditor and the audited entity"

independent agent For capital gains tax purposes, "in relation to a non-UK resident ("X") means a person who is the UK representative of X in respect of any agency in which the person is acting on behalf of X in an independent capacity" (TCGA1992 s271J(2)).

independent assessor Person who conducts an independent report on poll as requested by sufficient members of a quoted public company. The appointment of such a person is governed by CA 2006 ss343-345.

Independent Barring Board (IBB) Body corporate established under Safeguarding Vulnerable Groups Act 2006 s1(1) to keep a register of people barred from working with children or vulnerable adults. It has now been replaced by Disclosure and Barring Service.

independent broker "Person, who independently of the director or any person connected with him, selects the person with whom the transaction is to be effected" (CA 2006 s194(2)(a)). Under company law, members' approval is required for a substantial property transaction involving a director. There are exceptions, including a transaction on a recognised investment exchange through an independent broker.

independent broker conditions For the income of non-residents, this term is defined in ITA 2007 s817.

independent business review Statement made by a professional adviser in connection with a Time To Pay request involving more than £1 million.

independent examination (IE) An alternative to a full audit for charities with income of less than £500,000 a year (from February 2008). There are some restrictions when a full audit is still required, particularly in Scotland. The two main differences between IE and full audit are:

- the scrutiny of the accounts is less detailed; and

- the assurance is just that nothing has been found that needs reporting.

independent expert For the definition of a knowledge-intensive company for enterprise investment scheme and other schemes, this term is defined in ITA 2007 s252A as inserted by Finance (No 2) Act Sch 5. For venture capital trusts, the same definition is used in ITA 2007 s331A as inserted by Finance (No 2) Act 2015 Sch 6.

Independent Family Returns Panel Body established by Borders, Citizenship and Immigration Act 2009 s54A as inserted by Immigration Act 2014 s3. Its function is to consider how to deal with the children of a person deported from the UK.

independent financial adviser (IFA) A broker or other intermediary authorised to sell or advise on the policies offered by any insurance company, as well as other financial service providers.

independent investment manager conditions For the purposes of income of non-residents, this term is defined in ITA 2007 s818.

independent mental health advocate Person who acts on behalf of mental patients under the provisions of Mental Health Act 1983 s130A.

independent personal budget In relation to a local authority's care of an adult, means "a statement which specifies what the cost would be to the local authority concerned... of meeting the adult's eligible needs for care and support" (Care Act 2014 s28(1)).

index In mathematics, a number which indicates a relative change in a financial measure. An index is often applied by treating the number as half a fraction. For example if an item was bought when an index of inflation (such as RPI or CPI) was at 105, and the item was sold when the index was at 120, the inflated purchase price can be calculated by multiplying the actual price by 120/105.

There are also indices for investment, such as the various FT-SE, and other indices for other purposes.

The Retail Prices Index and FT-SE 100 index are given in section 3 of this dictionary.

indexation allowance Amount that could be added to the acquisition cost to reflect general inflation between acquisition and disposal, and thus reduce the amount of capital gain. The allowance was designed to stop capital gains tax being a tax on inflation. The allowance could be claimed by individuals on capital gains between April 1982 and April 1998, but not for gains that arise from 6 April 1998, when the rate was reduced. Companies could claim the allowance against corporation tax on chargeable gains between April 1982 and December 2017. From January 2018, a company may claim indexation allowance for periods up to December 2017. The allowance may be calculated either by using the retail prices index (reproduced in section 3 of this dictionary) or by using indexation factors produced by HMRC. (Factors for December 2017 are in section 3 of this dictionary). If using the retail prices index, the acquisition cost is increased by the index for the month of disposal divided by the index for the month of acquisition.

indexation loss Loss created by applying indexation to a capital gain/loss. From 29 November 1993, no relief is given for an indexation loss, subject to a two-year transitional period.

index-linked Description of something that relates to a published index, such as a savings product linked to the retail prices index.

index-linked pension Pension where payments increase each year. Such a pension may have:

- full indexation: it increases by the full amount of an index, such as retail prices index
- limited indexation: it increases by the lower of inflation and a fixed percentage, often 5%
- escalation: it increases by a fixed percentage each year, often 3%, regardless of inflation.

An occupational pension scheme sets out any indexation in the scheme details. For a private pension, the pensioner can choose what level of indexation to have. Annuity rates are given in section 3 of this dictionary.

index of members Alphabetical list of shareholders or guarantors which a limited company must keep in addition to its register of members if there are more than 50 members (CA 2006 s115).

India Eastern country. Its currency is the rupee of 100 paise. The UK has a double taxation agreement of 2013, a double taxation agreement of 1993 and a memorandum of understanding on Article 27 mutual agreement procedure. Payments of a pension made under Pensions (India, Pakistan and Burma) Act 1955 may be exempt from income tax under ITEPA 2003 s654.

indicative seal A trader seal that can withstand a force of between 250 and 1000 kilograms. A seal that can withstand a greater force is called a security seal. Further details are given in Customs notice 205.

indirect agent Customs agent who makes Customs declarations in the agent's own name (Taxation (Cross-border Trade) Act 2018 s21(1)(b)).

indirect benefit Any form of consideration provided indirectly to someone, such as from an employer to employee. An example is when an employee receives a benefit which arises indirectly from work such as winning a prize from an external body. In general such benefits are taxable as a benefit in kind unless it can be shown that the nature was unrelated to work such as a personal testimonial.

indirect shareholding percentage For entrepreneur's relief in a joint venture company, part of the shareholding test that must be satisfied. Details are given in TCGA1992 Sch 7ZA para 6.

indirect taxation Tax that is not paid directly to the tax authority but to someone else to pass on. Examples include Customs duties, excise duties and VAT.

individual risk In relation to resolution of tax disputes, "means a particular transaction (or series of transactions) or an item in a return or declaration which causes risk to past, or present or future revenue flows" (HMRC Notice of 20 December 2013).

individual savings account (ISA)

Definition

Tax-advantaged scheme whereby individuals may hold shares in companies. Shares held in an ISA have no income tax charged on their dividends, and no capital gains tax when sold. They were introduced on 6 April 1999, as a replacement for personal equity plans and tax-exempt special savings accounts.

Main provisions

The main provisions are:

- there is an annual limit per investor. Details are given under Individual Savings Accounts in section 3 of this dictionary
- every taxpayer has his or her own limit, so a husband's limit is separate from his wife's
- from April 2015, an ISA may be inherited tax free
- a withdrawal from an ISA may be made at any time, but funds withdrawn cannot be replaced once the limit has been reached in a tax year.

There are many rules which must be followed. These rules have changed many times since ISAs were introduced.

Law

The main law on ISAs is SI 1998 No 1870, issued under ICTA 1988 s151, TCGA1992 s151 and FA 1998 ss75-76. These regulations have been amended many times.

The statutory authority is ICTA 1988 ss333-333B, TCGA1992 s151, and FA 2008 ss75-76. Many details are given in regulations as SI 1998 No 1870 as amended.

The statutory provisions are now largely contained in ITTOIA 2005 ss694-701.

From 1 July 2014, ISAs are replaced by New ISAs (NISAs) when the annual limit was increased from £11,880 to £15,000, and has been subsequently indexed. NISAs largely abolished restrictions on what types of investment qualify for a NISA.

From 1 November 2011, it is possible to take out a junior ISA for UK-resident children under 18. Junior ISAs replace the child's trust fund. In addition to this general savings product, there are also junior ISAs and help-to-buy ISAs.

Previous provisions and history

- 6 April 1999: ISAs were classified as maxi-ISAs and mini-ISAs with separate limits
- 13 December 2000: an ISA may hold a depositary interest
- 6 April 2001: age limit for holders reduced from 18 to 16
- 8 January 2003: provision introduced to repair certain ISAs issued from 2001
- 17 November 2003: ISA may include shares in a UCITS
- 6 April 2004: 10% credit is no longer paid on savings
- 6 April 2005: ISAs became indefinite and would not end in 2005/06
- 6 April 2005: classification of maxi-ISAs and mini-ISAs is dropped
- 13-19 September 2007: special provisions introduced for Northern Rock
- 6 April 2008: half of an ISA may be invested in a cash ISA
- 30 June 2014: removal of restriction about holding half allowance in cash
- 6 April 2015: ISA can be inherited tax free.

individual savings account policy "A policy of life insurance which is an investment of a kind specified by regulations made by virtue of section 695(1) of ITTOIA 2005" (ICTA 1988 s431BB(2)).

individual voluntary arrangement (IVA) Legally binding arrangement between a debtor and creditors for paying at least 25% of the debts. An IVA is flexible to meet the needs of the debtor, but should not be seen as a quick and easy way to be shot of inconvenient debts.

Main points

The main points are:

- an IVA must be set up by an insolvency practitioner. The debtor usually appoints the practitioner.
  A list is available from www.insolvencydirect.bis.gov or by contacting the Official Receiver's office. An accounting firm may be able to advise
- it is normal for the debtor to have an informal meeting with the insolvency practitioner before appointment
- it is not necessary, and often undesirable, to use a debt management company. A debtor can approach an insolvency practitioner directly
- the insolvency practitioner often gets an interim order from a court to stop creditors taking action to recover their debts
- an IVA covers arrears of tax and national insurance, council tax, tax credit and benefit overpayments, personal loans, credit card balances, overdrafts, debts to family and friends, and many other debts and bills
- an IVA does not protect a debtor from secured debts. So, a mortgage could be enforced by the lender taking the property unless the creditor agrees to be part of the IVA, which is unlikely in practice
- a debtor may be required to remortgage a home to raise extra funds, provided there is sufficient net value. If this is not possible, the IVA may be extended by an extra year
- a creditor is expected to give up all savings
- a creditor who receives a windfall, such as an inheritance, is generally allowed to keep the first £500 but must give up the rest
- a lump sum withdrawal from a pension fund counts as a windfall, but the disguised remuneration cannot be compelled to make such a withdrawal
- income from work and pension income must be applied to the IVA.
- an IVA prevents creditors taking enforcement action against the debtor
- an IVA has a life, typically of 5 or 6 years
- during the life of an IVA, the debtor makes payments to be shared among creditors
- the insolvency practitioner looks at assets owned by the debtor to see if any could be sold to realise funds. A debtor may exclude particular assets, such as a car, but this could make it less likely that creditors will agree
- the insolvency practitioner draws up a proposal to put to the creditors. This covers how much of the debt they will receive and when they will receive it
- the insolvency practitioner calls a creditors' meeting, usually at their offices. The debtor is not required to attend, but it is usually advisable to do so

- a proposal requires the acceptance of 75% of the creditors by value. If a creditor is owed 26% of the debts, that creditor has 26% of the votes which means the creditor in effect has a veto
- creditors may suggest alternative provisions. These require the agreement of the debtor. If no agreement can be reached, the IVA cannot proceed. Alternative arrangements such as bankruptcy will be followed
- if a proposal is accepted, the IVA becomes immediately binding on all parties, including on creditors who voted against
- there is no limit to the number of debts or the total amount that may be covered by an IVA. An IVA is not appropriate if the debtor owes money to only one person
- an IVA can be expensive, and so is unlikely to be appropriate for debts below £10,000. In 2020, an IVA costs an average of between £4,000 and £5,000 to set up
- an IVA only covers one person, so joint debts may not be included. As the other person will often become liable for the whole debt, a possible solution is for both people to have IVAs that are connected, called interlocking IVAs
- a debtor who works in accountancy, law or financial services may find that he or she cannot keep their job if they take out an IVA. Other jobs are unlikely to be affected
- an IVA is recorded and will adversely affect the disguised remuneration's credit rating.

Alternatives to an IVA are bankruptcy, a debt relief order, debt management plan, and (from 2021) Breathing Space.

Debts not covered by an IVA

Some debts are not covered by an IVA. These are:

- maintenance payments ordered by a court
- child support arrears
- student loans
- fines imposed by the magistrates' court
- Social Fund loans
- TV licence arrears.

Indonesia State comprising an island group bound by Indian Ocean, Pacific Ocean and South China Sea. Its currency is the rupiah of 100 sen. The UK has a double taxation convention of 1994.

indulgence clause Clause in a guarantee that allows the lender to vary the terms of the loan without affecting the guarantee.

industrial action Organised protest by workers, including a strike. Any tax refunds due under PAYE are withheld during such action. Periods taking industrial action are also excluded in determining length of employment for employment rights.

industrial and provident society Legal entity that provides benefits to its members. Many are old co-operatives, working men's clubs, allotment societies, mutual investment companies, friendly societies, housing associations and similar. They are currently regulated by Co-operatives and Community Benefit Societies

Act 2003 which replaced 19th century laws. They are generally only taxed on their income from trading outside their membership, as set out in CTA 2010 s47. The taxation of their dividends is set out in CTA 2009 s132. Their payments are taxed under CTA 2009 from s499.

industrial building Structure that attracted its own capital allowance until April 2011. Such buildings may still qualify if in an enterprise zone, or may now qualify for structures and buildings allowance.

industrial development grants The tax implications are given in CTA 2009 s102 and ITTOIA 2005 s105. For an investment company, the provision is given in CTA 2009 s1252.

industrial injuries benefit (IIB) Social security benefit payable to someone who suffers from a personal injury sustained at work or from an industrial illness. The injury must lead to a loss of faculty. The main element of the benefit is disablement benefit. It may also include reduced earnings allowance or retirement allowance. The latter is only payable for accidents or diseases that happened before October 1990. The benefit may only be claimed by an employee who paid class 1 national insurance. The benefit is payable under Social Security Contributions and Benefits Act 1992 s94. This benefit is not subject to income tax (ITEPA 2003 s677).

inflation Measure of how much prices have increased. This is now generally measured by the consumer prices index, though the older retail prices index is used for some purposes, such as for index-linked securities.

informal correction Term used in CA 2006 s1075 in relation to a minor change to a document that may be made at Companies House.

informant Person who informs an authority of unlawful activity. HMRC does use informants and is allowed to pay them (Commissioners of Revenue and Customs 2005 s26). The right of a newspaper to deduct the cost of entertainment to informants was established in the case *Fleming v Associated Newspapers Ltd [1972] 48 TC 382*. This is discussed in HMRC Manual at BIM45030.

information notice Document served on a taxpayer or other person requiring them to provide details of a person's tax affairs. For many tax purposes, these are issued under FA 2008 Sch 36. There are other sections for specific tax issues.

infrastructure charges Charges made under Water Act 1989 towards costs of providing sewerage services. Such charges are standard-rated for VAT and do not come within the scope of zero-rating for sewerage charges (VAT notice 701/16).

Ingram Leading inheritance tax case on lease carve out schemes. Its full citation is *Ingram v Palmer-Tomkinson [1998]*. Under the scheme the transferor granted herself a lease from a trust she had set up. The House of Lords held that this was not a gift with reservation. Such a scheme has now been blocked by FA 1999 s104.

inheritance tax

Definition

Tax paid on the estate of someone who has died. It can also be charged on transfers of funds into certain types of trust. It was introduced in 1986 as a replacement for capital transfer tax. A loan to pay inheritance tax may qualify for income tax relief under ITA 2007 s403. The tax is collected under Inheritance Tax Act 1984.

Main points

The main points of inheritance tax are:

- it is paid by individuals on death or on transfer to a relevant property trust
- on death, there is a nil rate band on which the estate is taxed at 0%, and the excess is generally taxed at 40%. The nil rate band has been £325,000 since 2010
- the rate of tax is reduced to 36% if at least one tenth of the estate is left to charity
- the lifetime rate on payments to certain trusts is 20%
- no inheritance tax is payable on money that passes to a husband, wife or civil partner, unless that person is not domiciled in the UK when the tax-free limit is the same as the nil rate band
- on the death of a widow, widower or bereaved civil partner, the nil rate band of the former partner may be increased to a figure up to double the nil rate band otherwise applying
- from 2017, there is a residence nil rate band that may also be claimed when a main residence, or proceeds from one, are passed to children or remoter descendants
- there are some transfers that are exempt, such as to charity or for public benefit
- a lifetime transfer may be added back to the estate if it was made up to seven years before death. Some of the gift may be relieved if made more than three years before death
- some lifetime gifts are not added back. This includes normal expenditure, gifts up to £3,000 per year, and up to £250 per person per year
- there are special provisions for gifts with reservation, potentially exempt transfers and pre-owned assets
- a lifetime transfer to a trust may attract a 20% inheritance tax charge on amounts above the nil rate band, a ten-yearly charge of 6%, and an exit charge when the trust ends. Some types of trust are excluded from this provision. If the death rate of 40% subsequently applies, the 20% already paid is deducted
- quick succession relief may be claimed if a person dies within seven years of inheriting
- the tax is charged on a transfer of value
- the beneficiaries may be able to vary the terms of a will or intestacy under a deed of variation to an arrangement that is more tax-efficient

- businesses and farms may benefit from the 100% or 50% business property relief or agricultural property relief.

Inheritance Tax Act 1984 Act of Parliament originally enacted as Capital Transfer Tax Act 1984. It was renamed by FA 1986 s100(1)(b).

Inheritance Tax Direct Payment Scheme Scheme introduced from 31 March 2003 to allow inheritance tax to be paid from a bank account promptly. The personal representatives apply to HMRC for form IHT423. This is signed by the personal representatives and sent to the bank who will arrange payment without waiting for probate or letters of administration.

initial allowance A capital allowance that applied for the first year of ownership. All forms of this allowance had generally been abolished by 1993.

initial extra accessory In the context of taxing company cars, a qualifying accessory which is a non-standard accessory and is available with the car when it is first made available to the employee (ITEPA 2003 s126(2)).

initial payment In relation to capital allowances, "in the case of a plant or machinery lease, means a payment by the lessee –

(a) at or before the time when the lease is entered into, and

(b) in respect of the plant or machinery which is the subject of the lease"

(CAA 2001 s70YI(1)).

initial period Period of two years from when a company receives its trading certificate (CA 2006 s598(2)). This term is used to state a period that restricts a public company from making certain arrangements relating to transfers for non-cash assets. For tax, the term applies to a period for which one tax provision (usually beneficial) applies. An example is given in ITEPA 2003 s534 in relation to enterprise management incentive.

initial public offering (IPO) First offering of shares in a company to the public. It is often known as a flotation.

initial recognition The first time that an item is recognised in the accounts. FRS 102 requires that this be based on historical cost unless FRS 102 specifically requires fair value (FRS 102 section 2.46).

initial repairs Repairs to an asset to bring it into a useable condition. Such expenditure is generally regarded as revenue and not capital (*Law Shipping Co Ltd v IRC [1924] 12 TC 621).*

inland clearance depot Export clearance facilities for goods exported or imported through the Channel Tunnel. The UK depot is at Ashford in Kent.

Inland Revenue Body that existed between 1849 (from a merger of bodies formed from 1665) and 2005. In 2005, it merged with HM Customs and Excise to form HM Revenue and Customs (HMRC). It is charged with collecting most UK taxes and with other functions such as national minimum wage, property valuation and tax credits.

in loco parentis Latin: in the place of a parent.

innovation condition One of the conditions for enterprise investment scheme and other tax-advantaged schemes to qualify as knowledge-intensive which allows a higher level of investment. The condition is broadly that the company is engaged in producing intellectual property which it intends to exploit within ten years (ITA 2007 s252A(5). For venture capital trusts, the same condition is given in ITA 2007 s331A.

input tax VAT paid or payable by taxable persons on goods or services supplied to them (or acquired by them from another European Union (EU) Member State), which is used, or to be used, for the purpose of their business. VAT registered persons can reclaim input tax. Under VATA 1994 s24(1), input tax is:

"(a) VAT on the supply to him [registered taxpayer] of any goods or services;

(b) VAT on the acquisition by him from another member state of any goods, and

(c) VAT paid or payable by him on the importation of any goods from a place outside the member states,

being (in each case) goods or services used or to be used for the purpose of any business carried on or to be carried on by him".

VAT Notice 700 says that input tax "is the VAT you are charged on your business purchases and expenses, including:

- goods and services supplied to you in the UK
- goods you import from outside the EU
- goods you acquire from a taxable person in another EU member state (see Notice 725 The Single Market)
- goods you remove from a warehouse
- any services supplied in the UK which you receive from abroad, and
- overheads and research and development".

Following sub-sections provide further details.

in re Latin: in the matter of.

insider dealing When a person uses privileged information to make an investment, such as a director who knows something about their company which is not widely known. It is a criminal offence under Criminal Justice Act 1986.

insolvency

Definition

Financial status of owing more than you own. It is not a legal status. In itself, insolvency imposes no restrictions on the individual or business and has no legal consequences. Insolvency only incurs legal consequences when a procedure such as bankruptcy or liquidation is started.

Company insolvency

"(1) A company is deemed unable to pay debts –

(a) if a creditor to whom the company is indebted in a sum exceeding £750 then due has served on the company, by leaving at the company's registered office, a written demand requiring the company to pay the sum so due and the company has for 3 weeks thereafter neglected to pay the sum or to secure or compound for it to the reasonable satisfaction of the creditor, or

(b) the execution or other process issued on a judgement, decree or order of any court in favour of a creditor of the company is returned unsatisfied in whole or in part, or

(c) if it is proved to the satisfaction of the court that the company is unable to pay its debts as they fall due.

(2) A Company is also deemed unable to pay its debts if it is proved to the satisfaction of the court that the value of the company's assets is less than the amount of its liabilities, taking into account its contingent and prospective liabilities."

(Insolvency Act 1986 s123)

The £750 limit became £5,000 from 1 October 2015.

Capital gains tax

Capital gains tax implications are explained in TCGA1992 s66.

Charities

Relevant provisions are given in Charities Act 2011 from s113.

Value added tax

Guidance is given in VAT Notice 700/56

Position of HMRC

From 1 December 2020 (postponed from 1 April 2020) HMRC is a secondary preferential creditor for taxes owed by a business which that business has collected from other parties. These are VAT, income tax from PAYE, employer's national insurance, student loan deductions, and construction industry scheme deductions. For other taxes, such as corporation tax and employer's national insurance, HMRC ranks as an unsecured creditor. The law is FA 2020 from s98. This amends Insolvency Act 1986 Sch 6 Category 9. In Scotland, it amends Bankruptcy (Scotland) Act 2016 s129(2). In Northern Ireland, it amends Insolvency (Northern Ireland) Order 1989 No 2405 article 346.

From 5 September 2003, HMRC ranks as an unsecured creditor for all sums owed. The previous preferential creditor status was repealed by Enterprise Act 2002.

The change in 2003, was part of a package of reforms that saw some of the insolvent's assets reserved for unsecured creditors. This amount was 50% of assets up to £10,000, and 20% of the balance to a maximum of £800,000 (£600,000 before 6 April 2020). The maximum of £800,000 is likely to be reached on assets of £2,985,000.

Between 29 December 1986 and 4 September 2003, HMRC was a preferential creditor in respect of (broadly) 12 months' tax, and as an unsecured creditor for the balance.

insolvency practitioner Accountant who is licensed by his or her professional body to do insolvency work.

Insolvency Service Part of Department for Business, Energy and Industrial Strategy, or its predecessors, that deals with insolvencies.

inspector of taxes Official entrusted with ensuring the correct amount of tax is payable.

inspector's manuals Guidance issued by Inland Revenue (now HMRC) to its inspectors. It was originally regarded as confidential, but between 1990 and 1996 they were progressively published. They can be accessed free from HMRC's website. They contain useful advice on how HMRC deals with certain matters. Some parts are redacted.

instalment option Provision allowing inheritance tax to be paid in ten annual instalments in certain circumstances (IHTA 1984 s277).

instalment payments Arrangement whereby larger businesses must pay their tax in instalments.

For corporation tax, there are two regimes. Each require four payments calculated as a quarter of expected corporation tax liability for the year. These provisions are amended from 1 April 2019.

"Large companies" must pay the first instalment 6 months and 13 days from the start of the accounting period. The following payments are paid at three-monthly intervals. This means that payments are made in months 6, 9, 12 and 15 with any balance due nine months after the year-end, that is month 21. A large company is one whose profits exceed £1.5 million. If the corporation tax for the year does not exceed £10,000, quarterly payments are not required.

Very large companies have profits above £20 million. They are required to pay instalments four months earlier than a large company. The first instalment is due 2 months and 13 days after the start of the accounting period. The instalments are paid in months 2, 5, 8 and 11. If any accounting period is less than 12 months, the £1.5 million and £20 million limits are proportionately reduced.

Institute for Apprenticeships (IfA) Body established under Enterprise Act 2016 s22 and Sch 4. It supervises the apprenticeship scheme from 1 April 2017 under the apprenticeship levy. The body is renamed Institute for Apprenticeships and Technical Education by Technical and Further Education Act 2017 s1(1).

Institute of Chartered Accountants in England and Wales Professional body formed in 1870 and given its Royal Charter in 1880.

Institute of Chartered Accountants of Ireland Professional body for accountants in Northern Ireland and the Republic, founded in 1888.

Institute of Chartered Accountants of Scotland Oldest professional body for accountants, dating back to 1853.

Institute of Indirect Taxation Professional body established in 1991.

Institute of Legal Executives Professional body established in 1963.

instrument A written document that has legal consequences, such as a will or deed.

instrument of transfer Document that transfers or transmits ownership of shares (CA 2006 s755).

insurable interest Right to insure something, which generally requires the policy holder to demonstrate the risk of loss. The requirement to show an insurable interest in another person's life is given in Life Assurance Act 1774 s1.

insurance An agreement under which individuals, businesses, and other organisations, in exchange for payment of a premium, are guaranteed indemnity for losses resulting from certain risks specified in a policy. Where the risk is certain, such as a policy paying on death at any time, the term assurance is more accurate, though this distinction is not always made. The policyholder must have an insurable interest. Insurance policies may be subject to insurance premium tax. For value added tax, insurance is an exempt supply. Details are given in VAT Notice 701/36.

Insurance premiums are allowed as a business expense under the normal "wholly and exclusively" rules as explained in HMRC Manual from BIM45501. Relief may be given in full even when the policy offers "new for old" replacement.

Life insurance policy premiums once qualified for income tax relief.

There are detailed provisions in ICTA 1988 on how to tax insurance companies. The capital gains tax provisions are given in TCGA 1992 from s204.

insurance company Company that provides insurance. Corporation tax provisions are given in CTA 2009 from s386. Provisions for mutual companies are given in CTA 2009 s634.

insurance contract Contract between an insurance company and a policy holder. The accounting treatment is set out in UK standards as FRS 105 and in international accounting standards (from 2022) by IFRS 17.

insurance premium tax (IPT) Tax introduced on 1 October 1994 on many insurance premiums (FA 1994 ss48-74 and SI 1994 No 1774). The rates have increased many times since. From April 1997 there is a higher rate, set at the same rate as the standard rate of VAT. Rates are given in section 3 of this dictionary.

insurance reserve Sum set aside by an entity to pay its own insurance claims up to a limit. For accounting, this is treated as a reserve. For tax purposes, a payment from the reserve will usually be treated as a tax-deductible expense; the transfer to the reserve is not. The matter is explained in HMRC Manual at BIM45565.

insurance special purpose vehicle "Any undertaking which assumes risks from insurance or reinsurance undertakings and which fully funds its exposure to such risks through the proceeds of a debt issue or some other financing mechanism where the repayment rights of the providers of such debt or other financing mechanism are subordinated to the reinsurance obligations of the undertaking" (ICTA 1988 s431(2)).

intangible asset Asset that has no physical form, such as a patent, brand name or goodwill. For corporation tax, a definition is given in CTA 2009 s712. For capital gains tax, a definition is given in TCGA 1992 s275A.

intangible income Benefit provided to a body, usually a church or charity, other than in cash. Examples include free accounting, printing or office space. For accounting and any tax purposes, this is not included in the accounts unless the benefit provider specifically paid for the benefit.

intellectual property Intangible asset representing a right. Forms include copyright, patents, technical designs, trademarks, know-how and similar.

integral features Parts of a building otherwise called features integral to a building. From 1 April 2008, these attract a capital allowance as plant and machinery in the special rate pool (CAA 2001 from s33A).

integration stage Third stage in a money laundering offence. It is when the money is returned to the criminal. The first two stages are the placement stage and layering stage.

integrity Personal character required for accountants and others. For tax professionals, "a member must act honestly in all his dealings with his clients, all tax authorities and other interested parties, and do nothing knowingly or carelessly that might mislead either by commission or omission" (Professional Conduct in Relation to Taxation. May 2015). For auditors, the characters are fairness, candour, courage, intellectual honesty and confidentiality (Auditing Practices Board ES 1 para 7).

intellectual property The rights a person has over created works. This covers copyright, patents, technical designs, trademarks, plant breeders' rights, licences and know-how. A definition is given in CTA 2009 s172. For income tax, there are provisions in ITA 2007 s907(1). Customs may seize imported goods that breach such rights under SI 2004 No 1473 and explained in Customs notice 34.

For corporation tax, the term is defined as meaning –

(a) any patent, trade mark, registered design, copyright or design right, plant breeders' rights or rights under section 7 of the Plant Varieties Act 1997,
(b) any right under the law of a country or territory outside the United Kingdom corresponding or similar to a right with paragraph (a),
(c) any information or technique not protected by a right within paragraph (a) or (b) but having industrial, commercial or other economic value, or
(d) any licence or other right of anything within paragraph (a), (b) or (c)

(CTA 2009 s712(3)).

For income tax in relation to shares in a research institution spin-out company, the term is defined in ITEPA 2003 s456. Customs may seize goods that infringe trademarks and copyright under Goods Infringing Intellectual Property Rights (Customs) Regulations SI 2004 No 1473 (as amended). These rights are explained in Customs notice 34. In relation to deduction of income tax at source, the terms "means –

(a) copyright of literary, artistic or scientific work,
(b) any patent, trade mark, design, model, plan, or secret formula or process,
(c) any information concerning industrial, commercial or scientific experience, or
(d) public lending right in respect of a book"

(ITA 2007 s907(1) as replaced by FA 2016 s40).

intending supplies Supplies a person intends to make in the course of a business. It is a basis on which a person may register for VAT.

intense pulse light (IPL) Type of laser machine used in medical treatment. Generally, its use in treatment drawn up by a registered medical professional is exempt from VAT. Its use for cosmetic reasons is generally standard-rated. Further guidance is given in VAT Notice 701/31.

intention of testator Legal principle of interpreting a will according to the testator's intention. For example a testator's gifts to "mother" was held to mean his wife when it was shown that that was how he referred to his wife.

intent test Test introduced in July 2018 by the International Ethics Standards Board for Accountants in its revised code of ethics. It relates to the extent to which an inducement or hospitality offered to an accountant may be considered unethical.

intercepted goods Imports temporarily held by Customs while it investigates whether any law has been broken.

interest Sum charged for the use of capital, among other meanings.

interested third party Person who has a beneficial interest in a bank account from which HMRC has seized funds (F2A 2015 Sch 8 para 8(11)).

interest in land Any form of right over land. The main forms are fee simple (freehold), lease, easement and licence. A definition appears in CAA 2002 s175(1).

interest in possession (IIP) Form of trust where a beneficiary has an immediate right to income or use of a property, and another beneficiary has other rights. A common example is to allow a person to live in a house until they die when the property passes to someone else. The first person is the life tenant; the second is the remainderman. Inheritance tax is charged as if property had been wholly inherited by the life tenant. The law is IHTA 1984 s49. The status of an IIP trust was changed by FA 2006 s156 under which they are now generally taxed more severely as a relevant property trust.

interest in settled property Any interest created by or arising under a settlement. A definition and the tax treatment are set out in TCGA 1992 Sch 4A.

interest rate swap Agreement between two organisations to exchange borrowings. A common example is when a fixed interest borrowing is exchanged for a variable interest borrowing, known as a pure vanilla swap. For accounting and tax purposes, an interest swap is treated as two transactions: the loan agreement and the swap agreement.

interim accounts Accounts prepared partway through an accounting period. The extent to which they justify an interim dividend is explained in CA 2006 s1212(1).

interim dividend Share of company profits to its shareholders as an advance of the final dividend. Old articles of association may prohibit payment of an interim dividend.

intermediate rate Rate of 21% income tax introduced in Scotland from April 2018.

internal auditor Person employed by an organisation to audit its finances. Guidance is provided by International Standard on Auditing ISA 510.

internal rate of return Figure that represents the interest rate that corresponds to the profitability of an entity. This cannot be calculated but can be determined mathematically by iteration.

Internal Revenue Service (IRS) Tax collecting body of the USA.

internal transit When goods pass through the UK on their way to another foreign country. Such goods may be excused Customs duty and some Customs formalities.

international accounting standard Accounting standard issued by the International Accounting Standards Board (CA 2006 s474). Generally an entity may choose to prepare its accounts using either UK standards or international accounting standards. Accounts of companies listed on the London Stock Exchange or Alternative Investment Market must be prepared using international accounting standards.

international development Commitment to move towards 0.7% of gross national income (International Development (Reporting and Transparency) Act 2006 s3. An annual report must be issued on how far this target is being met. In 2020, the figure was reduced to 0.5%.

International Monetary Fund (IMF) Bank formed in 1945, which is part of United Nations. In 2010 it was thus an organisation of 186 countries. It provides loans and assistance to countries which get into financial difficulties. Such loans are usually conditional on the government abandoning bad economic practices. The UK government applied to the IMF in 1976.

international services This generally refers to goods imported for work to be done on them before being re-exported. They are zero-rated for VAT under VATA 1994 Sch 8 Group 7.

Internet Global network by which computers communicate. It includes the world wide web, user groups, email and similar. It is being increasingly used for tax purposes, such as under Making Tax Digital.

Internet sales Sale of goods or services effected on the Internet. They are regulated by the Distance Selling Regulations and E-Commerce Regulations. An Internet service provider can be made jointly and severally liable for VAT that is otherwise unpaid from an overseas seller using its platform. Internet companies may be liable for digital services tax.

Interpretation Act Law of 1978 which sets out how Acts of Parliament are to be understood.

interpretation Service Facility of HMRC to provide guidance in languages other than English and Welsh.

intervening year Tax year that falls between the year of departure and year of return for a temporary non-resident for capital gains tax purposes (TCGA 1992 s10A(8)).

intestacy State of having no valid will at time of death. The estate is administered under provisions of Administration of Estates Act 1925.

intimate search Search that involves the physical examination of a person's body orifices, such as to detect goods at Customs. Such a search may only be conducted by a medical practitioner or a registered nurse. The suspect may require the search to be authorised by a justice of the peace or a senior Customs officer. The law for Customs officers is CEMA 1979 s164; for police officers it is Police and Criminal Evidence Act 1984 from s55.

intra-EC supplies Supplies between businesses in different EU states. These are generally free of VAT and Customs duties, provided the procedure in VAT Notice 725 is followed.

Intrastat Statistics collected on trade in goods between EU states.

intra-union dues Customs duties and other import charges on supplies between EU states. Original member states had phased out such duties by 31 December 1969. The UK phased them out by 30 June 1977.

introducer Person who makes a marketing contact in relation to a notifiable tax avoidance scheme (FA 2004 s307(1A)). An introducer is not required to report the scheme to HMRC but may be required to provide information under FA 2004 s313C.

Inuit Eskimo. An Inuit who kills a seal in a traditional hunt for sustenance may be issued with a seal attestation allowing the seal, or its products, to obtain Customs clearance.

invalid care allowance Social security benefit paid to those who provided care for a disabled person. It was replaced by carer's allowance from 1 April 2003.

invalidity allowance One of two elements of invalidity benefit paid between 1971 and 1995.

invalidity benefit Social security benefit paid from 1971 to 1995, when it was replaced by incapacity benefit which was itself replaced by employment and support allowance.

invention A new and not obvious idea for which a patent may be issued. A capital allowance may be claimed for the patent. A company that exploits a patent may benefit from the patent box.

investment Asset held for the main purpose of generating income or a capital gain. Investment businesses are taxed less generously than trading businesses, which has been litigated in terms of property.

investment allowance Capital allowance paid between 1954 and 1966. The term is still used with a different meaning for the oil industry (CTA 2010 s332C).

investment bank Bank that deals with such areas as underwriting new share issues. It is given a specific meaning in CTA 2009 s133H. In the USA, the term is often used less specifically to mean a merchant bank.

investment bond Form of investment that has more than one element, such as a life assurance policy funded by a single premium. The term is given a specific meaning in CTA 2009 s133H.

investment bond arrangement One form of alternative finance. The capital gains tax provisions are TCGA 1992 s151N. The income tax provisions are ITA 2007 s564G.

investment club Group of up to 20 individuals who collectively invest funds. Each individual is potentially subject to income tax on the share of dividends and capital gains tax on disposals. In practice, these are often covered by annual allowances. HMRC provides guidance in HMRC Manual at CG20600. It provides form 185 which may be used for tax. A club is only required to make a return to HMRC on request under TMA 1970 s24 or FA 2011 Sch 23 para 65.

investment company Company whose shares may be traded on a stock exchange, and whose business is trading in shares of other companies. In relation to distributions, the term is defined in CA 2006 s833(1).

investment gold coin For VAT, this is a gold coin minted after 1800 that:

- is of a purity of not less than 900 thousandths
- is, or has been, legal tender in its country of origin, and
- is of a description of coin that is normally sold at a price that
- does not exceed 180% of the open market value of the gold contained in the coin.

Alternatively, it is a coin listed in VAT notice 701/12A Section 3.

investment income Income previously called unearned income. Until 1984, it was subject to investment income surcharge, an addition to income tax. Under modern thinking, investment income is subject to many tax reliefs.

investment income surcharge Additional income tax charged on investment income between 1973 and 1984.

Investment Management Association Trade body for investment industry formed in 2002 from a merger of existing bodies.

investment trust Company that invests in other companies. Investors buy shares in the investment trust, which is legally not a trust at all. Specific corporation tax provisions are given in CTA 2009 s395. A definition is given in CTA 2010 s1158. Provisions relating to profits or losses of a capital nature are given in CTA 2009 s637. For child trust funds, the term "refers to a company that is such a trust for the purposes of the CTAs, or would be such a trust but for section 1158(3) of the CTA 2010" (Child Trust Funds Regulations SI 2004 No 1450 reg 2(1)(b)).

Investors in People UK national standard for good practice in the training and development of people to achieve business goals.

invisible exports Exports of services such as banking and insurance.

invoice Document which confirms that a supplier has provided goods or services, and which states the amount charged. An invoice is not necessarily a demand for payment. There are strict provisions for a VAT invoice (VATA 1994 s96(1)).

involved third party In relation to HMRC powers, this term is defined, with the help of a table, in FA 2008 Sch 36 para 61A(1). In Scotland, "means a person who is, or a category of persons who are, specified by the Scottish Ministers by order" (Revenue Scotland and Tax Powers Act 2014 s142(3)). Such a person may have their business premises inspected by Revenue Scotland in relation to another person.

inward investment support Assistance in the form of advice provided by HMRC to overseas investors who seek to invest at least £30 million in the UK (statement of practice SP2/2012).

inward processing Temporary import of goods for a procedure such as repair or repackaging. There are procedures to avoid or refund Customs duties.

in-work conditionality Provision of universal credit where a claimant in work may be required to look for more work, such as longer hours.

IR 35 Arrangement whereby a worker provides his or her services through a limited company in circumstances where they would otherwise be regarded as an employee. From 6 April 2000, the company must operate PAYE (FA 2000 s60). and collect class 1 national insurance (SSCBA 1992 s4A) for the worker. From 6 April 2017, a public sector body decides whether IR 35 provisions apply. From 6 April 2021 (postponed from 2020), a private sector employer must make a similar decision.

Iran Arab state. Its currency is the rial of 100 dinar. The UK had no double taxation treaty but has an air transport agreement of 1960. The country is subject to UK sanctions, as are designated persons of the country.

Iraq Arab state. Its currency is the Iraq dinar of 1,000 fils. The UK has no double taxation treaty. The country is subject to UK sanctions, as are designated persons of the country.

Ireland Second largest island of British Isles. It comprises Northern Ireland which is part of the United Kingdom, and the Irish Republic which became independent in 1921.

Irish Republic Part of Ireland that became independent from the UK in 1921, and became a republic under a constitution of 1937. Its currency was the Irish pound or punt which was kept at par with sterling until 1978. Its currency is now the euro. The republic switched to decimal currency in 1971 and joined what is now the EU in 1973, both at the same time as the UK.

irregularity In relation to tax returns, the term "is intended to include all errors whether the error is made by the client, the member, HMRC or any other party involved in a client's tax affairs" (Professional Conduct in Relation to Taxation para 5.1). Subsequent paras set out the tax adviser's responsibilities for irregularities.

ISA withdrawal charge Amount deducted from a lifetime individual savings account when a payment is taken other than as set out in the scheme. The charge is 25%, except during the coronavirus outbreak when it was reduced to 20% by SI 2020 No 506.

Islamic finance Financial arrangements that are consistent with Sharia law for Muslims. The main difference is that payment of interest is not allowed. Various forms of alternative finance have been devised to get round this restriction. There are tax provisions for such arrangements designed to ensure that these are taxed on the same basis as the arrangement they seek to copy. Any taxpayer may use alternative finance.

Isle of Man Part of British Isles that is not part of the United Kingdom. For the purposes of VAT, the Isle of Man is treated as if it were part of the UK. The island uses currency based on UK currency and at par value, though its currency is not legal tender in the UK. The UK has a double taxation arrangement of 1991 as amended by an arrangement of 2008. In 2013, there was an exchange of letters for a double taxation agreement that is not yet in force. Tax provisions between UK and the Isle of Man are governed by Isle of Man Act 1979.

ISO codes Three-letter codes which identify currencies and **stores of value.** These are allocated by the International Organization for Standardization (ISO) under their standard ISO 4217. For most currencies, the code typically comprises two letters denoting the country and one letter denoting the currency, so the US dollar, British pound and Japanese yen are respectively USD, GBP and JPY. The euro is EUR. Stores of value are often denoted by X followed by two letters (such as the atomic symbol) so gold and silver are XAU and XAG. There are some symbols for currencies for particular applications, such as special drawing rights and the US dollar for next day funding.

isolated transaction Unique transaction that is not repeated. Such a transaction can still be regarded as trading as in the case *CIR v Fraser [1924] 24 TC 498*. The matter is discussed in HMRC Manual at BIM20230.

isolation note Form of fit note or sick note introduced from 23 March 2020 saying that the person is required to self-isolate because of coronavirus. The person may be eligible to claim statutory sick pay.

Israel Middle East nation mentioned in the Bible and reconstituted in 1948, though not recognised by most Arab states with whom Israel has fought many wars. Its currency is the shekel of 100 agora. The UK has a double taxation convention of 1962 as amended by a 1970 protocol.

issued shares Shares that have been issued to shareholders as against authorised share capital which includes shares yet to be issued (CA 2006 s546(1)(a)).

issue requirement Conditions which must be met by the terms of an issue of shares for them to qualify for tax such relief, such as for EIS relief under ITA 2007 s173A-174.

Italian Uplift claims VAT claims that were based on an argument that payments by HMRC in relation to Italian Republic claims had been based on average margins which were too low. In 2009 HMRC did not accept that argument, and there was a lead case proceeding in the Tribunal known as *Bristol Street Motors*. It was discovered that HMRC had made a repayment claim to Blake Holdings in 2013, but was resisting further claims. The history is explained in the case *Rolls Group [2015] TC 4581*.

Italy European state that is a member state of European Union, for which purpose these territories are excluded: Campion d'Italia, the Italian waters of Lake

Lugano, and Lvigno. The currency is the euro of 100 cents, prior to which the currency was the lira. The UK has a double taxation convention of 1988.

itemised pay statement Payslip which gives details of gross salary or wages, the amount of any variable element, the net amount payable, and a breakdown of any part which is paid differently from the rest. Such a statement must be provided with every payment (Employment Rights Act 1996 s8). From 6 April 2018, this right is extended to other workers. From the same date, it is also a requirement that a worker paid at an hourly rate must have the number of hours covered by the payslip stated. In practice, most payslips provide much more information than these minima.

items subject to legal privilege Term used in TMA 1970 s20C(4A) to describe documents which cannot be taken by HMRC when they enter premises with a warrant. The same term is used in Police and Criminal Evidence Act 1984 s10 in relation to police searches.

iteration Mathematical method for solving problems which can be defined but not calculated. An example is determining the internal rate of return. Iteration works by guessing at an answer and then refining it with subsequent answers.

itinerant worker Person whose work involves them in travelling to different wok locations. Such a worker is generally entitled to claim tax relief for food and drink under ITTOIA 2005s57A. An itinerant employee is able to claim tax relief under the normal employment rules.

ivory Material from the tusks of elephants. It is a valuable material that has led to poaching of elephants and made them an endangered species. Ivory and goods made from ivory may be seized by Customs if brought into the UK unless the holder has a CITES permit. From 2016, it is generally illegal to sell any ivory unless it predates 1947. Dealing in ivory is now generally prohibited under Ivory Act 2018 s1(1). This includes products that have ivory in them.

There are exceptions for:

- items that originated before 1918 and for which an exemption certificate has been issued on grounds of high artistic, cultural or historical value (Ivory Act 2018 s2):
- pre-1918 portrait miniatures where the surface areas is less than 320 square centimetres (Ivory Act 2018 s6)
- pre-1947 items where the ivory content is less than 10% and all the ivory is integral to the whole product (Ivory Act 2018 s7)
- musical instruments made before 1975 (Ivory Act 2018 s8) where the ivory represents less than 20% of the material used.

There are some other exceptions, such as for museums. The restrictions on ivory relate to that from elephant tusks. The restrictions do not apply to teeth, nor to tusks of other animals (such as walruses, mammoths, hippopotami, whales, narwhals and warthogs). In 2019, the government launched a consultation as to whether ivory from these animals should be included.

Ivory Coast English name of African state now generally known as Cote d'Ivoire. Ivory Coast is the name of the UK double taxation convention of 1985.

iXBRL Protocol for identifying financial data. From 2011, corporation tax returns must identify items according to this protocol.

Jaffa cake Product comprising a small piece of sponge cake covered in orange jam and coated with chocolate. The VAT tribunal held that this was a zero-rated cake and not a standard-rated chocolate biscuit as:

- the sponge element of a Jaffa cake is virtually identical to a zero-rated sponge cake
- the Jaffa cake was moist like a cake
- the sponge was an essential part of the cake; it was more than a base for the jam and chocolate

(United Biscuits (UK) Ltd. [1991] VTD 6344).

Jamaica Caribbean nation. Its currency is the Jamaican dollar of 100 cents. The UK has a double taxation agreement of 1973.

jam jar accounting Simple form of cash budgeting where amounts are put aside for specific bills, originally as cash in different jam jars. Some banks now offer this service.

jam jarring Service provided by some financial bodies for low income households. It allocates part of regular income to outgoings such as council tax, hire purchase, telephone etc. The term comes from jam jar accounting.

Japan Nation comprising islands in the Pacific Ocean. Its currency is the yen of 100 sen. The UK has a double taxation convention of 2006, amended by a protocol of 2013, and a memorandum of understanding on Article 25 mutual agreement procedure.

Japanese knotweed Plant that can be very destructive. It is the only plant that qualifies for land remediation relief from landfill tax (HMRC Business Brief 62/2008].

jeans These are zero-rated for VAT if designed for young children. Further details are given in VAT Notice 714. The matter has been heard by the tribunals in the cases *VF Corporation (UK) Ltd [1979] VTD 898* and *R Kaur Singh [1986] VTD 2433).*

Jersey The largest of the Channel Islands. It owes allegiance to the British crown but is an independent democracy with its own legal system and tax rules. It has its own currency based on UK currency and valued at par, but Jersey currency is not legal tender in the UK. Jersey is not a member of the European Union but is part of its Customs union. The UK has a double taxation arrangement of 1952 amended by an arrangement of 2009.

jet aircraft A jet aircraft is plant for the purposes of capital allowances. A problem arises in determining whether it is a long-life asset as much of the aircraft is replaced quickly. British Air Transport Association (BATA) estimates that only 39% (by value) of an original jet remains after 25 years. An agreement was been reached on the matter between HMRC and BATA in 1999 and applied until 2003. The current provisions are given in HMRC Manual at CA23782. Broadly, a jet with fewer than 60 seats is not a long-life asset. Similarly, a turbo-prop airliner with a maximum take-off weight above 5,700 kilograms is not a long-life asset.

Executive jet aircraft are generally regarded as long-life assets. This also includes fixed wing turbo prop or piston-driven aircraft with a maximum take-off weight above 2,730 kilograms. If either type of jet aircraft is used for more than 600 flying hours a year, it comes within the 50:50 rule. For other jet aircraft, the 50:50 rule applies. This regards half the cost of the jet as a long-life asset and the other half as normal plant and machinery.

jetsam Goods jettisoned from a ship and then washed up on shore. Some authorities limit the term to goods washed up from a ship that has sunk.

jizya Tax historically imposed on non-Muslim men in Muslim countries. Some reports suggest it is still imposed. It is variously seen as a tax, a licence or protection money.

Jobcentre Plus Body formed in 2002 which is now part of the Department of Work and Pensions. Its function is to provide work-related support to people in the UK.

Job Release Government scheme that ran from 1977 to 1988 which gave tax-free payments to encourage older employees to retire early to create job vacancies.

job retention bonus Sum of £1,000 that was to be paid in respect of every worker who had been furloughed under Coronavirus Job Retention Scheme but was kept on the payroll from November 2020 to 31 January 2021. This was scrapped when the Coronavirus Job Retention Scheme was extended to 31 March 2021 (and later 30 April 2021).

jobseeker's allowance Social security benefit paid for six months for someone who is unemployed and seeking work (Jobseekers Act 1995). It is usually paid to someone with sufficient national insurance record, though there is an income-based jobseeker's allowance. Payments are subject to income tax (ITEPA 2003 s660(1)). In addition to contribution-based jobseeker's allowance, there is also a means-tested version known as income-based jobseeker's allowance. This is being replaced by universal credit (WRA 2012 s33(1)(a)).

jobseeker's allowance adjustment Revised figure of jobseeker's allowance after a previous figure has been advised. The responsibility of the Department of Work and Pensions is given in PAYE regulations SI 2003 No 2682 reg 160.

job support scheme Coronavirus support scheme announced on 24 September 2020. It was to run for six months from 1 November 2020 and subsidise payroll workers. The scheme was dropped when the Coronavirus Job Retention Scheme was extended into spring 2021.

joint account Account which is shared by two or more people, such as bank account held by a married couple. HMRC's power to seize funds in a bank account is restricted to a proportionate share of a joint account (F2A 2015 Sch 8 para 7(4)).

joint and several liability Legal right to sue any member of a couple or group when a sum is owed by that group. This liability only arises in specific situations, such as in a partnership. For VAT, such a liability may arise under Value Added Tax 1994 s77A.

joint claimant Person who claims a benefit as a member of a couple. A joint claim may be made for tax credits (Tax Credits Act 2002 s3(8) or universal credit (WRA 2012 s40).

Joint Fraud Taskforce Initiative launched on 10 February 2016 by the Home Secretary . It brings together the police, payment providers, banks and regulatory bodies to tackle fraud.

joint offer In the context of a takeover bid, means an "offer by two or more persons jointly" (CA 2006 s987(1)). The section continues with the relevant company law.

joint property Property that is owned by two or more people. The legal and tax treatment can depend on whether it is owned as a joint tenancy or as a tenancy in common.

joint stock company Public company whose shares are owned by many people (CA 2006 s1041). This term is still found in company law though such a body is now more commonly called a public company.

joint tenancy Arrangement where two people co-own a property, as against a tenancy in common whereby each person has a half interest in the property. The main consequence is that only a tenant in common may leave his or her interest in their will.

joint venture Project undertaken by two separate businesses working together. It is not a separate legal entity. Profits must be apportioned between the businesses for tax purposes. There are specific provisions for entrepreneur's relief in TCGA 1992 Sch 7ZA.

Jones v Garnett The 2007 case otherwise known as *Arctic Systems*. The case was notorious for its novel use of trust legislation to attack a husband and wife company. HMRC eventually lost.

journal (1) Prime book of account which records financial transactions. In practice, routine transactions such as sales, purchases and payrolls are recorded in separate day books. The journal is used for non-routine transactions such as depreciation and accruals.

(2) Any publication produced at least once a year. It is generally zero-rated for VAT under VATA 1994 Sch 8 Group 3. Details are given in VAT notice 701/10.

journal entry Record in a journal. In double-entry bookkeeping, it records a transaction as one or more debits and one or more credits. The total debits must equal total credits. By convention, the debits are indented to the left in manuscript journals.

journalistic material Material collected by a journalist for his or her work. This is explicitly excluded from the scope of what HMRC may require under an information notice (FA 2008 Sch 36 para 19(2)). It is defined by reference to Police and Criminal Evidence Act 1984 s13. Similar provisions apply in Scotland under RSTPA 2014 s136(2).

journey For air passenger duty, this is defined as the travel from the original place of departure to the final place of destination (FA 1994 s43(1A)). The consequence is that two flights may be regarded as a single journey.

judgment Decision of a court, such as confirming that a sum of money is owed.

judgment in litigation judgment of a county court or higher court when HMRC is one of the parties. Under HMRC Notice of 19 March 2010, HMRC will honour the terms of a judgment. Previously HMRC had not always complied with an order to refund tax when the matter was under appeal.

judicial associated operations rule Term used to mean the decisions of *Burmah Oil [1982], Ramsay [1982]* and *Furniss v Dawson [1984]* where judges extended the scope of the law to establish the principle that where a transaction is effected by a series of steps, intermediate steps could be ignored if they served no commercial purpose other than tax avoidance.

Concern was expressed that judges were making the law rather than interpreting it. In *Furniss v Dawson,* Lord Roskill said "the ghost of the Duke of Westminster has haunted the administration of this branch of the law for too long". This was checked by later decisions, such as *Craven v White [1989]* where Lord Oliver said the rule was simply an exercise in statutory construction. In *MacNiven v Westmoreland [2001],* Lord Nicholls commented that the Ramsay principle was no more than a useful aid and did not introduce a new legal principle.

Judicial Committee Part of the Privy Council that acts as a court of appeal.

judicial review Power of a court to review a decision for which there is no other appeal procedure. Although judicial review has been used in tax cases, these have usually failed as there are tax appeal procedures. The upper tier tribunal has some review functions (Tribunals, Courts and Enforcement Act 2007 s15). Judicial review in Scotland is permitted by RSTPA 2014 from s40.

juke box Coin-operated machine that plays music. It is specifically exempted from amusement machine licence duty. For VAT, it is treated as an amusement machine (VAT Notice 701/13).

junior capital Deferred shares and similar forms of a company's capital that rank after other forms of capital.

junior ISA (JISA) Tax-advantaged savings product similar to an individual savings account (ISA). Its main provisions are:

- the beneficiary must be aged under 18;
- the beneficiary must be UK-resident;
- there must be no child trust fund for the beneficiary;
- the ISA is administered by the person with parental responsibility until the beneficiary is 18;
- contributions up to a limit a year (see below) may be made into the fund by anyone, including parents;
- a beneficiary may have one cash ISA and one shares ISA, but the annual limit applies to the two together;

- all returns on the ISA are tax-free;
- no amount may be withdrawn until the age of 18, except on terminal illness or death;
- at age 18, the junior ISA becomes an ordinary ISA.

The limit for 2020/21 is £9,000; in 2019/20 it is £4,368; and in 2018/19 is £4,260. Junior ISAs were introduced on 1 November 2011, replacing the previous child trust fund (CTF). From April 2015, CTF funds may be transferred into a junior ISA. Junior ISAs are regulated by SI 2011 No 1780.

Junior Tax Facts Teaching material produced by HMRC to explain tax to children aged between 8 and 11.

junk bond Bond that offers a high rate of return but also has a high risk of becoming worthless.

jury service Requirement of a person up to the age of 75 (70 before 1 December 2016) to serve on a jury unless excused. An employer must allow an employee to serve but need not pay the employee. The juror may claim for expenses and loss of earnings, to set limits, from the court, as explained in section 3 of this dictionary.

Just About Managing (JAM) Description of households that are just about able to pay their bills and have a reasonable standard of living. The term started to be used from autumn 2016 to describe people earning between £18,000 and £30,000 a year.

Käibemaks Estonian: value added tax.

kak One tenth of a riel, currency of Cambodia.

kangaroo For VAT, live kangaroos are standard-rated, but kangaroo meat prepared for human consumption is zero-rated (VAT notices 701/14 and 701/15).

kangaroo court Irregular court or tribunal that lacks authority and flouts proper procedure.

Kazakhstan Eastern state that gained its independence from Russia in 1991. Its currency is the tenge of 100 tiyn. The UK has a double taxation convention of 1994 amended by a protocol of 1997.

K code PAYE code that comprises the letter K, SK or CK followed by a number. The letter is in effect a minus sign. It means that the employee is taxed on a sum *greater* than his or her gross pay. This can happen if the employee has arrears of tax or generous benefits. K codes were introduced in 1993.

keeping in touch (KIT) Day when a woman on maternity leave may attend work without this ending her maternity pay period (SSCBA 1992 s165(4) and Statutory maternity pay Regulations SI 1986 No 1960 reg 94). She is allowed ten KIT days. They were introduced in 2007. She is entitled to be paid statutory maternity pay unless the employer agrees to pay her more. There are also 10 KIT days for statutory adoption pay and 20 days for statutory shared parental pay.

kelp Type of seaweed. There are restrictions on its removal under Scottish Crown Estate Act 2019 s15.

Kenya African state. Its currency is the Kenyan shilling of 100 cents. The UK has a double taxation convention of 1973 amended by a 1976 protocol.

kept hot In relation to food, means put in an environment where the temperature is maintained or the rate of cooling is slowed down. An item such as a sausage roll that is sold hot simply because it has not cooled down from cooking may be zero-rated as food. From 1 October 2012, if it is kept warm, it is standard-rated as hot take-away food (VATA 1994 Sch 8 Group 1 Note (3D).

kerosene For hydrocarbon oil duty, means heavy oil of which more than half distils at 240⁰ or less (HODA 1979 s1(8)).

khoum One fifth of a ourgiya, currency of Mauritania.

Kickstart scheme Government scheme started on 2 September 2020 during the coronavirus outbreak. It provides funds for a business to take on young workers. The main points are:

- the worker must be aged between 18 and 24
- the job must be for at least 25 hours a week
- the job must provide training
- the government pays all the wages plus employer's national insurance and pension costs for six months at a total cost of about £6,500 per worker
- there is no cap on the number of places
- an employer making 30 or fewer placements must make its bid via an intermediary
- the scheme runs to 2021 but may be extended.

The employer may also claim £1,500 for set-up costs.

killed in action Description of two schemes of estate duty relief for service personnel. Both schemes have now lapsed but could still be relevant for claiming transferable nil rate band for inheritance tax. Someone killed on active service is exempt from inheritance tax. These schemes are separate from the exemption from inheritance tax for those killed on active service under IHTA 1984 s154. From 19 March 2014, this exemption is extended by FA 2015 to emergency responders, such as paramedics and fire fighters, who die in the course of their work. The exemption is also extended by IHTA 1984 s154A to police officers who die in the course of duty.

kilning Heating in a kiln during brewing when barley steeped in water is kilned to stop germination.

kilogram Unit of weight equal to a thousand grams, about 2.2 pounds (Weights and Measures Act 1985 Sch 1). It is now defined by reference to Planck's constant and caesium atom by SI 2020 No 586 which made no practical difference.

kilometre Unit of length equal to 1,000 metres.

Kimberley Process Certificate Document needed to import rough diamonds from outside the EU.

Kindertransport Efforts made in the nine months before the second world war to remove Jewish children from German held territory. In 2019, the German government agreed to pay compensation to those affected. Such payments are tax free and exempt from inheritance tax (IHTA 1984 Sch 5A Item 10).

kindred and affinity Table of people to whom a person may not be married. The table is published by the Church of England as Canon B31 and has statutory authority under Marriage (Prohibited Degrees of Relationship) Act 1986 as amended.

kink test Capital gains tax provision that related to shares held on 6 April 1965 that were disposed of before 31 March 1982. It allowed the acquisition price to be substituted for 1965 value if greater. This is discussed in HMRC Manual ay CG51601.

kinnikinick Mixture of plant material used by native American as a substitute for tobacco. Should it be sold in the UK, it is subject to tobacco duty.

kip Currency of Laos.

Kiribati Island nation in the Pacific Ocean. Its currency is the Australian dollar of 100 cents. The UK has a double taxation arrangement of 1950 amended by an arrangement of 1974.

Kittel principle VAT rule from a 2008 case that a trader can be denied genuine input tax recovery if the trader knew, or should have known, that the transactions were connected to fraud. The name comes from the European case *Kittel v Belgium C-439/04 [2008] STC 1537.* This is commonly known as carousel fraud.

knitwear For VAT on children's clothing, knitted material is considered a stretch fabric. This issue was considered in the case *Jeffrey Green & Co Ltd [1974] VTD 69.*

know-how Knowledge or skill in a particular field. It is an intangible asset that attracts its own capital allowance (CAA 2001 from s452 Income tax provisions are given in ITTOIA 2005 s192(1) and corporation tax provisions from CTA 2009 from s176. Capital gains provisions are given in TCGA 1992 s261A.

knowledge-intensive company Company for whom the enterprise investment scheme and similar schemes have more generous qualifying conditions. The definition of such a company is contained in ITA 2007 s252A as inserted by Finance (No 2) Act Sch 5. For venture capital trusts, the same definition is given in ITA 2007 s331A as inserted by Finance (No 2) Act 2015 Sch 6. Broadly such a company must meet both an innovation condition and skilled employee condition.

Know Your Client Requirement that accountants, banks and other providers of professional services must know who their clients are. This is to prevent money laundering and other crimes.

koi carp Ornamental fish that is standard-rated for VAT. The VAT tribunal held that it could not be zero-rated as food in *J R Chalmers [1982] VTD 1433.* Although it was palatable, there was no evidence of any person eating one.

kopek One hundredth of a rouble, currency of Russia. The word can also be spelled kopeck or copeck.

kopiyka One hundredth of a hryvna, currency of Ukraine.

Korea Peninsula of China that has in effect been two hostile states since a war in 1953. The North state is known as the Democratic People's Republic of Korea. It is the world's only necrocracy as its president is still Kim Il-Sung who died in 1994. The de facto leader is his grandson. The currency is the North Korean won of 100 chon. The UK has no double taxation treaty. The country is subject to UK sanctions, as are designated persons of the country. The South state is the Republic of Korea. Its currency is the South Korean won of 100 jeon. The UK has a double taxation convention of 1996 which refers to South Korea simply as Korea.

korun (Kc) Plural of koruna, currency of the Czech Republic. Gold coins from 1,000 to 10,000 korun may be regarded as gold investment coins for VAT purposes (VAT notice 701/12A).

koruna (Kc) (1) Currency of Czech Republic. The plural is korun.
(2) Currency of Slovakia.

Kosovo East European state that gained its independence from Serbia in 2008. Its currency is the euro of 100 cents, though the Serbian dinar is also used. The UK has a double taxation convention of 2015.

Kretztechnik European court case *Kretztechnik AG v Finananzant Linz Case C-465 [2005].* which held that the issue of shares by a public limited company in return for capital investment is not a supply for VAT purposes. HMRC produced Guidance Note 8 in January 2010 explaining how this applies in the UK.

kronur Currency of Iceland. Gold coins for 500 or 10,000 kronur may be regarded as gold investment coins for VAT purposes (VAT notice 701/12A).

kroon Currency of Estonia.

Krugerrand Bullion gold coin issued by South Africa. It contains one troy ounce of fine gold, and bears a portrait of President Paul Kruger (1825-1904).

Kuwait Middle East state. Its currency is the Kuwaiti dinar of 1,000 fils. The UK has a double taxation agreement of 1999.

kwacha (1) Currency of Malawi.
(2) Currency of Zambia.

kwanza Currency of Angola.

kyat Currency of Burma.

Kyoto Protocol International agreement to reduce emissions of greenhouse gases. The protocol came into effect on 16 February 2005. One of its consequences was the creation of emissions allowances for which there are special tax provisions.

Kyrgyzstan Eastern state that became independent from Russia in 1991. Its currency is the som of 100 tyiyn. The UK has no double taxation treaty in effect, though one was signed on 13 June 2017 awaiting adoption.

label For VAT, a label is an item of stationery and is generally standard-rated unless ancillary to a supply taxed at a different rate. The VAT tribunal has ruled that an adhesive label containing text is not zero-rated as a leaflet.

Lady Day English quarter day on 25 March.

lagan Wreckage or goods from a ship that sink, as against flotsam and jetsam which float.

land Area of the earth's surface. Under English law, someone who owns land also owns everything under it and above it, with some exceptions. Transactions in land may attract stamp duty land tax or devolved equivalent. A supply of land is generally exempt from VAT, but construction work is subject to other provisions. The word "land" is defined in Interpretation Act 1978 Sch 1 and in many other statutory contexts.

land and buildings transaction tax (LBTT) Tax charged in Scotland from April 2015 instead of stamp duty land tax. The law is Land and Building Transaction Tax (Scotland) Act 2013.

landfill disposals tax Tax charged in Wales from April 2018 instead of landfill tax.

landfill tax Tax introduced on 1 October 1996 on material dumped in landfill sites (FA 1996 ss39-71 and Landfill Tax Regulations SI 1996 No 1527). It is charged at a higher rate for most material, and a lower rate for inert material. Many materials, such as water, are exempt. This tax is now devolved in Wales and Scotland.

landfill whole site expenditure Expenditure on a landfill site so it may receive waste material for many years. This is tax-deductible under ITTOIA 2005 s165 and CTA 2009 s142. It is discussed in HMRC Manual at BIM67516.

landing For Customs purposes, "in relation to aircraft, include[s] landing on water" (CEMAs1(1)).

landing charges Payment for getting goods from a ship or aircraft on to land, including through Customs.

landing order Permit which allows goods to be unloaded into a bonded warehouse without paying Customs duty.

land remediation relief Allowance equal to 150% of the costs of cleaning contaminated land bought from a third party (CTA 2009 from s1143). The relief from corporation tax was introduced in April 2009. Details of the relief are discussed in HMRC Manual at CIRD60051 and BIM45799.

landside Area controlled by Customs at an airport, as against airside.

land tax Tax charged from 1688 based on earlier taxes. In the 20th century, most taxpayers had redeemed their liability. The tax was finally abolished in 1963.

land transaction tax Tax introduced in Wales on 1 April 2018 as a replacement for stamp duty land tax under Land Transaction Tax and Anti-avoidance of Devolved Taxes (Wales) Act 2017 s6.

Large Business Service Large Case Management Board Board of HMRC. Its composition and function is set out in HMRC Notice of 20 December 2013.

large business tax notification Provision announced in 2020 Budget, possibly to start in April 2021, that requires a large business to notify HMRC if it takes a tax position which HMRC is likely to challenge.

large company Company whose profits exceeded £1.5 million in the previous year or £20 million in the current year (£10 million before 1 April 2019). Such a company must pay corporation tax in four instalments plus a final payment.
A company with profits above £1.5 million but not above £20 million pays in four instalments starting 6 months and 13 days after the start of the accounting period, and every three months thereafter. A company with profits above £20 million pays in instalments four months earlier, with the first payment due 2 months and 13 days after the start of the accounting period.

large fuel retailer Such a retailer may be required to provide public charging points or refuelling points under Automated and Electric Vehicles Act 2018 s11. Details and further definitions are contained in regulations.

large goods vehicle Vehicle that weighs more than 3,500 kilograms.

large pack For beer duty, a container of between 10 and 400 litres. It includes most kegs and casks.

lasting power of attorney (LPA) Arrangement that may be made by a person aged 18 or more with full mental capacity to allow someone to deal with their affairs should they lose mental capacity (Mental Capacity Act 2005). On 1 October 2007, they replaced enduring powers of attorney, though existing enduring powers of attorney may continue. An LPA may express the person's wishes for either or both of personal welfare and property and affairs.

Latakia Syrian form of tobacco.

late accounting date rules Provisions in ITTOIA 2005 from s208. They treat an accounting date that ends between 31 March and 4 April for income tax as if it were 5 April so as not to create an overlap period.

late night working When an employee works later than usual. An employer may pay for transport home without this being a taxable benefit in kind if four conditions are met (ITEPA s248). The conditions are:

- the employee works later than usual and until at least after 9pm
- this late night working is irregular, not part of a regular pattern of working, and happens on no more than 60 days
- by the time the employee has ceased work either public transport has ceased or it is not reasonable to expect the employee to use public transport
- the journey home is by taxi or similar transport.

These provisions are discussed in HMRC Manual from EIM21831.

latent allowance Amount by which the written down value of a fixed asset for tax purposes exceeds the net book value in the balance sheet. Under FA 2010 s26 and Sch26 and other law, the latent allowance of an acquired company may not be allowable against the tax liability of an acquiring company. This provision is an anti-avoidance measure to prevent companies reducing taxes by acquiring loss making companies.

latent ambiguity Expression that proves to have more than one meaning. An example is a provision in a will leaving a bequest to "my nephew John" when the testator has two nephews called John. The matter may be resolved by external evidence, such as a letter to one of the nephews.

late payment Paying a bill after it was due. There are various laws to deal with this, including the right to charge a fee plus interest at 8 percentage points above the base rate (Late Payment of Commercial Debts (Interest) Act 1988).

late payment interest Amount charged by HMRC for late payment of tax. Unlike penalties, there is no appeal against interest.

late registration penalty Penalty imposed by HMRC when someone registers for VAT after they should have done. Guidance is given in VAT Notice 700/41.

later accessory An accessory added to a company car after its acquisition and which cost at least £100 (ITEPA s126(3)). This is generally added to the list price of the car in calculating the taxable benefit.

late stamping For stamp duty, stamping a document after the due date. This includes stamping the document for insufficient amount and then further stamping the document. Late stamping may attract interest and penalties under Stamp Act 1891 s15A and s15B respectively.

Latvia East European state that is a member of the European Union. Its currency is the euro of 100 cents. The UK has a double taxation agreement of 1996.

laundering Process of taking "dirty" money such as from crime and making it appear clean. There are laws designed to counter this.

law lords Judges of the Supreme Court.

Law Society Body that licenses solicitors in the UK.

layering stage Second of three stages of money laundering. This is where an effort is made to dissociate the funds from the underlying crime.

lay justices' allowances Amounts paid to magistrates for discharging their duties. The allowance has three elements:

- travelling allowance;
- subsistence allowance; and
- financial loss allowance.

(Courts Act 2003 s15(1)).

lay rector Land owner who is liable to repair the chancel of a Church of England building.

lead case Case that is selected to establish a point of law where more than one case has been started on that point. Other cases are stayed (or sisted in Scotland) until the lead case has been determined. This procedure is permitted under SI 2009 No 273 rule 18.

leading and principal object The purpose for which a document is subject to stamp duty. It does not need to be stamped again for a subsequent transaction that is merely incidental.

leading question Question that is phrased so as to suggest the answer. In court, such questions are generally prohibited in examining a witness, but not in cross-examination.

leaflet Document that may be zero-rated for VAT under VATA 1994 Sch 8 Group 3. VAT notice 701/10 identifies these characters of a zero-rated leaflet:

- no larger than A4 page size when folded
- intended for reading rather than display
- conveys information
- not part of a larger work
- supplied in at least 50 copies for distribution
- printed on limp paper
- either is intended to be thrown away after reading or accompanies a product or service.

leap year Year that has 366 days by adding 29 February. This is any year that is divisible by 4 but not by 100 unless it is also divisible by 400. So 1900 was not a leap year but 2000 was.

These provisions are given in Calendar (New Style) Act 1750 s2 with effect from 1752. One practical consequence is that week 53 for PAYE purposes has two days instead of one.

lease Arrangement whereby someone retains ownership of an item and someone else uses it for a charge. A definition is given in CTA 2009 s937. For all but short-term and low value hires, accounting standards now treat the asset as if belongs to the lessee rather than the lessor. IFRS 16, effective from 2019, extends the scope of balance sheet reporting. The tax consequences of this are given in FA 2019 Sch 14 as amended by FA 2020 s35. A lease of land is treated as a fixed asset. There are several tax provisions for valuing leases.

leaseback A method of raising finance in which an organization sells its land or buildings to an investor (usually an insurance company) on condition that the investor will lease the property back to the organization for a fixed term at an agreed rental. This releases capital for the organization, enabling it to be used for other purposes. For stamp duty land tax purposes this is regarded as a single transaction.

leased car From April 2009, only 85% of the cost of leasing a car is tax-deductible unless the car has low emissions.

lease for life A lease that is granted for the remainder of a person's life, when the property passes to another person. For inheritance tax purposes, this is regarded as an interest in possession (IHTA 1984 ss49-50).

leasehold Ownership of property but not of the land it stands on. The leaseholder pays a ground rent to the owner of the land. From 27 June 2019, it is announced that all new-build houses must be sold freehold and not leasehold.

lease premium Sum paid in addition to a lease to secure the premises. There are tax provisions to determine how much of the premium is regarded as revenue and how much is capital. Income tax provisions are given in ITTOIA 2005 from s276; corporation tax provisions are given in CTA 2009 s217. Tables are given in section 3 of this dictionary.

lease purchase Arrangement in which a person leases an asset for a primary period during which the lessor recoups the capital cost of the asset. After this, the lessee has the option to buy the asset, usually for a nominal sum. For tax purposes, it is treated in exactly the same manner as a hire purchase agreement.

leasing of ships Activity which excludes a company from the scope of EIS relief or venture capital trusts. It is defined for this purpose in ITA 2007 s194 (EIS) and s305 (VCT).

least developed country County that benefits from a scheme of preferences for Customs purposes. For import duty, the scope is set out in Taxation (Cross-border Trade) Act 2018 Sch 3 Part 1. A list is given in appendix C to Customs notice 830.

leave travel Travel by a member of the armed forces while on leave. The provision of facilities for such travel is exempt from income tax under ITEPA 2003 s296.

Lebanon Middle East state. Its currency is the Lebanese pound of 100 piastres. The UK has no double taxation treaty but has an air transport profits agreement of 1963. The country is subject to UK sanctions, as are designated persons of the country.

Lebanese pound Currency of Lebanon.

ledger Record of transactions. Apart from the nominal ledger, all ledgers are outside the scope of double-entry bookkeeping.

legacy Gift of cash or personal property left in a will.

legacy benefits Social security benefits that are no longer paid to new claimants but may continue to be paid to existing claimants.

legacy duty A death duty charged under Legacy Duty Act 1796. It was repealed in 1949.

legal charge Claim on property, such as when a mortgage is secured on land. The charge is evidence by a legal document held at the Land Registry. This identifies who has a claim on the property. For a mortgage, the main lender is normally be identified as the first charge. There may be other charges registered.

legal costs Expenses incurred in asserting a legal right to defending a claim. The extent to which such expenses are tax-deductible is discussed in HMRC Manual at BIM37955.

legal entity A legal person; the body to whom the funds belong. In relation to people with significant control, the term means "a body corporate or a firm that is a legal person under the law by which it is governed" (CA 2006 s790C(5)).

legal obligation In accounting, an obligation that arises from a contract, legislation or other operation of law. FRS 102 section 2.20 gives it as one of the two types of obligation that creates a liability. The other is constructive obligation.

legal person Entity that is separately recognised in law but is not an individual. Examples of legal persons include companies and trusts.

legal privilege The right of confidentiality between a lawyer and his or her client. Communications between them cannot be ordered to be disclosed. Definitions appear in Criminal Justice and Police Act 2001 s65 and CA 2006 s1129. There is no legal privilege between an accountant and client, so it may be necessary for the accountant to advise a client via a lawyer.

legal tender Notes and coins which form the generally accepted currency. In the UK this comprises notes from the Bank of England and coins from the Royal Mint. These currently comprise four notes: £5, £10, £20 and £50; and eight coins: 1p, 2p, 5p, 10p, 20p, 50p, £1 and £2. Although other bank notes and other forms of exchange are widely accepted, they are not legal tender. There is no concept of legal tender in Scotland. Other coins are legal tender, though not used as such. These include:

- Britannia coins in gold and silver
- sovereigns, half sovereigns, quarter sovereigns and tenth sovereigns
- £2 and £5 gold coins minted from 1838
- double florins (1887-1890) for 20p
- commemorative coins for £5
- silver coins for £20, £50 and £100
- Maundy money
- 1 kilogram gold and silver coins minted from 2012

Bank notes, and £1 and £2 coins are legal tender to any amount; 20p and 50p coins to £10; 5p and 10p coins to £5; and 1p and 2p coins to 20p (Decimal Currency Act 1969 s1).

legatee Someone to whom a legacy is left. For capital gains tax, a definition is given in TCGA 1992 s64. For the accrued income scheme, a definition is in ITA 2007 s636(4).

Leghorn Cableseal wire seal One of two official types of Customs seal. The other is the Acme T lock. The Leghorn seal comprises a body and a wire. The body is painted aluminium with the legend "Customs GB". This is attached to a steel wire 1mm in diameter and 180mm long. Details of these seals are given in Customs notice 205.

legitim In Scots law, the right of a child has to share in the parent's estate regardless of what is written in a will.

legitimacy State of being born in wedlock. All legal bars of illegitimacy have now been removed except that an illegitimate child cannot take an inherited title. For all other purposes, there is no longer any distinction between legitimate and illegitimate children.

An illegitimate child may inherit property under Family Law Reform Act 1969. Until 1969, tax relief was not available for an illegitimate child unless the parents married (Finance (1909-1910) Act 1910 s68(1)).

Legitimacy Act 1976 s1 makes a child legitimate if the parents subsequently marry.

For tax purposes, legitimate and illegitimate children are treated the same.

legitimise Make legitimate.

Lennartz accounting Form of accounting for VAT that may be used from November 2007. Where an asset is acquired for both business and non-business use, this method allows the trader to claim all input tax and then to invoice itself and charge VAT for non-business use. This is an alternative to the usual arrangement of taking a portion of input tax.

leone Currency of Sierra Leone.

le roy le vault Normal French: the king wills it. Words of Royal Assent.

Lesotho African country that is landlocked in South Africa. Its currency is the loti of 100 lisente, though the rand is also used. The UK has a double taxation convention of 1997.

lessee Person who leases land or another asset from a lessor.

lessee's incremental borrowing rate "The rate of interest the lessee would have to pay on a similar lease or. if that is not determinable, the rate that, at the inception of the lease, the lessee would incur to borrow over a similar term, and with a similar security, the funds necessary to purchase the asset" (FRS 102 glossary).

less likely need For social security, a person whose situation is such that alternative payment arrangements need to be considered, but whose circumstances do not make them high likely needy. Examples of someone who is *not* a less likely need may include a claimant:

- without a bank account
- who has deduction orders in place
- who is a refugee or asylum seeker
- who has a history of rent arrears
- who was recently homeless or in care
- who has recently left prison
- who has a physical disability
- who does not understand English.

lessor Person who leases land or another asset to a lessee. There are definitions in ITA 2007 s614DG and CAA 2001 s70YI(1).

lessor company Company that leases equipment. There are provisions in CTA 2010 Part 9 to stop such companies being sold for tax avoidance purposes.

less than a container load Quantity of goods that is less than one full shipping container. It is used to calculate the VAT adjust figure on the delivery element of the cost of imported goods.

Let Property Campaign Campaign launched by HMRC in 2019 to ensure that overseas landlords pay tax on rent from UK property.

letter Communication in written form on any kind of physical material to be conveyed to a person or address indicated on the items itself or its wrapping, including a postal packet (Postal Services Act 2011 s65(1)).

letter of comfort Letter from a holding company to a bank in respect of a loan to a subsidiary. The letter usually seeks specific assurances from the holding company.

letter of credit Document issued by a bank requiring it to make payment when documents are presented to it.

letter of engagement Letter sent by an auditor or other professional person to a new client, setting out what services are being provided and the basis of charges.

letter of renunciation In a rights issue of shares, a letter sent with an allocation notice that allows the shareholder to indicate they do not wish to take up the rights issue. The shareholder may sometimes be able to sell the letter and the rights.

letter of weakness Term once used for a letter sent by the auditors to the directors setting out matters to which they should pay attention. The auditors' responsibility for such matters is now set out in International Standards on Auditing ISA 260 and 265.

letter of wishes Document issued by a member of a pension scheme saying who that member wishes to receive any benefits of the scheme on his or her death. This cannot be put in a will as the member does not own the pension fund assets.

letters of administration Legal appointment of an administrator for an intestate, someone who dies without leaving a will.

lettings relief Relief from capital gains tax for a residential property that is fully let (TCGA 1992 s223(4). The main points are:

- the maximum relief is £40,000 per owner
- lettings relief may not be claimed in addition to main residence relief for the same property
- from 6 April 2020, the owner must also live at the residence.

leu Currency of Romania, more accurately called the new leu.

lev Currency of Bulgaria. The plural is leva. Gold lev coins, from 1 to 20,000 leva, may be regarded as gold investment coins for VAT purposes (VAT notice 701/12A).

leva Plural of lev, currency of Bulgaria.

level annuity Annuity whose amount does not change. Its value therefore declines in line with inflation.

leverage American term for gearing.

levy allowance Amount of £15,000 that may be offset against the apprenticeship levy. As this levy is charged at 0.5% of payroll, it means the levy is payable only by payrolls of more than £3 million a year.

levy ceiling Maximum amount of pension levy that may be charged in a year (Pensions Act 2004 s178).

liability Obligation to make a payment; the opposite to an asset. Accounting standard FRS 102 glossary defines it as "a present obligation of the entity arising from past events, the settlement of which is expected to result in an outflow from the entity of resources embodying economic benefits". A definition appears in CA 2006 s831(3).

liability limitation agreement "An agreement that purports to limit the amount of a liability owed to a company by its auditor in respect of any negligence, default, breach of duty or breach of trust, occurring in the course of audit of accounts, of which the auditor may be guilty in relation to the company" (CA 2006 s534(1)). Unless such an agreement meets all the conditions set out in the Act, the agreement is void under s532. The main conditions are that the agreement:

- is only for one financial year which must be stated,
- does not include provisions which are prohibited under separate regulations,
- does not inhibit competition,
- is approved by ordinary resolution of members.

The agreement does not have to specify an exact amount, nor contain a formula by which such amount may be calculated (ibid s535(4)).

liability method Method of calculating deferred tax, based on what the rate of corporation tax is expected to be. This term was used in former accounting standard SSAP 15. It is now the standard method.

liability order

(1) Notice issued by a magistrates' court that a person is liable to pay rent or council tax. If the council can demonstrate that council tax is payable but has not been paid, the court *must* issue a liability order. The only defences are that the person is not liable, the council tax has been paid, or that the council has not followed the proper procedure. A liability order may be issued while a claim for council tax benefit or local equivalent is being considered. Once the council has the liability order, it may enforce it by distress, a council tax attachment of earnings order, deductions from benefits or insolvency procedures.

(2) Order from a magistrates' court that rent is owed. This allows the landlord to continue proceedings.

liable not liable concession VAT concession that allows HMRC to charge VAT on periods that briefly exceed the registration threshold but not when they return below the threshold. It is not listed among VAT concessions but is set out in HMRC Manual at VATREG28050 and VATREG28550 where it is redacted to members of the public but accessible to HMRC staff. This concession was considered in the case *Tim Hughes [2018] TC 6609.*

libel Defamation in permanent recorded form. This can be a tax-deductible expenses as explained in HMRC Manual at BIM38530.

Liberia African state. Its currency is the Liberian dollar of 100 cents. The UK has no double taxation treaty.

Liberian dollar Currency of Liberia.

Libid London interbank bid rate.

LIBOR **London interbank offered rate.** This is widely used as a basis for determining almost all interest rates. For the purposes of calculating the capital allowance on the net present value of a lease, LIBOR "means the London interbank offered rate on the relevant day for deposits for a term of 12 months in the relevant currency" (CAA 2001 s228MB(4)).

Libra Name for electronic currency proposed by Facebook in June 2019.

library Place which lends or hires items. Libraries principally lend books but there are also libraries for CDs, DVDs, games and toys. Local authorities are required to run book libraries without charge to its residents under what is now Public

Libraries and Museums Act 1964. Under s8, the library may make charges for late returned items. Late return payments are not subject to VAT. Any sales by libraries, such as refreshments or photocopying, are subject to VAT, though sales of books are zero-rated.

It is a criminal offence to bet or gamble in a library (Libraries Offences Act 1898 s2(3)).

For VAT, a library service is not a zero-rated supply of books *(UU Bibliotech Ltd [2006] VTD 19764).*

Libya North African state. Its currency is the Libyan dinar of 1,000 dirhams. The UK has a double taxation convention of 2008.

licence Permission to do something. In particular it relates to temporary occupation of premises. Such occupation does not trigger a liability to stamp duty land tax, unless the licence in truth represents a lease.

licence event In relation to oil and gas licences, this term is defined in Energy Act 2016 s30(3).

licence fees A business established to receive licence fees is an excluded activity for venture capital trust purposes under ITA 2007 s306.

licence year "In relation to an excise licence issuable annually, means the period of 12 months ending on the date on which that licence expires in any year" (CEMAs1(1)).

licensable activities Activities which require a local authority licence under Licensing Act 2003 s1. These are the sale of alcohol, regulated entertainment and late night (11pm to 5am) sales of refreshments.

licensed deposit taker Body that is licensed to accept deposits from members of the public and to pay interest on those deposits. It is a form of junior bank.

licensed user For hydrocarbon oil duty, "means an annual rebate payment person or a quarterly rebate payment person" (Hydrocarbon Oil Duties (Payment of Rebates) Regulations SI 1996 No 2313 reg 3(1)).

licensee Person who is licensed. In relation to capital allowances for the oil industry, the term is given a specific meaning in CAA 2001 s554(4).

licensing committee Body established by a local authority to grant licences (Licensing Act 2003 s6).

licensing hours order Order issued under Licensing Act 2003 s172 which permits licensed premises to remain open outside their licensed hours for the duration of a celebration period.

licit Lawful, allowable.

Liechtenstein Small European principality that is part of the European Economic Area but not the European Union. It was widely used for tax avoidance. Those who so avoided tax were given a chance to regularise their tax position under the Liechtenstein Disclosure Facility that ran from 1 September 2009 to 31 March 2016.

lien Common law right that repairers, innkeepers have to keep possession of someone's goods until their bill has been paid.

life annuity A contract that provides an income during the remaining lifetime of the purchaser.

life annuity loan Loan to buy an annuity. Certain loans taken out before 9 March 1999 may attract tax relief under ICTA 1988 s365.

life assurance Policy that pays on the death of a person. It differs from life *insurance* in that assurance always pays whereas insurance is conditional, such as a person dying before the age of 65.

life assurance relief Income tax relief in respect of a life assurance policy taken out before 14 March 1984. This relief is abolished from 2014/15.

lifeboat Boat for rescuing those in peril on water. Such a boat may be zero-rated under VATA 1994 Sch 8 Group 8. The scope has been progressively widened:

- 1 April 1973: RNLI lifeboat
- 1 May 1990: non-RNLI lifeboats; slipways
- 1 April 2002: life-saving equipment on lifeboats
- 1 April 2006: fuel for charity-operated lifeboat.

life expectancy Number of years a person can expect to live, as determined by their age and sex, from life expectancy tables, as in section 3 of this dictionary.

life insurance Insuring a person's life. Strictly speaking, life insurance is when someone dies and is therefore always payable eventually, whereas life assurance is only payable if someone dies by a certain date and is therefore not always payable. In practice, this distinction is not always made. Life assurance is now more commonly called term insurance. Life insurance and assurance is subject to Life Assurance Act 1774 which prescribes that:

- no-one may insure a life unless they have an insurable interest (s1);
- the names of the person having such insurable interest must be stated on the policy (s2); and
- no-one may insure someone else's life for a sum greater than their insurable interest (s3).

There is a special inheritance tax provision for life insurance contracts made before 22 March 2006 (Inheritance Tax Act 1984 s46A).

life interest Benefit a person can enjoy for the rest of their life but which they cannot pass on to anyone else. A life interest commonly arises when a will allows a person to continue living in a house but on their death, the property passes to someone else.

life interest trust An interest in possession trust with one or more fixed interests in the income. Under FA 2006, these are generally regarded as discretionary trusts for inheritance tax purposes. Exceptions are transitional serial trusts, immediate post-death interest trusts and trusts for a disabled beneficiary.

life peer Person who has a peerage for the duration of his or her life, but where the peerage does not devolve on death, as for a hereditary peer. Life peerages were created by Life Peerages Act 1958.

life policy Policy of life assurance. It is a form of property and may therefore be assigned to another person, such as to a bank when used as a collateral security for a mortgage.

For inheritance tax, a life policy taken out by a person on their own life becomes part of their taxable estate. This can be avoided by someone else taking out the policy (assuming they have sufficient insurable interest), or holding the policy in a trust.

lifestyling For child trust funds, "means the process beginning from a date on or before the child is 15 years of age, or from when the account is opened, whichever is later, and continuing until the child is 18 years of age, by which the account provider, and any relevant person, adopts an investment strategy which aims progressively to minimise the variation or potential variation in capital value of the account caused by market conditions from time to time" (Child Trust Fund Regulations SI 2004 No 1450 Sch para 2(6)).

life tenant Person who has a right to income, occupation of property or similar benefit for the rest of their life, after which the property or other asset passes to the remainderman.

lifetime allowance charge Maximum amount an individual may contribute to a pension fund in his or her lifetime and claim tax relief (FA 2004 from s214). This charge was introduced in 2006 since when it has both increased and decreased in amount. The rates are given under Pensions in section 3 of this dictionary.

lifetime allowance excess lump sum Lump sum benefit paid to a member of a registered pension scheme because they have used up their lifetime allowance. Tax provisions are given in FA 2004 Sch 29.

lifetime allowance protection Measure of relief from the pension lifetime limit when it reduced. The protection applied to those who had already exceeded the limit when it was reduced.

lifetime annuity Annuity contract purchased under a money purchase arrangement and which meets the conditions of FA 2004 Sch 28 para 3.

lifetime exemptions Payments that are not regarded as lifetime transfers for inheritance tax. They include the annual exemption, small gifts exemption, normal expenditure out of income, wedding presents, gifts to spouse or civil partner, and gifts to charities and political parties.

lifetime gift Gift made during the lifetime of the donor. If the donor dies within seven years, all or part of the gift may be added back to the donor's estate for inheritance tax purposes.

lifetime ISA Individual savings account available from 6 April 2017 (Savings (Government Contributions) Act 2017. It allows a person under 40 to save up to £4,000 towards a first home, and receive a £1,000 bonus from the government. It is subject to many conditions. It is sometimes abbreviated to LISA.

lifetime mortgage Form of regulated mortgage contract whose main terms are:

- the mortgagor is above a specified age,

- the loan is not repaid while the mortgagor is alive and occupying the property.

lifetime rate Rate of inheritance tax that can be payable during the donor's lifetime. It is charged at half the death rate, that is 20%.

lift For capital allowance purposes, a lift is treated as an integral feature, which means that it is included in the special rate pool and is subject to capital allowance at 6% on the writing down basis, and not the usual 18% for plant and machinery (CAA 2001 s33A).

lift the veil of incorporation When the court departs from the principle that a limited company has a separate identity from its owner. The principle is known as the veil of incorporation. The veil is lifted when it is being abused. An example was *Gilford Motor Company v Horne [1933].* An employee agreed to a restraint of trade clause not to approach his employer's customers. He left, and set up a company which made such approaches. The corporate structure could not be used to defeat legal responsibilities.

In USA, the term is piercing the veil of incorporation. This term is increasingly being used in the UK.

light agricultural vehicle Vehicle weighing up to 1,000 kilograms used for agriculture, forestry or horticulture. It may use red diesel (HODA 1979 Sch 1 para 3).

light crude oil Naturally occurring oil before processing which contains a high concentration (up to 97%) of the more valuable hydrocarbons.

lighterage Transference of goods from a large ship to a smaller ship that can reach harbour.

light oil For hydrocarbon oil duty, oil where at least 90% by volume distils at a temperature of no more than 21^{0}C and which gives off an inflammable vapour below 2^{0}C (HODA 1979 s1(3)).

light touch Period when HMRC enforces new regulations gently, seeking to advise taxpayers rather than penalise them.

light vehicle For vehicle excise duty, a vehicle with an unladen weight of up to 550 kilograms.

lilangeni Currency of Eswatini (formerly Swaziland). The South African rand is also used.

Limean London interbank mid price. This is the average of Libid and LIBOR.

limitation period Period in which action must be taken. Generally this is 6 years for contract, 3 years for personal injury, and 12 years for land issues (Limitation Act 1980). For many tax matters, the general limit is now 4 years, subject to many specific provisions and exceptions.

limited administration Administration of the estate of a deceased person for limited purposes specified by the court in the letters of administration. A common example is the grant of administration when the executor is a child.

limited by guarantee A company is so described if the liability of its members is limited to paying a defined sum, often a nominal figure such as £1 each, if the company is wound up (CA 2006 s3(3)). Since 22 December 1980 (1 July 1983 in

Northern Ireland), a company limited by guarantee may not have a share capital (CA s5(1)). However, companies already so formed may remain in that form.

limited by shares A company is so described if the liability of its members is limited to any unpaid amount on their shares, which is usually zero (CA 2006 s3(2)).

limited capability for work A person may be so assessed for the purposes of employment and support allowance (WRA 2007 s8) or universal credit (WRA 2012 s37(1)).

limited cost trader A VAT-registered business that uses the flat rate scheme but where costs are less than 2% of turnover (or £1,000 if higher). From 1 April 2017, such a trader must use the flat rate of 16.5% or revert to the usual basis of output tax minus input tax.

limited executorship In law, arrangement when a person is appointed in a will to act as executor for some property, but not all of it.

limited liability Limit on the liability of a member of a limited company or limited liability partnership or limited partner of a limited partnership. Their liability is limited to the amount of shares or partnership interest they have contributed.

limited liability partnership (LLP) Legal entity created from 6 April 2001 (13 September 2004 in Northern Ireland) and now widely used by law and accountancy firms. It is a body corporate where the liability of all members is limited. For tax purposes, it is fiscally transparent, which means that profits are generally taxed on the partners and not the partnership itself. The law is Limited Liability Partnership Act 2000. The taxation of LLPs is discussed in HMRC Manual at BIM72110 to BIM72155.

limited partnership Partnership formed under Limited Partnerships Act 1907. It is not the same as a limited liability partnership. It is an ordinary partnership where one or more partners has limited liability. There must be at least one partner with unlimited liability. There are limits on the amount of tax relief a limited partner may claim.

limited period annuity Annuity that does not last for the death of the annuitant but for a limited period, usually a fixed number of years. If the annuitant lives beyond that period, he or she may take out another annuity from what remains in the pension fund.

limited price indexation Indexation that is capped. It is widely used for pensions. This may, for example, index-link a pension to the lower of retail prices index and 5%.

limited prize machine Gaming machine which offers no opportunity to win a prize other than having a refund of the sum paid (Gambling Act 2005 s249).

limited probate Arrangement whereby an executor is appointed to deal with certain parts of an estate but not the whole of it.

link company Company that is both a member of a group and a consortium.

linked assets In relation to taxation of life assurance companies, "means assets of an insurance company which are identified in its records as assets by reference to the value of which benefits provided for under a policy or contract are to be determined and in a case where only part of an asset is so identified, references to a linked asset are references to that part" (ICTA 1988 s432ZA). Following sections expand this definition.

linked bingo Another name for combined bingo.

linked dwellings Two dwellings that have private access between them, and where there is some common ownership. The implications for annual tax on enveloped dwellings are given in FA 2013 s117.

linked entity In relation to corporation tax on banks, this term is defined in CTA 2009 s133F(6) as inserted by Finance (No 2) Act 2015 s18. It is also defined in CTA 2010 s269BC(3).

linked loan Loan that is made to a company because a taxpayer has subscribed for shares (ITA 2007 s164(2)). Such a loan prevents the taxpayer from subscribing for shares under enterprise investment scheme.

linked PIW For statutory sick pay, a period of incapacity of work that starts less than eight weeks after a previous period ended. The consequence is that the two periods are treated as one.

linked supplies concession VAT concession that relates to a minor article that is subject to a different rate of VAT from a main article to which it is linked. No apportionment is required if:

- the minor article is not charged for separately
- the minor article costs less the 20% of the combined supply (including VAT), and
- the minor item costs no more than £1 if the item is for retail sale, or £5 otherwise. (VAT Notice 700/7 para 6.2).

linking letter Letter provided by Jobcentre Plus or its equivalent to people who have recently received certain benefits. This may affect the maximum linked PIW for which statutory sick pay may be payable.

linking period Gap between periods that is sufficiently short for the periods to be regarded as one continuous period. For statutory sick pay the linking period is 8 weeks. For employment and support allowance, it is 12 weeks.

link papers In tax, "those papers which show how the figures in the return are derived from the figures in the prime records, are held by the agents, but are available to the taxpayer" (Inland Revenue Tax Bulletin of 2 August 1997).

Linux A computer operating system.

lipa One hundredth of a kuna, currency of Croatia.

liquefied petroleum gas (LPG) Form of road fuel and heating fuel. It is usually a mixture of propane and butane. It attracts a lower rate of duty than hydrocarbon oils. Company cars using LPG attract a lower rate of taxable benefit. It is subject to the reduced rate of VAT when supplied as domestic fuel, as explained in VAT Notice 701/19.

liquid In accounting, this refers to how easily an asset can be turned into cash. The most liquid asset is cash, followed by prepayments, debtors, stock and fixed assets.

liquidation Formal process of ending a company. The start of liquidation automatically starts a new accounting period for corporation tax (CTA 2010 ss626-633; CTA 2009 ss9-12). It is not possible to claim group relief between a solvent and insolvent company.

liquidation committee Committee appointed by the creditors to oversee a liquidation (Insolvency Act 1986 ss101, 141).

liquidator Insolvency practitioner whose task is simply to close down a business and sell what he can for as much as he can (Insolvency Act 1986, s91, ss135-140).

liquidity ratio Liquid assets divided by current liabilities, where liquid assets are current assets minus stock. This ratio is sometimes called the acid test. A ratio below 1 could suggest financial problems, though this depends on the nature of the business. A cash positive business such as a supermarket can safely trade with a low ratio. Conversely a business with a liquidity ratio much above 1 could indicate a business with excess cash.

liquor Strictly, this means any drink, though it almost always means alcoholic drink. Such drink is subject to alcoholic liquor duty and VAT.

lira (1) Unit of currency in Italy before it adopted the euro.
(2) Currency of Turkey.
The plural for both meanings is either liras or lire.

lis Suit or action where there is a dispute between the parties.

LISA Lifetime ISA.

Lisbon Treaty Agreement of the European Union. It was agreed on 13 December 2007 and came into force on 1 December 2009. It amended the Maastricht Treaty of 1993 and the Treaty of Rome of 1958. It replaced the Treaty of Amsterdam. It extended the scope of majority voting into 45 new areas, and made many administrative changes to the European Union.

lisente One hundredth of a loti, currency of Lesotho.

lis pendens Latin: pending suit. The term particularly applies to disputes about land.

listed place of worship Church, temple or other building set aside for worship under any religion and which is also a listed building. From April 2001, a grant may be obtained equal to the VAT on certain categories of work, or for some of that sum. The grant is paid in arrears by the Department of Culture Media and Sport (DCMS). It is now run by the company Topmark on behalf of DCMS.

Listing Agreement Document which a company signs outlining the conditions it must follow to be listed on the New York Stock Exchange.

Listing Rules Issued by the UK Listing Authority of the Financial Services Authority to regulate companies listed on the UK Stock Exchange. It includes rules on accounting information in annual reports.

list price The price at which an item is offered for sale, before any discounts, commissions or part-exchanges are consideration. The list price of cars is used to calculate the taxable benefit of a company car (ITEPA 2003 s123(1)).

litas Currency of Lithuania.

literal rule One of the methods for interpreting an Act of Parliament. It basically states that words are to be given their ordinary dictionary meaning if they are precise and unambiguous. The rule was summarised in the court case *Sussex Peerage Case [1844]*. The literal rule is not necessarily followed when interpreting other documents, such as wills *(Perrin v Morgan [1943]*).

literary work Any piece of writing. Where the author has spent more than one year creating it, he or she may be able to claim averaging of profits for income tax (ITTOIA 2005 s221(3)).

Lithuania Eastern European country, and member of the European Union. Its currency is the litas of 100 cents, which is pegged to the euro. The UK has a double taxation convention of 2001 amended by a protocol of 2002.

litigant Party to legal proceedings

litigation Legal proceedings where one party is suing another.

Litigation and Settlement Strategy (LSS) Procedure introduced by HMRC in 2007 to settle disputes with taxpayers, and to avoid the expense and delay of a trial in court. LSS uses a third party as a facilitator to move towards an agreed resolution.

litigious Description of a person or organisation that is fond of suing.

litre Metric unit of capacity, defined in 1901 as the volume of a kilogram of water at 4C under standard atmospheric pressure. There are about 4½ litres to a gallon. The litre is the standard measure for vehicle engine sizes.

Littlewoods case Long-running case on whether interest on tax refunds should be calculated on a simple interest or compound interest basis. In 2017, the Supreme Court finally ruled that it was simple interest.

littoral Belonging to the seashore; that part of land which is visible between high and low tides.

live performance The televising of a live performance is specifically excluded from television production relief (CTA 2009 s1216AD).

livery For VAT, livery services are generally standard-rated, though stabling may be exempt. VAT notice 701/15 gives details. A livery business qualifies for business property relief from inheritance tax (*M Vigne [2017] TC 6068)*. The tribunal rejected the argument that it was an investment from use of land. This decision was upheld by the upper tribunal in *Personal representatives of the estate of Maureen M Vigne [2018] UKUT 0357*.

livestock Cattle, horses, asses, mules, hinnies, sheep, pigs, goats and poultry. It also includes deer when not in a wild state, and pheasants, partridges and grouse in captivity (Animals Act 1971 s11). Livestock benefits from a special low rate of VAT in the Irish Republic.

live-work unit Term used in VAT Notice 708 for a property that comprises workspace and living accommodation in a single planning application. The extent to which VAT input tax relief may be claimed was considered in the tribunal case *Adrian Richard Railton Holden and Jane Elisabeth Holden [2012] TC 2043.*

living over the shop Living in accommodation when required to be near a workplace, not necessarily a shop. Generally expenditure on such accommodation is not tax-deductible, however commercially justified. A leading case on this is *Mason v Tyson [1980] 53 TC 333.* The matter is discussed in HMRC Manual at BIM37928.

living separately When a married couple live separate lives even though they may still live in the same home and co-operate in some matters. A leading tax case is *Holmes v Mitchell [1990] Ch D. 63 TC 718.* Generally tax law treats such a couple as if they were not married, e.g. TCGA 1992 s282.

living together Co-habiting. This can affect certain entitlement to social security payments. Even for a married couple, living together can be a further requirement, such as in TCGA1992 s282.

Lloyd's London-based insurance market founded in 1689. It funds insurance in syndicates of individuals known as Names. From 1992, limited companies may also be members. There are some special tax provisions for Names, e.g. FA 2007 Sch 11.

LLP Limited liability partnership.

Llywodraeth Cymru Welsh for "Welsh Government". This is one of the two official names of the body under Wales Act 2014 s4(1).

loading In business, the extent to which an individual is charged more than the "standard" or "average" rate for a product or (more usually) a service. An example is an additional insurance premium for a high risk customer.

loading list A commercial document which may be used when more than one item is being shipped. It may be used instead of continuation sheets to supplement Single Administrative Document (SAD) Community Transit (CT) documents.

loading pass Document for the purpose of obtaining authority to load Local Export Control (LEC) goods boarding a ship or aircraft, after they have been removed from the trader's approved premises.

loan Sum lent to a person. In general, there are no tax implications when a loan is made nor when it is repaid. If a loan is made by an employer, there may be a tax charge if the loan is for more than £10,000 and is either interest-free or charged at a low rate (ITEPA 2003 s173). Loan interest for the purpose of a trade is generally tax-deductible.

loan capital Funding for a business which has been acquired by borrowing.

loan charge Term for the new tax charge for disguised remuneration loans. It applies when a tax avoidance scheme is used whereby funds that represent earnings are paid to an offshore trust or similar body and then "lent" to the worker with no expectation that the loan will be repaid.

The charge imposes income tax on the amount of the outstanding loan on 6 April 2019. In December 2019, the charge was relaxed in three respects:

- the cut-off date was brought forward from April 1999 to September 2010. Loans made before this date avoid the charge,
- the payment date was deferred from April 2019 to September 2020
- those who used the scheme between 9 December 2010 and 5 April 2016 and disclosed this on their tax returns will not be charged.

The scheme was widely used by freelancers, footballers and celebrities, many of whom did not realise it was avoidance. The loan charge is imposed by Finance (No 2) Act 2017 Sch 11-12. The 2019 changes are given effect by amending these Schedules by FA 2020 ss15-21.

loan creditor "In relation to a company, means a creditor in respect of any debt of the incurred by the company:

(a) for any money borrowed or capital assets acquired by the company; or
(b) for any right to receive income created in favour of the company; or
(c) for consideration the value of which to the company was (at the time when the debt was incurred) substantially less than the amount of the debt (including any premium thereon);

or in respect of any redeemable loan capital issued by the company." (ICTA 1988 s417(7)).

loan guarantee Payment made on a loan by a guarantor rather than by the borrower. Generally such a payment is not tax-deductible as it is not wholly and exclusively for the guarantor's business. The case *Garforth v Tankard Carpets Ltd [1980]* held that a company could not claim for a guarantee to an associated company even though the court accepted that there was a genuine commercial reason for making it. The matter is discussed in HMRC Manual at BIM45301.

loan interest Interest charged on a loan.

Before 6 April 1969, interest on almost all loans was tax-deductible. From 6 April 1969 to 5 April 1972, loan interest was tax deductible only to the extent that it related to a mortgage, acquiring an interest in a partnership or close company, or for a qualifying trade purpose.

From 6 April 1972 to 27 March 1974, interest relief was granted on most payments to banks and similar UK bodies.

From 27 March 1974, loan interest was generally restricted to mortgages and business loans. Mortgage interest relief ended on 6 April 2000.

loan notes A method of borrowing from commercial institutions such as banks. A loan note may itself be tradeable on a stock exchange.

loan obligation In the context of a transfer of value by trustees linked with trustee borrowing, this term is given a specific meaning in TCGA1992 Sch 4B para 4(1).

loan on ordinary commercial terms This is an exception to the benefit in kind tax charge when an employer provides a low-interest of more than £10,000 to an employee. The condition is that the terms of the loan are equivalent to those offered to the employer's ordinary customers (ITEPA 2003 s176(2)).

loan relationship Loans incurred by a company to fund trading. Broadly, this totals all interest received and subtracts all such interest paid to give a single figure (CTA 2009 from s292). This is either subject to corporation tax as item a separate income stream, or allowed as taxable deduction.

loan society Body established to lend money on terms similar to friendly societies. The last society closed in 1996, and the relevant tax law was repealed in 1998.

loan to own Form of investment whose tax treatment is given in ITA 2007 s809FZV as inserted by FA 2016 s37.

loan to participators Money lent by a company to a participator, which usually means a shareholder. If the company is close company, a tax charge may arise under ICTA 1988 s419.

loan to value Amount of mortgage advanced as a percentage of the property's value.

local authority Council or similar body. There are definitions in Local Government Act 1972 and Localism Act 2011 s8(1). A local authority collects council tax and business rates.

A definition for company law is given in CA 2006 s1193(2).

Local authorities were extensively reorganised in 1974 under Local Government Act 1972. A local authority is exempt from VAT on statutory services such as fees for planning permission (VATA 1994 s96(4) but not for commercial services such as hall hire. So a local authority may be required to register for VAT (s42) but may be able to claim refunds (s33).

local charity A charity established for purposes which are by their nature or by the trusts of the charity directed wholly or mainly to the benefit of that area or of part of it"(Charities Act 1960 s45(1)). This definition was introduced from 1 August 1993. The definition is repeated in Charities Act 2011 s293.

local clearance procedure Arrangement where, with Customs approval, an exporter may control exports from his or her own premises.

local currency Currency of the area where a business or branch is operating, as against the currency in which the business prepares its accounts.

local enterprise agency Body established by local authorities, local companies and other parties to promote the economic life of their community. Donations to an agency qualify for relief from corporation tax (CTA 2009 s82) or income tax (ITTOIA 2005 s82).

local housing allowance (LHA) Benefit available to private sector tenants in Scotland, introduced in 2008. In effect, it is a different way of calculating housing benefit. Claimants must be in private sector rented accommodation and receiving means-tested benefits.

The allowance was based on the 30th percentile of local rented accommodation for broad rental market areas (BRMAs). Restrictions have since been introduced. These figures are published. For example, the LHA for Aberdeen and Shire in 2020/21 ranges from £97.81 in 2020/21 for a 1-bedroom property to £230.14 for a 4-bedroom property. Rates can be found online at:
https://www.gov.scot/publications/local-housing-allowance-rates-2020-2021/.

local land charges (LLC) Various records about properties. From 11 July 2018, the Land Registry is creating a Local Land Charges Register which will progressively record details. It is starting with Warwick District Council. These can be accessed from the register instead of the local council.

local lockdown When a defined area of the UK is subject to coronavirus lockdown restrictions. The first was Leicester from 29 June 2020. Later in 2020, local lockdowns were replaced by a Tier system of restrictions.

locally administered assistance Social security provision administered by local authorities in England from April 2013, as a replacement for the Social Fund. The devolved administrations of Scotland and Wales have similar arrangements. Each local authority decides how best to administer welfare beyond the statutory provisions. This includes use of food banks and furniture re-use projects.

local welfare assistance Welfare provisions offered by local authorities, particularly from 2013. There are national schemes in Scotland and Wales. Each authority sets its own rules.

Locata Website that helps people find social housing in particular areas.

location of assets Inheritance tax rules that determine whether assets are in the UK. They are given in IHTA 1984 s275. A non-domiciled taxpayer is not liable to pay inheritance tax on assets outside the UK.

Lochgelly principle Principle that a member of a trade protection organisation may claim part of the subscription as tax-deductible expenditure. The name comes from the case *Lochgelly Iron & Coal Company Ltd v Crawford [1913] 6 TC 267.* It is discussed in HMRC Manual at BIM24805.

lockdown Any arrangement whereby people are subject to restrictions of movement. The term was particularly used in relation to coronavirus restrictions. There was a national lockdown in England from 23 March 2020 and subsequently, local lockdowns from 29 June 2020, and a tiered system was introduced on 15 October 2020. Similar provisions were made in other parts of the UK.

lockdown job support scheme Another name for the expanded job support scheme.

locked in Situation where a person is unable or disinclined to realise a capital gain. Examples include soon after a flotation when directors may agree not to sell shares, or when a person does not wish to sell an asset because of capital gains tax.

lockstep Provision that applies in Wales from 2019 and did apply in Scotland between 1998 and 2017. It allows the devolved governments to vary each rate of income tax by the same number of percentage points.

The provision has never been used. It has been repealed in Scotland but remains in force in Wales.

locum insurance Insurance taken out by a professional person, usually operating as a sole trader or in a small business, to pay for someone to do their work should they become unable to do so. From 1 October 1996, such insurance premiums qualify for tax relief as a business expense. The matter is discussed in HMRC Manual at BIM45570.

locum tenens Latin for "one holding a place". The term means someone standing in for a professional person, where it is often abbreviated to "locum". Locum insurance premiums are tax-deductible.

locus in quo Latin for "place in which". This expression usually means the place where a crime was committed.

locus standi Latin for "the place of standing". It means the right to be heard in court.

lodger Person who lives at premises owned by another person, such as a spare bedroom in a family home. The once common practice became much less common from 1974 when the Rent Act and other legislation gave lodgers security of tenure.

HMRC may serve a notice under TMA 1970 s14 requiring the owner of a dwelling to list all lodgers.

Income from lodgers is taxed as property income. There is a tax allowance known as rent-a-room which can be offset against income from lodgers.

log book Term sometimes used for the V5C vehicle registration document. This is in allusion to the fact that registration was by a book from 1921 to 1965, and that the books remained legal until 1983. Vehicles are registered by the Driver and Vehicle Licensing Authority (DVLA) in the name of the vehicle's keeper, who is not necessarily the vehicle's owner. The current multi-coloured V5C form was introduced on 15 August 2010 with tear-off sections to provide a simple system for registering sales and other disposals.

The term log book simply means a record of events. As such there are many other forms of log book, including for other vehicles.

Lomé Convention Treaty signed in Lomé in Togo in 1975, followed by subsequent treaties of 1979, 1984 and 1989. It provided a free trade agreement between the EU (and previous bodies) and African, Caribbean and Pacific countries. It ended in 1996 and is now replaced by other forms of agreement.

London Clearing House (LCH) Organisation founded in 1888 to clear sugar and coffee trades in London. In 2003, it merged with Clearnet SA to become Central Counterparty Clearing House.

London Gazette Official publication of the UK government, first produced in 1665.

London Interbank Offered Rate (LIBOR) Rate of interest at which banks lend money to each other. In 2012, it was found that LIBOR had been fraudulently manipulated, leading to tighter regulation. From 2021, it is intended that countries will replace LIBOR with their own risk-free interest rates. In the UK this is the Sterling Over Night Index Average (SONIA).

London Metal Exchange (LME) International market for trading non-ferrous metals, particularly aluminium, copper, lead, nickel, tin and zinc. Its origins can be traced back to 1571.

London Stock Exchange The main stock exchange of the UK. It also runs the Alternative Investment Market.

long bond Bond that will mature in 10 or more years' time.

long chargeable period Period of more than one year. There are specific provisions regarding how the annual investment allowance is used for assets acquired in such a period (CAA 2001 s51M).

long dated stocks Government stocks which mature in 15 or more years' time.

longevity swap Financial instrument used by defined benefit pension funds. In effect it insures the fund against the risk of staff living longer than the age used to calculate their pension.

long funding lease Lease that, from April 2006, either lasts for seven years or lasts for five years and meets some other conditions (CAA 2001 s70G). The main consequence is that any capital allowance is claimed by the lessee and not the lessor.

long lease For capital allowances generally, this is a lease of land that lasts for at least 50 years (CAA 2002 s360I(2)).

long life asset Broadly, plant and machinery with an expected life of more than 25 years and a cost of at least £100,000 (CAA 2001 s91). Such plant must be put in a special rate pool where it attracts the lower rate of writing down allowance.

long service award Tax-free award that may be made to an employee with at least 20 years' service (ITEPA 2003 s323). The limit is £50 for each year of service, unchanged from 2003.

long-term debt Accounting term for a debt due in more than one year's time.

long-term insurance The term is defined in Financial Services and Markets Act 2000 s22. In relation to realised profits and losses, there are special provisions in CA 2006 s843.

long-term resident Someone who has been, or is expected to be, resident in a care home for at least three months (TCGA 1992 s225E(5)). Such a person is entitled to final absence relief of 36 months in relation to main residence relief from capital gains tax, instead of the 9 months that would otherwise apply.

long ton Term used for the ton in the UK equal to 2,240 pounds as against the short ton in the USA equal to 2,000 pounds.

look-back Description of a tax provision that considers circumstances in previous tax years. The patent box is an example.

look back period In accounting, a period of three to five years before adopting International Accounting Standards in which the entity should consider whether the standards then adopted require change on adoption (IFRS 1, para BC17).

looked after child For child trust funds:

(a) in England and Wales has the meaning given in section 22(1) of the Children Act 1989, extended to include a child accommodated by a local authority under section 17 of that Act, and

(b) in Northern Ireland, means a child accommodated under Part 4 of the Children (Northern Ireland) Order 1995

(Child Trust Funds Regulations SI 2004 No 1450 reg 33A(6)).

Lord Chancellor Head of the judiciary. Until 2006, the office holder was also Speaker in the House of Lords, and a Cabinet minister. The former function has now been made a separate office, and the latter office combined with Minister of Justice. As such the holder of the latter office has moved from the House of Lords to the House of Commons. For tax tribunals, the Lord Chancellor has certain protected functions as set out in Tribunals, Courts and Enforcement Act 2007 s144.

Lords of the Treasury Term used since 17th century for the people who run HM Treasury and who are, in effect, signatories on the nation's bank account. The First Lord of the Treasury is the prime minister. The Second Lord is the Chancellor of the Exchequer. There are usually four or five more who are now generally government whips.

lords spiritual Bishops who sit in the House of Lords.

lords temporal Members of the House of Lords other than bishops.

lorry driver There are some special provisions relating to accommodation and subsistence for lorry drivers, including a subsistence allowance agreed between the Road Hauliers Association and HMRC. They are explained in HMRC Manual at BIM37670.

loss The opposite of a profit or gain where, for example, expenditure has exceeded income. When incurred by a trade, it may be eligible for loss relief. The loss must be calculated on the same basis as profit (ITTOIA 2005 s26; CTA 2009 s47).

loss buying Acquiring a business to utilise its losses. This is generally restricted by provisions of TCGA 1992 from s184A.

loss-making year Year in which a trade makes a loss (ITA 2007 s64 and s120(1)).

loss of profits Insurance policy when a business is prevented from continuing for an insurable risk, such as fire. Premiums on such policies are normally allowable as a tax-deductible expense, as explained in HMRC Manual ay BIM45510.

loss relief Offsetting a loss against taxable profits. From 1 April 2017, loss relief for corporation tax is restricted when the company's profits exceed £5 million (CTA 2010 s269ZL). The restriction is £5 million plus half the excess. There are five types of loss relief:

- carry forward: a loss may be carried forward indefinitely against profits of the same trade (CTA 2010 s45; ITA 2007 s83). From 1 April 2017, there is a limit of how much profit may be offset by brought forward losses. This form of relief is the default position unless another form of relief is specifically claimed
- sideways loss relief (CTA 2010 s37; ITA 2007 s64)). Profits are offset against other income in the same accounting period and, from 1 April 2017, for future periods
- carry back relief (CTA 2010 s37; ITA 2007 s64). Losses may be offset against profits of the previous 12 months, usually resulting in a tax refund

- group relief (CTA 2010 Part 5). A loss may be offset against the profits of another company in the group as defined. This is broadly where one company owns at least 75% of the other, or where both are 75% owned by a third company. There is a similar consortium relief
- terminal loss relief (CTA 2010 s45A; ITA 2007 s89). A loss in the last accounting period may be offset against profits of the three previous years.

For income tax, losses may be offset in the same way except for group relief. There is also a provision in ITA 2007 s72 that allows losses in the first four years to be offset against profits of the three previous years. From 6 April 2013, some income tax loss reliefs are restricted to the greater of £50,000 or 25% of income (ITA 2007 s24; FA 2013 s16 and Sch 3).

There are some specific provisions for losses that arise from creative industries. There are also specific provisions for capital losses.

loss to the estate Basis of valuing gifts for inheritance tax, rather than value to the donee (IHTA 1984 s3(1)).

lost document Where a stamped document is lost, the stamp duty implications are as set out in Stamp Duties Management Act 1891 s12A.

lottery Form of gambling where participants pay a sum in return for a number of similar identification, and the prizes are awarded by lot. In law, a lottery is either a simple lottery or complex lottery (Gambling Act 2005 s14). A lottery run by a charity may be exempt from income tax under ITA 2007 s530.

Lottery prizes are exempt from income tax, and from capital gains tax. If a group of people collectively buy lottery tickets they should have an agreement on how any prizes will be dividend, who acquires the tickets, and the suchlike. The VAT position on lotteries is explained in VAT Notice 701/29.

lottery duty Specific betting duty charged on a lottery (FA 1993 from s24).

louma One hundredth of a dram, currency of Armenia.

lowballing Putting in a very low quote to buy business.

low earnings limit Figure used to calculate state second pension until 5 April 2016. Someone eligible for this pension but with earnings below the threshold was deemed to have income at this threshold. Figures are given in section 3 of this dictionary.

low emission car Car with carbon dioxide emissions below (from April 2018) 50 grams per kilometre. Higher limits applied for periods between April 2002 and April 2014. Such a car qualifies for a 100% first year allowance. Details are given under Capital Allowances in section 3 of this dictionary.

Low Emission Zone Area, roughly corresponding to Greater London, where heavier polluting vehicles must pay a charge for driving in it. The scheme was introduced in February 2008 for vehicles over 12 tonnes, and has since been extended to other vehicles but not to ordinary cars. The charge is additional to the congestion charge. There is also a separate ultra-low emission zone for central London. Rates are given under Congestion Charge and Other Road User Charges in section 3 of this dictionary.

lower earnings limit The amount of earnings that count towards a class 1 national insurance record for the state pension and some other benefits. National insurance is not actually paid until earnings have reached the earnings threshold, which is a higher figure. The figures are given under National Insurance in section 3 of this dictionary.

lower-income charity Charity whose gross income does not exceed £25,000 a year (Charities Act 2011 s145). Such a charity has a reduced requirement for its accounts to be independently examined.

low-income household For periods from 1 April 2016, the Secretary of State must publish data on such households under Welfare Reform and Work Act 2016 s4. For this purpose, low-income households are split between those where equivalised net income is less than 60% of the median, and those where it less than 70%.

lower limit annual accounting VAT scheme which is an alternative to annual accounting for businesses with an annual turnover below £100,000. This allows the business to make three quarterly payments each equal to 20% of the previous year's VAT liability. If the liability for any quarter is less than £2,000, no payment need be made. The business makes one annual return within two months of the end of the year when any balance is paid.

lower-paid employment Employment where the wages plus benefits do not exceed £8,500 a year (ITEPA s217)). Before 6 April 2016, such an employee paid less income tax on the value of some benefits in kind. From 6 April 2016, that distinction is only made for domestic staff and ministers of religion.

lower rate Rate of income tax below the basic rate that applies to the first small slice of income. Such a rate applied between 1992/93 and 1998/99, and for 1978/79 and 1979/80.

lower paid employment as a minister of religion A minister of religion whose earnings are less than £8,500 a year (ITEPA 2003 s290D(1)).
From 6 April 2016, such ministers continue to be exempt from the tax charge for accommodation and other expenses, even though the P11D limit is otherwise abolished.

lower relevant maximum amount (LRMA) The lower threshold for corporation tax. Between 1972 and 2015, corporation tax was charged at two rates. A small profits rate (previously known as small companies' rate) applied up to the LRMA, and higher rates above. The LRMA was £300,000 from 1999 to 2015.

lower strength beer Beer with an alcoholic strength of between 1.2% and 2.8% (ALDA 1979 s1AA). From 1 October 2011, such beer attracts a lower rate of duty.

low income exemption Relief for income tax given by Republic of Ireland.

low value invoice Invoice where VAT requirements are less strict. The limit has been £250 since 2004.

low vision leaflet (LVL) Document obtainable by or for a person of poor sight from a hospital or clinic. It can be the first step towards being registered as blind and able to claim blind person's allowance against income tax.

low wines "Weak spirits obtained from the distillation of wash" (Customs notice 39).

loyalty penalty When companies charge existing customers more than new customers. On 18 June 2019, the Competition and Markets Authority said it would investigate this as a sharp commercial practice.

LPG Liquid petroleum gas as road fuel.

ltd Abbreviation for "limited" which must be part after the name of a limited company unless it is a public company or it is a non-commercial company that has permission not to use it (CA 2006 s59). A Welsh company may use "cyf" instead.

LTT Land transaction tax.

Lucozade tablets A VAT tribunal held that these were zero-rated as food and not standard-rated as confectionery. Although naturally sweet from the glucose used, no sweetening material had been added. *(Smith Kline Beecham plc. [1993] VAT 10222).*

Lucy bond Financial instrument where the return is based on something fanciful, such as the weather or sporting results. It takes its name from The Beatles' fanciful song *Lucy in the Sky With Diamonds.*

lump sum An amount provided as a single payment rather than as regular income. The term is widely used for a payment usually equal to 25% of a pension fund that a person may take when they crystallise their pension entitlement. Provisions are set out in ITEPA 2003 from s636A.

lump sum death benefit Lump sum benefit paid by a pension scheme on the death of a member (FA 2004 s168(1)). Such a benefit may be paid before the member has crystallised any benefits or, in limited circumstances, after such benefits have crystallised. In the latter case, the benefit is treated as a drawdown lump sum death benefit and is taxed.

lunar month Period of four weeks. The moon actually takes about 29½ days to revolve around the earth.

lunatic Person who has periods of lucidity and periods of illucidity, as against an idiot who has no periods of lucidity. Both terms are now seen as pejorative and have been removed from tax legislation without any change in the law.

There is still in force the Trial of Lunatics Act 1883 s2 which allows the special verdict of not guilty by insanity. The term comes from the old belief that lunacy was prompted by a full moon.

lunch break Period of about 45 minutes to an hour in the middle of the day to allow workers to have lunch. Since 1 October 1998, a worker must have at least one 20 minutes break every six hours under Working Time Regulations SI 1998 No 1833.

luncheon voucher Document provided to workers that could be exchanged for food. They were introduced in 1946 and increased in 1948 to 3 shillings or 15p per day. They remained at that figure until the tax relief was abolished in 2013. They became subject to national insurance in 1999. Tax relief remains for some voucher-based canteen facilities under ITEPA 2003 s317.

Lunn case Leading case on the relationship between HMRC and a tax agent when the former has serious concerns about the latter's work such that HMRC believes significant amounts of revenue may be lost.

The case relates to when HMRC may refuse to work with the agent, and notifies his customers of this. As a result of this case, guidance was produced by HMRC in conjunction with professional bodies. The full citation is *Denis Christopher Carter Lunn and others v HMRC [2011] EWHC 240.*

Lunn was prosecuted in September 2013 on six counts of cheating the public revenue. He was acquitted on two counts. The jury could not decide on the other four. At a retrial, he was found guilty of the four counts. Lunn's clients were given the chance to pay the tax with interest, and avoid penalties.

The relationship has now been clarified in legislation.

Luxembourg Small European state which is a member of the European Union. Its currency is the euro of 100 cents. The UK has a double taxation convention of 1967 amended by a protocol of 2009. The country is widely seen as a tax haven.

LuxLeaks Name given to a cache of documents leaked in 2014 showing secret tax deals negotiated in Luxembourg.

luxury goods Term used for VAT between 18 November 1974 and 1976. Items that fell within this description paid a higher rate of VAT of 25%, reduced to 12.5% from 12 April 1976, until subsumed into the standard rate of (then) 15%.

Maastricht Treaty European treaty signed in February 1992 which changed the name of the European Economic Community to the European Community, and paved the way for the euro (European Communities (Amendment) Act 1993 s1(2)). It has been amended by further treaties.

Macedonia East European state which became independent of Yugoslavia in 1993. It was first known as Former Yugoslav Republic of Macedonia to distinguish it from the ancient kingdom of Macedonia. From 2019, it is known as North Macedonia. Its currency is the denar of 100 deni. The UK has a double taxation agreement of 2006.

Macfarlane Trust Trust established to provide ex gratia help to people who have been infected with HIV through contaminated blood or blood products used in the NHS. These payments are now made by MFET Ltd. Such payments are disregarded when determining entitlement to means-tested social security benefits. They are also exempt from income tax.

machine games duty Tax that is payable on machine games that give prizes.

machinery Item of equipment that has a moving part, not necessarily mechanically powered. Such an item qualifies for capital allowance for plant and machinery.

machine tools Machine tools that remain in the UK may be zero-rated if used to manufacture goods for export. Details are given in VAT Notice 701/22.

macro-economics Study of economics on a large scale, such as for an entire country or for the whole world.

"The study of overall economic headlines e.g. inflation, trade, output and the level of employment" (HM Treasury glossary).

Madagascar Island state in Indian Ocean. Its currency is the ariary of five iraimbilanja. The UK has no double taxation treaty.

Madbid Company that sells auction credits which are then used to bid for items. In the case *Marcandi Ltd [2018] CJEU Case 5-44/16,* it was held that the sale of auction credits was a supply of services for VAT purposes, and not a sale of goods.

mad money Emergency stash to protect a person from dependency, such as a person planning to leave their spouse.

made-wine Term which is no longer used, but which has been used in different contexts for alcoholic liquor duty. It now means any alcoholic drink made by fermentation rather than distillation which has a strength of more than 5.5% and is not cider (ALDA 1979 s1(5); Customs leaflet 163).

Before 15 March 1988, made-wine meant any drink made from fermenting a fruit other than grapes, apples or pears.

Between 1 January 1997 and 26 April 2002, the term was used for any drink made from mixing spirits with non-alcoholic drinks (commonly known as mixers). Examples of these made-wines include alco-pops and ready mixed gin and tonic.

magazine Periodical, of which a different edition is produced at least once a year. It may be zero-rated under VATA 1994 Sch 8 Group 3. From 1 May 2020, electronic versions are also zero-rated. Details are given in VAT Notice 701/10. A magazine distributor who bought magazines from publishers and sold them to wholesalers was making a zero-rated supply of magazines for VAT purposes, and not a standard-rated supply of marketing and distribution services *(Oldhams Distribution Pergamon Holdings Ltd [1990] VTD 6295).*

Magnitsky sanction Sanction against a person rather than a state. It is named after Russian accountant Sergei Magnitsky who was put to death after exposing Russian fraud. The USA passed a law in 2012 punishing the individuals responsible. The EU and other countries have passed similar laws. The UK allows for it in Sanctions and Anti-Money Laundering Act 2018, and imposed its first Magnitsky sanctions in June 2020.

maggots Soft-bodied larvae of flies widely used as fish bait. For VAT, these cannot be zero-rated as food for edible animals, as they are used to catch fish rather than to feed them. *Fluff Ltd (t/a Mag-It). QB [2000] STC 674.*

magistrates' court Court presided over by magistrates (Interpretation Act 1978 Sch 1). It is the lowest level of the criminal courts. They deal with some tax offences.

Magna Carta Document that barons forced King John to sign in 1215. It was enacted as an Act of Parliament in 1297, parts of which remain law. Its principles include that only Parliament may levy tax, which remains law though now stated in later legislation.

magnum Champagne bottle with the capacity of two standard bottles.

maiden name Original surname of a married woman. There is no legal requirement for a woman to take her husband's surname on marriage, though the practice remains common.

mail pack Package comprising a letter and leaflets. In a VAT case, the tribunal held that the cost could be apportioned between the zero-rated leaflets and the standard-rated letter *(Charterhill Marketing Ltd [2004] VTD 18144).*

main compensating product Product which results from processing of goods imported duty-free under inward processing relief.

main duty In the context of a large company's senior accounting officer, "to take reasonable steps to ensure that the company established and maintains appropriate accounting arrangements" (Inspector's Manual at SAOG 24000). The main duty is explained further at SAOG 14000.

mainly trading subsidiary "Subsidiary which, apart from **incidental purposes,** exists wholly for the purpose of carrying on one or more qualifying trades..." (ITA 2007 s137(7) and 181(8)).

main market The stock exchange operated by London Stock Exchange for companies which comply with its strict admittance rules, as opposed to the Alternative Investment Market.

main objects rule In company law, the main purpose for which a company was formed, as set out in the memorandum of association. Other objects are regarded as subsidiary. If the main object no longer exists, the company may be wound up. Modern practice avoids this either by making all objects independent, or by registering the company as a general trading company.

main phase Period for which employment support allowance is paid after the assessment period, usually of 13 weeks. During the main phase, the basic allowance may be supplemented by either the support component or work-related activity component.

main primary percentage Rate of class 1 national insurance payable by an employee on earnings between the earnings threshold and upper earnings limit.

main purpose rule Rule for interpreting an exclusion clause in a contract. The clause must not be interpreted to defeat the main purpose of the contract. A leading case is *Glynn v Margetson [1893].*

main rate car Car that was first registered before 1 March 2001, that has low carbon dioxide emissions or is electrically propelled (CAA 2001 s104AA).

main residence A person's principal home which is qualifies for main residence relief from capital gains tax (TCGA 1992 s222). The Court of Appeal ruled that the residence must show some permanence, some degree of continuity or some expectation of continuity *(Goodwin v Curtis [1998] CA. STC 475).*

main secondary percentage Rate of class 1 national insurance payable by an employer on earnings between the earnings threshold and upper earnings limit.

mainstream contractor Under construction industry scheme, someone who carries on the business of construction operations and who must therefore register with HMRC under the scheme, regardless of turnover.

mainstream corporation tax Corporation tax that excluded advance corporation tax (which was abolished in 1999).

maintenance Payment to a former spouse or to support a child.

The general rule (from 1988) is that the payment is neither tax-deductible by the payer not taxable in the hands of the payee. Payments of maintenance are excluded from inheritance tax (IHTA 1984 s11).

A tax reduction equal to 10% of the payment to a limit may be allowed under ITA 2007 s453 if the taxpayer pays maintenance to a former spouse or civil partner and either of them was born before 6 April 1935. The maximum is £3,260 a year, so the maximum income tax relief is £326.

Before 6 April 2000, the payer could claim some income tax relief.

maintenance calculation Calculation made to determine the amount of maintenance payable for a child (ITA 2007 s454(8)).

maintenance funds for historic land and buildings Form of discretionary trust established for the maintenance of specified lands and buildings. Such funds are relieved from the various tax charges that would otherwise apply to such a fund.

major audit Audit which is either of a listed company or where "there is a major public interest" (CA 2006 s525(2)). A major public interest is determined by guidance from the Secretary of State.

major change in nature of trade Event that can stop loss relief being carried forward. Guidance is given in statement of practice SP10/91.

major interest For companies, "A has a major interest in B at any time, if at that time

(a) A and one other person (C), taken together, have **control** of B, and

(b) A and C each have interests, rights and powers representing at least 40% of the holdings, rights and powers as a result of which A and C are taken to have control of B"

(CTA 2009 s473).

The section continues to explain how a major interest can exist when there are subsidiaries.

major interest in land This means either a freehold interest or a lease on which there is at least 21 years to run. For VAT, "in relation to land, means the fee simple or a tenancy for a term certain exceeding 21 years, and in Scotland means the interest of the owner, or the lessee's interest under a lease for a period of not less than 20 years" (Value Added Tax 1994 s96(1)). Such a supply may be zero-rated for VAT under Group 5. For corporation tax relief for land remediation, this term is defined in CTA 2009 s1178A.

majority shareholder Shareholder who owns or controls at least 50% of the company's shares. It should be noted that this can include someone who holds less than 50% of the shares if control is exercised, such as by the use of A-shares.

major sporting event The Treasury may make regulations under FA 2014 s48 to exempt participants from liabilities to pay income tax and corporation tax. Previously, tax exemptions were given for specific events.

Making Tax Digital HMRC publication of December 2015, setting out plans to reform the administration of taxes, including greater use of online facilities. VAT guidance is given in VAT Notice 700/22.

mala fides Latin: bad faith.

Malawi African country. Its currency is the kwacha of 100 tambala. The UK has a double taxation agreement of 1955 amended by a protocol of 1978. A pension paid from this country may be exempt from income tax under ITEPA 2003 s643.

Malaysia Eastern country. Its currency is the Malaysian dollar or ringgit of 100 sen. The UK has a double taxation agreement of 2010 amended by a protocol of 2010.

Malaysian dollar Currency of Malaysia.

Malaysian ringgit Another name for the Malaysian dollar.

Mali African country. Its currency is the CFA franc of 100 centimes. The UK has no double taxation treaty. The country is subject to UK sanctions, as are designated persons of the country.

Mallalieu v Drummond Leading case from the House of Lords on allowability of personal expenditure. It concerned the plain skirts and blouses that a female barrister was obliged to wear in court. It held that the clothes had a dual purpose and so were not allowable. It was not relevant that she chose not to wear such ordinary clothing other than for court appearances. Its full citation is *Mallalieu v Drummond [1983] HL. 57 TC 330.*

Malta European country and member of the European Union. Its currency is the euro of 100 cents. The UK has a double taxation convention of 1994.

Maltese lira Currency of Malta.

malt extract Regulations regarding the grading and marking of such extract is still governed by SI 1936 No 309.

Mammon God of this world, as personified by a desire for wealth. The Bible teaches "you cannot serve God and Mammon" (Matthew 6:24; Luke 16:13).

managed currency Currency whose exchange rate is not determined solely by market forces but is influenced by actions from a government, central bank or similar authority.

managed fund A pooled investment fund which is actively managed by a fund manager. Often, investment is only possible through a linked life insurance policy issued by the insurance company which is managing the fund.

managed migration Term used by Department of Work and Pensions to refer to the migration of claimants to universal credit from other means-tested benefits. The process runs from 2013.

managed payment plan Scheme introduced in April 2011 allowing payment of tax to be made over several months instead of in a single payment. Some payments are made in advance of the due date and some in arrears. Provided the plan has been followed, no penalty is charged for late payments after the due date.

managed service company (MSC) A company where:

(a) its business consists wholly or mainly of providing (directly or indirectly) the services of an individual to other persons,

(b) payments are made (directly or indirectly) to the individual (or associate of the individual) of an amount equal to the greater part of all the consideration for the provision of the services,

(c) the way in which those payments are made would result in the individual (or associates) receiving payments of an amount (net of tax and national insurance) exceeding that which would be received (net of tax and national insurance) if every payment in respect of the services were employment income of the individual, and

(d) a person who carries on a business of promoting or facilitating the use of companies to provide the services of individuals ("an MSC provider") is involved with the company

(ITEPA 2003 s61B(1)).

PAYE provisions are given in PAYE regulations SI 2003 No 2682 from reg 97ZA. This term was introduced on a change in the law in 2007. This extends the scope of IR35 regulations to a company that provides the personal services of individuals to other companies on the basis that would otherwise be similar to employment. The allowable expenses for such a company are given in CTA 2009 s141.

management Collective term for those persons responsible for the day-to-day running of a business. Accounting standards distinguish between management and control. Both involve running a business or, to be more precise, power over assets. The distinction is that a person exercise management when this power is exercised for someone else's benefit, and control when exercised for his own benefit. Management developed during the 19th century when railway companies, and later banks, became too large to be run by the people who owned them. Business management is now a separate discipline.

management accounting Reporting accounting information within a business, for management use only.

management buy-in (MBI) Purchase of a company by outsiders who provide new management.

management buyout (MBO) Acquisition of a business by people who work there. Such an acquisition is often funded externally. As the new management will intimately know the business, this can be an attractive prospect for investors and lenders. For accounting and tax purposes, an MBO is simply a takeover of an existing business.

management charges Charges made for running a business, such as may be charged by a holding company to a subsidiary. These are tax-deductible provided they are reasonable and commercially justified. If the charges are paid to another jurisdiction, they could be investigated for transfer pricing, as explained in HMRC Manual at BIM38230.

management expenses The term has a specific meaning in relation to loss relief in CTA 2010 s103.

management fee In investment, charges made by the managers of a fund. In relation to disguised investment management fees, this term is specifically defined in ITA 2007 s809EZB as inserted by FA 2015 s21. Management fees have also been used for tax avoidance of profit-shifting.

management letter Letter often sent by accountants to a business before issuing an audit report, setting out suggestions as to how the accounting and internal control procedures could be improved.

management receiver Person appointed under a restraint order to receive property (Proceeds of Crime Act 2002 s48).

Managing Deliberate Defaulters Scheme introduced by HMRC in 2011. It applies to someone who has incurred a penalty for tax evasion. Their tax affairs are monitored more closely for a period of between two and five years. Further details are given in HMRC factsheet CC/FS14.

managing director Person who is the most senior manager in a business.

managing trustees Trustees who manage an organisation on a day-to-day basis, unlike holding trustees.

manat Currency of Turkmenistan.

mandamus Writ ordering a person to discharge a legal duty. An order cannot be made on the Crown (government) itself, but can be made against a minister. An example of this is *R v Secretary of State for Social Services, ex parte Grabaskey. The Times 15 December 1972.* A mandamus order can only direct that a duty be carried out; it cannot direct *how* that duty is to be discharged.

mandarin Colloquialism for a senior servant, particularly one who is pompous and officious. The term was originally a Portuguese term for Chinese officials.

mandate (1) Instructions to the bank on who may sign cheques.

(2) Authority claimed by a successful political party to implement its manifesto after winning an election.

mandatory bid Compulsory bid, particularly the requirement to mount a takeover bid when someone owns 30% or more of the shares of a listed company.

mandatory e-filing Requirement that certain tax returns must be filed electronically and not on paper. The power to require this is FA 2002 s135.

Man Friday Faithful, willing and versatile attendant. The term comes from a character of that name in *Robinson Crusoe.*

man hour Work done by one man (or woman) in one hour.

manifest List of passengers or cargo carried on an aeroplane or ship. The term can refer to an invoice for cargo.

manifesto Public declaration of the policies of a political party or other person seeking office.

Manninen claim Claims for tax relief on cross-border dividends paid within the EU. The name comes from the leading case C-319/02.

mansion tax Wealth tax proposed by Liberal Democrats in 2009 and Labour party in 2014. Neither was introduced.

manual tagging Insertion of iXBRL tags on corporation tax other than automatic tagging. Tags are entered from a list either from that supplied free by HMRC for simple companies, or from commercial software. The use of these tags is compulsory from 1 April 2011.

manufactured dividend Payment due under a contract to replace a dividend the recipient would otherwise have received. There have been tax provisions to deal with this since 1960. The current provisions were introduced from 29 June 1992. The main provision is that the manufactured dividend is taxed as if it were a real dividend. Income tax provisions are in ITA 2007 from s573; capital gains tax provisions from TCGA 1992 s263D.

manufactured interest Payment made which is the equivalent to interest on loan without legally being such. The corporation tax implications are set out in Corporation Tax Act 2009 from s539; the income tax implications in Income Tax Act 2007 from s578.

manufactured payments Payments that are the equivalents of dividends and other distributions, but without being within the definition. Income tax provisions are set out in ITA 2007 from s572 and from s918.

manufactured payments contract For the purposes of the **accrued income scheme,** this term is defined in ITA 2007 s647.

manufacturing accounts Financial accounts that reflect the manufacture of goods as opposed to selling them. The latter functions are reflected in trading accounts. While this practice was once common, it is now rare. Such matters as profit from manufacture are better determined by management accounts.

If separate manufacturing accounts are prepared, the accounts in effect treat the entity as two separate parts. This means that a policy is needed regarding the sales figure in the management accounts. One choice is to transfer the goods at cost, so all the profit is shown in the trading accounts. The other is to transfer them at another figure, such as market value. This has the effect of splitting the profit between the two sets of accounts.

Keeping separate accounts may also require an adjustment to reflect unrealised profit in the manufacturing accounts.

For tax purposes, there is still one entity. This means that any profit which is split between the two sets of accounts must be aggregated when determining taxable profit.

manuscript paper Paper that is ruled with five-lined staves for writing music. As blank paper, it is standard-rated as stationery. If sold as finished music, it may qualify for zero-rating under VATA 1994 Sch 8 Group 3 as explained in VAT notice 701/10.

maps For VAT, maps are zero-rated under VATA 1994 Sch 8 Group 3, provided that they are designed to present the natural or artificial features of countries, towns, seas or the heavens. They may be produced on any material, and may be a single sheet, in a book or folded. Framed maps and decorative maps are standard-rated. Further details are given in VAT notice 701/10.

Mareva injunction Order of a court that prevents assets being transferred abroad. It is now more commonly called a freezing order. The name comes from the case *Marevia Compania Naviera SA [1980]. CA. 1 All ER 213.*

margin In accounting, the difference between the purchase price and selling price.

marginal cost The cost of one more item. This differs from direct costing which includes overheads such as business rates and insurance. The landmark case *Pepper v Hart [1992] 65 TC 421* held that the cost of providing a benefit to an employee was the marginal cost and not the direct cost. The case concerned a private school where staff could send their own children if there were unfilled places. It was held that the cost of this benefit was the cost of an additional pupil, such as the food, laundry and similar expenses. It was not the much higher direct cost which had to include overheads. HMRC issued a press release on 21 January 1993 explaining its position following this case.

marginal items of pay Expenses and other elements of a remuneration package of which the payroll department had no knowledge at the time. HMRC guidance generally allows such items to be taxed and subject to national insurance in the period when discovered, provided this does not affect the employee's entitlement to benefit.

marginal rate of tax Rate of tax that would be paid for every extra pound earned or spent. For example, income tax on earnings between £100,000 and £125,000 are subject to a marginal rate of 60%. This is 40% income tax plus 20% from the loss of personal allowance. Marginal rates are widely used in tax planning. Until 2015, the term was widely used for the rate of corporation tax on adjusted profit between (from 1994) £300,000 and £1.5 million. The marginal rate was the main rate plus one quarter of the difference between the main rate and small profits rate. So if the main rate was 26% and the small profits rate 20%, the marginal rate was 27.5%.

marginal relief Relief that reduced the full rate of corporation tax for smaller profits before 2015.

marginal retention rate Amount of income a taxpayer keeps after paying tax on an extra £1 of income. For an employee liable to pay 20% income tax and 12% national insurance, the rate is 68%.

margin call Request to a purchaser of an option or futures contract to make a further payment because a fall in the value of the underlying security has reduced the value of the original margin deposited.

margin scheme Any scheme that is based on the profit margin rather than turnover. In particular, it refers to the VAT scheme for second-hand goods (VATA 1994 s50A).

marine pilots' benefit fund This means –

(a) a fund established under section 15(1)(i) of the Pilotage Act 1983, or

(b) any scheme replacing such fund. (FA 2004 s191(8)).

marine voyage For hydrocarbon oil duty, "means a voyage in which the ship is at all times –

(a) within the limits of a port, or

(b) outside the United Kingdom"

(Hydrocarbon Oil Duties (Marine Voyages Reliefs) Regulations SI 1996 No 2536 reg 2).

marital acquest Property acquired by a couple during their marriage. When the couple divorce, there is an assumption that the marital acquest will be divided equally unless there is good reason to the contrary. Assets brought by the parties to the marriage are usually viewed differently, though the court can order them to be shared also.

marital status Whether a person is married. Strictly there are only two statuses: married or unmarried. It is usual to consider five: single (never married), married, widowed, divorced or separated, or in a civil partnership. An unmarried couple have no marital status and cannot, for example, benefit from the spousal exemption for inheritance tax. This applies even if they live together and have children. An unmarried couple may, however, be treated as a single household for social security purposes.

marked gas oil (MGO) Gas oil on which hydrocarbon oil duty has not been paid. Customs notice 75 imposes conditions on its storage and use.

It is a heavy oil of which not more than 50% by volume distils at a temperature not exceeding 240 degrees C and of which more than 50% by volume distils at a temperature not exceeding 340 degrees C. Marked gas oil also contains the prescribed markers Quinizarin and Solvent Red 24 to allow for rebated off-road use. Customs Notice 75 gives more details.

market Any place, forum or similar where people buy and sell from each other. Profits from selling rights in a market are subject to income tax (ITTOIA 2005 s12) or corporation tax (CTA 2009 s39).

market capitalisation The value of a company as measured by the total stock market price of its issued and outstanding shares. This is calculated by multiplying the number of shares by the current market price of a share. It is also widely used as a definition of company size.

market condition "A condition upon which the exercise price, vesting or exercisability of an equity instrument depends that is related to the market price of the entity's equity instruments, such as attaining a specified share price or a specified amount of intrinsic value of a share option, or achieving a specified target that is based on the market price of the entity's equity instruments relative to an index of market prices of market prices of equity instruments of other entities" (FRS 102 glossary).

market gardening Production of crops or flowers conducted more as a hobby than a business. For the first five years, a loss from this activity may only be offset against other profits to the extent that the activity was run commercially (ITA 2007 ss67-68; CTA 2010 s48). If it is run commercially, it is taxed as a trade (ITTOIA 2005 s9; CTA 2009 s36).

marketing assets return figure Term used in relation to taxation of intellectual property in Corporation Tax 2010 s357BK as inserted by FA 2016 s64(3). It is also used in Corporation Tax 2010 s357CN.

marketing authority Body that is responsible for marketing a product or commodity. Corporation tax provisions are given in CTA 2009 from s153.

marketing board Statutory board entrusted with the sales of a particular commodity or food product. Subscriptions to such a body are generally tax-deductible as is discussed in HMRC Manual at BIM24850.

market overt An open market where a buyer obtained good title to goods even if they were stolen. The right originated in 13th century as a means of allowing markets to sell goods without fear that someone will claim them as their property. Goods had to be sold between sunrise and sunset. The thinking was that someone who had goods stolen was negligent if they did not check their local market. This ancient right was abolished from 3 January 1995 by Sale of Goods (Amendment) Act 1994.

marketplace transaction In relation to digital services tax, "means a transaction on the online marketplace between users" (FA 2020 s41(11)).

market research reports When these are bound, they may qualify for zero-rating for VAT as a book *(City Research Associates Ltd [1984] VTD 189)*.

market value Price that may be expected when an item is sold between a seller and unconnected buyer in full knowledge of relevant facts. Such a figure is often determined by looking at prices for comparative goods or services. There are more specific definitions for some tax purposes. For options, the market value rule may be required for determining the capital gains tax.

For pensions, the market value of an asset held for the purposes of a pension scheme is to be determined in accordance with section 272 of the TCGA1992 and section 278(2) to (4) FA 2004 (where dealing with a right or interest in respect of money lent directly or indirectly to certain parties). The same definitions are used in relation to employment income (ITEPA 2003 s421).

market value rule For capital gains tax, a rule used to calculate the gain on an option (TCGA1992 s144ZA).

mark to market Basis of stock valuation based on market value. A legal definition is given in FA 2002 s65(2). Corporation tax provisions are given in CTA 2009 from s185. The tax consequences of moving to this basis from the realisation basis are given in ITTOIA 2005 s236.

markka Currency of Finland, before it adopted the euro in 2002. Gold coins for 1,000 or 2,000 markkaa may be regarded as gold investment coins for VAT purposes (VAT notice 701/12A).

markkaa Plural of **markka,** former currency of Finland.

mark of the beast The number 666 assigned to a beast representing the Antichrist, as stated in Revelation 13:15-18 in The Bible. The European Court of Human Rights held that the Russian tax authorities had not breached a Christian taxpayer's freedom of religion under Article 9 of the European Convention on Human Rights when it assigned her a 12-digit taxpayer number containing three consecutive 6s. *(T Skugar v Russia [2009]. ECHR. Case 40010/04.)*

Marrakech Accords Agreements that followed on from the Kyoto Protocol on implementing Clean Development Projects to reduce emissions of greenhouse gases.

Marren v Ingles Court case from 1980. It established that there is a capital gains tax liability on ascertainable deferred consideration, such as when part of the consideration is based on future profits in an earn-out.

marriage Union of one man to one woman, or from 13 March 2014, between two people of the same or opposite sex. In practice, civil partnerships have the same treatment as marriage. There are many tax provisions that relate to marriage such as transferable marriage allowance, spousal exemption from inheritance tax, tax-free transfers under capital gains tax, being connected person, and some provisions relating to employment benefits. It is illegal for an employer to discriminate against an employee on the grounds that they are or they are not married (Equality Act 2010 s8).

Gifts in contemplation of marriage enjoy an exemption from inheritance tax of up to £5,000 (unchanged since 1968) under IHTA 1984 s22.

Transfers between spouses are exempt from inheritance tax (IHTA 1984 s18).

For deaths from 9 October 2007, a person's nil rate band for inheritance tax may be increased by a figure based on the transferable nil rate band for a previously deceased spouse or civil partner (IHTA 1984 s8A).

Transfers between spouses are regarded as being on a no gain/no loss basis for capital gains tax (TCGA 1992 s58(1)).

From April 2015, a party to a marriage may pass 10% of their personal allowance to the other party (ITA 2007 ss55A-55E).

Travel to see a spouse working overseas is generally not a taxable benefit in kind (ITEPA 2003 s371).

Marriage automatically revokes a will unless the will states that is made in contemplation of marriage to an identified person and is intended to continue after the marriage (Wills Act 1837 s18).

marriage of convenience Marriage that is legal but has been entered into to give one of the parties a right of residence. A spouse who is married in another EU state may claim UK residence under Immigration (European Economic Area) Regulations SI 2006 No 1003 reg 17, unless the marriage is one of convenience. The Court of Appeal ruled in the case *Rosa v Secretary of State of the Home*

Department [2016] that the onus of proof that the marriage was one of convenience lay with the Home Secretary.

marriage relief Relief from Customs duty when goods are brought into the UK as a consequence of marriage. It is explained in Customs Notice 3.

marriage settlement Settlement made between husband and wife before or after the marriage. The terms of such a settlement may be considered in any divorce proceedings.

marriage value Latent increase in value of property when the leasehold and freehold interests are combined. Such a combination is usually effected by creating an RTE company. The marriage value is shared equally by the landlord and RTE company. It should be noted that the marriage value may be much greater than the freeholder's existing interest. The longer the term of the lease, the lower is the marriage value. For a very long lease, the marriage value may be a nominal sum.

married couple's allowance Additional personal allowance that may be claimed by a married individual born before 6 April 1935 (ITA 2007 s45). Other more generous allowances had all been abolished by 2000.

married woman's election (MWE) The right of a married woman to elect to pay a lower rate of class 1 national insurance contribution in return for receiving a lower level of benefit entitlement. The election could be made under the National Insurance (Married Women) Regulations 1948, or SI 1948 No 220 in Northern Ireland. The rules were explained in leaflet NI1.

The current right to pay the reduced rate is given in SI 2001 No 1004 regs 127-131. This right was ended from 11 May 1977 for women who had married before 6 April 1977. Women who had already established this right are allowed to continue, subject to conditions. A woman loses this right if she divorces or remarries. She does not lose it on widowhood. A woman may give up the right at any time.

The election is indicated in the contribution letter. A woman who would otherwise be on letter A has reduced contributions deducted using letter B.

An election was made by completing a form, commonly CF9. The employer was given a tear-off portion from the 1974/75 stamp card then used to record national insurance. These tear-offs were replaced by certificates of election in 1979 and 1980. There were two types of election: an actual election for women who so elected from 6 April 1975, and a deemed election for women who made the election before 6 April 1975 but after 5 April 1948. An actual election ceases to have effect after two years in which the woman was not working. She then becomes liable to pay class 1 national insurance at the full rate. There is no such cessation for a deemed election.

The CF9 forms were held by the national insurance office for six years and then destroyed. Details were transferred to a machine card MF15. This was in turn replaced by form RF1. This means that HMRC can no longer produce the woman's signed declaration.

There have been many cases when women dispute making the election. The first tier tribunal has to decide whether the woman's memory or HMRC's records are at fault. It has usually found in favour of HMRC.

marshalling Finding, identifying and valuing property, particularly in an insolvency.

Marshall Islands Country of islands in Pacific Ocean. Its currency is the US dollar of 100 cents. The UK has no double taxation treaty.

marshmallow cone Cone similar to an ice cream cone but pre-filled with marshmallow and with a sugar topping. The VAT tribunal held that these were biscuits and not confectionery *(Kathy's Kones Ltd (No 2) [1996] VTD 14880).*

Martens clause Clause in an international treaty. It states that anything not specifically provided in the treaty is subject to international law and is therefore not necessarily permissible. It was first used in the Hague Conventions of 1899 and 1909 at the behest of the Russian delegate Friedrich von Martens (1845-1909).

Martinmas Christian festival on 11 November. Before 1991, it was one of the four Scottish quarter days.

Martland criteria Criteria for determining whether to accept a late tax appeal, as set out by the upper tier tribunal in the case *William Martland v HMRC [2018] UKUT 178.* The basic criteria are:

- whether the delay is very short
- why the delay occurred
- whether, considering all the facts of the case, there would be prejudice to either side.

masculine gender Tax law generally refers to all taxpayers as "he". This includes female taxpayers by virtue of Interpretation Act 1978 s6.

mash Mixture of crushed malt and hot water used for brewing.

mashing-tub In brewing, where ingredients are mashed to make beer.

mash-tun In brewing, a vessel with a perforated bottom in which grist is placed with hot water to form the wort.

master For Customs purposes, any person in charge or command of a ship (CEMA 1979 s1(1)).

MasterCard A credit card system formed in the USA. Its predecessor came to the UK as the Access Card in 1968. In 1979, the name MasterCard was generally adopted as the clearing system for cards provided by various issuers.

Master of the Rolls Judge who presides over the Civil Division of the Court of Appeal. The name comes from the original responsibility of looking after charters, patents and import judgments that were written on rolls of parchment.

Master Trust scheme In relation to pension schemes, this term is defined in FA 2004 s279(1B) as inserted by FA 2018 Sch 3.

match Simple stick to create fire. Before 1992, they were subject to matches and mechanical lighters duty.

matches and mechanical lighter duty Excise duty charged on matches from 1853 to 1860, and on matches and mechanical lighters from 1916 to 1992.

matching Accounting transaction that expenses are matched against revenues in the period they are incurred. It is part of the accruals concept. This principle is also used in foreign exchange following the Midland Marine case, are discussed in HMRC Manual at BIM39520.

matching concept In accounting, another term for the accruals concept. This means that income and expenditure should be matched for each period.

maté Form of tea from Paraguay. It is specifically zero-rated for VAT by VATA 1994 Sch 8 Group 1 Items Overriding the Exception 4.

material In accounting, description of an amount which is sufficiently large to affect the overall financial picture.

material increase For council tax, this means an increase in the value of a property that justifies revising its council tax band from the next sale (Local Government FA 1992 s24).

materiality Accounting principle that financial statements should not be cluttered with detail that does not affect the overall financial picture (FRS 102 para 2.6).

Other than the general rule that tax computations must follow accounting standards, the concept of materiality is not imported into tax law, though there are many de minimis limits which have a similar purpose. This matter is discussed in HMRC Manual at BIM31045. The concept of materiality is addressed in Professional Conduct in Relation to Taxation from para 3.8 to 3.10. This makes clear that the concept of materiality applies only to the accounts, and not to the tax computation based on those accounts.

The Institute of Chartered Accountants in England and Wales has issued guidance in various technical papers, including TECH 03/08 in June 2008 which consolidated and expanded TECH 32/96. In September 1997 the Tax Faculty of the Institute of Chartered Accountants in England and Wales and Inland Revenue published a joint minute Tax 18/97 which states "the Revenue said that the usefulness generally of accounts was limited by the concept of materiality". The matter is discussed in HMRC Manual at BIM31045.

For auditing, provisions are given in International Standard on Auditing ISA 320.

material reduction Reduction in value of a domestic property that can justify its immediate moving to a lower council tax band (Local Government FA 1992 s24).

maternity The period of pregnancy, childbirth and immediately after childbirth. Adoption is not regarded as pregnancy, though employees have some similar adoption rights. A female employee has these rights in respect of maternity:

- maternity leave;
- paid leave for ante-natal care;
- statutory maternity pay if the relevant conditions are met, and maternity absence in some cases if they are not;

- the right not be unfairly dismissed or to suffer any other employment detriment because of maternity
- (from April 2020) the right to statutory parental bereavement leave and statutory parental bereavement pay if her child dies under the age of 18 or if her baby is stillborn after 24 weeks of pregnancy.

A man has some equivalent paternity rights. Apart from statutory maternity pay, there is no minimum qualifying period for any of these rights.

From 1 December 1994, employers must make an assessment of how employment conditions affect a new or expectant mother. There are separate regulations about specific processes, chemicals and other activities from which a pregnant employee must be protected.

maternity allowance Social security benefit that may be made to a pregnant woman who is not eligible for statutory maternity pay, such as by being self-employed or having low earnings (SSCBA 1992 s35). It is not subject to income tax (ITEPA 2003 s677).

maternity leave When a female employee is absent from work because of maternity. The law prescribes three types of maternity leave:

- compulsory maternity leave, where a woman may not return to work for two weeks after the birth (four weeks if she works in a factory, under Public Health Act 1936 s205);
- ordinary maternity leave, a period of 39 weeks (from 1 April 2007) which usually coincides with the maternity pay period;
- additional maternity leave, a period which brings the total maternity leave to 52 weeks. The woman is not entitled to any pay or statutory maternity pay during additional maternity leave.

Some of this leave is now replaced by shared parental leave. Other than pay, a woman is entitled to all other benefits under the contract of employment. So she is entitled to keep a company car and use any social facilities. Her pension payments continue to accrue. An employer and employee are entitled to agree to provide more maternity leave or for additional maternity pay to be made on whatever terms they wish.

If a woman becomes pregnant again during maternity leave, a fresh set of maternity leave starts even though it overlaps with the existing leave. This appears to be the ruling in the European Court of Justice case *Busch v Klinikum Neudstadt GmbH und Co Betriebs-KG [2003]*.

maternity pay Money paid to a woman who is absent from work during pregnancy, childbirth and the period immediately after childbirth. There are two types of maternity pay:

- statutory maternity pay, which is paid by the employer under rules laid down by the government; and
- occupational maternity pay, which may be paid by the employer under its own rules.

maternity pay period (MPP) Period for which statutory maternity pay is payable. This is 39 weeks for births expected from 1 April 2007, and 26 weeks for births expected before this date. The maternity pay period is not necessarily the same as a woman's entitlement to maternity leave. In general, the employee may choose when to start the MPP. This may be no earlier than 11 weeks before the expected week of childbirth (EWC) and no later than the day after the actual birth. If a woman contracts a pregnancy-related illness in the four weeks before the EWC, the start of that illness automatically starts the MPP. The MPP ends on the earliest of:

- 39 weeks after it started;
- when she returns to work, other than as an allowed keeping in touch day;
- when her employment ends;
- when she is imprisoned or taken into legal custody;
- the Saturday after she dies.

Before 1996, a MPP also ended if a woman went outside Europe. This rule has been repealed, so a MPP may continue wherever she is in the world.

If a woman becomes entitled to a pay rise before the end of her MPP, her SMP must (from 6 April 2005) be recalculated in accordance her new pay. This is known as the Gillespie ruling. A woman remains an employee during her MPP. That means she is entitled to all rights of employment (such as any company car) other than payment of normal salary or wages.

Matrix Churchill Company that makes machines tools. In 1992, it was the victim in a scandal when Customs prosecuted them for illegal exports to Iraq when the company had been authorised by the Ministry of Defence. The government issued public immunity certificates to prevent evidence being heard, until the judge overturned them. This led to the Scott Report which criticised the government. Among its findings, was that Customs had trespassed when they used an ostensible VAT inspection to check on the use of components. The scandal led to changes in the law on government powers.

Matthew, Saint Patron saint of tax collectors and accountants.

Maundy money Set of four silver coins with nominal values of 1p, 2p, 3p and 4p (and similar amounts of old pence before 1971). Under a tradition dating from 1725, the monarch distributes a bag of such coins to some elderly citizens on Maundy Thursday, the day before Good Friday. Although the coins are legal tender, in practice they are sold to collectors.

Mauritania West African country. Its currency is the ouguiya of 5 khoums. The UK has no double taxation treaty.

Mauritius Country in Indian Ocean. Its currency is the Mauritius rupee of 100 cents. The UK has a double taxation convention of 1981 as amended in 2011, and protocols of 2003 and 2011.

maxi-ISA Term used between 6 April 1999 and 5 April 2008 in relation to individual savings accounts. A taxpayer could only hold one maxi-ISA but many mini-ISAs.

maximum amount For means-tested social security benefits, this is the amount a claimant will receive if he or she has no income or capital. The term is also given a specific meaning for capital gains tax in TCGA 1992 s261C.

maximum potential adjustment HMRC defined this as the amount that would arise if the individual risk to which it relates was conceded in full to HMRC (HMRC Notice of 20 December 2013). It is determined without reference to prospects of success.

Maxwell pension scandal In 1991 it was discovered that the late entrepreneur Robert Maxwell had raided £460 million of his companies' pension funds to prop up his businesses, many of which failed, meaning that many workers faced not receiving their pension. This scandal led to a tightening of laws on occupational pension schemes, particularly with regard to who may be trustees. These provisions were contained in Pensions Act 1995.

may This auxiliary verb connotes discretion. So if tax law says that HMRC "may" do something, that means it can exercise discretion in deciding whether to do so. In the case *Scofield [2011] TC 1068,* HMRC was criticised for saying that "may" means "must". This was in relation to FA 2004 s66(1) which says HMRC "may" cancel a gross payment registration under the Construction Industry Scheme.

McKenzie friend Someone who is not legally trained but who the court is prepared to allow to sit and help a party in a case. The name comes from the case *McKenzie v McKenzie [1971].*

McMafia law Nickname given to unexplained wealth orders. The name comes from a British crime drama.

mea culpa Latin: by my own fault. It is an acknowledgment by someone of their mistake.

meal deal Sales promotion where several items may be selected for one price to make a meal, usually a light snack. A typical example is a sandwich, crisps and soft drink. This may involve apportionment for VAT. (VAT Notice 700/7).

meal-ticket Voucher for a meal. By extension, the term has come to mean a provider for a person's essentials of life.

meal voucher Non-cash voucher which:

(a) can only be used to obtain meals,

(b) is not transferable, and

(c) is not of the kind in respect of which no liability arises under section 266(3)(e) (subsidised meals)" (ITEPA 2003 s89(3)).

The limit was 15p a day from 1948 to abolition of the tax-free allowance from 6 April 2013.

meals There is generally no tax charge when an employer provides subsidised meals to workers in a canteen (ITEPA 2003 s317). This includes free or subsidised tea and coffee (ibid s317(6)).

mean In mathematics, the commonest form of average. There are two means: arithmetic mean and geometric mean.

The more common arithmetic mean adds up *n* numbers and divides by *n*.

The geometric mean multiplies the numbers and takes the *nth* root. The geometric mean tends to produce lower numbers, as can be illustrated by a simple example of considering the numbers 2 and 8. The arithmetic mean is 5, namely half of 10. The geometric mean is 4, the square root of 16.

The geometric mean is used for the FT-SE 100 index and in calculating the consumer prices index (CPI). The retail prices index (RPI) uses the arithmetic mean which is the main reason why CPI tends to give higher figures than RPI.

It is sometimes thought that the geometric mean gives a better indication of mood as being less influenced by changes. If the 8 in the example above rose to 9, the arithmetic mean would increase from 5 to 5.5, whereas the geometric mean increases from 4.0 to 4.243.

mean hourly output rate For national minimum wage, quantity of units that a worker could reasonably produce in one hour. This applies when a worker is paid per unit of production, such as lampshades assembled or envelopes stuffed. Such a worker must be paid at a rate of at least 120% this rate.

means of exchange One of the two traditional functions of money. The other is as a store of value. The use of money avoids the need for coincidence of supply in a barter transaction. The prerequisite is that the parties to a transaction both accept the form of money.

means-testing Determination of a person's income and wealth to see if they qualify for a means-tested benefit. Similar elements appear in some tax provisions. For example, the transferable marriage allowance only applies if neither party to a marriage or civil partnership pays higher rate income tax.

measurement basis Means by which a figure is determined. In accounting, the two commonest bases are historical cost and fair value (FRS 102 section 2.34).

meat The term now usually means animal flesh eaten as food. The word originally simply meant food, which meaning remains in words such as "mincemeat" and expressions such as "meat and drink".

Meat is generally zero-rated when sold as food, and standard-rated when sold as catering, that is cooked and ready to eat. Drink made from meat is specifically zero-rated for VAT. Under Value Added Tax 1994 Sch 8 Group 1, food is generally zero-rated. Excepted Item 3 standard-rates beverages. Items Overriding The Exception 6 reverses the exception, thus reinstating the zero-rating. Further guidance is given in VAT Notice 701/14.

mechanical effect In relation to tax policy, this measures the mathematical effect of a change in policy without considering changes in behaviour. So if a tax rates doubles, it assumes that the revenue will double. It does not consider whether the policy will reduce demand, encourage avoidance or lead to a change in another tax.

medal Small portable object, often circular and metallic, that is worn to indicate an achievement. Where a medal has been awarded for valour or gallant conduct, the disposal of such a decoration by the person to whom it was awarded is not taxable as a capital gain (TCGA1992 s268). The sale by a subsequent owner is not covered by this exemption and so may be taxable.

median Average which is the middle item in a list ranked in order. The median is widely used as the average for earnings as the more usual arithmetic mean would be distorted by high earners.

Mediation Process whereby two disputants attempt to resolve their dispute with the help of a third person. HMRC may offer alternative dispute resolution (ADR) as a form of mediation. A first tier tribunal may offer it under Tribunals, Courts and Enforcement Act 2007 s24.

medical check-up "Means a physical examination of the employee by a health professional for (and only for) determining the employee's state of health" (ITEPA 2003 s320B(3)). Such a check-up is usually exempt from tax.

medical courier charity Charity whose main purpose is "to provide services for the transportation of items intended for use for medical purposes. including in particular –

(a) blood

(b) medicines and other medical supplies

(c) items relating to people who are undergoing medical treatment" (Value Added Tax 1994 s33D(10)).

Ibid s11 extends the scope to a body whose main purpose is to support, develop and promote the activities of a medical courier charity. From 1 April 2015, such a charity may claim VAT input tax.

medical courier vehicle A vehicle used primarily for transporting medical items, which is owned by a charity registered for such work and which has the word "Blood" marked on both sides. From 1 April 2020, such a vehicle is exempt from vehicle excise duty under VERA 1994 Sch 2 para 6A(1). From 1 April 2015, a charity engaged in such work may claim VAT input tax (VATA 1994 s33D(11)).

medical expenses Generally medical expenses are not tax-deductible as they are not incurred wholly and exclusively for the trade or employment. A leading case is *Norman v Golder [1944] 26 TC 293* relating to treatment on the hand of a shorthand typist. This is discussed in HMRC Manual at BIM27940.

This extends to surgery, even when this is commercially justified as in the case *Prince v Mapp [1969] 46 TC 169* where a guitarist had private surgery on his finger to return to playing sooner. This is discussed in HMRC Manual at BIM37945.

Medical expenses paid by an employer for an employee may not be taxed as a benefit in kind if it comprises recommended medical treatment (ITEPA 2003 s320C(7), or is provided to an overseas employee (ITEPA 2003 s325).

There is also no benefit in kind charge for employment medicals or for corrective glasses for computer screen users.

medical insurance for the elderly From 6 April 1990 to 2 July 1997, income tax relief was given on medical insurance premiums for those aged 60 or over. From 6 April 1994, relief was restricted to the basic rate of tax.

medical items In relation to vehicle excise duty exemption for medical courier vehicles from 1 April 2020, this term "means items intended for medical purposes, including in particular –

(a) blood;
(b) medicines and other medical supplies
(c) items relating to people who are undergoing medical treatment.
'Item' includes any substance".(Vehicle Excise and Registration Act 1994 Sch 2 para 6A(2) as inserted by FA 2020 s87(3)).

medicinal product For VAT, "a substance presented as a medicine, or an ingredient for a medicine, capable of being administered to people or animals for a medicinal purpose" (VAT leaflet 701/1). Such a product may be zero-rated for VAT.

medicinal purpose For VAT purposes, this "means:

- treating or preventing disease;
- diagnosing disease, or ascertaining the existence or degree of a physiological condition;
- contraception;
- inducing anaesthesia:
- otherwise preventing or interfering with the normal operation of a physiological function, whether permanently or temporarily, and whether by terminating, reducing or postponing, or increasing or accelerating the operation of that function, or in any other way" (VAT leaflet 701/1).

The existence of a medicinal purpose, can establish that a substance is a medicinal product and may therefore qualify for zero-rating for VAT.

medicine For VAT, the tax treatment depends on how the medicine is supplied. For Customs control, details are set out in Customs notice 4. There are no restrictions on medicines sold without prescription. For prescription drugs, imports are restricted to 15 days' supply unless a Home Office licence permits a larger quantity.

medium-sized company Company that is neither small company nor large. (CA 2006 s465). Some companies are excluded from the scope even though they meet these conditions. The criteria are given under Small and Medium-Sized Companies in section 3 of this dictionary.

medium term bond Generally, a government bond that matures in 5 to 15 years' time.

meeting In tax administration. a meeting between HMRC and a taxpayer, usually with the taxpayer's tax adviser. If HMRC requests a meeting with a taxpayer or adviser, the tax adviser should establish the nature of the meeting (Professional Conduct in Relation to Taxation para 11.4).

mega-centre Term used by HMRC for its premises in Edinburgh from 2020. It is a seven-storey building housing 2,600 HMRC staff.

meltith Scottish term for the yield from one cow at one milking.

member Person who belongs to an organisation. In company law, a person who holds shares in a company limited by shares or who undertakes to provide a guarantee in a company limited by guarantee (CA 2006 s3). Under the company has been formed, the (future) member is called a subscriber (CA 2006 s10). A company must keep a register of its members (CA 2006 ss112-128). A company may have only one member (CA 2006 s123). For pensions, this means someone who is covered by an occupational pension scheme (FA 2004 s151). Typically, this includes current employees, former employees who have yet to retire, and former employees who have retired.

Under EU law, the term is used to mean a member state (European Communities Act 1972 Sch 1 Part II, now repealed).

member-nominated trustee Trustee of an occupational pension scheme nominated by its members (Pensions Act 2004 s241). At least one third of the trustees must be member-nominated.

Member of Parliament Person elected to the House of Commons. They have some special tax exemptions set out in ITEPA 2003 ss291-295. Some of these exemptions also apply to elected members of devolved bodies.

Member of the Legislative Assembly (MLA) Member of the devolved assembly in Northern Ireland.

members' club A club run by and for its members is subject to corporation tax on its profits, even if the club is not constituted as a company. This does not apply to a community amateur sports club, which is treated as a charity.

In practice, many clubs have not taxable profits. Transactions which involve only members and the club are not taxable. So subscriptions and bar takings, for example, are not included. Profits are therefore largely restricted to such items as bank interest and transactions with non-members, such as hall hire. Strictly, these are taxable however small. By concession, HMRC does not require a return or payment if the corporation tax is not expected to exceed £100 a year (HMRC Manual at COM23110).

A club that becomes dormant is not expected to submit returns, though dormancy is reviewed every five years.

members' voluntary winding-up Winding up of a solvent company by its members.

memorandum account Financial accounting records that are outside the double entry bookkeeping system. Examples include the sales ledger and purchase ledger.

memorandum of association Document that sets out basic details of a company (CA 2006 s8(1)). Modern memoranda contains just a list of subscribing founders. Older and more detailed memoranda contain more provisions which remain binding.

For VAT, a bound copy of the memorandum of association and articles of association was not separately zero-rated as a book. It was part of a supply of company formation *(JP Company Registrations Ltd [1986] VTD 2249).*

memorandum of understanding (MOU) Agreement between parties defining their roles in relation to each other. An MOU is not legally enforceable.

memorandum of wishes Another name for a letter of wishes. This is issued by a member of a pension scheme saying who they wish to receive any benefit after their death. It is not binding on the trustees but is usually followed in practice.

memorandum rule For stamp duty, the rule that a memorandum evidencing an oral contract may need to be stamped as if it were the original document. This was established in the case *Associated British Engineering Ltd v IRC [1941] 1 KB 15.*

memorial Statue, plaque or other structure or device to remind people of a person, people or event. The reasonable cost of a memorial is allowed as reasonable funeral expenses which reduces an estate for inheritance tax purposes (IHTA s172).

A memorial is standard-rated for VAT. It does not come within the scope of exemption for burial. Guidance is given in VAT Notice 701/32.

There is a specific provision allowing a crematorium to claim the cost of providing a memorial, provided receipts are treated as taxable profits (ITTOIA 2005 s172ZC).

memorial book A memorial book bought by a church to record the deaths of parishioners was not zero-rated for VAT as a book because its pages were blank when supplied *(Ormesby St Michael Parochial Church Council [2001] VTD 17375).*

memory Part of the computer where data are stored. A computer usually has two memories: the random access memory (RAM) that handles data being used, and secondary storage such as on a hard disk and on external devices such as compact discs and memory sticks. Computer memory is measured in bytes:

- kilobyte = 1000 bytes
- megabyte = 1000 kilobytes
- gigabyte = 1000 megabytes
- terabyte = 1000 gigabytes
- petabyte = 1000 terabytes.

mental capacity Ability to make decisions for oneself. This is governed by Mental Capacity Act 2005. This assumes everyone has mental capacity unless the contrary is shown (s1(1)). A contract is binding to the extent that the person understands its nature. For other cases, a trustee is usually appointed. This is often a family member or close friend. Otherwise the Office of the Public Guardian will appoint a trustee. This may require an application to the Court of Protection. The trustee may sign a tax return and deal with the patient's tax affairs as if they were the patient. A person is still liable to pay their tax and can be subject to enforcement action. HMRC has a policy of sympathetic treatment set out in HMRC Manual at DMBM585185. A trust for a mentally incapacitated person is subject to some exemptions from inheritance tax. People who have severe mental impairment are not counted for the purposes of council tax.

mens rea Latin for a guilty mind. It is a condition for most criminal offences, namely that the person intended to commit the offence.

mental capacity Ability to make decisions for oneself. Since 2007 this is governed by the Mental Capacity Act 2005. It assumes that every adult has full mental capacity until the contrary is shown. Agreements by a person of limited capacity are valid to the extent that the person is capable of understanding it. Tax returns may need to be submitted by an authorised trustee, either appointed by the person or appointed by the Court of Protection.

mental disorder Any disorder or disability of the mind (Mental Health Act 2007 s1(2)). Dependence on drugs or alcohol is not considered a disorder of the mind (Mental Health Act 1983 s1(3).

mental impairment Term used in Mental Health Act 1983. This term is dropped under Mental Health Act 2007 s1(3)(a).

Although a person has sufficient mental impairment under the Act, that person does not necessarily come within the scope of Disability Discrimination Act 2005 *(McDougall v Richmond Adult Community College [2007]*).

The term is defined differently under Disability Discrimination Act 1995 s68 and Sch 1 para 1(1) as "an impairment resulting from or consisting of a mental illness only if the illness is a clinically well-recognised illness".

mental incapacity Lack of mental capacity as shown by an inability of a person to manage their own affairs because of some mental illness or injury or similar. A taxpayer who lacks mental or physical capacity may appoint someone to administer his or her tax affairs. Some forms of mental illness can mean that a person is incapable of appointing someone. This situation was considered in the case *The appellant [2016] TC 5564.*

mentally disabled person In relation to capital gains tax on settled property, "means a person who by reason of mental disorder within the Mental Health Act 1983 is incapable of administering his property or managing his affairs" (TCGA1992 Sch 1 pars 1(6)).

menu List of items offered at a restaurant. By extension, it applies to any list from which a user may make a selection. The term is used in computing for a list of functions that can be accessed in a program.

mercantile Pertaining to merchants or trade.

merchandise in baggage Goods commercially imported in a person's luggage. This is legal but may need declaring as explained in Customs notice 6. From 1 January 2021, commercial goods brought into or out of the UK to or from the EU in baggage must be declared if the value exceeds €1,500, or €1,000 in Northern Ireland. This can be done online.

merchant bank Bank which deals with companies rather than individuals. They particularly deal with funding new issues of shares.

merger ***Definition***

Combination of two or more businesses into one. For public companies there are specific provisions in CA 2006 from s904. There are also specific accounting provisions and a Stock Exchange code.

Law

A merger can be effected in different ways. A merger by absorption is when one undertaking is taken into a public company (CA 2006 s904(1)(a)). Alternatively, a new company may be formed into which the existing companies are merged (CA 2006 s904(1)(b)).

Provisions for merger relief relax the rules that would otherwise apply to protect the share premium account (CA 2006 from s612). A merger is subject to EU Merger Directive 90/434/EEC, now given effect in UK law as FA 2007 s110

Accounting standard

"An entity combination that results in the creation of a new reporting entity formed from the combining parties, in which the controlling parties of the combined entities come together in a partnership for the mutual sharing of risks and benefits of the newly formed entity and in which no party to the combination in substance obtains control over any other, or is otherwise seen to be dominant.

"All of the following criteria must be met for an entity combination to meet the definition of a merger:

(a) no party to the combination is portrayed as either acquired or acquiree, either by its own board or management or by that of another party to the combination;
(b) there is no significant change to the classes of beneficiaries of the combining entities or the purpose of the benefits provided as a result of the combination; and
(c) all parties to the combination, as represented by the members of the board, participate in establishing the management structure of the combined entity and in selecting the management personnel, and such decisions are made on the basis of a consensus between the parties to the combination rather than purely by exercise of voting rights" (FRS 102 glossary).

Tax

Capital gains provisions are given in TCGA 1992 ss140E-140L. Generally, there is an exemption from stamp duty for transfers of companies, and from stamp duty land tax on transfers of properties, that arise from a merger. Provisions in relation to venture capital trusts are given in ITA 2007 s323(1).

Mervardeskatt (MOMS) Swedish: value added tax.

mesaj Rare form of bond whose terms have been arranged to make it appear exciting and capable of significant recovery from desperate situations.

Mesher order Court order that a divorced spouse holding an interest in the matrimonial home should hold it on trust for a limited period, such as when the youngest child reaches 18. It is named after a 1978 case. The home remains entitled to main residence relief from capital gains tax, but creates a discretionary trust that can trigger inheritance tax liabilities.

mesne profits Money that a landlord may claim from a tenant who remains in occupation after the tenancy has ended.

mess allowance Sum that may be paid to a member of the armed forces. It may be exempt from income tax under ITEPA 2003 s297.

messuage House with associated garden, outbuildings and orchard.

Methuselah Champagne bottle with a capacity of eight standard bottles.

methylated spirits Alcohol-based liquid that is made undrinkable. It is therefore not subject to alcoholic liquor duty (ALDA 1979 s75). It is now classified as denatured alcohol.

metre Unit of length, originally defined as one ten millionth of the distance between pole and equator. It is widely used to determine lengths, areas, capacities and densities in tax law. A metre is about 3.28 feet. The legal definition of a metre changed on 13 June 2020 by SI 2020 No 584 to a reference to a caesium atom. This change has no practical relevance.

metric carat Unit of weight equal to one fifth of a gram.

metric hundredweight 50 kilograms. This is a little under the imperial hundredweight which equates to 50.804 kilograms.

metric system System of units or length, mass etc that use the base ten, as against old imperial system that used historic measures of other multiples. The exception is time, which uses traditional measures of 60 seconds to a minute, 24 hours to a day etc.

The main metric units are the metre for length, litre for capacity and gram for weight. Other units include the ampere for electric current, Kelvin for temperature, candela for luminosity, radian for plane angle and steradian for solid angles.

Under Measurement Regulations SI 1995 No 1804, almost all measures must be expressed in metric units with some exceptions for pints and miles.

It was intended to make it illegal to quote imperial units, even for comparison purposes, from 1 January 2010, but that law was repealed in 2007.

Mexico South American state. Its currency is the peso of 100 centavos. The UK has a double taxation convention of 1994 and a protocol of 2011.

mezzanine floor Floor between two storeys of a building. Free-standing mezzanine floors have been held to be plant and machinery.

mezzanine finance Finance provided to a company after it has started up.

mezzanine level Stage of a company's development before it goes public.

MFET Ltd Company formed by the government to make payments to individuals who contracted AIDS from contaminated blood. Payments are tax-free (SI 2010 No 673), and are disregarded when determining means-tested social security benefits.

Michaelmas English quarter day of 29 September.

micro-business Business that generally meets at least two of these three conditions:

- turnover below £632,000
- balance sheet total below £316,000
- no more than 10 employees.

(Small Business, Enterprise and Employment Act 2015 s33(3)).

Such a business may submit simpler accounts.

microfinance Financial provision of small amounts, usually too small to be economically worthwhile for the main providers of financial services. The two most common forms of microfinance are:

- relationship-based banking such as a credit union or hawala where finance is arranged by people who know and trust each other
- group-based arrangements, where entrepreneurs come together to share overheads and facilities.

microgeneration Facility for homes to produce electricity from renewable sources like solar panels (Energy Act 2004 s82; Climate Change and Sustainable Energy Act 2006 s26(1)). A gain on the disposal of microgeneration is not a disposal triggering a tax liability (TCGA s263AZA).

microlettering Very small letters that look like dots to the naked eye. This is used as a security feature on modern Bank of England notes. Using a strong lens, the dots under the Queen's portrait appear as letters and numbers indicating the note's value. Dots on the pound coin are also microlettering.

Micronesia Nation of federated states in Pacific Ocean. They became independent in 1986. The currency is the US dollar of 100 cents. The UK has no double taxation treaty.

Micropal star ratings Rating system for unit trusts. Micropal continually monitor all UK unit trusts, measuring the balance between each fund's performance over three years against the up or down movements in its unit price (i.e. the volatility). They then award stars on a scale from 0 to 5, with the highest number going to those funds with the lowest volatility – and therefore risk – in relation to their overall performance. Five stars is the top award.

Midas touch The apparent ability of someone to succeed financially in any undertaking. Midas was a king of Phyrgia who supposedly turned everything he touched to gold.

middle date Fourth day of a week in which an accounting period ends. An accounting period need not end on a defined date (ITTOIA 2005 s211). It may, for example, end on the last Friday of March. This means that the end of the accounting period could be on any of the last seven days of March, between 25 and 31 March. For tax purposes, it is treated as always ending on the fourth day, which is 28 March.

Middle East Generally reckoned as the Arabic-speaking countries around the eastern end of the Mediterranean, plus Greece, Turkey, Cyprus, Iran and much of north Africa.

Midland Marine Leading court case on the matching of foreign exchange assets and liabilities. Its full citation is *Pattison v Marine Midland Ltd [1983] 57TC219*. It is discussed in HMRC Manual at BIM39520-39521.

Midsummer Day English quarter day of 24 June.

MiFID European Parliament and Council Directive on markets in financial instruments, as given effect in UK by SI 2004 No 39.

migrant settlement Trust that ceases to be UK resident. The tax implications are given in TCGA 1992 s89.

migrating trustee Trustee who ceases to be UK-resident. The capital gains tax implications are given in TCGA1992 s82.

milch-cow Cow yielding milk. By extension, the term means to any source of ready financial gain.

mile Unit of distance, still widely used. It is equal to 1,760 yards which is about 1,609.3 metres.

mileage allowance Payment that may be made tax-free and national insurance-free when an employee uses his or her own vehicle for business, such as visiting a customer or delivering goods (ITEPA 2003 s251). The limit is 45p a mile for a car, 24p for a motorcycle and 5p for a bicycle. The car allowance may be increased by 5p if carrying a passenger. The car allowance reduces to 25p after 10,000 business miles for income tax purposes but not for national insurance.

Military Cross Award for bravery. Payments of pension or annuity in respect of the award are free of income tax (ITEPA 2003 s638).

Military End Use Council Regulations Name for SI 2003 No 150. This requires authorisation by HMRC for Customs procedures. These procedures changed from 1 May 2016 as explained in Customs Information Notice 44 of 2 November 2015.

Military Medal Award for bravery. Payments of a pension or annuity in respect of this award are not subject to income tax (ITEPA 2003 s638).

milk This is zero-rated for VAT (VATA 1994 Sch 8 Group 1 Excepted Item 3 Items Overriding the Exception 6). Further guidance is given in VAT Notice 701/14. The addition of milk to a soft drink is not regarded as adding sugar to a drink for the purposes of soft drinks industry levy (FA 2017 s29(4)).

milk quota Right to sell a fixed amount of milk each year. It is an asset in its own right and, from 1994, may be sold separately from the land (Dairy Produce Quota Regulations 1994). For VAT, the sale of a quota with the land is regarded as part of the exempt supply of land. The sale of the quota alone is a standard-rated supply. For capital gains tax, it is possible to claim rollover relief. The tax position is given in TCGA 1992 s248D.

milkshake powder Chocolate flavoured milkshake powder is zero-rated for VAT as a form of cocoa. Strawberry and banana flavours are standard-rated. *Nestlé Ltd [2018] UKUT.*

milk substitute drink "Means a soft drink which –

(a) contains at least the specified quantities of calcium, and

(b) meets such other conditions as may be specified"

(FA 2017 s30(3)).

Such a drink is exempt from soft drinks industry levy.

millennium Period of 1000 years. The term popularly referred to the year 2000, though, strictly, the millennium did not start until 2001.

milling In brewing, a process where the malted barley is broken open to utilise the starchy inner parts of the malt corms to produce grist.

mine Profits from a mine are taxed as a trade (ITTOIA 2005 s12; CTA 2009 s39).

miner Person who extracts minerals from under the ground. A coal miner or former miner is entitled to free coal or an allowance in lieu (ITEPA 2003 s306).

mineral asset Mineral deposits, land including such deposits, or any interest or right over such land (CAA 2001 s97). Minerals are said to be won (picked up from the ground), quarried (removed from digging a hole in the ground) or mined (extracted from tunnels under the ground).

mineral deposits For the purposes of capital allowances, this includes all natural deposits capable of being lifted from the earth, and includes geothermal energy (CAA 2001 s394(3) and 452(3)). The tax implications for exploration and access are given in CTA 2009 s137 and ITTOIA 2005 s161.

Mineral Oil Reliefs Centre (MORC) Office of HMRC that allows rebated oil to be used in vehicles on payment of the duty.

mineral resource "Means a solid, liquid or gaseous mineral resource" (Deep Sea Mining Act 2014 Sch para 2(3)).

mineral royalties Payment to someone for extracting or winning minerals. Its provisions for income tax are given in ICTA 1988 s122(5). Its provisions for corporation tax are given in CTA 2009 s135. Corporation tax provisions for relief in respect of such royalties is given in CTA 2009 s258. Relief for expenses is given in s272.

mineral water For VAT, this is standard-rated. It does not benefit from the zero-rating for water.

minibus For licensing, a vehicle with between 9 and 16 passenger seats. For the purposes of works transport, it is a vehicle with between 9 and 11 passenger seats. The provision of such transport is not a taxable benefit in kind (ITEPA 2003 s242(3)).

mini-ISA Term used between 6 April 1999 and 5 April 2008 to distinguish individual savings accounts between maxi-ISAs and mini-ISAs. An investor was allowed to invest in only one maxi-ISA but could invest in more than one mini-ISA which had a separate cash limit.

minimum consideration rule Rule where an arm's length price is substituted for the actual consideration in a pre-completion transaction for stamp duty land tax (FA 2013 Sch 39 para 12-14).

minimum funding requirement (MFR) Rule introduced by Pensions Act 1995, effective from 1997, which broadly requires pension funds to have sufficient assets to meet their liabilities.

minimum guarantee The lowest amount of total income received by a person receiving a tax credit.

minimum income floor (MIF) For universal credit, the assumption that a self-employed claimant is receiving weekly income of 35 times the national minimum wage, regardless of what the claimant may actually be receiving. This applies from the second year of claiming. Some of the provisions were suspended during the coronavirus lockdown.

minimum income guarantee (MIG) Benefit provided by the government to top up low pensions. It was replaced by pension credits in 2003.

minimum lease payment For capital allowances, this is defined in CAA 2001 s70YE(1)).

minimum share capital The smallest legal amount of share capital that a limited company may have. There is no lower limit for a private company. For a public company, the lower limit is £50,000 or the equivalent in euros (CA 2006 s763(1)). This amount is known as the authorised minimum.

minimum value This term is used in relation to civil recovery of personal property under Proceeds of Crime Act 2002 s303Y as inserted by Criminal Finances Act 2017 s15. The minimum value is £1,000.

Mini One Stop Shop (MOSS) VAT system available from 1 January 2015. It allows a business that makes supplies of telecommunication, broadcasting or e-services to register in one EU state and make supplies in other member states at their rate of VAT.

miniskirt Short skirt that stops above the knee. It became fashionable in the 1960s and has been fashionable since. From 1 January 1966, existing purchase tax law had to be changed as skirts shorter than 24 inches were considered to be tax-exempt children's clothing. This led to a change in the law where skirts are defined according to waist size and how they are held out for sale. These provisions were continued when VAT replaced purchase tax in 1973. The miniskirt is also a fanciful economic measure known as the hemline theory.

minister of religion Vocation that is taxed as income under ITTOIA 2005 s159. For tax, ministers are regarded as employees, regardless of how they may regarded for other purposes. Ministers may be exempt from a benefit in kind for their accommodation (ITEPA 2003 s290) and some other expenses (ITEPA 2003 s351).

mini umbrella company Employment intermediary that is not an employment agency. HMRC said in Employers Bulletin 87 of December 2020 that such companies are widely used for fraud. The fraud involves splitting up a workforce into many small limited companies set up solely to exploit incentives for small businesses, such as the employment allowance and VAT flat rate scheme. The workers provided may be unaware of the arrangement. HMRC warns both employers and employees of the dangers of using such a company. Employers are asked to be careful about who supplies them with staff.

minor (1) Person under the age of 18. There are some special tax provisions for minors, such as trusts for bereaved minors and signing tax returns.

(2) Of small amount. Provisions for minor benefits for employees are given in PAYE Regs 2003 reg 186(3)(a), It should be noted that tax law makes a distinction between a minor benefit and a trivial benefit.

minor benefits Benefit that the Treasury may exempt from being a taxable benefit in kind (ITEPA 2003 s210). Orders have been issued exempting some travel and subsistence, pensions advice, recreational facilities and other benefits.

MIRAS Mortgage interest relief at source, as operated between 1983 and 2000.

minority participator For inheritance tax, "is a participator of the transferor company who is not, and is not a person connected with, a participator of the principal company of the group or of any of the principal company's participators" (Inheritance Tax Act 1984 s97(2)(b)).

mint Produce coins. The Mint or Royal Mint is where British coins are produced. From 1968, it is based in Llantrisant in Wales.

minuend In arithmetic, the number from which another is subtracted.

MIRAS Mortgage Interest Relief at Source. Although this is no longer available, tax relief may still be claimed for some old years under ICTA 1988 s369. The scheme operated from 1983 to 2000.

mirror legislation When text in one Act is reproduced in the same or similar terms in another Act. There are many examples where text in ITA 2007 is mirrored in CTA 2009 or CTA 2010.

mischief rule A method for interpreting an Act of Parliament. It asks for what purpose the Act was passed. A leading case is *Hayden's case [1543].* The rule is now usually only followed when words are ambiguous. In the tax case *Pepper v Hart [1992],* the House of Lords decided that they could look at parliamentary proceedings to see the purpose of a provision. In the case *Madeley v HMRC [2006] SpC 547,* the Special Commissioners made reference to an HMRC press release.

misdeclaration penalty (MP) VAT penalty that dealt with large misdeclarations. It was imposed under VATA 1994 s63 and explained in VAT Notice 700/42. For mistakes from 1 April 2009, it is replaced by an inaccuracy penalty.

misdirection Wrong advice given by someone who should know the correct answer. In tax law, the term usually applies when an officer of HMRC gives wrong advice to a taxpayer.

VAT notice 700 states "if [an HMRC] officer, with the full facts before him or her, has given a clear and unequivocal ruling on VAT in writing or, knowing the full facts, has misled a taxable person to that person's detriment, any assessment of VAT due will be based on the correct ruling from the date the error was brought to the taxable person's attention".

missing trader fraud VAT fraud that involves importing goods into the UK free of tax. They are then sold with VAT at the standard rate. The importer than absconds with the VAT collected.

misleading statement Statement which is expressed to make a person believe that it says something which is untrue. It is a criminal offence for a director to make a false statement in the directors' report, directors' remuneration report or summary financial statement (CA 2006 s463(1)).

mismatch condition Term used in relation to diverted profits tax, and which is defined in FA 2015 s86(2).

Missing in Action (MIA) Scheme of relief from estate duty suffered by those killed in the war. Details are given in the entry for **killed in action.** These provisions can still be relevant if claiming **transferable nil rate band** for inheritance tax where the first death was before 12 March 1952. This relief is quite separate from the inheritance tax relief for those killed on **active service.**

missing person A person:

- who is absent from their usual place of residence,
- who is absent from their usual day-to-day activities, and

- whose whereabouts are either not known at all or are known with insufficient precision to make contact (Guardianship (Missing Persons) Act 2017 s1).

After 90 days a person may apply to the court for an order to appoint a guardian to look after that person's financial and administrative affairs.

mistake There is limited culpability if HMRC makes a mistake, whereas a taxpayer is generally liable to a penalty for a mistake. A taxpayer may correct a mistake in a tax return within one year.

misunderstanding A type of extra-statutory concession applied in exceptional circumstances. It allows tax relief, where VAT is undercharged by a registered business on account of a bona fide misunderstanding. Conditions apply. VAT notice 700 states "in certain circumstances, we may exceptionally take no further action about VAT undercharged by a taxable person as a result of a genuine misunderstanding which does not concern anything clearly covered in our published guidance, or in specific instructions given to that taxable person".

misused stamp For stamp duty, when too much duty has been paid. It is treated as a spoiled stamp. The tax provisions are in Stamp Duties Management Act 1891 s10.

mitigation Reduction in penalty because of circumstances, such as a taxpayer being co-operative.

mixed expenditure Spending that contains two or more elements that are taxed differently. The general rule is that the elements should be separated and taxed accordingly. In relation to mutual trading, the matter is discussed in HMRC Manual at BIM24460.

mixed funds Funds that contain elements subject to different tax provisions, such as a mixture of capital and revenue, or taxable and non-taxable funds. This consideration is particularly relevant to non-domiciled taxpayers. In relation to the remittance basis, there are provisions in ITA 2007 s809Q.

mixed holding A single holding including shares that qualify for share loss relief and shares that do not. The tax treatment is addressed in CTA 2010 s76.

mixed income In relation to patent box, "means the proceeds of sale where an item falling within subsection (2) of section 257BH and an item not falling within that subsection are sold together as, or as part of, a single unit for a single price" (Corporation Tax 2010 s357BHC(2)).

mixed loan Loan that has more than one purpose in relation to qualifying for tax relief. Tax provisions are given in ITA 2007 s386.

mixed partnership Partnership where at least one partner is a company.

mixed supply For VAT, a supply whose elements are subject to different rates. The issue is whether these elements are taxed separately or whether the supply should be treated as a single supply.

mobile catering Sale of food from a van. For VAT, this has sometimes created a problem in determining whether the supply is zero-rated food or standard-rated catering.

In the case *C&E v B H Cope [1981] STC 532,* a supply at a racecourse was held to be catering as the premises were discernible. In *B R Jones [1977] VATTR 155,* a supply in an open space was held to be food.
Note that hot take-away food and drink is now always standard-rated.

mobile home For VAT, this may come within the definition of a zero-rated caravan. Guidance is given in VAT notice 701/20.

mobile phone Small portable device capable of sending and receiving telephone calls. From April 2006, the provision of one mobile phone to an employee is not a taxable benefit (ITEPA 2003 s319). HMRC now accepts that this includes Smartphones which have many other features, but it does not extend to tablets and other devices even whey have telephony ability.

mobility component One of the elements of the personal independence payment (WRA 2012 s79).

moccasin Type of footwear. It was held that moccasins from size 3 did not qualify for VAT zero-rating as children's clothing in the case *Brays of Glastonbury Ltd [1978] VTD 650.*

modern slavery The criminal offence of holding a person in slavery or servitude and often forcing them to do labour (Modern Slavery Act 2015 s1). The Act largely came into force on 31 July 2015. The International Labour Organisation estimated that 40.3 million people worldwide are held in modern slavery, of whom 24.9 million are in forced labour. There were an estimated 10,00-13,000 victims in the UK in 2013.
Under s52, anyone who suspects that someone is the victim of modern slavery or human trafficking must report it.
Under s54, a business with a turnover above £26 million must publish a statement on modern slavery within six months of the end of the business's accounting period. This requires businesses to check on their supply chains. Guidance is produced by the Home Office.

modified cash equivalent In relation to accommodation provided to an employee, this term is defined in ITEPA 2003 s106(2A) as inserted by FA 2017 Sch 2. In relation to cars, the term is defined in ITEPA 2003 s121B as inserted by FA 2017 Sch 2.

modified PAYE System of PAYE no longer used. It allowed in some circumstances, PAYE to be operated on a week 1 basis for two weeks with a cumulation in the third week.

Moldova Eastern country. Its currency is the Moldovan leu (plural is lei) of 100 bani. The UK has a double taxation convention of 2007.

Monaco Principality in Europe. It is not a member of the European Union but is part of its Customs union. Its currency is the euro of 100 cents. The UK has no double taxation treaty but does have a tax information exchange agreement of 2014.

Monagasque Pertaining to **Monaco.**

money Means of exchange and store of value. It is expressed in a currency, such as pounds, dollars or euros.

money bill Public bill that the Speaker of the High Court has certified contains only provisions dealing with finance and taxation (Parliament Act 1911 s1). The House of Lords debates the bill but cannot delay it.

monetarism

(1) Accounting principle that the accounts only reflect items to which a value in money terms may be ascribed.

(2) Economic principle that markets determine economic policy.

Monetary Policy Committee (MPC) Committee of nine people chaired by the Governor of the Bank of England. It is independent of the government. It meets monthly to set the level of interest rates in the economy. They set interest rates according to the targets they have been set for inflation. If they feel inflation is set to rise they may increase interest rates and vice-versa.

money Means of exchange and store of value. In 1875, the English economist William Stanley Jevons (1836-1882) also saw it as a measure of value and a standard of value. The four functions were summarised in the couplet:

Money's a matter of functions four,
A medium, a measure, a standard, a store.

Within a defined area, money takes the form of currency which may be regarded as legal tender.

Sometimes the word is used in a narrower sense, such as to means banknotes and coins rather than sums in a bank account. The word can also be used in a broader sense to mean wealth, including illiquid assets. In economic terms, the various measures of money are indicated as M0, M1, M3 etc.

For VAT, "money includes currencies other than sterling" (Value Added Tax 1994 s96(1)).

money advice Professional or expert advice offered to a debtor in relationship to a debt payment programme in Scotland (Debt Arrangement and Attachment (Scotland) Act 2002 s3). A debtor may not enter such a programme until he or she has received money advice.

moneyboxing Practice of holding excess cash in a company so that, when it is wound up, the shareholders get a tax advantage as the funds are treated as capital rather than income. Sometimes the funds are included as part of the disposal proceeds and subject to the even lower tax rate of 10% under entrepreneur's relief. The term is used in an HMRC consultation document of 9 December 2015. This makes it clear that HMRC sees moneyboxing as tax avoidance. When a company is wound up by a members' voluntary liquidation, HMRC will check to see if the cash is excessive for the company's commercial requirements.

There is no precise formula for determining how much cash is excessive, leading to concerns that a company could be caught when the directors were merely cautious rather than seeking a tax advantage.

There is a specific provision that income tax is paid on any distribution from a close company if a shareholder is involved in a company within two years of the first company's liquidation. This is to stop phoenixism.

The legislation is ITTOIA 2005 s396B and s404A, both inserted by FA 2016 s35. It applies from 6 April 2016. Where a deliberate attempt has been made to avoid income tax, a penalty of up to 60% of the tax involved can be imposed.
HMRC gives more details in Spotlight 47 of 4 February 2019.

money debt Term used for loan relationship in corporation tax. It means a debt that is settled by payment of money.

money earnings Term used in ITEPA 2003 s18 in relation to salaries and wages paid in money rather than in benefits in kind.

MoneyGram International funds transfer system operated through Post Offices which allows funds to be provided within minutes.

money laundering Any process which is designed to take dirty money (such as from crime) and make it look clean. It is a crime not to report suspicion of money laundering. Money laundering involves at least two offences:

- the crime which generated the funds
- steps to try to legitimise (or launder) those funds.

The three stages of laundering are:

- placement stage, when funds make their first entry into the financial system
- layering stage, when efforts are made to cut any ties that link the funds to crime
- integration stage, when funds are returned to the criminal.

The main law is Money Laundering, Terrorist Financing and Transfer of Funds (Information on the Payer) Regulations (SI 2017 No 692) issued under the authority of Financial Services and Markets Act 2000. These regulations apply from 26 June 2017.

Proceeds of Crime Act 2002 s340(11) extends this to include attempts, conspiracy, incitement, aiding, abetting, counselling and procuring of the offence.

moneylender Person who lends money as a business by charging interest. Such a business requires a licence under Consumer Credit Act 1974.

money market Any market where money may be borrowed and lent, usually for large amounts for a short term.

money purchase An alternative term to describe a defined contribution pension scheme (FA 2004 s152(2)).

money purchase benefits Benefits provided under a defined contribution pension scheme (FA 2004 s227C).

money service business Business that handles money and is not covered by other provisions. Examples include bureaux de change and third party cheque clearers. From 1 June 2002, they must register with HMRC.

money supply Total amount of money in the economy at any time. There are many measures from narrow money, designated M0, which measures notes and coins, to M4 which includes all deposits held in banks and elsewhere.

money's worth Term used for PAYE to mean something that represents money and is used as a substitute (ITEPA 2003 s62(3)). Examples include gold ingots and

National Savings certificates. Such items are taxed as cash earnings. Guidance is given in HMRC Manual at EIM00570.

Mongolia Eastern country between Russia and China. Its currency is the tugrik of 100 mongo. The UK has a double taxation convention of 1996.

monies Old term, still sometimes used for legal purposes, meaning amounts of money.

monkey (1) Endangered animal. Imports of the animal and its products are generally prohibited under Convention on International Trade in Endangered Species.
(2) Slang term for £500 or $500.

monopoly Supply by one person, who is then a position to dictate prices in a manner which may not be in the interests of competition. Under Fair Trading Act 1973 ss6-7, a monopoly existed when a supplier controlled at least 25% of the market. Control by two people is called duopoly. Control by a small number of people is oligopoly.
Where one, two or a small number people control the markets or demand, the terms are respectively monopsony, duopsony and oligopsony.

monosodium glutamate Flavour enhancer. When supplied alone, it is standard-rated for VAT. It is not zero-rated as food because it has no nutritional value (VAT notice 701/14).

Monte Carlo simulation Mathematical method for determining an outcome when a problem can be defined but not calculated. For example, a business may know the probability of certain eventualities happening and the outcome of each eventuality. The eventuality may be allocated a series of numbers, so a 40% probability could be represented by the numbers 1 to 40, and another 23% probability by the number 41 to 63, and so on.
Random numbers are then used to consider what happens. This process is repeated until a consistent pattern emerges.
In tax, its most likely use is to test the credibility of a pattern of trading.

Montenegro East European country which became independent from Yugoslavia in 1996. It is not a member of the European Union but its currency is the euro of 100 cents. The UK double taxation convention of 1981 with Yugoslavia continues to apply.

month Period of between 28 and 31 days (Interpretation Act 1978 Sch 1). This provision has applied since 1850. A time limit of one month therefore means by one less than the day in the following month. This is known as the corresponding day **rule.** This has been demonstrated in cases such as *re O'Connor Utilities Ltd [2009] EWHC 3704 (Admin)* where it was held that the time of one limit specified in CEMA 1979 Sch 3 para 3 from 4 November 2008 expired on 3 December 2008. The consequence was that a notice served on 4 December 2008 was held to be late.
Alternatives to the calendar month are the tax month which runs from the 6th of one month to the 5th of the next (PAYE Regs 2003 reg 2(1). These are numbered, so tax month 1 is 6 April to 5 April, and so on.

There is also a lunar month which is four weeks. There are 13 lunar months in a year.

monthly PAYE threshold Amount that a monthly paid worker may earn before becoming liable to have income tax deducted under the PAYE scheme. (PAYE Regulations SI 2003 No 2682 reg 9(8)).
The amount is one twelfth of the personal allowance.

Montserrat UK Overseas Territory near St Kitts and Nevis. The currency is the East Caribbean dollar.

moonlighter Person who works a second job. HMRC uses the term to mean such a person whose second income is not declared for tax purposes.

moonshine Illicitly produced liquor.

mooring Tying or otherwise securing a boat to dry land. For VAT, this is generally a standard-rated supply, even for a houseboat. Further guidance for ships is contained in VAT leaflet 744c, and for houseboats in leaflet 701/20.

morality tax Situation where behaving morally is tax-disadvantageous. It particularly referred to the tax provisions in the 1960s and 1970s when there could be tax disadvantages by marrying.

moral rights In relation to copyright, means the right of a creator of the work to be identified as such, and not to have his work subjected to derogatory treatment (Copyright Designs and Patents Act 1988 s77).

moral test Test used by the Irish court in *Hayes v Duggan [1926]* where the Irish Supreme Court held that profits from illegal fruit machines could not be taxed because it was immoral for the state to profit from what it forbids. This view was specifically disavowed in the UK, particularly in *Mann v Nash [1932]*. The matter is discussed in HMRC Manual at BIM22008.

moratorium Temporary cessation of payments while a company in difficulty attempts to sort itself out. This is now permitted in UK insolvency law under Insolvency Act 1986 from sA1 as inserted by Corporate Insolvency and Governance Act 2020 from s1.

more than 50% test Requirement in tax law that replacement expenditure for an integral feature qualifies for a capital allowance, provided that more than 50% of the asset is replaced within a 12-month period.

more than one document Principle of stamp duty that where a transaction is given effect by two or more documents, only one needs to be stamped.

more than one transaction Principle of stamp duty that where one document gives effect to two or more stampable transactions, it must be stamped for each of them.

Morocco African country. Its currency is the dirham of 100 centimes. The UK has a double taxation convention of 1981.

mortality tables Tables produced of how long people are expected to live, according to their sex and current age. A summary is given in section 3 of this book.

mortgage Secured loan to buy an asset, such as a home. From 2000, there is no tax relief on mortgage interest for a home.

mortgagee Lender who provides funds under a mortgage.

mortgage holiday Period when a mortgagor is allowed not to make repayments. The lender may agree a holiday at any time. A general holiday was agreed between 1 May 2020 and 31 October 2020 as a coronavirus-related provision. Interest continues to accrue during the holiday.

mortgage prisoner People who are trapped in mortgages with high interest rates and are unable to switch to a lower rate mortgage. In July 2020, the BBC said there were 170,000 such people.

Mortgagor Borrower who secures funds under a mortgage.

Morton's fork Argument advanced by John Morton (c1420-1500) who was Archbishop of Canterbury and a minister of Henry VIII. He argued that if a person appeared rich, he could afford to pay tax. If he appeared to be poor, he was concealing his wealth, and could afford to pay tax.

most recent return For real time information for PAYE, this term is given a specific meaning in PAYE regulations SI 2003 No 2682 s67G(6).

MOT Compulsory annual test for most mechanical road vehicles that are at least three years old. It is not possible to pay vehicle excise duty for a vehicle that needs an MOT test but does not have one. The letters stand for Ministry of Transport, now replaced by the Deposit of Transport.

motor caravan For VAT, this does not come within the scope of a zero-rated caravan (VAT leaflet 701/20). Vehicle excise duty provisions are set out in Vehicle Excise and Registration Act 1994 Sch 1 which provides a definition.

motorcycle Two-wheeled mechanically propelled vehicle, subject to vehicle excise duty. An employee who uses his or her motorcycle for the employer's business may be paid 24p a mile tax-free.

motor home Vehicle that has facilities for everyday living. This is standard-rated for VAT as it does not come within the scope of zero-rated caravans. Guidance is given in VAT Notice 701/20.

motor spirit Old name for petrol. It is sometimes still used to distinguish it from aviation fuel.

motor vehicle A mechanically propelled vehicle which is intended or adapted for use on roads. Such a vehicle is subject to vehicle excise duty.

mouse Computer device to move a cursor round a screen, and which may be clicked to perform certain functions.

moving-in time The time when a person moves into a dwelling that becomes the person's main residence for capital gains tax purposes (TCGA 1992 s223ZA(1)(b) as inserted by FA 2020 s24(4)).

moving to a higher cost housing area Tax-free allowance that an employer could make to an employee who relocated to an area where houses were more expensive. It was abolished in 1993.

moving walkway This is a feature integral to a building and so qualifies for a writing down allowance of 6% a year (CAA 2001 s33A).

mowing machine Powered machine for cutting grass. It is an exempt machine for oil duty under HODA 1979 Sch 1 para 6.

Mozambique African country. Its currency is the new metical of 100 centavos. The UK has no double taxation treaty.

mudaraba Limited partnership and profit-sharing agreement under Sharia law. It is taxed according to the arrangement it seeks to imitate.

mud money In acting, payment to extras who are unable to work because the ground is too muddy.

mufawada Joint venture partnership under Sharia law. It is taxed according to the arrangement it seeks to imitate.

multiple birth When more than one baby is born in one birth. Only one amount of statutory maternity pay is payable. Child benefit may be claimed for each child.

multiple dwellings A single interest in more than one dwelling. From 2011, it may be possible to calculate stamp duty land tax on the basis of the tax payable on one dwelling, and multiplying it by the number of dwellings (FA 2011 Sch 22). This can avoid the higher rates of duty otherwise payable.

multiple PAYE schemes The regulations are in PAYE regulations 2003 from reg 98.

multiplier(1) For council tax, the amount by which the rateable value of a non-domestic property is multiplied to determine the business rates payable.

(2) For company car fuel benefit, a figure that is multiplied by a percentage related to the car's emissions. Details are given under Company Cars in section 3 of this dictionary.

multisave Sales promotion method widely used in retail, such as "3 for the price of 2". VAT is charged at the amount charged to the customer. This may require apportionment where the items are not all subject to the same VAT rate. Multisave schemes are often funded by manufacturers, who make repayments to the retailers. The manufacturer may reduce its output tax by the amount of VAT included in the payments. If different rates apply, this may require apportionment. The retailer must include the VAT element of these payments in their own VAT returns. (VAT Notice 700/7 para 6.3).

multi-year contract Term used in relation to taxation of corporate members of Lloyd's (FA 2012 s25(4)).

multure Scots term for a fee, originally for grinding grain.

mum For alcoholic liquor duty, a form of black beer which is exempt from duty (Alcoholic Liquor Duties Act 1979 s4(1)).

Munro Inheritance tax case that helps to determine whether a gift is a gift with reservation. In particular, the case established the principle of shearing where an outright gift may be made of less than the whole property. The case was a Privy Council case on stamp duty in Australia, but is still regarded as a valid precedent. The full name is *Munro v Commissioners of Stamp Duties (New South Wales) [1934].*

mural Wall painting. Producing murals is not regarded as construction work for the Construction Industry Scheme. A mural may be regarded as plant when used to create ambience.

museum Place that exhibits artefacts to enable learning. Such a body is able to reclaim VAT input tax under VATA 1994 s33A even though it has not made supplies. The list of such bodies is given in SI 2001 No 2789 Sch. Museums are allowed to charge admission under Museums and Galleries Admission Charges Act 1972 s1.

museum and galleries exhibition tax relief Relief from corporation tax that may be claimed by a museum or gallery from 1 April 2017 under CTA 2009 from s1218ZA.

mushroom kits For VAT, these are specifically zero-rated as being an item to prepare food for human consumption. A reusable container for this purpose is standard-rated. It was held that the kit was a mixed supply in *Cheshire Mushroom Farm [1974] VTD 71.*

music Sheet music is zero-rated for VAT under VATA 1994 Sch 8 Group 3 whether in book form or loose leaf form. This does not extend to manuscript paper, text books about music, piano player rolls, commissioning of music, musical performance or recorded music. A musical composition is a creative work for which the composer may be able to claim averaging of profits for income tax under ITTOIA 2005 s221(3).

An opera, musical or similar work may benefit from corporation tax relief for dramatic productions (CTA 2009 s1217FA(2)).

An orchestra may benefit from orchestra relief from corporation tax (CTA 2009 s1217RG).

Musical performance can be either a taxable vocation or a tax-free hobby, depending on how it is pursued. If the former, the musician or musical group may need to register for VAT. An orchestra or other ensemble may be exempt from VAT under VATA 1994 Sch 9 Group 13 Note 29(c). This did not apply when an orchestra employed a full-time managing director *(Bournemouth Symphony Orchestra [2006] EWCA Civ 1281).*

mutatis mutandis Latin: the necessary changes being made.

Mutual Assistance Recovery Directive (MARD) EU Council Directive 2008/55/EC that requires member states to co-operate in recovering tax. This is given effect in UK law by FA 2002 s134 and Sch 39.

mutual debt When two people each owe money to the other. In normal accounting, these figures should not be netted off. If A owes B £100, and B owes A £20; the accounts should show that A owes B £100 and not £80. A and B may agree that both debts will be settled by a single payment of £80, but that requires them both to agree and for two accounting entries to be made for the one payment.

mutual exclusivity Principle of taxation that income assessed as from one source cannot also be assessed under another. A case on this is *Edon v Ross [1961]*. It is discussed in HMRC Manual at BIM14005. Similarly income tax, corporation tax and capital gains tax are mutually exclusive. If an income or profit falls to be taxed under one of these taxes, it cannot also be taxed under another.

mutual insurance company Insurance company owned by its members. The tax provisions are given in CTA 2009 s634.

mutuality of obligation The duty of two parties to provide a benefit to each other as part of a contract. This is no longer regarded as a factor in determining whether a worker should be taxed as an employee, as almost all contracts involve mutuality.

mutual recognition principle Legal requirement that goods legally produced in one part of the UK must be freely available in all parts of the UK (United Kingdom Internal Market Act 2020 s2).

mutual trading Arrangement whereby members of a club or similar trade with each other. Such activities are not taxable (CTA 2009 s633).

Myanmar Eastern country formerly known as Burma. Its currency is the kyat of 100 pyas. UK has a double taxation convention of 1951 still in the name of Burma. Payments of a pension made under Pensions (India, Pakistan and Burma) Act 1955 may be exempt from income tax under ITEPA 2003 s654. The country is subject to UK sanctions, as are designated persons of the country.

NACE classification "The first level of the common statistical classification of economic activities in the European Union established by Regulation (EC) No 1893/2006 of the European Parliament and the Council of 20 December 2006 (as that Regulation has effect from time to time)" (CAA 2001 s51G(7)). A company engaged in such activity may have a restricted right to claim annual investment allowance.

Na h-Eileanan an Iar Scottish constituency formerly known as Western Isles. The term is Scottish Gaelic for Western Isles. There are some special provisions under Islands (Scotland) Act 2018 s18.

naked In finance, description of any arrangement which is not hedged or otherwise protected.

nakfa Currency of Eritrea.

nama al-mal Capital accumulation under Islamic finance.

Name Member of Lloyd's insurance market who underwrites insurance policies.

name Words by which a person, company or other entity is known. There are few restrictions on what an individual chooses to call himself or herself, unless it is used for fraud. Company names must be registered.

name and shame Provision introduced from April 2010. It allows HMRC to publish the name and other details of tax defaulters who attempted to evade at least £25,000 in tax (FA 2009 s94). There is a similar provision for employers who fail to pay the national minimum wage.

Namibia African country. Its currency is the Namibian dollar of 100 cents which is kept at parity with the South African rand. The UK has a double taxation convention of 1962 amended by a protocol of 1967.

nanny Person who is paid to look after a child, usually while the parents are away working. A nanny is an employee who must be paid under the PAYE system, usually, with class 1 national insurance deducted. A nanny is also entitled to all benefits under employment law, such as holidays and sick pay.

If an employer pays for an employee to have a nanny, the employee is subject to tax and the employer to class 1A national insurance on the cost of the nanny, including the employer's national insurance.

nappies These are regarded as clothing for young children and so are zero-rated for VAT.

narrative reporting Part of a business's annual accounts, expressed in words rather than figures, such as the directors' report (CA 2006 s417).

NASDAQ National Association of Securities Dealers Automated Quotation System. It is pronounced as nazz-dak. NASDAQ is the largest electronic securities trading system in the world. It started on 8 February 1971 as the first electronic exchange. It is now owned and operated by NASDAQ OMX Group which is itself listed on NASDAQ. In 2006 it became a national securities exchange.

National Advice Service Part of HMRC that deals with general enquiries on tax. It cannot deal with taxpayer-specific enquiries. The telephone number is 0845 010 9000. There is a textphone for the hard of hearing on 0845 000 0200, and a service in Welsh on 0845 010 0300. It can also be contacted online at https://www.gov.uk/contact-hmrc.

National Audit Office Independent body that audits the accounts of government departments and other bodies. Its functions are governed by the Budget Responsibility and National Audit Act 2011 s20 and Sch 2.

national broadcasting company In relation to capital allowances on shared transmission facilities, "means a body corporate engaged in the broadcasting for general reception by means of wireless telegraphy of radio or television services or both on a national basis" (FA 1991 s78(8)).

National Clearance Hub (NCH) Part of HMRC. It is a single national site that has replaced entry processing units at major airports and ports.

National Crime Agency Body formed on 7 October 2013 to replace the Serious Organised Crime Agency.

National Cyber Security Centre (NCSC) Government body, part of GCHQ, that provides guidance and other assistance in dealing with threats from cyber attacks. It was formed in October 2016 from predecessor bodies.

national debt "The total amount of debt owed by a government, raised through borrowing from individuals and institutions. It is the sum total of all previously incurred deficits that have not been paid" (HM Treasury glossary).

National Employment Savings Trust (NEST) Government provider of workplace pensions. it was established in October 2012 and is governed by Pensions Act 2008. More details are given under Workplace Pensions in section 3 of this dictionary.

National Export Scheme An electronic system of managing declarations to Customs officers in HMRC. It was introduced in 2003.

national health insurance Health service insurance scheme that started in 1913. It provided entitlement to medical service. It was funded by deductions from wages similar to national insurance. It ended when the current National Health Service was created in 1948.

National Health Service Publicly funded health care service introduced in 1948 to replace existing schemes.

national insurance Charge on earnings that funds social security and pensions, first introduced in 1912 under National Insurance Act 1911. Strictly speaking, it is not a tax but a compulsory insurance premium (SSCBA 1992). In its evolution from 1912, it has gradually lost the nature of insurance and assumed the nature of taxation. It is collected under several classes, of which class 1 is paid by employees and their employers, and classes 2 and 4 by the self-employed. Class 3 comprises voluntary payments that may be made to complete contribution years and ensure the contributor's entitlement to a state pension. Employers may be liable to pay class 1A and 1B. There was also briefly a class 3A, allowing those who reached state pension age by 6 April 2016 to make an additional payment to secure a higher state pension.

Class 1 is assessed on earnings whereas income tax is assessed on income arising. While efforts have been made to harmonise the two taxes, some differences remain in that class 1 does not apply to all sources subject to it. It does not apply to employment benefits in kind, for example.

There is no tax relief for national insurance except that employers may claim relief for employer's national insurance.

A taxpayer cannot claim income tax relief for national insurance (ITTOIA 2005 s 360A) but an employer may claim tax relief for employer's national insurance (ITEPA 2003 s53).

national insurance holiday Short-term government help to businesses by excusing them from paying some employer's national insurance. Two such schemes have been introduced: from 2010 to 2013, and from 1996 to 1999.

national insurance number Unique number allocated to UK residents when they are 15 and to non-residents when they need one. The number stays with the person for life, regardless of changes in their circumstances. It is now used for many other purposes. The number comprises two letters, three pairs of digits and what is now a final check letter in the form: AB 12 34 56 C.

national insurance surcharge Addition to national insurance charged between 1977 and 1985. It provided no additional entitlement to state pension or any social security benefit and was, in reality, another income tax.

National Islands Plan Plan prepared for Scottish islands under Islands (Scotland) Act 2018 s3.

National Living Wage Higher rate of national minimum wage payable from April 2016 for workers aged 25 or more. Rates are given under National Minimum Wage in section 3 of this dictionary.

National Lottery National lottery introduced in November 1994 under National Lottery Act 1994. Winnings are tax free, but profits are subject to lottery duty.

national minimum wage (NMW) A minimum wage that an employer must pay a worker, including an employee (National Minimum Wage Act 1998 s1(1)).

The wage was introduced in April 1998 and has been revised many times since. There is a national living wage for workers aged 25 or over, other rates. Some points to note are:

- NMW is administered and enforced by HMRC
- the right to NMW extends to workers which is wider than just employees. It includes agency workers, homeworkers and outworkers, casual labour, piece workers and commission-only workers, zero hours workers, and seconded staff
- there are different rates for different age groups
- the rate was introduced from 1 April 1998 at £3.60 an hour. It increases each year, now in April
- the national minimum wage applies to basic pay only. An employer may not include bonuses, commission, overtime premium and tips in the reckoning
- NMW does not apply for hours when a person is on call but not otherwise working
- there are strict penalties for non-compliance. The employer is required to make up the shortfall to the employee, pay a penalty, and may be named and shamed
- benefits in kind do not count toward NMW with the sole exception of accommodation for which a small accommodation offset may be included
- NMW is considered for a pay reference period. This means that the pay for that period must exceed the number of hours multiplied by the appropriate NMW rate. An employer may pay some of those hours at below the NMW, provided that the average for the whole period exceeds the rate
- an employer has not breached NMW rules if some of a worker's pay is put aside into a Christmas fund or holiday fund which reduces pay to below the NMW rate. The employee must have control over the fund, and the payment before deduction must comply with NMW rules
- NMW is determined for each worker on one of four bases: time work, salaried-hours work, output work and unmeasured work.

Rates are given in section 3 of this dictionary.

national purpose Purpose considered of benefit to the country as a whole. A gift for such purpose is exempt from inheritance tax (Inheritance Tax Act 1984 s25). The scope of relevant bodies is set out in Sch 3 of this Act. There is a separate scheme where works of art may be accepted in lieu of inheritance tax.

National Savings and Investments (NSI) Part of the Exchequer which borrows from the public in the form of low value investments such as National Savings certificates. Interest rates are given in section 3 of this dictionary.

National Savings certificate (NSC) Savings product issued by the National Savings Bank as a safe low cost investment for ordinary citizens and as a means of raising funds for the government. Typically they comprise either fixed interest or index-linked investments for between two and five years. These certificates are issued in accordance with National Debt Act 1972 s8.

National savings stamps Stamps and similar tokens issued from 1861 as a form of investment in the government. They were issued under the authority of National Debt Act 1972 s10. The National Savings Stamps Regulations SI 1969 No 1343, appear still to be in force. The legal definition of the stamp was given in FA 1961 s35(1) as amended by Post Office Act 1969 s112. Stamps are no longer issued, but existing stamps may still be redeemed at face value. They may now be worth more to a stamp collector.

natural gas Gas with a methane content of at least 80%.

natural justice Rules and procedures that must be followed by every court, tribunal or other body exercising a judicial function. This imposes a duty to:

- to act fairly, in good faith, without bias, and in a judicial temper;
- to give each party the opportunity to present his case, and to correct anything in the other party's case;
- not to hear one side of a case behind the back of the other party;
- not be a judge in your own case, and to declare any personal interest;
- to give everyone notice of what they are accused;
- to disclose all relevant documents to both parties.

The rules of natural justice must be followed in tax appeals (HMRC Manual at AH3935).

national security Such provisions that the government puts into place to protect the country from such risks as war, terrorism, espionage, cyber attacks and similar. "The government works to identify the most pressing risks to our security, and put in place the ways and means to address them" (government website).

These provisions can include exclusion of material that would otherwise be available, such as evidence in court or data protection. In 2020, national security was added to the list of factors that may be considered in approving a company merger.

national security and defence exemption For the purposes of data protection, this is set out in Data Protection Act 2018 s26.

National Service Compulsory conscription into the armed forces. The UK had two periods of conscription for the world wars from 1916 to 1920, and from 1939 to 1960. The last conscripted soldier was demobilised in 1963, 18 years after the end of the war. The laws were Military Service Act 1916, and Military Training Act 1939 replaced by National Service (Armed Forces) Act 1939, and then National Service Act 1948.

national security certificate Document issued by a Minister of the Crown that prevents disclosure of information on grounds of national security. Data protection provisions are set out in Data Protection Act 2018 ss 27, 79, 111 and 130.

National Sports Councils For corporation tax relief for grassroots sport, "means –

(a) the United Kingdom Sports Council,

(b) the English Sports Council,

(c) the Scottish Sports Council,

(d) the Sports Council for Wales, and

(e) the Sports Council for Northern Ireland"

(CTA 2010 s217C(5) as inserted by Finance (No 2) Act 2017 s22).

National Will Register On-line facility for registering the existence of a will. It is run by a company called Certainty.co.uk. For a fee, a will can be registered. For another fee, it is possible to search the database to see if a person left a will. The company can also search for a will that has not been registered.

NATO North Atlantic Treaty Organisation. This is an alliance of 30 countries in Europe and North America, including the United Kingdom, established on 4 April 1949 with the purpose of safeguarding the freedom and security of all its members by political and military means. An external attack on any member country is regarded as an attack on all member countries.

natural capital Value of the natural world. This looks at green spaces and trees and values them according to their recreation value, carbon dioxide removal and pollution removal. In June 2019, the Office of National Statistics valued the UK's natural capital at £791 billion. The World Bank did a similar exercise and concluded that the planet's natural resources are worth $100 billion.

natural child

(1) A child produced from one's body, as against an adopted child or foster child.

(2) Until 1969, the term was sometimes used to mean an illegitimate child.

natural gas Combustible gas which is found naturally in the earth, as against producer gas which is created by a process. For hydrocarbon oil duty, it is defined as "gas with a methane content of not less than 80%" (HODA1979 s23C(5)(b)).

natural justice Rules and procedures that must be followed by any court, tribunal or other body charged with adjudicating the rights of others. This includes an employer disciplining an employee, or a club disciplining a member. A decision may be set aside by a court if these rules or procedures have not been followed. The principles of natural justice include a duty:

- to act fairly, in good faith, without bias, and in a judicial temper;
- to give each party the opportunity to present his case, and to correct anything in the other party's case;
- not to hear one side of a case behind the back of the other party;
- not to be a judge in your own case, and to declare any personal interest;
- to give everyone notice of what they are accused;
- to disclose all relevant documents to both parties.

The rules of natural justice must be followed in tax appeals (HMRC Manual at AH3935).

natural person Living individual, as against a corporate person such as a company.

natural road fuel gas "Is road fuel gas with a methane content of not less than 80%" (HODA1979 s5(2)). This definition was added from 1 September 2004.

nature of income condition One of the conditions that must be met for an investment to qualify for venture capital trust relief, as set out in ITA 2007 s274. The condition is that the company's income is derived wholly or mainly from shares or other securities.

Nauru Island state that became independent in 1968. Its currency is the Australian dollar of 100 cents. The UK has no double taxation treaty.

nautical mile Imperial measure of length used at sea. Since 1970, it has been defined as 1,852 metres. Previously it was 1,853.184 metres which is the equivalent of 6,080 feet or 1.056 miles.

Nazi compensation Compensation paid in respect of suffering at the hands of the Nazi government of Germany (1933-1945). Originally such payments were only tax-free if paid by the German or Austrian government and were tax-free under their laws. The scope was gradually widened, many decades after the event:

- 6 April 1986: the requirement for the payment to be exempt under German or Austrian law was abolished;
- 8 May 2000: compensation paid on dormant accounts of Holocaust victims became tax-free;
- 18 January 2001: compensation paid to owners or heirs of assets seized by the Nazis became tax-free;
- 19 July 2005: tax exemption for payments to Holocaust victims and their descendants under the Restore UK scheme.

The law is ITEPA 2003 s642.

Similar provisions apply for capital gains tax on the disposal of the right to receive compensation (TCGA1992 s268A), inserted in 2006 with retrospective effect from 1996.

nearest relative Person who is most closely related to a person for whom an application may be made under Mental Health Acts 1983 and 2007. Such a person may be asked to act for the patient, in which case they become the acting nearest relative.

near money Assets such as money market instruments and time deposits which are readily convertible into cash.

Nebuchadnezzar Champagne bottle with a capacity of 20 standard bottles.

necessary expenses In relation to possible taxation of advances to an employee, "are expenses (including travelling expenses) which –

(a) the employee is obliged to incur and pay as holder of the employment, and

(b) are necessarily incurred in the performance of the duties of the employment" (ITEPA 2003 s179(5)).

necessity Legal defence that what would otherwise be a criminal offence is justified on ground of public policy. An example is smashing a window to rescue a person in a house on fire, or shooting a dog which is savaging sheep. Necessity cannot justify a private need, such as shoplifting when hungry.

née French: born. The term is used of a woman to indicate her maiden name, thus Mary Jones (née Smith).

negative carry Situation where the cost of finance is greater than the return on an investment.

negative cash flow Situation where an organisation's expenditure is greater than its income.

negative clearance Procedure that assumes that something notified to an authority is permissible unless the contrary is determined.

negative equity When the amount owed in a mortgage or other secured loan is less than the value of the secured asset.

negative goodwill When the amount paid for a business is less than the value of its net assets. The corporation tax consequences are addressed in CTA 2009 s724.

negative pregnant In law, an evasive response that answers a question in court while avoiding the substantive issue. An example is a witness who says he did not receive £1,000 from a person, and does not admit receiving £999.

negative taxation When the rate of taxation is such that a person receives a benefit rather than make a payment. Although negative taxation has often been considered as a means of integrating taxation with social security, the problems of harmonising two different objectives and establishing realistic rates have always led to such plans being abandoned. Despite this, there are some elements of negative taxation in the UK system, such as the enhanced research and development tax credits and land remediation relief. In both cases, the tax relief exceeds the expenditure.

neglect In law, the tort of failure to exercise a duty of care properly. The term is particularly applied to parents or guardians who do not look after their children properly.

For a personal liability notice served on a director for unpaid national insurance, the term is more narrowly defined than for the tort. In the case *O'Rorke [2013] All ER (D) 150 (Dec)*, the Upper Tribunal held that neglect had to be considered subjectively. In that case, a director who suffered serious mental illness had not been neglectful.

negligence Failure to exercise the standard of care reasonably expected. A legal discourse was given in the non-tax case of *Blyth v Birmingham Waterworks [1859] All ER 478*. For tax, an error due to negligence can lead to a penalty.

negligible value Description used in capital gains tax for shares or other securities whose value is close to zero (TCGA 1992 s24(2)). A taxpayer may treat this as a disposal and reacquisition for zero, which will usually trigger a capital loss.

nemine contradicente Latin: no-one saying otherwise. It is often abbreviated to nem con.

net A figure derived from deducting an element from a gross figure, so net profit is gross profit minus expenses; net pay is gross pay minus income tax and national insurance.

net asset restriction Restriction on a public company paying a dividend when the value of its net assets is less than the aggregate of its called-up share capital and its undistributable reserves, or where payment of the divided would so reduce the value of its net assets (CA 2006 s831). There is no such restriction for a private company.

net assets Value of all of an entity's assets, including fixed assets, of an entity, minus its liabilities (CA 2006 s831(2)).

net book value In accounting, value of a fixed asset after depreciation has been subtracted. This is generally not relevant for tax as depreciation is not tax-deductible. For leases, there is a specific provision in CAA 2001 s228H(1).

net borrowings Amount of money an organisation has borrowed minus amounts of cash it holds.

net cash flow Difference between the amount of money coming in and money going out of an organisation.

net cost of the demolition For capital allowances for plant and machinery, "means the amount, if any, by which the cost of the demolition exceeds any money received for the remains of the plant and machinery" (CAA 2001 s26(4)).

For qualifying buildings, "means the amount, if any, by which the cost of the demolition exceeds any money received for the remains of the qualifying building" (CAA 2001 s360S(3)).

For capital allowance for an assured tenancy, "means the amount, if any, by which the cost of the demolition exceeds any money received for the remains of the property" (CAA 2001 s528(3)).

net cost of the restoration In relation to mineral extraction, this term is defined in CAA 2001 s416(7). For ring-fence activities, a different definition is given in CAA 2001 s416ZA(9).

net current assets Current assets of an organisation minus liabilities.

net current liabilities Current liabilities of an organisation minus its current assets.

net division approach Method of apportioning an estate when the residue of the estate is shared between exempt and non-exempt beneficiaries (such as a charity) so that they each receive the same net figure after deducting inheritance tax. This can require double grossing up. The matter was considered in the case *re Ratcliffe [1999] STC 262.*

net earnings In accounting, profit after all interest, taxes and other costs and expenses have been deducted.

Netflix effect Term coined in 2018 for the practice of not paying for a television licence because the premises occupier does not watch terrestrial television, but only watches subscription services such as Netflix, Amazon, BT and Sky.

Netherlands European state and member state of European Union, sometimes called Holland. "Netherlands" originally included Belgium. For EU purposes, the current state excludes the Netherlands Antilles. Netherlands' currency from 2002 is the euro of 100 cents. Previously, it was the guilder.

The UK has tax treaties of 2008 with the Netherlands that was amended by protocols in 2013 and 2014. There is a separate double taxation convention of 2013 on bank taxes.

Netherlands Antilles Autonomous region of the Caribbean, belonging to Netherlands. It was widely used for tax planning. It ceased to exist in 2010, when the islands were given separate relationships with the Netherlands.

Netherlands Benefit Act for Victims of Persecution 1940-45 Scheme that makes payments to victims of wartime persecution under Dutch law. Payments from this scheme are exempt from income tax under ITEPA 2003 s642A as inserted by FA 2016 s23(1). The exemption applies from 2016/17.

N-Ethyl-N[2-(1-isobutoxy)ethyl]-4-(phenylazo)aniline Approved marker for hydrocarbon oils under Hydrocarbon Oil (Designated Markers) Regulations SI 1996 No 1251 para 2(2). It is yellow.

net income For tax, total income less reliefs.

net interest Gross interest less tax.

net liabilities Value of liabilities minus assets.

net liquid funds Organisation's cash plus marketable investments, minus its short-term borrowings.

net loss Loss after deducting overheads, expenses, depreciation and tax.

net margin Difference between sales price and total cost of an item, including its share of overheads. The difference is usually expressed as a percentage, but may be expressed as an amount.

net monthly account (NMA) A form of settlement terms where the customer is supposed to pay the invoice by the end of the month following that in which it was issued.

net off Process of deducting a liability from an asset and showing a single figure as an asset or liability. For example if A owes B £6,000, and B owes A £4,000, they could agree to net off these transactions and settle them by A paying B £2,000. In normal accounting, figures should not be netted off. In this example, A owes B £6,000.

There are some exceptions. For loan relationship for corporation tax, interest receivable and interest payable are netted off to a single figure. In terms of repaying tax, HMRC has the right to net off tax owed.

net overseas hours All hours worked overseas during a tax year.

It is used in the third automatic overseas residence test under the statutory residence test. Details are given under Statutory residence test in section 3 of this dictionary.

net pay Pay after tax and national insurance have been deducted. For some purposes, pension contributions are also deducted.

net PAYE income Income subject to PAYE minus allowable pension contributions and allowable donations to charity (PAYE Regulations 2003 reg 3(1)).

net pay pension scheme "Means a pension scheme in the case of which some or all of the members of the pension scheme are entitled to be given relief in accordance with section 193 in respect of the payments of contributions by them under the pension scheme" (FA 2004 s191(9)).

net premiums written In relation to taxation of corporate members of Lloyd's "means gross premium written net of reinsurance premiums payable under reinsurance ceded" (FA 2012 s28(6)).

net present value (NPV) Value of a future cashflow reduced by a succession of reducing factors to represent inflation. For tax, this is required to calculated stamp duty land tax on a lease. Sample rates are given in section 3 of this dictionary.

net profit Turnover of a business minus costs and expenses. The figure is usually quoted before tax has been deducted. A tax computation for a trading entity starts with "net profit per the accounts". This figure is then adjusted in accordance with tax law.

net profit ratio Ratio of an organisation's net profit to its net sales.

This ratio may be compared with organisations of similar size and activity to see which is the most efficient.

net realisable value Proceeds of selling an item, less the costs of selling.

For accounting, stock is usually valued at lower of cost and net realisable value. Tax follows the accounting standard.

net receipts Amount of money received after deductions for the cost of collection.

net relevant earnings (NRE) A definition of pensionable income that was once used in determining the maximum contributions to a retirement annuity or personal pension scheme that qualify for tax relief. It was defined in ICTA 1988 s646.

net residual value (NRV) Expected proceeds from disposing of an asset at the end of its life, less the cost of disposing of it. Disposal may be by sale or salvage. If an asset has an NRV, depreciation is calculated on the difference between acquisition cost and NRV. For example, a press cost £1,000 and is expected to be disposed of for £100 after five years. The depreciation charge for the five years is £900. On the straight line basis, that is £180 per year.

net return Return on an investment after tax and any expenses.

net salary Salary after deduction of tax, national insurance and other permitted deductions.

net sales Value of sales less returns from customers, discounts, commission and similar expenses of sales.

net taxable earnings (NTE) Total of taxable earnings less deductions. This is expressed in the formula TE – DE in ITEPA 2003 s11(1).

net taxable pension income (NTPI) Amount of pension income chargeable to income tax (ITEPA 2003 s567).

net taxable specific income (NTSI) Taxable specific income less specific deductions from that income. This is expressed in the formula TSI – DSI in ITEPA 2003 s12(1).

net turnover Income from turnover or sales, after discounts have been subtracted, and excluding VAT and any other duties or sales taxes.

net worth How much a person or organisation is worth. It represents how much they own minus how much they owe.

net yield Profit from investments less tax, expressed as a percentage of the value of the investments.

Net Zero Transport Board Body launched on 7 July 2020 to help decarbonise UK transport.

neutral One of the five requirements for accounts to meet the requirement for reliability. This in turn is one of the four requirements for accounting information required by Statement of Principles. Accounts are neutral if they are free from deliberate or systematic bias, such as presenting the accounts to resist a takeover bid or to assist in raising finance. In practice, it can be difficult to differentiate between deliberate bias and undue optimism.

neutral citation Citation for law reports that is given by the courts themselves and not by the publishers of law reports. These citations were introduced in 2001 for the House of Lords (now Supreme Court), Court of Appeal and Privy Council. They were extended to the High Court in 2002. Such cases can be accessed on the bailii website free.

Nevada corporation US corporation incorporated in the state of Nevada, widely seen as the USA's main corporate haven after Delaware.

new accessory In the context of taxing company cars, a replacement accessory. Provision of a new accessory does not increase the taxable benefit of the car if it is no superior to the old accessory. If it is superior, the *whole* cost of the accessory is added to the list price for calculating the taxable benefit (ITEPA 2003 s131).

new affordable home Means a starter home "made available for people whose needs are not adequately served by the commercial housing market" (Housing and Planning Act 2016 s74(7)).

new annuity In relation to the taxation of general annuity businesses, "means any annuity, so far as paid under a contract made by an insurance company in an accounting period beginning on or after 1st January 1992 and so far as referable to the company's basic life assurance and general annuity business" (ICTA 1988 s437(1C)).

new area In relation to relocation expenses, this is defined in ITEPA 2003 s281(6).

new dwelling Dwelling that has been created from an existing dwelling. The implications for annual tax on enveloped dwellings are set out in FA 2013 s125. For starter homes, the term "means a building or part of a building that –

(a) has been constructed for use as a single dwelling and has not been previously occupied, or

(b) has been adapted for use as a single dwelling and has not been occupied since its adaptation"

(Housing and Planning Act 2016 s(2) and s74(7)).

new enterprise allowance (NEA) "Scheme designed to assist unemployed people who wish to start their own business" (Commons Standard Note of 27 June 2014). It has some similarity to the New Deal programme offered between 1997 and 2011, when they were replaced by welfare-to-work schemes, following a change of government.

The scheme is available to individuals aged 18 or over in Great Britain who are claiming jobseeker's allowance, employment and support allowance or are a lone parent claiming income support.

The scheme pays £65 a week for 13 weeks, and £3 for the next 13 weeks, giving a total of £1,274. Participants may also be able to access a loan of up to £2,500.

NEA was initially piloted in Merseyside in January 2011 before being rolled out nationally between April and August 2011. The scheme was initially restricted to those who had been unemployed for at least six months. The scope was widened in October 2012.

Initial contact is via a local Jobcentre Plus work coach.

new employee Person who starts employment (PAYE Regs 2003 from reg 41).

new-for-old Insurance cover for property or equipment where an item lost or destroyed is replaced by the equivalent new item without deduction for age or wear and tear of the old item, and regardless of price inflation.

Where an insurance policy qualifies as a tax-deductible business expense, the existence of a new-for-old clause does not reduce the allowability of the expense, as explained in HMRC Manual at BIM45501.

new land In a compulsory acquisition, land that is provided in compensation for the taking of old land.

The capital gains tax provisions are given in TCGA1992 s247.

new leu Currency of Romania.

new means of transport (NMT) VAT term for some types of ships, aircraft and motorised land vehicles for the transport of passengers or goods which, when bought new in one member state for removal to another, can be bought VAT free.

The law is VATA 1994 s40.

The definition is given in Value Added Tax 1994 s95. A means of transport is new if the period from acquisition in another member state to first entry into service is less than:

- three months for a ship or aircraft
- six months for a land vehicle, and
- if in that period it has travelled under its own power for less than:
- 100 hours for a ship
- 40 hours for an aircraft
- 6000 kilometres for a land vehicle.

(Value Added Tax 1994 s95(3)).

new oil Oil after it has been charged under HODA1979 s6, as oil of one description becomes oil of a different description as a result of approved mixing in a pipeline with other oil which has been charged with duty.

new pence One hundredth of a pound from when the UK adopted decimal currency in 1971. The word "new" was dropped in 1982.

new pensioner Person who becomes a member of a pension payroll. The PAYE implications are set out in PAYE regulations SI 2003 No 2682 from reg 54.

new product In relation to alcoholic liquor duty, wine or made-wine that is diluted after the post-duty point as a means of reducing total excise duty payable. This is outlawed from 1 April 2020 by Alcoholic Liquor Duties Act 1979 s55ZA as inserted by FA 2020 s81.

new sol Currency of Peru.

newspaper Publication issued at least once a week in a continuous series under the same title (VATA 1994 Sch 8 Group 3). They must contain a substantial amount of news and be national, international or local. It is zero-rated for VAT. Guidance is given in VAT Notice 701/10.

newspaper advertisements These were zero-rated for VAT before 1 May 1985. They are now standard-rated.

newspaper publishing company In relation to inheritance tax and newspaper trusts, the term "means a company whose business consists wholly or mainly in the publication of newspapers in the United Kingdom" (Inheritance Tax Act 1984 s87(3)).

New Taiwan dollar Currency of Taiwan.

newton Unit of force.

New Zealand Country in Pacific Ocean. Its currency is the New Zealand dollar of 100 cents. The UK has a double taxation convention of 2003 amended by a protocol of 2007.

ngultrum Unit of currency in Bhutan, comprising 100 chetrum. Indian currency is also legal tender in Bhutan.

ngwee One hundredth of a kwacha, currency of Zambia.

Nicaragua South American country. Its currency is the córdoba of 100 centavos. The UK has no double taxation treaty. The country is subject to UK sanctions, as are designated persons of the country.

niche Among other meanings, a form of memorial to the dead. The tax provisions are given in ITTOIA 2005 from s172ZA, with effect from 1 March 2012.

Nicotania Genus of tobacco plants. Tobacco duty is payable on the cured leaves of any plant in this genus, and on any product designed to imitate such leaves.

Niger African landlocked country, pronounced "knee-share" where the SH is like the S in treasure. Its currency is the CFA franc of 100 centimes. The UK has no double taxation treaty.

Nigeria African country. Its currency is the naira of 100 kobo. The UK has a double taxation convention of 1987.

night For Customs purposes, the period between 11pm and 5am (CEMA 1979 s1(1)).

Nijjar conditions Ruling by Judge Jonathan Richards in the case *Nijjar v HMRC [2017]* which set out the conditions for upholding a penalty for not paying an accelerated payment notice (APN). The four conditions are:

- the APN was served on the taxpayer
- it was issued in accordance with FA 2014 s219(2)
- payment of the APN had not been made by the date given in TMA s59C
- the penalty has been correctly calculated.

Nikkei Most widely used Japanese share index as published in its newspaper *Nihon Keizai Shimbun* since 7 September 1950. It measures Japanese share prices of the 225 leading companies.

nil cash benefit Term used in ITEPA 2003 s151 when an employee is not assessed to income tax on the value of road fuel provided for a company car because either:

- the car may only be used for business, or
- the employee is required to refund the cost of fuel used for private journeys.

nil rate band Slice of estate on which inheritance tax is charged at 0% (IHTA 1984 Sch 1). The band has been £325,000 since 2009.

This band may be increased by a transferable nil rate band from a spouse or by the residence nil rate band (IHTA 1984 s8A-8C). This applies where the second death occurs on or after 9 October 2007.

From 6 April 2017, there is also a residence nil rate band (IHTA 1984 s8D-8M) where a property, or proceeds of a property, pass to the child or other descendant of the deceased. This allowance was phased in over four years, reaching £175,000 in 2020/21. With the transferable nil rate band, it is now possible for £1 million to be taxed at 0%.

It should be noted that the nil rate band band is taxed at 0% and is not exempt from the tax. This is not a semantic difference, as it has implications for reporting and can have for capital gains tax.

The nil rate band should be indexed in line with the consumer prices index unless Parliament decides otherwise (IHTA 1984 s8). Parliament has decided otherwise every year since 2009.

Rates of inheritance tax are given in section 3 of this dictionary.

nil rate band trust Trust commonly used before 2008 to utilise the nil rate band that would otherwise be lost when one spouse died, leaving his or her estate to the surviving spouse. The amount of estate above the nil rate band would be transferred to a trust, using the nil rate band. The trust was created by the will.

The use of these trusts became largely redundant when the transferable nil rate band was introduced in 2008 under FA 2008 s10 and Sch 4. In some cases, the introduction of this transfer meant that the trust could be disadvantageous.

There is still a role for such trusts. For example, they can be used when a widow or widower remarries. The trust will protect the nil rate band of the previous spouse which would otherwise be lost.

nil return Any return which reports an amount of zero for the period.

nil tax code For PAYE, a code that indicates that no tax is to be deducted or refunded in the current or future pay period. The code operates on a non-cumulative basis unless HMRC specifically directs otherwise (PAYE Regulations SI 2003 No 2682 reg 33). Its definition is a special code "which requires no deduction of tax" (ibid reg 7(3)(c)). The code is NT.

NI rate activity In relation to capital allowances in Northern Ireland, this term is defined in CAA 2001 s6C.

nitrogylcerine Substance included in the list of explosives (Explosives Act 1875 s3(1)) for which there are special Customs provisions.

no-counteraction notice Notice issued by HMRC under ITA 2007 s698A stating that no counteraction is required in relation to anti-avoidance provisions relating to transactions in securities, as set out in ITA 2007 Part 13 Chapter 1, as amended by FA 2016 s34.

node For blockchain, a node is a computer that is participating in a blockchain, by posting transactions and maintaining a copy of the ledger. Nodes may or may not be data miners.

no effective loss rule The rule that shareholders in a company may not bring an action for damages merely because the company in which they hold shares has suffered damage. The shareholders cannot claim for a reduction in the market value of their shares, nor for a lower rate of dividend receipts. The company itself may have a claim for damages, but the shareholders cannot enforce this nor take action on their own behalf. In other words, a shareholder cannot sue for a reduction in the value of his or her shares that merely reflects the loss suffered by the company.

The legal principles were set out in the case *Johnson v Gore Wood [2002] 2 AC 1.*

In the case *Marex Financial Ltd v Sevilleja [2020] SC. The Times 22 July 2020,* the Supreme Court held that the courts had tended to widen the scope of the rule too much. It held that a creditor could bring an action when a director asset-stripped the company to prevent a judgment being paid. The creditor could bring such an action, even though the liquidator could have done.

no gain/no loss basis For capital gains tax, a disposal that is regarded as creating neither a gain nor a loss.

no hours rule Element of universal credit in that the claimant is restricted to the number of hours worked in a week to qualify for a particular benefit. Universal credit is paid for any number of hours worked.

no linked loans requirement Requirement under tax law that an investor must not have a linked loan with a company in whose shares he or she wishes to claim EIS relief (ITA 2007 s164).

nolle prosequi Acknowledgment of undertaking by the prosecution not to proceed with a case.

nominal ledger In bookkeeping, the record where debit and credit balances are recorded against various accounts, and from which a trial balance can be extracted.

nominal share capital Total amount of share capital that a company is allowed to issue.

nominal trust fund Trust that contains a nominal sum (often £10) solely for the purpose of establishing the trust. This is done in readiness for receiving the substantive trust fund, such as to receive inherited funds. Such trusts are often set up to be referred to in a will when the substantive funds are transmitted on death.

nominal value Amount stated on a share certificate as the value of the share when first issued. The value which must be ascribed to each share of a UK company (CA 2006 s542(1)).

nominated partner Another term for representative partner. It is the member of a partnership who is responsible for submitting details of the partnership's profits and capital gains to the tax authorities.

In the context of digital reporting and record-keeping, a nominated partner "is a partner nominated for the purposes of this Schedule –

(a) by the partners, or

(b) by the Commissioners"

(TMA 1970 Sch A1 para 5(2) as inserted by Finance (No 2) Act 2017 s60(2)).

nominee shareholder Person listed as a shareholder but who in reality holds them for the benefit of another. HMRC may ask a shareholder whether he or she is the beneficial owner or a nominee (TMA 1970 s26).

non-active partner Member of a partnership who plays no part in its day-to-day management, sometimes called a sleeping partner. There are restrictions on how much of the partnership loss such a partner may claim against taxable income (ITA 2007 s103B).

non-advanced education Education at a level below the highest level.

The term is relevant for claiming social security benefits. For example, child benefit may be claimable for a young person in non-advanced education but is not claimable for a young person in advanced education.

Non-advanced education includes GCSEs, A-levels and AS levels, NVQ level 3 and below, National Diploma or Ordinary National Diploma, and Scottish equivalents.

non-advisor One of the tests that a tax avoidance scheme designer must meet not to be regarded as a promoter of the scheme.

no names basis Approach to HMRC to ascertain the tax position on a matter without disclosing the name of the taxpayer.

In some cases, such as the Liechtenstein Disclosure Facility, this is permitted. However, payment of tax, submission of returns and disclosure of underpayments always require disclosure of taxpayer's identity.

non-business activity Activity that is not predominantly concerned with making a supply for consideration and so is outside the scope of VAT. Examples given in VAT Notice 700 include the provision of free information; maintaining parks and similar; and publicising political or religious views.

non-business day A Saturday, Sunday or public holiday (Bills of Exchange Act 1882 s192). Public holidays are as set out in Financial Dealings Act 1971.

non-cancellable period Period in which a lease may only be determined by the occurrence of a remote contingency or by an additional payment that appears unlikely to be paid at the inception of the lease (CAA2001 s70YF4(1)).

non-commercial society Term used in Gambling Act 2005 s19 to describe a charity, sports or arts body or other non-commercial body. This description exempts the body from some of the requirements of the Act, which allows churches and charities to run raffles and tombolas, provided there is no private gain.

non-contributory Description of a social security benefit that does not depend on having sufficient national insurance contributions.

non-controlling interest Another term for minority interest.

"The equity in a subsidiary not attributable, directly or indirectly, to a parent" (FRS 102 glossary).

Non-controlling interest is now the favoured term. The accounting treatment is set out in FRS 102 sections 9.20 to 9.22.

non-cooperating country or territory Country or territory listed by the Financial Action Task Force as either unable or unwilling to co-operate in addressing problems of money laundering or terrorism funding. In 2000 and 2001, there were 23 such territories. Since 2006, there are none.

non-cooperation route Decision of a taxpayer who is invited to settle his or her tax affairs under the contractual disclosure facility. This broadly means that the taxpayer will pay a civil penalty for any tax offence and avoid criminal charges. A taxpayer who does not agree within 60 days is considered to have rejected the offer which means HMRC may investigate the taxpayer under criminal powers (COP 9 para 2.8).

non-corporate distribution rate (NCDR) Charge imposed on companies between 1 April 2004 and 31 March 2008 who paid corporation tax at the starting rate of zero, and paid dividends.

The NCDR was set at 19%. This meant that companies only enjoyed the benefit of the zero starting rate on retained profit.

non-cumulative basis Method of operating PAYE as if every pay period were the first in the tax year. It is an exception to the normal cumulative rule. It may only be used when specifically required by regulations or directed by HMRC (PAYE Regulations SI 2003 No 2682 reg 26).

non-current assets Any asset that does not meet the definition of a current asset. Also described as fixed assets.

"Assets of the entity which –

(a) it does not expect to realise, or intend to sell or consumer, in its normal operating cycle;
(b) it does not hold primarily for the purpose of trading;
(c) it does not expect to realise within 12 months of the reporting period;
(d) are cash or cash equivalents restricted from being exchanged or used to settle a liability for at least 12 months after the reporting period"

(FRS 102 glossary).

The term "non-current assets" is preferred by international accounting standards.

non-current liabilities Any liability that does not meet the definition of a current liability. Also described as long-term liabilities.

"Liabilities of the entity which are not current liabilities" (FRS 102 glossary).

The term "non-current liabilities" is preferred by international accounting standards.

non-cumulative preference share Preference share where any interest not paid in one year is lost. The interest is not added to the amount payable in any future year.

non declarable transaction Transaction where there is no obligation to pay stamp duty or to notify HMRC. Details are given in FA 2003 Sch 11.

non-deferred annuity "Means an annuity –

(a) which is not granted under a contract for a deferred annuity, and

(b) which is granted in the ordinary course of a business of granting annuities on the life of a person"

(TCGA1992 s204(9)).

non-domiciled spouse Husband, wife or civil partner who does not have a UK domicile. For inheritance tax, the spousal exemption for such a spouse is limited. From April 2012, the limit is of the same amount as the nil rate band. Previously the limit was £55,000 from 1982.

non est Contraction of non est inventus, Latin for "not to be found". The term means that the sheriff cannot find the person.

non-established taxable person Person who is registered for VAT in the UK but who is not UK-resident. From 1 January 2002, HMRC has the right to require such a person to appoint a representative.

non-food additives Term used in VAT notice 701/14 for such products as "bicarbonate of soda, saltpetre and other single chemicals for use in brining or other processing of meats or fish". They are standard-rated for VAT.

non-intimate sample "Means –

(a) a sample of hair other than pubic hair;

(b) a sample taken from a nail or from under a nail;

(c) a swab taken from any part of a person's body other than part from which a swab taken would be an intimate sample;

(d) saliva;

(e) a skin impression"

(Police and Criminal Evidence Act 1984 s65 as amended).

non-life policy of insurance "Means –

(a) a contract made in the course of a capital redemption business, within the meaning of Chapter 1 of Part 12 of the Taxes Act, and

(b) any policy of insurance which is not a policy of insurance on the life of any person"

(TCGA1992 s204(10)).

non-money earnings Term used in ITEPA 2003 s19 to mean benefits in kind and similar reward for employment other than money earnings.

non-natural person Term used for annual tax on enveloped dwellings to mean a legal person who is not a human person. Examples include companies and trusts.

non-operational In relation to the remittance basis, this term is given a specific meaning for a target company in ITA 2007 s809VH(6).

non-participating funds Term used in ICTA 1988 s432C in relation to determining the tax liability of life assurance companies.

non-primary purpose trading When a charity decides "to use trading activities as a way of raising money" such as selling goods in a shop or through a catalogue (VAT notice 701/1). Such activities must be conducted through a subsidiary trading company.

non-priority order Attachment of earnings order issued under Attachment of Earnings Act 1971 for sums owed other than unpaid fines and child maintenance. These are now rare.

The employer must deduct a sum stated from each payslip and pay it to the court which issued the notice. A non-priority order must only be deducted when all priority orders have been dealt with.

non-profit company In relation to taxation of insurance companies, means "a company carrying on long-term business where, at the end of the period:

(a) none of the liabilities of that business, or

(b) none but an insignificant proportion of those liabilities"

(ICTA 1988 s431(2)).

non-profit making Description of an entity that is established for a purpose other than trading or investing. In terms of taxing directors, a definition is given in ITEPA 2003 s223(8). For VAT, the matter is discussed in VAT Notice 701/5.

non-resident Person who is not regarded as UK-resident for tax purposes (ITA 2007 from s810). This is now determined by the statutory residence test which is summarised in section 3 of this dictionary. In general terms. a non-resident is liable only to UK tax on income earned in the UK or remitted to the UK. If this results in double taxation, the non-resident may be able to claim double taxation relief.

non-resident company Company that is not regarded as UK resident. Its liability for corporation tax is set out in CTA 2009 from s19.

non-resident corporate landlord Non-resident company or other corporate body that owns property in the UK.

This was a common way to avoid inheritance tax until the law was changed in 2017. From April 2019, such landlords are liable to pay income tax. From April 2020, they pay corporation tax. Such a landlord must be registered with HMRC but need not be registered at Companies House.

non-resident group Group of companies where either no company is UK-resident, or where at least two companies are not UK-resident (TCGA 1992 s14(4)).

non-residential pitch In the context of the VAT exemption for land in seasonal caravan accommodation "means a pitch which –
(a) is provided for less than a year, or
(b) is provided for a year or more and is subject to an occupation restriction and which is not intended to be used as the occupant's principal place of residence during the period of occupancy"
(Value Added Tax 1994 Sch 9 Group 1 Note (14A) as inserted by Value Added Tax (Land Exemption Order) SI 2012 No 58 with effect from 1 March 2012).

non-resident insurance company Insurance company that is not resident in the UK (SI 2003 No 2715 reg 2).

non-resident parent Parent who does not live with a child, particularly in relation to someone who pays maintenance for the child.

non-resident period Period for which a migrating settlement was not UK resident (TCGA1992 s89).

non-savings, non dividend (NSND) Category of income. Such income remains subject to UK rates of income tax when Scottish rate of income tax is introduced from April 2016.

non-smoking material (NSM) Material developed to imitate smoking tobacco but without nicotine and other harmful materials. It was still subject to tobacco duty. NSM products were manufactured in June 1977, but the imposition of duty meant that they did not achieve their purpose. They were withdrawn from sale a few months later and all stocks incinerated.

non-standard accessory In the context of company cars for tax purposes, any accessory which is not a standard accessory (ITEPA 2003 s125(4)).

non-tariff barrier Barrier to international trade other than Customs duty or any form of ban or legal restriction. Examples include excessive documentation and requirements to pay in an expensive currency.

non-trade business Business activity that is not within the scope of a trade. The term is specifically used in ITTOIA 2005s609 in relation to exploitation of film rights.

non-traded company "Is a company none of whose shares were, at any time during the confirmation period concerned, shares admitted to trading on a relevant market or on any other market which is outside the United Kingdom" (CA 2006 s853F(2)).

non-trading deficit Corporation tax provisions are given in CTA 2009 from s456.

non-trading income Interest paid by a company on loans that do not fund the business. Such interest is not tax-deductible under the loan relationship rules of CTA 2009 Part 5.

non-UK profits Term used in CTA 2010 s108 in relation to restrictions on loss relief.

non-UK registered scheme In relation to the overseas transfer charge for pensions, "means a registered pension scheme established in a country or territory outside the United Kingdom" (FA 2004 s242A as inserted by FA 2017 Sch 4 para 14).

non-UK resident "Means a person who is not resident in the United Kingdom" (TCGA1992 s271D(1) and s271J(1)).

non-UK tax In relation to corporation tax and group relief, "means a tax chargeable under the law of a territory outside the United Kingdom which –

(a) is charged on income and corresponds to United Kingdom income tax, or

(b) is charged on income or chargeable gains or both and corresponds to United Kingdom corporation tax"

(CTA 2010 s187).

no offset principle Accounting concept that assets and liabilities must be shown separately in the accounts and not be netted off.

no possibilities test Requirement that a company may only obtain UK tax relief for overseas losses when there is no possibility of tax relief being claimed overseas. This follows litigation brought by Marks and Spencer in 2005. HMRC issued a press release setting out its views on 22 May 2013.

no pre-arranged exits requirement Requirement under ITA 2007 s177 that enterprise investment scheme relief against income tax depends on the investor not having pre-arranged an exit, or for the disposal of his shares at the time of acquiring them.

no prize machine Gaming machine which provides no opportunity to win a prize (Gambling Act 2005 s248). For these purposes, a free replay is not regarded as a prize.

no recourse The condition that a person whose migration status is under query must have "no recourse to public funds". The legislation is Immigration Act 1971 and subordinate regulations.

In practice, this means that they cannot claim social security benefits. In the case *R v Hilton. [2020] SC. The Times 13 July 2020,* it was held that no recourse was illegal where it imminently leads to destitution.

no reflective loss rule Rule under company law that a shareholder cannot bring an action against the company or directors for a loss. On 15 July 2020, the Supreme Court ruled that a claim could be brought by creditors in the case *Marox Financial Ltd v Sevilleja [2020] SC. The Times 22 July 2020.*

Norfolk reed Plant that is standard-rated. VAT Notice 701/38 specifically excludes this from zero-rating as it is grown for thatching and not for food.

normal and necessary Term used in VAT notice 700 in relation to packaging.

Normal and necessary packaging is regarded as part of the packaged product.

normal car For income tax on employment income, the car normally provided to an employee, as against a replacement car (ITEPA 2003 s145(1)).

normal commercial loan For corporation tax, this term is used in relation to the taxation of distributions. It is defined in CTA 2010 s162. Such a loan must be for new consideration and must meet four conditions.

normal employee costs Expenses normally paid to an employee, such as remuneration, sick pay, holiday pay and redundancy pay.

Such expenses are tax deductible even when paid in circumstances that would otherwise make them non-deductible, such as on cessation of business. This matter is discussed in HMRC Manual at BIM38315.

normal employment period In relation to statutory parental bereavement pay "is the requirement that any period of paid parental bereavement leave is to be treated as if it were a period throughout which the member in question works normally and receives the remuneration likely to be paid for doing so" (Social Security Act 1989 s5D(4) as inserted by Parental Bereavement (Leave and Pay) Act 2018 Sch para 7).

normal expenditure out of income For inheritance tax, such expenditure is excluded when determining tax liability (Inheritance Tax Act 1984 s21). So if a father provides an allowance for a child at university, that is not regarded as a taxable gift should the father die within seven years.

normal minimum pension age This is age 50 for the period before 6 April 2010; and age 55 on or after 6 April 2010.

normal rent "That amount is the amount that L [the lessor] would, apart from this Part, bring into account as rent from the lease that arises to L in that period of account for the purpose of determining L's liability to income tax for the related tax year or years" (ITA 2007 s614AA(2)). A similar definition appears in CTA 2009 s896.

normal rental excess For finance leases, this term is defined in ITA 2007 s614BJ(1).
In relation to anti-avoidance provisions about leases, the term is defined in CTA 2009 s909(1).

normal selling price In relation to VAT on investment gold coins, the price that may be commanded for a particular coin (VAT notice 701/12A).
Provided that coins of that kind are sold for no more than 180% of their gold value, a specific coin may still be regarded as an investment coin even if sold for more because of a special factor for a particular coin, such as being from a rare year.

normal writing-down allowance Term used in CAA 2001 s126 to means the writing down allowance that applies when there are no restrictions on the rate because of overseas leasing.

Northern Ireland Northern area of Ireland which is part of the UK (Government of Ireland Act 1920). Generally tax and social security laws there are the same, though this is sometimes given effect by separate legislation. Corporation Tax (Northern Ireland) Act 2015 allows Northern Ireland to charge a different rate of corporation tax. The expectation is that this will reduce the rate to 12½%, the same as the Republic. There are provisions in FA 2015 to apportion corporation tax between UK and Northern Ireland rates.
VAT is refunded to Northern Ireland under VATA 1994 s99.
As Northern Ireland adjoins another state, there are special Customs provision in CEMA 1979 s26 and s68B. The post-Brexit position from 2021 is not yet clear.
Northern Ireland does not charge council tax but uses a system of rates.
Air passenger duty is devolved to Northern Ireland where it has been set at zero.

Northern Ireland has its own devolved Assembly that meets at Stormont. The Assembly was suspended for about three years until 11 January 2020.

From 1 January 2021, Northern Ireland is still governed by some EU rules (European Union (Withdrawal Agreement) Act 2020 ss21-24). There are new procedures for goods passing between Northern Ireland and Great Britain.

Residents of Northern Ireland are entitled to an Irish passport which means they retain freedom of movement within the EU.

Northern Ireland additional deduction In relation to film tax relief for corporation tax in Northern Ireland, this term is defined in CTA 2010 s357RA.

For television tax relief, the term is defined in CTA 2010 s357SA.

For video games tax relief, the term is defined in CTA 2010 s357TA. For theatrical productions, the term is defined in CTA 2010 s357UA.

Northern Ireland Assembly Devolved legislature of **Northern Ireland.** It was formed in 1998, but its powers were subsequently suspended several times. The Assembly appoints the **Northern Ireland Executive.** It has 108 members known as **Members of the Legislative Assembly (MLAs).** The Assembly ceased to function for three years until it was restored on 11 January 2020.

Northern Ireland authority In relation to apprenticeships, "means –

(a) a Northern Ireland department, and

(b) any body or other person that is prescribed, or of a prescribed description"

(Apprenticeships, Skills, Children and Learning Act 2009 s40B(3) as inserted by Enterprise Act 2016 s26).

Northern Ireland banknotes Banknotes issued by banks in Northern Ireland (Currency and Bank Notes Act 1928).

Strictly speaking, these notes are not legal tender anywhere, not even in Northern Ireland, but they are widely accepted as currency and may be paid into UK banks.

Notes are issued by:

- Bank of Ireland from 1929, including National Bank from 1929 to 1959
- Danske Bank from 2013, and previously Northern Bank from 1929 to 2012
- First Trust Bank from 1994, previously Allied Irish Banks 1982 to 1993, and Provincial Bank of Ireland from 1929 to 1982
- Ulster Bank from 1929.

Notes are issued for £5, £10, £20, £50 and £100. By agreement, all banks use the same colours for different denominations.

Northern Ireland bank notes were subject to stamp duty until 1 January 1992.

Northern Ireland Contributions and Benefits Act "Means Social Security Contributions and Benefits (Northern Ireland) Act 1992" (Social Security Administration Act 1992 s176(5)).

Northern Ireland Department In relation to co-operation with HMRC and the Department of Work and Pensions in social security fraud, "means any of the following –

(a) the Department for Social Development;

(b) the Department of Finance and Personnel;

(c) the Department for Employment and Learning."
(WRA 2012 s127(7)).

Northern Ireland element In relation to corporation tax, this term is defined in CTA 2010 s357OP.

Northern Ireland employer In relation to corporation tax, this term is defined in CTA 2010 s357KD.

Northern Ireland Executive The executive part of the Northern Ireland Assembly, established under Northern Ireland Act 1998. It comprises a First Minister and other departmental ministers.

Northern Ireland expenditure In relation to corporation tax relief for research and development "means expenditure incurred in a trade to the extent that the expenditure forms part of the Northern Ireland profits or Northern Ireland losses of the trade" (CTA 2010 s357P(2)(a)).

Northern Ireland firm In relation to corporation tax, the term is defined in CTA 2010 s357WA. For capital allowances, the term is defined in CAA 2001 s6B.

Northern Ireland friendly society "Means a friendly society, not being a collecting society, which is registered in Northern Ireland for purposes corresponding to the Friendly Societies Act 1974" (SI 1977 No 1143, as amended).

Northern Ireland intangibles credits In relation to corporation tax, this term is defined in CTA 2010 s357OP.

Northern Ireland intangibles debits In relation to corporation tax, this term is defined in CTA 2010 s357OP.

Northern Ireland legislation This comprises:

(i) Acts of the Parliament of Ireland;
(ii) Acts of the Parliament of Northern Ireland;
(iii) Orders in Council under section 1(1) of the Northern Ireland (Temporary Provisions) Act 1972;
(iv) Measures of the Northern Ireland Assembly established under section 1 of the Northern Ireland Assembly Act 1973;
(v) Orders in Council under Schedule 1 to the Northern Ireland Act 1974;
(vi) Acts of the Northern Ireland Assembly; and
(vii) Orders in Council under section 85 of the Northern Ireland Act 1998.

(Interpretation Act 1978 s24(5)).

Northern Ireland long haul rates of duty Rates of air passenger duty from Northern Ireland, as set out in FA 1994 s30A.

Northern Ireland SME company For the purposes of capital allowance in Northern Ireland, this term is defined in CAA 2001 s6A.

Northern Ireland supplementary deduction In relation to film tax relief in Northern Ireland, this term is defined in CTA 2010 s357RC.
For television tax relief, the term is defined in CTA 2010 s357SA.
For video games tax relief, the term is defined in CTA 2010 s357TB.
For theatrical productions, the term is defined in CTA 2010 s357UB.

Northern Ireland workforce conditions In relation to corporation tax, these are defined in CTA 2010 s357KE.

Northern Rock British bank that failed in 2007, having converted from a building society in 1997. It led to the first run on a British bank for more than 150 years. It was bailed out by the government. The tax consequences are set out in SI 2009 No 3227.

North Korea Generally used name for the Democratic People's Republic of Korea.

Norway European country that is not in the European Union but is in EFTA. Its currency is the krone of 100 ore. The UK has a double taxation convention of 2013.

no-show payment Payment made for a supply of goods or services which the payer does not take up.

From March 2019, this is treated as a supply for VAT purposes, as the supplier had made the supply. This means that VAT is chargeable at the appropriate rate for the goods or serviced.

Previously a no-show was regarded as not a supply and therefore outside the scope of VAT.

no tax avoidance requirement Requirement that entitlement to a tax relief depends on there being a genuine commercial reason other than tax avoidance. This requirement is set out in ITA 2007 s165 for EIS relief.

notary public Lawyer who has authority to witness documents and spoken statements, usually for a fee. Most solicitors are notaries public.

notch Term used for the point in a scale where an increase leads to a much higher rate of tax under the slab basis. This applied to stamp duty land tax before 2014. It also applied to class 1 national insurance in the 1980s.

It was also used in Pakistan for employment income, leading to a situation where an increase in gross pay led to a reduction in net pay.

The notch formula is:

$$P = T(H - L)/(1 - H)$$

where P is the additional pay above the threshold needed to compensate for the higher rate of tax, T is the threshold, L is the rate of tax below the threshold, and H is the rate of tax above the threshold. Rates of tax must be expressed as a decimal.

notes to the accounts Additional information in either narrative or numerical form to a set of accounts. These are usually printed in sequentially numbered sections, some of which are cross-referenced to the main financial statements. For all purposes, the notes are regarded as part of the accounts (CA 2006 s47(2)). The accounting requirements are detailed in FRS 102 section 8.

not guilty by insanity Verdict that may be given under the unrepealed Trial of Lunatics Act 1883 s2.

notice case When an employment ends by the employer or employee giving notice to the other (ITEPA 2003 s402E(3)). This applies regardless of whether the notice is more or less than the statutory or contractual minimum. A termination payment is subject to tax and national insurance regardless of notice periods or which party gave notice.

notice of appeal Notice issued by one party stating that he intends to appeal against a decision by the other party.

In particular, the term is used when a taxpayer contests a tax assessment or a tax code. The procedure is given in TMA 1970 s31A. The main conditions of such a notice is that it must be in writing and sent within 30 days to the HMRC officer who issued the contested assessment or code.

notice of coding Notice which informs a person of a code that has been issued. The term often applies to the P2 form from HMRC advising an employee of a tax code.

notice of correction Document sent to an individual or trust when HMRC has corrected "obvious errors or omissions" in a personal return or trustee's return. The procedure is set out in TMA 1970 s9ZB.

The notice has the effect of amending the tax return as stated unless the taxpayer sends a notice of rejection within 30 days.

notice of enquiry Document sent by HMRC to a taxpayer of an intention to enquire into an aspect of a tax return.

notice of objection In relation to HRMC's powers to seize funds from a taxpayer's bank account without needing the authority of any court, a notice given by the taxpayer or other interested party to HMRC objecting to the seizure on one of the permitted grounds (Finance (No 2) Act 2015 Sch 8 para 10).

Notice of Vehicle Arrivals (NOVA) Customs scheme introduced in April 2013 for new and used vehicles brought into the UK. It requires the vehicle to be notified to HMRC within 14 days.

notice period Amount of time an employer or employee must give the other to end an employment. This is stated in the contract of employment, though statutory minimum periods of notice are set out in Employment Rights Act 1996 s86.

notifiable contribution arrangements Arrangements designed "to enable... any person to obtain an advantage in relation to a [national insurance] contribution" (Social Security Administration Act 1992 s132A(3)).

Such arrangements must be disclosed to HMRC under SI 2007 No 785 as amended.

notification obligation Duty to notify HMRC of a matter relating to VAT where non-compliance leads to a penalty under Value Added Tax 1994 s77(4C).

notification of senior accounting officer details "Formal provision of SAO details to HMRC by a qualifying company" (Inspector's Manual at SAOG 24000). Details of the provision are given at SAOG 13000.

notified sum Amount that a bank has taken from a taxpayer's bank account and passed to HMRC under a hold notice. The bank is obliged to notify the customer of the amount. (Finance (No 2) Act 2015 Sch 8 para 7(8)).

notional benefit Benefit where the amount is deemed rather than calculated. An example is the taxable benefit of a company car.

notional land transaction Concept used in connection with pre-completion transactions and SDLT. The concept is set out in FA 2013 Sch 39 para 5.

notional loan Term used in relation to the taxation of certain employment-related securities (ITEPA 2003 s446S).

notional marketing royalty (NMR) Term used in relation to taxation of intellectual property. It is defined in Corporation Tax 2010 s357BKA as inserted by FA 2016 s64(3).

notional PAYE amount Term used in relation to disguised remuneration (ITEPA 2003 s554H(9)).

notional payment For national insurance, payment that an employee is treated as having made when earnings exceed the lower earnings limit but where no national insurance has actually been paid because the earnings threshold has not been reached (Social Security Contributions and Benefits Act 1992 s6A).

For income tax on earnings, the term means a sum regarded as pay though not provided directly by the employer (ITEPA 2003 s222).

The PAYE provisions are given in PAYE regulations SI 2003 No 2682 from reg 62.

notional PE profits Term used in relation to diverted profits tax and defined in FA 2015 s88(5).The definition is amended by FA 2016 s43(3).

notional price Term used to determine the value of a company car when there is no readily available list price. The procedure is broadly to use the list price of an equivalent car. (ITEPA 2003 s124(1)).

In relation to priority share allocations to employees, the term is defined in ITEPA 2003 s545(5).

notional relief In relation to an anti-avoidance provision on R&D credits, this term is defined in CTA 2009 s1118. This definition is amended by FA 2016 s48(3).

notional remitted amount In relation to the remittance basis, this term is given a specific meaning in ITA 2007 s809Z5.

notional replacement cost Method of stock valuation that is generally not accepted for tax purposes *(BSC Footwear Ltd v Ridgeway [1971] 47TC495).* The matter is discussed in HMRC Manual at BIM33125.

notional royalty For patent box, this term is defined in Corporation Tax 2010 s357BHA.

notional royalty election Term used in relation to taxation of intellectual property. Details are given in Corporation Tax 2010 s357BNA.

notional value Amount for which a business may claim a capital allowance for plant and machinery it has produced itself (CAA 2001 s13(2)). The value is the market value of buying an equivalent asset.

not proven In Scots law, a verdict that a case has been neither proved nor disproved.

novation Agreement by which the two parties to a contract agree that one of them shall be replaced by a new party. So a novation would allow A and B both to agree that a contract between them may become a contract between A and C.

For leases, there are some tax provisions set out in CAA 2001 s70W.

novelist An artist, sculptor, novelist, author, composer or other creator of art may average profits over three years under certain conditions (ITTOIA 2005s221).

nuclear site Such a site does not come within the scope of contaminated land. It is therefore excluded from the scope of tax relief for contaminated land under CTA 2009 s1145B.

nude contract A contract where there is no consideration.
Unless the contract was made under seal, a nude contract cannot be enforced.

nudge letter Letter from HMRC designed to prompt action, such as to submit or check a tax return. The letter does not necessarily indicate that anything is wrong with the taxpayer's affairs, nor that the taxpayer is under investigation.

numbercard Plastic card that was issued before 2011 to tell someone their national insurance number. This is now done by letter.

number of employees requirement Condition which must be satisfied by a company for investment in it to qualify for EIS relief. The requirement is basically that the company must not have more than 250 employees (50 before 6 April 2012) (ITA 2007 s186A). The same provision applies to VCT relief (ITA 2007 s297A).
The number is increased to 500 employees for knowledge-intensive company from 1 April 2016.

number plate Combination of numbers and letters that are unique to each motor vehicle. They must usually be displayed at the front and back in accordance with regulations. Number plates were introduced in 1904. The number plate may indicate the age of the vehicle as explained under Number Plates in section 3 of this dictionary.

Numismatism Collection or study of coins.

nuncupative will Will made without writing. Such a will is valid if made by a serving member of the armed forces (Wills Act 1837 s11; Wills (Soldiers and Sailors) Act 1918).

nuptial agreement Agreement between the parties to a marriage or civil partnership. The most common form is the prenuptial agreement which sets out how assets will be divided should the marriage fail. A postnuptial agreement is a similar agreement between partners who are already married. The Supreme Court held in *Radmacher v Granatino [2010] UKSC 42*, that the court should give weight to a nuptial agreement. Subsequent cases have made clear that the agreement must be fair.

nursery ground In relation to agricultural use, such ground is exempt from non-domestic rates from 1 April 2015 in England, and from 1 April 2017 in Wales. This law is given in Local Government FA 1988 Sch 5 para 39c) as inserted by Non-Domestic Rating (Nursery Grounds) Act 2018 s1(1).

nursing home This activity is excluded from the tax relief for venture capital trusts by ITA 2007 s309. For this purpose s309(2) defines a nursing home as "any establishment which exists wholly or mainly for the provision of nursing care:
(a) for person suffering from sickness, injury or infirmity, or
(b) for women who are pregnant or have given birth".

Expenses incurred in nursing a taxpayer back to health are generally not tax deductible, according to Inspectors' Manual at BIM37950.

A nursing home is excluded from the scope of enterprise investment scheme (ITA 2007 s198).

nursing shawl This was held not to be a garment, and so did not qualify for VAT zero-rating as children's clothing *(W G Jones & Sons [1974] VTD 117).*

nuts These are zero-rated as food "if raw and unprocessed for human consumption" or if "roasted or salted nuts in their shells, however supplied bulk or retail" (Value Added Tax 1994 Sch 8 Group 1 Excepted Item 5). The matter is further explained in VAT notice 701/14.

oath Declaration in court to tell the truth. It "include[s] affirmation and declaration" (Interpretation Act 1978 Sch 1).

obiter dicta Comments made by a judge which do not settle the case but may provide a persuasive precedent for subsequent cases.

objectivity Requirement for an auditor. It is the state of mind that excludes bias, prejudice and compromise, and gives a fair and impartial consideration to all relevant matters.

obscenity Material that tends to deprave and corrupt (Obscene Publications Act 1959 s1(1)). The material does not have to be distasteful. Customs may seize imported obscene goods if such goods may not be lawfully sold in the UK.

obscuration The extent to which a hydrometer reading of the strength of alcoholic liquor known as spirits is reduced by the presence of sweetening, colouring, or other matter.

obstruction Obstruction of an officer of HMRC without lawful excuse is an offence under Commissioners for Revenue and Customs Act 2005 s31. It may also be an offence under the general criminal law.

obtaining services dishonestly Crime of fraud committed by a person who dishonestly obtains services for himself or another. This applies when services attract a charge, the person knew that or knew that may be so, and deliberately fails to make payment (Fraud Act 2006 s11).

occupancy restriction "Any covenant (for example, agreement or term in a contract), statutory planning consent, site licence or similar permission, the terms of which prevent the person to whom the pitch is provided from occupying it by living in a caravan at all times throughout the period for which the pitch is provided (such as a condition that says 'no caravan shall be lived in during February'). (VAT leaflet 701/20).

The existence of such a restriction means that the provision of a caravan pitch is likely to be standard-rated for VAT rather than exempt. The matter is fully explained in VAT leaflet 701/20.

occupation

(1) Physical possession and control of land.

Under Land Registration Act 1925, the proprietary rights of a person in actual occupation may be an overriding interest that binds a purchaser of registered land unless inquiry is made of that person and the rights are not disclosed. The occupier of a property is liable to pay council tax or business rates. In marriage, occupation established a right over the matrimonial home which may be protected as a land charge (Family Law Act 1996).

(2) How a person earns his or her living. "References to an occupation, in relation to an individual, are references to any activities of a kind undertaken in a profession or vocation, regardless of whether the individual –

(a) is carrying on a profession or vocation on the individual's own account, or

(b) is an employee or office-holder" (ITA 2007 s774).

occupational maternity pay Pay during maternity that derives from a contract of employment or is voluntarily paid by an employer, rather than deriving from statute.

occupational pension scheme (OPS) A pension scheme set up by an employer for employees. It is run by Trustees and usually provides life insurance as well as pension benefits. The pension earned by the employees is usually based on a percentage of final salary or on the amount paid in (money purchase basis). An occupational pension can either be contributory (where members contribute to the fund) or non-contributory, which is entirely paid for by the employer.

A statutory definition is "a pension scheme –

(a) that –

(i) for the purpose of providing benefits to, or in respect of, people with service in employments of a description, or

(ii) for that purpose and also for the purpose of providing benefits to, or in respect of, other people, is established by, or by persons who include, a person to whom subsection (2) applies when the scheme is established or (as the case may be) to whom that subsection would have applied when the scheme was established had that subsection then been in force"

(Pension Schemes Act 1973 s1(1)).

HMRC defines it as "a pension scheme set up by an employer (known as a sponsoring employer) to provide benefits for, or in respect of

- any or all of his own employees
- any or all of the employees of any other employer"

(Inspectors' Manual at RPSM02200040). This mirrors the wording of FA 2004 s150(5).

occupational sick pay Payment during sickness other than statutory sick pay. It derives from the contract of employment or may be paid voluntarily by the employer.

occupier Person who occupies a building but may not own it. Liability for council tax and business rates is with the occupier.

OECD Organization for Economic Co-operation and Development. Body founded in 1961, succeeding a similar body founded in 1948. The UK is a member. Its original purpose was to promote financial policies that discourage war. Its current work includes efforts to prevent international tax avoidance, for which it produced a widely used tax convention in 2010.

OECD model tax convention Document produced by OECD in 2010 and widely used since then (CTA 2010 s357GE(1)).

OECD transfer pricing guidelines "Has the same meaning as 'the transfer pricing guidelines' in section 164 of TIOPA" (Corporation Tax 2010 s357GE(1)).

OEIC Pronounced as "oiks", this stands for Open-Ended Investment Companies. Although not dissimilar to unit trusts and investment trusts, an OEIC is basically a company which can be self-contained or it can form an "umbrella" over a range of individual funds (sometimes referred to as sub-funds). Instead of units, an OEIC issues shares and these can be of different classes – for example, for income accumulation, for income distribution, or classes where income is paid gross or net of lower-rate income tax.

OEIC Regulations Open-Ended Investment Companies (Tax) Regulations SI 1997 No 1154.

oersted Unit of magnetic field strength.

offal For VAT, offal sold for human consumption or for use in animal feeds is zero-rated. Most other offal is standard-rated. Full details are given in VAT notice 701/15.

off-balance-sheet finance An arrangement to keep matching assets and liabilities away from the entity's balance sheet.

offer A step in making a contract. The contract is made when an offer by one party is accepted by the other.

offer document Formal document in which a company offers to buy shares held by another, usually as part of a takeover bid.

Such a document must be in accordance with rules as set out in CA 2006 from s962 and the Takeovers Directive.

The term "offer document" is defined in CA 2006 s953(9) as being a document that complies with Article 6.2 of the Directive.

offer document rules "Rules designated as rules that give effect to Article 6.3 of that [Takeovers] Directive" (CA 2006 s953(9)).

offer period This usually refers to an offer to buy shares for more than market value in a takeover. The term is defined by CA 2006 s971(1) by reference to the Takeover Code.

offertory Collection of money in a church.

offer to the public An offer of shares or other securities for purchase by members of the public (CA 2006 s756).

This is subject to many legal restrictions. In general, such an offer must be by a public company and in accordance with a prospectus.

Office for Budget Responsibility Body established in 2010 to examine and report on the sustainability of public finances (National Audit Act 2011 s3 and Sch 1).

Office for Legal Complaints (OLC) Body corporate established by Legal Services Act 2007 s114.

Office for National Statistics (ONS) Government agency which produces statistics. It was formed in 1966 by a merger of two bodies.

Office for Professional Body Anti-Money Laundering Supervision (OFBAS)

Body announced formed in 2018 to identify and address weaknesses in bodies charged with enforcing money-laundering rules.

Office for Students (OfS) Body established by Higher Education and Research Act 2017 s1. The Act sets out its functions. The Office started on 8 January 2018.

Office for Tackling Injustices (OfTI) Body created by the government on 12 July 2019 to inform and challenge government on addressing disparities between certain groups in society.

office holder Person who holds an office. There are corporation tax provisions in CTA 2009 s969.

Office of Civil Nuclear Security (OCNS) Part of the Health and Safety Executive. One of its functions is to regulate the import of nuclear material.

Office of Financial Sanctions Implementation (OFSI) Body established within the Treasury on 31 March 2016 to "provide a high-quality service to the private sector, working closely with law enforcement to ensure that financial sanctions are properly understood, implemented and enforced" (OFSI website).

Office of the Internal Market (OIM) Body formed under UK Internal Market Act 2020. It monitors the UK internal market following the UK's withdrawal from the EU.

officer In relation to a company, this means a director, manager or secretary (CA 2006 s1173(1)).

In HMRC, it means a person so appointed under Commissioners for Revenue and Customs Act 2005 s2.

Officers of Revenue and Customs Official term for tax officers appointed by the Commissioners for Her Majesty's Revenue and Customs (Commissioners for Revenue and Customs Act 2005 s2).

official agent "Means a person who is not a consul... but is employed on the staff of —

(a) a consulate, or

(b) an official department or agency of a foreign state"

(ITEPA 2003 s301(5)).

official custodian Officer whose function is to act as trustee for charities in circumstances prescribed by Charities Act 2011 s21. The custodian is appointed by the Charity Commission.

official development assistance (ODA) Target of overseas aid to be provided by the UK government. This is set at 0.7% of gross national income under Development (Official Development Assistance Target) Act 2015 s1(1)). In 2020, the government announced it would reduce the figure to 0.5%.

official liquidator Liquidator appointed by a government department when no such appointment is made by the members or creditors (Insolvency Act 1986 s136).

Official Property Holder Person appointed under Audit, Investigations and Community Enterprise) Act 2004 s29 to hold property belonging to a community interest company under the terms of Sch 5 of the Act. The office is a corporation sole.

official rate of interest Rate published by HMRC, usually annually, that is used to determine the taxable benefit of a beneficial loan, accommodation provided to employees, and the charge for a previously owned asset (ITEPA 2003 s181). Rates are given under Beneficial Loans in section 3 of this dictionary.

Official Receiver Government officer who deals with a person who has become bankrupt or an insolvent business (Insolvency Act 1986 ss399-401).

Official Solicitor Person appointed to act for the government in the courts under various enactments, particularly Supreme Court Act 1981 s90.

official statistics Statistics produced by the Office of National Statistics or by another government or government-appointed body (Statistics and Registration Service Act 2007 s6).

off-line For Customs purposes, the onward carriage of a through inter-airport removal or a through transit, by a carrier who is not the inward carrier of the goods.

off-market purchase In company law, term used for when a company buys shares in itself other than from a recognised stock market.
Generally this is prohibited under CA 2006 s694.

off-plan purchase Purchase of a building on the basis of plans, when the building work is not completed (or may not even have started). Such a purchase may qualify for sub-sale relief from stamp duty land tax under the provisions of FA 2013 s195. The implications for annual tax on enveloped dwellings are given in FA 2013 s113.

off-season letting Letting of holiday accommodation outside the normal holiday season. This can have VAT implications for caravan letting, as explained in VAT Notice 701/20.

offset When an asset and liability are netted off to a single figure. Under accounting standards, this should not happen when the figures relate to separate transactions.

offset account Bank account where savings and borrowings are netted off. For a business account, tax relief is usually given on the net figure, as explained in HMRC Manual at BIM45695.

offset method Method set out in accounting standard SSAP20 (now repealed) regarding foreign exchange. The tax implications are discussed in HMRC Manual at BIM39522.

offshore evasion Evasion of tax using offshore facilities. From January 2017, this is subject to a tougher penalty equal to the greater of 100% of the tax involved and £3,000.

Offshore Funds (Tax) Regulations Name of SI 2009 No 3001.

offshore installation Oilrig or similar (ITA 2007 s1001). Travel expenses to and from the mainland are not taxed as a benefit in kind (ITEPA 2003 s305). An offshore installation is specifically excluded from the scope of seafarers' deduction.

offshore matter In relation to tax penalties, the term is defined in FA 2007 Sch 24 para 4A(4).

offshore waters "Means –

(a) the waters comprising the territorial sea of the United Kingdom, and
(b) the sea in any areas for the time being designated under section 1(7) of the Continental Shelf Act 1964"

(Energy Act 2016 s18(1)).

off-shoring Practice of relocating a business function overseas, usually to avoid having to comply with UK laws and regulations.

oil Organic substance that occurs naturally in the earth and can be made from plant material. A definition appears in CTA 2010 s356LA(4) by reference to the Petroleum Act 1988.

There are many tax provisions, including hydrocarbon oil duty and VAT when used as road fuel. Production of oil may be subject to petroleum revenue tax.

Oil used for residential heating may be subject to the 5% reduced rate (VATA 1994 Sch 7A Group 1). This is explained in VAT Notice 701/19. HMRC accepts that a supply of up to 2,300 litres is for domestic used.

Corporation tax provisions for the oil industry are in CTA 2010 s278 and ITTOIA 2005 s225E).

Oil Act Common name for Hydrocarbon Oil Duty 1979.

oil activities Trading activities whose taxation is set out in ITTOIA 2005 from s225ZH.

Oil and Gas Authority Body formed in April 2015 to regulate the oil and gas industries. It has power to impose levies on licence holders.

oil contractor activities For corporation tax purposes, this term is defined in CTA 2010 from s356L.

oil extraction This is considered as a separate trade in its own right for tax purposes (CTA 2010 s272; ITTOIA 2005 s225A).

oil field Area of land or sea from which oil is extracted. Such activities are usually subject to a special rate of corporation tax which is ring-fenced from other trading activities. From 1974, each oil field is treated as a separate trade.

oil field licensee In relation to PAYE for UKCS workers, "means the holder of a licence under Part 1 of the Petroleum Act 1998 in respect of the area in which the duties of the continental shelf worker's employment is performed" (PAYE regulations SI 2003 No 2682 ref 84D).

oil licence Licence to drill for oil. Such a licence cannot give rise to rollover relief (TCGA1992 s193). A licence is excluded from the degrouping charge (CTA 2009 s809). From 29 March 2011, this term includes goodwill and any related intangible asset (CTA 2009 s809(1A).

oil production sharing contract Contract between an oil company and a country (or its representative) where oil is or may be produced. There are some special capital allowance provisions for such contracts as set out in CAA 2001 from s167.

oil-related activities Oil extraction and related activities in the acquisition, enjoyment or exploitation of oil rights (CTA 2010 s274).

oilrig An oilrig or similar installation qualifies for capital allowances as plant and machinery. From 7 August 2000, this includes the cost of preparing the oilrig for use. The relevant provisions are CAA 2001 ss163-164. Transport of workers from the UK mainland to an oilrig is exempt from tax as a benefit in kind under ITEPA 2003 s305.

oil residues "Any waste consisting of, or arising from, oil or a mixture containing oil" (Prevention of Pollution Act 1971 s29(1)).

oil rights The right to extract oil and the rights of interest in the oil (CTA 2010 s273).

oilseed rape Plant that is zero-rated when used as food, usually for animals, but standard-rated for other uses. Guidance is given in VAT Notice 701/38.

Oireachtas Legislature of the Irish Republic.

old annuity contract General annuity contract made before 1 January 1992 (FA 2001 Sch 7 para 16(7)).

old asset Asset that is realised for the purpose of reinvestment (CTA 2009 s754(2)).

old code scheme Superannuation fund approved before 1970 which has not been re-approved under later pension scheme legislation. Such schemes retain their tax advantages, provided no further contributions have been made since 5 April 1980. The matter is discussed in HMRC Manual at RPSM02100020.

old contract costs In relation to fair value accounting for life insurance contracts, the term is defined in CTA 2009 s568(2).

old dwelling Dwelling from which a new dwelling is created. The implications for annual tax on enveloped dwellings is given in FA 2013 s125.

Old Lady of Threadneedle Street Poetic description of the Bank of England. The term dates back to a ballad of 1797, but may have been current before then. The Bank is still based in Threadneedle Street, London.

old pence Term for currency before decimalisation in 1971. There were 240 old pennies to the pound, denoted by the letter d as in 6d.

old Scottish term days The Scottish equivalent to quarter days before 13 June 1991.

old state pension Category A or B retirement pension payable by the state before 6 April 2016 (Pensions Act 2014 s21).

old-style secure tenancy Tenancy that may be provided under Housing Act 1985 s81B.

old vehicles exemption Exemption from vehicle excise duty (road tax) for old vehicles (Vehicle Excise and Registration Act 1994 Sch 2). From 1 April 2016, the exemption applies to vehicles constructed before 1 January 1976.

oligopoly Control similar to monopoly but exercised by a family or a small group of people.

oligopsony When a small number of people control the demand or market for a product or service.

Olin v Scorer Name of a leading tax case whose full citation is *Olin Energy Systems Ltd v Scorer [1982] Ch D, 58 TC 592.* The case held that interest is allowable only if used for the trade for which the loan was taken out. This case is discussed in HMRC Manual at BIM45665.

Because of the appeals, this case is sometimes quoted with the parties reversed.

Oman Arab state. Its currency is the Omani rial of 1,000 biasas. The UK has a double taxation convention of 1998 as amended by a protocol of 2009.

ombudsman An independent official to whom grievances can be aired, free of charge. Ombudsman is a Swedish word meaning citizen's representative. The Insurance Ombudsman Bureau aims to increase confidence in Insurance by offering an independent resource for resolving disputes between insurance companies and their customers. There are other ombudsmen.

Ombudsman for the Board of the Pension Protection Fund Commissioner appointed under Pensions Act 2004 s209 to perform the task of the job title.

ombudsman scheme Scheme which the Office for Legal Complaints must operate (Legal Services Act 2007 s115).

omission Leaving out something or failing to do something which should be done. In law the word action usually includes an omission in failing to act.

omnishambles "A situation that has been comprehensively mishandled". This definition was provided by Oxford English Dictionary when they accepted the word in October 2019. The term was first used for the 2012 Budget, several of whose provisions were promptly reversed.

Omsaetningafgift Danish: value added tax.

Omzetbelasting (OB) Dutch: value added tax.

on all fours Legal expression referring to a situation which is strictly analogous to another. It has been used by HMRC such as in describing the extent to which a previous decision binds them in the future.

on approval Where goods are supplied to a customer on the basis that they may be accepted and paid for, or rejected. VAT is charged on the earlier of when the customer accepts the goods or 12 months after they were supplied (HMRC Brief 5 (2018)). Any delivery charge is considered a separate supply.

One Click Process that allows a business to register at Companies House, and with HMRC for PAYE, corporation tax and self-assessment in a single operation. It was introduced in April 2012.

onerous contract Contract where the unavoidable costs of meeting obligations exceeds the economic benefit derived from it (FRS 102 glossary). A liquidator has the right to disclaim an onerous contract.

one-way exchange effect Term used in relation to exchange gains and losses and derivatives. Corporation tax provisions are given in CTA 2009 s328A, where the term is defined. Financial derivatives provisions are given in CTA 2009 s606A.

ongoing compliance obligations Duties of a taxpayer to be honest in declaring taxable income after previous frauds have been addressed under the Contractual

Disclosure Facility (CDF). Having concluded the civil investigation into a tax fraud, HMRC will usually arrange a subsequent check to ensure that the taxpayer's affairs are now being dealt with honestly. Further details of these obligations are set out in code of practice COP 9 as issued on 19 January 2012.

online financial marketplace "An online marketplace is an 'online financial marketplace' for a relevant accounting period if more than half of the revenues arising to the provider in the accounting period in connection with the online marketplace arise in connection with the provider's facilitation of the trading of financial instruments, commodities or foreign exchange" (FA 2020 s45(2)).

online market place Facility such as eBay or Amazon whereby goods may be purchased online from different suppliers. From 2018, the online market place is jointly and severally liable for VAT that should be charged by sellers (VATA 1994 s77BA). Online market places may be liable for digital services tax from April 2020 (Finance Act 2020 from s39).

Online Tax Registration Service (OTRS) Facility set up in April 2012 that allows a business to register once on-line for all the major business taxes. From April 2013, this is the default method for so registering. It will also then include registering for class 2 national insurance.

on or before Term used for real time information when operating PAYE.

The expression means that an employer must notify HMRC on or before the employee is paid. For a micro-business with nine or fewer employees, this requirement was relaxed until 5 April 2016. Such an employer may report paying an employee by the last pay day in the tax month.

For casual workers, such as those engaged by a farm to bring in the harvest, there is a separate relaxation where payments must be notified no later than a week after payment.

on-sales only licence "Means a premises licence which –

(i) authorises the sale by retail of alcohol for consumption on the licensed premises, but

(ii) does not authorise off-sales" (Licensing Act 2003 s172 F (10) as inserted by Business and Planning Act 2020 s11).

onshore allowance Allowance on capital expenditure for extracting shale gas.

The allowance has effect from 5 December 2013. It exempts 75% of capital expenditure from the corporation tax supplementary charge on ring-fence profits.

Provisions are given in CTA 2010 from s356C.

onshore oil-related activities In relation to oil and gas companies, this term is defined in CTA 2010 from s356B.

onshore wind closure date "Means the date on which the Energy Act 2016 is passed" (Electricity At 1989 s32LC as inserted by Energy Act 2016 s79(3)).

onshore wind generating station "Means a generating station that –

(a) generates electricity from wind, and

(b) is situated in England, Wales or Scotland, but not in waters in or adjacent to England, Wales or Scotland up to the seaward limits of the territorial sea" (Electricity Act 1968 s32LC(3) as inserted by Energy Act 2016 s79).

on similar terms This expression is defined in ITEPA 2003 s546 in relation to priority share allocations to employees. It means that shares allocated to employees of that company are not regarded as a benefit in kind if the employees acquire them on similar terms to non-employees.

onward transfer In relation to overseas transfer charge for pensions, "is a transfer of sums or assets held for the purpose of, or representing accrued rights under, an arrangement under a QROPS or former QROPS in relation to a member so as to become held for the purpose of, or to represent rights under, an arrangement under another QROPS in relation to that person as a member of that other QROPS" (FA 2004 s244A(3) as inserted by FA 2017 Sch 4 para 11).

opaque Term used by HMRC to describe transactions whose real nature is concealed from it. The term is widely used in connection with offshore funds and tax avoidance schemes.

opaquing liquid Liquid which is used to cover text on a document, such as Tippex and Liquid Paper. Opaquing liquids should not be used on manual accounting records which must always indicate what has been written and when any mistakes were corrected.

op cit The book previously cited.

OPEC Organisation of Petroleum Exporting Countries. It was founded in 1960 by 11 states to control the supply and price of petroleum.

open cheque Cheque which has no crossing and which may therefore be cashed by the holder. Open cheques are now very rare as they have little more security than cash.

open contract Contract for property that specifies only the names of the parties, the identity of the property and the price. Certain obligations are then placed on the purchaser and seller to complete the transaction.

open ended investment company (OEIC) Collective investment scheme with wider scope than a unit trust (Financial Services Act 1986 s75(8)). Gains from an OEIC (pronounced "oik") are exempt from capital gains tax. Income tax provisions are given in ITTOIA 2005 s373.

Open Government Licence Licensing arrangement which allows users fair use of government publications, such as free downloading of Acts of Parliament from the Internet. A list of free websites is provided under Website Addresses in section 3 of this dictionary.

opening accounts Financial records at the start of an accounting period. They must be the same as at the end of the immediately previous period.

opening balance Balance on an account at the start of an accounting period. It is the same balance as at the end of the previous accounting period.

opening compliance check letter Letter sent by HMRC to a taxpayer at the start of any form of compliance check.

opening entry In accounting, first entry made to an account.

opening market value In relation to occupational pension schemes, this term is defined in FA 2004 s185C(2).

opening price Price of a share or similar security at the start of a day's trading.

opening stock Value of stock held by a business at the start of an accounting period. This is the same figure as at the end of the previous accounting period, which figure should already be in the nominal ledger. The business calculates cost of goods sold as:

cost of goods sold = opening stock + purchases – closing stock.

Closing stock is per the stock check and is entered in the nominal ledger as a journal entry. A business's gross profit is turnover minus cost of goods sold.

open item statements Statement sent to customers listing only the invoices that remain unpaid. This contrasts with statements that are simply a copy of the sales ledger that lists all invoices issued and payments received. The term has largely fallen into disuse as modern practice is always to send open item statements, something that is easily achieved with modern accounting software.

open market Market where anyone may buy and sell without restriction.

open market option The rule which requires a pension provider to allow a person to obtain a pension from any company, and is not restricted to taking a pension from the company where the funds were accrued. The Financial Services Authority has found that companies can vary in their pension rates by as much as 25%, particularly for the less usual forms of annuity.

opera Dramatic performance with music. It may qualify for theatrical productions tax relief (CTA 2009 s1217FA(2)).

An opera company was held to be a non-commercial supplier of cultural services, and therefore making VAT exempt supplies under VATA 1994 Sch 9 Group 13 Note 2(C) in the case *Loughborough Festival Opera [2006] Ch D EWHC 40 (Ch).*

operating activities The principal revenue-producing activities of the entity, and other activities that are not investing or financing activities.

"The principal revenue-producing activities of the entity and other activities that are not investing or financial activities" (FRS 102 glossary).

"Ordinary activities are any activities which are undertaken by a reporting entity as part of its business and such related activities in which the reporting entity engages in furtherance of, and incidental to, or arising from, those activities. Ordinary activities include any effects on the reporting entity of any event in the various environments in which it operates, including the political, regulatory, economic and geographical environments, irrespective of the frequency or unusual nature of the events"
(FRS 102 section 5.10).

For statements of cash flow, "operating activities are the principal revenue-producing activities of the entity" (FRS 102 section 7.4). This goes on to list those activities that produces inflows and outflows.

operating costs For the definition of a knowledge-intensive company for enterprise investment scheme and other schemes, this term is defined in ITA 2007 s252A as inserted by Finance (No 2) Act 2015 Sch 5.

operating currency In relation to foreign exchange transactions, this term is defined in CTA 2009 s606D.

operating lease Any lease that is not a finance lease (FRS 102 glossary). In practice, this means any hire where the amount paid does not substantially meet the purchase price of the asset hired. The practical consequence is that operating leases are treated as revenue expenditure in the personal allowance and not as fixed assets on the balance sheet.

operating profit Profit from an entity's normal activities. It is sometimes shown separately on the profit and loss account, though this is not a strict requirement (FRS 102 section 5.9B).

operating segment "An operating segment is a component of an entity:

(a) that engages in business activities from which it may earn revenues and incur expenses (including revenues and expenses relating to transactions with other components of the same entity);
(b) whose operating results are regularly reviewed by the entity's chief operating decision maker to make decisions about resources to be allocated to the segment and assess its performance; and
(c) for which discrete financial information is available"

(FRS 102 glossary).

operating system The program that manages a computer's resources and performs basic tasks, e.g. recognising keyboard input, sending output to the display screen or printer, managing files and directories, controlling peripheral devices, and allocating system resources to other software programs running on the computer.

operational allowance Additional payment to members of the armed forces involved in certain theatres of military action. It is exempt from income tax (ITEPA 2003 s297A).

operational research Study of how a business works to see where any efficiencies can be made.

Operation Magnify HMRC campaign launched in October 2015 against tax fraud in the construction industry.

Operation Maypole Customs operation against carousel fraud.

operator (1) Person who operates a piece of equipment, particularly a machine or telephone switchboard.
(2) For air passenger duty, "in relation to any aircraft, means the person having the management of the aircraft for the time being" (FA 1994 s43(1)).

(3) In relation to peer-to-peer lending, this term is given a specific meaning in ITA 2007 s412J and s888E(4).

(4) Whoever has responsibility for a wrecked ship (Wrecks Convention article 9).

opportunity cost The cost of not pursuing the next best alternative. It applies when there is a constraint, such as limited manpower, materials or quota.

opportunity pricing Exploiting a situation by raising prices such as when goods or services are in short supply or suddenly become needed.

opted-in company A company that has passed an opting-in resolution in relation to a takeover bid and where the relevant conditions continue to apply (CA 2006 s971(1)).

opted-out creditor In relation to insolvency, this term is defined in Insolvency Act 1986 s248A.

optical character recognition (OCR) System of stylised numbers printed in a special magnetic ink which can be read directly into a computer. Such numbers appears on cheques.

The first patent on such a system was taken out in 1929. Such equipment was developed from 1955 to read numbers on coupons. The US postal system adopted OCR in 1965.

optician Person who checks eyes. Such a business is taxed as a trade. For VAT, it is likely to be partially exempt as eye tests are exempt while providing glasses and contact lenses are standard-rated.

opting out When a person elects not to continue with a right, in particular the right of a worker to opt out of the workplace pension.

option For investment, an agreement that allows a person to buy or sell shares, securities, commodities or other assets at a particular price on or before a specific date. If the option is not exercised, it becomes worthless. The option is a security in its own right. A call option gives the holder the right to buy a particular number of shares (or other securities) at a particular price by a certain date. A put option is the opposite, giving the holder the right to sell shares or securities. If the option is not exercised, the option becomes worthless.

In relation to exchange gains and losses, the term is defined in CTA 2009 s328F.

In relation to employee share schemes, the term is defined in CTA 2009 s1005.

For derivatives, it is defined in CTA 2009 s606F.

See also the separate entry for option to tax.

optional remuneration arrangement (OpRA) An arrangement where an employee may choose elements of his or her remuneration. This often takes the form of salary sacrifice where the employee gives up part of his or her salary for a benefit. This was often done when the benefit was not taxed or was taxed more leniently.

The tax advantage of this is largely lost from 6 April 2017 (ITEPA 2003 s69A). An employee is now taxed on the higher of the value of benefit and the amount forgone. The new rule applies even if the benefit is not otherwise taxable.

An arrangement made before 6 April 2017 in relation to accommodation or school fees retains its tax advantage until 5 April 2021, provided it has not been varied.

option to pay Principle of taxation which states that people should be able to choose whether to pay tax according to what transactions they choose to make. This principle applied to the many 19th century excise duties and 20th century purchase tax, where the rates were much higher on those items considered luxuries.

This principle has now generally been replaced by the principle of ability to pay, though vestiges of option to pay can be found in current provisions for excise duty and VAT.

option to tax Right of a landlord to choose whether to charge VAT on commercial rent which would otherwise be exempt (VATA 1994 Sch 10). The proper name for this option is the election to waive exemption. This allows the landlord to claim input tax on expenses. In practice, the option is most likely to be exercised when the tenants are VAT-registered businesses which are not partially exempt. The main points are:

- the option applies to land, buildings and civil engineering works, and to buildings within the curtilage
- the option can apply to complexes of units separated by internal links such as covered walkways
- the landlord choose what property to opt in
- an extension to an opted building is automatically included within the option, but a separate building on newly acquired land is not, even if later connected to opted property
- the option applies to sales as well as rent
- the option applies to service charges from the landlord
- there is a six-month cooling off period when the landlord can change his or her mind, provided the landlord has not claimed input tax, or the landlord refunds any input tax claimed
- an option lasts for 20 years when it may be renewed or cancelled
- the option does not apply to residential property. If a premises has both commercial and residential elements, they must be apportioned with the option applying only to the commercial element
- if the landlord has already made an exempt supply to a tenant, the landlord needs HMRC permission to exercise the option. This permission takes about a month during which time the landlord may not exercise the option
- the option applies to sales of property as well as rent
- the landlord may choose when to make the election. In practice, this is often when input tax is about to be incurred. For a new buildings, it is common to apply for option after construction
- a housing association may serve a notice on form VAT 1614D which disapplies the option to tax and makes the supply VAT exempt. This means that input tax already claimed can be retrospectively disallowed

- the capital goods scheme applies to property costing more than £250,000. It can require input tax to be repaid if a property changes its nature within ten years of supply. The option to tax can avoid such repayment
- VAT may be added to opted rent under VATA 1994 s89, but if the lease expressly excludes VAT (as the tenant should have ensured), the rent is regarded as VAT-inclusive. This means that the net amount received by the landlord is reduced by one sixth
- a VAT invoice must be issued for each charge where VAT is applied
- there are anti-avoidance rules to prevent the option being used to avoid tax.

oral declaration Spoken statement affirming a truth. Oral declaration supported by an inventory document may be used for Customs duty relief under the temporary admission procedure.

Orcadian Pertaining to the Orkney Islands of Scotland.

orchestra Body of 12 or more musicians, at least half of whom are not electrically amplified (CTA 2009 s1217PA(1)). This is wide enough to include many brass band, wind bands and dance bands. Such a body may, from 1 April 2016, be eligible to claim orchestra tax relief from corporation tax in respect of certain concerts.

orchestral concert A concert by an orchestra (as defined), ensemble, group or band consisting wholly or mainly of instrumentalists who are the primary focus of the concert (CTA 2009 s1217PA(1)). Section 1217PA(2) says a concert does not qualify if:

- its main purpose is to advertise or promote any goods or services
- the concert comprises a contest or competition, or
- the concert is to make a commercial recording.

orchid Endangered plant. The importation of the plant or its products is generally prohibited under CITES convention.

order The many meanings of this word include a statutory instrument that provides legislation as allowed by an Act of Parliament.

order for sale of shares Order made by a court requiring that shares in a public company must be sold because of unlawful restrictions imposed on them (CA 2006 s801).

order of discharge In insolvency, an order that a bankrupt may obtain from the court. This releases the bankrupt from all debts other than those that arose from fraud and from certain other debts (Insolvency Act 1986 ss280-281).

Orders in Council Orders issued by the privy council under the royal prerogative.

ordinary benefits Benefits provided by an community amateur sports club which do not trigger a tax liability. The matter is discussed in HMRC Manual at BIM24340.

ordinary commuting "Means travel between –

(a) the employee's home and permanent workplace, or

(b) a place that is not a workplace and a permanent workplace" (ITEPA 2003 s338(3)).

Ordinary commuting is not a deductible expense from employment income.

ordinary contribution The normal rate of class 2 national insurance (Social Security Contributions and Benefits Act 1992 s11), as against higher-rate contributions paid by share fishermen and volunteer development workers.

ordinary maternity leave A period of (from 1 April 2007) 39 weeks for which a female employee is entitled to be absent from work. If she meets the relevant conditions, she will receive statutory maternity pay during this period. This is provided by Employment Rights Act 1996 s71.

ordinary residence One of the concepts that, before 6 April 2013, determined whether a taxpayer was UK resident. Although now repealed, some elements of it are contained in the statutory residence test. Details can be found under Statutory residence test in section 3 of this dictionary.

ordinary resolution In company law, a decision of shareholders passed by a simple majority, that is more than half of those who voted (CA 2006 s282(1)).

An ordinary resolution may be taken by a show of hands unless a ballot is required. An ordinary resolution deals with all issues except those for which a special resolution or unanimous **resolution** is required.

ordinary share Financial instrument given to those who own a company (CA 2006 s560(1)).

ordinary statutory paternity pay (OSPP) Paternity pay for one or two weeks that may be claimed by a father or other partner of person who gives birth to or adopts a child. The entitlement is set out in Social Security Contributions and Benefits Act 1992 s171ZA.

The payment is subject to income tax (ITEPA 2003 s660(1)).

From 6 April 2011, this term replaces statutory paternity pay in recognition that additional statutory paternity pay may be claimed from that date.

ordinary trust assets In the context of a transfer of value by trustees linked with trustee borrowing, this term is given a specific meaning by TCGA1992 Sch 4B para 7(1).

ordinary UK overseas property business "Means a UK property business except so far as it is a UK furnished holiday lettings business" (CTA 2009 s748(5)).

ore (1) Rock from which metal or other mineral may be extracted. (2) One hundredth of the krona, currency of Sweden.

organ For medical transplants, "means a differentiated and vital part of the human body, formed by different **tissues,** that maintain its structure, vascularisation and capacity to develop physiological functions with an important level of autonomy" (Directive 2003/23/EC article 3).

organist An organist in the Church of England has been held to be an employee of the incumbent and parochial church council. A paid organist should therefore be paid on a PAYE payroll.

For VAT, the services of an organist are standard-rated if the organist is registered *and* the supply is made as part of a business. A VAT-registered person who plays the organ as a hobby does not charge VAT.

For VAT, the services of an organist at a funeral are exempt. Further details are given in VAT notice 701/32.

original appellant For VAT, "means the person who made the appeal to the tribunal under section 83" (Value Added Tax 1994 s85B(8)).

original book value In relation to capital allowances and leases, this term is given a specific meaning in CAA 2001 s222B and subsequent sections.

original borrower In relation to interest on peer-to-peer lending "in relation to any credit, means the person to whom the credit is originally provided" (ITA 2007 s888E as inserted by FA 2017 Sch 5 para 3).

original consideration In relation to capital allowances and leases, this term is given a specific meaning in CAA 2001 s222B and subsequent sections.

original contract In relation to certain embedded derivatives, this term is given a specific meaning in CTA 2009 s616(7).

original gravity For beer duty, gravity of the liquid before fermentation (ALDA 1979 s3(1)C). Guidance is given in Customs notice 226.

original lender In relation to interest on peer-to-peer lending "in relation to any credit, means the person who originally provides the credit" (ITA 2007 s888E as inserted by FA 2017 Sch 5 para 3).

original master version In relation to sound recordings, means "the master tape or master audio disc of the recording" (CTA 2009 s152(1)(b)).

original place of departure For air passenger duty, this is as indicated on the ticket (FA 1994 s43(2)).

original relevant transfer For overseas pensions, this term is defined in FA 2004 Sch 34 para 1(6B) as inserted by FA 2017 Sch 4 para 2.

original right For national insurance on share options, term used in Social Security Contributions (Share Options) Act 2001 s3.

original shares Share originally held but now replaced in a reorganisation (TCGA 1992 s116). The main provision is that there is no disposal of shares when they are replaced solely in a reorganisation.

original supplier For VAT, person who supplied goods to a customer in another EU state via a third party (VATA 1994 s14).

originating application Process by which legal proceedings are started. For tax tribunal hearings, the process is set out in SI 2009 No 273 rule 21.

ornamental fish Term used in VAT notice 701/14 for tropical fish and similar. Such fish are standard-rated. They are not zero-rated as food, even when such fish are edible.

ornamental vegetable Term used in VAT notice 701/14 to describe such products as ornamental cabbage. These products are standard-rated if they are sold for their appearance, even if the product is edible.

ostrich For VAT purposes, ostriches and their eggs are zero-rated as food from 1 April 1995. Previously they were standard rated as non-edible animals.

ouguiya Currency of Mauritania.

Outer House Part of the Court of Session in Scotland. It comprises all but eight of its judges.

outgoing auditor Auditor whom the company wishes to replace (CA 2006 s514(1)). If the auditor does not agree to the replacement, he or she has the right to make representations to members of the company.

outgoing partner Person who is leaving or has left a partnership. Such a person is not liable for any debts of the partnership which arose after he left (Partnership Act 1890 s17).

outline disclosure Admission by a taxpayer that he or she has deliberately underpaid tax. The admission includes a summary of how. If this disclosure is made under the Contractual Disclosure Facility, the taxpayer will usually avoid criminal charges.

outplacement services Services of counselling and similar to assist an employee into a new job (CTA 2009 s73 and ITTOIA 2005 s73).

output tax VAT charged on supplies made. The VAT return usually shows output tax minus input tax, and is accompanied by a payment equal to this figure.

output work For national minimum wage, when a person is paid according to what they have achieved, such as per lampshade assembled or per 100 envelopes stuffed. From 2005, such a worker must be paid at least 120% of the national minimum wage for average output (SI 1999 No 584 para 5).

outside the scope For VAT, activities that are outside the scope of the tax. Examples include performing a statutory function and transfer of a business as going concern. They are outside the scope of VAT as they are not legally regarded as a supply. Further details are given in VAT Notice 701/1.

outstanding VAT "A person has outstanding VAT for a prescribed accounting period if some or all of the VAT for which he is liable in respect of that period has not been paid by the last day on which he is required (as mentioned in subsection (1) above) to make a return for that period; and the reference in subsection (4) above to a person's outstanding VAT for a prescribed accounting period is so much of the VAT for which he is so liable as had not been paid" (Value Added Tax 1994 s59(6)). A person is liable to a default surcharge on the amount.

outward processing relief System of Customs relief when goods are temporarily exported, such as for repair, and are then re-imported.

overdraft The situation when a person has withdrawn more money from his or her bank account than is in there. An overdraft is either an:

- authorised overdraft; or
- unauthorised overdraft.

An authorised overdraft is one agreed in advance with the bank, whereas an unauthorised overdraft is not agreed but which the bank is prepared to tolerate. A bank has no obligation to allow an unauthorised overdraft and may dishonour payment rather than allow an account to become overdrawn.

overfill tolerance For beer duty, the maximum amount that a large pack, such as a keg or cask, may depart from the stated quantity. This is usually around 1%. More details are given in Customs notice 226.

overgeared Description of a company that has large borrowings relative to its equity (basically share capital). The consequence is that the company's shareholders suffer in a poor year but benefit in good years.

overhedged Description of a financial risk where the hedging is excessive. Where this is done as part of a risk transfer scheme, it may be caught by an anti-avoidance provision of FA 2010 s46 and Sch 16.

overlap period Period at the beginning of trading which falls within two basis periods and where profits may have been taxed twice (ITTOIA 2005 s204), This often happens at the start of a business. This amount may be deducted from final profits when the trade ceases, though with no allowance for inflation.

overlap profit Profit for a period which is covered by two basis periods for income tax. The profits for one of these periods qualifies for overlap relief when the business ceases.

The term "means profit which arises in an overlap period" (ITTOIA 2005 s204).

overlap relief

(1) Reclaim of income tax paid twice because of the overlap period.

(2) Relief given for main residence relief from capital gains tax when a person acquires a new residence before disposing of the old. Such a period is treated as if it were a period of occupation (TCGA 1992 s223(2)(a)).

overlapping period For group relief, the period which is common to the claim period and surrender period (CTA 2010 s142(1)).

overpayment When a customer pays more than required and the trader does not refund it. Such overpayment is taxed as trading income. This was upheld in the case *Pertemps Recruitment Partnership Ltd v HMRC [2011] UKUT 88.*

Similar provisions apply for VAT. For example, a person incurs a £3.40 parking charge but does not have the right coins for the machine, so he pays £4 and gets no charge. That is regarded as a VAT-inclusive charge of £4.

Overpayment Recovery (OPREC) HMRC computer system that "provides IT support for the collection, recovery and accounting of overpaid amounts of child benefit" (Inspectors' Manual at DMBM100120).

overriding limit In PAYE, the rule that income tax may not exceed 50% of gross pay for any pay period (PAYE Regulations 2003 reg 2(1)).

overseas conference The ability to deduct such expenses from taxable profits follow the normal wholly and exclusively rule. How they apply to this item is discussed in HMRC Manual at BIM42525.

overseas dividend In relation to manufactured payments means "any interest, dividend or other annual payment payable in respect of overseas securities" (CTA 2009 s814(2)).

overseas freezing order "An order:

(a) for protecting, pending its transfer to the participating country, evidence which is in the United Kingdom and may be used in any proceedings or investigation in the participating country, and

(b) in respect of which the following requirements of this section are met" (Crime (International Co-operation) Act 2003 s20(2)).

The conditions are broadly that it the order is issued by a court under its criminal law in a country which participates in these arrangements.

Overseas Pensions Act Pensions paid under this Act of 1973 may be exempt from income tax under ITEPA 2003 s651.

overseas pension scheme Pension scheme, other than a registered scheme, which is established outside the UK and satisfies HMRC's requirements (FA 2004 s150(7)). HMRC provides helpsheet HS344.

overseas property business "A company's overseas property business consists of —

(a) every business which the company carries on for generating income from land outside the United Kingdom, and

(b) every transaction which the company enters into for that purpose otherwise than in the course of such a business"

(CTA 2009 s206).

An identical definition for income tax is given in ITTOIA 2005 s265.

overseas securities "Means shares, stock or other securities issued by —

(a) a government, local authority or other public authority of a territory outside the United Kingdom, or

(b) another non-UK resident body of persons"

(ITA 2007 s567(2)).

The same definition appears in CTA 2009 s814(3).

Overseas Service Act Act of 1958 that may provide a pension for those who worked overseas. Such a pension may be free of income tax under ITEPA 2003 s652.

Overseas Service Pension Fund Pension fund established under Overseas Aid Act 1966 s7(1).Payments of pensions from this fund may be free of income tax under ITEPA 2003 s653.

overseas shares "Means shares in a non-UK resident company" (ITA 2007 s567(1A).

Oversea Superannuation Scheme Payment made under the Oversea Superannuation Scheme (formerly known as the Colonial Superannuation Scheme). Such a payment may be free of income tax under ITEPA 2003 s650.

overseas tax Tax paid in another country which may qualify for double taxation relief. In relation to manufactured payments, means "tax under the law of a territory outside the United Kingdom" (CTA 2009 s814(4)).

overseas transfer charge Income tax charge that may be made from 9 March 2017 when assets of a pension fund are transferred to a QROPS (FA 2004 s244A).

overtime Sum paid to an employee for additional working. This is sometimes paid at a higher rate. It is taxed on the same basis as normal salary or wages. If overtime is paid at a higher rate, the additional element, or overtime premium, is not counted towards the national minimum wage.

owner Person who has legal title to land or goods though he may not have occupation or possession of them. For Customs purpose, owner "in relation to an aircraft, includes the operator of the aircraft" (CEMAs1(1)), and owner "in relation to a pipe-line, means (except in the case of a pipe-line vested in the Crown which in pursuance of arrangements in that behalf is operated by another) the person in whom the line is vested and, in the said excepted case, means the person operating the line" (CEMAs1(1)).

ownership Description of having legal title to property or other asset, as against possession which means having custody.

Oxford comma Comma placed before the word "and" to disconnect the following term from the adjective or adverb that qualifies preceding terms. So the expression "fixed plant and machinery, and loose tools" would mean that "fixed" applied to "plant" and "machinery" but not to "loose tools". Although this is a common practice, it is not supported by authoritative text books on English grammar. For its relevance in interpreting tax law, see **comma.**

P2P Peer to peer lending, a description whereby individuals lend to each other, often through an Internet platform.

P11D Form completed at the end of the tax year by an employer setting out what taxable benefits have been provided to employees (PAYE Regulations 2003 from reg 85). Until 5 April 2016, the form only applied to employees who earned at least £8,500 in salary and benefits. That amount is unchanged from 1979. That limit now only applies to ministers of religion. The form requires a return of all taxable benefits provided for director and employees during the tax year unless (from 2016) these benefits have been payrolled.

P45 Form issued to an employee with a copy sent to HMRC when an employment ends.

P60 Annual certificate issued by an employer to an employee stating how much the employee has earned in the tax year, and how much tax and national insurance was deducted.

PACE Police and Criminal Evidence Act 1984.

package test VAT term for a test which may allow a printer to zero-rate an entire consignment of material for a charity even though some of it would be standard-rated if supplied separately. Details are given in VAT Notice 701/10.

packaging For VAT, "normal and necessary" packaging is regarded as part of the product and is not separately taxed, as explained in VAT Notice 700. This does not apply when the packaging is a product in its own right, such as a food product provided in a reuseable storage jar. For patent box, the term has a specific meaning in CTA 2010 s357BH(4).

packaging premises For soft drinks industry levy, where the drinks are packed. The levy is charged when the drinks are removed from such premises (FA 2017 s32).

packed lunch Food prepared for eating later, as often supplied by hotels. From 1 July 1991 it was put beyond doubt that this is a VAT standard-rated supply of catering and not a zero-rated supply of food.

paid or incurred basis Term for informal arrangements sometimes agreed with tax inspectors before 1999. It allowed expenses to be claimed in the period when paid rather than when occurred. These arrangements have now been ended, though a similar effect can be achieved by using the cash basis. The matter is discussed in HMRC Manual at BIM42220.

paisa One hundredth of a rupee, currency of India.

Pakistan Eastern country. Its currency is the Pakistan rupee of 100 paisa. The UK has a double taxation convention of 1986. Payments of a pension made under Pensions (India, Pakistan and Burma) Act 1955 may be exempt from income tax under ITEPA 2003 s654.

Palau Island state in Philippine Sea that became independent in 1994. Its currency is the US dollar of 100 cents. The UK has no double taxation treaty.

palladium Element that is a precious metal.

palliative care charity Charity whose main purpose is to care for terminally ill people (VATA 1994 s33D(1)). From 1 April 2015, such a charity may claim back VAT input tax.

Panama South American country. Its currency is the balboa of 100 centésimos, though the US dollar is also widely used. The UK has a double taxation convention of 2013.

Panama papers Set of more than 11 million documents leaked from a Panamanian law firm in 2016, showing widespread international tax evasion.

panini For VAT, the issue is whether this is intended to be eaten hot, making it standard-rated as hot takeaway food, or cold, making it zero-rated as food. The VAT tribunal has made opposite decisions on similar facts finding it standard-rated in *Coffee Republic plc [2006] VTD 20150* but zero-rated in *R J Warren]2006] VTD 19902.* The former decision is probably the better one.

pannage The right to pasture swine in a forest.

panty liner This is reduced-rated or (from 1 January 2021) zero-rated for VAT as sanitary protection but standard-rated for incontinence (VATA 1994 Sch 7A Group 4). The matter is explained in VAT Notice 701/18.

paper people Fictitious people created for illegal purposes, such as to claim social security.

paper profit Profit or gain that arises from an accounting adjustment but which is not reflected as additional cash. An example is revaluing an asset.

Papua New Guinea Country in Pacific Ocean. Its currency is the kina of 100 toea. The UK has a double taxation agreement of 1991.

para Abbreviation: paragraph. The term is widely used for sections of a Statutory Instrument or of a Schedule to an Act of Parliament.

Paraguay South American country. Its currency is the guarani of 100 céntimos. The UK has no double taxation treaty.

parent For childcare, a person who either has parental responsibility or care of a child (Children Act 2016 s1(9)). A parent may not be biologically related to the child. For inheritance tax provisions for trusts for a bereaved minor, a parent is someone who had parental responsibility (IHTA 1984 s71H).

parental bereavement leave (PBL) A statutory right for a parent to take two weeks paid leave if they have a child under 18 who dies or a baby who is stillborn after 24 weeks of pregnancy. The right applies to deaths from 6 April 2020. The right is given in Employment Rights Act 1996 s80EA as inserted by Parental Bereavement (Leave and Pay) Act 2018 Sch para 1. The following points were clarified in November 2018:

- parent means the child's primary carer
- the leave may be taken in one block of two weeks, or as two separated periods of one week
- the leave must be taken within 56 weeks of the death
- notice periods will be flexible, with less rigorous requirements for notice taken soon after death
- evidence requirements will largely follow those for other forms of family leave.

parental bereavement pay Payment provided to an employed parent for up to two weeks payment during parental bereavement leave when a child under 18 dies. The right is given in Social Security Contributions and Benefits Act 1992 s171ZZ6 as inserted by Parental Bereavement (Leave and Pay) Act 2018 Sch para 5.

parental leave Right of a parent to take unpaid leave from 15 December 1999 to deal with certain matters relating to their child, such as taking a child to an emergency babysitter or dealing with an issue at school (Employment Rights Act 1996 ss76-79).

parent company Company that owns other companies (CA 2006 s1173(1)).

parent with care Parent who looks after a child. The term is often used in relation to maintenance where a parent with care receives payments from an absent parent.

Pareto principle Observable phenomenon that in many situations, 80% of the effects come from 20% of the causes. An example is a company that earns 80% of its profits from 20% of its products. It is a widely used rule of thumb in business management. The term comes from the Italian economist (1848-1923) who first postulated the principle in 1906.

pari passu Latin for "with equal step". It is the principle that, for example, requires creditors of the same rank to be paid the same percentage of their debt in an insolvency.

parish District that has its own church. It is still used as the basic unit of area in the Church of England. It may also be used for civic administration. From 1 July 1837, the church's vestry became separate from the civil parish under

Registration Act 1836. There are 10,479 civil parishes and 12,557 ecclesiastical parishes in England.

parking fine Fine for illegal parking of a vehicle, such as not paying, exceeding the time limit, not parking in a proper space, and similar. Where an employer pays a parking fine incurred by an employee, HMRC says this is a taxable benefit to the employee if the fine was handed to the employee at the time or if the car belongs to the employee. It is not a taxable benefit if the fine was paid by the employer as registered owner (Inspectors' Manual at BIM42520).

parking space The provision of a parking space near work is not a taxable benefit (ITEPA 2003 s266(1)).

Parliament House of Commons and House of Lords. It is the place where statutes are made and matters of national importance discussed.

Parliamentary annuities Annual amounts paid to individuals on the instructions of Parliament. The main recipients were members of the Royal Family other than the Queen herself. From 1993, the Queen reimbursed the Treasury. From 2011, these annuities are abolished with the sole exception of that for the Duke of Edinburgh which is paid directly from the Consolidated Fund.

Parliamentary Partnership Assembly Body that may be set up under Article INST 5 of the EU/UK withdrawal agreement of 24 December 2020. The assembly comprises members of the European Parliament and UK Parliament as a forum to exchange views.

Parliamentary pension funds Funds set up under House of Commons Members' Fund Act 1939. Its tax treatment is set out in ICTA 1988 s613.

parochial charity Charity that relates to a parish or property within it. Legal provisions are contained in Charities Act 2011 from s298.

parrot Endangered bird. The importation of the bird or its products is generally prohibited under CITES convention.

Part 4 charges Taxes on savings and investment income as set out in Part 4 of ITTOIA 2005 from s365.

Part 4 TIOPA amount In relation to transfer of intangible assets not at arm's length, "means the amount which, following the application of Part 4 of TIOPA [Taxation (International and Other Provisions) Act 2010] in relation to the consideration for the transfer, is brought into account in respect of the consideration for the purposes of corporation tax" (CTA 2009 s846(1C) as inserted by Finance (No 2) Act 2015 s42(1)).

Part 5 one-way exchange effect provisions Provisions set out in CTA 2009 ss328A-328H.

Part 6 asset In relation to a fixture for which research and development allowance has been claimed, the asset represented by such fixture (CAA 2001 s187(1)(b))

Part 6 expenditure In relation to a fixture for which research and development allowance has been claimed, the amount of such claim (CAA 2001 s187(1)(a)).

Part 7 one-way exchange effect provisions Provisions set out in CTA 2009 from s606H.

Part 36 offer Offer made by one party to litigation (which can be HMRC) to the other under Part 36 of Civil Procedure Rules. This puts pressure on the other party to settle the case, and can restrict their claim to costs if they do not. Such offers are often preferred to Calderbank letters.

part disposal For inheritance tax provisions, the term "means a disposal of property which does not consist of or include the whole of each property which is one of associated properties and of which there has been a conditionally exempt transfer" (Inheritance Tax Act 1984 s32A(6)).

For capital gains tax, "there is a part disposal of an asset where an interest or right in or over the asset is created by the disposal, as well as where it subsists before the disposal, and generally, there is a part disposal of an asset where, on a person making a disposal, any description of property derived from the asset remains undisposed of" (TCGA1992 s21(2)(b)).

Provisions for capital gains tax are given in TCGA1992 from s242. Part disposals of long-funded plant and machinery are given in TCGA1992 s42.

part exchange Sales method which involves taking in an old item as part payment for a new item. This method is particularly common for selling cars, where the old car may be accepted as part payment of a new car. The old car is often accepted at a value above its second-hand price as a means of clinching the sale.

For the purposes of income tax or corporation tax, the car must be valued as part of the purchase price. From August 1994 this may be at the car's trade value and need not be at a higher price allowed to clinch the sale.

partial closure notice Notice of closure in respect of some items under enquiry by HMRC while leaving others. Such notices are permitted under Finance (No 2) Act 2017 s63 and Sch 15. The notices must relate to an enquiry under:

- TMA 1970 s9A, 12ZM or 12AC, or
- FA 1998 Sch 18.

partial exemption (PE) In VAT, the procedure which may be required when a VAT-registered trader makes both taxable and exempt supplies. Taxable supplies include zero-rated supplies. Partial exemption seeks to restrict the amount of input tax which the trader may claim on the VAT return, either as a deduction from the output tax payable or as a repayment from, HMRC. Banks and other financial institutions are always partially exempt.

The principle is simple. Suppose a trader has taxable supplies of £200,000 and exempt supplies £100,000 and incurs input tax of £60,000. Two-thirds of the output is taxable, so only two-thirds of the input tax may be claimed. In this example, £40,000. The other £20,000 is an additional cost to the trader. While the principle is simple, the operation is notoriously complex.

Some small traders may be excused partial exemption if:

- their average monthly input tax does not exceed £625 (unchanged from 1994); and
- the exempt input tax does not exceed 50% of VAT on all purchases (introduced to counter the toothbrush scheme).

Such traders may claim back all their input tax and need not be concerned about partial exemption. For other traders, the standard method is normally used unless a special method can be justified.

Supplies and their related purchases are excluded if they can be exactly matched, such as if a bank sells money boxes. Some other supplies are also excluded (such as leases). From this a percentage is calculated according to a detailed procedure based on previous figures. The percentage determines how much input tax may be claimed back. This is subject to an annual adjustment which amends the input tax claimed in the light of figures for the current year.

Where the standard method is not appropriate, a special method may be agreed with HMRC. From 17 April 2002, HMRC may use the standard method override where, exceptionally, the trader is using the standard method and it does not give a fair apportionment of tax.

Partial exemption has been part of the VAT system since the tax was introduced in 1973. The present system was introduced on 1 May 1992. There was another revision in 1987. In particular, it should be noted that what is now called the standard method was known as the special method between 1987 and 1992.

partial intestacy When not all a person's property can pass on their death under the terms of a will. This is usually because property has been overlooked (such as when there is no residuary legatee), or when a provision fails for any reason.

The property which does not pass in accordance with the will passes under the provisions of the Administration of Estates Act 1925 and subsequent legislation.

partially sighted Person who has very poor sight but who is not severely sight impaired. Such a person may be registered as blind, and be eligible for blind person's allowance and other disability provisions.

participating equity holders In relation to distribution rights of a company being wound up, means "the equity holders of company B [being wound up] –

(a) to whom the profit distribution would be made, or

(b) who would be entitled to participate in the notional winding up"

(CTA 2010 s169(2)).

participator For companies, "a person having a share or interest in the capital or income of the company, and, without prejudice to the generality of the preceding words, includes:

(a) any person who possesses, or is entitled to acquire, share capital or voting rights in the company;

(b) any loan creditor of the company;

(c) any person who possesses, or is entitled to acquire, a right to receive or participate in distributions of the company... to loan creditors by way of premium on redemption;

(d) any person who is entitled to secure that income or assets (whether present or future) of the company will be applied directly or indirectly for his benefit." (ICTA 1988 s417(1)).

The definition includes an associate of the participator.

[Note that the word "participant" is used in other contexts for someone who participates in something.]

partner Person with whom one is associated in some way.

partner payment notice Notice issued to a partner to pay tax when a tax avoidance scheme has failed. It is the equivalent of an accelerated payment notice. Such notices are issued under FA 2014 Sch 32. The legal consequences of such a notice were considered in *Eamonn Dunne and Vincent Gray v CRC. QBD [2015]*

partnership

(1) Various types of relationship between two or more people. For business purposes, there is:
- an ordinary partnership under Partnership Act 1890;
- a limited partnership under Limited Partnership Act 1907;
- a limited liability partnership under Limited Liability Partnership Act 2000.

  Generally, the profits of a partnership are taxed in the hands of the partners.

(2) In the sense of a partnership under the 1890, a partnership is defined as "the relationship which subsists between persons carrying on a business in common with a view to making a profit" (Partnership Act 1890 s1(1)).

Under English law, a partnership is not a legal person, but is in effect two or more sole traders working together. A partnership is a legal person under Scots law.

For capital gains tax, partners are assessed separately (TCGA1992 s59).

For VAT, a partnership may register as a body separate from its partners (VATA 1994 s45).

A partnership may trade under the surnames of the partners, with or without initials or first names, under the provisions of CA 2006 s1192(3).

partnership at will Partnership that has no fixed term for its duration. Any partner may end the partnership simply by giving notice to the other partners (Partnership Act 1890 s26(1)).

Partnership Council Body established under Article INST 1 of the EU/UK withdrawal agreement of 24 December 2020. It is co-chaired by a member of the EU and a representative of the UK government. It meets as required and at least once a year. Its agenda is set by mutual consent. Its function is "to oversee the attainment of this Agreement and any supplementing agreement. It shall supervise and facilitate the implementation and application of this Agreement and of any supplementing agreement". Subsequent paras set out its powers and procedures.

partnership deed Document setting out the agreement of the partners on how the partnership is to be conducted (including the arrangements for sharing profits and losses).

partnership return Tax return which must be submitted by a partnership under TMA 1970 s12AA.

partnerships involving companies Corporation tax provisions are given in CTA 2009 from s380. Special provisions for certain embedded derivatives are given in CTA 2009 from s619.

partnership statement Document stating amounts of taxable income received by a partnership. TMA 1970 s12AB requires such a statement to be sent to HMRC with the partnership return.

part work Series of publications that builds up into a book. By concession, such works are zero-rated for VAT under VATA 1994 Sch 8 Group 3, as explained in VAT notice 701/10. Amendments to part works are also zero-rated. Where the part work comprises a magazine, it may be separately zero-rated as such.

party plan selling Scheme under which a company appoints distributors who in turn, appoint sub-distributors who act as hosts or hostesses of a party to supply company goods. The sub-distributor makes the sale, and pays the distributor a percentage of the proceeds, keeping the balance as commission. In a case concerning Tupperware parties, the Court of Appeal held that the supplier was the sub-distributor, and not the distributor. The significance of the case is that sub-distributors' sales figures were typically below the VAT registration threshold. *(P & R Potter v Customs and Excise. CA [1985] STC 45).*

party trays Tray with food provided for immediate consumption with little if any additional preparation by the customer.
For VAT, this is generally regarded as a supply of food and not of catering. A leading case is *C&E v Safeway Stores plc. QB [1996] STC 163.*

par value The nominal value of a share. It is usually the price at which the share was first issued. It usually bears little relationship to the market value.

passenger For air passenger duty, this is any person carried on an aircraft who is not a member of the flight crew, not a cabin attendant and not within the scope of any other requirement that may be made (FA 1994 s43(1)).

passenger payment An additional 5p a mile that, from 2002, may be made to an employee using his or her own transport for business purposes and who carries a passenger while doing so (ITEPA 2003 s233). Unlike the tax-free expense of an employee using their own transport on business, an employee cannot make a claim for tax relief if the employer does not make this payment.

passenger transport For VAT, zero-rated transport in a vehicle that carries at least 10 people, so taxis are excluded (VATA 1994 Sch 8). The transport must be to another place, so ski lifts and fairground rides are excluded. Passenger vehicles are specifically exempt from capital gains tax under TCGA 1992 s263.

passenger transport undertaking "An undertaking whose business consists wholly or mainly in the carriage of passengers or a subsidiary of such an undertaking" (ITEPA 2003 s86(3)).

passenger vehicle This is specifically exempt from capital gains tax under TCGA1992 s263.

passported benefit Social security or similar benefit where entitlement depends on already receiving another benefit.

past owner Someone who previously owned an asset. A specific definition is given in CAA 2001 s187A(2). An income tax charge can arise on a pre-owned, such as when a parent gives an asset to a child and the parent continues to use it.

pataca Currency of Macao.

patent Intellectual property in a registered invention. From 1986, this lasts for 20 years. There is a special capital allowance for patents (CAA 2001 s464). A company that exploits a patent may be able to save corporation tax by using the patent box. A company may claim tax relief for expenses connected with patents (CTA 2009 s89).

Customs may seize imported goods that breach a patent, as explained in Customs notice 34. Payment of patent royalties is usually a tax-deductible expenses, and receipts are usually taxable income. Such income may be spread over more than one tax year under ITA 2006 s461.

patent box Provision of corporation tax that allows a company to make deductions from its corporation tax liability to the effect that it pays an effective rate of 10% on the exploitation of an invention (CTA 2010 from s357A). Claiming the patent box is voluntary. This provision was phased in between 2013 and 2017.

patent infringing goods "Any goods that will infringe a patent under UK law or a supplementary protection certificate (SPC) under EC law" (Customs notice 34). Customs may seize such goods.

paternity In law, acknowledgement of being a father. This gives the father various rights and duties. The father is assumed to be the husband of the mother unless otherwise stated, this is known as the presumption of legitimacy. A man is also regarded as the father if he has agreed for his name to appear on the birth certificate.

If paternity is disputed, a DNA test may be carried out. This can be 100% conclusive in establishing that a man is *not* the father, and 99.9% conclusive in establishing that a man is. This rises to 100% if the mother co-operates.

A court may order a DNA test. This requires a swab from the child under Human Tissue Act 2004. This requires either the assent of the person having care and control of a child under 16, an order of the court, or the agreement of the child when 16 or over. The court's usual attitude is summarised by Lord Justice Ward in the Court of Appeal in *Re G (Parentage: Blood Sample) [1997]:* "It is essential for the ultimate well-being of this child, both that she knows the truth about who her father is, and that she knows it sooner rather than later."

A paternity test may be requested under Family Law Reform Act 1969 ss20-23.

Paternity rights include:

- paternity leave from work
- paternity pay during paternity leave
- parental leave
- statutory parental bereavement leave and statutory parental bereavement pay.

paternity leave Up to two weeks leave by the partner of a person who gives birth to or adopts a child. The partner can be female. The partner is entitled to statutory paternity pay during that leave. From 5 April 2015, a partner may also take shared parental leave.

pathfinder prospectus Prospectus published by a company before its flotation.

patronymic In Iceland and Slavic countries, a middle name based on the father's first name. So if Ivan Vaslov has a son Edvard and a daughter Raisa, their names will be Edvard Ivanovich Vaslov and Raisa Ivanova Vaslov.

pawnbroker Person who lends money on the security of goods left. It is a quick way to borrow money, and does not depend on having a good credit rating. The main points of pawnbroking are:

- goods (often jewellery) left are said to be pledged. The receipt for them is called a ticket
- the pawnbroker asks the borrower to sign a pre-contract credit form. This may be waived if the borrower has used that pawnbroker in the previous three years
- the amount lent is usually a fraction of the item's real value, perhaps half. Amounts as little as £5 may be borrowed. There is no upper limit
- the pawnbroker must state what rate of interest is charged. This must also be expressed as an APR. The rate is usually more than a bank loan but less than a payday lender
- there is a 14-day cooling off period during which the borrower may withdraw but must pay interest charged during that period
- goods must be kept by the pawnbroker for six months
- goods may be recovered at any time by repaying the pledge plus interest, or paying the interest and pledging them again
- if the pledge is not repaid, the pawnbroker may sell the goods and use the proceeds to reduce the debt
- if the ticket is lost and the amount borrowed was less than £75, the pawnbroker may allow the borrower to complete a standard form. If the amount is more than £75, the borrower must swear an oath before a magistrate or commissioner of oaths, for which a fee is often charged
- if the pledge is not redeemed and the borrowed sum is more than £100, the pawnbroker must notify the borrower before selling the goods
- if the sum realised from sale is greater than the amount of the loan and interest, the balance is paid to the borrower
- a borrower is not liable for any shortfall should the sale not fully cover the loan and interest.

Many pawnbrokers are members of the National Pawnbroker's Association which has a code of conduct for its members. Pawnbroking is regulated by Consumer Credit Act 1974 as amended. Guidance on the tax implications of pawnbroking may be found in HMRC Manual at MLR3C2111.

Pawnbroking originated in China in about 1000 BC. In the UK, it became very common in the late 19th century. The nursery rhyme *Pop Goes the Weasel* is believed to be about pawnbroking.

Pay As You Earn System of collecting taxes from employment, introduced in 1944. Its use is compulsory. Tax is collected by reference to a tax code issued to each employee. National insurance is collected by reference to a contribution letter. These amounts are collected for tax months (6th of a calendar month to 5th of next month) and usually passed to HMRC by 22nd electronically or by 19th otherwise. There may also be adjustments for such things as statutory maternity pay. The employer must also make annual returns. PAYE is now administered electronically under Real Time Information.

PAYE **Pay As You Earn.**

payee Person to whom a payment is made. For PAYE, "means an employee, agency worker, pensioner or other payee" (PAYE Regulations SI 2003 No 2682 reg 2(1)).

PAYE income Income subject to the Pay As You Earn scheme (ITEPA 2003 s683(1)). There are three such sources of income:

- employment income
- pension income
- social security income.

payer Person who makes a payment.

PAYE records "Means the following documents and records —

(a) all wage sheets, deductions working sheets, documents completed under regulation 46 (Form P46), information provided under regulation 40A(1) (duty of employee to assist with completion of new employee fields in returns under regulations 67B and 67D) and any other documents and records relating to —

(i) the calculation of the PAYE income of the employees,

(ii) relevant payments to the employees, or

(iii) the deduction of tax from, or accounting for tax in respect of such payments, and

(b) all documents relating to any information which an employer is required to provide to HMRC under regulation 85 (Forms P11D and P9D)."

(PAYE regulations SI 2003 No 2682 reg 97(3) as amended)

PAYE refund Amount of tax that may be refunded to an employee under the PAYE system, such as when earnings are low late in the tax year, or the employee's tax code is adjusted. From 1996, no permission is needed to refund PAYE.

PAYE regulations Details rules for operating PAYE. They are statutory instrument SI 2003 No 2682, as amended.

PAYE settlement agreement (PSA) Agreement whereby the employer pays tax on the grossed-up value of benefits provided to employees that are minor, irregular or where apportionment to specific employees is impractical (ITEPA 2003 ss703-707). They were introduced in 1996. From 6 April 2018, a PSA lasts indefinitely until cancelled by HMRC or the employer. The employer is liable to pay class 1B national insurance on a PSA.

PAYE threshold Amount at which an employee starts to be liable to pay income tax under the PAYE scheme (PAYE Regulations 2003 reg 9).

payment for loss of office Payment to a person who gives up an office, such as director, voluntarily or otherwise. The term is widely construed to include compensation payments of all sorts, including of associated companies and payments on retirement, other than pensions.

Under CA 2006, such a payment may require the approval of members under CA 2006 s217. For tax, the first £30,000 may be tax-free.

payment holiday When a borrower is allowed to stop making payments for a period. There was a payment holiday of at least six months for mortgages and loans during the coronavirus of 2020. Interest continues to accrue during the holiday.

payment on account Some tax provisions require tax to be paid in advance of the underlying accounts being finalised. The self-assessment for income tax generally requires a payment to be made on 31 January in the tax year. Larger companies are required to pay corporation tax in instalments. Large VAT payers are required to make monthly payments (VATA 1994 s28). They still make quarterly returns.

payment period Period for which a payment relates for PAYE (PAYE Regs 2003 reg 25(6)).

payment protection insurance (PPI) Insurance policy sold with other financial products such as mortgages or bank accounts. They were sold from the 1970s, with most sold between 1990 and 2010.

The Financial Conduct Authority found that the policies were widely missold. A deadline of 29 August 2019 was set for policyholders to claim. About £33 billion was repaid with interest. The repayment bears no tax as it is simply a refund. Any interest paid with it, which was often more than the refund, is taxable as income.

payment via employer Term used for a benefit provided to an employee via the payroll. Although statutory maternity pay and similar could be so regarded, the term generally refers to working tax credit which was so paid between 2003 and 2006.

pay period Length of time to which a payslip relates. It is of particular relevance in calculating national insurance.

payphone Coin-operated telephone. For VAT purposes, this is a supply of a service at a VAT-inclusive price (VAT notice 700). The VAT fraction must be used to calculate the VAT element. For a standard rate of 20%, this means that one sixth of the payphone takings are VAT output tax.

pay reference period Period for which a worker must be paid the national minimum wage.

payroll The function of paying staff, with related duties.

payroll error Mistake in calculating the amount an employee should receive in his payslip. If the mistake is an underpayment, this should be corrected promptly. An employee may be willing to wait to the next pay period for a small underpayment to be corrected, but does not have to. Any underpayment comprises an unlawful deduction from wages. It is usually sufficient to make an advance equal to the underpayment, and to reclaim this on the corrected next payslip.

If the mistake is an overpayment, the law does not always allow it to be recovered.

If the mistake relates to tax or national insurance, the mistake must be corrected in accordance with those regulations. In general, the mistake must be corrected on the next payslip. The PAYE system usually sorts out any miscalculations of income tax. For an under-deduction of national insurance, the sum may be recovered in the current tax year or the following tax year, but not later. If the mistake cannot be corrected, HMRC must be so advised.

payroll giving Method by which workers may make tax-relieved donations to charities through the payroll (ITEPA 2003 s713). It was introduced in 1987. The scheme is voluntary for both employer and employees. From 2000, there is no limit to the maximum donation.

Approval of payroll giving schemes is set out in SI 1986 No 2211. The amount of giving is deducted from gross pay under PAYE, thus giving the employee income tax relief at source. Note that the donation does not reduce the amount of national insurance payable.

payroll ID Code used to identify an employee in a payroll package and in correspondence with HMRC. The ID must be unique for each employee. A new employee must not be given the ID for a former employee (HMRC Employer Bulletin 87 of December 2020).

payrolling Practice of accounting for tax on benefits through the payroll. The value of the benefit is added to gross pay and the same value is subtracted from net pay. This allows the benefit to have tax deducted at the correct rate. It should be noted that most benefits are not subject to class 1 national insurance, and so this adjustment is not made to calculate NI.

Payrolling is not part of the PAYE system though it is known that there are some arrangements agreed with HMRC that allows it to happen. Suggestions for using payrolling as an alternative to the current P11D system have been made frequently.

From 6 April 2016, payrolling is put on a statutory but voluntary basis under FA 2016 s15. An employer may choose to payroll the benefits of company cars, car fuel allowance, memberships, and private medical insurance. Payrolling may not be used for other benefits, such as beneficial loans.

Benefits have their values added to gross pay for income tax purposes (but not for national insurance). PAYE income tax is calculated for gross pay including benefit value. The same figure for value is then subtracted from net pay. Thus the benefit has been taxed at source. Such a benefit is excluded from the P11D form.

payslip Document that must be legally given to each employee (Employment Rights Act 1996 s8). From 6 April 2019, it must also be given to other workers, providing basic details of how their pay has been calculated.

PD1 HMRC department that deals with government ministers, senior civil servants and royalty.

P/E ratio Accounting ratio widely used for investment. It divides the value of a company's ordinary share by its earnings per share. The number represents the market expectation of the company's future performance.

peat Organic material extracted from a bog. When used as domestic fuel, it may be reduced rated for VAT under VATA 1994 Sch 7A Group 1. Further details are given in VAT Notice 701/19.

pecuniary Pertaining to money.

pecuniary liability principle Tax principle that there is a possible taxable benefit when an employer pays a personal liability of an employee (ITEPA 2003 s62(3)(a). The matter is discussed in HMRC Manual at EIM005800.

pedlar Itinerant vendor of household goods. Such a person must be at least 17 years old, of good character and have a pedlar's licence issued by the police under Pedlars Acts 1871 and 1881. In 2015, the government decided not to repeal these Acts.

peer to peer (P2P) Lending between individuals rather than between an individual and a financial institution. P2P lending platforms are regulated by the Financial Conduct Authority under Financial Services and Markets Act 2000 Part 4A. Losses from P2P lending may be offset only against P2P profits, under the provisions of ITA 2007 Part 8 Chapter 1A inserted by FA 2016 s32. Guidance is given in HMRC Manual at SAIM 12010. The definition of a peer-to-peer loan is given in ITA 2007 s412I. Provisions relating to income tax on interest is given in ITA 2007 s888E as inserted by FA 2017 Sch 5 para 3.

Penalties Consistency Panel Part of HMRC to which other officers may refer cases for guidance on what penalty should be imposed. It is referred to the in HMRC Manual at SAOG19200, for example.

penalty Charge incurred as a consequence of doing something wrong. For tax allowability, a penalty intended as a punishment is not tax-deductible. A penalty that has the nature of compensation is generally allowable. This general principle was established in *McKnight v Sheppard [1999] 71TC419* and is discussed in HMRC Manual at BIM38500.

Rates are given under Penalties in section 3 of this dictionary.

penalty charges Charges imposed by HMRC or similar body in respect of non-compliance with a law. Such penalties are generally not themselves tax-deductible (ITTOIA 2005s54).

The law on penalties for failure to make a return is given in FA 2009 s106 and Sch 55.

The law on penalties for failure to pay tax is given in FA 2009 s107.

penalty proceedings Legal proceedings brought against a taxpayer (TMA 1970 ss100C-100D).

pendente lite Latin: when litigation is pending. This refers to the period when a legal action has started but the matter has not been concluded.

penny Unit of value or coin of which there are 100 in a pound from 1971, and 240 previously. The penny was introduced around 775 AD. On 2 May 2019, the government abandoned plans to demonetise the little used 1p and 2p coins.

penny share Ordinary share in a company that trades for a low amount, usually less than £1.

pennyweight Old unit of weight still used for some jewels and precious metals. There are 240 pennyweight to a pound. A pennyweight is about 1.55 grams.

pension *Overview*

Regular payment in retirement generally funded by contributions put aside during the pensioner's working life.

Pensions are broadly funded in one of three ways:

- via the state
- through an employer's occupational pension scheme
- by the taxpayer himself or herself.

State pension

The state provides a basic pension and additional pension.

The basic pension is payable from state pension age (details in section 3 of this dictionary) provided the taxpayer has, from 6 April 2016, 35 years of national insurance contribution records. This means that the taxpayer has paid class 1, 2 or 3 national insurance for 35 whole years. Gaps in contribution record may be plugged by paying class 3 contributions, though there are time limits for doing so. If there are fewer than 35 years, a proportionately reduced pension is paid.

The additional pension comprises:

- graduated pension earned between 1961 and 1975
- state earnings-related pension scheme (SERPS) from 1978 to 2002, and
- state second pension earned between 2002 and 2016.

Each of these earns additional entitlement that is payable with the state pension.

For taxpayers who reach state pension age from 6 April 2016, they will receive a single tier pension unless the state pension plus additional pension gives a higher amount.

Someone with no entitlement may benefit from having contributions credited to them to create an entitlement.

Someone with no entitlement is entitled to receive a smaller state pension from the age of 80.

Occupational pension

An occupational pension scheme operates on one of two bases:

- defined benefit
- defined contribution.

A defined benefit scheme, sometimes called a final salary scheme, states in advance how much pension a person will receive. Typically a scheme will offer perhaps 1/60 of final salary for each year of service, so someone who works for 20 years will receive a pension of one third of their final salary. These schemes are generous to the employee and expensive to the employer (several businesses have been bankrupted by their pension schemes), and so these are now generally restricted to the public sector and some larger companies.

A defined contribution scheme, also known as money purchase, collects funds from the taxpayer, his or her employer, plus earnings from the invested fund as interest or dividends. This builds up a pot. When the taxpayer decides to start his or her pension, they can choose what type of pension they want, according to what the pot will buy.

Private pension

A person may, from 1978, take out a private pension. This is a defined contribution scheme. It works on the same basis as a defined contribution occupational pension scheme except that there is no employer's contribution.

Contracting out

From 1978, an occupational pension scheme could "contract out". That means that scheme members stopped building up an entitlement under SERPS or state second pension. They and their employers paid a little less national insurance. That stopped in 2012 for defined contribution schemes, and from 2016 for defined benefit schemes.

From 1978, an approved private pension scheme could similarly benefit. The taxpayer paid the full rate of national insurance but had part of it credited to his or her pension scheme pot. This stopped in 2012.

Tax relief

There is no limit to the amount a person may contribute to a pension scheme. The limit is on the amount that qualifies for income tax relief. There is no national insurance relief. So an employee earning £3,000 a month who pays £200 into a pension fund, pays income tax on £2,800 but national insurance on £3,000.

A person may contribution up to 100% of their earnings, or £3,600 if more, to a pension scheme each year. Otherwise pension contributions are subject to an annual limit and a lifetime limit. For occupational pension scheme, these limits include the employer's contributions.

Payment of pension

The pension fund is used to buy an annuity, which simply means that the lump sum is converted to a regular income. This is often for the rest of a person's life, so those who die young subsidise those who die old. Alternatively, it may be for a finite number of years, after which the remaining pot can buy another annuity.

A pension is not just paid for retirement. A pension can, for example, be paid to someone who is disabled at any age.

In general, up to 25% of a pension fund may be taken as a tax-free lump sum between the ages of 55 and 74. Someone with a defined contribution fund may now take sums out at any age.

Payments or regular pension are taxable, regardless of whether the taxpayer has taken out a lump sum. This includes the state pension which is paid without deduction of tax. The income tax is collected by some other means, such as by deduction from other income.

Payments from an occupational pension scheme or private pension scheme have income tax deducted at source by the pension provider. This is done under PAYE via a pension payroll. The pensioner is given a tax code and income tax charged accordingly.

If payments are made from a pension fund other than within the legal limits, they may be subject to high rates of income tax.

National insurance is not deducted from pension payments.

There are many other provisions relating to pensions. Some details and rates are given in section 3 of this dictionary.

pensionable earnings Earnings on which the contributions and benefits of a pension scheme are calculated (Superannuation Act 2010 s3(7)).

pension benefits Entitlements that arise from a pension. The main benefit is a regular income. This is subject to income tax on the same basis as earnings and (if the pensioner is still under state pension age) class 1 national insurance. Generally, the pensioner may receive up to one quarter of the pension fund tax free. Occupational pension schemes may also provide life insurance, and a pension to dependants.

pension cold calling Making unsolicited calls to members of the public about their pensions. This is outlawed from 9 January 2019 by SI 2018 No 1396.

pension credit Social security benefit introduced in 2003 to pensioners on a low income (State Pension Credit Act 2002; State Pension Credit Regulations SI 2002 No 1792). It is tax free and is not subject to the benefit cap. It has two elements. The guarantee credit is designed to ensure that the pensioner has a minimum level of income. The savings credit rewards pensioners who have savings. The savings credit is phased out from 2016.

pension debit Amount by which a person's pension entitlement is reduced by pension-splitting on divorce under Welfare Reform and Pensions Act 1999 s29.

pensioner Person in receipt of a pension. For PAYE, the term "means a person receiving PAYE pension income" (PAYE Regulations SI 2003 No 2682 reg 2(1)).

pensioner's Christmas bonus A sum of £10 paid each Christmas to each person receiving a state pension (SSCBA 1992 s148). This sum has not changed since its introduction in 1971. It is not taxed (ITEPA 2003 s677).

pension fund Fund established by an employer, company, trade union or other body to collect and invest funds, paid by one or both of the employer and employee. Pension funds are major investors in shares. In relation to staffing costs for research and development expenditure, the term is defined in CTA 2009 s1123(8).

pension guarantee Period (often five years) for which pension payments are guaranteed even if the pensioner dies.

pension income Regular income from a pension as against a lump sum. The income is subject to income tax (ITEPA 2003 from s565).

pension input period Period for which pension contributions are measured against the annual limit (FA 2004 s280(2)). Since 2015, this period has been the same as the tax year.

pension lump sum Single payment that a pension member may receive, typically up to one quarter of the pension fund. The payment is usually tax-free.

pension payer For PAYE, "means a person making payments of PAYE pension income" (PAYE Regulations SI 2003 No 2682 reg 2(1)). Regulation 11 explains how such a payer should operate the PAYE regulations.

Pension Protection Fund Body designed to protect members of defined benefit pension schemes that become insolvent (Pensions Act 2004 s107). It started in 2005, and is funded by a levy on defined benefit pension schemes. Its rates are given in section 3 of this dictionary.

pension protection levy Levy made on pension funds under provisions of Pensions Act 2004 s175. Its rates are given in section 3 of this dictionary.

pensions advice allowance Tax allowance introduced from 6 April 2017 (ITEPA 2003 s308C). It allows a pension scheme member to draw up to £500 from his or her pension fund for advice on pensions.

Pensions Advisory Service, The Body established to provide advice to members of an occupational pension scheme. It is grant-funded from the Department of Work and Pensions.

pension scheme A means by which an individual can make pension provision. This may be either collective or individual and with or without the involvement (by means of contributions or otherwise) from the individual's employer.

HMRC defines a pension scheme as a scheme "set up to provide benefits for/in respect of any of the following circumstances

- retirement,
- death,
- attaining a particular age,
- serious ill-health or incapacity, or
- in similar circumstances."

(Inspectors' Manual at RPSM02200020). This mirrors the wording of FA 2004 s150.

Such a scheme may be registered or unregistered. A registered pension scheme attracts particular tax advantage.

pension scheme member Someone who has rights under a pension scheme, particularly an occupational pension scheme. There are four types of member:

- active member: someone who is accruing benefits under the scheme (usually a current employee);
- deferred member: someone who is no longer accruing benefits (usually a former employee) though benefits already accrued may continue to grow by being indexed;
- pension credit member: someone who has rights under the scheme from pension credits (usually someone who has transferred from another pension scheme but who is not an active member); and
- pensioner member: someone who is receiving a regular pension (usually a retired employee).

Only an active member is entitled to tax relief on contributions to the pension fund, though this point is largely academic as only active members would be contributing anyway.

Pensions (India, Pakistan and Burma) Act Act passed in 1955 that may provide a pension to those who worked there. Payments paid under this Act may be free of income tax under ITEPA 2003 s654.

pension splitting Provision where a divorced person may be entitled to have part of a former spouse's pension fund transferred to him or her (WRA 1999). This provision is introduced from 1 December 2000.

Pensions Regulator Body corporate established under Pensions Act 2004 s1 with effect from 6 April 2005.

Pensions Regulator Tribunal Tribunal established under Pensions Act 2004 s102 to deal with disputes between pension funds and the Pensions Regulator.

pension tax relief Tax relief on contributions to a pension fund. Note that there is no equivalent relief for national insurance. This means that an employee earning £2,000 a month and paying £100 to a pension fund pays tax on £1,900 but national insurance on £2,000.

People's Budget David Lloyd George's highly controversial Budget of 1909. He sought to increase taxes and introduce national insurance. It led to a constitutional crisis and restrictions on the House of Lords.

personal equity plan Tax-advantaged investment scheme from 1987 to 1999, when it was replaced by ISAs.

peppercorn Trivial sum that still is adequate as consideration to ensure that what is really a gift counts as a contract. At 2020 prices, a peppercorn is worth about a fortieth of one penny. In the case *Chappell v Nestlé [1960] AC 67*, Somervell LJ said "a peppercorn does not cease to be good consideration if it is established that the person does not like pepper and will throw away the corn".

peppercorn option An option in an insurance policy that allows the policyholder to reduce the premiums to a nominal amount after ten years or more, and is then able to make part-surrenders of the policy. The insurance premium tax implications are discussed in HMRC Manual at IPTM8180.

Pepper v Hart Leading tax case which was finally settled by the House of Lords in 1992. It established an important legal principle, and clarified an area of tax law. The legal principle established is that the courts may look to Hansard, the record of Parliamentary proceedings to see what the purpose of an Act was in deciding how to interpret it. This is a modern form of what is known as the mischief rule. The case clarified the tax law on what constitutes the cost of an employee benefit. A teacher of a private school was allowed to have his son educated there for a much reduced fee. It was accepted that this was a taxable benefit in kind to the extent that the cost of the education exceeded the sum paid by the teacher. The dispute was whether the cost was the marginal cost of educating one extra pupil (basically food, stationery, laundry etc for one pupil) or was the direct cost which includes all the school's overheads divided by the number of pupils. All the courts up to the Lords held that the Act was written so that the direct cost had to be used, which resulted in a much larger figure. The Lords held they could look to the Parliamentary debate, and held it was the marginal cost.

per annum Latin: per year.

P/E ratio Important financial indicator for investors. It takes the price of the share, as shown on a stock market for a listed company, and divides it by the earnings per share (EPS). The EPS is itself an indicator representing net profit after tax divided by the number of shares in issue. So if a company makes a net profit of £4 million and has 2 million shares in issue. the EPS is £2. If the share is trading at £10, the P/E ratio is 5. For listed shares, the P/E ratio is published with share prices in *The Financial Times* and other newspapers.

percentage point The number of a percentage. The term is commonly used to avoid ambiguity when percentages change. The statement that an interest rate of 10% has increased by 5% could be regarded as meaning that the new interest rate is either 15% or 10.5%. Ambiguity is avoided by saying that it has moved by five percentage points or half a percentage point, as appropriate.

One hundredth of a percentage point is a basis point.

percentage threshold scheme Scheme that operated between 1995 and 2014, whereby an employer could recover statutory sick pay (SSP) from the state for any period when SSP exceeded 13% of total national insurance. Since 6 April 2014, the scheme has been scrapped and the employer bears the whole cost of SSP, apart from a special scheme that applied during the coronavirus outbreak.

perch Imperial unit of length equal to 5½ yards, about 5.03 metres.
A square perch is 30¼ square yards, about 25.3 square metres
In stonemasonry, the term is a cubic measure of 24¾ cubic feet or 0.7 cubic metres.

per contra Latin: to the opposite. Accounting term, now rarely used, referring to the opposite side of a bookkeeping double entry.

percussion caps Items in the list of explosives for which there may be special Customs provisions (Explosives Act 1875 s3(1)).

per diem Latin for "daily". The term is sometimes used to mean a daily allowance, such as additional pay for working overseas.

perfect entry "Entry made in accordance with regulation 5 of the Customs Controls on Importation of Goods Regulations 1991 or warehousing regulations, as the case may require" (CEMAs1(1)).

performance In accounting, "the relationship of the income and expenses of an entity, as reported in the statement of comprehensive income" (FRS 102 glossary). "Performance is the relationship of the income and expenses of an entity during a reporting period" (FRS 102 section 2.23).

performance bond Form of guarantee from an insurance company given by a seller in a contract. If the seller fails to honour a commitment and make adequate compensation, the buyer may claim under the bond.

performance-related condition "A condition that requires the performance of a particular level of service or units of output to be delivered, with payment of, or entitlement to, the resources conditional on that performance" (FRS 102 glossary).

performance-related pay Another term for profit-related pay.

period for filing In company law, the period allowed for the filing of company accounts (CA 2006 s441(2)).

periodical Publication circulated at regular intervals. It is generally zero-rated under VATA 1994 Sch 8 Group 3. A publication can qualify even when it largely comprises posters to be unstapled *(EMAP Consumer Magazines Ltd [1994] VTD 13322).* It also includes a single edition when there had been an intention to produce further editions *(European Publishing Consultants Ltd [1994] VTD 13841).*

periodic charge Another name for the ten-yearly charge to inheritance tax on a relevant property trust.

periodic payment For stamp duty, periodic payments may generally be regarded as part of the transaction value for a period of up to 20 years. For maintenance, this "does not include an instalment of a lump sum" (ITA 2007 s454(9). The consequence is that this did not qualify for the 10% tax relief for maintenance payments.

period of absence In relation to private residence relief for capital gains tax, "means a period during which the dwelling-house or the part of the dwelling-house was not the individual's only or main residence and throughout which he had no residence or main residence eligible for relief under this section" (TCGA1992 s223(7)).

period of account Period for which a set of accounts are made up. In effect, it is the same as an accounting period. The term is given a specific meaning for capital allowances (CAA 2001 s6(2)).

period of default Period when tax remained unpaid after the due date. It runs from the due date to the day before the tax was paid (TMA 1970 s59C(12)).

period of importation In relation to the temporary importation rule under the remittance basis, this term is defined in ITA 2007 s809Z4(10).

period of incapacity for work (PIW) Absence that qualifies for statutory sick pay, for which a PIW must last for at least four days. The person must generally be absent for a recognisable sickness or injury, including necessary convalescent. If a person starts a new PIW within eight weeks of a previous one ending, the two PIWs are treated as one.

period of no public access In relation to the temporary importation rule for the remittance basis, this term is defined in ITA 2007 s809Z4(10).

period of ownership In relation to private residence relief from capital gains tax, this "does not include any period before 31 March 1982" (TCGA1992 s223(7)). The Court of Appeal ruled that the period starts from completion in the case *Higgins v HMRC [2019].*

perishable goods Goods that will deteriorate quickly and naturally, such as fruit. There are many legal provisions that allow the possessor to deal with such items, such as disposal by a Customs officer.

perjury The criminal offence of lying under oath or of making a false statement on a tax return (Perjury Act 1911 s5). This was defined as a "false statement to the prejudice of the Crown and public revenue" in the case *R v Hudson [1956] CA 36 TC 561*. Summary proceedings can be brought in Scotland under TMA 1970 s107.

perk Abbreviation of perquisite, a benefit from work.

permanent difference In relation to deferred tax, a difference between a person's profit per the accounts and their taxable profits, where that difference will not reverse. An example is the disallowance of entertainment or personal expenditure. A permanent difference is not reflected in the amount of deferred tax.

permanent establishment Maintaining a trading presence in a country. There are many tax provisions relating to this, particularly regarding VAT.

permanent home The country where a person intends to live for the rest of his or her life. It is a factor in determining domicile for inheritance tax.

permanent interest bearing shares (PIBS) Shares often issued by building societies for which there are special provisions for capital gains tax (TCGA 1992 s117(8A)).

permanent overpayment (POP) Small excess payment of £2 or less created as a result of a charge amendment or a payment being applied to a charge record" (Inspectors' Manual at DMBM121055". A POP is not reallocated even where there are outstanding liabilities from the taxpayer.

permanent residence For capital gains tax, this means main residence.

permanent workplace In relation to travel in employment, means "a place which –

(a) the employee regularly attends in the performance of the duties of the employment, and

(b) is not a temporary workplace"

(ITEPA 2003 s339(2)).

per mille Per Thousand. The premium rate for some types of group insurance is quoted per £1000 of benefit.

permitted limit In relation to enterprise investment scheme, the maximum number of employees that may be employed by an investee company. This is 500 for a knowledge-intensive company and 250 for other companies (ITA 2007 s186A(3A) as inserted by Finance (No 2) Act Sch 5).

permitted maximum age requirement In relation to enterprise investment scheme, this term is defined in ITA 2007 s175A as inserted by Finance (No 2) Act 2015 Sch 5.

permitted period In relation to residence nil rate band for inheritance tax, this term is defined in Inheritance Tax Act 1984 s8L(2) as inserted by Finance (No 2) Act 2015 s9.

permitted work Work a person may do without it affecting their entitlement to employment and support allowance.

permitted work higher limit Work for which an employment support allowance may be paid, provided it is arranged by a local authority or other body entrusted with assisting claimants back into work. A claimant may do such work for up to 52 weeks.

permitted work lower limit Work for which an employment support allowance claimant is paid no more than £20 a week.

perpetual bond In investment, a bond that has no maturity date and no provision for repaying the principal. It therefore pays interest indefinitely.

perpetual debenture Debenture that cannot be redeemed, or where redemption is after a long time or on the happening of an unlikely contingency. Such debentures are generally legal under CA 2006 s739.

perpetual succession Attribute of a company that it can live for ever, after its founders have died.

perpetuity (1) Term for an attempt to dictate how property is held a long time into the future. It is regarded as contrary to public policy for someone to be able to tie up property for centuries.

The present law is contained in Perpetuities and Accumulations Act 2009 which came into force on 6 April 2010. It creates a maximum perpetuity period of 125 years. A will or trust deed may specify a shorter period, but not a longer one. All pension schemes are exempted from this limit (as previously a few pension schemes were caught).

The 2009 Act only applies to newly created trusts and estates. Existing trusts and estates remain governed by Perpetuities and Accumulations Act 1964, though trustees may opt into the 2009 provisions but with a 100-year accumulation period. The 1964 Act generally imposes a limit of 80 years. Trusts and estates created before 16 July 1964 are governed by common law provisions against perpetuities. These provisions were developed from the end of the 17th century. They generally restrict the perpetuity period to the life of the settlor plus 21 years.

(2) British government security that the government is not obliged ever to repay but may continue paying interest indefinitely.

perquisite (perk) Incidental benefit from employment. It is taxed as a benefit in kind.

perry Cider made from pears, and subject to the same rates of alcoholic liquor duty.

persistent poverty In Scots law, from 2017 this is defined as when a child has lived in a household with income of less than 60% of median income for three out of four consecutive years (Child Poverty (Scotland) Act 2017 s6).

person Someone recognised by law. This can be a normal human individual or a recognised corporate body such as a company or trust (Interpretation Act 1978 Sch 1).

person abroad For the purposes of anti-avoidance on transfer of assets abroad, the term means "a person who is resident or domiciled outside the United Kingdom" (ITA 2007 s718(1)).

personal allowance Amount an individual may earn in a tax year before becoming liable to pay income tax. (ITA 2007 s35). For 2020/21, the allowance is £12,500 a year. Rates for other years and other income tax allowances are given in section 3 of this dictionary.

From 1990, this applies to all individual taxpayers including married women.

This allowance is reduced by £1 for every £2 by which adjusted net income exceeds £100,000 (FA 2009 s4). The consequence of this is to create a marginal income tax rate of 60% on the slice of income up to £100,000 plus twice the personal allowance. For 2020/21 (when the personal allowance is £12,500), this 60% rate applies to income between £100,000 and £125,000, after which the marginal rate returns to 40%.

From April 2015, it is possible for a spouse or civil partner to transfer 10% of their personal allowance to their partner, provided the partner is not liable to the higher rate of tax (FA 2014 s11). For a personal allowance of £12,500, this means that one partner will have an allowance of £13,750, and the other partner £11,250.

personal company For capital gains tax on gifts of business assets, a company where at least 5% of the voting rights are vested in an individual (TCGA 1992 s165(8)).

person already connected with the company Term used in CA 2006 s756(5). Such a person is not regarded as a member of the public for the purposes of an offer to acquire shares or other securities in a private company.

personal applicant "A person who is applying for a grant of representation without the help of a solicitor or other agent" (HMRC inheritance tax glossary).

personal capacity Legal ability which it is assumed all adults have to manage their affairs until the contrary is demonstrated.

personal chattels Movable items; same as chattels. The term "shall mean goods, furniture, and other articles capable of complete transfer by delivery, and (when separately assigned or charged) fixtures and growing crops, but shall not include chattel interests in real estate, nor fixtures (except trade machinery as herein-after defined), when assigned together with a freehold or leasehold interest in any land or building to which they are affixed, nor growing crops when assigned together with any interest in the land on which they grow, nor shares or interests in the stock, funds, or securities of any government, or in the capital or property or incorporated or joint stock companies, nor choses in action, nor any stock or produce upon any farm or lands which by virtue of any covenant or agreement or of the custom of the country ought not to be removed from any farm where the same are at the time of making or giving of such bill of sale" (Bills of Sale Act 1878 s4).

For inheritance purposes, "means tangible movable property, other than such property which –

- consists of money or securities for money, or
- was used at the death of the intestate solely or mainly for business purposes, or
- was held at the death of the intestate solely as an investment."

(Administration of Estates Act 1925 s55(1)(x) as amended by Inheritance and Trustees' Powers Act 2014 s3(1)).

personal company For capital gains tax on gifts of business assets, a company where at least 5% of the voting rights are vested in the individual (TCGA1992 s165(8)).

personal contract purchase Means of acquiring personal goods, such as a car. It is a cross between hire purchase and leasing.

When the item is acquired, the seller states the price at which he is prepared to buy back the item after a stated number of years. This price is known as the minimum guaranteed future value (MGFV). Until then the car is leased. When the time arrives, and assuming the goods are still in fair condition, either the seller pays the MGFV and the lease ends, or the possessor pays the dealer and the MGFV and acquires the vehicle outright.

personal credit agreement Agreement between an individual and another person by which that other person provides the individual with credit of any amount (Consumer Credit Act 1974 s8(1)).

personal effects For Customs purposes, items that a person reasonably requires for a journey. This includes clothing, toiletries, personal jewellery and pets. Such effects are exempt from Customs duty but must be notified to Customs.

personal employee Domestic staff who could be taxed under the simplified PAYE deduction scheme. This scheme was closed to new employees from 6 April 2012 and to existing employees from 6 April 2013. All personal employees must now be accounted for under normal PAYE rules with reporting under real time information.

personal equity plan (PEP) Tax-advantage savings scheme that applied between 1987 and 1999. It is now replaced by the individual savings accounts (ISAs).

personal estate Property other than land and buildings that a person owned at death (Wills Act 1837 s1).

personal identification number (PIN) Code, typically of four digits, which allows the holder of a card to access the funds to which the card relates. The number is commonly referred to as a PIN number (even though the N of PIN stands for number).

personal incidental expenses (PIE) Original name for incidental overnight expenses.

personal independence payment (PIP) Social security payment to help with the additional costs of long-term disability. It replaces **disability living allowance.** Its main features are:

- it may be claimed by or for anyone who is at least 16 years old and who has not reached state pension age
- it is not means-tested
- there are two elements: a daily living component for those who have difficulty with everyday life, and a mobility component for those who have mobility problems
- a claimant may receive one or both of these components

- eligibility is assessed on a point basis. Someone needs 8 points for a PIP at basic rate, or 12 points for the enhanced rate
- points depend on how the disability affects the claimant, not on the nature of the disability itself. For example, a person who cannot use an oven but can use a microwave scores 2 points. A person who cannot prepare or cook food at all scores 8 points
- the disability must have been met for three months and expected to last for another nine months
- an award is usually made for 2 years, but can be made for 5 or 10 years
- PIP may be claimed by calling 0800 917 2222.

The relevant law is WRA 2012 from s77.

personal information Information that relates to a person's health, welfare or spiritual support. HMRC is generally not allowed to see such information about a taxpayer (FA 2008 Sch 36 para 19(3)). Similar provisions apply in Scotland (Revenue Scotland and Tax Powers Act 2014 s136(6)). There are some exceptions. For example, if a taxpayer argues that they have reasonable excuse for late payment or filing because of a health condition, they will usually be expected to provide evidence of this.

personal liability notice (PLN) Notice that HMRC may serve on a culpable company officer requiring them personally to pay any shortfall of national insurance (Social Security Administration Act 1992 from s121C). From 6 April 2014, there are circumstances when a PLN may be served on a director for unpaid PAYE (ITEPA 2003 s97ZA).

personal licence For alcohol, "a licence which:

(a) is granted by a licensing authority to an individual, and
(b) authorises that individual to supply alcohol, or authorise the supply of alcohol, in accordance with a premises licence"

(Licensing Act 2003 s111(1)).

For gambling, a licence which authorises an individual to perform functions in connection with gambling facilities (Gambling Act 2005 s127).

personal loan Money lent to an individual. For peer-to-peer loans, the term is defined ITA 2007 s412(7). This restricts loss relief on such loans.

personal pension Pension plan that an individual may take out for himself or herself from July 1988 and for which he or she may receive tax relief up to an annual allowance and lifetime allowance. Such a scheme must be set up in accordance with FA 2004 s154(1).

personal pension scheme A pension scheme previously approved by the Board of Inland Revenue under ICTA 1988 s361. Such a pension scheme must be established in accordance with FA 2004 s154(1). A personal pension scheme is one so established which is not an occupational pension scheme (Pension Schemes Act 1993 s1(1)).

personal portfolio bond Tax avoidance scheme that was rendered ineffective from 6 April 1999. It was an insurance policy that invested in assets already owned by the policy holder.

personal protective equipment Equipment to protect an individual from external risks. The term was particularly used in 2020 for equipment to protect health and care workers during the coronavirus outbreak. These items were temporarily zero-rated from 1 May 2020 under SI 2020 No 458 which created a new Group 20 in VATA 1994 Sch 8. On 9 July 2020, HMRC expressly stated that personal protective equipment provided by an employer is not a taxable benefit in kind of the employee.

personal records Records that relate to an individual rather than to his or her business, financial or tax affairs. HMRC is generally restricted from requesting such records in an information notice (FA 2008 Sch 36 para 19(3)). This largely follows police law (Police and Criminal Evidence Act 1984 s12). For Scotland, similar provisions are given in Revenue Scotland and Tax Powers Act 2014 s136(6).

personal representative Person who deals with the estate of a person who has died. The personal representative is an executor if the deceased left a will, or administrator otherwise.

personal return Declaration an individual is required to make to HMRC to allow his liability for income tax and capital gains tax to be calculated. The general requirement is contained is TMA 1970 s8.

personal savings allowance Additional allowance against income tax available from 6 April 2016 for savings income. The amount is £1,000 for a basic rate taxpayer; £500 for a higher rate taxpayer; and zero for an additional rate taxpayer.

personal security Expenditure that relates to protecting people, rather than property. From 6 April 1989, tax relief may be claimable for such expenditure (ITEPA 2003 s377 and ITTOIA 2005 s81.

Expenditure may qualify for a capital allowance (CAA 2001 s33).

An Inland Revenue press release dated 13 April 1989 gave examples as including alarm systems, bulletproof glass in windows, and floodlighting. The press release suggested that the tax relief applied only to persons who "face a special threat of injury or death from terrorists and other extremist groups who resort to violence".

In the case *Lord Hanson v Mansworth [2004] SpC 410*, the Special Commissioners held that Lord Hanson was one of the few people who qualified. Hanson had received death threats from the IRA against whom his company incurred high expenditure to protect him.

personal service company (PSC) Company that provides the services of a worker who would otherwise be regarded as an employee. From 6 April 2000, the PSC is generally required to collect tax and national insurance under the IR 35 provisions (ITEPA 2003 ss48-61).

personal welfare LPA A form of lasting power of attorney that may be made from 1 October 2007 by a person who is at least 18 and has mental capacity (Mental Capacity Act 2005). It appoints someone called the attorney who may make decisions about the person's welfare should that person lose mental capacity. Such decisions include giving consent for medical treatment.

person with significant control (PSC) Person who exercises significant control over a company but is not necessarily a director.

From 1 January 2016, every company must keep a register of PSCs. The law is contained in CA 2006 from s790A as inserted by Small Business, Enterprise and Employment Act 2015 from s81.

per stirpes Latin for "by branches". It relates to how property is divided between descendants. If a parent leaves property to his or her children, one of whom has died, that child's inheritance is divided between that child's own children.

persuasive precedent Decision of a court or tribunal that influences future decisions without binding courts or tribunals to follow it. Examples of persuasive precedents include decisions of a first tier tribunal, decisions of courts in other countries with similar systems of law, and obiter dicta in other cases.

Peru South American country. Its currency is the new sol of 100 centimos. The UK has no double taxation treaty.

pervasive recognition Procedure to be followed in measuring amounts in financial statements. The procedure is set out in accounting standard FRS 102 para 2.35.

perversity Unreasonable wrongness, usually capricious. It is the only ground of appeal on a point of fact from a decision of a tribunal.

The leading case on this is the House of Lords decision in *Edwards v Bairstow & Harrison [1955] 36 TC 207.* A leather manufacturer bought a cotton spinning plant with a view to selling it quickly. In the event, it sold the plant in five lots. The general commissioners and Chancery Division of the High Court held this was an isolated transaction and not taxable. The Lords decided that "the only reasonable conclusion on the evidence before the Commissioners was that the transaction was an adventure in the nature of trade". It held that "the Commissioners have acted without any evidence or upon a view of the facts which could be reasonably entertained".

HMRC discusses the matter in HMRC Manual at BIM20075.

pesewa One hundredth of a cedi, currency of Ghana.

peso Currencies of Argentina and Chile.

pesticides tax A proposed tax suggested in 1999 to deal with environmental concerns. In the event, those concerns were addressed without the need to introduce this tax.

Peterhead principle Principle that establishes when a mutual trading organisation is engaged in mutual trading. The name comes from the case *British Legion Branch, Remembrance and Welcome Home Fund v CIR [1953] 35 TC 509.* The matter is discussed in HMRC Manual at BIM24475.

pet food Food specifically prepared for pets. It does not benefit from the exemption for some animal feed (such as for farm animals) in VATA 1994 Sch 8 Group 1. The matter is discussed in VAT Notice 701/15.

petition principii Latin for "inclining towards the beginning". In logic and advocacy, a false argument that assumes what it is trying to prove.

Pet Passport Scheme by which a cat, dog or ferret could move between EU states without having to stay in quarantine.

From 1 January 2021, such UK passports cease to be valid. Such pets from Great Britain need an animal health certificate (AHC). This confirms that the pet has been microchipped and vaccinated against rabies. A certificate is needed 10 days before travelling and is valid for four months. The first such certificate is available from 22 December 2020. The traveller must enter the UK or EU at a designated travellers' point of entry.

The same process applies to a pet travelling between Northern Ireland and Great Britain.

In addition, a pet travelling to Northern Ireland, Finland, Irish Republic or Malta must be treated against tapeworm five days before arrival.

The new provisions apply to all pets including guide dogs and other assistance dogs.

petrol Common form of road fuel. It is subject to hydrocarbon oil duty (HODA 1979 s6) and VAT.

Petrol provided to an employee for private use in a company car is a taxable benefit, in addition to the benefit of the car itself (ITEPA 2003 s149). The employer is liable to pay class 1A national insurance. Provision of such fuel may require an adjustment to the VAT return.

petroleum gas For hydrocarbon oil duty, this is a hydrocarbon that is gaseous at a temperature of 15^{0}C and a pressure of 1013.25 millibars, and which is not natural gas (HODA 1979 s23C(5)(a)).

petroleum revenue tax Addition to corporation tax payable in respect of petrol production (Oil Taxation Act 1975). It was introduced in 1974. The tax was not applied to fields approved from 16 March 1993. Its rate was set to zero from 1 January 2016.

petrol pump A petrol pump (and other road fuel delivery equipment) is sometimes supplied by an oil company on a deferred payment basis. The tax treatment for the different methods is explained in HMRC Manual at BIM45365.

petty cash Ready cash in the form of bank notes and coins kept by an entity to pay for small items of incidental expenditure. Payments are usually recorded in a petty cash book and supported by vouchers. The expenses side of this book is a prime book of account for bookkeeping purposes.

PFI Private finance initiative. This is an arrangement whereby a private enterprise provides a public facility such as a hospital or prison, and receives payments from the state. Such arrangements are generally exempt from stamp duty land tax (FA 2003 Sch 4 para 17).

phantom shares Financial arrangement whereby a person receives payment from a company as if he or she owned shares in the company. Such "shares" are sometimes used in employee schemes. Guidance is given in HMRC Manual at BIM44002.

phased retirement "When the deceased has divided their pension entitlement into a series of segments and has agreed a plan of retirement with their pension provider to take so many segments each year" (HMRC inheritance tax glossary).

pheasants Game birds. These are zero-rated as food even when bred for shooting *(N C D Carter [2000] VTD 17288).*

Philippines Island state in the Pacific Ocean. Its currency is the Philippine peso of 100 centavos. The UK has a double taxation convention of 1976.

Philippine peso Currency of the Philippines.

phishing Practice of pretending to be HMRC or a bank or other body when sending emails in large numbers. The object is to obtain personal details and bank account numbers.

HMRC has a department that deals with phishing. HMRC asks those who receive suspicious emails, text messages or phone calls to contact them at phishing@hmrc.gov.uk or by text message to 60599.

phoenix company Company that "rises from the ashes" of another company that has become insolvent with unpaid debts. The phoenix company is usually in the same business and run by the same people.

photobook A bound book comprising photographs taken by a customer. Such a book can come within the scope of VAT zero-rating for books (*Harrier LLC. TC 1562 [2011]).*

phytosanitary certificate Document required for the importation of some plants. The certificate relates to how far the plant will grow and spread.

piano rolls Rolls of perforated paper which operate a pianola or other type of player piano. It is standard-rated according to VAT notice 701/10, and does not benefit from the zero-rating for printed music under VATA 1994 Sch 8 Group 3.

piece rate Method of paying employees or other workers according to what has been produced, such as £2 for each item assembled.

piece worker A person who is paid according to units of production rather than time. A piece worker must be paid the national minimum wage on the time work basis.

pig ark Piece of curved material to make a simple kennel-like protection for outdoor pigs. This qualifies as plant and machinery (at the higher rate) in the pig industry (HMRC Brief 03/2010 issued on 23 February 2010).

Pigovian tax Tax imposed to reduce demand for a product for social reasons. Taxes on alcohol, tobacco and petrol are examples.

pig tent Form of protection for outdoor pigs. This qualifies as plant and machinery (at the higher rate) in the pig industry (HMRC Brief 03/2010 issued on 23 February 2010).

Pilcher The case that determined the tax treatment for crops on land. The full name of the case is *CIR v Pilcher [1949] 31TC314.* It is discussed in HMRC Manual at BIM35410.

pilotage The act of steering a boat, particularly through difficult waters or between structures, or the fee for doing so. Pilotage is generally zero-rated under VATA 1994 Sch 8 Group 8.

pilot scheme Scheme that is tried out on an experimental basis in a limited area to identify practical issues. Many social security benefits are first subject to a pilot scheme.

pinball machine For VAT purposes, this is regarded as an amusement machine (VAT notice 701/13). Such a machine is specifically excluded from the scope of amusement machine licence duty.

pinniped Category of animal that includes seals, sea-lions and walruses. The import of the fur or other products of such animals is generally prohibited from 20 August 2010.

PIN number Personal identified number, particularly the four-digit number to authorise a payment against a debit or credit card.

pint Imperial unit of liquid capacity. It is equal to 568.26 millilitres. There are 8 pints in a gallon. Milk and some drinks are still sold in pints.

pipeline Method of importing gas or liquid whose treatment is given in CEMA 1979 s3.

pirated goods Goods produced in contravention of copyright laws or patents. Customs may seize such goods.

Pitcairn Islands UK Overseas Territory comprising islands in the South Pacific Ocean. It was settled in 1790 by mutineers from the Bounty and their Tahitian companions. The currency is the New Zealand dollar.

pitch agreement Lease, agreement or similar arrangement that allows a person to park a caravan on a site. The terms of such an agreement can determine the VAT liability for the supply of a site, as explained in VAT leaflet 701/20.

pitching In brewing, the re-using of yeast from a previous brew.

Pivotal Enterprise Resilience Fund Fund launched in Scotland in May 2020 to help small and medium-sized businesses in Scotland.

pizza For VAT, the supply of a takeaway pizza is standard-rated as hot takeaway food. The tribunal did not accept that a pizza was only hot as a result of having not cooled down, and could be eaten cold. *Domino's Pizza Group Ltd (No 2) [2002] VTD 18866.*

placement stage First of three stages of money laundering. This is when funds from crime first enter the financial system. The next two stages are layering stage and integration stage. **place of business**Where a business, trade, profession or vocation is carried on, or the head office when there is more than one place (TMA 1970 Sch 3 para 2(5)).

place of residence A person's usual place of residence or, if unknown, the person's last known place of residence (TMA 1970 Sch 3 para 2(4)).

place of supply Country which is regarded as from where a supply is made for VAT purposes (VATA 1994 s7-7A).

plainly unfair Grounds on which a penalty may be set aside. An example is the case *Hok Ltd [2011] TC 1286.* There have been many cases where harsh and disproportionately penalties have been upheld by tribunals, so this would seem to be limited to the most extreme cases.

plain vanilla In investment, a description of a derivative or other security with standard exercise terms and no special clauses. For derivatives, the term is defined in CTA 2009 s708.

Plan Green Unsuccessful tax avoidance scheme. It sought to reduce an employee's income tax liability for car benefit by purchasing carbon credits to set off against the carbon dioxide emission from which the benefit is calculated. The scheme does not work as carbon credits do not affect car benefit. Further details are given in HMRC Spotlight 16.

planning blight Loss in value of land because of a proposed development nearby.

planning contribution Scheme of allowing planning authorities to collect a sum from developers in their area as an additional source of revenue (Planning and Compulsory Purchase Act 2004 s46).

planning gain supplement Proposed charge that local authorities would have been able to impose on planning permissions. The idea was suggested in 2005 and dropped in 2006. It was replaced by community infrastructure levy from 6 April 2010.

planning permission Permission from a local authority allowing certain building works to proceed. This can be relevant for determining VAT liability. From April 2010, the authority may impose a community infrastructure levy on developments.

For VAT recovery for a DIY housebuilder, it is essential that the builder complies strictly with the terms of the planning permission (VATA 1994 Sch 8 Group 5 Note 2).

plant Items with which a business is carried out, such as machinery, furniture and computers. The definition comes from the case *Yarmouth v France [1887] 4 TRL 1,* which is not a tax case but one for compensation when a workman was injured by his boss's plant — a horse. The judge defined plant as "whatever apparatus is used by a businessman for carrying on his business — not his stock in trade which he buys or makes for resale, but all goods and chattels, fixed and movable, live or dead, which he keeps for permanent employment in the business".

The exact scope of plant has been much litigated, particularly with regard to what is premises rather than plant. Plant qualifies for capital allowances for plant and machinery. It is exempt from capital gains tax.

plant and machinery Although this is a single category of capital allowance (CAA 2001 from s11), it represents two categories of assets. Plant is as separately explained and has been much litigated. In contrast, machinery simply means something with a moving part, not necessarily powered, and seems to have caused no problems. Plant and machinery count as wasting assets, which mean they are excluded from capital gains tax (TCGA 1992 s44(1)(c)).

Plant Health Movement Certificate (PHMC) Certificate that may be needed to import certain plants and plant products.

plants For VAT purposes, plants are zero-rated if used for human or animal consumption. Other plants, such as those for ornamentation, are standard-rated.

plant variety rights The intellectual property in new breeds of flowers or plants. it is governed by an international convention of 1961, as revised. Customs may seize goods that breach these rights.

plastic packaging tax Tax that the government intends to introduce in April 2022 on plastic packaging that has a low content of recycled plastic. The tax is charged when packaging contains less than 30% recycled plastic.

platinum Naturally occurring element which is regarded as a precious metal. It has a white lustre. As an element it has the atomic symbol Pt and the atomic number of 78. It is widely used in jewellery and as a store of value. Platinum bullion has the ISO currency code of XPT.

Platinum also has some industrial uses such as for electrical contacts and in emission controllers on car exhausts.

play For the purposes of theatrical productions tax relief, this may qualify as a dramatic production if the conditions are met (CTA 2009 s1217FA(2)).

playgroupThe supply of this service is generally standard-rated for VAT. The Court of Appeal refused to allow a playgroup to zero-rate the element that related to a child's T-shirt in the case *Tumble Tots (UK) Ltd v HMRC. Ch D [2007] STC 1171.*

playing cards Pack of 52 cards, possibly plus jokers, used for many games. They were subject to a special excise duty until 1960 as evidenced by an elaborate design on the ace of spades. Some card games are subject to betting and gaming duties.

plc Abbreviation that follows the name of a public limited company from 1980. In Wales, the abbreviation "ccc" may be used instead.

pleasure craft In relation to excluded leading activities for venture capital trusts, the term means "any ship of a kind primarily used for sport and recreation" (ITA 2007 s305(8)).

Customs implications are set out in Customs notice 8.

pleating Process in making a type of skirt. For VAT, pleating of material so that it may only be used to make girls' skirts was sufficient to bring the supply within the scope of zero-rating of children's clothing *(Ali Baba Tex Ltd [1992] STC 590).*

plene administravit Latin for "administered in full". It is a defence by an executor to a late claim against an estate which has been fully settled and where there are no more assets.

plug and play Colloquial term for a tax avoidance scheme that uses standard documents. All such schemes must be reported to HMRC from 1 August 2006 under disclosure of tax avoidance scheme.

Plumbers Tax Safe Plan (PTSP) Scheme run by HMRC from 1 March 2011 to 31 May 2011 to encourage voluntary disclosure of undeclared tax by plumbers, gas fitters and similar. Those who use the scheme incur a lower penalty.

plural In a statute, the singular includes the plural unless the contrary intention appears (Interpretation Act 1978 s6).

plutonium Radio-active metal element. A licence is needed from the Office of Civil Nuclear Security to import this metal. Customs clearance cannot be obtained without this licence.

Podatek od towarów i uslug Polish: value added tax.

poet A poet may be able to average profits over three years under ITTOIA 2005 s221.

point of sale scheme VAT scheme for retailers. This usually involves a check-out system that scans a bar code on an item's packaging (or from a separate card for items such as fruit and vegetables sold loose) and which can identify the correct rate of VAT.

poisha One hundredth of a taka, currency of Bangladesh.

poker dice This game is specifically listed in Betting and Gaming Duties Act 1981 s13(3) as coming within the scope of gaming licence duty.

Poland East European country that is a member of the European Union. Its currency is the zloty of 100 groszy. The UK has a double taxation convention of 2006.

police Law enforcement agency. For deaths from 19 March 2014, the estate of a police officer is free of inheritance tax if the death was either in the course of police work or where the person was targeted because of being in the police.
The relevant laws are Inheritance Tax Act 1984 ss154A and 155B respectively, both inserted by FA 2015.

Police and Criminal Evidence Act (PACE) Law passed in 1984 that provides a legislative framework for police investigations. Some provisions apply to tax investigations, such as the right to be cautioned before being charged with a criminal offence. HMRC officers can be bound by some of its provisions in tax investigations.

police bail Release of an arrested person subject to conditions imposed by the police. The relevant law is Police and Criminal Evidence Act 1984 from s30A.

police detention The right of the police to detain a person in connection with police duties. This is subject to limitations set out in Police and Criminal Evidence Act 1984 s34.

police organisation "Means an organisation of persons in police service" (ITA 2007 s458(5)). Payments to such a body are tax-deductible to the extent that they relate to superannuation, life insurance or funeral benefits.

police pension There are three schemes of police pension in England and Wales, depending on when the officer joined.
Up to 5 April 2006, an officer joined the Police Pension Scheme established under the Police Pensions Regulations 1987. This is a final salary scheme based on the highest salary in the last three years of service.

Between 6 April 2006 and 31 March 2015, the New Police Pension Scheme applies under Police Pensions Regulations 2006. This is a final salary scheme based on the highest salary in the last ten years of service.

From 1 April 2015, the scheme is under Police Pensions Regulations 2015. This is based on 1/55.3 of each year's salary, indexed each year to retirement.

Police Regulations Regulations issued under Police Act 1996 s50. Current regulations are SI 2003 No 527.

policy holder participation fund "A fund in the case of which an amount equal to the amount shown in line 34 of Form 58 for the fund is allocated to policy holders for the relevant period" (ICTA 1988 s444AJ(8)).

political donation Sum given to a political party or candidate in an election. A company must disclose any such donation in its accounts (CA 2006 ss362-379) and needs authorisation from members if it exceeds £5,000 in any 12-month period.

Generally. such donations are not taxable. A leading case is *Boarland v Kramat Pulai Ltd [1953] 35 TC 1.* The matter is discussed in HMRC Manual at BIM42528.

political levy Part of a trade union subscription that is donated to a political party. A trade union member has the right not to pay this levy under Trade Union and Labour Relations (Consolidation) Act 1992 s86.

politically exposed person Someone entrusted with prominent public functions by a state other than the UK or an EEA country, or a member of their family or close associate (Proceeds of Crime Act 2002 s362B(7)). Additional measures may be needed for financial dealings with such a person.

political party Body formed to support candidates in a political election. A sum left to a political party is exempt from inheritance tax, if the party at the last general election either elected two or more MPs, or elected one MP and received at least 150,000 for all its candidates.

poll tax Popular name for the unpopular community charge, applied from 1990 (1989 in Scotland) to 1993. It is also the name of taxes levied in the 14th and 17th centuries.

polyandry Having more than one husband. In the UK, this is the crime of bigamy.

polygamy Having more than one wife. In the UK, this is the crime of bigamy (Offences Against the Person Act 1861 s57). It is legal in some other countries. UK law generally recognises only the first marriage. A wife in a polygamous marriage is recognised for tax purpose even if she is not the first wife *(Nabi v Heaton [1938] CA. 57 TC 292).*

polymer banknotes Bank of England notes produced on polymer plastic rather than paper. Notes replaced are £5 in 2016; £10 in 2017; £20 in 2020; £50 in 2021. The notes are more durable and harder to forge.

pomace Crushed apples used to make cider.

pontage Charge to cross a bridge, or to raise funds to repair a bridge.

pony Slang term for £25.

Ponzi fraud Common investment fraud, typically promising high returns. Early "investors" are paid from later investors until the promoter disappears with the money. It was first used in 1919.

pool Collection of assets treated for accounting or tax purposes as if they were a single asset. An example is capital allowances for plant and machinery where there is a main pool, one or more single asset pools, and one or more class pools.

pool betting Form of gambling where the prize money is a share of the sum staked (Gambling Act 2005 s12). This figure is usually after the organiser's commission has been deducted. Customs notice 147 makes clear that this includes when:

- the winners share the stakes paid;
- the winners share a fixed amount; or
- the winnings are at the discretion of the promoter or some other person.

The betting must not be at fixed odds. Pool betting usually means the football pools, but it can extend to other forms of betting, including fantasy football competitions.

The Tote (Successor Company) Ltd held the exclusive licence to offer pool betting in respect of horse racing in Great Britain, until mid-2018. Such betting is subject to pool betting duty. It requires a licence from the Gambling Commission.

pool betting licence Licence issued by Gambling Commission to someone who provides facilities for pool betting (Gambling Act 2005 s65(2)(d)).

pooled car Car that is kept at business premises for business use by staff generally and not for one particular person. Provided conditions are met, such a car does not give rise to a benefit in kind charge (ITEPA 2003 s167).

pooled van Van provided by an employer for business use only. Ordinarily an employee is not assessed to tax on the benefit of using such a van (ITEPA 2003 s168).

poor law Provisions to relieve poverty that applied from 1601 to 1948.

popcorn For VAT purposes, unsweetened popcorn is zero-rated food; sweetened popcorn is standard-rated confectionery. This was determined in the old purchase tax cases of *C & E v Clark's Cereal Products Ltd [1968] 3 All ER 778* and *C & E v Popcorn House Ltd [1968] 3 All ER 782*.

pornography Images and other material of an indecent nature. Imported material that cannot be legally produced in the UK may be seized by Customs. Under Digital Economy Act 2017 s14 it is an offence to make pornography accessible by someone under 18.

port (1) Place approved by Customs where goods may legally be offloaded from ships. The port must be approved by Customs under CEMA 1979 s19.

(2) Alcoholic drink made from blending wines with spirits. It is an exception to the blending rules for alcoholic liquor duty (ALDA 1979 s71(2)).

Portugal European country which is a member state of the European Union, which includes the Azores and Madeira. Its currency is the euro of 100 cents. The UK has a double taxation convention of 1968.

POS safe Cash tray or similar for use with modern tills. It has two sets of keys. One opens the safe while the other locks it into position.

possession Physical custody rather than ownership. Customs duties may be charged on the possessor of goods, as explained in Customs Notice 3.

post Send mail. An item is regarded as having been posted if sent to the correct address with the proper amount of postage having been prepaid (Interpretation Act 1978 s7). Such mail is regarded as having been delivered in the ordinary course of post. HMRC usually allows one day for first class post, and three days for second class. Where a penalty is charged for a return or payment received by post late, a penalty may be imposed unless the taxpayer can demonstrate that there was a postal delay. The first tier tribunal has recommended that a taxpayer gets a free certificate of posting for a tax return sent near a due date.

postage Charge made for sending items by mail. Postage charged by Royal Mail for regulated services are exempt from VAT. Other services provided by Royal Mail are standard-rated. A charge for delivery is standard-rated even if the item, such as a book, is zero-rated. Booksellers often offer free delivery to avoid this charge. Further guidance is given in VAT Notice 700/24.

postage stamp Adhesive label indicating that postage has been paid, currently regulated by Postal Services Act 2011 s62. Historically, postage stamps could be used to pay stamp duty, particularly on receipts until 1971.

UK and Isle of Man postage stamps for postal use are exempt from VAT, provided they sold for face value or less. Used stamps and all foreign stamps (even if valid for postage abroad) are subject to VAT. Further details are given in VAT Notice 701/8.

postal order Document that can be bought for amounts between 50p and £250 at a Post Office and sent by post. They have the advantage that the recipient does not get the sender's financial details. They are subject to a charge given in section 3 of this dictionary.

post-balance sheet event Something that happens between the end of an accounting period and when those accounts are approved. The accounting treatment is now given in accounting standard-rated FRS 102 section 32, which is broadly the same as previous standards.

If the event is an "adjusting event", the accounts must be adjusted. This must refer to something that was extant before the end of the accounting period. The example given in HMRC Manual at BIM31040 is of a farmer whose crops were destroyed by a disease that was present but undetected in the accounting period. A non-adjusting event would be if the crops were destroyed by fire after the accounting period.

The tax position follows the accounting provisions.

post-cessation Description of income received and expenses incurred after a trade has ceased. This is taxed as non-trading income (ITTOIA 2005 from s241; CTA 2009 from s188).

post-cessation receipts Corporation tax provisions are given in CTA 2009 from s188. The term is defined in s190 and s282. Their charge to tax is given from s280.

For income tax, details are given in ITTOIA 2005 from s241. A definition is given in s246. For property businesses, the tax provisions are given in ITTOIA 2005 from s349. A definition is given in s353.

post clearance demand note Notice issued by HMRC for customs duty and VAT for goods that cleared Customs as duty-free but subsequently became dutiable.

postcode Combination of letters and digits to identify an address. They were first introduced on 11 October 1959, and nationally between 1967 and 1974.

post-commencement period of account In relation to capital allowances for plant and machinery subject to a lease and finance leaseback, "means any period of account ending on or after 6th December 2006" (FA 2007 Sch 5 para 17(6)).

post-commencement rental In relation to capital allowances for plant and machinery subject to a lease and finance leaseback, "means –

(a) any amount receivable on or after 6th December 2006 in respect of any period beginning on or after that date, or
(b) the appropriate fraction of any amount receivable on or after that date in respect of any period beginning before, and ending on or after, that date,

but does not include any amount received before that date"
(FA 2007 Sch 5 para 17(6)).

post-commencement supplement provisions In context, "means this section and sections 323 to 329" (CTA 2010 s321(4)).

postdated Given a later date, usually on a cheque. Such a cheque may not be paid in until that later date. Postdating does not affect the validity of the cheque or bill of exchange (Bills of Exchange Act 1882 s13(2)).

post-employment benefit plan "Formal or informal arrangements under which an entity provides post-employment benefits for one or more employees" (FRS 102 glossary). Any plan designed to confer a benefit on former employees. FRS 102 section 9.12 states that such a plan is not be accounted for as a special purpose vehicle.

post-employment earnings Earnings received by someone after they cease to be an employee. Such earnings are taxable (ITEPA 2003 s563) under PAYEE (PAYE Regs 2003 from reg 37).

post-employment notice pay (PENP) In relation to termination pay, this term is defined in ITEPA 2003 s402D as inserted by Finance (No 2) Act 2017 s5(3)).

post-employment notice period In relation to employment termination pay, "is the period –

(a) beginning at the end of the last day of the employment, and
(b) ending with earliest lawful termination date".

(ITEPA 2003 s402E(5)).

post-entitlement enhancement In relation to pension funds, "is an increase in the annual rate of a scheme pension under the arrangement, at a time after the member has become entitled to the scheme pension" (FA 2004 s236A(2)).

poster For VAT purposes, a poster is not within the scope of books and therefore is not zero-rated under VATA 1994 Sch 8 Group 3, according to VAT notice 701/10. However zero-rating was allowed to a quarterly publication of a 32-page magazine called *Just Seventeen Posters* which consisted almost entirely of posters that could be displayed when the magazine was unstapled. It was held to be within the ordinary meaning of a zero-rated "periodical" despite having little text *(EMAP Consumer Magazines Lid [1994] VTD 13322).*

post-free Arrangement whereby the postage for mail is paid by the addressee and not the sender. It is sometimes used for marketing. Post-free supplies are sometimes used to avoid VAT on zero-rated goods. For example a £20 book subject to £2 postage would incur 40p VAT on the postage charge, whereas a book sold post-free for £22 incurs no VAT.

postgraduate loan Student loan for a postgraduate degree. From 6 April 2019, such a loan is repaid at 6% on earnings above £21,000. This may be in addition to other student loans. Details are given in section 3 of this dictionary.

post-grant contravention Where a person who is has a limited right to rent continues to rent property after that right has expired (Immigration Act 2014 s22(10)).

post-nuptial After the marriage, as in a settlement between a married couple regarding what should happen to their property should they separate. A court may be guided by such an agreement, but is not bound by it.

post office Premises that provides postal services as defined in Postal Services Act 2011 s15(1). Tax may be paid at a post office using an HMRC paying-in slip. This is regarded as an electronic payment by HMRC.

postponed accounting VAT arrangement whereby imported goods are not taxed on import but on the next regular VAT return.

postponed debt In Scotland, a debt that ranks after other debts (Bankruptcy (Scotland) Act 1985 s51).

postponed entry Delay in the importation of goods. The Customs implications are set out in CEMAs37B.

post-war credits Additional tax imposed during the second world war by reducing the personal allowances (FA 1941 s7). This tax was repaid between 1959 and 1973 (Income Tax (Repayment of Post-War Credits) Act 1959), though some still remains unclaimed. They are repaid with interest at 138% (FA 1972 s131(1)). The repayment is not subject to repayment supplement (ICTA 1988 s824(7)).

potato crisps These are standard-rated for VAT when packaged for human consumption without further preparation. They are excepted from the scope of zero-rating food by Value Added Tax 1994 Sch 8 Group 1 Excepted Item 5.

potato puffs These are standard-rated for VAT when packaged for human consumption without further preparation. They are excepted from the scope of zero-rating food by Value Added Tax 1994 Sch 8 Group 1 Excepted Item 5.

potential lost VAT In relation to transactions connected with VAT fraud, "is –

(a) the additional VAT which becomes payable by T [party to the transaction] as a result of the **denial decision,**

(b) the VAT which is not repaid to T as a result of that decision, or

(c) in a case where as a result of that decision VAT is not repaid to T and additional VAT becomes payable by T, the aggregate of the VAT that is not repaid and the additional VAT"

(VATA 1994 s69C(8) as inserted by Finance (No 2) Act 2017 s68(2)).

potentially exempt transfer (PET) "A transfer of value –

(a) which is made by an individual on or after 18th March 1986 but before 22nd March 2006, and

(b) which, apart from this section, would be a chargeable transfer (or to the extent to which, apart from this section, it would be such a transfer), and

(c) to the extent that it constitutes either a gift to another individual or a gift into an accumulation and maintenance trust or a disabled trust. (Inheritance Tax Act 1984 s3A(1)).

Also, "a transfer of value –

(a) which is made by an individual on or after 22nd March 2006,

(b) which, apart from this section, would be a chargeable transfer (or to the extent to which, apart from this section, it would be such a transfer), and

(c) to the extent that it constitutes –

(i) a gift to another individual,

(ii) a gift into a disabled trust,

(iii) a gift into a bereaved minor's trust on the coming to an end of an immediate post-death interest"

(Inheritance Tax Act 1984 s3A(1A)).

These definitions are further explained in later sections. In practice, a PET is any donation made during a person's lifetime that is not immediately exempt. (Such exempt donations include a gift to a spouse, and amounts covered by the annual exemption or small gifts exemption).

poultry "Domestic varieties of the following, that is to say, fowls, turkeys, geese, ducks, guinea-fowls, pigeons and quails" (Animals Act 1971 s11). For VAT, poultry for food is zero-rated; ornamental breeds are standard-rated. The exact scope is set out in VAT notice 701/15.

pound (1) Unit of currency in the UK, and the oldest currency still in use anywhere in the world. It was based on a pound weight of silver in the Middle Ages. From 1971, it is divided into 100 pence. The currency took the form of:

- a gold sovereign from 1838
- a bank note from 1914 to 1988, the last of which was demonetised on 11 March 1988;
- a round coin from 1985 to 2015, demonetised on 15 October 2017

- a 12-sided from 28 March 2017

(2) Unit of weight comprising 16 ounces and equivalent to 453.6 grams. There are 2,240 pounds in a ton, and 2.2046 pounds in a kilogram.

poverty Insufficiency of funds for normal living. The commonest measure is relative poverty, generally defined as less than 70% of median earnings. There are other measures.

Poverty and Inequality Commission Scottish body established under Child Poverty (Scotland) Act 2018 s8.

poverty trap Situation where a person cannot escape from **poverty.** An example is where means-tested social security benefits are withdrawn as a person earns more.

power of attorney Right a person gives to someone else to act on their behalf.

power of maintenance Power provided by a will or deed giving trustees the power to spend income of trust property on the maintenance and education of children who will be the ultimate beneficiaries. The power is given by Trustee Act 1925 s31.

practice directions Directions for hearings before a court or tribunal. Tax tribunals provide such direction under Tribunals, Courts and Enforcement Act 2007 s23.

prayer card For VAT, prayer cards and cards containing bible verses are not zero-rated as leaflets *(Christian Art Ltd [1990] VTD 5940).* A leaflet must be limp.

precedent Decision of a court that binds or influences subsequent courts or tribunals where the facts are sufficiently similar. Traditionally, judges made the law, which established common law. The courts no longer make law but clarify existing law.

A binding precedent is a decision that establishes a principle which binds lower courts and tribunals when presented with the same facts.

A persuasive precedent is a decision that influences decisions of other courts and tribunals but without binding them. Examples include decisions of first tier tribunals, of courts of other countries which have a similar system of law, and of passing comments (obiter dicta) made by judges but which do not go to the heart of the matter then being tried.

precept Order requiring someone to take money from someone else. In particular, it refers to the principle in local authority taxation where, for example, a borough council may collect council tax for itself and under precepts from the county council and police authority.

precious metal Metal that is regarded as of intrinsic value and is therefore used as a means of exchange and store of wealth. The former was usually in the form of coins; the latter remains in the form of bullion. Gold and silver are precious metals. Other metals are included according to context. Proceeds of Crime Act 2002 s303B(4)(a) defines precious metals as gold, silver and platinum.

pre-completion transaction Term used in relation to stamp duty land tax from 17 July 2013. Its provisions are contained in FA 2013 Sch 39. It replaces the previous "transfer of rights" provisions. HMRC issued a guidance note on 17 July 2013.

pre-contract expense When this incurred by a company in connection with a derivative contract, it qualified for tax relief as if had the expense had been occurred in connection with the derivative (CTA 2009 s607).

predictive value The quality of accounting information in helping users to evaluate past, present and future events. The information does not need to have the nature of a forecast; indeed, it includes evaluating past information. Predictive value is one of the two factors of relevance set out in Statement of Principles. The other is confirmatory value. Relevance is one of the four qualities of accounting information required by Statement of Principles.

predominant activity For VAT on water, test to determine whether the customer is engaged in industrial activities. Water to such a customer is generally standard-rated rather than zero-rated. Details of the test are given in VAT notice 701/16.

pre-emption right Right of an existing shareholder to have the opportunity to buy new shares before they are offered to others.

preference share Form of financial instrument. A holder of a preference share is a creditor of the company, not a part-owner. The preference share holder is entitled to a dividend, usually expressed as a fixed percentage, before ordinary shareholders receive their dividends. A definition for tax purposes is given in ICTA 1988 s210(4).

preferential creditor Person who is entitled to be paid before other creditors.

preferential rate of duty Special low rate of Customs duty agreed with a country. Details are given in Customs notice 826.

pre-fermentation mixture In relation to cider and perry, this is the mixture of juice and other ingredients from which fermentation takes place (ALDA 1979 s1(6)(i)).

pregnancy-related illness Illness caused by pregnancy, but not one that is merely exacerbated by pregnancy. If a woman contracts such an illness in the four weeks before the expected birth, this triggers the start of the maternity pay period unless it has already started.

pre-incorporation contract Contract made on behalf of a company before it is formed (CA 2006 s51). The person who makes the contract is personally liable under it unless the company agrees to ratify the contract.

preliminary issue In tax cases, a matter dealt with before the hearing on the substantive issue. A preliminary issue is often on an administrative matter such as whether a claim was in time, or if the tribunal has authority to hear the issue.

preliminary notice For diverted profits tax, a notice given by an HMRC office to a company where the former suspects that tax has been avoided by the diversion of profits. The law is FA 2015 from s93.

premium bond National Savings product introduced in 1956. Instead of paying interest, equivalent amounts are allocated as randomly selected prizes. These prizes are tax-free. Rates are given under National Savings in section 3 of this dictionary. Premium bonds are not subject to capital gains tax (TCGA 1992 s121).

prenuptial agreement Agreement made between two people before they marry on what happens if they separate. Such agreements are common when one party is already wealthy at the time of the marriage. Although a pre-nuptial agreement cannot be upheld under English law, it will be considered by a judge when making a divorce settlement.

pre-owned asset (POA) An income tax charge introduced from 6 April 2005 when a person gives away an asset which they continue to use, such as living in a house given to a child. This charge is an anti-avoidance provision for inheritance tax. The law is contained in Finance Act 2004 Sch 15, and in Finance Act 2007 s66. Regulations are contained in SI 2005 No 724. Guidance is given in leaflet IHT 500. The main elements are:

- POA can apply to land, chattels and intangible property
- it is an inheritance tax anti-avoidance provision to plug a gap in gift with reservation law. POA therefore does not apply to gifts with reservation
- very little tax has been raised by POA rules as it is a deterrent. It has in effect ended lease carve-outs, settlements on interest in possession trusts (also known as Eversden schemes), reversionary lease schemes and double trust or lifetime trust schemes
- the income tax charge (not inheritance tax) is based on the benefit a former owner receives from using the asset.

There are de minimis limit, such as when a parent stays for a short while with a son or daughter in a home the parent donated to them. Examples of what comes within the scope of POA is discussed in HMRC Manual at IHTAM44005.

prepared drink For soft drinks industry levy, a drink produced by dilution, including squashes and similar (FA 2017 s27(1)).

prepayment When a payment is made in one **accounting period** all or some of which relates to a later period. The opposite is called an accrual. For example, a business which makes its accounts up to 31 March, pays six months' rent of £1,200 in advance on 1 February. Four months of this relates to the following accounting period, so an adjustment is made (usually as a journal entry) whereby £800 is charged to the later accounting period. The double entry is to debit prepayments and to credit the relevant expense heading in the profit and loss account, such as rent.

In bookkeeping, this is the opposite to an **accrual.** Prepayments require a journal entry at the end of the accounting period. The amount of the prepayment which relates to a future accounting period is calculated. The double entry is: debit prepayments, credit the relevant expense. This journal needs to be reversed at the start of the next accounting period.

Usually the accounting treatment determines the tax treatment (Inspectors' Manual at BIM42210).

prepayment certificate In medicine, an annual season ticket for prescription charges. Such a ticket is issued for three months or 12 months. It is usually cost effective to buy such a certificate if the patient would otherwise pay for four prescriptions in three months or 14 in 12 months.

The legal definition is "a certificate which confers on the person to whom it is granted exemption from charges otherwise chargeable under the regulations in respect of drugs, medicines and appliances supplied during such period as may be prescribed" (National Health Service Act 2006 s174). The amount is given under Prescription Charges in section 3 of this dictionary.

pre-return banding check (PRBC) Check undertaken by HMRC to confirm that a residential property is in the correct value band for the purposes of annual tax on enveloped dwellings.

prescription charge Charge made to dispense a doctor's prescription. It is subject to many exceptions. The charge was introduced in 1952, and was abolished between 1965 and 1968. Any food, drug, toiletry or cosmetic may be prescribed by a doctor unless it appears on a list of excluded items (NHS (General Medical Services Contracts) (Prescription of Drugs etc) Regulations SI 2004).

It is possible to buy a certificate that covers all prescriptions for 3 months or 12 months (National Health Service Act 2006 s174).

Details of the charges and exemptions are given in section 3 of this dictionary.

presentation currency Currency in which accounts are prepared.

present gravity Current gravity of beer that may be used to determine strength for alcoholic liquor duty. Details are given in Customs leaflet 226.

present value Future amount expressed at the value of today's currency. This is achieved by multiplying by a discounted cashflow factor. For 5%, this is 100/105 which is 0.9524. So £100 receivable in a year's time at that interest or inflation rate is worth £95.24 today. Present value is used to calculate stamp duty land tax on lease income. Factors and tables are given in section 3 of this dictionary.

Preston factors Factors used in calculating pension entitlement for part-time workers. The factors are produced each month by the government.

presumption of continuity In tax investigations, the presumption that a business is run in the same way in each tax year, unless the contrary is shown. A leading case is *Jonas v Bamford [1973] Ch D. 51 TC 1.*

presumption of death General rule that a court may declare someone dead if they have been missing for seven years and there is no evidence to suggest they are still alive. From 1 October 2014, the law is codified to a single set of rules for all purposes, including tax (Presumption of Death Act 2013). The same provision is given in Civil Partnership Act 2004 s55.

Under Guardianship (Missing Persons) Act 2017, from 31 July 2019 a guardian may be appointed to look after the financial and administrative affairs of someone who has been missing for 90 days.

presumption of legitimacy Legal presumption that the husband of a wife is the father of her child unless the contrary is shown.

presumption of validity For the purposes of mutual assistance in recovering tax between member states, the presumption that a request from a state has been "duly made in accordance with MARD unless the contrary is proved" (FA 2011 Sch 25 para 14).

presumptive charge Beer duty calculated according to the amounts of malt and sugar used.

pre-tax Description of an amount before any tax has been deducted.

pre-tax net income American term for a corporation's annual net income before it has paid taxes.

pre-tax profit Another name for profit before tax. It is the main measure of profit for investment purposes.

pre-trading expenditure Expenditure incurred in relation to a trade before it commences. For income tax and corporation tax, such expenditure is tax deductible if (from 1 April 1993) incurred in the previous seven years. Previous limits were five years from 1 April 1989; three years from 1 April 1980, before which pre-trading expenditure was not allowable. Income tax relief for such expenditure incurred in the seven years before commencement may be claimed under ITTOIA 2005s57 and CTA 2009 s61.
The implications for loan relationship are given in CTA 2009 s330.
For VAT, input tax may be claimed for goods purchased in the previous four years and still held at registration, and for services acquired in the six months before registration.

prevailing market rate In accounting, "the rate of interest that would apply to the entity in an open market for a similar financial instrument" (FRS 102 glossary).

prevention procedures Procedures designed to prevent someone for helping another person in evading tax (Criminal Finances Act 2017 s45(3)).

previous total tax In relation to direct collection or special arrangements for collecting tax on employment earnings outside PAYE, this term is defined in PAYE regulations SI 2003 No 2682 reg 144(1).

previous total tax to date Under PAYE, the amount of cumulative tax an employee has had deducted before the current pay period. The term is defined in PAYE Regulations SI 2003 No 2682 reg 23(8) and 23(9).

previous year basis Method of determining the basis period for income tax, used before 1994.

previous year income Figure that may be used in the income test in determining entitlement to a tax credit (Tax Credits Act 2002 s7(5)).

price cap For starter homes, the maximum value of the property. This is £450,000 in Greater London and £250,000 elsewhere (Housing and Planning Act 2016 s2(6)). The scheme started in 2016 though no homes had been built under it by 2019.

price cash flow ratio Financial ratio calculated as current share price divided by cashflow per share.

price-earnings ratio This is now generally known as the P/E ratio.

price fixing Agreement between suppliers to control the prices at which they offer their goods or services. This is generally an offence under competition law. The case *Guest Keen & Nettlefolds Ltd v Fowler [1910] 5 TC 511* established that expenditure incurred on price-fixing is tax-deductible.

price to sales ratio (PSR) Financial ratio of a company calculated as its current share price divided by sales per share.

Pridetines vertes mokestis (PVM) Lithuanian: value added tax.

prima facie Latin: at first sight.

primary adviser The professional person who provides tax advice directly to the taxpayer, as against a person who devises an avoidance scheme.

primary financial statements The balance sheet, profit and loss account, statement of total recognised gains and losses and cash flow statement.

primary lease period First period of a finance lease where the payments usually cover the cost of the leased item.

primary poverty Poverty where a person has insufficient income to provide for the basics of life. It has a similar meaning to absolute poverty, but makes a distinction from secondary poverty.

prime minister (PM) Political leader of the country. The position also connotes First Lord of the Treasury.

priming For beer duty, adding sugar solution to encourage secondary fermentation and increased alcoholic strength. Customs notice 226 gives more details.

Prince v Mapp Leading case on the general tax disallowance of surgery. The full citation is *Prince v Mapp [1969] 46TC169.* It relates to a guitarist's injured finger and is discussed in HMRC Manual at BIM37945.

principal (1) Sum of money that attracts interest or other periodic payments. (2) Person for whom an agent acts.

principal acting trustee Under the trust registration service, the one trustee so designated. It should be noted that all trustees remain accountable for the tax liability of the tax.

principal charge Another name for the ten-yearly charge to inheritance tax, payable by discretionary trusts and other relevant property trusts.

principal private resident relief Another name for main residence relief from capital gains tax.

printing money Colloquialism for quantitative easing. This is in allusion to a country printing more bank notes without a matching increase in national wealth.

prior charge percentage Proportion of a company's profits which is paid to preference shareholders and holders of similar security before it is possible to make a distribution to ordinary shareholders. It is also known as the priority percentage.

priority of debts Order in which debts of an insolvent company are to be paid. Provisions are set out in Insolvency Act 1986 s59. Provisions are noted under Insolvency in section 3 of this dictionary.

priority rule In relation to consideration for a lease, "is a rule (however expressed) to the effect that particular provisions have effect to the exclusion of, or otherwise in priority to, anything else" (ITA 2007 s809ZFA(7) as inserted by FA 2016 s68).

prior period errors "Omissions from, and misstatements in, an entity's financial statements for one or more prior periods arising from a failure to use, or misuse of, reliable information that:

(a) was available when financial statements for those periods were authorised for issue; and

(b) could reasonably be expected to have been obtained and taken into account in the preparation and presentation of those financial statements" (FRS 102 section 10.19).

prior period of loss Period of up to five years for which special conditions apply for a loss from hobby farming or market gardening to be available for loss relief (ITA 2007 s68(5)).

prior tax year For resident nil-rate band in inheritance tax, this term is defined in Inheritance Tax Act 1984 s8D(6) as inserted by Finance (No 2) Act 2015 s9.

prior year adjustment Adjustment made in an accounting period to reflect an amendment to the accounts of an earlier accounting period.

privacy Legal concept that individuals and businesses are entitled not to have certain information disclosed. This is a separate concept from the quasi-contractual duty of confidentiality, and from the state ordered secrecy. Tax details are generally confidential.

private company Company that does not come within the scope of a public company (CA 2006 s4(1)).

Private Company Price Index (PCPI) Index of capitalisation factors that can be used to value private companies. It is produced by the accounting firm Stoy Hayward. Its use was considered in the tax case *Foulser [2015] TC 4413.*

private finance initiative Method of funding public buildings and projects by a private company financing it and being paid a royalty. It was first used in the UK in 1992 and was widely used by the government between 1997 and 2010. In 2018, the government said it would not use this method again. There are some special provisions for stamp duty land tax.

private hearing For tax tribunals, a hearing to which the public is not admitted. A private hearing may only be ordered for reasons set out in The Tribunal Procedure (First-tier Tribunal) (Tax Chamber) Rules SI 2009 No 273 rule 32(2). The VAT tribunal ruled that "whenever possible, decisions of these tribunals should be given in public so that they could be published for general guidance". A hearing should only be in private "when a hearing in public would defeat the ends of justice, or would be likely to harm the appellant in the course of his business" *(Guy Butler (International) Ltd (No 1) [1974] VTD 106A.*

private medical insurance Insurance that pays for private medical insurance under the terms of its policy. Between 1990 and 1997, some tax relief was given for insurance for taxpayers aged 60 or more. This is a taxable benefit in kind if provided to an employee.

private residence relief Another term for main residence relief from capital gains tax (TCGA 1992 s222).

private travel Travel between two places, neither of which is a workplace (ITEPA 2003 s338(5). This is not generally tax-deductible.

private use In tax, description of expenditure that is for personal use and not for business use. For VAT, the input tax cannot be reclaimed even though the trader is registered for VAT and has a VAT invoice. VAT Notice 700 says "private use includes:

- your own personal use of business assets, and
- use outside the business by anyone else, such as an employee, a relative or a friend".

For income tax, such expenditure is not allowed as a tax deduction. It should be noted that it is not necessarily wrong for personal expenditure to be shown in a business's profit and loss account. But if it is, such expenditure must be added back in determining **adjusted profit.**

In the context of whether a car or van is so available by an employee for tax purposes, means "any use other than for the employee's business travel" (ITEPA 2003 s118(2)).

For a heavy goods vehicle, the definition is "use other than for travel which the employee is necessarily obliged to do in the performance of the duties of the employment" (ITEPA 2003 s238(4)).

For an asset owned by an employer and used by an employee, there is a 20% tax charge. The law is ITEPA 2003 s205. The tax charge is extended to when an asset is made available to an employee's family member by ibid s205(1A) inserted by FA 2017 s8(2).

If part of a trader's stock is taken for personal use, it must be added back at its *selling price* and not its purchase price. For example, if a grocer takes stock that he bought for £10 but sells for £16, he must add £16 to his taxable profits.

For Customs and other import purposes, there are restrictions on the amount of goods that may be brought in for private use. For vehicles, personal use is defined as "the use of a road vehicle, trailer or caravan (whether or not motorised) for other than business" (Customs notice 3).

privileged communication Communication between a lawyer and client that HMRC may not access (FA 2008 Sch 36 para 23; in Scotland: Revenue Scotland and Tax Powers Act 2014 s138).

privileged trust Trust that is exempt from the stricter tax provisions introduced in 2006, when many trusts were reclassified as relevant property trusts and taxed on the same basis as discretionary trusts. These trusts are:

- charitable trusts
- pre-2006 accumulation and maintenance trusts where the beneficiaries inherit absolutely at 18
- age 18-25 trusts
- trusts for a bereaved minor
- employee trusts.

privileged will Will that may be made by a soldier on active service or a sailor at sea. It need not be in writing; it does not need two witness; it may be made by someone under 18 (Wills Act 1837 s11; Wills (Soldiers and Sailors) Act 1918).

privity of contract The general legal rule that only the parties to a contract may sue on it. There are many exceptions to this rule, such as third parties to a contract in addition to some exceptions relating to land.

Privy Council "means the Lords and others of Her Majesty's Most Honourable Privy Council" (Interpretation Act 1978 Sch 1). The Privy Council comprises leading politicians and other leading figures. Membership is for life. Members style themselves "Rt Hon".

prize Its many meanings include winnings from a competition or bet. Such prizes are not subject to income tax, though a betting or gaming duty may have been paid.

prize competition Competition for which a prize is awarded and which is not gaming, betting or a lottery (Gambling Act 2005 s339). This is not regarded as gambling. In gambling, this includes something which requires a guess, such as the outcome of a race, regardless of whether any money is staked (Gambling Act 2005 s11).

prize salvage Payment for services in retaking a ship, aircraft or goods from the enemy. From 21 January 1944, such a claim needs the consent of the Admiralty or Secretary of State (Prize Salvage Act 1944).

prize total In relation to children's television, means the amount of any money prize plus the cost of providing any non-money prize (CTA 2009 s1216ASA(3) as inserted by FA 2015 s30).

From 1 April 2015, there is a special tax relief for making children's programmes other than quiz shows and game shows where the prize total exceeds £1,000.

"The prize total for a programme is the total of –

(a) the amount of each relevant prize that is a money prize, and
(b) the amount spent on each other relevant prize by, or on behalf of, its provider" (CTA 2009 s1216DA(3)).

Relevant prize "means a prize offered in connection with participation in a quiz, game, competition or contest in, or promoted by, the programme" (ibid).

probability The mathematical likelihood of something happening. This is usually expressed as a number between 0 representing impossibility to 1 representing certainty.

In accounting, probability is one of two factors in recognising an item in the accounts (FRS 102 section 2.29). The other factor is reliability of measurement.

probate Legal recognition of a will.

probate fee Charge for admitting a will to probate. The rates are given in section 3 of this dictionary. The government dropped plans in 2019 to replaced fixed fees with a sliding scale. The fees are given in section 3 of this dictionary.

pro bono Expression that means "for the public good", particularly when a professional person agrees to work for no fee.

procedural fairness Principles of natural justice that relate to the proper conduct of a criminal investigation or equivalent. This includes matters such as providing adequate notice to the affected party, allowing the party to make amends (where appropriate) or take other effective action (such as resigning), providing details of the charge, and being given the right to be heard. Judicial guidance has been provided on fairness.

processed under Customs control Process whereby goods are imported for processing as previously agreed with Customs. Duty is charged according the product it becomes.

process now, check later Underlying philosophy behind most tax returns. The taxpayer provides information to HMRC which initially accepts it and then has a period in which to raise any queries.

procuration fee Fee charged by a lender to secure a loan. It is also known as a commitment fee. Under normal allowability rules, such a fee is not allowable if it is incurred as part of the cost of obtaining capital, but is allowable if the borrowings are temporary. A leading case on this is *Ascot Gas Water Heaters Ltd v Duff [1942] 24 TC 171.* The matter is discussed in HMRC Manual at BIM 45825.

production animal Animal kept for a trade purpose. A capital allowance may not be claimed (CAA 2001 s38).

production company In relation to special reliefs for theatrical productions, the term is defined in CTA 2009 s1217FC.
For orchestra tax relief, the term is defined in CTA 2009 s1217PB.

production herd Collection of animals kept for the products obtained from them while alive (ITTOIA 2005 s112(1)(c); CTA 2009 s110(1)(c)). The herd basis may be used.

production order Order which a sheriff may make under Proceeds of Crime Act 2002 s380. The order requires a person who has possession of goods to produce them to the sheriff.

profession Occupation that involves some substantial exercise of intellectual skill (HMRC Manual at BIM14090). Generally a profession is now taxed on the same basis as a trade. In relation to VAT, guidance is given in VAT leaflet 701/5.

Professional Conduct in Relation to Taxation (PCRT) Guidance for accountants and other tax agents produced by the main accounting bodies. The latest guidance was issued in March 2017, effective from March 2019.

professional enquiry Enquiry from a tax adviser, or prospective adviser, from a former tax adviser. The former tax adviser should seek permission from the client before disclosing any information. If permission is refused, the new adviser should be informed of that fact and left to make his or her own decision on whether to act for the client. If permission is granted, the former adviser should disclose "all the information needed and reasonably requested by the prospective adviser to enable him to decide whether to accept the work" (Professional Conduct in Relation to Taxation paras 5.37 to 5.39).

professional indemnity insurance Insurance that protects professionals from liability arising from their work. Premiums are usually tax-deductible. This is discussed in HMRC Manual at BIM45515.

profit Wealth generated by commercial activity. It is usually distinguished between gross profit and net profit. The former is the difference between price and cost, whereas net profit further deducts overheads and other expenses.

Another distinction is between operating profit and non-operating profit. The former is the profit from the business's normal activities whereas the latter includes such things as interest on deposits, rent from letting surplus space and similar.

Profit is subject to income tax for sole traders, partnerships and trusts, and to corporation tax for companies and other corporate entities.

The tax is charged on adjusted profit. This is the net profit per the accounts which are adjusted in accordance with tax law. This adds back disallowed items such as depreciation, personal expenses and fines. It then deducts amounts for capital allowances, research and development and other items. The profit must have been determined in accordance with accounting standards.

profit and loss account Financial statement showing how much profit or loss has been made by a commercial entity over a stated period.

Companies have been required to produce such an account since 1929. Acceptable formats are given in SI 2008 No 410.

Income tax or corporation tax is computed from the net profit taken from this account to which adjustments are made.

profit extraction How a person takes profit from a commercial body. For a company, the main choices are profit or dividends, though there are other choices.

profit-related expense An expense of a business whose amount is related to the profits of the business. For tax, the issue is whether the expense is in truth a dividend or share of the profit, in which case it is not tax-deductible. However, relation to profits is not fatal to tax-deductibility as was shown in the case *British Sugar Manufacturers Ltd v Harris [1937] 21TC528*. The matter is discussed in HMRC Manual at BIM37830.

profit-related pay Amount of pay related to how much profit was earned by a commercial entity or part of such entity. Between 1987 and 1999, such pay attracted tax relief.

profits and assets test In relation to entrepreneur's relief and partnership involvement in a joint venture company, this term is defined in TCGA1992 Sch 7ZA from para 15.

profit-seeking motive Desire for an organisation to make a profit for its owners or operators. The presence of such a motive will usually make any profit or surplus taxable. The absence of such a motive does not necessarily mean that any surplus avoids tax. The matter is discussed in HMRC Manual at BIM24345 and elsewhere.

profit sharing This term may be used in a general sense for one of several tax-advantaged schemes such as share incentive plan. It also specifically applied to a tax-advantaged scheme that operated between 1979 and 2002.

profit shifting Tax avoidance that involves transferring profits to lower taxed countries. This is often done by paying interest, royalties or management charges. The OECD has been developing methods to counter this.

profits of a trade Amount on which a trade is subject to income tax (ITTOIA 2005 s25) or corporation tax (CTA 2009 s46).

profits tax Tax on commercial profits charged between 1946 and 1965 when corporation tax was introduced.

pro forma invoice Document issued before goods or services are supplied, seeking payment. Although it is laid out as an invoice, it is not so regarded for accounting purposes, nor is it a VAT invoice.

programme For VAT, a printed programme supplied on its own is zero-rated as a brochure. Where it is supplied in connection with a fair, sporting event, concert or similar, it may be possible to apportion the consideration. An early case of apportionment was *M H Jarmain [1979] VTD 723* where 25% of the admission to a stamp fair was attributed to the programme. This was followed in the case *J C Thomas [1985] VTD 1862* when 15% of the charge for a greyhound race was attributed to the programme. However no apportionment was allowed for almost identical facts relating to a greyhound race in *Town & Country Factors Ltd (No 2) [2002] VTD 18569.*

progressive tax Tax that takes an increasing proportion of income as income rises. Income tax is an example.

prohibited allowance CAA 2001 s114 gives this a specific meaning in relation to a capital allowance that has been wrongly claimed for overseas leasing of plant and machinery. The section provides a mechanism for recovering the allowance. This mechanism is explained in HMRC Manual at CA24350.

prohibited or restricted goods Classes of goods where specific provisions apply for Customs (CEMA 1979 s1(1)). Prohibited goods may not be imported at all, while restricted goods require some form of clearance or licence.

Project Blue Long-running tax case finally heard in the Supreme Court on 13 June 2018. It related to the sale of Chelsea Barracks in 2007 using an SDLT avoidance scheme.

Project Zephyr Tax avoidance scheme that sought to create allowable losses. The scheme was the subject of the tax appeal *Fidex [2011] TC 1550.*

promise not to resign Such a payment made to a director or employment is taxed as employment income. In the case *Prendergast v Cameron [1940] 23TC122,* Viscount Caldicott said "I can see no difference between a promise not to resign and a promise to continue to serve as a director".

Promoter of Tax Avoidance Scheme (POTAS) Tax adviser who promotes a scheme, particularly one who operates secretly and does not co-operate with HMRC. Regulations were introduced in 2014 to deal with POTAS.

Prompt Payment Code Code of practice designed to encourage fair dealings. It is administered by the Chartered Institute of Credit Management on behalf of the Department for Business, Energy and Industrial Strategy. Departmental responsibility has now passed to the Office of the Small Business Commissioner. Signatories to the code agree:

- to pay invoices within the terms agreed
- to pay 95% of invoices within 60 days
- not to try to change payment terms retrospectively
- not unreasonably to change payment terms to smaller companies
- to provide suppliers with clear guidance on payment procedures
- to have a system to deal with complaints and disputes
- to advice suppliers promptly if an invoice cannot be paid within agreed terms
- to encourage suppliers to seek compliance with the code through their own supply chains.

Companies may apply to be signatories to the Code, and may publicise acceptance. Companies are publicly named if they do not comply.

prompt payment discount Reduction in price if the customer pays promptly. From 1 April 2015, VAT is charged on the discounted amount only if the discount was actually given.

proof of earnings Statement made by an employer on how much an employee earns. Such a statement should only be made when the employee has authorised it or the law requires it. Employers routinely provide payslips and P60 annual certificates which an employee may show to anyone.

proof spirit Old measure of alcoholic strength now replaced by alcohol by volume. Pure alcohol was 175.25 degrees proof. 100 degrees proof was 57.3% alcohol by volume.

propaganda expenses Expenses incurred to publicise an opinion or to further a campaign. The extent to which such expenses are tax-deductible depends on how far the opinion or campaign relates to the business. They were allowed in the case *Morgan v Tate & Lyle Ltd [1954] 35 TC 367* which related to a campaign to prevent a loss of the business. The matter is discussed in HMRC Manual at BIM42528.

property Anything which is capable of being owned, particularly land and buildings. It also includes intangible property such as copyright and trademarks. In tax, the term is sometimes given a specific meaning. For example, in HMRC Manual at BIM14070, the term "extends to anything capable of being owned" for business tax purposes.

Property Acts 1925 Series of laws passed in 1925 that made major changes to the land law. These were supplemented by further laws in 1926. The six Acts of 1925 are:

- Administration of Estates Act

- Law of Property Act
- Land Registration Act
- Land Charges Act
- Settled Land Act
- Trustee Act

property allowance Income tax allowance provided by FA 2017 s17 and Sch 3. It allows a taxpayer to earn up to £1,000 a year without having to pay income tax. If this is the taxpayer's sole source of income, they need not complete a tax return. This is additional to rent-a-room relief, but the property allowance may not be used to augment that relief. If a taxpayer has property income of more than £1,000, they may either deduct actual allowable expenditure, or may deduct £1,000. The allowance may be claimed in respect of property in the UK or overseas. It may not be claimed by a partnership, nor by an employee in respect of sums paid by an employer.

property and affairs LPA A form of lasting power of attorney (LPA) that may be made from 1 October 2007 under Mental Capacity Act 2005. It is also possible to make a personal welfare LPA. An individual who is 18 and has mental capacity may make a property and affairs LPA appointing someone (the attorney) to make decisions on his or her behalf should the individual lose mental capacity. This LPA allows the attorney to take such actions as paying bills, collecting debts, claiming benefits, and selling property.

property arrangements In relation to reverse premiums, "means the property transaction and any arrangements entered into in connection with it (whether before it, at the same time as it or after it)" (ITTOIA 2005 s103(b)).

property authorised investment fund (PAIF) Form of tax-advantaged property investment company introduced from 6 April 2008. It is an open-ended investment company authorised by the Financial Conduct Authority to hold property.

The idea of a PAIF is that investors are taxed in the same way as if they had invested directly in the property. The income has three separately identified streams: property income, dividend income, and other income (such as interest). The law is SI 2006 No 964, as amended.

The PAIF provides an income gross from 6 April 2017, with no tax deducted. This income is taxed in the hands of the investor. It is therefore popular with tax-exempt investors such as charities, pension funds and ISA holders.

The main points about a PAIF are:

- it must be an open-ended investment company incorporated in the UK
- it must derive at least 60% of its income as property income
- it is authorised and regulated by the Financial Services Authority
- there is no need for the PAIF to be listed on a stock exchange
- a PAIF may be used by both individual and institutional investors in the UK and overseas
- all capital gains are tax exempt

- all income distributions are tax exempt, except for a withholding tax for some foreign shareholders
- special tax charges are imposed on a PAIF that carries excessive debt or makes distributions from exempt income to any company that holds more than 10% of its shares
- PAIFs generally benefit from double taxation treaties.

property business Business that consists of renting property, and buying and selling property. It is not regarded as a trade unless it provides additional services, as for a hotel. Such a business is subject to income tax under ITTOIA 2005 from s263 or corporation tax under CTA 2009 from s203.

property developer Person who develops land for sale. For annual tax on enveloped dwellings, there are some special provisions in FA 2013 from s128.

property development Activity which excludes a company from the scope of EIS relief. It is defined for this purpose in ITA 2007 s196. For venture capital trust purposes, this is defined as "the development of land:

(a) by a company which has, or at any time has had, an interest in the land, and

(b) with the sole or main object of realising a gain from the disposal of an interest in the land when it is developed" (ITA 2007 s307(2)).

Section 307(3) defines interest in land.

property-embedded fixtures and fittings Fixed asset that attracts a capital allowance as features integral to a building. When the building is sold, the buyer and seller must agree a figure for the asset's value which they both use for tax purposes.

property income Rent and similar payments from property. They are subject to income tax (ITTOIA 2005 from 260) or corporation tax (CTA 2009 from s202).

property management company Company that looks after the common parts of a building in multiple occupation. It is often taxed as a mutual trading organisation as is discussed in HMRC Manual at BIM24782.

property, plant and equipment (PPE) Term for tangible fixed assets now widely used in financial accounting, such as in FRS 102 section 17.

"Tangible assets that:

(a) are held for use in the production or supply of goods or services, for rental to others, or for administrative purposes; and

(b) are expected to be used for more than one period"

(FRS 102 glossary).

property trading business For annual tax on enveloped dwellings, means "a business that –

(a) consists of or includes activities in the nature of a trade of buying and selling dwellings, and

(b) is carried on on a commercial basis and with a view to profit" (FA 2013 s141(3)).

propone In Scots law, to put an argument before the court.

proposed dividend Dividend that the directors recommend to shareholders they accept as their share of the profits.

Under UK accounting standards, such unpaid dividends are shown as a current liability.

Under international accounting standards, they are not shown on the balance sheet on the grounds that there is no liability until the shareholders accept the directors' recommendation (which they almost always do in practice). Instead the proposed dividend is disclosed in a note to the accounts.

proprietor's interest Term sometimes used to mean the capital contributed by a sole trader.

pro rata In the same ratio.

prospectus Financial statements and supporting detailed descriptions published when a company is offering shares for sale to the public. A prospectus must comply with requirements set out by the Financial Conduct Authority.

prostitution Offering sexual services for money. It is a taxable trade, as was held in *CIR v Aken [1990] 63 TC 395.*

protected animal Animal which is neither commonly domesticated nor under the control of man (Animal Welfare Act 2006 s2).

protected benefits Benefits in kind that are excluded from the salary sacrifice rules introduced from 6 April 2017. The new rules generally tax benefits received from salary sacrifice at the higher of the benefit's value or amount of salary sacrificed. Protected benefits are excluded from this provision. If taxed, the amount is of the benefit. Protected benefits are:

- pension contributions and advice
- childcare
- outplacement counselling and retraining
- bicycles and bicycle equipment
- cars with emissions below 76gm/km
- annual leave.

protected building Building which is listed because of its age or merit. Adaptations to such a building may be zero-rated for VAT.

protected disclosure Lawful disclosure by an employee of unlawful conduct in the employer's business (Employment Rights Act 1996 s43B). A disclosure is lawful if made to the employer, to obtain legal advice and in some other circumstances. The protection from employment detriment is wider than for whistle-blowing.

In relation to proceeds of crime, provisions are given in Proceeds of Crime Act 2002 s337.

protected earnings Income up to which an attachment of earnings or arrestment of earnings cannot be operated for an employee in that pay period.

protected leasing Leasing of plant and machinery to a person overseas on terms which avoid tax provisions that would otherwise apply. Those provisions restrict the right to claim capital allowances (CAA 2001 s10595)).

protected pension input amount Amount paid to a pension fund before 22 April 2009. Such a payment is excluded from the annual allowance charge.

protectionism Political policy of protecting home markets by imposing import restrictions and import duties. These are outlawed between EU member states, and are discouraged in various world trade agreements.

Protection of Vulnerable Groups Scheme in Scotland (PVGS) A scheme introduced in Scotland to control employment where this involves access to vulnerable individuals. The law is Protection of Vulnerable Groups (Scotland) Act 1997. Where an employer pays the registration fees for an individual to belong to the scheme, those fees are not a taxable benefit in kind (FA 2011 s39).

protective boots Boots for industrial use, such as on building sites. If the boots meet the appropriate standard they can be zero-rated for VAT, as explained in VAT Notice 701/23. Boots for other uses, such as riding horses or for motorcycles, are standard-rated.

protective claim Claim made in a tax appeal by either the taxpayer or HMRC to ensure that the deadline is not missed. This is common when the same issue is being litigated with regard to another taxpayer and the claim is paused until that decision is known.

protective equipment Protective boots and helmets, motorcycle helmets, pedal cycle helmets, and children's car seats and travel systems. The children's car seats etc may be reduced-rated for VAT under VATA 1994 Sch 7A Group 5. The other items are zero-rated under VATA 1994 Sch 8 Group 16. Details are given in VAT Notice 701/23.

protective helmet Hard hat or similar for industrial use, such as on a building site. If the helmet meets the British Standard or European standard, it may be zero-rated. Details are given in VAT Notice 701/23. Zero rating does not apply if the helmets are provided to an employer for use by employees.

protective trust

(1) An interest in possession trust that ends if the life tenant becomes bankrupt or otherwise alienates his interest. The trust then becomes a discretionary trust (IHTA 1984 s88).

(2) A more general term for a trust established for a person who cannot look after his or her financial affairs.

provenance Check on the weight and quality of an item, particularly items such as gold bullion.

provision Part of the funds set aside to meet a liability. Accounting standard FRS 102 defines it as a liability of uncertain amount or timing.

provisional collection of taxes Law that allows taxes to continue to be collected temporarily while an Act is going through Parliament for more permanent collection. The current Act dates from 1968.

provision for doubtful debts An estimate of the risk of not collecting full payment from credit customers, reported as a deduction from trade receivables (debtors) in the balance sheet. A provision for doubtful debts is not tax-deductible, though bad debts are tax-deductible.

proximity premium Additional value of a property because it is close to an amenity.

prudence Accounting concept that requires a degree of caution, but not bias, in inclusion of uncertain amounts in accounts.

In 1971, accounting standard SSAP 2 broadly required assets to be understated and liabilities to be fully stated.

In 2001, this was replaced by FRS 18 which sought a more realistic approach where assets and liabilities were treated with the same degree of prudence. Uncertainty was expressed in more detail in the notes to the accounts.

FRS 102 made this more explicit: "the exercise of prudence does not allow the deliberate understatement of assets or the deliberate understatement of liabilities or expenses. In short, prudence does not permit bias" (FRS 102 extract from section 2.9)

Prudential Regulation Authority Body formed in 2013 and now part of the Bank of England. Its objectives are to promote the safety and soundness of firms, and to ensure protection for holders of insurance policies.

Public Accounts Committee Committee of the House of Commons which investigates spending by each government department.

public benefit One of the tests for a body to qualify as a charity (Charities Act 2011 s2).

public bus service A bus service that all may use, though an employer may subsidise it to maintain the service for its employees. Such subsidy is not taxed as a benefit in kind to the employees (ITEPA 2003 s243).

public company A company whose certificate of incorporation states that it is a public company (CA 2006 s4(2)). Broadly, this is a company that may offer its shares to the public.

Public Guardian Officer appointed by the Lord Chancellor under Mental Capacity Act 2005 s57. The duties include oversight of lasting powers of attorney.

public hearing A hearing to which the public is admitted. This is the normal arrangement for tax cases.

public holiday Day when certain employees need not work. The term now means the same as a bank holiday. There are 8 public holidays in England and Wales; a slightly different 8 in Scotland; and 11 in Northern Ireland.

public house Premises open for the sale of alcoholic drink on the premises, commonly called a pub. As pubs often have living accommodation for the publican or manager, issues can arise on the allowability of property expenses. This is discussed in HMRC Manual at BIM37930.

public interest Set of criteria that must be considered by a prosecutor before bringing criminal proceedings.

public interest immunity (PII) Common law principle that a court can prevent a litigant disclosing information if doing so is contrary to the public interest. PII is usually sought by the government which issues a certificate, colloquially known as a gagging order. The court usually allows PII unless there is reason to doubt its appropriateness. Such a case was the Matrix Churchill trial in 1991.

Public Interest Unit (PIU) Part of the office of the Official Receiver. The unit reports irregularities discovered during insolvency investigations to the appropriate authority. Tax irregularities are reported to HMRC. An example of them doing this is in the case *Michael Rangos. TC 01893 [2012].*

public lending right Scheme where authors and other copyright holders may receive royalties on books lent from libraries (Public Lending Right Act 1979). It was introduced in 1979, and extended to e-books in 2018.

public limited company Limited company that may offer its shares to the public.

public offer When shares in a company are offered to the general public. If an employee buys shares in his or her company in a public offer, there is no taxable benefit in kind (ITEPA 2003 s421F). If the employee is given free shares, discounted shares, or a greater allocation of shares, that may be a taxable benefit unless it comes within a tax-advantaged scheme.

Public Sector Audit Appointments Ltd (PSAA) Company limited by guarantee formed under Local Audit and Accountability Act 2014. It is responsible for appointing auditors to local public bodies including local authorities.

public sector exit payment Payment made to an employee who leaves his or her job in the public sector. Rules about the maximum payment that may be made are given in regulations made under Small Business, Enterprise and Employment Act 2015 s154. The limit is set at £95,000 under s155A of the Act as inserted by Enterprise Act 2016 s41. This took effect from 4 November 2020 under SI 2020 No 1122.

public transport strike There is no taxable benefit in kind when an employer provides certain assistance to employees affected by such a strike (ITEPA 2003 s245).

Publishing Details of Deliberate Defaulters Formal name for naming and shaming tax offenders (FA 2004 s94). The provisions were introduced in 2010. They allow HMRC to disclose for one year details of taxpayers who deliberately concealed a tax liability of at least £25,000.

pulp Fruit and vegetable pulp is usually zero-rated for VAT as food (VAT notice 701/14).

punt Its meanings include the pound used in the Republic of Ireland before it adopted the euro.

purchase and resale arrangement One of the five forms of alternative financial arrangements. Its provisions for income tax are given in ITA 2007 s564C; and for capital gains tax in TCGA 1992 s151J.

purchased goodwill Goodwill bought with an acquired company, as opposed to goodwill generated within a business.

purchased life annuity Income for life bought from an insurance company (CTA 2009 s561(2)). The part of the annuity representing a return of capital is tax-free. The balance is treated as interest and is taxed.

purchase tax Tax charged on goods, particularly luxuries, from 1940 to 1973 when replaced by VAT.

pure income profit Term used to define those payments that benefit from the tax treatment for annual payments. The term was used in the case *Comiskey v Hanbury. CA [1939] 38TC588.*

purported partner In relation to an LLP run not for profit, this term is defined in TMA 1970 s12ABZAA (5) as inserted by FA 2020 s104(1).

purpose test Factor in deciding how a business is taxed on a payment for compensation or damages. The matter is discussed in HMRC Manual at BIM42955.

purpose trust Trust established for a stated purpose, as against a trust merely for possession and distribution of assets.

putative treaty Double taxation treaty agreed by both countries but not yet put into effect. This was a problem with the treaty for Ghana.

put option Arrangement where the holder has the right, but not the obligation, to sell shares or other securities on predefined terms.

pyx Box at the Royal Mint to test the weight and fitness of coins. The trial has been conducted since 1282. The current legal requirement for it is in Coinage Act 1971 s8. The trial is now purely ceremonial as coins are checked by more sophisticated modern machinery.

Qatar Arab country. Its currency is the Qatar royal of 100 dirhams. The UK has a double taxation agreement of 2009 amended by a protocol of 2010. There is a double taxation agreement, consolidated version, of 2010.

Qatar riyal Currency of Qatar.

QROPS Qualifying recognised overseas pension scheme. From April 2017, there is generally a 25% tax charge when a UK pension is transferred to a QROPS.

quadruple entry bookkeeping Term coined for the phenomenon where two trading parties each record the same transaction using double-entry bookkeeping. Blockchain has been suggested as a means of eliminating this duplication.

qualec Qualifying low emission car. The term was used before 2012.

qualified audit opinion Statement from the auditors that the accounts do not represent a true and fair view either wholly or with regard to particular matters. This does not automatically trigger a tax investigation but makes this more likely.

qualifying accessory Additional item added to a company car and which may increase the value on which the employee pays tax (ITEPA 2003 s125(1)).

qualifying change Term used in FA 2010 s26 to cover the sale, part-sale, change of ownership and similar changes in ownership of a business that could prevent an acquiring company being able to claim the capital allowances of the acquired company.

qualifying co-production In relation to television production relief, "means a relevant programme that is eligible to be certified as a British programme under section 1216CB as a result of an agreement between Her Majesty's Government in the United Kingdom and any other government, international organisation or authority" (CTA 2009 s1216AI).

qualifying corporate bond (QCB) A financial instrument that evidences a loan relationship (TCGA 1992 from s117). It is generally exempt from capital gains tax.

qualifying creative work A literary, dramatic, musical or artistic work which provides a particularly large revenue in one tax year.

From 6 April 2001 there is a special tax provision which helps to prevent the writer, playwright, composer or artist being highly taxed in one year. The provision considers two consecutive years. The provisions is triggered when either:

- the profit for one year is less than 70% of an adjacent year; or
- the profit for one year is nil.

In such a case, the profits may be averaged according to a specific formula. The total profits of all years are fully taxed; the scheme simply evens up the income between the relevant years.

qualifying earnings factor (QEF) Amount calculated from national insurance contributions in a tax year to determine certain benefits (SSCBA 1992 s122(1)).

qualifying employment share trust (QUEST) An employee share ownership trust (ESOT) that meets certain conditions when the trust is established. These are set out in FA 1989 Sch 5. Tax relief is provided by FA 1989 s67.

qualifying interest in possession (QIIP) Type of trust that is exempt from the ten-yearly charge (IHTA 1982 from s59). The main points are that the trust was set up before 22 March 2006 under a will or intestacy as an interest in possession trust.

qualifying recognised overseas pension scheme (QROPS) A recognised overseas pension scheme is a qualifying recognised overseas pension scheme if it satisfies certain HMRC requirements. The scheme manager must notify HMRC that the scheme is a recognised overseas pension scheme and provide evidence to HMRC where required. The scheme manager must also sign an undertaking to inform HMRC if the scheme ceases to be a recognised overseas pension scheme and comply with any prescribed information requirements imposed on the scheme manager by HMRC. The recognised overseas pension scheme must not be excluded by HMRC from being a qualifying recognised overseas pension scheme.

qualifying week The 15th week before expected week of childbirth. An employee who was working in that week may be entitled to statutory maternity pay.

qualifying work In relation to the fixed rate deduction for use of home for business premises, the term "means –

(a) work done by the person, or any employee of the person, in the person's home wholly and exclusively for the purposes of the trade, or

(b) where the person is a firm, work done by a partner or any employee of the firm, in the partner's home wholly and exclusively for those purposes" (ITTOIA 2005 s94H(4A) as inserted by FA 2016 s24(5).

qualifying young person Term used in social security legislation to describe someone for whom child benefit may be claimed. A qualifying young person is basically someone aged 16 to 18 (and in limited circumstances 19) who is in full-time education or training and for any extension period thereafter. For tax credits, the term is defined in Tax Credits Act 2002 s8(4).

qualitative characteristics Requirements of published accounts of a reporting entity as set out in FRS 102 from para 2.4. The characteristics are:

- understandability
- relevance
- materiality
- reliability
- substance over form
- prudence
- completeness
- comparability
- timeliness
- balance between benefit and cost.

quantitative analysis In investment, process of valuing a share or other security by numerical information such as sales and profit margins. Analysis from non-numerical information is known as qualitative analysis.

quantitative easing Monetary policy where the Bank of England buys government bonds or other financial assets to inject money into the economy to expand economic activity.

It is sometimes called "printing money", as in effect it is like printing banknotes without underlying assets. This would have the effect of a small devaluation of the currency, thus increasing inflation. In practice, the policy has been followed when inflation and interest rates are low, and the country has economic problems. Quantitative easing is also called asset purchase.

Quantitative easing has a similar effect to a sales tax.

A list of quantitative easing occasions is given in section 3 of this dictionary.

quarantine Compulsory isolation for a period, such as on bringing animals into the UK. The term was also used during the coronavirus outbreak to mean a period when a person from overseas may have to remain at home for 7 to 14 days.

quarantine kennels These qualified for capital allowance as plant if constructed between 1 April 1972 and 14 March 1988.

quarry Profits from a quarry run as a business are subject to income tax (ITTOIA 2005 s12) or corporation tax (CTA 2009 s39).

quart Imperial unit of liquid capacity equal to 2 pints, 69.355 cubic inches or 1.136 litres. There are four quarts in a gallon.

quarter In tax, this usually means a period of three months such as for VAT returns (VATA 1994 s94(1)) or payments from a bank (ITA 2007 s947(4)).

The word can also mean a quarter of a hundredweight, i.e. 28 pounds (25 in USA), eight bushels of corn, or a 25 cent coin in USA.

quarter day One of four dates in the year when rent is traditionally paid. In England and Wales the dates are 25 March, 24 June, 29 September and 25 December. In

Scotland, from 1991, the dates are 28 February, 28 May, 28 August and 28 November. These are also given in section 3 of this dictionary.

quarterly PAYE The right to pay PAYE quarterly rather than monthly if the employer reasonably believes the amount will be less than £1,500 (unchanged from 2000) a month (PAYE Regulations 2003 reg 3(1)). The scheme was introduced in 1991. Note that the right to pay quarterly remains for the year even if the PAYE exceeds £1,500 a month.

quarterly rebate payment person For hydrocarbon oil duty, "means a rebate payment person permitted by the Commissioners, in the licence issued by them to him as a rebate payment person, to furnish an estimate (governed by the Regulations) in relation to any quarterly period in any year beginning 1st January, 1st April, 1st July and 1st October" (Hydrocarbon Oil Duties (Payment of Rebates) Regulations SI 1996 No 2313 reg 3(1)).

quartile In statistics, those items that fall into one of the four quarters of a range, such as the richest quartile, second richest quartile etc.

quash In law, extinguish or annul completely.

quasi-cash collateral "In relation to a stock lending arrangement or quasi-stock lending arrangement, means —

(a) any money which is payable for a relevant purpose, and
(b) any other property which is transferable for a relevant purpose" (ITA 2007 s600(4)).

Section 600(5) defines "relevant purpose" as meaning part of a stock-lending or quasi-stock lending arrangement.

quasi-contract An obligation that does not arise from a contract but is similar to one that does. The implications have been considered in the cases *Sinclair v Brougham [1914]* and *Nelson v Larholt [1951]*.

quasi-debt Term used by international accounting standards in relation to preference shares.

quasi-derivative "A contract or asset having the effect of a derivative contract" (FCA glossary).

quasi-distribution Loan by a company to a shareholder. This was a common tax avoidance scheme that has now been made ineffective.

quasi-easement Implied right of a tenant to enjoy all easements which are necessary to enjoy the property rights granted. The issue was considered in the case *Wheeldon v Burrows [1879]*.

quasi-loan Transaction with the nature of a loan arranged through a third party. If a quasi-loan is arranged between a company and one of its directors, the approval of members may be required. The statutory definition is:

"A transaction under which one party (the creditor) agrees to pay, or pays otherwise than in pursuance of an agreement, a sum for another (the borrower) or agrees to reimburse, or reimburses otherwise than in pursuance of an agreement, expenditure incurred by another party for another (the borrower):

(a) on terms that the borrower (or a person on his behalf) will reimburse the creditor; or

(b) in circumstances giving rise to a liability on the borrower to reimburse the creditor" (CA 2006 s199(1)).

quasi-loan payment information In relation to trading income provided through third parties by a loan outstanding on 5 April 2019, the term is defined in Finance (No 2) Act 2017 sch 12 para 23 as inserted by FA 2018 Sch 2.

quasi-stock lending arrangements "Means so much of any arrangements between two or more persons as are not stock lending arrangements, but are arrangements under which –

(a) a person ("the lender") transfers securities to another person ("the borrower") otherwise than by way of sale. And

(b) a requirement is imposed on a person to transfer any or all of the securities, or any other property, back to the lender or any other person otherwise than by sale"

(ITA 2007 s600(2)).

quasi-subsidiary "A quasi-subsidiary of a reporting entity is a company, trust, partnership or other vehicle that, though not fulfilling the definition of a subsidiary, is directly or indirectly controlled by the reporting entity and gives rise to benefits for that entity that are in substance no different from those that would arise were the vehicle a subsidiary" (FRS 5 para 7, now repealed). A different definition is given in CTA 2010 s32(3) in relation to whether dividends from such a company are franked investment income.

quasi-uniform When an employee's clothing is so prescribed by the employer that it serves a similar function to a uniform. Unlike a uniform, such clothing is not tax deductible by the employee. The leading case is *Mallalieu v Drummond [1983] 57 TC 330*. The matter is discussed in HMRC Manual at BIM37910.

Queen Elizabeth II Monarch of the UK (1926-) who acceded to the throne on the death of her father King George VI in 1952. Her image appears on coins, banknotes and stamps. All taxes are collected in her name. The Queen is exempt from tax though she agreed to pay it voluntary in 1993.

Queen's counsel (QC) Senior barrister or solicitor during the reign of a Queen.

quetzal Currency of Guatemala, named after the country's national bird. It is divided into 100 centavos. Gold coins for 5, 10 or 20 quetzales may be regarded as gold investment coins for VAT purposes (VAT notice 701/12A).

quick response mechanism Provision of an EU directive to counter VAT fraud, introduced in 2011. It allows a member state to impose a reverse charge without needing a derogation.

Quick Shoe Leading tax case on the extent to which the purchaser of a business may claim tax relief for discharging liabilities of the seller. The full citation is *Cooke v Quick Shoe Repair Service [1949] 30TC460*. The capital element of the consideration is discussed in HMRC Manual at BIM35655; the revenue element at BIM38330.

quick succession relief Relief from inheritance tax when property is inherited for a second time within five years (IHTA 1984 s141). Further details are given in section 3 of this dictionary.

quid Colloquialism for a pound in money. The term dates from 1688.

quiet possession Right to use one possessions freely. In consumer contracts, this right is given by Consumer Rights Act 2015 s17(6).

quindraka One hundredth of a lek, currency of Albania.

quintal Unit of weight equal to 100 kilograms, or one tenth of a metric tonne.

Quinizarin Colouring agent that may be used to indicate that hydrocarbon oil duty has not been paid on oil.

quire Old term for 24 or 25 sheets of paper. A ream is 20 quires, and thus comprises 480 or, more usually, 500 sheets.

quiz machine Machine which asks questions for the paying user to select a correct answer. Such a machine is specifically excluded from the scope of amusement machine licence duty.

quorum Minimum number of members who must be present at a meeting for it to transact business. The size of the quorum is usually stated in the body's constitution.

The quorum is usually expressed either as a number or as a percentage of the membership. If insufficient people attend, the meeting is inquorate and cannot transact business. Where a meeting is inquorate, the rules should allow the meeting to be reconstituted at a later date subject to proper notification and notice period, when the meeting may transact its business regardless of whether it is quorate.

In company law, a single member can be a quorum (CA 2006 s318(1)).

quota Limit on number. Some Customs duties may be relieved by a quota pertaining to a particular product from a specific country (Taxation (Cross-border) Trade Act 2018 s11).

quotation A statement of how much a contractor or supplier will charge for providing goods or a service. A quotation is legally binding for a stated period, unlike an estimate.

quoted company A company whose shares are listed on the London Stock Exchange, the official list of any EEA state, or the New York Stock Exchange or NASDAQ in USA (CA 2006 s385(2)).

quoted option Option quoted on a recognised exchange. The term is so defined in TCGA1992 s144, which deals with the capital gains tax implications.

quotient In mathematics, the answer from a division calculation. In the calculation:

$$12 \div 4 = 3,$$

12 is the dividend, 4 is the divisor and 3 is the quotient.

R Reinfection rate of an infectious disease. It represents the number of people who can be infected by a single carrier. This number became particularly important during the coronavirus outbreak in 2020. The coronavirus R number without countering measures is between 2 and 6, and was often quoted as 3. Various draconian measures were taken to push the R number below 1. Many tax and financial provisions were introduced to help those financially affected.

rabbit (1) Colloquialism for a surprise announcement, such as those sometimes given by the Chancellor of the Exchequer at the end of a Budget speech. It is an allusion to the old magic trick of producing a white rabbit from a seemingly empty top hat.

(2) Possible form of goodwill as a fourth category of cat, dog and rat.

racehorse owners' scheme Special VAT scheme whereby a person or group of people may register for VAT if they own at least 50% of a horse registered at Weatherbys. Details are given in VAT leaflet 700/67.

Rachmanism Exploitation of tenants by an unscrupulous landlord for his financial benefit. The term comes from Peter Rachman (1919-1962) who employed such methods against tenants in Notting Hill in the 1950s and 1960s. This included driving out tenants who had legal protection by violence or threats of violence. He was exposed in 1963. The Rent Act 1965 was passed to address such concerns.

racial discrimination Discriminating against a person because of their colour, race, nationality or ethnic or national origin. It is generally unlawful under Race Relations Act 1976 or Equalities Act 2010.

rack rent The amount of rent that can be legally charged according to what could be obtained in the open market. Colloquially, it has come to mean a high rent. For local authority action against insanitary housing, it means a rent which is at least two-thirds of the full net annual value of the house (Housing Act 1936 s9(4)).

racking For alcoholic liquor duty, a term given a specific meaning in Alcoholic Liquor Duties Act 1979 s16 in relation to storage of spirits.

racking line For beer duty, collection of kegs or casks filled at the same time. It is relevant in determining quantities subject to beer duty, as explained in Customs notice 226.

radial chord Curvature in the sides of a many-sided coin, such as the UK's 20p, 50p and (from 2017) £1 coins. It allows the coin to roll.

radian Unit of circular measure, approximately equal to 57.3 degrees.

radio licence Tax charge for a licence required between 1927 and 1971 to use a radio.

radio transmitter Customs may seize imported radio transmitters that are not authorised for use in the UK. This includes CB radios and cordless telephones.

raffle Lottery for goods.

rag trade Colloquialism for the clothing industry.

railway Profits from a railway run as a trade are subject to income tax (ITTOIA 2005 s12) or corporation tax (CTA 2009 s39). The definition of a railway is as given in Railways Act 1993. Capital allowances for railway assets are explained in CAA 2001 s95.

railway asset Means –

(a) a locomotive, tram or other vehicle, or a carriage, wagon or other rolling stock designed or adapted for a railway;
(b) anything which is, or is to be, comprised in any railway station, railway track or light maintenance depot or any apparatus which is, or is to be, installed in association with such a station, track or depot" (CAA 2001 s95(2)).

Capital allowance provisions are given in CAA 2001 s95.

Ramsay Leading tax case of 1981. It basically allows intermediary steps in a series of transactions to be ignored if they have no commercial purpose other than tax avoidance. Its scope was extended by Furniss v Dawson.

ranking In insolvency, the order in which different classes of debt are paid.

rand Currency of South Africa.

random number Number arbitrarily chosen, usually from a predefined range such as between 1 and 100. It can be used in simulation. A random number may be produced from random number tables, a scientific calculator or a spreadsheet. A number is not random if simply made up by the user.

rank In insolvency, a class of debt determining the order in which it is paid relevant to other classes.

ransom Payment to a criminal for such purpose as releasing a kidnapped purpose or preventing products being contaminated. Such payments are not illegal in themselves, but as criminal payments, they are not tax-deductible (CTA 2009 s1304). The matter is discussed in HMRC Manual at BIM43180.

rapid reclaim Scheme announced by the government in 2017 to allow personal independence payment (PIP) claimants to resume receiving PIPs more quickly after being overseas for 13 weeks.

rappee Coarse snuff made from dry tobacco.

rappen One hundredth of a Swiss franc, currency of Switzerland. It is also known as a centime.

rate applicable to trusts (RAT) Rate of income tax applied to discretionary trusts from 2005. It is the same as the UK additional rate of income tax.

rateable value Value placed on property by HMRC's Valuation Office Agency. This figure is used to determine business rates, and may be used to determine taxable benefit of employee accommodation.

rated output work Basis for ensuring that the national minimum wage (NMW) is paid for output work, where a person is paid according to work done rather than time spent. Examples include homeworkers who assemble items or put literature into envelopes. Compliance with the NMW regulations requires either a record to be kept of hours worked, or for a system of rated output work which calculates a piece rate based on 120% of the NMW for the mean hourly output rate, as explained in the entry for output work.

rate of return Total income from an investment expressed as a percentage of the amount invested.

rates Term widely used for the local taxation of residences from 1694 until the community charge was introduced in Scotland in 1989 and in England and Wales in 1990, now replaced by council tax in 1993. The rates are still levied in Northern Ireland.

rated output work Method for ensuring that the national minimum wage is paid when an employee is paid according to work done rather than time spent.

ratio The relationship one figure has to another. It is usually expressed as a single digit from dividing one number by another. In accounts, many of these ratios are used for management and investment purposes. Common examples include the price/earnings ratio, earnings per share and working capital ratio.

ratio decidendi Latin for "the reason for the decision". It is the deciding factor in a court case. As such it becomes binding on similar cases in the same or lower courts until it is either reversed by a higher court or overturned by legislation. Other comments made by a court are called obiter dicta, which may establish a persuasive precedent.

Raw Tobacco Approval Scheme Scheme introduced from 1 April 2017 under which anyone who intend to carry on any activity involving raw tobacco must register with HMRC. The scheme was introduced to prevent tax evasion.

RDE2 Real driving emissions 2 standard, also known as Euro 6d. From 6 April 2018, company cars with diesel engines that comply with this standard are not subject to a 4% addition to the percentage rate which otherwise applies. The addition is added to the percentage taken from tables relative to carbon dioxide emissions. This is multiplied by the car's list price to give the taxable benefit to the employee.

read In relation to company documents, "a document or information can be read only if –

(a) it can be read with the naked eye, or

(b) to the extent that it consists of images (for example, photographs, pictures, maps, plans or drawings), it can be seen with the naked eye."

(CA 2006 s1168(6)).

readies Colloquialism for money, particularly in the form of banknotes.

readily convertible asset (RCA) Asset that can easily be turned into cash, such as a gold ingot or National Savings certificate. If such an asset is provided to an employee, it is regarded as gross pay subject to PAYE income tax and class 1 national insurance. It is not treated as a benefit in kind.

real In relation to amounts, this usually refers to a figure that has been adjusted for inflation, taxation or a similar factor.

real estate Property which consists of land and buildings. For wills, the term "shall extend to manors, advowsons, messuages, lands, tithes, rents, and hereditaments whether corporeal, incorporeal or personal, and to any undivided share thereof, and to any estate, right or interest (other than a chattel interest) therein" (Wills Act 1837 s1).

real estate investment trust (REIT) Company which provides a collective investment in commercial property. From 1 January 2007, a special regime operates at the option of the company. Under the REIT scheme, the company pays an entry fee of 2% of the value of the property. This property is then ring-fenced from any other activities of the company. The property rental business of the REIT is not subject to corporation tax. However a loss made by the REIT may be offset against profits of the non-REIT business. The REIT must meet various conditions. The legislation is CTA 2010 Part 12.

realisation In accounting, the process of turning an asset into cash.

realisation basis For taxation of certain securities, means "not recognising a profit or loss on any asset until it is realised" (FA 2002 s65(2)). The provisions for moving to mark to market are given in ITTOIA 2005 s236.

realisation concept Accounting principle that increases in value should only be recognised when the asset is sold. UK accounting standards depart from this concept for land and buildings which should be periodically revalued.

realised loss Loss arising from revenue which has been suffered by the entity. Further guidance for companies is contained in CA 2006 s841.

realised profit Profit arising from revenue which has been earned by the entity and for which there is a reasonable prospect of cash being collected in the near future. Further guidance for companies is contained in CA 2006 s841.

real property Term sometimes used to mean land and buildings rather than other types of property.

real terms This expression when related to an amount means adjusted to reflect inflation.

real time Where a computer reacts immediately to instructions from the user.

real time information (RTI) Scheme introduced in 2012 for PAYE that requires the employer to provide to HMRC full details of each payslip at or before the employee is paid. In practice, this is done automatically by payroll software. The scheme became compulsory from 6 October 2013 (PAYE Regulations 2003 reg 2A(1)).

real time returns Returns made under real time information. The statutory provisions are given in PAYE regulations SI 2003 No 2682 from reg 67B and Schedule A1, with effect from 6 April 2012.

real world driving emissions System adopted in 2015 to measure emissions from vehicles under normal driving rather than under test conditions. This followed the vehicle emissions scandal when it was discovered that some vehicles had devices fitted that gave a false reading.

reasonable care Standard expected of a taxpayer when completing a tax return. Failure to exercise reasonable care can make the taxpayer liable for a penalty based on carelessness.

reasonable care, skill and diligence The qualities which a company director is expected to exercise (CA 2006 s174(1)). This requires "the general knowledge, skill and experience that may reasonably be expected of a person carrying out the functions carried out by a director" (ibid s174(2)(a)) plus "the general knowledge, skill and experience that the director has" (ibid s174(2)(b)).

reasonable excuse

General

Reason why a taxpayer should not be penalised for non-compliance with a tax obligation. This includes grounds for an appeal against filing or payment of tax. There is no appeal for interest charged on late payment. There are different legal provisions for different taxes though, in practice, the standard is the same. Appeals on grounds of reasonable excuse are routinely heard by tribunals. HMRC has produced guidance on its website, though reasonable excuse has been held to wider than that guidance. The Chartered Institute of Taxation also produced guidance on 22 February 2012.

Insufficiency and reliance

For VAT, two reasons are given as *not* comprising reasonable excuse. These are insufficiency of funds, and reliance on another person (VATA 1994 s71(1)). However these are not what they may seem. The case *C & E Commrs v JB Steptoe [1992] CA. STC 757* held that there was reasonable excuse when a shortage of funds was due to reasons beyond the business's control. In this case, Steptoe was an electrical contractor, 95% of whose work was for the London Borough of Redbridge who routinely paid him two months late. Having lost three times, the Commissioners announced their changed of policy in a press release of 6 June 1991. It should be noted that Steptoe could have avoided the problem by using cash accounting, which Customs and Excise pointed out to him in 1989. The fact that Steptoe did not was not in itself sufficient reason to deny him reasonable excuse.

Similarly reliance on another person is not what it may seem. Of many cases on this, in *Barrett [2015] TC 4514,* a tribunal found that a builder had reasonable excuse when a builder engaged an accountant who failed to use the construction industry scheme. A builder was entitled to believe that a practising accountant was competent.

Scope of reasonable excuse

There has been a long conflict between HMRC and the tribunals on what constitutes reasonable excuse. HMRC has routinely said "Our view is that a reasonable excuse is normally an unexpected or unusual event, either unforeseen or beyond your control". The tribunals have said that reasonable excuse is wider than that. In the *Steptoe* case, the upper tribunal said ([2018] UKUT 156 at para 83) that reasonable excuse "is far wider than those remarks implied might be the case". It suggested that if HMRC continues to use that "mantra", costs could be awarded against it.

In the case *J & L Benson Building Services [2018] TC 6546,* said that HMRC's position was a "discredited argument" (para 50) whose continued was "unforgiveable" (para 48). In the case *HMD Response International [2011] TC 1322,* the judge slated HMRC for a £500 late filing penalty imposed on a charity. He said (para 4) "such high-handed threatening action was not justified. It smacks more of the conduct of a disreputable debt collector than of responsible conduct by an organ of the state".

Examples of reasonable excuse being upheld other than for unexpected events include:

- reliance on an HMRC officer *(Evans Transport [1987] VTD 2974)*
- a reasonable belief that a return had been accepted by HMRC's computer *(Robert Morris [2017] TC 6160)*
- ignorance of the law *(Christine Perrin [2018] UKUT 156).* This applies when the law is unusual and HMRC has not done enough to publicise it.

Where there is a national or other significant factor affecting returns, the government will often grant a blanket relaxation of penalty rules. This happened, for example, for flooding, foot and mouth disease, and coronavirus.

Some general principles

Some general principles of reasonable excuse can be discerned from tribunal decisions:

- it is HMRC's job to prove that a penalty is payable. It is not enough for HMRC to assert facts and then require the taxpayer to disprove them *(Mr Richard Jones [2018] TC 6560 para 23)*
- the matter should be considered on the basis of what a reasonable taxpayer would have done *(Nigel Barrett [2015] UKFTT 0329).* The test is objective *(The Clean Car Company Ltd [1991] VTD 5695)*
- a belief that HMRC acted outside the law is not reasonable excuse *(Francis Chapman [2017] TC 6206)*
- the normal vicissitudes of trade are not reasonable excuse. A business should have provisions to deal with normal levels of staff sickness, computer glitches, and late payments from customers
- it is unlikely that reasonable excuse will be upheld if the taxpayer ignored communications from HMRC *(John McFarlane [2018] TC 6512)*
- a combination of factors may collectively be reasonable excuse even though each factor alone is not *(Scott Building Contractors [2017] TC 6066)*
- a tribunal can be more compassionate than HMRC *(Sandpiper Car Hire Ltd [2018] TC 6497)*
- a trader is expected to help himself or herself, such as by deregistering for VAT when turnover declines sharply *(Philip Ashley Legg [2018] TC 6488).* A business is not penalised because it could use Time To Pay or cash accounting but did not. There was reasonable excuse when HMRC refused even to consider a Time To Pay request *(WeR Your IT [2013] TC 3116)*
- action by a bank such as incorrectly entering a cheque *(Premier Roofing Systems Ltd [1991] VTD 6338)* or suddenly reducing an overdraft facility *(Kingston Craftsmen (1981) Ltd [1991] VTD 5409)* are reasonable excuse
- there can be reasonable excuse when HMRC has delayed a tax refund to the same taxpayer, even if for another tax *(G T Shaw & M A Whitlock [1988] VTD 3530)* or even when owed by another country *(DPC European Transport [1988] VTD 16177)*

- a mistake is not reasonable excuse, however innocent *(Garnmoss Ltd [2012] TC 2001)*
- there is usually a time limit for reasonable excuse. What is reasonable excuse for one or two penalties ceases to be reasonable excuse after sufficient time has passed *(Alan Peter Metcalfe [2018] TC 6510)*
- any false statement in a claim for reasonable excuse is likely to be fatal to the claim *(Albert Guest House [1990] VTD 5524)*
- claims based on illness of the taxpayer will usually require evidence. They are not reasonable excuse if the taxpayer could have engaged help *(G G Wright [1990])*
- absence from work is unlikely to be reasonable excuse *(Pip Systems [1988] VTD 3413).*

Unusual reasons

Reasonable excuse has produced many unusual excuses. There was reasonable excuse when an accounts clerk was found to have kept accounting records in Chinese *(P Jennings & Sons Ltd [1991] VTD 6696).* There was no reasonable excuse when a taxpayer wrongly believed that the Canary Islands were part of the EU *(Ian Neave [2018] TC 6437).* HMRC has also reported that excuses routinely include "my dog ate my tax return". Another taxpayer claimed that his mother-in-law was a witch who cast an evil spell on him. Neither was accepted.

rebasing When the base is changed, such as for an index or value. The term is particularly used for capital gains.

For individuals, from 6 April 1988, the base for acquisition costs was moved from 6 April 1965 to 1 April 1982 (TCGA 1992 ss35-36, Sch3-4). This means that for disposals from 6 April 1988 of assets acquired before 1 April 1982, the market value as at 1 April 1982 is substituted for the acquisition cost. In other words, gains before 1982 are not taxed.

For companies, they have the *option* not to make such a rebasing election. They may use the acquisition cost instead. This election must be made within two years after the end of the future year of disposal. This election does not apply to plant and machinery for which capital allowances have been claimed. If the election is made to use a value from 1965, the position can be more complicated as there were different valuation provisions in effect, particularly for quoted securities and land with development value.

rebasing relief Relief introduced in 2017 for taxpayers who have a deemed domicile from being UK resident in 15 of the previous 20 years. The relief allows the taxpayer to pay capital gains tax using asset value as at 5 April 2017 for acquisition cost (ITA 2007 s835BA).

rebated oil Oil that bears a lower level of hydrocarbon oil duty than normal. There are restrictions on use of such oil (HODA 1979 ss11 and 14).

rebate payment person For hydrocarbon oil duty, "means subject to paragraph (3) below of this regulation, a person –

(a) who applies in writing to the Commissioners for a licence authorising him to make payments in accordance with the provisions of these Regulations for the purposes of section 12(2) or section 13AA(3) and (4) of [HODA1979], as specified in his application, and

(b) to whom a licence is issued by the Commissioners".

(Hydrocarbon Oil (Payment of Rebates) Regulations SI 1996 No 2313 reg 3(1)).

rebuttable presumption Something which is assumed to be true until evidence is found which suggests otherwise. Rebuttable presumptions are widely used in auditing. An audit starts with the rebuttable presumptions that the accounts have been prepared honestly but may contain mistakes.

recapitalisation Change in the capital structure of a company when new shares are issued to restore the value of the capital towards the amount it was previously. Recapitalisation is often undertaken by a struggling company seeking to avoid insolvency.

receipt (1) Money received.

(2) Document evidencing money paid. HMRC no longer routinely issues receipts but will provide one on request.

receipt of insignificant value

In the context of EIS relief, this means a receipt of no more than £1,000 (ITA 2007 s215(2)). Such a receipt disapplies the rule in s213 which requires the relief to be reduced if the investor receives value from the investee company.

receive In relation to anti-avoidance provisions for intellectual property, this word "means receive —

(a) directly or indirectly;

(b) by one payment or a series of payments"

(ITA 2007 s917A(4) as inserted by FA 2016 s41).

receiver Person dealing with the affairs of a person or other legal entity, usually when that person or entity is insolvent or otherwise not able to look after their own affairs.

receivership When an insolvent company is taken over by an insolvency practitioner who may run parts of it, sell parts of it and liquidate what remains.

receiving education In relation to universal credit, is a description of someone in full-time education, study or training. The general rule is that such a person may not claim universal credit, with some exceptions for disabled people and for young people without parental support. If a couple claims universal credit and one is receiving education, the other person may be able to claim.

recession Two consecutive quarters when the nation's gross domestic product contracts. Recent UK recessions have been:

- 2020 from first quarter, due to coronavirus
- 2008 quarter 2 to 2009 quarter 2, banking crisis
- 1990 quarter 3 to 1991 quarter 3, savings and loans crisis
- 1980 quarter 1 to 1981 quarter 1, deflationary policies
- 1975 quarters 2 and 3, oil crisis

- 1973 quarter 3 to 1974 quarter 1, oil crisis.

reciprocal agreement Agreement between two parties where each agrees to provide similar assistance to the other. In tax, this particularly applies to international agreements on national insurance and social security, of which there are many. The statutory authority is contained in Social Security Administration Act 1992 s179.

reciprocal holdings Situation where two companies each own shares in the other. This may be done to frustrate takeover bids.

reckonable service In relation to overseas pensions, this term is defined in ITEPA 2003 s574A(6) as inserted by FA 2017 Sch 3.

reckonable year For the state pension, a year that counts towards the 35 qualifying years needed to secure a pension under Pension Act 2014 s4(5)).

reclaim fund Fund established by a bank or building society to meet claims from individuals who are found to be the rightful owners of bank or building society accounts that have been declared dormant. A full definition is given in Dormant Bank and Building Society Accounts Act 2008 s5.

recognised stock exchange Stock exchange whose valuations are accepted for tax purposes (FA 2007 Sch 26).

recognised transfer Transfer of a member's accrued rights in a pension scheme to another scheme (FA 2004 s169).

recognition In accounting, the process whereby an item is included in the accounts. "The process of incorporating into the statement of financial position [balance sheet] or statement of comprehensive income [profit and loss account] an item that meets the definition of an asset, liability, equity, income or expense" and satisfies the two recognition criteria. These are the probability of future economic benefit, and reliability of measurement (FRS 102 glossary and section 2.27).

"The process of incorporating an item into the primary financial statements under the appropriate heading. It involves depiction of the item in words and by a monetary amount and inclusion of that amount in the statement totals" (FRS 5 para 6).

Guidance on recognition of assets and liabilities is given in FRS 18 para 9 and FRS 5 from para 20. Detailed provisions are given in IFRS 1.

recommended medical treatment Treatment that is to assist the employee to return to work after an absence of 28 days or more due to injury of ill health (ITEPA s320C(3)). This must be made under the provisions of Employment and Training Act 1973 s2, or by an occupational health service under arrangements made by the employer.

From 1 January 2015, such treatment is not a taxable benefit in kind up to £500 per tax year per employee, nor is it subject to national insurance.

recomputation Preparing a tax computation for a second or subsequent time because of an error or change of practice from the first computation.

Reconciliation In accounting, process of agreeing financial statements, particularly the bank statement to the entity's own records.

reconditioning For VAT, reconditioning goods is a service (VAT notice 700). Small components that are replaced, such as batteries, filters and oil, are not regarded as a separate supply.

reconstruction and acquisition reliefs Various reliefs from stamp duty land tax in respect of the reconstruction and acquisition of companies. They are given in FA 2003 Sch 7.

reconversion of stock Process of turning stock (meaning equity capital) back into ordinary shares. The company law is contained in CA 2006 s620. The right to convert shares to stock was given in CA 1985 s121(2)(c). This right has now been repealed by the 2006 Act though previous stock conversions remain legal. Reconversion of stock requires an ordinary resolution of the shareholders but no longer requires prior authority in the articles of association.

reconveyance Right of a seller to have property sold back by the buyer. CTA 2009 s224 contains provisions for when a lease is sold with a right to reconveyance. Similar provisions for income tax are given in ITTOIA 2005 s284.

record-keeping Basic financial records that must be kept for tax purposes. Guidance for the self-employed is provided by HMRC at http://www.hmrc.gov.uk/sa/rec-keep-self-emp.htm. Guidance for VAT is given in VAT Notice 700/21. All taxpayers are required to prepare and retain sufficient records for their tax return. This general duty is given in TMA 1970 s12B as inserted by FA 1994 s196 and Sch 19.

For companies, this requirement is explicitly given in CA 2006 ss386-389.A penalty may be imposed for failure to keep proper records. HMRC's policy for such policies is given in the Inspectors Manual at EM4650. These provisions state what records must be kept, but generally do not specify how these records should be kept. This changes under Making Tax Digital. HMRC is given power to direct what records must be kept in electronic form under TMA 1970 sA1 para 11 as inserted by Finance (No 2) Act 2017 s60(2).

recovered debt Bad debt that is subsequently paid after being written off. The accounting, VAT and tax treatment is simply to treat it as income in the period when paid.

recovery condition One of two conditions that a universal credit claimant must satisfy to receive a budgeting advance. The condition is that the DWP is satisfied that the claimant is able to repay the advance. The other condition is the earnings condition.

recovery plan Plan made by a business to recover from adverse trading or financial position. For financial institutions, the Financial Services Authority has certain powers and duties as set out in Financial Services and Markets Act 2000 s139B.

recovery provisions Provisions that allow tax relief to be retrospectively denied. The main recovery provisions are TMA 1970 Sch 1AB and FA 1998 Sch 18. This term is so defined in CAA 2001 s70H(3).

recovery of benefit order Order made under Social Security Administration Act 1992 s101 to recover the cost of providing benefit from the person who should have been paying child maintenance. The tax treatment is set out in ITA 2007 s456.

recovery provisions Provisions in law that allow tax relief to be retrospectively disallowed. The main provisions are in TMA 1970 Sch 1AB; FA 1998 Sch 18 and CAA 2001 s70H(3).

recreational benefits Sports facilities and similar provided by an employer for employees. These may be exempt from taxation as a benefit in kind under ITEPA 2003 s261.

recreational trust Trust that provides recreation or other leisure activities. Such a trust may be charitable (Charities Act 2011 s5).

rectification In contract law, when the parties or a court clarifies what the parties meant by a particular expression in a contract. Extrinsic evidence may be used. In inheritance tax, the term is used when the court corrects a faulty deed of variation to give effect to what the beneficiaries intended. This must be supported by adequate evidence. In law, correction of a mistake in a document by the court (Supreme Court Act 1981 s61(1) and Sch 1).

rectifier "May not distil or extract feints or spirits from any other material than spirits on which duty has been duly paid" (Alcoholic Liquor Duties Act 1979 s21). A rectifier is severely restricted on what other trades he may follow (ibid s24).

rectifier's licence Licence which is required for compounding or rectifying spirits (Alcoholic Liquor Duties Act 1979 s18).

recycled pension When a pension lump sum is used to fund a new pension scheme. This is generally legally when the taxpayer is aged between 55 and 74, but tax relief may be limited from 2006 if certain conditions are met.

red channel Part of a port or airport where a traveller should go if he or she has goods on which duty needs to be declared.

red diesel Diesel oil stained with a red dye to indicate that it attracts a lower rate of hydrocarbon oil duty. It may be used for certain non-transport vehicles such as tractors and gritters.

redeemable Description of a preference share or other security that a company may buy back from the holder.

redenomination Changing the currency or nominal value of an asset or liability. CA 2006 ss623-628 contains provisions relating to the redenomination of ordinary shares. In particular, a company's share capital may not be reduced by more than 10% (ibid s626(4)).

redenomination reserve Capital reserve that a company must create when its share capital is reduced by a **redenomination** of share values (CA 2006 s628).

red point Place in a port or airport where a person bringing in dutiable goods may speak to a customs office by telephone.

In the case *Mark Bowes [2017] TC 6163*, it was suggested that goods could not be said to have been smuggled into the UK until a person has either spoken to a customs officer or passed the red point.

reduced payment In an annuity, a payment which is significantly less than an earlier payment under the same annuity. This may make the annuity a steep-reduction annuity, for which there are special tax provisions (ICTA 1988 s437A).

reduced pollution certificate (RPC) Certificate that a vehicle first registered before 1 October 2001 meets the exhaust emission standard that exempts it from paying the charge for the Low Emission Zone.

reduced rate Any rate that is lower than normal. In particular, it refers to the 5% rate of VAT that applies to a limited range of goods. The law is VATA 1994 s29A. The list of reduced rated items is given in VATA 1994 Sch 7A.

reducing balance method Method of calculating depreciation where each year's figure is calculated as a percentage of *the previous year's* net balance, as against the more common straight line method where each year is calculated as a percentage of the original cost. Under the reducing balance method, an asset never reaches a value of zero. For example, an asset costing £10,000 and written off over ten years on the straight line method would simply have £1,000 charged to profit and loss account each year and be worth nothing after ten years.

reduction of share capital When a limited company reduces its amount of share capital (CA 2006 s64(1)). For a private company, this requires a special resolution. For other companies, it requires a special resolution and confirmation by the court.

redundancy pay Sum paid to an employee whose job has been made redundant. Employment law requires a statutory payment to such a worker with at least 2 years' service (Employment Rights Act 1996 1996 from s135). This statutory redundancy pay is tax free. An employer may make a further termination payment. Generally, this payment, including statutory redundancy pay, is free of tax and national insurance up to £30,000 (ITEPA 2003 s309).

The employer may deduct the cost of redundancy pay from profits subject to income tax (ITTOIA 2005 s76) or corporation tax (CTA 2009 s76). The matter is discussed in HMRC Manual at BIM38385.

Redundancy Support Service for Apprentices (ReSSA) Government-backed online and telephone support service launched on 1 August 2020 for apprentices who lost their jobs during the coronavirus outbreak.

re-engagement order An order made by an employment tribunal or other body requiring an employer to re-engage an unfairly dismissed employee on equivalent terms. An employer cannot be forced to comply with the order, but will have to pay compensation if he or she does not.

re-examination Court procedure of a witness being questioned a second time by the side that called him or her to give evidence.

referendum Ballot of UK voters (or some of them) other than in an election. There have been 13 referendums since 1973. A list of referendums will be found under Elections in section 3 of this dictionary.

referential bid Bid that refers to the amount of another bid, such as "£10,000 more than any other bid". The House of Lords held that such a bid is invalid in *Harvela Investments Ltd v Royal Trust Co of Canada Ltd [1985]*. It observed that two referential bids would lead to an impossible situation.

refer to drawer (RD) Expression written on a cheque that has been dishonoured, usually because there are insufficient funds to pay the amount.

refinery (1) Premises approved by HMRC for treatment of oil (ALDA 1979 s27) (2) Place where oil is refined (HODA 1979 s19A).

refrigeration For VAT, a supply of refrigeration is treated as a supply of goods (VATA 1994 Sch 4 para 3). Supplies to residences are reduced-rated (VATA 1994 Sch 7A Group 1), but otherwise standard-rated. The matter is explained in VAT Notice 701/6.

Regional Comprehensive Economic Partnership (RCEP) Free trade agreement signed by 15 Asian and Pacific countries on 15 November 2020. The countries are Australia, Brunei, Cambodia, China, Indonesia, Japan, Laos, Malaysia, Myanmar, New Zealand, Philippines, Singapore, South Korea, Thailand, and Vietnam. These countries account for 30% of the world's population and $26.2 trillion in GDP. RCEP is expected to eliminate about 90% of trade tariffs between these countries within 20 years.

Registered Exporter System (REX) System of self-certification of origin of goods. It is an EU system in which the exporter must be registered.

registered friendly society Incorporated body that provides insurance cover. It may also provide other benefits such as payment of discretionary benefits or running a working men's club. The law is Friendly Societies Act 1974 of 1992. They are regulated by the Financial Conduct Authority, Their tax provisions are given in ICTA 1988 ss460-466.

registered items service "Means a service of conveying postal packets from one place to another by post which provides –

(a) for the registration of the packets in connection with their conveyance by post, and

(b) for the payment of an amount determined by the person providing the service in the event of the theft or loss of or damage to the packets"

(Postal Services Act 2011 s32(4)).

registered medical practitioner "Means a fully registered person within the meaning of the Medical Act 1983 who holds a licence to practise under that Act" (Interpretation Act 1978 Sch 1).

registered office Address to which communications to a company are sent (CA 2006 s86).

registered pension scheme Pension scheme that is registered with HMRC (or Inland Revenue before 2005) or has acquired registered status by being approved on 5 April 2006. Registration is under FA 2004 Part 4 Chapter 2.

From 6 April 2007, a pension scheme is approved by the Financial Conduct Authority under Financial Services and Markets Act 2000.

registered social landlord Housing association or other not-for-profit body that provides social housing for people in need. They are registered under Housing and Regeneration Act 2008. From 1 January 2000, short-term tenancy agreements made by such landlords may be exempt from stamp duty land tax.

registered society Friendly society that is mutual and not incorporated (TCGA 1992 s217A).

registered sports club Sports club registered under CTA 2010 Part 13 Chapter 9. Such a club cannot be a charity (Charities Act 2011 s6). They are treated in a similar manner for tax.

register of interests Record that a public company must keep of all information received by it in relation to interests in its shares other than ownership (CA 2006 s808).

register of members List of shareholders or other members of a limited company. Every company must keep such a register (CA 2006 ss113-121).

register of prohibited trustees Register kept by the Pensions Regulator of persons not allowed to be trustees of a pension fund (Pensions Act 2004 s66).

registrable Liable to be registered. For VAT, this term is used in VATA 1994 Sch 1 para 18.

registrant discount Discount on shares that may be offered to subscribers in a share issue. If offered to employees, the position is explained in ITEPA 2003 s547.

registration certificate Document which shows that something has been registered, particularly document V5C which shows that a vehicle has been registered to a particular keeper.

registration threshold Amount at which a person or other body must register. In particular, it refers to the turnover limit of £85,000 a year when a trader must register for VAT (VATA 1994 Sch 1 para 1(1)).

regressive tax Tax that is unrelated to earnings and therefore takes a higher share of earnings for lower earnings. Road tax is an example.

Regular Reserve Name given to what was the Army Reserve. The name change is effected by Defence Reform Act 2014 s44(1).

regulated market Term used in EC directive 2004/39/EC article 4.1(14). It is quoted in CTA 2010 s1158 in relation to investment trusts. The same definition is extended to company law by CA 2006 s1173(1), except where the EEA state has not implement the Directive. In such case, the term "has the same meaning as it has in Council Directive 93/22/EEC on investment services in the securities field" (CA 2006 s1173(2)).

Regulatory Policy Committee (RPC) Government body that provides independent scrutiny of the assessments which departments and regulators prepare when proposing new regulatory measures.

rehabilitation Process to allow people who have served sentences to resume normal life in society. The main law is the Rehabilitation of Offenders Act 1974. The law has been amended several times, most recently from 10 March 2014.

From 1 November 2020, there are shorter rehabilitation periods in Scotland under Management of Offenders (Scotland) Act 2019.

The Act introduces the concept of spent and unspent convictions. All sentences of up to four years imprisonment become spent after a rehabilitation period. That means that the person may be allowed not to disclose the sentence for such purposes as employment, insurance, housing applications and attending educational courses. A conviction becomes spent if the person has not offended again during the rehabilitation period. A prison sentence of four or more years is never spent. A public protection sentence is also never spent.

There are some exceptions where spent sentences must be disclosed. These are listed in the Rehabilitation of Offenders Act 1974 (Exceptions) Order 1975. This Act is to be amended to shorten rehabilitation periods.

rehearing Second hearing of a case on which a court has already pronounced. An example is an appeal.

rehearsal money Payment to performers while rehearsing. If the performers are employees, they are entitled to such payment which must be of a least the national minimum wage. It is subject to tax and national insurance as gross pay.

Rehoboam Champagne bottle with a capacity of six standard bottles.

reimbursement Money given to someone who has incurred an expense on someone else's behalf. The tax implications of reimbursement of employees' expenses is set out in ITEPA 2003 s334.

reimbursement arrangements Arrangements to reimburse customers amount of overcharged VAT (Value Added Tax 1994 s80A(2)).

reinstatement When an employee is re-engaged having been suspended or dismissed. During suspension, an employee is entitled to normal salary. In 2020, the Court of Justice of the European Union held that an employee's annual leave entitlement continued to accrue between dismissal and reinstatement (*QH v Varhoven kasatsionen sad na Republika Bulgaria [2020]. Case C-762/)*

reinsurance contract In accounting, "an insurance contract issued by one issuer (the reinsurer) to compensate another insurer (the cedant) for losses on one or more contracts issued by the cedant" (FRS 102 glossary).

reinsurance treaty In relation to taxation of annuity business "means a contract under which one insurance company is obliged to cede, and another (in this paragraph referred to as a "reinsurer") to accept, the whole or part of a risk of a class or description to which the contract relates" (FA 1991 Sch7 para 16(7)).

REIT See **Real estate investment trust.**

related base unit In relation to the reduced rate of VAT for a child's **safety seat,** means "a base unit which is designed solely for the purpose of attaching a safety seat securely in a road vehicle by means of anchorages that form part of the base unit and which, when in use on a road vehicle, can be restrained in one or more of the following ways —

(a) by a seat belt fitted in the vehicle, or

(b) by permanent anchorage points in the vehicle, or

(c) by belts attached to permanent anchorage points in the vehicle"

(Value Added Tax 1994 Sch 7A Group 5 para 2A as inserted by SI 2009 N 1359 from 1 July 2009.)

related employments Two or more employments that are treated as being one employment for determining whether a person is in lower-paid employment. The provisions are set out in ITEPA 2003 s220.

related party transaction Financial transaction between two connected persons, such as between a company and one of its directors. Accounting standard FRS 102 makes clear that this includes transactions where no price is charged. Such transactions must be disclosed in the accounts.

related person For residence nil rate band for inheritance tax, this is given a specific meaning in Inheritance Tax Act 1984 s8G as inserted by Finance (No 2) Act 2015 s9.

related property For inheritance tax, "related property is property that is in the estate of a spouse or civil partner, or belonging to a charity of one of the political, national or public bodies to which exempt transfers may be made. There are special rules for valuing related property" (HMRC inheritance tax glossary).

related settlement Trust established on the same day as another trust by the same settlor (IHTA 1984 s62(1)).

related third party Person who in reality is providing a benefit to an employee on behalf of the employer. Such a benefit is treated as if provided by the employer (PAYE Regulations 2003 reg 86(4)).

relationship breakdown Divorce, separation or other event that causes two people to stop living together, whether married or not. Where the arrangements following such breakdown include the creation of a fixed interest trust, it may be taxed under the more generous rules that applied before 22 March 2006.

relative Person to whom someone is related. The exact scope depends on the context. A narrow context is ancestors, descendants, brothers and sisters in ITEPA 2003 s61(6) and TCGA 286. A wider definition includes uncles, aunts, nieces and nephews in IHTA 1984 s270.

relative bargaining power The extent to which two parties to an agreement have equal power over the other. For an arm's length contract, it is assumed that the power is approximately equal. Employment law and consumer law gives statutory rights to employees and consumers to address perceived inequality in bargaining power. Relative bargaining power was considered in the Autoclenz decision in determining whether a worker was an employee for tax purposes.

relative poverty Being financially disadvantaged relative to one's peer group. This is often taken to mean earning less than 70% of median average earnings. In Scotland, the figure is 60% (Child Poverty (Scotland) Act 2017 s3).

release for free circulation Commonest Customs procedure of imported goods being legally saleable in the UK after payment of any import VAT and other duties.

release of goods When Customs allows an importer free access to imported goods, having ensured that the relevant Customs procedures have been completed and any duty paid.

relevant dilution rate The amount of water a manufacturer of squash or similar drink says should be added to make a drink (FA 2017 s23(2)). This determines how much soft drinks industry levy is charged.

relevance One of the four requirements for accounting information. Statement of Principles states "information is relevant if it has the ability to influence the economic decisions of users and is provided in time to influences those decisions" (Chapter 3).

It can be seen that materiality is an implied condition. Two characteristics of relevance are predictive value and confirmatory value. FRS 102 includes this as a qualitative characteristic of information in financial statements. Its definition there is "the information provided in financial statements must be relevant to the decision-making needs of users, Information has the quality of relevance when it is capable of influencing the economic decisions of users by helping them evaluate past, present of future events or confirming, or correcting, their past evaluations" (FRS 102 section 2.5).

relevant dilution ratio For soft drinks industry levy, the ratio of water to liquid to produce a drink. This is as stated on the drink packaging. In the absence of such information, the ratio is determined by HMRC. (FA 2017 s27(2)).

relevant event Change in details about a company which must be reported in a confirmation statement (CA 2006 s853B). For VAT and call-off stock, the term is given a specific meaning in VATA 1994 Sch 4B para 7.

relevant property trust Classification of trust introduced on 22 March 2006. It includes all discretionary trusts and many other types of trust that had previously been treated more leniently for inheritance tax. In effect, this change in the law treats most trusts as if they were discretionary trusts for inheritance tax purposes. This means, for example, that they are liable to the ten-yearly charge.

reliability One of the qualitative characteristic of information in financial statements. "The quality of information that makes it free from material error and bias and represents faithfully that which it either purports to represent or could reasonably be expected to represent" (FRS 102 glossary). In previous standards, it is defined as the qualitative characteristic of being free from material error and bias, representing faithfully. This is one of the four requirements of accounting information required by Statement of Principles. Reliability is itself broken down into five elements:

- faithful presentation
- neutral
- free from material error
- complete
- prudence.

relief Provision that reduces the amount of tax otherwise payable.

relief declaration return Annual return for Annual Tax on Enveloped Dwellings stating that a property or properties qualifies for relief from the tax (FA 2013 s159A as inserted by FA 2015 s73).

religion System of belief, such as Christianity or Islam. It has many financial implications. A religion may qualify as a charity provided it passes the public benefit test. So relief from suffering qualifies but private prayer does not. For the purposes of charity law, religion includes one which believes in more than one god or which does not involve any belief in a god (Charities Act 2006 s2(3)) and Charities Act 2011 s3(2)(a)). For tax purposes, religion requires a belief in a supreme being, so atheistic bodies do not qualify.

In May 2018, ACAS published guidance on discussing religion in the workplace.

religious community Monastery, convent or similar establishment where people live under religious vows. These usually include sharing property on a communal basis. Members of religious communities are exempt from the national minimum wage provided:

- the community is a charity or established by a charity;
- the purpose of the community is to practise or advance a religious belief;
- all or some members live together for that purpose.

Guidance is provided in HMRC Manual at EIM69700.

religious exemption Provision that allows someone to submit tax returns on paper if their religion forbids them from using a computer. This applies only to individuals, not to companies. The only known such religions are Ultra-Orthodox Jews, Closed Brethren and Seventh Day Adventists.

religious order Monastery, convent or similar establishment where members live together to practise their religion. Members of the order are subject to tax and national insurance in the normal way, even when they have taken a vow of poverty. The matter is discussed in HMRC Manual at EIM69700. Members of an order may be exempt from the national minimum wage.

relinquishing spouse or partner Husband, wife or civil partner who had transferred part of their personal allowance before their death (ITA 2007 s6(3)).

relocation expenses Expenses incurred in relocating an employee to a different part of the country. In such a case, the employer may provide up to £8,000 (unchanged since 1993) tax-free towards certain relocation expenses (ITEPA 2003 from s271).

remainderman Person who inherits property in an interest in possession trust when the life tenant dies or their interest otherwise expires. All remaindermen must be named rather than just identified; it is not sufficient to describe them as "my grandchildren" for example.

remaining useful life In relation to capital allowances of leased assets, means the period from the commencement of the lease to when the asset is no longer used, and no longer likely to be used, as an asset of the business (CAA 2001 s70Y(1)).

remediation of contaminated land The special tax provisions for this are given in CTA 2009 from s1143.

remedial order Order of a court or other body that remedies a defect, particularly one that reverses the sale of shares or other security in a private company to a member of the public (CA 2006 s759(1)).

Remembrance, Responsibility and Future English name for German compensation scheme for anyone who was a slave or forced labourer during the second world war. In 2015, it was stated that such payments are exempt from inheritance tax.

remittance Sending of a payment. A non-resident individual who remits money to the UK may be liable to pay UK income tax on the remittance.

remittance advice Document that may accompany a payment. They are usually numbered, file and cross-referenced to the accounting records.

remittance basis Provision that applies when income is earned by a UK resident who is not UK domiciled (ITA 2007 from s809A). The basis broadly means that the income is taxed to the extent that it is remitted to the UK.

remote gambling This is allowed under Gambling Act 2005. Law on licensing is amended by Gambling (Licensing and Advertising) Act 2014 s1.

remote gaming duty Tax on gaming from a terminal operating a computer remote from the operator. Details are given in HMRC Notice 455A.

remoteness test Rule on whether expenditure is tax-deductible. This generally restricts the allowability to the direct purpose of the payment and not to indirect benefits. A leading case is *Union Cold Storage Ltd v Jones [1924] 8 TC 725.* It is discussed in HMRC Manual at BIM37200.

remote operating licence Licence issued by the Gambling Commission to someone who offers remote gambling or who offers services by remote communications (Gambling Act 2005 s67). Further details are provided in HMRC leaflet 455A.

remote transit shed Approved place situated within an airport but outside the HMRC approved area. Non-EU goods may be stored there until assigned a Customs approved treatment or use.

removable contents In relation to a caravan, such contents are standard-rated though the caravan itself may be zero-rated. Guidance on the scope of removable contents was provided by the First Tier Tribunal in *Colaingrove Ltd. TC 2715 [2013].*

removal Sending goods to another EU state. Under the single market, this is not considered an export. This provision no longer applies from 1 January 2021.

removal expenses The expenses of relocating a business are generally tax-deductible as explained in HMRC Manual at BIM42530.

The expense of relocating an employee may also be tax-deductible as explained at BIM42531. Such expenses are not taxable as a benefit in kind up to £8,000 (ITEPA 2003 from s271).

remuneration All salaries, wages, commissions, bonuses, benefits, expenses and similar payments paid to an employee. HMRC gives a definition in leaflet 480. For national insurance, a definition is given in SI 1978 No 1689 reg 1(2). A business may claim remuneration of its staff as a business expense unless the remuneration remains unpaid nine months after the year-end (ITTOIA 2005 s36; CTA 2009 s1288).

renaming loans Unsuccessful tax avoidance scheme that renamed loans as sums held in a fiduciary capacity. Spotlight 39 gives more details.

renewable energy certificate (REC) Certificate that a company may buy when it cannot sufficiently offset its non-renewable energy consumption. For VAT, the reverse charge applies to such certificates. Further details are given in VAT Notice 735 and HMRC Brief 4(2019).

renewables obligation certificate Certificate issued under Electricity Act 1989 s32B or equivalent Northern Ireland law. No tax is paid on the receipt of such a certificate (ITTOIA 2005 s 782A). No capital gains tax is payable on its disposal (TCGA 1992 s263AZA).

renewable source electricity Electricity produced from renewable sources such as waves, sunlight and wind. From 1 August 2015, such electricity is subject to climate change levy.

renewables obligation certificate Certificate issued under Electricity Act 1989 s32B or equivalent Northern Ireland law. No tax is payable on receipt of such a certificate under ITTOIA 2005s782A as inserted by FA 2007 s21. Nor is capital gains tax payable (TCGA1992 s263AZA).

renewable source electricity (RSE) Electricity that is produced from renewable sources such as wind, waves and sunlight. RSE is subject to climate change levy from 1 August 2015, with a transitional period to 31 March 2018, under Finance (No 2) Act 2015.

renewable source heating system The grant-funded installation of such a system may qualify for reduced rate of VAT under Value Added Tax 1994 Group 3. A definition is given in para 4B.

renewable sources Sources of energy which are not finite. A list of such sources is given in Climate Change and Sustainable Energy Act 2006 s26(2) as follows:

(a) biomass;
(b) biofuels;
(c) fuel cells;
(d) photovoltaics;
(e) water (including waves and tides);
(f) wind;
(g) solar power;
(h) geothermal sources;
(i) combined heat and power systems.

renewal Replacement of a fixed asset. Generally, this is treated as capital expenditure and not as the revenue cost of repair and maintenance.

As most repairs involve some new material, the difference is one of degree. In the case *Brown v Burnley Football Athletic Co Ltd [1980] 53 TC 357*, the judge said "renewal, as distinguished from repair, is reconstruction of the entirety, meaning by the entirety not the whole but substantially the whole subject-matter under discussion".

renewals accounting Where the estimated level of expenditure required to maintain the operating capacity of an asset (or group of assets treated as one asset) involves continual replacement of parts according to an asset management plan, and those costs are shown as depreciation in the accounts. Renewals accounting was permitted by old accounting standard FRS 15, but is not now permitted under FRS 102 and other current standards. Consequently, it is not allowed for tax purposes. The matter is discussed in HMRC Manual at BIM31065.

renewals allowance Allowance that could be claimed before April 2016. This allowance had been in existence for decades, predating capital allowances. It allowed for the cost of replacing implements, utensils and other articles used in a business. From April 2016, relief for such expenditure is given by capital allowance or landlord relief for replacing furnishings and appliances.

renouncing probate When a person appointed executor in a will refuses to accept the office.

rent Arrangement whereby one person pays money to another to use that person's property. In relation to a lease, the word is defined by reference to the definition of lease in ITA 2007 s614DG.

rent-a-room Tax relief for letting a room in one's house. The scheme was introduced in 1992. The annual limit is (from 2016) £7,500 a year. From April 2019, it is a condition that the property owners shares occupancy for at least some of the time. The amounts are given in section 3 of this dictionary.

rent repayment order Order that a tribunal may make against a landlord or property agent under Housing and Planning Act 2016 s40.

rent tribunal Body that settles disputes between landlords and tenants on the amount of rent payable.

renvoi Rules governing arrangements when the courts of one country seek to impose the laws of another. Renvoi allows the court to send back such a case.

reorganisation Restructuring of a company or other organisation for administrative convenience. This is not treated as a disposal for capital gains tax (TCGA 1992 s127).

repair (1) A repair of a business asset is generally a tax-deductible expenses, but its replacement is not (see "renewal").

(2) When HMRC amends an obvious error in a tax return within 9 months from its receipt. HMRC notifies the taxpayer of its correction which the taxpayer may accept or reject.

repatriation Returning a person, money or assets to the original country.

repayment interest Interest that is added to an amount of tax refunded to a taxpayer. The main legal provision is FA 2009 s102. The rate of interest has been 0.5% since 29 September 2009.

Repayment of Teachers' Loan Scheme Scheme run from 1 July 2002 to 30 June 2005 to encourage teachers to take posts in subjects where there is a shortage. The teacher was provided with an income contingent loan. This is written off over ten years provided the teacher remains in eligible employment. The amount written off each year is a benefit in kind potentially subject to income tax and national insurance. The government pays this amount, so the teacher incurs no charge. Where it is not written off, the loan is collected under the student loan deduction scheme.

repayment interest Sum added to a repayment of tax by HMRC.

repayment return For VAT, a return that leads to a repayment of VAT. This often happens when the business makes zero-rated supplies. The return is checked by computer against credibility checks. Most pass. If they do not, they are checked manually, sometimes with further investigation. Details are given in VAT Notice 700/58.

repayment supplement Interest paid by HMRC on a tax refund. This term is now confined to VAT, with the term repayment interest used for other taxes. A return supplement is paid if a VAT refund is not made within 30 days of the repayment return. These 30 days exclude days when reasonable enquiries are being made. The matter is explained in VAT Notice 700/58.

repeal Revocation of a law, rule, regulation or similar. A repeal of a repeal does not revive the original law (Interpretation Act 1978 s15).

repeated benefit fraud Criminal offence when a person is found to have committed an offence (known as a disqualifying event) within five years of a similar offence (Social Security Fraud Act 2001 s7 as amended by WRA 2012 s119).

repeated prosecution Offence under Article 6 of the European Convention on Human Rights, which requires a fair trial. In 2006, the European Court of Human Rights found that Ukraine had breached this right when it prosecuted a Customs official for smuggling and tax evasion solely because the court president did not agree with the first two decisions.

replacement Person, business, asset or funds which are used in place of such item which is no longer available. In relation to capital allowances on feature integral to a building, the term is defined in CAA 2001 s33B.

replacement car In relation to employment, a car that replaces a company car that is unavailable for up to 30 days (ITEPA 2003 s145(1)(b). Provided the car is not materially better than the one it replaces, there is no additional tax charge. HMRC Manual at EIM25135 makes clear that the provision of a better car does not trigger a benefit in kind tax charge unless that was one of the main purposes of the replacement. An example is given at EIM25180.

replacement expenditure Expenditure to replace a fixed asset. In bookkeeping, this is regarded as an expense and so is charged to the profit and loss account and not capitalised. In tax, replacement expenditure on an integral feature may attract a capital allowance, provided the expenditure meets the more than 50% test.

replacement instrument Document that replaces a stamped document that has become damaged or destroyed. The stamp duty implications are set out in Stamp Duties Management Act 1891 s12A.

replacement loan The general rule is that the tax deductibility of a replacement loan follows that of the original loan. This is explicitly stated for a business loan in ITA 2007 s408, and for an employment-related loan in ITEPA 2003 s186.

repo Sale of securities with the right to buy them back later, almost always for a higher price. Details are given in CTA 2009 s547 and FA 2007 Sch 13 para 15(9). Income tax provisions are given in ITA 2007 s 569. Capital gains tax provisions are given in TCGA 1992 from s261F and from s542.

reportable account Account whose information may be shared by tax jurisdictions under international agreements. This is given statutory effect in the UK under SI 2015 No 878 para 2.

reporting date The end of the last period covered by financial statements (FRS 102 glossary).

reporting entity Person, business, organisation or other entity to which a set of accounts relates. Defining exactly what the entity comprises can be unclear for bodies such as churches and schools. The question to ask is who owns the funds. So a church flowers fund is probably part of the entity whereas a Friends of the Church fund probably is not.

reporting period The period to which a set of accounts relates (FRS 102 section 3.10). Before FRS 102, the term was sometimes used to mean the period after the end of the accounting period in which all transactions for the accounting period must be finalised.

representative member Company that is nominated to submit VAT returns and payments when there is a group registration.

representative partner Member of a partnership who is responsible for declaring the income and gains of the partnership. Each partner is ordinarily expected to use this figure in his or her own tax return. A partner is usually expected to accept the figure and to resolve any disagreement within the partnership. If this proves impossible, the partner may report a different figure and should specifically disclose this fact to HMRC.

Republic of Ireland Independent state comprising the island of Ireland minus Northern Ireland. It started as Irish Free State in 1922 and became a republic completely free of UK in 1949. There remain special provisions between UK and the Republic. It has its own tax system, some of which is modelled on the British system. The Irish income tax system uses Schedules similar to those once used in the UK. The PAYE system is similar, with P45 certificates (for example) performing the same purpose. An Irish P45 may not be accepted in the UK. The Republic joined the EU in 1973 at the same time as the UK. It has no plans to leave the EU. The Republic adopted the euro as its currency in 2002. Since 2002, the tax year is the calendar year and no longer starts on 6 April.

- Income is subject to income tax and an income levy from 2009

- Corporation tax is charged at lower rates of 10% and 12.5%
- Capital gains tax is charged at 22% or 25%
- VAT is charged at rates between 0% and 21%.

There is a capital acquisitions tax at 25% above a threshold which corresponds to inheritance tax.

The Republic also charges withholding taxes, relevant contracts tax, dividend withholding tax, excise duties, plastic bag levy, vehicle registration tax, non-principal private residence levy, motor tax and local taxes.

repurchase agreement Agreement between a company and its shareholder whereby arrangements are made to buy back the shares. The tax implications are given in ICTA 1988 s231AB.

repurchase price Amount payable under a repo contract. The capital gains tax implications are given in TCGA 1992 from s261F.

reputation The extent to which tax relief may be claimed for protecting one's reputation is discussed in HMRC Manual at BIM37965. A leading case is *McKnight v Sheppard [1999] 71TC419.*

required information Information that HMRC may require from a third party, particularly under TMA 1970 s20(7AC).

requirement to correct Legal obligation for those with undeclared tax obligations from overseas to declare them to HMRC by 30 September 2018.

research and development Research is acquiring new knowledge while development is the commercial application of research. The tax treatment is generous, and closely follows the accounting treatment. In accounting, research is always treated as an expense, and is not capitalised (FRS 102 section 18.8E). Research is defined as one of:

- activities aimed at obtaining new knowledge
- search for, evaluation, and final selection of, applications of research findings
- and other knowledge
- search for alternatives for materials, devices, products, processes, systems or services
- formulation, design, evaluation and final selection of possible alternatives for new or improved materials, devices, products, processes, systems or services (FRS 102 section 18.8G).

Development may be capitalised as an intangible fixed asset if the business can demonstrate all of the following:

- technical feasibility to complete the development to a saleable product
- intention to complete the product
- ability to sell the product
- how the product will pay for itself, such as by demonstrating a market
- availability of resources to complete the development
- ability to measure the development expenditure (FRS 102 section 18.8H).

Note that there is no longer any distinction between pure development and applied development.

For capital allowances, the term is defined in CAA 2001 s437(2). The expense can be subject to an enhanced capital allowance of up to 230% of expenditure (CTA 2009 from s1039). W here a small company has insufficient profits to utilise a capital allowance, it may instead receive a credit. Details and rates are given in section 3 of this dictionary.

Generally expenses are deductible from taxable income (ITTOIA 2005 s87; CTA 2009 s87).

There is also a special capital allowance for patents.

Income from exploiting a patent can be subject to corporation tax at an effective rate of 10% under the patent box.

research and development expenditure credit An alternative to research and development tax relief, that is of value to companies that do not yet pay corporation tax. Such a company may claim a payment equal to a sum up to (from 1 April 2020) 13%. See section 3 of this dictionary for more details.

research institution An educational or non-profit-making body engaged in research. Payments by a company to such a body are tax-deductible (CTA 2009 s88). A university, institution or similar body may form a spin-out company to exploit such research. Where someone who had been engaged in that research is given shares in such a company, the benefit in kind tax charge that would otherwise apply may be excluded by provisions in ITEPA 2003 from s451. The capital gains tax implications are given in TCGA 1992 s149AB.

reservation of title Condition of sale in which ownership of the goods remains with the seller until the bill has been paid. This means that the seller can take back the goods if the buyer becomes insolvent, rather than ranking as an unsecured creditor. This is also known as a Romalpa clause.

reserve Allocation of retained profit held by a business for a particular purpose. For tax purposes, reserves are simply treated as part of the taxable profit.

reserved Schedule D status Special tax provision introduced by HMRC in 1990. It broadly held that actors, musicians and other performers who had already established self-employed status could keep it. Following legal actions in 1993, HMRC now accepts that whether performers are employed or self-employed is a matter of law. The position is discussed in the HMRC Tax Manual at ESM4122.

reservist Person in civilian occupation who can be called up for military duty. They are protected from detriments in their civilian employment by Reserve Forces (Safeguard of Employment) Act 1985 and Reserve Forces Act 1996. It is a criminal offence to terminate an employment because the employee is a reservist.

Their training allowance is not a taxable benefit (ITEPA 2003 s298).

Their earnings from the Ministry of Defence are subject to PAYE and class 1 national insurance (PAYE Regulations 2003 reg 122(2)).

reset bond Bond issued to reset an interest rate (CTA 2009 s454).

residence Country in which a person lives or from which a company operates. The tax position for individuals is given in ITTOIA 2005 from s17.

It is possible to have two or more residences. From 2013, residence is determined by the statutory residence test, summarised in section 3 of this dictionary.

Broadly, a UK resident is subject to tax on earnings from anywhere in the world. There are other tax implications.

Residence is a status exclusive to tax. It may not be the same as domicile, nationality or citizenship.

For companies, details of residence are given in CTA 2009 from s13 and in statement of practice SP 1/90. A company is UK resident if either it was incorporated in the UK or its main place of business is in the UK.

residence nil rate band (RNRB) An addition to the nil rate band for inheritance tax that may be claimable when a family home passes to the children or other descendants of the deceased. This provision is enacted in Inheritance Tax Act 1984 ss8D-8M by Finance (No 2) Act 2015 s9. It applies for deaths from 6 April 2017. The main provisions are:

- the property must have been used as a residence and not, for example, as a buy-to-let property
- the deceased must have owned the property or had another "qualifying residential interest"
- where the property has previously passed to a surviving spouse, it may be added to the amount of transferable nil rate band on the second death
- the property must pass to a child or remoter descendant of the deceased. This includes a stepchild, adopted child, foster child and grandchild
- RNRB may be claimable when the property has been held in a trust.

The rates are given under Inheritance Tax in section 3 of this dictionary.

residence status Whether someone is regarded as resident in a country. This can determine their liability to tax and entitlement to benefits. In the UK, from 2013 this is determined by the statutory residence test, as detailed in section 3 of this dictionary.

residential address Where a person lives. A company director once had to disclose his home address in the register of directors. It is now permissible for the director to give a service address which may be the company's registered office (CA 2006 s163(5)).

residential care home This is taxed as a business, but is specifically excluded from some tax-advantaged investment schemes, such as venture capital trust (ITA 2007 s309).

residual amount In relation to a lease, means so much of the fair value of the plant and machinery that the lessor cannot reasonably be expected to recover from the lease payments (CAA 2001 s70YE(3)).

residual input tax In a business that is partially exempt for VAT, input tax that cannot be wholly allocated to taxed or to exempt supplies. The business may claim a proportion of residual input tax (VAT Regulations SI 1995 No 2518 reg 101).

residual or scrap value In relation to wasting assets, means "the predictable value, if any, which the wasting asset will have at the end of its predictable life" (TCGA1992 s44). Other parts of this section indicate how this is to be calculated.

residual profit For patent box, additional income generated by a patent as determined by the calculation method specified by HMRC.

residual subsidy A subsidy that could be paid by central government to a housing authority under Housing FA 1972 s1.

residual value Expected value of a fixed asset at the end of its useful life, minus any costs of disposal. It can be relevant in determining the tax liability of a long-funded lease, For lessees of long-funded leases, the term is defined in ITTOIA 2015 s148J(2).

residuary devisee Person entitled to what remains of the land and buildings owned by someone who died and left a will (Wills Act 1837 s25).

residuary estate Part of the estate of a deceased person that has not been specifically bequeathed or devised (Administration of Estates Act 1925 s33(4)).

residuary legacy Legacy of whatever is left over from an estate after other legacies have been paid.

residue of the suggestion maximum Amount that may be paid tax-free to an employee as a suggestion award when a previous payment has been made.

res ipsa loquitur Latin: the thing speaks for itself. This term is particularly used in cases of negligence, as in *Byrne v Boodle [1863].*

res judicata Latin for "a thing adjudicated". It is the legal principle that a decision of the court or tribunal stands unless overturned by a higher court. It also means the matter cannot be litigated again.

resolution Motion to be debated by a board, committee or similar body.

A company may pass an ordinary resolution (CA 2006 s282) or a special resolution (CA 2006 s83). The former requires more than 50% of vote by value of shareholding, whereas the latter requires 75%. The following sections give details on how the resolutions are to be passed.

A resolution by members to wind up a company is governed by Insolvency Act 1986 s84(1).

resources Those things which are necessary for an entity to function. It always includes money. It may also include one or more of premises, labour, material and infrastructure.

When one resource is restricted, that is a constraint. This becomes the determining factor in quantifying an opportunity cost.

respite care Care for a person provided by someone other than the usual carer, so that the carer may have a break.

respondent Person in a hearing against whom proceedings are brought by the appellant. In most tax cases, the respondent is HMRC (SI 2009 No 273 rule 1(3)).

responsibility for children and young persons One of the additions that may be made to the standard allowance for universal credit (WRA 2012 s10).

rest break Break from work, usually when an employee may eat and drink. Minimum rest breaks are specified in the Working Time Directive. This Directive, effective from 1 October 1998 under SI 1998 No 1833, specify these rest breaks:

- 11 consecutive hours in every 24 hours
- short break every 6 consecutive hours
- one rest day each week
- four weeks paid holiday per year (increased to 5.6 weeks under UK law).

For the national minimum wage, rest breaks do not count as working hours.

restitutionary claim Right of someone to reclaim money such as when an overpayment has been made. The fact that such a right exists does not stop the overpayment being taxable income (*Pertemps Recruitment Partnership Ltd v HMRC [2011] UKUT B8).*

restitution interest Interest paid by HMRC in respect of overpaid corporation tax. From 21 October 2015, this is subject to a special 45% rate of corporation tax (CTA 2010 s357YA).

restoration fee Amount payable to Customs to have seized goods returned. The matter is explained in Customs leaflet 12A.

restraint order Order by a court that prevents a person from doing something. In particular, it refers to an order restricting a person from dealing with any realisable property under Proceeds of Crime Act 2002 s41.

restricted funds Funds held by a church or charity which may only be used for a specific purpose, usually because that was a condition imposed by the donor or by the church or charity when the funds were raised. Such funds must be shown separately in the accounts.

restricted goods Goods for which a licence or certificate is required as a condition of importation (CEMA 1979 s1(1)). Such goods include explosives, firearms, live animals, products from endangered species, and radio transmitters. More information is given in Customs notice 3.

restricted occupancy When the right to live somewhere is limited to certain times of the year. Such occupancy can affect the VAT treatment of caravan sites, as explained in VAT leaflet 701/20.

restricted shares In relation to certain schemes for employees, these are shares that can be forfeited if a performance condition is not met (CTA 2009 s1005). The matter is discussed in HMRC Manual at BIM44010.

restricted stock units Deferred share awards made overseas, as defined in HMRC Manual at EIM70450. These units are usually structured to give an employee shares in a business if certain conditions are met. They are taxed as earnings under ITEPA 2003 Chapter 5 Part 2.

restrictive covenant Clause in a contract which prevents someone from doing something. Common examples are covenants restricting a seller of a business from starting a new competitive business or restricting an employee from working for a competitor. Most covenants have a time limit. Not all such covenants are legally enforceable.

Where a payment has been made for such a covenant, the issue arises as to whether that is capital or revenue. The matter is discussed in HMRC Manual at BIM35595.

In terms of payments to former directors or employees, the tax liability is unaffected by whether the covenant is enforceable (ITEPA 2003 s225(8); CTA 2009 s69).

restructuring Programme that changes the scope of business undertaken by an entity or the manner in which that business is conducted (FRS 102 glossary).

resulting trust Trust which arises from the conduct of the parties.

retail price maintenance When a manufacturer determined the selling price of retail goods. Shops were not allowed to sell the goods for less than that price. This has generally been illegal since 1964, though exceptions for books and medicines continued for longer.

Retail Prices Index (RPI) Measure of inflation using figures produced by Office of National Statistics. The index was fixed at 100 in January 1987. Indices are produced for months before and after this date. In January 2020, the index was 290.6. This means that consumer goods that cost £100 in January 1987 will, on average, cost £290.60 in January 2020.

Consumer goods do not increase in price uniformly so there are many indices for individual products and groups of products. For example. the index for broccoli was 173 in January 2020.

The index started in 1947 when it replaced the cost of living index introduced in 1914. The index and inflation rates are given in section 3 of this dictionary.

For economics, from 2013 it has now generally been replaced by the consumer price index (CPI), which is considered to be more accurate and tends to produce lower figures (for reasons explained under Mean). It is also used by other countries, making inflation rates more comparable. RPI is still used to index tax allowances, for corporation tax chargeable gains indexation, social security payments, rail fares and National Savings products.

The government has announced plans to phase out retail prices index from 2030.

retailer vouchers Document, card, token or similar issued by a trader who will either redeem it for goods or services or who will reimburse another trader who does so. The form of the voucher is irrelevant, so it includes both paper tokens and electronic cards.

For VAT, the question is when the supply has occurred: whether it is when the voucher is issued (whether or not it was sold) or when the voucher is redeemed. The law has changed several times. There is also a complication if the voucher can be exchanged for either standard-rated or zero-rated goods or services. The current position applies to vouchers issued from 1 January 2019. VAT is generally charged on the supply of the voucher if all the goods or services for which it can be used are subject to the same rate of VAT. If the voucher can be used for both standard-rated and zero-rated goods and services, VAT is charged when the voucher is redeemed.

Before 1 January 2019, the distinction was whether the voucher could be used for only one purpose, such as a telephone card, or could be used for more than one, such as a store voucher.

This is a complex area, particularly when more than two parties are involved.

The law is VATA 1994 s51B-51D and Sch 10A-10B. Guidance is given by HMRC information sheet 09/18 and in VAT Notice 700/7.

Retail Scheme A method of arriving at the value of VAT due on retail sales where this is not separately identified at the point of sale.

Historically there have been many such schemes. Modern developments such as bar codes and scanners on tills have made many of these otiose. There are now three standard VAT retail schemes:

- point of sale scheme
- apportionment scheme
- direct calculation scheme.

If turnover is more than £130 million a year, the retailer must agree a bespoke scheme with HMRC.

A retail scheme may be used with cash accounting or annual accounting. It may not be used with the flat rate scheme.

retained case law UK case law and EU case law (European Union (Withdrawal) Act 2018 s6(7)). EU case law remains as a precedent after Brexit but may be overturned by a UK court.

retained direct principal legislation EU law that is regarded as UK law after Brexit. This includes many provisions relating to VAT and Customs duties.

retained profit That element of profit that a company keeps for its future use and does not distribute as dividends.

retainer Fee paid to someone for being available to work rather than for the work itself. A retainer is taxed as income.

retention payment Portion of a contract price that is withheld from payment pending confirmation that the work has been properly carried out and any faults rectified.

retirement annuity Financial arrangement similar to a personal pension. No new retirement annuities may be written from 1 July 1988, but existing ones may continue.

retiring partner Partner who leaves a partnership. Such a partner remains liable for debts and other obligations incurred before retirement (Partnership Act 1890 s17(2)) unless an agreement has been reached with the new partnership under ibid s17(3).

For tax, a retirement ends a partnership and creates a new one unless the old and new partners sign an election to treat them as one continuing partnership.

retraining course Course funded by the taxpayer's employer. Provided the course is relevant to the employee's work and other conditions are met, the course is not a taxable benefit in kind.

The expense is tax-deductible by the employer (ITTOIA 2005 s74; CTA 2009 s74). Provided conditions are met, it is not a taxable benefit in kind to the employee (ITEPA 2003 s311).

retrospection Applying law to things that have already happened. Generally tax law seeks to avoid this on the principle that a taxpayer is entitled to know his or her tax liabilities at the time of a particular action and not have that subsequently changed. Tax law generally does not introduce provisions that apply retrospectively unless:

- it is to the taxpayer's advantage
- the Chancellor of the Exchequer has announced the change and the retrospection applies from that date
- it corrects an error or unintended consequence of a previous enactment, or
- it is to counter blatant tax avoidance.

It is arguable that tax law on accelerated payment notices, pre-owned assets and loan charge each represent retrospective taxation.

retrospective earnings Earnings that apply to work previously done, such as a backdated pay rise. These are treated as income when paid, not when earned, under the PAYE system (PAYE Regulations 2003 reg 50A).

return (1) Total amount received from an investment. This usually comprises capital growth plus dividends.

(2) Form that must be submitted, such as a tax return (TMA 1970 s118(1)).

return amendment Change to a tax return that has already been submitted to HMRC. A taxpayer may amend a return within 12 months of the due date. HMRC may amend a return within 9 months with the taxpayer's agreement.

return on capital employed Financial measure of how far the profits of a business represent value for investors. It takes the operating profit before interest deductions and taxation, and divides it by share capital plus long-term loans.

return to work credit Social security payment paid for a year before 1 October 2013 when someone came off benefits to start work. It is now replaced by allowing universal credit or other benefit to continue for a short period.

revaluation Attributing a different value to an asset. Depreciation is a form of revaluation, though the term is more usually restricted to a non-gradual change. There are special tax provisions for revaluing an intangible asset in CTA 2009 s723.

Revenue, The Term sometimes used to mean Inland Revenue or (from 2005) the departments of HMRC that deal with direct taxes.

revenue Income, as distinguished from a capital gain. Similarly revenue expenditure is distinguished from capital expenditure where the whole amount of the former may be deductible from taxable profits.

FRS 102 glossary defines revenue as "the gross inflow of economic benefits during the period arising in the course of the ordinary activities of an entity when those inflows result in an increase in equity, other than increases relating to contributions from equity participants"

Revenue and Customs Prosecutions Office Body formed in 2005 to deal with tax prosecutions. It was independent of HMRC. In 2010, it was merged with the Crown Prosecution Service.

Revenue Decision Statement from HMRC seeking to clarify a point of law. Some were issued in 1983, since when no more have been issued.

Revenue Interpretation Statement from HMRC setting out its view on a particular topic. The first of 268 such Interpretations was issued in 1983. The last was issued in 2006.

revenue-neutral Description of a change in taxation policy that seeks not to change the amount of tax revenue raised.

revenue recognition Point at which income and expenditure is included in the accounts. Recognition is usually when an invoice is issued or received, unless a business has opted for cash accounting.
The UK accounting standard is FRS 102 section 23. The international accounting standard is IFRS 15 which is more detailed and will be reflected in a revision to FRS 102.
Tax practice follows the accounting standard.
Revenue recognition is discussed in HMRC Manual at BIM40075.

Revenue Scotland Body formed in 2015 to collect devolved taxes in Scotland (Revenue Scotland and Tax Powers Act 2014 s2(1)).

revenue trader Person who deals with goods subject to excise duty (CEMA 1979 s1(1)).

revenue vessel Ship, boat or similar used by Customs to detect and prevent smuggling (CEMA 1979 from s82).

reverse burden of proof Situations in law where the burden of proving something falls on the party opposite to the one who would otherwise have the burden. Generally the law places the onus of proof on the prosecutor or the applicant in a civil action.

reverse charge For VAT, when the customer accounts for the tax. Such provisions have been introduced from 2007 to help counter tax fraud on some supplies, such as mobile phones and computer chips. It can apply to some intra-EU supplies. The reverse charge for wholesale gas and electricity is set out in VATA 1994 s9A.
From 1 March 2021 (postponed from 1 October 2019), it applies to some construction work. It is also possible for a supplier and customer to agree a reverse charge for any supply.
It is also possible for a buyer and seller voluntarily to agree a reverse charge on any supply. This is sometimes used for author's royalties and sales of scrap materials where it is the buyer who determines the price.

reverse factoring Factoring of invoices but arranged by the customer rather than the supplier. There is no specific accounting standard on reverse factoring, where figures are often shown as trade payables or other creditors. The use of reverse factoring was considered a significant element in the collapse of Carillion in 2018.

reverse premium Payment by a landlord to a tenant to lease a property. From 1999, such premiums are taxed as revenue receipts of the tenant (ITTOIA 2005 s311; CTA 2009 from s250). The matter is discussed in HMRC Manual at BIM35610.

reverse takeover Arrangement when a company that is taken over becomes the owner of the acquiring company. This is usually achieved by the shareholders of the acquiring company exchanging those shares for ones in the acquired company.

The arrangement is used when the acquired company is considered as a more appropriate vehicle for the new group, such as when the acquired company already has a Stock Exchange listing.

reverse vending machine Machine that accepts empty plastic bottles, drink cans and similar used packaging, and exchanges it for cash or, more usually, a cash voucher. The first such machine in the UK was installed in 2018.

reversing entry Entry made in the financial records to correct a double entry originally entered the wrong way round. The reversing entry must be made twice: one to reverse the original entry, and again to make the correct entry.

reversion When property returns to a previous owner, such as when a leased asset returns to the lessor (ITTOIA 2005 s307(3)).

reversionary annuity An annuity paid to someone on the death of someone else, such as to the husband or wife of the annuity holder.

reversionary interest Future interest in property, usually from reversion or remainder. It may be contingent, such as when a property will pass to a person when someone else has died (IHTA 1984 s47).

review In relation to tax disputes, it means the process whereby a taxpayer may ask for a matter to be looked at by another tax officer who has not been involved the issue for an independent opinion. A request for such a review is at the discretion of the taxpayer, and does not compromise his right to proceed to start proceedings. The right for VAT is given in VATA 1994 from s83A.

revived will Will that has been revoked, and then made effective again by a codicil withdrawing the revocation.

revised accounts In company law, accounts which are issued after accounts for the same period have been published (CA 2006 s454).

revocation notice Document that revokes something, particularly from HMRC to an employer, revoking a provision that allows the employer to provide tax-free benefits to employees (ITEPA 2003 s289C(1)).

reward Term that means almost any kind of payment, particularly a payment for assistance given. HMRC may pay a reward for information given (Commissioners for Revenue and Customs Act 2005 s26).

reward for services Term used in cases concerning the tax liability of employment income. For example, in the case *Hochstrasser v Mayes [1960]*, Upjohn J said that a profit from employment "must be in the nature of a reward for services, past, present of future". HMRC Manual at EIM00610, however, states that "the words 'reward for services' should not be taken too literally".

Reynaud Leading case from 1999 on associated operations for discretionary trusts. The full citation is *Reynaud v CIR [1999] SpC 196.*

rhinoceros Endangered animal. The importation of the animal or its products is generally prohibited under CITES convention.

riba Islamic term for usury. In this context this means all charging of interest, which is forbidden under Sharia law. There are two types of riba:

- increase in capital without providing any services; and
- commodity exchanges of unequal amount.

rider An amendment to an insurance policy that modifies the policy by expanding or restricting its benefits or excluding certain conditions from coverage.

riding hat Up to size 6.5, this is zero-rated for VAT as children's clothing. This was unsuccessfully challenged in the case *Charles Owen & Co (Bow) Ltd [2003] VTD 11267.*

right holder "The holder of a trade mark, copyright, right in a performance, design right, patent, supplementary protection certificate, plant variety right, protected designation of origin, geographical designation, any person authorised to use those rights or an authorised representative" (Customs notice 34). Customs may seize goods where the rights of the right holder are infringed.

right of audience The right to be heard in court, other than as a witness. The right is given to:

- barristers
- solicitors who have been admitted or enrolled to conduct litigation
- anyone who is a party to the case
- (at tax tribunals) a qualified accountant.

right of way The right to pass over land. Profits from this are taxed as if it were a trade (ITTOIA 2005s12).

rights issue Issue of new shares in a company where the existing shareholders are offered shares in proportion to their existing holding. A rights issue usually offers the shares for less than their market value to encourage their purchase.

right to be heard Legal right of natural justice that a person accused of crime or other wrongdoing should have the opportunity to make representations before suffering any penalty or detriment. This is not a precisely defined right. The issue was discussed in *Ridge v Baldwin [1964] AC 40* and in *Russell v Duke of Norfolk [1949] 1 All ER 109.*

right to manage (RTM) Description of a company formed to manage property (Leasehold Reform Act 2002 s7). It gives leaseholders the statutory right to take over the management of their property from the landlord.

right to reside Right to live in the UK. This is a condition for claiming some social security benefits. The right is held by all UK nationals, and by nationals of other EU states who (from 1 January 2021) have established residence rights.

ring fence Process by which financial transactions in an area are considered separately from other areas. For corporation tax, banking and oil exploitation are ring-fenced, and merchant shipping may be if the company so chooses.

ring fence asset In relation to provisions of oil taxation "means a qualifying asset which is, or has been, used wholly or partly for the purposes of ring fence trade" (CTA 2009 s291A(2) as inserted by FA 2018 s22(3)).

ring fence amount Figure used to calculate corporation tax on ring fence profits, as explained in CTA 2010 s22.

ring fence trade Trade whose income is ring-fenced for tax purposes and not mixed with other income (ITA 2007 s87). The most common example is oil extraction. Provisions relating to capital allowances are given in CAA 2001 s45F. For corporation tax and the oil industry, the term "means activities which –

(a) are within the definition of oil-related activities in section 274, and

(b) constitute a separate trade (whether because of section 279 or otherwise)" (CTA 2010 s277 and ITTOIA 2005 s225D).

riot When 12 or more people engage in or threaten violence. The conduct must be such that a reasonable person fears for his or her safety. If property is damaged, destroyed or stolen in a riot, an uninsured person may claim from the police. For an insured person, the insurance company may claim from the police. The law is now Riot Compensation Act 2016, which replaces Riot (Damages) Act 1886. A riot is defined in Public Order Act 1986 s1, except that the 2016 Act s1(6) excludes the compensation provisions from an enclosed place, such as a prison, hospital, asylum centre or young offender institution.

riot claims bureau Body that may be established by the Secretary of State to deal with claims for riot compensation. (Riot Compensation Act 2016 s6(1)).

riparian Pertaining to a river or to land adjacent to a river.

risk Chance that an adverse event will happen. Businesses need to consider all risks in determining whether they are a going concern. Risk management is a business discipline in its own right.

risk-adjusted Description of a profit or return on capital which has been adjusted to reflect the risk of achieving the desired figure. This is typically achieved by multiplying the desired figure by a factor between 0 and 1.

risk finance investment In relation to enterprise investment scheme, this term is defined in ITA 2007 s164A(3) as inserted by Finance (No 2) Act 2015 Sch 5.

risk-reward ratio In investment, the requirement for a risky venture to offer a higher return than a safe investment.

risk-to-capital condition Requirement of tax-advantaged investment schemes that the investor must bear some risk. It applies to enterprise investment scheme (ITA 2007 s157A), seed enterprise investment scheme (ITA 2007 s257AA), and venture capital trusts (ITA 2007 s286ZA).

risk transfer Any arrangement by which a financial risk is transferred to another person. FA 2010 s46 and Sch 19 contain provisions to restrict tax relief to the underlying economic reality. Where the arrangement is designed to avoid tax, it may be caught by CTA 2009 from s937A.

ritual slaughter The ritual slaughter of animals according to Jewish law was held to be zero-rated as part of the process of providing zero-rated meat for human consumption. *The London Board for Shechita [1974] VATD 52.*

riyal Currency of Yemen.

road construction vehicle For oil duty, this was a category of except vehicle under HODA1979 Sch 1 para 12. From 1 April 2008, the exception comes within the scope of road surfacing vehicles under ibid para 12A as inserted by SI 2007 No 93.

road-friendly suspension Suspension system in a heavy goods vehicle where at least 75% of the spring effect is caused by an airspring (VERA 1994 Sch 1 para 11C). Under vehicle excise duty regulations, from 1 April 2011, such a vehicle may be licensed to carry a heavier load.

road fuel Petrol, diesel, liquid petroleum gas and similar used to drive a vehicle. Such fuel is subject to hydrocarbon oil duty and VAT. Electricity is not regarded as a road fuel.

road fuel gas "Means any substance which is gaseous at a temperature of 15ºC and under a pressure of 1013.25 millibars, and which is for use as fuel in road vehicle" (HODA1979 s5 and ITEPA 2003 s171(1)).
Excise duty is charged under HODA1979 s8.
In the UK there are two types of such gas in use: compressed natural gas (CNG) and liquid petroleum gas (LPG). Company cars which run on this fuel may attract a lower rate of tax for the employee.
For employment income, there is a special provision in ITEPA 2003 s146.

road haulage Free travel across the EU by member states is guaranteed by EU Regulation (EC) 1072/2009 of 21 October 2009.
From 1 January 2021, this is replaced for UK hauliers by the model licence in Appendix Road A.1.3 to Annex Road-1 in the EU/UK withdrawal agreement of 24 December 2020.. This is given effect in UK law by European Union (Future Relationship) Act 2020 s2s23-25.

road pricing Additional tax on motorists for each mile driven on certain roads at certain times. No such systems exist in UK at present.

road roller Road vehicle which is category G on a driving licence. For oil duty, "a road roller is an excepted vehicle" and may use rebated oil (HODA1979 Sch 1 para 13).

road surfacing vehicle Vehicle primarily designed to build or repair roads (HODA 1979 Sch 1 para 13A).

road tax Common name for vehicle excise duty.

road vehicle Any vehicle constructed or adapted for use on roads and which is not an excepted vehicle (HODA 1979 s27(1)).

robot For tax administration, software that checks data inputted by taxpayers. They were introduced in 2010 and check millions of data. The advantages are that they are much faster than humans, they are less prone to error, and they free HMRC staff from boring work.

rod (1) For length, an old unit of length equal to 5½ yards or 16½ feet.
(2) For brickwork, 272½ cubic feet.

rolled gold Metal coated with a very thin layer of gold.

rolled-up coupons Interest coupons on securities where no payment is made, but the value is added to the capital.

rolled-up holiday pay When payment for holiday is not made at the time of the holiday but as an addition to pay for all weeks that the employee is at work with no payment at all for the weeks on holiday.
The Working Time Directive specifies a minimum period of paid leave to which all workers are entitled. The European Court of Justice has made it clear that it would like to see rolled-up holiday pay outlawed, however it has also been held that it does not contravene the directive provided the rolled-up holiday pay is made "transparently and comprehensively". Useful guidance on this has been provided by the Employment Appeal Tribunal in *Lyddon v Englefield Brickworks. EAT [2007]*
A limited exception to the rules on holiday pay was made during the coronavirus outbreak.

rolled-up indexation For capital gains tax, indexation on a rolled-over disposal (TCGA1992 s55(9)).

rollover relief Relief from capital gains tax (or chargeable gains corporation tax) when the proceeds from disposal of a building or certain other assets are used to acquire another asset (TCGA 1992 s152). There is generally a four-year window of one year before disposal and three years after. The two periods are then treated as one for the tax. Mode details are given under Capital gains tax in section 3 of this dictionary.

Romalpa clause Reservation of title in a contract for sale of goods. The name comes the case *Aluminium Industrie Vasseen BV v Romalpa Aluminium Ltd [1976] 2 All ER 577. CA.*

Romania East European country that is a member of the European Union. Its currency is the new leu (plural lei). The UK has a double taxation convention of 1975.

roof For VAT purposes, a roof can be differently defined depending on context.
A roof as an integral part of a building follows the VAT rate for the building. In other contexts, guidance was given in the case *Pinevalue Ltd [2014].*
The case *Wetheralds Construction Ltd [2016] TC 5552* held that insulating materials added to a roof were reduced-rated insulation and not standard-rated building work.

Rooker-Wise amendment Requirement introduced in 1977 that the main tax allowances must increase each year in line with inflation. It is now ITA 2007 s21. It is named after Labour MPs Geoff Rooker and Audrey Wise. Although it is still law, it has been widely ignored.

rotational land Land that is used for different crops each year and is allowed to lie fallow for some years, as a means of maximising overall crop yields. Such land will usually qualify for agricultural property relief from inheritance tax under Inheritance Tax Act 1984 s117.

rouble (1) Currency of Russia.
(2) Currency in Belarus.

roulette Gambling game of chance where punters bet on a number selected by spinning a wheel with a ball on it. It is listed in Betting and Gaming Duties Act 1981 s13(3) as subject to gaming duty.

rounding Mathematical process of adjusting a figure to express it with sufficient accuracy. The general rule for rounding is that decimals of .5 or above are rounded up, and decimals of below .5 are rounded down. So 134.5 and 134.7 would be rounded to 135, but 134.2 and 134.4 would be rounded down to 134. For tax, the general rule is that amounts of income are rounded to the nearest pound, and tax to the nearest penny. The rounding is always in the taxpayer's favour, so a taxable income of £24,269.98 is regarded as £24,269.

In a parliamentary statement of 18 May 1993, it was stated that Inland Revenue (now HMRC) would accept computations for corporation tax rounded to the nearest £1,000 provided:

(a) the turnover of the business is at least £5 million in the current year or previous year;

(b) the company accounts are prepared to the nearest £1,000;

(c) the rounding is fair, unbiased, defined in the accounts and consistently used; and

(d) any program or software used in the rounding is identified.

The limit of £5 million in (a) relates to the company and not to a group of companies.

For VAT, the European Court of Justice has ruled that the UK is free to make its own rules on rounding: *re Wetherspoon [2009] Case C-302/07.*

round sum allowance Fixed amount added to an employee's pay. Unless this is covered by a dispensation or exemption, the allowance is added to gross pay for the purposes of tax and class 1 national insurance.

round-the-world scheme Tax avoidance scheme. It involved holding shares in an offshore trust that accrued gains and were migrated to a low-rate or no-rate tax jurisdiction where the UK has a tax treaty, where the gain was crystallised with little or no tax paid. The trust is then repatriated to the UK where the funds may be used free of tax. The scheme was held not to work by the first-tier tribunal in the cases *R Lee; N Bunter [2017] TC5757* as the trust's place of management was held to be UK, so the trust had never migrated.

roup Scottish term for an auction.

routine deduction Term used in relation to taxation of intellectual property, used in Corporation Tax 2010 s357BJA as inserted by FA 2016 s64(3).

routine domestic tasks Term used in VAT Notice 701/2. It includes housework, simple odd jobs, shopping and collecting prescriptions. An organisation that provides such services for someone who cannot perform them himself or herself may exempt them as a welfare service under VATA 1984 Sch 7 Group 9.

Royal Assent When the monarch signs an Act of Parliament, or another procedure is followed under Royal Assent Act 1967. The monarch signifies Assent by letters patent under the Great Seal and signed in her own hand. An Act becomes law when it is either so declared in the House of Lords or is notified to each House of Parliament. It is not known what would happen if the monarch refused assent as this has not happened since 1707.

Royal Bank of Scotland Bank formed in Scotland by royal charter in 1728 as a rival to the Bank of Scotland which was suspected of having Jacobite sympathies. It took over NatWest Bank in 2000. It is one of three Scottish banks allowed to issue banknotes. It changed its name to NatWest Group in 2020.

royal charter Decree by the monarch which remains one of the ways in which a company comes into existence. Today, the procedure is generally reserved for non-commercial entities such as professional bodies.

royal jelly Secretion from bees that feeds the larvae and queen bee. It is edible by humans. For VAT, this was held to be standard-rated and not zero-rated as food. *Grosvenor Commodities Ltd [1990] VTD 7221.*

Royal Mail Company that oversees the national postal service (Postal Services Act 2011 s4). Its regulated services are exempt from VAT. Services where it competes with other couriers are standard-rated.

Royal Mail Steam Packet case The name often given to the landmark auditing case of *R v Kylsant [1931]*. The company reported trading losses by transferring from reserves accumulated during the first world war. This was not explained in the accounts. Chairman Lord Kylsant was arrested and imprisoned for issuing a company prospectus that was "false in a material particular" even though every word of it was true.

Royal Mint Body responsible for producing Britain's coins, founded in 866 AD. It also produces medals and coins for more than 100 other countries. From 1 March 1966, it is based in Llantrisant in Wales. The Mint is under the control of the Master of the Mint who is Chancellor of the Exchequer (Coinage Act 1971 s4(1)). In practice, the Mint's daily operations are managed by the deputy master (Coinage Act 1971 s4(2)). Each issue of coins is authorised by a royal proclamation under Coinage Act 1971.

Royal Naval Reserve One of the classes of reservists (PAYE regulations SI 2003 No 2682 reg 122(2)).

royalties Sums paid for use of intellectual property, such as a copyright or patent. Royalties are taxed as income. The term is defined in CTA 2009 s714). A business established to receive royalties is excluded from the scope of a venture capital trust (ITA 2007 s306).

RTM company "A company is a RTM [right to manage] company in relation to premises if –

(a) it is a private company limited by guarantee, and
(b) its memorandum of association states that its object, or one of its objects, is the acquisition and exercise of the right to manage the premises"

(Commonhold and Leasehold Reform Act 2002 s73(2)).

This definition is extended to company law by CA 2006 s1181(4).

rub-down search Search which is neither an intimate search nor a strip search (CEMA 1979 s164(5)). It may be made a Customs officer, for good reason, who is of the same sex as the person being searched. The person to be searched may require the officer to refer the matter to his or her superior officer (CEMA 1979 s164(3)).

rufiyaa Currency of Maldives.

rugby Sport played in two forms: Rugby Union and Rugby League.
It was originally an amateur game with 15 players a side; the latter is the main professional game with 13 players a side.
The tax case *Jarrold v Boustead [1964]* held that a player was not liable to pay employment tax on a signing-on fee when joining a Rugby League side from Rugby Union. The payment was compensation for giving up his amateur Rugby Union status which then barred him for life from Union. HMRC Manual at EIM00710 states that this precedent is unlikely to be followed now as a result of changes in the status of Rugby Union players.
The extent to which a rugby club is a mutual trade is discussed in HMRC Manual at BIM24365.

rule 18 Rule that allows a tax tribunal to hear separate cases together when they relate to the same issue (The Tribunal (First-Tier Tribunal) (Tax Chamber) Rules Si 2009 No 273 rule 18). One of the cases is selected as the lead cases. Any other case relating to the same issue is stayed until the lead case has been determined.

rule of 72 Rule of thumb that 72 divided by an interest rate will tell you approximately how many years it takes for money to double. So 6% compound interest doubles the money in 12 years. More details are given in section 3 of this dictionary under Compound Interest.

rule of 78 Method of depreciation, also known as sum of the digits. If an asset has an estimated useful life of four years, the numbers 1 to 4 are added to give 10. Four tenths of the asset is depreciated in year 1, three tenths in year 2 and so on. The method was considered appropriate for assets where the value is lost most heavily in early years. It was allowed under old accounting standard SSAP 21 but is not listed as an acceptable method in FRS 102 section 17.22. The "78" is the sum of the digits 1 to 12.

rule of 85 Generous pension provision that applied to local government schemes. A person could take a full pension if their age plus years of service were 85 or more. Someone starting work at 16 could thus retire at 51. The provision was scrapped for new starters from 1 October 2006 and for existing members from 1 April 2008, subject to some transitional provisions.

rule of 97 Algorithm used in allocating VAT numbers. A VAT number has nine digits of which the last two are check digits. The first seven digits are each multiplied by 8, 7, 6, 5, 4, 3 and 2 respectively. These products are totalled. The two check digits are the number that must be added to the total to make it divisible by 97.

rules of court Rules made by Act of Parliament, statutory instrument, by a higher court or otherwise binding on courts (Interpretation Act 1978 Sch 1).

running costs Costs of using an asset rather than of owning it. The term is particularly used for cars.

running tank Auxiliary fuel tank on a vehicle. Fuel in such a tank must be duty-paid, as explained in Customs notice 75.

running total Total to which further figures will be added later.

running yield Estimate of the annual rate of interest paid by fixed income investments. It does not take into account any increases or decreases in the capital value of the investment.

run-off period In relation to the payment of pension benefits as part of a termination settlement, this is the period from the end of the employment to the last day of the sixth tax year following the tax year in which the tax year started (ITEPA 2003 s409(6)).

rupee Currency of India.

rupiah Currency of Indonesia.

rural fuel duty Reduced rate of road fuel duty for rural areas. It reduces the duty on road fuel by 5p a litre. The reduction is designed to eliminate the additional cost of road fuel for those areas. Retailers are required to reduce their prices to customers by 5p a litre.

The provision was introduced in March 2012 for fuel purchased from 1 January 2012. It was extended by area from 1 April 2015. It was introduced by regulation under HODA 1979 s20AA.

The reduction applies to the Inner and Outer Hebrides, islands in the Clyde, the Isles of Scilly and the post town of Hawes in North Yorkshire. It also applies to postcodes EX35, LA17, IV14, IV21, IV22, IV26, IV27. IV54, KW12, PA80, PH19, PH23, PH36 and PH41.

Before 1 April 2015, the relief was only available for Inner and Outer Hebrides, Northern Isles, islands in the Clyde, and Isles of Scilly.

Retailers of road fuel in these areas must register with HMRC. This allows them to claim the relief on a monthly basis. The scheme is not available to businesses who buy road fuel in bulk for their own use.

The scheme required a derogation from the EU which was provided. The government confirms that the provisions will continue after Brexit.

Guidance is given in Revenue and Customs Brief 3 (2015)

rural rate relief Relief from business rates for the last village shop, post office, petrol station or pub in an area with a population below 3,000. The shop or post office must have a rateable value up to £8,500. and a pub or petrol station must have a rateable value up to £12,500. Relief is given by application to the local authority. Businesses may qualify for other forms of rate relief.

This relief is additional to other rates reliefs.

Rwanda African country. Its currency is the Rwanda franc of 100 centimes. The UK has no double taxation treaty.

Rwanda franc Currency of Rwanda.

Rysaffe Tax effective arrangement where several discretionary trusts are established on different days. The name comes from the case *Rysaffe Trustee Company (CI) Ltd v CIR [2003].*

Saba One of the islands of what was known as the Netherlands Antilles, a tax haven.

sabbatical Period of leave, usually paid and usually lasting for months, allowing a person to study or rest. This is common in the fields of education and the church. The income continues to be taxed in the normal way.

sabbatical officer Person engaged in running a body, usually on a voluntary basis, while on a sabbatical. This was an issue in the VAT case *Keele University Students Union [2009] TC 82*. They claimed VAT exemption for attending cultural events under VATA 1994 Sch 9 Group 13 Note 2(c). A condition is that the event must be run by unpaid volunteers. The sabbatical officers received a bursary which was below the market rate but was not nominal. That meant the union was not run on a voluntary basis and so could not claim VAT exemption.

sabotage Crime of deliberate damage to another person's property or activities. Payments to buy off a saboteur are disallowed by CTA 2009 s1304. The matter is discussed in HMRC Manual at BIM43180.

SA Donate Scheme that ran from 2005 to 2012 under which self-assessed taxpayers could nominate a charity to receive any tax refund. Very little use was made of it.

sack Dismissal from employment. The term comes from the old practice of giving the worker a sack in which to remove his belongings.

SAFE Strategic Accounting Framework, HMRC computer system.

safeguarded amount Amount of £5,000 that must be left in a bank account when HMRC has seized funds under the direct recovery rules of F2A 2015 Sch 8.

safeguarded rights For pensions, the rights as set out in Pension Schemes Act 1993 s68A.

safe harbour A provision that automatically provides protection. An example is activities from 2012 that protect controlled foreign companies from additional tax.

safety seat Car seat designed for a child under 14. It is reduced-rated for VAT under VATA 1994 Sch 7A Group 5 para 2. Further information is given in VAT Notice 701/23.

sailaway boat Vessel that is used to export itself. There is a special provision to zero-rate it for VAT if exporting outside the EU. Details are given in VAT Notices 703/2 and 703/3.

sailing The Customs implications of sailing to and from the UK are set out in Customs notice 8. The special VAT provisions for sailaway boats are given in VAT notices 703/3 (intra-EU) and 703/2 (outside EU).

Saint Helena UK Overseas Territory comprising a volcanic island in the South Atlantic Ocean. The currency is the St Helena pound.

Saint Helena pound Currency of St Helena.

Saint Kitts and Nevis Caribbean country. Its currency is the East Caribbean dollar of 100 cents. The UK has a double taxation arrangement of 1947.

Saint Lucia Caribbean country. Its currency is the East Caribbean dollar of 100 cents. The UK has no double taxation treaty.

Saint Matthew Disciple of Christ who wrote the first book of the New Testament. He is the patron saint of accountants and tax collectors.

Saint Vincent and the Grenadines Caribbean country. Its currency is the East Caribbean dollar of 100 cents. The UK has no double taxation treaty.

salami slicing Advocacy technique of reducing evidence or argument to a series of narrow propositions, each of which can be challenged.

salaried hours One of the bases for determining national minimum wage (SI 1999 No 584 para 4). The salary or wages must be paid at the hourly rate for all contracted hours.

salaried partner Partner who receives a salary rather than a share of the profits. Such a partner in a limited liability partnership may be taxed as an employee through the payroll and not be regarded as self-employed.

salary Payment to an employed worker, usually on an annual basis. It is subject to PAYE income tax and class 1 national insurance.

salary premium Additional sum paid to a salaried worker, such as for working during the night or on a bank holiday. Such premium is included in salary for the purposes of PAYE income tax and class 1 national insurance. It is not considered as part of the national minimum wage (SI 2020 No 339).

salary sacrifice Arrangement whereby an employee gives up part of his or her salary in lieu of a benefit, usually one which is either tax free or which is subject to a lesser amount of income tax or national insurance or both.

From 6 April 2017. the tax advantage is removed as the benefit is taxed on the amount of the income sacrificed.

For previous periods, a salary sacrifice scheme worked only if the contract of employment was changed and could not be further varied unilaterally by the employee.

The exemption for trivial benefits does not apply if the benefit is provided as part of a salary sacrifice scheme (ITEPA 2003 s323A(8) as inserted by FA 2016 s13).

sale and finance leaseback Arrangement whereby an entity sells an asset and then leases it back. The provisions for capital allowance are given in CAA 2001 from s221.

Income tax provisions are given in ITA 2007 from s681A and ITTOIA 2005 s285.

Corporation tax provisions are given in CTA 2009 s225 and from s834.

Before 2 July 1997, this was a tax avoidance scheme whereby a non-taxable body such as a local authority sold its assets to a commercial company which could claim capital allowances which was then reflected in lower lease premiums.

sale and repurchase Form of trading where the seller agrees to buy back the goods, such as when a book fails to sell in a shop.

The accounting treatment depends on whether the title to the goods has passed to the buyer under the terms of the contract. Current accounting standard FRS 102 at section 23.12 says that the sale should not be recognised by the seller if the sale is conditional on the buyer selling the goods or where the buyer may rescind the purchase for a specific reason or for any reason, and the seller is uncertain about the probability of the return.

The tax treatment follows the accounting standard.

There are separate provisions for the accrued income scheme in ITA 2007 s263A.

sale at undervalue A sale of an asset for less than the sum that would be expected.

Such sales commonly arises in domestic arrangements and in tax planning. There are usually tax provisions to substitute market value in such cases.

For the disposal of a short lease, there is a specific provision in CAA 2001 s88.

sale or return When goods are provided on the basis that the recipient may either return them or buy them. For accounting purposes, the sale is not recorded until the recipient has accepted the goods (FRS 102 section 23.10). The tax treatment follows the accounting standard.

VAT is charged from the earlier of when the customer either accepts the goods or 12 months after they were supplied.

sales Turnover, or gross charge for goods and services supplied in a defined period. It is usually stated without reclaimable VAT.

sales incentive scheme Scheme that rewards employee or other person for achieving a performance that is to the business's advantage. Typically the scheme offers a prize, not usually in cash but in a perceived luxury items such as a holiday. The cost of the scheme and its prizes is tax-deductible if three conditions are met:

- the reward has been genuinely earned by the recipient,
- there is an obligation upon the trader to provide the gift, and
- the gift is provided as part of a genuine business scheme

(Inspector's Manual at BIM45080).

sales journal Book in which sales are recorded. Such a journal is usually restricted to non-cash sales. Entries from it are later posted to the sales ledger, and totals from the sales journal are posted to the nominal ledger.

sales ledger Record of how much each individual customer owes. It is a memorandum account, in that it is outside the scope of double-entry bookkeeping.

sales of lessors expense Term defined in FA 2000 s79A(3) in relation to tonnage tax, as added by FA 2012 s24(3). [The Act does not include any apostrophe in the first word.]

Salmanezah Champagne bottle with a capacity of 12 standard bottles.

Salomon v Salomon Court case from 1897 which clarified the existing law that a limited company is a separate legal entity from its owners.

salt When sold for culinary use, this is zero-rated for VAT as food. This requires it to be sold in packs of up to 12.5 kilograms. Salt sold for other purposes, such as for dishwashers, is standard-rated. The matter is explained in VAT Notice 701/14.

salt spring When run commercially, profits are specifically subject to income tax (ITTOIA 2005 s12) or corporation tax (CTA 2009 s39).

salvage Recovering value from a damaged asset. This is generally zero-rated for VAT under VATA 1994 Sch 8 Group 8. Under maritime law, a salvor may claim up to 10% of the value of salvaged material from a ship (Maritime Insurance Act 1906 s65(2)).

Samaritans Charity founded in 1953 that provides comfort to the suicidal and despairing. It derives its name from a parable in Luke 10:30-37 in the Bible. Contact details can be found under Addresses in section 3 of this dictionary.

same-day rule Capital gains tax rule for identifying the acquisition cost of a share. The rule assumes that shares sold on the day of acquisition are ranked first.

same premises test In tax, a test for eligibility for the annual investment allowance. Companies are eligible if they are within the same business classification and operate from the same premises at both the beginning and end of the chargeable period.

same roof rule Rule that a victim cannot claim compensation for sexual abuse suffered from someone living under the same roof for periods before 1 October 1979.

This rule was abolished with retrospective effect from 13 June 2019.

Samoa Island country in Pacific Ocean. Its currency is the tala of 100 sene. The UK has no double taxation treaty.

sample The supply of a sample worth more than £50 is subject to VAT on its value, even though no charge is made for it. From 2012, this limit applies to each sample and is not an annual limit. The matter is discussed in VAT Notice 700/7.

An imported sample to obtain orders may be exempt from Customs duty and import VAT.

sample product Product supplied solely for the purpose of obtaining orders. There is a special Customs procedure under which samples may be exempt from Customs duty and import VAT. The three conditions are:

- once imported, the item can only be used as a sample
- it is of negligible value (typically less than £20, though this is not a statutory or regulatory limit)
- it is supplied solely to gain further orders for the product.

Customs are more likely to accept an import as a sample product if it is so marked, and if the importer or user is required to destroy the sample after examination.

Samurai sword Customs may seize any such sword with a curved blade exceeding 50cm in length unless it is imported for participation in martial arts events or religious ceremonies (Customs notice 1).

sanction Financial restriction imposed on a regime. This may be a country, business, organisation or person.

For the UK, sanctions were imposed by the EU. These remain in force until 11pm on 31 December 2020, after which they are expected to continue under UK law. Sanctions are usually imposed for either internationally unacceptable behaviour, or for breaching money laundering regulations.

For the former, the UK usually follows the United Nations list. The latter are usually imposed by Sanctions and Anti-Money Laundering Act 2018.

Countries which have sanctions as at 1 January 2021 are Afghanistan, Belarus, Bosnia and Herzegovina, Burma (Myanmar), Burundi, Central African Republic, Democratic Republic of the Congo, Guinea, Guinea-Bissau, Iran, Iraq, Lebanon, Libya, Mali, Nicaragua, North Korea, Russia, Somalia, South Sudan, Sudan, Syria, Venezuela, Yemen and Zimbabwe.

A full list of sanctioned countries and persons, and the exact scope of the sanctions, can be founded on the government's website.

sanctionable benefit Social security benefit to which a sanction may be applied for non-compliance with a condition (WRA 2012 s117).

sanctions order Order that bans or restricts the export of certain military or other sensitive products to a particular state.

sandwich Food product whose VAT treatment depends on how it is supplied. If sold to be taken away before eating, it is zero-rated as food. If sold to be eaten on the premises, it qualifies for the 5% hospitality rate during coronavirus provisions. If provided as part of an event, like a wedding reception or corporate event, it is standard-rated.

sandwich relief One of the absence reliefs for main residence relief from capital gains tax (TCGA 1992 s323). It allows certain absences to be disregarded. These include a period of any length while the taxpayer worked outside the UK, and a period of up to four years where the taxpayer worked in the UK but where it was reasonable for the employee to live elsewhere.

sanitary protection Such products are zero-rated from 1 January 2021. Before then, the products are reduced-rated under VATA 1994 Sch 7A Group 4. The exact scope is summarised in VAT Notice 701/18. From 2015, the Treasury has donated to women's charities a sum equal to the VAT collected on these products.

Sao Tome and Principe Island country in the Gulf of Guinea. Its currency is the dobra of 100 centimos. The UK has no double taxation treaty.

sasine in Scots law, the act of giving possession to legal property.

satang One hundredth of a baht, currency of Thailand.

Saturday fund Mutual insurance fund as originally set up in the 1870s, when workers were traditionally paid on a Saturday and contributed to a fund to insure them against illness. Some of these funds still exist where they are treated as a mutual body. The matter is discussed in HMRC Manual at BIM24685.

sausage casings These were held to be zero-rated as food in the case *Devro Ltd [1991] VTD 7570*. The argument that they would not be eaten on their own was dismissed. Flour, sugar and salt are not eaten on their own but are zero-rated as food.

save as you earn (SAYE) This term now usually means a tax-advantaged option scheme for employees of a commercial company. A scheme requires HMRC approval.

The employee may save between £5 and £500 per month (£250 between September 1991 and April 2014) usually as a deduction from pay.

The scheme is subject to many rules, as set out under Employee Schemes in section 3 of this dictionary.
Before 1994, there was an ordinary SAYE scheme for any investor.

savings basic rate The rate of income tax applied to savings income in accordance with ITA 2007 s6C as inserted by FA 2016.

savings certificate Document showing how much an individual has saved with the organisation issuing the certificate. For corporation tax, a definition is given in CTA 2009 s1281(3).

savings credit One of two elements of the pension credit (State Pension Credit Act 2002 s3). It is paid only if the claimant or their partner reached state pension age by 6 April 2016.

savings income Income that arises from interest on savings and similar, and not from other sources. Until 1984, this was taxed more heavily than earned income as unearned income or as investment income. From 1996, the opposite position has been taken in that savings income is often taxed less heavily. The two main provisions are the starting rate for savings and the savings nil rate.

The starting rate for savings allows up to £5,000 to be taxed at 0% (ITA 2007 s12A). For this purpose, savings income is regarded as the highest slice of income after any dividend income. Most pension lump sums and social security benefits may also be disregarded. The consequence is that the band is only available if other income does not exceed the personal allowance by £5,000.
The savings rate allows £1,000 tax relief for basic rate taxpayers and £500 for higher rate taxpayers (ITA 2007 s7). There is no allowance for additional rate taxpayers. This may be claimed by taxpayers as a deduction from savings income except to the extent that such income has already been relieved by the personal allowance or dividend allowance.
All this means that a person can earn £18,500 tax-free: £12,500 personal allowance, £5,000 starting rate plus £1,000 savings allowance.

Savings Income Information Regulations (SIR) Name of SI 2003 No 3297, in force from 1 July 2005. It transposes into English law the European Savings Directive. It sets out the duties of paying agents in reporting savings income to HMRC.

savings rate Low or zero rate for savings income for those who have no other or little other income (ITA 2007 s7). From 2014, it charges 0% on income up to £5,000. Savings income is regarded as the top slice of taxable income, so only someone with a low income can benefit.

savoury snacks Some snacks are standard-rated for VAT. These include potato products (including crisps), cereal snacks and nuts that are roasted and salted. The exact scope is given in VAT Notice 701/14.

SAYE option scheme Tax-advantaged savings scheme for employees (ITEPA 2003 from s516). Details are given in Employee Schemes in section 3 of this dictionary.

sayonara tax Departure tax introduced by Japan in January 2019.

scale charges Table of figures to be used for tax purposes. Many such tables are produced such as for calculating company car benefit, VAT on fuel benefit, and expenses for business accommodation.

schedule (1) An appendix giving detailed provisions in an Act of Parliament. (2) System of determining liability to income tax (1803-2005) and corporation tax (1965-2009). The original schedules were A property; B farming; C investment; D trading; E employment.

Schedule 1AB claim Claim for error and mistake relief as provided in TMA 1970 Sch 1AB. Guidance is provided in HMRC Manual at SACM12085.

Schedule 23 While there are many Acts that have 23 or more Schedules, this term probably means FA 2001 Sch 23 which refers to the data gathering powers of HMRC.

schedule 36 This usually means Finance Act 2008 Sch 36 which gives details of HMRC's powers of information and inspection.

scheme administration member payment Payments made by a registered pension scheme to or in respect of a member or a former member for the purposes of administration or management of the scheme.

The tax provisions are set out in FA 2004 s171.

scheme administrator The person(s) appointed in accordance with the pension scheme rules to be responsible for the discharge of the functions conferred or imposed on the scheme administrator of the pension scheme by and under Part 4 of FA 2004. This person must be resident in an EU member state or in Norway, Liechtenstein or Iceland (EEA states which are not EU states). The person must have made the declarations to HMRC required by section 270(3) FA 2004.

scheme designer Person who helps design a tax avoidance scheme but is not the scheme promoter.

scheme of reconstruction In the context of capital gains tax "means a scheme of merger, division or other restructuring that meets the first and second, and either the third or fourth, of the following conditions" (TCGA1992 Sch 5AA para 1).
The four conditions relate to:

(1) issue of ordinary share capital
(2) equal entitlement to new shares
(3) continuity of business
(4) compromise or arrangement with members

Scheme Reference Number (SRN) Number allocated to a reported tax avoidance scheme. This must be quoted on the tax returns of all scheme users.

Schengen Convention Convention on border controls in Europe. By 2016 it applied to all EU countries except UK and Denmark. From 2021, it includes Gibraltar.

schilling Currency of Austria before it adopted the euro in 2002. For VAT, gold investment coin issued by Austria and listed in VAT notice 701/12A.

scholarship When provided by an employer to an employee or a member of the employee's family, this may be a taxable benefit under ITEPA 2003 s211.

school photograph In the VAT case *Customs v P L A Paget [1989] QB STC 773*, the Court held that a school which sold photographs was not acting as the agent of the photographer.

school uniform This may be zero-rated for VAT when of a size and design for children under 14, as explained in VAT Notice 714. It is not sufficient that the clothes are held out for sale as for children under 14.

scientific research Any research in the fields of natural or applied science for the extension of knowledge (ITTOIA 2005 s88(3); CTA 2009 s88(3)). A capital allowance may be claimed under CAA 2001 ss437-452.

scot Old term for a local property tax charged in the 10th century. This meaning lives on in the expression "scot free".

Scotch whisky Whisky that has been distilled and matured in Scotland (Customs notice 39).

Scotland Country that forms Great Britain with England and Wales from 1707 (Union With Scotland Act 1706). Some taxes, including aspects of income tax, have been devolved to Scotland from 2015.

From 2018, Scotland has replaced the 20% basic rate band with three bands: 19% starter rate, 20% basic rate and 21% intermediate rate. Other rates are 1 percentage point higher than in UK.

Scotland has a different legal system. Its Parliament was revived in 1998.

Scottish additional rate Provision of ITA 2007 s10(4) that allowed the Scottish Parliament to vary the basic rate of income tax from 6 April 2016. The power was never used. It is replaced by new powers under Scotland Act 2016 which gives greater freedom for setting income tax rates in Scotland.

Scottish banknotes These are issued by the Bank of Scotland, Clydesdale Bank and Royal Bank of Scotland. They are not legal tender anywhere in the UK, but as the Bank of England will accept them, they are treated as if they were legal tender (Bank Notes (Scotland) Act 1845).

Scottish basic rate Provision of ITA 2007 s10(4) that allowed the Scottish Parliament to vary the basic rate of income tax from 6 April 2016. The power was never used. It is replaced by new powers under Scotland Act 2016 which gives greater freedom for setting income tax rates in Scotland.

Scottish child payment Social security benefit due to be introduced in Scotland in February 2021 giving an extra £10 a week for a family with a child.

Scottish Consolidated Fund Fund into which Revenue Scotland pays the tax it collects (Revenue Scotland and Tax Powers Act 2014 s5(1)).

Scottish Enterprise Body formed in 1991 to promote business in Scotland.

Scottish Fiscal Commission Body that prepares forecasts and assessments in relation to taxes devolved to the Scottish Parliament (Scottish Fiscal Commission Act 2016 s1).

Scottish higher rate Provision of ITA 2007 s10(4) that allowed the Scottish Parliament to vary the basic rate of income tax from 6 April 2016. The power was never used.

It is replaced by new powers under Scotland Act 2016 which gives greater freedom for setting income tax rates in Scotland.

Scottish island marine area "Means such part of the Scottish marine area (within the meaning of Part 1 of the Marine (Scotland) Act 2010) which is –

(a) adjacent to an island, and

(b) up to 12 nautical miles from that island, measured from the low water mark of the ordinary spring tide"

(Islands (Scotland) Act 2018 s23).

Scottish Job Start A single payment of £250 (£400 if the claimant has a child) made in Scotland from 17 August 2020 to a person aged between 16 and 24 (25 for a care leaver) to help with starting a new job.

Scottish landfill tax Scottish equivalent to landfill tax, introduced from April 2015.

Scottish Legal Complaints Commission Body established under Legal Profession and Legal Aid (Scotland) Act 2007 s1 to hear complaints of professional conduct or unsatisfactory professional conduct by members of the legal profession in Scotland.

Scottish limited partnership (SLP) A limited partnership formed under Scots law. It is formed under Limited Partnerships Act 1907. This means that one or more partners can limit their liability but cannot participate in the management of the partnership.

An SLP is not a limited liability partnership, which is a separate legal entity that may be established in the UK, including Scotland. Unlike limited partnerships in the rest of the UK, a Scottish limited partnership has legal personality of its own. This gave them advantages for investment and in avoiding money laundering rules. From 26 June 2017, an SLP must disclose a person with significant control to Companies House.

Scottish Parliamentary Standards Commissioner Person appointed under Scottish Parliamentary Standards Commissioner Act 2002 s1.

Scottish partnership In Scotland, unlike England, a partnership is recognised as a separate legal entity from the partners (Partnership Act 1890 s4(2)).

There is also a Scottish limited partnership.

Scottish rate of income tax (SRIT) Rates of income tax that are charged on earned income of Scottish residents from April 2017. Investment income is charged at UK rates.

These rates are given under Income Tax in section 3 of this dictionary.

Scottish rate resolution "Means a resolution of the Scottish Parliament under section 80C of the Scotland Act 1998" (ITA 2007 s989 as amended by Scotland Act 2016 s14(3)(c)).

Scottish social security charter This is produced under Social Security (Scotland) Act 2018 s15.

Scottish social security principles These are set out in Social Security (Scotland) Act 2018 s1. The principles "are –

(a) social security is an investment in the people of Scotland,

(b) social security is itself a human right and essential to the realisation of other human rights,
(c) the delivery of social security is a public service,
(d) respect for the dignity of individuals is to be at the heart of the Scottish social security system,
(e) the Scottish social security system is to contribute to reducing poverty in Scotland,
(f) the Scottish social security system is to be designed with the people of Scotland on the basis of evidence,
(g) opportunities are to be sought to continuously improve the Scottish social security system in ways which—
  (i) put the needs of those who require assistance first, and
  (ii) advance equality and non-discrimination,
(h) the Scottish social security system is to be efficient and deliver value for money".

Scottish social security system This is defined in Social Security (Scotland) Act 2018 s23.

Scottish taxpayer Person who is liable to pay income tax at Scottish rates (Scotland Act 2012 s25). This is broadly any Scottish politician, anyone who resided in Scotland for at least 183 days in the tax year, and anyone who resided in Scotland for more days than in any other country.

Scottish tax tribunals Bodies that hear tax appeals in Scotland (Revenue Scotland and Tax Powers Act 2014 from s20).

Scottish term dates Quarter days in Scotland. They are given in section 3 of this dictionary.

Scottish variable rate (SVR) The original right of the Scottish parliament to vary the basic rate of income tax by adding or subtracting 3p in the pound for all residents in Scotland. This right has never been used, though it was once considered as a means of scrapping the council tax.

The provision is replaced by Scottish Rate of Income Tax from April 2016.

Scott schedule Schedule used in litigation. It sets out a list of issues to be determined by the judge. This is often in the first of four or five columns. The second column may indicate the cost of resolving the issue. The next two columns allow for responses.

Scott undertaking Undertaking by HMRC that it will not use tax investigations for covert purposes. This followed the Matrix Churchill scandal of 1992 when the company was illegally checked under the guise of a VAT visit. The undertaking was replaced in 2011 by provisions in Regulation of Investigatory Powers Act 2007.

scrap *Definition*

Material left over from manufacturing activities, but which still has a value. A common example is metal left over from machining. It can be sold to a scrap metal dealer who melts it down for re-use.

In accounting, care must always be taken to ensure that scrap sales are accounted for as turnover. Where a scrap dealer is VAT-registered, it is common for the reverse charge method to be used.

Law

Scrap metal dealing is now governed by Scrap Metal Dealers Act 2013, which replaces Scrap Metal Dealers Act 1964.

A licence is required to trade as a dealer.

It is generally an offence to pay for scrap metal in cash, or otherwise than by cheque, bank transfer, debit card or credit card (Scrap Metal Dealers Act 2013 s12). This is to deter theft of metal by ensuring that the seller can be traced.

scrappage Government scheme to give someone an allowance for scrapping an old car, introduced in 2009. A similar scheme was introduced for old boilers.

scratch card Card made of cardboard or plastic which contains concealed information that becomes legible when a surface (usually made from a form of latex) is scratched away, often using the edge of a coin. The card must be provided with this information covered. Its uses include topping up mobile phones, gaming and software. In the former, the area reveals a code which can be sent to the phone company to add credit to the telephone.

Another use is for gaming. If the revealed area displays a winning combination or code, the holder is entitled to an instant prize. The first such cards were issued in 1974 by Scientific Games Corporation. The modern method was patented in the USA in 1987 by Astro-Med Inc.

Where a scratch card is offered as a promotional prize by a business, the card may be allowable as a low value business gift, provided the supplier's name is conspicuously displayed.

Whenever a scratch card, lottery ticket or similar is provided as a benefit in kind to an employee, its taxable value is the list price that would have been charged to buy the ticket or card. Any prize won is tax-free and does not represent an additional benefit. Conversely, not winning a prize does not reduce the value of the card or ticket to zero (see Inspector's Manual at BIM45085).

scrip dividend Dividend paid in the form of new shares rather than cash.

scrip issue Bonus issue of shares.

scroll Manuscript written on a roll of paper or other material. It is standard-rated for VAT. It does not come within the scope of VAT zero-rating of books *(The Hall of Names Ltd [1991] VTD 8806).*

sculptor Person who may apply for profits to be averaged over three years under ITTOIA 2005 s221.

Sea Cadet Corps Officers, adult instructors and adult warrant officers of this corps are a class of reservists (PAYE regulations SI 2003 No 2682 reg 122(2)).

seafarer Person whose duties are on an ocean-going ship (ITEPA 2003 s40(5)). Such a person is entitled to a measure of income tax relief (ITEPA 2003 s372) and special rates of national insurance (SSCBA 1992 s117).

seal (1) Impression made on a document, usually either using sealing wax or by making an impression using a device similar to pliers. The latter style was often made using an adhesive red wafer in the shape of a starburst. The requirement for a company to have a seal was abolished from 31 July 1990. Seals are now generally only used for ceremonial documents.

(2) Animal. The import of the animal or products is generally prohibited from 20 August 2010.

seal attestation Document issued by a state authority that a seal has been killed in a traditional hunt by Intuits (Eskimos) as part of a national cull to maintain the animal population. Such a document allows seal products to be imported through Customs. Otherwise a seal is a protected animal from 20 August 2010.

sealed will Will that has been granted probate by a judge by being sealed and not made public as most wills are. Wills of the royal family have been sealed since 1910.

sea wall Embankment or other provision to protect an area from encroachment or flooding from the sea or a tidal river. It is excluded from the scope of plant and machinery, but there are specific corporation tax and income tax reliefs that may be claimed.

search (1) For Customs purpose, the examination of a person to see if they are smuggling goods (CEMA 1979 s164). There are three types of search: rub-down search, strip search and intimate search.

(2) In computing, finding documents and text by entering a keyword. In information notices issued by HMRC, the parties are expected to agree the keywords to identify documents. If they cannot agree, the matter is determined by a tribunal.

search and rescue charity Charity whose main purpose is to conduct search and rescue operations in the UK or its marine area, or to develop such a charity. From 1 April 2015, such a charity may claim VAT input tax under VATA 1994 s33D(5)-33D(8).

search and seizure warrant Warrant which may be issued under Proceeds of Crime Act 2002 s352.

search warrant Permission given by a magistrate to a police officer to search premises (Police and Criminal Evidence Act 1984 s8).

seasonal pitch Non-residential pitch for a holiday caravan. From 1 March 2012, it may be exempt from VAT under VATA 1994 Sch 9 Group 1 Note (14).

Seasonal Workers Pilot Scheme that allows workers from outside the EU to enter the UK for up to six weeks for harvesting work. The scheme was introduced in 2019. The number of workers has been expanded from 10,000 in 2020 to 30,000 in 2021.

sea wall Embankment or similar designed to protect an area from flooding by the sea or other tidal water. A sea wall is explicitly excluded from the scope of plant and machinery (CAA 2001 s22(1) List B).

Tax relief may be given for such expenditure under other provisions (ITTOIA 2005 s315; CTA 2009 s254).

second abolition date The date of 6 April 2016 when the reduced rate of national insurance ended for members of a defined benefit pension scheme (Pension Schemes Act 1993 s7A).

secondary contributor Person who is liable to pay the secondary rate of class 1 national insurance (SSCBA 1992 s7). This is usually the employer.

secondary funds In relation to the taxation of derivatives, this term is given a specific meaning in ITA 2007 s809FZP(5) as inserted by FA 2016 s37.

secondary lease period Period of a lease when payments have already been made to cover the cost of the leased asset, and only nominal payments are now made.

secondary threshold Threshold at which an employer becomes liable to pay class 1 national insurance. The rates are given under National Insurance in section 3 of this dictionary.

second-hand goods Goods that have been owned by someone else. The scope under EU law was defined in the Dutch case *(Sjelle Autogenbrug I/S v Skatteministeriet. [2017] All ER (D) 10 (Feb) Case C-471/15)*. This held that it included goods that needed repair, but excluded scrap, gems and works of art. The decision meant that the goods benefited from a special scheme for VAT.
In the UK, there is an optional scheme for such goods which allows VAT to be charged on the profit margin rather than on the whole price (SI 1995 No 1268). A business must register with HMRC to use the scheme. The goods must have been bought from someone who is not VAT-registered or who is a business also registered under the scheme. Further details are given in VAT Notice 718.

second purchase price Term used in relation to the alternative finance arrangement known as purchase and resale arrangements (TCGA1992 s151J).

second reduced rate In Irish Republic, rate of VAT that is lower than the reduced rate. In 2017/18, when the Republic's standard rate is 23%, the reduced rate is 13.5% and the second reduced rate is 9%. It applies to horses not intended for use in foodstuffs or agricultural production.

second tax year For income tax, the basis period for the second tax year in which a person carries on a trade (ITTOIA 2005 s200). Tax is charged for the period to the accounting date in the tax year, provided this is at least 12 months. If not, the basis period is the first 12 months of trade. As some of this will have already been taxed in the first tax year of trading, the trader is entitled to overlap relief for the profit that has been taxed twice. This relief may be deducted when the trade ceases, with no allowance for inflation, or possibly when it changes its accounting date.

Secretary of State "Means one of Her Majesty's Principal Secretaries of State" (Interpretation Act 1978 Sch 1).

secret reserves Reserves which are concealed so as not to be evident from a balance sheet. A distinction is usually drawn between secret reserves and hidden reserves, where the latter are shown on the balance sheet but may not be obvious.

Bookkeeping and Accounts by Spicer and Pegler identifies nine methods for creating secret reserves in accounts:

(1) Writing down assets below their market value by excessive provision for depreciation.
(2) Writing off assets altogether, although they are still of value
(3) Creating excessive provisions for bad debts
(4) Charging capital expenditure to revenue
(5) Omitting goodwill from the accounts
(6) Overstating liabilities in the balance sheet
(7) Treating reserves for contingencies as provisions for specific liabilities
(8) Grouping free reserves with liabilities, so as to inflate the liabilities on the balance sheet
(9) Crediting exceptional or non-recurring profits direct to a contingencies reserve, and including such reserves in the liabilities on the balance sheet.

It should be realised that most of these methods now contravene accounting standards.

secret trust Trust created in a will in accordance with provisions not stated in the will.

section 12 kerosene "Means heavy oil of the description given by paragraph (c) of section 11(1) of the [HODA1979]" (Hydrocarbon Oil (Payment of Rebates) Regulations SI 1996 No 2313 reg 3(1)).

section 13 pension Pension entitlement that arises under Pensions Act 2014 s13. The term is used in Pensions Act 2014 Sch 9.

section 13AA kerosene "Means kerosene of the description given by sections 13AA(5) of the [HODA1979] for the purposes of sections 13AA and 13AB of the Act" (Hydrocarbon Oil (Payment of Rebates) Regulations SI 1996 No 2313 reg 3(1)).

section 24 duty Requirement for a trade union to maintain a register of its members under Trade Union and Labour Relations (Consolidation) Act 1992 s24.

section 30 disposal For capital gains tax, a disposal of an asset where value shifting has taken place (TCGA 1992 s30).

section 32 policy A buyout policy used to transfer a pension settlement.

section 33 refund Refund of VAT that may be claimed by a local authority or other public body.

section 38 contribution notice Notice sent by the Pensions Regulator under Pensions Act 2004 s38 where there is evidence that steps have been taken to avoid recovery of a debt owed by an employer to a final salary (or defined benefit) pension scheme.

section 42(7) claim Claim made in accordance with TMA 1970 s42(7). This section lists provisions in other Acts under which a claim may be made for tax relief.

section 45A allowance First year allowance for environmentally friendly plant (CAA 2001 s45A-45H).

section 45H expenditure Expenditure on some environmentally-friendly equipment that may qualify for a first year allowance.

section 61 expenses Expenses incurred by **tenants under taxed leases,** as set out in ITTOIA 2005s61.

The term is used in ibid s63.

section 104 holding Holding of shares under the provisions of TCGA 1992 s104. This regards shares of the same class and company as being a single asset.

section 106 money Amounts paid under Town and Country Planning Act 1990 s106 as a condition of receiving planning permission. The funds must be to address a matter without which the permission could not be granted, such as improved transport facility.

section 114 notice Notice issued under Local Government FA 1988 s114, as amended. This section requires the chief finance officer of a local authority to make a report if a council or similar body has made or is about to make a financial decision that is unlawful. The report must be sent to every member of the authority.
A notice is also required if the authority is about to produce an unbalanced budget.
The authority must convene a full council meeting within 21 days to consider the notice. Until that meeting has been held, the council may not agree any new spending, though it may continue with already agreed spending.
Several such notices were issued in the 1990s. Nottinghamshire County Council issued one in 2018.

section 131 rights Inheritance rights of a civil partner and their children, as conferred by Civil Partnership Act 2004 s131. These rights are generally identical to those of a husband or wife. In Scotland, these rights also apply to legitim.

section 148 In relation to pensions, refers to Social Security Administration Act 1992 s148. This deals with revaluations of pension benefits.

section 172 statement Statement that a company may be required to produce setting out how the directors have sought to promote the success of the company, as required by CA 2006 s172.

section 176 allowance For long funding leases, an allowance given in accordance with the provisions of CAA 2001 s176.

section 338 expenses Travelling expenses that may be paid to an employee tax-free under ITEPA 2003 s338.

section 390 scheme Term used in relation to disguised remuneration (ITEPA 2003 s554X(12).

secured loan Loan where a failure to repay means that the lender may take an identified asset. A mortgage is a form of secured loan.

securities Another name for stocks and shares but also applies to any approved or registered financial instrument, such as bonds.
For company law, the term is defined in CA 2006 s783.
For employment income, the term is defined in ITEPA 2003 s420.
The tax treatment for dealers in securities is given in CTA 2009 from s128.
For the accrued income scheme, a definition is given in ITA 2007 s619.

Securities and Exchange Commission (SEC) American official body which regulates the securities markets.

Securities and Futures Association (SFA) A regulatory body which polices investment businesses, such as stockbrokers.

Securities and Investments Board Regulator of financial services, now replaced by Financial Conduct Authority.

Securities Directive EU directive 2001/34/EC of 28 May 2001 regarding the admission of securities to official listings. It is given effect in the UK by SI 2003 No 3297.

Securities Institute Professional body of securities and investment professionals formed in 1992. In 2009, it received a royal charter and is now called the Chartered Institute for Securities and Investment (CISI).

It offers five classes of member: affiliate, student, associate, member and fellow. The last three may use the designatory letters ACSI, MCSI and FCSI.

securities transactions In relation to HMRC data-gathering powers, "means –

(a) transactions in securities
(b) transactions under which a representative payment has been, is to be or may be made, or
(c) the making or receipt of a **representative payment**"

(FA 2011 Sch 23 para 19(3)).

security For tax, the main meaning is a deposit that HMRC may require for registering a taxpayer for VAT or PAYE.

security feature Feature on a company car to meet a threat to the employee's personal security (ITEPA 2003 s125A). From April 2011, this is not a taxable benefit.

security for payment of PAYE This may be required under the provisions of PAYE regulations SI 2003 No 2682 from reg 97M, which is effective from 6 April 2012.

security for VAT VAT law allows HM Revenue & Customs to require the provision of an amount of security where it is considered that a business represents a risk to the collection of VAT.

security seal A trader seal that can withstand a force of 1000 kilograms. Further details are given in Customs notice 205.

sederunt book In Scotland, register of sequestrations.

sediment Solid matter that settles from a suspension in liquid.

For some beer this may produce undrinkable sediment on which beer duty may be relieved.

seed A seed may be zero-rated for VAT if used to produce plants for human consumption or as animal feeding stuff (Value Added Tax 1994 Sch 8 Group 1 Item 3). Details are given in VAT Notice 701/38.

Seed Enterprise Investment Scheme (SEIS) Tax-advantaged investment scheme for investments in newly formed businesses. The law is ITA 2007 from s257A.

It complements enterprise investment scheme (EIS) while being more restrictive in scope but more generous in tax relief. SEIS uses many of the rules of EIS.

The main elements of the scheme are:

- relief is given for purchase of ordinary shares
- the shares must have first issued from 6 April 2012
- income tax relief is given at 50% of the cost of the shares to a maximum of annual investment of £100,000
- the shares must be held for three years or the relief is clawed back
- there is a carry-back provision where SEIS investment can be offset against income of the previous tax year, but not to before 6 April 2012
- capital gains tax is charged on only half the gain if the proceeds of an SEIS investment are reinvested in a way that also qualifies for tax relief. (This provision was originally intended to apply only in 2012/13 for the whole gain, but has been extended in scope and halved in value)
- any reinvestment of an SEIS gain must still be within the £100,000 annual limit
- capital gains tax is not charged on the disposal of shares held for at least three years
- a company that has raised funds under SEIS may raise further funds under EIS or a venture capital trust.

Help is provided by HMRC is helpsheet HS393.

see through Description of a tax provision that looks beyond the structure of a transaction or relationship in determining the tax liability.

A simple example is a bare trust where the beneficiary is taxed rather than the trust. Other examples can include controlled foreign companies and some tax avoidance schemes.

sefdydliad elusennol corfforedig Welsh: charitable incorporated organisation.

segmental reporting Reporting revenue, profit, cash flow assets, liabilities for each geographical and business segment within a business, identifying segments by the way the organisation is managed.

seignorage The difference between the face value of a note or coin, and its cost of production. This is sometimes seen as a tax.

seise Old spelling of seize, which is still used in some legal contexts.

seized money Money that is claimed under Proceeds of Crime Act 2002 s67.

For Scotland, the term is also given a specific meaning in Proceeds of Crime Act 2002 s131ZA as inserted by Criminal Finances Act 2017 s28.

seizure Forcible removal of property, such as when tax is owed or a crime has been committed. Police powers are set out in Police and Criminal Evidence Act 1984 s19. Customs' powers are explained in leaflet 12A.

seizure information notice Notice sent by Customs in respect of goods seized when the owner was not present. If the owner was present, a notice of seizure is issued instead.

selective employment tax Tax charged between 1966 and 1973 on certain businesses and paid to others. This tax and purchase tax were abolished when VAT was introduced.

self-assessment Requirement for a taxpayer to report and determine his or her own tax liability. This is now used for almost all taxes (TMA 1970 s9).

self-assessment autocoding Procedure whereby a person's tax code is automatically adjusted from data entered on a self-assessment tax return. This procedure was introduced from September 2011.

self-billing Arrangement where a customer makes out tax invoices for his or her VAT registered supplier and sends a copy to the supplier, usually with the payment. This arrangement is used in areas where it is the customer who knows the amount to be billed, such as for scrap metal and publishing royalties.

Details are given in VAT Notice 700/62.

self-certification When a person signs a certificate about himself or herself. An example is form SC2 that may certify an employee's sickness for up to seven days.

self-contained unit For council tax, a building or part of a building that has been constructed or adapted for separate living accommodation. It can include a caravan or boat.

The unit should usually contain provisions for sleeping, cooking and washing.

self-employed Description of someone who works for himself or herself. Care needs to be shown to ensure that the person is not really an employee.

A self-employed person pays income tax on earnings which are usually reported to HMRC under self-assessment. The person is generally liable to national insurance under classes 2 and 4.

self-employed earner For national insurance, "means a person who is gainfully employed in Great Britain otherwise than in employed earner's employment (whether or not he is also employed in such employment)" (Social Security Contributions and Benefits Act 1992 s2(1)(b)).

self-employment income support scheme Scheme introduced by the government in 2020 to provide funding to self-employed people affected by coronavirus. A summary is provided in Coronavirus in section 3 of this dictionary.

self-investment Extent to which a pension fund may invest in its sponsoring employer. From 1992, this is generally limited to 5% of funds.

self-isolation When a person must stay at home because they have symptoms of coronavirus in 2020. The isolation period was originally seven days for the person and 14 days for members of their household, to allow for any incubation. The seven days was extended to ten days from 31 July 2020. An employee who self-isolates may be able to claim statutory sick pay.

self-isolation payment One of two schemes announced by the government during the coronavirus outbreak. The first was announced on 1 September 2020 and offered £13 a day for someone receiving universal credit or working tax credit, who must self-isolate and cannot work from home.

The second, called Test and Trace Support, was introduced on 28 September 2020 makes a single payment of £500 to such a person.

self-liquidating loan Short-term loan secured against something that will generate funds for the repayments, such as on growing crops.

self-propulsion In relation to the VAT position for a **houseboat,** "refers to any vessel that is either:

- independently propelled, or
- not independently propelled but could be readily adapted to be capable of self-propulsion, for example by installing an engine, propeller or mast." (VAT leaflet 701/20).

self-representation When a person is representing himself or herself and not acting as an agent for someone else. Tax law assumes that everyone is self-representing unless the opposite is expressly stated.

self-sequestration Insolvency proceedings started in Scotland by the debtor.

self-supply When a business uses its own products. Generally, there is no VAT on such a transaction. Exceptions are when:

- a motor dealer takes a car for his or her own use
- a car on which VAT may be reclaimed (such as a hire car) is put to another use
- when someone uses their own labour to construct a non-residential building or to increase floor space by more than 10%.

These exceptions are listed in VAT Notice 700.

For income tax or corporation tax, any tax is determined on the normal selling price, not the cost price.

seller In relation to a transfer of stock in the course of a trade, means "the person who makes the transfer" (CTA 2009 s170 and ITTOIA 2005 s181(2)).

selling plate Horse race where the owners agree that the winners will be sold at a pre-agreed price.

sell to cover Instruction to sell shares to realise finds to meet a liability, particularly a tax liability. The term is used in relation to employee schemes (ITEPA 2003 s222) under which a tax charge may arise.

semble It appears. The word is sometimes used in law reports to indicate something that appears to be a legal argument but where there is still some doubt.

Sen (1) One hundredth of a riel, currency of Cambodia.
(2) One hundredth of a rupiah, currency of Indonesia.
(3) One hundredth of a yen, currency of Japan.
(4) One hundredth of a ringgit, currency of Malaysia

send (1) In relation to postal services, means to entrust delivery to the service. If it can be shown that the letter or package was properly provided to the postal service, correctly addressed and with the correct amount of prepaid postage, the letter or package is assumed to have been delivered unless the contrary can be shown (Interpretation Act 1978 s7). When sending a return or payment to HMRC, it is advisable to get a certificate of posting.
(2) In computing, this means to transmit data to another person. For tax purposes, this is complete when the person has received it not when it was sent. Most computer systems generate an acknowledgment when data have been received.

sender In relation to electronic filing, "means –

(a) in relation to a statement to which regulation 2 applies, the company making the qualifying distribution, or person acting on its behalf;

(b) in relation to a statement to which regulation 3 applies, the person under the duty to furnish the certificate, or another person acting on his behalf; and

(c) in relation to statement, notice, certificate or voucher to which regulation 4 applies, the person required or authorised, under the relevant provision mentioned in paragraph (2) of that regulation, to deliver that statement, notice, certificate or voucher, or another person acting on his behalf"

((Income and Corporation Taxes (Electronic Certificates of Deduction of Tax and Tax Credit) Regulations SI 2003 No 3143 reg 1(3)).

sene One hundredth of a tala, currency of Samoa.

Senedd Welsh term for the National Assembly of Wales.

Senegal African country. Its currency is the CFA franc of 100 centimes. The UK has agreed a double taxation convention in 2015 which came into force in 2016.

senior accounting officer (SAO) "Director or officer of a company who, in the company's reasonable opinion, has overall responsibility for the company's financial arrangements" (Inspector's Manual at SAOG 24000).

The duty to designated an SAO is only required for a company with an annual turnover above £200 million.

These obligations apply for financial years that start on or after 21 July 2009.

The duties are set out at SAOG 12000.

The statutory authority is FA 2009 Sch 46 which sets out the duties of the SAO.

Senior President of Tribunals Person so appointed under Tribunals, Courts and Enforcement Act 2007 s2.

senior capital Capital in the form of secured loans which is repaid before junior capital if the business is liquidated.

senior statutory auditor The individual in an accounting firm who is so identified under either an EU standard or statutory guidelines (CA 2006 s504(1)). The senior statutory auditor must sign the audit report for all audits conducted by his or her firm.

seniti One hundredth of a pa'anga, currency of Tonga.

sensitive case Term used by HMRC in a notice of 20 December 2013 for a case whose decision could have a significant and far-reaching impact on HHMRC policy, strategy or operations. HMRC refers such a case to its Tax Disputes Resolution Board.

sensitive interest Personal interest which, if disclosed, could lead to the person being subject to violence or intimidation (Localism Act 2011 s32(1)).

sensitive risk Term used in HMRC Notice of 20 December 2013 about resolving tax disputes. Where the risk in a case is sensitive, the case should be referred to the Tax Disputes Resolution Board for guidance.

The term means an individual risk "where a decision to resolve a dispute might have a significant and far-reaching impact on HMRC policy, strategy or operations. In consequence, they may also be likely to prompt significant national publicity".

sensitivity In management accounting, the ratio of output to input. If a small increase in price leads to a large decrease in sales, the product or service is price sensitive.

The word has a similar meaning in the abstract as when a person reacts more strongly than would otherwise be appropriate.

sente One hundredth of a loti, currency of Lesotho.

sentence Punishment imposed by a court for breach of criminal law. Courts Act 1971 s57 states that the term includes hospital orders and recommendations for deportation.

Sentencing Code Statement of guidelines and procedures for passing sentences for criminal offences. This is now contained in Sentencing Act 2020.

sents One hundredth of a kroon, currency of Estonia.

Seoul Declaration Agreement reached in September 2006 between various national administrations on tax co-operation under the auspices of OECD. This work has continued to expand in subsequent years.

separate enterprise principle Principle used to determine corporation tax payable by a non-resident company (CTA 2009 s21).

For Northern Ireland, the principle is given in CTA 2010 s357NC.

separate use Term used in VATA 1994 Sch 8 Group 6 Item 2 in relation to zero-rating for approved alterations to a protected building.

The meaning of these words was considered by the upper tier tribunal in the case *HMRC v Lunn [2009] UKUT 244* in relation to a building within the curtilage of a protected building. It held that the words meant separate from other uses.

separation When a married couple or a civil partnership live apart without divorcing or formally ending the civil partnership. This does not require any legal proceedings. A couple may be separated even though they live in the same home, and when they co-operate in some areas, such as finance and their children.

A deed of separation may be made to formalise such an arrangement. The couple remain married or in a civil partnership.

A decree for separation may be granted by a court under Matrimonial Causes Act 1973 s17.

A court may order separation under Matrimonial Proceedings (Magistrates' Court) Act 1960 s2.

A separation order may be made for a civil partnership (Civil Partnership Act 2004 s179).

A separated couple are treated as two single people for most tax purposes.

The couple may still be regarded as part of the same household for social security purpose, depending on the facts of each case. In practice, if either party regards the marriage or civil partnership as finished, they will usually be regarded as separate households even when the other party hopes for reconciliation.

separation order The equivalent to divorce in a civil partnership (Civil Partnership Act 2004 s179).

sequestration

(1) Process of seizing the bank account or other assets as a legal procedure.
(2) Form of bankruptcy in Scotland.

Serbia East European country. Its currency is the Serbian dinar of 100 paras. The UK's double taxation convention with Yugoslavia of 1981 continues to apply.

serial tax avoidance regime (STAR) Anti-avoidance legislation introduced from 15 September 2016. It applies to a taxpayer who used a defeated tax avoidance scheme. Its main points are:

- STAR can apply to a single instance of tax avoidance
- STAR applies to all taxes including national insurance, apprenticeship levy, soft drinks industry levy and excise duties
- STAR applies in relation to any new tax avoidance scheme entered into from 15 September 2016, or entered into before then and defeated after 5 April 2017
- STAR applies to any scheme covered by general anti-abuse rule (GAAR) or disclosure of tax avoidance schemes (DOTAS)
- within 90 days of the defeat of an avoidance scheme, HMRC may issue a warning letter to the taxpayer that additional tax-geared penalties will apply if further avoidance schemes are used within the next five years
- during the warning period, the taxpayer is required to submit an annual information notice stating what, if any, avoidance arrangements have been used
- if a further scheme is defeated within the warning period, a penalty will be imposed of 20% of the tax avoided for the first defeat, 40% for a second, and 60% for a third or subsequence
- a defeat in the warning periods starts another five-year warning period
- an arrangement is defeated when all legal procedures have been concluded and it is determined that the arrangement does not work as the taxpayer intended
- a taxpayer who has suffered three further defeats may be publicly named, and will be restricted in relation to certain tax reliefs
- a taxpayer may receive a warning letter if associated with a taxpayer whose avoidance scheme has been defeated. Associated means in a partnership or a group of companies
- STAR does not apply if the taxpayer has settled the matter with HMRC before 6 April 2017.

Serious Fraud Office Government body formed in 1988 under Criminal Justice Act 1987 to investigate serious fraud, bribery and corruption in England, Wales and Northern Ireland, but not in Scotland. It is superintended by the attorney-general.

serious ill-health lump sum Lump sum paid to a member of a pension scheme where a doctor has certified that the member has less than one year to live. Such a lump sum may be paid at any age.

For a defined contribution scheme, the amount is the member's fund or pot. For a defined benefit scheme, the amount is a capitalised amount as calculated by the pension trustees.

The lump sum only applies to the part of the fund that has not crystallised as a benefit such as pension payments or drawdown, even if those benefits have not yet commenced. Details are given in SI 2006 No 572. The position is slightly different for payments before 16 September 2016.

If a member was in receipt of a pension from a scheme before 6 April 2006, a lump sum may only be paid for prospective rights on 6 April 2006.

If the payment exceeds the lifetime allowance, the excess is subject to income tax at 55%.

Otherwise, the lump sum is tax-free to a member who receives it before his or her 75th birthday. Where the sum is received by someone who is 75 or older, the amount is taxed as pension income, at the person's marginal rate of income tax. Before 16 September 2016, this payment was taxed at 45% (55% before 6 April 2015).

The relevant law is ITEPA 2003 s205A; FA 2004 s216(1) and Sch 32 para 15 and Sch 29 para 4.

Guidance is given in HMRC Manual at PTM063400.

serious loss of capital When the net assets of a company are worth less than half of its called-up share capital. A public company in such a situation must call a general meeting (CA 2006 s656).

Serious Organised Crime Agency Body established under Serious Organised Crime and Police Act 2005 s1. It was replaced by the National Crime Agency from 7 October 2013.

SERPS State earnings-related pension scheme. Government-backed additional pension arrangement which ran from 6 April 1978 to 2002, when it was replaced by the similar state second pension (S2P).

Under SERPS, employees pay some additional national insurance to secure more pension from the government. As originally planned, an employee who was a member of SERPS for his or her entire working life and who earned more than the upper earnings limit for national insurance would receive additional pension of 25% of band earnings. This would be a significant sum which could more than double the state pension.

In fact, the scheme did not last long enough for anyone to receive such a high figure, though state second pension is broadly similar. In 1999, the scheme was reduced in terms of benefits provided. The maximum benefit was progressively reduced to 20% of band earnings, among other changes.

More details are given under State Pensions in section 3 of this dictionary.

servant The term originally meant someone who worked for another person (the master or mistress) whether as an employee or in another capacity. The term now is more usually restricted to people in domestic services such as butlers, maids and gardeners.

It remains an offence for a master or mistress not to provide food, clothing and lodging so that the servant's life is endangered (Offences Against the Person Act 1861 s26). In practice, such a case is now more likely to be prosecuted under modern slavery laws.

serve In relation to postal services, "Where an Act authorises or requires any document to be served by post (whether the expression "serve" or the expression "give" or "send" or any other expression is used) then, unless the contrary intention appears, the service is deemed to be effected by properly addressing, pre-paying and posting a letter containing the document and, unless the contrary is proved, to have been delivered at the time at which the letter would be delivered in the ordinary course of post" (Interpretation Act 1978 s7).

service For VAT, a supply which is not of goods.

In many cases, it does not matter much whether a supply is regarded as of goods or services because the VAT rates and most of the rules are the same. The differences relate to a few provisions such as place of supply rules and pre-registration supplies received.

In other countries in the EU, there are different rates for services, which means the matter has been more litigated there.

The following have been held to be supplies of services rather than goods:

- repairs of items (*Van Dijk's Boekhuis BV v Staatssecretaris van Financiën [1985] ECJ Case 139/84)*
- catering *(Faaborg-Gelting Linien A/S v Finanzamt Flensburg [1996] ECJ Case C-231/94)*
- customised software *(Levob Verzekeringen BV v Staatssecretaris van Financiën [2006] ECJ Case C-41/04)*
- reprographic services of documents *(Grpahic Procédé v Ministère du Budget des Comptes publics et de la Fonction Publique [2010] ECJ Case C-88/09).*

service address Address at which a company director may be contacted (CA 2006 s1141(6)). This is either the director's home address or the company's registered office (CA 2006 s163(5)).

The company must know the residential addresses of all its directors and must convey this to Companies House. A director may request that his or her address is not made public (CA 2006 s1088). Statutory bodies, such as the police, have the right to know the address.

service by post This is generally regarded as having been completed when a properly addressed letter is sent in a postage-paid package, and sufficient time has passed for the letter to have been delivered in the ordinary course of post.

service charge

(1) Amount added to a bill, such as for waitering services in a restaurant. For VAT purposes, this is regarded as part of the catering service.

(2) Charge to tenants for maintenance of common parts.

service person Member of the armed forces or a civilian subject to service discipline under Armed Forces Act 2006.

If such a person dies from 19 March 2014 from being targeted because of their service status, their estate is free of inheritance tax (IHTA 1984 s155A). This is in addition to the long-standing exemption for those who die in military action.

Services Directive European directive 2009/2299 effective from 28 December 2009. It sets out the information which service providers must provide to clients and prospective clients.

service user number Reference number used by customers of banks who are authorised to collect payment by direct debit.

set off When a debt owed by A to B is reduced by a debt owed by B to A. This is not normal accounting practice.

HMRC may use this procedure in UK apart from Scotland, unless insolvency proceedings have been started (FA 2008 s130).

set rate A fixed amount, as against an amount relative to a variable figure. The term is used for statutory maternity pay after the first six weeks.

settled land Land that is limited by way of succession (Settled Land Act 1925). An example is where land is left to A for the rest of his life, and then to B.

settled property Assets put into a trust.

The term is defined specifically for capital gains tax in TCGA 1992 s68; for income tax in ITA 2007 s466; and for inheritance tax in IHTA 1984 from s43.

settled status Residence status offered to citizens of other EU citizens who have been UK resident for five years by the end of 2020. It does not apply to the Irish Republic where existing provisions continue. It is extended to citizens of Iceland, Liechtenstein, Norway and Switzerland.

A citizen of one of these countries already legally in the UK may remain until 30 June 2021, which is the deadline for applying for status. No fee is charged.

Application must be made for each person, including partners and children.

Someone with serious criminal convictions may be refused.

A successful applicant is given either settled status or pre-settled status. Settled status is given to someone who had been living in the UK for five years and was started living before 31 December 2020. Generally, this means a continuous period of five years though some absences are allowed. Pre-settled status is given to someone who was living in the UK on 31 December 2020 but does not have five years' residence. Such a person may apply for settled status when they have five years' residence.

Someone with settled status may work in the UK, claim benefits, use the NHS without charge and enrol in education.

settlement Financial arrangement where one party, the settlor, provides money or other assets for use by a beneficiary (which may include the settlor). All trusts are settlements, but "settlement" is wider and also includes such arrangements as a joint bank account.

There is no definition for tax purposes, except one for the limited purpose of tax avoidance. This defines a settlement as "any disposition, trust, covenant, agreement, arrangement or transfer of assets" (ITTOIA 2005 s620(1)).
For inheritance tax, a full definition is given in Inheritance Tax Act 1984 s43(2).

settlement day When the purchase of a security must pay for it. For the accrued income scheme, a definition is given in ITA 2007 s674.

settlement power For inheritance tax, "means any power over, or exercisable (whether directly or indirectly) in relation to settled property or a settlement" (Inheritance Tax Act 1984 s47A).

settlor Person who provides property in a trust and thereby creates the trust.
For capital gains tax, the term means "the person, or any of the persons, who has made, or is treated for the purposes of this Act as having made, the settlement" (TCGA1992 s68A(1). The section goes on to define settled property.
For income tax, an equivalent definition is given in ITA 2007 s467.
For inheritance tax, the term "includes any person by whom the settlement was made directly or indirectly, and in particular (but without prejudice to the generality of the preceding words) includes any person who has provided funds directly or indirectly for the purpose of or in connection with the settlement or has made with any other person a reciprocal arrangement for that person to make the settlement" (Inheritance Tax Act 1984 s44(1)).

settlor-interested Description of a trust where the settlor retains a benefit. Such a trust is subject to special capital gains tax provisions from 2008 (TCGA 1992 Sch 4A para 7(4)).

settlor's threshold amount The first slice of a trust's income that is generally exempt from income tax (ITA 2007 ss491-492). This is £1,000, divided by the number of trusts created by the settlor but never below £200.

severally Description of a liability that applies individually. In law, the expression "jointly and severally" is often used to mean that a liability may be enforced against a partnership, group or similar collectively or against any one member.

severance pay Another term for termination pay.

severe disablement allowance Social security benefit for severely disabled claimants (SSCBA 1992 s68). It is tax-free (ITEPA 2003 s677). The allowance is closed to new claimants from 2001, who instead may receive employment and support allowance.

severe disfigurement This can amount to a disability (Disability Discrimination Act 1995 Sch 1 para 3).

severe impairment of intelligence This is a factor that can determine eligibility for social security, such as disability living allowance. The criterion is generally accepted as an IQ of 55 or less.

severely sight impaired Description of a person with such limited vision that they are registered as blind. They qualify for blind person's allowance for income tax and may qualify for benefits.

Severn Bridges Two bridges that cross the River Severn on the M4 and M48 motorways. On 8 January 2018, they returned to public ownership which meant that VAT was no longer charged on the tolls. The tolls were scrapped on 17 December 2018.

Sewel convention Political convention that the UK government will not legislate on Scottish matters without the consent of the Scottish Parliament (Scotland Act 2016 s2 as amended). It is named after Lord Sewel.

sewerage Disposal of foul water. For domestic use, this is zero-rated under VATA 1994 Sch 7 Group 2. From 1 July 1990, it is standard-rated for business premises. Guidance is given in VAT Notice 701/16.

sex Whether a person is male or female. Changes in tax and national insurance law since 1970 mean that a person's sex is much less relevant and so it is now usual to allow a person not to say.

sex discrimination Treating one sex less favourably than the other. This has generally been illegal since 1975. The current law is Equality Act 2010 s11.

Sex discrimination includes discrimination on grounds of marital status or pregnancy.

It also includes indirect discrimination unless this can be justified.

From 2017, an employer with 250 or more employees must publish details of their gender pay gap (Equality Act 2010 (Gender Pay Gap Information) Regulations SI 2017 No 172.

sex industry Although legal, there are restrictions on its use of Jobcentres and government-sponsored employment programmes (Employment and Training Act 1973 s2A). Profits of the industry, legal or otherwise, are taxable.

sexual harassment Unwanted conduct of a sexual nature (Equality Act 2020 s26(3)). This includes inappropriate touching, comments of a sexual nature (even if intended as a joke), and displaying explicit pictures. ACAS produced guidance on the subject in June 2018.

sexual orientation Whether a person is homosexual or heterosexual. Since 2007, it is generally illegal to discriminate against a person on such grounds. The current law is Equality Act 2010 s12.

In 2011, HMRC produced booklet Pride 1 on issues for LGBT taxpayers. In it, HMRC says it will not accept a sex change without a gender recognition certificate but will accept a change of name and title by telephone. There are no specific tax provisions for LGBT taxpayers.

Seychelles Island republic in the Indian Ocean. Its currency is the Seychelles rupee. The UK has no tax treaty.

Seychelles rupee Currency of the Seychelles.

shadow ACT Unrelieved advance corporation tax that built up before April 1999. There are provisions whereby this may still be set off against corporation tax liabilities (SI 1999 No 358).

shadow Chancellor Member of the opposition party in Parliament who shadows the Chancellor of the Exchequer.

shadow director Person who acts as a director of a company even though he does not officially hold that position. Such a person usually has all the duties and liabilities of a director.

The statutory definition is "a person in accordance with whose directions or instructions the directors of the company are accustomed to act" (CA 2006 s251(1)).

Someone is not a shadow director just because he provides advice in a professional capacity (ibid s251(2)).

There are further legal provisions in Small Business, Enterprise and Employment Act 2015 s89, for which purpose a definition is given in s90.

shale gas Naturally occurring gas found in large amounts in shale formation. Its extraction is by a process known as fracking which must be licensed (Infrastructure Act 2015 ss43-48). From 5 December 2013, an offshore allowance was introduced to exempt 75% of capital expenditure from the corporation tax supplementary charge for ring-fenced profits.

Although fracking remains legal, on 2 November 2019, the government said it would not issue any more hydraulic fracturing consents.

sham civil partnership Civil partnership arranged solely or primarily to obtain UK residence (Immigration Act 2014 s55).

sham marriage Marriage arranged solely or primarily to obtain UK residence (Immigration Act 2014 s55).

sham transaction Transaction that is not genuine, though it may be legal. Under company law, the veil of incorporation may be lifted for a sham transaction.

The nature of a sham transaction is that documents do not represent the real nature of the transaction. This can apply when such documents are presented to HMRC as in *Hitch's Executors v Stone [2001] CA. STC 214.*

For VAT, input tax may not be claimed for a sham transaction. It is not necessary for HMRC to show fraud; it is sufficient that it demonstrates that the documented transaction is not genuine. Examples include *Plasma Trading Ltd v HMRC [2006]* and *Senergy (UK) Ltd [2006].*

shandy Mixture of beer with either lemonade or ginger beer. It is subject to alcoholic liquor duty only if its strength exceeds 1.2%.

share Part ownership of a company (CA 2006 s540(1)). The shareholders collectively own the company. It should be noted that this ownership is usually restricted to ordinary shares. A-shares and preference shares do not normally provide the element of ownership.

In the context of derivatives, a definition is given in CTA 2009 s710.

There are some tax-advantaged schemes relating to shares for both investors and employers, as noted in section 3 of this dictionary.

share capital Name given to the total amount of cash which the shareholders have contributed to the company.

share coupon Detachable part of a share warrant by which the bearer may claim a div (CA 2006 ss779-781).

shared car Company car that is shared by two or more employees (ITEPA 2003 s148).

share disposal Process by which a person no longer owns shares. The three methods are

- transfer: giving or selling them
- transmission: passing on death
- forfeiture: shares are lost such as for non-payment of a call.

share dividend Amount paid to shareholders in proportion to their holding. A company does not have to pay a dividend, even if profitable. A dividend declared on the basis of published accounts is a final dividend. A dividend paid between accounts is an interim dividend. Some old articles of association do not allow an interim dividend to be paid.

shared lives Scheme whereby an individual may look after an adult in a way similar to fostering. From April 2010, the tax provisions for fostering apply also to shared lives.

Shared Ownership and Affordable Home Programme (SOAHP) Full name of the Affordable Homes Programme. This broadly allows government funds to be used to provide affordable homes between 2016 and 2023.

shared parental leave Provision introduced in 2015 that basically allows a partner to share maternity leave and maternity pay. It replaced additional paternity leave.

share exchange Where shares in one company are exchanged for shares in another. If the company is a transparent entity, provisions of TCGA 1992 s140H apply. The matter was considered in the case *Ansyz v CIR [1977] Ch D 53 Tc 601.*

ShareGift Charity to which small holdings may be donated without any fees charged by registrars. These low value holdings, often of collapsed companies, are aggregated and sold. The proceeds go to charity.

shareholder Person who owns a share or shares in a company.

shareholders' funds Name given to total of share capital and reserves in a company balance sheet.

shareholding test For entrepreneur's relief, a test for a joint venture company. The test is broadly that the taxpayer owns 5% of the shares. The full test is set out in TCGA1992 Sch 7ZA paras 5-6.

share incentive plan (SIP) Tax-advantaged arrangement for employees to hold shares in their employer, introduced on 28 July 2000. They were previously known as all employee share option plans (AESOPs) or employee share plans (ESOPs) or employee share option trusts (ESOTs). The main points are:

- all employees must generally be eligible to participate. This may include directors and senior staff
- the plan must be approved by HMRC
- the plan must not contain any provision that is unnecessary to the scheme
- the employee may be issued with free shares with a value of up to £3,600 in a tax year (£3,000 before April 2014)
- the employee may then, if he or she wishes, buy partnership shares of up to £1,800 a year (£1,500 before April 2014)

- partnership shares must be bought by deduction from gross pay through the payroll. Thus income tax and national insurance relief is given at source
- matching shares may be issued by the employer at a ratio of two matching shares to one partnership share. Thus an employee may acquire £9,000 worth of shares for £1,800 (or less if tax relief is considered)
- the shares are held in a trust for between three and five years
- shares released to the employee after five years incur no tax charge
- dividends on shares paid to employees are taxed on the same basis as other dividends.

Details of tax implications for employees are given in ITEPA 2003 from s488.

Details of tax implications for employers are given in CTA 2009 from s983.

The position for trustees is given in ITA 2007 s488.

Capital gains tax provisions are given in TCGA1992 s236A and Sch 7A.

share loss scheme Unsuccessful tax avoidance scheme that seeks to produce losses to offset against taxable profits. Spotlight 15 explains why these schemes do not work.

share matching Capital gains tax rules for matching share disposals against acquisitions. Shares are ranked in the order of those bought on the same day; those bought in the previous 30 days; other shares.

share number Number allocated to a share certificate or shareholding. It is a legal requirement (CA 2006 s543).

share option Right to buy or sell shares at a future date for a fixed price.

"A contract that gives the holder the right, but not the obligation, to subscribe to the entity's shares at a fixed or determinable price for a specific period of time" (FRS 102 glossary).

There are two types of share option. The traditional option is simply buying the right. A traded option is a right which is itself a saleable security. Share options are sometimes provided free to directors and senior managers as an incentive.

A share option is a highly-geared form of investment. Suppose a person pays 20p for an option to buy a share for £2 in a year's time. If the share is then worth £1.99, the option is worth zero as it is cheaper to buy the shares on the open market. If the share is then worth £2.40, the investor makes an immediate profit of 40p per share, which is a return of 200%.

National insurance provision is given in Social Security Contributions (Share Options) Act 2001.

share premium Amount paid by a shareholder for a share above its nominal value. The company law is given in CA 2006 from s610.

share split When one share is divided into several share of smaller value to make trading them easier.

Share the Joy Government campaign launched in February 2018 to promote shared parental leave which has a low take-up rate.

share value The value of a share. Ultimately this is simply the amount someone else will pay for it. For listed shares, the value can be looked up in a newspaper. For unlisted shares, this is a matter of negotiation with HMRC.

For inheritance tax, listed shares are usually valued at the "quarter up" rule, where the value is the lower figure plus one quarter of the difference. So if a share has a list of 240-244, it will be valued at 241.

share warrant Rare form of share certificate where ownership is vested in whoever possesses the document (CA 2006 s779). Payment is made by presenting the company with a coupon that is detached from the certificate.

Sharia law Law and code of conduct for Muslims. One of the provisions is a ban on charging interest. Various alternative finance products have been designed to get round this ban. The general principle is that they are taxed on the same basis as the financial product they copy. Any taxpayer, regardless of religion, may use alternative finance products.

Sharkey v Wernher Leading House of Lords case from 1955. It decided that when goods are removed from a trader's business for the trader's personal use, this must be accounted for at the selling price and not cost price. This rule is now contained in statute law (ITEPA 2005 ss172A-172F; CTA 2009 from s156). The matter is discussed in HMRC Manual at BIM33630.

shearing For inheritance tax, when a person makes a disposition of less than the whole property, particularly for land. The principle was established in the case *Munro v Commissioners of Stamp Duties (New South Wales) [1934].*

Shed identity A 3-letter code that provides a unique identity for a transit shed located at a Cargo Community System (CCS-UK) airport.

shekel Currency of Israel.

shellfish For VAT, shellfish are only zero-rated if for food. VAT notice 701/15 defines this as "oysters, mussels, whelks etc".

In another context, "shellfish includes crustaceans and molluscs of any kind" (Diseases of Fish Act 1937 s10).

sheltered accommodation Living accommodation where assistance is available on site, such as from a warden.

There is an exemption from the national minimum wage where work and sheltered accommodation are provided as part of a programme to assist people back into normal life. The conditions for this exemption are:

- the worker is at least 26 years old;
- the shelter is provided as part of the rehabilitation programme;
- the worker is provided with training as part of the programme.

sheriff Court officer who oversees bailiffs.

sherry Alcoholic drink made from blending wine with spirits. It is an exception to some of the excise rules about blending of liquors (ALDA 1979 s71(2)).

shielding In relation to coronavirus, this was the requirement that extremely vulnerable people were required to stay at home for 12 weeks from 22 March 2020.

Arrangements were made to ensure that shielded people received food and medicine.
Such people received a shielding note. This allows them to claim statutory sick pay and to get priority home delivery from supermarkets.
For the second lockdown from 5 November 2020 to 2 December 2020, they were advised to stay at home.

shilling (1) Pre-decimal coin worth one twentieth of a pound, or 5p.
(2) Unit of currency in Kenya, Somalia, Tanzania and Uganda.

ship Large watercraft that sails oceans and deep waterways. There are many specific tax provisions for ships.
Seafarers may claim a special tax deduction (ITEPA 2003 s40). This does not include an offshore installation, even if it has floated there (ITEPA 2003 s40(5)(b) and s385).
A merchant shipping company may elect to use tonnage tax as an alternative to corporation tax on its shipping activities (FA 2000 s82 and Sch 22: SI 2000 No 2303). Details are given in section 3 of this dictionary.
For VAT, a supply of a ship is zero-rated if it is of at least 15 tonnes, is a lifeboat, a houseboat or a boat adapted for a disabled person (VATA 1984 Sch 8).
Capital gains tax provisions are given in TCGA 1992 from s94 The capital allowance provisions are given in CAA 2001 from s127. There is a special provision for claiming excess allowances for ships leased overseas (CAA 2001 s113).

shipbuilding This activity is excluded from eligibility for venture capital trust under ITA 2007 s307A.
This section defines shipbuilding as set out in EU Framework to State Aid on Shipbuilding 2003/C 317/06, where para 10 states: "'shipbuilding' means the building, in the Community, of self-propelled seagoing commercial vessels".

SHIP code of practice Code for businesses which offer various equity release schemes.

shop Place where the public may enter to buy goods. A definition is given in Employment Rights Act 1996 s43ZB(2) with regard to Sunday working.
Most shops were required to shut during the coronavirus lockdown from 26 March 2020 (SI 2020 No 350).

shoplifting Stealing goods from a shop. It is a criminal offence of theft under Theft Act 1968 s1.
A shoplifter may be arrested and taken into custody. If convicted by a court, the shoplifter may be imprisoned for up to six months for taking items up to £200, and for seven years for £200 or more.
If the goods stolen are worth less than £200, the offence may be dealt with under Anti-Social Behaviour, Crime and Policing Act 2014. For thefts below £200, a shoplifter may plead guilty by post.
About 80,000 cases of shoplifting come before the courts each year. Some shops have to increase prices by up to 10% to cover the losses from shoplifting. It is believed that there are about 1 million instances of shoplifting each year, with small convenience stores particularly vulnerable.

In 2017, the Metropolitan Police unilaterally decided they would not investigate shoplifting of goods below £50 unless a suspect was identified.
Supermarkets usually have cameras and security staff. They may apprehend a suspected shoplifter and detain them until the police arrive. The shoplifter will usually be banned from the store. Those convicted say they get away with it about nine times out of ten.

shore power Power supplied from the shore to a moored boat. HMRC takes the view that shore power is not sufficient in itself to establish that the boat is a main residence and exempt from CGT.

shortcake Food that is zero-rated for VAT. However, in the case *North Cheshire Foods Ltd VTD 2709*, the tribunal held that a small chocolate decoration of about 1% of the biscuit's content was enough to make it standard-rated.

short chargeable period Period of less than one year in which the annual investment allowance may be proportionately reduced (CAA 2001 s51L).

short-dated gilt Government security that is payable within five years.

short lease Lease which lasts for a short period, typically up to three years. In tax law, a term that applies to a **funding lease** where the term is either:

- less than five years; or
- between five and seven years *and* the lease meets three further conditions (CAA 2001 s70 I)

These conditions are that:

- the lease is treated as a finance lease in the books of the lessor;
- the residual value of the finance lease is less than 5% of the market value of the plant at the start of the lease term: *and*
- total rentals in the first year are no lower than 90% of the rentals in the second year. and rentals in any year after the second year are no greater than 110% of those in the second year.

The third of these conditions is to exclude leases where a large payment is made on the first day for tax avoidance purposes.

short life asset For capital allowance purposes, an asset which is plant and machinery but which is not a long life asset. The statutory definition is in CAA 2001 s83.
Broadly this is an asset that the business chooses to put outside the main pool of plant and machinery, with the consequence that a balancing allowance can be claimed for the full written down value when disposed of.
The asset must have an expected life of no more than eight years from 1 April 2011, or four years previously.

short payment period For PAYE, a payment period that is shorter than normal. This often happens for the employee's final pay period, or when pay day falls on 5 April (PAYE Regs 2002 reg 25(8)).

short position Situation where an investor sells short, that is he sells he does not yet own in the hope that he will be able to buy them more cheaply later.

short return Tax return form SA200 with accompanying notes on SA211. It may be used for self-assessment by taxpayers whose affairs are simple and straightforward.

short rotation coppice Method or planting willow which is cut back each year for fuel. From 2 November 1994, this is treated as farming and not as commercial occupation of woodlands. From 6 April 1995, land used for such purpose may qualify for agricultural property relief from inheritance tax.

shorts (1) Trousers that stop above the knee.
These are zero-rated for VAT if they qualify as clothing for young children. The matter is explained in VAT Notice 714. A case concerning elasticated sports shorts was *Falcon Sportswear Ltd [1985] VTD 2019.*
(2) Short-dated gilts, typically with a maturity of less than five years.

short selling Selling a security that the seller does not own, in the hope that it may be bought in time at a lower price. The Financial Conduct Authority has the power to stop short selling under Financial Services and Markets Act 2000 s131B.

short service benefit Term used for money purchase pension schemes in which the taxpayer was a member for a short period. Provisions are given in Pension Schemes Act 1993 s71 as amended.

short service refund lump sum Refund of pension contributions to someone who has less than two years' qualifying service (FA 2004 Sch 29 para 5).
From 1 October 2015, this is reduced to 30 days for those in defined contribution schemes (FA 2014 s36), but not for defined benefit schemes. The lump sum is taxed at (from April 2010) 20% up to £20,000, and 50% on the excess.
If the contributions did not attract tax relief, perhaps because the contributions exceeded the lifetime allowance, there is no tax on that element of any refund (ITEPA 2003 s636A).
Any interest paid on a refund is taxed separately.
The matter is discussed in HMRC Manual from PTM045000.

short skirt The VAT and economic implications are explained under miniskirt.

short-term advance Temporary loan that may be made to a social security claimant. They replaced alignment payments in 2013.

short-term annuity An annuity contract purchased from a member's unsecured pension fund held under a money purchase arrangement that provides that member with an unsecured pension income for a term of no more than five years (not reaching to or beyond their 75th birthday), and which meets the conditions imposed through paragraph 6, Schedule 28 to the FA 2004.

short-term assistance Money or other assistance that may be provided in Scotland under Social Security (Scotland) Act 2018 s36.

short-term benefit Contributory social security benefit paid for a short period. These are defined as short-term incapacity benefit and maternity allowance (SSCBA 1992 s202(2)). It also included jobseeker's allowance but this has been removed (WRA 2007 s67).

short-term capital Capital needed by a business for less than 12 months to fund its business activities.

short-term creditor Person to whom money is owed payable within next 12 months.

short-term debtor Person who owes you money payable within the next 12 months.

short-term employment Employment for a period of three months or less (Trade Union and Labour Relations (Consolidation) Act 1992 s282). Such an employee does not have protection against redundancy.

short-term hiring in Hire of a car for less than 45 days (CTA 2009 s58A). Such a hire is generally wholly tax-deductible and not limited to 85% of the hire charge.

short-term lease Generally, a lease of land with less than 50 years to run.

short-term leasing Leasing of plant and machinery for less than 30 consecutive days, or for no more than 90 days in a 12-month period (CAA 2001 s121(1). Such a lease avoids restrictions on capital allowance that would otherwise apply (CAA 2001 s105). The matter is discussed in HMRC Manual at CA24100.

short-term security Any form of security that matures within five years.

short ton American measure of weight equal to 2000 pounds. This is less than the British ton of 2240 pounds or metric ton (or tonne) of 2204 pounds. The British ton is 12% heavier, the short ton is 11.72% lighter. The short ton weights 907.185 kilograms.

showcasing Arrangement where someone in the arts arranges an exhibition, concert or similar to demonstrate their talent. Provided this has a genuine commercial motive, it is tax-advantaged.
A leading case is *Lunt v Wellesly [1945] 27 TC 78.*
The matter is discussed in HMRC Manual at BIM37785.

show of hands Common method of voting. It is allowed at general meetings of companies under CA 2006 s284(2). The vote is of the number of shareholders regardless of their shareholdings. Members may request a written ballot, in which case the vote is according to the size of shareholdings.

showroom tax Informal term for the higher rate of vehicle excise duty for the first year of a new car, introduced in 2008.

shrinkage Amount by which something reduces in size. In finance, it particularly refers to losses from shoplifting and staff theft.

shrinkflation Term coined in 2017 to mean when consumer goods are reduced in size for the same price rather than having the price increased.

shroff Far Eastern money lender, particularly one who evaluates coins.

shroud For VAT, this is exempt if provided as part of a funeral service. Further details are given in VAT notice 701/32.

shuttle mediation Form of mediation where the parties are not together. The mediator moves between them conveying each side's position to the other. This is a slow and inefficient process which is discouraged, but may be necessary if the parties cannot or will not be together.

Shylock Grasping money lender, from the character in the play *Merchant of Venice* by Shakespeare.

sibling Brother or sister.

sic bo Chinese dice game that from 23 April 2002 is specifically listed as subject to gaming licence duty (BGDA 1981 s13(3)).

sickie Colloquial term for when a worker pretends to be sick to get a day off work.

sickness benefit Social security benefit once paid to those who were sick. It has now been replaced by other benefits such as statutory sick pay, universal credit, and employment and support allowance.

sideways loss relief When a loss from a trade may be offset against other income of the same year or previous year (ITA 2007 s64; CTA 2010 s37). From 1 April 2017, it may be carried forward to a later year. This relief is subject to several anti-avoidance provisions introduced from 2007.

From April 2013, relief is generally capped at the greater of £50,000 and 25% of income (FA 2013 s16 and Sch 5). From 12 March 2008, the relief is restricted to £25,000 for individuals who conduct a trade but spend less than ten hours a week on commercial activities (FA 2008 s60 and Sch 21).

Sierra Leone East African country. Its currency is the leone of 100 cents. The UK has a double taxation agreement of 1947 amended by a protocol of 1968.

sight draft Bill of exchange which is payable when presented.

signature Stylised form of writing one's name which is widely used to signify assent to a document.

A paper tax return must be signed (TMA 1970 s8(2)). An unsigned paper return is automatically rejected. For online returns, equivalent security comes from the use of a password and activation code.

Accounts sent with a tax return need not be signed. In the case *Codu Computer Ltd [2011] TC 1055,* a late filing penalty was cancelled when the accounts, submitted by the due date, were sent back for signature.

For someone who cannot sign on their own behalf, an attorney may sign for them, under statement of practice A13 of 18 June 1979.

The signature does not have to be legible or even based on the person's name. An identifying mark can be a signature. Legible signatures are often considered to be harder to forger.

A signature is valid if signed by a rubber stamp or machine, or is pre-printed such as on a cheque. A handwritten signature is called a wet ink signature.

Copying a signature can be the criminal offence of forgery (Forgery Act 1913 s1). It may also be fraud, depending on what is being signed.

Detecting forged signatures is difficult. A survey in 2002 found that experts rejected 5% of genuine signatures and 71% of forged signatures.

signed accounts The accounts of a company must be approved by the directors (CA 2006 s414(1)). The balance sheet must be signed on behalf of the directors (s414(2). If the accounts are prepared on the basis for small companies, a statement to that effect must appear immediately above the signature (s414(3)).

The auditor's report is also signed. In practice, a few copies of the accounts are hand signed with "wet ink signatures". Other copies of the accounts have the name printed or a facsimile of the signature.

There is no requirement for business accounts submitted with a tax return to be signed. HMRC lost a case where they imposed a penalty for late submission because the accounts were returned for signature *(Codu Computer Ltd [2011] TC 1055).*

significant This is an accounting concept. Accountants and auditors should be concerned about significant amounts and not be bothered about insignificant ones. A figure is considered significant if it changes the picture painted by the accounts. Former accounting standard-rated FRS 5 attempted a definition that the term "should be judged in relation to those benefits and risks that are likely to occur in practice, and not in relation to the total possible benefits and risks".

significant accounting transaction For the purposes of a dormant company, this means a transaction that is required to be entered into the accounting records under CA 2006 s386 (CA 2006 s1169(2)). In practice, simply receiving income such as bank interest and payment of an audit fee are not regarded as significant.

significant difference In statistics, a difference which indicates a relationship between results. This is usually regarded as being around 20%.

If a test to see if there was any correlation between A and B showed average results of 1.03 with B and 1.07 without B, there is no significant difference, as such a difference could just be down to statistical sampling. If the results were 1.03 and 1.27, there is an indication that there probably is some significant different. This leads on to considerations of causation.

significant equity stake investment In relation to the taxation of derivatives, this is given a specific meaning in ITA 2007 s809FZL(3).

significant influence In relation to associated companies, this is the power to participate in the financial or operating policy of the association which stops short of control (FRS 102 glossary).

The term is also used in deciding whether a member of an limited liability partnership should be taxed under PAYE (HMRC Technical Note of 10 December 2013).

significantly below cost This term is used in relation to VAT on welfare services. These are treated as not being a business supply if the charge is less than 85% of the cost to the welfare provider (VAT Notice 701/1).

significant pain or discomfort Term used in VAT notice 701/2 in relation to the supply of welfare services.

If a person cannot perform routine domestic tasks without significant pain or discomfort, an organisation performing such tasks for such a person may be providing a zero-rated supply.

significant people function One of three conditions for a controlled foreign company to come within the scope of UK tax.

significant tax dispute Term used in two Notes issued by HMRC on 27 and 28 February 2012. They relate to transparency and to management of the dispute. Neither Note defined the term, though the former refers to disputes involving at least £100 million in tax.

signing-on fee Fee paid to someone to join an organisation. It is widely used in sport. The fee is now almost always taxed as income. The matter is discussed in HMRC Manual at EIM00700 and EIM00710.

silk Term for a senior barrister who is a Queen's Counsel (QC). They wear silk gowns.

Silk v Fletcher Leading tax case relating to the allowability of interest paid. Its full citation is *Silk v Fletcher [1999] PC 201,* and *[2000] SPC 262.*
The case is discussed in HMRC Manual at BIM45725.

silo Airtight chamber or pit used for storing grain or similar. This qualifies for capital allowance as plant and machinery.

silver Precious metal traditionally regarded as second to gold. It has the atomic symbol Ag. It has been used for coins since 600 BC. In the UK, silver coins were made of sterling silver (92.5% silver, 7.5% copper) until 1925. It was then replaced with a 50% alloy until 1940. From 1940, only commemorative coins use real silver. Coins for 5p to 50p are made from cupro-nickel to 2011 and nickel-plated steel from 2012. Cupro-nickel coins are now being removed from circulation.
The pound currency was originally the value of a pound weight of silver. Unlike gold, there is no special VAT provision for silver.

simalcrum Sham arrangement.

SIM card Small electronic card that stores data and can be put into a mobile phone or similar device. The letters stand for Subscriber Identification Module.

simony Offence of buying or selling a spirituality. The term comes from Simon Magus in chapter 8 of Acts of Apostles in the Bible. It is no longer a criminal offence under English law, but can invalidate a contract, and justify dismissal and excommunication of a priest. It is also a serious offence under canon law.

simple assessment Assessment raised by HMRC on the basis of what HMRC knows about the taxpayer. The taxpayer may pay the assessment or may appeal within 60 days. A simple assessment is issued on form P800 or PA 302. The latter is a simple assessment letter. A taxpayer who pays a simple assessment, knowing that it understates the tax that is owed, is liable to a penalty.
The law is contained in FA 2016 s167, effective from 6 April 2017. The first simple assessments were issued on 22 September 2017.

simple interest When interest is charged on a principal amount but not also on interest previously added. So 10% of £100 earns interest of £10 for each year indefinitely. Under the alternative of compound interest, the interest for year 1 would again be £10. For year 2, the 10% interest would be calculated on £110, including the previous interest, and so would be £11 rather than £10. Tables of compound interest factors are given in section 3 of this dictionary.
On 25 July 2018, the Supreme Court finally ruled that interest payable by HMRC was calculated on a simple interest basis and not compound interest (*Prudential Assurance Company Ltd v HMRC [2018] SC).*

simple lottery Lottery where all the prizes are awarded by chance (Gambling Act 2005 s14(2)). This covers almost all lotteries, including the National Lottery.

Simplified Administrative Accompanying Document (SAD) Tax form C88 for duty paid goods moving between European Union (EU) and EEA Member States.

It was introduced in 1987, and extended to include Turkey in 2012 and North Macedonia in 2015.

Its legal basis is EU council regulation 2013/952 and subsequent laws.

For goods despatched from the UK on or after 1 January 2021, exporters no longer used a SAD but must use the excise movement and control system (EMCS). An export declaration may also be required.

simplified deduction scheme Modified form of PAYE that could be used for domestic staff before April 2014. Such staff must now have income tax and national insurance deducted under the normal PAYE system.

simplified declaration procedure Scheme that allows exporters to submit abbreviated details of exports to Customs at export, and provide further details within 14 days.

simplified deduction scheme Variation of the PAYE scheme that could be used for domestic staff before April 2014. It may no longer be used.

simultaneous or later disposal value For disposals under a finance lease, this term is defined in ITA 2007 s614BS(6).

For anti-avoidance, the term is defined in CTA 2009 s918(6).

simulation Mathematical method of solving problems that can be quantified but not calculated. It involves the use of random numbers, such as may be generated on a scientific calculator, Excel spreadsheet or taken from random number tables.

A simple example is that there are three eventualities whose probabilities are 60%, 30% and 10%. These can be allocated the numbers 1 to 60, 61 to 90, and 91 to 100. Random numbers are generated and the consequences noted. This exercise is repeated until a consistent result or range of results is discerned.

Such methods can be used to check the credibility of trading revenue for tax purposes.

sine die Latin: without day. Expression used to refer to a case that is adjourned indefinitely.

Singapore Eastern country. Its currency is the Singapore dollar of 100 cents. The UK has a double taxation agreement of 1997, a protocol of 2010 and two protocols of 2012.

Extra-statutory concession A49 applies to the widow of a man of Singapore nationality who was resident in the UK and worked as a public official for the government of Singapore.

Singapore dollar Currency of Singapore.

singer The European Court of Justice ruled in a German case that the performance of solo singers did not come within the scope of VAT exemption for cultural services under what was the Sixth Directive Article 13A(1)(n), as that referred only to "bodies" and did not apply to individual performances. *(Hoffmann. ECJ Case C-144/00 [2004] STC 740).*

single administrative document (SAD) Tax form C88 that must be produced for Customs in respect of imported goods. It is used in the EU and some other countries from 1987. It is an eight-part document.

single asset pool Pool for capital allowances which only contains one asset. (CAA 2001 s54(3)). Assets that must be put into such a pool are:

- short life assets (CAA 2001 s86)
- ships (CAA 2001 s127)
- plant and machinery for a non-qualifying activity (CAA 2001 s206)
- partial depreciation subsid (CAA 2002 s211)
- contribution allowances for plant and machinery (CAA 2001 s538).

single claim Claim for tax credits by a single person, as against a joint claim. (Tax Credits Act 2002 s3(8)).
Similar claim for universal credit (WRA 2012 s40).

single compliance process Arrangement between HMRC and a small or medium-sized enterprise or its tax agent to establish in advance the tax risks to the enterprise. It was launched on 7 February 2012 with a view to ending later that year, but is continuing. It involves several steps starting with an initial review, asking the taxpayer for more information, processing that information and discussing it with the taxpayer, and then resolving the issue.

single currency Name used for the EU currency that became the euro.

single dwelling interest Term for a single property within the scope of annual tax on enveloped dwellings (FA 2013 s108).

single dwelling transaction For stamp duty land tax, a transaction whose "main subject matter consists of –
(a) an interest in a single dwelling, or
(b) an interest in a single dwelling and other property"
(FA 2003 Sch 6B para 3(2)).

single entry bookkeeping Method of recording transactions without using double entry bookkeeping. Although not illegal, it is not recommended.

Single Finance Guidance Body Body created by the Department of Work and Pensions to give advice to the public from January 2019 on pensions, money matters, debt, and consumer protection.

single-income claimant In relation to incapacity benefit, this term is specifically defined in PAYE regulations SI 2003 No 2682 reg 173.

single investment project In relation to the cap on first year allowances for plant and machinery in designated assisted areas, "has the same meaning as in Commission Regulation (EU) No 651/2014 (General Block exemption regulations)". (CAA 2001 s212U(5)).

Single Market Term used from 1993 for the market of the European Union. It became a reality in 2003.

single member company Limited company which has one shareholder (CA 2006 s123).

single payment scheme (SPS) Scheme for paying farmers under common agricultural policy until 2015 when it was replaced by the basic payment scheme.

single person For the purpose of the benefit cap for social security, "means a person who is not a member of a couple" (WRA 2012 s96(10)).

single premium bond Life assurance policy sold as an investment (ITTOIA 2005 s484). Each year, 5% cumulative of the sum deposited may be withdrawn without triggering a tax liability. The whole sum is taxed at the end. There is no capital gains tax on such a bond.

single ship pool Balance of expenditure for a ship that must be kept separate from other capital expenditure for capital allowance purposes under the provisions of CAA 2001 s127. An explanation is provided in HMRC Manual at CA 25150.

single statement approach Accounting option that produces a single profit and loss account (or statement of comprehensive income), and does not replace it with two statement where income is shown separately. The accounting requirements are given in FRS 102 section 5.

single taxable person For VAT, one person who runs a business or businesses. If the businesses is artificially split, HMRC has power to aggregate them (VAT notice 700).

single-tier adviser Financial adviser who advises on the financial products of only one company and is usually and employee of that company.

singleton brewery Brewery that has one premises (ALDA 1979 s36D-36F).

single total remuneration figure Total amount received by the chief executive of a company with 250 or more employees. From 1 January 2019, it is required for disclosure of the CEO pay ratio.

singular In legislation, a singular word includes the plural unless the context indicates otherwise (Interpretation Act 1978 s6).

sinking fund Money put aside to meet a future requirement. Details are given in section 3 of this dictionary.

sinking stone Large stone with a hole cut in it to accommodate a rope. It is used by smugglers to keep goods below the sea.

Sint Eustatius One of the islands of what was known as the Netherlands Antilles.

Sint Maarten One of the islands of what was known as the Netherlands Antilles.

SIP Share incentive plan.

sister company Company that is part of the same group but is not the holding company.

site of the old dwelling In relation to annual tax on enveloped dwellings, means "the land on which the dwelling stood and that counted as part of the dwelling" (FA 2013 s127(5)).

site preparation Making ground ready for a new building. There are provisions on tax deductions for disposal of waste materials (ITTOIA 2005 from s165; CTA 2009 from s143).

site restoration Payment to restore a site that has been used for disposing of waste. From 6 April 1989, such a payment is generally tax-deductible (ITTOIA 2005 s168(3)); CTA 2009 s145).

site-wide operation Arrangement whereby someone who operates an amusement arcade may account for VAT on the basis of all machines rather than for each machine separately (VAT notice 701/13). HMRC permission must be obtained.

sitting day In relation to tax administration, means a day when the House of Commons is sitting (Provisional Collection of Taxes Act 1968 s1(5C)).

sitting places Where a tribunal may sit (Tribunals, Courts and Enforcement Act 2007 s26).

six counties The counties of Northern Ireland.

sixpence Pre-decimal coin worth six old pence, half a shilling or one fortieth of a pound, or 2½p in decimal currency. It was demonetised on 30 June 1980.

skilled employee condition The condition for a knowledge-intensive company that at least 20% of the workforce has a master's degree or doctorate (ITA 2007 s252A). Such a company is eligible for more generous investment under enterprise investment scheme and venture capital trust.

For venture capital trusts, the same provisions are given in ITA 2007 s331A(9).

skill machine Machines that provides quizzes or otherwise tests the user's knowledge. They are not regarded as gaming machines (VAT Notice 701/13).

skimming pricing Pricing policy which starts at a high price which is then reduced to make the product available to a wider market.

skirting In relation to a caravan, the supply of a skirting is regarded as an integral part of the supply of a caravan. For VAT, the treatment of the skirting is the same as for the caravan.

slab basis Where a tax charge increases but applies to the whole charge not to slices. This basis was used for stamp duty land tax before 2015 (2016 for commercial property). It still applies in some limited areas of tax, such as for determining the benefit of a staff party.

slatted flooring area This qualifies as plant and machinery (at the higher rate) in the pig industry when used in connection with a slurry system (HMRC Brief 03/2010 issued on 23 February 2010).

slaughter Tax provisions for the compulsory slaughter of animals are given in ITTOIA s225ZA, effective from 1 March 2012.

slavery Ownership of one person by another. It was formally abolished in the UK in 1807 having been held to be illegal by the courts in 1772. The current law is Trade Union and Labour Relations (Consolidation) Act 1992 s236. There are separate laws for modern slavery, particularly Modern Slavery Act 2015.

slavery contract Contract whereby an entertainer sells his or her services to a company in exchange for a regular income.

Such income is generally assessable as employment income, except that the broadcaster David Frost managed to maintain his self-employed status in a case in 1980 when he sold his services to an American company.

sleep-in shift Where a worker sleeps on the premises while on-call. In 2017, the employment appeal tribunal had held that such workers were entitled to the national minimum wage for the whole period while on-call, even while asleep. This decision was reversed by the Court of Appeal in 2018 in the case *Mencap Society v Tomlinson-Blake [2018] EWCA Civ 1641.*

sleeping partner Member of a trading business who has contributed finance but plays no part in the management of the business. There are limits on the amount of tax relief a sleeping partner may claim for losses.

slice basis Determining a tax liability where different rates are charged on different slices of income. Income tax and most other taxes now use this basis.

slimming products These are standard-rated for VAT and do not benefit from the zero rating for food. Details are given in VAT Notice 701/14.

slippers These are zero-rated for VAT as children's clothing below size 3 *(R v Spencer (Cosy Comfort Slippers) Ltd [1991] VTD 7945).* They could not benefit from zero-rating for girls' shoes up to size 5½, as slippers are generally suitable for either sex.

slot length In relation to television product relief, "means the period of time which the programme is commissioned to fill" (CTA 2009 a1216AB(7)).

Slovakia European country that is a member of the European Union. Its currency is the euro of 100 cents. The UK double taxation convention of 1990 with Czechoslovakia continues to apply.

Slovenia European country that is a member of the European Union. Its currency is the euro of 100 cents. The UK has a double taxation convention of 2007.

slow moving stock Inventory that takes longer to sell than was expected. HMRC may be willing to accept that its net realisable value is less than cost, as discussed in HMRC Manual at BIM33145.

slow payer Customer who is habitually late in making payment. In itself this does not make sums owed into tax-deductible bad debts unless there is evidence of the customer's poor financial health. The matter is discussed in HMRC Manual at BIM42710.

sludge dewatering system This qualifies as plant and machinery (at the higher rate) in the pig industry (HMRC Brief 03/2010 issued on 23 February 2010).

slurry storage Place where farmers (and some others) are required to store fertilisers under The Control of Pollution (Sludge, Slurry and Agricultural Fuel oil) Regulations 1991. The regulations are tightened up in Nitrate Vulnerable Zones from 1 January 2009. Slurry storage typically comprises a tank or pit, with pipes or channels.

Guidance on the right to claim capital allowances for slurry storage was given by HMRC in *HMRC Brief 66/2008.* Broadly this allows the facilities to claim allowances as plant and machinery, except to the extent that they comprise buildings.

slurry storage systems This qualifies as plant and machinery (at the higher rate) in the pig industry (HMRC Brief 03/2010 issued on 23 February 2010).

small brewery beer Beer produced in quantities of less than 60,000 hectolitres a year (ALDA 1979 s36D). Such beer attracts a lower rate of beer duty, as explained in Customs notice 226.

small business An entity below a certain size, given in section 3 of this dictionary. It has reduced duties for accounting, and benefits from some tax provisions, such as for research and development. Statutory definitions are given in Small Business, Enterprise and Employment Act 2015 s33(2) and Enterprise Act 2016 s2(1).

Small Business Commissioner (SBC) Position created by Enterprise Act 2016 s1(1). The function is:

"(a) to provide general advice and information to small businesses..., and

(b) to consider complaints from small businesses relating to payment matters in connection with the supply of goods and services to larger businesses..." (ibid s1(2)).

small business rate relief Scheme introduced in 2005 to provide relief for small businesses in premises with a low rateable value. The scheme has been much extended.

small company Company that meets two of these three conditions: turnover up to £10.2 million; balance sheet total to £5.1 million; no more than 50 employees. These limits apply from 1 January 2016. More details are given in section 3 of this dictionary.

small craft Sea-going vessel of up to 100 tons. They may be given a Customs licence which exempts them from some Customs regulations.

small disposal Small disposal on a capital distribution (TCGA 1992 s122(2)), a share reorganisation (ibid s116(3)), conversion of securities (ibid s133(2), or compulsory acquisition of land (ibid s32(1)(a)). In such cases, the amount received is treated as a reduction of acquisition cost for capital gains tax, and not as a disposal.

The law does not define "small", but HMRC has said it will accept the greater of £3,000 or 5%, and will consider higher figures.

Guidance has also been given in the case *O'Rourke v Binks [1992] STC 703.*

small earnings exemption Annual income below which a self-employed person need not pay class 2 national insurance (SSCBA 1992 s11(4)). The limit is now the same as the annual primary threshold for class 1 national insurance, which is £9,500 for 2020/21.

The taxpayer with low earnings may choose to pay class 2 to maintain his or her national insurance record for the state pension. It costs less than class 3 that would otherwise need to be paid. Paying class 2 also entitles the taxpayer to some benefits that class 3 does not, such as employment and support allowance.

small employer's relief (SER) Additional amount of statutory maternity pay and related benefits that may be recovered from the state by a small employer. A small employer is one whose national insurance in the previous year did not exceed £45,000 (unchanged since 2004).

Such an employer may claim 100% plus a compensation rate to reflect the employer's national insurance. The compensation rate for 2020/21 is 3%, so the employer claims 103% of statutory maternity pay. Other employers may claim only 92% (SSCBA 1992 s167).

Further details of rates are given in section 3 of this dictionary.

small gift exemption For inheritance tax, a gift of up to £250 per person per year (IHTA 1984 s20). Such gifts are not added back to the estate.

There is no limit to the number of people who may receive small gifts under this exemption. If a gift to a person exceeds £250, this whole exemption is lost. It cannot be used to reduce the value of the gift.

This exemption cannot be combined with other exemptions.

A gift that does not meet the conditions for this exemption may be exempt under other provisions, such as the annual exemption or normal expenditure out of income.

small gift from third party Gift of up to £250 that an employee may receive from a third party without it counting as a taxable benefit (ITEPA 2003 s324).

small holding

(1) Plot of agricultural land that is not big enough to be called a farm. It was defined in Small Holdings and Allotments Act 1926 as being between 1 and 50 acres.

(2) A holding of securities up to £5,000. Such a holding is generally excluded from tax provisions for accrued income scheme (ITA 2007 s639).

small LLP Regulations The Small Limited Liability Partnerships (Accounts) Regulations SI 2008 No 1912.

small loan In relation to peer-to-peer lending, this means a loan of £25,000 or less (ITA 2007 s412I(8).

small maintenance payment Maintenance paid for a child or former spouse of up to £48 a week. This was paid gross before 6 April 1988.

Generally maintenance payments from then are regarded as non-taxable income in the hands of the recipient (ITA 2007 s453) and not tax-deductible in the hands of the payer.

small non-commercial consignments relief Relief that was once available for small quantities of excisable goods. It was abolished from 19 July 2007.

small or medium-sized enterprise (SME) An entity below a certain size, given in section 3 of this dictionary. It has reduced duties for accounting, and benefits from some tax provisions, such as for research and development.

small pack For beer duty, a container of up to 10 litres. For such packs, the average size rules apply, as explained in Customs notice 226.

small part disposal Disposal of part of land with a value up to £20,000 (TCGA 1992 s242). In some circumstances, this may be regarded as a reduction of acquisition cost rather than a disposal for capital gains tax.

small pension pot Personal pension pot which contains no more than £30,000, or up to three pension pots, each of which contains no more than £10,000. The member may receive the whole amount in cash. The first 25% is tax free.

small pool balance Amount in a capital allowance pool that has fallen below £1,000. From 2008, a capital allowance may be claimed for the whole amount (CAA 2002 s56A).

small producer For soft drinks industry levy, someone who produces up to one million litres of soft drink in a year (FA 2017 s38(7)).

small profits rate Lower rate of corporation tax that applies to smaller companies for periods before 1 April 2015 (CTA 2010 s3).

small ship For Customs purposes, means a ship with a registered tonnage of up to 100 tons, or a hovercraft of any size (CEMA 1979 s81(1)).

small works contract Contract for building work of fairly small amount, typically less than £500,000.

smart charge point Charging point for an electric vehicle that can receive and process information as set out in Automated and Electric Vehicles Act 2018 s15.

smart contract Blockchain that includes program code in addition to data. The code can automatically generate journal entries and ledger entries in the accounting records.

smart phone Mobile phone that has additional functions such as camera, Internet access and games.

Under HMRC Brief 02/12, HMRC now accepts that such a telephone comes within the scope of a mobile phone that an employer may provide to an employee without its being a taxable benefit in kind (ITEPA 2003 s319).

The mobile phone exemption does not apply to laptops, tablets and similar devices even if they have telephony facilities.

HMRC has said it will keep this matter under review as technological developments may blur the distinction between a computer and a mobile phone.

[Smartphone is sometimes written as a single word.]

smell test Term used by Exchequer Secretary David Gauke MP in a speech on 23 July 2012 about artificial tax avoidance schemes. If the "arrangements stink", advisers should "stay well clear".

smishing Impersonating HMRC or a reputable body in a text message as a means of obtaining personal details. (Oxford Dictionary accepted this as a word in 2017.)

Smith, Adam Scottish philosopher (1723-1790) who developed theories of the political economy that are still widely quoted.

His most popular work is *The Wealth of Nations* published in 1776 and subsequently reprinted with amendments.

smokeless fuel Alternative to coal. A miner may receive free such fuel or an allowance in lieu of such fuel. The fuel or allowance is tax free under ITEPA 2003 s306. A similar provision applies for former miners under ibid s646.

smoking Burning tobacco or similar, and inhaling the smoke for pleasure. It is now discouraged by the government because of its negative impact on health.

Smoking in buildings (other than a private home) was generally banned from:

- 26 March 2006 in Scotland
- 2 April 2007 in Wales
- 30 April 2007 in Northern Ireland
- 1 July 2007 in England.

Other restrictions have been introduced to discourage smoking:

- 1 August 1965: TV cigarette advertisements are banned
- 1971: first health warnings appear on cigarette packets
- 1991: all tobacco advertising banned on television
- December 2002: large health warnings appear
- 14 February 2003: all forms of tobacco advertising are banned
- 14 May 2003: sponsorship by tobacco companies is banned
- May 2004: advertising in tobacconists is banned
- 21 December 2004: large adverts in shops and pubs are banned
- 2006: limits imposed on exports of tobacco
- 1 October 2007: minimum age for purchase raised from 16 to 18
- 1 October 2008: pictorial images added to health warnings
- 1 October 2011: cigarette machines are banned
- 6 April 2015: cigarette displays must be covered in shop
- 1 October 2015: illegal to smoke in a car with anyone under 18
- 20 May 2016: illegal to sell packets of less than 20 cigarettes
- September 2016: plain packaging starts to be phased in
- 20 May 2020: ban on menthol cigarettes.

Tobacco products are subject to tobacco products duty under TPDA 1979. Rates are given in section 3 of this dictionary. The products are also subject to VAT.

A first tier tribunal has held that a gazebo in the grounds of a pub to provide rain cover for smokers outside was plant and not premises, and so qualified for a capital allowance *(Mrs C A Andrew [2011]. TC 799).*

smuggling Importing goods and avoiding Customs controls and taxes. The practice has been known since 13th century.

Customs' power to deal with smuggling is now found in CEMA 1979 ss19-51 and other statutes.

snipe Bid placed at the last moments of an online auction with a view to preventing any higher bids.

snowballing When two or more companies "trade" with each other when they are under the control of the same person, to create the illusion that the companies have high turnover.

snow clearing machine "A vehicle is an excepted vehicle when it is —

(a) being used, or

(b) going to or from the place where it is to be or has been used, for the purpose of clearing snow from public roads by means of a snow plough or similar device (whether or not forming part of the vehicle)" (HODA1979 Sch 1 para 7).

snuff Tobacco powder. It is traditionally taken in a small amount by pinching some between a finger and thumb and inhaling it. It may be scented. Snuff is exempt from tobacco products duty but subject to value added tax. Nasal snuff product is banned from sale in the UK under the Tobacco for Oral Use (Safety) Regulations 1992.

Social Fund Part of the social security system that provides one-off loans and payments for particular circumstances.

It provides budgeting loans, Sure Start maternity grants, funeral expenses payments, cold weather payments, and winter fuel payments. From 2013, some of the discretionary forms of help are covered by local welfare assistance.

social care compliance scheme Scheme operated by HMRC between 2016 and 2018 in relation to the national minimum wage for sleep-in duties.

In 2016, the employment appeal tribunal ruled that a worker was entitled to be paid national minimum wage for all hours on call, even if asleep. This created a large liability for the social sector. The scheme allowed such employers to register with HMRC where they were given time to pay the backdated arrears. In July 2018, the Court of Appeal overturned the tribunal decision. The scheme was closed on 31 December 2018.

Social Chapter Part of the EU Maastricht Treaty of 1991, ratified in 1993, which helped create the European Union. The Chapter deals mainly with workers' rights.

social distancing Space required between people during the coronavirus outbreak. This is generally two metres (SI 2020 No 350).

social engineering Implementing policies, such as by adjusting tax rates and reliefs, to achieve a desired social outcome.

social enterprise Business that is run for its benefit to society rather than for profit.

Social Fund Part of the social security system. It comprises budgeting loans which must be repaid, and grants which are not repaid. The main points about budgeting loans are:

- they are available in England, Scotland and Wales (not Northern Ireland)
- they are not available to someone receiving universal credit. They should seek a budgeting advance of universal credit instead
- the claimant must be receiving a qualifying benefit, broadly income support, jobseeker's allowance, employment and support allowance or pension credit
- the benefit must have been received for at least 26 weeks before making the application
- the amount of loan is reduced if the claimant has capital of more than £1,000, or £2,000 if over 63
- the loan must be for specific necessary expenditure such as clothing, furniture, bills, rent, and expenses in seeking or re-entering work
- the minimum loan is £100

- the maximum loan for 2020/21 is £348 for a single person, £464 for someone with a partner, £812 for someone with a child
- loans must be repaid within 104 weeks, usually by deduction from benefits.

The other element of Social Fund comprises various grants that are not repaid. These are:

- Sure Start maternity grants, payable to some social security claimants who are pregnant or have given birth in the last six months
- funeral expenses payment, payable to some social security claimants who have accepted responsibility for paying for a funeral
- cold weather payments, payable to some social security claimants when the temperature in their area is below 0C for seven consecutive days
- winter fuel payments.

social housing Accommodation that is provided on the basis of need rather than price.

"Social housing is let at low rents on a secure basis to those who are most in need or struggling with their housing costs. Normally councils and not-for-profit organisations (such as housing associations) are the ones to provide social housing." (Shelter website).

The policy for who qualifies is now made by local authorities under provisions of Localism Act 2011.

Provisions relating to annual tax on enveloped dwellings are given in FA 2013 s150.

social investment In relation to charities, the term is defined in Charities Act 2011 s292A as inserted by Charities (Protection and Social Investment) Act 2016 s15.

social investment tax relief (SITR) Tax relief introduced in 2014 and revised in 2017. The relief was due to end on 5 April 2019 but has been extended to 5 April 2021. The law is ITA 2007 Part 5B and SI 2014 No 3066.

social investment In relation to charities, the term is defined in Charities Act 2011 s292A as inserted by Charities (Protection and Social Investment) Act 2016 s15. It gives tax relief to individuals for investment in social projects. The individual may claim 30% of the investment against his or her income tax liability. There are other tax benefits, and conditions. The main elements are:

- it is only available to individual, not companies
- the individual may claim 30% of the sum invested against their income tax
- the investment must be held for three years or the tax relief is lost
- there is no capital gains tax on the disposal
- any dividends paid are subject to income tax
- the investee must be for a defined and regulated social purpose
- the investee organisation must have fewer than 250 employees (500 before 6 April 2017) excluding volunteers, and assets of no more than £15 million
- an investee organisation must be cleared by HMRC before accepting investment under SITR
- an individual may invest in more than one social enterprise provided the total of all such investments does not exceed £1 million
- from 2015, it is possible to invest through a social venture capital trust.

For investments from 6 April 2017, the limit for the same raised by the investee increases to £1.5 million (F2A 2017 s14 and Sch 1). Other changes are made.

social media service Body that may be liable to pay digital services tax (FA 2020 s43(3)).

social security Arrangements whereby the state makes payments to citizens according to their circumstances. These fall into three broad categories:

- contributory benefits that depend on the claimant having sufficient national insurance contributions, such as jobseeker's allowance
- non-contributory benefits that are paid regardless of contribution record or income level, such as child benefit
- means-tested benefits that are paid to claimants on a low income, such as universal credit.

Payments that replace income are generally taxed as income (ITEPA 2003 s661). Payments that meet need are generally not taxed (ITEPA 2003 s656).

social security co-operation Co-operation between the UK and EU on social security is provided for in EU/UK withdrawal agreement of 24 December 2020. The relevant provisions are given effect in UK law by European Union (Future Relationship) Act 2020 s26.

social security fraud Deliberately claiming social security benefits to which the person is not entitled. The claimant can have a financial penalty imposed, or be sanctioned. During the sanction period, either no benefit is paid, or the benefit is paid at a reduced rate. Where there has been no deliberate fraud but negligence, the claimant is liable to a civil penalty (from October 2012) of £50.
Social security fraud is also a criminal offence.

social wage Economic term for the value of publicly-funded facilities provided to citizens at no direct cost, such as health services, emergency services, roads, parks, libraries and the police.

Societas Europaea (SE) Form of European company created under EU Council Regulation 2157/2001 article 8 from 2004. Such companies are intended to be able to trade freely in any EU state. By April 2018, only 3,015 registrations have been made, of which most are in the Czech Republic. It may be registered in the UK when it becomes UK resident for corporation tax (CTA 2009 s16).
The tax provisions for a group that includes an SE are given in CTA 2009 s770.

Society of Trust and Estate Practitioners (STEP) Professional body for trust and estate practitioners. STEP "is a unique professional body providing members with a local, national and international learning and business network focusing on the responsible stewardship of assets today and across the generations" (STEP website). Full members use the designatory letters TEP.

soft drink For the purposes of soft drinks industry levy, "means —

(a) a beverage of an alcoholic strength not exceeding 1.2%;
(b) a liquid which, when prepared in a specified manner, constitutes a beverage within paragraph (a)" (FA 2017 s26(1)).

"A liquid is prepared in a specified manner if it is —
(a) diluted with water

(b) combined with crushed ice, or processed as to create crushed ice,
(c) combined with carbon dioxide, or
(d) prepared by way of a process that involves any combination of the processes mentioned in paragraphs (a) to (c)"
(FA 2017 s26(2)).

soft drink industry level Tax introduced on 6 April 2018 on the soft drinks industry on products containing 5 or more grams of added sugar per 100 millilitres of drink (FA 2017 from s26). A higher rate applies for more than 8 grams. The tax only applies where sugar has been added. It does not apply to drinks where sugar occurs naturally as in orange juice or milk.

software Programs and similar that run computers. If bought outright, software can qualify as plant and machinery for capital allowances (CAA 2001 from s71). For research and development, there are provisions from CTA 2009 from s1125. As Customs duty is charged on goods and not services, there is no duty on software alone. Duty can be charged on a tangible product, such as a CD, on which software is supplied.
In accounting, software is treated as part of the computer and is depreciated on the same basis as hardware.

solar panel Device that converts sunlight to electricity. When fitted to a residential or charitable building, it may qualify for the reduced rate of VAT under VATA 1994 Sch 7A Group 2. This is a form of microgeneration for which there are various tax reliefs.

solar shading This is a feature integral to a building and so qualifies for the lower rate of writing down allowance (CAA 2002 s33A).

sold loose Term used by retailers for items which are not pre-packaged but where the customer selects the quantity, such as fresh fruit and vegetables which are traditionally sold by weight.
For VAT, such items must be capable of ready identification by the check-out staff, who can weigh the item and enter an appropriate code to determine the price.

solera System of blending wines to make sherry.

sole trader Simplest form of trading entity, simply consisting of an individual. For income tax, a sole trader is taxed on all his or her profits.

solicitor Lawyer who deals directly with clients. They are regulated by the Solicitors Regulation Authority from 2007.

Solicitors Regulation Authority (SRA) Body launched on 29 January 2007 to regulate solicitors. It was previously the Law Society Regulation Board. The change of name reflects its greater independence.

solid fossil fuels Coal, petroleum coke, lignite, coke, and semi-coke of coal or lignite. The carbon price support rate of climate change levy is payable when these are used to produce electricity.

solid fuel When supplied for domestic use, this is reduced-rated for VAT under VATA 1994 Sch 7A Group 1. Further details are given in VAT Notice 701/19.

solidum In Scots law, a complete sum of money.

Solomon Islands Island country in Pacific Ocean. Its currency is the Solomon Islands dollar of 100 cents. The UK has a double taxation arrangement of 1950 as amended by an arrangement of 1974.

Solomon Islands dollar Currency of Solomon Islands.

solus account Term sometimes used to mean accounts of an entity rather than one that pertains to its client. There is a restriction in an entity hedging certain foreign exchange in a solus account. This is discussed in HMRC Manual at BIM39522.

solvency The financial status of being able to pay bills as they fall due.

Solvent Yellow 124 Dye used in EU states to indicate road fuel on which hydrocarbon oil duty has not been paid.

som Currency of Kyrgyzstan.

Somalia West African country. Its currency is the Somali shilling of 100 cents, though other currencies are also widely used. The UK has no double taxation treaty. The country is subject to UK sanctions, as are designated persons of the country.

Somali shilling Currency of Somalia.

Somerset House Large building in London by Waterloo Bridge. HMRC (and its predecessor bodies) used some of it between 1789 and 2013.

somoni Currency of Tajikistan.

son's or daughter's services allowance Additional tax allowance between 1935 and 1988 when a taxpayer was dependent on a son or daughter. Before 1978, it could only be claimed for a daughter.

SORN Statutory off-road notice. Such a notice can be filed with the DVLA to confirm that a vehicle is not being used on public roads and is therefore exempt from vehicle excise duty.

SORP Statement of recommended practice. This is a non-binding accounting standard for a particular sector, such as charities or the oil industry.

sort code Code that indicates each branch of each bank, introduced from 1957. The code comprises six digits, usually represented as three pairs in the form 12-34-56.

sou An old French coin worth 5 centimes. By extension, any low value coin or small amount of money.

sound recording Corporation tax provisions are given in CTA 2009 from s150.
"Sound recording does not include a film soundtrack" (ibid s152(1)(a)).
Such expenditure is excluded from a degrouping charge under CTA 2009 s811.
Income tax provisions are set out in ITTOIA 2005 from s130.

source doctrine Principle that income tax is charged according to its source. This was considered by the Court of Appeal in the case *Ardmore Construction Ltd v HMRC [2018] EWCA Civ 1438*. The principle is explained in HMRC Manual at BIM14065.

source fund In relation to overseas pensions, this is a ring-fenced transfer fund as explained in FA 2004 Sch 34 para 1(6D).

source principle Tax principle that UK tax can be determined according to the source of the funds. The matter was considered by the Court of Appeal in the case *Ardmore Construction Ltd v HMRC [2018] EWCA Civ 1438.*

South Africa African country. Its currency is the rand of 100 cents. The UK has a double taxation convention of 2002 and a protocol of 2010. It also has a double taxation agreement of 2002 amended by a protocol of 2010.

South Georgia UK Overseas Territory administered from the Falkland Islands. It uses UK currency.

South Sudan African country that gained independence from Sudan in 2011. Its currency is the South Sudanese pound of 100 piastres. The UK has no double taxation treaty.

The country is subject to UK sanctions, as are designated persons of the country.

sovereign (1) Gold bullion coin first minted in 1489. Those minted from 1838 are legal tender for £1, though worth much more as bullion. They ceased to be used as everyday currency in 1914. An attempt to avoid tax by paying low wages but paying them in sovereigns for pounds failed in *Jenkins v Horn [1979].* Sovereigns come within the special VAT scheme for gold coins.

(2) The office of the monarch (Interpretation Act 1978 s10).

sovereign debt Money owed by a state or government. From 20 March 1990, banks are limited in the amount of tax relief they may claim for such debts.

Sovereign Grant State funding of the monarch and royal family from 2013, replacing the previous Civil List (Sovereign Grant Act 2011).

space activity This is launching or procuring the launch or the return to earth of a space object or aircraft carrying a space object, operating a space object, or any activity in outer space (Space Industry Act 2018 s1(4)).

spacecraft It is possible to claim capital gains rollover relief for spacecraft (TCGA 1992 s155 Class 3).

space heater This qualifies as a feature integral to a building and thus for the lower rate of capital allowance for plant and machinery (CAA 2002 s33A).

Spain European country that is a member state of the European Union. The state includes the Balearic Islands, but excludes the Canary Islands, Ceuta and Melilla. Its currency is the euro of 100 cents, before which it was the peseta. The UK has a double taxation convention of 2013.

spare part Although these are often regarded as accessories for normal trading purposes, they are not so regarded for tax. The stock and sale of spare parts is treated the same as for main products. The fitting of a spare part usually comes within the scope of a repair which means it is wholly tax-deductible. It is a matter of fact and degree when such fitting becomes a replacement which is treated as capital expenditure.

sparkling Description of wine that is fizzy, which is defined as having carbon dioxide making the pressure at 20ºC at least 3 bars in excess of atmospheric pressure (ALDA 1979 s59). Sparkling wine with alcoholic content above 5.5% is taxed more heavily than still wine. There are also provisions for sparkling cider (ALDA 1979 s62A(2)). These are noted in section 3 of this dictionary.

spear phishing Phishing that is aimed at a particular person, company or small group, rather than a mass audience.

special administrative region The Hong Kong or the Macao Special Administrative Region of the People's Republic of China (ICTA 1988 Sch 25 para 5(4)).

special annual allowance charge Income tax charge that may be imposed when a person's pension contributions have exceeded a limit (FA 2009 Sch 35).

special auditor's report Statement from the company's auditors that the company may submit abbreviated accounts to Companies House (CA 2006 s49). The statement must be submitted with the accounts.

special case exemption Exemption from the provisions of optional remuneration arrangements (ITEPA 2003 s228A).

special codes PAYE tax codes that do not follow the usual form of a number and a letter (PAYE Regulations 2003 reg 7(3)). Special codes are BR, D0, D1, NT and emergency codes.

Special Commissioners Trained tax professionals who heard tax appeals until replaced by tax tribunals in 2009. Special Commissioners' decisions from March 1995 have been published, providing an additional body of tax law.

special crossing Crossing on a cheque with a place or name of bank indicated. The cheque may be cashed only at that place or bank (Bills of Exchange Act 1882 s76(2)).

special cumulation The hypothetical total used to calculate the ten-year charge of relevant property trusts for inheritance tax (IHTA 1984 s68). The total is the sum of the settlor's chargeable transfers in the seven years before the commencement of the settlement, plus the amounts on which the exit charge has been imposed in the previous ten years.

special Customs procedure One of a storage procedure, a transit procedure, inward processing or an authorised use procedure or temporary admission procedure (Taxation (Cross-border Trade) Act 2018 s3(5)).

special destination Provision under Scots law whereby a person automatically inherits jointly owned property from a spouse or civil partner (Family Law (Scotland) Act 2006 s19). The provision ceases to apply if the marriage or civil partnership ends (Succession (Scotland) Act 2016 s2).

special drawing rights An international reserve asset of the International Monetary Fund, first created in 1969 to supplement member countries' official reserves. It is not a currency though it is similar in operation to one. Its value is based on a basket of five currencies: US dollar, euro, Chinese yuan, Japanese yen and pound sterling.

special film relief In relation to provisional entitlement to film loss relief, the term is defined in CTA 2009 s1212(1).

special guardian Person appointed by a court to be a child's guardian (Children Act 1989 s14A).

special indorsement When a cheque or bill of exchange has been indorsed to a specified person (Bills of Exchange Act 1882 s34(2)).

special leasing Leasing other than as part of a business. There are special provisions for capital allowances (CAA 2001 s190). Special leasing of plant and machinery is set out in CAA 2001 from s258. Further provisions are given in statement of practice SP 3/91.

special licence

(1) One of three types of licence that was required for amusement machine licence duty. These provisions are now replaced by machine games duty,

(2) Licence issued by the Archbishop of Canterbury under Canon B34 to allow a person to marry in a church without banns being called.

Special Liquidity Scheme Government-backed scheme introduced in April 2008 by the Bank of England during the banking crisis.

special lump sum death benefits charge Charge to income tax that arises when certain types of lump sum death benefit are paid in respect to someone who had reached the age of 75. It is generally subject to the income tax charge of 45% (FA 2004 s 206(4)).

For payments from 6 April 2016 to an individual, the 45% charge is replaced by using the emergency tax code under PAYE for that individual. If the individual as a result pays too much income tax, he or she may claim a rebate.

special method In relation to VAT partial exemption, a method for working out how much residual input tax a business may claim if the standard method does not give a fair and reasonable result. Use of a special method requires HMRC approval.

special mixed funds rules Rules that allow employees who do some work overseas to use a simpler system than the normal mixed funds rules. The rules are given in ITA 2007 ss809RA-809RD. HMRC produced Guidance on 27 June 2013.

specialist printing equipment Equipment that may be used to produce a counterfeit banknote or a document such as a passport. It is an offence or provide such equipment without authority (Specialist Printing Equipment and Materials (Offences) Act 2015 s2.

special procedure rule Business records and journalistic material that are protected from police seizure under Police and Criminal Evidence Act 1984 s14.

special purpose vehicle A company, trust or other body set up for a particular financial transaction. The accountancy treatment is given in FRS 102 sections 9.10-9.12.

special rate pool For capital allowances, the pool for long-life assets (CAA 2001 s104C). Assets in the pool are written down by 6% a year (8% before April 2019; 10% before April 2012).

special relief Relief that can allow an excessive tax assessment or determination to be displaced after the normal time limit has expired (F2A 2015 s52). In 2011, it was introduced to replace equitable liability.

special repayment rate Rate of interest that may be applied to a tax judgment debt under Finance (No 2) Act 2015 s52. It is two percentage points above the base rate.

special resolution Decision where company law requires a 75% vote in favour (CA 2006 s283(1)).

special seal A trader seal that HMRC may allow a trader to use as an alternative to an official Customs seal. Details are given in Customs notice 205.

special tax credit Provision that relates to aggregates levy in Northern Ireland (FA 2001 s30B).

special television relief "Means –

(a) television tax relief, or

(b) relief under section 1216DC (transfer of terminal losses from one relevant programme to another"

(CTA 2009 s1216E(1)).

Special Territories Countries or areas that are not part of the EU, but are treated as part of its Customs Union. It includes the Channel Islands.

special trust For charities, property that is held for a specific purpose (Charities Act 2011 s287).

special verdict Verdict that a person committed a criminal offence but was insane at the time (Trial of Lunatics Act 1883 s2). Acquittals on the ground of insanity may be made under Criminal Procedure (Insanity and Unfitness to Plead) Act 1991 s1. Procedures are governed by Criminal Procedure (Insanity) Act 1964 s5.

special video games relief In relation to video games tax relief, "means –

(a) video games tax relief, or

(b) relief under section 1217DC (transfer of terminal losses from one video game to another)" (CTA 2009 s1217E(1).

specific bequest Provision in a will that leaves a specific item to a person, such as leaving an item of jewellery to a named grandchild.

specific devise In executorship, a specific piece of land that is left in a will.

specific duty Customs duty that is charged according to quantity, such as so much per kilogram or litre.

specific gravity Ratio of weight of a liquid to the same quantity of water. Before 1993, this was used to calculate beer duty.

specific legacy When a particular item of property is left in a will.

specific purpose financial statement Document containing financial information which is prepared for a particular purpose and is not normally available to a wider audience.

specified percentage Figure used in the calculation of the default surcharge for VAT. The term is defined in Value Added Tax 1994 s59(5).

specimen charges Legal practice that a person who has committed a large number of offences is charged just with a few of them. This applies to tax law as to other branches of criminal law.

speculative cost Any cost incurred without knowing whether it will lead to a return. If the cost does not lead to a return, it is known as an abortive cost. For VAT, these terms are specifically used to mean the cost of finding sites for possible building development. A speculative cost is regarded as a genuine business expense on which input tax may be reclaimed. If a developer later decides to proceed with an aborted scheme, it may be necessary to apportion the abortive cost between business and non-business use and disallow the latter.

spent conviction A conviction for a criminal offence where sufficient time has passed for that conviction to be considered irrelevant for such purposes as seeking insurance or employment (Rehabilitation of Offenders Act 1974, amended in 2014). A period of imprisonment of four or more years is never spent.
There are some exceptions, such as working in finance.
The rehabilitation periods have been reduced in Scotland from 1 November 2020 under Management of Offenders (Scotland) Act 2019. Similar reductions are proposed for the rest of the UK.

spes succesionis Latin for "hope of succession". It relates to the next of kin where someone did not leave a will.

spillage Accidental loss of liquid. There are special reliefs from alcoholic liquor duty for spillages.

spinner device Any device fitted to a car to enable a disabled person to turn the steering wheel. It can be as simple as fixing a knob to the wheel.
The presence of such a device is sufficient to justify the zero-rating of a vehicle as for the disabled under Value Added Tax 1994 Sch 8 Group 12 Item 2A.
This was held in the case *Dennis George Bunning and Christina Denise Bunning. TC 1730 [2012].* This case also held that the restrictions quoted by HMRC in VAT notice 701/59 were stricter than the law allowed.

spiral binding The use of spiral binding can determine whether a product comes within the scope of a VAT zero-rated book. An example is in the case *Harrier LLC. TC 1562 [2011].*

spirits Liquor produced by distillation and which is subject to the highest rates of alcoholic liquor duty. It includes such liquors with an alcoholic strength above 1.2% or which are mixed with such liquors (ALDS 1979 s1(2)). From April 2006, all spirits must display a duty stamp.

spirits of wine Plain spirits of a strength not less than 80% manufactured in the United Kingdom (ALDA 1979 s4(1))

spirits receiver Part of the still in which spirits are distilled. Customs notice 39 states that, unless the receiver is approved as a warehouse vat, remnants in a spirit receiver must be collected and removed before any newly produced spirits are put in.

spiritual welfare A form of welfare service that may be VAT exempt. Details are given in VAT leaflet 701/2 and in HMRC Manual at VATWELF4050.

split level trust Unit trust where the capital growth and income streams are split and sold separately.

splitting of supplies When a single supply for VAT is split into two, so that one part can benefit from a lower rate. Such splitting was generally made ineffective from 19 July 2011 by VATA 1994 Sch 8 Part 2 Notes (2) and (3).

split year treatment Arrangement where, exceptionally, a taxpayer may be regarded as UK resident for part of a tax year instead of for a whole tax year. From April 2012, this is included in the statutory residence test, summarised in section 3 of this dictionary. Previously the treatment was allowed by extra-statutory concessions.

spoilage When liquor is spoiled or has become unfit for use. Alcoholic liquor duty may be reclaimed for spoilt beer (ALDA 1979 s46), spoilt cider (ALDA 1979 s64(1)) or spoilt wine (ALDA 1979 s61(1)).

spoiled stamp For stamp duty, a provision that allows repayment when the document fails to achieve its purpose. The procedure is given in Stamp Duties Management Act 1891 s9.

spoilt beer Beer which "has become spoilt or otherwise unfit for use" (Alcoholic Liquor Duties Act 1979 s46). Such beer may have its beer duty remitted or repaid.

spoilt cider Cider which "has accidentally become spoilt or otherwise unfit for use and.... has been returned to the maker" (Alcoholic Liquor Duties Act 1979 s64(1)). Cider duty may be remitted or repaid on spoilt cider.

spoilt wine Wine or made-wine which "has accidentally become spoilt or otherwise unfit for use and... has been returned to the producer" (Alcoholic Liquor Duties Act 1979 s61(1)). Wine duty may be remitted or repaid on spoilt wine.

sponsored walk Walk organised to raise funds. For VAT, this is generally regarded as outside the scope of tax. VAT Notice 701/1 says that incidental benefits such as a free T-shirt may be ignored.

sponsoring employer Employer who provides an occupational pension scheme for staff (FA 2004 s150(6)). Further information is given in HMRC Manual at RPSM02200040.

sponsorship Commercial arrangement whereby a business provides funds in return for a benefit. This is a commercial arrangement similar to advertising, and not a charitable one. HMRC will want to see evidence of the commercial value, and that the sponsorship is not in reality the proprietor indulging a private interest. The matter is discussed in HMRC Manual at BIM42555.

sport For charity law, activities and games that promote health by physical or mental skill or exertion (Charities Act 2011 s3(2)(d)).

For tax purposes, such as community amateur sports clubs, the definition is narrower, largely being confined to physical activities.

sports drinks For VAT, sports drinks are zero-rated as food unless marketed as products to enhance physical performance or similar (VATA 1994 Sch 8 Group 1 Note 4A, effective from 1 October 2012. Guidance is given in VAT Notice 701/14.

sports facilities When provided by an employer, this is generally not regarded as a taxable benefit in kind (ITEPA 2003 s261).

sports grounds Safety at such grounds may qualify for a specific capital allowance under CAA 2001 from s30.

sports league For VAT, such services are generally standard-rated, as explained in HMRC Brief 4/11. The leagues are not providing an exempt supply of land use.

sports testimonial Sports event or similar held to raise funds for the benefit of a particular person, such as on their retirement. As such funds are considered a gift, they had not been taxable. This was the decision in *Reed v Seymour]1927]*. From 6 April 2017, testimonials are subject to income tax and national insurance on the amount above £100,000 where the testimonial had been announced after 24 November 2015. The tax charge is given in ITEPA 2003 Part 7A; the national insurance charge by National Insurance (Termination Awards and Sporting Testimonials) Act 2019 from s3.

Spotlight Information published by HMRC explaining why it believes a tax avoidance scheme is ineffective. A list is given in section 3 of this dictionary.

spousal exemption Exemption from inheritance tax when an estate is inherited by a husband, wife or civil partner (IHTA 1984 s18). It is unlimited unless the spouse was not UK domiciled when, from 2013, the exemption is limited to £325,000.

This provision only applies to couples who are legally married or in a civil partnership. There have been several unsuccessful challenges by unmarried couples.

spouse Husband or wife. Although this term does not include a civil partner, tax law generally treats a civil partner as a spouse. There many tax consequences of marriage. These include:

- transfers between the parties are exempt from inheritance tax
- transfers between the parties are treated as no gain/no loss for capital gains tax
- they are associated persons or connected persons for many tax provisions
- one partner may transfer one tenth of their personal allowance to the other.

spread Difference between buying and selling prices, particularly of financial products. Depending on context, this is also known as turn or gross profit.

spreading election Election made by a taxpayer under FA 2002 Sch 22. Where there has been a change of tax law affecting an accounting period start ends after 31 July 2001, the taxpayer may be able to make an election to spread the consequential adjustments over six accounting periods. The matter is discussed in HMRC Manual at BIM34120.

spreadsheet Computer-based table on which data are stored and tabulated. The most popular form is the Excel spreadsheet produced by Microsoft. It is ideal for tax computations as it avoids arithmetical errors and makes adjustments and corrections easy.

spring statement Statement made in spring, usually March, when the Budget was in autumn. In 2016, it was announced that a November Budget and spring statement was to be the norm. In 2019, there was no Budget at all. In 2020, the

Budget was in March with a further Budget planned for November 2020 cancelled.

spritzer Mixture of white wine and soda water. If sold already mixed, it is subject to alcoholic liquor duty as wine.

squeeze-out Term for when a shareholder has acquired 90% of the shares in a coronavirus and requires the remaining shareholders to sell to him (CA 2006 from s979).

squirrel Hide money away for later use, in a similar way that squirrels hide nuts.

Sri Lanka Island country in the Indian Ocean, formerly known as Ceylon. Its currency is the Sri Lankan rupee of 100 cents. The UK has a double taxation convention of 1979 amended by an exchange of notes in 1980. Britain gave independence under Sri Lanka Republic Act 1972.

Sri Lanka rupee Currency of Sri Lanka.

SSS islands Sint Maarten, Saba, and Sint Eustatius. This is an island group in the eastern Caribbean sea to the east of Puerto Rico. Before 2010, they were part of Netherland Antilles, widely used for international tax planning.

stabling Accommodation for a horse or other animal. For VAT, an exclusive right is an exempt supply of land. The lessor may charge VAT if he or she has exercised an option to tax. Any other supply, such as animal feed, is standard-rated. Details are given in VAT Notice 701/15.

staff Collective term for a workforce. Wages, salaries and other staff expenses are generally tax-deductible for income tax or corporation tax. There are specific tax provisions for staffing costs in relation to research and development (CTA 2009 s1123) and land remediation (CTA 2009 s1170).

staff bureau Business that provides staff for other businesses. They are generally treated for tax as an employment agency. VAT guidance is provided by VAT Notice 700/34.

staff entertainment This includes Christmas parties, staff outings and similar events. These are generally tax-deductible by the employer.

They are not a taxable benefit in kind to the employee unless the cumulative annual cost exceeds £150 per person attending (not necessarily an employee). If they do, the whole cost of the one that breaches the limit is a taxable benefit. So if an employer provided three parties that each cost £60, the first two would not be taxed while the whole £60 of the third would be. The cost includes VAT even if the employer can reclaim this as input tax.

For VAT, VAT Notice 700 says "you may recover VAT incurred on staff entertainment to the extent that the expenditure relates to the purpose of your business".

staffing costs In relation to tax relief for research and development, this term is defined in CTA 2009 s1123.

In relation to land remediation expenditure, the term is defined in CTA 2009 s1170.

staff provider In relation to externally provided workers engaged in research and development, this term is defined in CTA 2009 s1127.

staff provision payment In relation to externally provided staff for research and development, this term is defined in CTA 2009 s1127.

stage gate Point in a process where a particular matter must be addressed. HMRC used the term in its guidance notes on transfer pricing issued on 10 July 2008.

stage manager Person who supervises the technical aspects of a dramatic performance. Sometimes stage managers also stand in for absent actors. On 5 March 2010, HMRC issued Guidance Note 5 regarding the extent to which stage managers may be taxed on the same basis as Equity contract actors, that is paying income tax as self-employed but national insurance as employees.

stage payments Payments made during the course of a contract, particularly in construction. For VAT, there is a tax point in respect of each stage payment at the earlier of when an invoice is issued and when payment is made.

stagger Schedule of months for which VAT and insurance premium tax are payable. Generally, the taxpayer may choose his or her own series of stagger months.

staging date Date by which an employer is required to have arranged auto-enrolment for employees in a workplace pension.

staircase tax Informal name given to the additional business rates that could be payable following the Supreme Court decision *Woolways v Mazars [2015]*. This held that two parts of a building must be separately rated if separated by a common part, such as a staircase or corridor. The decision was reversed in legislation by Rating (Property in Common Occupation) and Council Tax (Empty Dwellings) Act 2018 s1.

staircasing Practice of making payments by a co-owner of a property to gain a larger stake. Stamp duty land tax provisions were amended in March 2008.

These give the co-owner the option of paying SDLT on the whole price at the outset, in which case no further SDLT becomes payable.

Alternatively, SDLT can be paid on the amount paid for the co-owner's interest in the property plus the net present value of rent payable. In practice, SDLT is often not payable on the rent element. No further SDLT is then payable until the person owns at least 80% of the property.

stake (1) interest or investment in an organisation, asset or activity.

(2) Amount placed as a bet or wager.

stakeholder pension Personal defined contribution pension introduced in April 2001 (Welfare Reform Pensions Act 1999 s2). An employer of five or more people had to offer a stakeholder pension but does not have to contribute to it, unlike workplace pensions.

A stakeholder pension may still be taken out by someone who is employed, self-employed or unemployed. It has the advantage of low charges.

stale cheque Cheque which the payee has not paid into his account and where the time limit for doing so (usually six months) has expired.

staleness In tax, the doctrine that a discovery assessment can become stale, and thus unenforceable, by the passage of time.

This principle was expressly stated by the first tier tribunal in the case *Bashir Ahmed Jafari [2019] TC 7465.* HMRC issued a discovery assessment under Taxes Management Act 1970 s29 when it was issued 30 months late and nothing new had been discovered in that period.

HMRC argued that staleness was "unsound and devoid of statutory authority". Although the term is not used in the Act, the doctrine of staleness has been upheld by the Court of Appeal in the case *Tooth v HMRC [2019] EWCA Civ 825.* It had also been upheld by the upper tribunal in *Beagles v HMRC [2018] UKUT 38 (TCC).*

The taxpayer had not raised the issue of staleness; the tribunal did so on its own volition. The tribunal criticised HMRC for its refusal to accept the doctrine.

stall In terms of a stand at an exhibition at an exhibition or fair, or similar arrangement, this is standard-rated for VAT as a supply of a service. There have been some cases where it was held to be exempt as use of land.

stamp Means of marking a document such as by impression, printed mark or paper impression.

For stamp duty (but not stamp duty land tax), stamp is defined by Stamp Act 1891 s27.

Stamp Act Law of 1891, amended many times, giving the law on stamp duty.

stamp album Folder or similar that contains (usually) used postage stamps.

HMRC regards this as standard-rated stationery and not zero-rated book unless no more than 25% of the space is reserved for mounting stamps. A folder, originally produced by the Post Office, and containing stamps was held to be zero-rated in the case *S P Schusman [1994] VTD 11835.*

stamp duty ***Overview***

Tax charged on documents from 1694, in. Originally there was no penalty as such for non-payment of stamp duty; the penalty is that an unstamped document may be ineffective in its purpose. The first stamp duty was imposed in the Netherlands in the early 17th century.

Types of stamp

The stamps were of three types:

- adhesive stamps, either specially produced by Inland Revenue or (sometimes) using an ordinary postage stamp
- embossing of paper using a die in a press
- producing the document on pre-stamped paper.

From 25 May 2000, provisions are introduced to allow for electronic stamping. Most transactions are now "stamped" using the CREST settlement system. A report by the Office of Tax Simplification (OTS) in 2017, found that 103,000 documents a year still involved embossing pieces of paper, the only extant form of physical stamping.

There is now only one office that can do it, based in Birmingham. This uses presses dating from 1870s with special coloured inks. This stamps 70% of straightforward stock transfer forms within five days and more complicated forms within 15 days. These time limits are in addition to time in the post. There is a limited facility where, by arrangement, same day stamping can be effected. Fewer than 50 such arrangements are made each year. OTS recommends that paper stamping be abolished and replaced by issuing a unique transaction reference online.

From 22 April 2019, a stamp may also be produced by computer under provisions in SI 2019 No 719.

Bases of stamp duty

Stamp duty is assessed on two bases:

- a fixed duty of a set amount per document
- ad valorem duty based on the value of the underlying transaction.

The fixed duties extended to a wide range of documents, including the common 2d duty on cheques until 1971. In 1965 there were more than 50 heads of documents requiring stamping. Most other fixed duties were abolished from 26 March 1985. The provision remains in vestigial form in that some such documents must still be presented to ensure that no ad valorem duty is payable. The fixed £5 charge for transactions of shares was abolished from 13 March 2008.

Ad valorem duty is (since 2003) in practice only charged on transactions in shares and some other securities, though it can still be charged for other documents where there is a need formally to register a title.

In 1990, it was announced that this duty would also be abolished with the introduction of the TAURUS system of share dealing. These provisions were enacted in FA 1990 ss107-111 from a date to be announced. TAURUS collapsed on 11 March 1993 and with it the abolition of the ad valorem duty. The 1990 Act provisions are still law but uncommenced.

Development of stamp taxes

Stamp duty dates from 1694. The main laws are now Stamp Duty Act 1891 and Stamp Duty Management Act 1891. Both Acts have been modified by FAs. In 1983, a proposal to consolidate the Acts was abandoned.

FA 1999 changed the heads of charge, and FA 2003 removed land transactions completely and made them subject to stamp duty land tax (SDLT). This tax has now been devolved and replaced in Scotland and Wales. Colloquially SDLT is still often referred to as stamp duty, even though it is a completely different tax.

There is also a separate stamp duty reserve tax, introduced in 1986.

Collectively these are known as stamp taxes, although two of the three have never involved stamps of any kind, and the original stamp duty rarely does.

stamp duty land tax (SDLT) Tax paid on transactions in land and buildings from 2003, when it replaced stamp duty on such transactions (FA 2003). SDLT is still often called stamp duty, although it is a completely different tax. The tax was replaced in Scotland by land and buildings transaction tax in April 2015, and in Wales by land transaction tax from April 2018.

There are different rates for residential and commercial property. There is a threshold below which SDLT is not payable.

The rates are given in section 3 of this dictionary.

stamp duty reserve tax (SDRT) Tax charged on agreements to transfer chargeable securities that are not otherwise subject to stamp duty (FA 1986 ss86-99). The tax was introduced on 1 July 1986.

standard accessory In relation to a company car, this is an accessory equivalent to one assumed to be available with cars of the same price" (ITEPA 2003 s125(4)).

standard allowance The main element of universal credit (WRA 2012 s1(3)).

standard basis One of the two bases for awarding **costs** in a tribunal decision. The other basis is indemnity basis.

standard beneficiary country Country that benefits from a General System of Preferences for Customs purposes. The list is given in Customs notice 830 Appendix B.

standard case For tax tribunals, a case that is more involved than a basic case and requires a hearing (SI 2009 No 273 rule 23(2)(c)).

standard cider For alcoholic liquor duty, cider which is not sparkling and has a strength not exceeding 7.5%.

standard class travel For air passenger duty, the only or lowest class of travel available (FA 1994 s30(10)).

standard debt In personal finance, a sum owed that causes concern to the debtor but is not too serious.

standard deviation Mathematical measure of how far a series of numbers departs from their average. It can be used to determine the risk element in an negligible value portfolio. The steps in calculating are:

- calculate the average (arithmetic mean)
- subtract the average from each number
- take the square of each difference
- add up all these squares
- take the square root of the total.

As an example, consider two series of five numbers:

- 20, 21, 22, 23, 24
- 2, 12, 22, 32, 42

Each has an average of 22 but the latter clearly has a wider range. The standard deviation of the former is 1.58114; and of the latter 15.81139.

standard exchange scheme Scheme that may be used for outward processing to provide relief from Customs duties. It deals with goods that are imported having been exported for a process, such as repair.

standard fraction Fraction used to calculate marginal relief from corporation tax before 2015 (CTA 2010 s19(3)).

standard hour In management accounting, the amount of work that can be achieved in one hour by a worker under normal conditions of efficiency.

standard import values Customs system for valuing seasonal imports, such as fruit where the value changes during the year.

standard letter Letter that is pre-written with only a few details left to be completed. These are widely used in finance, such as audit reports, letters of engagement and credit control letters.

standard lifetime allowance The lifetime allowance for pension contributions (FA 2004 s218). The rates are given in section 3 of this dictionary.

standard litre For oil duty, "shall mean a litre of any liquid at a temperature of 15 degrees C" (Hydrocarbon Oil Regulations SI 1973 No 1311 reg 2).

standard method For VAT, a means of calculating input tax in partial exemption. This means does not need HMRC approval. Other methods do.

standard rate Rate which applies unless another rate is specified. The term is particularly used for:

(a) rate of national minimum wage for all workers aged 22 to 24;
(b) rate of VAT which is charged on a supply unless another rate is specified;
(c) (sometimes) basic rate of income tax. It was the official term between 1907 and 1973.

For beer duty, the standard rate is paid by brewers who produce more than 60,000 hectolitres annually.

standard-rated Description of supplies that are subject to VAT at the standard rate. There is no schedule of such supplies, as all supplies are standard-rated unless there is a specific provision applying the zero rate, reduced rate or exemption.

standby Arrangement when a worker is required to be available for work at short notice. Such a worker is entitled to be paid the national minimum wage when:

- actually working having been called out
- required to be at or near the work premises
- not allowed to sleep.

This issue has been litigated several times.

stand good Term used when a tax assessment from HMRC is regarded as correct because the taxpayer cannot displace it (TMA 1970 s50(6)). The Court of Appeal commented in the case *T Haythornwaite & Sons v Kelly [1927] 11 TC 657.*

standing charges The cost of owning a car rather than of using it. Standing charges typically include vehicle excise duty, MOT, insurance, and cost of capital.

standing order Arrangement whereby a bank is instructed to make regular payments of a fixed amount from an account. The amount may only be varied by the account holder.

standing statement of fixed deductions Statement provided by an employer to an employee listing deductions made from every payslip and which therefore do not need to be detailed on the payslip itself (ERA 1996 s9).

stapled entity For digital services tax, an arrangement where shares in one company impact on shares in another (FA 2020 s60(3)).

star The service of having a star named after you was held to be standard-rated for VAT in the case *Schoemann ISR (UK) Ltd [1993] VTD 11713,* though it is not clear what is being supplied. None of the companies offering star naming are recognised by NASA or other recognised space or astronomical bodies.

starch Polycarbonate substance found in potatoes, rice and some other plants. For VAT, it is zero-rated when sold as a food product but standard-rated when sold for other purposes, such as stiffening shirt collars (VAT Notice 701/14).

stardust Name sometimes given to the metallic strip in a banknote.

stare decisis Latin: stated decision. The principle that a precedent is binding in law.

starter home The term "means a building or part of a building that—

(a) is a new dwelling,
(b) is available for purchase by qualifying first-time buyers only,
(c) is to be sold at a discount of at least 20% of the market value,
(d) is to be sold for less than the price cap, and
(e) is subject to any restrictions on sale or letting specified in regulations made by the Secretary of State (for more about regulations under this paragraph, see section 3)."

(Housing and Planning Act 2016 s2(1)).

starting rate Income tax rate below the basic rate, and generally applied to a thin slice of income. It applied to income tax between 2001/02 and 2007/08, and to corporation tax between 2000 and 2008. In April 2018, Scotland introduced a starter rate of income tax of 19%.

starting travelling expenses Expenses incurred by an employee in travelling from the UK to take up employment (ITEPA 2003 s341(8)). It is generally tax-deductible if the employment is overseas.

State Earnings Related Pension Scheme See **SERPS** above, and **State Pensions** in section 3 of this dictionary.

statement Document that summarises facts, particularly one from a supplier listing invoices that remain unpaid and sent to a customer.

statement for the account Term used in relation to child trust funds, and explained in Child Trust Funds Regulations SI 2004 No 1450 reg 10.

statement of accuracy Statement that HMRC may certify under administrative provisions for leases (ITTOIA 2005 s300; CTA 2009 s237).

statement of affairs Formal statement provided to court to support an individual voluntary agreement proposal.

statement of allocation Notice given to HMRC by a building society in relation to the bank levy (CTA 2010 s269CI(3) as inserted by FA 2015 Sch 2).

statement of assets and liabilities Such a statement may be produced by a body that prepares a receipts and payments account. The statement is the equivalent to a balance sheet.

Statement of Auditing Standard (SAS) UK auditing standard produced by the Auditing Practices Board.

statement of capital Statement made by directors about the company's share capital. Such a statement may be required for a reduction in share capital. The contents of such a statement are set out in CA 2006 s644(2).

statement of case Summary of the main facts and arguments in litigation.

statement of cash flows Financial statement that sets out where an entity received its funds and how it spent them. Unlike other financial statements, this statement is factual and not an opinion. Details on preparing such a statement are given in FRS 102 section 7.

statement of changes in equity

(1) Financial statement reporting all items causing changes to the ownership interest during the accounting period. This is generally required by an entity that uses international accounting standards but does not produce a statement of recognised income and expenditure.

(2) Statement in relation to the taxation of derivatives (CTA 2009 s710).

statement of compliance Document submitted by a company to Companies House to say that the requirements of Companies Act 2006 have been met (CA 2006 s13). For a public company, such a statement may be accepted in issuing a trading certificate (CA 2006 s762(3)).

statement of comprehensive income (SCE) Statement that combines the income statement with other gains and losses recognised in an accounting period. It is basically the same as the profit and loss account.

state of emergency Declaration by the King or Queen in Council which allows Parliament to take emergency action under Emergency Powers Act 1920.

statement of financial position New alternative name for the balance sheet.

statement of high net worth Statement made by an individual that he or she has assets above a specified value (Consumer Credit Act 1974 s16A; SI 2005 No 1529). The statement must be signed by a qualified accountant. Such a person is exempt from some of the provisions of the Act.

The Financial Conduct Authority defines high net worth as either having net income of at least £150,000 a year or net assets of at least £500,000. The figure for net assets does not include the value of the individual's main home nor any rights under an insurance contract.

statement of initial significant control Document that a company must file at Companies House on incorporation (CA 2006 s12A).

statement of practice Document issued by HMRC and predecessor bodies explaining how it understands a tax provision, and how it will apply it. HMRC will not challenge a taxpayer who follows a statement of practice. A taxpayer may argue that a statement of practice is not in accordance with the law.

statement of recognised gains and losses (STRGL) Financial statement that summarises all gains and losses in an accounting period, regardless of whether those gains and losses are reflected in the profit and loss account or balance sheet. Typically such a statement analyses gains and losses as:

- profit

- revaluation of assets
- actuarial gains or losses on pension scheme
- currency translation differences
- hedges against cashflow and investments.

statement of recommended practice (SORP) A non-compulsory set of accounting standards for particular sectors, such as charities or the oil industry. A list of SOPRS is given under Accounting Standards in section 3 of this dictionary.

statement of rights In company law, a statement outlining the rights of members to vote or appoint a proxy. Such a statement must be sent with all notices of meeting (CA 2006 s325(1)).

statement of standard accounting practice (SSAP) UK accounting standard issued between 1971 and 1990, when replaced by financial reporting standards.

statement of total recognised gains and losses (STRGL) Another name for the statement of recognised gains and losses.

statement of truth Statement made to provide evidence in an application sent to the Land Registry in relation to an application. Examples include an application to:

- be registered as proprietor of land on the basis of adverse possession;
- be registered where there are no extant documents to prove title;
- register a right acquired by prescription;
- apply for an entry to protected an undocumented interest in land: or
- cancel a restriction protecting a trust in land that has come to an end.

Before November 2008, such evidence was provided by a statutory declaration. From November 2008, the evidence is provided by a statement of truth. From 29 June 2015, form ST5 is used to cancel a restriction.

state pension An amount paid by the state to its older citizens. It is payable under Social Security and Contributory Benefits Act 1992 from s44.

Categories of pension

There are three categories of state retirement pension:

- Category A, paid at state pension age based on the person's national insurance contributions record
- Category B, paid at state pension age based on a spouse's contributions, and paid at a rate of about 60% of Category A
- Category D, paid at the age of 80 at the same rate as Category B for someone without sufficient national insurance record for A or B.

(Category C was for those who had retired before July 1948 or who were married to someone who was. This category is now extinct.)

Taxation

The pension is subject to income tax but is not taxed at source.

The tax is often collected by adjusting the tax code for another pension in payment.

Qualifying age

The qualifying ages are now the same for men and women. These ages are given under state pension age in section 3 of this dictionary.

National insurance conditions

A person is eligible for the pension if they have paid sufficient national insurance contributions for 35 years before they reach state pension age.

A pension forecast should be obtained, ideally while the taxpayer is still in his or her 40s or 50s, to check. Any gaps in the current year or six previous tax years can be filled by paying class 3 national insurance contributions.

Between 2012 and 2016, the requirement was for 30 years. Before April 2012, it was nine years of every ten years of working life.

If someone does not have a full record, they will receive a pro rate reduced pension.

A married or widowed person may be able to claim a smaller pension on the basis of their partner's contributions. All pensioners receive a pension at the age of 80.

Other information

The amount of pension is usually increased each April to allow for inflation.

The pension may be supplemented by additional pension.

A pensioner with low income may be entitled to claim pension credit.

state second pension Additional pension provided by the state. It was introduced in 2002 to replace the similar SERPS and was itself replaced by the single tier pension in 2016. The main changes were to restratify the earnings factors so that those on lower incomes received a greater pension, and to extend its scope to full-time carers.

state succession Principle that a double taxation treaty continues to apply when there is a change in sovereignty. For example, when the USSR was dissolved in 1991, the UK regarded its treaty as effective with the constituent states unless they decided otherwise, as five states did.

static caravan For VAT, this may come within the definition of a zero-rated caravan, as explained in VAT Notice 701/20.

stationery For VAT, this is generally standard-rated even if in the form of a book. Where a book contains information, as most diaries do, it is still zero-rated. There is an exception when the book has been completed. So a completed diary or ship's log may be zero-rated under VATA 1994 Sch 8 Group 3, as explained in VAT Notice 701/10.

status bar Part of a screen, often at the top, which indicates what is being worked on.

status discount Term used in relation to people who are ignored for the purposes of determining liability to council tax. Such people include full-time students and people who have severe mental impairment.

status quo Latin: state as it is.

statute Piece of written law, usually an Act of Parliament.

statute-barred When a right has expired through passage of time. Most debts have a limit of six years under Limitation Act 1980. Tax has a time limit of 20 years for fraud, six years for carelessness, and four years otherwise.

Statute of Frauds Law passed in 1677 requiring certain contracts to be in writing. Section 4 regarding sales of land and guarantees remain in force, though it is disapplied for financial collateral arrangements under SI 2003 reg 4(1).

statutory adoption pay (SAP) Social security benefit paid through the payroll to an employee who adopts a child (SSCBA 1992 from s171ZL).

SAP was introduced in 2003 and is paid at the same rate as statutory maternity pay. It is taxable as gross pay. Where a couple adopts, they may choose who claims statutory adoption pay. Their partner may be able to claim statutory paternity pay (even if female).

statutory apprenticeship "Means any course or training that is, or is to be, provided under –

(a) an approved English apprenticeship;

(b) an apprenticeship agreement within the meaning of section 32;

(c) an arrangement to undertaken any other kind of working –

(i) in relation to which alternative English completion conditions apply under section 1(5), and

(ii) in connection with which training is to be provided in accordance with an apprenticeship framework within the meaning given in section 12; or

(d) arrangements made under –

(i) section 2 of the Employment and Training Act 1973,

(ii) section 17B(1)(a) of the Jobseekers Act 1995.

(iii)section 2(3) of the Enterprise and New Towns (Scotland) Act 1990, or

(iv)section 1 of the Employment and Training Act (Northern Ireland) Act 1950,

that are identified by the person making the arrangements as arrangements for the provision of apprenticeships"

(Apprenticeships, Skills, Children and Learning Act 2009 sA11 as inserted by Enterprise Act 2016 s25).

It is an offence to describe any other form of training as an apprenticeship.

statutory debt repayment plan Scheme the government announced on 19 June 2019 to be introduced in England and Wales from 2021. It allows an individual with problem debt to repay the amount under an appropriate plan. It has since been renamed Breathing Space.

statutory declaration Declaration made before a magistrate or commissioner of oaths under Statutory Declarations Act 1835. Making a false statement is the crime of perjury (Perjury Act 1911 s5).

statutory demand Formal notice sent by a creditor to a disguised remuneration before starting bankruptcy proceedings (Insolvency Act 1986 s268(1)).

statutory funding objective Requirement that every pension scheme has sufficient and appropriate assets to cover its liabilities (Pensions Act 2003 s222(1)).

statutory instrument (SI) Form of delegated legislation, usually made by a government minister under provisions in an Act of Parliament. Many tax provisions are made by statutory instrument, such as PAYE Regulations.

statutory maternity pay (SMP) Payment made through the payroll to a female employee who is absent from work because of childbirth. It was introduced in 1987. It is subject to income tax and class 1 national insurance. The woman must have sufficient qualifying service and earn at least the lower earnings limit for national insurance.

The qualifying service is 26 weeks into the qualifying week which is 15 weeks before the expected birth. In practice, this means that SMP is payable only to a woman who became pregnant while in that employment.

A woman who does not meet those conditions may qualify for maternity allowance instead.

SMP is paid for 39 weeks. For the first six weeks, it is usually of 90% of normal earnings, followed by payment at a set rate. The employer eligible may reclaim 103% of SMP through the PAYE scheme if within the scope of small employer's relief, or 92% otherwise.

From April 2015, some maternity leave and pay may be passed to a partner under the provisions of shared parental leave.

Rates are given in section 3 of this dictionary.

statutory parental bereavement leave Legal right of a parent to take two weeks off work if they suffer the death of a child under 18 or a stillborn baby after 24 weeks of pregnancy from 6 April 2020. The leave may be taken as one block of two weeks, two blocks each of one week, or one block of one week.

The main provisions are in SI 2020 No 249. Administrative regulations are in SI 2020 No 246.

This right applies from the first day of employment.

statutory parental bereavement pay Payment to a parent who suffers the death of a child under 18 or stillborn baby after 24 weeks of pregnancy from 6 April 2020. Entitlement depends on the employee having at least 26 weeks' continuous employment up to the week of the death. It is paid during statutory parental bereavement leave. It also depends on the employee earnings at least the lower earnings limit for national insurance.

The pay is the same as the set rate for statutory maternity pay or 90% of average weekly earnings if lower.

statutory paternity pay Social security payment introduced in 2003, and paid through the payroll. It is subject to income tax and class 1 national insurance. It is paid to the partner (not necessarily male) of a person receiving statutory maternity pay or statutory adoption pay. It is paid at a set rate for one whole week or two whole weeks.

From 2011, some maternity leave and pay may be transferred to a partner as additional statutory paternity pay. From 2016 that is replaced by shared parental leave.

statutory payment One of statutory sick pay, statutory maternity pay, statutory paternity pay, statutory adoption pay or statutory parental bereavement pay. Rates are given under Statutory Payments in section 3 of this dictionary.

statutory residence test Sets of rules introduced in April 2013 to determine whether someone is UK resident. It considers a series of tests which, in order, are automatic overseas tests, automatic UK tests, and the sufficient ties test. The test is set out in section 3 of this dictionary.

statutory review Procedure introduced by HMRC as part of the reform of tax appeals.

If a taxpayer disagrees with HMRC, the taxpayer may ask for the matter to be reviewed by another HMRC officer who has not been involved.

In Employer Bulletin 87 of December 2020, HMRC said that it conducted 28,000 statutory reviews in 2018/19 of which 14,000 were altered as a result. The majority of reviewed cases do not proceed to tribunal.

A review does not prejudice a subsequent tribunal hearing. The taxpayer has 30 days from the review to appeal to a tribunal.

statutory sick pay (SSP) Social security benefit provided through the payroll and subject to income tax and class 1 national insurance (SSCBA 1992 ss151-154).

Statutory sick pay is subject to income tax (ITEPA 2003 s660(1) and class 1 national insurance. It was introduced in 1983 and has changed significantly since then. SSP is now optional, provided the employer provides employees with at least the amount of SSP they would have received.

SSP is paid for a diagnosed illness or injury, including necessary convalescence. It is generally paid from the fourth calendar day of illness for a maximum of 28 weeks at a set rate. The employee must be earning at least the lower earnings limit. Two absences are said to be linked if there is less than 8 weeks between them. This means that the two or more periods of at least four days will be treated as one in determining whether the 28-week limit has been reached.

From 2014, the employer generally bears the whole cost of statutory sick pay with no reclaim from the government.

Some separate provisions were made for statutory sick pay during the coronavirus outbreak in 2020.

Rates of statutory sick pay are given in section 3 of this dictionary.

statutory travel concession permit Bus pass issued to anyone who is of state pension age (Concessionary Bus Travel Act 2007). It is valid throughout the United Kingdom.

statutory trust Trust that is created under operation of the law. An example is when a person dies intestate (Administration of Estates Act 1925 s47).

staying In law, temporary suspension of a legal action, often while a point of law is settled in another case about the same issue.

stealth tax Informal term for any arrangement that increases tax in a way that is not immediately obvious.

An example is the reduction in personal allowance for incomes above £100,000. This in effect creates a marginal income tax rate of 60%.

Other examples similarly restrict reliefs for savings income, childcare vouchers and pension contributions for higher earners.

steam Water as a gas from heating. If the supply is of steam itself, it may be zero-rated as a supply of water under VATA 1994 Sch8 Group 2. If the steam is supplied as heat, it may be reduced rated when supplied to homes or charities, or standard-rated when supplied to businesses. The matter is explained in VAT Notice 701/16.

steep-reduction annuity An annuity where:

"(a) the amount of any payment in respect of the annuity (but not the term of the annuity) depends on any contingency other than the duration of a human life or lives;

(b) the annuitant is entitled in respect of the annuity to payments of different amounts at different times; and

(c) those payments include a payment (a reduced payment) of an amount which is substantially smaller than the amount of at least one of the earlier payments in respect of that annuity to which the annuitant is entitled" (ICTA 1988 s437A(1)).

stellar contribution Term sometimes used in a divorce settlement. If one party has a particular talent that generates income, the other party has a reduced claim on such income.

STEM Science, technology, engineering and mathematics.
These four disciplines can attract favourable treatment. For example, someone qualified in one of these areas may earn extra points under immigration law.

stencil In tax investigations, an outline document which is completed by HMRC as a means of recording evidence.

stepped Description of a financial instrument where the interest or repayment increases over time.

steps In relation to mutual assistance in recovering tax between member states, the term "includes any legal or administrative steps, whether by way of legal proceedings, distress, diligence or otherwise"
(FA 2011 Sch 25 para 6(4)).

steradian Unit of a solid angle.

sterling Another name for the pound as the unit of currency.

sterling index Index which shows the value of UK currency against a basket of other currencies.

sterling silver An alloy of silver and base metal (usually copper) with at least 92.5% silver.

stet Mark in accounts or text that removes a correction, leaving the original entry or text.

stewardship Taking care of resources owned by another person and using those resources to the benefit of that person. The term can also mean the wise use of collective assets, such as the natural environment.

Stichting MarorGelden Overheid Dutch name for Dutch Maror Fund, set up to pay compensation to victims of the Holocaust. On 16 December 2015, it was announced that payments under this scheme are exempt from UK inheritance tax.

sticky keys In computing, a facility to assist disabled people by letting the keys take longer to perform their function.

Stiftung EVZ German scheme known in English as Remembrance, Responsibility and Future. It compensates those used as forced labour in the second world war. On 16 December 2005, it was announced that payments under the scheme are exempt from inheritance tax.

Stigma damages Damages that may be paid to a worker for a connection with a disgraced business. The first such damages were paid to an employee who worked for the failed bank BCCI in 1991.

Still Apparatus in which alcoholic spirits are distilled (Customs notice 39).

Stillbirth Birth of an already dead child. If the pregnancy lasted for at least 24 weeks, the mother may be able to claim statutory maternity pay and statutory parental bereavement pay.

Still licence Licence required to keep and use stills for making spirits (ALDA 1979 s82).

Stipend Regular payment to a minister of religion or other person not to work but to be available for pastoral or other duties. A stipend is subject to income tax and national insurance as if it were salary.

Stock (1) Goods held as inventory.

(2) Equity of a company expressed in value rather than number of shares. It is favoured in USA.

Stockbroker Person who buys and sells shares and other securities for customers.

Stock deficiency In relation to shops, the loss of stock for reasons that cannot be identified but are believed to be shoplifting or pilferage by staff. The shopkeeper may deduct the cost of stock so lost from the shop assistant's wages provided this does not exceed 10% of those wages (ERA 1996 s17).

Stock dividend When a dividend is paid in the form of additional shares. Such a dividend is treated as if paid in cash (ICTA 1988 s249). The capital gains tax treatment is given in TCGA 1992 s142.

Stock exchange Forum for buying and selling shares and other securities. The main UK exchange is the London Stock Exchange.

Stock lending Practice of lending shares to another company.

The income tax provisions are given in ITA 2007 s568.

Corporation tax provisions are given in TCGA 1992 s263B.

The deemed manufactured dividend rules are given in CTA 009 s812.

Stock lending is generally outside the scope of accrued income scheme (ITA 2007 s653).

Stock market value Value of a listed company calculated by multiplying its ordinary shares by the share's market value.

Stock relief Tax relief available to businesses between 1974 and 1984 to reflect the effect of inflation on stock held.

Stocktaking Exercise, usually performed at the end of the accounting period, of physically counting goods in stock, usually with the auditor in attendance.

These items are then valued to give a figure for closing stock. This figure is entered into the accounts as a journal entry which is reversed at the start of the next accounting period.

The closing stock is used to calculate the cost of goods sold from which gross profit is determined.

Stock turnover Accounting ratio which measures how long stock is held by a business before being sold. It is calculated as the total value of stock sold in the year divided by the average value of goods held in stock.

Stone Unit of weight equal to 14 pounds, widely used for weight of people. There are 8 stone to a hundredweight and 160 stones in a ton. A stone equals 6.3505 kilograms.

Stop In banking, an instruction that countermands a previous instruction, such as directing that a cheque not be paid.

Stop and search The right of police to stop people and vehicles to search them (Police and Criminal Evidence Act 1984 s1).

Stop over Interruption of a journey, such as for an overnight break.

A stopover in itself does not convert commuting into business travel. A leading case is *Sargent v Barnes [1978] 52 TC 335.* This is discussed in HMRC Manual at BIM37935. For air passenger duty, a stopover breaks a journey so that each part is taxed separately. Details are given in Customs notice 550.

Stopped cheque Cheque that has been issued but where the issuer subsequently tell the bank not to pay it, usually because the cheque has been lost or misappropriated.

Storage jar Jar that is intended and designed for repeated use. If sold on its own, this is standard-rated. If sold containing food, this is a mixed supply where each element is subject to its own rate of VAT.

Store of value Any item which is widely regarded as being valuable and which is therefore the basis of currency. Precious metals and gems are stores of value, as can be land, antiques, and works of art.

The term is also used as one of the two functions of money. The other function is as a means of exchange.

Stormont Place where the Northern Ireland Assembly meets and which is sometimes used to mean the Assembly.

stotinka One hundredth of a lev, currency of Bulgaria. The plural is stotinki.

stout Dark beer. It is subject to beer duty.

stove From 1 January 2006, a stove that burns wood or straw may qualify for the reduced rate of VAT under VATA 1994 Sch 7A Group 2.

straddling period Accounting period that straddles a date when a tax provision changes. In relation to the supplementary charge for ring-fenced profits of the oil industry, this is an accounting period that straddles 24 March 2011 (FA 2011 s7(3)). For ring-fenced losses, it means an accounting period that straddles 1 January 2006 (CTA 2010 s327).

In relation to diverted profits tax, the term is explained in FA 2015 s116(2).

In relation to loss-related tax avoidance, it means a period that spans 1 April 2017 (Finance (No 2) Act 2017 s19(11)).

In relation to hybrid mismatches, it "means an accounting period or payment period (as the case may be) beginning before 13 July 2017 and ending on or after that date" (Finance (No 2) Act 2017 s24(12)).

straight line method Method of calculating depreciation or capital allowance where the figure for each year is a percentage of the original figure. This is used for structures and buildings allowance, but not for plant and machinery which uses the reducing balance method.

stratified When an amount is sliced into strata subject to different treatments. An example is class 1 national insurance which is stratified for the purpose of calculating state second pension.

Strategic Accounting Framework (SAFE) Computer system introduced by HMRC in phases during 2006/07 "for the collection and accounting of the miscellaneous charges previously dealt with by the Network Units in Cumbernauld and Shipley" (Inspectors' Manual at DMBM100110). It also provides IT support for pension simplification charges and legal costs.

strategic plan for England In relation to dormant accounts, "means a statement containing the [Big Lottery] Fund's policies for the distribution of dormant account money for meeting English expenditure" (Dormant Bank and Building Society Accounts Act 2008 Sch 3 para 1(2)).

strategic plan for Northern Ireland In relation to dormant accounts, "means a statement containing the [Big Lottery] Fund's policies for the distribution of dormant account money for meeting Northern Ireland expenditure" (Dormant Bank and Building Society Accounts Act 2008 Sch 3 para 4(2)).

strategic plan for Scotland In relation to dormant accounts, "means a statement containing the [Big Lottery] Fund's policies for the distribution of dormant account money for meeting Scottish expenditure" (Dormant Bank and Building Society Accounts Act 2008 Sch 3 para 3(2)).

strategic plan for Wales In relation to dormant accounts, "means a statement containing the [Big Lottery] Fund's policies for the distribution of dormant account money for meeting Welsh expenditure" (Dormant Bank and Building Society Accounts Act 2008 Sch 3 para 2(2)).

strategic report A report that a company produces providing a fair review of its business and description of the principal risks it faces (CA 2006 s414C(2)). Small companies are exempt. The Financial Reporting Council produced guidance in July 2018.

strategy "The direction and scope of an organisation over the long term: ideally, which matches its resources to its changing environment, and in particular its markets, customers or clients so as to meet stakeholder expectations" (*Exploring Corporate Strategy*, G Johnson and K Scholes, Prentice Hall).

stratification Banding of an amount where each band is treated differently. The term was used when the state second pension replaced SERPS in 2002. Instead of all band earnings accruing entitlement on the basis of 20%, those earnings were stratified with the lowest accruing at 40%, the middle at 10% and the top at 20%. The consequence was that someone with maximum band earnings still accrued entitlement at 20%, but those with less than the maximum band accrued entitlement at an overall rate between 20% and 40%.

straw For VAT, this is generally standard-rated, as explained in VAT notice 701/15. Straw-burning stoves may, from 1 January 2006, qualify for the reduced rate of VAT under Value Added Tax 1994 Sch 7A Group 2.

straw man Man with little or no financial means, particularly when put up for a purpose such as fighting a legal action knowing that the other side cannot recover any award of costs. The term man of straw is also used. Someone who fights a legal action using a straw man may be liable under the rules of champerty.

stream (1) Small water course. Profits from trading activity are subject to income tax (ITTOIA 2005 s12) or corporation tax (CTA 2009 s39).
(2) A source of income.

streaming An alternative method of taxation in relation to intellectual property. Details are given in Corporation Tax 2010 from s357D as inserted by FA 2016 s64(6) and Sch 9.

strength In relation to alcoholic liquor duty, how much alcohol by volume there is in a drink. It is the ratio of the volume of alcohol to total drink (ALDA 1979 s2(2)(c)).

stress test Analysis of how far a bank can withstand an economic crisis.

stretcher Device for carrying an injured person. In some circumstances this may be zero-rated for VAT. In May 2004, the minimum statutory length was reduced from 2.28 metres to 1.95 metres. VAT law reflects this change of size.

stretch fabric Fabric that can be stretched to a larger size when made into clothing. Common examples include Spandex and Lycra. In determining whether a garment meets the size requirement to be zero-rated as children's clothing, the size must be measured with the fabric fully stretched.
The issue of stretchability was considered in the VAT case *Jeffrey Green & Co Ltd [1974] VTD 69.*

strictly In tax practice, this word indicates what the letter of law requires though a more reasonable approach may apply in practice.

strike Deliberate stoppage of work (Trade Union and Labour Relations (Consolidation) Act 1992 s246).
Periods on strike are deducted from periods of continuous employment for establishing employment rights.
Workers on strike are not paid. Any strike pay from a trade union is not taxed as it is regarded as a refund of contributions.
Any PAYE refunds due to strikers must be withheld until the strike has ended (PAYE Regulations 2003 para 64).

strike off Process of removal from a register, particularly the process by which a defunct company may be removed from the register at Companies House without the need for a formal liquidation.

Such an application may be made by the registrar under CA 2006 s1000 if the registrar believes that no business is being carried on and has written to the company to enquire.

Alternatively an application may be made by the company itself under s1003. In such a case, the company is usually struck off the register three months later.

striking price Price at which a security is sold by tender. Bidders make offers of varying amounts. The striking price is the figure that ensures sufficient sale is made.

strip Form of tradeable security, usually comprising two puts and one call on a share or other security. There are some tax provisions such as TCGA 1992 s47.

stripped bond scheme Tax avoidance scheme where banks sold bonds stripped of their interest coupons. It was held to be ineffective in 2013 for reasons explained by HMRC in Spotlight 18.

strip search Search by a Customs officer requiring the removal of clothes next to the skin (CEMA 1979 s164(5)). The search must be conducted by a person of the same sex.

strip tease In a Norwegian case *Fylkesskattsjefen v Diamond GoGo Bar. Langmannsrett. The Times 7 December 2006,* the tax authorities held that a strip tease show was artistic and therefore exempt from VAT under EU law. Although Norway is not an EU country, its VAT law is modelled on EU law.

This precedent is unlikely to be followed in the UK as the VAT exemption for culture in VATA 1994 Sch 9 Group 13 is restricted to non-profit-making bodies.

strong cider For alcoholic liquor duty, cider that is not sparkling and has an alcoholic strength of more than 7.5% (ALDA 1979 s62B(4)(b)).

structural deficit One of two elements of the Budget deficit. The other is the cyclical deficit. HM Treasury glossary says that structural deficit "occurs when government spending exceeds tax receipts. A government can run a structural deficit even if the economy is growing strongly. Consequently, it can only be tackled by reducing government spending or raising taxes."

structured settlement Damages set out as a lump sum and an annuity, as allowed for in Damages Act 1996.

structures and buildings allowance (SBA) Capital allowance introduced for structures and buildings where expenditure has been incurred from 29 October 2018. The legal provisions are contained in Treasury regulations issued under FA 2019 s30. These do not use the term "structures and buildings allowance" but call it "construction expenditure on buildings and structures". An HMRC technical note of 29 October 2018 gives these main details:

- SBA applies to non-residential buildings and structures in commercial use. The scope is therefore wider than the old industrial buildings allowance
- SBA may be claimed for offices, shops, warehouses, factories, walls, bridges, and tunnels
- SBA is claimed separately for each building and structure
- if a business has an accounting period of less than one year, the SBA is proportionately reduced

- SBA may not be claimed for any expenditure which is deductible from taxable profits, such as routine maintenance
- expenditure on features integral to a building continue to qualify for plant and machinery capital allowance rather than SBA. This includes using the annual investment allowance (AIA) for such expenditure. SBA expenditure does not qualify for AIA
- SBA may be claimed only if the taxpayer uses it for a trade, profession, vocation, or (subject to some restrictions) a property business or investment business
- SBA may not be claimed where the owner does not pay UK tax. If such a person sells the property to a taxpayer who does qualify, that taxpayer may claim SBA for the remainder of the original term
- SBA may be claimed for overseas buildings if the business is subject to UK tax
- SBA cannot be claimed for the cost of land nor for dwellings, but may be claimed for a hotel business
- where a building includes dwellings, SBA may only be claimed for the non-residential element, provided this is at least 10%
- SBA may not be claimed for communal areas used for both residential and commercial use
- SBA may be claimed for demolition and other work to land necessary for a qualifying building or structure
- SBA may not be claimed for rights over land, nor for the cost of obtaining planning permission
- SBA may be claimed for new work, converting buildings to commercial use, and to improving existing buildings
- SBA applies to expenditure incurred from 29 October 2018 unless the contract was agreed before that date
- SBA is given at 2% on a straight line basis. This is increased to 3% from 1 April 2020 for both new structures and existing structures erected from 29 October 2018
- where a property is leased, both the lessor and lessee may claim SBA for their expenditure. There are other provisions for leases
- SBA may be claimed for when the building first comes into use
- a taxpayer need not claim SBA in any year, but any SBA not claimed is lost. It cannot be rolled over to a later year
- if a property is sold, the new owner may continue claiming SBA at 3% of original expenditure. There is no balancing allowance
- if subsequent work is done on a property for which SBA is being claimed, the existing SBA continues at the same amount. A new claim for SBA may be made for the subsequent work. This means that several SBAs may be claimed for the same property, with each ending in a different year
- if a building for which SBA is claimed ceases to be used for a qualifying purpose, the SBA stops. There is no clawback of relief previously given

- if a building for which SBA has stopped is then brought back into commercial use, SBA may resume but no allowance is given for the non-qualifying period. In other words, SBA stops after 33⅓ years
- if a building is demolished, SBA stops
- if a building is damaged and cannot be used, SBA may be claimed for two years to allow for reconstruction. In limited circumstances this may be extended to five years
- SBA is subject to anti-avoidance provisions.

The 2% annual rate was increased to 3% from 1 April 2020 by FA 2020 s29 which amended CAA 2001 s270AA. This increase is retrospective, which means that an additional 1% may be claimed pro rata for the period from 29 October 2018 to April 2020. This is given by CAA 2001 s270GD as inserted by FA 2020 s29(5).

student Person engaged in studying. Before 2015, there was a special scheme using form P38(S) whereby a student could earn during the three main holidays without paying tax, but that is no longer available.

student loan Loan provided to a student in tertiary education. The loan is repaid from subsequent earnings as a percentage above a threshold, similar to a tax. There are three types of student loan. Plan 1 loans apply to students who started their course between September 1998 and August 2012. Plan 2 loans apply to students who started from September 2012. From April 2019, there are also postgraduate loans. From 6 April 2021 Scotland is introducing Plan 4 loans.
Details and rates are given in section 3 of this dictionary.

students' union A university students' union was not allowed to claim exemption from VAT for cultural entertainments under Value Added Tax 1994 Sch 9 Group 13 Note 2(c). Its officers received bursaries which meant that it was not run on a voluntary basis. (*Keele University Students Union [2009] TC 82).*

subcontractor Person engaged by a contractor to do some of the work. In the construction industry, a contractor must deduct a sum for tax from the labour element of payments to a subcontractor unless that subcontractor has a certificate from HMRC. The rates are given under construction industry scheme in section 3 of this dictionary.

sub-division In relation to shares, means splitting the nominal value into a larger number of lower value shares, such as splitting each £1 share into ten 10p shares. The company law is found in CA 2006 s618. The opposite process is known as consolidation.

sub-fund Part of a settlement that the trustees may elect to be treated separately for capital gains tax.

subgroup Group of companies that is itself part of a larger group. In relation to the substantial shareholding exemption, there are provisions in TCGA 1992 Sch 7AC para 26(2).

subject access request (SAR) Term used by HMRC for a request by an individual for information it holds about that individual. It is a right under Data Protection Act. It also includes national insurance details from 1975/76.

A request through an accountant, solicitor or other professional requires written authorisation from the subject. A request for a person who has died may be made by someone entitled to settle the tax and national insurance affairs of the deceased.

subject to contract Term used in negotiation indicating an *intention* to create contractual relations but not doing so yet. The legal authority for this comes from the case *Chillingworth v Esche [1924]*. The term is widely used in purchases of land and property.

sub-sale When a buyer acquires goods to sell to another buyer. Normally there are no legal consequences as the sub-sale is simply regarded as a second contract for sale. There are some special provisions regarding sub-sale as it affects seller's lien in Sale of Goods Act 1979 s47.

For stamp duty land tax, the sale of a property by a purchaser to a subpurchaser. A subsale can be relieved from duty. This commonly applies when builder A sells to developer B who sells to buyer C, such as when units are sold off-plan. For SDLT purposes, this is treated as a sale from A to C. The provisions were amended by FA 2013 to counter avoidance schemes. Under the 2013 Act, relief is given on the same basis subject to many anti-avoidance provisions, but B must now file a return to HMRC.

sub-sale relief Relief from stamp duty land tax given on a sub-sale. The relief is given by FA 2013 s195.

subscribing employee Employee who subscribes for shares in the company that employs him. The definition includes directors. In relation to priority share allocations, the term is defined in ITEPA 2003 s547(6).

subscription

(1) Payment and application to buy shares in a new company.

(2) Money paid in advance for a time-based service, such as membership of an organisation or to buy a series of publications.

The VAT position for subscriptions to a club or association are given in VAT leaflet 701/5.

subsidiary Company wholly or largely owned by another company. For company law, this is defined in CA 2006 s1159(1). For accounting, a parent company and its subsidiaries may have their accounts consolidation as group accounts as set out in FRS 102 section 9. The two steps of consolidation are:

- remove transactions between companies within the group
- add all like accounts together.

If a holding company owns less than 100% but more than 50%, the whole amount is still added, but a figure for minority interest is shown on the balance sheet with capital.

For group relief from corporation tax, a company is a subsidiary if the parent company owns 75% of the company (CTA 2009 s765).

subsidiary trading company Trading company owned by a charity. It is taxed as a trading company and not as a charity, though that is easily overcome by Gift Aiding the profits.

subsistence Payment for accommodation and food. Where an employee is away on business, subsistence payments may be made tax-free. The limits are given under Travel and Subsistence in section 3 of this dictionary.

subsisting interest in possession For inheritance tax, this term is defined in Inheritance Tax Act 1984 s80(7) as inserted by Finance (No 2) Act 2015 s13.

substance of the document For stamp duty, examination of a document to ascertain its nature to determine the amount of duty payable.

substance over form Accounting concept that financial records reflect the reality in preference to the legality (FRS 102 section 2.8). An example is a leased asset. Legally, it belongs to the lessor, but accounting shows it as an asset of the lessee. It appears on the balance sheet of the lessee and not the lessor.

substantial acquisition In relation to annual tax on enveloped dwellings, this broadly means an addition that costs at least £40,000 (FA 2013 s103(1)).

substantial donor Someone who has donated to charity at least:

- £25,000 in the last year, or
- £150,000 in the last six years (ICTA 1988 ss506A-506C; ITA 2007 ss549-557).

Such a donor is subject to an anti-avoidance provision from 2006. This withdraws tax relief to the extent that the donor received any significant benefit from the charity.

substantial non-cash asset In company law, an asset other than cash whose value exceeds either:

- £100,000, or
- 10% of the company's value plus £5,000.

If a transaction for such an asset is made with a director, the company usually requires approval from the members (CA 2006 s190).

substantial shareholder exemption (SSE) Exemption from capital gains tax on the disposal of shares where the seller has owned at least 10% of the shares for a sufficient period.

For disposals from 1 April 2017, that continuous period is 12 months in the previous six months. Previously, it was 12 months of the previous 24 (TCGA 1992 s192A and Sch 7AC).

The company must have been a trading company for that period. HMRC's understanding of what is meant by a trading company was given in HMRC Brief 29/2011.

This exemption was introduced for periods after 31 March 2002.

This provision is extended to situations where:

(a) at least 25% of the ordinary share capital is held by institutional investors,

(b) the investing company holds ordinary shares with an acquisition cost of at least £20 million,

(c) the investing company is entitled to a proportionate share of profits.

These provisions are contained in Transfer of Capital Gains Act 1992 Sch 7AC para 8A The provisions apply to disposals made from 1 April 2017.

substantial shareholding Any shareholding of more than 3% of the company's ordinary shares. The name of the shareholder and size of their holding must be disclosed in the accounts.

substantively enacted In terms of accounting for deferred tax, this refers to tax provisions which are known to be coming into effect even though they may not have yet done so. Such tax provisions must be reflected in the calculation for deferred tax.

substantive trust fund Trust fund containing the funds for which it was set up, as against a nominal sum (often £10) held merely to establish the trust.

substituted remuneration Lump sum received instead of normal pay. HMRC Manual at EIM00670 says this should be taxed as normal remuneration under ITEPA 2003 s62. A leading case on this is *Bolam v Muller [1947] 28 TC 471.*

substantive issue The main issue in dispute in legal proceedings. This contrasts with a preliminary issue that deals with such matters as procedure or hardship applications.

substantively enacted In relation to the accounting treatment for deferred tax: "tax rates shall be regarded as substantively enacted when the remaining stages of the enactment process historically have not affected the outcome and are unlikely to do so.

"A UK tax rate shall be regarded as having been substantially enacted if it is included in either:

(a) a Bill that has been passed by the House of Commons and awaiting only passage through the House of Lords and Royal Assents; or
(b) a resolution having statutory effect that has been passed under the Provisional Collection of Taxes Act 1968. (Such a resolution could be used to collect taxes at a new rate before that rate has been enacted. In practice, corporation tax rates are now set a year ahead to avoid having to invoke the Provisional Collection of Taxes Act for the quarterly payment system.)

"A Republic of Ireland tax rate can be regarded as having been substantively enacted if it is included in a Bill that has been passed by the Dail"
(FRS 102 glossary).

substantive trust fund Trust which contains the funds for which it was set up, as against a nominal trust fund which holds a small amount to allow the trust to be set up. It is common practice to create a trust with a nominal sum such as £10. This means that the trust is ready when the more valuable assets are ready to be settled into the trust.

substantive law Law as it relates directly to matters, as opposed to procedural matters. Such law is known as adjectival law.

substitute value Value that may be used when stock is transferred between businesses. The matter is discussed in HMRC Manual at BIM33500.

substitution effect Consideration of the effect of a change in tax law that reflects a change in behaviour. It complements the income effect.

If the income tax rate is reduced by one tenth, the income effect says that income tax revenue will be reduced by one tenth.
The substitution effect would note that a reduction in income tax means that taxpayers have more disposable income to spend, which will have the effect of boosting VAT receipts.

substantive law Law as it relates directly to matters in hand, as against adjectival law which deals with procedures.

subtotal Total to which further sums are added.

subtraction Mathematical process of reducing one number by another.
In the equation: 10 – 3 = 7
10 is the minuend, 3 is the subtrahend, and 7 is the difference.

succession duty A death duty charged under Succession Duty Act 1853 until repealed by FA 1949 s27 from 30 July 1949.

successive life interests Arrangement where a life interest trust nominates a series of beneficiaries so that when the interest of one beneficiary expires, the benefit passes to the next beneficiary.

successors' annuity In relation to taxation of pensions, the term is defined in FA 2004 Sch 28 para 27FA(1) as inserted by FA 2015 Sch 4 para 5.

sucre Currency of Ecuador.

Sudan Country of West Africa. Its currency is the Sudanese pound of 100 piastres. The UK has a double taxation convention of 1975.
The country is subject to UK sanctions, as are designated persons of the country.

Sudanese pound Currency of Sudan.

sufficient ties test Series of tests to determine UK residence under the statutory residence test when previous tests have established neither UK residence nor non-residence. The test considers four ties, or five if the taxpayer has been UK resident within the previous three years. The number of ties established for the taxpayer are then compared to the number of days of UK residence. Residence or non-residence is then determined from tables. Details can be found in section 3 of this dictionary.

sugar Sweetening material. If added to a soft drink, it may trigger a liability to soft drinks industry levy (FA 2017 s29). Sugar was subject to excise duty until 1962. For VAT, sugar is generally zero-rated as food.

suggestion award Tax-free sum that may be paid tax-free to an employee in respect of a suggestion (ITEPA 2003 s322). It is also free of national insurance. The maximum sum depends on whether the suggestion is take up by the employer. If it is, the award is known as a financial benefit award. This is tax-free up to the greater of:

- 50% of the expected saving in the first year of adopting the suggestion, and
- 10% of the expected saving in the first five years.

The maximum is capped at £5,000.

An encouragement award of £25 may be paid tax-free for a good suggestion, whether or not taken up, or to reward an employee for a special effort.

sukuk Form of investment bond which avoids paying interest while replicating its effect (ITA 2007 s564R). It is an alternative finance arrangement. It is designed to be compliant with Sharia law, though any taxpayer may use the bond; it is not restricted to Muslims. It is taxed on the same basis as the bond whose effect it seeks to replicate.

sulphur Non-metallic element. There are lower rates of hydrocarbon duty on petrol and diesel that have low sulphur content.

sum (1) In mathematics, the total of a series of numbers.
(2) An amount of money.

summary dismissal When an employee is dismissed instantly without notice or payment in lieu of notice. The employee is entitled to payment for work done up to the point of dismissal. Summary dismissal is only justified when the employee's conduct is such that it undermines the trust and confidence that is implied in every contract of employment.

summary warrant In Scots law, an order granted to a government body or local authority to recover a debt. Provisions for its use to recover tax are given in FA 2008 s128.

Summer Economic Statement Statement given in Parliament by Chancellor of the Exchequer Rishi Sunak MP on 8 July 2020 setting out a further package of measures to deal with coronavirus.

sumptuary tax Tax that is imposed partly or wholly to reduce demand, such as on tobacco products. It is also called a **Pigovian tax**.

sundry In bookkeeping, a category of income or expenditure for which there is no other account. If the amount becomes large, separate categories should probably be created.

sunk cost In management accounting, an expense that has already been incurred and which is therefore ignored in decision making. For example, a lorry has £2,000 work done on it. It is then found that it either needs another £2,500 of work or can be replaced for £3,000. The £2,000 is a sunk cost, so, in the absence of any other factor, the lorry is repaired rather than replaced.

sunset clause Clause in a law, contract or similar that states when the provisions will cease. Many short-term tax incentives contain sunset clauses.

superannuation Pension paid to someone who is too old or ill still to work.

super profit Profit greater than that expected. Such figures are sometimes used to calculate commission or goodwill.

superstitious uses Object of a trust for the propagation of a rite not permitted by law. Such an object invalidates the trust.

supertax Addition to income tax charged between 1909 and 1920. It was replaced by surtax, which was itself replaced by higher rate tax from 1973.

supervening trade Trade which is created after a non-commercial activity. An example is when someone inherits an asset and sells it as part of a trade. The matter is discussed in HMRC Manual at BIM20315.

support component Element of the social security benefit employment and support allowance paid when someone has limited capacity for work.

supplementary petrol duty Addition to petroleum revenue tax imposed in 1981 and 1982.

supply Provision of goods or services. VAT is a tax on supplies made in the course of furtherance of a business by some who is, or should be, registered for VAT. While most supplies are sales, the two are not synonymous. Free gifts and barter transactions are supplies for VAT.

supply and demand Basic principle of economics that any imbalance between supply and demand affects the price of goods or services in a free market.

supply VAT The VAT due on supplies of goods and/or services deemed to be made in the UK.

support component An element of the social security benefit employment and support allowance. This component is paid when someone has a limited capacity for work. It is paid in the main phase of the benefit, which is usually after an assessment phase of 13 weeks.

Support for Mortgage Interest Social security scheme to assist in repaying a mortgage. From 6 April 2018, it is replaced by repayable loans.

supporting documents In relation to tax disputes, this is defined as any written material that indicates the truth of a statement. TMA 1970 s12B(6)(b) defines supporting documents as including "books, deeds, contracts, vouchers and receipts".

supra Latin for "above". It is sometimes used in legal documents to indicate a matter already referred to.

Supreme Court Final court of appeal in the UK, replacing the House of Lords from 1 October 2009 (Constitutional Reform Act 2005 s23).

In certain cases, the term can mean the Supreme Court and lower courts (Courts Act 1971 s1).

surcharge allowance In relation to corporation tax surcharge on banks, a form of group relief that may be claimed. Details are given in CTA 2010 s269DA(3).

surcharge on banking companies Additional 8 percentage points added to the rate of corporation tax charged to banks from 1 January 2016 (CTA 2010 from s269D).

Sure Start maternity grant Social Fund payment to a woman on means-tested benefit who gives birth to:

- her first child, or
- twins or other multiple birth when she already has at least one child.

The amount is £500. This is tax-free and does not affect entitlement to other benefits. In Scotland it is replaced by Pregnancy and Baby Payment.

surgery Generally surgery is unlikely to be tax-deductible as it will not meet the "wholly" condition. A leading case is *Prince v Mapp [1969] 46 TC 169*. A professional guitarist was not allowed to claim tax relief for private surgery to his finger so he could return to work sooner than waiting for NHS treatment. The matter is discussed in HMRC Manual at BIM37945.

Suriname South American country. Its currency is the Suriname dollar of 100 cents. The UK has no double taxation treaty.

Suriname dollar Currency of Suriname.

surplus Excess of income over expenditure by a non-commercial entity. It is the equivalent to profit.

surplus business accommodation Accommodation that has been used in the taxpayer's trade, or was acquired for use in the trade, in the last three years. Income from letting such accommodation for up to three years may be taxed as trading income and not as property income (ITTOIA 2005 s21).

surplus earnings rule Provision of universal credit introduced from April 2018 to prevent earnings patterns being manipulated to maximise benefit payable. If earnings for a month exceed £2,500, the earnings are carried forward to the next month. If that month's earnings then exceed £2,500, universal credit stops.

surrenderable amount Amount of loss that a company may pass to another company in the same group as group relief (CTA 2020 s139).

surrender period Accounting period in which group relief is claimed for a loss (CTA 2010 s142).

surrogacy Arrangement in which a woman (surrogate) bears a child with the view that another woman shall be regarded as the mother (Surrogacy Arrangements Act 1985).

The surrogate or birth mother is entitled to maternity rights such as statutory maternity pay and maternity leave even though she does not keep the baby.

The other mother is regarded as adopting the child, and so may be eligible for statutory adoption pay and adoption leave.

Surrogacy is legal in the UK, but agreements are not enforceable. It is an offence to pay a surrogate any fee though reasonable expenses may be reimbursed.

surtax Addition to income tax on higher incomes charged between 1909 and 1973 when replaced by higher rate income tax.

surviving spouse A partner to a marriage who outlives the other. From 1 January 1996, a surviving spouse must live for 28 days after their partner's death to inherit. This provision is contained in Administration of Estates Act 1925 s46(2A) as inserted by Law Reform (Succession) Act 1995 s1.

survivorship When someone outlives someone else. This is particularly relevant when a person dies soon after inheriting.

For deaths from 1 January 1996, a surviving spouse of an intestate only inherits if the spouse lives for 28 days after the death (Administration of Estates Act 1925 s46(2A) as inserted by Law Reform (Succession) Act 1995 s1.

For testates, a survivorship clause may be explicitly contained in the will.

survivorship clause Condition in a will that someone must live for a certain period (typically one month) after the death to inherit.

For inheritance tax, the disposition is treated as made when the potential entitlement arises, unless that is more than 12 months later. In such a case, the disposition is not treated as made until then (IHTA 1984 s92).

suspended beer Term used in Customs notice 226 to mean beer subject to suspended duty.

suspended duty When excisable goods are allowed to move freely within the EU area. This usually requires financial security.

suspense account In bookkeeping, an account to which part of a double entry may be temporarily posted. This allows the records to remain balanced until the correct account is identified. An example is a payment received where the payer is not known. All reasonable efforts should be made to identify amounts in a suspense account.

suspension

(1) When Customs duty is deferred, such as under inward processing or drawback.

(2) When an employee is temporarily removed from their work, such as pending an investigation into misconduct. Generally the employee is entitled to his or her full pay during suspension.

suspension of penalties Provision introduced in April 2010 to allow penalties to be suspended when they arise from carelessness. No penalty is payable if the taxpayer complies with HMRC's directions for two years.

suspicious activity report (SAR) Report that must be filed by anyone, including a professional adviser, who has suspicion that financial activities relate to crime, money-laundering or terrorism (Proceeds of Crime Act 2002; Terrorism Act 2000). It is an offence not to report reasonable suspicion.

swamping When a controlled foreign company attempts to shelter large amounts of income from UK tax. The term was used in an HMRC consultation document of June 2011.

Swaziland African country. Its currency is the lilangeni (plural emalageni) of 100 cents. This is kept at par with the South African rand which is also used as currency. The UK has a double taxation agreement of 1968. On 19 April 2018, King Mswati III announced that the country would be renamed Eswatini to mark the 50th anniversary of its independence.

sweatpants These may be zero-rated if they qualify as children's clothing, as explained in VAT Notice 714. The issue was considered in the case *BG Supplies (Birmingham) Ltd [1993] VTD 11663.*

sweat shop Place of work where a person is made to work very hard for minimal wages, often in poor conditions.

Sweden European country that is a member of the European Union. Its currency is the Swedish krona of 100 ore. The UK has a double taxation convention of 2015.

Swedish marshmallow Sweet product similar to marshmallow. The VAT tribunal held that it was confectionery in *E Round & Son Ltd, VTD 2069.*

sweeper Term sometimes used for what was Schedule D Case VI income. The term means a provision that sweeps up income not taxed under other schedules. This meaning is used in BIM14030.

sweepstake Form of betting (particularly in racing) where each punter chooses an entrant and the winner takes all amounts staked, sometimes less a cut for the organiser. A sweepstake is generally exempt from betting duties.

sweet Item of confectionery. It is standard-rated for VAT as it specifically excluded from the scope of zero-rated food. VAT Notice 714 gives specific details. Sweets have been defined as "sweetened prepared food which is normally eaten with the fingers" in the case *Unibev [2004] VTD 18437*. In old excise Acts, the word meant a sweet wine.

sweetheart deal Arrangement where one customer or taxpayer apparently receives preferential treatment.

sweet wort In brewing, mixture formed by mixing the grist with hot water. The sweet wort has material added to remove unwanted solid material and provide the wort for brewing.

SWIFT Bank Identifier Code Series of letters and numbers that are the equivalent of the sort code in international banking.

swipe card Plastic card that gives access to premises or stores money. VAT notice 701/5 gives advice on when such cards are used for bar purchases in a club.

Swiss bank Bank in Switzerland which is renowned for protecting customer privacy. Under an agreement between the UK and Swiss authorities in 2011, Swiss banks will deduct withholding tax on payments to UK residents, unless those residents have authorised the Swiss bank to disclose details to the UK authorities.

Swiss Bank Settlement Arrangement whereby Swiss banks made payment to people used as slaves or forced labourers in the second world war. On 16 December 2015, it was announced that payments under this scheme are exempt from inheritance tax.

Swiss franc Currency of Switzerland.

syllogism In logic, a proposition from which a proof may be inferred. The simplest example is if A = B and B = C, then we may infer that A = C. Tax cases are full of syllogisms.

Syria Arab country. Its currency is the Syrian pound of 100 piastres. The UK has no double taxation treaty. The country is subject to UK sanctions, as are designated persons of the country.

Syrian pound Currency of Syria.

syrup Syrups used to make drinks are standard-rated for VAT. They are specifically excepted from the scope of zero-rating for food by Value Added Tax 1994 Sch 8 Group 1 Note 4.

T1 status HMRC term for goods not in free circulation.

Table A Set of tax tables to determine the free pay (or pay adjustment) for a payslip subject to PAYE.

Table B Set of tax tables to determine the amount of tax payable on a payslip after using Table A.

table football game Such a machine is specifically excluded from the scope of amusement machine licence duty.

tablets Medicinal tablets are subject to VAT as medicine. Food tablets are not zero-rated as food, even if palatable and nutritious. Fruit and vegetable tablets were denied zero-rating in the case *National Safety Association of America (UK) Ltd [1995] VTD 14241.*

tabular Description of accounting records that are kept in columns.

T-account Historic method of drawing up an account in bookkeeping. It involves drawing a large capital T. The name of the account is written above the horizontal line. The debits are recorded on the left of the vertical line, and the credits on the right. At the end of an accounting period a debit or credit balancing entry is made so that both sides balance. The balancing entry is taken to the trial balance.

tachograph Device installed in some vehicles to keep an automatic record of journeys. This may be used as be evidence about the tax allowability of journeys.

tacit relocation Provision under Scots law whereby a tenant of agricultural property may remain if neither party terminates a lease and the tenant inherits the property from its previous owner. This is not subject to inheritance tax (IHTA 1984 s177).

tagging Identifier attached to something. From 1 April 2011, items in a corporation tax return must be tagged using iXBRL.

tail swallowing Sale of sufficient rights to buy shares in a rights issue. For example, a shareholder is offered 110 shares at 100p or a payment of 10p for the rights for each share. If the shareholder sells 100 rights, he realises £10, enough to buy 10 shares. Tail swallowing is subject to special tax provisions in relation to share incentive plans. Under ITEPA 2003 Sch 2 para 77, the trustees have the power to sell sufficient rights to buy shares. This is subject to any direction given by the participant.

tainted charity donation Donation to a charity where the donor receives a significant personal benefit (ITA 2007 s809ZJ; CTA 2010 s939C). The capital gains tax implications are given in TCGA 1992 s257A. These rules apply from 1 April 2011. The rules are an anti-avoidance measure to ensure that tax relief for charities is not abused by making arrangements so that the donation provides financial benefits to the donor.

tainted gift Gift made within six years of the offence which funded it (Proceeds of Crime Act 2002 s77).

Taiwan Island country in Pacific Ocean. It originally claimed sovereignty over the whole of China. Conversely, China claims sovereignty over Taiwan. Its currency is the New Taiwanese dollar of 100 cents. The UK has a double taxation agreement of 2002 with an annex.

Tajikistan Eastern country. Its currency is the somoni of 100 dirams. The UK has a double taxation agreement of 2014 which came into force on 16 March 2015.

taka Currency of Bangladesh.

take-home pay Amount of salary or wages that an employee actually receives. Although this term is not defined, net pay usually means pay from which tax, national insurance, student loan repayments and pension contributions have been deducted. Take-home pay is where further deductions have been made, such as for trade union dues or loan repayment.

take-off weight For air passenger duty, the weight of an aircraft including people and contents at the time the aeroplane takes off (FA 1994 s29(2)). This weight is relevant for determining liability to air passenger duty.

takeover One business acquiring another. There is a special tax provision for employee share schemes (CTA 2009 s1023(3)).

takeover bid Attempt by one company to acquire another. The former is the acquirer; the latter is the target. Such bids are regulated by provisions of the Takeovers Directive and Takeover Code (CA 2006 s953(9)). The expenses of such a bid are generally treated for tax as capital expenditure rather than revenue expenditure.

Takeovers Directive EC Directive on Takeover Bids 2004/25/EC. Compliance with this Directive is a function of the Panel on Takeovers and Mergers (CA 2006 from s942).

taking control of goods Process to secure payment of tax. The procedure is contained in Tribunals, Courts and Enforcement Act 2007 Sch 12. Its application for tax is given in FA 2008 s127.

tala Currency of Samoa.

talking books for the blind CDs, cassettes, tapes or similar where a book is read. These are zero-rated for VAT if provided by a charity to blind people (VATA 1994 Sch 8 Group 4).

tambala One hundredth of a kwacha, currency of Malawi.

tampon For VAT, this is subject to the reduced rate of 5% from 1 January 2001 under VATA Sch 7A Group 8. The exact scope is explained in VAT notice 701/18. The government has said they will be zero-rated from 1 January 2021.

tampon tax Popular name for the 5% rate of VAT charged on sanitary products from January 2001, the lowest rate permitted under EU law. From 2015, the government had made donations equal to the sum collected to women's charities. Sanitary products are zero-rated from 1 January 2021.

tangible asset Fixed asset which has a physical form, such as building, vehicle, furniture or machine, as against intangible assets such as goodwill and brand name.

Tanzania African country. Its currency is the Tanzanian shilling of 100 cents. The UK has no double taxation treaty.

Tanzanian shilling Currency of Tanzania.

tapered reduction In relation to pensions allowance, this is the amount to which the annual allowance is reduced for those earning more than £150,000 a year. The reduction is set out in FA 2004 s228ZA as inserted by Finance (No 2) Act 2015 Sch 4 para 10.

taper relief

(1) Method of granting quick succession relief for inheritance tax. Details are given under Inheritance Tax in section 3 of this dictionary.

(2) Reduction in amount of capital gains tax according to how long an asset had been owned. It applied from 1998 to 2008, when it was replaced by entrepreneur's relief.

taper threshold (TT) Maximum amount for which **residence nil-rate band** applies for inheritance tax (Inheritance Tax Act 1984 s8D(5) as inserted by Finance (No 2) Act 2015 s9(4)).

tare Weight of an empty vehicle or vessel. The tare is deducted from a loaded vehicle or vessel to determine the weight of freight.

TARGET In banking, cross-border euro settlement system that links CHAPS in the UK with equivalent systems in EU countries.

targeted anti-avoidance rule (TAAR) Provision of tax law designed to counter the exploitation of tax rules to gain an unintended tax advantage. An example is FA 2010 s25 which is a TAAR for annual investment allowance.

tariff code Ten-digit number used to classify imported goods to determine what Customs duty is payable. From 1 January 2011, the UK replaces the EU Code with the UK code.

tariff income For social security, the amount of income assumed to arise from capital.

tariff suspension Temporary relief from import duty (Taxation (Cross-border Trade) Act 2018 s12).

tar sprayer Vehicle used in road-building and repair. It may use rebated fuel (HODA 1979 Sch 1 para 13B).

tax Compulsory charge imposed by a government or similar body to fund public expenditure.

The distinction between taxes, levies and other charges is not clear. It has been suggested that a tax is a payment where nothing is directly received back in return, but this definition is not met by the television licence (a tax), nor conversely by class 4 national insurance (not a tax). There are over 30 taxes in the UK, depending on how you count the various excise duties.

The word is defined in relation to information powers in FA 2008 Sch 36 para 63(1).

For VAT, the word "tax" means VAT (VATA 1994 s96(1)).

taxable earnings Earnings subject to income tax (ITEPA 2003 s175(2)).

taxable employment and support allowance "Means any amount of employment and support allowance which is chargeable to tax under Chapter 2 of Part 10 of

ITEPA (tax on social security income)" (PAYE regulations SI 2003 No 2682 reg 184A).

taxable incapacity benefit "Means any amount of incapacity benefit which is chargeable to tax under Chapter 2 of Part 10 of ITEPA (tax on social security income)" (PAYE regulations SI 2003 No 2682 reg 173).

taxable income elasticity (TIE) The percentage change in total taxable incomes in response to a 1% change in the net-of-tax rate.

This reflects such changes as mechanistic effect, behavioural effect and general equilibrium effects.

Detailed research of the TIE for Scottish rate of income tax has been published.

taxable income support "means any amount of income support which is chargeable to tax under Chapter 2 of Part 10 of ITEPA (tax on social security income" (PAYE regulations SI 2003 No 2682 reg 181).

taxable jobseeker's allowance "Means any amount of jobseeker's allowance which is chargeable to income tax under Chapter 2 of Part 10 of ITEPA (tax on social security income)" (PAYE regulations SI 2003 No 2682 reg 148).

taxable payments For employment income, the amount of gross pay as reduced by free pay or increased by additional pay under the PAYE system (PAYE Regulations 2003 reg 2(1)).

taxable person

(1) For employment income, the person to whom the earnings or benefits relate (ITEPA 2003 s13(3)).

(2) For VAT, the person registered, particularly an importer who re-imports goods (VATA 1994 s3).

taxable specific income Amount of specific income subject to tax (ITEPA 2003 s10(3)).

taxable supply Supply of goods or services which is not exempt from VAT. It bears VAT at the standard rate, reduced rate or zero rate. It "is a supply of goods or services made in the United Kingdom other than an exempt supply" (VATA 1994 s4(2)).

taxable turnover For VAT, total revenue from supplies that are taxable at the standard rate, reduced rate or zero rate. Exempt supplies are excluded.

taxable unit The person or group subject to tax. In general this is the individual person or company. An exception is council tax which is charged on households. Before 1990, a married couple were regarded as one unit for income tax.

tax accountant Person who offers tax advice to clients. Such a person need not be qualified. Under TMA 1970 s20A, HMRC may require a tax accountant to provide papers about a client if the *tax accountant* has been convicted of a tax offence or paid a penalty for assisting in the preparation of a false tax return (under TMA 1970 s99). There are further provisions for a tax adviser.

tax accounting arrangements In relation to a senior accounting officer:

- the framework of responsibilities, policies, appropriate people and procedures in place for managing tax compliance risk, and

- the systems and processes which put this framework into practice (HMRC Manual at SAOG24000).

tax adjustment

(1) Any adjustment required or authorised by law in calculating the profits of a trade for corporation tax purposes (CTA 2009 s180(5)).

(2) Any change in the accounts that arise from a change in tax law (FA 1998 s42(1).

This is discussed in HMRC Manual at BIM34095.

tax advantage Any provision or arrangement that results in a taxpayer paying less tax. In the context of anti-avoidance, the term is variously defined in TCGA 1992 s16A(2); ITTOIA 2005 s23D(3) and Revenue Scotland and Tax Powers Act 2014 s65(1).

tax-advantaged Description of a scheme that reduces a person's tax.

tax advice This is defined in the Professional Conduct in Relation to Taxation from para 4.1. It covers advising a client of choices under tax law and explaining the tax implications of proposed transactions or eventualities.

tax adviser Person who gives tax advice (TMA 1970 s20B(10)). Generally HMRC cannot compel a tax adviser to produced papers owned by the adviser and which relate to tax advice to a client.

tax agent Accountant or other person who assists people with complying with their tax responsibilities, such as preparing and submitting tax returns. HMRC said in 2010 that it values tax agents.

The role of a tax agent was considered by the High Court in the case *Lunn v HMRC [2011] EWHC 240, particularly para 13.*

From 1 April 2013, legislation allows HMRC to investigate dishonest conduct by tax agents, impose civil penalties of between £5,000 and £50,000, and publish their name and address (FA 2012 Sch 38). Where there is evidence of dishonesty, HMRC can require production of working papers. These provisions are discussed in HMRC Manual from CH180000.

Tax and Prices Index Index produced by the Office of National Statistics between 1987 and 2017. Its aim was to show improvement in consumer incomes when inflation was high and tax rates were being cut.

tăxa pe valoarea adăugată Romanian: value added tax.

tax arrangements In relation to tax avoidance, these are arrangements where it is reasonable, in all the circumstances, to conclude that obtaining a tax advantage was the main purpose or one of the main purposes (HMRC Guidance on Follower Notices and Accelerated Payments 2014).

tax assessment Statement from HMRC on how much tax it believes is owed by the taxpayer.

Tax Assurance Commissioner Senior HMRC official. The role was created in 2013 following criticism of how HMRC had negotiated settlements of tax disputes. The Commissioner scrutinises settlements involving £100 million or more tax or which are sensitive.

taxation matters In relation to judgment debts, means anything for which HMRC is responsible other than national insurance (F2A 2015 s52(15)).

Taxation (Post-Transition) Bill Bill introduced to Parliament on 8 December 2020 to regulate UK tax affairs after the end of the Brexit transition period on 31 December 2020.

tax avoidance Act of diminishing one's tax liability within the law, as against the illegal act of tax evasion. This distinction is not always clear cut.

While tax planning remains acceptable to HMRC and the government, artificial avoidance is not. Various provisions have been implemented in the last 40 years, including disclosure of tax avoidance schemes (DOTAS) and more powers for HMRC. HMRC has also published hallmarks of avoidance scheme, set out in section 3 of this dictionary.

The distinction was noted thus: "tax avoidance involves bending the rules of the tax system to gain a tax advantage that Parliament never intended. It often involves contrived, artificial transactions that serve little or no purpose other than to produce this advantage. It involves operating within the letter — but not the spirit — of the law" (HMRC publication *Tackling Tax Evasion and Avoidance. March 2015).*

tax avoidance arrangements In the context of related national insurance avoidance, "includes arrangements which enable, or might be expected to enable, a person to obtain an advantage in relation to any tax (within the meaning of Part 7 of the FA 2004)" (Social Security Administration Act 1992 s132A(7)). In relation to taxation of intellectual property, the term is given a specific definition in ITA 2007 s917A as inserted by FA 2016 s41.

Tax Avoidance Scheme Regulations The name for Statutory Instrument SI 2004 No 1864 as amended.

tax break Provision that allows a taxpayer to reduce his or her tax.

Tax Bulletin Publication produced by HMRC up to 2006. From 2007 it is replaced by HM Revenue and Customs Briefs.

tax burden In politics, how the obligation to pay tax falls on the individual or business. There are different ways to classify tax burden. A common method is direct taxation and indirect taxation. The former is where tax is paid direct to the state body (such as income tax, corporation tax and capital gains tax) whereas the latter is paid to someone else to pay to the state (such as excise duties and VAT). Tax burden may also be determined according to how it is calculated. This may be seen as one of four methods:

- proportionate: where tax paid is directly related to amount spent and does not vary by size. VAT is an example
- progressive: where tax is paid at a higher rate for larger amounts, such as higher rates of income tax
- regressive: where tax is paid at a lower rate for larger amounts, such as employee's national insurance
- fixed amount: where tax is paid at a fixed amount, such as vehicle excise duty.

tax code For PAYE, a combination of numbers and letters that indicates how an employee is to be taxed. These are listed in section 3 of this dictionary.

tax collector HMRC official whose duties are to collect tax rather than assess it.

tax concession Strictly relaxation from tax rules in circumstances. Such concessions are made by HMRC. They are known as extra-statutory concessions.

tax conditiality Term coined in the Budget 2020 to mean making the issue of approvals, licences and grants by the government conditional on tax compliance.

tax credit For social security, a means-tested benefit that has nothing to do with tax (Tax Credits Act 2002). There are currently two forms of tax credit: child tax credit and working tax credit. They are both being replaced by universal credit. Tax credits are administered by HMRC. The tax credit functions of HMRC are given in FA 1989 s182(2ZA).

tax-deductible Description of an expense or liability that may be deducted from taxable income.

tax deed Agreement between two parties (usually a contract to buy a business) whereby one party agrees to accept the benefit or detriment of a tax issue that was not settled at the time of the agreement. A tax deed has the effect of adjusting the price paid for a business which can itself affect the parties' tax liabilities. The case *Teesside Power Holdings Ltd v Electrabel International Holdings BV [2012] EWHC 33* held that a tax deed agreeing to pay a refund does not require payment of interest in the absence of a specific clause to that effect.

tax disc Circular piece of paper produced to be attached to a vehicle from 1 January 1921 to 30 September 2014, to indicate that vehicle excise duty (road tax) had been paid. The last tax disc expired on 30 September 2015 since when records are kept online and can be checked by anyone.

At the same time, the duty attached to the keeper of the vehicle rather than to the vehicle itself. This means that a new owner must tax the car. The former owner automatically receives a rebate when the vehicle's ownership is re-registered at DVLA. As duty is paid or repaid for whole months only, it usually means that duty is paid twice for the month of transfer.

Tax Disputes Resolution Board Board established by HMRC in 2013 to:

- make decisions and recommendations about proposals for resolving significant tax disputes
- the selection and oversight of cases within the High Risk Corporates Programme
- serve as the escalation point for cases from the Case Boards within Lines of Business.

Further details were given in an HMRC Notice of 20 December 2013.

Taxes Act 1970 Income and Corporation Taxes Act 1970.

Taxes Act 1988 Income and Corporation Taxes Act 1988.

Taxes Impact Assessment Statement on how a proposed change to the tax system is expected to affect different groups of taxpayer.

taxe sur la valeur ajoutée French for "value added tax". This can appear on invoices from France or Belgium. This was originally a different French tax which became the basis for VAT in UK and EU.

tax evasion Illegal act of suppressing or falsifying information to reduce a tax burden. It is a criminal offence.

The Professional Conduct in Relation to Taxation from para 9.1 says that a tax adviser must not be involved in tax evasion other than to assist a taxpayer in regularising his or her tax affairs.

Tax Evasion Hotline Free telephone service to report suspected tax evasion or other fraud (such as falsely claiming coronavirus support). The number is 0800 788 887. Suspicions may also be reported from the HMRC website.

tax exempt Not subject to tax. This usually refers to bodies that have diplomatic immunity and some international organisations. It can also be applied to charities.

tax exempt special savings account (TESSA) Tax-advantaged savings account available between 1 January 1991 and 5 April 1999 (ICTA 1988 s326A(1)) when they were replaced by individual savings accounts.

Tax Faculty A faculty of the Institute of Chartered Accountants in England and Wales that is open to members and non-members.

tax fraud Offence of being knowingly concerned in the fraudulent evasion of tax or duty by the person or another person (code of practice COP 9 para 8.1).

tax-free childcare Scheme introduced from November 2017 whereby the government pays 20% of the cost of childcare to a limit of £10,000 a year. The main elements are:

- the parents must be in work, which includes self-employment
- the parents must not be paying tax at a higher rate
- funds are paid into a special bank account
- funds may only be used for qualifying childcare
- the state pays £2 for every £8 paid by the parents.

The scheme was available for children:

- under 6 from 24 November 2017
- under 9 from 15 January 2018
- under 12 from 14 February 2018.

tax functions Range of duties performed by HMRC as defined in FA 1989 s182(2) and FA 2011 Sch 23 para 47.

tax gap Difference between amount of tax collected and amount of tax that should be collected. The current methodology was devised in 2015/16. The tax gap was 7.5% in 2005/06, and fell to a record low of 4.7% for tax year 2018/19. Most of the gap is due to insolvency.

tax-geared penalty Any tax penalty that is calculated by reference to an amount of tax (TMA 1970 s127B).

tax harmonisation Provisions designed to align either two taxes or taxes in two countries. Efforts have been made to align provisions of income tax and class 1 national insurance. Less successful efforts have been made to align VAT and corporation tax rules in the EU.

tax haven Country or territory where tax rates are low, or where tax rules are less onerous.

Tax Health Plan Limited tax amnesty offered to doctors and other medical practitioners. On 11 January 2010, it was announced that if they voluntarily disclosed untaxed income by 31 March 2010, tax penalties would be discounted by 10%.

tax holiday Period when a business or person is excused from paying tax. Such holidays have been declared for business rates during the coronavirus outbreak. There have also been some employer's national insurance holidays.

taxi Motor cab in which a fare-paying passenger is driven. The term originally referred merely to the meter that recorded the charge. VAT guidance for taxis is given in VAT Notice 700/25.

taxi fares These are generally standard-rated for VAT. They do not come within the scope of zero-rated passenger transport under VATA 1984 Sch 8 Group 8 unless, exceptionally, they can carry more than 10 passengers. VAT guidance for taxis is given in VAT Notice 700/25.

tax incentive Provision in tax law that reduces a tax liability to encourage taxpayers to follow a desired course. UK tax law is full of such incentives.

tax increment financing Method of financing government expenditure from tax revenue streams. It is widely used in the USA. In the 2011 Autumn Statement, the government ruled out using it in the UK.

taxing master Former name for a court officer who deals with disputes on legal fees. The officer is now called a costs judge.

taxing officer Person appointed by each House of Parliament to calculate the costs of moving certain Bills (Parliamentary Costs Act 2006 s1).

tax inspector Official of HMRC who deals with tax assessments.

Tax Inspectors Without Borders Joint initiative of OECD and United Nations established in 2015 to help developing nations with their tax administration.

tax invoice Invoice that meets the conditions for VAT rules.

tax it or lose it Campaign launched by DVLA on 3 November 2017, warning drivers that untaxed cars could be seized.

Tax Justice Network Independent body formed in 2003 to study international tax and promote reform.

tax leaks Leaks of information about tax avoidance and tax evasion. Such information is often leaked by a whistleblower. The information is illegally obtained, usually by the whistleblower transferring millions of documents to investigative journalists.

The four biggest leaks of recent years, with the number of pages of documents, are:

- Cook Islands: 2.5 million
- Panama Papers: 11.5 million
- Bahamas: 1.5 million

• Paradise Papers: 13.4 million.

Although obtained illegally, the tax authorities including HMRC have used the data, though there have been few prosecutions. The Panama Papers became a national news story, as details on more than 200,000 individuals and entities were made public. They included political leaders. The prime minister of Iceland, Sigmundur Davíð Gunnlaugsson resigned.

The papers provided much useful information on how tax avoidance schemes worked.

tax lock commitment Commitment made in 2015 that the government would not raise the rates of income tax, VAT or national insurance during the lifetime of the Parliament (F2A 2015 ss1-2). The commitment was not renewed in legislation after the 2017 and 2019 elections.

tax loophole Unintended provision of tax law.

tax loss Loss made by a business which may be offset against taxable income.

Taxman Song written by George Harrison and recorded in 1966 by The Beatles on their album *Revolver.* It laments that tax rates then could reach 19 shillings in the pound: "let me tell you how it will be, there's one for you, nineteen for me".

In 1966, the standard rate of income tax was 8s 3d in the pound and surtax could add another 10 shillings. In 1965/66, surtax rates were increased by 10%.

tax month For PAYE, a period from the 6th of one calendar month to the 5th of the next month (PAYE Regs 2003 reg 2(1)).

tax morality Term coined by then Inland Revenue chairman Sir Nick Montagu in 2002 to suggest that tax avoidance was immoral.

In 1992, Lord Templeman said in the case *Ensign Tankers (Leasing) Ltd v Stokes [1992],* "there is no morality in a tax and no illegality or immorality in a terms and conditions scheme".

tax neutral Description of a transaction or a change in tax law that is intended not to change the amount of tax collected, but may change how it is calculated and who pays it.

tax not deducted because of the overriding limit For PAYE, means "any tax –

(a) which is due at the relevant date in accordance with the appropriate tax tables in respect of any taxable payments or local taxable payments to date, but

(b) which has not been deducted because of the overriding limit"

(PAYE Regulations SI 2003 No 2682 reg 2(1)).

taxonomy Classification according to principles. Corporation tax accounts must from 2011 have details encoded according to the iXBRL taxonomy.

tax paid Description of goods where all necessary duties and taxes have been paid and will not be refunded.

"All taxes due on the goods wherever purchased have been paid and have not been, nor will be, refunded" (Customs notice 3).

tax payable Amount of tax which a person or organisation must pay.

tax payable under the assessment In relation to PAYE and self-assessment, this is given a specific meaning in PAYE regulations SI 2003 No 2682 s188(7).

taxpayers' charter Documents produced by the tax authorities from 1990, setting out their basic standards of service. The latest charter was published on 5 November 2020. The duty to produce a charter is Commissioners of Revenue and Customs Act 2005 s16A. It promises that HMRC will:

- help taxpayers meet their tax responsibilities
- ensure that taxpayer get any benefits, tax credits, refunds and other support that may be claimed
- provide accurate, consistent and clear information
- advise taxpayers of options if they disagree with HMRC
- work with taxpayers to reach an appropriate outcome quickly and simply
- provide services that are designed around what a taxpayer needs to do
- provide services that are accessible, easy and quick to use, minimising costs to the taxpayer
- ensure that the people who deal with a taxpayer have the right level of expertise
- answer questions and resolve things first time, as quickly as it can
- explain what happens next in any issue
- put right any mistake as soon as possible
- explain how to make a complaint
- assume the taxpayer is telling the truth unless it has good reason to believe otherwise
- listen to taxpayer's worries and be responsive to the taxpayer's personal situation
- provide extra support to taxpayers who need it
- allow someone else to deal with a taxpayer's affairs
- treat taxpayer information as confidential
- only use tax information fairly and lawfully
- treat taxpayers with respect, professionalism and integrity.

Few of these provisions are legally enforceable though they may be quoted to HMRC.

tax period For VAT, period covered by a VAT return. This is usually three months, but can be one month, one year, or sometimes other periods. For PAYE, the term "means –

(a) tax quarter [for simplified deduction scheme] or regulation 70 (quarterly tax periods) applies, or

(b) tax month, in every other case"

(PAYE Regulations SI 2003 No 2682 reg 2(1)).

tax planning Legal activity of organising one's affairs so as to reduce the amount of tax payable. HMRC said "tax planning involves using tax reliefs for the purpose for which they were intended, for example, claiming tax relief on capital investment, or saving via ISAs or for retirement by making contributions to a pension scheme. However, tax reliefs can be used excessively or aggressively, by others than those intended to benefit from them or in ways that clearly go beyond the intention of Parliament" (*Tackling Tax Evasion and Avoidance*, HMRC publication of March 2015, which seeks to distinguish tax planning from tax avoidance.) Similar views are given in Professional Conduct in Relation to Taxation para 4.3).

tax point Date that fixes the liability for VAT on a supply (VATA 1984 s6). This is generally when the supply took place. It may be up to two weeks later when an invoice is issued, or earlier when payment is made.

tax policy Policy established by a Treasury committee in November 2018. It said that tax should:

- be fair
- support growth and competitiveness
- be certain
- be stable
- be practical
- be coherent.

tax pool Record of income tax paid by the trustees of a discretionary trust plus any tax deducted at source on income they receive. This pool is reduced by the tax credit on income distributed to beneficiaries. If the balance in the tax pool is less than the tax credit, the beneficiaries must pay the balance to HMRC (ITA 2007 s497).

tax position General term for the status of someone's tax affairs. In Scotland, the term is defined in Revenue Scotland and Tax Powers Act 2014 s120(1).

tax presence For PAYE, the state of an employer being in the UK and therefore obliged to operate PAYE.

tax quarter For quarterly payment of PAYE one of the following three-month periods:

- 6 April to 5 July
- 6 July to 5 October
- 6 November to 5 January
- 6 January to 5 April

(PAYE Regs 2003 reg 2(1)).

tax rates Percentage or amount at which a tax is charged.

tax rebate Refund of tax previously paid, particularly when provided by an employer under the PAYE system.

tax reduction Reduction in income tax given in addition to personal allowances and other reliefs (ITA 2007 s26).

tax relief Any form of allowance or similar that may be deducted from otherwise taxable income.

tax return Form or online equivalent that a taxpayer is obliged to complete for the tax authorities. For individuals, it discloses liabilities to income tax, capital gains tax and class 4 national insurance. For companies, it disclose liability to corporation tax. There are separate returns for VAT, inheritance tax and other taxes.

tax revenue Amount of tax received by the government.

tax schedules Categories of income and the rules governing their taxation. They were first introduced in 1803 for income tax and adopted for corporation tax when introduced in 1965. They were discontinued from 2005 for income tax and for corporation tax from 2009. For income tax, the Schedules were:

- Schedule A (1803-2005) land and buildings
- Schedule B (1803-1998) farming, later woodlands
- Schedule C (1803-1996) public securities
- Schedule D (1803-2005) trading and miscellaneous
- Schedule E (1803-2005) employment
- Schedule F (1965-2005) share dividends.

Schedules D and E were further divided into cases.

tax shelter Arrangement where income or gain can be protected from the tax otherwise payable. A limited company can be a tax shelter.

tax tables Tables produced by HMRC for payroll use (ITEPA 2003 s685; PAYE Regs 2003 reg 2(1)).

tax treaty Agreement between the UK and a foreign territory relating to tax. It resolves issues where otherwise the same income or gain may be taxed twice. A treaty thus avoids double taxation.

Under international law a treaty is "an international agreement concluded between states in written form and governed by international law, whether embodied in a single instrument, or in two or more related instruments, and whatever its particular designation" (Vienna Convention on the Law of Treaties 1969 article 2 para 1(a)).

The UK has more than 100 tax treaties, some of which are limited in scope.

tax value The amount on which VAT is charged.

tax volatility The extent to which a country's tax income is vulnerable to small changes, such as when tax comes from a few sources. In 2018, the Irish Republic considered its corporation tax income to be volatile.

tax warehouse Another name for a Customs warehouse.

tax wedge The difference between the cost of employing someone and what that person receives. Using 2020/21 rates, someone earning £26,000 a year would normally have take-home pay of £21,322 after deduction of £2,698 tax and £1,980 national insurance. The employer pays employer's national insurance of £2,375.

This means that the employer has spent £28,375 to give the employee £21,322. The difference is £7,053. This is 24.8% of £28,375, which is the tax wedge.

Sometimes, employer's national insurance is excluded.

The term has been defined by OECD.

TaxWatch An organisation that defines itself as "a UK charity dedicated to compliance and sound administration of the law in the field of taxation".

tax week Period of seven days starting on 6 April and every seventh day thereafter (PAYE Regulations 2003 reg 2(1)). It is used to determine the PAYE payable by weekly employees. It is also used for national insurance for which a similar definition appears in SSCBA 1992 s122(1).

As a calendar year comprises 1 day (or 2 days in a leap year) more than 52 weeks, a pay day on 4 or 5 April may fall in what is known as week 53.

tax year Period from 6 April to the next 5 April for which income tax and capital gains tax are assessed. This year is used for income tax, capital gains tax and inheritance tax. It is not used for corporation tax or VAT.

Before 1752, the calendar year started on Lady Day, 25 March. Calendar (New Style) Act 1750 moved from the old Julian calendar to the more accurate Gregorian calendar. This meant that 11 days were lost, so 2 September 1752 was followed by 14 September 1752. While this Act also made 1 January, the first day of the calendar year, the tax year still started on Lady Day.

As 11 days had been lost, the tax year was extended by 11 days so that it ended on 4 April.

Under the new calendar, every 100th year was not a leap year unless it was a 400th year. So 1800 was not a leap year. An extra day was added so that the tax year ended on 5 April. No extra day was added in 1900, so the tax year has ended on 5 April since 1800.

A Parliamentary answer in 1972 confirmed that the government had no intention to change the date. The Irish Republic replaced this tax year with the calendar year from 2002.

Taylor Report Report produced on 11 July 2017 by a group chaired by Matthew Taylor on the gig economy. It noted that employment law has three categories of worker whereas tax law only has two. The Report suggested the creation of a new category called dependent contractor. This has not been adopted.

TC (1) Citation of cases as reported in the official guide to tax cases started in 1875.
(2) First tier tribunal tax cases from 2003.

tea Beverage that is specifically zero-rated under VATA 1994 Sch 8 Group 1 Items Overriding The Exception 4. Further guidance is given in VAT Notice 701/14. It was subject to excise duty from 1660 to 1962.

Teach-a-steach Alba Scots Gaelic for Revenue Scotland (Revenue Scotland and Tax Powers Act 2014 s2(2)).

technical provisions

(1) Term used in Pensions Act 2004 s222(2) to mean the amount required on the basis of an actuarial calculation of the liabilities of a pension scheme.
(2) Term used in FA 2007 Sch 11 para 3(7) in relation to detailed tax provisions for insurance businesses.

teeming and lading Employee fraud that involves falsifying figures in one period and correcting them in the next.

tein One hundredth of a tenge, currency of Kazakhstan.

teind Scottish term for a tithe, or to take a tithe.

telecommunications wholesale From 1 February 2016, a reverse charge for VAT is introduced for business wholesaling telecommunication services. Further guidance is given in HMRC Brief 1 (2016). This should be read with VAT Notice 735.

teleology Interpretation according to purpose. VAT and Customs laws are largely interpreted teleologically. Other tax law is interpreted literally.

Teleos European case *R (on application of Teleos plc) v HMRC (C-409/04} [2007]* on the evidence needed to show that goods have been exported. It held that a business should not be penalised for relying on seemingly legitimate proof of export which proves to be false. As a consequence, HMRC amended its practice as stated in statement of practice SP1/20.

telephone Instrument for relaying sound, particularly conversation, over a long distance. HMRC has published statement of practice SP1/2010 on its policy in doing business by telephone. This statement was amended on 7 February 2012.

television This is subject to VAT at the standard-rated. Between 1957 and 1963, it was subject to a specific excise duty. For shared transmission services, there are specific tax provisions in FA 1991 s78, and capital gains tax provisions in TCGA 1992 s267.

Some television programmes may qualify for tax discount as explained under Creative Industries Relief in section 3 of this dictionary.

television advertisement duty Duty charged on television advertisements between 1961 and 1964.

television entertainer An issue was whether such an entertainer is taxed as employed or self-employed. The issue was largely settled by the Court of Appeal decision in *ITV Services Ltd v HMRC [2013] EWCA Civ 867*. This broadly held that an entertainer booked for a single performance may be self-employed, while others are generally employed. HMRC set out its practice in Briefs 29/13 and 11/14. Similar issues continue to arise with regard to IR 35 liability.

television guide The publication of a television guide by a television channel is now generally considered to be part of the standard-rated broadcasting service and not a separate supply of a zero-rated publication. Such a separate ruling had been given in the case *British Sky Broadcasting Group plc [1999] VTD 16220*, but was not followed in the case *The Angel Foundation Ltd [2003] VTD 18818*.

television licence Licence required since 1946 to watch terrestrial television channels, currently required by Communications Act 2003 s363.

From September 2016 this includes watching catch-up services such as iPlayer. The licence is legally a tax. One licence covers any number of sets at the premises.

From 2000, the licence was free to households where someone over 75 lives. From 1 Aug 2020, that is restricted to over-75s who are receiving pension credit. There is a reduction for someone with a severe vision impairment.

Under provisions of SI 2020 No 160, those who have problems in paying the licence can be allowed to make weekly or monthly payments.

The licence is needed in the UK and Crown dependencies.

Since 1991, it is collected by the BBC. The BBC is authorised to use surveillance and detection to identify licence evaders. The licence fee provides about 75% of the BBC's income. The rest comes from hire of studio facilities and selling programmes to other channels internationally.

Watching or recording television without a licence is a criminal offence that can attract a penalty of up to £1,000. The Office of National Statistics changed its classification of the licence in 2006 from a service charge to a tax.

television tax relief Relief from corporation tax from 2013 in respect of making certain television programmes. Details are given under Creative Industries Relief in section 3 of this dictionary.

telling, giving and helping Three elements of disclosure in a tax investigation. The term was used in a consultation document in July 2011 about dishonest tax agents.

Tell Us Once Government provisions so that government bodies only need to be told once of a change in circumstances. It is a heading for WRA 2012 s135 in relation to social security.

temping Common term for someone provided as a temporary worker by an employment agency. Since 1975, such a worker must have income tax and national insurance deducted on a payroll run by the agency.

temporal condition One of two conditions that must be met for a connected flight to be regarded as part of one journey for the purposes of air passenger duty. The other condition is the ticketing condition. The temporal condition restricts the number of hours between flights. Details of this are set out in Customs notice 550.

temporarily imported vehicle For Customs purposes, this means a vehicle brough into UK for use here for up to six months. Such a vehicle is generally exempt from VAT and Customs duty. If the vehicle complies with the licensing and registration of its home country, it is also exempt from vehicle excise duty.

temporary admission When goods are brought into the UK for a short time, such as to exhibit a picture. Such goods may be relieved of Customs duty.

temporary building For VAT purposes, the supply of a temporary building is generally regarded as a standard-rated supply of a service or goods, and not as an exempt supply of an interest to occupy land. A recent case on what constitutes a temporary building is *Sibcas Ltd [2017] All ED 207 (Jul). UKUT 298.*

temporary deemed employee When someone is sufficiently under the control of an employer to be regarded as an employee, creating a vicarious liability for the employer. The term was used by the Court of Appeal in the case *Hawley v Luminar Leisure plc [2006].* The case concerned a door supervisor of a night club who attacked a customer.

temporary event notice Form of licence needed from local authority to sell alcohol at a local function such as a church fete (Licensing Act 2003 s100). Such a notice is issued routinely subject to conditions and no objection from the police.

temporary hard standing Area near a landfill site designed to allow landfill operations to take place. Material so used is not subject to landfill tax.

temporary importation rule Provision that provides relief under the remittance basis. The rule is defined in ITA 2007 s809Z4.

temporary non-resident Person who is resident for a tax year in which he returns to original country and who was not resident for the previous year. Their capital gains tax liability is set out in TCGA1992 s10A.

temporary site haulage road Road constructed from waste material to give access to a landfill site. Material so used is not subject to landfill tax.

temporary storage For Customs duty, there is a special procedure for goods so imported. There are also specific provisions for beer duty as explained in Customs notice 199A.

temporary tax "A tax which has been imposed, or renewed or reimposed, for a limited period not exceeding eighteen months, and was in force or imposed during the previous financial year" (Provisional Collection of Taxes Act 1968 s2(2)). Income tax is a temporary tax, even though it has been charged every years since 1842.

temporary workplace In relation to travel in employment, "means a place which the employee attends in the performance of the duties of the employment –

(a) for the purpose of performing a task of limited duration, or

(b) for some other temporary purpose"

(ITEPA 2003 s339(3)).

This expression is further clarified in following sub-sections.

Travel to a temporary workplace is generally tax deductible for up to 24 months. The limit was 12 months before 6 April 1998.

tenancy Agreement by which one person pays a landlord to occupy their property. For pubs, a statutory definition is given in Small Business, Enterprise and Employment Act 2015 s6(2).

tenancy deposit "In relation to a tenancy, means any money intended to be held (by the landlord or otherwise) as security for –

(a) the performance of any obligations of the tenant arising under or in connection with the tenancy, or

(b) the discharge of any liability of the tenant arising under or in connection with the tenancy"

(Housing and Planning Act 2016 s62).

tenancy strategy Strategy that every local authority must prepare and publish (Localism Act 2011 from s150).

Tenant Fees Act An Act of 2019 which protects tenants from unfair charges from landlords. The Act takes effect from 1 June 2019. The Act:

- caps most tenancy deposits at five weeks' rent
- restricts administrative and renewal fees to a reasonable amount
- limits charges for such things as lost keys to a reasonable amount for which the landlord must provide evidence
- gives tenants the right to recover sums wrongly paid
- gives trading standards officers and first tier tribunals the power to order repayments.

tenant for life Person who holds an estate for life and has wide powers under Settled Land Act 1925. They are being phased out under provisions of Housing and Planning act 2016 Sch 7.

Tenant Hardship Fund Fund established in Scotland in 2020 to assist tenants struggling to pay rent because of coronavirus.

tenant in common When two people co-own land and property such that each person can leave their interest in a will.

tenant pur autre vie Tenant during the life of another person.

tenant right Rights of a tenant of an agricultural property to compensation on the end of the tenancy in respect of unexhausted improvements on the holding (Agricultural Holdings Act 1986).

tender (1) Offer to provide goods or services for a stated price, and often subject to stated conditions.
(2) Offer money in the form of bank notes and coins for payment. Legal tender is given in section 3 of this dictionary.

tenendum Latin: to be held. Clause in a conveyance which states that land is to be held by the grantee.

tenge Currency of Kazakhstan.

tennesi One hundredth of a manat, currency of Turkmenistan.

ten pence coin Coin minted from 1968 as a decimal replacement of the florin worth two shillings. It was made from cupro-nickel until 2012 when it was replaced by nickel-plated steel. Its diameter reduced from 24mm to 18mm in 1990.

ten pound note Banknote worth £10. The current issue depicts Jane Austen, is printed on polymer plastic and was issued on 14 September 2017.

ten shilling note Banknote worth 10 shillings or half a pound. It was issued between 1914 and 1970 when replaced by the 50p coin.

ten-yearly charge Inheritance tax charge imposed on discretionary trusts, and, from 22 March 2006, other relevant property trusts (IHTA 1984 s61(1)). It is charged every ten years.
This charge is 30% of the lifetime rate of inheritance tax. As the lifetime rate is 20%, this means the charge is a maximum of 6% of the trust's value. The calculation can be complicated. It divides the ten years into 40 quarters and calculates for each quarter, excluding assets added during that quarter.

terabyte In computing, storage capacity equal to 1 trillion bytes.

teraflop In computing, unit of speed equal to 1 trillion floating-point operations per second.

term deposit Money placed on deposit for a fixed period at the end of which it is returned to the lender with interest.

terminal bonus Additional bonus which may be paid when a claim arises under a with-profit life insurance policy, either at maturity or on death of the policyholder.

terminal illness Description of a person suffering from a physical condition from which there is no likelihood of avoiding death. Such a person automatically qualifies for the highest rate of the care component of the disability living allowance and can be a factor in determining entitlement to the mobility component of the same allowance. There are special provisions allowing for a lump sum payment from a pension fund. Provisions relating to the personal independence payment to someone who is terminally ill are set out in WRA 2012 s82.

For child trust funds, the term is defined according to the definitions for terminal illness for social security purposes (Child Trust Funds Regulations SI 2004 No 1450 reg 18A(6)).

terminal loss relief Provision whereby a loss in a final accounting period may be offset against profits in the three previous periods (ITA 2007 s90; CTA 2010 s37).

terminal market Place where commodities are traded. There are special VAT provisions in VATA 1994 s50. These are explained in VAT Notice 701/9.

termination In relation to leases this occurs when a predetermined period ends or when the lease ends by a party exercising a right to do so or by operation of the law (CAA 2001 s228H(1).

termination award Payment to someone on their leaving employment. This may be tax-free up to £30,000 (unchanged from 1988). The law is ITEPA 2003 s401(1) as amended.

A similar definition for social security appears in SSCBA 1992 s10(12).

From 6 April 2018, these provisions apply to payment in lieu of notice. Previously this was taxable if it arose from a provision in the contract of employment, but not if there was no such provision. The latter was considered to be compensation for wrongful dismissal.

Statutory redundancy pay is exempt from income tax but must be included to see if the £30,000 limit has been reached.

From April 2020, the employer must pay class 1A national insurance on payments above £30,000.

term insurance Insurance policy that runs only for a defined period. It particularly applies to life insurance where a payment is only made if a person dies before a predetermined date or age.

terms of audit appointment Conditions under which an auditor is engaged (CA 2006 s493).

Territorial Army The Territorial Army is renamed the Army Reserve under Defence Reform Act 2014 s44(2). They are one of the classes of reservists (PAYE regulations SI 2003 No 2682 reg 122(2)).

territorial waters Waters that extend into the sea up to 12 miles from land (Territorial Sea Act 1967). Internationally this is governed by a Geneva Convention of 1958.

terrorism Use of violence and fear. Not only is this a crime itself, but failure to report evidence is itself a crime. This overrides any duty of client confidentiality. Tax authorities may disclose confidential information to intelligence services under Anti-Terrorism, Crime and Security Act 2001 s19.

Payments to terrorists are not tax-deductible as they are criminal payments. The matter is discussed in HMRC Manual at BIM43120.

TESSA Tax exempt special savings account available between 1991 and 1999, now replaced by individual savings accounts (ISAs).

testacy The state of having a valid will.

testamentary capacity Ability to make a will. Generally this means that the person is aged 18 or more and has sufficient mental capacity (Wills Act 1837). Soldiers and mariners on actual military service may make a will at any age, which may be verbal (Wills Act 1837; Wills (Soldiers and Sailors) Act 1918).

A person has sufficient mental capacity if he or she understands what a will is, how it affects their property, and that "no disorder of mind shall poison his affections, pervert his sense of right, or prevent the exercise of his natural faculties — that no insane delusion shall influence his will in disposing of his property and bring about a disposal of it which, if the mind had been sound, wo uld not have been made" (*Cockburn C J in Banks v Goodfellow [1870] LR 5 QBR 549, 565).*

testamentary disposition Freedom of an individual to leave his or her property in a will as he or she wishes.

testamentary guardian Person appointed in a will to look after a testator's child who is still under 18.

testamentary intention Principle that the intention of the testator determines how a will is to be interpreted.

testamentary trust Trust that is created by a will.

testate State of having a valid will.

testator Person who has made a will.

testatrix Term now rarely used for a female testator.

test case Case brought before a court to establish a legal principle.

test day Day used to determine whether there is a one-way exchange effect in exchange gains and losses and derivatives. The term is defined in CTA 2009 s328C for exchanges and s606C for derivatives.

testimonium Clause at the end of a deed or will which commences "in witness whereof..."

Test in Live Facility provided in some on-line tax-filing facilities on HMRC website. It allows a user to test the compatibility of their data and software without making a real tax return.

test return Dummy tax return that may be sent to HMRC to ensure that the connection is working properly.

tests of truth In evidence, the three tests of whether a witness is being truthful are demeanour, consistency and background.

tetri One hundredth of a laria, currency of Georgia.

Thailand Eastern country. Its currency is the baht of 100 satang. The UK has a double taxation convention of 1981.

Thalidomide Trust Trust established on 10 August 1973 for children born with disabilities because of the drug Thalidomide. Under SI 2004 No 1819, payments from the trust are not taxed.

thalweg German: valley way. The boundary of lands separated by a river as being the centre of its navigable waters.

thank you In April 2011, HMRC asked taxpayers not to send them thank you letters.

theatre tax credit Surrenderable loss that may be converted to a payment by a theatrical company under CTA 2009 s1217K. Details are given under Creative Industries in section 3 of this dictionary.

theatrical artist Actor or other entertainer who primarily works in theatres. The case *Madeley v HMRC SpC 547 [2006]* established that this term also applied to television presenters. The case concerned Richard and Judy Madeley who presented a daytime television programme.

theatrical production For the purposes of theatrical productions tax relief, "means a dramatic production or a ballet (and any ballet is therefore a theatrical production, whether or not it is also a theatrical production), But see section 1217FB [which excludes some types of production]" (CTA 2009 s1217FA(1)).

A theatrical production may qualify for a special corporation tax relief from 22 August 2014 under provisions set out in CTA 2009 from s1217F. Details are given under Creative Industries in section 3 of this dictionary.

A production is not regarded as theatrical if:

(a) its main purpose is advertising
(b) the performances include a competition or contest
(c) a wild animal is used in any performance,
(d) the production is of a sexual nature, or
(e) its main object is to make a film.

(CTA 2009 s1217FB(1)).

theatrical release For the purposes of corporation tax relief on film production, "means exhibition to the paying public at the commercial cinema" (CTA 2009 s1196(2)). It is a condition for film tax relief that the film be intended for theatrical release.

the Bar Term used to mean barristers collectively. Barristers qualify when they are "called to the bar". This was once a physical bar in a court which only a barrister was allowed to pass.

thebe One hundredth of a pula, currency of Botswana.

theft Dishonest appropriation of "property belonging to another with the intention of permanently depriving the other of it" (Theft Act 1968 s1). The term theft includes offences of larceny, robbery, burglary, blackmail, obtaining goods by deception, receiving and handling stolen property, unlawful abstraction of electricity, and related offences.

Theft Act 1978 added the offences of making off without payment.

Losses of cash or goods from theft are generally tax deductible, unless made by a director or proprietor of the business. A leading case on this latter point is

Curtis v J & G Oldfield Ltd [1925] 9 TC 319. The matter is discussed in HMRC Manual at BIM37810.

Theft can be a reasonable excuse for being late with filing a tax return or paying tax.

Thellusson Act Accumulations Act 1800, now replaced. This was prompted by the case *Thellusson v Woodford [1799]* where the deceased left a will tying up his estate for decades so that no living person could benefit.

therm Unit once used for calculating payment for gas. It is equal to 100,000 British thermal units. It is equal to 1.055×10^8 joules.

thermal insulation For capital allowances, this is regarded as a features integral to a building and so qualifies for a 6% writing down allowance in a special pool (CAA 2001 from s27).

The Times National newspaper that publishes law reports. The citation is simply *The Times* followed by the date that it appeared.

thin capitalisation Form of tax avoidance similar to transfer pricing. It operates when a group company charges a much higher or lower interest rate on interest as a means of shifting profit to a lower taxed country.

From April 2004, there are specific provisions to counter this. They broadly disallow the payment of interest to a connected company to the extent that the rate exceeds that of a commercial lender.

thing In relation to an online marketplace in things and digital services tax, the word "means any services, goods or other property" (FA 2020 s43(6)(a)).

third company For consortium relief, "a company that is not... a member of the same group of companies as the trading company" (CTA 2010 s155(4)).

third country Country or territory outside the European Union.

In relation to savings income, "means a territory other than a member State" (Importing of Savings Income Information Regulations SI 2003 No 3297 reg 2(2)).

In relation to merchandise in baggage, "any country or territory that is not part of the EU" (Customs notice 6).

third country goods fulfilment business When a person stores goods from a country outside the European Union for which there has been no supply of goods in the UK for VAT purposes, but where they are offered for sale in the UK.

VAT provision are given in Finance (No 2) Act 2017 ss48-59 which implements EU directive 2016/112/EC and regulation 282/2011 of 15 March 2011.

A person carrying on such a business needs approval from HMRC under Finance (No 2) Act 2017 ss49. It is an offence to run such a business without approval. Penalties include fines, imprisonment and confiscation of the goods.

The provisions take effect from 1 April 2019 under The Finance (No 2) Act 2017 Part 3 (Appointed Days) Regulations SI 2018 No 298.

These provisions are designed to deal with VAT avoidance when goods are sold in UK through Internet platforms such as Amazon.

third party acquisition In relation to goodwill acquired from a related party, the term is defined in CTA 2009 s849B(7) as inserted by FA 2015 s26.

third party entertainment When an employee is entertained in the course of employment by someone other than the employer. Such entertainment is generally exempt from tax up to £150 under ITEPA 2003 s265.

third party funding Arrangement whereby an organisation is funded by another to provide a service, such as when a local authority funds a charity to provide a specific service. Third party funding is subject to VAT, but grant funding is not (VAT notice 701/1).

third party insurance Insurance to protect people who are not parties to the insurance policy. It is an offence to take a vehicle on to a British road without such insurance (Road Traffic Act 1988 s143(1)(a)).

third party notice

(1) Notice that HMRC may serve to someone other than the taxpayer to obtain information about the taxpayer (FA 2008 Sch 36 para 2; previously TMA 1970 s20). In Scotland there are similar provisions under Revenue Scotland and Tax Powers Act 2014 s125.

(2) Notice served by the Pensions Regulator on a third party under Pensions Act 2014 s14.

third party payment Trading payment made through someone who is not a party to the trade (ITTOIA 2005 s23C(2)).

Third World Developing countries of Africa, Asia and South America.

Threadneedle Street Road in London that houses the Bank of England, and which is sometimes used to mean the Bank.

three-card poker From 23 April 2002, this card game is specifically added to the list in Betting and Gaming Duties Act 1981 s13(3) as coming within the scope of gaming licence duty.

three certainties Conditions for a valid express trust. The certainties are of words and intention, subject matter, and beneficiaries. These conditions were established in the court case *Knight v Knight [1840].*

three-fourteenths trust Trust sometimes found in the Church of England. It is based on the old practice of allowing church school premises to be used by the church on Sundays and Saturday mornings: three-fourteenths of the week.

three line accounts Simplified tax reporting for a small business whose turnover (from 2009) does not exceed the VAT threshold. Such a taxpayer need only report turnover, costs and expenses, and net profit.

threepence coin Silver coin minted for regular use from 1547 to 1937 and still minted as part of Maundy money, or brass coin minted from 1937 to 1967. It was worth three old pence, one eightieth of a pound.

threshold Amount at which a tax provision takes effect.

through airway bill An airway bill where the final destination is not the airport of receipt (AOR). The goods have arrived at the AOR to be routed on.

tick box Method of inspection, audit or similar which simply requires that a series of simple tests are undertaken as evidenced by a tick in a box on a form.

ticket Document providing evidence, such as of admission. For VAT, the supply is the right to attend, so the supply is made when the ticket is acquired not when the event happens. For air passenger duty, a ticket is evidence of carriage of a person by air (FA 1994 s43(1)).

tidal waters Any part of the waters that naturally ebb and flow (Merchant Shipping Act 1894).

tidying up Term, not a colloquialism, meaning to make existing provisions clearer without changing them. The term is used in FA 2007 Sch 10 para 5 in relation to provisions in TCGA 1992.

tied oil Oil which has been delivered as conditionally relieved of duty (SI 2002 No 1471 reg 3).

tied financial adviser Person who has been authorised by the relevant body as a financial adviser, but who is only allowed to promote products of one company.

tied premises Accommodation provided to an employee as part of the job. With some exceptions, this is a taxable benefit in kind.

tier 1 capital In banking, a core measure of a bank's financial strength from the perspective of the regulator. The term is defined in according with an accord agreed at Basel I. Tier 1 capital primarily comprises shares and retained earnings. It may contain non-cumulative preference shares.

tiger Endangered animal. The importation of the animal or its products is generally prohibited under CITES convention.

tiger economy Emerging economies of Asian countries.

tights Single garment of pantihose. If an employer pays for tights for employees, such as when they get laddered, this counts as a taxable benefit in kind. Historically, it is known that these were not regarded as a taxable benefit, though there was no law exempting them. Current government advice is clear that such provision is now taxable.

till Machine for keeping cash, particularly in a shop. They can keep a running total of sales.

Modern tills can also print out a list of items purchased with prices. HMRC allows such till receipts to be treated as if they were VAT invoices for amounts up to £250. This means that input tax may be claimed on purchases used for a registered business.

The usual way of doing this is for goods to have a simple code, such as letters A, B and C corresponding to the different VAT rates. Thus it is possible to identify which items bore VAT. The amount is shown separately on the till receipt.

time In any Act of Parliament, a time is Greenwich mean time unless the Act specifically states otherwise (Interpretation Act 1978 s9).

For dates, the law usually does not concern itself with times of day. So a provision that takes effect from 6 April does so from the first second of that day. A person whose birthday is 19 November comes of an age in the first second of the day, regardless of at what time they were born. Similarly a tax return due on 31 January is submitted on time up to midnight on that day. There are some exceptions. Changes in rates of excise duty are often effective from 6pm.

Care needs to be taken when counting days such as for time limits for tax compliance. The corresponding day rule should be noted. There is a day counter in section 3 of this dictionary.

time dumping Unlawful practice of inflating the numbers someone has worked and expects payment.

time for print Arrangement between photographers and models. Instead of either paying the other, they agree to license each other to use the photographs subject to conditions, allowing each to build up their portfolios at little cost. For tax purposes, this is not regarded as a barter transaction, so neither party has to account for VAT or income.

time immemorial "From when the memory of man runneth not to the contrary". Statute of Westminster 1275 fixed this as being before 6 July 1189, the start of the reign of Richard I. Any custom that has existed from time immemorial has the force of law.

timeliness One of the qualitative characteristics of accounts. FRS 102 defines it as "providing the information in financial statements within the decision time frame" (FRS 102 glossary).

timely use Reasonably prompt use of information by HMRC. This is usually taken to mean within 12 months. Extra-statutory concession A19 allows a taxpayer to be excused an unexpected tax demand where HMRC did not make timely use of information.

time of accrual Time when a chargeable gain accrues to a company that wishes to claim group relief (TCGA 1992 s171A(3)).

time off for dependants The right of an employee to take unpaid time off work to look after a dependant (ERA 1996 s57A).

time off for public duties The right of an employee to take unpaid time off work to perform a public duty such as councillor or magistrate (ERA 1996 s50).

time of supply For VAT, when a supply is made (VATA 1994 s5). This can determine the tax point.

time order Order by a court allowing a debtor more time to pay where the debt is governed by Consumer Credit Act 1974. This generally means that, from 1 May 1988, the debt is below £25,000.

timeshare Form of licence over property typically where the licensee has the right to use the property for the same one or two weeks each year. It is widely used for holiday accommodation.

Such properties are regarded as business premises and so are subject to business rates rather than council tax.

time-shaving Practice of paying time workers only for whole hours or whole parts of an hour, such as in multiples of 10 minutes or 15 minutes. This means that the worker is paid for less than the time worked.

Time To Pay (TTP) Scheme introduced in December 2008 to taxpayers with a cashflow problem extra time to pay any tax. It is not intended to provide an enduring subsidy.

Penalties for late payment are suspended during TTP (FA 2009 s108).

TTP can often be arranged by a single telephone call to 0300 200 3835. From 29 January 2020, it is also possible to make application online.

From 3 August 2015, the taxpayer is normally expected to set up a direct debit. Provided the terms are honoured, the taxpayer does not incur interest or penalties for late payment.

HMRC guidance in 2014 says that TTP arrangements are expected to last a few months. It is rare for an arrangement last for more than a year.

Further guidance is provided in HMRC Manual ay DMBM800010.

time work Basis used for determining whether the national minimum wage (NMW) regulations have been followed. This is the commonest of the four bases used. Under the time work basis, the worker must be paid at least the NMW multiplied by the number of hours worked in a pay reference period. For this purpose, hours at work generally include:

- time at work actually working;
- time spent at work when available for work but prevented from doing so;
- training during normal working hours;
- travelling in the course of work (but not normal commuting); and
- when on standby or on-call at or near the place of work and must stay awake.

Hours at work generally do not include:

- rest breaks, including tea breaks;
- when the worker is on standby or on-call at home;
- when the worker is on standby or on-call anywhere, but is allowed to sleep;
- normal commuting to and from work;
- training outside working hours.

Time work is defined in SI 1999 No 584 para 3.

timing difference Differences between when tax is paid on profits and the profits for the period multiplied by the tax rate. A fuller definition is given in FRS 102 glossary. The timing difference is reflected in the accounts as deferred tax.

A timing difference most commonly happens for depreciation. Suppose a business has profits of £250,000 before capital expenditure and in that period spends £100,000 on machinery expected to last 10 years.

The business will charge £10,000 depreciation in its profit and loss account and report profits of £240,000. However, the business can claim annual investment allowance for the whole £100,000 in the period of acquisition and so will pay tax on only £150,000. The tax on the timing difference of £90,000 is deferred tax.

In the following nine years with the same profit, the company will report profits of £240,000 but pay tax on £250,000. This £10,000 a year for nine years in effect claws back the £90,000 in the first year.

timing rule For disclosure of tax avoidance scheme, this is the date on which the arrangements were made (HMRC leaflet DOTAS of January 2016, para 7.4.3).

tip Gratuity such as paid to a hairdresser, waiter or taxi driver. These are subject to income tax as employment income, regardless of how the tip is paid.

Where the employer passes the tip to the employee, the employer must operate PAYE (PAYE Regs 2003 reg 100(7)).

For national insurance, a tip is subject to class 1 national insurance only if it is paid via the employer. So handing a £5 note to a waiter is national insurance-free whereas putting it in a jar by a till or adding it to a bill makes it subject to national insurance.

A tip is not included in determining whether a worker has received the national minimum wage.

For VAT, a voluntary tip is not part of the standard-rated supply of catering but service charges are (VAT Notice 700).

tipping off Giving advance disclosure to a person. For money laundering, this is a criminal offence under Proceeds of Crime Act 2002 s333A.

Titanic clause Provision in a will setting out how an estate should be distributed if several members of a family die together.

tithe Traditional payment of one tenth of income or produce to the church or other authorities. These were the earliest taxes. Many Christians and adherents of other religions still tithe their income.

From around 786AD, tithes became compulsory in England. They were paid to the Church (of England) which then was responsible for many public services.

In 1836, tithes in kind were replaced by cash payments called rentcharge. Tithe Acts of 1918 and 1925 allowed rentcharge to be redeemed by annuities of up to 60 years. Rentcharge was abolished by Tithe Act 1936 s13. Compulsory tithes were abolished by FA 1977.

tithe rentcharges Sum from merging tithes under provisions of Tithe Act 1838 and previous legislation. Under s2 of the Act, such merger is exempt from stamp duty. Tithe rentcharges were abolished by Tithe Act 1936, which Act was itself repealed by Statute Law (Repeals) Act 2004 s1(1).

T-level Technical qualification at level 3, equivalent to an A-level. The first three were introduced on 11 October 2017, to be taught from 2020. It is planned that a complete range will be taught from 2022.

tobacco Cured leaves of any plant of the Nicotania species. Tobacco products have generally been subject to tobacco duty since 1565. The current law is Tobacco Products Duty Act 1979. Tobacco products are also subject to the standard-rated rate of VAT.

The government has introduced many provisions to discourage tobacco use, see **smoking**.

From 1 April 2017, businesses or individuals that intend to deal in raw tobacco must be approved by HMRC under the Raw Tobacco Approval Scheme.

tobacco allowance Amount of tobacco products that an individual may personally import without having to pay duty. Further details are given in Duty Free Allowances in section 3 of this dictionary.

tobacco duty Excise duty on four types of tobacco product: cigarettes, cigars, hand-rolling tobacco, and other tobacco (TPDA 1979). Snuff is exempt. From 1 April 2001. all packets of cigarettes and hand-rolling tobacco must have a fiscal mark to show that duty has been paid.

tobacco for heating Sticks of tobacco that are heated but not burned and whose smoke is inhaled. From 1 July 2019, this product is within the scope of tobacco products duty (SI 2003 No 1471).

tobacco products manufacturing machine Machinery designed primarily for manufacturing tobacco products. From 1 August 2018, such machines must be licensed.

Tobin tax Tax on foreign exchange transactions proposed by US economist James Tobin (1918-2002). It has not been implemented.

toea One hundredth of a kina, currency of Papua New Guinea.

toffee apple For VAT, this was held in a purchase tax case to be zero-rated as food and not standard-rated as confectionery in *Candy Maid Confectionery Ltd [1968] 3 All ER 773.*

Togo African country. Its currency is the CFA franc of 100 centimes. The UK does not have a double taxation treaty.

token amount Nominal figure, often £1. Payment of a token amount may be necessary to ensure that a transaction is legally a contract.

Tokyo Round Round of talks under General Agreement on Tariffs and Trades in Tokyo in 1970. It led to large reductions in international customs duties and to the creation of customs unions.

tolar Currency of Slovenia, before it adopted the euro in 2007.

tolerance In relation to PAYE, this means a small amount whose collection HMRC does not pursue. This has been £50 for many years. Between September 2010 and March 2011, it was increased to £300 to help clear a backlog of tax reconciliations.

toll Charge to use a facility, such as a bridge or tunnel. For private operators, this is regarded as a trade. Some details of tolls are given under Congestion Charge and Road User Charges in section 3 of this dictionary. Profits from tolls when run as a trade are taxable under ITTOIA 2005 s12.

Tolley tax annuals Series of tax annuals published by Tolley Publishing Ltd.

tomb Place of burial of a deceased person. From 15 July 1987, the cost of a tombstone or gravestone is allowed as a reasonable funeral expense within the meaning of Inheritance Tax Act 1984 s172.

tombola Form of lottery, usually of low value, where tickets are issued and prizes given for winning tickets, randomly drawn.

Tomlin order Court order that gives legal effect to a compromise agreement between the parties. The name comes from such a direction issued by Mr Justice Tomlin in 1927.

TOMS Tour operator's margin scheme, for VAT.

Ton Imperial unit of weight equal to 20 hundredweight or 2,240 pounds. It is equivalent to 1,016 kilograms.

Tonga Island country in Pacific Ocean. Its currency is the pa'anga of 100 seniti. The UK does not have a double taxation treaty.

tonnage tax Optional method of corporate taxation for shipping companies. Instead of using the normal method of corporation tax, the company may elect for their shipping activities to be taxed according to the tonnage of their ships. Rates are given in section 3 of this dictionary.

tonne Metric weight of 1000 kilograms. This is about 2204 pounds, slightly less than imperial ton of 2240 pounds.

tontine Rare form of collective annuity where the last survivor receives the whole amount.

too big to fail Term coined in 2007 when the collapse of private banks would have led to disastrous consequences, forcing the government to intervene.

too good to be true One of the hallmarks of a tax planning scheme of which taxpayers are advised to be wary.

tool In relation to trade tools, this means any implement, utensil or article (ITTOIA 2005 s68(3)).

tools of trade Those items a trader needs for his or her trade. Such items may not be seized in a bankruptcy.

toothbrush scheme VAT avoidance scheme that was ended in 1 December 1994. Under it, dentists sold toothbrushes to avoid the partial exemption rules that then applied.

top-slicing relief Income tax relief that allows a large amount earned in one year to be spread over more than one year. It is now largely restricted to assignments of life assurance policies (ITTOIA 2005 from s535). There are similar tax provisions for such areas as farming profits and creative works.

tort In law, a civil wrong for which compensation may be claimed. An example is negligence.

tortfeasor Person who commits a tort.

total Sum arrived at by addition.

total additional pay to date In relation to K codes used in the PAYE system, to be added to taxable pay to date to calculate tax on a payslip (PAYE Regs 2003 reg 2(1)).

total amount of income treated as received This is given a specific meaning in ITA 2007 s794(1).

total amount of the debt In relation to PAYE, the total amount owing to HMRC which may be recovered by adjusting a tax code (PAYE Regs 2003 reg 14D(3)).

total compensation profit Term used in relation to compensation for compulsory slaughter of animals (ITTOIA 2005 s225ZB).

total comprehensive income Change in equity during an accounting period resulting from transactions and other events, other than transactions with equity participants (FRS 102 glossary).

total comprehensive income and profit or loss Arithmetical difference between income and expenses. It is not a separate element of the financial statements (FRS 102 section 2.43).

total dwellings consideration For stamp duty land tax, this is the total consideration for dwellings plus so much of the chargeable consideration for any of the linked transactions (FA 2011 Sch 22 para 5).

total free pay to date For PAYE, the amount of the personal allowance and any other allowances or adjustments to which an employee is entitled at the time a payslip is produced (PAYE Regs 2003 reg 2(1)). This is subtracted from the taxable pay to the same time, from which the tax is calculated.

total income Total of all income subject to income tax (ITA 2007 s23).

total intestacy State where no property can pass on a person's death because the person left no will or the will is not valid. The property passes under provisions of Administration of Estates Act 1925. Intestacy provisions are given in section 3 of this dictionary.

totalisator For pool betting duty, a machine or instrument used for pool betting calculations (Customs notice 147).

total litre capacity Capacity of a vehicle's fuel tanks. From 1 November 2012, the penalty for improperly using rebated fuel is based on this capacity (HMRC Brief 29/12).

total loss In shipping, where a ship has been lost and nothing salvaged (Marine Insurance Act 1906 s68).

total net tax deducted For PAYE, the total tax deducted from payments to an employee plus any tax accounted for as notional payments less any tax repaid to the employer (PAYE Regs 2003 reg 2(1)).

total payments to date For PAYE, the sum of all payments made by the employer to the employee since the start of the tax year (PAYE Regs 2003 reg 2(1)).

Total Quality Management (TQM) Forms of business initiative developed by Western countries in response to competition from Japan. Work started in the 1970s and peaked in 1993. Various attempts have been made to codify TQM, such as the international standard ISO 9000.

total R & D aid This term is used in CTA 2009 s1113(3) in relation to an anti-avoidance provision regarding research and development.

total relevant turnover amount Term used for enterprise investment scheme in relation to tax limits (ITA 2007 s175A(8)) and the same definition for venture capital trusts (ITA 2007 s280C(9)).

touring company Travelling theatrical company. If they give 14 theatrical performances in at least 6 different premises, they may qualify for theatrical productions tax relief.

touring exhibition Exhibition of museum or gallery items held at two or more venues where at least 25% of the items in the first display are shown in subsequent exhibitions, and there is no more than six months between exhibitions. This may qualify for museums and galleries exhibition tax relief from corporation tax.

Tourism Kickstart Package of measures from the government introduced on 3 July 2020 to help the tourism industry during the coronavirus lockdown.

tour operators' margin scheme (TOMS) Special VAT scheme that may be used by tour operators, who buy in and resell travel, accommodation and related supplies (VATA 1994 s53).

towage Fee for towing. It is generally zero-rated under VATA 1994 Sch 8 Group 8.

toxicity charge Also known as T-charge. It was introduced in central London on 23 October 2017 at a rate of £10 a day. It has been replaced by the ultra-low emission zone.

tracing value Provision in relation to taxation of UK land transactions. Details are given in CTA 2010 356OM.

tractor Category of road vehicle that may, under conditions, use diesel on which hydrocarbon oil duty has not been paid (HODA 1979 Sch 1: Customs notice 75).

trade Commercial activity, as against hobbies or capital gains. The term has never been defined in tax law. Instead the six "badges of trade" set out in a Royal Commission report of 1954 are widely used. They are:

(a) subject matter of realisation;
(b) length of ownership;
(c) frequency of transactions;
(d) supplementary work;
(e) circumstances which were responsible for the realisation; and
(f) motive.

A single transaction can be a trade.

TMA 1970 s118(1) says that a trade includes every trade, manufacture, adventure or concern in the nature of a trade.

A definition is given in CTA 2009 s298 regarding loan relationship. There has been much case law.

trade association Organisation formed to further the interests of its members (CA 2006 s375(2). Payments to such organisations are not regarded as political donations HMRC has reached agreement on VAT with several trade bodies as listed in VAT Notice 700/57.

trade classification Four-digit code that classifies the nature of a business. From 1990, the code is allocated when the company registers at Companies House. The code is also used for VAT purposes.

The first two digits indicate the group of the activity. For example, 00 indicates agriculture, forestry and fishing. Trade classification 0011 is livestock farming.

trade dispute Dispute between an employer and workers (Trade Union and Labour Relations (Consolidation) Act 1992 s218 and s244). An employee engaged in a trade dispute is not entitled to any rebates generated under the PAYE scheme (PAYE Regulations 2003 reg 64).

traded option Option that is a security in its own right. The capital gains tax implications are given in TCGA 1992 from s143.

trade income relief Carry-forward trade loss relief plus terminal trade loss relief (ITA 2007 s95(3)).

trade mark Logo, symbol or other visual identification of a product or brand (Trade Marks Act 1994). A company may usually claim tax relief for expenses related to a trade mark (CTA 2009 s90).

trade or professional fund For inheritance tax, a fund that compensates its members for losses (IHTA 1984 s58(3).

Trade Partnership Committee Body form under article INST 2 of the EU/UK withdrawal agreement of 24 December 2020.

Many specialist committees are set up under the same article, including the Trade Specialised Committee on Customs Cooperation and Rules of Origin.

trade preference scheme A preferential rate of import duty unilaterally established by the UK government under Taxation (Cross-border Trade) Act 2018 s10.

trade profits Profits from a trade run by a sole trader or partnership (ITTOIA 2005 from 25). They are subject to income tax.

trade related property Property whose nature is essential for the trade. Examples include pubs, hotels, cinemas, theatres, petrol stations, care homes and restaurants.

HMRC takes the view that where such a property is sold, a distinction should be made between the goodwill of the business and the enhanced value of the property.

trader seal Seal of an authorised trader that HMRC may allow the trader to use instead of an official Customs seal. Details are given in Customs notice 205.

trade tools Tools used in a trade. Income tax provisions are explained in ITTOIA 2005 s68; corporation tax provisions in CTA 2009 s68.

trade union Organisation that deals with workers' rights (Trade Union and Labour Relations (Consolidation) Act 1992 s1).

Subscriptions are not tax-deductible (ITA 2007 s457).

The VAT liability of a trade union is explained in VAT leaflet 701/5.

trading account Financial statement that shows income, costs and expenses from trading activities. It is a subset of the profit and loss account.

trading allowance An amount that a person may earn from 6 April 2017 from trading income without having to declare that income or pay income tax on it (FA 2017 s17). The amount is £1,000. If a trader has more income, they may either declare their taxable profits in the usual way, or deduct £1,000 from their income. If a trader has more than one source of income, he or she may choose how to allocated this amount between trades.

trading certificate Document issued by Companies House to a public company (CA 2006 s761). A public company may not transact any business or borrow any money until it has this certificate.

trading company Company set up to pursue a trade, as against a property company, investment company, or non-commercial company.

Definitions appear in ITA 2007 s397(6) for employee-controlled companies; in CTA 2018 s185; and for the oil industry in CTA 2010 s279H(4).

trading disclosures Matters that an overseas company may be required to disclose under regulations (CA 2006 s1051).

trading group Group of companies whose members collectively carry on a trade or trades (ITA 2007 s151(1)).

For employee-controlled companies, a definition appears in ITA 2007 s397(6).

trading income Profits from a trade. For corporation tax, it is defined in CTA 2009 from s34. The term is also used in HMRC Manual from BIM40051. It says that in marginal cases, two questions should be asked:

- does the sum at issue arise from the trade at all?
- if it does, is it a capital or revenue item?

trading interest Interest paid by a company on loans to fund its training. Such interest is an allowable tax deduction in the loan relationship rules of CTA 2009 Part 5.

trading loss Loss that a business sustains from its trading activities. In relation to group relief, the term is defined in CTA 2010 s100(1).

trading requirement One of the conditions for enterprise investment scheme (ITA 2007 s181).

trading stamp Stamp issued by a shop according to the value of purchases made. These are stuck into books which could be redeemed for goods. They were popular in the 1960s. Green Shield Stamps were the most popular. They lost much popularity in 1977 when Tesco stopped issuing them, and were completely discontinued from 1991. Stores now prefer loyalty cards.

They were governed by Trading Stamps Act 1964, which was repealed in 2005. There remains a special VAT provision in VATA 1994 s52.

From 1 June 1996, trading stamps are treated as any other discount voucher.

trading stock Stock and property used to make the goods or services of a business (ICTA 1988 s100(2); CTA 2009 s156).

A long definition is given in CTA 2009 s1632(2) and ITTOIA s172A(2).

trading stock appropriated by trader Where a trader takes stock for his or her own use, the trader must account for it on the basis of its selling price, not its cost (ITTOIA 2005 s172B). This is the statutory enactment of the decision in the case *Sharkey v Werner [1956].*

trading test Test to see if an activity is a trade for tax purposes. This is particularly relevant for illegal trades. The matter is discussed in HMRC Manual at BIM22007.

traditional option Right to acquire a share or security at a future date, usually at a price already agreed. A traditional option is not itself a saleable security, unlike the traded option.

training Activities designed to help a person perform their duties or occupation better.
A distinction is made from education in that training is related to specific work. This distinction was made by an official of the Department of Education and Science in the case *Barry v Hughes [1971] 48 TC 586.* He defined training as "the systematic development of the attitude/knowledge/skill pattern required by an individual in order to perform adequately a given task or job". This was accepted by the court.
Workplace training is generally not a taxable benefit in kind to an employee (ITEPA 2003 from s250).
Training may be exempt from VAT if provided by a non-commercial eligible provider of tuition, funded by the government (VATA 1994 Sch 9 Group 6). Further details are given in VAT Notice 701/30.

training and enterprise council Local body established in 1989 and abolished in 2001. Between 1 April 1990 and 31 March 2000, a company could claim tax relief for contributions to a council.
Such councils were replaced in 2001 by Learning and Skill Councils, which have themselves been replaced in 2009 by Young People Learning Agency.

training course If related to work, this is a tax-deductible expense for the employer and not a taxable benefit in kind for the employee. The matter is discussed in HMRC Manual at BIM42526. The allowability of food and accommodation is discussed at BIM45047.

training levy Levy that a training body may impose on businesses in its area under Industrial Training Act 1982.

Rates for the Construction Industry Training Board levy and Engineering are given in section 3 of this dictionary.

training materials Stationery, books and other written material, audio and video material, computer files and similar. If provided as part of work-related training, they are usually not a taxable benefit in kind (ITEPA 2003 s254(3)).

training mode Facility on electronic point of sales systems such as check-out tills at supermarkets. This mode allows staff to be trained without data entered being included as genuine sales.

training-related asset Asset used in work-related training. Its provision by an employer is usually not a taxable benefit in kind of the employee (ITEPA 2003 s254(2)).

transaction Any activity or adjustment that requires an entry in the accounting records.

transaction connected with VAT fraud A person who enters into such a transaction, and where other conditions are met, may be subject to a tax penalty under VATA 1994 s69C as inserted by Finance (No 2) Act 2017 s68(2).

transaction costs Costs which are directly related to specific transactions, particularly buying and selling assets. Such costs include delivery, installation, instruction into use and commissions.

In relation to accounting for financial instruments, "incremental costs that are directly attributable to the acquisition, issue or disposal of a financial asset or financial liability, or the issue or reacquisition of an entity's own equity instrument. An incremental cost is one that would not have been incurred if the entity had not acquired, issued or disposed of the financial asset or liability, or had not issued or reacquired its own equity instrument" (FRS 102 glossary).

transaction in securities Purchase, sale or exchange of securities; issue of new securities; applying or subscribing for securities; and altering the rights of securities. Corporation tax provisions are given in CTA 2010 ss 682-687; income tax provisions in ITA 2007 from s682.
HMRC has data-gathering powers under FA 2011 Sch 23 para 19(4).

transaction value Value used to determine the amount on which a tax, such as Customs duty, is payable (Taxation (Cross-border Trade) Act 2018 s16(3)).

transaction with connected persons For capital gains tax or chargeable gain corporation tax, this means a transaction between two parties who have an existing relationship. For individuals, this means a parent or remoter ancestor, a child or remoter descendant, a brother or sister, or the partner of one of these people. For companies, this means another company controlled by the same person or someone connected with them. The consequences of such a transaction are that:

- market value may be substituted for disposal proceeds
- any loss may not be set off against other capital gains generally, but only against gains with the same person, and
- where assets (such as shares) are disposed of to the same person over six years, and their value taken together is greater than taken separately, each disposal is treated as a proportion of the aggregate value. (TCGA 1992 ss18-20 and s286).

transfer Moving something from one place to another. It particularly applies to a transfer of company shares (CA 2006 s776) on which stamp duty may be payable.

transferable tax allowance Part of the personal allowance that may be transferred between members of a marriage or civil partnership (ITA 2007 ss55A-55E). From April 2015, one tenth of the personal allowance may be transferred by a basic rate taxpayer.

transfer controls "In relation to any technology, means the prohibition or regulation of its transfer:

(a) by a person from a place within the United Kingdom to a person or place outside the United Kingdom;
(b) by a person or from a place outside the United Kingdom to a person who, or a place which, is also outside the United Kingdom (but only where the transfer is by, or within the control of, a United Kingdom person);
(c) by a person or from a place within the United Kingdom to a person who, or a place which, is also within the United Kingdom (but only where there is reason to believe that the technology may be used outside the United Kingdom); or

(d) by a person or from a place outside the United Kingdom to a person or place within the United Kingdom (but only where the transfer is by, or within the control of, a United Kingdom person and there is reason to believe that the technology may be used outside the United Kingdom).

(Export Control Act 2002 s2(2)).

transferee Person to whom something is transferred.

transferee company Company to which the whole or part of its undertaking or property is transferred in an amalgamation or reconstruction (CA 2006 s900(1)). For inheritance tax and close companies, the term is given a specific meaning in Inheritance Tax Act 1984 s95.

transfer fee Fee paid to secure the services of a sports person, particularly a footballer. The fee is treated as an intangible asset for accounting purposes. For tax, clubs were allowed to treat such fees as revenue expenditure before 1999. It is now treated as capital.

transfer freight manifest Removal authority for air freight consignments which are to be transferred from one transfer shed to another before going to their final destination.

transfer journal Term sometimes used for the journal used to make double entries in bookkeeping, to distinguish it from other books of account.

transfer lump sum death benefit A lump sum benefit paid from a money purchase arrangement for the benefit of another member of the same pension scheme following the death of a member (or dependant) who is over 75.Provided there is no surviving dependant of the member, a lump sum pay be paid under FA 2004 Sch 29 para 19.

transfer notice Notice from HMRC transferring the PAYE liability of a management service company (PAYE Regs 2003 from reg 79C).

transfer of a going concern (TOGC) When a business is taken over but run as before. For VAT, this is regarded as outside the scope of tax (VATA 1994 s49). This is because the transfer is not regarded as a supply. Further provisions are given in SI 1995 No 1268.

Care should be taken as VAT may be payable on the transfer of assets without the business, or on the transfer of a business that is not a going concern.

Guidance is given in VAT Notice 700/9. Explanations are provided in HMRC Briefs 30/2012 and 27/2014.

The directors of a company that is transferred may make special provisions for their employees under CA 2006 s247.

When a business is transferred, the employees' accumulated rights are protected by Transfer of Undertakings (Protection of Employment) Regulations 1981.

transfer of an income stream The income tax provisions are given in ITA 2007 from s809ZA.

transfer of assets abroad This is a common tax avoidance procedure. There is anti-avoidance legislation in ITA 2007 from s714.

transfer of nil rate band For deaths from 9 October 2007, an increase on the inheritance tax nil rate band of up to 100% based on the percentage of unused nil rate band by a former spouse or civil partner. For example, a widow dies on 1 January 2021. Her husband died on 1 February 2008 when the nil rate band was £300,000. He left £100,000 to their children and the rest to his wife. As the bequest to his wife is exempt anyway, that means that two-thirds of his nil rate band was unused. The transfer allows the wife's nil rate band to be increased by two-thirds, so that the £325,000 becomes £433,333.

The residence nil rate band may be similarly transferred. This is now £175,000 meaning that a person may have a total nil rate band of £500,000. With a 100% transfer, it is possible to leave £1 million worth of estate to one's children free of income tax.

If a person dies having had two or more former spouses or civil partners at the time of their deaths, the percentages for each may be added but are capped at 100%.

There is no action needed on the first death, which may be before, on or after 9 October 2007. A list of nil rate bands is given in section 3 of this dictionary.

transfer of property In relation to capital gains tax of trusts, this is given a specific meaning in TCGA 1992 s688(2). An equivalent meaning for income tax is given in ITA 2007 s470(3).

transfer of residence Customs term for when a person relocates to the UK. Generally, goods (including cars) that accompany a relocated person are free of duty, subject to some conditions (Customs notice 3).

transfer of shares Process by which the ownership of shares pass. This requires three steps: a contract to sell, delivery of certificate or electronic equivalent, and change of entry in the company register. The transfer is complete at the third stage.

Note that a transfer usually requires action by the shareholder. If a shareholder dies, the shares are said to be transmitted as part of the estate.

transfer on death Occasion on which property becomes subject to inheritance tax (IHTA 1984 s266(2)).

transferor Person who transfers something.

transferor company Company which is wholly or partly transferred to another company in a reconstruction or amalgamation (CA 2006 s900(1)). Tax law generally does not impose a charge in such circumstances. For close companies, there is a specific provision for inheritance tax in IHTA 1984 s95.

transfer pricing Price charged when two entities under the control of the same person pass goods between them. The commonest example is a group with companies in countries with significantly different tax rates.

There are tax provisions to ensure that the price is not set so as to shift profit to the lower tax country. They replace the price with an arm's length market value (ITTOIA 2005 s172F).

transfer scheme Any arrangement whereby the assets, liabilities, undertaking, profits or losses of one entity are legally passed to another. This may be effected by a legal document or by statute. An example of the latter is given in Postal Services Act 2011 s8.

A more general power is given in Public Bodies Act 2011 from s23. The tax provisions are given in s25.

transfer value The value that has built up in one pension scheme and which may be transferred to another. An occupational pension scheme is not obliged to accept a transfer value.

transgender Person who identifies as neither male or female. Under English law, including tax law, a person is the sex of their birth until given a gender reassignment certificate. A review in 2020 decided not to change the basic law though it made some procedural simplifications.

Transit Accompanying Document (TAD) Document that must travel with exported goods.

transit day Day spent in the UK while travelling between two other countries. It is not regarded as a day in the UK for the purposes of the statutory residence test, provided the person leaves the UK on the day after arriving, and does not engage in any activity that is significantly unrelated to the person's work.

transit duty Customs duty that may be imposed on goods passing through one territory on its passage to another territory.

transitional Term widely used in tax to mean provisions to ease a change in tax law.

transitional period Period from the UK leaving the EU to concluding a new trading relationship with the EU. This was 1 February 2020 to 31 December 2020. During this period, the UK continued to follow EU rules.

transitional protection Addition to universal credit paid when someone is migrated from previous benefits that paid more.

transitional provision Any provision which allows a new rule to be phased in to minimise its impact. Transitional provisions are widely encountered in tax law to minimise a significantly larger tax burden which could fall on some taxpayers on a change in the tax system.

transitional rate Rate at which a state pension may be paid to someone who has at least one qualifying year between 1978 and 2016 (Pension Act 2014 s4).

A qualifying year is one in which the person has a full national insurance record. A person needs 35 such years for a full state pension from 6 April 2016.

transitional relief Informal term for the provisions of IHTA 1984 s7(4). This is the relief for potentially exempt transfers. Details are given under Inheritance tax in section 3 of this dictionary.

transitional serial interest Form of trust that is inheritance tax-advantaged.

transit procedure A Customs procedure that allows goods to move freely within the EU without payment of Customs duty until they have reached their final destination. It can also allow goods to pass through a third country.

transit shed Place near an approved wharf where imported goods may be held pending payment of customs duties. It must be approved by HMRC under CEMA 1979 s25.

translate Express an amount in a different currency. Note that a currency is only converted when it has been exchanged for another currency.

transliteration Restating characters into those of the English alphabet, such as when the company uses the Cyrillic or Greek alphabet. A company submitting a document using non-English characters may be required to re-submit using English characters (CA 2006 s1109).

transmission Change of share ownership other than by transfer or forfeiture. The commonest example is on death.

transmission facilities The taxation relating to facilities shared by broadcasting companies is given in FA 1991 s78. The capital gains tax implications are given in TCGA 1992 s267.

transparency State where tax is applied as if an entity did not exist. In other words, for tax, we look through the entity. The word is also used to mean that something is what it appears to be.

Consumer contracts are transparent if expressed in plain and intelligible language (Consumer Rights Act 2015 s69).

transparent entity The term particularly means an entity that is resident in a EU state outside the UK which has no ordinary share capital. It falls outside the Mergers Directive.

A full definition is given in TCGA 1992 s140L(1)(c). For embedded derivatives, a definition is given in CTA 2009 s680(2).

transport Means of moving people and goods. There is a vast amount of legislation, both relating to tax and other matters, on transport.

Some forms of transport are zero-rated for VAT under VATA 1994 Sch 8 Group 8. This zero rates public transport in a vehicle that carries at least ten passengers, and international transport in a vehicle of any size. The same Group also zero rates some vehicles:

- a ship weighing at least 15 tons and which is not primarily used for recreation or pleasure,
- a lifeboat, houseboat or boat adapted for a disabled person
- hovercraft of any size that is not for recreation or pleasure
- aircraft of at least 8000 kilograms which are not primarily for recreation or pleasure.

Some services are zero-rated, including repairs to zero-rated ships and aircraft.

transport container Standard-sized re-usable metal container for the bulk shipment of goods. They were developed from 1957, becoming widely used from 1968 and of a standard size from 1972.

Their cross section is a square of 8ft 6in (2.59 metres). The length is 40 feet (12.2 metres), though some are half that length. They have a patent-free twistlock in the corners for secure lifting and stacking

They are subject to special provisions regarding leasing (CAA 2001 s124). Guidance is given in HMRC Manual at CA24130.

Transports Internationaux Routiers (TIR) System whereby road hauliers are given a carnet which allows them to cross national borders with minimum Customs formalities.

transport strike An employer may provide certain assistance for employee's travel during a public transport strike without that assistance being taxed as a benefit in kind (ITEPA 2003 s245).

transport voucher Ticket, pass or similar to allow a person to use passenger transport services (ITEPA 2003 s245).

travaux préparatoires French: preparatory works. particularly in relation to passing laws. These can be useful in interpreting an international treaty. This was referred to in the case *Fothergill v Monarch Airlines Ltd [1981] HL. AC 251*

travel Moving from place to place. The extent to which travel constitutes a tax-deductible expense depends on circumstances.

Normal commuting between home and work is not normally tax-deductible as it is not "in the course" of the duties of employment but to get to the place where the duties may start (ITEPA 2003 s338).

Travel in the course of work usually is a tax-deductible expense, such as when an employee collects goods or visits a customer (ITEPA 2003 s337).

travel concession Any provision that allows a person to use public transport for less than the full fare. A common example is the bus pass provided under Concessionary Bus Travel Act 2007.

traveller's cheques Documents bought from a bank in different pre-set amounts. They may be exchanged in foreign banks for the local currency, or even used as a form of currency.

treason Criminal offence of conspiring against the state. it is an offence under Treason Act 1351, which is still law.

Anyone who discovers treason must report it. This overrides any duty of client confidentiality. It is an offence not to report it. The last treason trial in Britain was in 1948.

Treasury Government department responsible for the nation's finances.

Treasury Bills Form of short-term government borrowing, usually for up to 91 days. They are offered to the money market by weekly tender.

Treasury cat Cat kept by the Treasury to keep down mice. The Treasury issued a statement in November 2018, saying the cat is called Gladstone. He costs nothing, as costs and care are met by staff and voluntary donations He is not on the payroll nor subject to IR 35 provisions.

Treasury directions Orders from the Treasury that are binding on HMRC (Commissioners of Revenue and Customs Act 2005 s11).

Treasury secretary Government Cabinet minister who is second in command at the Treasury to the Chancellor of the Exchequer.

Treasury shares Shares in a company that the company holds with a view to resale (CA 2006 from s724). Such shares were introduced in 2003. They may not exceed 10% of share capital. Otherwise a company acquiring shares in itself means those shares are cancelled.

Treasury Solicitor Solicitor who:

- advises the Treasury on legal matters
- instructs parliamentary counsel on Bills
- appears for the Crown in civil proceedings, and
- acts as the Queen's Proctor.

treaty International agreement between states or territories. They are governed by the Vienna Convention on the Law of Treaties 1969.

A treaty has also also been defined as a contract between two states in the case *R v Governor of Ashford Remand Centre, ex parte Beese [1973] All ER 250.*

A tax treaty deals with issues that stop the same income or gain being taxed twice, once in each country. It may impose a tax equal to the higher rate, and then determine how that is shared between them.

The UK authority for making tax treaties is ICTA 1988 s788(1). This was modified from 25 July 2002 by FA 2002 s88(1) so the UK could make a treaty with Taiwan.

A treaty comes into effect when it has completed the formalities of each state. In 1977 a treaty with Ghana was made replacing that of 1947. Inland Revenue announced it was effective from 6 June 1978. In 1991, it was discovered that it had never been ratified in Ghana, so it ceased to be of effect and the UK reverted to the 1947 treaty.

Most modern treaties follow a model drafted by the OECD.

The UK has more than 100 such treaties on tax. Originally they were with countries in the British Empire or Commonwealth. The first non-Commonwealth country with a treaty was USA in 1945.

Treaties can be interpreted so as to deal with changed circumstances. When the USSR split in 1991, the UK regarded the treaty as being in effect with each separate state until they each declined (as some did) or negotiated a new treaty.

References in old treaties to surtax can apply to higher rate income tax. In addition to treaties on taxation itself, the UK has separate treaties on sharing tax information, and on social security.

Treaty of Accession Document signed by then prime minister Edward Heath in 1972 taking Britain into the European Economic Community on 1 January 1973. This became the European Union which the UK left in 2020.

Treaty of Amsterdam European Union treaty with replaced the Treaty of Rome on 1 May 1999 and was itself replaced by the Lisbon Treaty from 1 December 2009.

Treaty of Rome Original agreement between six European countries (Belgium, France, Germany, Italy, Luxembourg, Netherlands) on 25 March 1957 which expanded in scope and size to become the European Union. It was replaced by the Treaty of Amsterdam from 1 May 1999.

Treaty on European Union The Maastricht Treaty.

treaty shopping Practice of establishing residence in a state to benefit from its treaties.

treble Three times as much, as against triple which means three times as many.

treeness of the tree Quotation from *Correggiosity of Correggio* by Laurence Sterne (1713-68) to mean the essential qualifies which define the nature of an item. The quotation has been used in tax cases to distinguish between capital and revenue. Capital is like the tree, enduring from year to year, while revenue is like the fruit.

trente et quarante Game that is specifically listed in Betting and Gaming Duties Act 1981 s13(3) as coming with the scope of duty.

Treth Welsh for "tax".

Treth ar Werth Welsh for "value added tax".

trial balance List of debits and credits taken from the nominal ledger, from which the final accounts are prepared. The debits and credits should equal the same total. The trial balance is then used to produce the final accounts. At its simplest each debit and credit is allocated either to the balance sheet or profit and loss account.

triangulation For VAT, when goods are moved between one EU state and another by instructions from a third. The EU procedure is set out in VAT Notice 725. For employee travel when an employee travels from home direct to a place for business such as to a customer. From 6 April 1998, the whole of that journey may be treated as business travel and none of it is regarded as commuting.

tribunal Forum for resolving issues that do not require the formality and expense of a court hearing. They are regulated by Tribunals and Inquiries Act 1971.

Tax tribunals deal with tax disputes from 2009 when they replaced General Commissioners and Special Commissioners.

In relation to PAYE, the term means the first tier tax tribunal (PAYE Regs 2003 reg 2(1)).

Tribunals Service Body that was created on 3 April 2006 under Constitutional Reform Act 2005. It is responsible for a two-tier tribunal system that came into being on 3 November 2008 under Tribunals Courts and Enforcement Act 2008.

This arrangement absorbed 20 existing tribunals into the system.

Tribunals are divided into chambers, of which the tax chamber is one.

There is a first tier tribunal whose decision on a point of fact is final, unless perverse. Appeals lie to the upper tier tribunal. Further appeals on points of law may then be made to the courts.

tribute In ancient times, gifts to priests. They are sometimes regarded as the oldest forms of tax.

trick clause Clause that does not mean what it seems to say. A notorious example is the doubling clause used in some leases. It says something like "each year the rent shall increase by an amount equal to the rent plus inflation". This appears to say that the rent increases by inflation. So if the rent is £1,000 and inflation is 2%, the rent increases to £1,020. That is not what it says. The rent increases *by* £1,020 to £2,020, and so on. By year 10, the rent is £571,166.

triennial Every three years.

trigger In tax law, an event or circumstance that brings a tax provision into effect. For example, there is no tax on the increase in value of certain assets. The trigger for capital gains tax is when there is a disposal of such asset.

trigger date In relation to taxation of termination payments, the date is –

(a) if the termination is not a **notice case**, the last day of the employment, and
(b) if the termination is a notice case, the day the notice is given

(ITEPA 2003 s402E(2)).

trillion One thousand billion, or one million times one million. It is 1 followed by 12 noughts.

Trinidad and Tobago Island country. Its currency is the Trinidad and Tobago dollar of 100 cents. The UK has a double taxation convention of 1982.

A pension paid from this country may be exempt from income tax under ITEPA 2003 s643.

Trinidad and Tobago dollar Currency of Trinidad and Tobago.

triple Three times as many, as against treble which means three times as much.

triple assessment Tax introduced in 1798 which is seen as a precursor to income tax, first introduced in 1799.

triple lock Guarantee that, from 2012, the state pension will increase each year by the highest of price inflation, wage inflation and 2.5%.

triple witching hour Final hour of a period of trading when three types of future and options contracts expire, making the financial market volatile.

Tristan da Cunha UK Overseas Territory of an island in the South Atlantic Ocean. Its uses British currency. It also produces its own coinage, mainly for collectors.

trivial Of such small amount as not worth bothering about. In accounting this is called immaterial. Care should be taken in tax as no amount ceases to be payable just because it is small. HMRC has a policy of tolerance where it does not chase small amounts owed under the PAYE system, but a taxpayer should not rely on this.
The guide Professional Conduct in Relation to Taxation says in para 5.17 says "in the opinion of the professional bodies it is reasonable for a member to take no steps to advise HMRC of isolated errors where the tax effect is no more than minimal, say up to £200, as these will probably cost HMRC and the client more to process than they are worth to the Exchequer".
There are many de minimis provisions in tax law designed to avoid the expense and inconvenience of following a tax procedure for a small amount.

trivial benefit Benefit in kind provided to an employee of such small amount that it may be ignored (ITEPA 2003 s323A).
From April 2016, the limit is £50 per employee per year. For a close company, there is a further employer limit of £300 a year.
A trivial benefit should not be confused with a minor benefit. The latter is taxable but where the tax is usually paid by a PAYE settlement agreement.

trivial pension Pension of a small amount and which may be paid as a single lump sum. From 2018, the limit is £30,000 for one pension pot, or £10,000 for each of three pots.

Previously, from 6 April 2011, it was £18,000 for all pension pots. From 6 April 2006, it was 1% of the lifetime allowance.

The consequence is that the whole of the pension fund may be paid as a lump sum. Generally, 25% is tax-free and the balance is taxed as income.

tronc System whereby tips and gratuities are shared out among staff. It is operated by a troncmaster, who must operate PAYE and class 1 national insurance.

troncmaster Person who operates a tronc.

Troubles Permanent Disablement Payment Scheme Government-backed scheme announced on 24 February 2020 to pay compensation to people who were permanently disabled in "The Troubles" in Northern Ireland between 1 January 1966 and 12 April 2010.

The person must have been disabled in the UK as a consequence of Northern Ireland troubles. Payments are backdated to December 2014.

troy ounce Old measure of weights still used for jewels and precious metals. A troy ounce equals 31.1 grams.

Truck Acts Laws passed from 1831, based on older laws, that outlawed the practice of paying workers in tokens that could only be spent in the employer's shops. They also disallowed unlawful deductions from wages. They were repealed by Payment of Wages Act 1960.

The law on unlawful deductions from wages is now found in Employment Rights Act 1996 s13.

truck tokens Tokens for small amounts resembling coins. They were often produced by traders when low value coins were scarce. It led to an abuse whereby workers were paid in such tokens which could only be used in an employer's shop where prices could be inflated. This was outlawed by Truck Acts 1831 to 1940 which required wages to be paid in coins of the realm.

true and fair The overriding objective of all accounts since 1947. True means in accordance with accounting records. Fair means that the picture painted by the accounts reflects the financial reality.

For companies, the requirement is now CA 2006 s393.

This provision was adopted by the EU in the Fourth Council Directive on company law 78/660/EEC.

Statement of Principles for Financial Reporting says in para 10: "The concept of a true and fair view lies at the heart of financial reporting in the UK and the Republic of Ireland. It is the ultimate test for financial statements and, as such, has a powerful, direct effect on accounting practice. No matter how skilled the standard-setters and law-makers are, it is the need to show a true and fair view that puts their requirements into perspective." Points to note about "true and fair" include:

- its scope changes over time;

- it requires financial statements to contain information "sufficient in quantity and quality to satisfy the reasonable expectation of the readers to whom they are addressed" (Statements para 12).

HMRC can reject accounts that are not true and fair, even if they comply with accounting standards (FA 1986 s84). The only known example of this is *GDF Suez Teesside Ltd (formerly Teesside Power Ltd) v HMRC [2015] TC 4590.*

true copy Exact copy of a document. It is usually a photocopy which an accountant or lawyer confirms is a true copy of an original that he or she has seen.

true gravity Gravity of beer as calculated rather than measured. This is accepted for the purposes of determining beer duty.

true interest cost Cost of interest in a financial transaction when all fees and other considerations are taken into account.

true-up Term sometimes used to mean to bring a value into line with a predetermined criterion or process. An example in finance is replacing an expected value with a realised value.

Trussell Trust Network of food banks established in Salisbury in 1997. By 2021, it had more than 1,200 food banks. The basic scheme is that a doctor, social worker, priest, Citizen's Advice Bureau worker or similar person provides a voucher that can be redeemed for food, usually for three days. Food is donated by individuals, companies and supermarkets.

trust Arrangement whereby one person holds property for the benefit of another or others. There are many different types subject to different tax treatments. A trust is a legal entity that is liable to pay income tax, and may be required to pay inheritance tax. A trust requires three parties:

- a settlor, who provides the funds or asset
- trustees, who legally own the property
- beneficiaries, who receive the beneficial interest of the property.

A trust also requires property, such as cash, land, buildings or other asset. Sometimes a trust is created by a nominal amount, often £10, while awaiting the main assets.

An authoritative definition is "an equitable obligation, binding a person (called a trustee) to deal with property (called trust property) owned by him or a separate fund, distinct from his own private property for the benefit of persons (called beneficiaries or, in old cases cestuis que trust), of whom he may himself be one and any one of whom may enforce the obligation: any act or neglect on the part of a trustee which is not authorised or excused by the terms of the trust instrument, or by law, is called a breach of trust." (*Law of Trusts and Trustees,* by Underhill and Layton).

HMRC gives "a simple definition from a legal viewpoint" in the inspectors' manual at TSEM1010:

"A trust is a disposition of property to a person (trustee) or persons jointly (trustees) in whom the legal title then vests in the confidence that the benefits will be applied to the advantage of one or more other persons (beneficiaries) or some other object permitted by law."

Trusts pay income tax on profits, such as interest on an account (ITA 2007 from s479).
Capital gains tax implications are given in TCGA 1992 s65.
There are many inheritance tax provisions for different types of trust, such as accumulation and maintenance trusts, bare trusts, discretionary trust, interest in possession trusts, relevant property trusts, serial interest trusts and trusts for a bereaved minor.

trust corporation Company set up to act as a trustee. Such companies are often subsidiaries of banks and insurance companies. A trust corporation may act alone where otherwise two or more trustees would be required.

trust deed (1) Legal document that formally creates a trust. This is not a legal requirement but is normal for all but the simplest trusts. A trust may also be created by a will.
(2) In Scotland, a voluntary arrangement for payment of creditors by an insolvent person.

trustee Person who holds property in trust for another. In general, a trustee may be an individual aged 18 or over, or a company.
There must always be at least one trustee, but there is no general upper limit. For land, there must be two trustees unless the trustee is a trust corporation. For a trust of land, there is a maximum of four trustees.
The duties of trustees are now largely set out in Trustee Act 2000. The duties will also usually be in a trust deed. This Act replaces the Trustee Investments Act 1961, even for existing trusts.
A definition for inheritance tax is given in IHTA 1984 s45.

trustee bank Bank offering savings facilities for small investors, typically run by unpaid trustees. Such banks are regarded as trading for tax purposes from 21 November 1979.

trustee borrowing Where there is a transfer of value by trustees linked with trustee borrowing, the capital gains tax provisions are given in TCGA 1992 Sch 4B.

trustee in bankruptcy Insolvency practitioner who deals with the property of a bankrupt.

trustee savings bank British financial institutions formed from 1817 that originally accepted deposits from poorer people who could not open an account with other banks. At a time when many banks crashed causing losses for customers, the trustee savings banks were strictly regulated in that they dealt with government bonds or Bank of England deposits.
To promote their use, interest on such bank accounts was tax-free up to a limit for many years.
In 1975, the banks were nationalised into one bank. This merged with Lloyds Bank in 1995 and was demerged in 2013.

trustees' return Tax return which trustees may be required to make under TMA 1970 s8A.

trust for a bereaved minor (TBM) Trust where the beneficiary is under 18 where one or more parent or guardian has died. It is specifically excluded from the inheritance tax provisions for a relevant property trust introduced from 22 March 2006 (IHTA 1984 s71A). A TBM is created:

- under the will of a deceased parent of the minor
- under a statutory trust arising on intestacy, or
- under the Criminal Injuries Compensation Scheme.

Such a trust qualifies as an 18-25 trust provided all the capital and income passes outright to the beneficiary at the age of earlier. There is no inheritance tax charge if the assets are paid before the age of 18, and a reduced charge if paid between 18 and 25.

trust for saying masses Trust established to say masses when someone has died, particularly in the Roman Catholic church. As there is no beneficiary, this is regarded as a trust of imperfect obligation.

trust for the disabled Such a trust is subject to inheritance tax as an interest in possession trust and not as a relevant property trust (IHTA 1984 s89). The definition of a disabled person is given in FA 2005 Sch 1A.

trust instrument A trust deed, will or other document that creates a trust.

trust of life assurance policies A trust whose property is a life assurance policy. Such a trust may be created to insure a life without the proceeds forming part of the person's estate. From 22 March 2006, such a trust is taxed as a relevant property trust.

trust or company service provider (TCSP) Firm or person who provides the services of company formation, directorship, registrar, business trustee, recruitment agency or personal service company. From 1 April 2008, such a firm may be required to register with HMRC under money laundering regulations.

trust period Period for which a trust may exist. Charitable trusts may live for ever. Other trusts are usually limited to 125 years if created from 6 April 2010, and 80 years if created before (as explained under perpetuities).

trust property Money, land and buildings or other assets held by trustees in a trust for the benefit of the trust's beneficiaries.

trust protector In tax evasion, a person who nominally controls a trust as a means of concealing the identity of the true settlor. A trust protector typically transfers funds on the basis of verbal instructions, that are not documented.

trust registration service (TRS) A government scheme that requires a trust to be registered with HMRC if the trust has any tax implications. There are some exceptions, such as for pension schemes and bare trusts.

Trusts that had a liability for income tax or capital gains tax in 2016/17 should have registered by 5 January 2018 (put back from 5 October 2017). Subsequently a trust must register by 5 October after the end of the tax year in which the first tax liability arose. There is a penalty for late registration.

If there are two or more trustees, one must be designated as the principal acting trustee.

The registration includes information that may not be immediately available to the trustee, such as the national insurance number of each individual beneficiary. Where beneficiaries cannot be individually identified, it is sufficient to report a class of beneficiaries.
Registration requires an agent services account. This provides a user ID and password. Someone without such an account will be provided with these items on first registration.

tuck shop In the case *St Benedict Trading Ltd [1993] VATTR 12915*, it was held that a tuck shop was supplying food, some of which was zero-rated for VAT. It was not supplying catering.

tugrik Unit of currency of Mongolia.

tun Large cask, particularly for holding beer during brewing.

Tunisia African country. Its currency is the Tunisian dinar of 1,000 millimes. The UK has a double taxation convention of 1982.
The country is subject to UK sanctions, as are designated persons of the country.

TUPE Transfer of Undertakings (Protection of Employment) Regulations SI 2006 No 246, which replaced regulations from 1981.
These ensure continuity of employment when a business is taken over. An employee has his or her employment rights protected as if the two employments were one.

Tupperware case The VAT case in the Court of Appeal of *P & R Potter v Customs and Excise [1985] STC 45*. This held that, for VAT, the supplier was the sub-distributor who held the party and not the main distributor who provided the goods.

turf accountant Bookmaker or betting shop.

Turkey Eastern country. Its currency is the Turkish lira of 100 kurus. The UK has a double taxation agreement of 1988.
Turkey is not a member of the European Union, but has equivalent Customs union provisions under the Ankara Agreement. These are set out in Customs notice 812.
The country is subject to UK sanctions, as are designated persons of the country.

turkey Edible fowl. The VAT position depends on whether the fowl is to be eaten (zero-rated) or is ornamental (standard-rated).
In VAT Notice 701/15, the former comprises the breeds of Beltsville White, British White, Broadbreasted White, Bronze, Norfolk Black, and derivatives and crossbreeds of these.

Turkmenistan Eastern country that became independent from Russia in 1991. Its currency is the manat of 100 tennesi.
The UK has a double taxation convention of 2016 that takes effect from 1 January 2017. It replaced one signed in 1985 with the USSR.

Turks and Cacos Islands UK Overseas Territory in Atlantic Ocean. Its currency is the US dollar.

turn Difference between the rates for equivalent services, such as borrowing and lending money.

turnover Income from the commercial activities of a business. It is also called income or revenue.

Company law defines the term in CA 2006 s539.

Accounting standards define it in FRS 102 glossary. The requirement for this to be stated on the face of the accounts is in FRS 102 section 5.7C.

Turnover is relevant for many tax provisions, including:

- whether a business should register for VAT
- whether a business is classified as small, medium-sized or a micro-entity
- whether a business may use cash accounting
- whether a business may use any of several schemes for smaller businesses.

Turnover excludes VAT charged by the business.

turnover aggregation When the turnover of two or more entities need to be added. here are several tax provisions where this is required. For companies, turnover is net of trade discounts, VAT and sales taxes (CA 2006 s539).

In practice that applies to all businesses and not just companies. It is required to see if a business has a turnover of £200 million or more and so needs a senior accounting officer. Details are given in HMRC Manual at SAOG24000. It can be required for enterprise investment scheme (ITA 2007 s175A(8) or venture capital trusts (ITA 2007 s280C(9)).

Turnover determines many tax provisions, such as cash accounting, annual accounting and the flat rate scheme for VAT.

turtle Endangered animal. The importation of the animal or its products is generally prohibited under Convention on International Trade in Endangered Species.

Tuvalu Island country in the Pacific Ocean. Its currency is the Tuvalu dollar of 100 cents, though the Australian dollar is widely used. The UK has a double taxation arrangement of 1950 as amended by a 1974 arrangement.

twenty pence coin Legal tender coin first issued on 9 June 1982. It is a cupro-nickel coin with a higher copper content than used for other cupro-nickel coins. The double florin and tenth ounce silver Britannia coin are also legal tender for 20p, though not used as such.

twenty pound note Bank of England note for £20. The current note is a polymer plastic note issued from 20 February 2020 depicting the artist J W Turner. The previous paper notes are expected to be demonetised in 2021.

twin unit caravan "Such a caravan can fall within this definition [of caravan] if composed of no more than two sections designed to be assembled on site by means of bolts, clamps and other devices, as long as, once assembled, it is physically capable of being moved from one place to another"

(VAT leaflet 701/20).

two pence coin Coin worth 2p first produced in 1968 and legal tender from 1971. The coin is minted in copper-plated steel from 1992 and in bronze previously.

two-stage verification Additional level of security introduced by HMRC from September 2017 when submitting an online return. The number changes for each submission.

In addition to the 12-digit Gateway number and the taxpayer's password, HMRC sends a message to a mobile phone or landline giving a six-digit number that must be entered by the taxpayer. This number must be entered on the online form within 15 minutes.

two-statement approach In accounting, when an entity decides to produce and income statement and a separate statement of comprehensive income. The alternative is the single-statement approach.

Details are given in FRS 102 Section 5.

two-stroke Description of a small engine for a vehicle (such as a motorcycle) whose cycle comprises two piston strokes.

two-year discretionary trust A discretionary trust that lasts for between three months and two years, to exploit the provisions of IHTA 1984 s188.

This trust disapplies the exit charge otherwise payable by a discretionary trust, provided there has been no interest in possession. Any distribution made during this period is, in effect, backdated to the date of death.

Tynwald Governing body of the Isle of Man.

type A equity Form of bank equity, as are types B, C and D.

It is relevant for the bank levy. The types are defined in FA 2011 Sch 19 para 17.

UAE dirham Currency of United Arab Emirates.

uberrimae fidei Latin for "of utmost faith".

This is an exception to the general legal rule that a party to a contract does not have to make any representations to the other party.

The exceptions apply to contracts of insurance, family settlement, partnership, suretyship, and allotment of shares.

UCITS Undertakings for collective investments in securities.

UCITS Directive "Means Council Directive 85/611/EEC of 20th December 1985 on the co-ordination of laws, regulations and administrative provisions relating to undertakings for collective investment in transferable securities as amended" (Importing of Savings Income Information Regulations SI 2003 No 3297 reg 2(1)).

Udal tenure Ancient form of tenure that applies to Orkney and Shetland Islands and is still recognised by Scots law provided it was registered by 1 April 2003. One of the main differences is that Udal tenure extends to the tide at low water mark rather than high water mark. This affects rights such as of pipelines and buried cables.

UEFA Financial Fair Play Regulations Financial rules regarding football clubs in Europe. They were introduced in 2009 to stop clubs spending more than they can afford to buy good players, and then getting into financial difficulties. Clubs that breach these rules, such as Manchester City, face sanctions.

Uganda African country. Its currency is the Uganda shilling of 100 cents. The UK has a double taxation convention of 1992.

Uganda shilling Currency of Uganda.

UITF abstract 7 Statement from the Urgent Issues Tax Force that has the force of an accounting standard but dealt with an issue that could not wait for a new standard. They are abolished for accounting periods that start on or after 1 January 2015.

UK activity Term used in relation to diverted profits tax and defined in FA 2015 s87(5).

UK approval certificate In relation to VAT on road fuel provided to employees, this "means a certificate issued under:

(a) section 58(1) or (4) of the Road Traffic Act 1998; or

(b) Article 31A(4) or (5) of the Road Traffic (Northern Ireland) Order 1981

(Value Added Tax 1994 s57(9)).

A similar definition is used for the taxation of company cars, this is defined in ITEPA 2003 s171(1).

The same definition is used in relation to capital allowances in CAA 2001 s268C(4).

UK-based earnings Income from employment in the UK by an employee who also has overseas earnings (ITEPA 2003 s25).

UK Border Agency (UKBA) Body set up on 1 April 2008 to protect the UK from illegal immigration. It was closed in 2013 and replaced by UK Visas and Immigration. Before 2008, this was undertaken by HMRC or its predecessor body, HM Customs and Excise. HMRC retains responsibility for taxes on imported goods.

UK companies not formed under companies legislation Term used in CA 2006 from s1040. It refers to companies registered overseas, unregistered companies, companies registered before 1862, and companies registered by other means such as letters patent or royal charter.

UK continental shelf That part of the waters surrounding the UK where the water is shallow. The UK claims mineral rights, particularly oil, for this area (Continental Shelf Act 1964). An agreement has been reached with Norway, Denmark, Germany and Netherlands on their respective boundaries of the shelf.

UKCS continental shelf certificate Certificate issued by HMRC to an employee working on the UK continental shelf (PAYE Regs 2003 reg 84A).

UK digital services revenues In relation to digital services tax, "a group's 'UK digital services revenues' for a period are so much of its digital services revenues for that period as are attributable to UK users" (FA 2020 s41(2)). Section 41 continues by setting out five Cases when revenues are so attributable.

UK-established Term used for VAT to describe a person who has a business establishment or other fixed establishment in the UK for their business (VATA 1994 Sch 1 para 1(10)).

UK expenditure For the purposes of corporation tax relief on film production, this term is defined in CTA 2009 s1185 and s1216AH.

UK financial instrument Financial instrument that is admitted to trading on a market in the UK (Financial Services and Markets Act 2000 s131C(6)).

UK furnished holiday lettings business UK property business so far as it consists of the commercial letting of furnished holiday accommodation (CTA 2009 s748(5)).

UK GAAP UK generally accepted accounting principles (ITA 2007 s997(2); CTA 2010 s1127(2)).

UK Government Investments Ltd Company registered on 11 September 2015 to hold investments for the government. Grants, loans and other payments may be made under the provisions of Enterprise Act 2016 s36.

UK-linked Tax term for a description of debt subject to tax provisions in ITEPA 2003 s33.

UK permanent establishment For loss relief, any permanent establishment through which a company carries on a trade in the UK (ICTA 1988 s403G(6)).

UK property business "A company's UK property business consists of –

(a) every business which the company carries on for generating income from land in the United Kingdom, and

(b) every transaction which the company enters into for that purpose otherwise than in the course of such a business"

(CTA 2009 s205).

An identical definition for income tax is given in ITTOIA 2005 s264.

Ukraine Eastern country that become independent from Russia in 1991 though territorial disputes between the countries remain. Its currency is the hryvnia of 100 kopiykas. The UK has a double taxation convention of 1993. The country is subject to UK sanctions, as are designated persons of the country.

UK-registered company For consortium relief, a company that is UK resident or trades in the UK through a permanent establishment (CTA 2010 s134).

UK-relieved funds Term used in relation to overseas transfer charge for pensions. It is defined in FA 2004 s242B as inserted by FA 2017 Sch 4 para 14.

UK sector of the continental shelf "The areas designated under section 1(7) of the Continental Shelf Act 1964" (ITEPA 2003 s41(2)).

UK securities "Means securities of –

(a) the government of the United Kingdom,

(b) a local authority in the United Kingdom,

(c) another public authority in the United Kingdom, or

(d) a UK resident company or other UK resident body"

(ITA 2007 s566(3)).

Sub-section (4) adds "but UK securities does not include UK shares".

The same definition appears in ITA 2007 s919(6) in relation to manufactured payments.

UK shares "Means shares in a UK resident company" (ITA 2007 s566(1)).

UK tax evasion offence "Means –

(a) an offence of cheating the public revenue, or

(b) an offence under the law of any part of the United Kingdom consisting of being knowingly concerned in, or in taking steps with a view to, the fraudulent evasion of a tax"

(Criminal Finances Act 2017 s45(4)).

UK tax evasion facilitation offence "Means –

(a) being knowingly concerned in, or in taking steps with a view to, the fraudulent evasion of a tax by another person,

(b) aiding, abetting, counselling or procuring the commission of a UK tax evasion offence, or

(c) being involved art and part [sic] in the commission of an offence consisting of being knowingly concerned in, or in taking steps with a view to, the fraudulent evasion of a tax"

(Criminal Finances Act 2017 s45(5)).

ullage Difference between the amount of liquor a barrel can contain and the amount it does contain.

Ulster The northernmost part of Ireland, comprising nine counties. Six counties are in Northern Ireland (and thus in the UK), namely: Antrim, Armagh, Down, Fermanagh, Londonderry and Tyrone. Three are in the Irish Republic: Cavan, Donegal and Monaghan.

Ulster Savings Certificates "Means savings certificates issued or treated as issued under section 15 of the Exchequer and Financial Provisions Act (Northern Ireland) 1950" (CTA 2009 s1282(6)).

ultimate holding company Company that owns all the subsidiaries and their parent companies. The ultimate holding company must be named in the accounts.

ultimus haeres Latin: ultimate heir. This refers to the state or crown. The term is particularly used in Scots law for someone who dies intestate or without next of kin.

ultra-low emission zone (ULEZ) Areas of London where, from 8 April 2019, polluting vehicles must pay a charge to enter.

Details are given under Congestion Charge and Road User Charges in section 3 of this dictionary.

ultra-low sulphur diesel oil Gas oil where:

- the sulphur content does not exceed 0.005% by weight
- the density does not exceed 835 kilograms per cubic metre at 15C, and
- at least 95% by volume distils at a temperature not exceeding 345C (HODA 1979 s1(6).

ultra-low sulphur petrol Unleaded petrol of which the sulphur content does not exceed 0.005% by weight and the aromatics content does not exceed 35% by volume.

ultra-violet feature Security feature on Bank of England notes. If a modern note is put under a light with a frequency around 365 nanometres, the value of the note appears in red and green.

ultra vires Latin for "beyond the powers". It refers to act that is beyond the powers of a body. The consequence is that the act is void. Historically, a company could

trade only for the purpose stated in its memorandum of association. Any contract outside that purpose was ultra vires.
Companies Act 1965 s20 repealed the ultra vires doctrine to protect third parties.
The doctrine remains valid in some other countries and in other contexts.

umbrella scheme Authorised unit trust where participants' contributions are put into separate pools and where the participant may transfer between pools.
The capital gains tax provisions are given in TCGA 1992 s99A.
There is a similar definition in relation to child trust funds in SI 2004 No 1450 reg 2(1)(c).

Umsatzsteuer (Umst) German term for "value added tax".

unable or virtually unable to walk Term used in determining the amount of mobility component that may be paid to a claimant for disability living allowance. Someone who meets this condition qualifies for the higher rate of mobility component.
The claimant must be either unable to walk at all, or be very limited in distance, speed or time for which the claimant can walk. The higher rate may also be claimed where, although walking is possible, the exertion in doing so is detrimental to the claimant's health.
For speed and distance, the law sets no formal limits. In practice, though, this can mean a maximum limit of 50 metres at a speed of 60 metres per minute.
Someone who has no feet because both legs are missing from above the ankle qualifies for the higher rate, even if they are able to walk using prostheses.

unadministered estate For inheritance tax, all the property held by the personal representative for the time being, excluding property which is the subject of a specific disposition or which is held for paying debts (IHTA 1984 s91(2)(a)).

unallocated cash Entry on a statement recording money received from a customer which has not been allocated against outstanding invoices.

unallocated precious metals For VAT, there is a supply when the buyer has the right to call for the metal but has not been specifically allocated any. The scheme originally applied to gold, silver and platinum. From 1 December 1994, it also applies to rhodium, ruthenium, osmium and iridium.

unallowable purpose In relation to tax avoidance and loan relationship, this term is defined in CTA 2009 s442.

unappropriated profits Profits which have yet to be allocated as dividends or retained profit.

unappropriated surplus Term used in ICTA 1988 s444AL(3) in relation to the taxation of mutual life assurance business.

unaudited accounts Description of accounts which have not been audited yet. Such accounts may be provided on a provisional basis, provided it is stated that they are unaudited. Unaudited accounts may not be put to members of a company or organisation (which requires an audit) for approval.

unauthorised deduction This term particularly applies to wages. An employer may only deduct money required by law (such as tax and student loan deductions) or where the employee has authorised it (such as trade union dues or loan repayments). Any other deduction is unlawful under Employment Rights Act 1996 s13. The employee may bring an action against the employer before the employment tribunal.

unauthorised employer payment Payment by a registered pension scheme that is an occupational pension scheme to or in respect of a sponsoring employer or a former sponsoring employer which is not an authorised employer payment, or anything which is treated as being an unauthorised payment to a sponsoring employer or former sponsoring employer under Part 4 of FA 2004. The term is defined in FA 2004 s160(3).

unauthorised payments charge Tax imposed at a high rate on payments from a pension fund to a member outside the permitted limits.

unauthorised unit trust Unit trust that has not been authorised under Financial Services and Markets Act 2000. Such a unit trust is legal but may not be offered to the public, and is subject to different regulation.

The tax provisions for such unit trusts from 6 April 2014 is given in SI 2013 No 2819.

unbalanced Not balanced. Description of accounts where the figures do not add up as they should. This indicates an error. An unbalanced figure may be accepted if:

- the difference is small;
- there is no reason to believe that the difference is from two larger amounts;
- there is no reason to believe that the difference indicates a failure to keep proper records; and
- the cost of finding the difference is disproportionate to the amount involved.

unborn widow Problem that once arose under the law for perpetuities. A person may leave estate to a son then living, then to his wife (not yet known), and then to their children. The wife may not even be born at the time, and may outlive other beneficiaries by more than 21 years. Before the law changed in 1964, such a bequest would be void.

uncalled Description of the share price which has not been fully paid (CA 2006 s547). Sometimes new shares are sold where payment is required in instalments known as calls. For example, a £1 share may have three calls of 40p, 30p and 30p. Many of the privatisations of the 1980s were funded in this way. If a call is not paid when required, the share is forfeited with no refund of any previous calls. The various tax-advantaged schemes for company investment all require the investment to be in fully paid shares or in options for them.

uncertainty In accounting, this usually refers to uncertainty about the tax treatment of an item or transaction. Guidance on how to deal with this is provided in international accounting guidance IFRIC 23 from 1 January 2019.

unclaimed allowance This usually refers to part of a capital allowance that a business has chosen not to claim (CAA 2001 s442(4)). Sometimes a business may not claim the full allowance, so that they do not lose entitlement under another provision, such as loss relief.

uncleared effects Amounts paid into a bank account but which have yet to appear on a bank statement. These items must be identified in a bank reconciliation.

uncommercial trade Trade which is not run on a commercial basis, such as a hobby. Losses from such activity may not be offset against other profits (ITA 2007 s66).

unconscionable Term used in tax law to mean completely unreasonable, unreasonably excessive or inordinate or outrageous. HMRC may grant special relief when not to do so would be unconscionable.

This is one of the conditions set out in TMA 1970 Sch 1AB para 3A to allow HMRC to grant special relief. For example, it may be unconscionable to require a taxpayer to pay tax twice even though tax law may require or allow this. In practice, this provision is sparingly used.

The meaning of the word was considered by a tax tribunal in the case *Clark [2015] TC 4509*. This held that the dictionary definition should be used, namely completely unreasonable, unreasonably excessive, inordinate or outrageous.

uncrystallised In tax, this refers to a gain that is not yet taxed. The commonest example is the increase in the value of an asset that is not subject to capital gains tax until crystallised by a disposal.

uncrystallised funds Funds held in a money purchase pension scheme that have yet to be used to provide benefits to the member. A full definition is given in FA 2004 Sch 28 para 8(3). These provisions were amended from 6 April 2015 by Taxation of Pensions Act 2014 s53.

uncrystallised funds lump sum death benefit Lump sum benefit paid from a money purchase pension scheme following the death of a member before the age of 75 (FA 2004 Sch 29 para 15).

uncrystallised funds pension lump sum Amount of a money purchase pension fund that is tax-free when taken as a lump sum. From 6 April 2015, there is no restriction on the amount that may be so taken. In general, 25% of the fund is tax-free, and the balance is added to the person's taxable income.

undated bond Financial instrument that has no maturity date. Such a bond is usually redeemed at any time of the holder's choice.

undercapitalised Description of a business or venture that has insufficient capital. Such a business may still survive and even prosper, but will probably have difficulties in trading in its early years.

underhedged Description of a risk for which there is insufficient hedging, such as when a business is over-exposed to currency fluctuations. Where underhedging is part of a risk transfer scheme, it may be caught by anti-avoidance provisions of FA 2010 s46 and Sch 16.

underlease Lease granted by someone who is himself or herself a lessee.

underlying chain payment In relation to worker's services provided to the public sector by a person with significant control, this term is defined by ITEPA 2003 s61S(5).

underlying income or gain In relation to the remittance basis, this is given a specific meaning in ITA 2007 s809VM(5).

underlying subject matter Property to which a future, option, contract for difference or similar financial instrument relates (CTA 2009 s583).

under-occupied Domestic property that is not fully utilised, particularly by having more bedrooms than are needed for the household. From April 2013, this can lead to a restriction on housing benefit or universal credit under what is commonly called the bedroom tax.

underpants A fanciful measure of economic prosperity, based on the theory that people buy more underwear when the economy is booming.

understandability One of the qualitative characteristics of financial statements.
"The presentation of information in a way that makes it comprehensible by users who have a reasonable knowledge of business and economic activities and accounting and a willingness to study the information with reasonable diligence" (FRS 102 glossary).
Guidance on how to present information is given in FRS 102 section 2.4.

undertaking

(1) Any corporate body pursuing activities, whether or not for profit (CA 2006 s1161(1)).
(2) The business of funeral directors, which may be exempt from VAT as explained in VAT Notice 701/32.

undervalue Value below the market value. CTA 2009 s222 contains provisions relating to a lease at undervalue.

underwater option Share option whose exercise price is higher than the current market value of the share (HMRC Manual BIM44001 glossary). Such an option is worthless unless the position is reversed.

underwrite Accept responsibility for something, such as agreeing to make up a loss if a venture or share raises insufficient cash.

underwriting year Same as the calendar year (FA 2007 Sch 11 para 3(9).

undeveloped market value of the interest For capital allowances of mineral extraction, this term is defined in CAA 2002 s404(2) and 424(2).

undischarged bankrupt Person who has been declared bankrupt and is still bound by its restrictions.

undistributable reserve Funds held by a business which it may use for its business but which cannot be distributed to shareholders. This comprises the share capital and capital reserves. For net asset restriction, the term is defined in CA 2006 s831(4).

undrinkable sediment This is produced in cask conditioned beer. Relief from beer duty may be claimed (Customs notice 226).

undue influence When one person has power to influence another to make a contract in the first person's favour. This can have the effect of invalidating the contract.

unearned income Term used before 6 April 1984 for investment income.

unemployment benefit Social security benefit paid to the unemployed. It was replaced by jobseeker's allowance from 1996.

unexplained wealth order Order that may be made by the High Court from 31 January 2019 on application from HMRC or other enforcement agency against a politically exposed person (Proceeds of Crime Act 2002 s362A as inserted by Criminal Finances Act 2017 s1). Subject to conditions, it requires an individual to identify the source of their apparent wealth. In the absence of satisfactory explanation, their property may be seized. The conditions are:

- there are reasonable grounds for suspecting that a person holds property
- the property has a value of at least £50,000
- the Court is satisfied that the known sources of lawfully obtained income are insufficient to obtain the property
- the person is a politically exposed person
- there are reasonable grounds to suspect that the person has been involved in serious crime, not necessarily in the UK.

As at 31 December 2020, only three such orders had been made, none by HMRC.

unfair contract terms A printed term in a consumer contract which the business person seeks to impose on the consumer. It does not apply to business contracts. Under Unfair Contract Terms Act 1977, such a provision is of no effect if the contract term seeks to:

- avoid liability for death or personal injury (s2);
- avoid liability when the business is at fault (s3);
- unreasonably indemnify a third party (s4);
- restrict statutory liability for faulty goods (s5).

unfair dismissal Dismissal of an employee for an unfair reason. It has been illegal since 1971. The current law is ERA 1996 s94. Note that dismissal in the wrong *manner* is wrongful dismissal. It is possible for a dismissal to be both unfair and wrongful.

unfair evidence "Evidence on which the prosecution proposes to rely to be given if it appears to the court that, having regard to all the circumstances, including the circumstances in which the evidence was obtained, the admission of the evidence would have such an adverse effect on the fairness of the proceedings that the court ought not to admit it" (Police and Criminal Evidence Act 1984 s78).

unfair prejudice Action taken by majority shareholders against the interest of minority shareholders who have statutory protection under CA 2006 from s994.

unfair terms Terms in a consumer contract that are unfair. The law is Unfair Contract Terms Act 1977.

A definition is given in Consumer Rights Act 2015 s62(4), which strengthens consumer rights.

unfinished beer Beer that is not yet ready to drink but where **beer duty** may be payable (Customs notice 226).

unfitness In relation to disqualification of company directors, unfitness is determined in accordance with Disability Discrimination Act 1995 from s12, including s12C as added by Small Business, Enterprise and Employment Act 2015 s105.

unfunded debt Debt which requires no particular measures for its repayment. The term is commonly used for short-term borrowing where the amount is recoverable from an insurance claim.

unfurnished letting This is usually held not to be a trade but property income, even when some administrative work is done. A leading case is *Pairceir v EM. [1971] Irish Case. HC(1).*

ungeared Description of a business that has no borrowings to fund its business. Its funding comes from shareholders and retained profit.

unicorn Term that gained currency from 2015 for a fast-growing privately-owned business.

unified business rate Local taxation of business premises that are not subject to council tax. They were introduced by Local Government Finance Acts 1988 to 1990. From 1 April 2013, a new system of business rates is introduced.

unified tax Income tax system introduced from 1973 that replaced the previous system.

uniform Form of clothing that identifies the occupation of its wearer. This usually requires the clothing to have the name or logo of the employer visible.

Provided this does not comprise normal clothing, it is a tax-deductible expense of the employee, or a non-taxable benefit if provided by the employer.

A leading case is *Mallalieu v Drummond [1983] 57 TC 330.* This allowed a female barrister to claim for gown, wig and tabs that she had to wear in court, but not for white blouses and black skirts that she bought to wear in court but which could be worn outside. The case is discussed in HMRC Manual at BIM37910. The manual gives as examples a nurse's uniform and waiter's tailed coat.

Many workers, particularly manual workers, may be able to claim a fixed allowance that covers uniform expenses. These Expense Allowances are given in section 3 of this dictionary.

There is no VAT liability when an employer provides a uniform. The case *French Connection Ltd [2015] TC 4367* held that this did not extend to a fashion company requiring staff to wear clothes from its latest range, even though this had a commercial purpose.

It is a criminal offence to wear a uniform falsely to indicate a police or military rank (Official Secrets Act 1920 s1) or to wear a uniform in connection with a political objective (Public Order Act 1936 ss1-2).

unincorporated association Group of people working together who are not in a formal partnership, trust or company. Such an association is liable to corporation tax on any profits.

union flag National flag of the United Kingdom adopted by Order in Council of 1801. Otherwise the flag has not been legally adopted. In a Parliamentary answer of 1933, it was stated that any British subject may fly the flag.

At sea, its use is restricted to military vessels (Merchant Shipping Act 1995). It is not true that the flag is called the Union Jack on ships; union flag and Union Jack are synonyms.

Other vessels may fly an ensign, which is a blue or red flag with the union flag in one corner.

Under CEMA 1979 s91(2) any "vessel in the service of Her Majesty" flying the correct ensign may order a vessel suspected of smuggling to heave to. If it does not, the British vessel may give chase, fire a warning shot, and ultimately open fire.

union learning representative Trade union official whose function is to identify and help meet the learnings needs of its members. Such an official has the right to paid leave for such duties (Trade Union and Labour Relations (Consolidation) Act 1992 s168A).

unique selling point (USP) In marketing, quality of goods or services that identify why a customer should favour those of one supplier over another. Examples of USPs include cheaper price, prompter delivery, greater durability, better support services, readier availability, greater ease of use, and more attractive design.

unique tax reference (UTR) Number allocated to a taxpayer by HMRC, and which should be quoted in all correspondence with HMRC. It usually comprises two sets of five digits.

Unique Ticket Number (UTN) Number that may be allocated to each ticket by an event organiser. From April 2018, resellers of tickets must state the UTN if one has been issued. This is designed to prevent touting.

unissued capital Capital that a company is authorised to issue, usually as shares, but has not done so.

unitary authority Part of the UK where there is one local authority rather than having two authorities at different levels, such as a borough council and a county council covering the same area. Birmingham is the UK's largest unitary authority.

unitary taxation System of income tax introduced in 1973, replacing the previous system where 2/9 of income was usually tax-free, and various rates of income tax and supertax applied on taxable income.

United Kingdom (UK) Term adopted on 1 January 1801 for the union of England, Wales, Scotland and Ireland (now just Northern Ireland).

From 12 April 1927, it was legally defined as "Great Britain and Northern Ireland" (Interpretation Act 1978 Sch 1).

The UK does not include Isle of Man or the Channel Islands.

United Kingdom securities "Any securities issued by or on behalf of Her Majesty's Government in the United Kingdom or the Government of Northern Ireland and any securities of a body corporate incorporated in any part of the United Kingdom" (TMA 1970 s24(4)).

United Nations International organisation established in 1944 to discuss and regulate international relations.

United States of America (USA) Federal republic of 50 states which developed from 1783 when it gained independence from Great Britain. Its currency is the US dollar of 100 cents. The UK has a double taxation convention of 2001 amended by a protocol of 2002.

unit holder Person who holds a unit, usually in a unit trust.

unit load Any load, including groupage, which leaves the approved premises as a single, identifiable unit intended for exportation.

unit of account In accounting, the unit of the currency in which the accounts are prepared.

unit trust Popular collective investment scheme. It comprises a portfolio of investments in which an investor buys units. It allows someone to have a diverse portfolio for lower amounts of investment.

The capital gains tax implications are given in TCGA 1992 ss99-103A.

universal credit Means-tested social security benefit introduced from 2013 to replace six existing means-tested benefits (WRA 2012 s1). The migration was due to have been completed by 2017 but has been deferred several times.

The benefits it replaces are called legacy benefits. They are child tax credit, housing benefit, income support, income-based jobseeker's allowance, income-related employment and support allowance, and working tax credit.

Unlike previous benefits, a claimant remains on universal credit as he or she moves between employment, self-employment and unemployment.

This has the advantage that a claimant does not lose benefit and have to claim afresh every time his or her employment status changes. It also resolves some problems with previous benefits, such as the sharp reduction in benefit when a claimant works between 16 and 24 hours a week.

The main elements of universal credit are:

- it is paid monthly in arrears
- it is paid to households with little income and without significant savings
- it must be claimed online or by calling 0800 328 5644; it is not given automatically
- the claimant must either be 18 or more years old, or 16-17 and meet certain conditions
- universal credit comprises a standard allowance and additions for children, disability and housing
- the first payment is paid after five weeks, though claimants may receive an advance from the first day
- circumstances are reviewed each month
- as income increases by £1, benefit is reduced by 63p
- there is a work allowance which is ignored in determining amount of universal credit
- self-employed claimants must comply with a minimum income floor to demonstrate that they really are running a commercial business.

From 16 November 2020, the earnings periods rules are amended so that earnings may be allocated to the period when earned and not when paid (SI

2020 No 1138). This follows the Court of Appeal decision in *Secretary of state v Johnson [2020] EWCA Civ 778.*

The scheme has been amended several times since its introduction to deal with issues as they arose.

More details are given under Social Security rates in section 3 of this dictionary.

Universal Credit Transition Fund Fund established from April 2020 to assist vulnerable people to claim universal credit.

universal dummy The code QQ999999 that must be used by a paying agent when reporting savings income that does not have its own identification reference number for the security involved. Use of this number will lead to the paying agent being audited by HMRC.

Universal Jobmatch Website that connects jobseekers with job vacancies. It was renamed Find a Job from 14 May 2018.

universal postal service Arrangements that ensure that mail is delivered to every address in the UK.

universal service provider (USP) For postal services, Royal Mail. Its status as USP allows its services to be exempt from VAT, though this was restricted from 31 January 2011. Broadly, postal services are exempt from VAT where Royal Mail has a monopoly, but subject to VAT when competing with commercial couriers.

unjust enrichment Provision in VAT law that restricts a refund of VAT if this is likely to be kept by the business and not passed to its customers. (VATA 1994 ss80A-80B).

It sometimes happens that a business finds it has charged VAT on a supply that is zero-rated. It may then claim a refund of VAT from HMRC to pass on to customers. A business does not have to do this. Unjust enrichment refers to when a business claims a VAT refund without passing it on to customers. The matter was tested in the series of cases *Marks and Spencer plc v Customs and Excise [2000].* The matter is discussed in HMRC Manual at VRM12220.

unjustified enrichment This is the Scottish equivalent to unjust enrichment found in Revenue Scotland and Tax Powers Act 2014 from s109. In Scotland this applies to direct taxes as well as VAT.

unlawful Contrary to the law. A distinction is sometimes drawn from "illegal" in that unlawful acts incur no penalty.

unlawful deduction from wages Deduction from wages for a reason which is not permitted. Only these items may be legally deducted from wages:

- income tax and national insurance;
- contributions to an occupational pension scheme or workplace pension of which the employee is a member;
- corrections of an overpayment on a previous payslip, subject to conditions;
- attachments of earnings which been authorised by a court or other authority;
- amounts which are authorised by the contract of employment;
- amounts which the employee authorised *before* the deduction was made; and

- retail deductions for shortfalls of stock or cash in the retail trade, subject to restrictions.

It should be remembered that any other deduction is unlawful even if the employee owes the money. An employee may take a claim to an employment tribunal for an unlawful deduction.

In particular, an employer has no right of sight-off against wages such as for such items as damage caused to company property or amounts outstanding for purchases from the company.

unlawful dismissal Dismissal of an employee in an improper manner, such as by not following a discipline procedure or not giving proper notice. It is a breach of contract. It is different from unfair dismissal which is dismissal for an unfair reason.

unlawful distribution Dividend or similar distribution made by a company other than as permitted under company law, such as by having insufficient profits. If a shareholder knows that the distribution is unlawful, it must be immediately repaid to the company (CA 2006 s847).

unleaded petrol Petrol that contains less than 0.13 grams of lead per litre of petrol (HODA 1979 s13A). Before 1 April 1990, the limit was 0.20 grams.

unlimited company Company where the liability of its members is not limited. Such companies are now rare.

Unlisted Securities Market A junior stock market run by the London Stock Exchange between 1980 and 1996. A similar facility is now provided by the Alternative Investment Market.

UNLOCODE Identification scheme for locating goods to be exported or imported. It is used for Customs duty purposes.

unmarked gas oil Heavy oil which does not contain a dye. This indicates that duty has been paid.

unmarked kerosene A heavy oil of which more than 50% by volume distils at a temperature not exceeding 240 degrees C, but which does not contain the prescribed marker coumarin. Unmarked kerosene is usually called AVTUR or aviation turbine fuel, as it is used in aircraft engines.

unmarried couple For pension credit, two people who are living other as husband and wife, but who are not married (State Pension Credit Act 2002 s17(1).

unmeasured work A base for determining whether national minimum wage has been paid (SI 1999 No 584 para 6). It is only used for workers where the other bases do not apply. It requires the employer and worker to agree how long a piece of work is expected to take, and ensure that the national minimum wage is paid for those hours.

unnecessary material Term used in company law to mean items submitted to Companies House in excess of that required and which cannot readily be separated from the rest of the document. The presence of such material may mean that the document is regarded as not having been submitted (CA 2006 s1074).

unpaid amount In relation to PAYE, "means any amount of tax or interest which –

(a) an employer is liable to pay under regulation 75A(10), 76(2), 77(6), 78(8) or 79(2)(b);

(b) an employee is liable to pay under regulation 72(7) or regulation 81(6)." (PAYE regulations SI 2003 No 2682 reg 84(1)).

unpaid contributions National insurance contributions that have not been paid when they should have been. The offences are dealt with in Social Security Administration Act 1992 from s119.

unpaid expense Bad debt for which a trade had claimed tax relief when it ceased trading (ITA 2007 s99(1)). Should the debt subsequently be paid it is treated as a qualifying payment and becomes taxable.

unpaid leave Absence from work for which an employee is not paid. The employee generally remains entitled to any tax refunds generated by the PAYE system unless taking industrial action (PAYE Regs 2003 reg 63).

The PAYE allocates the personal allowance (with any adjustments) on an equal basis throughout the year. So, in broad terms, one twelfth of the personal allowance is allowed each month. If the personal allowance is £12,500, This is £1,041 a month. For a basic rate taxpayer this is equivalent to £208 tax. Provided the employee has already paid at least this amount of tax since 6 April, a payslip with gross pay of zero can generate net pay.

unpaid remuneration Pay to directors or other employees that has been included in the accounts but not paid. If remuneration has not been paid nine months after the end of the accounting period, it is not deductible from taxable profits (ITTOIA 2005 s36; CTA 2009 s1288). For an investment company, the same provision is given in CTA 2009 s1250.

unpaid rent condition A condition that must be met for a landlord to end a shorthold tenancy for abandoned premises (Housing and Planning Act 2016 s58(1)).

unpaid amount PAYE or interest that is owed and has not been paid. A specific definition is given in PAYE Regs 2003 reg 84(1).

unpaid seller A seller of goods who has provided the goods as required under the contract and has either not been paid the whole price, or where payment was made by a bill of exchange which has not been honoured (Sale of Goods Act 1979 s38(1)).

Under s39 of the Act, an unpaid seller has the right of seller's lien on any goods still in the seller's possession, a limited right of re-sale, and the right to stop goods in transit. These are in addition to his or her right to sue for payment.

unpaid work requirement Element of a criminal sentence that an offender must perform unpaid work (Criminal Justice Act 2003 s199).

unprompted In relation to tax penalties, this refers to a disclosure that has not been prompted by any investigation or query from HMRC. A tax penalty may be reduced if disclosure was unprompted.

unprotected trust deed In Scotland, a trust deed which is not registered and therefore does not stop a creditor starting sequestration proceedings.

unqualified report Report, particularly by an auditor, in which there was no aspect of the business that caused concern and needed reporting.

unquoted company Company whose shares are not listed on a stock exchange. This is a condition for employee-controlled companies (ITA 2007 s397(6)).

unquoted shares Shares that are not listed on a stock exchange. Their capital gains tax position is given in TCGA 1992 s273.

unquoted status requirement Requirement that entitlement to tax relief in some circumstances depends on the company not being listed on a stock exchange. This applies under the enterprise investment scheme (ITA 207 ss143 and 184); venture capital trust relief (ITA 2007 s295) and share loss relief (CTA 2010 s85).

unrealised capital gain Investment or asset which has grown in value but has not been turned into cash.

For capital gains tax, there is no tax liability for an unrealised gain such as continuing to own an asset whose value is increasing. The liability to tax usually arises when the gain is crystallised on a disposal.

unrealised profit Profit that has been earned but not turned into cash. A common example is a debt awaiting payment. There are some legal restrictions on the use of unrealised profits (CA 2006 ss846 and 849).

unrealised profit account In traditional bookkeeping, this is needed if a company keeps separate manufacturing accounts and trading accounts. This is now very rare.

The account is needed to ensure that stock is valued correctly and does not include unrealised profit. It applies when goods are transferred from the manufacturing account to the trading account at a sum in excess of cost.

The double entry is similar to a provision, and is usually made in the journal. The debit is to the account with the carried forward sum and the credit to the brough forward figure, with the balance written off to the profit and loss account.

unredeemed pledge Pledge which a borrower has made but has not redeemed. An example is when a personal item is pledged or pawned, and the person cannot raise the cash to redeem the pledge to get it back.

unreduced amount Term used in CTA 2009 s230 and ITTOIA 2005 s290 in relation to the additional calculation rule for leases.

unregistered company Generally this is a body corporate that has a principal place of business in the UK but is not registered in the UK. Company law provisions are given in CA 2006 s1043. It pays corporation tax as if it were a registered company.

unrelieved loss Loss where no tax relief has been claimed for the current year and where the loss may carried forward to future years (ITA 2007 s83(2)).

unremittable amounts Sums that cannot be sent to the UK, usually because of restrictions in another country (ITTOIA 2005 from s187; CTA 2009 from s1272). The general principle is that sums are not included in taxable income until they can be remitted.

unrestricted fund Fund that a charity may use for any purpose, unlike a designated fund or restricted fund.

unsecured creditors People to whom money is owed but where they hold no security. Their ranking in an insolvency is set out under Insolvency in section 3 of this dictionary.

unsecured pension Payment of income withdrawals direct from a money purchase arrangement, or income paid from a short-term annuity contract purchased from such an arrangement, to the member of the arrangement (who is aged under 75) and that meet the conditions laid down in FA 2004 Sch 28 para 6-10.

unsecured pension fund Funds, whether sums or assets, held under a money purchase arrangement that have been designated to provide a scheme member (who is aged under 75) with an unsecured pension, as identified in FA 2004 Sch 28 para 8. Once sums or assets have been designated as part of an unsecured pension fund any capital growth or income generated from such sums or assets are equally treated as being part of the unsecured pension fund.

Similarly where assets are purchased at a later date from such funds, or sums generated by the sale of assets held in such funds, those replacement assets or sums also fall as part of the unsecured pension fund (as do any future growth or income generated by those assets or sums).

unsigned accounts Set of financial statements which lack a signature on the balance sheet. HMRC lost a case where they imposed a penalty for late submission because the accounts were returned for signature *(Codu Computer Ltd [2011] TC 1055.*

unsocial hours Hours when most people prefer not to work. This typically includes nights, weekends and public holidays. Working unsocial hours often attracts a premium, though this is a matter of contractual negotiation between employer and employee. An employee has no automatic right to a higher rate of payment.

unsolicited "Means, in relation to goods sent to any person, that they are sent without any prior request made by him or on his behalf" (Unsolicited Goods and Services Act 1971 s6(1)).

The broad implications are that:

- the recipient should notify the sender and invite them to collect the goods. The recipient is not obliged to send them back
- the recipient must take reasonable care of the goods as an involuntary bailee
- if the sender does not collect the goods within three months, the goods become the property of the recipient who may do with them whatever he or she wishes.

Untelraab Case that helped establish legal precedent that the residence of the company is where its decisions were made. The full name is *Untelraab Ltd v McGregor. SpC 55 [1995].*

untrue declaration False declaration for Customs purposes. It is an offence for which penalties are prescribed by CEMAs167.

unwritten law Law that is not written down, though it may be subsequently recorded. It includes common law, equity and custom.

upfront fee Fee paid in advance of receiving any service or benefit. It is one of the hallmarks of an artificial tax avoidance scheme.

upper accruals point Limit for class 1 national insurance that existed between 2009 and 2016. Pay above this point was subject to the full rate of national insurance but did not earn any extra entitlement to state second pension.
The upper accruals point for the whole period was £770 a week, which is £3336 a month or £40,040 a year.

upper earnings limit Maximum earnings on which the full rate of class 1 national insurance is payable (SSCBA 1992 s5(1)(a)). It was originally fixed at seven times the amount of state pension.
From 2008, this is linked to the threshold for paying higher rate income tax. The rates are given under National Insurance in section 3 of this dictionary.
From 1975 to 1984, this was the limit at which the employer and employee paid no further class 1 national insurance. From 1984 to 2003, it was the limit to which the employee (but not employer) paid no further class 1 national insurance.

Upper House House of Lords.

upper secondary threshold Limit of earnings to which employer's national insurance is not payable for an employee under 21 (SSCBA 1992 s9A(3)). It was introduced in 2015, and has been the same as the upper earnings limit.

upper tribunal Tax tribunal to which an appeal may be made on a point of law from a decision by the first tier tribunal (Tribunals, Courts and Enforcement Act 2007 s3). Some complex cases may go straight to the upper tribunal.

There is a separate upper tribunal for Scotland (Revenue Scotland and Tax Powers Act 2014 s21(4)).

upset price Reserved price of goods at auction. If no-one bids a higher amount, the goods are sold at the upset price.

upstream loan Loan made by a subsidiary to its parent company.

uranium Radioactive metal element. A licence is needed from the Office for Civil Nuclear Security to import it. Customs needs to see this licence.

urban regeneration company Body set up by the government to assist in regenerating cities Contributions by companies to such bodies may qualify for corporation tax relief (ITTOIA 2005 s86; CTA 2009 s82; ICTA 1988 s79B).

ure In Orkney and Shetland Isles, an area of land whose feu duty is one eighth of a mark.

urgency condition Provision under Guardian (Missing Persons) Act 2017 s3(3)(b). This allows a court to appoint a guardian for a missing person where a decision is needed, or likely to be needed, in relation to the missing person's property for financial affairs without waiting the usual 90 days.

Urgent Issues Task Force Part of the Financial Reporting Council that issued brief statements of accounting practice which could not wait for the development of a full accounting standard. The Task Force was abolished in 2014.

urn An urn provided as part of a funeral service comes within the scope of VAT exemption for burial. Otherwise, it is standard-rated. Details are given in VAT Notice 701/32.

Uruguay South American country. Its currency is the Uruguay peso. The UK has a double taxation convention of 2016.

Uruguayan Peso Currency of Uruguay.

usage method Method of calculating depreciation, particularly for mines, quarries and similar. It calculates depreciation by how much of the asset has been used in the period.

usage segmentation Classifying users of products according to their usage of a product or service. The classification is usually a simple one such as heavy, medium and light.

USB datastick Small device, typically about 7cm long and 1cm wide with a standard rectangular plug for USB connectors on computers. It can hold many gigabytes of data. Tax data may be submitted to HMRC on a datastick, though it should be realised that HMRC then destroys the datastick and does not return it.

use class order In planning law, a category of building uses for which planning permission may be given, such as an office or a shop.

used-up amount Term used in relation to ring-fence allowances in CTA 2010 s330A(3).

useful economic life Period for which an organisation expects to derive economic benefit from an asset (FRS 102 glossary). This is the basis of depreciation. It can also be relevant for determining the tax liability on a finance lease. For finance leases, there is a test set out in CAA 2001 s70P.

use of information Rules that govern what HMRC may do with information received from and about taxpayers (Commissioners of Revenue and Customs Act 2005 s17).

use of the money raised requirement Condition for enterprise investment scheme (ITA 2007 s175)and venture capital trusts (ITA 2007 s293). The broad requirement is that at least 80% of the funds must be used within a year of being raised.

user name Customer's name in stylised form or similar which a person uses to access a password-protected computer file. The person must usually then enter a password that is registered to the user name.

Usher Tax case on the remoteness test for tax allowability of expenditure. The full name is *Usher's Wiltshire Brewery Ltd v Bruce [1914] 6 TC 399*. The issue is discussed in HMRC Manual at BIM37200.

USSR Union of Soviet Socialist Republics, disbanded in 1991.

usual place of residence For VAT place of supply rules, "in relation to a body corporate, means the place where it is legally constituted" (VATA 1994 s9(6)). For VAT registration, the same definition is used in ibid Sch 1 para 10(4)(b)).

usury Term now means extortionately high interest. Historically, usury was considered the unacceptable practice of charging interest on loans to relieve need rather than to fund a commercial enterprise.

utilities Basic services provided to a household or the businesses that provide them. The services are usually regarded as gas, electricity, water, sewerage, telephone and broadband.

Utility scheme Government scheme from 1941 to 1952 where clothing and household items were manufactured to the same standard and price as a wartime economy measure. Utility goods were exempt from purchase tax.

utmost good faith Term used by insurance companies requiring full disclosure by customers under the uberrimae fidei principle.

Uzbekistan Eastern country, formerly part of USSR. Its currency is the som of 100 tiyms. The UK has a double taxation convention of 1993, amended by a protocol of 2018.

V5C Registration certificate (similar to log book) for a motor vehicle. It is a multi-coloured two page form used to record changes of ownership, and to identify who is liable to tax it.

V11 Reminder issued by DVLA when vehicle excise duty needs renewing.

vacant possession Description of a building where there are no sitting tenants.

vaccine research relief Tax relief between 22 April 2003 and 31 March 2017 for research into vaccines (CTA 2009 from s1039). Its scope was reduced in 2011 and abolished in 2017 (FA 2016 s47). Fewer than ten companies claimed it. It is replaced by direct funding such as through the Ross Fund.

vagrant Criminal offence of being an "idle and disorderly person", a "rogue and vagabond" or an "incorrigible rogue", as defined in Vagrancy Act 1824.

vague Insufficiently detailed. A vague clause can invalidate a clause or legacy. Whether a clause is vague is ultimately for the courts to decide.

Vallambrosa Leading tax case from 1910 on whether expenditure is capital or revenue. The full name is *Vallambrosa Rubber Company Ltd v Farmer [1910] 5 TC 529*. The case related to the costs of looking after rubber trees for five years before they provide rubber. The matter is discussed in HMRC Manual at BIM35305.

valour An award for valour is exempt from income tax (ITEPA 2003s638). The disposal of a decoration by a person to whom the award was made is exempt from capital gains tax (TCGA 1992 s268). The disposal by someone else is not covered by this exemption.

valuable consideration In contract, a consideration capable of supporting a contract. A contract for a nominal value is therefore a valid contract. Under Law of Property Act 1925 s205(1), valuable consideration includes marriage but not nominal amounts.

valuation assumptions This term is particularly used in specific circumstances. For pensions, there are assumptions if the person has not reached such age (if any) as must have been reached to avoid any reduction in the benefits on account of age, that the person reached that age on the date, and that the person's right to receive the benefits had not been occasioned by physical or mental impairment.

For council tax, the assumptions are that:

- the property has vacancy possession,
- a house was sold freehold, and a flat with a 99-year lease,
- the property if free of any rent charge (or Scottish equivalent),
- the property is of the same size and layout as when valued,
- the dwelling is in reasonable repair,
- fixtures for disabled people are excluded from valuation,
- the premises is restricted to private residence,
- the premises have no development value.

valuation bands Bands reflecting the value of domestic property for the purposes of determining council tax. Properties are banded A to I in Wales, and from A to H in England and Scotland. Details are given under Council Tax in section 3 of this dictionary.

valuation declaration For Customs purposes, a statement that an importer may be required to make in relation to goods above a certain value.

valuation list List kept by a local authority listing residential properties and their valuation band for council tax (Local Government Finance Act 1992 s23).

valuation of benefits In relation to employee benefits, this is determined according to ITEPA 2003 s415.

Valuation Office Part of HMRC that values properties (Commissioners of Revenue and Customs Act 2005 s10).

valuation tribunal In relation to non-domestic rates means a body set up under Local Government Finance Act 1988 s55(8).

value Worth ascribed to an asset, person or organisation. Value must be based on assumptions that are appropriate to the circumstances.

value added tax (VAT) Tax introduced in 1973 on the supply of goods or services by registered traders. It replaced purchase tax and selective employment tax. It was first enacted in FA 1973. It is now enacted by VATA 1994 s1(1).

VAT is charged on supplies, which are not necessarily sales. A charge to VAT arises when:

- a supply is made
- in the course or furtherance of a business
- by a person who is, or should be, registered for VAT.

The Act has Schedules of supplies that are zero-rated, reduced-rated or exempt for VAT. There are also some supplies that are regarded as outside the scope of VAT. Otherwise, VAT is charged at the standard rate of 20%.

Generally, a supply must be supported by a VAT invoice.

The name comes from the fact that the tax is charged on the value added by the business. Suppose a registered business buys £200 worth of goods to sell for £300. The business pays £240 to its supplier, which is £200 plus 20% VAT. It sells the goods for £360 which is £300 plus 20%. On its VAT return, it pays the £60, called output tax, and subtracts the £40 paid to its supplier, called input tax, and pays £20 to HMRC. That £20 is 20% of the £100 value added.

For VAT, no distinction is made between capital and revenue. Provided capital expenditure is related to the business, VAT may generally be claimed for capital expenditure. So a shop may claim back VAT on a new till on the same basis as VAT for its stock.

VAT may be shown on credit notes where they represent a genuine reduction of value, such as a retrospective discount.

value chain In management accounting, a description of the series of activities that bring a unit of production of goods or services from its initial stages to delivery to the customer.

value in use Accounting term for the present value of cash flows expected to be derived from an asset or cash-generating unit (FRS 102 glossary).

value judgment Determination of the rightness or wrongness of someone or something. This typically involves comparison with a set of values based on a value system. A value judgment typically determines culpability.

For tax, this can be determinative of the amount of penalty, which is higher for deliberate concealment as against carelessness. The value system for tax penalties is what a responsible taxpayer would do.

value of supply of goods or services Amount on which VAT is charged (VATA 1994 s19).

value-protected annuity Form of pension that is available from 6 April 2006. It operates as a normal annuity except that if a member dies before the age of 75 (or any pre-agreed age), a sum will be paid equal to the balance of the pension fund.

Suppose a man aged 65 starts to receive a pension of £5,000 a year from a fund of £100,000 and dies aged 72. He has received £35,000. This means that £65,000 remains in the fund, possibly plus interest. That will be paid to his estate from which income tax is deducted.

value received by the investor This term is used in relation to enterprise investment scheme. If an investor receives any benefit from a company in which he or she has invested under the scheme, the tax relief may be reduced under provisions of ITA 2007 s213 unless the amount is of insignificant value.

value shifting Tax avoidance scheme that seeks to reduce capital gains tax by shifting value of the disposed asset. There are anti-avoidance measures to counter such schemes, such as TCGA 1992 from s29 as amended by FA 2011 Sch 9. There are separate provisions for pension funds under FA 2006 from s181.

van Vehicle weighing up to 3,500 kilograms and which is primarily designed to carry goods or burden, rather than passengers. This can determine the taxable benefit in kind when provided to an employee (ITEPA s115(1) and s235(3)). Details can be found under Company Cars and Van Benefits in section 3 of this dictionary.

In marginal cases, HMRC gives guidance on its website. This is guidance and may be challenged at a tribunal.

Note that a vehicle may be differently regarded for different taxes. In the case *County Pharmacy [2005]*, the Special Commissioners held that a motor home was a car for income tax purposes even though it was treated as a van for VAT. Rates of van benefit are given in section 3 of this dictionary.

van benefit Taxable benefit in kind of providing an employee with a van that may be used for personal use. A van is taxed less heavily than a car. Rates are given under Van Benefit in section 3 of this dictionary.

Van den Berghs Leading case on whether expenditure is capital or revenue. Its full name is *Van den Berghs Ltd v Clark [1935] 19 TC 390.* The matter is discussed in HMRC Manual at BIM35530.

van fuel benefit The amount that an employee is taxed on the benefit in kind of being provided with fuel for a van for private use. It is additional to the tax on the van itself. Rates are given under Van Benefit in section 3 of this dictionary.

vanilla In relation to financial products, this means simple and conservative. The term is an allusion to ice cream.

vanity publishing When an author pays a publisher to publish his or her book. For VAT, if the publisher sells the books to the author, it is zero-rated as a supply of books. If the publisher retains possession of the books, it is regarded as a mixed supply of zero-rated books and standard-rated publishing (VAT Notice 701/10).

Arrangements have been made with trade bodies on how to apportion the supply (VAT Notice 700/57).

Vanuatu Island country in Pacific Ocean that became independent in 1980. Its currency is the vatu. The UK has no double taxation treaty.

vapour recovery unit Device that is legally required at oil terminals to ensure that vaporised oil does not enter the atmosphere. There are provisions to ensure that the recovered oil is not taxed twice.

Vardy Unsuccessful stamp duty land tax scheme. A property was purchased by a UK unlimited company formed for the purpose and passed to the shareholder as a dividend. It was held that this unlawful as the dividend did not arise from company profits. The case was *Vardy Properties v Vardy Properties Ltd [2012].* It is explained by HMRC in Spotlight 13.

variation Departure from what is expected. A significant variation in a tax return may prompt an enquiry from HMRC.

VAT Value added tax.

VAT code Number that corresponds to a rate of VAT, as used by modern tills.

VAT co-operation Co-operation between the UK and EU on VAT matters from 1 January 2021 is provided for in EU/UK withdrawal agreement of 24 December 2020. This is given effect in UK law by European Union (Future Relationship) Act 2020 s22.

VAT credit Amount of VAT refundable by HMRC when input tax exceeds output tax.

VAT fraction Fraction used to determine the VAT element of a VAT-inclusive price. For the 20% rate, the fraction is 1/6. For 5%, it is 1/21. So if an item costs £120 including VAT at 20%. the VAT element is one sixth, namely £20. The fraction is calculated as R/(100+R) where R is the rate of VAT as a percentage.

VAT group Group of bodies that may register for VAT as if they were a single entity.

VAT Guide VAT Notice 700 which provides general guidance on VAT.

VAT invoice Invoice which shows VAT and meets the requirements of VAT regulations. Under SI 1995 No 2518, a VAT invoice must generally show:

- a unique sequential invoice number
- the time of supply or other tax point
- the date of issue of the invoice
- the trader's name and address
- the trader's VAT registration number
- the customer's name and address
- a description of the goods or services supplied, and to which the invoice relates
- for each item supplied, the VAT-exclusive charge, and the rate of VAT applied
- for countable items, the quantity supplied and unit charge (such as per item or per hour)
- the total amount of the invoice, excluding VAT
- the total amount of VAT charged, and the total value of the invoice
- any discount offered, such as for prompt payment
- additional details if the supply is made under special provisions such as a margin scheme, reverse charge or tour operators' margin scheme.

If the supply is zero-rated to a business in another EU state, the invoice must also give the customer's VAT number with the appropriate country prefix code. Less detailed invoices are permitted for supplies below £250.

The right to claim input tax depends in part on having a valid VAT invoice. An invoice may be issued electronically.

VAT notice Publication from HMRC about VAT. There are more than 100 such notices, some of which have legal effect.

VAT number Unique nine-digit number that identifies a business registered for VAT.

VAT period Period for which a VAT return must be submitted. This is usually three months.

VAT registration Process whereby a business is registered for VAT and given a registration number. VAT Notice 700/1 sets out who should register. VAT Notice 700/2 explains group registration and divisional registration.

VAT repayment supplement Amount, equivalent to interest, which may be added to a refund of VAT under the provisions of VATA 1994 s79. The supplement is specifically excluded from corporation tax by CTA 2009 s1286.

VAT representative Someone in the UK who acts on VAT matters for someone based overseas.

VAT return A standard form completed at regular intervals, usually every three months, stating how much VAT is payable. Guidance on completing a VAT return is given in VAT Notice 700/12.

VAT right For transactions connected with fraud, the term "includes the right to deduct input tax, the right to apply a zero rat to international supplies and any other right connected with VAT in relation to a supply" (VATA 1994 s69C(5) as inserted by Finance (No 2) Act 2017 s68(2)). For these purposes s69C(6) establishes that the EU case law to determine such matters are:

(a) joined Cases C-439/04 and C-440/04 *Axel Kittel v. Belgian State; Belgium v. Recolta Recycling* (denial of right to deduct input tax), and

(b) Case C-273/11 *(b)Mecsek-Gabona Kft v Nemzeti Adó- és Vámhivatal Dél-dunántúli Regionális Adó Főigazgatósága* (denial of right to zero rate).

The penalty under these provisions is 30% of the potential lost VAT.

VAT surcharge Penalty for being late with a VAT return or payment (VATA 1994 s59). This is not deductible against trading profits for income tax (ITTOIA 2005s54).

VAT value adjustment Figure used to calculate VAT on the delivery element of imported goods. VAT is charged on the whole cost of importing goods including the delivery charge to the UK address. As goods delivered next to airport have a lower UK delivery cost than those delivered hundreds of miles away, the delivery charge is calculated as the cost of delivery to the port plus an average figure for delivery within the UK. In 2015, sea freight had a charge of between £170 and £550. Airfreight had a minimum charge of £100.

VCT approval Approval by HMRC that a company is a venture capital trust (ITA 2007 s259(2)).

VCT-in-liquidation The tax provisions for a venture capital trust in liquidation are set out in Chapter 5 of ITA 2007, that is from s314. The term is fully defined in s320.

vegan truffle balls These were held to be VAT standard-rated confectionery in *Corte Diletto UK Ltd [2020] TC 7570.*

vegetable fat Means "a triglyceride of vegetable origin" (HODA1979 s23C(5)(d)).

vegetable juice The addition of this to a soft drink is not taken as adding sugar for the purposes of soft drinks industry levy (FA 2017 s29(3)).

vegetables These are usually zero-rated as food. Vegetable oils may also be zero-rated "even if they are used as massage or cosmetic oils, provided they are of a type and grade suitable for culinary purposes, and they do not contain any substance, such as perfume, that would make them unsuitable for culinary use" (VAT notice 701/14).

vehicle Any means of transport. Most law relates to motor vehicles, which are defined as mechanically propelled vehicles designed or adapted for use on the roads (Road Traffic Acts). A passenger vehicle is exempt from capital gains tax (TCGA1992 s263).

Vehicle and Operator Services Agency (VOSA) Government body that oversees transport regulations.

vehicle battery charging From 6 April 2018, there is no income tax liability when an employer provides this service at the workplace for a car or van used by an employee. The exemption from tax is given by ITEPA 2003 s237A as inserted by FA 2019 s8(1). The main conditions are:

- the facility is at the workplace. This exemption does not cover recharging at other locations
- the facility is generally available to all employees at that workplace.

The car or van must be used by the employee, who need not be the driver. The exemption can apply when the employee is a passenger. The exemption applies solely to the recharging. It does not cover any ancillary parking charge.

vehicle excise duty (VED) *General*

Tax charged for using a mechanical vehicle on a public road. It thus includes petrol and diesel vehicles, electric vehicles and steam vehicles. It does not include bicycles, boats, aircraft or horse-drawn vehicles. The tax is sometimes called road tax or car tax, though the latter term refers to a different tax.

The tax is charged under Vehicles Excise and Registration Act 1994 and other legislation, including Passenger Vehicles Act 1981 and Road Traffic Act 1988.

The tax is administered by the Driver and Vehicle Licensing Authority (DVLA). From 2014, vehicles in Northern Ireland are administered by DVLA rather than by a separate body. The amount is set by regulation, usually announced in advance in the Budget. The system changed for vehicles registered from 1 April 2017. The main categories of vehicle are:

- cars and vans up to 3.5 tonnes
- motorcycles
- light goods vehicles up to 3.5 tonnes
- tricycles to 450 kilograms.

There are separate charges for passenger vehicles and heavy goods vehicles. There is also a facility for trade plates used by motor dealers. Heavy goods vehicles are taxed according to their size, and their weight per axle.

Zero emission vehicles and electric vehicles are generally taxed at zero. There are also exemptions for many types of service vehicles, such as ambulances, snow ploughs, road gritters, farm tractors, trams, and vehicles that do not carry people.

From 1 April 2014, vehicles manufactured before 1 January 1974 are exempt. This has been changed to a rolling 40-year exemption, so in 2021, pre-1981 vehicles are exempt.

From 1998, a vehicle that has been taxed since 31 January 1988 but is now not parked or used on public roads must be covered by a statutory off road notification (SORN). This is administered in a similar manner to VED.

Basis of charge

The basis of charge depends on whether the vehicle was first registered from 1 April 2017.

For such vehicles, for the first year, the charge is a higher figure based partly on carbon dioxide emissions and what fuel is used. This has been called the showroom tax. From the second year, the charge is a fixed figure. This is £140 for most cars. An additional charge is payable if the vehicle has a list price of more than £40,000. This is paid for five years from years 2 to 6.

For vehicles first registered between 1 March 2001 and 31 March 2017, VED is charged according to the amount of carbon dioxide emitted. There were seven bands indicated A to F, to which a seventh G was added from 23 March 2006. From 1 April 2009, there are 13 bands indicated by the letters A to M. From 1 April 2010, there was a higher rate of VED for the first year for the lowest four and highest six bands. This has been called the showroom tax.

The change in 2001 was part of a policy to reduce vehicle emissions which then averaged 178 grams per kilometre. In 2003, a zero rate was introduced for vehicles with emissions below 100 g/km. For vehicles first registered before 1 March 2001, the tax is based on engine size.

Payment

VED is usually paid in advance for 12 months or 6 months. A small discount is offered for paying by direct debit.

Until 1 October 2014, the tax was evidenced by a circular tax disc which had to be displayed on the vehicle's windscreen. Obtaining the tax disc acted as a check that the vehicle is insured and has a valid MOT certificate. The tax disc has now been replaced by on-line records.

In the month before renewal, the DVLA issues a reminder letter with a code number. This allows the tax to be renewed online. MOT and insurance are centrally recorded and checked against these records. These records can now be accessed online at no charge.

Details of vehicle excise duty rates are given in section 3 of this dictionary.

vehicle scrappage scheme Scheme which provides a sum to a person for scrapping an old car to buy a new one. In the UK, the scheme was introduced from 1 June 2009. It paid £2,000 to anyone who scrapped a car at least ten years old and bought a new one. Of this, £1,000 came from the government and the other £1,000 had to come from the car dealer. The scheme was intended to help the troubled car industry and to promote more environmentally-friendly vehicles.

veil of incorporation Rule that a company is a separate legal entity from its owners. The veil may be lifted in some cases.

vellum Specially treated goatskin on which Acts of Parliament are traditionally printed. Two copies are so produced, one for the House of Lords and one for the Public Records Office. These contain vellum Acts from 1497. Private Acts have been printed on archive paper since 1956. On 2 November 2015, it was decided that the Public Records Office copy of all Acts may also be printed on archive paper.

Veltema A case on the powers of HMRC regarding a discovery assessment. A taxpayer was liable to tax on the value of a property transferred to him from a company which was professionally valued at £100,000. This was disclosed on the tax return and was not challenged. The company submitted its return showing the same valuation, but this time it was challenged as a discovery assessment after the deadline for an ordinary assessment. The value was eventually agreed at £145,000. The taxpayer appealed on the grounds that there was nothing to discover as the amount had already been disclosed. The matter depended on whether the inspector could be "reasonably aware" of an insufficiency on a return. In this case, the Court of Appeal held that the inspector could not be so aware, so the discovery assessment was allowed. The full citation is *Langham v Veltema [2004] 76 TC 259*. HMRC's view was subsequently set out in statement of practice SP1/06.

vending machine Machine that sells goods on insertion of sufficient coins. Modern machines may also give change. The presence of a machine creates a unilateral contract when used by a purchaser.

For VAT, a person who allows a vending machine on their premises is regarded as making a standard-rated supply of services. It is not a zero-rated supply of use of land unless the contract specifies the exact area for the machine.

For a supply of food and drink, a vending machine is regarded as a supply of catering for consumption on the premises where the machine is situated. *Burnham Radio Recreational & Welfare Club [1977] VTD 518.* and *Macklin Services (Vending) West Ltd [1979] VTD 688.*

In accounting, the cash and goods held in a machine are part of the cash and stock of a business on balance sheet date.

A vending machine is specifically excluded from the scope of amusement machine licence duty.

Venezuela South American country. Its currency is the bolivar fuerte of 100 céntimos.

The UK has a double taxation agreement of 1996.

The country experienced hyperinflation in 2017.

The country is subject to UK sanctions, as are designated persons of the country.

ventilation For VAT, a supply of ventilation is treated as a supply of goods (VATA 1994 Sch 4 para 3). As such, supplies for residential use are generally reduced-rated under Sch 7A Group 1, but standard-rated for other supplies. Details are given in VAT notice 701/19. For capital allowances, this may qualify as a feature integral to a building (CAA 2001 s33A).

venture capital trust (VCT) Form of tax-advantaged vehicle for investment in companies, often high-risk companies. A VCT is itself a company whose shares are traded on stock markets. The Financial Conduct Authority suggests that buyers of such shares should be sophisticated investors with an annual income of at least £100,000 or investments of at least £250,000. Finance companies often recommend that a VCT should not be more than 10% of an investor's portfolio.A VCT is defined in ITA 2007 s259(1) as being not a close company which is approved as a VCT by HMRC. The scheme allows immediate tax relief equal to 30% of the sum invested (this was 40% for 2004/05 to 2005/06, and 20% previously). Also, capital gains tax liabilities may be rolled over. The shares must be held for five years (three years before 6 April 2006).

The VCT must be quoted on the Stock Exchange, invest at least 70% of its funds in unquoted companies, invest at least 30% of its funds in new unquoted companies, and invest no more than 15% of its funds in any one company. There are other conditions.

Capital gains tax law is contained in TCGA1992 from s151A.

Specific provisions for the taxation of the trust itself are given in CTA 2009 s396.

Verify System used to access government websites, including tax sites from 2015. It gives the user a password which simplifies logging in.

vermouth Blended alcoholic drink. If it has used the same name from before 1932, it is exempt from some provisions for alcoholic liquor duty.

vertebrate "Means any animal of the Sub-phylum Vertebrata of the Phylum Chordata" (Animal Welfare Act 2006 s1(5)). This definition is used for "wild animal" in CTA 2009 s1217FB(5). The section disallows theatrical productions tax relief if a wild animal is used in a performance. A wild animal is defined as a "vertebrate other than man" in Animal Welfare Act 2006 s1(1).
The use of animals in circuses was generally banned in 2019.

very large company Term used for a company with profits exceeding £20 million in an accounting period of 12 months, or pro rata for a shorter period. Such a company must, from 1 April 2019, pay corporation tax in four instalments. The first is due 2 months and 13 days after the start of the accounting period. The next three are due every 3 months thereafter.

vessel For oil duty, "includes any tank or container for storing oil and any still or utensils in which oil may be processed" (Hydrocarbon Oil Regulations SI 1973 No 1311 reg 2).

vest (1) Deliver to a person the full possession of land, and so clothe him with its legal estate.
(2) For accounting, "become an entitlement. Under a share-based payment arrangement, a counterparty's right to receive cash, other assets or equity instruments of the entity vests when the counterparty's entitlement is no longer conditional on the satisfaction of any vesting conditions" (FRS 102 glossary).

vesta Wax-stemmed match.

vest bag Term sometimes used by a supermarket for a single use carrier bag. So called because it looks a little like the garment vest.

vesting assent Instrument whereby a personal representative vests land in a tenant for life under Settled Land Act 1925 s117(1).

vesting order Court order vesting property in a person stated. This commonly happens when trustees are unwilling or unable to act in such a capacity. Under company law, a court may make such an order when a claim is made by a person against disclaimed property of a struck off company (CA 2006 s1017).

veteran car Car made before 1905.

veterans Person who has served in the UK armed forces. For the purposes of employer's national insurance, the person must have completed at least one day of basic training in the forces. The government proposes to grant employers of veterans exemption from employer's national insurance from 6 April 2021 to 5 April 2024. For the 2021/22 tax year, employer's national insurance will be paid and then reclaimed. The relief applies up to upper earnings limit.

vexatious litigant Person who repeatedly brings legal actions. It is possible to get an order against such a person who must then obtain permission from the court before commencing any further legal actions.

vicarious liability When one person is legally held liable for the actions of another. An employer can be vicariously liable for actions of an employee.

Victims' Information Service (VIS) Government scheme launched in 2015 to assist victims of serious crime.

Victoria Cross Award for bravery. Payments of pension or annuity in respect of the award are free of income tax (ITEPA 2003 s638).

vide Latin: see.

videlicet (viz) Latin: that is to say.

video evidence When evidence is presented in court by means of a pre-recorded interview on video tape or similar (Criminal Justice Act 2003 s137).

video game For the purposes of video games relief, this term is defined in CTA 2009 s1217AA. In particular it excludes anything produced for gambling or promotion.

video games tax relief Relief from corporation tax introduced in 2010 on a similar basis to tax relief for films.

video hearing and language A system whereby parties may participate in a tribunal hearing using a video link. Its first use at a tax tribunal case was in *Ewa Gondek [2018] TC 6440* on 8 March 2018.

Vienna Convention

(1) Vienna Convention on Diplomatic Relations signed in 1961. In the UK, the convention is implemented by Diplomatic Privileges Act 1964. Goods and services provided to those with diplomatic immunity are exempt from duties and tax. The Convention is given as Sch 1 of the Act. The immunity from taxation is given in Article 23.

(2) Vienna Convention on the Law of Treaties 1969. This requires treaties to be interpreted in good faith in accordance with the ordinary meaning of words used, in the light of their context and the object and purpose of the treaty.

Vietnam Eastern country. Its currency is the dong of 10 ho or 100 xu. The UK has a double taxation agreement of 1994.

village hall Provisions of facilities at a village hall may meet the conditions of a recreational trust as set out in Charities Act 2011 s3(4)(a). The construction of a village hall may qualify for zero-rating. However, this is a much litigated area, particularly where the hall is also used for another purpose, such as a sports club.

vinasse Residue from alcohol distillation.

vinegar Condiment and pickling medium with a bitter taste from containing acetic acid. It is traditionally made from brewing and fermentation and is therefore subject to some controls in relating to alcohol liquor duty, while not being subject to the duty itself.

vinegar-maker Such a person is exempt from some of the legal restrictions of manufacturing spirits without a licence (Alcoholic Liquor Duties Act 1979 s25).

vingt-et-un This game is specifically listed in Betting and Gaming Duties Act 1981 s13(3) as coming within the scope of gaming licence duty.

vintage car Car made between 1919 and 1930.

virement Authorised transfer of funds from one budget to another, such as when an organisation reallocates a surplus in one fund to another fund.

virtual currency "A digital representation of value, not issued by a central bank, credit institution or e-money institution, which in some circumstances can be used as an alternative to money" (European Central Bank). Virtual currency is also called cryptocurrency.

virtually Term used frequently in tax law to qualify "all" or "none", or equivalent terms. Its meaning is to disallow only a very small amount. So someone has "virtually no benefit" if the actual benefit is trivial. The matter was expressed by Lord Hoffman in relation to gifts with reservation in *Ingram* as: "for one thing, it is in one sense a penal section. Not only may you not have your cake and eat it, but if you eat more than a few de minimis crumbs of what was given, you are deemed for tax purposes to have eaten the lot".

virtually to the exclusion of Term used in inheritance tax in relation to gifts with reservation (GWR) , where it is a condition that the gift is to the exclusion or "virtually the entire exclusion" of benefit to the donor to avoid the GWR provisions. HMRC has stated that this means that the benefit to the donor is "small".

Where a donor has given a house to a donee, HMRC accepts that there is no GWR if the donor subsequently:

- stays with the donee for up to two weeks a year;
- stays at the house without the donee for up to one month a year;
- makes purely social visits staying for one night;
- stays for a temporary reason, such as for medical care or convalescence (of either donor or donee);
- stays for a domestic reason, such as baby-sitting;
- visits up to five times a year to use the library.

Other examples include using a donated motor car no more than three times a month, or using donated land to ride a horse or exercise a dog but not so as to restrict the donee's use.

virtual party Online party where a traditional party is not possible because of the coronavirus lockdown. HMRC confirmed that the tax relief for Christmas parties and other staff entertainment applies to virtual parties.

virtual witness Where someone sees something online rather than in person. For wills, virtual witnessing is legal from 31 January 2020 to 31 January 2022. This is considered second best to witnessing in person. The video and sound quality must be adequate for the witness to see what is happening.

visa Endorsement on a passport permitting the holder to enter or leave a country, or to work or undertake other activities while there.

visible exports/imports In economics, exports or imports of goods, as against invisible exports or imports of such things as insurance and financial services.

vision print Photographic record of a document. Vision prints are made of all paper VAT returns and may be submitted as evidence when a paper copy is no longer available.

visiting book Record of people who have visited a place. It can be an evidential document in a tax investigation.

visiting forces A body, contingent or attachment of the armed forces of another country, stationed in the UK on the invitation of the British Government. This includes NATO forces.

They are generally exempt from UK income tax. The provisions are set out in ITA 2007 s833.

Their accommodation is specifically excluded from council tax.

VAT relief may be claimed for supplies to:

- NATO forces based in the UK
- NATO military headquarters and personnel based in UK
- US military cemeteries at Brookwood and Madingley.

  Details of the VAT relief are set out in VAT Notice 431.

visiting performer Entertainer or sports person who is non-resident in a tax year but visits the UK and earns income (ITTOIA 2005s13 and CTA 2009 s1309).

visor A visor supplied as part of a zero-rated helmet is also zero-rated. If supplied separately, it is generally standard-rated. VAT Notice 701/23 gives details.

viz Abbreviation of videlicet, Latin for "that is to say".

vocation For income tax purposes, how "a person passes his or her life and indicates a calling, although not necessarily one related to religion or high-minded service to others. A bookmaker and a jockey have been held to engage in vocations and authors, dramatists and professional singers have all been dealt with by the Courts on the basis that they carried on vocations." (Inspectors' Manual BIM14090). Vocation "means the way in which a person passes his life" *(Denman J in Partridge v Mallandaine [1896] 2 TC 179).*

vocational training

Income tax

From 6 April 1992 to 5 April 2000, a taxpayer could claim tax relief for vocational training. This was subject to many conditions, particularly that it should lead to an NVQ qualification or Scottish equivalent. From 6 April 1999, tax relief was restricted to the basic rate of income tax.

Value added tax

"Vocational training covers training or re-training and work experience for:

- paid employment

- voluntary employment in areas beneficial to the community as a whole, education, health, safety, welfare, and charity work in general" (VAT Notice 701/30 para 5.3).

The VAT implications are set out in VAT Notice 701/30.

Voice over Internet Protocol (VoIP) Protocol that allows spoken telephony over the Internet by Skype or similar provider.

The provision of such a service comes within the scope of the reverse charge for the VAT place of supply rules from 1 January 2015.

void Of no legal effect. Such a contract is regarded as never having happened. Any consideration provided must be returned.

voidable Agreement or other act which one party may choose to make void. Until such an election has been made, the agreement remains legally valid.

voidable marriage Marriage which could be declared invalid, usually because there has been no consummation. Such a declaration is regarded as an annulment which means that the marriage is regarded as never having existed. However, for the purposes of tax and benefits, the marriage is regarded as having existed until the date of annulment.

void period Period in which something did not happen, such as an unoccupied rented property.

voiding key Provision in an EPOS system whereby a transaction can be cancelled such as when a check-out operator makes a mistake while checking out goods.

Volkswagen Car manufacturer. The Volkswagen Transporter Kombi was held to be a car, but the Volkswagen Vivaro was held to be a van in the case *Coca-Cola Enterprises Ltd and others [2017] TC6082.*

voluntary annual payment Voluntary payment made to a former employee. It is similar in nature to a pension and is broadly taxed as one (ITEPA 2003 from s633).

voluntary arrangement In insolvency, an arrangement made by an individual or by the directors of a company to creditors. Typically such an agreement includes payment of part of the debts by a stated date. Provisions for such arrangements are set out in Insolvency Act 1986 from s1.

voluntary conveyance Conveyance of property other than for valuable consideration (Law of Property Act 1925 s173).

voluntary deduction from pay A deduction from wages or salary which the employee has authorised. Such deductions are often made to repay a loan, for trade union dues or a subscription to a social club. The authorisation must be made *before* the event which causes the deductions. In the case *Discount Tobacco & Confectionery Ltd v Williamson [1993],* the Employment Appeal Tribunal held that an agreement to repay a deficiency of cash was an unlawful deduction from wages as the agreement was made after the deficiency arose. The employer should bring proceedings in the county court.

An involuntary deduction is not permissible under Employment Rights Act 1996. It should be noted that an employer may not deduct a sum from wages just because the employee owes a sum to the employer. An employee may appeal to the employment tribunal against an unlawful deduction from wages, even if the sum is owed by the employee to employer.

The authorisation must be genuinely voluntary. In the case *Fairfield Ltd v Skinner EAT [1992]*, the Employment Appeal Tribunal held that it could look behind the ostensible reason to see if the authorisation really was voluntary.

voluntary deregistration When a business chooses to have its VAT registration cancelled. A business must have a turnover below the deregistration threshold which is different from the registration threshold.

voluntary direct payment When an employee elects to pay HMRC directly for an underpayment of tax that arose under the PAYE system. This is an alternative to coding out that HMRC may otherwise use.

voluntary disclosure A way of correcting errors discovered on a previous tax return. The position of a tax adviser in relation to such disclosure is set out in Professional Conduct in Relation to Taxation from para 7.1.

voluntary liquidation Ending of a solvent company by its members.

voluntary mutual Popular name for a mutual health insurer. Their tax treatment is discussed in HMRC Manual at BIM24685.

voluntary or community body For the purposes of business activities for the business impact target, this term is defined in Small Business, Enterprise and Employment Act 2015 s27(5).

voluntary redundancy When an employee agrees to be made redundant from his work, usually on the basis of a generous package.

voluntary registration When a person or business chooses to register, particularly when a business registers for VAT even though its turnover is below the registration threshold.

voluntary revision of accounts In company law, procedure whereby the directors of a company may issue accounts to replace those already published (CA 2006 s454). Such a revision is confined to correcting the accounts to the extent that they did not previously comply with company law or accounting standards.

voluntary severance For public pensions, means "any other loss of office or employment" that is not **compulsory severance** (Superannuation Act 2010 s3(6)(b)).

voluntary striking off When a company itself requests that it be removed from the register at Companies House. The procedure is set out in CA 2006 s1003.

voluntary worker Someone who agrees to work for no payment, usually for a church, charity or other non-profit-making body. Such a worker does not have to be paid the national minimum wage (NMW). They may be paid genuine expenses. A worker cannot agree to be paid less than the NMW; they are either paid nothing or the full NMW.

volunteer reserve force "The Royal Navy Reserve, the Royal Marines Reserve, the Territorial Army or the Royal Auxiliary Air Force" (Armed Forces Act 2006 s374).

voting rights The right of someone to vote, such as a shareholder in a company. There are many tax provisions which either require or restrict a person according to how much control they have over a company. An example is the provision for entrepreneur's relief in TCGA 19992 Sch 72A para 9. In the context of a takeover bid, the term is defined as "rights to vote at general meetings of the company in question, including rights that arise only in certain circumstances" (CA 2006 s953(9)).

voucher Any document which gives details of a financial transaction.
There are special VAT provisions for face-value vouchers in VATA 1994 Sch 10A. Originally, if a voucher can be used for only one purpose (such as operating a telephone), VAT is charged on the sale of the voucher. If the voucher can be used for more than one purpose (such as a store card), VAT is only charged when the card is used, if buying items subject to VAT. From 1 January 2019, a VAT is standard-rated if it can be used for more than one purpose, each of which is standard-rated.
A VAT tribunal has ruled that a book of vouchers is not a zero-rated book but a supply of services *(Graham Leisure Ltd [1981] VTD 1304).*

voyeurism Person who derives gratification by secretly watching other people, particularly when they are undressed. For statutory sick pay purpose, this is expressly excluded as an illness.

vulnerable adult A person under the age of 18, or a person over 18 but who, for physical or mental reasons is unable to look after himself or herself, or their finances.
For inheritance tax, there are special provisions for trusts for such people. These generally exclude the trust from the additional charges for a relevant property tax. Those who work with vulnerable adults, including volunteers, must be cleared by the Disclosure and Barring Service.
Vulnerable adults must still meet their tax and other obligations. If they cannot do this themselves, a trustee may be appointed. This is often a family member, but can be a person appointed by the Court of Protection.

vulnerable person For the purposes of restrictions during the coronavirus outbreak, "includes –
(i) any person aged 70 or older;
(ii) any person under 70 who has an underlying health condition, including but not limited to, the conditions listed in Schedule 1;
(iii)any person who is pregnant"
(The Health Protection (Coronavirus, Restrictions) (England) Regulations SI 2020 No 350 para 1(3)(c)).
Schedule 1 lists:
(1) chronic (long-term) respiratory diseases, such as asthma, chronic obstructive pulmonary diseases, emphysema or bronchitis
(2) chronic heart disease, such as heart failure
(3) chronic kidney disease
(4) chronic liver disease, such as hepatitis

(5) chronic neurological conditions, such as Parkinson's disease, motor neurone disease, multiple sclerosis, a learning disability or bronchitis
(6) diabetes
(7) problems with the spleen, such as sickle cell disease or removal of the spleen
(8) a weakened immune system as the result of conditions such as HIV and AIDS, or medicines such as steroid tablets or chemotherapy
(9) being seriously overweight, with a body mass index of 40 or above.

wadiah Safe-keeping of valuables, as permitted under Islamic financing.

wafers For VAT purposes, edible wafers are zero-rated as food unless sold with ice cream when they are standard-rated (VAT notice 701/14).

waffle cone Product similar to an ice cream cone but lined with chocolate. It is not eaten on their own but filled with ice cream or a similar product. The VAT tribunal held that they were not biscuits as they were not intended to be eaten on their own *(Marcantonio Foods Ltd. VTD 15486 [1997]).*

wages Payment for work done. Generally, income tax and national insurance must be deducted at source by the employer.

wages councils Bodies originally established by Trade Boards Act 1909 to ensure that workers were not exploited by low wages. Their scope was considerably extended in 1945. Their powers were restricted in 1986 before being abolished in 1993. Since 1999, the issue of low pay has been addressed by the national minimum wage.

waiter Person who attends to customers in a restaurant. Originally the term also meant a watchman or Customs officer, whose duties included waiting for something to happen. All tips paid to a waiter (or waitress) are subject to income tax. A tip is only subject to class 1 national insurance if paid via an employer or troncmaster, such as when the tip is added to a card payment or put in a jar by the till. There is no national insurance if the tip is given directly to the waiter.

waiting day Day for which a benefit is not paid while entitlement is established. There are three waiting days for statutory sick pay and employment and support allowance. Before 14 February 2018, there were seven waiting days for universal credit.

waiver or remuneration When a director or employee forgoes payment due to his or her. Such amounts are not included in the person's estate for inheritance tax.

Wales Principality that adjoins England to form Britain. It now has its own Assembly with limited devolved powers over tax.

walking possession agreement For VAT, "means an agreement under which, in consideration of the property distrained upon being allowed to remain in the custody of the person in default and of the delaying of its sale, the person in default –

(a) acknowledges that the property specified in the agreement is under distraint and held in walking possession, and
(b) undertakes that, except with the consent of the Commissioners and subject to such conditions as they may impose, he will not remove or allow the

removal of any of the specified property from the premises named in the agreement"

(Value Added Tax 1994 s68(2)).

wall chart This item is not regarded as a map or chart for VAT purposes, and is therefore not zero-rated under VATA 1994 Sch 8 Group 3. Further details are given in VAT notice 701/10.

wall panelling For tax, the case *JD Wetherspoon plc v HMRC [2008] SpC 657* held that wall panelling in a pub was not plant. This issue was debated at length, implying that similar items could be held to be plant. The deciding factor in this case was that the panelling was not exceptional.

Wall Street New York Stock Exchange, from the name of the road in Manhattan where it is located.

walrus Large marine mammal with prominent tusks. The import of the fur or other products of such animals is generally prohibited from 20 August 2010.

waqf An inalienable religious endowment under Sharia law.
[It is also spelled wakf.]

war Armed conflict between nations, or between groups within a nation. The latter is usually called a civil war. There are many tax and legal consequences of war.

war disablement pension Payment made to someone who has been injured or disabled as a result of past service in the armed forces. If disablement is assessed at 20% or more, the person receives a pension. Otherwise they receive a lump sum.

warehouse A place for storing goods, particularly one approved by HM Customs and Excise for the storage of goods without the payment of certain duties or taxes which would normally be due on those goods. The main types of warehouse are Customs Warehouses; Excise Warehouses; and Customs and Excise Warehouses.

The application for VAT is given in VATA 1994 s18.

warehouse vat Spirits receiver that HMRC has approved as a place where spirits may be stored as well as manufactured.

warehousing system Arrangement agreed with HMRC or Customs which allows goods to be stored in a warehouse before duty or VAT is paid.

The VAT provisions are given in VATA 1994 s18.

war loan Government gilt issued to provide funds to pay for a war. Some of these are exempt from capital gains tax. A list is provided under Gilts in section 3 of this dictionary.

warning pack Details about pension schemes provided to scheme members at the ages of 50, 55 and 60. The idea is to prevent members making unwise decisions about their pensions. Details of the packs were announced by the Financial Conduct Authority in June 2018.

warning period In relation to serial tax avoidance regulations, a period of five years from when a taxpayer's avoidance scheme was defeated.

war orphan Child suffering from neglect or want of care as a result of the death of a parent from 3 September 1939. The Department of Work and Pensions is obliged to provide for such a child until the age of 21.

warrant Its meanings include an instrument that entitles its holder to subscribe for shares in a company, or for assets representing a loan relationship with the company (CTA 2009 s710).

warrant of attachment Warrant which allows goods to be seized.

warrant to cite In Scotland, an order for a debtor to attend court in sequestration proceedings.

war savings certificates Certificates issued by the government before 1972 to fund a war and which may continue to be held on the same conditions (National Debt Act 1972 s9).

war service Service in the armed forces during war. Under various laws passed at the time, such service usually counts as part of a person's employment for the purposes of building up a superannuation or pension entitlement. Certain pensions for war service are exempt from income tax (ITEPA 2003 s639).

war widow's pension Pension payable to a widow, widower, surviving civil partner, or child in respect of someone killed while in the armed forces, or who died as a result of an illness or injury while serving. The illness or injury must have occurred before 6 April 2005.

A definition for pension credit is given in State Pension Credit Act 2002 s17(1). HMRC provides guidance on the taxation of such pensions in helpsheet HS344.

wash For spirits duty, this refers to wort in which fermentation has begun. More details are given in Customs leaflet 39.

wash charger In brewing, "a vessel in which wash is collected from the wash back for removal to the still" (Customs notice 39).

waste-book Day book or journal in which financial transactions are recorded, prior to them being entered in a prime book of account. This practice is now rare.

wasted costs In litigation before a tribunal, "means any costs incurred by a party —

(a) as a result of any improper, unreasonable or negligent act or omission on the part of any legal or other representative or any employee of such a representative, or

(b) which, in the light of any such act or omission occurring after they were incurred, the relevant Tribunal considers it reasonable to expect that party to pay"

(Tribunals, Courts and Enforcement Act 2007 s29(5)).

waste disposal Corporation tax provisions are given in CTA 2009 s142; income tax provisions in ITTOIA 2005 from s165.

waste disposal site In relation to tax allowance for site preparation, a full definition appears in ITTOIA 2005 s167(1).

wasting asset An asset that has an expected life of less than 50 years and is therefore exempt from capital gains tax under TCGA 1992 s44. All animals, plant and machines are regarded as wasting assets.

water For VAT, water is zero-rated when supplied to domestic premises under VATA 1994 Sch 8 Group 2. It is standard-rated to business premises from 1 July 1990.
The zero-rating extends to supplies of ice, steam, metered water, and abstraction of non-potable water.
Zero-rating does *not* extend to distilled or deionised water, dry ice, mineral and table water and infrastructure charges under Water Act 1989.
Bottled water for drinking is standard-rated. It is specifically excepted from the scope of zero-rating for food by Value Added Tax 1994 Sch 8 Group 1 Note 3.

water bailiff Customs officer who inspects vessels as they reach or leave port.

watercourse Easement that allows for a flow of water over someone else's land.

water gavel Rent paid for water or fishing rights.

water ice This is standard-rated for VAT. It is excluded from the scope of zero-rated food by Value Added Tax 1994 Sch 8 Group 1 Excepted Item 1.

Waterloo decision Rule that "where a parent company allows the employees of its subsidiaries to participate in its share schemes, the arm's length principle requires that the subsidiaries make a contribution to the parent" (Inspector's Manual at BIM44235).
The name comes from the case *Waterloo plc v CIT. SpC301.*

water meter Device fitted in premises to monitor water usage so that the charge is based on usage and not on water rates. The installation of a meter is usually voluntary, though generally encouraged by water companies.
Some meters have automated meter readers which automatically send readings to the company.
For VAT, costs relating to these meters are not within the scope of the zero-rating for water (VAT notice 701/16). They may be zero-rated when installed as part of a zero-rated residential construction.

water rates Charge for water supply and sewerage facilities that is based on the rateable value of the property rather than the amount of water used.

water supply licence Licence issued under Water Industry Act 1991 s17A as inserted by Water Act 2014 s1(1).

water system For capital allowance purposes, this is treated as an integral feature, which means that it is included in the special rate pool and is subject to capital allowance at 8% on the writing down basis, and not the usual 18% for plant and machinery (CAA 2001 s33A).

water turbine Device that turns the flow of water into electricity. From 1 October 2019, VAT on water turbines increases from 5% to 20%.

waterworks Profits from this, when run as a trade are subject to income tax (ITTOIA 2005s12) or corporation tax (CTA 2009 s39).

Wates principles Principles of corporate governance in private companies published by the Financial Reporting Council in December 2018. They follow a report from a committee chaired by James Wates.
The six principles relate to:
- purpose and leadership
- board composition
- board responsibilities
- opportunity and risk
- remuneration
- stakeholder relationships and engagement.

watt (W) Unit of power.

watt-hour Use of one watt of power for one hour.

waveson Floating wreckage or flotsam.

way-going crop Crop that is sown during one tenancy but cannot be harvested until after the tenancy has expired. The first tenant often has the rights to the crop.

wayleave Right of way over someone else's land, such as to remove minerals or to carry water or electricity. Tax provisions are given in ITTOIA 2005 s22 and CTA 2009 s45.

wealth tax Tax imposed on how much a person is worth. The UK has no such tax.

weapons Customs are likely to seize any offensive weapons carried by a traveller to the UK.

wear and tear allowance Allowance equal to 10% of rent that a landlord could deduct before 6 April 2016. The landlord may now deduct only actual costs from taxable income.

Weatherbys English company established in 1770 and based in Wellingborough, Northamptonshire. It provides the central administration for the horse racing industry, maintains the Thoroughbred breed register and acts as the bank to the British Horseracing Authority. A person or group that owns at least 50% of a horse registered with Weatherbys may use the special racehorse owners' scheme for VAT. Details are given in VAT Notice 700/67.

Web Usually means the worldwide web where websites are hosted and may be accessed.

webinar Seminar conducted on a website. Those on tax may be conducted by HMRC or a commercial company. HMRC started running webinars in February 2012. It runs two types:
- live webinars at predetermined times which allow for on-line questions and answers, and
- pre-recorded webinars that can be watched at any time.

The webinars are free but taxpayers must register in advance.

website Place where information can be accessed on the Internet. Websites in section 3 of this dictionary gives addresses for websites that may be of interest to tax practitioners.

website invoice Invoice which is produced on a website rather than as a separate document. This is legal for all purposes, including tax and VAT, provided there is adequate security and recording.

wedding albums The VAT tribunal has ruled that an album of wedding photographs is not a zero-rated book *(D A Draper [1980] VTD 1107).*

wedding gift For inheritance tax, this is tax exempt up to £5,000 from a parent; £2,500 from a remoter ancestor; and £1,000 from anyone else. These limits have not changed since 1986. A wedding gift from an employer to an employee is tax-free (HMRC Manual at EIM00600). Wedding gifts are generally exempt from Customs duty, as explained in Customs Notice 3.

week Period of seven days. For statutory sick pay and statutory maternity pay, it is seven days starting with Sunday.

week 53 For PAYE purposes, 5 April or (in a leap year) 4 and 5 April. These come after week 52.

week's pay Amount set by the government as a maximum figure for calculating statutory redundancy pay or how much of unpaid wages ranks as a preferential debt. The amount is given under Employment Limits in section 3 of this dictionary.

weighbridge Device for weighing loaded vehicles.

weighted age Person's actual age to which years are added or subtracted to reflect their health. It is used to calculate pensions.

welfare Provision of finance and support to someone in need.

welfare advice Service that may be reduced-rated for VAT under VATA 1994 Sch 7A Group 9, as explained in VAT leaflet 701/2. Note that is *advice* that is reduced-rated; welfare services may be zero-rated.

Reduced-rated welfare advice is "advice or information that directly relates to the:

- care or protection of children or young people or
- physical or mental welfare of elderly, sick, distressed or disabled people"

(VAT notice 701/2).

Advice that relates to a *specific* person (of any age) is usually zero-rated as welfare services.

welfare services Category of services that may be exempt from VAT under VATA 1994 Sch7 Group 9. Advice is given in VAT Notice 701/2.

Welfare State Term applied to the UK from 1942 with regards to its commitment to care for citizens throughout their lives in the forms of benefits, free services and other forms of assistance. Formal provision of state welfare dates back to 16th century.

well-being "In relation to an individual, means that individual's well-being so far as relating to any of the following —

(a) personal dignity (including treatment of the individual with respect)

(b) physical and mental health and emotional well-being

(c) protection from abuse and neglect

(d) control by the individual over day-to-day life (including over care and support, or support, provided to the individual and the way in which it is provided)
(e) participation in work, education, training or recreation
(f) social and economic well-being
(g) domestic, family and personal relationships
(h) suitability of living accommodation
(i) the individual's contribution to society"
(Care Act 2014 s1(2)).
Local authorities have a duty to promote individuals' well-being under s1(1).

Welsh Language spoken by some people in Wales. Many official documents may be submitted in Welsh, though often an English transaction is required.
Laws in Wales Act 1535 s20 made it illegal to use Welsh in courts and legal documents. That provision was repealed by Welsh Language Act 1993.

Welsh additional rate Additional rate of income tax that the Welsh Assembly may impose under ITA 2007 s6B(10). It has yet to be imposed.

Welsh Assembly Common name for National Assembly for Wales.

Welsh basic rate Basic rate of income tax charged in Wales, as defined in ITA 2007 s6B(10).

Welsh body In relation to exchanges of information in connection with social security administration, "means –
(a) a local authority in Wales,
(b) a person authorised to exercise any function of such an authority in relation to **welfare services,**
(c) a person providing to a local authority in Wales services relating to welfare services, or
(d) a person prescribed or of a description prescribed by the Secretary of State" (WRA 2012 s131(12)).

Welsh Church funds These funds may have been allocated under a scheme under Welsh Church Act 1914. Where these funds were vested in a county or county borough in Wales before 1 April 1974, they are re-vested in the county council which comprises the greater part of the previous county (Local Government FA 1972 s211).

Welsh company "Company as to which it is stated that its registered office is to be situated in Wales" (CA 2006 s88(1)). Such a company has the right to issue documents and returns in Welsh rather than in English, though it must file an English translation.

Welsh Government Administration of the Welsh Assembly. Under Wales Act 2014 s4(1) this name replaces the previous Welsh Assembly Government.

Welsh higher rate Higher rate of income tax charged in Wales, as defined in ITA 2007 s6B(10).

Welsh land transaction Acquisition of land in Wales for which the Welsh Assembly may be given taxation powers under Government of Wales Act 2006 s116L as inserted by Wales Act 2014 s15(1).

Welsh list In relation to non-domestic rates, "means —

(a) a local non-domestic rating list that has to be compiled for a billing authority in Wales, or

(b) the central non-domestic rating list that has to be compiled for Wales"

(Local Government FA 1988 s55(8) as inserted by Enterprise Act 2016 s32).

Welsh rate resolution Resolution passed by the Welsh Assembly with regard to income tax (Government of Wales Act 2006 from s116D).

Welsh Revenue Authority (WRA) Body established to collect taxes devolved to the Welsh Assembly from 2018.

Welsh taxpayer Person who is liable to pay income tax under a Welsh rate resolution. Such a person is defined in Government of Wales Act 2006 s116E. A Welsh taxpayer is someone with a "close connection" with Wales as further defined in s116G. For PAYE purposes, a Welsh resident has a tax code prefixed C. Wales has the right to vary income tax rates from 6 April 2019.

Westminster Area of London where Parliament is situated, and therefore sometimes used to mean Parliament.

Westminster doctrine Doctrine that decisions of the courts are equally binding on the taxpayer and the tax authorities, regardless of how inconvenient this is for the tax authorities. The term comes from the successful tax avoidance case *IRC v Duke of Westminster [1936] 19 TC 490.*

wet ink signature Hand-signed signature as against an electronic signature.

wet money In acting, money paid to extras who cannot work because it is raining.

Wet uitkeringern vervolgingsslachtoffers 1940 to 1945 Scheme run by Dutch government to provide compensation for victims of Nazi and Japanese aggression in the Netherlands between 1940 and 1945. Such payments are exempt from UK income tax from 6 April 2016.

WEU Western European Union. Japanese aggression in the Netherlands between 1940 and 1945. Such payments are exempt from UK income tax from 6 April 2016

white diesel Diesel to which no colouring agent has been added. This indicates that hydrocarbon oil duty has been paid.

wharf Place by a river or similar to land goods transported by water.

For capital allowances, this is specifically excluded from the scope of plant and machinery (CAA 2001 s22(1) List B).

For customs duties, goods transported by sea must be landed at a wharf approved under CEMAs20.

wharfinger Owner of a wharf.

wheel of fortune This game is specifically listed in Betting and Gaming Duties Act 1981 s13(3) as coming within the scope of gaming licence duty.

whereabouts unknown Description of someone whose current address is not known. There is a specific tax provision for paying agents of savings funds for such people. If the agent made payment, details must be reported but with "whereabouts unknown" as the payee's address. If no payment was made, there is nothing to report. If arrears of payment when the address is subsequently discovered, the payment of all arrears is reported for the period of payment.

whiskey Traditional spelling for whisky made in Ireland. It is also sometimes used in USA and elsewhere.

whisky Alcoholic drink classified as a spirit for purposes of alcoholic liquor duty. A fuller description is given in Customs notice 39.

The law on duty on spirits is given in Alcoholic Liquor Duties Act 1979 ss5-35 and Spirits Regulations Si 1991 No 2563.

Whisky has been subject to liquor duty since 1644. In 1823, the law was reformed to introduce an annual licence as a means of stamping out illegal distilleries.

Whisky Export Refund Scheme A system of refunds on EC cereals used in the manufacture of whisky for export outside the EU. Details are given in Customs notice 39.

Whitebox Tax avoidance scheme that tried to save income tax by exploiting a perceived mismatch in the legislation on accrued interest and that of manufactured interest. The scheme was also known as Project Corbiere. The scheme was rendered ineffective by the decision in *Barnes [2011] TC 972.*

white-collar crime Financial crime such as fraud and embezzlement.

white-collar worker Someone who works in an office, unlike a blue-collar worker who works in a factory.

white diesel Diesel oil that does not contain any colouring agent, indicating that hydrocarbon oil duty has been paid.

Whitehall Area of London where many government offices are based. The term is therefore sometimes used to mean the civil service.

white list Term widely used for the lists of investment transactions held by HMRC for two purposes:

- to identify activities that may qualify for the Investment Manager Exemption, and
- to specify that transactions are not treated as trading transactions for UK tax purposes.

These lists are compiled under the provisions of Statutory Instruments SI 2006 No 924, SI 2009 No 3021 and SI 2011 No 2999.

White Paper Government document setting out is policies and proposals in a particular area.

white space Common name for the "other information" box on a tax return. Sufficient disclosure in this box prevents HMRC from raising a discovery assessment.

Whit Monday The day after Pentecost Sunday. It was a bank holiday until 1967.

wholly One of the conditions that must be met for trading expenditure to be tax-deductible. The word relates to the amount of money. The purpose of the payment is governed by the word exclusively.

wholly and exclusively Conditions necessary to claim an expense against trading income for income tax (ITTOIA 2005 s 54) or corporation tax (CTA 2009 s54).

wholly-owned subsidiary Company all of whose shares are owned by another company. "A company is a wholly-owned subsidiary of another company if it has no members except that other and that other's wholly-owned subsidiaries or persons acting on behalf of that other or its wholly-owned subsidiaries" (CA 2006 s1159(2)).

Widening Access Training Scheme (WATS) Training scheme in nursing, midwifery and other medical and health disciplines. From 1 September 2019, income tax and class 1 national insurance is due on this benefit. This is administered by the employer, usually an NHS trust, through the PAYE scheme. Some workers were subject to tax and NI before this date. Such workers may claim a refund from their employer.

widget (1) For beer duty, "device inserted into cans and bottles which recreates the effect of draught beer when it is poured" (Customs notice 226).
(2) In management accounting, an unspecified manufactured object.

widow Woman whose husband has died. Her marital status is the same as a single person.
For the purpose of claiming benefits this means that the couple were either legally married at the time of the husband's death or their marriage was considered valid under UK law. In Scotland (but not elsewhere in the UK) a person may be considered a wife "by cohabitation with habit and repute" even if there has not been a marriage ceremony provided the reputation began before 4 May 2006 (Family Law (Scotland) Act 2006 s3).

widowed mother's allowance Social security benefit paid to a woman whose husband died before 9 April 2001 and who either had custody of a child or was pregnant by him at the time. This is now replaced by bereavement support payment.

widower Man whose wife has died.

widow's bereavement allowance Addition to the income tax personal allowance allowed to a widow (but not a widower) in the year of husband's death and the following year between 1980 and 2000.

wife Woman to whom a man is married, or (from 2013) to whom another woman is married.
The meaning of the term was considered in the case *Nabi v Heaton. CA [1983] 57 TC 292* which held that "his wife" meant "a person being his wife". This was relevant for a polygamous marriage or where a person had the misfortune of two wives dying in the same tax year.
A wife must be a person where there is evidence of a legal marriage (*Rignell v Andrews. Ch D [1990] 63TC312).*

wife's earned income relief Tax relief that a husband could claim in respect of his wife's earnings before 6 April 1990.

wild animal For the purposes of theatrical productions tax relief, "means an animal of a kind which is not commonly domesticated in the British Islands (and in this definition animal has the meaning given by section 1(1) of the Animal Welfare Act 2006")" (CTA 2009 s1217FB(5)).

"Animal means a vertebrate other than man" (Animal Welfare Act 2006 s1(1)). A vertebrate "means any animal of the sub-phylum Vertebrata of the Phylum Chordata" (ibid s1(5)). A performance that uses a wild animal cannot qualify for this tax relief. There are many restrictions on importing animals and animal products under the Convention on International Trade in Endangered Species.

wildcat strike Sudden stoppage of workers taken by the workers themselves and not organised by a trade union.

Wilkinson case The case *ex parte Wilkinson [2005]* heard by the House of Lords. It held that HMRC had exceeded its authority in many of the extra-statutory concessions it had introduced. This led to many of them being replaced by legislation.

will Document which states what a person wishes to happen to his or her property on their death. It can also appoint an executor, say who you wish to look after your children under 18, and how you wish your remains to be disposed of.

The term includes a codicil a testament and any other of testamentary disposition (Wills Act 1837 s1).

A person who makes a will is said to be the testator, and his or her estate is said to be testate.

The main requirements for a will are that:

- it is in writing
- it is identifiable as a will
- it is signed by the testator
- the testator was aged 18 and had mental capacity
- the signature is signed by two witnesses who are not beneficiaries. The witnesses' partners must also not be beneficiaries.

Some of these requirements are relaxed for people on military service. The will must be kept safe and where it can be found, such as with a solicitor, bank, will storage company or the London Probate Service. Beneficiaries should be told where the will is.

It is advisable for the deceased to record where his or her assets are and for this to be kept up to date and readily findable by the executor. The government recommend that a will is reviewed every five years.

A will can be revoked or amended at any time before death while the testator retains sufficient mental capacity. An amendment may be made by a codicil or by making another will. A later will replaces an earlier will to the extent that they conflict.

If there may be doubt whether a person had sufficient mental capacity to make a will, it is advisable for a doctor either to act as witness or to write a letter to that effect to be kept with the will.

While making a will is a simple process, it is advisable to use a solicitor or professional will writer in drafting it. There are numerous examples of wills prepared that have been held to mean something different from what the testator probably intended.

A will ensures that the testator's wishes are followed. If a person dies intestate, without a will, the estate passes under the laws of intestacy. Wills should be reviewed periodically to ensure that it still reflects the wishes of the testator.
A will can be challenged on the grounds that it does not make adequate provision for a person who was dependent on the deceased, or that the deceased lacked mental capacity.
Marriage revokes a will unless the will was made in contemplation of marriage and identifies the husband or wife. Divorce does not revoke a will but excludes the divorced party as a beneficiary. The deceased may make a further will including a former spouse as a beneficiary.
Inheritance tax is payable on the estate of someone who has died. It is possible to draft a will in ways that minimise that tax liability.

win For minerals, this means obtaining other than by quarrying or mining, such as simply picking up rocks or stones from the ground. For tax purposes, it is regarded as exploitation of land, and is taxed on the same basis as mining operations. A leading case is *Golden Horeshoe (New) Ltd v Thurgood [1933] 18TC280.* The matter is discussed in HMRC Manual at BIM35405.

windfall clause Term common in an IVA which provides that any windfall, such as inheritance or win, must be given to creditors.

windfall tax Tax charged only in the year 1997 on the profits made by utility companies when they were privatised (Finance (No 2) Act 1997 ss1-5 and Sch 1-2).

winding-up Process of ending a company's existence as set out in company law. These are given in CA 2006 from s1000. Provisions for charities are given in Charities Act 2011 from s113.

winding-up petition Petition presented to the court to wind up a company.

window tax Tax charged on the number of windows in a building between 1696 and 1851.

Windrush compensation scheme Provision whereby compensation is paid to victims who legally came to the UK from West Indies between 1948 and 1973 but who were improperly denied benefits and other rights. The scandal broke in 2018. Compensation is paid under Windrush Compensation Scheme (Expenditure) Act 2020. It is exempt from tax under Finance Act 2020 s102 and Sch 15.

wine Alcoholic liquor made from the fermentation of any fruit except apples or pears and which has an alcoholic strength of at least 1.2%. It is subject to alcoholic liquor duty (ALDA 1979 s1(4)) and VAT.

winning Gaining minerals without mining, drilling or quarrying. It is taxed on the same basis as mining. The matter is discussed in HMRC Manual at BIM35405.

winter economy plan Package of measures announced on 24 September 2020 to provide financial help during the coronavirus lockdown.

winter fuel payment Payment given to older people, regardless of income or wealth, made automatically between mid-November and Christmas to assist with extra costs of winter heating. The person must have reached state pension age and meet other conditions. The amount is £200 per person or couple, or £300 if over

80. Payment is made under Social Fund Winter Fuel Payments Regulations SI 2000 No 729. There are other means-tested benefits that may be claimed. The payment is not taxable.

winter heating assistance Benefit that may be provided in Scotland under Social Security (Scotland) Act 2018 s30.

with costs Term used in legal judgments indicating that the winner is entitled to recover their legal costs from the loser.

withdrawal rate Rate at which an entitlement is withdrawn. It applies to means-tested benefits such as tax credits and universal credit, and tax-advantage schemes such as lifetime ISAs.

withering on the vine Allowing the value of a fixed sum to reduce over a long period through inflation.

withholding foreign partnership (WP) Partnership that assumes responsibility for administering a withholding tax on non-USA investments held by American investors under Foreign Account Tax Compliance Act 2010 of USA.

withholding foreign trust (WT) Trust that assumes responsibility for administering a withholding tax on non-USA investments held by American investors under Foreign Account Tax Compliance Act 2010 of USA.

withholding responsibility Power assumed by a non-US investment business (or equivalent) to administer the withholding tax under Foreign Account Tax Compliance Act 2010 of USA.

withholding tax Tax that is deducted by a payer of interest, rent or similar from a sum paid to a person in another tax jurisdiction. The amount deducted is passed to the tax authority of the payer's country.

without prejudice Comment on a letter which generally stops it being shown to a judge. It is used to conduct separate negotiations while a court case is proceeding.

without profits Description of a life insurance policy where the holder is not entitled to any share of the company's profits. The sum payable is only the amount guaranteed in the policy however profitable the insurance company may be.

with profits Description of a life insurance policy where the holder is entitled to a share of the insurance company's profit. Each year a bonus is added to the guaranteed sum insured to reflect the company's profit. Usual practice is to 'smooth' such bonuses so that a comparatively unsuccessful year will not necessarily lead to a lower bonus but a succession of poor years will be reflected by a gradual reduction of bonus rate (and conversely for a series of successful years).

with profits endowment A fixed term investment with life cover. The guaranteed sum insured is increased by bonuses, representing a share of the profits of the life fund.

with-profits fund For child trust funds, a definition is given in Child Trust Fund Regulations SI 2004 No 1450 Sch para 2(6).

witness Person who appears in court or at a tribunal to give evidence on what they know. For crime, the law is largely contained in Criminal Evidence Act 1898.

wizard Piece of computer software used to load other software.

woman Female adult. Whether a person is a woman was considered in the tax case *M [2010] TC 638*. Since 1975, it is illegal to discriminate against a woman on grounds of her sex (Equality Act 2020 s11).

wood For VAT, wood sold as fuel may be reduced rated under VATA 1994 Sch 7A Group 1 when supplied for domestic use. Further details are given in VAT notice 701/19. The wood must be held out for sale as fire wood.

wood-burning stoves These may qualify for the reduced rate of VAT under Value Added Tax 1994 Sch 7A Group 2, from 1 January 2006.

woodlands Managing woodlands is not a trade subject to income tax (ITTOIA 2005 s11) and is not subject to capital gains tax (TCGA 1992 s250). Commercial occupation of woodlands may be subject to corporation tax (CTA 2009 s38). Inheritance tax relief may be claimed for growing timber under IHTA 1984 s125.

words There have been several judicial comments on how to determine the meaning of words used in tax law:

- judges may look at any provision of any statute *(Colquhoun v Brooks [1889] 2 TC 490)*
- words and phrases should follow their legal meaning if they have acquired one, and the ordinary dictionary definition when they have not *(Heaslip v Hasemer [1927] 13 TC 212)*
- where there is more than one meaning, the judge should choose the one which harmonises with the general intention of the legislation *(CIR v Wilson's Exors [1934] 18 TC 465).*

The Office of Tax Simplification has extensively looked at the issue of how tax law is drafted.

work allowance For universal credit, this is an amount that a claimant is allowed to earn before the amount of credit is reduced. If a person earns more than this allowance, the credit is reduced by 63% of the excess. Each claimant is entitled to one, and only one, work allowance. The amount depends on whether the claimant:

- is a single person or a couple
- is responsible for one or more children
- has limited capacity for work.

workaround Temporary provisions which allows a provision to be completed when necessary information is not to hand. An example includes an all-purpose code which may be used when the proper code is not known. The dummy UTR for tax purposes is an example. Another example in 2017 was when it was discovered that it was not possible to make an online report of a no gain/no loss for capital gains tax. The workaround was to report a gain or loss of 1p.

work availability requirement For universal credit, this "is a requirement that a claimant be available for work" (WRA 2012 s18(1)).

work capability assessment (WCA) Assessment of how far a person is not able to work and thus entitled to benefit. The WCA was revised on 28 March 2011 under SI 2011 No 228.

worker Person who works for someone else but who may not be an employee. Such workers have some employment rights such as national minimum wage, Working Time Directive rights and protection from discrimination.

workfare Form of welfare where recipients must do some work.

work-focused health-related assessment Assessment made of a person under WRA 2007 s11 with a view to making a payment of employment support allowance. For universal credit, a similar definition appears in WRA 2012 s16(4).

work-focused interview Interview to determine entitlement to employment support allowance. The law is contained in WRA 2007 s12.

work-focused interview for partner Interview with a partner of a benefit claimant where both the claimant and partner are under the age of 60, with a view to seeing if either could support the other. Entitlement to benefit can depend on the partner agreeing to attend such an interview (Social Security Administration Act 1992 s2AA).

work-focused interview requirement For universal credit, "is a requirement that a claimant participate in one or more work-focused interviews as specified by the Secretary of State" (WRA 2012 s15(1)).

workhouse Place where poor could find accommodation and work, often under harsh conditions. They were provided from 17th century, were a duty on parishes from 1845, and finally abolished in 1930.

Workie Puppet used in television commercials from 21 October 2015 to promote workplace pensions.

working capital Finance provided to meet short-term needs of an entity. In bookkeeping, it is defined as current assets minus current liabilities.

working capital ratio Current assets divided by current liabilities.
Most companies will seek a ratio between 1 and 3, though this depends heavily on the nature of the business. Cash positive businesses, such as supermarkets can prosper on ratios below 1.

working day This is variously defined for different purposes. For employment taxation it is a day that an employee is at work (ITEPA 2003 s89(3)). For company law, it is any day except a weekend or bank holiday (Companies Act 2006 s1173(1)). The same definition is used for tax tribunals (SI 2009 No 273 rule 12(3)) and small company protection (Regulatory Enforcement and Sanctions Act 2008 s30D(2)).

working dog Sheep dog, guard dog, gun dog, racing greyhound or dog for the blind. Specially formulated food for such dogs is zero-rated whereas dog food for pets is generally standard-rated (VAT notice 701/15).

working families tax credit (WTFC) Means-tested social security benefit introduced on 5 October 1999, and payable through the payroll from 6 April 2000. From 7 April

2003, this was replaced by the working tax credit which is paid by DWP directly to the claimant.

Working Groups Various bodies established under Articles INST 3 of the EU/UK withdrawal agreement of 24 December 2020. They assist committees set up under the agreement.

working hours "Any time when under [a worker's] contract of employment, or their contract personally to do work or perform services, he is required to be at work" (Trade Union and Labour Relations (Consolidation) Act 1992 s246).

working life For pension purposes, this is from when a person reaches 16 until they reach state pension age (Pensions Act 2004 s282).

working papers Documents used in the preparation of any accounts, tax return or similar. These must be neatly written and filed, clearly stating the entity and dates to which they relate, and to what they refer.

working tax credit Means-tested social security benefit to supplement low wages of employees. They are paid under Tax Credits Act 2020 from s10. They are not taxed (ITEPA s677). This benefit is being replaced by universal credit under Welfare Reform Act 2012 s33(1).

Working Time Directive EU directive 2003/88/EC issued on 23 June 2000 and binding on all members. It replaced a previous directive from 1993. It is given effect in UK law from 1 October 1998 under SI 1988 No 1833. Its provisions are set out in section 3 of this dictionary.

work in progress Value assigned to partially completed work at the end of an accounting period. It is a current asset added to stock in the balance sheet. The income tax provisions are given in ITTOIA 2005 from s182 and are discussed in HMRC Manual at BIM33020.

Work Life Balance Directive EU directive 2010/18/EU adopted on 21 June 2018.

work of art Painting, drawing, engraving, sculpture or similar. There are special VAT rules (VATA 1994 s21). There are some exceptions and special provisions for inheritance tax. A work of art may be excluded from capital gains tax (TCGA 1992 s258).

workplace Place where an employee's attendance is necessary for the duties of the employment (ITEPA s339(1)). This can be relevant in determining the income tax liability for travelling expenses.

workplace parking Provision of a parking place at or near an employee's workplace. It is generally not a taxable benefit in kind (ITEPA s237(3)), though from 6 April 2017 it may be taxed if provided under optional remuneration rules.

workplace parking levy Charge that a local authority may impose for workplace parking. Edinburgh, Glasgow and Nottingham have done so or plan to do so. In Scotland, the levy is imposed under Transport (Scotland) Act 2019.

work preparation requirement Requirement for a universal credit claimant to attend a course or take other action to make themselves more likely to secure employment (Welfare Reform Act 2012 s16(1)).

work-related activity Activity that a claimant may be required to undertake as a condition of receiving employment and support allowance (Welfare Reform Act 2007 s13). Such activity may include training or voluntary work.

work-related requirement Requirement that a claimant must meet as a condition of receiving universal credit (Welfare Reform Act 2012 s13) or jobseeker's allowance (Jobseekers Act 1995 s6(2)).

work search requirement Requirement that a claimant must make efforts to find employment as a condition of receiving universal credit (Welfare Reform Act 2012 s17(1)) or jobseeker's allowance (Jobseekers Act 1995 s6D).

works transport service When an employer provides a bus or minibus to bring employees to work (ITEPA 2003 s242(2)). Provided the vehicle has nine seats, it will usually not be taxed as a benefit in kind.

work trial When a job applicant is asked to do some work to test their ability. Under government guidelines produced in December 2018, this must be reasonable for the purpose and not used as a source of free labour. Where it is unreasonable, the employer risks prosecution under national minimum wage laws.

work tie One of the sufficient ties test to determine UK residence for tax purposes. It is met if the person works in the UK for at least three hours on each of 40 or more days in the tax year.

World Health Organisation (WHO) Specialised agency of United Nations. It was established on 7 April 1948 under a constitution agreed in 1946, and is based in Geneva, Switzerland. It took over the Office International d'Hygiène Publique from the League of Nations. Donations of medical supplies to WHO are usually allowable as a business expenses even if the donation does not otherwise meet the requirement for an allowable business gift. Further guidance is provided in HMRC Manual at BIM45200.

worldwide debt cap Tax provisions set out in Taxation (International and Other Provisions) Act 2010 Part 7 and brought into effect from 1 January 2010. The provisions can serve to restrict the amount of UK tax relief that may be claimed by an international group of companies.

worldwide light vehicle test procedure Method of testing vehicle emissions used internationally from 2017 after it was found that some emission figures from tests were false. The procedure is adopted in UK from 1 April 2020 under Vehicle Excise and Registration Act 1994 Sch 1 para 1GA.

wort Any infusion, solution or mixture intended to be fermented to make spirits, as explained in Customs notice 39.

wounds pension Pension paid in respect of a wound suffered in military service or during war. It may be exempt from income tax under ITEPA 2003 s641.

WRA charter Charter issued by the Welsh Revenue Authority in March 2018.

wreath Arrangement of flowers and other plant materials to form a ring. They are commonly used as decorations or as tributes to the deceased. For VAT, this is a standard-rated supply. A funeral wreath is not within the scope of the exemption for funeral services. Further details are given in VAT notice 701/32.

wreck For merchant shipping "following a maritime casualty, means:
(a) a sunken or stranded ship; or
(b) any part of a sunken or stranded ship, including an object that is or has been on board such a ship; or
(c) any object that is lost at sea from a ship that is stranded, sunken or adrift at sea; or
(d) a ship that is about to, or may reasonably be expected, to sink or to strand, where effective measures to assist the ship or any property in danger are not already being taken"
(Wrecks Convention article 4).

Wrecks Convention "Means the Nairobi International Convention on the Removal of Wrecks 2007 done in Nairobi on 18 May 2007" (Merchant Shipping Act 1995 s255A as inserted by Wreck Removal Convention Act 2011 s1). The text of the Convention is given in Sch 11ZA of the 1995 Act.

wristband For VAT, these items are not clothing and so do not come within the scope of zero-rating when supplied for children *(Vidhani Brothers Ltd [2004] VTD 18997).*

writ Legal or formal document by which a person is required to do something, such as attend court.

write off Process for removing a balance from the accounts, such as when a business accepts that a bad debt will not be paid.
This is usually made by an entry in the journal. The double entry is debit bad debts (an expense), and credit debtors (an asset). Such an entry usually requires a high level of authorisation.
Corporation tax provisions for writing off assets are given in CTA 2009 s184.

writing down allowance Capital allowance which is calculated as a percentage of an asset's written down value. It is used for plant and machinery. The rates are given under Capital Allowances in section 3 of this dictionary.

wrongful disclosure Improper disclosure of information by HMRC of a taxpayer's information. It is an offence under Commissioners for Revenue and Customs Act 2005 s19. There is an exception for public interest disclosure.

wrongful dismissal Termination of employment contrary to law or the contract of employment, such as not giving a warning or sufficient notice. It is actionable as a breach of contract. Note that this is different from unfair dismissal.

wrongful trading Offence of allowing a business to continue when it is obvious that it cannot meet its liabilities (Insolvency Act 1986 s214(2)).
These provisions were suspended during the coronavirus lockdown. If the business was *set up* with the intention of defrauding customers and suppliers, the more serious offence of fraudulent trading is committed.

X-ray Police powers to take an x-ray of a detained person who may have swallowed a Class A drug are given in Police and Criminal Evidence Act 1984 s55A.

xu One hundredth of a dong, currency of Vietnam.

yacht VAT leaflet 701/20 notes that a yacht is unlikely to qualify for zero-rating as a houseboat.

yard Imperial unit of length equal to 3 feet, 36 inches or 0.9144 metres. There are 1,760 yards in a mile.

year Time taken for the earth to revolve round the sun. This is 365.24 days. For convenience the year is treated as 365 days with leap years of 366 days. The term is often qualified. A calendar year means 1 January to 31 December. The financial year for corporation tax runs from 1 April to 31 March. The tax year runs from 6 April to 5 April.

year of assessment Year whose income or profit is subject to income tax or corporation tax.

year of departure Last tax year of assessment before a temporary non-resident leaves the UK (TCGA1992 s10A(8)).

year of expected first production In relation to oil and gas companies, this term is defined in CTA 2010 s332FB(5).

year of return Tax year in which a temporary non-resident leaves the UK (TCGA1992 s10A(1)) and ITTOIA 2005 s368A(3)).

year of transfer In relation to attribution of gains to beneficiaries, "means the tax year in which the transfer occurred" (FA 2008 Sch 7 para 121(2)).

year-to-date Cumulative figures used to calculate income tax under PAYE.

yeast Micro-organisms that are used to ferment sugar into alcohol. The commonest species used for this purpose is Saccharomyces cerevisiae.
When sold as a product for use in food, yeast is generally zero-rated. A preparation or extract of yeast is specifically zero-rated for VAT. Under Value Added Tax 1994 Sch 8 Group 1, food is generally zero-rated. Excepted Item 3 standard-rates beverages. Items Overriding The Exception 4 reverses the exception, thus reinstating the zero-rating.
Further guidance is given in VAT Notice 701/14.

Yemen Arab state. Its currency is the riyal of 100 fils. The UK has no double taxation treaty. The country is subject to UK sanctions, as are designated persons of the country.

yen Currency of Japan. It comprises 100 sen.

yield Return seen as a percentage on the investment.

yogurt For VAT, this is zero-rated as food except when sold to be eaten while frozen (VAT notice 701/14). Yogurt to be eaten when frozen is excepted by Value Added Tax 1994 Sch 8 Group 1 Excepted Item 1. Yogurt to be eaten unfrozen, though it may have been frozen for storage, is standard-rated under Item Overriding The Exception 1 in the same section.

young carer "Means a person under 18 who provides or intends to provide care for an adult" (Care Act 2014 s63(6)).

young carer grant Social security payment in Scotland for claimants aged between 16 and 18 who do not qualify for carer's allowance. It is exempt from income tax under ITEPA 2003 s677(1).

young carer's assessment An assessment a local authority may be required to make for a young carer under the provisions of Care Act 2014 s64.

young child In relation to free childcare, means a child under the age of 5 (Childcare Act 2016 s1(9)). For VAT, clothing for young children may qualify for zero-rating under VATA 1994 Sch 8 Group 16, as explained in VAT notice 714.
It was unsuccessfully argued that the term should mean children under the age of 16 in the case *NA Gura (t/a Vincent Footwear) [2001] VTD 978.*

young person In law, someone aged between 14 and 17.

youth club For VAT, "a club is a youth club if it meets all of the following conditions:

- its members are mainly under 21 years of age
- it has been established to promote the social, physical, educational or spiritual development of its members
- it provides a range of activities
- it has its own constitution
- it is able to produce its own accounts
- it cannot and does not distribute any profit
- it applies any profit made to provide or enhance the service to its members". Services of a youth club are generally exempt from VAT under VATA 1994 s31 and Sch 9 Group 6 Item 6, as amended.

The exemption includes associations of youth clubs.
Further guidance is given in VAT Notice 701/35.

yuan Unit of currency in China. Gold coins from 5/20 to 1,000 yuan may be regarded as gold investment coins for VAT purposes (VAT notice 701/12A).

Yugoslavia East European country created in 1918 which broke up into separate states from 1993.

Zaire Former name of the Congo, used between 1970 and 1997.

zaire Currency used in Zaire.

zakat Islamic tax of 2½% paid by Muslims on property transactions.

Zambia African country. Its currency is the kwacha of 100 ngwee. The UK has a double taxation convention of 1972 amended by a protocol of 1981. It also has a double taxation agreement of 2014. A pension paid from this country may be exempt from income tax under ITEPA 2003 s643.

zero-based budget Budget where all figures of expenditure are reset to zero unless expenditure is justified. It does not simply uplift figures from the previous year.

zero-carbon home Dwelling that produces no net amount of carbon dioxide. Such dwellings attracted stamp duty land tax relief between 1 October 2007 and 30 September 2012.

zero-coupon bond In investing, a bond that pays no interest but is sold at a discount allowing a capital gain to be made when it is redeemed.

zero-hours contract (ZHC) Contract of employment where the employer only pays the worker for the hours actually worked. Where the contract prevents the worker working for someone else, this is known as exclusivity. This is generally outlawed under Employment Rights Act 1996 s27A as inserted by Small Business, Enterprise and Employment Act 2015 s153(2).

zero-rating When VAT is charged at 0% (VATA 1994 s30). It differs from exemption, when VAT is not charged, as input tax may be claimed in respect of zero-rated supplies but not for exempt supplies. The scope of zero-rating is given in VATA 1994 Sch 8, which is summarised under VAT Schedules in section 3 of this dictionary.

zillmerising "Method known by that name for modifying the net premium reserve method of valuing a long-term insurance contract by increasing that part of the future premiums for which credit is taken so as to allow for initial expenses" (FCA glossary).

Zimbabwe African country formerly known as Rhodesia. Its currency was the Zimbabwe dollar which became worthless in 2009 from hyperinflation. Other currencies such as US dollar and South African rand are used in practice. The UK has a double taxation convention of 1982. The country is subject to international sanctions, which also apply to designated persons of the country.

Zimbabwe dollar Currency of Zimbabwe. The currency in effect became worthless and was largely abandoned from 12 April 2009. Various stable currencies were used instead. On 24 June 2019, the Reserve Bank of Zimbabwe replaced these multiple currencies with the Real Time Gross Settlement dollar.

zombie business Term coined in 2012 for a business that has failed but where it is not liquidated for ulterior reasons, such as a bank not wishing to record its loss.

zone Area which has been designated for a particular purpose, such as an enterprise zone.

zoo Admission to a zoo can be exempt from VAT as supply of a cultural service under Value Added Tax 1994 Sch 9 Group 13 Note 2. The extent to which input tax may be reclaimed for animal feed was considered in the case *Twycross Zoo (No 1) VTD 19548 [2004].*

zymurgy Science of fermentation.

Section 2: Abbreviations

A (1) annual allowance
(2) attendance allowance
A&A additions and amendments
AAAI Associate of the Institute of Administrative Accountants
AAD accompanying administration document
AAE Actuarial Association of Europe
AAG Anti-Avoidance Group (part of HMRC)
AAL additional adoption leave
AAM agent account manager
AAR advance assurance request
AAT Association of Accounting Technicians
ABAB Administrative Burden Advisory Board
ABB activity-based budgeting
ABC activity-based costing
ABCP asset-backed commercial paper
ABCUL Association of British Credit Unions Ltd
ABI Association of British Insurers
ABIST autonomous built-in self test (in computers)
ABP alternative banking platform
ABTA Association of British Travel Agents
abv alcohol by volume
ABWOR absent by way of representation
AC Appeal Court (part of case citation)
a/c account
ACA Associate member of the Institute of Chartered Accountants in England and Wales or Institute of Chartered Accountants of Ireland
ACAS Advisory, Conciliation and Arbitration Service
ACAT Association of Church Accountants and Treasurers
ACCA Association of Chartered Certified Accountants. (It is also used as designatory letters for its associate members)
ACE asset confiscation enforcement
ACF Association of Charitable Foundations
ACH automated clearing house
ACIE Association of Charity Independent Examiners
ACIS associate member of the Chartered Institute of Secretaries
ACL access control list
acn all concerned notified
ACP African, Caribbean and Pacific States
ACRS accelerated cost recovery system

ACS	authorised contractual scheme
ACSI	associate member of the Chartered Institute for Securities and Investment
ACT	(1) advance corporation tax (2) Association of Corporate Treasurers
ACTA	Anti-Counterfeiting Trade Agreement
actg	acting
ACU	Asian currency unit
acv	actual cash value
acy	average crop yield
AD	anaerobic digestion, turning waste food into electricity
ADB	accidental death benefit
ADD	(1) anti-dumping duty (2) accidental death and dismemberment (for insurance)
ADF	additional disagreement factor
ADI	accumulation/distribution indicator
ADIT	Advanced Diploma in Taxation (qualification offered by Chartered Institute of Taxation)
ADLs	activities of daily living (term used for social security)
ADOC	actual date of childbirth
ADP	automatic data processing
ADR	(1) alternative dispute resolution (2) American depositary receipt
ADT	air departure tax
adv	advised that (used in HMRC communications)
AE	(1) Accountancy Europe (2) auto-enrolment
AEA	annual exempt amount (for capital gains tax)
AEO	attachment of earnings order
AEOI	automatic exchange of information
AER	annual equivalent rate (of interest paid)
AESOP	all employee share ownership plan, now known as a share incentive plan
AFA	(1) Általános Forgalmi Adó, Hungarian for "value added tax" (2) Armed Forces Act, of 2006 or 2016
afaik	as far as I know
AFBD	Association of Futures Brokers and Dealers
AFC	advance fixing certificate
AFGX	Affarsvarlden Index (index for the Stockholm Exchange)
AFIP	Air Forces Independence Payment
AFPC	Advanced Financial Planning Certificate
AFPRB	Armed Forces' Pay Review Body
AFPS	Armed Forces Pension Scheme

AFR	advisory fuel rate
AFRS	Agricultural Flat Rate Scheme (for VAT)
AFS	available for sale
AG	Aktiengesellschaft, German limited company
A-G	Attorney-General
Ag	atomic symbol for silver
AGI	adjusted gross income (US tax term)
AGM	annual general meeting
agt	agent
AHC	animal health certificate
AI	artificial intelligence
AIA	annual investment allowance
AIB	(1) Accountant in Bankruptcy (Scottish law officer)
	(2) Allied Irish Bank
AIF	(1) approved investment fund
	(2) authorised investment fund
AIFM	alternative investment fund manager
AIIB	Asian Infrastructure Investment Bank
AIIT	associate member of the Institute of Indirect Taxation
AIM	Alternative Investment Market
AIR	alcohol ingredients relief
AITC	Association of Investment Trust Companies
AKLS	Automated Lane Keeping System
Aktb	Aktiebolaget (Swedish joint stock company)
AL	apprenticeship levy
Al	aluminium
ALCS	(1) aggregates levy credit scheme
	(2) Authors' Licensing and Collecting Society
ALDA	Alcoholic Liquor Duties Act 1979
ALI	American Law Institute
ALLA	audit liability limitation agreement
All ER	All England Law Reports
ALT	alternate key on computer
ALU	arithmetic logic unit (in computer)
ALKS	Automated Lane Keeping System
ALV	Arvonlisavero, Finnish for "value added tax"
ALVS	automatic licence verification system
AM	account manager
am	ante meridian, morning
A&M	accumulation and maintenance , form of trust
AMAP	approved mileage allowance payment

AMC	annual management charge
AME	annually managed expenditure, Treasury term
AMHB	appropriate maximum housing benefit
AMHP	approved mental health professional
AML	anti-money laundering
AMP	asset management plan
AMR	(1) actual marketing royalty
	(2) automated meter reader
AMRA	Access to Medical Records Act 1988
AMT	alternative minimum tax
ANCT	assumed notional council tax
ANPR	automatic number plate recognition
A/O	account of
AOB	any other business
AOP	(1) adjusted operating profit
	(2) annual operating plan
AOR	airport of receipt
AOSS	Agent Online Self Service
AP	(1) accounting period
	(2) additional pension
	(3) accounts payable
APA	(1) advance pricing agreement (or arrangement)
	(2) additional personal allowance (now abolished)
APB	Auditing Principles Board
APD	air passenger duty
APEC	Asia-Pacific Economic Co-operation
API	application program interface
APM	(1) alternative performance measure
	(2) Association of Project Managers
APN	accelerated payment notice
APP	authorised push payment (form of fraud)
app	Computer application, such as for mobile devices. Now regarded as not an abbreviation
APR	(1) agricultural property relief
	(2) annualised percentage rate
APRT	advance petroleum revenue tax
APS	approved profit-sharing
AQL	acceptable quality level
AR	(1) all risks, for insurance
	(2) accounts receivable
	(3) administrative review, by Home Office for immigration

a/r	as required
ARA	Assets Recovery Agency
arb	arbitrageur
ARC	Accounting Regulatory Committee
ARD	accounting reference date
ARGA	Audit, Reporting and Governance Authority
ARM	adjustable rate mortgage
ARPS	adjustable rate-preferred stock
ARPU	average revenue per user
ARR	(1) accounting rate of return
	(2) age-related rebate
AS	(1) Aktieselskab, Danish for "public company"
	(2) Aksjeselskap, Norwegian for "public company"
ASA	(1) accommodation service accountant, in armed forces
	(2) agent services account
ASAP	as soon as possible
ASB	Accounting Standards Board
ASC	Accounting Standards Committee
ASCLA	Apprenticeships, Skills, Children and Learning Act 2009
ASCN	appropriate scheme number, of pension
ASEAN	Association of South-East Asian Nations
ASF	Adoption Support Fund
ASORP	actuarial statement of recommended practice
ASP	(1) accountancy service provider
	(2) Act of the Scottish Parliament
	(3) alternatively secured pension
	(4) average selling price
ASPP	additional statutory paternity pay
asst	assistant
AST	automated screen trading
ATA	Admission Temporaire Carnet (for Customs)
ATAD	Anti Tax Avoidance Directive
ATCA	advance thin capitalisation agreement
ATED	annual tax on enveloped dwellings
ATF	authorised treatment facility
ATII	associate member of the Chartered Institute of Taxation
ATK	available tonne kilometres (measure of an aircraft's carrying capacity)
ATL	above the line
ATM	automated teller machine
AToS	age-based terms of service (in armed forces)
ATR	Admission Temporaire Roulette (for Customs)

ats	at the suit of
ATT	Association of Tax Technicians
ATX	Austrian Traded Index
AU	approved user
Au	atomic symbol for gold
AUDDIS	automated direct debit instruction service
AUT	authorised unit trust
AUTIF	Association of Unit Trusts and Investment Funds
AVC	additional voluntary contribution
AWB	air waybill
AWE	average weekly earnings
AWOL	absent without leave
AWRS	Alcohol Wholesalers Registration Scheme
AWW	army welfare worker
B2B	business to business
B2C	business to consumer
B2G	business to government
BA	banker's acceptance
BAA	British Accounting Association
BACS	Bankers' Automated Clearing System
BADR	business asset disposal relief
BALO	Bulletin des Annonces Légales Obligatoires (French government publication)
BALRM	basic arm's length return method
BAME	black, African and minority ethnic
BASIS	Business Angel Seed Investment Scheme
BATA	British Air Transport Association
BATR	business asset taper relief
BAU	business as usual
BBA	British Bankers Association
bboe	billions of barrels of oil equivalent
BBSI	bank and building society interest
BC	(1) balancing charge
	(2) basis for conclusions (used in international accounting standards)
	(3) British Council
B&C	benefits and credits
BCA	business current account
BCC	(1) British Chamber of Commerce
	(2) British Company Cases (series of law reports)
BCD	Banking Consolidation Directive
BCE	benefit crystallisation event

BCM	Better Case Management
BCOBS	Banking Conduct of Business Sourcebook
BCS	British Compounded Spirits
BEN	Business Economic Notes
BEP	breakeven point
BERR	Department for Business, Enterprise and Regulatory Reform (now Department for Business, Energy and Industrial Strategy)
BERTI	Binding European Retrieval of Tariff Information
BES	Business Expansion Scheme
BESA	Bond Exchange of South Africa
BEST	Business Education and Support Team (part of HMRC)
BF	Border Force
bfa	British Franchising Association
BFH	Bundesfinanzhof (German supreme court for taxation matters)
BFOC	bona fide occupational condition
b/fwd	brought forward
B&G	betting and gaming
BGC	bank giro credit
BGDA	Betting and Gaming Duties Act 1981
BHC	bank holding company
BIC	bank identifier code
BID	business improvement district
BIFEX	Baltic International Freight Futures Exchange
BIMBO	buy-in management buy-out
BIN	bank identification number
BIOS	Basic input/output system
BIOT	British Indian Ocean Territory
BIP	border inspection post
BIPRU	Prudential source book for banks, building societies and investment firms
BiRiLiG	Bilanzrichtliniengesetz, German law on accounting directives
BIS	(1) Bank for International Settlements (2) Department for Business, Innovation and Skills (now Department for Business, Energy and Industrial Strategy)
BIT	business impact target
B/L	bill of lading
BLAGAB	basic life assurance and general annuity business
bldg	building
BME	black and minority ethnic
bn	billion
BNPL	buy now, pay later
BOBL	Bundesobligationen, German bonds

BoE	Bank of England
BOGOF	buy one, get one free
BOM	bill of materials
BOP	balance of payments
BOT	bought
bpd	barrels per day
BPO	business process outsourcing
BPP	Budget Payment Plan
BPR	(1) business property relief
	(2) brief project report
BPRA	business premises renovation allowance
BPS	Basic Payment Scheme, under Common Agricultural Policy
BPSS	Business Payment Support Service
BPT	Basic Payroll Tools
BPV	bank payment voucher
BR	basic rate (used as a tax code)
BRC	(1) Budget Responsibility Committee
	(2) Business Records Checks
BRD	business requirements document
BRMA	broad rental market area, for local housing allowance in Scotland
BRO	bankruptcy restriction order
BRP	biometric residence permit
BRRD	Banking Recovery and Resolution Directive
BRS	business rates supplement
BRU	bankruptcy restriction undertaking
BRV	bank receipt voucher
BS	British Standard
B/S	balance sheet
BSE	Bombay Stock Exchange
BSI	British Standards Institution
BSL	British Sign Language
BSP	bereavement support payment
BSR	benchmark scale rate
BST	British standard time
BSUS	business start-up scheme
BSV	balance sheet value
BSVP	balance sheet value pool
Bt	baht, currency of Thailand
BTA	business tax account
BTAN	Bons à taux annuel nomalisés, French government bond
BTC	British Tax Cases

BTI	(1) Binding Tariff Information (2) British Trade International
BTN	Brussels Tariff Nomenclature
BTR	British Tax Review
BTW	Belasting over de Toegevoegde Waarde, Dutch for "value added tax"
btw	by the way
BU	business unit
BV	Besolten Vennootschap, Dutch for "limited company"
BVC	bona vacantia dissolved company
BVD	bona vacantia division, of Department for Business, Energy and Industrial Strategy
BVI	British Virgin Islands
BVPI	best value performance indicator
BVPS	book value per share
BVR	best value review
c	About, approximately
CA	(1) Chartered accountant. Designatory letters for members of Institute of Chartered Accountants of Scotland (2) Companies Act (3) Court of Appeal, particularly in case citations (4) Carer's allowance
CAA	Capital Allowances Act 2001
CAAT	Central-Agent Authorisation Team, of HMRC
CAB	(1) Citizens Advice Bureau (2) Careers Advice Board, in armed forces
CAC	(1) Customs Action Code (2) Central Arbitration Committee
CAD	(1) Cash against documents (2) Capital Adequacy Directive
CAF	Charities Aid Foundation
CAFCASS	Children and Family Court Advisory and Support Service
CAGR	compound annual growth rate
CAMEL	Capital adequacy, asset quality, management quality, earnings, liquidity. Five principles for evaluating a bank
CAO	(1) chief accounting officer (2) chief administrative officer
CAP	(1) Common Agricultural Policy, of European Union (2) chargeable accounting period
CAPA	Confederation of Asian and Pacific Accountants
CAPEX	capital expenditure

CAPM	capital asset pricing model
CAR	(1) Customer accounting record, held by HMRC
	(2) Compound annual return
CARD	Consolidated Admissions and Reporting Directive
CASC	community amateur sports club
CAT	(1) Competition Appeal Tribunal
	(2) Customs Action Text
	(3) Cumbernauld Accounting Team, HMRC dep
	(4) comparable adjustable transaction
	(5) certified accounting technician
CATO	Company Accounts and Tax Online
CATS	certificate of accrual on Treasury securities
CAV	cur adv vult: the court wishes to be advised
c/b	Call back. Abbreviation used in HMRC notes
CBA	cost benefit analysis
CBC	Cwmni buddiant cymunedol, Welsh for community interest company.
CbC	country by country, form of financial reporting
CBO	collateralised bond obligation
CBOE	Chicago Board Options Exchange
CBOT	Chicago Board of Trade
CBR	cost benefit ratio
CBT	computer based training
cc	(1) carbon copy, now any form of copy to a third party
	(2) cubic centimetre
CCA	(1) climate change agreement
	(2) current cost accounting
	(3) Court of Criminal Appeal
CCAB	Consultative Committee of Accounting Bodies
CCAEO	community charge attachment of earnings order
CCAMLR	Convention of the Conservation of Antarctic Marine Living Resources
CCAV	Centre for Connected and Autonomous Vehicles
CCC	(1) Community Customs Code
	(2) Commodity Credit Corporation
CCCTB	common consolidated corporation tax base
CCEP	Customs civil evasion penalty
CCFS	Care Case Fee Scheme
CCG	Customs Comprehensive Guarantee
CCH	CCH Editions Ltd, publisher
CCLI	Commonwealth Climate and Law Initiative
CCLN	Consignment Control Label Number
CCMS	client and cost management system, used in courts

CCN	County Council Network
CCP	(1) cross country pipeline
	(2) central counterparty
	(3) common commercial policy
CCR	counterparty credit risk
CCS	(1) carbon capture and storage
	(2) Crown Commercial Service
CCS-UK	Cargo Community System
CCT	company car tax
CCTO	Central Community Transit Office
CCW	Countryside Commission for Wales
CD	(1) certificate of deposit
	(2) compact disc
Cd	command paper, produced by government
CD and G	Crown dependencies and Gibraltar
CDC	(1) collective defined contribution, form of pension scheme
	(2) Council for Disabled Children
CDE	Centre for Defence Enterprise
CDF	contractual disclosure facility
CDFI	community development financial institution
CDM	(1) clean development mechanism, for environmental protection
	(2) change and data management
CDO	collateralised debt obligation
CDOT	Crown dependencies and overseas territories
CD-R	compact disk, recordable
CD-ROM	compact disk-read only memory
CDRP	Crime and Disorder Reduction Partnership
CDS	(1) Customs Declaration Service
	(2) credit default swap
CDT	compulsory drug testing
CE	compliant with EU directives on electromagnetism
C&E	Customs and Excise
CEA	(1) continuity of education allowance
	(2) capital expenditure amount
CEAS	Children's Education Advisory Service, part of Ministry of Defence
CEC	Commodities Exchange Center Inc
CED	common entry document
CEECs	Central and Eastern European Countries
CEFAS	Centre for Environment, Fisheries and Aquaculture Services
CEG	Careers Employment Group, in armed forces
CEMA	Customs and Excise Management Act 1979

CEO	chief executive officer
CEP	(1) civil evasion penalty
	(2) contributions equivalent premium, for pensions
CER	certified emission reduction
CESR	Council of European Securities Regulators
CET	Common External Tariff
cf	compare
CFA	(1) chartered financial analyst
	(2) conditional fee agreement
CFAB	Certificate in Finance, Accounting and Business
CFC	(1) controlled foreign company
	(2) Common Fund for Commodities
	(3) consumption of fixed capital
CFCT	cash flow cycle time
CFD	contract for difference
CFE	Confédération Fiscale Européene
CFF	(1) Children's Funeral Fund
	(2) Crime Fighting Fund
CFI	code for classification of financial instruments
CFM	certified financial manager
CFO	chief finance [or financial] officer
CFP	(1) Common Fisheries Policy
	(2) capital fulcrum point
CFS	consolidated financial statement
CFSP	(1) Customs Freight Simplified Procedure
	(2) common foreign and security policy
CFTC	Commodity Futures Trading Commission
c/fwd	carried forward
CGBR	Central Government Borrowing Requirement
CGNCR	Central Government Net Cash Requirement
CGT	capital gains tax
Ch	Chancery, division of High Court
CHAI	Commission for Healthcare Audit and Inspection
Ch D	Chancery Division, of High Court
CHIEF	Customs Handling of Import and Export Freight
CHIPS	Clearing House Inter-bank Payments System
CHP	combined heat and power
CI	(1) Channel Islands
	(2) Cayman Islands
CIArb	Chartered Institute of Arbitrators
CIB	Chartered Institute of Bankers

CIC	community interest company
CICA	Criminal Injuries Compensation Authority
CICM	Chartered Institute of Credit Management
CID	(1) criminal investigation department, of police
	(2) case information database, for immigration
CIF	carriage, insurance and freight
CIG	Criminal Investigations Group, part of HMRC
CII	Chartered Insurance Institute
CIL	community infrastructure levy
CILA	Chartered Institute of Loss Adjusters
CILEX	Chartered Institute of Legal Executives
CILIP	Chartered Institute of Library and Information Professionals
CILOCT	Contribution in lieu of council tax, in armed forces
CILT	Chartered Institute of Logistics and Transport
CIM	Chartered Institute of Marketing
CIMA	Chartered Institute of Management Accountants
CIO	(1) charitable incorporated organisation
	(2) chief information officer
CIOB	Chartered Institute of Building
CIOBS	Chartered Institute of Bankers in Scotland
CIOT	Chartered Institute of Taxation
CIP	(1) Customs information paper
	(2) carriage and insurance paid
CIPA	Chartered Institute of Payment Attorneys
CIPD	Chartered Institute of Personnel and Development
CIPFA	Chartered Institute of Public Finance and Accountancy
CIPP	Chartered Institute of Payroll Professionals
CIPR	Chartered Institute of Public Relations
CIPS	Chartered Institute of Procurement and Supply
CIR	Commissioners of Inland Revenue
CIS	(1) construction industry scheme
	(2) collective investment scheme
CISI	Chartered Institute for Securities and Investment
CISO	chief information security officer
CITES	Convention on International Trade in Endangered Species
CITIC	China International Trust and Investment Corporation
CITOPS	Customs and International Trade Operations
CITR	community investment tax relief
CIU	collective investment undertaking
CJ	chief justice
CJA	Criminal Justice Act

CJIA	Criminal Justice and Immigration Act
CKM	customer knowledge management
CLF	central liquidity facility
CLO	(1) collateralised loan obligation
	(2) chief legal officer
CLS	(1) contractor loan scheme
	(2) continuous linked settlement
CLSO	contractor loan settlement opportunity
CLT	chargeable lifetime transfer, for inheritance tax
Cm	command paper
c&m	care and maintenance
CMA	(1) Competition and Markets Authority
	(2) certified management accountant
CMCC	Cheque Card Management Committee
Cmd	command paper
CME	Chicago Mercantile Exchange
CMEA	Council for Mutual Economic Assistance
CMI	Chartered Management Institute
Cmnd	command paper
CMO	(1) collateralised mortgage obligation
	(2) chief marketing officer
CMR	Convention Merchandises Routiers
CN	combined nomenclature
C/N	credit note
CNC	customer-nominated contact
CNCD	combined consignment note and Customs declaration
CNCOM	concentration risk capital component
CNG	compressed natural gas
CNMV	Comisión del Mercado de Valores, the Madrid stock exchange
CNR	Centre for Non-Residents, part of HMRC
CO	(1) certification officer, for trade unions
	(2) commanding officer, in armed forces
co	company
CO2	carbon dioxide
COA	chart of account
COB	(1) closure of business, or close of business
	(2) conduct of business, in investment
COBS	Conduct of Business Sourcebook
COC	(1) cost of capital
	(2) cost of credit
COCIS	contracted-out contribution information service

COD	(1) cash on delivery
	(2) contracted out deduction
	(3) cost of debt
CoD	certificate of destruction
COE	centre of excellence
COFACE	Compagnie Française pour l'Assurance du Commerce Exterieur, the French equivalent to the Export Credits Guarantee Department.
COF	cost of funds, index of Treasury bills
COGS	cost of goods sold
COIN	continuously offered intermediate note
COLA	cost of living adjustment
COLTS	continuously offered longer-term securities
COMB	contracted out mixed benefit, form of occupational pension scheme
COMEX	Commodity Exchange of New York
COMP	contracted-out money purchase, form of pension scheme
COMPS	contracted-out money purchase scheme
COMPSHP	contracted-out money purchase stakeholder pension
COO	(1) country of origin
	(2) chief operating officer
COP	code of practice
COR	customer organisation representative
cor	coram, Latin for "in the presence of"
corp	corporation
CoS	certificate of sponsorship, for immigration skills charge
COSA	cost of sales adjustment
COSR	contracted-out salary-related, form of occupational pension scheme
COSRS	contracted-out salary-related scheme
COT	customer operations team, of Companies House
CP	commercial paper
CPA	(1) cost per action, or cost per acquisition
	(2) certified public accountant, in USA
	(3) Civil Partnership Act 2004
CPAG	Child Poverty Action Group
CPC	(1) Customs procedure code
	(2) cost per click
CPCT	Civil Penalty Compliance Team
CPD	continuing professional development
CPE	continuing professional education
CPEI	Customs Procedures with Economic Impact
CPF	carbon price floor
CPI	(1) consumer price index

	(2) comparable profit interval
CPL	cost per lead
CPM	cost per thousand
CPO	chief procurement officer
CPP	current purchasing power
CPR	contract profit rate
CPS	(1) Crown Prosecution Service
	(2) Carbon Price Support mechanism
CPT	Cuideachta phoibli' theoranta, Gaelic for public limited company
CPU	(1) central processing unit, of computer
	(2) Central Planning Unit, of HMRC
CPVO	Community Plant Variety Office
CQI	Chartered Quality Institute
CQS	consolidated quotation service
cr	credit
CRA	credit reference agency
CRC	(1) carbon reduction commitment
	(2) community rehabilitation company
CRCA	Commissioners for Revenue and Customs Act 2005
CRD	(1) Central Registration Depository
	(2) Capital Requirements Directive
CRM	customer relationship management
CRN	Customs Registered Number
CRO	Companies Registration Office
CROIC	cash returned on invested capital
CRR	(1) Capital Requirements Regulations
	(2) community and race relations
CRT	composite rate tax
CS	Countryside Scheme
CSA	(1) Child Support Agency
	(2) cost-sharing arrangement, in relation to patent box
CSC	composite service company
CSCE	Coffee, Sugar and Cocoa Exchange Inc of New York
CSCI	Commission for Social Care Inspection
CSDR	Community system of duty reliefs
CSE	certificate of secondary education
CSFA	Children, Schools and Families Act 2010
CSG	(1) cost sharing group, for VAT
	(2) community safety group
CSJ	Centre for Social Justice
CSO	child support order

CSOP	company share option plan
CSP	community systems provider
CSR	(1) Customs statistical reference
	(2) corporate social responsibility
CSSF	Conflict Stability and Security Fund
CST	community security trust
csv	comma separated variables, in spreadsheets
CT	(1) corporation tax
	(2) common transit, or community transit
CTA	(1) Corporation Tax Act, 2009 or 2010
	(2) call to action
CTAEO	council tax attachment of earnings order
CTB	council tax benefit
CTC	(1) child's tax credit
	(2) cost to company
CTCG	corporation tax on chargeable gains
CTD	(1) certificate of tax deposit
	(2) cheapest to deliver
CTF	(1) child trust fund
	(2) counter-terrorism finance
CTFO	Child Trust Fund Office
CTIS	Director of Corporation Tax, International and Stamps, a Northern Ireland office
CTO	Capital Taxes Office
CTQU	Central Tariff Quota Unit
CTSA	corporation tax self-assessment
Ct Ses	Court of Session
CTT	capital transfer tax
CU	currency unit
Cu	atomic symbol for copper
cu	cubic
CUSIP	Committee on Uniform Securities Identification Procedure
CV	curriculum vitae
CVA	company voluntary agreement
CVC	certificate of veterinary clearance
CVD	countervailing duty
CVED	common veterinary entry document
CVP	cost-volume-profit
CVS	corporate venturing scheme
CW	Customs warehousing
CWA	Chemical Weapons Authority

cwt	hundredweight
CWTS	Central Warrants Trading System
cyf	cyfyngedig, Welsh for limited
d	(old) pence
DAC	(1) European Council directive 2011/06 on co-operation for tax enforcement (2) dispending appliance contractor, in NHS
DAN	deferment approval number
DAS	(1) pipeline duty adjustment statement (2) debt arrangement scheme
DAX 30	widely quoted German share index
DB	defined benefit, pension scheme
dba	doing business as
DBS	Disclosure and Barring Service
DC	defined contribution, pension scheme
DCF	discounted cashflow
DCLG	Department for Communities and Local Government
DCS	Digital Case System
DD	direct debit
D/D	direct debit
DDA	Disability Discrimination Act 1995
DDC	dealer deposit contribution
DDI	direct debit instruction
DDP	deemed direct payment
DDS	digital disclosure service
DDV	Davek na dodano vrednost, Slovenian for "value added tax"
DEB	denatured ethanol B
DECC	Department for Energy and Climate Change
DEP	designated export place
DERV	diesel engine road vehicle, mainly used to mean the oil
DExEU	Department for Exiting the European Union
dFM	Deputy First Minister, of Northern Ireland Executive
DfID	Department for International Development
DFPNI	Department of Finance and Personnel, Northern Ireland
DG	director-general
DGN	dangerous goods notice
DH	dirham, currency of Morocco
DHCP	dynamic host configuration period
DHP	discretionary housing payment
DHSC	Department of Health and Social Care
DI	dispatch information

DIE	designated investment exchange
DIFOT	delivery in full on time
DIP	direct input provider
disc	discount
DIT	Department for International Trade
DITMO	deep in the money option
DIY	do it yourself
DJF	Djibouti franc
DKr	Danish krone
DM	Deutschmark
DMA	(1) Direct Marketing Association
	(2) direct market access
DMB	Debt Management and Banking, team in HMRC
DMHEF	Debt and Mental Health Evidence Form
DMI	debt market integrator
DMO	Debt Management Office
DMV	deemed market value
DN	deficiency notice
DNA	deoxyribonucleic acid
D/NI	deduction/no inclusion
DNS	domain name system
D&O	directors and officers, insurance term
do	ditto
DOA	dead on arrival
DOB	date of birth
DOE	depending on experience
DOL	Daily Official List
DORA	Defence of the Realm Act 1914
DOTAS	disclosure of tax avoidance schemes
DoV	deed of variation
DPA	(1) Data Protection Act
	(2) deferred prosecution agreement
DPF	Deposit Protection Fund
DPH	Daň z přidané hodnoty, Czech for "value added tax"
DPO	(1) documentary proof of origin
	(2) days payable outstanding
DPP	Director of Public Prosecutions
DPT	diverted profits tax
DPTC	disabled person's tax credit
DR	depositary receipt
dr	debit

DRA	default retirement age
DRC	Democratic Republic of Congo
DRD	Direct Recovery of Debts
DRIP	dividend re-investment plan
DRT	detonation resistance test certificate
DSE	display screen equipment
DSMEG	duty suspended movements of excise goods
DSO	day sales outstanding
DSP	(1) director of service prosecutions (2) delivery service provider
DSR	debt service ratio
DSS	Department of Social Security, now Department of Work and Pensions
DT	double taxation
DTA	double taxation agreement
DTB	Deutsche Terminböurse
DTC	depository trust company
DTCC	depositary trust and clearing corporation
DTI	(1) Department of Trade and Industry (now Department for Business, Energy and Industrial Strategy) (2) direct trader input
DTP	desktop publishing
DTR	(1) double taxation relief (2) disclosure rules and transparency rules
DTTO	drug testing and treatment order
DTTP	double taxation treaty passport
DUCR	declaration unique consignment reference
DUS	distinct, uniform and stable (for plant variety rights)
DVLA	Driver and Vehicle Licensing Authority
DVO	District Valuer's Office
DVP	delivery vs payment
DVSA	Driver Vehicle and Standards Agency
DWP	Department of Work and Pensions
E&A	exploration and appraisal, in oil industry
EAC	(1) Economic Affairs Committee (2) Environmental Audit Committee
E&B	Ellis and Blackburn, law reports
E&F	error and fraud
EA	(1) Environment Agency (2) Education Act
ea	each

EAA	European Accounting Association
EAEC	European Atomic Energy Community
EAGGF	European Agricultural Guidance and Guarantee Fund
EAIG	excise assessments interim guidance, HMRC manual
EANDCB	equivalent annual net direct costs to business
EAR	effective annual rate
EARN	Euro Area Reference Note
EAS	(1) Enterprise Allowance Scheme
	(2) Employment Alignment Submission
EASDAQ	European Association of Securities Dealers Automated Quotations
EAY	effective annual yield
EBIT	earnings before interest and taxes
EBITA	earnings before interest, taxes and amortisation
EBITDA	earnings before interest, taxes, depreciation and amortisation
EBM	earn back model
EBQ	economic batch quantity
EBRD	European Bank for Reconstruction and Development
EBT	employee benefit trust
EBTI	European Binding Tariff Information
EBTSO	employee benefit trust settlement opportunity
EC	(1) European Community
	(2) European Commission
	(3) early conciliation
E&C	enforcement and compliance
ECA	(1) enhanced capital allowance
	(2) European Court of Auditors
	(3) electronic commerce activity
	(4) European Communities Act 1972
ECAI	external credit assessment institution
ECB	European Central Bank
ECD	Electronic Commerce Directive (in UK SI 2002 No 1775)
ECDBR	Enforcement and Compliance Dispute Resolution Board
ECEP	EC export preference, HMRC manual
ECGD	Export Credit Guarantees Department
ECHR	European Court of Human Rights
ECIU	Energy and Climate Intelligence Unit
ECJ	European Court of Justice (now Court of Justice of the European Union)
ECL	expected credit loss
ECO	energy company obligation
ECOFIN	Economic and Financial Affairs Council, of European Union
ECON	employer's contracting out number

ECOS	employee car ownership scheme
ECP	(1) Euro commercial paper
	(2) excise civil penalties, HMRC manual
ECPET	EC preferences on exports to Turkey, HMRC manual
ECPIT	EC preferences on imports from Turkey, HMRC manual
ECR	(1) European Court Reports
	(2) enhanced capital requirement
ECS	(1) employer compliance system
	(2) electronic clearing system
ECSC	European Coal and Steel Community
ECSL	EC sales list
ECU	European currency unit
ED	exposure draft
ED(DP)R	Excise Duties (Deferred Payment) Regulations 1992
EDCS	electronic data capture service
EDDC	excise due diligence guidance, HMRC manual
EDF	European Development Fund
EDGAR	electronic data gathering, analysis and retrieval system
EDI	electronic data interchange
EDIFACT	electronic data interchange for administration, commerce and transport
EDO	extremism disruption order
EDQ	electronic documents questionnaire
EDR	(1) effective date of registration
	(2) energy demand reduction
	(3) Euro depositary receipt
EDSP	exchange delivery settlement price
EE	enhanced exports
EEA	European Economic Area
EEC	European Economic Community (now European Union)
EEE	electrical and electronic equipment
EEIG	European economic interest grouping
EEO	equal employment opportunity
EEOC	Equal Employment Opportunity Commission
EF	earnings factor, for national insurance
EFA	Education Funding Agency
EFO	economic and financial outlook, in spring or autumn statement
EFP	exchange for physicals
EFRAG	European Finance Reporting Advisory Group
EFRBS	employer-financed retirement benefit scheme
EFSM	European Financial Stabilisation Mechanism
EFT	electronic funds transfer

EFTA	European Free Trade Association
Eftpos	electronic financial transactions at the point of sale
EG	(1) Enforcement Guide
	(2) Estates Gazette
e.g.	exampli gratia, Latin for "for example"
EGAD	excise goods accompanying documents
EGDR	Excise Goods (Drawback) Regulations 1995
EGLBAGL	Exchange Gains and Losses (Bringing into Account Gains and Losses) Regulations SI 2002 No 1970
EGLR	Estates Gazette Law Reports
EHC	Export Health Certificate
EIA	Education and Inspections Act 2016
EIB	European Investment Bank
EIC	Excise and Inland Customs
EIDR	entry in declarant's records
EIGA	Export and Investment Guarantees Act 1991
EIK	eat-in kitchen
EIM	Employment Income, HMRC manual
EIR	earned income relief (now abolished)
EIRIS	Ethical Investment Research Service
EIS	enterprise investment scheme
EISA	Enterprise Investment Scheme Association
EJRA	employer justified retirement age
EJSS	expanded job support scheme
EL	expected loss
ELG	eligible liabilities guarantee scheme
ELM	Electronic Money Sourcebook
ELPS	Equity Life payment scheme
ELS	electronic lodgements service
ELV	end of life vehicle
EMA	(1) European Monetary Agreement
	(2) exponential moving average
EMBI	emerging markets bond index
EMH	efficient market hypothesis
EMI	(1) enterprise management incentive
	(2) European Monetary Institute
	(3) equated monthly instalment
EMIR	European Markets Infrastructure Regulations
EMPS	energy market participants
EMS	(1) European Monetary System
	(2) Electromagnetic signature, in coins

EMTR	effective marginal tax rate
EMU	European Monetary Union
EO	economic operator
EOB	end of business
EOC	Equal Opportunities Commission, now abolished
EOD	end of day
EOE	European Options Exchange
EOHOS	Eat Out to Help Out Scheme
EOI	expression of interest
EOM	end of message
EOQ	economic order quantity
EORI	Economic Operator Regulation Identification
EOTC	Equal Opportunities Training Centre
EOV	existence, ownership and valuation
EOY	end of year
EPA	enduring power of attorney
EPB	(1) Economic Prosperity Board
	(2) Export Promotion Board, of Singapore
EPC	Export Promotion Council
EPCAP	Enemy Property Compensation Advisory Panel
EPE	expected positive exposure
EPLI	employment practices liability insurance
EPN	escalating penalty notice
EPOS	electronic point of sale
EPP	executive pension plan
eps	earnings per share
EPSS	Excise Payment Security System
EPU	(1) Entry Processing Unit
	(2) European Payments Union
EPW	externally provided worker
Eq	(1) Equity Cases, published between 1865 and 1875
	(2) Equity Reports, case reports published between 1853 and 1855
EQIA	Equality Impact Assessment
ER	(1) Monogram of Queen Elizabeth II
	(2) English Reports, case reports from 1220 to 1865
	(3) Entrepreneur's relief
ERA	Employment Rights Act 1996
ERDF	European Regional Development Fund
ERG	Efficiency and Reform Group
ERIC	European Research Infrastructure Consortia
ERISA	Employment Retirement Income Security Act 1974, US law

ERL	Export Reception List
ERM	exchange rate mechanism
ERN	Export Reference Number
ERNIE	Electronic Random Number Indicator Equipment, for premium bonds
ERODG	HMRC manual on excise repayment of duty
ERP	enterprise resource planning
ERS	(1) employment-related securities
	(2) employment recognition scheme
ERSM	HMRC manual on employment-related securities
ERSS	electronic return storage system
ERTS	enhanced remote transit shed
ERU	emission reduction unit
ES	(1) Ethical Standard
	(2) Country prefix code for Spain
ESA	employment and support allowance
ESC	(1) extra-statutory concession
	(2) European Social Chapter (or Charter)
	(3) employer-assisted childcare
ESCB	European System of Central Banks
ESD	European Savings Directive
ESFA	Education and Skills Funding Agency
ESI	employment status indicator
ESIM	HMRC Manual on excise statutory interest
ESL	(1) European Sales List
	(2) English as a second language
ESM	HMRC Manual on employment status
ESOP	employee share (or stock) ownership plan
ESOS	Energy Savings Opportunity Scheme
ESOT	employee share ownership trust
Esq	esquire
ESRA	Ethical Standards for Reporting Accounts
ESS	(1) Export Safety and Security
	(2) employee self-service
	(3) employment status service
	(4) electronic suppression of sales
ESSA	Employee and Share Schemes Act 2002
EST	Eastern Standard Time, in USA
ET	(1) employment tribunal
	(2) earnings threshold
ETA	estimated time of arrival
ETC	exchange traded commodity

ETD	estimated time of departure
ETF	(1) exchange traded fund
	(2) electronic transfer of funds
ETL	expected tail losses
ETS	(1) Emissions Trading System
	(2) enhanced thinking skills
ETSSB	Employment Tribunal System Steering Board
EU	European Union
EUA	EU Allowance Unit
EU ETS	European Union Emissions Trading Scheme
EUIPO	European Union Intellectual Property Office
EURES	European Employment Service
EUSD	European Union Savings Directive
EUTM	European Union trade mark
EUUT	exempt unauthorised unit trust
EV	expected value
EVA	economic value added
EVPI	expected value of perfect information
EVR	electronic version of the tax return
EWER	Excise Warehousing (Etc) Regulations
ex	without, former
EXC	HMRC Manual on excise competent official guidance
Ex D	Exchequer Division, series of law report between 1865 and 1875
ex div	without dividend
exes	expenses
exor	executor
expat	expatriate
EXS	exit summary declaration, for Customs duty
ExTRA	Export/Transit Project
EYU	earlier year update
EZ	enterprise zone
EZA	enterprise zone allowance
EZPUT	enterprise zone property unit trust

F	degrees Fahrenheit
FA	Finance Act
FAB	flavoured alcoholic beverage
FAE	final admitting exam
FAFTS	financing-arrangement-funded transfers to shareholders, for life assurance
FAIFA	Fiscal Assurance in the Freight Area
Fam D	Family Division, of the High Court

FAQ	frequently asked questions
FAR	fixed assets ratio
FAS	(1) flexible accounting system
	(2) Family Advocacy Scheme
FASB	Financial Accounting Standards Board, of USA
FAT	financial activity tax
FATCA	Foreign Accounting Tax Compliance Act 2010, of USA
FATF	Financial Action Task Force
FB	foreign body, as used on sick notes
FBSC	Finance Bill Sub-Committee
FBu	Burundi franc
FC	Congolese franc
FCA	(1) Financial Conduct Authority
	(2) Fellow of the Institute of Chartered Accountants in England and Wales
FCBA	foreign currency bank account
FCCA	Fellow of the Association of Chartered Certified Accountants
FCDO	Foreign Commonwealth and Development Office
FCIE	Fellow of the Association of Charity Independent Examiners
FCIM	HMRC Manual on fraud civil investigation
FCIPP	Fellow of the Chartered Institute of Payroll Professionals
FCL	full container load
FCM	futures commission merchant
FCO	Foreign and Commonwealth Office
FCP	Fonds Commun de Placement, Luxembourg fund structure
FCPE	finance company partial exemption
FCR	(1) Family Court Reports, law reports published from 1987
	(2) Federal Court Reports, US law reports
FCRA	Fair Credit Reporting Act 1969, US law
FCSI	Fellow of the Chartered Institute for Securities and Investment
FCU	file checking unit, in police
FDA	First Division Association, Civil Service trade union
FDC	(1) fleur de coin, high state of collectable coin
	(2) first day cover, of a stamp
FDF	Food and Drink Federation
FDI	foreign direct investment
FDIC	Federal Deposit Insurance Corporation
FDR	family dispute resolution
FE	further education
Fe	atomic symbol for iron
FEC	licensed family entertainment centre
Fed	Federal Bank of USA

FEE	Fédération des Experts Comptables Européens
FEES	Financial Conduct Authority manual on fees
FERA	Food and Environment Research Agency
FES	front end scanning, Companies House term
ff	and following pages
f & f	fixtures and fittings
FFI	foreign financial institution, US term
FFP	Financial Fair Play Regulations, of football body UEFA
Fgas	fluorinated greenhouse gases
FHDDS	Fulfilment House Due Diligence Scheme
FHL	furnished holiday lettings
FHLMC	Federal Home Loan Mortgage Corporation, US body known as Freddie Mac
FHTP	Forum on Harmful Tax Practices
FI	(1) country prefix for Finland
	(2) financial intermediary
	(3) financial institution
	(4) financial instrument
FIA	Futures Industry Association
FICA	Federal Insurance Contributions Act, of USA
FICC	Fixed Income, Currency and Commodities
FICN	fake Indian currency note
FICO	form of credit scoring
FID	(1) foreign income dividend
	(2) foreign income distribution
Fid Def	Fidei Defensor, Latin for "Defender of the Faith, coin obverse legend
fi fa	fieri facias, Latin for "cause to be made", used in warrant to seize goods
FIFO	first in first out. method of stock valuation
FII	franked investment income
FIIT	Fellow of the Institute of Indirect Taxation
FILEX	Fellow of the Institute of Legal Executives
FIMBRA	Financial Intermediaries Managers and Brokers Regulatory Association, abolished in 1984
FINROF	Funds Investing in Non-reporting Offshore Fund
FIO	free in and out, marine carriage term
FIOD	Dutch Fiscal and Investigation Service
FIS	(1) Fraud Investigation Service
	(2) family income support
FISMA	Financial Services and Markets Act 2000
FIT	(1) feed-in tariffs
	(2) Part of Financial Conduct Authority handbook on tests for fit and proper persons

FL	financial leverage
FLO-CERT	Fairtrade Labelling Organization body that issues certificates
FLR	(1) Family Law Reports, published from 1980
	(2) Federal Law Reports, Australian law reports from 1956
FLS	Funding for Lending Scheme
FM	First Minister, of Northern Ireland Executive
FMB	Federation of Master Builders
FMC	flat management company
FMed3	medical certificate
FMU	Forced Marriage Unit, part of Home Office
FMV	fair market value
FNMA	Federal National Mortgage Association, US body known as Fannie Mae
FO	foreign office
FOB	free on board; freight on board
FOBT	fixed odds betting terminal
FOC	free of cost
FOF	fund of funds
FOI	Freedom of Information
FOIA	Freedom of Information Act 2000
FOK	fill or kill, investment term
forex	foreign exchange
FOS	Financial Ombudsman Service
FOTRA	free of tax to residents abroad
FP	fraud protection, in relation to pensions
FPA	Arithmos Forologikou Mitroou, Greek for "value added tax"
FP&A	financial planning and analysis
FPC	(1) Financial Planning Certificate
	(2) HMRC Manual on film production company
FPCF	finite population correction factor
FPCS	fixed profit car scheme
FPI	Family and Parenting Institute
FPN	fixed penalty notice, for motoring offence
FPO	(1) fast parcel operator
	(2) follow on public offer
FPS	(1) full payment submission, for real time information
	(2) Faster Payment Service
	(3) financial and professional services
FR	(1) Country prefix code for France
	(2) Fully reportable, under European Savings Directive
FRA	forward rate agreement
FRAA	flat rate accrual amount, of state second pension

FRB	future revenue benefit
FRC	Financial Reporting Council
FRED	Financial Reporting Exposure Draft
FRF	Farming Recovery Fund
FRN	floating rate note
FRRP	Financial Reporting Review Panel
FRS	financial reporting standard
FRSSE	Financial reporting standard for smaller enterprises, now replaced
FRT&MAU	Financial Reporting Team and Management Account Unit, for immigration skills charge
FRU	free representation unit
FRY	final relevant year
F&S	Fox and Smith law reports
FSA	Financial Services Authority
FSAVC	free-standing additional voluntary contribution
FSC	(1) Financial Securities Centre
	(2) fire-safe cigarette
FSCS	Financial Services Compensation Scheme
FSD	final supplementary declaration
FSMA	Financial Services and Markets Act 2000
FSR	Fleet Street Reports, law reports from 1963
F Supp	Federal Reporter Supplement, US law reports
FT	Financial Times
FTA	(1) Freight Transport Association
	(2) Federation of Tax Administrators
	(3) free trade agreement
FTE	(1) full time employment
	(2) First Time Exporters
fte	full time equivalent
FTII	Fellow of the Institute of Taxation
FTLR	Financial Times Law Report, published between 1986 and 1988
FTP	file transfer protocol
FTPA	Fixed Term Parliament Act 2011
FTR	film tax relief
FTRS	Full Time Reserve Service, in armed forces
FTSE	Financial Times and Stock Exchange, used for indices
FTT	first tier tribunal
FTWA	full time working abroad
F/U	follow up
FUD	fear, uncertainty and doubt
FV	future value

FVA	fair value of assets
FWO	farewell offering
FX	foreign exchange
FY	financial year
FYA	(1) first year allowance
	(2) for your action
FYI	for your information
FYROM	Former Yugoslav Republic of Macedonia, used between 1993 and 2019
FZ	free zone
G	guarani, currency of Paraguay
G$	Guyana dollar
GAAP	generally accepted accounting practice/principles
GAAR	(1) general anti-abuse rule, from 2012
	(2) general anti-avoidance rule, before 2012
GAAS	generally accepted audit standards
GACV	HMRC Manual on guidance on audit of Customs values
GAD	Government Actuary's Department
GAS	Government Accounting Service
GATT	General Agreement on Tariffs and Trade
GAYE	Give As You Earn, now more commonly called payroll giving
GBD	general betting duty
GBER	General Block Exemption Regulations
GCA	Groceries Code Adjudicator
GCCR	Goode Consumer Credit Reports, first published from 1882
GCFP	Government Counter Fraud Profession
GCR	group capital resources
GCRR	group capital resources requirement
GDL	Graduate Diploma in Law
GDO	genuine diversity of ownership, in collective investment scheme
GDP	gross domestic product
GDPR	General Data Processing Regulation(s)
GDR	global depositary receipt
GEN	Financial Conduct Authority handbook of general provisions
GENPRU	General Prudential Sourcebook
GEO	Government Equalities Office
GFCF	gross fixed capital formation
GFCR	gross finance costs relief
GHG	greenhouse gas
GI	geographical indication, on spirits
GIB	Green Investment Bank

GICR	general insurance capital requirement
GIM	HMRC Manual on general insurance
GISC	General Insurance Standards Council
GIV	gift inter-vivos, a lifetime gift
GL	general ledger
GLA	Gangmasters Licensing Authority
GLD	Government Legal Department
GLO	group litigation order
GM	gross margin
gm	gram
gm/km	grams per kilometre
GMP	guaranteed minimum pension
GMV	gross merchandise volume
GMW	guaranteed minimum wage
GNMA	Government National Mortgage Association, US body known as Ginnie Mae
GNP	gross national product#
GNSS	global navigation satellite system
GOMC	gas oil marker concentrate
GP	(1) general practitioner, doctor
	(2) gross profit
GPE	general purpose exemption
GPhC	General Pharmaceutical Council
GPM	graduated payment mortgage
GPO	(1) group purchasing organisation
	(2) General Post Office, replaced in 1969
Gr8	great, texting abbreviation
GRA	Gender Recognition Act 2004
GRB	graduated retirement benefit, also known as graduated pension
GRC	Gender Recognition Certificate
GREIT	HMRC Manual on real estate investment trusts
GRI	global reporting initiative
GRN	goods received/receipt note
GSP	generalised system of preferences, for Customs duties
GST	goods and services tax
GSV	gross sales value
GTC	good till cancelled
GTCE	General Teaching Council for England
GTS	gambling tax service
GU	gastric ulcer, used on sick notes
GUI	graphical user interface
GVC	global value chain

GVS	general value statement, for Customs
HAWB	house air waybill
HB	housing benefit
HBLB	Horserace Betting Levy Board
HC	(1) High Court
	(2) House of Commons
HCO	hydrocarbon oils
HCOBIG	HMRC tax manual on biofuels and substitutes
HCOGAS	HMRC tax manual on gas for road fuel use
HCOS	HMRC tax manual on hydrocarbon oil strategy
HCOTEG	HMRC tax technical manual on oils
HDPE	high density polyethylene. Milk containers are made from it
HE	higher education
HEAG	Hidden Economy Advisory Group
HEE	Health Education England
HEFCE	Higher Education Funding Council for England, now abolished
HEI	higher education institution
HFEA	Human Fertilisation and Embryology Authority
HFSS	high in fat, salt or sugar, description of food
HGCA	part of Agriculture and Horticulture Board that charges a levy on cereals and oilseeds
HGV	heavy goods vehicle
HICBC	high income child benefit charge
HICP	harmonised index of consumer prices, also abbreviated to CPI
HIERC	higher income excess relief charge
HIP	home information pack
HIPC	heavily indebted poor country
HIT	housing investment trust
HK	Hong Kong
HK$	Hong Kong dollar
HL	House of Lords
HLIG	High Level Implementation Group
HLP	Housing Law Reports
HM	Her Majesty, or His Majesty
H&M	Hemming and Miller's Law Reports
HMAG	HMRC Manual on holding and movements assurance guidance
HMASA	HMRC Manual on holding and movements alcohol strategy
HMC	hospital management committee
HMCE	HM Customs and Excise, part of HMRC since 2005
HMDS	HMRC Manual on holding and movements: duty stamps

HMRC	HM Revenue and Customs
HMRCC	HM Revenue and Customs Commissioners
HMWARE	HMRC Manual on warehouse guidance
HNWI	high net worth individual
HNWU	High Net Worth Unit
HO	Home Office
HOC	Home Office Circular
HODA	Hydrocarbon Oil Duties Act 1979
hols	holidays
Hon	honorary
Hons	Honours, part of a degree
Hon Sec	honorary secretary
HOR	Hydrocarbon Oil Regulations 1973
HP	hire purchase
hp	horsepower
HQ	headquarters
HQLA	high quality liquid assets
HR	human resources
HRA	Health Research Authority
HRD	human resources development
HRM	human resources management
HRP	home responsibilities protection
HRT	hand-rolling tobacco
HS	harmonised system, of Customs duties
HS2	high speed railway line being built in UK
HSBC	name now used by Hongkong and Shanghai Banking Corporation
HSC	Harmonised System Committee
HSEN	Harmonised System Explanatory Notes
HSI	Hang Seng Index
HST	high speed transmission
HSWA	Health and Safety at Work Act 1974
HTA	Human Tissues Authority
HU	country prefix for Hungary
HVA	high volume agent
HVAC	heating, ventilation and air conditioning
IA	(1) initial allowance
	(2) international assistance
	(3) impact assessment
IAASB	International Auditing and Assurance Standards Board
IACS	International Association of Classification Societies

IAG	Investor Advisory Group
IAS	international accounting standard
IASB	International Accounting Standards Board
IASC	International Accounting Standards Committee
IATA	International Air Transport Association
IB	tax code for an employee entitled to blind person's allowance
IBAN	international bank account number
IBAP	Intervention Board for Agricultural Produce, now the Rural Payments Agency
IBB	Independent Barring Board
IBEA	Intervention Board Executive Agency
IBNR	insurance business not required
IBR	Independent Business Review
IBRD	International Bank for Reconstruction and Development
ICA	(1) International Co-operative Alliance
	(2) individual capital assessment
ICAAP	internal capacity adequacy assessment process
ICAEW	Institute of Chartered Accountants in England and Wales
ICAI	Institute of Chartered Accountants of Ireland
ICANZ	Institute of Chartered Accountants of New Zealand
ICAS	Institute of Chartered Accountants of Scotland
ICB	industry classification benchmark
ICD	(1) inland clearance depot
	(2) investor compensation directive
ICE	in case of emergency
ICES	Chartered Institution of Civil Engineering Surveyors
ICG	individual capital guidance
ICMA	International Capital Markets Association
ICN	(1) Intrastat Combined Nomenclature
	(2) international consignment note
ICO	Information Commissioner's Office
ICOBS	Insurance: New Conduct of Business sourcebook
ICR	(1) intelligent character reading
	(2) Industrial Cases Report
	(3) Income Contingent Repayment
ICS	import control system
ICSID	International Centre for Settlement of Investment Disputes
ICT	(1) immediately chargeable transfer
	(2) intra-company transfer
ICTA	Income and Corporation Taxes Act 1988 (or 1970)
ICVC	investment company with variable capital

ID	identity
IDAS	identity authentication system, introduced in 2009 for tax credit claimants
IDG	HMRC Manual on information disclosure
IDK	internal derangement of knee, used on sick notes
IE	(1) country prefix code for Ireland
	(2) independent examination
	(3) interest expense
i.e.	id est, Latin for "that is"
IEIM	HMRC Manual on international exchange of information
IESBA	International Ethics Standards Board for Accountants
IET	international emissions trading
IFA	(1) intangible fixed asset
	(2) independent financial adviser
	(3) Institute of Financial Accountants
IfA	Institute for Apprenticeship
IFAW	International Fund for Animal Welfare
IFC	international finance corporation
IFIAR	International Forum of Independent Audit Regulators
IFO	German index of short-term economic indicators
IFP	Institute of Financial Planning
IFRIC	International Financial Reporting Interpretations Committee
IFRS	International Financial Reporting Standard
IFT	Insurance Fraud Taskforce
IG	implementation guidance, used by International Accounting Standards Board
IGA	inter-governmental agreement
IH	Inner House, of Court of Sessions in Scotland
IHD	ischaemic heart disease, used on sick notes
IHS	immigration health surcharge
IHT	inheritance tax
IHTA	Inheritance Tax Act 1984
IHTM	HMRC Manual on inheritance tax
IIA	Chartered Institute of Internal Auditors
IIB	industrial injuries benefit
IICSA	Independent Inquiry into Child Sexual Abuse
IIEDS	Individual Investor Express Delivery Service
IIF	Institute of International Finance
IIP	interest in possession, type of trust
IIS	(1) inward investment support
	(2) investment income surcharge
ILA	individual learning account

ILEX	Institute of Legal Executives, now Chartered Institute
ILG	index-linked gift
IMA	(1) initial maintenance assessment
	(2) Investment Managers Association
IMD	insurance mediation
IME	internationally mobile employee
IMEXPG	HMRC Manual on import and export pipelines
IMF	International Monetary Fund
IMO	International Maritime Organisation, part of UN
IMPAC	International Merchants Purchase Authorisation Card
IMPS	HMRC Manual on imports
IMRO	Investment Management Regulatory Organisation
IMS	industrial methylated spirits
IN	prefix to introductory paragraphs of International Financial Reporting Standards
in	inch, inches
INACE	HMRC Manual on administrative co-operation in excis
Inc	Incorporated
INCHP	HMRC Manual on import and national clearance hub procedures
INN	international non-proprietary name, of drugs
in re	in the matter of
INRIX	organisation that analyses traffic data in different countries
INS	Immigration and Naturalization Service, of USA
INSPRU	Prudential sourcebook for insurers
INTM	HMRC international tax manual
IOB	Insurance Ombudsman Bureau
IOM	(1) International Organization for Migration
	(2) Isle of Man
IOP	index of production
IOPC	Independent Office for Police Conduct
IORP	Institutions for Occupational Retirement Pension
IOSCO	International Organisation of Securities Commissions
IoT	Internet of things
IOU	personal loan authorised by the borrower
IP	(1) insolvency practitioner
	(2) intellectual property
	(3) inward processing
IPA	individual pension account
IPCC	Independent Police Complaints Commission, now replaced by Independent Office for Police Conduct
IP D	inward processing drawback

IPDI	immediate post-death interest
IPE	International Petroleum Exchange
IPGN	HMRC Manual on import preference guidance notes
IPI	income protection insurance
IPL	intense pulse light
IPO	(1) Intellectual Property Office
	(2) initial public offering, of shares
IPR	(1) inward processing relief
	(2) intellectual property rights
IPR/CS	inward processing relief/Continental Shelf
IPRU	Interim Prudential sourcebook
IPSASB	International Public Sector Accounting Standards Board
IPSE	Association of Independent Professionals and Self-employed
IPT	(1) insurance premium tax
	(2) HMRC Manual on insurance premium tax
	(3) item per transaction
IP&T	Butterworth Intellectual Property and Technology Cases
IPTM	HMRC Manual on insurance policyholder taxation
IPV	intimate partner violence
IR	(1) Inland Revenue
	(2) Insolvency Rules
	(3) interest rate, particularly of a derivative product
IR 35	provisions relating to personal service companies
IRA	individual retirement account
IRAM	Inland Revenue approved mileage rate
IRC	(1) Internal Revenue Code
	(2) Inland Revenue Commissioner
IRLR	Industrial Relations Law Reports
IRM	Institute of Risk Management
IRP	Independent Reconfiguration Panel
IRR	internal rate of return
IRS	Internal Revenue Service, US taxation authority
IRTC	individual resettlement training costs, in armed forces
IRU	(1) Union Internationale des Transports Routiers (International Road Transport Union) – an international trade organisation for the road transport industry.
	(2) indefeasible right of use.
IS	information systems
ISA	individual savings account
ISBN	international standard book number
ISC	immigration skills charge

ISD Investment Services Directive

ISDN (1) integrated services digital network
(2) income support deduction notice

ISG Intermarket Surveillance Group

ISIN international securities identification number

ISLA International Securities Lending Association

ISM Institute of Supply Management

ISMA International Securities and Markets Association

ISO International Organization for Standardization, which issues codes for currencies and similar

ISPV insurance special purpose vehicle

ISSN international standard serial number, given to publications

IT (1) country prefix code for Italy
(2) information technology

ITA (1) Income Tax Act 2007
(2) intelligent telephone automation

ITCLR intention to create legal relations, a condition for a contract

ITDLO international trade development liaison officer

ITEPA Income Tax (Earnings and Pensions) Act 2003

ITLR International Tax Law Reports

ITP (1) international trade prototype
(2) illicit trade protocol

ITR individual turnover report

ITS intermarket trading system

ITSA income tax self-assessment

ITT invitation to tender

ITTOIA Income Tax (Trading and Other Income) Act 2005

IVA (1) individual voluntary agreement
(2) invalidity addition, to certain state benefits
(3) Imposta sul valore Aggiunto, Italian for "value added tax".
(4) Imposto sobre o Valor Ascrescentado, Portuguese for "value added tax".
(5) Impuesto sobre el Valor Anadidio, Spanish for "value added tax"

IWC in-work credit

iXBRL inline extensible business reporting language

IYR in-year revenue

J (1) judge, or justice
(2) journal

J5 UK, Australia, Canada, Netherlands and USA, formed as a body in 2018 to gather tax intelligence

J$ Jamaican dollar

JAM	just about managing
JBL	Journal of Business Law
JC	Justiciary Cases, Scottish law repots
JCCC	Joint Customs Consultative Committee
JCT	form of contract for building contracts
JCVI	Joint Committee on Vaccination and Immunisation
JD	Jordanian dinar
JDI	just do it
JEB	Judicial Executive Board
JGB	Japanese government bond
JISA	junior individual savings account
JIT	just in time
Jnr	junior
JP	(1) justice of the peace
	(2) series of law reports
JPA	joint personnel administration
JR	judicial review
JRC	Jersey Royal Court
JSA	jobseeker's allowance
JSP	Joint Service Publication
JSS	Job Support Scheme
JST	joint supervisory team
JTASSG	Joint Tax Agent Strategy Steering Group
JV	joint venture
JVCC	Joint VAT Consultative Committee
K	(1) tax code where taxable pay is greater than gross pay
	(2) thousand
KBC	Dutch bank
KBD	King's Bench Division, part of High Court during the reign of a king
Kc	korun or koruna, currency of the Czech Republic
KD	Kuwaiti dinar
KDB	knowledge development box
KIA	killed in action
KIBOR	Karachi interbank offered rate
KM	convertible mark, currency of Bosnia and Hercegovina
Km	kilometre, kilometres
KMC	kerosene marker concentrate
KPI	key performance indicator
Kr	Icelandic kronur
kWh	kilowatt hour

kyc	know your customer
L	Roman numeral for 50
L£	Lebanese pound
LA	levy allowance
LAA	Legal Aid Agency
LAEF	lifetime allowance enhancement factor
LAGB	Linguistics Association of Great Britain
LAPFF	Local Authority Pension Fund Forum
LAPR	life assurance premium relief
LASAAC	Local Authority (Scotland) Accounts Advisory Committee
lb	pound in weight
LBG	Lloyd's Banking Group
LBM	London Bullion Market
LBMA	London Bullion Markets Association
LBO	leveraged buyout
LBTT	land and buildings transaction tax, in Scotland
LC	(1) Lord Chancellor
	(2) local compliance
L/C	letter of credit
LCE	London Community Exchange
LCH	London Clearing House
LCJ	Lord Chief Justice
LCL	less than a container load
LCM	(1) lower of cost or market
	(2) Legislative Consent Motion, of Scottish Parliament
LCP	Local Clearance Procedure, for Customs
LD	Libyan dinar
LDC	least developed country
LDF	Liechtenstein Disclosure Facility
LDPE	low density polythene
LDT	(1) land disposals tax
	(2) licensed deposit taker
Le	leone, currency of Sierra Leone
LEC	(1) Local Export Control, Customs term
	(2) low emissions certificate
LECD	Landelijk Expertise Centrum Diversiteit, National Expertise Centre for Diversity, Netherlands.
LED	light emitting diode
LEL	lower earnings limit, for national insurance
LETB	Local Education and Training Board

LFR	live facial recognition
LFS	Living Costs and Food Survey
LFT	landfill tax
LGBT	lesbian, gay, bisexual and transgender
LGC	Laboratory of the Government Chemist
LGR	Butterworth's Local Government Reports
LHA	local housing allowance
LIBOR	London Interbank Offered Rate
LIC	local import control
LIFFE	London International Financial Futures and Options Exchange
LIFO	last in first out, method of stock valuation
LIT	life interest trust
LITRG	Low Incomes Tax Reform Group
LJ	(1) Lord Justice of Appeal
	(2) Law Journal Newspaper County Court Reports
LJ(OS)	Law Journal Old Series law reports
Lk	lek, currency of Albania
LL	lower limit
LLA	long-life assets
LL B	Bachelor of Law degree
LLC	(1) local land charges
	(2) limited liability company
LL D	Doctor of Law degree
LLM	HMRC Manual on Lloyd's insurance market
LL M	Master of Law degree
LLP	limited liability partnership
LME	London Metal Exchange
LMIL	London Market Information Link
LMO	London Mint Office
LMS	learning management system
LNA	liquidity needs analysis
LNG	liquid natural gas
LO	local office, of DVLA
LOCOG	London Organising Committee of the Olympic Games Ltd
LOI	lost on ignition
LoU	letter of undertaking
LP	limited partnership
LPA	(1) lasting power of attorney
	(2) local planning authority
LPG	liquid petroleum gas
LPOG	HMRC Manual on labour provider guidance

LPP	legal professional privilege
LPS	local pharmaceutical services, in NJHS
LR	(1) listing rules
	(2) Law reports
LRC	Law Reports of the Commonwealth
LRMA	lower relevant maximum amount, for corporation tax
LRR	land remediation relief
LRS	Learning Records Service
LRT	lower rate tax
LS	locus sigilli
LSC	Learning and Skills Council
LSD	old term for pounds, shillings and pence
LSE	(1) London Stock Exchange
	(2) London School of Economics
LSS	Litigation and Settlement Strategy, HMRC policy
LT	(1) country prefix for Lithuania
	(2) life tenant, of a trust
	(3) Law Times Reports
LTAHAW	living together as husband and wife
LTC	long-term care, insurance term
ltd	limited, or limited company
LTICR	long-term insurance capital requirement
LTIP	long-term incentive plan
LTT	land transaction tax
LTV	loan to value, mortgage term
LU	country prefix for Luxembourg
LV	(1) country prefix for Latvia
	(2) luncheon voucher
LVL	low vision leaflet
LVT	leasehold valuation tribunal
LY	last year
M	Roman numeral for 1,000
M0	measure of narrow money, notes and coins in circulation
M1	(1) measure of money, namely M0 plus overnight deposits
	(2) indication that a tax code is used on a month 1 basis
M2	measure of money, comprising M1 plus short-term deposits
M3	measure of money, comprising M2 plus debt securities and some other instruments
M4	measure of money, comprising M3 and all bank and similar deposits
MA	(1) Master of Arts degree

	(2) Marketing Authorisation
M&A	mergers and acquisitions
MAC	membership audit certificate
MACD	moving average convergence/divergence
MAD	(1) Market Abuse Directive
	(2) mean absolute deviation
MAFF	Ministry of Agriculture, Fisheries and Food, now part of DEFRA
MAFR	mandatory audit firm rotation
MAIB	Marine Accident Investigation Branch
MAMA	Models and Managers Association
MAPPA	Multi-Agency Police Protection Arrangements
MAR	(1) mileage allowance rate
	(2) Market Conduct sourcebook
MARD	Mutual Assistance Recovery Directive
MAWB	master air waybill
max-fac	maximum facilitation, term used in Brexit negotiations
MB	megabytes
MBI	management buy-in
MBO	management buyout
MBS	mortgage-backed security
MC	minimum contribution, to a pension fund
MCAS	Mortgage Code Arbitration Scheme
MCD	miscellaneous cash deposit
MCOB	Mortgages and Home Finance: Conduct of Business sourcebook
MCR	minimum capital requirement
MCSI	Member of the Chartered Institute for Securities and Investment
MCT	mainstream corporation tax
MD	managing director
MDA	Misuse of Drugs Acy 1971
MDB	multilateral development bank
MDD	Managing Deliberate Defaulters
MDR	Misuse of Drugs Regulations 2001
m/e	month ending
Meg	Megone's Company Cases
MEGS	Music Export Growth Scheme
MEP	Member of the European Parliament
Mer	Merivale's Reports
MERV	minimum efficiency reporting value
MFDS	more frequent data sharing, by Student Loans Company
MFET Ltd	company set up by Department of Health to make payments to AIDS victims
mfg	manufacturing

MFI	money flow index
MFR	minimum funding requirement
MGA	ariary, currency of Madagascar
MGO	marked gas oil
MGP	manufactured gas plant
MHCLG	Ministry for Housing, Communities and Local Government
MHRA	Medicines and Healthcare products Regulatory Agency
MI	myocardial infarction, used on sick notes
MIA	missing in action
MIB	(1) Motor Insurers Bureau
	(2) merchandise in baggage
MIC	marker identification code
MICEX	stock exchange, recognised by HMRC in 2011
MID	Measuring Instruments Directive
MIF	minimum income floor
MiFID	European directive on markets in financial instruments
MIG	minimum income guarantee
MIIC	Motor Insurers' Information Centre
MILA	Integrated Latin American Market
MILE	maximum impact, little effort
MIME	multipurpose mail extensions
MIRAS	mortgage interest relief at source
MIT	(1) minimum income threshold
	(2) market-if-touched
MKO	marked kerosene
MLA	Member of the Legislative Assembly, of Northern Ireland
MLAR	Mortgage Lending and Administration Return
MLC	Meat and Livestock Commission
MLR	various HMRC tax manuals on money laundering
MLRO	money laundering reporting officer
MMA	married man's allowance
MMC	(1) Money Markets Committee, of Bank of England
	(2) Monopolies and Mergers Commission, now abolished
MMO	Marine Management Organisation
MMS	(1) mineralised methylated spirits
	(2) multi-media messaging service
MNE	multi-national enterprise
MNI	Ministry of National Insurance, now abolished
MO	modus operandi
MOC	market-on-close
MOD	(1) Ministry of Defence

	(2) manufactured overseas dividend
MoM	month on month
MOO	(1) market-on-opening
	(2) mutuality of obligation
MOP$	pataca, currency of Macau
MOQ	minimum order quantity
Mor	Morrison's Decisions, law reports
MORC	Minerals Oil Relief Centre, part of HMRC
MOSS	mini one stop shop, used for VAT
MOT	annual test required for most road vehicles
MOTPO	mechanical output, total power output, climate change levy term
MOU	memorandum of understanding
MP	(1) Member of Parliament
	(2) misdeclaration penalty
	(3) military police
MPA	Major Projects Authority
MPAA	money purchase annual allowance
MPC	marginal propensity to consume
mpg	miles per gallon
mph	miles per hour
MPR	monthly progress report
MPS	Metropolitan Police Service
Mr	title used for adult man
MR	(1) Master of the Rolls, senior judge in Court of Appeal
	(2) main rate, of corporation tax
	(3) ringgit, currency of Malaysia
	(4) mutual recognition
MRO	(1) market rent only
	(2) maintenance, repair and operations
MRP	maximum retail price
Mrs	title used by a married or widowed woman
MS	multiple sclerosis, term used on sick notes
Ms	title used by woman who does not wish to identify as to whether married
ms	manuscript
M&S	(1) Maule and Selwyn's law reports
	(2) Marks and Spencer, supermarket chain
MSB	money services business
MSC	management service company
MSc	master of science degree
MSCI	index of world share prices produced by Morgan Stanley Capital International

MSF	most similar forces, military term
MSOD	monthly statement of select operational data
MSP	Member of the Scottish Parliament
MT	(1) country prefix code for Malta
	(2) new metical, currency of Mozambique
	(3) empty, used to identify cylinder of other container
MTA	mirrored terms agreement
$MtCO_2$	million tons of carbon dioxide
MTD	(1) Making Tax Digital
	(2) month to date
MTF	multilateral trading facility
MTIC	missing trade intra-community fraud, VAT offence
MRM	mark to market
MTN	medium-term note
MUC	mini umbrella company
MUUT	mixed unauthorised unit trust
MV	(1) motor vehicle
	(2) market value
MV82	market value as at 1982, capital gains tax term
MVL	members' voluntary liquidation
MVNO	mobile virtual network operator
M&W	Meeson and Welsby law reports
MWC	managerial working capital
MWE	married women's election, for national insurance
Mx	title used by people who do not wish to identify their sex
My & Cr	Mylne and Craig's law reports
N	atomic symbol for nitrogen
NACE	statistical classification under an EU regulation, used for capital allowances
NACUE	National Association of College and University Entrepreneurs
NAD	no abnormality detected, term used on sick notes
NADFAS	National Association of Decorative and Fine Arts Societies
NAEA	National Association of Estate Agents
NAFD	National Association of Funeral Directors
NAFTA	North American Free Trade Association
NAIC	National Association of Investors Corporation
NALC	National Association of Local Councils
NAO	National Audit Office
NAPF	National Association of Pension Funds
NAPM	National Association of Purchasing Management
NAREIT	National Association of Real Estate Investment Trusts, US body

NAS National Advice Service, part of HMRC
NASD National Association of Securities Dealers
NASDAQ National Association of Securities Dealers Automated Quotation system
NASES National Association of Student Employment Services
NATO North Atlantic Treaty Organisation
NAV net asset value
NAVC National Approval and Verification Centre, for excise warehousing
NAWI Non-Automatic Weighing Instructions directive
nb nota bene, Latin for note well
NBV net book value
NC Nomenclature Committee
NCA National Crime Agency
NCB no claims bonus, in insurance
NCBO no change in beneficial ownership
NCCT non-cooperating country or territory
NCDR non-corporate distribution rate
NCH National Clearance Hub
NCIS National Criminal Intelligence Service
NCS National Crime Squad
NCSC National Cyber Security Centre
NCTS (1) New Community Transit System
(2) New Computerised Transit System
ND (1) North Dakota, USA
(2) non-discrimination
NDA (1) non-disclosure agreement
(2) Nuclear Decommissioning Agency
NDPB non-departmental public body
NEA new enterprise allowance
NEM New Employment Model
nem con nemine contradicente, Latin for no-one saying otherwise
nem dis nemine dissentiente, Latin for none dissenting
NES (1) National Export System (from 2007)
(2) New Export System (before 2007)
(3) Needs Enhanced Support, part of HMRC
NEST National Employment Savings Trust
NESTA National Endowment for Science, Technology and the Arts
NETA New Electricity Trading Arrangements
NEPT non-established taxable person
NEU National Education Union
NEUUT non-exempt unauthorised unit trust
NFA National Futures Association

NFFC	National Film Finance Corporation
NFI	National Fraud Initiative
Nfk	nafka, currency of Eritrea
NFO	new fund offer
NFPI	National Family and Parenting Institute
NFTS	National Film and Television School
NGFS	Network for Greening the Financial System
NH	new holding
NHS	(1) National Health Service
	(2) nugatory health expenditure, in armed forces
NI	(1) national insurance
	(2) Northern Ireland
NIA	Northern Ireland Assembly
NIAUR	Northern Ireland Authority for Utility Regulation
NIC	(1) national insurance contribution
	(2) National Infrastructure Commission
NICA	National Insurance Contributions Act 2014
NIC&EO	National Insurance Contributions and Employer Office, part of HMRC
NICT	Northern Ireland corporation tax
NID	Iraqi dinar
NIDAC	National Import Duty Adjustment Centre
NIE	Northern Ireland Executive
NIF	note issuance facility
NIHP	National Institute for Health Protection
NII	net interest income
NIM	(1) HMRC Manual on national insurance
	(2) net interest margin
NIP	(1) non-investment product
	(2) notice of intended prosecution, for motoring offence
NIR	Northern Ireland rate
NIRE	Northern Ireland regional establishment
NIRU	National Imports Relief Unit
NIS	new Israeli shekel
NIT	negative income tax
NL	country prefix code for Netherlands
NLGS	National Loan Guarantee Scheme
NLJ	New Law Journal
NLW	national living wage
NMD	non-ministerial department
NMRO	National Measurement and Regulation Office
NMS	normal market size

NMT	new means of transport
NMW	national minimum wage
NMWM	HMRC Manual on national minimum wage
NNP	non-natural person, such as a company or trust
NNTO	no need to open
No	number
NOA	net operating assets
NOI	net operating income
NOK	next of kin
NOL	notice of liability
NOMAD	nominated adviser
NOPAT	net operating profit after tax
NOPL	notice of potential liability
NOR	not ordinarily resident
Nov	November
NOVA	notice of vehicle arrivals
NP	no problem
NPA	(1) normal pension age
	(2) non-performing asset
NPG	natural petroleum gas
NPIA	National Policing Improvement Agency
NPL	non-performing loan
NPO	non-profit organisation
NPR	number of pieces received
NPV	(1) net present value
	(2) no par value
NPX	number of pieces expected
NRA	(1) normal retirement age
	(2) National Roads Authority, Irish body
NRB	nil rate band, of inheritance tax
NRBW	National Resources Body for Wales
NRCGT	non-resident capital gains tax
NRCL	non-resident corporate landlord
NRD	(1) normal retirement date
	(2) non-financial reporting directive
NRE	net relevant earnings
NRV	(1) net realisable value
	(2) net residual value
NSB	National Savings Bank
NSC	National Savings Certificate
NS&I	National Savings and Investments

NSM	non-smoking material
NSND	non-savings, non-dividend
NSPCC	National Society for Protection of Cruelty to Children
NSR	national insurance contributions settlement return
NSWLR	New South Wales Law Reports
NSWR	New South Wales Reports
NT	tax code indicating that no tax is to be deducted
NT$	New Taiwan dollar
NTBs	non-tariff barriers
NTC	national tax credits
NTE	not to exceed
NTI	net taxable income
NTO	national training obligation
NTPI	net taxable pension income
NTSI	net taxable specific income
Nu	ngultrum, currency of Bhutan
NURS	non-UCITS retail fund
NV	Naamioze Vennootschap, a Dutch company.
NVQ	national vocational qualification
NVR	national insurance verification request
NW	North Western Reporter
NWTSG	National Working Together Steering Group
NWTT	National Working Together Team, part of HMRC
NYBOT	New York Board of Transport
NYD	not yet diagnosed, use on sick notes
NYMEX	New York Mercantile Exchange
NYSE	New York Stock Exchange
NZ$	New Zealand dollar
NZBLC	New Zealand Business Law Cases
NZCLC	New Zealand Company Law Cases
NZLR	New Zealand Law Reports
O	(1) order, in legal judgments
	(2) tax code used before 1973
OA	osteoarthritis, used on sick notes
oao	on account of
OAP	old age pensioner
OARS	Opening Automated Reporting Service
OBD	Office of Budget and Delivery
OBR	Office of Budget Responsibility
OC	opportunity cost

OCC	Options Clearing Corporation
OCD	Officers' Career Development, in armed forces
OCF	operating cashflow
OCG	organised criminal group
OCI	other comprehensive income
OCNS	Office of Civil Nuclear Safety
OCO	one cancels other
OCR	optical character recognition
OCT	overseas countries and territories
Oct	October
OD	overdraft
ODA	official development assistance
ODPM	Office of the Deputy Prime Minister
ODS	ozone depleting substances
OECD	Organization for Economic Co-operation and Development
OEEC	Organisation of European Economic Co-operation
OEIC	open-ended investment company
OEM	original equipment manufacturer
OFCOM	Office of Communications
OFEX	Independent stock exchange
Ofgem	Office and Gas Electricity Markets
OFI	Office for Investment
OFM	HMRC Manual on offshore funds
OFSI	Office of Financial Sanctions Implementation
OFMDFM	Office of the First Minister and Deputy First Minister, in Northern Ireland
OfS	Office for Students
OFSTED	Office for Standard in Education
OFT	Office of Fair Trading, now abolished
OfTI	Office for Tackling Injustices
OG	original gravity, of beer
OGA	Oil and Gas Authority
OGDs	other government departments, term used by Customs
OI	other interest
OIBDA	operating income before depreciation and amortisation
OIE	overnight incidental expenditure
OIM	Office of the Internal Market
OIML	Organisation of Legal Metrology
OISC	Office of the Immigration Services Commissioner
OJEC	Office Journal of the European Communities
OKR	objectives and key results
OLC	Office for Legal Complaints

OLEV	Office of Low Emission Vehicles
O&M	organisation and management
OMB	Office of Management and Board, US body
OML	occupational maternity leave
OMP	occupational maternity pay
OMRLP	Official Monster Raving Loony Party
OMS	other member state, of the European Union
O/N	overnight
ONSCG	HMRC Manual on other non-statutory clearance guidance
OOO	out of office
OPAS	Occupational Pension Advisory Service, now Pensions Advisory Service
OPB	Occupational Pensions Board
OPBAS	Office for Professional Body Anti-Money Laundering Supervision
op cit	the book previously cited
OPEC	Organisation of Petroleum Exporting Countries
OPEX	operating expenditure, operational expenditure
OPLR	Occupational Pension Law Reports
OPR	onward processing relief, for Customs duty
OPRA	Occupational Pensions Regulatory Authority
OpRA	optional remuneration arrangement
OPREC	overpayment recovery, HMRC computer term
OPS	(1) occupational pension scheme
	(2) operational planning system
OPT	outward processing trade
OR	(1) ordinary residence
	(2) operational research
ORR	Office of Rail Regulation
ORS	open, random and support, modern form of management
O/S	outstanding
OSHA	Occupational Safety and Health Administration, in USA
OSP	occupational sick pay
osp	obit sine prole, Latin for died without issue
OSPP	ordinary statutory paternity pay
OSR	overseas scale rate
OT	(1) overtime
	(2) HMRC Manual on oil taxation
OTA	Oil Taxation Act 1975
OTC	(1) Operations Tariff Classification
	(2) over the counter
OTIF	on time in full

OTR	(1) orchestra tax relief
	(2) HMRC Manual on orchestra tax relief
OTRS	online tax registration scheme
OTS	Office of Thrift Supervision, US government department
OVA	Office of Veterans' Affairs
oz	ounce(s)
P	(1) National insurance contribution letter for mariner under 21 with deferred contributions
	(2) pula, currency of Botswana
	(3) Philippine peso
p	(1) penny, pence
	(2) page
P2B	platform to business
P2P	peer to peer
PA	(1) per annum, i.e. per year
	(2) personal assistant
	(3) public addresss, amplification system
	(4) purchasing agent
PACAC	Public Administration and Constitutional Affairs Committee, of MPs
PACE	Police and Criminal Evidence Act 1984
PAH	polycyclic aromatic hydrocarbon
PAIF	property authorised investment fund
PAP	production account point
PAR	Practice Assurance Regulations
para	paragraph
PAS	(1) pipeline adjustment statement
	(2) Planning Advisory Service
	(3) penalties and appeals system
PAT	profit after tax
PAYE	Pay As You Earn
PAYG	pay as you go
Pb	atomic symbol for lead
PBD	pool betting duty
PBEC	Pacific Basin Economic Council
PBF	planning, budgeting and forecasting
PBGC	Pension Benefit Guaranty Corporation
PBIK	payrolling benefits in kind
PBIT	profit before interest and tax
PBL	parental bereavement leave
PBR	(1) pre-Budget review

	(2) plant breeders' rights
PBT	profit before tax
PC	(1) personal computer
	(2) Privy Council
	(3) pension credit
	(4) Police Constable
PCA	personal current account
PCAOB	Public Company Accounting Oversight Board
PCB	Pensions Compensation Board
PCC	(1) processing under Customs control for free circulation
	(2) Police and Crime Commissioner
	(3) parochial church council
PCDN	post clearance demand note
PCF	Police Consultative Forum
PCLS	pension commencement lump sum
PCm	HMRC Manual on personal contact
PCO	primary care organisation, in the National Health Service
PCPI	private company price index
PC&R	Property and Compensation Reports
PCRT	Professional Conduct in Relation to Taxation
PCS	Parliamentary Commissioner for Standards
PCSO	Police Community Support Officer
PCT	primary care trust, in National Health Service
PCTR	post-cessation trade relif
PCU	professional court user
PD	(1) personnel development
	(2) Probate Division law reports
	(3) Prospectus Directive
P&D	Probate and Family law report
PDA	(1) personal digital assistant
	(2) Probate, Divorce and Admiralty, old division of High Court
PDBD	pay day by day
PDDD	publishing details of deliberate defaulters
PDMR	person discharging managerial responsibilities
PDP	personal development portfolio
PDR	(1) personal development review, particularly in police
	(2) personnel development record, in armed forces
PE	(1) permanent establishment
	(2) partial exemption, for VAT
	(3) private equity
P/E	price/earnings ratio

PEACE	prepare and plan, engage, account, challenge, explain. Traditional interview technique
PEACH	system for electronic application of certificates by Rural Payments Agency
PED	PIN entry device
PEFF	property-embedded fixtures and fittings
PEG	price to earnings growth ratio
PENP	post-employment notice pay
PEP	personal equity plan
PEPP	pan-European personal pension
PERG	Perimeter Guidance manual of Financial Conduct Authority
PES	personal export scheme
PET	potentially exempt transfer, for inheritance tax
PETA	People for the Ethical Treatment of Animals
PEX	public expenditure
PFEW	Public Federation of England and Wales
PFFI	participating foreign financial institution
PFI	private finance initiative
PG	(1) Professional Group, that discusses tax matters with HMRC (2) present gravity, for beer duty (3) personal guarantee
PGL	postgraduate loan
PGS	person who has given security for PAYE
pH	measure of acidity
PHE	Public Health England
PHMC	plant health movement certificate
PHSI	Public Health and Seeds Inspectorate
PI	proprietor's interest
PIA	Personal Investment Authority
PIBOR	Paris interbank offered rate
PIBS	permanent interest bearing shares
PIC	prior informed consent
PICNIC	problem in chair, not in computer
PID	prolapsed intervertebral disc, used on sick notes
PIDA	Public Interest Disclosure Act 1998
PIE	(1) personal incidental expenses (2) public interest entity
PII	professional indemnity insurance
PIM	HMRC Manual on property income
PIP	(1) pension input period (2) personal independence payment (3) protected investment product

PIR	post-implementation review
PIS	(1) perpetual inventory system
	(2) payment initiation service
PISA	OECD programme for international student assistance
PIU	Public Interest Unit, part of office of Official Receiver
PIW	period of incapacity for work, for statutory sick pay
P&L	profit and loss
PL	country prefix code for Poland
plc	public limited company
PLN	(1) penalty liability notice
	(2) personal liability notice
PLR	(1) Estate Gazette Planning Law Reports
	(2) potential lost revenue
	(3) public lending right
PLU	price look up code
PM	(1) prime minister
	(2) particulate matter
	(3) project management
pm	post meridian, afternoon
PMA	plant and machinery allowance
PMAC	period moving average cost
PMI	(1) performance market indicator
	(2) purchasing manager's index
PNR	passenger number reference
PNT	position, navigation and timing
PO	(1) Post Office
	(2) profit objective
	(3) purchase order
POA	(1) pre-owned asset
	(2) price on application
POAO	products of animal origin
POB	Professional Oversight Board
POCA	Proceeds of Crime Act 2004
POD	payment on demand
POEM	place of effective management
POP	permanent overpayment
POS	point of sale
POTAM	Panel on Takeovers and Mergers
POTAS	promoter of tax avoidance scheme
POTUS	President of the United States
PP	(1) personal pension

	(2) product placement
pp	per pro
PPA	(1) Professional Publishers Association
	(2) power purchase agreement
PPBS	planning programming budget system
PPC	prescription prepayment certificate
PPD	prompt payment discount
PPE	(1) plant, property and equipment
	(2) politics, philosophy and economics, university course
	(3) personal protective equipment
PPERA	Political Parties, Elections and Referendums Act 2000
PPF	Pension Protection Fund
PPFM	Principles and Practices of Financial Management
PPI	(1) protection plan insurance
	(2) Pensions Policy Institute
PPIA	protected pension input amount
PPIAFRC	payment protection insurance additional fully reportable countries
ppl	pence per litre
PPOB	principal place of business
PPP	(1) personal pension plan
	(2) purchasing power parity
	(3) public private partnership
	(4) purchasing power parity
	(5) public-private partnership
PPS	Police Pension Scheme
PPV	pay per view
PQE	post-qualification experience
PR	(1) personal representative
	(2) Prospectus Rules handbook
	(3) public relations
	(4) proportional representation
	(5) purchase requisition
PRA	(1) Prudential Regulation Authority
	(2) position risk adjustment, insurance term
PRAG	Pensions Research Action Group
PRAU	Performance Reporting and Analysis Unit, of Home Office
PRBC	pre-return banding check, for annual tax on enveloped dwellings
PRIF	Plastic Research Innovation Fund
PRN	packaging waste recovery note
PRO	Excise Duties (Personal Reliefs) Order 1992
PROF	Professional Firms sourcebook, of Financial Conduct Authority

PRP	profit-related pay
PRR	(1) private residence relief
	(2) position risk requirement
PRS	(1) premium rate services, telephone term
	(2) Performing Rights Society
PRSA	personal retirement savings account
PRT	petroleum revenue tax
PRTA	Petroleum Revenue Tax Act 1980
PRU	(1) Police Resources Unit
	(2) Integrated Prudential sourcebook
PSA	(1) PAYE settlement agreement
	(2) Pension Schemes Act 1993
	(3) public service agreement
	(4) personal savings allowance
	(5) pension scheme administrator
	(6) HMRC Manual on PAYE settlement agreements
PSAA	Public Sector Audit Appointments Ltd
PSBR	public sector borrowing requirement
PSC	(1) person with significant control
	(2) personal service company
PSE	public sector entity
PSNB	public sector net borrowing
PSNI	Pharmaceutical Society of Northern Ireland
PSO	Pension Schemes Office
PSP	performance share plan
PSR	price to sales ratio
PST	Pacific Standard Time, in USA
PSV	passenger service vehicle
PT	(1) primary threshold, for national insurance
	(2) country prefix code for Portugal
	(3) prescribed territories
Pt	(1) Part, of an Act of Parliament
	(2) atomic symbol for platinum
	(3) point, particular as a type size
PTA	(1) Prevention of Terrorism (Temporary Provisions) Act 1989
	(2) personal tax account
	(3) parent teacher association
PTM	(1) Panel on Takeovers and Mergers
	(2) HMRC Manual on pensions tax
PTO	(1) Pupillage Training Organisation, for barristers
	(2) please turn over

	(3) project to date
PTRAS	pension tax relief at source
PTSP	Plumbers Safe Tax Plan
PTVC	post transaction value check
Pty	proprietary company, US term
PUO	pyrexia of unknown origin, term for sick notes
PV	(1) present value
	(2) photovoltaic, pertaining to solar panels
PVD	Principal VAT Directive
PVE	payment via employer
PVGS	Protection of Vulnerable Groups Scheme in Scotland
PVM	Pridetines vertes mokestis, Lithuanian for "value added tax"
PVR	plant variety rights
PVRO	Plant Variety Rights Office
PVS	permanent vegetative state
PWC	post-war credit
PwC	Name now used by accounting firm PriceWaterhouse Coopers
PWLB	Public Works Loan Board
P Wms	Peere Williams' law reports
PYA	prior year adjustment

Q	question
Q1	first quarter
Q2	second quarter
Q3	third quarter
Q4	fourth quarter
QA	quality assurance
QAD	Quality Assurance Department
QB	Queen's Bench Division, of High Court
QBD	Queen's Bench Division, of High Court
QC	(1) Queen's Counsel
	(2) prefixes to paragraphs in chapter 3 of the conceptual framework of International Financial Reporting Standards
	(3) quality control
QCB	qualifying corporate bond
QCF	Qualifications and Credit Framework
QE	qualifying expenditure
QED	quod erat demonstrandum, Latin for "which was to be demonstrated"
QEF	qualifying earnings factor
QI	qualifying intermediary
QIIP	qualifying interest in possession

QIP	quarterly instalment payment, of corporation tax
QIS	qualified investor scheme
QLR	qualifying loan relationship
QOPS	qualifying overseas pension scheme
QOQ	quarter on quarter
QRC	quarantine release certificate
QR	Quick Response, pattern of black squares that can be read by a mobile phone
QRM	Quick Response Mechanism
QROPS	qualifying recognised overseas pension scheme
QRP	qualifying residual profit
QST	Quebec sales tax
QTD	quarter to date
QUEST	qualifying employment share trust
R	(1) rex (king) or regina (queen), as used in court case citations
	(2) reinfection rate of coronavirus and other diseases
	(3) Indian rupee
	(4) Nepalese rupee
	(5) rand, currency of South Africa
r	(1) figure used to calculate climate change levy
	(2) radius
R$	real, currency of Brazil
RA	(1) recovered amount
	(2) reciprocal agreement
	(3) residents association, ratepayers association
RAC	(1) retirement annuity contract
	(2) Royal Automobile Club
RAD	Royal Association for Deaf People
RADA	Royal Academy of Drama and Art
RAG	regulated activity group
RAP	rupees, annas and pies, old currency of India
RAS	relief at source
RAT	rate applicable to trusts
RAVTPA	relevant accounting value of third party acquisitions
RBA	Reserve Bank of Australia
RBI	Reserve Bank of India
RBS	Royal Bank of Scotland
RCA	(1) readily convertible asset
	(2) root cause analysis
RCB	Regulated Covered Bond sourcebook
RCEP	Regional Comprehensive Economic Partnership

RCH	recognised clearing house
RCMM	registered competitive market maker, US term
RCPO	Revenue and Customs Prosecution Office
RCS	(1) receipts clearing system, part of HMRC
	(2) regulated capital securities
RCTU	Revenue and Customs Trade Union
RD	refer to drawer, banking term
R/D	refer to drawer, banking term
R&D	research and development
RD$	Dominican Republic peso
RDC	Regulatory Decisions Committee
RDCO	registered dealer in controlled oil
RDE	real world driving emissions
RDEC	research and development expenditure credit
RDPR	refer to drawer, please re-present
RDRM	HMRC Manual on residence, domicile and remittance basis
RDS	relevant discounted security
RE	(1) residual expenditure
	(2) retained earnings
REA	relevant earnings amount
REC	(1) Recognised Investment Exchange and Recognised Clearing House sourcebook
	(2) Recruitment and Employment Confederation
	(3) renewable energy certificate
REDCENT	Accounting Centre for Registered Excise Dealers and Shippers
REQAE	HMRC Manual on requesting assistance in relation to excise
RES	(1) retail export scheme
	(2) race equality scheme
RESA	Regulatory Enforcement and Sanctions Act 2008
RESACE	HMRC Manual on responding to requests for co-operation in excise
REX	registered exporter scheme
RFC	released for free circulation
RFI	request for information
RFU	Rugby Football Union
RFTU	road fuel testing unit
RGA	Remote Gambling Association#
RGD	remote gaming duty
RGR	returned goods relief
RHA	Road Haulage Association
RHDI	real household disposable income
RHI	Renewable Heat Incentive

RI	(1) Republic of Ireland
	(2) Revenue Interpretation
RIBA	Royal Institute of British Architects
RIDDOR	Reporting of Injuries, Diseases and Dangerous Occurrence Regulations SI 2013 No 1471
RIE	recognised investment exchange
RIF	(1) risk information form
	(2) realistic imitation firearm
RIH	right ingual hernia, found on sick notes
RILOR	recompense in lieu of relocation, in armed forces
RIPI	relevant intellectual property income
RIS	regulatory information service
RM	HMRC Manual on repayment claims
RMAR	Retail Medication Activities Return
RMB	remnimbi, a currency of China
RMBS	residential mortgage-backed security
RMP	(1) remote marking premises
	(2) repeated misdeclaration penalty
RMPP	Royal Mail Pension Plan
RNG	random number generator
RNIB	Royal National Institute for Blind People
RNLI	Royal National Lifeboat Association
RNRB	residence nil rate band
RO	country prefix code for Romania
ROA	return on assets
ROAS	return on ad spend
ROCE	return on capital employed
ROCH	recognised overseas clearing house
ROCU	regional organised crime unit
ROE	return on equity
ROI	return on investment
ROIC	return on invested capital
ROIE	recognised overseas investment exchange
ROL	remote operating licence
RONA	return on net assets
ROS	return on sales
RP	(1) retail price
	(2) initials used by HMRC for forename when taxpayer is not an individual
Rp	rupiah, currency of Indonesia
RPA	(1) receipts and payments account
	(2) Rural Payments Agency

	(30 responsible paying authority, for pensions
RPB	(1) recognised professional body
	(2) regional planning body
RPC	(1) reduced pollution certificate
	(2) Regulatory Policy Committee, government body
RPI	retail prices index
RPM	retail prices maintenance
RPPD	FCA regulatory guide on responsibility of providers and distributor
RPSM	HMRC Manual on registered pension schemes
RQF	regulated qualifications framework
RR(A)A	Race Relations (Amendment) Act 2000
RRMPR	Registered Remote Marking Premises Regulations 2002
RRR	rural rate relief
RS	repayment supplement
RSC	Rules of the Supreme Court
RSE	renewable source energy
RSRB	regulated sale and rent back
RSL	registered social landlord
RSP	retail selling price
RSS	really simple syndication
RSTPA	Revenue Scotland and Tax Powers Act 2014
RSU	restricted stock units
RTAR	Revenue Traders (Accounts and Records) Regulations 1992
RTC	requirement to correct
RTE	right to collective enforcement, of a leasehold
RTFO	Renewable Transport Fuels Obligation
RTI	real time information, of PAYE
RTL	Repayment of Teacher's Loan scheme
RTM	right to manage, type of company
RTP	registered tobacco premises
RTR	Revenue Traders (Accounts and Records) Regulations 1992
RTWDV	relevant tax written down value
rUK	rest of UK
RV	rateable value
RVF	relevant valuation factor
RVI	referral of vision impairment
RVM	reverse vending machine
RWA	risk weighted average
S	(1) Shaw, Scottish law reports
	(2) south

s	(1) section, particularly of an Act of Parliament
	(2) shilling
S£	Syrian pound
S$	(1) Singapore dollar
	(2) tala, currency of Samoa
S2P	state second pension
SA	(1) self-assessment
SAAD	simplified administration accompanying document
SAARC	South Asian Association for Regional Cooperation
SAAS	Student Awards Agency Scotland
SAB	Safeguarding Adults Board
SAC	Summary Appeal Court
SAD	single administrative document
SAFE	Strategic Accounting Framework, of HMRC computer
SAIL	single alternative inspection location
SAIM	HMRC Manual on savings and investment
SALR	South Australian law reports
SAM	social accounting matrix
SaMBA	small and micro business assessment
SAP	statutory adoption pay
SAR	suspicious activity report
SARL	Société à Responsibilité Limité. French: limited company
SAS	statement of auditing standards
SASP	single authorisation for simplified procedures
SASR	South Australian State Reports
SATR	self-assessment tax return
SAV	shares and assets valuation, department of HMRC
Sav	Savile's law reports
sav	stock at valuation
SAWS	seasonal agricultural workers scheme
SAYE	save as you earn
SB	supplementary benefit
SBA	(1) structures and buildings allowance
	(2) small business administration
SBAT	supplementary benefit appeals tribunal
SBC	(1) standard beneficiary country
	(2) small business commissioner
SBEE	Small Business, Enterprise and Employment Act 2015
SBLC	standby letter of credit
SBRR	small business rate relief
SBU	strategic business unit

SC	(1) Supreme Court
	(2) Court of Sessions law reports
SCBA	social cost benefit analysis
SCCS	social care compliance scheme
SCE	European co-operative society
SCF	Save the Children Fund
SCG	Serbia and Montenegro
SCH	secure children's home
Sch	Schedule, particularly of an Act of Parliament
SCIO	Scottish Charitable Incorporated Organisation
SCL	student of civil law
ScLR	Scottish Law Reporter
SCM	(1) state certified midwife
	(2) supply chain management
SCN	St Kitts and St Nevis
SCON	scheme contracted-out number
SCOTVEC	Scottish Vocational Education Council, now replaced
SCP	(1) single compliance process
	(2) simplified clearance procedure
SCR	senior common room
SCS	Scottish Court of Session
SCSI	small computer systems interface
SCT	small claims threshold
SCTS	Scottish Courts and Tribunal Service
SD	(1) supplementary declaration
	(2) South Dakota, USA
sd	sine die, Latin for "without a day", such as when no date has been fixed for an adjournment
SDA	service delivery agreement
SDBL	sight draft bill of lading
SDC	supervision, direction and control
SDI	(1) simplified declaration of imports
	(2) strategic defence initiative
SDIL	soft drinks industry levy
SDL	share and deposit liabilities
SDLP	Social and Democratic Labour Party, Northern Ireland political party
SDLT	stamp duty land tax
SDLTM	HMRC Manual on stamp duty land tax
SDMA	Stamp Duties Management Act 1891
SDP	simplified declaration procedure
SDR	(1) special drawing rights

	(2) Spirit Drinks Regulations 2008
SDRT	stamp duty reserve tax
SDSL	Symmetric Digital Subscriber Line
SDVS	Spirit Drinks Verification Scheme
SDW	simplified declaration warehouse
SE	(1) south east
	(2) Societas Europaea, form of company
	(3) country prefix code for Sweden
	(4) stock exchange
	(5) Society of Engineers
SEA	Single European Authorisation
SEAC	School Examination and Assessment Council
SEAQ	Stock Exchange Automated Quotation system
SEC	Securities and Exchange Commission, of USA
sec	(1) second, measurement of time
	(2) section
	(3) secretary
SECR	streamlined energy and carbon reporting
sec reg	secundum regulam, Latin for "according to the rule"
SED	(1) Single European Declaration
	(2) seafarer's earnings deduction
SEE	small earnings exemption, for class 2 national insurance
SEED	(1) System for Exchange of Excise Data
	(2) Scottish Executive Education Department
SEF	structured enquiry form, used in payroll
SEFT	South East Flexible Ticketing
SEIS	seed enterprise investment scheme
SEN	special educational needs
Sen	senator
SENA	special educational needs addition, in armed forces
SEND	special educational needs and disability
SEO	(1) senior executive officer
	(2) search engine optimisation
seoo	Sauf erreur ou omission. French equivalent to "error and omissions excluded"
SEPA	Scottish Environmental Protection Agency
SER	(1) special export refund
	(2) small employer's relief
SERPS	state earnings-related pension scheme
SERV	Handbook guide for service companies
SES	standard exchange system, for Customs duties

SET	(1) secure electronic transition
	(2) selective employment tax
SETS	Stock Exchange Electronic Trading Service
SF	Sinn Féin, Irish political party
SFA	(1) Securities and Futures Authority, now replaced by FCA
	(2) Skills Funding Agency
	(3) sweet Fanny Adams, or sweet f*** all, ie nothing
SFAS	Statement of Financial Accounting Standards, US term
SFD	simplified frontier declaration
SFGB	Single Finance Guidance Body
SFO	Serious Fraud Office
SFP	sulphur-free petrol
SFr	Swiss franc
SFT	securities financing transaction
SG	(1) solicitor-general
	(2) HMRC Manual on securities guidance
SGAAR	Scottish general anti-avoidance rule
sgd	signed (by)
SGML	Standard Generalized Markup Language, computer term
SGSAROA	HMRC Manual on strategic goods and services: assessment of risk and offence action
SGSELSG	HMRC Manual on strategic goods and services: BIS export licensing and sanctions – general
Sgt	sergeant
S/H	(1) shorthand
	(2) second-hand
SHA	strategic health authority
SHEFC	Scottish Higher Education Funding Council
SHP	stakeholder pension
ShPP	shared parental pay
SHRC	Scottish Human Rights Centre
SI	(1) statutory instrument
	(2) country prefix code for Slovenia
	(3) Système International d'Unités. International system of metric units of measure.
	(4) South Island, of New Zealand
SIB	Securities and Investment Board
SIC	prefix for interpretation of international accounting standards before May 2004
SID	senior independent director

SIFA	part of Financial Conduct Authority's handbook on how small IFA firms should use the handbook
SIM	subscriber identification module, as in SIM card for mobile phone
Sim	Simon's law reports
SIMM	single in-line memory module
SIO	senior investigating officer, in police
SIOG	HMRC Manual on special investigations operational guidance
SIP	share incentive plan
SIPP	self-invested personal pension scheme
SIR	(1) standard for investment reporting
	(2) Savings Income Information Regulations 2003
	(3) Savings Income Return
SIS	special import scheme, for veterinary medicines
SITPRO	Simplified International Trade Procedures Board
SITR	social investment tax relief
SIV	(1) standard import values
	(2) structured (or special) investment vehicle
SJ	Solicitors' Journal
SJC	Supreme Judicial Court, US term
SK	(1) country prefix code for Slovakia
	(2) koruna, currency of Slovakia
	(3) Canadian province of Saskatchewan
Skr	skipper
S&L	savings and loans
SLA	(1) short-life asset
	(2) service level agreement
SLC	Student Loans Company
SLfT	Scottish landfill tax
SLP	Scottish limited partnership
SLRP	supervisory liquidity review process
SLT	(1) Scots Law Times
	(2) speech and language therapist
SM	(1) sergeant-major
	(2) short metre
SME	small and/or medium-sized enterprise
SMI	support for mortgage interest
SMMT	Society of Motor Manufacturers and Traders
SMO	senior medical officer
SMP	statutory maternity pay
SMR	standardised mortality rate
SMS	sponsor management system, for immigration skills charge

SMTP	simple mail transfer protocol
Sn	atomic symbol for tin
sn	secundum naturam, Latin for "according to nature"
SNCCR	small non-commercial consignment relief
SNCF	Société Nationale des Chemins de fer Français, the French national railway
SNG	syngas
SNO	senior nursing officer
SNP	Scottish National Party
Snr	senior
SO	(1) senior officer
	(2) special order
	(3) signal officer
	(4) sales order
	(5) standing order
	(6) staff officer
So	south
s.o.	seller's option or shipping order
SOAHP	Shared Ownership and Affordable Homes Programme
SoC	statement of case
Soc	(1) society
	(2) socialist
SOCA	Serious and Organised Crime Agency
SOE	special operations executive
SOFA	statement of financial activities
Sol Gen	Solicitor General
Solr	solicitor
SONIA	sterling overnight interbank average rate
SOP	(1) significant other person
	(2) standard operating procedure
SOR	sale or return
SORIE	statement of recognised income and expenditure
SORN	statutory off-road notice
SORP	statement of recommended practice
SOS	international call sign for help
SOT	(1) share option trust
	(2) stay-on tab
sov	sovereign (coin), or colloquialism for one pound
SP	(1) statement of practice
	(2) starting price
sp	(1) sine prole, Latin for "without issue"
	(2) special

S&P	Standard and Poor's, US stock index
SPA	(1) state pension age
	(2) special protection area
spA	Societa per Azione, Italian limited company
SPAB	Society for the Protection of Ancient Buildings
SPAD	signal passed at danger
SpAd	special adviser
SPBL	statutory parental bereavement leave
SPBP	statutory parental bereavement pay
SPC	(1) special commissioners
	(2) supplementary protection certificate
	(3) single person company
SPD	(1) supplementary petroleum duty
	(2) Sozialdemokratische Partel Deutschlands, German Social Democrat Party
SPDS	simplified PAYE deduction scheme
SPE	(1) special purpose entity
	(2) HMRC Manual on Customs special procedures
SPF	significant people function
SPFL	Scottish Professional Football League
SPG	Special Patrol Group
spgr	specific gravity
SPI	Survey of Personal Incomes
SPIC	simplified procedure for import clearance, no longer used
SPICe	Scottish Parliament Information Service
SPIR	HMRC Manual on spirits production
SPL	shared parental leave
SPM	HMRC Manual on statutory payments
spm	strokes per minute, typing speed
SPOC	single point of contact
SPR	(1) small profits rate, of corporation tax
	(2) Society for Physical Research
SPS	single payment scheme, for farmers
SPUC	Society for the Protection of the Unborn Child
SPV	(1) special purpose vehicle
	(2) simplified procedure values, for Customs purposes
	(3) super priority visa
sp vol	specific volume
sq	square
SQA	Scottish Qualifications Authority
SQC	Scottish Qualifications Certificate
sq ft	square foot

sq in	square inch
SQL	structured query language
sq m	square metre
sqn	squadron
Sqn Ldr	squadron leader
sq yd	square yard
SR	(1) starting rate, of income tax
	(2) tax code used before 1973
	(3) Special Reserve
	(4) Saudi riyal
	(5) Southern Region
Sr	(1) senior
	(2) Señor, Spanish equivalent to "Mr"
sr	steradian, a measure of angle
SRA	(1) Solicitors Regulation Authority
	(2) Strategic Rail Authority
SRAM	static random access memory
SRB	sale and rent back
SRC	student representative council
SRCh	state registered chiropodist
SREP	supervisory review and evaluation process
SRFI	strategic rail freight interchange
SRFN	strategic rail freight network
SRIT	Scottish rate of income tax
SRN	(1) scheme reference number, for avoidance schemes
	(2) state registered nurse
SRO	(1) self-regulating organisation
	(2) standing room only
SR&O	standing rules and orders
SRS	scheme reconciliation service
SRT	statutory residence test
Srta	Señorita, Spanish equivalent to "Miss"
SRU	Scottish Rugby Union
SS	(1) secretary of state
	(2) steamship
SSA	standard spending assessment, of local authority
SSAFA	Soldiers, Sailors, Airmen and Families Association
SSAP	statement of standard accounting practice
SSAS	small self-administered scheme, of pension
SSB	(1) state sickness benefit
	(2) single sideband transmission

SSC	Solicitor before the Supreme Courts, of Scotland
SSCBA	Social Security Contributions and Benefits Act 1992
SSC(NI)A	Social Security Contributions and Benefits (Northern Ireland Act 1992
SSD	social services department
SSDP	South Sudanese pound
SSE	substantial shareholder exemption
SSI	Scottish statutory instrument
SSL	secure sockets layer, computing term
SSN	(1) standard shipping note
	(2) social security number, in USA
	(3) standard serial number
SSP	(1) statutory sick pay
	(2) Scottish Socialist Party
SSPE	securitisation special purpose entity
SSR	Soviet Socialist Republic
SSRB	review body on senior salaries
SSRO	Single Source Regulations Office
SSSI	site of special scientific interest
SSS	Sint Marten, Saba and Sint Eustatius, part of Netherlands Antilles
SST	supersonic transport
ST	(1) secondary threshold, for national insurance
	(2) standard time
St	(1) saint
	(2) street
Sta	station
Staffs	Staffordshire
STAR	serial tax avoidance regime
STD	(1) subscriber trunk dialling, for telephones
	(2) sexually transmitted disease
std	standard
STEM	science, technology, engineering and mathematics
STEP	Society of Trust and Estate Practitioners
STFC	Scientific and Technology Facilities Council
STFR	single total figure of remuneration
stg	sterling
Sth	south
STI	sexually transmitted infection
STICS	sterling investment in capital securities
stip	stipendiary
Stir	Stirlingshire
STOL	system to allow aircraft to take off and land over short distances

stp	standard temperature and pressure
Stra	Strange's King's Bench Reports, law reports
STRB	School Teachers' Review Body
STRGL	statement of recognised gains and losses
STSMS	HMRC Manual on stamp taxes on shares
STTG	HMRC Manual on Scottish taxpayer technical guidance
STUC	Scottish Trades Union Congress
STV	single transferable vote
SUA	start-up agreement
sub nom	sub nomine, Latin for "under the name of"
SUCB	single use carrier bag
SUD	single use device
SUDS	sudden unexplained death syndrome
Suff	Suffolk
SUN	service user number, used for direct debits
Sun	Sunday
Sup Ct	Supreme Court
SURF	spent unreprocessed fuel
SUV	sports utility vehicle
SVA	(1) single vehicle approval
	(2) shareholder value analysis
	(3) strategic value analysis
SVD	Shares Valuation Division, of HMRC
SVGA	super video graphics array
SVM	HMRC Manual on shares and asset valuation
SVO	straight vegetable oil
svp	s'il vous plais. French for "if you please"
SVQ	Scottish Vocational Qualification
SVR	Scottish variable rate, of income tax
SW	(1) south west
	(2) short wave radio
SWA	South West Africa, now known as Namibia
SWAT	special weapons and tactics
SWF	(1) shared wealth fund
	(2) single white female
SWIFT	international equivalent to banking sort code
SWL	safe working load
SWM	single white meal
SWOT	strengths, weaknesses, opportunities and threats
SWP	(1) skills with prizes, type of amusement machine
	(2) Socialist Workers Party

SWR	Scotch Whisky Regulations 2009
SYHA	Scottish Youth Hostels Association
SYSC	Financial Conduct Authority handbook on senior management arrangements
T	tesla, unit of magnetic flux
T$	(1) pa'anga, currency of Tonga
	(2) Trinidad and Tobago dollar
TA	(1) Territorial Army
	(2) training agency
	(3) temporary admission, Customs term
	(4) telegraphic address
TAAR	targeted anti-avoidance rule
TAB	Technical Assistance Board, of United Nations
TAC	(1) trades advisory council
	(2) tobacco advisory committee
	(3) total allowable catches, fishing term
TACOS	terms and conditions of service
TAD	transit accompanying document
TAFE	technical and further education
TAM	(1) telephone answering machine
	(2) television audience measurement
TAP	total allocated to policyholders
TAPS	trader account payment system
TARGET	Euro settlement system that links CHAPS with similar EU systems
TARIC	tariff code, for Customs
TARP	troubled assets relief programme
TAVRA	Territorial and Army Volunteer Reserve, replaced in 1979
TAWB	through air waybill
TB	(1) tax bulletin
	(2) tuberculosis
	(3) Treasury Bill
	(4) trial balance
TBA	to be advised
TBC	to be continued/completed
TBE	territorial business exemption
TBM	trust for a bereaved minor
TBS	Teachers Benevolent Society
TBTF	too big to fail
TC	(1) tax case
	(2) Financial Conduct Authority manual on technical competence

	(3) travellers' cheque
TCA	technician in costing and accounting
TCB	Thames Conservancy Board
TCD	Trinity College, Dublin
TCEA	Tribunals, Courts and Enforcement Act 2007
TCF	to be called for
TCFD	Task Force on Climate-related Financial Disclosures
TCEx	Tariff Commune Express consignment note
TCGA	Taxation of Chargeable Gains Act 1992
T-charge	toxicity charge, in low emission zone of London
TCLS	trivial commutation of lump sum, of a pension
TCM	HMRC Manual on tax credits
TCO	total cost of ownership
tCO_2	tons of carbon dioxide
TCP/IP	transmission control protocol/internet protocol
TCRM	HMRC Manual on tax compliance risk
TCS	Tariff Classification Service
TCV	total contract value
TD	(1) Teachta Dala, Gaelic for "deputy to the Dail"
	(2) technical drawing
TDA	(1) taking and driving away
	(2) Training and Development Agency
TDMA	time division multiple access, in telephones
TDO	training development officer
TDP	trainer development programme
TDR	total of disposal receipts, for capital gains tax
TDRB	Tax Disputes Resolution Board
TDSI	tax deduction scheme for interest
TEC	training and enterprise council
TEE	Trans-Europe Express
TEFL	teaching English as a foreign language
TEFU	Treaty on the Functioning of the European Union
TEI	total employment income
TEP	designatory letters of a full member of the Society of Trust and Estate Planners
TES	(1) targeted employment support
	(2) temporary employment subsidy
	(3) Times Educational Supplement
TESL	teaching of English as a second language
TESSA	tax-exempt special savings account, now abolished
TEU	Treaty on European Union

Tex	Texas
TFE	trader front end, Customs term
TFEU	Treaty of the European Union
TfL	Transport for London
TFP	time for print
TFS	transfrontier shipment of waste
TGO	Timber Growers' Organisation
TGWU	Transport and General Workers Union, now part of Unite
Th	Thursday
THI	temperature humidity index
TI	temporary importation
TIC	true interest cost
TIE	taxable income elasticity
TIEA	tax information exchange agreement
TIF	tax increment financing
TIFF	tagged-image format filing, standard computer format for pictures
TIOPA	Taxation (International and Other Provisions) Act 2010
TIR	Transports Internationaux Routiers
TIS	(1) technical interface specification
	(2) transactions in securities
TIWB	Tax Inspectors Without Borders
Tk	taka, currency of Bangladesh
TL	Turkish lira
TLA	(1) three-line account
	(2) three-letter acronym
TLC	tender loving care
TLR	Times Law Reports
TMA	(1) Taxes Management Act 1970
	(2) Theatrical Managers Association
	(3) Tobacco Manufacturers' Association
TMI	too much information
TMO	telegraphic money order
TMT	technology, media and telecommunications
TMW	taxable maximum for a week, social security term
TN	Tennessee, US state
TNC	trans-national company or corporation
TNE	tolerable negative error, for weights and measures
TNR	temporary non-resident
TNRB	transferable nil rate band
TO	(1) telegraphic office
	(2) telegraphic order, of money

	(3) turn over
TOBCSC	HMRC Manual on tobacco control of supply chains
TOC	(1) table of contents
	(2) train operating company
TOGC	transfer of a business as going concern
TOMS	tour operator's margin scheme, for VAT
TOR	Treaty of Rome
ToR	terms of reference
TP	(1) taxpayer
	(2) third party
TPA	transfer of personal allowance
TPAS	The Pensions Advisory Service
TPC	HMRC Manual on television production company
TPD	(1) tobacco products duty
	(2) Transvaal Provincial Division Reports, law reports
	(3) HMRC Manual on tobacco products duty
TPDA	Tobacco Products Duty Act 1979
tph	trains per hour
TPI	tax and prices index
TPIM	Terrorism Prevention and Investigation Measure
TPO	(1) total power output
	(2) tree preservation order
TPS	transaction processing system
TPUK	Trade Partners UK
TQ	tariff quota
TQM	total quality management
TQSN	tariff quota serial number
TR	trust rate
tr	transaction
TRA	(1) Trade Remedies Authority
	(2) Tobacco Retailers Alliance
TRD	temporarily relieved of duty
TRF	transfer
TRG	tax return guide
TRH	their royal highnesses
TRID	Trade Remedies Investigations Directive
TRIO	the responsibility is ours, church giving scheme
TRIPS	trade related aspects of international property rights
TRL	transport research laboratory
TRP	taxed receipt payment
TRS	Trust registration service

TRT	total revenue from tax
TS	Treasury solicitor
T&S	travel and subsistence
TSA	Training Service Agency
TSAD	HMRC Manual on temporary storage and approved depositaries
Ts & Cs	terms and conditions
TSB	Trustee Savings Bank, though now an independent bank called TSB
TSEM	HMRC Manual on trusts, settlements and estates
TSI	transitional serial interest
TSO	(1) town sub-office
	(2) The Stationery Office
TSP	Tax Specialist Programme
TSR	(1) terminate and stay resident, computer term
	(2) total shareholder return
TT	(1) telegraphic transfer
	(2) technical training
	(3) teetotal
	(4) taper threshold, for inheritance tax
TTC	tax type code
TTF	tax transparent fund
TTIP	Transatlantic Trade and Investment Partnership
TTM	HMRC Manual on tonnage tax
TTOG	HMRC Manual on technical teams operational guidance
TTP	(1) Time To Pay
	(2) trusted third party
TTR	HMRC Manual on theatre tax relief
TTS	text to speech
TU	trade union
TUC	Trades Union Congress
TUCC	Transport Users' Consultative Committee
TUI	true-up interest
TUPE	Transfer of Undertakings (Protection of Employment) Regulations SI 2006 No 246
TURN	Trader's Unique Reference Number
TV	television
TVBS	true value at balance sheet
TVEI	Technical and Vocational Education Initiative
TVM	time value of money
TWOC	taking without owner's consent
TX	Texas, US state
TY	thank you

TYVM	thank you very much
UAE	United Arab Emirates
UAP	upper accruals point
UAR	United Arab Republic, Egypt and Syria between 1958 and 1961
UART	Universal Asynchronous Receiver/Transmitter, a computer component that manages serial communication
UB	unemployment benefit
UBR	unified business rate
UC	universal credit
UCAS	Universities and Colleges Admissions Service
UCATT	Union of Construction, Allied Trades and Technicians, now part of Unite
UCC	Union Customs Code
UCITS	undertakings for collective investments in transferable securitis
UCL	University College, London
UCO	used cooking oil
UCR	unique consignment reference
UDA	Ulster Defence Association
UDC	universal decimal classification
UDI	unilateral declaration of independence
UDM	Union of Democratic Mineworkers
UDT	United Dominions Trust
UEFA	Union of European Football Associations
UEL	upper earnings limit, for national insurance
UFC	Universities Funding Council, now replaced
UFEC	unlicensed family entertainment centre
UFPLS	uncrystallised funds pension lump sum
UHF	ultra-high frequency
UHT	ultra-high temperature
UITF	Urgent Issues Task Force, pre-2015 accounting standards setter
UJD	Utriusque Juris Doctor, a doctor of both canon and civil law
UK	United Kingdom
UKAEA	United Kingdom Atomic Energy Authority
UKAR	UK Asset Resolution
UKBA	United Kingdom Border Agency
UKCES	United Kingdom Commission for Employment and Skills
UKCF	United Kingdom Community Foundation
UKCIS	United Kingdom Council for Internet Safety
UKCN	United Kingdom Competition Network
UKCS	United Kingdom Continental Shelf
UKFI	United Kingdom financial institution

UKFTT	United Kingdom first tier tribunal
UK GAAP	United Kingdom generally accepted accounting principles
UKIP	United Kingdom Independence Party
UKITA	UK IT Association
UKLA	United Kingdom Listing Authority
UK(NOR)	not ordinarily resident in the UK
UKOITC	United Kingdom Oil Taxation Committee
UKPE	United Kingdom permanent establishment
UKQI	UK quality infrastructure
UKRI	United Kingdom Research and Innovation
UKSC	United Kingdom Supreme Court
UKUT	United Kingdom upper tribunal
UKVI	UK Visas and Immigration
UL	(1) upper limit (2) Underwriters Laboratories
ULEV	ultra-low emission vehicle
ULEZ	ultra-low emission zone
ULS	unduly lenient sentence
ULSD	ultra low sulphur diesel
ULSP	ultra low sulphur petrol
UM	ouguiya, currency of Mauritania
UMGO	unmarked gas oil
UMIST	University of Manchester Institute of Science and Technology
UMKO	unmarked kerosene
Umst	Umsatzsteuer, German for "value added tax"
UMTS	Universal Mobile Telecommunications System
UN	United Nations
UNCTAD	United Nations Council on Trade and Development
UNDP	United Nations Development Programme
UNDRO	United Nations Disaster Relief Organisation
UNECA	United Nations Economic Commission for Africa
UNECE	United Nations Economic Commission for Europe
UNEDIFACT	United Nations Electronic Data Interchange for Administration, Commerce and Transport
UNEP	United Nations Environment Programme
UNESCAP	United Nations Economic and Social Commission for Asia and the Pacific
UNESCO	United Nations Educational, Scientific and Cultural Organisation
UNGC	United Nations Global Compact
UNHCR	United Nations High Commission [or Commissioner] for Human Rights
UNICEF	United Nations Children's Fund
UNIDO	United Nations Industrial Development Organisation

univ (1) universal
(2) university
UNIX Computer operating system
UNLOCODE Identification scheme for locating goods to be exported or imported
UNMOVIC United Nations Monitoring, Verification and Inspection Commission
UNO United Nations Organisation
UNRRA United Nations Relief and Rehabilitation Administration
UNRWA United Nations Relief and Works Agency
UNSCOM United Nations Special Commission
UO unattached officer
UOM Union of Myanmar
UPOV international convention on plant variety rights
UPP unsatisfactory performance procedure, police term
UPS uninterruptable power supply
UR repayment user, excise duty term
URA usual residential address
URC United Reformed Church
URI (1) uniform resource identifier
(2) upper respiratory infection, used on sick notes
URL Unique Resource Locator, computer term
URTI upper respiratory tract infection, used on sick notes
US (1) United States of America, commonly used as an adjective
(2) under-secretary
(3) United Services
US$ US dollar
us ut supra, Latin for "as above"
u/s unserviceable [or occasionally, useless]
USA United States of America
USAF United States Air Force
USAID United States Agency for International Development
USB universal serial bus, computer term
USDAW Union of Shop, Distributive and Allied Workers
US GAAP United States generally accepted accounting principles
USIA United States Information Agency, now replaced
USM Unlisted Securities Market, now replaced by Alternative Investment Market
USNX United States Navy Exchange
USO universal service operator, particularly Royal Mail
USP (1) universal service provider
(2) unique selling point
USS United States ship [or steamer]
USSR Union of Soviet Socialist Republics, now disbanded

UST	upper secondary threshold, in national insurance
usw	und so weiter, German for "and so forth"
UT	(1) universal time
	(2) Utah, US state
UTC	universal time co-ordinated
UTCCRs	Unfair Terms in Consumer Contracts Regulations 1999
UTI	urinary tract infection, used on sick notes
UTID	unit trust investment duty
UTN	unique ticket number
UTR	unique tax reference
UU	Ulster Unionist
UUP	Ulster Unionist Party
UUT	unauthorised unit trust
UVF	Ulster Volunteer Force
UWIST	University of Wales Institute of Science and Technology
UWO	unexplained wealth order
UZ	Uzbekistan
V	(1) Roman numeral for 5
	(2) volt(s)
v	against or versus
V5C	registration document for a vehicle
VA	(1) vice-admiral
	(2) Royal Order of Victoria and Albert
	(3) Virginia, US state
vac	(1) vacation
	(2) vacancy
	(3) vacuum cleaner, including use as a verb
VAD	(1) Voluntary Aid Department
	(2) value added distributor
VAEC	HMRC Manual on VAT assessments and error correction
VAR	value added reseller
VaR	value at risk
var	(1) variable
	(2) various
	(3) variety
VAS	Voluntary Advisory Service
VAT	value added tax
VATAAS	HMRC Manual on VAT annual accounting scheme
VATAC	HMRC Manual on VAT accounting
VATAFRS	HMRC Manual on VAT agricultural flat rate scheme

VB	(1) visual basic, computer term
	(2) very best, salutation
VBRA	Vehicle Builders and Repairers Association
VC	(1) Victoria Cross
	(2) vice-chancellor
	(3) venture capital
V-C	vice-chancellor
VCLT	Vienna Convention on the Law of Treaties 1969
VCOAD	Voluntary Committee on Overseas Aid and Development
VCP	vehicle check point
VCR	video cassette recorder
VCRA	Violent Crimes Reduction Act 2006
VCT	venture capital trust
VCU	VAT Central Unit, part of HMRC
VDQS	Vin Délimite Qualité Supérieure, French classification of fine wine
VDR	voyage data recorder
VDT	visual display terminal
VDU	visual display unit
VE	(1) vocational education
	(2) Victory in Europe, end of war in 1945
VED	vehicle excise duty
Ven	Venerable, title of archdeacon
VERA	Vehicle Excise and Registration Act 1994
Vern	Vernon's Reports, law reports
VESA	Video Electronics Standards Authority
Ves Jun	Vesey's junior Chancery Reports
Vet MB	Bachelor of Veterinary Medicine
VF	video frequency, or voice frequency
VFM	value for money
vg	very good
VGA	video graphics array
VHCC	very high cost care
VHF	very high frequency, radio term
VHR	veterinary homeopathic remedy
VHS	video home system
VI	(1) Virgin Islands
	(2) vehicle inspectorate
	(3) Vancouver Island
VIB	visual information board
VIC	vehicle identity check
VIES	VAT Information and Exchange System

VIN	vehicle identification number
VIP	very important person
VIR	vulcanised India rubber
VIS	Victims' Information Service
viz	videlict, Latin for "that is to say"
VJ	(1) voluntary jurisdiction
	(2) Victory over Japan, end of war in 1945
VLCC	very large crude carrier
VLF	very low frequency
VLO	valuation liaison officer
VLR	Victorian Law Reports
VLSI	very large scale integration, computer term
VMD	(1) Veterinary Medicines Directorate
	(2) Doctor of Veterinary Medicine
VMH	Victoria Medal of Honour
VMI	vertical motion index, computing term
VO	(1) veterinary officer
	(2) Royal Victorian Order
VOA	Valuation Office Agency
VOD	video on demand
VODG	Voluntary Organisations Disability Group
VOIP	voice over internet protocol
vol	volume
VOSA	Vehicle and Operator Services Agency
VOSS	Voluntary Organisation for Social Services
VP	vice president
VPN	virtual private network
VR	(1) Victorian Law Reports
	(2) variant reading
VRAM	video random access memory
VRML	virtual reality markup language
VRN	VAT regulation number
VRR	(1) victim's right to review
	(2) vaccine research relief
VRS	(1) video rating system
	(2) video relay system
VRU	vapour recovery unit
VS	veterinary surgeon
VSA	variable shift arrangement
VSO	(1) Voluntary Services Organisation
	(2) voluntary services overseas

VSS	victim support scheme
VSU	voluntary services unit
VT	(1) vatu, currency if Vanuatu
	(2) Vermont, US state
VTC	vocational training centre
VTR	video tape recorder
vv	(1) vice versa
	(2) volumes
VVs	varicose veins, used on sick notes
VW	Volkswagen, make of car
W	(1) west
	(2) watt
W1	week one, used for PAYE codes
WA	(1) West Africa
	(2) Western Australia
	(3) Withdrawal Agreement, from European Union
WAAC	Women's Army Auxiliary Corps
WAAF	Women's Auxiliary Air Force
WACC	weighted average cost of capital
WAES	Workshop on Alternative Energy Strategy
WAG	Writers and Artists Guild
wag	wives and girlfriends
WAIS	wide area information server, computer term
Wal	Walloon
WAN	wide area network
WAP	wireless application protocol
WASP	(1) white Anglo-Saxon protestant
	(2) weighted average selling price
WATS	Widening Access Training Scheme
WAV	standard computer format for audio files
WB	World Bank
Wb	Weber, unit of magnetic flux
WBA	widow's bereavement allowance
WBD	work breakdown structure
WC	(1) water closet, i.e. toilet
	(2) working capital
wc	without charge
WCA	work capability assessment
WCC	World Council of Churches
W/Cdr	wing-commander

WCO	World Customs Organization
WCS	World Conservation Strategy
WD	(1) waiting day
	(2) War Department
	(3) Welfare Department
	(4) Works Department
WDA	(1) writing down allowance
	(2) Welsh Development Agency
WDIC	wholesale dealer import certificate
WDM	(1) worldwide dispatch manager, postal service
	(2) World Development Movement
WDP	war disablement pension
WDV	written down value
WE	(1) War Establishment
	(2) Women's Equality Party
WEA	Workers Educational Association
WEC	World Employment Conference
WED	World Environment Day
WEEP	Work Experience on Employer's Premises
wef	with effect from
WERS	Whisky Export Refund Scheme
WET	West European Time
WEU	Western European Union
WFA	White Fish Authority
WFC	World Food Council
WFH	wages for housewives
WFP	(1) winter fuel payment
	(2) World Food Programme, United Nations body
WFTC	working families tax credit
wg	wire gauge, or water gauge
WHO	World Health Organisation
WHT	withholding tax
WI	(1) Women's Institute
	(2) West Indies
	(3) Wisconsin, US state
WIG	widely imported goods
wilco	will comply
Wilts	Wiltshire
WIMAX	worldwide interoperability for microwave access
WIP	work in progress
WIPO	World Intellectual Property Organisation

WIRA	Wool Industry Research Association
WISP	WAP Internet service provider
WJEC	Welsh Joint Education Committee
wk	(1) week
	(2) work
wkly	weekly
WLA	Women's Land Army, disbanded in 1950
WLL	with limited liability
WLR	Weekly Law Reports
WLTP	Worldwide Harmonised Light Vehicles Emissions Test Procedure
WMA	weighted moving average
WMC	working men's club
WML	wireless mark-up language
WMS	written ministerial statement
WN	Law Reports Weekly Notes
WNP	Welsh National Party
WO	(1) War Office
	(2) Warrant Office
	(3) Welfare Officer
	(4) work order
wo	without
WOB	white on black
WOCCU	World Council of Credit Unions
WOLTS	withdrawal of legal tender status
WOM	whole of market
WOO	window of opportunity
WOSB	War Office Selection Board
WOW	waiting on weather
WOWGR	Warehousekeepers and Owners of Warehoused Goods Regulations 1999
WP	(1) without prejudice
	(2) word processor
	(3) withholding foreign partnership
	(4) Warsaw Pact
	(5) weather permitting
WPC	Woman police constable, term discontinued in 1999
WPICC	with profits insurance capital component
WPL	workplace parking levy
wpm	words per minute
WR	(1) Weekly Reporter, law reports
	(2) Western Region
WRA	(1) Welsh Revenue Authority

	(2) Water Research Association
WRAC	Women's Royal Army Corps
WRAF	Women's Royal Air Force
WRI	Women's Rural Institute
WRNS	Women's Royal Naval Service
WRP	Worker's Revolutionary Party
wrt	with respect to
WRU	who are you?
WRVS	Women's Royal Voluntary Service
WT	(1) working together
	(2) withholding foreign trust
wt	weight
WTD	week to date
WTO	World Trade Organization
WTSG	Working Together Steering Group
WV	Western Virginia, US state
WVS	Women's Voluntary Service
WW	worldwide
WWF	Worldwide Fund for Nature
WWI	world war 1, 1914-1918
WWII	world war 2, 1939-1945
www	worldwide web
WY	Wyoming, US state
WYSIWYG	what you see is what you get
X	(1) Roman numeral for 10
	(2) unknown, in algebra
	(3) first character in payment reference from HMRC
xa	ex all
XB	Christmas Bonus
XD	ex dividend
XE	currency authority
XL	extra large
XML	extensive mark-up language
XMS	extended memory system
XXL	extra extra large
Y	(1) yuan, currency of China
	(2) yen, currency of Japan
YB	year book
YC	Young Conservative

Y&CC	Younge & Collyer's Company Cases
yd	yard, unit of length
YHA	Youth Hostels Association
YJB	Youth Justice Board
YM	you're welcome
YMCA	Young Men's Christian Association
Yn	yen
YOP	Youth Opportunities Programme
YOS	Youth Offending Scheme
YOY	year on/over year
YPLA	Young People's Learning Agency
yr	year
YT	Yukon Territory, in Canada
YTC	yet to confirm
YTD	year to date
YTS	Youth Training Scheme
YWCA	Young Women's Christian Association

Z$	Zimbabwe dollar
ZCYC	zero coupon yield curve
ZEV	zero-emission vehicle
ZHC	zero hours contract
Zhr	zero hour
zl	zloty, currency of Poland
Z list	list of transactions as produced by modern till
ZR	zero-rated
ZRE	Democratic Republic of Congo
ZST	zone standard time

Section 3: Tax rates and other data

Accommodation charge

When an employer provides accommodation for an employee which is not tax-exempt, the employee is generally liable to pay income tax on

- the property's rateable value, plus
- the amount by which the property cost more than £75,000 (unchanged from 1984) multiplied by the official rate of interest, the same as the beneficial rate (2.25% for 2020/21), plus
- expenses paid by the employer, such as insurance and utility bills.

Accounting standards

Accounts used for tax preparation must comply with UK or international accounting standards.
These lists refer to standards that were current or prospective in 2020.
It should be noted that many standards have been amended since first issued.

UK accounting standards

- Forward to accounting standards
- FRS 100 application of financial reporting requirements
- FRS 101 reduced disclosure framework
- FRS 102 financial reporting standard applicable in the UK and Republic of Ireland
- FRS 103 insurance contracts
- FRS 104 interim financial reporting
- FRS 105 financial reporting standard applicable to the micro-entities regime
- Overview of financial reporting framework

Financial reporting standards FRS 1 to 30, statement of standard accounting practices (SSAPs), UITF abstracts and N statement have all been repealed.

FRS 102 sections

The main UK accounting standard FRS 102 is divided into sections, each of which is a mini-standards:

Section	Subject
1	Scope
1A	Small entities
2	Concepts and pervasive principles
3	Financial statement presentation
4	Statement of financial position
5	Statement of comprehensive income and income statement
6	Statement of changes in equity and statement of income and retained earnings
7	Statement of cash flows
8	Notes to the financial statements
9	Consolidated and separate financial statement
10	Accounting policies, estimates and errors
11	Basic financial instruments
12	Other financial instruments

13	Inventories
14	Investments in associates
15	Investments in joint ventures
16	Investment property
17	Property, plant and equipment
18	Intangible assets other than goodwill
19	Business combinations and goodwill
20	Leases
21	Provisions and contingencies
22	Liabilities and equity
23	Revenue
24	Government grants
25	Borrowing costs
26	Share-based payment
27	Impairment of assets
28	Employee benefits
29	Income tax
30	Foreign currency translation
31	Hyperinflation
32	Events after the end of the reporting period
33	Related party disclosure
34	Specialised activities
35	Transition to this FRS

Statements of recommended practice (SORP)

These are produced by other bodies but are confirmed by the Financial Reporting Council.

Sector	*Issued by (main body)*
Authorised funds	Investment Association
Charities	Charity Commission
Further and higher education	Universities UK
Investment trust companies	Association of Investment Companies
Limited liability partnerships	CCAB
Pension schemes	Pensions Research Accountants Group
Social housing providers	National Housing Federation

International accounting standards

Preface to IFRS standards

Conceptual framework for financial reporting

IAS 1	Presentation of financial statements
IAS 2	Inventories
IAS 7	Statement of cash flows
IAS 8	Accounting policies, changes in accounting estimates and errors
IAS 10	Events after the reporting period
IAS 11	Construction contracts
IAS 12	Income taxes
IAS 16	Property, plant and equipment
IAS 17	Leases

IAS 18	Revenue
IAS 19	Employee benefits
IAS 20	Accounting for government grants and disclosure of government assistance
IAS 21	The effects of changes in foreign exchange rates
IAS 23	Borrowing costs
IAS 24	Related party disclosures
IAS 26	Accounting and reporting by retirement benefit plans
IAS 27	Separate financial statements
IAS 28	Investments in associates and joint ventures
IAS 29	Financial reporting in hyperinflationary economies
IAS 32	Financial instruments: presentation
IAS 33	Earnings per share
IAS 34	Interim financial reporting
IAS 36	Impairment of assets
IAS 37	Provisions, contingent liabilities and contingent assets
IAS 38	Intangible assets
IAS 39	Financial instruments: recognition and measurement
IAS 40	Investment property
IAS 41	Agriculture
IFRS 1	First-time adoption of International Financial Reporting Standards
IFRS 2	Share-based payment
IFRS 3	Business combinations
IFRS 4	Insurance contracts
IFRS 5	Non-current assets held for sale and discontinued operations
IFRS 6	Exploration for and evaluation of mineral resources
IFRS 7	Financial instruments: disclosures
IFRS 8	Operating segments
IFRS 9	Financial instruments
IFRS 10	Consolidated financial statements
IFRS 11	Joint arrangements
IFRS 12	Disclosure of interests in other entities
IFRS 13	Fair value measurement
IFRS 14	Regulatory deferral accounts
IFRS 15	Revenue from contracts with customers
IFRS 16	Leases
IFRS 17	Insurance contracts

Acts of Parliament

In the UK, a tax may only be charged under the authority of an Act of Parliament. The main Acts for UK taxes are given below.

Tax	**Act or acts**
Alcoholic liquor duty	Alcoholic Liquor Duties Act 1979
Capital gains tax	Taxation of Chargeable Gains Act 1992
Corporation tax	Corporation Tax 2009
	Corporation Tax 2010

Hydrocarbon oil duty	Hydrocarbon Oil Duty Act 1979
Income tax	Income Tax Act 2007
	Income Tax (Earnings and Pensions) Act 2003
	Income Tax (Trading and Other Income) Act 2005
Inheritance tax	Inheritance Tax Act 1984
National insurance	Social Security Contributions and Benefits Act 1992
	National Insurance Contributions Acts of 2002, 2006, 2008, 2011
Petroleum revenue tax	Oil Taxation Act 1975, 1983
Stamp duty	Stamp Act 1891
	Stamp Duties Management Act 1891
Tobacco products duty	Tobacco Products Duty Act 1979
Value added tax	Value Added Tax Act 1994
Taxes in general	Capital Allowances Act 2001
	Customs and Excise Management Act 1979
	Taxes Management Act 1970
	Taxation (International and Other Provisions) Act 2010

Addresses and telephone numbers

This is a selection of contact details that may be useful for tax accountants.

• Association of Accounting Technicians, 140 Aldersgate Street, London EC1A 4HY. 020 3735 2468.

• Association of Chartered Certified Accountants. 0141 582 2000

• Association of Tax Technicians, 30 Monck Street, London SW1P 2AP. 020 7340 0551

• Chartered Institute of Payroll Professionals, Goldfinger House, 245 Cranmore Boulevard, Solihull, West Midlands. B90 4ZL. 0121 712 1000

• Chartered Institute of Taxation, 30 Monck Street, London SW1P 2AP. 020 7340 0550

• Child benefit queries: HMRC helpline 0300 200 3100

• Companies House, Crown Way, Maindy, Cardiff CF14 3UZ. 0303 123 4500

• Department for Business, Energy and Industrial Strategy, 1 Victoria Street, London SW1H 0ET.

• Department of Work and Pensions, Caxton House, Tothill Street, Westminster, London SW1H 9NA

• Financial Conduct Authority, 12 Endeavour Square, London E20 1JN. 0300 500 8082

• Financial Reporting Council, 125 London Wall, Barbican, London EC2Y 5AS. 0300 500 0597

• HMRC Central Agent Authorisation Team, such as for forms 64-8. HMC BX9 1AN. Completed forms should be set to HMRC, Benton Park View, Longbenton, Newcastle, NE98 1ZZ

• HMRC inheritance tax payments: HM Revenue and Customs, CAT 1, Room B1-25/26, St Mungo's Road, Cumbernauld, G67 1YZ.

• HMRC new employer helpline. HMRC, BX9 1BX. 0300 200 3211

• HMRC newly self-employed helpline: PO Box 4000, CF14 8HR. 0300 200 3504

• HMRC payments: HMRC Accounts Office, Bradford BD98 1GG. 0300 200 3200. For apprenticeship levy: 0300 200 3200

• Institute of Chartered Accountants in England and Wales, Chartered Accountants' Hall, Moorgate Place, London EC2R 6EA. 01908 248250

• Institute of Chartered Accountants of Scotland, CA House, 21 Haymarket Yards, Edinburgh EH12 5BH. 0131 347 0100

• Institute of Chartered Accountants of Ireland (Belfast). 32-38 Linenhall Street, Belfast, County Antrim, BT2 8BG. 0353 1637 7200

• Institute of Chartered Accountants of Ireland (Dublin). Chartered Accountants House, 47-49 Pearse Street, Dublin 2. 028 9043 5840

• Institute of Company Secretaries and Administrators. 6-10 Kirby Street, London EC1N 8TS. 020 7580 4741

• Legal Aid general queries. 0300 200 2020. Email: contactcivil@justice.gov.uk

• Low Pay Commission: 020 7211 8119

• National Insurance Helpline, HMRC, BX0 1AN. 0300 200 3500

• Office for National Statistics: 0845 601 3304

• Passport Office, PO Box 767, Southport PR8 9PW. 0300 222 0000

• Pensions Regulator, Napier House, Trafalgar Place, Brighton BN1 4DW. 0345 600 1011

• Pension tracing service: The Pensions Service 9, Mail Handling Site A, Wolverhampton WV98 1LU. 0800 731 0193

• Revenue Adjudicator, PO Box 10280, Nottingham, NG2 9PF. 0300 057 1111

• Samaritans: For those needing help: Chris, Freepost RSRB-KKBY-CYJK, PO Box 9090, Stirling, FK8 2SA. 24-hour helpline service; 116 123

• Society of Trust and Estate Practitioners: 11-19 Artillery Row, London SW1P 1RT. 020 3752 3700

• Taxed Award Scheme. HMRC Incentive Award Unit, BX9 1BX. 0300 200 3200

• Time To Pay: 0300 200 3835

• VAT helpline, HMRC, 123 Vincent Street, Glasgow G2 5EA. 0300 200 3700

See also Helplines at HMRC; Website addresses

Advisory fuel rates

These rates are revised every three months. They were introduced in 2002.

The rate of 4p per mile for electric cars was introduced on 1 June 2018.

The employer may use the rates at the date shown or up to one month later.

This is the tax-free amount in pence per mile which either:

- *an employee may reimburse the employer for private use of a company car without becoming subject to car fuel benefit*
- *an employer may reimburse the employee for business use of a company car where the employee is not subject to car fuel benefit.*

From	Petrol cars			Diesel cars			LPG cars			Electric cars
	up to 1400cc	1401-2000cc	over 2000cc	up to 1600cc	1601-2000cc	over 2000cc	up to 1400cc	1401-2000cc	over 2000cc	
1,12,20	10	11	17	8	10	12	7	8	12	4
1.9.20	10	12	17	8	10	12	7	8	12	4
1.6.20	10	12	17	8	9	12	6	8	11	4
1.3.20	12	14	20	9	11	13	8	10	14	4
1.12.19	12	14	21	9	11	14	8	9	14	4
1.9.19	12	14	21	10	11	14	8	10	14	4

1.6.19	12	15	22	10	12	14	8	9	14	4
1.3.19	11	14	21	10	11	13	7	8	13	4
1.12.18	12	15	22	10	12	14	8	10	15	4

Aggregates levy

The rate is £2 per tonne from when the tax was introduced in 2009.

Air passenger duty

This tax is charged at rates for Band A destinations up to 2,000 miles; and Band B destinations above 2,000 miles. Before 1 April 2015, there were also Band C and Band D destinations.
The duty is charged per passenger per flight, subject to many detailed provisions.
The reduced rate applies for aeroplanes with seat pitches of less than 1.016 m (40 inches) The standard rate applies for greater seat pitches.
The higher rate applies for aeroplanes of 20 tonnes or more that carry fewer than 19 passengers.
From 1 January 2013, this tax is devolved in Northern Ireland where the rate is zero.
In Scotland, the tax will be replaced by air departure tax from a date yet to be advised.

Reduced rate

From	*Band A*	*Band B*
1 April 2020	£13	£80
1 April 2018	£13	£78
1 April 2017	£13	£75
1 April 2016	£13	£73
1 April 2015	£13	£71

Standard rate

From	*Band A*	*Band B*
1 April 2020	£26	£176
1 April 2019	£26	£172
1 April 2018	£26	£156
1 April 2017	£26	£150
1 April 2016	£26	£146
1 April 2015	£26	£142

Higher rate

From	*Band A*	*Band B*
1 April 2020	£78	£528
1 April 2019	£78	£515
1 April 2018	£78	£468
1 April 2017	£78	£450
1 April 2016	£78	£438
1 April 2015	£78	£426

Alcoholic liquor duty

Rates of duty are per hectolitre (100 litres).

Drinks with a strength below 1.2% (alcohol by volume) are not subject to duty. VAT is charged on the price of liquor plus duty.

Type of drink	1 Feb 2019	13 March 2017
General beer duty	£19.08	£19.08
High strength beer (above 7.5%)	£24.77	£24.77
Low strength (1.2% - 2.8%)	£8.42	£8.42
Lower rates apply for small breweries		
Still cider: 1.2% - 6.9%	£40.38	£40.38
Still cider: 6.91% - 7.5%	£50.71	£40.38
Still cider: 7.51% - 8.5%	£61.04	£61.04
Still cider above 8.5%	taxed as wine	taxed as wine
Sparkling cider: 1.2% - 5.5%	£40.38	£40.38
Sparkling cider: 5.51% - 8.5%	£288.10	£279.46
Sparkling cider above 8.5%	taxed as wine	taxed as wine
Wine: 1.2% - 4.0%	£91.68	£88.93
Wine: 4.01% - 5.5%	£126.08	£122.30
Wine: 5.51% - 15%	£297.57	£288.65
Wine: 15.01% - 22%	£396.72	£384.82
Sparkling wine: 5.5% - 8.5%	£288.10	£279.46
Sparkling wine: 8.51%-15%	£381.15	£369.72
other strengths as for still wine		
Spirits: rate per litre of pure alcohol	£28.74	£28.74

Anniversaries

This list notes some significant anniversaries in 2021 and 2022.

LANDMARK ANNIVERSARIES IN 2021

Date	Year	Ago	Event
4 January	2011	10	Standard rate of VAT is increased to 20%
31 January	1971	50	Radio licences are abolished
4 February	1971	50	Rolls-Royce is declared bankrupt and is nationalised
15 February	1971	50	Britain adopts decimal currency
13 March	1961	60	White fivers cease to be legal tender
29 March	1971	50	Court rules that a prize for passing exam is taxable
1 April	1971	50	Restrictions are lifted on citizens owning gold
7 April	1941	80	Basic rate of income tax increased to record 50%
10 April	2001	20	Tesco is first supermarket with turnover above £1b
24 April	1981	40	IBM launches first personal computer
28 April	1961	60	Britain makes first application to join Common Market
1 May	1961	60	Betting shops become legal
4 May	2001	20	Merger between Halifax and Bank of Scotland
9 May	1671	350	Thomas Blood dresses as a clergyman to try to steal the Crown Jewels
19 May	1991	30	Soviet Union ceases to exist
29 May	1871	150	First bank holiday in Britain
21 June	1971	50	Britain starts successful negotiation to join Common Market (now EU)

23 June	2016	5	Britain votes to leave European Union
29 June	1871	150	First legal recognition of trade unions in Britain
20 July	1971	50	House of Lords gives ruling in *Greenberg* on taxation of dividend strips
6 August	1921	100	Germany introduces large tax rise to pay war reparations
11 August	1911	110	House of Lords is banned from amending Finance Acts
12 August	1961	60	Start of building Berlin Wall
15 August	1971	50	USA in effect ends Bretton Woods agreement
1 September	1921	100	Nine councillors in Poplar are arrested for refusing to set a rate
11 September	2001	20	Terrorist attack on World Trade Center, New York
16 September	1861	160	Start of Post Office Savings Bank
4 October	1921	100	Germany imposes 100% tax on imports to pay war reparations
21 October	1971	50	House of Lords rules that dividend stripping is not a trade
23 October	2001	20	Accounting firm Arthur Andersen starts shredding Enron documents
2 November	1896	125	First motor insurance policy written in Britain
11 November	1921	100	First poppy day organised by British Legion
19 November	1901	120	Telephone system in London is completed
1 December	2001	20	Death of George Harrison of The Beatles, who wrote the song *Taxman*
2 December	2001	20	Enron files for bankruptcy
6 December	1921	100	Ireland is partitioned. Irish Free States comes into being
19 December	1961	60	Government decides to adopt decimal currency

LANDMARK ANNIVERSARIES IN 2022

Date	**Year**	**Ago**	**Event**
1 January	1772	250	First travellers cheques issued, in USA
1 January	1947	75	Coal mines are nationalised
1 January	2012	10	5p and 10p coins are now made from nickel-plated steel
14 January	1962	60	First European Common Agricultural Policy is agreed
14 January	1992	30	Bank of Credit and Commercial International is liquidated
31 January	1992	30	Trading floor of London Stock Exchange is used for last time
1 March	1947	75	International Monetary Fund comes into existence
15 March	1972	50	High Court rules in *McMann v Shaw* that payments for loss of office are taxable
22 March	1972	50	House of Lords rules in *Helical Barr* on tax consequences of a change of accounting date
16 May	1972	50	Opening of first derivatives exchange, in Chicago
10 June	1942	80	Economist John Maynard Keynes is given a peerage
13 June	1922	100	Austria says that it is bankrupt
23 June	1972	50	The pound is allowed to float against other currencies
2 July	1947	75	Britain accepts US aid under Marshall Plan
16 August	1922	100	First licence issued to use a franking machine

7 September	1862	160	First life assurance policy issued based on life expectancy
15 September	1947	75	Government starts spending gold reserves to buy imports
16 September	1992	30	Black Wednesday as sterling loses 16% of value and is forced out of the Exchange Rate Mechanism
23 October	1972	50	Access cards are introduced in UK
30 October	1947	75	General Agreement on Tariffs and Trades founded
1 November	1922	100	German mark falls to £1 = 20,000 marks
1 November	1922	100	Radio licences are introduced at 10 shillings a year
1 November	1947	75	Belgium, Luxembourg and Netherlands form a customs union
6 November	1972	50	Government introduces 90 day freeze on prices and incomes
13 November	1947	75	Hugh Dalton resigns as Chancellor of the Exchequer when part of his Budget is leaked
14 November	1947	75	First time share prices are telegraphed between two cities
14 November	1972	50	Dow Jones index goes above 1000
1 December	1942	80	Publication of Beveridge Report on social security

Annual tax on enveloped dwellings

Property value	2020/21	2019/20	2018/19	2017/18
Below £500,000	nil	nil	nil	nil
from £500,000	£3,700	£3,650	£3,600	£3,500
from £1 million	£7,500	£7,400	£7,250	£7.050
from £2 million	£25,200	£24,800	£24,250	£23,550
from £5 million	£58,850	£57,900	£56,550	£54,950
from £10 million	£118,050	£116,100	£113,400	£110,100
from £20 million	£236,250	£232,350	£226,950	£220,350

Annuity and sinking fund rates

The annuity fund rate shows how a fund will grow if £1 is paid in every month.
The sinking fund shows how much needs to be deposited each month to reach £1
The present worth is what £1 in the future is worth today if that amount were compounded each month at the nominal annual rate.
These figures assume monthly payments equal to one twelfth of the rate.

Rate	Years	Annuity	Sinking	Present worth
1%	1	12.055 153	0.082 952	0.990 053
	2	24.231 411	0.041 268	0.980 207
	3	36.529 923	0.026 623	0.969 549
	4	48.952 124	0.020 428	0.960 805
	5	61.499 048	0.016 260	0.951 249
	10	126.149 874	0.007 927	0.904 875
	15	194.114 004	0.005 151	0.860 761
	20	265.561 242	0.003 766	0.818 799
	25	340.670 084	0.002 936	0.778 882
	30	419.628 215	0.002 383	0.740 911

2%	1	12.110 613	0.082 572	0.980 214
	2	24.465 671	0.040 873	0.960 821
	3	37.070 108	0.026 224	0.940 245
	4	49.928 959	0.020 028	0.923 177
	5	63.047 355	0.015 861	0.904 913
	10	132.719 660	0.007 534	0.818 867
	15	209.713 055	0.004 768	0.741 003
	20	294.796 834	0.003 392	0.670 543
	25	388.821 125	0.002 572	0.606 783
	30	492.725 387	0.002 029	0.549 085
3%	1	12.166 382	0.082 194	0.970 481
	2	24.702 818	0.040 481	0.941 835
	3	37.620 560	0.025 830	0.914 033
	4	50.931 208	0.019 634	0.887 053
	5	64.646 712	0.015 469	0.860 869
	10	139.741 418	0.007 156	0.741 095
	15	226.972 690	0.004 406	0.637 986
	20	328.301 998	0.003 045	0.549 222
	25	446.007 823	0.002 242	0.472 808
	30	582.736 884	0.001 716	0.407 026

The formulae are: Annuity: $((1 + r)^n - 1)/r$

Sinking fund: $r/((1 + r)^n - 1)$

Present worth: $1/(1 + r)^n$

where r is the rate of interest expressed as a decimal (so 2.4% is 0.024) and n is the number of years.

Where payments are made more frequently than once a year, r must be divided by the number of payments a year, and n by the number of payments. So for monthly payments at an annual rate of 2.4% over 3 years, r is 0.002 and n is 36.

For an Excel spreadsheet, the formulae are entered as:

Annuity: =((1+R)^N-1)R

Sinking fund: = R/((1+R)^N-1)

Present worth: =1/(1+R)^N

where appropriate numbers must be entered for R and N.

See also the savings depletion tables.

Annuity market rates

These figures indicate the standard annual annuity rates for a pension fund of £100,000 (defined as a fund of £133,333 from which the 25% lump sum of £33,333 has been paid).

These figures were taken from the Sharing Pensions website https://www.sharingpensions.co.uk/annuity_rates.htm#text5 as at 1 October 2020.

SINGLE LIFE

Age	Level rate no guarantee	Level rate 10 year guarantee	3% escalation no guarantee
55	£3,688	£3,662	£2,088
60	£4,143	£4,101	£2,531
65	£4,848	£4,793	£3,254
70	£5,706	£5,551	£4,061
75	£6,819	£6,397	£5,170

JOINT LIFE

Age	Level rate 50% joint life	Level rate 100% joint life	3% escalation 50% joint life
55	£3,364	£3,167	£1,885
60	£3,853	£3,579	£2,293
65	£4,439	£4,095	£2,893
70	£5,166	£4,718	£3,570
75	£6,192	£5,472	£4,656

Single life means that only the pension member receives a pension. Joint life means that a surviving partner continues to receive 50% or 100% of the member's pension.

The table assumes that the partner is the same age as the member. If he or she is younger, the rate is reduced.

Level rate means that the pension never increases in amount. 3% escalation means that it increases by 3% each year.

The 10 year guarantee is that the pension will be paid for 10 years even if the member dies before then. Without the guarantee, the pension stops when the member dies.

These figures are based on a central London postcode. Other areas could be up to 4% higher.

The figures assume no medical adjustments, such as for a smoker or someone with an impaired life.

Apprenticeship levy

This levy was introduced in April 2017 at a rate of 0.5% of payroll subject to an annual allowance of £15,000. This means it is only paid by payrolls of more than £3 million.

Approved mileage rates

These are the rates at which an employer may reimburse an employee for using his or her own transport on the employer's business without creating a tax liability. If an employer reimburses at a lesser amount, the employee may claim tax relief for the shortfall.

From April 2011, the rates per mile are:

Car up to 25,000 miles:	45p
Car above 25,000 miles	25p
Motorcycles	24p
Bicycle	20p.

These rates are also used for national insurance, except that the rate remains at 45p for all mileage.

From April 2002, the rates were as above except that the car rate of 45p was 40p.
In addition, there is a 5p a mile rate if the employee takes a passenger. This is not an allowance, so the employee cannot claim tax relief for any shortfall.

Arrestment of earnings

These are deductions from earnings that may be made in Scotland.
Rates last revised from 6 April 2019.

Weekly earnings	Attachment
up to £122.28	nil
to £442.00	greater of £4 or 19% of earnings above £122.28
to £664.50	£60.75 plus 23% of earnings above £442.00
above £664.50	£111.92 plus 50% of earnings above £664.50
Monthly earning	**Attachment**
up to £529.90	nil
to £1,915.32	greater of £15 or 19% of earnings above £529.90
to £2,879.52	£263.23 plus 23% of earnings above £1,915.32
above £2,879.52	£485.00 plus 50% of earnings above £2,879.52
Daily earnings	**Attachment**
up to £17.42	nil
to £62.97	greater of 50p or 19% of earnings above £17.42
to £94.67	£8.65 plus 23% of earnings above £62.97
above £94.67	£15.95 plus 50% of earnings above £94.67

Attachment of earnings orders

These are orders made outside Scotland for sums to be deducted from wages. There are 17 different types of order subject to three sets of tables.

Council tax attachment of earnings orders. Rates from 1 April 2007

The table shows rates for maximum income

Weekly	Monthly	Daily	Deduction rate
£75	£300	£11	nil
£135	£550	£20	3%
£185	£740	£27	5%
£225	£900	£33	7%
£355	£1,420	£52	12%
£505	£2,020	£72	17%
above	above	above	17% to its limit, plus 50% of excess

Deductions of earnings orders. Rates from 2014

These orders were suspended from April 2020

Weekly	Monthly	Daily	Deduction rate	
			Lower	Higher
£100	£430	£15	nil	5%
£160	£690	£23	3%	6%
£220	£950	£32	5%	10%
£270	£1,160	£39	7%	14%
£375	£1,615	£54	11%	22%

£520	£2,240	£75		15%	30%
above	above	above	20%	40%	

Attachments of earnings issued by court. Rates from 5 April 2004

Weekly	**Monthly**	**Daily**	**Deduction rate**
£55	£220	£8	nil
£100	£400	£15	3%
£135	£540	£20	5%
£165	£660	£24	7%
£260	£1,040	£38	12%
£370	£1,480	£53	17%
above	above	above	17% to its limit, plus 50% of excess

Bank base rates

From	**Rate**
19 March 2020	0.10%
11 March 2020	0.25%
2 August 2018	0.75%
2 November 2017	0.50%
4 August 2016	0.25%
5 March 2009	0.50%
5 February 2009	1.00%
8 January 2009	1.50%

Bank holidays

England and Wales	**2020**	**2021**	**2022**
New Year's Day	1 January	1 January	2 January
Good Friday	10 April	2 April	15 April
Easter Monday	13 April	5 April	18 April
May bank holiday	8 May	3 May	2 May
Spring bank holiday	25 May	31 May	30 May
Summer bank holiday	31 August	30 August	29 August
Christmas Day	25 December	27 December	26 December
Boxing Day	28 December	28 December	27 December

Scotland	**2020**	**2021**	**2022**
New Year's Day	1 January	1 January	2 January
2 January	2 January	2 January	3 January
Good Friday	10 April	2 April	15 April
May bank holiday	8 May	3 May	2 May
Spring bank holiday	25 May	31 May	30 May
Summer bank holiday	3 August	2 August	1 August
St Andrew's Day	30 November	30 November	30 November
Christmas Day	25 December	27 December	26 December
Boxing Day	28 December	28 December	27 December

Northern Ireland	2020	2021	2022
New Year's Day	1 January	1 January	2 January
St Patrick's Day	17 March	17 March	17 March
Good Friday	10 April	2 April	15 April
Easter Monday	13 April	5 April	18 April
May bank holiday	8 May	3 May	2 May
Spring bank holiday	25 May	31 May	30 May
Battle of the Boyne	13 July	12 July	12 July
Summer bank holiday	31 August	30 August	29 August
Christmas Day	25 December	27 December	26 December
Boxing Day	28 December	28 December	27 December

Additional bank holidays may be proclaimed by the Queen under Banking and Financial Dealings Act 1971. The monarch may also move the date of an existing bank holiday. She is advised by the Department for Business, Energy and Industrial Strategy.

Scotland includes St Andrew's Day under St Andrew's Day Bank Holiday (Scotland) Act 2007.

Christmas Day and Good Friday are old common law holidays.

Additional bank holidays have been:

- 14 March 1968: to close the London gold market to stem losses on the pound
- 14 November 1973: wedding of Princess Anne and Captain Mark Phillips
- 7 June 1977: Queen's silver jubilee
- 29 July 1981: wedding of Prince Charles and Lady Diana Spencer
- 31 December 1999: to mark the millennium
- 3 June 2002: Queen's golden jubilee
- 29 April 2011: wedding of Prince William and Catherine Middleton
- 5 June 2012: Queen's diamond jubilee.

Bank levy

This tax is charged on banks from 1 January 2011 on their total equity and liabilities reported on their balance sheet. It is being phased out.

Rate charged on	Short-term liabilities	Long-term liabilities and equity
From 1 January 2020	0.14%	0.07%
1 January 2019	0.15%	0.075%
1 January 2018	0.16%	0.08%
1 January 2017	0.17%	0.085%
1 January 2016	0.18%	0.09%
1 January 2015	0.21%	0.105%

Beneficial loan rates (official rate of interest)

An employee may be liable to income tax if the employer provides an interest-free or low-interest loan of more than £10,000 (£5,000 before April 2014).

In determining whether a loan is low-interest, and to calculate any tax due, these official rates of interest are used

Tax year	Official rate
2020/21	2.25%
2019/20	2.5%
2018/19	2.5%
2017/18	2.5%
2016/17	3.0%
2015/16	3.0%
2014/15	3.25%

Benford's law

Benford's law is the observation that in any random selection of numbers from real life, such as from a set of accounts, the frequency of the digits 1 to 9 follows the order of the digits, so 1 is the commonest and 9 the least common.

It is named after the mathematician Frank Benford (1883-1948).

This law can be used to indicate fraud. When numbers are made up, they tend to be more equally distributed, with each digit having a frequency of around 11%.

The full table is

Digit	Frequency
1	39.1%
2	17.6%
3	12.5%
4	9.7%
5	7.9%
6	6.7%
7	5.8%
8	5.1%
9	4.6%

Betting and gaming duties

In most cases, small-scale betting and gaming is exempt from duty.

Bingo duty from 1 April 2015

10% of profits.

Gaming duty from 1 August 2020

Gross gaming yield	*Rate*
First £2,471,000	15%
next £1,703,500	20%
next £2,983,000	30%
next £6,296,500	40%
remainder	50%

General betting duty (such as betting shops) from 6 October 2001

Fixed odds and totalisator bets	15%
Financial spread bets	3%
Other spread bets	10%
Commission charges by betting exchanges	15%

Lottery duty

12% of stake money

Machine games duty

Percentage of takings minus prizes of highest rated game.

Cost to play	*Prize*	*Rate*
20 pence or less	£10 or less	5%
21 pence to £5	£11 or more	20%
more than £5	any	25%

Pool betting duty from 31 March 2002

15% of bookmaker's profits

Remote gaming duty

21 % from April 2019

15% previously

Bicycle transfer

HMRC allows a bicycle to be transferred to an employee at a percentage of its price without triggering a tax liability. The percentage depends on the age of the bicycle, and whether it originally cost more than £500.

Age of bicycle	**Below £500**	**£500 or more**
1 year	18%	25%
18 months	16%	21%
2 years	13%	17%
3 years	8%	12%
4 years	3%	7%
5 years	-	2%
6 or more years	-	-

Business rates

Business rates for non-residential premises in England are calculated by multiplying the rateable value as at 1 April 2015 by the standard multiplier, or, if the rateable value is below the figure under "small business rateable", the small business multiplier.

Year	**Standard multiplier**	**Small business multiplier**	**Small business rateable**
2020/21	0.512	0.499	£51,000
2019/20	0.504	0.491	£51,000
2018/19	0.493	0.480	£51,000
2017/18	0.479	0.466	£51,000
2016/17	0.497	0.484	£18,000 (£25,500 in London)

In the **City of London,** the multiplier for 2020/21 is 0.520, or 0.507 for small businesses.

The City is levying a further 0.02 on all properties with a rateable value above £70,000 towards Crossrail.

In **Wales**, the multiplier for 2020/21 is 0.535

Premises with a rateable value below £6,000 receive 100% relief

Premises with a value between £6,000 and £12,000 receive tapered relief between 100% and 0%. There are other reliefs.

In **Scotland,** for 2020/21 the standard and small business multiplier is 0.498. It was 0.490 in 2019/20.

From April 2020, the small business bonus scheme is restricted to properties in active use.

From April 2020, the large business supplement is split into immediate property rate and higher property rate.

There are many other reliefs and provisions.

In **Northern Ireland,** the multipliers are set by local councils.

Business statistics

These statistics were produced by the Department for Business, Energy and Industrial Strategy for the beginning of 2020.

	Number of businesses
Total:	6.0 million
Small (up to 49 employees)	5.94 million
Medium (50 to 249 employees)	36,100
Large (250 or more employees)	7,800
Number who have employees:	4.6 million
Number with no employees:	1.4 million
Legal form	
Sole traders:	3.5 million
Trading companies:	2.0 million
Partnerships	414,000
Tax registration	
Registered for VAT or PAYE	2.7 million
Not registered for either:	3.3 million
Geography	
Businesses in England:	5.3 million
Scotland	370,000
Wales	209,000
Northern Ireland	148,000
Turnover (2019, excluding financial sector)	
All businesses	£4,346,969 million
SMEs (to 249 employees)	£2,270,229 million
Large businesses (250 + employees)	£2,076,740 million
Employment	
All businesses	27.732 million
SMEs (to 249 employees)	16.836 million
Large businesses (250 + employees)	10.896 million

Capital allowances

Category of expenditure	**Capital allowance**
Cars	See below
Dredging	4% (from 5 November 1962)

Features integral to a building	Treated as special rate plant and machinery
Know-how	25% writing down allowance (from 31 March 1986)
Mineral extraction (not oil)	10% on acquisition of asset (from 31 March 1986) 25% reducing balance otherwise
Patent rights	25% writing down allowance (from 31 March 1986)
Plant and machinery (see below)	Annual investment allowance 100% first year allowance for some assets 18% writing down allowance for general pool 6% writing down allowance for special rate pool (from 1/6 April 2019, previously 8%)
Research and development	100% (from 5 November 1962)
Structures and buildings allowance	3% reducing balance from 28 October 2018 (originally introduced at 2%)

Types of allowance

Annual investment allowance	Annual allowance for plant and machinery except cars. Unused allowance cannot be carried forward or back May be used with writing down allowance for same asset
First year allowance	Allowance claimed in tax year a qualifying asset was acquired Restricted to small range of goods (see below)
Straight line basis	Annual allowance based on original cost
Writing down allowance	Allowance on written down value of pool of assets. Known as the reducing balance method

Annual investment allowance

From	*Amount*
1 January 2021	£200,000
1 January 2019	£1 million
1 January 2016	£200,000
6 April 2014	£500,000
1 January 2013	£250,000
6 April 2012	£25,000
6 April 2010	£100,000
6 April 2008	£50,000 (when allowance was introduced)

Cars

Zero emission	100% first year allowance
Low emission	100% first year allowance (until April 2021) 18% writing down allowance
Medium emission	No first year allowance 18% writing down allowance (to April 2021) 6% writing down allowance (from April 2021)
High emission	6% writing down allowance (8% before April 2019)

Features integral to a building: scope
Electrical and lighting systems
Cold water systems
Space or water heating systems, powered systems of ventilation, air cooling or air purification, and any floor or ceiling comprised in such a system
Lifts, escalators and moving walkways
External solar shading.

Definitions of cars by emissions

Classification	*From*	*Rate of emission*
Low emission	April 2018	50 gm/km or less
	April 2015	75 gm/km or less
	April 2013	95 gm/km or less
	April 2009	100 g,/km or less
High emission	April 2018	above 110 gm/km
	April 2015	above 130 gm/km
	April 2013	above 130 gm/km
	April 2009	above 160 gm/km

Different provisions applied before April 2009.

First year allowances

A 100% first year allowance may be claimed in 2020/21 for these items. The final column give the section in Capital Allowances Act 2001.

Asset	*CAA*
Energy-saving plant or machinery on Energy Technology List	s45A
Cars with low carbon dioxide emissions (see above)	s45D
Goods vehicles with zero emissions	s45DA
Plant and machinery for gas refuelling station	s45E
Plant and machinery for electric charging points	s45EA
Plant and machinery for company in ring fence trade	s45F
Environmentally beneficial plant and machinery per Energy Technology List	s45H
Certain new investments in enterprise zones	s45K
Zero emission goods vehicles (from April 2021)	-

Capital gains tax

	2020/21	**2019/20**	**2018/19**	**2017/18**
Annual exempt amount	£12,300	£12,000	£11,700	£11,300
Exempt amount for trusts	£6,150	£6,000	£5,850	£5,650
Chattels exemption	£6,000	£6,000	£6,000	£6,000
Residential property higher rate	28%	28%	28%	28%
Residential property lower rate	18%	18%	18%	18%
Individuals on other assets higher	20%	20%	20%	20%
Individuals on other assets lower	10%	10%	10%	10%
Business asset disposal relief rate	10%	10%	10%	10%

Business asset disposal relief was known as entrepreneur's relief before 6 April 2020.

Share identification rules

Shares disposed of are regarded as acquired in this order

- on the same day
- within the last 30 days
- others as a single pool

RELIEFS AND EXCEPTION

This lists those items for which relief is given from capital gains tax or chargeable gains corporation tax. It should be noted that these reliefs and exceptions are subject to conditions.

Charities

Their gains are exempt provided the proceeds are used for a charitable purpose.

Disincorporation relief

This provided relief when an incorporated body disincorporated, such as a limited company becoming a sole trader. It only applies to disincorporations between 1 April 2013 and 31 March 2018.

Entrepreneur's relief/business asset disposal relief

From	*Lifetime limit*
11 March 2020	£1 million
6 April 2011	£10 million
23 June 2010	£5 million
6 April 2010	£2 million
6 April 2008	£1 million (when introduced)

Gifts to the nation

Gifts of pre-eminent property to the nation are exempt.
From 2012/13, such a gift also attracts income tax relief of 30% of the gift's value.
Note that this is a separate provision from inheritance tax rules on such gifts.

Gilts

The government has produced a list of gilts that are exempt, given later in this section.

Investors' relief

This is a relief from capital gains tax on the disposal of unlisted shares.
It reduces the rate of capital gains tax to 10%.
The disposal must be after 6 April 2016 for shares issued from 17 March 2016.
The shares must have been held for at least three years.
This may be claimed by individuals or trusts, but not companies.
The maximum amount that may be claimed is £10 million.
This is separate from entrepreneur's relief, though similar to it.

Lettings relief

- similar to main residence relief when a residential property has been let
- available for the period when taxpayer lived in it, and for last 9 months whether or not taxpayer lived there. This was 18 months between 6 April 2014 and 6 April 2020. It is 36 months (for all tax years) if it was the sole home and the taxpayer was disabled

• relief is restricted to the lowest of £40,000, chargeable gain, amount that would have been claimed as main residence relief
• for disposals from 6 April 2020, it is a condition that the taxpayer also lived in the home. For previous disposals it was sufficient that the taxpayer had lived in it at any time for any period.

Main residence relief (or private residence relief)

• the taxpayer's only or main home
• occupied by taxpayer from acquisition to disposal subject to absence reliefs
• includes garden of up to half a hectare, or larger if appropriate to property
• includes outbuildings within the curtilage
• the property has not been let, other than having a lodger
• if part has been used for a business, that part is excluded from relief
• the property was not bought with a view to making a gain.

Pre-1982 gains

Gains that accrued before 1/6 April 1982 are not taxed. This is usually achieved by substituting April 1982 value for acquisition cost.

Rollover relief

This allows the proceeds of a disposal to be applied to the acquisition of a new asset, not necessarily of the same class, with triggering a liability. The time window is one year before disposal to three years after disposal. The classes are:
• land and buildings used for a trade
• fixed plant and machinery, not forming part of a building
• ships, aircraft and hovercraft
• satellites, space stations and spacecraft
• goodwill
• milk quotas, potato quotas, ewe and suckler cow premium quotas, fish quotas
• entitlements under the single farm payments scheme
• entitlements under the basic payment scheme (from 20 December 2013)
• Lloyd's members' syndicate rights and assets treated as acquired by members.

Tax-advantaged schemes

There are many tax-advantaged schemes that provide relief from capital gains tax. These include enterprise investment scheme, seed enterprise investment scheme, employee-ownership trusts, shareholder employees, and social enterprise investment.

Wasting assets

Wasting assets are those with an expected life of less than 50 years.

This includes all animals, and all plant and machinery, even if already more than 50 years old.

It also includes part of a lease of lease than 50 years, as shown in the lease table later in this section.

Carrier bag charge

This is a charge a retailer must make for providing a single use carrier bag.

It is not a tax as the retailer may keep the charge, though most donate the proceeds to charity.

Where a retailer is VAT registered, the charge includes VAT. So a 5p charge is 4.17p for the bag and 0.83p VAT.
The 5p or 10p charge is a minimum; the retailer may charge more.
A retailer who is not compelled to make a charge may voluntarily do so.

The compulsory charge applies to a bag which is:
- new, not reused
- has a thickness of 70 microns or less
- has handles, an opening, and is not sealed.

The charge is not compulsory for:
- bags for life that are sold for more than 5p, including free replacements
- woven plastic bags
- bags solely used for uncooked fish and meat
- bags for unwrapped food such as chips where any existing package is not secure enough to prevent leakage
- bags for flowers, bulbs etc, and for goods contaminated by soil
- bags for unwrapped blades
- bags for prescription medicines
- bags for a service with no goods, such as dry cleaning
- bags for holding live fish or other aquatic creatures
- bags for goods in transit
- sealed bags for mail order and click-and-collect orders
- bags containing free promotional material.

Records must be kept. Premises may be inspected. Penalties may be imposed.

England

Until 31 March 2021, the charge is 5p per bag by a retailer who employs more than 250 staff.
From 1 April 2021, the charge is 10p per bag for all retailers of any size.
For a VAT-registered business, this is 8.33p per bag plus 1.67p VAT.

Scotland

From 20 October 2014, a 5p charge is made for bags.

Wales

From 1 October 2011, a 5p charge is made for bags for goods supplied from Wales, even if delivered outside Wales.

Northern Ireland

From 8 April 2013, a 5p charge is introduced for bags.
From 19 January 2014, the charge is also made for reusable carrier bags sold for less than 20p.

Coronavirus outbreak

During the coronavirus outbreak the charge was waived for online deliveries:
- in England between 21 March 2020 and 21 September 2020
- in Scotland between 1 April 2020 and 3 October 2020
- in Wales between 9 April 2020 and 30 December 2020.

Certificates of tax deposit

From 23 November 2017, no new certificates are issued, but existing certificates are honoured until 23 November 2023. The final rates of interest were fixed on 6 March 2009. No interest is paid for certificates below £100,000. Rates for certificates of £100,000 are:

Number of months held	**Used to pay tax**	**Cashed**
under 1	0%	0%
1 or more	0.75%	0.25%

Chancellors of the Exchequer

Name	**Party**	**Took office**
Rishi Sunak	Conservative	13 February 2020
Sajid Javid	Conservative	24 July 2019
Philip Hammond	Conservative	13 July 2016
George Osborne	Conservative	11 May 2010
Alistair Darling	Labour	28 June 2007
Gordon Brown	Labour	2 May 1997
Kenneth Clarke	Conservative	27 May 1993
Norman Lamont	Conservative	28 November 1990
John Major	Conservative	26 October 1989
Nigel Lawson	Conservative	11 June 1983
Sir Geoffrey Howe	Conservative	4 May 1979
Denis Healey	Labour	5 March 1974
Anthony Barber	Conservative	25 July 1970
Iain MacLeod	Conservative	20 June 1970

Charities associated benefit

A charity may provide a low value benefit to a donor by way of thank you without the tax relief being lost. Limits are set so that this provision cannot be exploited for tax avoidance.

From 6 April 2019, the limits are:

Value of gift	***Max value of benefit***
up to£100	25% of value of gift
above £100	£25, plus 5% of value above £100.

Before 6 April 2019, the limits are:

Value of gift	***Max value of benefit***
up to £100	25% of value of gift
between £100 and £1,000	£25
above £1,000	5% of value of gift.

For both periods, there is also a condition that the benefits associated with gifts do not exceed £2,500 (£500 before 6 April 2011).

Childcare

The cost of childcare is not tax-deductible under the normal rules of allowable expenses for employment as it is not incurred *in the performance of the duties* of the employment. However, some special provisions have been made.

Childcare vouchers	**from April 2005:** free of income tax to £50 a week; completely free of national insurance **from April 2006:** weekly income tax allowance increases to £55 **from April 2011:** weekly income tax allowance reduces to £28 a week for higher rate taxpayers, and £22 a week for additional rate taxpayers. It remains at £55 a week for basic rate taxpayers **from April 2013:** weekly income tax allowance for additional rate taxpayers increases to £25. Other rates unchanged **from April 2017:** Scottish taxpayers are subject to the additional rate allowance at the lower additional rate threshold for Scotland **from October 2018:** voucher scheme closed to new entrants but not for existing participants. New entrants restricted to tax-free childcare, generally of £2,000 a year, about £38.46 a week.
Free childcare	**from September 2017:** 30 hours of free childcare is provided to working parents up to £5,000 a year for 3- and 4-year olds. The previous limit was 15 hours **from 24 November 2017:** extended to children under 6 **from 15 January 2018:** extended to children under 10
Tax-free childcare	Available to a parent (or guardian) who need not be an employee. The parent must earn between £6,240 and £100,000 a year. The child must be under 12, or under 17 if disabled. They open an account into which they may up to £2,000 a year (£4,000 for a disabled child). At the end of the year, the government adds £2 for every £8 paid into the account.
Workplace nursery	Tax-free if provided by the employer.

Christmas parties

A Christmas party (or any staff social event at any time of the year) is a tax-free benefit in kind to employees, provided the cumulative cost per attendee during the tax year does not exceed:

From	**Amount**
6 April 2003	£150
6 April 1995	£75
6 April 1989	£50
Previously	£35

Note that an attendee does not have to be an employee.

The amount must include VAT even if the employer may recover it as input tax.

If an event exceeds the amount, the whole of that event ceases to be tax-free. So if an employer arranges three social events each costing £60, the first two will be tax-free but the whole of the third is taxable.

Climate change levy

This tax was introduced in 2001 as a charge on the commercial supply of energy. The charges for gas and electricity are per kilowatt hour.

The charges for oil and other taxable commodities are per kilogram
These rates are reduced when there is a climate change agreement on effect
Supplies of solid fuels, gas and liquefied petroleum gas used in electricity generation are also subject to carbon support rates.

From	Electricity	Gas	Oil	Other
1 April 2020	0.811p	0.406p	2.175p	3.174p
1 April 2019	0.847p	0.339p	2.175p	2.653p
1 April 2018	0.583p	0.203p	1.304p	1.591p
1 April 2017	0.568p	0.198p	1.272p	1.551p

Company car rates

An employee is taxed on the benefit of being provided with a car that may be used for private mileage. The benefit is the list price of the car multiplied by a percentage according to the car's carbon dioxide emissions.

Rates to 2019/20

Emission in gm/km	2019/20	2018/19	2017/18	2016/17
0	16%	13%	9%	7%
1-50	16%	13%	9%	7%
51-75	19%	16%	13%	11%
76-94	22%	19%	17%	15%
95-99	23%	20%	18%	16%
100-104	24%	21%	19%	17%
105-109	25%	22%	20%	18%
110-114	26%	23%	21%	19%
115-119	27%	24%	22%	20%
120-124	28%	25%	23%	21%
125-129	29%	26%	24%	22%
130-134	30%	27%	25%	23%
135-139	31%	28%	26%	24%
140-144	32%	29%	27%	25%
145-149	33%	30%	28%	26%
150-154	34%	31%	29%	27%
155-159	35%	32%	30%	28%
160-164	36%	33%	31%	29%
165-169	37%	34%	32%	30%
170-174	37%	35%	33%	31%
175-179	37%	36%	34%	32%
180-184	37%	37%	35%	33%
185-189	37%	37%	36%	34%
190-194	37%	37%	37%	35%
195-199	37%	37%	37%	36%
200 or more	37%	37%	37%	37%

Rates from 2020/21

From 6 April 2020, the rates use different break points.

For hybrid cars with emissions up to 50 gm/km, the rate depends on the maximum distance that may be travelled on electric power alone.

Emission	Mileage	2020/21	2021/22	2022/23
0		0%	1%	2%
1-50	over 130	0%	1%	2%
1-50	70-129	3%	4%	5%
1-50	40-69	6%	7%	8%
1-50	30-39	10%	11%	12%
1-50	below 30	12%	13%	14%
51-54		13%	14%	15%
55-59		14%	15%	16%
60-64		15%	16%	17%
65-69		16%	17%	18%
70-74		17%	18%	19%
75-79		18%	19%	20%
80-84		19%	20%	21%
85-89		20%	21%	22%
90-94		21%	22%	23%
95-99		22%	23%	24%
100-104		23%	24%	25%
105-109		24%	25%	26%
110-114		25%	26%	27%
115-119		26%	27%	28%
120-124		27%	28%	29%
125-130		28%	29%	30%
131-134		29%	30%	31%
135-139		30%	31%	32%
140-144		31%	32%	33%
145-149		32%	33%	34%
150-154		33%	34%	35%
155-159		34%	35%	36%
160-164		35%	36%	37%
165-169		36%	37%	37%
170 or more		37%	37%	37%

For diesel engine cars, the percentage is increased by 4 percentage points up to an overall maximum of 37%, unless (from 2018/19) the car meets the Real Driving Emissions Standard when no additional percentage points are added. If the employer also pays for the fuel, an additional car fuel benefit charge is made. There are separate rates for a company van.

Company car fuel benefit

If an employer provides fuel for the employee's private use, there is an additional tax charge. The taxable benefit is an annual multiplier which is multiplied by the same percentage as used for company car benefit.

Tax year	Multiplier
2020/21	£24,500

2019/20 £24,100
2018/19 £23,400
2017/18 £22,600
2016/17 £22,200
2015/16 £22,100
2014/15 £21,700
2013/14 £20,200
2010/11 – 2012/13 £18,800
2005/06 – 2009/10 £14,400

Compound interest

This table shows how £100 grows at different rates of compound interest over different numbers of years. Amounts above £10,000 are rounded to the nearest £1.

Rate %	1yr	2yr	3yr	4yr	5yr	6yr	7yr	8yr	9yr
1	101.00	102.01	103.03	104.06	105.10	106.15	107.21	108.29	109.37
1.5	101.50	103.02	104.57	106.14	107.73	109.34	110.98	112.65	114.34
2	102.00	104.04	106.12	108.24	110.41	112.62	114.87	117.17	119.51
2.5	102.50	105.06	107.69	110.38	113.14	115.97	118.87	121.84	124.89
3	103.00	106.09	109.27	112.55	115.93	119.41	122.99	126.68	130.48
3.5	103.50	107.12	110.87	114.75	118.77	122.93	127.23	131.68	136.29
4	104.00	108.16	112.49	116.99	121.67	126.53	131.59	136.86	142.33
4.5	104.50	109.20	114.12	119.25	124.62	130.23	136.09	142.21	148.61
5	105.00	110.25	115.76	121.55	127.63	134.01	140.71	147.75	155.13
5.5	105.50	111.30	117.42	123.88	130.70	137.88	145.47	153.47	161.91
6	106.00	112.36	119.10	126.25	133.82	141.85	150.36	159.38	168.95
6.5	106.50	113.42	120.79	128.65	137.01	145.91	155.40	165.50	176.26
7	107.00	114.49	122.50	131.08	140.26	150.07	160.58	171.82	183.85
7.5	107.50	115.56	124.23	133.55	143.56	154.33	165.90	178.35	191.72
8	108.00	116.64	125.97	136.05	146.93	158.69	171.38	185.09	199.90
8.5	108.50	117.72	127.73	138.59	150.37	163.15	177.01	192.06	208.39
9	109.00	118.81	129.50	141.16	153.86	167.71	182.80	199.26	217.19
9.5	109.50	119.90	131.29	143.77	157.42	172.38	188.76	206.69	226.32
10	110.00	121.00	133.10	146.41	161.05	177.16	194.87	214.36	235.79
10.5	110.50	122.10	134.92	149.09	164.74	182.04	201.16	222.28	245.62
11	111.00	123.21	136.76	151.81	168.51	187.04	207.62	230.45	255.80
11.5	111.50	124.32	138.62	154.56	172.34	192.15	214.25	238.89	266.36
12	112.00	125.44	140.49	157.35	176.23	197.38	221.07	247.60	277.31
12.5	112.50	126.56	142.38	160.18	180.20	202.73	228.07	256.58	288.65
13	113.00	127.69	144.29	163.05	184.24	208.20	235.26	265.84	300.40
13.5	113.50	128.82	146.21	165.95	188.36	213.78	242.64	275.40	312.58
14	114.00	129.96	148.15	168.90	192.54	219.50	250.23	285.26	325.19
14.5	114.50	131.10	150.11	171.88	196.80	225.34	258.01	295.42	338.26
15	115.00	132.25	152.09	174.90	201.14	231.31	266.00	305.90	351.79
15.5	115.50	133.40	154.08	177.96	205.55	237.41	274.20	316.71	365.80
16	116.00	134.56	156.09	181.06	210.03	243.64	282.62	327.84	380.30
16.5	116.50	135.72	158.12	184.21	214.60	250.01	291.26	339.32	395.31
17	117.00	136.89	160.16	187.39	219.24	256.52	300.12	351.15	410.84

17.5	117.50	138.06	162.22	190.61	223.97	263.16	309.22	363.33	426.91
18	118.00	139.24	164.30	193.88	228.78	269.96	318.55	375.89	443.55
18.5	118.50	140.42	166.40	197.18	233.66	276.89	328.12	388.82	460.75
19	119.00	141.61	168.52	200.53	238.64	283.98	337.93	402.14	478.54
19.5	119.50	142.80	170.65	203.93	243.69	291.21	348.00	415.86	496.95
20	120.00	144.00	172.80	207.36	248.83	298.60	358.32	429.98	515.98

Rate %	**10yr**	**11y**	**12yr**	**15yr**	**20yr**	**25yr**	**30yr**	**40yr**	**50yr**
1	110.46	111.57	112.68	116.10	122.02	128.24	134.78	148.89	164.46
1.5	116.05	117.79	119.56	125.02	134.69	145.09	156.31	181.40	210.52
2	121.90	124.34	126.82	134.59	148.59	164.06	181.14	220.80	269.16
2.5	128.01	131.21	134.49	144.83	163.86	185.39	209.76	268.51	343.71
3	134.39	138.42	142.58	155.80	180.61	209.38	242.73	326.20	438.39
3.5	141.06	146.00	151.11	167.53	198.98	236.32	280.68	395.93	558.49
4	148.02	153.95	160.10	180.09	219.11	266.58	324.34	480.10	710.67
4.5	155.30	162.29	169.59	193.53	241.17	300.54	374.53	581.64	903.26
5	162.89	171.03	179.59	207.89	265.33	338.64	432.19	704.00	1146.74
5.5	170.81	180.21	190.12	223.25	291.78	381.34	498.40	851.33	1454.20
6	179.08	189.83	201.22	239.66	320.71	429.19	574.35	1028.57	1842.02
6.5	187.71	199.92	212.91	257.18	352.36	482.77	661.44	1241.61	2330.67
7	196.72	210.49	225.22	275.90	386.97	542.74	761.23	1497.45	2945.70
7.5	206.10	221.56	238.18	295.89	424.79	609.83	875.50	1804.42	3718.97
8	215.89	233.16	251.82	317.22	466.10	684.85	1006.27	2172.45	4690.16
8.5	226.10	245.32	266.17	339.97	511.20	768.68	1155.83	2613.30	5908.63
9	236.74	258.04	281.27	364.25	560.44	862.31	1326.77	3140.94	7435.75
9.5	247.82	271.37	297.15	390.13	614.16	966.84	1522.03	3771.94	9347.73
10	259.37	285.31	313.84	417.72	672.75	1083.47	1744.94	4525.93	11739
10.5	271.41	299.91	331.40	447.13	736.62	1213.55	1999.26	5426.14	14727
11	283.94	315.18	349.85	478.46	806.23	1358.55	2289.23	6500.09	18456
11.5	296.99	331.15	369.23	511.83	882.06	1520.10	2619.67	7780.27	23107
12	310.58	347.85	389.60	547.36	964.63	1700.01	2995.99	9305.10	28900
12.5	324.73	365.32	410.99	585.18	1054.51	1900.26	3424.33	11120	36110
13	339.46	383.59	433.45	625.43	1152.31	2123.05	3911.59	13278	45074
13.5	354.78	402.67	457.04	668.25	1258.69	2370.81	4465.56	15843	56207
14	370.72	422.62	481.79	713.79	1374.35	2646.19	5095.02	18888	70023
14.5	387.31	443.47	507.77	762.22	1500.06	2952.14	5809.85	22502	87151
15	404.56	465.24	535.03	813.71	1636.65	3291.90	6621.18	26786	108366
15.5	422.49	487.98	563.62	868.42	1785.01	3669.02	7541.53	31862	134617
16	441.14	511.73	593.60	926.55	1946.08	4087.42	8584.99	37872	167070
16.5	460.53	536.52	625.04	988.30	2120.89	4551.43	9767.37	44982	207155
17	480.68	562.40	658.01	1053.87	2310.56	5065.78	11106	53387	256622
17.5	501.62	589.41	692.56	1123.49	2516.27	5635.68	12622	63316	317609
18	523.38	617.59	728.76	1197.37	2739.30	6266.86	14337	75038	392736
18.5	545.99	647.00	766.69	1275.78	2981.03	6965.60	16276	88866	485196
19	569.47	677.67	806.42	1358.95	3242.94	7738.81	18468	105167	598891
19.5	593.85	709.65	848.04	1447.17	3526.62	8594.05	20943	124370	738576
20	619.17	743.01	891.61	1540.70	3833.76	9539.62	23738	146977	910044

YEARS IT TAKES FOR A SUM TO REACH A MULTIPLE AT DIFFERENT RATES

Rate	*Double*	*Treble*	*Quadruple*
1%	69.7	110.4	139.3
1.5%	46.6	73.8	93.1
2%	35.0	55.5	70.0
2.5%	28.1	44.5	56.1
3%	23.4	37.2	46.9
3.5%	20.1	31.9	40.3
4%	17.7	28.0	35.3
4.5%	15.7	25.0	31.5
5%	14.2	22.5	28.4
5.5%	12.9	20.5	25.9
6%	11.9	18.9	23.8
6.5%	11.0	17.4	22.0
7%	10.2	16.2	20.5
7.5%	9.6	15.2	19.2
8%	9.0	14.3	18.0
8.5%	8.5	13.5	17.0
9%	8.0	12.7	16.1
9.5%	7.6	12.1	15.3
10%	7.3	11.5	14.5
11%	6.6	10.5	13.3
12%	6.1	9.7	12.2
13%	5.7	9.0	11.3
14%	5.3	8.4	10.6
15%	5.0	7.9	9.9
16%	4.7	7.4	9.3
17%	4.4	7.0	8.8
18%	4.2	6.6	8.4
19%	4.0	6.3	8.0
20%	3.8	6.0	7.6

Congestion charge and other road user charges

Congestion charge in London

This charge was introduced in 2003 to reduce congestion in central London.

A western section was added in February 2007 and removed on 4 January 2011.

From 22 June 2020, congestion charge applies between 7am and 10pm on every day.

Previously, the charge applies to vehicles entering the zone between 7am to 6pm, Monday to Friday.

Penalties are charged if the charge is not paid by midnight on the day of travel.

From	*Charge*
22 June 2020	£15
June 2014	£11.50
January 2011	£10
July 2005	£8

February 2003 £5

The charge was suspended from 23 March 2020 to 21 June 2020.

Low emission zone in London

A low emission zone came into effect on 4 February 2008 for almost the whole Greater London area.

It operates for 24 hours a day, 7 days a week.

A vehicle that meets the relevant emission standard does not pay the charge.

Otherwise, the charge is £100 per day for vans, diesel vehicles to 3.5 tonnes, and minibuses up to 5 tonnes; and £200 for other vehicles.

The standards are made tougher from 1 March 2021. The charge for larger vehicles increases to £300 a day.

Ultra-low emissions zone (ULEZ) in London

The ultra-low emission zone came into effect on 8 April 2019.

It covers the same area as the congestion charge.

It applies for 24 hours a day for every day except Christmas Day.

For vehicles that do not meet the emission standard, the charge is £12.50 for most vehicles; and £100 for vehicles over 3.5 tonnes, and buses or coaches over 5 tonnes.

Durham road user charge

This imposes a daily charge of £2 between 10am and 4pm Monday to Saturday,

M6 toll

The M6 toll road is an alternative to the normal M6 motorway around Birmingham.

The charge depends on whether the driver leaves at a midway junction.

For a car, the charge is:

Time	*Mainline*	*Junction*
Weekday 7am – 7pm	£6.70	£4.80
Off peak 5am-7am; 7pm-11pm	£6.60	£4.80
Night 11pm-5am	£4.20	£3.20
Weekend day 5am-11pm	£5.60	£4.20
Weekend night 11pm-5am	£4.20	£3.20

There are different rates for motorcycles, cars with trailers, vans, and lorries.

Dartford crossing

Vehicle	*One-off*	*With an account*
Motorcycles	free	free
Vehicles with two axles	£3.00	£2.63
Vehicles with more than two axles	£6.00	£5.19

The charge must be paid by midnight on the following day or a penalty will be incurred.

No charge is made for vehicles which are free of vehicle excise duty because of a disability.

There are discounts for residents of Dartford and Thurrock.

Severn Bridges

The two bridges are part of M4 and M48.

The tolls were scrapped on 17 December 2018.

Tolls

The M6 toll and Dartford crossing are the only tolls on UK motorways.

The following A-roads have tolls:

- A4 Batheaston Bridge

- A15 Humber Bridge
- A19 Tyne Tunnels
- A38 Tamar Bridge
- A41 Mersey Tunnels
- A57 Durham Bridge
- A59 Mersey Tunnels
- A533 Mersey Gateway
- A3025 Itchen Bridge

There are many other bridges, tunnels, B-roads and minor roads for which tolls are charged.

Construction industry scheme deductions

Status of subcontractor	Deduction
Registered for gross payments with HMRC	0%
Registered with HMRC but not for gross payments	20%
Not registered with HMRC	30%

Coronavirus schemes

The coronavirus outbreak in 2020 led to more than 200 pieces of legislation, touching almost every area of human activity, including tax. The government announced various schemes to provide support to individuals and businesses affected.

Apprentice scheme

- the scheme started on 1 September 2020
- the government pays £2,000 for each new apprenticeship up to the age of 24, and £1,500 from the age of 25

Bounce back loans

- scheme to help businesses that are too small for Coronavirus Business Interruption Loan Scheme to get a government-supported loan
- businesses may borrow up to 25% of turnover
- loan is a minimum if £2,000 and maximum of £50,000
- government guarantees 100% of the loan
- government pays interest for first 12 months
- after 12 months interest is fixed at 2.5% pa
- if a business applied for a loan less than the maximum allowed, it may apply for a top-up loan by 31 January 2021 (originally 30 November 2020)
- the business must be based in the UK, have been established before 1 March 2020 and been negatively impacted by coronavirus
- loan is for 6 years, but may be repaid earlier for no fee
- no repayments are due for first year
- before first payment is due, lender will offer to extend loan to 10 years
- the lender may allow an interest-free option for six months up to three times during the loan's lifetime
- the lender may allow one repayment holiday of 6 months once six repayments have been made
- scheme is offered by 29 participating lenders, including most retail banks.

Closed business grant

- where a business is told to close, the government provides a cash grant of £3,000 a month
- businesses in the hospitality, leisure and retail sectors that have suffered reduced demand due to local restrictions may claim backdated grants of up to £2,100 a month for the period between 1 August 2020 and 5 November 2020
- local authorities were provided with £1.1 billion to provide local help to businesses.
- further help has been provided.

Contain Outbreak Management Fund (COMF)

- central government provides local authorities with a sum equal to £8 per head of population for help for critically vulnerable people during lockdown from 5 November 2020 to 2 December 2021.

Coronavirus Business Interruption Loan Scheme (CBILS)

- available to businesses with annual turnover up to £45 million
- from 30 July 2020 a business in financial difficulties at 31 December 2019 may apply provided its turnover is below £9 million and it has fewer than 50 employees
- the deadline was put back from 30 September 2020 to 30 November 2020, and then again to 31 January 2021.

Coronavirus Job Retention Scheme (CJRS), furlough

- this scheme paid 80% of wages
- from 1 July 2020, employees may work part-time
- HMRC started to check compliance with scheme rules from 18 Aug 2020
- overpaid CJRS must be refunded by employer within 90 days to avoid a penalty
- deadline of 30 November 2020 was extended to 31 January 2021

Coronavirus Job Retention Scheme 2

- Coronavirus Job Retention Scheme was due to end on 31 October 2020, but a second furlough scheme was announced on 5 November 2020 to run from 1 November 2020 to 31 March 2020. on 17 December 2020, this was extended to 30 April 2021
- the scheme pays 80% of wages. This figure was to be reviewed in January 2021, but on 17 December, it was confirmed that it would remain at 80%
- a worker may be furloughed if he or she must stay at home such as for childcare
- a worker should not be furloughed because the worker is going on leave or it is a quiet time of year for a seasonal business. The worker or business must have been affected by coronavirus
- maximum payment by government is £2,500 a month
- the employer pays employer's national insurance and pension costs
- claims may be made from 11 November 2020
- an employer may claim even though the employer had not claimed under the previous scheme
- the employee must have been on the payroll on 30 October 2020
- a claim may be made for someone who was on the payroll on 23 September 2020 and is subsequently re-employed
- the employer must have made a PAYE real time information submission for the employee at any time between 20 March 2020 and 30 October 2020

- for claims after 1 December 2020, HMRC will publish from 1 February 2021, the names of employers who have claimed under this scheme and will indicate the approximate amount from 14 bands

Deferments

- changes to accounting standard IAS 1 on liabilities is put back by one year to 2023
- HMRC becoming a secondary preferential creditor is put back from 1 April 2020 to 1 December 2020
- Customs tariffs on coronavirus-related products are suspended from 1 January 2021
- the right to evict tenants has been suspended for periods that have been extended

Covid Winter Grant Scheme

- announced by government on 8 November 2020
- central government provides £170 million to local authorities to provide targeted help to residents in need
- at least 80% of these grants must be used to buy food or pay bills between December 2020 and March 2021

Direct earnings attachments

- these deductions from wages for overpayments of social security were suspended from April 2020 to June 2020, and then indefinitely

Eat out to help out

- subsidy for meals on Monday to Wednesday during August 2020
- government will refund half the cost of a meal up to £10, including children's meals, but not alcoholic drink
- the restaurant or other establishment must register with the government by 7 July 2020
- the discount is on the sale price after any other discounts have been offered
- with the reduction to 5% VAT, this means that meals can be 62.5% cheaper

Green Homes Grant Scheme

- pays for two-thirds of the cost of making homes more energy efficient up to £5,000 per home
- low income households could receive £10,000
- traders were invited to register from 12 August 2020
- homeowners and landlords can check their eligibility from 28 August 2020

Hospitality sector support

• a grant additional to existing grants for the hospitality, leisure and non-essential retail sector that are required to close because of lockdowns announced from December 2019

• the grant is an amount per property according to its rateable value. Up to £15,000, the grant us £4,000; between £15,001 and £51,000, the grant is £6,000; and above £51,000, it is £9,000

• the government has provided a further £594 million to local authorities for further discretionary support

Job retention bonus

This was announced as a £1,000 bonus for every worker who remains on the payroll for three months after the Coronavirus Job Retention Scheme ended on 31 October 2020.

As the scheme did not end then but was extended by five months, this scheme was not introduced.

Kickstart

• the scheme began on 2 September 2020
• provides placements for universal credit claimants aged between 16 and 24
• the placement lasts for six months during which time the government pays the wages, typically about £6,500 per worker
• the claimant must work for at least 25 hours a week
• the claimant must be paid the national minimum wage which the employer may top up
• the employer may also claim £1,500 to set up the scheme
• an employer making 30 of fewer placements must do so via an intermediary

Self-employment income support scheme (SEISS) 1

• this consisted of two payments
• could be claimed by a self-employed person who was trading in 2019/20
• the first claim could be made between 13 May 2020 and 13 July 2020
• the person must have submitted their 2018/19 tax return by 23 April 2020
• at least half their income must have come from self-employment
• their profits must have been no more than £50,000 averaged over three years
• the first payment was 80% of three months' profits to a maximum of £7,500 paid in a single payment
• the second payment could be claimed between 17 August 2020 and 19 October 2020
• the second payment was 70% of three months' profits to a maximum of £6,750

Self-employment income support scheme 2

• on 5 November 2020, the government announced a third period for which self-employment income support scheme would be paid
• this runs for three months from 1 November 2020 to 31 January 2021
• it is paid at 80% of annual profits to a maximum of £2,500 per month
• payments are made sooner than under SEISS 1 with first payment before Christmas 2020
• claims must be submitted by 30 November 2020
• a second payment will be made for months February 2021 to April 2021, details to be announced

Self-employment income support schemes 3

• scheme 3 was announced on 5 November 2020 for three months from 1 November 2020 to 31 January 2021
• it pays 80% of profits to a maximum payout of £2,500 a month
• claims must be made by 30 November 2020
• payments are made sooner than previous schemes

Self-employment income support scheme 4

- announced on 5 November 2020 for February 2021 to April 2021
- details not announced

Self-isolation payment

- scheme started on 1 September 2020
- claimant must be receiving universal credit or working tax credit, and be employed or self-employed
- payment is £13 a day in areas with a high incidence of coronavirus
- it appears to have been replaced by Test and Trace Support

Social security changes

- universal credit increased by £20 a week to April 2021.
- minimum floor rule for universal credit suspended until 30 April 2021

Stamp duty threshold

- the threshold for stamp duty land tax was increased from £125,000 to £500,000 in England Northern Ireland between 8 July 2020 and 31 March 2021
- the threshold for land and buildings transaction tax in Scotland increases from £145,000 to £250,000 between 15 July 2020 and 31 March 2021
- the threshold for land transaction tax in Wales increases to £250,000 between 27 Jul 2020 and 31 March 2021

Statutory sick pay (SSP)

- from 28 May 2020, an employee told to self-isolate may claim SSP
- from 5 August 2020 up to ten days' SSP may be claimed for self-isolation. The self-isolation period was extended from seven to ten days from 31 July 2020

Tax changes

- from 11 June 2020 to 5 April 2021, expenses incurred by an employer in arranging for home working by employees is not a taxable benefit in kind
- on 8 July 2020, HMRC confirms that coronavirus tests are not a taxable benefit in kind
- on 9 July 2020, HMRC confirms that personal protective equipment provided by an employer is not a taxable benefit in kind

Test and Trace Support

- pays a lump sum of £500 to someone on a low income who must self-isolate, is on a low income and cannot work from home
- scheme introduced from 12 October 2020, administered by the local authority, with payment backdated to 28 September 2020.

VAT hospitality rate

- from 15 July 2020 to 12 January 2021, the 20% rate of VAT is reduced to 5% for three new categories of hospitality: catering, holiday accommodation, and shows and attractions.
- given effect by new groups 14 to 16 in VATA 1994 Sch 7A
- flat rate scheme percentages reduced for same period

VAT other provisions

- personal protective equipment is zero-rated from VAT and exempt from Customs duty from 1 May 2020, initially to 31 July 2020 but then extended
- zero-rating of e-books was brought forward from 1 December 2020 to 1 May 2020

Corporation tax

From	*Rate*
1 April 2019	19%
1 April 2015	20%
1 April 2014	21%
1 April 2013	23%
1 April 2012	24%
1 April 2011	26%

Before 1 April 2015, there was a lower small profits rate.
Restitution interest is taxed at 45% from 21 October 2015.
The rate for ring-fenced profits in the oil industry has been 30% since 2014, with a lower rate of 19%.
The government abandoned plans to reduce the rate to 17% from April 2020.
Banks pay an additional 8 percentage points from 1 January 2016.
There are provisions, yet to be used, to allow Northern Ireland to charge a lower rate.
Merchant shipping may elect to pay tonnage tax instead of corporation tax on its fleet.
Loans to participators in a close company are subject to 32.5%.

Council tax bands

All residential properties are allocated a band based on their historic values. A band D property is considered the average. Council tax for other bands is determined as a multiple of band D. So if the council tax for a band D property is £1,800, the council tax for a band A property is £1,200, and for a band H property £3,600.
Council tax is not charged in Northern Ireland.

Band	Multiple
A	2/3
B	7/9
C	8/9
D	1
E	11/9
F	13/9
G	5/3
H	2
I	7/3 (only in Wales)

For **England,** properties are banded according to their sale value on 1 April 1991

Band	Maximum value
A	£40,000
B	£52,000
C	£68,000
D	£88,000
E	£120,000
F	£160,000
G	£320,000
H	no limit

For **Scotland,** properties are banded according to their sale value on 1 April 1991

Band	Maximum value
A	£27,000
B	£35,000
C	£45,000
D	£58,000
E	£80,000
F	£106,000

G £212,000
H no limit

For **Wales,** properties are now banded according to their market value on 1 April 2003

Band	Maximum value
A	£44,000
B	£65,000
C	£91,000
D	£123,000
E	£162,000
F	£223,000
G	£324,000
H	£424,000
I	no limit

Northern Ireland never adopted council tax or community charge but stayed with the rates.

In 2007, it changed to a system whereby each council sets a domestic rate poundage which is multiplied by the capital value of each home.

So a £100,000 home with a poundage of 0.008000 would give rates of £800.

Creative industry reliefs

For each of these reliefs, there are many conditions that must be met.

Animation

- the animation must be certified by the British Film Institute
- animation must be intended for broadcast
- at least 51% of core expenditure is on animation
- at least 10% of core costs relate to UK activities
- additional deduction is lower of 80% of core expenditure and amount of UK core expenditure
- animation relief may be surrendered for a 25% payable tax credit

Children's television

- programme must be certified by the British Film Institute
- programme must be intended for broadcasting, including online streaming
- primary audience for programme is for those under 15
- at least 10% of core costs must relate to UK activities
- quizzes, game shows, competitions and similar are allowed only if the prize total does not exceed £1,000
- additional deduction is lower of 80% of core expenditure and amount of UK core expenditure
- relief may be surrendered for a 25% payable tax credit

Films

- film must pass the cultural test or qualify as an official co-production
- film must be intended for theatrical release
- at least 10% of core costs must relate to UK activities
- may claim lower of 80% of core expenditure or total of UK core expenditure
- may surrender film relief for a payable tax credit of 25% of core expenditure

High-end television

- programme must be certified by the British Film Institute
- programme must be intended for broadcast to general public, including online streaming
- programme must be drama, comedy or documentary
- at least 10% of core costs must relate to UK activities
- average core expenditure is at least £1 million per hour of slot length
- slot length must be at least 30 minutes
- some programmes are excluded, such as current affairs, quiz shows, variety shows, competitions, contests, live events, and training programmes
- additional deduction is lower of 80% of total core expenditure or amount of UK core expenditure
- relief may be surrendered for a 25% payable tax credit

Museums and galleries

- may be claimed in respect of exhibitions at one or more places
- exhibition must be a curated display of an organised collection of objects or works considered to be of scientific, historic, artistic or cultural interest. An exhibition may be of a single item
- at least 25% of core expenditure must be in European Economic Area
- excluded are competitions, live performances, sales, and displays of living creatures
- additional deduction is lower of 80% of total core expenditure or amount of EEA core expenditure
- relief may be surrendered for a 20% payable tax credit, or 25% if touring
- a touring exhibition must be held in at least 2 venues; at least 25% of objects or works displayed in first exhibition must be displayed in subsequent exhibitions; there should not be a gap of more than 6 months between exhibitions.

Orchestra

- may be claimed by a musical group of at least 12 players, at least half of whom are not electronically amplified. This means that brass bands and dance bands can be included. The ensemble may play any style of music
- the group must perform live for the paying public or for educational purposes
- excluded are performances for advertising, competitions and recordings
- additional deduction is lower of 80% of total core expenditure or amount of UK core expenditure
- relief may be surrendered for a 25% payable tax credit

Theatre

- available for ballet, and for plays, operas, musical and dramatic pieces where performances are live and the performers play roles
- all or a high proportion of the performances are to paying members of the public
- at least 25% of core expenditure is within European Economic Area
- productions are excluded if it is mainly for advertising, uses a wild animal, is of a sexual nature, or has a main object of making a film
- additional deduction is lower of 80% of total core expenditure or amount of EEA core expenditure
- relief may be surrendered for a 20% payable tax credit, or 25% if touring

- touring means performance in at least 6 venues, and at least 14 performances in at least 2 venues

Video games

- game must be certified by British Film Institute
- game must be intended for supply to general public
- at least 25% of core expenditure is within European Economic Area
- additional deduction is lower of 80% of total core expenditure or amount of UK core expenditure
- relief may be surrendered for a 25% payable tax credit

Criminal fines

Many Acts on criminal law do not specify an amount for a fine but say that an offence attracts a fine at a Level between 1 and 5. These amounts are currently (from 12 March 2015):

Level	*Fine*
1	£200
2	£500
3	£1,000
4	£2,500
5	unlimited

Customs tariff

UK tariff applies from 1 January 2021. The full list of 11,830 items can be downloaded from https://www.check-future-uk-trade-tariffs.service.gov.uk/tariff?q=&n=100&p=1

In addition to these rates, goods from certain countries may be subject to countervailing duty or anti-dumping duty.

The following list gives a few, fairly random, samples from the full tariff list. It should be noted that many of these products have alternative codes and tariffs for product variations.

Code	Description	UK tariff
9105 11 00	Alarm clock (not electric)	4%
2827 10 00	Ammonium chloride	4%
0808 10 80	Apples	4% (Jan – Mar)
		0% (Apr – Jul)
		8% (Aug - Dec)
0803 90 10	Bananas	£95 per 1000 kg
1602 50 95	Beef	16%
2203 00 01	Beer, in bottles	0%
0106 41 00	Bees	0%
8712 00 30	Bicycles	14%
0106 31 --	Bird of prey, live	0%
0810 30 10	Blackcurrants	8%
4901 99 00	Books	0%
1905 90 30	Bread	8%
8703 21 10	Cars, new	10%
0406 90 21	Cheddar cheese, not grated or powdered	£139 per 100 kg

0306 39 90 Crustaceans for human consumption	12%
3204 12 00 Dyes, synthetic acid	6%
2529 10 00 Feldspar	0%
0304 89 90 Fish fillets, frozen	14%
9201 20 00 Grand piano	0%
2009 39 51 Lemon juice	14% plus £17 per 100 kg
0401 10 90 Milk, skimmed in packs of less than 2 litres	£10 per 100 kg
0603 13 00 Orchids, fresh cut	8%
1511 90 99 Palm oil	8%
0809 30 90 Peaches	16%
0804 30 00 Pineapples	4%
1602 49 19 Pork	£71 per 100 kg
0302 84 10 Sea bass, fresh or frozen	14%
6404 19 10 Shoes	16%
9402 10 00 Swivel chairs	0%
8528 72 40 Televisions, LCD screen	14%
0702 00 00 Tomatoes	8% (Nov – 14 May) 14% (15 May – Oct)
2903 23 00 Trichloroethylene	4%
3402 90 90 Washing powder	4%
2208 30 30 Whisky, single malt Scotch	0%

Day counter

This is a simple method to determine the number of days between two dates.

The number corresponding to the first date is subtracted from that for the second.

If the range of dates is inclusive, in that the first and late date should both be included, the answer is increased by 1.

If the range of dates spans 29 February, the answer should be increased by 1.

This table can be used to calculate pay for an irregular pay period, or to determine whether a condition for statutory residence test or furnished holiday lettings has been met.

For example, a person is not in the UK between 13 September and the following 10 March. The number of inclusive days this covers is 434 – 256 + 1 = 179.

Year 1

Day	Jan	Feb	Mar	Apr	May	Jun	Jul	Aug	Sep	Oct	Nov	Dec	
1	1	32	60	91	121	152	182	213	244	274	305	335	
2	2	33	61	92	122	153	183	214	245	275	306	336	
3	3	34	62	93	123	154	184	215	246	276	307	337	
4	4	35	63	94	124	155	185	216	247	277	308	338	
5	5	36	64	95	125	156	186	217	248	278	309	339	
6	6	37	65	96	126	157	187	218	249	279	310	340	
7	7	38	66	97	127	158	188	219	250	280	311	341	
8	8	39	67	98	128	159	189	220	251	281	312	342	
9	9	40	68	99	129	160	190	221	252	282	313	343	
10	10	41	69	100	130	161	191	222	253	283	314	344	
11	11	42	70	101	131	162	192	223	254	284	315	345	

12	12	43	71	102	132	163	193	224	255	285	316	346
13	13	44	72	103	133	164	194	225	256	286	317	347
14	14	45	73	104	134	165	195	226	257	287	318	348
15	15	46	74	105	135	166	196	227	258	288	319	349
16	16	47	75	106	136	167	197	228	259	289	320	350
17	17	48	76	107	137	168	198	229	260	290	321	351
18	18	49	77	108	138	169	199	230	261	291	322	352
19	19	50	78	109	139	170	200	231	262	292	323	353
20	20	51	79	110	140	171	201	232	263	293	324	354
21	21	52	80	111	141	172	202	233	264	294	325	355
22	22	53	81	112	142	173	203	234	265	295	326	356
23	23	54	82	113	143	174	204	235	266	296	327	357
24	24	55	83	114	144	175	205	236	267	297	328	358
25	25	56	84	115	145	176	206	237	268	298	329	359
26	26	57	85	116	146	177	207	238	269	299	330	360
27	27	58	86	117	147	178	208	239	270	300	331	361
28	28	59	87	118	148	179	209	240	271	301	332	362
29	29		88	119	149	180	210	241	272	302	333	363
30	30		89	120	150	181	211	242	273	303	334	364
31	31		90		151		212	243		304		365

Year 2

Day	Jan	Feb	Mar	Apr	May	Jun	Jul	Aug	Sep	Oct	Nov	Dec
1	366	397	425	456	486	517	547	578	609	639	670	700
2	367	398	426	457	487	518	548	579	610	640	671	701
3	368	399	427	458	488	519	549	580	611	641	672	702
4	369	400	428	459	489	520	550	581	612	642	673	703
5	370	401	429	460	490	521	551	582	613	643	674	704
6	371	402	430	461	491	522	552	583	614	644	675	705
7	372	403	431	462	492	523	553	584	615	645	676	706
8	373	404	432	463	493	524	554	585	616	646	677	707
9	374	405	433	464	494	525	555	586	617	647	678	708
10	375	406	434	465	495	526	556	587	618	648	679	709
11	376	407	435	466	496	527	557	588	619	649	680	710
12	377	408	436	467	497	528	558	589	620	650	681	711
13	378	409	437	468	498	529	559	590	621	651	682	712
14	379	410	438	469	499	530	560	591	622	652	683	713
15	380	411	439	470	500	531	561	592	623	653	684	714
16	381	412	440	471	501	532	562	593	624	654	685	715
17	382	413	441	472	502	533	563	594	625	655	686	716
18	383	414	442	473	503	534	564	595	626	656	687	717
19	384	415	443	474	504	535	565	596	627	657	688	718
20	385	416	444	475	505	536	566	597	628	658	689	719
21	386	417	445	476	506	537	567	598	629	659	690	720

22	387	418	446	477	507	538	568	599	630	660	691	721
23	388	419	447	478	508	539	569	600	631	661	692	722
24	389	420	448	479	509	540	570	601	632	662	693	723
25	390	421	449	480	510	541	571	602	633	663	694	724
26	391	422	450	481	511	542	572	603	634	664	695	725
27	392	423	451	482	512	543	573	604	635	665	696	726
28	393	424	452	483	513	544	574	605	636	666	697	727
29	394		453	484	514	545	575	606	637	667	698	728
30	395		454	485	515	546	576	607	638	668	699	729
31	396		455		516		577	608		669		730

Deadlines and due dates

Calendar dates

31 January
- Due date for tax returns submitted on-line
- First instalment of income tax for current year, and balance from previous year

1 February
- second 5% penalty imposed for unpaid tax and national insurance liabilities from year before last

14 February
- last day for an employee to apply for deferment of class 1 national insurance for current tax year

1 April
- Start of financial year for corporation tax

5 April
- Last opportunity to utilise income tax personal allowances, annual ISA allowances, and exemptions for capital gains tax and inheritance tax

6 April
- Start of tax year for income tax, national insurance, capital gains tax and inheritance tax

19 April
- Date for FPS (full payment submission) for previous tax year's PAYE

30 April
- Due date for inheritance tax on lifetime transfers between previous 6 April and 30 September.
- Daily £10 penalties start for outstanding self-assessment.
- ATED returns must be filed and any reliefs claimed

5 May
- Last day for a tax credits claim to be backdated to 6 April

19 May
- Date after which submission of full payment submission for PAYE attracts a penalty

31 May
- P60s must be issued to employees
- FATCA returns are due for period to previous 31 December

5 July
- PAYE settlement agreements must be agreed with HMRC
- Letting agents acting for non-resident landlords must make returns of rents paid to landlord

6 July
- P11D returns must be submitted
- Employers must provide employees with P11D information
- Annual returns for employee share schemes
- Report of termination payments above £30,000

	• Directors and employees must make good cost of certain benefits to avoid being taxed on them
7 July	• Return of non-cash benefits in previous tax year to retired employees
19 July	• Class 1A national insurance due for previous year
31 July	• Second instalment of income tax, capital gains tax and class 4 national insurance for tax year ended last 5 April
1 August	• Taxpayers who have not paid previous year's tax become liable to additional penalty of 5% of the tax
31 August	• latest date for HMRC to issue a tax self-assessment return form for completion by 31 October. A later issued form must be completed within two months of its issue
5 October	• date by which a taxpayer liable to income tax or capital gains tax must notify HMRC of liability if no notice has been issued
30 September	• Self-assessment due if HMRC is calculating the tax
19 October	• Settlement of PSAs (PAYE settlement agreements) and payment of class 1B national insurance
31 October	• Due date for self-assessment tax returns on paper
31 December	• Due date for self-assessment return if underpaid tax is to be collected by adjustment of tax code

Deadlines and due dates for specific taxes

Capital gains tax	• 30 days from the sale of a UK residence (before 6 April 2020, this only applied to non-resident taxpayers)
	• Otherwise, with income tax return
Corporation tax	• Nine months and 1 day after end of accounting period
	• Where payment is by instalments on 14th day of 7th, 10th, 13th and 16th month of the accounting period
Inheritance tax	• Lifetime transfers between 6 April and 30 September: next 30 April
	• Lifetime transfers between 1 October and 5 April: six months after the end of the month of transfer
	• Transfers on death: six months after end of month of death
PAYE	• 19th after end of tax month (5th of month) for non-electronic payments
	• 22nd after end of tax month if paid electronically
VAT	• end of month after end of quarter unless paid electronically
	• 7th after end of following month if paid electronically. If paid by direct debit, the return must be submitted by 7th but funds are taken on 10th.

Digital services tax

This is charged at 2% on UK revenues of digital platform companies with annual revenue above £500 million, from its introduction on 1 April 2020.

From 14 October 2020, the interest for late payment if 2.6%, and the repayment rate is 0.5% (SI 2020 No 995)

Discounted cashflow factors

This table gives the factors to represent net present value by which a future sum, expressed in years, is worth today at different percentage rates.

The 3.5% factors may be used to calculate stamp duty land tax on lease income, though HMRC provides an online calculator that may be more convenient.

Years	1	1.5	2	2.5	3	3.5	4	4.5	5
1	0.9900	0.9850	0.9800	0.9750	0.9700	0.9650	0.9600	0.9550	0.9500
2	0.9801	0.9702	0.9604	0.9506	0.9409	0.9312	0.9216	0.9120	0.9025
3	0.9703	0.9557	0.9412	0.9269	0.9127	0.8986	0.8847	0.8710	0.8574
4	0.9606	0.9413	0.9224	0.9037	0.8853	0.8672	0.8493	0.8318	0.8145
5	0.9510	0.9272	0.9039	0.8811	0.8587	0.8368	0.8154	0.7944	0.7738
6	0.9415	0.9133	0.8858	0.8591	0.8330	0.8075	0.7828	0.7586	0.7351
7	0.9321	0.8996	0.8681	0.8376	0.8080	0.7793	0.7514	0.7245	0.6983
8	0.9227	0.8861	0.8508	0.8167	0.7837	0.7520	0.7214	0.6919	0.6634
9	0.9135	0.8728	0.8337	0.7962	0.7602	0.7257	0.6925	0.6607	0.6302
10	0.9044	0.8597	0.8171	0.7763	0.7374	0.7003	0.6648	0.6310	0.5987
11	0.8953	0.8468	0.8007	0.7569	0.7153	0.6758	0.6382	0.6026	0.5688
12	0.8864	0.8341	0.7847	0.7380	0.6938	0.6521	0.6127	0.5755	0.5404
13	0.8775	0.8216	0.7690	0.7195	0.6730	0.6293	0.5882	0.5496	0.5133
14	0.8687	0.8093	0.7536	0.7016	0.6528	0.6073	0.5647	0.5249	0.4877
15	0.8601	0.7972	0.7386	0.6840	0.6333	0.5860	0.5421	0.5012	0.4633
16	0.8515	0.7852	0.7238	0.6669	0.6143	0.5655	0.5204	0.4787	0.4401
17	0.8429	0.7734	0.7093	0.6502	0.5958	0.5457	0.4996	0.4571	0.4181
18	0.8345	0.7618	0.6951	0.6340	0.5780	0.5266	0.4796	0.4366	0.3972
19	0.8262	0.7504	0.6812	0.6181	0.5606	0.5082	0.4604	0.4169	0.3774
20	0.8179	0.7391	0.6676	0.6027	0.5438	0.4904	0.4420	0.3982	0.3585
21	0.8097	0.7280	0.6543	0.5876	0.5275	0.4732	0.4243	0.3803	0.3406
22	0.8016	0.7171	0.6412	0.5729	0.5117	0.4567	0.4073	0.3631	0.3235
23	0.7936	0.7064	0.6283	0.5586	0.4963	0.4407	0.3911	0.3468	0.3074
24	0.7857	0.6958	0.6158	0.5446	0.4814	0.4253	0.3754	0.3312	0.2920
25	0.7778	0.6853	0.6035	0.5310	0.4670	0.4104	0.3604	0.3163	0.2774

Diverted profits tax

This is charged at 25% on diverted profits by UK companies from 1 April 2015, except for ring-fenced profits, where the rate is 55%.

Duty-free allowances

From January 2021

From 1 January 2021, duty-free allowances apply equally to EU and non-EU countries. The allowances are:

- 42 litres of beer
- 18 litres of still wine
- 4 litres of spirits or 9 litre of sparkling wine or fortified wine
- one of 200 cigarettes, 100 cigarillos, 50 cigars, 250 grams of tobacco, or 200 sticks of tobacco for heating
- £390 of other goods, or £270 if arriving by private plane or boat.

Each category may be split. So, for example, someone may bring in 100 cigarettes and 25 cigars.

If someone declares that they have exceeded the limit, they may pay duty under a simplified system up to the upper threshold, as set out in SI 2020 No 1412:

Description	*Excise duty*	*Upper threshold*
Beer	80p/litre	110 litres
Still wine	£2.97/litre	90 litres
Sparkling wine	£3.81/litre	60 litres
Cider	40p/litre	20 litres
Strong cider	£2.88/litre	20 litres
Made-wine	£2.97/litre	20 litres
Spirits	£10.66/litre	10 litres
Cigarettes	£320,90/1000	800 cigarettes
Hand-rolling tobacco	£271.40/kilo	1 kilogram
Other tobacco	£134.24/kilo	1 kilogram
Cigars	£305.23/kilo	200 cigars
Cigarillos	£305.23/kilo	400 cigarillos
Tobacco for heating	£75.48/100 sticks	800 sticks

Before January 2021: outside EU

The duty-free allowance for goods imported from outside the EU apply to goods imported by the traveller himself or herself and are for personal use, which includes giving away as a gift. The traveller must be at least 17 years old.

The limits are:

- 16 litres of beer
- 4 litres of non-sparkling wine
- either 1 litre of spirits (over 22% alcohol) or 2 litres of sparkling wine or fortified wine
- one of 200 cigarettes, 100 cigarettes, 50 cigars, 250 grams of tobacco

The last two allowances may be split.

- other gifts up to £390, or £270 if arriving by private plane or boat.

Customs duty on amounts above these limits is payable at 2.5% on goods up to £630, and at different rates above £630.

Import VAT may also be payable.

Before January 2021: from the EU

Until 31 December 2020, no duty is payable on goods brought in from an EU state provided the person transports the goods himself or herself, they are for personal use (including giving away as gifts) and duty was paid in the country where they were bought.

Duty is payable if the goods were brought in to resell.

There are indicative amounts above which Customs may ask for evidence of personal use. The indicative amounts are:

- 800 cigarettes
- 200 cigars
- 400 cigarillos
- 1 kilogram of tobacco
- 110 litres of beer
- 90 litres of wine

- 10 litres of spirit
- 20 litres of fortified wine, such as sherry or port

EC sales lists

All VAT-registered businesses are required to submit an EC sales list of supplies to other EU states for periods up to 31 December 2020. A sales list is not required for periods from 1 January 2021. The final EC sales list must be submitted by 21 January 2021.

A monthly sales list is required for supplies of goods above the threshold above.

For goods below the threshold, and where all supplies are of services, a quarterly return is required.

From	**Goods threshold**
1 January 2014	£35,000
1 January 2010	£70,000

Election results

UK GENERAL ELECTIONS

Date	*Prime minister*	*Con*	*Lab*	*LD*	*SNP*	*Other*	*Ruling party*
12.12.2019	Boris Johnson	365	202	11	48	24	Con
8.6.2017	Theresa May	317	262	12	35	24	Con/DUP
7.5.2015	David Cameron	330	232	8	56	24	Con
6.5.2010	David Cameron	307	255	59	6	23	Con/LD
5.5.2005	Tony Blair	198	355	62	4	23	Lab
1.5.2001	Tony Blair	166	413	52	5	19	Lab
1.5.1997	Tony Blair	165	418	46	6	24	Lab
9.4.1992	John Major	336	271	20	3	21	Con
11.6.1987	Margaret Thatcher	376	229	22	3	20	Con
9.6.1983	Margaret Thatcher	397	209	23	2	19	Con
3.5.1979	Margaret Thatcher	359	261	9	2	19	Con

In 1983 and 1987, the LD vote was of the alliance between SDP and Liberal party. In 1979 it was of the Liberal party.

The number of seats in the House of Commons is:

From	*Number*
2010	650
2005	645
1997	659
1992	651
1983	650
1974	635

Seats are allocated by geographical area under "first past the post".

Elections must be held at least once every five years.

The UK Parliament also comprises the House of Lords which is not elected.

EUROPEAN ELECTIONS

Date	*Brex*	*UKIP*	*Con*	*Lab*	*LD*	*SNP*	*Other*
23.5.2019	29	-	4	10	16	3	11
22.5.2014	-	24	19	20	1	2	7

4.6.2009	-	13	26	13	11	2	8
10.6.2004	-	12	27	19	12	2	6
10.6.1999	-	3	36	29	10	2	5
9.6.1994	-	-	18	62	2	2	3
15.6.1989	-	-	32	45	-	1	3

The UK had 73 seats from 2014; 72 from 2009; and 78 from 2007.

Members (MEPs) are elected by proportional representation from regional party lists.

Elections are held every five years. The UK ceased to be represented from 31 January 2020.

SCOTTISH PARLIAMENT

Date	*SNP*	*Lab*	*LD*	*Con*	*Grn*	*Other*
5.5.2016	63	24	5	31	6	0
5.5.2011	69	37	5	15	2	1
3.5.2007	47	46	16	17	2	1
1.5.2003	27	50	17	18	7	10
6.5.1999	35	56	17	18	1	2

The Scottish Parliament was revived in 1999.

It has 129 members (MSPs) of whom 73 are elected by constituencies under "first past the post" The other 56 are elected by eight regions each choosing seven members.

Elections are generally held every four years.

WELSH ASSEMBLY (Senedd)

Date	*Lab*	*Con*	*LD*	*PC*	*Other*
5.5.2016	29	11	1	12	7
5.5.2011	30	14	5	11	0
3.5.2007	26	12	6	15	0
1.5.2003	30	11	6	12	1
6.5.1999	28	9	6	17	0

The Welsh Assembly was created in 1999.

It comprises 60 members (MSs) comprising 40 constituency members and 20 from electoral regions. Elections are generally held every four years.

NORTHERN IRELAND ASSEMBLY

Date	*DUP*	*SF*	*UUP*	*SDLP*	*Allce*	*Grn*	*Other*
2.3.2017	28	27	10	12	8	2	3
5.5.2016	38	28	16	12	8	2	4
5.5.2011	38	29	16	14	8	1	2
7.3.2007	36	28	18	16	7	1	2
26.11.2003	30	24	27	18	6	0	3
25.6.1998	20	18	28	24	6	0	10
20.10.1982	21	5	26	14	10	0	2

The Assembly comprises 90 members (MLAs) elected under the single transferable vote.

The Assembly was suspended from January 2017 to January 2020

REFERENDUMS

Date	*Area*	*Proposition*	*Result*	*%*
23.6.2016	UK	Leave or remain in EU	Leave	51.89
18.9.2014	Scotland	Independence	No	5.30
5.5.2011	UK	Adopt alternative vote	No	67.90
3.3.2011	Wales	Assembly have law-making powers	Yes	63.49

4.11.2004	NE Eng	Creation of North East Assembly	No	77.93
22.5.1998	NI	Support Good Friday agreement	Yes	71.12
7.5.1998	London	Creation of a London Assembly	Yes	72.01
18.9.1997	Wales	Welsh Assembly	Yes	50.30
11.9.1997	Scotland	Scottish Parliament	Yes	74.29
1.3.1979	Scotland	Devolved Assembly	No[1]	48.38
1.3.1979	Wales	Welsh Assembly	No	79.74
5.6.1975	UK	UK remain in EC	Yes	67.23
8.3.1973	NI	Remain part of UK	Yes	98.90

[1] *Although a 51.62% majority voted yes in the 1979 referendum, it failed to secure the required 40% of all voters, achieving only 32.9%, and so failed.*

Other referendums have been held by local authorities since 1913.

Employee share schemes

These four schemes allow a director or employee to benefit from shareholders in the employing company, provided all the conditions are met.

Company share option plan

- Maximum of £30,000 in options on shares

Enterprise management incentive

- Company may offer if gross assets do not exceed £30 million and has fewer than 250 employees
- Maximum value of options: £250,000

Save As You Earn

- Minimum monthly contributions of £5 for 36 month scheme
- Maximum monthly contribution of £500 for 60 months.
- The scheme attracts interest which has been 0% since 2012.

Share incentive plan

- Employee must have worked for employer for at least 18 months
- Employer may issue up to £3,600 of free shares
- Employee may buy 1 partnership share for every 2 free shares held
- Partnership shares may not exceed 10% of annual salary
- Partnership shares may only be bought by payroll deduction.
- Deduction is from gross pay, giving income tax and national insurance relief at source
- Employer may provide matching shares at a rate of up to 2 for every 1 partnership share
- Shares must be held for three years from acquisition in a trust for the employee.

Other arrangements

Employee shareholder

Between 1 September 2013 and 30 November 2016, an employee could become an employee shareholder.

The employee gives up some employment rights as an employee shareholder.

The employee shareholder must be given at least £2,000 in shares tax-free. There is no upper limit.

From 1 September 2013, the shares have a capital gains tax exemption of £50,000 and a lifetime limit of £100,000. The lifetime limit was removed from 17 March 2016.

Employee ownership trusts

From 1 October 2014, an exemption from income tax applies to a bonus payment to an employee in such a trust up to £3,600 a year

Employee tax-free benefits

These benefits may be tax-free when provided to an employee, usually subject to conditions. The benefit may not be tax-free when provided under a salary sacrifice arrangement.

- **Accommodation:** if necessary for job, traditionally provided, or needed for security
- **Armed forces allowances**
- **Canteen facilities:** if available to all staff
- **Car accessories:** if needed for work or for disabled employee
- **Car parking:** free if at or near place of work
- **Commuting during a public transport strike**
- **Commuting for late night work or when car-sharing has broken down**
- **Cycling equipment** and facilities, subject to conditions
- **Diplomats' expenses**
- **Electric vehicle recharging:** if at place of work
- **Employee indemnity insurance**
- **Entertainers' agency fees**
- **Eye tests and corrective spectacles:** for workers who use computer screens
- **Incidental overnight expenses:** to limits while away on work
- **Loan interest:** on loans up to £10,000
- **Long service awards:** to limits
- **Medical check-ups**
- **Medical treatment:** up to £500 if recommended
- **Mobile phone:** one per employee. This includes a smart phone but not tablets and similar even if they have telephony functions
- **Oil rig workers transport** between rig and mainland
- **Outplacement counselling**
- **Parties:** up to a cumulative total of £120 per person per tax year
- **Pension advice:** to a limit
- **Pension contributions:** to workplace pension or occupational pension scheme
- **Political expenses** of members of Parliament, European Parliament, or devolved bodies
- **Pool car:** incidental use only
- **Professional subscription**
- **Relocation expenses:** up to £8,000
- **Retraining courses** when under notice of redundancy
- **Security assets:** to provide personal security to employee
- **Scholarship:** up to £15,480 a year from 2007 for certain educational courses
- **Suggestion scheme awards:** to limits
- **Tea and coffee:** provided at the workplace

- **Termination payment:** up to £30,000 (from 1998)
- **Third party gifts:** up to a limit
- **Training:** that is relevant to work
- **Travel:** in the course of business, and in a few other cases, but not commuting
- **Trivial benefits:** up to £50 per benefit, and £300 annual limit
- **Uniform, protective clothing or stage clothing**
- **Use of own transport:** reimbursement to 45p a mile for car; 24p for motorcycle; or 20p for bicycle
- **Workplace nursery:** subject to conditions

Employment limits

	2020/21	2019/20	2018/19	2017/18
Week's pay	£538	£525	£508	£489
Unlawful inducement re trade union	£4,294	£4,193	£4,059	£3,907
Basic award for unfair dismissal	£6,562	£6,408	£6,203	£5,970
Maximum award for unfair dismissal	£16,140	£15,750	£15,240	£14,670
Expulsion from trade union minimum	£10,022	£9,787	£9,474	£9,118
Expulsion from trade union maximum	£104,659	£102,194	£98,922	£95,211
Guarantee payment per day	£30	£29	£28	£27
Compensatory award unfair dismissal	£88,519	£86,444	£83,682	£80,541
Failure to reinstate or re-engage min	£13,988	£13,650	£13,208	£12,714
Failure to reinstate or re-engage max	£27,976	£27,300	£26,416	£25,428

Enterprise zones

These are 48 areas known as enterprise zones in the UK. 24 were created in 2012, and a further 24 added in 2016 and 2017.

A business locating in a zone qualifies for either:

- 100% business rates of up to £275,000 over five years, or
- 100% first year allowance for plant and machinery.

All zones qualify for simplified planning permission for new development.

A list of zones is given below. The exact boundary is identified by maps. The final column marked FYA indicates whether first year allowances are available in the zone or part of it.

Name of zone	**FYA**
Aerohub, Cornwall and Isles of Scilly	yes
Alconbury Enterprise Campus, Cambridge	no
Anglesey	no
Aylesbury Vale, Buckinghamshire	no
Birmingham Curzon Street	no
Black Country	yes
Blackpool Airport	yes
Bristol Temple Quarter, Bath, Somer Valley	no
Cambridge Campus	no
Cardiff Airport and St Athan	no
Carlisle Kingmoor Park, Cumbria	yes

Central Cardiff	no
Ceramics Valley, Stoke and Staffordshire	yes
Cheshire Science Corridor, Cheshire and Warrington	yes
Coleraine, Northern Ireland	yes
Deeside	yes
Didcot Growth Accelerator, Oxfordshire	no
Discovery Park, Kent	no
Dorset Green, Dorset	no
Dundee Claverhouse, Dundee City	yes
Dundee Port	yes
Ebbw Vale	yes
Enterprise M3 (Basingstoke & Deane, East Hampshire, Runnymede)	yes
Enviro-Tech, Hertfordshire	no
Great Yarmouth and Lowestoft	no
Greater Manchester Life Science, Manchester	no
Harlow	no
Haven Waterway, Wales	yes
Heart of South West, South West England	no
Hereford	no
Hillhouse International, North West England	yes
Humber	yes
Irvine, North Ayrshire	yes
Lancashire, Samlesbury and Warton	no
Leeds City Region	yes
Luton Airport	yes
M62 Corridor, Leeds region	no
Mersey Waters, Liverpool	no
MIRA Technology Park, Leicester	no
Nigg, Scottish Highlands	yes
Northampton Waterside	no
North East England	yes
Nottingham	yes
Nottingham and Derby	yes
Port Talbot, Wales	yes
Royal Docks, London	no
Sci-Tech Daresbury, Liverpool	no
Science Vale UK, Oxfordshire	no
Sheffield City Region	yes
Snowdonia, Wales	no
Solent, Gosport, Hampshire	no
Tees Valley	yes
York Central	no

European Union states

The European Union comprised 28 states from 1 July 2013 when Croatia joined to 31 January 2020 when the UK left.

Many tax provisions relate to whether a transaction involves an EU state. The following provides details.

Country	Joined	Territorial scope
Austria	1 January 1995	
Belgium	1 January 1958	
Bulgaria	1 January 2007	
Croatia	1 July 2013	
Cyprus	1 May 2004	Excludes northern areas not controlled by government. Includes UK bases of Akrotiri and Dhekelia
Czechia	1 May 2004	
Denmark	1 January 1973	
Estonia	1 May 2004	
Finland	1 January 1995	
France	1 January 1958	Includes Monaco, but excludes overseas departments Guadeloupe, Martinique, Reunion, St Pierre and Miquelon. Excludes French Guiana and Andorra.
Germany	1 January 1958	Excludes Büsingen and Heligoland
Greece	1 January 1981	
Hungary	1 May 2004	
Ireland	1 January 1973	
Italy	1 January 1958	Excludes Livigno, Campione d'Italia, the Italian waters of Lake Lugano, San Marino and Vatican
Latvia	1 May 2004	
Lithuania	1 May 2004	
Luxembourg	1 January 1958	
Malta	1 May 2004	
Netherlands	1 January 1958	
Poland	1 May 2004	
Portugal	1 January 1999	Includes Azores and Madeira
Romania	1 May 2004	
Slovakia	1 May 2004	
Slovenia	1 May 2004	
Spain	1 January 1986	
Sweden	1 January 1995	
United Kingdom	1 January 1973	Isle of Man is part of VAT area but not within scope of sales list. Excludes Channel Islands.

Åland Islands, Liechtenstein and Mount Athos are not part of EU.

The European Economic Area (EEA) comprises the EU plus Iceland, Liechtenstein and Norway.

Switzerland is not a member of the European Union or EEA but is part of the EU single market.

EU candidate countries are Albania, Montenegro, North Macedonia, Serbia and Turkey.

Exchange rates

This table shows spot exchange rates for £1 sterling according to Bank of England on the last available date in each month.

The currencies quoted are Australian dollar, Canadian dollar, euro, Japanese yen, Swiss franc and US dollar.

	Aus$	Can$	euro	yen	rand	SwFr	US$
31 December 2020	1.7634	1.7378	1.1118	140.667	20.0299	1.2022	1.3649
30 November 2020	1.8123	1.7305	1.1160	139.272	20.6488	1.2086	1.3353
30 October 2020	1.8418	1.7245	1.1104	135.227	21.0194	1.1854	1.2933
30 September 2020	1.8038	1.7266	1.1023	136.387	21.5702	1.1872	1.2924
28 August 2020	1.8146	1.7469	1.1205	140.396	22.1729	1.2054	1.3330
31 July 2020	1.8304	1.7589	1.1096	138.752	22.2617	1.1949	1.3126
30 June 2020	1.7953	1.6835	1.1002	133.391	21.4676	1.1711	1.2359
29 May 2020	1.8632	1.7090	1.1118	133.154	21.7893	1.1878	1.2368
30 April 2020	1.9268	1.7519	1.1515	134.871	23.1739	1.2166	1.2613
31 March 2020	2.0260	1.7651	1.1306	133.866	22.1530	1.1966	1.2403
28 February 2020	1.9783	1.7148	1.1630	137.917	20.0877	1.2371	1.2776
31 January 2020	1.9685	1.7429	1.1897	142.880	19.7626	1.2709	1.3179
31 December 2019	1.8834	1.7202	1.1765	143.421	18.5475	1.2770	1.3210
29 November 2019	1.9122	1.7182	1.1730	141.649	18.9538	1.2928	1.2936
31 October 2019	1.8785	1.7008	1.1598	139.858	19.4952	1.2768	1.2939
30 September 2019	1.8625	1.6313	1.1302	133.155	18.6787	1.2288	1.2320
30 August 2019	1.8084	1.6189	1.1061	129.298	18.4938	1.2049	1.2183
31 July 2019	1.7761	1.6081	1.0999	132.967	17.3556	1.2121	1.2246
28 June 2019	1.8139	1.6633	1.1176	137.144	17.9497	1.2411	1.2728
31 May 2019	1.8193	1.7037	1.1309	136.845	18.3407	1.2676	1.2602
30 April 2019	1.8525	1.7537	1.1632	145.195	18.6855	1.3281	1.3036
29 March 2019	1.8344	1.7409	1.1605	144.229	18.7990	1.2979	1.3030
28 February 2019	1.8693	1.7511	1.1680	148.042	18.6932	1.3247	1.3300
31 January 2019	1.8039	1.7275	1.1460	143.146	17.4445	1.3045	1.3152
31 December 2018	1.8092	1.7393	1.1149	140.395	18.3635	1.2561	1.2769
30 November 2018	1.7472	1.6957	1.1266	144.864	17.6854	1.2750	1.2760
31 October 2018	1.8028	1.6779	1.1277	144.237	18.8650	1.2853	1.2779
28 September 2018	1.8025	1.6858	1.1228	148.146	18.4498	1.2738	1.3041
31 August 2018	1.7980	1.6944	1.1169	144.078	19.0509	1.2569	1.2994
31 July 2018	1.7645	1.7081	1.1210	146.832	17.1784	1.2985	1.3117
29 June 2018	1.7876	1.7370	1.1308	146.223	18.1046	1.3108	1.3203
31 May 2018	1.7587	1.7263	1.1400	144.591	16.8563	1.3087	1.3308
30 April 2018	1.8251	1.7659	1.1402	150.765	17.1977	1.3637	1.3776
29 March 2018	1.8291	1.8093	1.1410	149.241	16.6239	1.3438	1.4033
28 February 2018	1.7687	1.7656	1.1299	147.074	16.2656	1.3022	1.3780

31 January 2018	1.7563	1.7448	1.1416	155.265	16.8839	1.3217	1.4221
29 December 2017	1.7276	1.6935	1.1270	151.974	16.6308	1.3179	1.3510
30 December 2016	1.7027	1.6576	1.1651	143.871	16.8797	1.2522	1.2303
31 December 2015	2.0264	2.0584	1.3605	178.406	23.1077	1.4726	1.4819
31 December 2014	1.9018	1.8074	1.2841	186.250	18.0327	1.5439	1.5608
31 December 2013	1.8484	1.7576	1.2004	173.478	17.3982	1.4728	1.6528
31 December 2012	1.5591	1.6084	1.2263	139.336	13.7202	1.4807	1.6168
30 December 2011	1.5195	1.5772	1.1950	119.637	12.5202	1.4535	1.5461
31 December 2010	1.5272	1.5558	1.1670	126.993	10.3649	1.4592	1.5655
31 December 2009	1.7958	1.6931	1.1255	150.322	11.8911	1.6691	1.6148
31 December 2008	2.0605	1.7744	1.0342	130.175	13.2906	1.5298	1.4376

Flat rate expense allowance

Agriculture	all workers	100
Airlines	pilots, co-pilots, helicopter pilots and uniformed flight deck crew	1,022
	cabin crew - stewards and stewardesses	720
Aluminium	a. continual casting operators, process operators, de-dimplers, driers, drill punchers, dross unloaders, firemen (engaged to light and maintain furnaces), furnace operators and their helpers, leaders, mould-men, pourers, remelt department labourers and roll flatteners	140
	b. cable hands, case makers, labourers, mates, truck drivers and measurers and storekeepers	80
	c. apprentices	60
	d. all other workers	120
Armed forces	all ranks in the: - army - Royal Air Force - Royal Marines	100
	- Royal Navy	80
Banks and building societies	uniformed doormen and messengers	60
Brass and copper	braziers, coppersmiths, finishers, fitters, moulders, turners and all other workers	120
Building	a. joiners and carpenters	140
	b. cement works, roofing felt and asphalt labourers	80
	c. labourers and navvies	60
	d. all other workers	120
Building materials	a. stone masons	120
	b. tilemakers and labourers	60
	c. all other worker	80

Clothing	a. lacemakers, hosiery bleachers, dyers, scourers and knitters, knitwear bleachers and dyers	60
	b. all other workers	60
Constructional engineering (includes buildings, shipyards, bridges and roads)	a. blacksmiths and their strikers, burners, caulkers, chippers, drillers, erectors, fitters, holders up, markers off, platers, riggers, riveters, rivet heaters, scaffolders, sheeters, template workers, turners and welders	140
	b. banksmen, labourers, shop-helpers, slewers and straighteners	80
	c. apprentices and storekeepers	60
	d. all other workers	100
Electrical and electricity supply	a. workers incurring laundry costs only	60
	b. all other workers	120
Trades ancillary to engineering	a. pattern makers	140
	b. labourers, supervisory and unskilled workers	80
	c. apprentices and storekeepers	60
	d. motor mechanics in garage repair shop	120
	e. all other workers	120
Fire service	uniformed fire fighters and fire officers	80
Food	all workers	60
Forestry	all workers	100
Glass	all workers	80
Healthcare staff in the National Health Service, private hospitals and nursing homes	a. ambulance staff on active service	185
	b. nurses, midwives, chiropodists, dental nurses, occupational, speech, physiotherapists and other therapists, healthcare assistants, phlebotomists and radiographers shoes and stockings or tights allowance (where everyone is required to wear the same colour or style)	125 12 shoes 6 tights or stockings
	c. plaster room orderlies, hospital porters, ward clerks, sterile supply workers, hospital domestics and hospital catering staff	125
	d. laboratory staff, pharmacists and pharmacy assistants	80
	e. uniformed ancillary staff - maintenance workers, grounds staff, drivers, parking attendants and security guards, receptionists and other uniformed staff	80

Heating	a. pipe fitters and plumbers	120
	b. coverers, laggers, domestic glaziers, heating engineers and all their mates	120
	c. all gas workers and all other workers	100
Iron mining	a. fillers, miners and underground workers	120
	b. all other workers	100
Iron and steel	a. day labourers, general labourers, stockmen, timekeepers, warehouse staff and weighmen	80
	b. apprentices	60
	c. all other workers	140
Leather	a. curriers (wet workers), fellmongering workers and tanning operatives (wet)	80
	b. all other workers	60
Particular engineering (work on commercial basis in a factory or workshop producing components such as wire, springs, nails and locks)	a. pattern makers	140
	b. chainmakers, cleaners, galvanisers, tinners and wire drawers in the wire drawing industry and toolmakers in the lock making industry	120
	c. apprentices and storekeepers	60
	d. all other workers	80
Police force	a. ranks of police officers up to and including chief inspector	140
	b. community support officers including Metropolitan Police	140
	c. other police employees (but not special constables)	60
Precious metals	all workers	100
Printing	a. letterpress section-electrical engineers (rotary presses), electrotypers, ink and roller makers, machine minders (rotary), maintenance engineers (rotary presses) and stereotypers	140
	b. bench hands (periodical and bookbinding section), compositors (letterpress section), readers (letterpress section) telecommunications and electronic section wire room operators, warehousemen (paper box making section)	60
	c. all other workers	100
Prisons	uniformed prison officers	80

Public service - docks and inland waterways	a. dockers, dredger drivers and hopper steerers	80
	b. all other workers	60
Public service - public transport	a. garage hands including cleaners	80
	b. conductors and drivers	60
Quarrying	all workers	100
Railways	See the appropriate category for craftsmen (for example engineers, vehicles) all other workers	100
Seamen	carpenters a. passenger liners	165
	b. cargo vessels, tankers, coasters and ferries	140
Shipyards	a. blacksmiths and their strikers, boilermakers, burners, carpenters, caulkers, drillers, furnacemen (platers) holders up, fitters, platers, plumbers, riveters, sheet iron workers, shipwrights, tubers and welders	140
	b. labourers	80
	c. apprentices and storekeepers	60
	d. all other workers	100
Textiles and textile printing	a. carders, carding engineers, overlookers and technicians in spinning mills	120
	b. all other workers	80
Vehicles	a. builders, railway vehicle repairers and railway wagon lifters	140
	b. railway vehicle painters, letterers, and builders' and repairers' assistants	80
	c. all other workers	60
Wood and furniture	a. carpenters, cabinetmakers, joiners, wood carvers and woodcutting machinists	140
	b. artificial limb makers (other than in wood), organ builders and packaging case makers	120
	c. coopers not providing their own tools, labourers, polishers and upholsterers	60
	d. all other workers	100

FT-SE 100 index

Date	Index
31 December 2020	6460.52
30 November 2020	6266.19
30 October 2020	5577.27
30 September 2020	5897.50
28 August 2020	5963.57
31 July 2020	5897.76

Date	Index
30 June 2020	6169.74
29 May 2020	6076.60
30 April 2020	5901.21
31 March 2020	5671.96
28 February 2020	6580.61
31 January 2020	7286.01

Date	Index
31 December 2019	7542.44
29 November 2019	7346.53
31 October 2019	7248.38
30 September 2019	7408.21
30 August 2019	7207.18
31 July 2019	7586.78
28 June 2019	7425.63
31 May 2019	7161.71
30 April 2019	7418.22
29 March 2019	7279.19
28 February 2019	7074.73
31 January 2019	6968.85
28 December 2019	6584.68
30 November 2018	6980.24
31 October 2018	7128.10
28 September 2018	7510.20
31 August 2018	7432.42
31 July 2018	7748.76

Date	Index
29 June 2018	7636.93
31 May 2018	7678.20
30 April 2018	7509.30
29 March 2018	7056.61
28 February 2018	7231.91
31 January 2018	7533.55
29 December 2017	7687.77
30 November 2017	7326.67
31 October 2017	7493.08
29 September 2017	7372.76
31 August 2017	7430.62
31 July 2017	7372.00
30 June 2017	7312.72
31 May 2017	7519.95
28 April 2017	7203.94
31 March 2017	7322.92
28 February 2017	7263.44
31 January 2017	7099.15

Gilts exempt from capital gains tax

The following gilts are exempt from capital gains tax under TCGA 1992 s16(2), 115(1) and Sch 9.

%	Title
2½%	Annuities 1905 or after
2¾%	Annuities 1905 or after
2½%	Consolidated Stock 1923 or after
3½%	War Loan 1952 or after
4%	Consolidated Loan 1957 or after
3½%	Conversion Loan 1961 or after
3%	Treasury Stock 1966 or after
2½%	Treasury Stock 1975 or after
3%	North of Scotland Electricity Stock 1989 to 1992
12¾%	Treasury Loan 1992
8%	Treasury Loan 1992
10%	Treasury Stock 1992
3%	Treasury Stock 1992
12¼%	Exchequer Stock 1992
13½%	Exchequer Stock 1992
10½%	Treasury Convertible Stock 1992
2%	Index-Linked Treasury Stock 1992

%	Title
12½%	Treasury Loan 1993
6%	Funding Loan 1993
13¾%	Treasury Loan 1993
10%	Treasury Loan 1993
8¼%	Treasury Stock 1993
14½%	Treasury Loan 1994
12½%	Exchequer Stock 1994
9%	Treasury Loan 1994
10%	Treasury Loan 1994
13½%	Exchequer Stock 1994
8½%	Treasury Stock 1994
8½%	Treasury Stock 1994 'A'
2%	Index-Linked Treasury Stock 1994
3%	Exchequer Gas Stock 1990-95
12%	Treasury Stock 1995
10¼%	Exchequer Stock 1995
12¾%	Treasury Loan 1995
9%	Treasury Loan 1992-96

%	Title
15¼%	Treasury Loan 1996
13¼%	Exchequer Loan 1996
14%	Treasury Stock 1996
2%	Index-Linked Treasury Stock 1996
10%	Conversion Stock 1996
10%	Conversion Stock 1996 'A'
10%	Conversion Stock 1996 'B'
13¼%	Treasury Loan 1997
10½%	Exchequer Stock 1997
8¾%	Treasury Loan 1997
8¾%	Treasury Loan 1997 'B'
8¾%	Treasury Loan 1997 'C'
8¾%	Treasury Loan 1997 'D'
8¾%	Treasury Loan 1997 'E'
15%	Exchequer Stock 1997
7%	Treasury Convertible Stock 1997
6¾%	Treasury Loan 1995-98
15½%	Treasury Loan 1998
12%	Exchequer Stock 1998
12%	Exchequer Stock 1998 'A'
9¾%	Exchequer Stock 1998
9¾%	Exchequer Stock 1998 'A'
7¼%	Treasury Stock 1998 'A'
7¼%	Treasury Stock 1998 'B'
12%	Exchequer Stock 1998 'B'
45/8%	Index-Linked Treasury Stock 1998
7¼%	Treasury Stock 1998
9½%	Treasury Loan 1999
10½%	Treasury Stock 1999
12¼%	Exchequer Stock 1999
12¼%	Exchequer Stock 1999 'A'
12¼%	Exchequer Stock 1999 'B'
2½%	Index-Linked Treasury Convertible Stock 1999
10¼%	Conversion Stock 1999
6%	Treasury Stock 1999
-	Floating Rate Treasury Stock 1999
9%	Conversion Stock 2000
9%	Conversion Stock 2000 'A'
9%	Conversion Stock 2000 'B'

%	Title
9%	Conversion Stock 2000 'C'
8½%	Treasury Loan 2000
8%	Treasury Stock 2000
8%	Treasury Stock 2000 'A'
13%	Treasury Stock 2000
13%	Treasury Stock 2000 'A'
7%	Treasury Stock 2001
7%	Treasury Stock 2001 'A'
14%	Treasury Stock 1998-2001
2½%	Index-Linked Treasury Stock 2001
9¾%	Conversion Stock 2001
10%	Treasury Stock 2001
9½%	Conversion Loan 2001
10%	Treasury Stock 2001 'A'
10%	Treasury Stock 2001 'B'
-	Floating Rate Treasury Stock 2001
12%	Exchequer Stock 1999-2002
12%	Exchequer Stock 1999-2002 'A'
9½%	Conversion Stock 2002
10%	Conversion Stock 2002
9%	Exchequer Stock 2002
7%	Treasury Stock 2002
9¾%	Treasury Stock 2002
9¾%	Treasury Stock 2002 'A'
9¾%	Treasury Stock 2002 'B'
9¾%	Treasury Stock 2002 'C'
13¾%	Treasury Stock 2000-2003
13¾%	Treasury Stock 2000-2003 'A'
2½%	Index-Linked Treasury Stock 2003
9¾%	Conversion Loan 2003
6½%	Treasury Stock 2003
8%	Treasury Stock 2003
8%	Treasury Stock 2003 'A'
10%	Treasury Stock 2003
10%	Treasury Stock 2003 'A'
10%	Treasury Stock 2003 'B'
3½%	Funding Stock 1999-2004
11½%	Treasury Stock 2001-2004
9½%	Conversion Stock 2004
10%	Treasury Stock 2004

%	Title
6¾%	Treasury Stock 2004
5%	Treasury Stock 2004
6¾%	Treasury Stock 2004 'A'
43/8%	Index-Linked Treasury Stock 2004
9½%	Conversion Stock 2004 'A'
12½%	Treasury Stock 2003-2005
12½%	Treasury Stock 2003-2005 'A'
10½%	Exchequer Stock 2005
9½%	Conversion Stock 2005
9½%	Conversion Stock 2005 'A'
8½%	Treasury Stock 2005
8%	Treasury Loan 2002-2006
8%	Treasury Loan 2002-2006 'A'
2%	Index-Linked Treasury Stock 2006
9¾%	Conversion Stock 2006
7½%	Treasury Stock 2006
7¾%	Treasury Stock 2006
11¾%	Treasury Stock 2003-2007
11¾%	Treasury Stock 2003-2007 'A'
7¼%	Treasury Stock 2007
4½%	Treasury Stock 2007
8½%	Treasury Loan 2007
8½%	Treasury Loan 2007 'A'
8½%	Treasury Loan 2007 'B'
8½%	Treasury Loan 2007 'C'
13½%	Treasury Stock 2004-2008
9%	Treasury Loan 2008
9%	Treasury Loan 2008 'A'
9%	Treasury Loan 2008 'B'
9%	Treasury Loan 2008 'C'
9%	Treasury Loan 2008 'D'
5%	Treasury Stock 2008
2½%	Index-Linked Treasury Stock 2009
5¾%	Treasury Stock 2009
8%	Treasury Stock 2009
4%	Treasury Stock 2009
8%	Treasury Stock 2009 'A'
4¾%	Treasury Stock 2010
6¼%	Treasury Stock 2010

%	Title
2½%	Index-Linked Treasury Stock 2011
4¼%	Treasury Gilt 2011
9%	Conversion Loan 2011
9%	Conversion Loan 2011 'A'
9%	Conversion Loan 2011 'B'
9%	Conversion Loan 2011 'C'
9%	Conversion Loan 2011 'D'
3¼%	Treasury Gilt 2011
5½%	Treasury Stock 2008-2012
9%	Treasury Stock 2012
9%	Treasury Stock 2012 'A'
5%	Treasury Stock 2012
5¼%	Treasury Gilt 2012
2½%	Index-Linked Treasury Stock 2013
8%	Treasury Stock 2013
4½%	Treasury Gilt 2013
2¼%	Treasury Gilt 2014
5%	Treasury Stock 2014
7¾%	Treasury Loan 2012-2015
2¾%	Treasury Gilt 2015
4¾%	Treasury Stock 2015
8%	Treasury Stock 2015
8%	Treasury Stock 2015 'A'
2½%	Treasury Stock 1986-2016
2½%	Index-Linked Treasury Stock 2016
2%	Treasury Gilt 2016
4%	Treasury Gilt 2016
2½%	Index-Linked Treasury Stock 2016 'A'
12%	Exchequer Stock 2013-2017
1%	Treasury Gilt 2017
1¼%	Index-Linked Treasury Gilt 2017
1¾%	Treasury Gilt 2017
8¾%	Treasury Stock 2017
8¾%	Treasury Stock 2017 'A'
1¼%	Treasury Gilt 2018
5%	Treasury Gilt 2018
0⅛%	Index-linked Treasury Gilt 2019
3¾%	Treasury Gilt 2019
4½%	Treasury Gilt 2019

%	Title
2%	Treasury Gilt 2020
2½%	Index-Linked Treasury Stock 2020
3¾%	Treasury Gilt 2020
4¾%	Treasury Stock 2020
1½%	Treasury Gilt 2021
3¾%	Treasury Gilt 2021
8%	Treasury Stock 2021
1¾%	Treasury Gilt 2022
0½%	Treasury Gilt 2022
1⅞%	Index-Linked Treasury Gilt 2022
4%	Treasury Gilt 2022
0⅛%	Treasury Gilt 2023
0¾%	Treasury Gilt 2023
2¼%	Treasury Gilt 2023
1%	Treasury Gilt 2024
0⅛%	Index-Linked Treasury Gilt 2024
2½%	Index-Linked Treasury Stock 2024
0⅝%	Treasury Gilt 2025
2%	Treasury Gilt 2025
5%	Treasury Stock 2025
0⅛	Index-Linked Treasury Gilt 2026
1½%	Treasury Gilt 2026
1¼%	Treasury Gilt 2027
1¼%	Index-Linked Treasury Gilt 2027
4¼%	Treasury Gilt 2027
6%	Treasury Stock 2028
1⅝%	Treasury Gilt 2028
0⅛%	Index-Linked Treasury Gilt 2028
0⅛%	Index-Linked Treasury Gilt 2029
0⅞%	Treasury Gilt 2029
0⅜%	Treasury Gilt 2030
4⅛%	Index-Linked Treasury Stock 2030
4¾%	Treasury Gilt 2030
1¼%	Index-Linked Treasury Gilt 2032
4¼%	Treasury Stock 2032
0¾%	Treasury Gilt 2034
4½%	Treasury Gilt 2034
2%	Index-linked Treasury Stock 2035
4¼%	Treasury Stock 2036
0⅛%	Index-linked Treasury Gilt 2036
1¾%	Treasury Gilt 2037
1⅛%	Index-Linked Treasury Gilt 2037
4¾%	Treasury Stock 2038
4¼%	Treasury Gilt 2039
0⅝%	Index-Linked Treasury Gilt 2040
4¼%	Treasury Gilt 2040
0⅛%	Index-Linked Treasury Gilt 2041
1¼%	Treasury Gilt 2041
0⅝%	Index-Linked Treasury Gilt 2042
4½%	Treasury Gilt 2042
0⅛%	Index-Linked Treasury Gilt 2044
3¼%	Treasury Gilt 2044
3½%	Treasury Gilt 2045
0⅛	Index-Linked Treasury Gilt 2046
4¼%	Treasury Gilt 2046
1½%	Treasury Gilt 2047
0¾%	Index-Linked Treasury Gilt 2047
0⅛%	Index-Linked Treasury Gilt 2048
4¼%	Treasury Gilt 2049
1¾%	Treasury Gilt 2049
0½%	Index-Linked Treasury Gilt 2050
0½%	Index-Linked Treasury Gilt 2050
0¼%	Index-Linked Treasury Gilt 2052
3¾%	Treasury Gilt 2052
1⅝%	Treasury Gilt 2054
1¼%	Index-Linked Treasury Gilt 2055
4¼%	Treasury Gilt 2055
0⅛%	Index-Linked Treasury Gilt 2056
1¾%	Treasury Gilt 2057
0⅛	Index- Linked Treasury Gilt 2058
4%	Treasury Gilt 2060
0½%	Treasury Gilt 2061
3½%	Treasury Gilt 2062
0⅛%	Index-linked Treasury Gilt 2065
2½%	Treasury Gilt 2065
0⅛%	Index-linked Treasury Gilt 2068
3½%	Treasury Gilt 2068
1⅝%	Treasury Gilt 2071

Gross domestic product (GDP)

This table gives the seasonally adjusted gross domestic product for different periods in millions of pounds, as determined by the Office of National Statistics.

BY YEAR

Year	*GDP*
2019	2,172,511
2018	2,141,792
2017	2,115,296
2016	2,079,113
2015	2,043,909
2014	1,996,725
2013	1,941,155
2012	1,899,626
2011	1,872,838
2010	1,849,247
2009	1,811,672
2008	1,889,401
2007	1,894,682
2006	1,850,989
2005	1,802,435
2004	1,750,690
2003	1,711,559
2002	1,656,531
2001	1,621,208
2000	1,578,121

Year	*GDP*
1999	1,524,662
1998	1,476,025
1997	1,423,254
1996	1355,798
1995	1,322,839
1994	1,290,179
1993	1,242,396
1992	1,212,206
1991	1,207,364
1990	1,220,831
1989	1,211,937
1988	1,181,481
1987	1,117,428
1986	1,060,255
1985	1,027,873
1984	987,166
1983	965,509
1982	926,621
1981	908,707
1980	915,042

BY QUARTER

Year	*Quarter 1*	*Quarter 2*	*Quarter 3*	*Quarter 4*
2020	528,287	429,219	497,909	
2019	541,195	541,944	544639	544,733
2018	532,104	534,140	537,326	538,222
2017	526,081	527,622	529,856	531,717
2016	516,456	518,794	520,379	523,484
2015	506,314	510,095	512,070	515,430
2014	484,629	497,849	503,589	503,589
2013	479,357	483,211	487,728	490,859
2012	472,809	472,114	477,869	476,834
2011	466,970	467,370	486,942	469,556
2010	457,058	461,765	465,134	465,290
2009	452,896	452,036	452,595	454,145
2008	480,523	477,834	470,368	460,676
2007	469,274	471,920	475,530	477,958
2006	461,059	462,305	462,734	464,891
2005	442,793	447,996	452,721	458,925

2004	435,802	437,406	438,191	439,291
2003	421,580	425,428	430,274	434,277
2002	410,434	412,445	415,187	418,465
2001	401,021	404,118	407,236	408,833
2000	391,937	394,312	395,469	396,403

Grossing up and netting down percentages

Grossing up percentage is the percentage by which a figure must be increased so that when the amount is deducted, the answer is the original figure. So for 20%, the grossing up percentage is 25%. So £1 grosses up to £1.25. 20% of £1.25 is 25p which, when subtracted, gives £1. In tax, this is used for Gift Aid, net pay arrangements and some inheritance tax computations.

Netting down percentage is the percentage by which a figure must be subtracted so that when the percentage is added, the answer is the original figure. So for 20%, the netting down factor is 16.7%. So £1 nets down to 83.3p. 20% of this is 16.7p, which, when added, gives a total of £1. This percentage is the VAT fraction.

Net down	Rate	Gross up
0.99010	1	1.01010
1.47783	1.5	1.52284
1.96078	2	2.04082
2.43902	2.5	2.56410
2.91262	3	3.09278
3.38164	3.5	3.62694
3.84615	4	4.16667
4.30622	4.5	4.71204
4.76190	5	5.26316
5.21327	5.5	5.82011
5.66038	6	6.38298
6.10329	6.5	6.95187
6.54206	7	7.52688
6.97674	7.5	8.10811
7.40741	8	8.69565
7.83410	8.5	9.28962
8.25688	9	9.89011
8.67580	9.5	10.49724
9.09091	10	11.11111
9.50226	10.5	11.73184
9.90991	11	12.35955
10.31390	11.5	12.99435
10.71429	12	13.63636
11.11111	12.5	14.28571
11.50442	13	14.94253
11.89427	13.5	15.60694
12.28070	14	16.27907
12.66376	14.5	16.95906

13.04348	15	17.64706
13.41991	15.5	18.34320
13.79310	16	19.04762
14.16309	16.5	19.76048
14.52991	17	20.48193
14.89362	17.5	21.21212
15.25424	18	21.95122
15.96639	19	23.45679
16.66667	20	25.00000
17.35537	21	26.58228
17.69547	21.5	27.38854
18.03279	22	28.20513
18.36735	22.5	29.03226
18.69919	23	29.87013
19.02834	23.5	30.71895
19.35484	24	31.57895
19.67871	24.5	32.45033
20.00000	25	33.33333
23.07692	30	42.85714
25.92593	35	53.84615
28.57143	40	66.66667
31.03448	45	81.81818
33.33333	50	100.00000

The grossing up formula is G=100R/(100-R)
The netting down formula is N=100R/(100+R)
where G is grossing up percentage; N is netting down percentage; and R is the original percentage rate.

Hallmarks of a tax avoidance scheme

HMRC says that the presence of any of these factors in a scheme indicates that it may be for tax avoidance, and therefore will probably not work.

- it sounds too good to be true
- artificial or contrived arrangements are involved
- it seems very complex for what you want to do
- there are guaranteed returns for apparently no risk
- there are secrecy or confidentiality agreements
- upfront fees are payable or the arrangement is on a no win/no fee basis
- the scheme is said to be verified by a top lawyer or accountant, but no details of their opinion are provided
- the scheme is said to be approved by HMRC (not true)
- taxation of income is delayed or tax deductions are accelerated
- tax benefits are disproportionate to the commercial activity
- offshore companies or trusts are involved for no sound commercial reason
- a tax haven or banking secrecy country is involved without any sound commercial reason

- tax exempt entities, such as pension funds, are involved inappropriately
- it contains exit arrangements designed to sidestep tax consequences
- it involves money going in a circle back to where it started
- low risk loans to be paid off by future earnings are involved
- the scheme promoter lends the funding needed.

Helplines at HMRC

General helpline

HMRC national advice service: 0300 200 3300

Specific helplines

- aggregates levy: 0300 200 3700 .
- agent dedicated line: debt management: 0300 200 3887
- agent dedicated line: self assessment: 0300 200 3311
- agent dedicated line: tax credits: 0345 300 3943
- air passenger duty: 0300 200 3700
- alcohol and tobacco warehousing: 0300 200 3701
- alcohol duty: 03000 592 688
- annual tax on enveloped dwellings: 0300 200 3510
- automatic exchange of information: 03000 576 748
- beer duty: 03000 583 920
- bereavement: 0300 200 3300
- capital gains tax: 0300 200 3300
- certificates of tax deposit: 03000 546 900
- change of address: 0300 200 3300
- charities: 0300 123 1073
- child care providers and working tax credit: 0345 300 3941
- child care services including tax-free childcare: 0300123 4097
- climate change levy: 0300 200 3700
- construction industry scheme: 0300 200 3210
- construction industry scheme payments: 0300 200 3401
- coronavirus generally: 0800 024 1222
- Coronavirus Job Retention Scheme: 0800 024 1222
- corporation tax forms: 0300 200 3411
- creative industry reliefs: 0300 123 3440
- Crown servants working abroad: 0135 535 9022
- debt collection, confirming identity of HMRC staff: 0300 3862
- deferred national insurance payments: 0300 200 3500
- duty deferment: 03000 594 243
- eat out to help out: 0300 322 9429
- employers: 0300 200 3200
- employers checking a tax code: 0300 200 3300
- employment related securities: 0300 322 7074
- employment status: 0300 123 2326
- excise duties: 0300 200 3700

- excise movements and control system: 0300 200 3700
- expatriate employees: 0300 533148
- flooding, tax problems caused by: 0800 904 7900
- fraud reporting: 0800 788 887
- gambling duties: 0300 200 3700
- guardian's allowance: 0300 322 9080
- help to save scheme: 0300 322 7093
- imports and exports: 0300 322 9434
- income tax generally: 0300 200 3300
- inheritance tax: 0300 123 1072
- insurance premium tax: 0300 200 3700
- international tax debt: 0300 322 9208
- IR 35: 0300 123 2326
- landfill tax: 0300 200 3700
- let property campaign: 0300 123 0998
- money laundering: 0300 200 3700
- national imports relief: 0300 322 7065
- national insurance: 0300 200 3500
- New Computerised Transit System: 0300 322 7095
- non-resident employees: 03000 533 148
- non-resident entertainers: 0300 322 7877
- non-resident landlords: 0300 322 9433
- non-residents income tax and capital gains: 0300 200 3300
- non-residents payments: 0300 322 9206
- offshore disclosure: 0300 322 7012
- online debit and credit payments: 0300 200 3601
- PAYE payments: 0300 200 3401
- payment problems: 0300 200 3835
- payments and penalties: 0300 200 3854
- pension schemes: 0300 123 1079
- probate: 0300 123 1072
- savings: 0300 200 3300
- seafarers national insurance: 03000 582 419
- seafarers tax: 0300 200 3300
- Secure Data Exchange Service: 03000 597 222
- self assessment: 0300 200 3600
- self-employed national insurance: 0300 200 3500
- seed enterprise investment scheme: 0800 024 1222
- shares and asset valuations: 0300 123 1082
- soft drinks industry levy: 0300 200 3700
- stamp duty land tax and stamp duty reserve tax: 0300 200 3510
- stamp taxes online services: 0300 200 3600
- statutory payment dispute team: 0300 322 9422
- statutory sick pay rebate scheme: 0800 024 1222
- support for new employers: 0300 200 3211

- tax avoidance, escaping from scheme: 03000 530 435
- tax credit payments: 0345 3-2 1429
- tax credits: 0345 300 3900
- technical problems using online facilities: 0300 200 3600
- trusts: 0300 123 1072
- VAT online queries: 0300 200 3701
- VAT option to tax: 0300 200 3700
- VAT payment slips ordering: 03000 519 206
- VAT reliefs for disabled and older people: 0300 123 1073
- VAT repayments for non-UK businesses: 0300 322 9279
- vehicle imports: 0300 322 7071
- Welsh speakers: 0300 200 1900
- yachts to or from UK: 0300 123 2012

For many issues, it may be quicker to send an email or use an online enquiry facility. More details on contacting HMRC can be found at https://www.gov.uk/government/organisations/hm-revenue-customs/contact

See also **Address; Website addresses**

Helpsheets

These helpsheets are produced by HMRC and may be accessed free from its website.

Number	Subject
HS201	Vouchers, credit cards and tokens
HS202	Living accommodation
HS203	Car benefits and car fuel benefits
HS204	Limit on income tax reliefs
HS205	Seafarers' earnings deduction
HS207	Non-taxable payments or benefits for employees
HS208	Payslips and coding notices
HS210	Assets provided for private use
HS211	Employment, residence and domicile issues
HS212	Tax equalisation
HS213	Payments in kind and asset transfers
HS220	More than one business
HS222	How to calculate your taxable profits
HS223	Rent a room scheme
HS224	Check reliefs and rules for farmers and market gardeners
HS227	Relief for trading losses
HS229	Information from your accounts
HS231	Calculating doctor's expenses
HS232	Farm stock valuation
HS234	Averaging for creators of literary or artistic works
HS236	Qualifying care relief for carers
HS237	Community investment tax relief
HS238	Revenue recognition in service contracts
HS240	Self-assessment tax return for Lloyd's underwriters

HS251	Agricultural land loss relief
HS252	Capital allowances and balancing charges
HS253	Furnished holiday lettings
HS260	Overlap relief
HS261	Foreign tax credit and capital gains
HS262	Income and benefits from transfers of assets abroad or from non-resident trusts
HS263	Relief for foreign tax paid
HS264	Paying tax on the remittance basis
HS270	Trusts and settlements – income treated as the settlor's
HS275	Entrepreneur's relief
HS276	Incorporation relief
HS278	Temporary non-residents and capital gains tax
HS281	Capital gains tax, civil partners and spouses
HS282	Capital gains tax when someone dies
HS283	Private residence relief
HS284	Shares and capital gains tax
HS285	Capital gains tax, share reorganisations and company takeovers
HS286	Negligible value claims and income tax losses on disposals of shares
HS287	Capital gains tax and employee share schemes
HS288	Partnerships and capital gains tax
HS290	Business asset rollover relief
HS292	Capital gains tax land and leases
HS293	Chattels and capital gains tax
HS294	Trusts and capital gains tax
HS295	Capital gains tax on gifts and similar transactions
HS296	Debts and capital gains tax
HS297	Venture capital trusts and capital gains tax
HS298	Venture capital trusts and capital gains tax
HS299	Non-resident trusts and capital gains tax
HS300	Non-resident savings and investment income
HS301	Beneficiaries receiving capital payments from non-resident trust
HS302	Dual residency
HS303	Non-resident entertainers and sportspersons
HS304	Non-residents tax relief under double taxation agreements
HS305	Employment-related shares and securities
HS307	Non-resident capital gains for land and property in the UK
HS308	Investors' relief
HS320	Gains on UK life insurance policies
HS321	Gains on foreign life insurance policies
HS325	Other taxable income for self-assessment
HS340	Interest and alternative finance payments eligible for relief on qualifying loans and alternative finance arrangements
HS341	Enterprise investment scheme: income tax relief
HS342	Charitable giving tax relief

HS343	Accrued income scheme
HS345	Pension savings: tax charges
HS380	Partnerships that operate partly overseas
HS390	Foreign credit relief for capital gains of trusts and estates
HS392	Trust management expenses
HS393	Seed enterprise investment scheme: income tax and capital gains tax reliefs

History of tax

Key dates in the development of current tax law

Year	**Event**
1055	• Customs duties are introduced
1083	• First national land tax imposed, called "mycel great gyld"
1202	• First attempt at introducing national rates of Customs duties
1207	• King John introduces tax called thirteenth, used as basis for future taxes
1215	• Magna Carta establishes that only Parliament may raise taxes
1254	• First Parliament where nobles had a say on taxes
1266	• End of local Customs duties
1297	• Confirmation of charters signed to restrict taxation of business
1311	• Customs duties paid to Parliament from which an allowance is made to the king
1377	• Introduction of first poll tax
1381	• Peasants' revolt against poll tax
1407	• Parliament takes over all responsibilities for tax
1436	• Introduction of "subsidie", early form of income tax
1450	• England's Treasurer is beheaded by mob over tax grievances
1451	• World's first known tax on income is introduced, in Florence, Italy
1487	• Coastal trade is banned without a certificate from the king
1489	• First tax commissioners who assess tax in addition to collecting it
1494	• Introduction of double-entry bookkeeping
1562	• All residents of a parish may be assessed to raise alms for the poor
1564	• New law requires ports to be inspected to ensure Customs duties are paid
1601	• Introduction of local rates to raise funds to look after the poor
1624	• First stamp duty imposed, on legal and official documents
1643	• First excise duty imposed, on domestic production and imports
1647	• Riots over new excise duties
1649	• Execution of king Charles I. One of the accusations against him was that he tried to raise taxes without Parliamentary approval.
1660	• Introduction of excise duty on alcoholic drink
1671	• End of practice of farming tax revenues
1680	• Britain joins the gold standard
1688	• Many more goods become subject to excise duties
1691	• Introduction of land tax
1694	• Introduction of stamp duty
1696	• Introduction of window tax
1698	• Last time that the poll tax was levied

1716 • Hefty increases in tax on gin and other spirits
1733 • First use of the word Budget in relation to national tax and spending
1739 • Report says that local collection of tax is unsatisfactory
1752 • Start of tax year moves from 21 March to 5 April
1765 • Britain imposes stamp duty on USA, leading to war of independence
1783 • Stamp duty introduced on bank notes of at least 1 guinea
1785 • Formation of Board of Taxes to collect tax in England and Wales
1787 • Customs duties are levied on individual items and not total value
1796 • Introduction of a tax on dogs
1798 • It becomes possible to redeem liability to land tax
1799 • First introduction of income tax
• Codified list of 3,000 categories of excise duty
1800 • Stamp duty is charged on all bank notes
• Truck Act gives workers the right to be paid wages in cash
1803 • Income tax introduced for second time
• Schedules of income tax introduced, not abolished until 2010
1806 • First attempt to simplify income tax in new Act
1816 • Income tax abolished for second, and final, time
1819 • Start of long-term reduction in excise duties
1838 • It becomes illegal to own a slave in Britain
• Metropolitan Police required to register carriages
1842 • Income tax is re-introduced as a temporary measure, which it still is
1844 • Formation of Companies House
• Income tax yield allows reductions and abolition of many excise duties
1845 • Income tax is announced as needed for three more years
1846 • Repeal of the Corn Laws
1849 • Inland Revenue is formed from merger of Board of Stamps and Taxes with Board of Excise
1851 • Window tax is replaced by assessed taxes and house duty
1853 • William Gladstone makes three-hour Budget speech. He defers abolition of income tax until 1860
• Excise duty imposed on matches
1860 • William Gladstone says he is unable to abolish income tax
• Excise duty on matches repealed until 1916
1870 • Freelance surveyors and assessors are no longer used to collect tax
• Chancellor of the Exchequer becomes Master of the Mint, and still is
1874 • Income tax is reduced to 2d in the pound, less than 1%. Widely seen as the last opportunity to abolish income tax
1890 • Partnership Act passed. It is still law
1891 • Stamp Act passed. It is still law.
1902 • Income tax now yields as much revenue as excise duties
1907 • Higher rates of income tax are introduced for higher incomes
1909 • Lloyd George introduces People's Budget, triggering a constitutional crisis
• Government temporarily loses right to collect income tax
• Old age pensions are introduced

	• Supertax is introduced
	• Responsibility for excise duties passes from Inland Revenue to HM Customs which is renamed HM Customs and Excise
	• Imposition of motor spirit duty at 3d on the 6d charge per gallon
1911	• National Insurance Act passed, introducing national insurance
1912	• National insurance is introduced
	• National Health Insurance is introduced
1913	• Provincial Collection of Taxes Act passed
1914	• income tax increased to 1s 6d in the pound (7.5%)
	• Start of first world war. Gold ceases to be used for currency
1915	• Special rate of income tax introduced for army pay
	• Income tax exemptions are reduced, leading to higher amounts of tax
	• Excess profits tax introduced to stop companies profiteering from war
	• Import duties yield £100 million for first time
	• Vehicle excise duty imposed on mechanically propelled vehicles
1916	• Excise duty re-imposed on matches
	• Farmers can be taxed as traders rather than under Schedule B
1918	• First consolidation of income tax law since 1842
1921	• Tax relief introduced for pension contributions
1926	• Introduction of betting tax
1927	• Introduction of radio licence
1928	• Hydrocarbon oil duty replaces motor spirit duty
1930	• Stamp duty no longer applies to conveyances between associated companies
1931	• Import duty of 100% imposed on all imports
1932	• Discovery of tax returns from 1802 to 1815, thought to have been destroyed
	• Import Duties Act passed which has the effect of ending international trade
1935	• House of Lords declares tax avoidance is legal in Duke of Westminster case
1937	• National defence contribution is introduced
1938	• Income tax increased to 5 shillings in the pound (25%)
1940	• Introduction of purchase tax
	• Government allows workers to pay income tax weekly
	• Tax case rules that high remuneration to family members is not tax-deductible
1941	• Income tax increased to 10 shillings in the pound (50%)
1942	• Publication of Beveridge Report on post-war social security
1943	• Purchase tax increased to 100% on luxury items
1944	• Pay As You Earn is introduced
1945	• Income tax rate reduced from 50% to 45%
	• First UK double taxation treaty with non-empire country: USA
1946	• Introduction of luncheon vouchers
	• National defence contribution is renamed profits tax
	• Introduction of television licence

	• First provisions of social security reforms are introduced
1947	• Profits tax is restricted to companies
1948	• Higher rates of income tax introduced for investment income
	• Reform of social security
1951	• First commercial computer capable of calculation and data handling
	• Purchase tax is doubled on consumer durables
1952	• National Insurance Fund is overfunded, so payments into it are stopped
	• Consolidation of customs and excise duties. This leads to repeal of more than 200 Acts
	• Introduction of television detector vans
1954	• Married women allowed to pay class 3 national insurance contributions
1955	• Tax case holds that goods taken for personal use are taxed on sale price
	• Tax case holds that a tribunal decision is final on a point of fact, unless perverse
1958	• Undistributed profits brought within scope of profits tax
1960	• Blind person's allowance for income tax is introduced
	• Betting shops become legal, and liable to pay betting taxes
	• Introduction of graduated pension scheme
1961	• Graduated pension contributions are introduced
1962	• Introduction of unit trust investment duty
	• Schedule D Case VII income tax introduced to tax short-term capital gains
	• Confectionery is subject to purchase tax
1964	• IBM launches first computer system to bridge scientific and business use
1965	• Introduction of capital gains tax
	• Corporation tax replaces profits tax, and income tax for companies
	• Definition of child's skirt is changed as miniskirts mean purchase tax is lost
1966	• Import duties abolished from EFTA countries
	• Selective employment tax is introduced
	• Introduction of 100% tax relief for research and development
	• Introduction of general betting duty
	• National insurance loses universality when supplementary contributions and benefits are introduced for unemployment and some other benefits
	• Introduction of capital allowance for dredging
1967	• First use of a computer by Inland Revenue
	• Taxes become subject to a 10% surcharge
1968	• Higher rate of television licence introduced for colour sets
	• All Customs barriers removed within European Community
	• Income tax charge introduced to claw back family allowance from higher earners
1970	• Income tax and corporation tax are consolidated in a new Act
1971	• Britain adopts decimal currency
	• Stamp duty is abolished on cheques and receipts
	• Abolition of the radio licence
1973	• Value added tax replaces purchase tax and selective employment tax

- UK joins Common Market, later European Union
- Capital duty introduced on forming a company
- Introduction of development gains tax

1974
- Capital transfer tax replaces estate duty
- Wealth tax is proposed but not introduced
- Introduction of petroleum revenue tax

1975
- Directors become subject to PAYE and class 1 national insurance
- National insurance ceases to be fixed amount and is calculated as a percentage of earnings
- National insurance ceases to be recorded by stamps on cards
- It becomes illegal to pay women less than men doing the same job
- End of graduated pension scheme

1976
- Development land tax replaces development gains tax

1977
- Married women lose the right to elect to pay a lower rate of national insurance
- Child allowance starts being phased out and replaced by child benefit
- First home computers go on sale: Commodore PET and Tandy TRS-80
- Introduction of national insurance surcharge

1978
- Rates of class 1 national insurance are reduced if employee is a member of an occupational pension scheme
- State earnings-related pension scheme (SERPS) is introduced

1979
- Replacement of many laws on excise duties
- Child relief against income tax is finally phased out
- Margaret Thatcher becomes prime minister and adopts monetarism rather than Keynesian economics

1981
- IBM launches its first personal computer
- Budget raises taxes in a recession, defying Keynesian theory

1982
- Leading case on tax avoidance: Ramsay

1983
- Introduction of statutory sick pay

1984
- Introduction of FT-SE 100 index
- Leading case on tax avoidance: Furniss v Dawson
- Tax relief for life assurance relief is abolished for new policies
- Abolition of investment income surcharge
- Police and Criminal Evidence Act 1984 introduced, also applies to tax investigations
- Data Protection Act becomes law

1985
- Employer's national insurance is payable on all earnings above lower earnings limit with no upper limit
- Abolition of national insurance surcharge
- Most fixed rates of stamp duty are abolished
- Development land tax is abolished
- Microsoft releases Windows 1.0

1986
- Writing down allowance for know-how changes to 25% straight line basis
- Stock Exchange radically changes under Big Bang
- Inheritance tax replaces capital transfer tax

- Introduction of stamp duty reserve tax
- Statutory sick pay period extended from 8 weeks to 28 weeks
- Single Market in EU
- Abolition of most excise licences
- Truck Acts are replaced by Wages Act

1987
- European Community introduces Common Customs Tariff
- Introduction of statutory maternity pay
- Introduction of payroll giving

1988
- Customs Common Tariff is revised, with products given a 15-digit code
- Abolition of unit trust investment duty
- Abolition of capital duty on company formation
- Introduction of £30,000 limit for termination payments
- Income tax and corporation tax law is consolidated in a new Act

1989
- Community charge (poll tax) introduced in Scotland
- Case establishes that a taxpayer may choose a commercial arrangement that saves tax

1990
- Community charge (poll tax) introduced in England and Wales
- Abolition of life assurance policy duty
- Income tax relief is given on private medical insurance premiums for those over 60
- Unified business rates replace local business rates
- Worldwide web comes into being
- Fixed Profit Car Scheme is introduced
- Husbands and wives are separately taxed
- Employers become liable to fund statutory sick pay

1991
- Introduction of class 1A national insurance

1992
- Black Wednesday when UK forced to leave Exchange Rate Mechanism
- Stamp duty abolished on Northern Ireland banknotes
- Abolition of matches and mechanical lighters duty
- Abolition of car tax on cars and caravans
- Starting rate of 20% income tax introduced

1993
- Class 1 national insurance becomes payable on marketable assets
- First "booze cruise" to buy lower taxed drink in France
- Late paid national insurance attracts an interest charge
- Goods in free circulation in one EU state are regarded as in free circulation in all EU states
- The Queen agrees to pay tax
- Community charge is replaced by council tax
- Basis of beer duty changes from original gravity to alcohol by volume
- Trade Union Reform and Employment Rights Act becomes law

1994
- Company cars are taxed according to emissions rather than engine size
- Class 1 national insurance is charged on gem stones and liquor
- Introduction of air passenger duty
- Introduction of insurance premium tax

1995
- Class 1 national insurance is charged on vouchers for marketable assets

• Statutory sick pay is paid at a fixed amount unrelated to earnings
• Customs duties are abolished on goods between Turkey and EU

1996 • Self-assessment is introduced for income tax
• Schedule C income tax is abolished
• Introduction of national insurance holidays
• Asylum and Immigration Act becomes law

1997 • New rates of duty are introduced for strong cider
• Windfall tax is imposed on privatised utilities

1998 • Data Protection Act is amended

1999 • Starting rate of income tax reduced from 20% to 10%
• Class 1 national insurance is payable from an earnings threshold rather than the lower earnings limit
• End of national insurance holidays
• Remaining fixed rates of stamp duty increased from 50p to £5
• National minimum wage is introduced
• Tax credits are introduced, though they are not related to tax
• Vehicle excise duty rates are determined by exhaust emissions
• Working Time Directive is adopted
• Government considers, but rejects, a pesticides tax

2000 • Age allowance restricted to taxpayers born before April 1935
• Starting rate of corporation tax is reduced to 10%
• Employers required to collect repayment of student loans
• Lower hydrocarbon oil duty is applied to low-sulphur fuels
• UK generally switches to metric units
• Family credit is replaced by working families tax credit and disabled person's tax credit, which is paid through the payroll

2001 • Enhanced rates of capital allowance introduced for energy efficient products
• Temporary scheme of stamp duty relief introduced for house sales in disadvantaged areas
• Cigarette packets must bear a fiscal mark
• Introduction of climate change levy

2002 • Starting rate of corporation tax is reduced to 0%
• Introduction of approved mileage rate of 40p a mile
• Advisory rates are introduced when employee uses own vehicle for business
• Many European states adopt the euro as currency
• Introduction of money-laundering laws
• Alco-pops are taxed as spirits
• Reduced rate of beer duty is introduced for small breweries
• Introduction of aggregates levy
• State second pension replaces state earnings-related pension scheme (SERPS)
• Law prevents part-time workers being treated less fairly

2003 • Stamp duty land tax replaces stamp duty on property sales

	• SERPS is replaced by state second pension
	• Statutory paternity pay and statutory adoption pay are introduced
	• Change in method of calculating fuel benefit to employees
	• Civil evasion penalties are introduced for less serious Customs offences
	• Introduction of working tax credit
	• National insurance charge of 1% is introduced on earnings above the upper earnings limit
	• Introduction of provisions regarding flexible working
	• Statutory adoption pay and statutory paternity pay are introduced
2004	• Introduction of non-corporate distribution rate of corporation tax
	• Debt Arrangement Scheme introduced in Scotland
	• Electronic payment of PAYE is compulsory for large employers
2005	• Introduction of child trust funds
	• Inland Revenue and HM Customs and Excise merge to form HM Revenue and Customs
	• HMRC discovers it has been charging interest on stamp duty with no authority
	• Electronic filing of PAYE year-end returns is compulsory for large employers
2006	• Abolition of 0% starting rate of corporation tax
	• Bottles of spirits must display a duty stamp
2007	• Nil rate band for inheritance tax becomes transferable between spouses
	• HMRC loses discs containing personal details of 25 million people
	• People coming to UK must declare cash above €10,000
	• End of rule allowing a litre of drink to be sent to UK duty-free
	• Introduction of remote gaming duty
	• Construction industry scheme is revised
2008	• Starting rate of 10% income tax is abolished
2009	• Stamp duty abolished where ad valorem duty does not exceed £5
	• Upper accruals point introduced for class 1 national insurance
	• Upper earnings limit for national insurance harmonised with income tax threshold
	• Online in-year filing of PAYE is compulsory for 50 or more employees
	• Civil partnerships become legal for same sex couples
	• Tax tribunals replace special and general commissioners
	• New penalty regime introduced for incorrect tax returns
	• Tips no longer count towards national minimum wage
2010	• Limits introduced on tax relief for pension contributions
	• Entitlement to state pension reduced to 30 years' contributions
	• Additional statutory paternity leave is introduced
	• Start of transition period to equalise men and women's state pension age
	• All employers are required to file PAYE returns online
	• In-year surcharges introduced for late payment of PAYE
	• Fit notes replace sick notes
	• Additional rate of 50% income tax introduced

• Personal allowance restricted on income above £100,000
• Adult rate of national minimum wage starts at 21, not 22.

2011 • Standard rate of VAT increased from 17.5% to 20%
• Triple lock introduced on state pensions
• Addition to national insurance above upper earnings limit increased from 1% to 2%
• Limits introduced on contributions to pension fund

2012 • Student loans treble from £3,000 to £9,000 a year. Plan 2 is introduced for loan repayments
• Real time information introduced for PAYE
• Workplace pensions introduced
• Contracting out of class 1 national insurance ends for money purchase pension schemes

2013 • Introduction of disincorporation relief
• Introduction of statutory residence test
• Tax relief abolished for luncheon vouchers
• General anti-abuse rule introduced for tax avoidance schemes
• Introduction of high income child benefit charge
• Major reforms to social benefits, including "bedroom tax"
• Parental leave period (unpaid) extended to 18 weeks
• Direct Earnings Attachments introduced to collect overpaid social security

2014 • Real time information from PAYE is used to calculate benefits entitlement
• Employment allowance introduced for employer's national insurance
• Accelerated payment notices introduced
• Government ends all reimbursement of statutory sick pay
• National insurance thresholds cease to be linked to state pension
• Stamp duty land tax moves from slab basis to slice basis
• Tax discs on vehicles are abolished
• Scotland votes in a referendum to remain in UK
• Further reductions in limits to contributions to pension funds

2015 • Corporation tax is charged at a single rate of 20%
• Introduction of transferable marriage allowance
• Final absence relief for main residence relief from capital gains tax is generally reduced from 36 months to 18 months
• Class 3A national insurance introduced
• Taxpayers given greater freedom to draw from their pension pots
• Scotland replaces stamp duty land tax with land transaction tax
• HMRC introduces robot software to check tax returns
• New shared parental leave and shared parental pay
• Employer's national insurance waived for employees under 21

2016 • Scotland is given power to introduce its own rates of income tax
• UK votes in a referendum to leave the EU
• State second pension is replaced by single tier pension for new pensioners
• Introduction of national living wage as higher rate of national minimum wage

- Statutory tax relief for trivial benefits of £50 a year introduced

2017
- Public sector employers must determine IR 35 rules
- Introduction of tax-free childcare
- Introduction of apprenticeship levy
- Trusts must register if they have tax implications
- Salary sacrifice schemes largely negated under optional remuneration rules
- Discontinuation of certificates of tax deposit
- Supreme Court rules that simple interest applies to tax refunds
- Introduction of simple assessments for tax
- Introduction of serial tax avoidance regulations
- Indexation of chargeable gains is frozen
- HMRC starts to use voiceprints as passwords
- Financial Crimes Act makes failure to prevent tax evasion a crime
- Employer's national insurance waived for apprentices under 25
- Salary sacrifice is replaced by stricter optional remuneration provisions

2018
- HMRC stops accepting payment of tax by personal credit card
- Wales replaces stamp duty land tax with land transaction tax
- Introduction of soft drinks industry levy
- CHIEF Customs system starts to be replaced by Customs Declaration Service
- Introduction of structures and buildings allowance
- VAT threshold is frozen at £85,000
- Scotland replaces basic rate income tax with three rate bands
- First tax tribunal case using video equipment
- Abolition of the £8,500 threshold for determining taxation of benefits in kind
- Introduction of payrolling certain benefits in kind
- Diesel company cars that meet Euro standard are exempt from extra 4%

2019
- Making Tax Digital becomes compulsory for VAT traders with a turnover above £85,000
- Introduction of loan charge
- Minimum period of share ownership for entrepreneur's relief extended from one year to two years
- VAT on solar panels and wind turbines increased from 5% to 20%

2020
- UK leaves the European Union
- Statutory parental bereavement leave and statutory parental bereavement pay introduced
- Extensive changes to tax and other systems caused by coronavirus outbreak
- Lifetime allowance for business asset disposal relief (formerly entrepreneur's relief) reduced from £10 million to £1 million

Homeworkers' additional household expenses

This amount may be paid to an employee tax-free for the additional expense of doing some work from home. This is allowed by ITEPA 2003 s316A, and explained in HMRC Manual at EIM01472.

From	Weekly amount
6 April 2020	£6
6 April 2012	£4
6 April 2008	£3
6 April 2003	£2

Hydrocarbon oil duty

These rates have generally remained unchanged since 23 March 2011.
These products are generally subject to VAT on the price plus duty.

Product	Duty
Petrol or diesel	57.95p per litre
Biodiesel or bioethanol	57.95p per litre
LPG used as road fuel	31.61p per kilo
Natural gas used as road fuel	24.70p per kilo
Red diesel	11.14p per litre
Fuel oil	10.70p per litre
Aqua-methanol	7.90p per litre (from 14 November 2016)

Immigration health surcharge

This charge may be made as part of an immigration application, unless the applicant is exempt. It was not charged for people coming to the UK from an EEA country before 1 January 2021.

Category of person	Amount (from 27 October 2020)
Student or Tier 5 migrant	£470 a year
Applicant under 18 when applying	£470 a year
All other applicants	£624 a year

Parts of a year are rounded up to the nearest half year.
The charge was introduced on 6 April 2015 at £200 a year.
From April 2018, it doubled to £400, with a student rate of £300.
The current figures apply from 27 October 2020.
From 27 October 2020, health and care workers are added to the exemptions. Any such worker who had already paid the surcharge may have it refunded.

Immigration skills charge

This is paid by the UK sponsor in respect of each foreign worker employed unless they are excepted. The charge was introduced from 6 April 2017. A foreign worker is one who comes from outside the EU or EEA.
The amount depends on the whether the sponsor is a charity/small sponsor or a medium or large sponsor.

The maximum relates to a period of five years which is the longest period for which a worker may be sponsored.

There are separate rates for some workers in the performing arts.

The payment is refunded if the application is unsuccessful or if the worker does not work for the sponsor.

Period	**Charity/small**	**Medium or large**
12 months	£364	£1,000
each extra 6 months	£182	£500
Maximum	£1,820	£5,000

The amount is fixed and is not reduced for shorter periods.

Incomes by percentile

This tables gives 2017/18 annual incomes per percentile for those who have some liability to income tax. The figure are before tax. This means that, for example, the poorest 10% had incomes up to £13,900.

These figures are from Table 3.1a produced by Office of National Statistics in March 2020.

1	11,700	27	17,800	53	25,600
2	12,000	28	18,100	54	25,900
3	12,300	29	18,300	55	26,300
4	12,500	30	18,600	56	26,700
5	12,800	31	18,800	57	27,100
6	13,000	32	19,100	58	27,500
7	13,200	33	19,300	59	28,000
8	13,500	34	19,600	60	28,400
9	13,700	35	19,900	61	28,900
10	13,900	36	20,100	62	29,300
11	14,100	37	20,400	63	29,800
12	14,400	38	20,700	64	30,300
13	14,600	39	21,000	65	30,800
14	14,800	40	21,300	66	31,300
15	15,100	41	21,600	67	31,900
16	15,300	42	21,900	68	32,400
17	15,500	43	22,200	69	33,000
18	15,800	44	22,500	70	33,600
19	16,000	45	22,800	71	34,200
20	16,200	46	23,100	72	34,900
21	16,400	47	23,400	73	35,600
22	16,700	48	23,800	74	36,200
23	16,900	49	24,100	75	37,000
24	17,100	50	24,400	76	37,800
25	17,400	51	24,800	77	38,500
26	17,600	52	25,200	78	39,400

79	40,200
80	41,100
81	42,100
82	43,100
83	44,100
84	45,000
85	46,100

86	47,500
87	49,000
88	50,600
89	52,600
90	54,900
91	57,700
92	61,000

93	65,000
94	70,200
95	76,800
96	86,000
97	98,600
98	121,000
99	175,000

Income tax

	2020/21	**2019/20**	**2018/19**	**2017/18**
Personal allowance	£12,500	£12,500	£11,850	£11,500
Married couple's allowance max	£9,075	£8,915	£8,695	£8,445
Married couple's allowance min	£3,510	£3,450	£3,360	£3,260
Income limit for married couple's allowance	£30,200	£29,600	£28,900	£28,000
Blind person's allowance	£2,500	£2,450	£2,390	£2,320

The personal allowance is reduced by £1 for every £2 income above £100,000. This means that there is a marginal rate of income tax of 60% on a slice of income which, for 2020/21, is between £100,000 and £125,000.

Rates (except in Scotland)

	2020/21	2019/20	2018/19	2017/18
20% basic rate on next slice of	£37,500	£37,500	£34,500	£33,500
40% higher rate on next slice to	£150,000	£150,000	£150,000	£150,000
45% additional rate above				

There is a savings rate of 0% for savings income up to £5,000

Scottish rates

	2020/21	2019/20	2018/19	2017/18
19% starter rate on next slice of	£2,085	£2,049	£2,000	-
20% basic rate on next slice to	£37,500	£37,500	£34,500	£33,500
21% intermediate rate to	£30,930	£30,930	£31,580	-
41% higher rate on income up to	£150,000	£150,000	£150,000	£150,000
46% top rate above				

The higher rate was 40% for 2018/19 and 2017/18

These rates only apply to earned income such as from employment or self-employed. Investment income is subject to UK rates.

Dividend rates

	2020/21	2019/20	2018/19	2017/18
Basic rate and non-taxpayer	7.5%	7.5%	7.5%	7.5%
Higher rate	32.5%	32.5%	32.5%	32.5%
Additional rate	38.1%	38.1%	38.1%	38.1%
Dividend allowance	£2,000	£2,000	£2,000	£5,000

Loss relief cap

From 6 April 2013, there is a cap on income tax relief for loss relief equal to the greater of £50,000 or 25% of adjusted total income.

Trust

Dividend income for discretionary trusts is generally taxed at 38.1% from 2016/17.

Other income is generally taxed at 45% from 2015/16.

For trusts made by the same settlor, the basic rate band is divided by the number of trusts subject to a minimum allowance of £200.

High income child benefit charge

This is charged on income of more than £50,000 in respect of a taxpayer responsible for a child for whom child benefit is claimed.

The charge is 1% of the child benefit for every £100 that income exceeds £50,000, so all child benefit is clawed back on incomes above £60,000.

Other reliefs

Age allowances were available for older taxpayers until 2015/16

From 2015/16, a taxpayer may transfer 10% of their personal allowance to a spouse or civil partner.

From 2016/17, there is a £1,000 allowance for trading income, and another £1,000 for property income.

There is a savings allowance of £1,000 for basic rate taxpayers, £500 for higher rate taxpayers, and £0 for additional rate taxpayers.

Life assurance relief of 12.5% of premiums was available to 2014/15 for policies taken out before 14 March 1984.

Rent-a-room limit is £7,500 a year from 2016/17, and £4,250 previously from 1997/98.

Historic rates of allowances

Year	Personal allowance	Blind person	Age 65-74	Age 75+	MCA 65-74	MCA 75+	Earnings Limit
2016/17	£11,000	£2,290	-	-	-	£8,335	£27,700
2015/16	£10,600	£2,290	-	£10,660	-	£8,335	£27,700
2014/15	£10,000	£2,230	£10,500	£10,660	-	£8,185	£27,000
2013/14	£9,440	£2,160	£10,500	£10,660	-	£7,915	£26,100
2012/13	£8,105	£2,100	£10,500	£10,660	-	£7,705	£25,400
2011/12	£7,475	£1,980	£9,940	£10,090	-	£7,295	£24,000
2010/11	£6,475	£1.890	£9,490	£9,640	-	£6,965	£22,900
2009/10	£6,475	£1,890	£9,490	£9,640	-	£6,965	£22,900
2008/09	£5,435	£1,800	£9,030	£9,180	£6,535	£6,625	£21,800
2007/08	£5,225	£1,730	£7,550	£7,690	£6,285	£6,365	£20,900
2006/07	£5,035	£1,660	£7,280	£7,420	£6,065	£6,135	£20,100
2005/06	£4,895	£1,610	£7,090	£7,220	£5,905	£5,975	£19,500
2004/05	£4,745	£1,560	£6,830	£6,950	£5,725	£5,795	£18,900
2003/04	£4,615	£1,510	£6,610	£6,720	£5,565	£5,635	£18,300
2002/03	£4,615	£1,480	£6,100	£6,370	£5,465	£5,535	£17,900
2001/02	£4,535	£1.450	£5,990	£6,260	£5,365	£5,435	£17,600
2000/01	£4,385	£1,400	£5,790	£6,050	£5,165	£5,255	£17,000

The married couple's allowance (MCA) was limited to 10% tax rate from 2000.

From 2000, the 75+ rate of MCA applied only if one partner was born before 6 April 1935.

The age allowance is reduced by £1 for every £2 that income exceeds the earnings limit but From 2010, the personal allowance reduces by £1 for every £2 that income exceeds £100,000.

Historic rates of income tax

Year	Starter rate	Starter limit	Basic rate	Higher rate	Higher threshold	Add'l rate	Additional threshold
2016/17	-	-	20%	40%	£32,000	45%	£150,000
2015/16	-	-	20%	40%	£31,785	45%	£150,000
2014/15	-	-	20%	40%	£31,865	45%	£150,000
2013/14	-	-	20%	40%	£32,010	45%	£150,000
2012/13	-	-	20%	40%	£34,370	50%	£150,000
2011/12	-	-	20%	40%	£35,000	50%	£150,000
2010/11	-	-	20%	40%	£37,400	50%	£150,000
2009/10	-	-	20%	40%	£37,400	-	-
2008/09	-	-	20%	40%	£34,800	-	-
2007/08	10%	£2,230	22%	40%	£34.600	-	-
2006/07	10%	£2,150	22%	40%	£33,300	-	-
2005/06	10%	£2,090	22%	40%	£32,400	-	-
2004/05	10%	£2,020	22%	40%	£31,400	-	-
2003/04	10%	£1,960	22%	40%	£30,500	-	-
2002/03	10%	£1,920	22%	40%	£29,900	-	-
2001/02	10%	£1,880	22%	40%	£29,400	-	-
2000/01	10%	£1,520	22%	40%	£28,400	-	-

Indexation allowance

For chargeable gains subject to corporation tax, the acquisition cost is uplifted by indexation to reduce to remove that element of gain which is due to inflation. There is no indexation for capital gains subject to capital gains tax.

The indexation may be calculated using either the retail prices index or the following indexation factors. The acquisition cost is multiplied by the factor and added to the cost. For assets acquired before March 1982, the acquisition cost is replaced by the asset's market value in March 1982. The indexation stopped from December 2017. This means that disposals from January 2018 are indexed only up to December 2017. These indexation factors may therefore be used for any disposal from December 2017.

Acquisition from 1982 to 1988; disposed from December 2017

	1982	1983	1984	1985	1986	1987	1988	
January	-	2.366	2.202	2.049	1.889	1.781	1.692	
February	-	2.352	2.189	2.025	1.879	1.770	1.682	
March	2.501	2.346	2.179	1.997	1.875	1.764	1.671	
April	2.432	2.300	2.137	1.934	1.847	1.732	1.629	
May	2.407	2.286	2.126	1.921	1.842	1.729	1.619	
June	2.398	2.278	2.118	1.915	1.844	1.729	1.609	
July	2.397	2.260	2.121	1.920	1.852	1.732	1.606	
August	2.396	2.246	2.092	1.912	1.843	1.724	1.577	
September	2.398	2.232	2.086	1.914	1.829	1.716	1.565	
October	2.381	2.220	2.067	1.909	1.825	1.703	1.540	
November	2.364	2.209	2.058	1.899	1.801	1.690	1.528	
December	2.371	2.200	2.060	1.895	1.792	1.692	1.521	

1989 to 1995	**1989**	**1990**	**1991**	**1992**	**1993**	**1994**	**1995**	
January	1.505	1.327	1.136	1.051	1.017	0.968	0.905	
February	1.487	1.314	1.125	1.040	1.004	0.957	0.893	
March	1.476	1.291	1.116	1.034	0.996	0.952	0.885	
April	1.433	1.223	1.089	1.004	0.978	0.929	0.866	
May	1.418	1.204	1.083	0.996	0.971	0.922	0.859	
June	1.410	1.195	1.074	0.996	0.972	0.922	0.856	
July	1.408	1.193	1.078	1.004	0.977	0.931	0.865	
August	1.402	1.171	1.074	1.002	0.968	0.922	0.855	
September	1.385	1.151	1.066	0.995	0.960	0.918	0.847	
October	1.367	1.134	1.058	0.988	0.961	0.915	0.856	
November	1.347	1.139	1.051	0.991	0.964	0.914	0.856	
December	1.341	1.141	1.049	0.998	0.960	0.905	0.845	
1996 to 2002	**1996**	**1997**	**1998**	**1999**	**2000**	**2001**	**2002**	
January	0.852	0.801	0.744	0.702	0.669	0.625	0.605	
February	0.843	0.794	0.735	0.699	0.660	0.617	0.600	
March	0.836	0.790	0.729	0.695	0.651	0.615	0.594	
April	0.822	0.779	0.710	0.683	0.635	0.607	0.583	
May	0.819	0.772	0.701	0.679	0.629	0.596	0.578	
June	0.818	0.766	0.702	0.679	0.625	0.595	0.578	
July	0.825	0.766	0.706	0.684	0.631	0.605	0.581	
August	0.816	0.755	0.699	0.680	0.631	0.598	0.577	
September	0.808	0.746	0.692	0.673	0.620	0.593	0.566	
October	0.808	0.744	0.691	0.670	0.621	0.596	0.563	
November	0.807	0.742	0.692	0.668	0.616	0.602	0.561	
December	0.801	0.738	0.692	0.662	0.615	0.604	0.558	
2003 to 2009	**2003**	**2004**	**2005**	**2006**	**2007**	**2008**	**2009**	
January	0.559	0.519	0.472	0.438	0.379	0.326	0.324	
February	0.551	0.513	0.467	0.432	0.369	0.316	0.316	
March	0.546	0.507	0.460	0.426	0.361	0.311	0.316	
April	0.535	0.498	0.451	0.415	0.354	0.300	0.315	
May	0.532	0.491	0.448	0.407	0.349	0.293	0.307	
June	0.534	0.489	0.447	0.401	0.342	0.283	0.303	
July	0.534	0.489	0.447	0.401	0.349	0.285	0.303	
August	0.531	0.484	0.444	0.396	0.342	0.280	0.297	
September	0.524	0.478	0.440	0.390	0.337	0.273	0.292	
October	0.523	0.475	0.439	0.388	0.331	0.277	0.288	
November	0.522	0.471	0.436	0.383	0.326	0.288	0.284	
December	0.516	0.464	0.433	0.372	0.319	0.306	0.276	
2010 to 2017	**2010**	**2011**	**2012**	**2013**	**2014**	**2015**	**2016**	**2017**
January	0.276	0.214	0.168	0.131	0.101	0.089	0.075	0.047
February	0.269	0.202	0.159	0.123	0.094	0.083	0.070	0.036
March	0.260	0.196	0.155	0.118	0.091	0.082	0.065	0.033

April	0.248	0.186	0.147	0.115	0.088	0.078	0.064	0.028
May	0.244	0.182	0.147	0.112	0.087	0.076	0.061	0.024
June	0.241	0.182	0.150	0.114	0.085	0.074	0.057	0.021
July	0.244	0.185	0.149	0.114	0.086	0.075	0.056	0.019
August	0.239	0.178	0.144	0.108	0.082	0.070	0.052	0.012
September	0.234	0.169	0.139	0.104	0.080	0.071	0.050	0.011
October	0.232	0.168	0.132	0.104	0.079	0.072	0.050	0.010
November	0.226	0.166	0.132	0.103	0.082	0.070	0.047	0.008
December	0.218	0.162	0.127	0.101	0.080	0.067	0.041	nil

Individual savings accounts (ISAs)

Maximum annual subscription	**Amount**	**Cash limit**
From 6 April 2017	£20,000	-
2015/16 and 2016/17	£15,240	-
From 1 July 2014	£15,000	-
From 6 April 2014	£11,880	£5,940
2013/14	£11,520	£5,760

Junior ISA limits	**Limit**
2020/21	£9,000
2019/20	£4,368
2018/19	£4,260
2017/18	£4,128
2015/16 and 2016/17	£4,080
From 1 July 2014	£4,000
From 6 April 2014	£3,840
2013/14	£3,720

Lifetime ISA

These were introduced from 6 April 2017.

It allows an individual aged between 18 and 40 to save up to £4,000 a year and receive a 25% bonus after one year. Contributions may continue until the holder reaches 50.

Funds may be used to buy a house or be withdrawn at the age of 60.

Earlier withdrawals attract a charge, usually of 25%.

Help to buy ISA

These were available between 1 December 2015 and 30 November 2019 for first-time home buyers. Contributions may continue to be made until 30 November 2029.

The maximum savings amount is £200 a month.

When the savings reach £1,600, the government adds 25% to a maximum of £3,000 on £12,000 of savings.

Inflation

This table shows what £1 in different years is worth at December 2019.

The figures are calculated using the consumer prices index by the Bank of England, except for the annual inflation figures which are from the Office of National Statistics and use a different index.

The tables means, for example, that £1 spent on consumer goods in 1970 would, on average, cost £15.59 in December 2019.

Over that period of 49 years, the inflation rate has been at an annual average of 5.8%.

During 1970, inflation was 6.37%.

It should be noted that reliable tables date only from, 1914.

These tables can be multiplied. So the value of £12 worth of goods in a particular year is 12 times the "worth" figure.

To find out what £1 in December 2019 is worth in a previous year, you use the reciprocal of "worth". So £1 was worth £1/15.59 = 6.4p at 1970 values.

Year	Worth	Average inflation	Annual inflation
2019	-	-	1.74%
2018	£1.03	2.8%	2.29%
2017	£1.06	2.8%	2.56%
2016	£1.10	3.2%	1.01%
2015	£1.12	2.8%	0.37%
2014	£1.13	2.4%	1.45%
2013	£1.15	2.4%	2.29%
2012	£1.19	2.5%	2.57&
2011	£1.23	2.6%	3.86%
2010	£1.29	2.9%	2.49%
2009	£1.35	3.1%	1.96%
2008	£1.37	2.7%	3.52%
2007	£1.40	2.8%	2.39%
2006	£1.46	2.9%	2.46%
2005	£1.50	3.0%	2.09%
2004	£1.55	3.0%	1.39%
2003	£1.59	3.0%	1.38%
2002	£1.64	2.9%	1.52%
2001	£1.67	2.9%	1.53%
2000	£1.70	2.8%	1.18%
1999	£1.75	2.8%	1.75%
1998	£1.77	2.8%	1.82%
1997	£1.83	2.8%	2.20%
1996	£1.89	2.8%	2.85%
1995	£1.94	2.8%	2.70%
1994	£2.00	2.8%	2.22%
1993	£2.05	2.8%	2.56%
1992	£2.09	2.8%	4.59%
1991	£2.16	2.8%	7.46%
1990	£2.29	2.9%	8.06%
1989	£2.51	3.1%	5.76%
1988	£2.70	3.3%	4.16%
1987	£2.83	3.3%	4.15%
1986	£2.95	3.3%	3.43%
1985	£3.05	3.3%	6.07%
1984	£3.24	3.4%	4.96%
1983	£3.40	3.5%	4.61%
1982	£3.56	3.5%	8.60%
1981	£3.86	3.6%	11.88%
1980	£4.32	3.8%	17.97%
1979	£5.10	4.2%	13.42%
1978	£5.78	4.4%	8.26%
1977	£6.26	4.5%	15.84%
1976	£7.25	4.7%	16.56%
1975	£8.45	5.0%	24.21%
1974	£10.50	5.4%	16.04%
1973	£12.19	5.6%	9.20%
1972	£13.29	5.7%	7.07%
1971	£14.24	5.7%	9.44%
1970	£15.59	5.8%	6.37%
1969	£16.58	5.8%	5.45%
1968	£17.47	5.8%	4.70%
1967	£18.29	5.7%	2.48%
1966	£18.77	5.7%	3.91%
1965	£19.51	5.7%	4.77%
1964	£20.42	5.6%	3.28%
1963	£21.10	5.6%	2.02%
1962	£21.50	5.5%	4.20%
1961	£22.43	5.5%	3.45%
1960	£23.20	5.5%	1.00%
1959	£23.44	5.4%	
1958	£23,54	5.3%	
1957	£24.29	5.3%	
1956	£25.15	5.3%	
1955	£26.43	5.2%	
1954	£27.59	5.2%	
1953	£28.13	5.2%	
1952	£28.99	5.2%	

1951	£31.65	5.2%	
1950	£34.52	5.3%	
1949	£35.60	5.2%	
1948	£36.63	5.2%	
1947	£39.42	5.2%	
1946	£42.20	5.3%	
1945	£43.48	5.2%	
1944	£44.68	5.2%	
1943	£45.94	5.2%	
1942	£47.47	5.1%	
1941	£50.86	5.2%	
1940	£56.40	5.2%	
1935	£71.65	5.2%	
1930	£65.86	4.8%	
1925	£61.25	4.5%	
1920	£45.03	3.9%	
1915	£103.57	4.6%	
1910	£118.68	4.5%	
1905	£122.51	4.3%	
1900	£123.84	4.1%	
1850	£135.63	2.9%	
1800	£84.39	2.0%	
1750	£223.39	2.0%	
1700	£206.99	1.7%	

Inheritance tax

	2020/21	**2019/20**	**2018/19**	**2017/18**
Nil rate band	£325,000	£325,000	£325,000	£325,000
Residence nil rate band	£175,000	£150,000	£125,000	£100,000
Rate of inheritance tax on death	40%	40%	40%	40%
Lifetime rate	20%	20%	20%	20%

The death rate reduces to 36% if at least one tenth of the estate is left to charity

There are many reliefs from and exceptions to inheritance tax.

Excepted estates

From 1 September 2006, an account need not be delivered if the estate is below all of these limits and meets other conditions.

Total chargeable transfers since 6 April:	£10,000
Total chargeable transfers in last 10 years:	£40,000
Total gross value of property outside UK:	£100,000
Aggregate value of transfers of cash, securities etc	£150,000
Settled property passing on death	£150,000

Exemptions

Annual exemption	£3,000
Small gift exemption	£250
Transfer to non-dom spouse	£325,000 (from 6 April 2013)
	£55,000 (from 9 March 1982 to 5 April 2013)
Gifts in consideration of marriage or civil partnership	
by parent	£5,000
by remoter ancestor	£2,500
by party to the marriage	£2,500
by anyone else	£1,000

Reliefs

Agricultural property relief	100%
in limited circumstances	50%
Business property relief	100%

land, plant and machinery	50%

Quick succession relief

Up to	*Relief*
One year	100%
to two years	80%
to three years	60%
to four years	40%
to five years	20%
more than five years	0%

Taper relief

Years between death and gift	*Percentage of tax due*
less than 3	100%
3	80%
4	60%
5	40%
6	20%
7	0%

Fall in value relief

The probate value of an asset may be replaced by the actual value if it falls in value after the death within these time limits:

interest in land	4 years
quoted security or qualifying investment	1 year

Transferable nil rate band

Where a married person or civil partner dies on or after 9 October 2007, all or part of a previously deceased spouse's or civil partner's nil rate band may be added. This can require a knowledge of the nil rate band when the previous partner died. This includes nil rate bands for capital transfer tax between 1977 and 1986, and estate duty between 1914 and 1972.

From	*Nil rate band*
6 April 2009	£325,000
6 April 2008	£312,000
6 April 2007	£300,000
6 April 2006	£285,000
6 April 2005	£275,000
6 April 2004	£263,000
6 April 2003	£255,000
6 April 2002	£250,000
6 April 2001	£242,000
6 April 2000	£234,000
6 April 1999	£231,000
6 April 1998	£223,000
6 April 1997	£215,000
6 April 1996	£200,000
6 April 1995	£154,000
10 March 1992	£150,000

6 April 1991	£140,000
6 April 1990	£128,000
6 April 1989	£118,000
15 March 1988	£110,000
17 March 1987	£90,000
18 March 1986	£71,000
6 April 1985	£67,000 [capital transfer tax]
13 March 1984	£64,000
15 March 1983	£60,000
9 March 1982	£55,000
26 March 1980	£50,000
27 October 1977	£25,000
13 March 1975	£15,000
22 March 1972	£15,000 [estate duty]
31 March 1971	£12,500
16 April 1969	£10,000
4 April 1963	£5,000
9 April 1962	£4,000
30 July 1954	£3,000
10 April 1946	£2,000
16 August 1914	£100

Interest on late paid tax

From 23 August 2016	2.75%
29 September 2009 to 22 August 2016:	3%

Personal representatives' allowable expenses (from 6 April 2004)

Gross value of estate	*Allowable expenditure*
up to £50,000	1.8% of probate value of assets sold
to £90,000	£900
to £400,000	1.0% of probate value of assets sold
to £500,000	£4,000
to £1 million	0.8% of probate value of assets sold
to £5 million	£8,000
above £5 million	0.16% of probate value of assets sold to maximum of £10,000

Insolvency ranking

The order of ranking for distribution of an insolvent company's debts is:

- pre-preferential creditors: the fees and expenses of the liquidator
- secured creditors
  - those who have a charge on property or plant
- fixed and floating charges
  - usually these are secured by a debenture
- fixed charge creditors
  - a bank or similar who has a charge on an asset
- floating charge creditors

    - a general charge over all the company's assets
- unsecured creditors to a limit
    - from 15 September 2003, some assets must be set aside for unsecured creditors. The amount is 50% of assets up to £10,000 and 20% of assets between £10,000 and £800,000 (£600,000 before 6 April 2020)
- preferential creditors
    - employees' wages to a limit of eight weeks to a maximum (which is £538 a week for 2020/21, giving a maximum preference of £4,304)
    - from 1 December 2020, VAT, employer's national insurance, construction industry scheme deductions and student loan repayments. (HMRC had a more general preferential ranking before 5 September 2003.)
- unsecured creditors (to the extent not already relieved)
    - including HMRC and employees to the extent that they are not preferential creditors
- associated creditors, such as where a director has lent money to the company
- shareholders, except holder of deferred shares. If any payment is made, the company was not actually insolvent
- holder of any deferred share, often a founder of the business.

Insurance premium tax

This is charged on most general insurance premiums. There is a higher rate for travel insurance, mechanical and electrical appliances, and some vehicle insurance.

From	Standard rate	Higher rate
1 June 2017	12%	20%
1 October 2016	10%	20%
1 November 2015	9.5%	20%
4 January 2011	6%	20%
Previously	5%	17.5%

Interest on overdue tax

These rates now apply to most taxes. A lower rate is paid for repayments from HMRC.

From	Rate	Repayment
7 April 2020	2.60%	0.50%
30 March 2020	2.75%	0.50%
21 August 2018	3.25%	0.50%
21 November 2017	3.00%	0.50%
23 August 2016	2.75%	0.50%
29 September 2009	2.50%	0%

Interest on underpaid or overpaid quarterly payments of corporation tax

From	Rate	Repayment
30 March 2020	1.10%	0.50%
23 March 2020	1.25%	0.50%
13 August 2018	1.75%	0.50%

13 November 2017	1.50%	0.50%
15 August 2016	1.25%	0.50%
16 March 2009	1.50%	0.25%
16 February 2009	2.00%	0.50%

Intestacy rules

This is how an estate devolves when the deceased has left no will, depending on what relations survive him. For these purposes, "spouse" includes a civil partner.

The term "whole blood" means with both parents in common; "half blood" means with one parent in common.

Where there is a valid will, that takes precedence, except that the deceased must make provision to support those who are dependent on him or her under Inheritance (Provision for Dependants) Act 1975.

These rules are set out in Administration of Estates Act 1925, as amended.

ENGLAND AND WALES

Surviving relations

Spouse, no children, parents or siblings

Spouse inherits everything.

Spouse and children

From 6 February 2020: Spouse inherits personal chattels, £270,000 absolutely, life interest in half the remainder. Children receive one half of residue on statutory trust, with other half on statutory trust on the death of spouse

From 1 October 2014: as above but £250,000 instead of £270,000

From 1 February 2009: Spouse inherits personal chattels, £250,000 absolutely, half the residue *absolutely* (not a life interest). Children receive half of residue on statutory trust

From 1 December 1993: As above but £200,000 absolutely

From 1 June 1987: As above but £125,000

From 1 March 1981: As above but £85,000

From 15 March 1977: As above but £55,000

From 1 July 1972: As above but £40,000

From 1 January 1967: As above but £30,000

From 1 January 1953: As above but £20,000

From 1 January 1926: As above but £1,000

Spouse, no children, but parent, sibling or niece/nephew

From 1 October 2014: Spouse inherits everything

From 1 February 2009: Spouse inherits personal chattels, £450,000 absolutely, one half of residue absolutely. Remainder to parents, or if not alive to siblings or their children

From 1 December 1993: As above but £125,000 absolutely to spouse

From 1 June 1987: As above but £75,000

From 1 March 1981: As above but £40,000

From 15 March 1977: As above but £25,000

From 1 July 1972: As above but £15,000

From 1 January 1967: As above but £8,750

From 1 January 1953: As above but £5,000

From 1 January 1926: As above but £1,000

No spouse or children

The estate passes to the highest listed survivor or equally to survivors

- Children
- Parents
- Siblings of the whole blood, or their children if already dead
- Siblings of the half blood, or their children if already dead
- Grandparents
- Uncles and aunts of the whole blood
- Uncles and aunts of the half blood
- The Crown.

SCOTLAND

Spouse with no children, parents or siblings

Spouse inherits everything

Spouse and children

Spouse takes dwelling house to value of £300,000, personal chattels to £24,000. If the remainder of the state is less than £42,000, it all passes to the spouse. If it exceeds £42,000, £42,000 passes to the spouse plus 7% interest from death. The remainder is divided one third to the spouse, and two-thirds between the children.

Spouse, no children but grandchildren

As for spouse and children, but with remainder shared between grandchildren

No spouse, but children or grandchildren

The children take the estate absolutely. If there are no children, the grandchildren take the estate absolutely.

No spouse, children or grandchildren

The estate passes to the highest living relative or relatives in this list:

- Parents
- Brothers and sisters, and their children if brother or sister is already dead
- Uncle and aunts
- Grandparents
- Brother and sisters of grandparents
- The Crown (which may benefit those with a moral rather than legal claim on the estate).

NORTHERN IRELAND

An intestate estate is administered in accordance with Administration of Estates Act (Northern Ireland) 1955, as amended. These rules apply from 1 January 2008.

Spouse, no children, parents or siblings

Spouse receives everything.

Spouse and children

Spouse gets personal chattels, £250,000 absolutely and half the remainder (if one child) or one third (if two or more children). The children receive the remainder.

Spouse, no children but parents

Spouse gets personal chattels, £450,000 absolutely and half the remainder. The balance is shared by parents.

Spouse, no children or parents, but brothers or sisters

Spouse gets personal chattels, £450,000 absolutely and half the remainder. The balance is shared by brothers and sisters.

No spouse

The estate passes to the highest listed survivor or survivors:

- Children
- Parents
- Brothers and sisters
- Nephews and nieces
- Grandparents
- Aunts and uncles
- Cousins
- The Crown.

Provision for those who were financially dependent on the deceased may be made under Inheritance (Provision for Family and Dependants) (Northern Ireland) Order 1979.

Intrastat reporting

Intrastat reporting requires a VAT-registered trader to report arrivals and dispatches (imports and exports) from other EU states if they exceed the threshold given below for a calendar year.

These reports are not required for imports from the EU to Great Britain from 1 January 2021, but are required for imports to Northern Ireland.

From	Arrivals	Dispatches	Delivery terms
1 January 2015	£1,500,000	£250,000	£24 million
1 January 2014	£1,200,000	£250,000	£24 million
1 January 2010	£600,000	£250,000	£16 million
1 January 2009	£270,000	£270,000	£16 million
1 January 2008	£260,000	£260,000	£14.5 million

Investment schemes

There are four tax-advantaged investment schemes that offer generous tax relief to investors in new companies or social enterprises.

An investee company may ask HMRC to confirm whether it is eligible for a scheme.

There are other conditions to those listed below.

Enterprise investment scheme (EIS)

This scheme was introduced on 1 January 1994 to replace similar schemes introduced from 1981. It provides generous tax relief for investors who buy shares in small trading companies. These limits apply from 2012.

Maximum individual investment	£1 million
Maximum raised by company per year	£5 million
Maximum raised by company during its lifetime	£12 million
Maximum number of company employees	250

The taxpayer receives 30% income tax relief up to maximum.

The taxpayer must not hold 30% or more of the existing shares

Any gain on the shares is exempt from capital gains tax if held for three years.

The subscription must be for cash.

Funds raised must be used for a trading purpose within two years.

Seed enterprise investment scheme (SEIS)

This scheme was introduced in 2012 to provide more generous tax relief than EIS for start-up companies.

The taxpayer receives 50% income tax relief up to £100,000.

Other rules are similar to EIS.

Venture capital trusts (VCTs)

This scheme started in 1995. It allows individuals to invest in small high-risk companies through a VCT.

Maximum gross assets of investee company	£15 million
Maximum number of employees	250

Investment is within seven years of first commercial sale.

Social investment tax relief (SITR)

This allows funds to be invested in a social enterprise, namely a charity, community interest company or community benefit society.

Maximum gross assets of enterprise	£15 million
Maximum number of employees	250

The taxpayer receives 30% income tax relief.

Jury service rates

Jurors are not paid for jury service but may be able to claim expenses.

A **self-employed** juror may claim for each day at court:

- up to £64.95 for loss of earnings and extra childcare costs
- £5.71 for food and drink
- the cost of travel to and from the court.

A person on **benefits** continues to receive benefit for up to 8 weeks of jury service.

If a trial lasts longer, the court provides a loss of earnings form.

An **employed** person may claim:

- £64.95 a day if more than 4 hours spent at court
- £32.47 a day if less than 4 hours at court

After 10 days:

£129.91 a day for more than 4 hours at court

£64.95 for less than 4 hours at court

Travel may be claimed at cost for public transport

- car or motorcycle: 31.4p a mile
- bicycle: 9.6p a mile
- car passenger: 4.2p a mile

Food and drink may be claimed at:

- £5.71 a day for up to 10 hours
- £12.17 a day for more than 10 hours.

Land and buildings transaction tax

Land and buildings transaction tax (LBTT) is charged on property sales in Scotland from 1 April 2015 where it replaces stamp duty land tax.

There is an additional dwelling supplement for a second home. This is 3% from 1 April 2016, and 4% from 25 January 2019.

The rates are temporarily reduced between 15 July 2020 and 31 March 2021.

Freehold residential property bought before 15 July 2020 or from 1 April 2021

Slice of property price	*Main rate*	*Higher rate to 24.1.19*	*Higher rate from 25.1.19*
up to £145,000	0%	3%	4%
£145,001 to £250,000	2%	5%	6%
£250,001 to £325,000	5%	8%	9%
£325,001 to £750,000	10%	13%	14%
over £750,000	12%	15%	16%

From 30 June 2018, a first time buyer pays duty at 0% on the first £175,000.

Freehold residential property bought between 15 July 2020 and 31 March 2021

Slice of property value	*Rate*
up to £250,000	0%
£250,001 to £325,000	5%
£325,001 to £750,000	10%
over £750,000	12%

Freehold residential property leased

There is no LBTT on leased residential property in Scotland unless the lease exceeds 175 years.

Non-residential property bought or leased

Slice of property price	*From 7.2.20*	*From 25.1.19*	*From 1.4.15*
up to £150,000	0%	0%	0%
£150,001 to £250,000	1%	1%	3%
£250,001 to £350,000	5%	5%	3%
over £350,000	5%	5%	4.5%

Non-residential property leased

NPV of rents	*From 7.2.20*	*From 1.4.15*
up to £150,000	0%	0%
£150,001 to £2 million	1%	1%
over £2 million	2%	1%

Where the annual rent for a lease exceeds £1,000 a year, there is no 0% band.

LBTT has many exemptions and reliefs.

Land transaction tax

Land transaction tax (LTT) is paid for property transactions in Wales from 1 April 2018 where it replaces stamp duty land tax (SDLT)

Like SDLT, it has different rates for residential and non-residential properties.

A higher rate, an additional 3%, is payable for a second property or where a company purchases a residential property costing more than £40,000. This rate increases to 4% for properties where the effective transfer date is 22 December 2020 or later.

The residential rates were temporarily reduced between 27 July 2020 and 31 March 2021.

Residential property bought before 27 July 2020 or from 1 April 2021

Slice of property price	*Main rate*	*Higher rate to 21.12.20*	*Higher rate from 22.12.20*
up to £180,000	0%	3%	4%
£180,001 to £250,000	3.5%	6.5%	7.5%
£250,001 to £400,000	5%	8%	9%
£400,001 to £750,000	7.5%	10.5%	11.5%
£750,001 to £1.5 million	10%	13%	14%
over £1.5 million	12%	15%	16%

Residential property bought between 27 July 2020 and 31 March 2020

Slice of property price	*Rate*
up to £250,000	0%
£250,001 to £400,000	5%
£400,001 to £750,000	7.5%
£750,001 to £1.5 million	10%
over £1.5 million	12%

Residential leases

There is no LTT on residential lease income in Wales.

Non-residential property bought

Slice of property price	*Rate*
Up to £150,000	0%
£150,001 to £250,000	1%
£250,001 to £1 million	5%
over £1 million	6%

Non-residential leases

NPV of rents threshold	*Rate*
up to £150,000	0%
£150,001 to £2 million	1%
over £2 million	2%

A non-residential lease is taxed on the net present value (NPV).

If the annual rent is more than £9,000 (including VAT), the 0% band is removed, so the first £250,000 is taxed at 1%.

Landfill tax

	2020/21	2019/20	2018/19	2017/18
Landfill tax (England and Northern Ireland)				
Active waste per tonne	£94.15	£91.35	£88.95	£86.10
Inert waste per tonne	£3.00	£2.90	£2.80	£2.70
Maximum credit	5.3%	5.3%	5.3%	4.2%
Scotland landfill tax (in Scotland)				
Standard rate per tonne	£94.15	£91.35	£88.95	£86.10
Lower rate	£3.00	£2.90	£2.80	£2.70
Maximum credit	5.6%	5.6%	5.6%	5.6%
Landfill disposals tax (in Wales)				
Standard rate per tonne	£94.15	£91.35	£88.95	-
Lower rate	£3.00	£2.90	£2.80	-
Unauthorised disposal rate	£141.20	£137.00	£133.45	-

Before 1 April 2018, landfill tax applied in Wales

Landlords' restriction on finance costs

A landlord of residential property is not able to claim the whole amount of finance costs against his or her highest rate of income tax. Instead they are allowed to claim against their marginal rate a percentage of costs. The balance gets tax relief at 20%.

Tax year	Percentage relieved at highest marginal rate
2020/21 and later	0%
2019/20	25%
2018/19	50%
2017/18	75%
2016/17 and earlier	100%

Lease depreciation table

This restricts the percentage of the capital gain for a lease that had less than 50 years to run at the date of disposal. The percentage is the number of whole years, plus the appropriate numbers of monthly increments for whole months. An odd 14 days or more is counted as one monthly increment.

Years	%	Monthly increment
50 or more	100	-
49	99.657	0.029
48	99.289	0.031
47	98.902	0.032
46	98.490	0.034
45	98.059	0.036
44	95.595	0.039
43	97.107	0.041
42	96.593	0.043

Years	%	Monthly increment
41	96.041	0.046
40	95.457	0.049
39	94.842	0.051
38	94.189	0.054
37	93.497	0.058
36	92.761	0.061
35	91.981	0.065
34	91.156	0.069
33	90.280	0.073

Years	%	Monthly increment
32	89.354	0.077
31	88.371	0.082
30	87.330	0.087
29	86.226	0.092
28	85.053	0.098
27	83.816	0.103
26	82.496	0.110
25	81.100	0.116
24	79.622	0.123
23	78.055	0.131
22	76.399	0.138
21	74.635	0.147
20	72.770	0.155
19	70.791	0.165
18	68.697	0.175
17	66.470	0.186
16	64.116	0.196

Years	%	Monthly increment
15	61.617	0.208
14	58.971	0.221
13	56.167	0.234
12	53.191	0.248
11	50.038	0.263
10	46.695	0.279
9	43.154	0.295
8	39.399	0.313
7	35.414	0.332
6	31.195	0.352
5	26.722	0.373
4	21.983	0.395
3	16.959	0.419
2	11.629	0.444
1	5.983	0.470
0	0	0.499

Lease premium

Where a short term lease of up to 50 years is granted, part of it is taxed as a gain and part as rent. The apportionment is as below where the term of the lease is the number of whole years.

Term in years	% as gain	% as rent
50	98	2
49	96	4
48	94	6
47	92	8
46	90	10
45	88	12
44	86	14
43	84	16
42	82	18
41	80	20
40	78	22
39	76	24
38	74	26
37	72	28
36	70	30
35	68	32

Term in years	% as gain	% as rent
34	66	34
33	64	36
32	62	38
31	60	40
30	58	42
29	56	44
28	54	46
27	52	48
26	50	50
25	48	52
24	46	54
23	44	56
22	42	58
21	40	60
20	38	62
19	36	64

Term in years	% as gain	% as rent
18	34	66
17	32	68
16	30	70
15	28	72
14	26	74
13	24	76
12	22	78
11	20	80
10	18	82

Term in years	% as gain	% as rent
9	16	84
8	14	86
7	12	88
6	10	90
5	8	92
4	6	94
3	4	96
2	2	98
1 or 0	0	100

Legal tender

Royal Mint coins are legal tender in the whole UK to these amounts:

Denomination	**Maximum amount**
£1 and above:	any amount
20p bur less than £1	£10
5p and 10p	£5
1p and 2p	20p

Coins are produced for general circulation in amounts of 1p, 2p, 5p, 10p, 20p, 50p, £1 and £2. Other coins are produced for collectors for these and other amounts, but shops and banks generally do not accept them.

Current coins for general circulation

Value	*Description*	*First issued*
1p	round copper	December 1968
2p	round copper	December 1968
5p	round silver	30 June 1993
10p	round silver	31 December 1990
20p	seven-sided silver	9 June 1982
50p	seven-sided silver	1 September 1997
£1	12-sided bimetallic	28 March 2017
£2	round bimetallic	15 June 1998

Bank of England notes are legal tender for England and Wales, but not for Scotland or Northern Ireland. They are produced for amounts of £5, £10, £20 and £50.

Current banknotes

Value	*Series*	*Depicting*	*First issued*
£5	F	Winston Churchill	13 September 2016
£10	F	Jane Austen	14 September 2017
£20	F	Adam Smith	13 March 2007
£50	E	Matthew Boulton and James Watt	2 November 2011

All notes from F series are produced on polymer plastic rather than paper.

The £50 series E note is to be demonetised in 2021 and replaced by a polymer note featuring Alan Turing.

Demonetised coins: decimal

Value	*Description*	*First minted*	*Demonetised*
½p	round copper	December 1968	28 February 1998
5p	large coin	23 April 1968	31 December 1990
10p	large coin	23 April 1968	31 December 1990
50p	large coin	1 September 1997	28 February 1998
£1	round coin	21 April 1983	15 October 2017

Demonetised coins: pre-decimal

Name	*Value*	*Decimal value*	*Demonetised*
half-crown	2s 6d	12½p	1 January 1970
florin	2s	10p	30 June 1993
shilling	1s	5p	31 December 1990
sixpence	6d	2½p	30 June 1990
threepence	3d	1.25p	31 August 1971
penny	1d	0.42p	31 August 1971
halfpenny	½d	0.21p	1 August 1969
farthing	¼d	0.10p	31 December 1960
half-farthing	⅛d	0.05p	31 December 1869

Demonetised bank notes

Value	*Series*	*Depicted on reverse*	*First Issued*	*Demonetised*
10 s	A	whorls	25 October 1948	29 October 1962
10 s	C	Britannia	12 October 1961	22 Nov 1970
£1	A	whorls	13 September 1948	28 May 1962
£1	C	Britannia	17 March 1960	31 May 1979
£1	D	Sir Isaac Newton	9 February 1978	11 March 1988
£5	white	blank	1793	1 March 1946
£5	B	lion	21 February 1957	27 June 1967
£5	C	Britannia	21 February 1963	31 August 1973
£5	D	Duke of Wellington	11 Nov 1971	29 Nov 1991
£5	E	George Stephenson	1 March 1993	21 Nov 2003
£5	E	Elizabeth Fry	21 May 2002	5 May 2017
£10	C	Britannia	21 February 1964	31 May 1979
£10	D	Florence Nightingale	20 February 1975	20 May 1994
£10	E	Charles Dickens	29 April 1992	31 July 2003
£10	V	Charles Darwin	7 November 2000	1 March 2018
£20	D	William Shakespeare	9 July 1970	19 March 1993
£20	E	Michael Faraday	27 September 1993	28 February 2001
£20	E	Edward Elgar	22 June 1999	30 June 2010
£50	D	Christopher Wren	20 March 1981	20 Sept 1996
£50	E	Sir John Houblon	20 April 1994	30 April 2014

All other Bank of England notes were demonetised in 1945.

Scottish and Irish bank notes are not legal tender anywhere. As the Bank of England accepts their notes for value, other banks and shops will usually accept them.

Life expectancy tables

These are the life expectancy tables, expressed as years left to live for men and woman of different ages from birth. They are based on tables from the Office of National Statistics for the years 2017-2019. The "age at death" figure is the age to which the person is expected to live according to their current age.

			Age at death	
Age	**Male**	**Female**	**Male**	**Female**
0	79.37	83.06	79	83
1	78.71	82.35	79	83
2	77.72	81.37	79	83
3	76.73	80.38	79	83
4	75.74	79.39	79	83
5	74.75	78.39	79	83
6	73.76	77.40	79	83
7	72.76	76.41	79	83
8	71.77	75.41	79	83
9	70.77	74.42	79	83
10	69.78	73.42	79	83
11	68.78	72.42	79	83
12	67.79	71.43	79	83
13	66.79	70.43	79	83
14	65.80	69.44	79	83
15	64.81	68.45	79	83
16	63.82	67.45	79	83
17	62.84	66.46	79	83
18	61.86	65.47	79	83
19	60.88	64.49	79	83
20	59.91	63.50	79	83
21	58.94	62.51	79	83
22	57.97	61.53	79	83
23	57.00	60.54	80	83
24	56.03	59.55	80	83
25	55.06	58.57	80	83
26	54.09	57.58	80	83
27	53.12	56.60	80	83
28	52.15	55.61	80	83
29	51.19	54.63	80	83
30	50.23	53.65	80	83
31	49.26	52.67	80	83
32	48.30	51.69	80	83
33	47.34	50.71	80	83
34	46.39	49.74	80	83
35	45.43	48.76	80	83

			Age at death	
Age	**Male**	**Female**	**Male**	**Female**
36	44.48	47.79	80	83
37	43.53	46.82	80	83
38	42.59	45.86	80	83
39	41.64	44.89	80	83
40	40.70	43.93	80	83
41	39.76	42.97	80	83
42	38.83	42.01	80	84
43	37.90	41.05	80	84
44	36.97	40.10	80	84
45	36.05	39.15	81	84
46	35.13	38.21	81	84
47	34.22	37.27	81	84
48	33.31	36.33	81	84
49	32.40	35.40	81	84
50	31.50	34.47	81	84
51	30.61	33.54	81	84
52	29.72	32.62	81	84
53	28.83	31.70	81	84
54	27.95	30.78	81	84
55	27.07	29.87	82	84
56	26.20	28.97	82	84
57	25.34	28.07	82	85
58	24.49	27.17	82	85
59	23.64	26.29	82	85
60	22.80	25.41	82	85
61	21.97	24.53	82	85
62	21.15	23.67	83	85
63	20.34	22.81	83	85
64	19.55	21.96	83	85
65	18.76	21.12	83	86
66	17.98	20.29	83	86
67	17.22	19.46	84	86
68	16.46	18.64	84	86
69	15.72	17.83	84	86
70	14.99	17.02	84	87
71	14.26	16.23	85	87

			Age at death	
Age	Male	Female	Male	Female
72	13.54	15.44	85	87
73	12.84	14.68	85	87
74	12.16	13.93	86	87
75	11.50	13.19	86	88
76	10.85	12.47	86	88
77	10.23	11.76	87	88
78	9.63	11.08	87	89
79	9.04	10.42	88	89
80	8.47	9.77	88	89
81	7.93	9.14	88	90
82	7.40	8.54	89	90
83	6.89	7.95	89	90
84	6.41	7.39	90	91
85	5.96	6.87	90	91
86	5.53	6.36	91	92

			Age at death	
Age	Male	Female	Male	Female
87	5.14	5.89	92	92
88	4.76	5.45	92	93
89	4.41	5.04	93	94
90	4.10	4.65	94	94
91	3.79	4.30	94	95
92	3.51	3.97	95	95
93	3.24	3.67	96	96
94	2.99	3.38	96	97
95	2.77	3.12	97	98
96	2.58	2.90	98	98
97	2.41	2.70	99	99
98	2.25	2.51	100	100
99	2.09	2.33	101	101
100	2.02	2.15	102	102

Metric conversion rates

Linear

1 inch = 2.54 millimetres
1 foot = 0.3048 metres
1 yard = 0.9144 metres
1 mile = 1.6093 kilometres

1 metre = 39.3701 inches
1 metre = 3.208 feet
1 metre = 1.0936 yards
1 kilometre = 0.6214 miles

Area

1 square inch = 645.2 square millimetres
1 square foot = 0.0929 square metres
1 square yard = 0.8361 square metres
1 acre = 0.4047 hectares
1 square mile = 2.59 square kilometres

1 square millimetre = 0.0015 square inches
1 square metre = 10.764 square feet
1 square metre = 1.196 square yards
1 hectare = 2.471 acres
1 square kilometre = 0.3861 square miles

Volume

1 cubic inch = 16.3871 cubic centimetres
1 cubic foot = 0.02832 cubic metres
1 cubic yard = 0.7646 cubic metres

1 cubic centimetre = 0.061 cubic inch
1 cubic metre = 35.315 cubic feet
1 cubic metre = 1.308 cubic yards

Capacity

1 pint = 0.5682 litres
1 gallon = 4.546 litres
1 fluid ounce = 28.41 millilitres

1 litre = 1.7598 pints
1 litre = 0.22 gallons
1 millilitre = 0.0352 fluid ounces

Angles

1 degree = 0.017453 radians

1 radian = 57.298 degrees

Weight

1 ounce = 28.35 grams
1 pound = 0.5359 kilograms
1 ton = 1.016 tonnes

1 gram = 0.035274 ounces
1 kilogram = 2.2046 pounds
1 tonne = 0.9842 tons

Mortgage repayments

This table gives the estimated monthly mortgage repayments in pounds for a £100,000 loan at various rates of interest over various terms.

This is for a mortgage which pays interest and repays capital. It excludes any fees.

These amounts may be multiplied pro rata. So, the repayment for a mortgage of £300,000 is simply three times the figure in the table.

Interest rate	15 years	20 years	25 years	30 years
1.0%	598	460	377	322
1.5%	621	483	400	345
2.0%	644	506	424	370
2.5%	667	530	449	395
3.0%	691	555	474	422
3.5%	715	580	501	449
4.0%	740	606	528	477
4.5%	765	633	556	507
5.0%	791	660	585	537
5.5%	817	688	614	568
6.0%	844	716	644	600
6.5%	871	746	675	632
7.0%	899	775	707	665
7.5%	927	806	739	699
8.0%	956	836	772	734
8.5%	985	868	805	769
9.0%	1,014	900	839	805
9.5%	1,044	932	874	841
10.0%	1,075	965	909	878
10.5%	1,105	998	944	915
11.0%	1,137	1,032	980	952
11.5%	1,168	1,066	1,016	990
12.0%	1,200	1,101	1,053	1,029
12.5%	1,233	1,136	1,090	1,067
13.0%	1,265	1,172	1,128	1,106
13.5%	1,298	1,207	1,166	1,145
14.0%	1,332	1,244	1,204	1,185
14.5%	1,366	1,280	1,242	1,225
15.0%	1,400	1,317	1,281	1,264

National insurance

Class 1 national insurance	2021/22	2020/21	2019/20	2018/19	2017/18
Lower earnings limit weekly	£120	£120	£118	£116	£113
Lower earnings limit monthly	£520	£520	£512	£503	£490
Lower earnings limit annual	£6,230	£6,240	£6,136	£6,032	£5,876
Primary threshold weekly	£184	£183	£166	£162	£157

Primary threshold monthly	£797	£792	£719	£702	£680
Primary threshold annual	£9,568	£9,500	£8,632	£8,424	£8,164
Secondary threshold weekly	£170	£169	£166	£162	£157
Secondary threshold monthly	£737	£732	£719	£702	£680
Secondary threshold annual	£8,840	£8,788	£8,632	£8,424	£8,164
Upper earnings limit weekly	£967	£962	£962	£892	£866
Upper earnings limit monthly	£4,189	£4,167	£4,167	£3,863	£3,750
Upper earnings limit annual	£50,270	£50,000	£50,000	£46,350	£45,000
Employee rate to UEL	12.0%	12.0%	12.0%	12.0%	12.0%
Employee rate above UEL	2.0%	2.0%	2.0%	2.0%	2.0%
Reduced rate	5.85%	5.85%	5.85%	5.85%	5.85%

The 2020/21 rates were given in a ministerial statement on 16 December 2020.

Employees pay class 1 national insurance at 12.0% on income between the primary threshold and upper earnings limit, and then at 2.0% on further income.

Employers pay 13.8% on all income above the secondary threshold without limit

Class 1A and 1B national insurance is paid by the employer only at the class 1 rate

Class 1 provisions

The right of an employer and employee to pay a reduced rate if the employee is a member of a **contracted out pension scheme** ended in 2012 for defined contribution schemes, and in 2016 for defined benefit schemes.

From 6 April 2015, employer's national insurance is not payable for employees **under 21.**

From 6 April 2016, employer's national insurance is not payable for apprentices **under 25.**

The government plans to exempt civilian employers of military veterans for the first year of civilian employment between 6 April 2021 and 5 April 2024.

Class 2 weekly	**2021/22**	**2020/21**	**2019/20**	**2018/19**	**2017/18**
Weekly amount	£3.05	£3.05	£3.00	£2.95	£2.85
Small profits threshold	£6,515	£6,475	£6,365	£6,205	£6,025
Share fisherman weekly	£3.70	£3.70	£3.65	£3.60	£3.50
Volunteer development worker	£6.00	£6.00	£5.90	£5.80	£5.65
Class 3 weekly	£15.40	£15.30	£15.00	£14.65	£14.25
Class 4					
lower profits limit annual	£9,568	£9,500	£8,632	£8,424	£8,164
Upper profits limit annual	£50,270	£50,000	£50,000	£46,350	£45,000
Rate between limits	9%	9%	9%	9%	9%
rate above upper profits limit	2%	2%	2%	2%	2%

HISTORIC RATES

Years	**LEL**	**ET**	**UEL**	**Ee**	**Er**	**Class 2**	**Class 3**
	£	**£**	**£**	**rate**	**rate**	**amount**	**amount**
2016/17	112	155	827	12.0	13.8	2.80	14.10
2015/16	112	155	815	12.0	13.8	2.80	14.10
2014/15	111	153	805	12.0	13.8	2.75	13.90
2013/14	109	149[1]	797	12.0	13.8	2.70	13.55
2012/13	107	146[1]	817	12.0	13.8	2.65	13.25
2011/12	102	139[1]	817	11.0	12.8	2.50	12.60

2010/11	97	110	844	11.0	12.8	2.40	12.05
2009/10	95	110	844	11.0	12.8	2.40	12.05
2008/09	90	105	770	11.0	12.8	2.30	8.10
2007/08	87	100	670	11.0	12.8	2.20	7.80
2006/07	84	97	645	11.0	12.8	2.10	7.55
2005/06	82	94	630	11.0	12.8	2.10	7.35
2004/05	79	91	610	11.0	12.8	2.05	7.15
2003/04	77	89	595	11.0	12.8	2.00	6.95
2002/03	75	89	585	10.0	11.8	2.00	6.75
2001/02	72	87	575	10.0	11.9	2.00	6.75
2000/01	67	-	535	10.0	12.2	2.00	6.55

LEL is lower earnings limit expressed as a weekly figure
ET is earnings threshold for employees expressed as a weekly figure
This was the same as the lower earnings limit before 2001/02.
[1] The employer had a lower earnings threshold for these years: 2013/14 - £148; 2012/13 - £144; 2011/12 -£136.
UEL is upper earnings limited expressed as a weekly figure.
From 2009/10 to 2015/16, there was also an upper accruals point (UAP) of £770 a week for each year.
The Ee rate is the percentage rate paid by the employee from the earnings threshold to the upper earnings limit.
There is reduced rate for married women of 5.85% from 2012/13; 4.85% from 2003/04; and 3.85% from 2000/01.
Employees in a contracted out pension and their employer both paid lower rates of national insurance up to 2015/16 for a defined benefit scheme, and to 2011/12 for a defined contribution scheme.
For years 2011/12 onwards, the employee pays 2% secondary rate on earnings above the upper earnings limit. Between 2003/04 and 2010/11, the secondary rate was 1%. Before 2003/04, there was no secondary rate.
The class 2 and class 3 rates are the amounts in pounds per week. There are different class 2 rates for share fishermen and volunteer development workers.

National insurance contribution letters

The appropriate rate of national insurance for an employee is indicated by a single letter. Those currently used are:

A standard rate
B married woman's reduced rate
C age exempt, so only employer's national insurance paid
G apprentice mariner under 25
H non-mariner apprentice under 25
J non-mariner deferment
M standard rate, under 21
Q mariner deferment
X under 16 so no liability
Z under 21 deferment.

Other letters have historically been used.

National minimum wage

	21/22	20/21	19/20	18/19	17/18
National living wage per hour	£8.91	£8.72	£8.21	£7.83	£7.50
age 21 to 22*	£8.36	£8.20	£7.70	£7.38	£7.05
age 18 to 20	£6.56	£6.45	£6.15	£5.90	£5.60
age 16 to 17	£4.62	£4.55	£4.35	£4.20	£4.05
apprentice rate	£4.30	£4.15	£3.90	£3.70	£3.50
accommodation offset per day	£8.36	£8.20	£7.55	£7.00	£6.40

* before 6 April 2020, the age range 21 to 22 was 21 to 24.

National savings rates

Direct ISA

From	*Rate*
24 November 2020	0.1%
1 March 2019	0.9%
24 September 2018	0.75%
1 December 2017	1.0%
1 May 2017	0.75%
6 June 2016	1.0%
16 November 2015	1.25%
27 February 2014	1.5%
5 November 2012	2.25%
19 August 2009	2.5%
18 March 2009	1.3%
19 February 2009	1.8%
21 January 2009	2.3%
7 November 2008	3.3%
8 October2008	4.8%
10 April 2008	5.3%

Payments are tax free.

Direct saver

From	*Rate*
24 November 2020	0.15%
1 October 2018	1.0%
1 December 2017	0.95%
1 May 2017	0.7%
6 June 2016	0.8%
12 September 2013	1.1%
25 January 2012	1.5%
19 July 2010	1.75%
8 March 2010	2.0%

The rate is variable, subject to tax, paid gross

Guaranteed growth bonds

The 6-month bond is no longer on sale.

The 52nd issue rate from 18 August 2010 is 1.55%. Paid gross, taxable

Rates for the 1-year bond:

From	*Issue*	*Rate*
24 November 2020	67	0.10%
1 May 2020	66	1.10%
2 September 2019	65	1.25%
1 May 2019	64	1.50%
11 June 2018	63	1.50%
1 December 2017	62	1.50%
20 November 2017	61	1.50%
13 November 2017	60	1.25%
1 April 2017	59	0.95%
1 July 2016	58	1.20%
20 October 2015	57	1.45%
9 December 2013	56	1.25%
5 July 2013	55	1.50%
27 February 2013	54	1.75%
5 October 2012	53	2.00%
20 September 2012	52	2.20%
27 September 2010	51	2.20%
18 August 2010	50	2.45%
17 February 2010	49	3.20%
26 October 2009	48	3.95%

Rates for the 18-month.

These are no longer on sale.

Income bonds

From	*Gross rate*	*AER*
24 November 2020	0.01%	0.01%
1 October 2018	1.15%	1.16%
1 December 2017	1.00%	1.00%
1 May 2017	0.75%	0.75%
6 June 2016	1.00%	1.00%
12 September 2013	1.25%	1.26%
6 April 2013	1.75%	1.76%

	to £24,999	*to £24,999*	*£25,000+*	*£25,000+*
	Gross rate	*AER*	*gross rate*	*AER*
19 July 2010	1.45%	1.46%	1.75%	1.76%
20 May 2009	1.70%	1.71%	2.00%	2.02%
18 March 2009	0.70%	0.70%	1.00%	1.00%
19 February 2009	1.20%	1.21%	1.45%	1.46%
21 January 2009	1.95%	1.97%	2.20%	2.22%
19 November 2008	2.45%	2.48%	2.70%	2.73%
6 November 2008	3.75%	3.82%	4.00%	4.07%

7 October 2008	4.25%	4.33%	4.50%	4.59%
6 May 2008	4.45%	4.54%	4.70%	4.80%

Subject to tax, paid gross. Minimum £500.

Interest is rounded up or down to nearest penny. So, from 24 November 2020, balances below £646 do not receive an interest payment every month.

Investment account

From	*Rate*		
24 November 2020	0.01%		
1 October 2018	0.80%		
1 December 2017	0.70%		
1 July 2016	0.45%		
21 May 2012	0.75%		
	Rate under £25,000	*Rate £25,000+*	*Rate £50,000+*
18 March 2009	0.20%	0.30%	0.30%
19 February 2009	0.30%	0.40%	0.50%
21 January 2009	0.35%	0.55%	1.90%

Subject to tax, paid gross.

Junior ISA

From	*Rate*
24 November 2020	1.50%
1 March 2019	3.25%
12 March 2018	2.50%
1 December 2017	2.25%
15 August 2017	2.00%

Tax free.

Premium bonds

Effective from	*Prize rate*	*Chances of winning to 1*
1 December 2020	1.0%	34,500
1 December 2017	1.4%	24,500
1 May 2017	1.15%	30,000
1 June 2016	1.25%	30,000
1 August 2014	1.35%	26,000
1 August 2013	1.3%	26,000
1 October 2009	1.5%	24,000
1 April 2009	1.0%	36,000
1 December 2008	1.8%	36,000
1 November 2008	2.85%	24,000
1 May 2008	3.4%	24,000

Prizes are tax-free.

Net pay table

This table shows the amount of income tax, national insurance and net pay for different amounts of annual employment gross income. It uses rates of income tax and national insurance for the UK (except Scotland) for 2020/21. The income tax rates are calculated as if from tax tables; other methods of calculation may differ by up to £4.

It assumes that the taxpayer is entitled to the full personal allowance and no other income tax allowances, and is liable to pay the full rate of national insurance.

The table allows for the reduction in personal allowance when income exceeds £100,000.

It makes no allowance for pension contributions, student loans or payrolled benefits.

It does not show employer's national insurance.

Gross pay	Tax	NI	Net pay
9,000	0	0	9,000
10,000	0	60	9,940
11,000	0	180	10,820
12,000	0	300	11,700
13,000	98	420	12,482
14,000	298	540	13,162
15,000	498	660	13,842
16,000	698	780	14,522
17,000	898	900	15,202
18,000	1,098	1,020	15,882
19,000	1,298	1,140	16,562
20,000	1,498	1,260	17,242
21,000	1,698	1,380	17,922
22,000	1,898	1,500	18,602
23,000	2,098	1,620	19,282
24,000	2,298	1,740	19,962
25,000	2,498	1,860	20,642
26,000	2,698	1,980	21,322
27,000	2,898	2,100	22,002
28,000	3,098	2,220	22,682
29,000	3,298	2,340	23,362
30,000	3,498	2,460	24,042
31,000	3,698	2,580	24,722
32,000	3,898	2,700	25,402
33,000	4,098	2,820	26,082
34,000	4,298	2,940	26,762
35,000	4,498	3,060	27,442
36,000	4,698	3,180	28,122
37,000	4,898	3,300	28,802
38,000	5,098	3,420	29,482
39,000	5,298	3,540	30,162
40,000	5,498	3,660	30,842
41,000	5,698	3,780	31,522
42,000	5,898	3,900	32,202
43,000	6,098	4,020	32,882

Gross pay	Tax	NI	Net pay
44,000	6,298	4,140	33,562
45,000	6,498	4,260	34,242
46,000	6,698	4,380	34,922
47,000	6,898	4,500	35,602
48,000	7,098	4,620	36,282
49,000	7,298	4,740	36,962
50,000	7,498	4,860	37,642
51,000	7,896	4,880	38,224
52,000	8,296	4,900	38,804
53,000	8,696	4,920	39,384
54,000	9,096	4,940	39,964
55,000	9,496	4,960	40,544
56,000	9,896	4,980	41,124
57,000	10,296	5,000	41,704
58,000	10,696	5,020	42,284
59,000	11,096	5,040	42,864
60,000	11,496	5,060	43,444
65,000	13,496	5,160	46,344
70,000	15,496	5,260	49,244
75,000	17,496	5,360	52,144
80,000	19,496	5,460	55,044
85,000	21,496	5,560	57,944
90,000	23,496	5,660	60,844
95,000	25,496	5,760	63,744
100,000	27,496	5,860	66,644
105,000	30,496	5,960	68,544
110,000	33,496	6,060	70,444
115,000	36,496	6,160	72,344
120,000	39,496	6,260	74,244
125,000	42,496	6,360	76,144
130,000	44,500	6,460	79,040
135,000	46,500	6,560	81,940
140,000	48,500	6,660	84,840
145,000	50,500	6,760	87,740
150,000	52,500	6,860	90,640
160,000	57,000	7,060	95,940
170,000	61,500	7,260	101,240
180,000	66,000	7,460	106,540
190,000	70,500	7,660	111,840
200,000	75,000	7,860	117,140
250,000	97,500	8,860	143,640
300,000	120,000	9,860	170,140

Gross pay	Tax	NI	Net pay
350,000	142,500	10,860	196,640
400,000	165,000	11,860	223,140
450,000	187,500	12,860	249,640
500,000	210,000	13,860	276,140
600,000	255,000	15,860	329,140
700,000	300,000	17,860	382,140
800,000	345,000	19,860	435,140
900,000	390,000	21,860	488,140
1 million	435,000	23,860	541,140
2 million	885,000	43,860	1,071,140
5 million	2,235,000	103,860	2,661,140
10 million	4,485,000	203,860	5,311,140
20 million	8,985,000	403,860	10,611,140
50 million	22,485,000	1,003,860	26,511,140
100 million	44,985,000	2,003,860	53,011,140

Non-dom charge

A taxpayer who is not UK-domiciled (a "non-dom") may elect to be treated as if UK domiciled.

Otherwise non-doms whose foreign income or gains are at least £2,000 a year must either pay tax on them (some of which may be reclaimable) or elect for the remittance basis. The latter means the taxpayer must pay an annual charge of:

Years in UK	From	Amount of charge
7 of last 9	2013	£30,000
12 of last 14	2013	£50,000
	2015	£60,000
17 of last 20	2013	£30,000
	2015	£90,000
	2017	not payable

From 2017, someone who is UK resident for 15 year out of the last 20 is taxed as if UK resident for all taxes, and so is not eligible to pay the charge.

Number plates

Tax provisions on cars can be based on their age.

This is indicated by the number plate from 1963.

From 1 September 2021

UK number plates take the form two letters, two digits and three letters in the form AB 12 CDE.

The two numbers indicate the year of registration.

Number 01 indicates the car was registered between September 2001 and February 2002

Numbers 02 to 50 indicate that the car was registered between March and August in that year of the 20th century.

Numbers 51 to 00 indicate that the car was registered between September and February in the year in which that period started if 50 is subtracted. So 70 indicates a car registered between September 2020 and February 2021.

A car may display an earlier number plate, such as a personalised plate, but not one which is later.

From 1963 to 2021

From August 1983 to September 2001, the number plate was a prefix of one letter, three digits and three letters in the form A 123 CDE.

From 1 January 1963 to 1983, the number plate was three letters, three numbers and a suffix of one letter in the form ABC 123 D. The suffix changed in August from 1967 and on 1 January previously.

Letter	*Prefix*	*Suffix*
A	1983/84	1963
B	1984/85	1964
C	1985/86	1965
D	1986/87	1966
E	1987/88	Jan 1967- July 1967
F	1988/89	Aug 1967/68
G	1989/90	1968/69
H	1990/91	1969/70
J	1991/92	1970/71
K	1992/93	1971/72
L	1993/94	1972/73
M	1994/95	1973/74
N	1995/96	1974/75
P	1996/97	1975/76
R	1997/98	1976/77
S	1998-Feb 1999	1977/78
T	Mar 1999-Aug 1999	1978/79
V	Sep 1999-Feb 2000	1979/80
W	Mar 2000-Aug 2000	1980/81
X	Sep 2000-Feb 2001	1981/82
Y	Mar 2001-Sep 2001	1982/83

In 1983, the letter Q was introduced for a car whose age is not known.

Before 1963

From 1930 to 1963, number plates took the form of three letters and up to three numbers in the form ABC 123, with no prefix or suffix. Some number plates in the 1950s had this reversed in the form 123 ABC.

In the early 1960s, some number plates were introduced with up to four digits followed by two letters in the form 1234 AB.

From the introduction of number plates on 1 January 1904 to 1930, numbers were allotted as one or two letters followed by up to four digits in the form A1 to YY9999.

Official Receiver fees

When the Official Receiver acts as trustee in a personal bankruptcy, these fees are payable:

Nature of fee	Amount
Administration fee (own petition)	£1,990
Administration fee (other petition)	£2,775
General fee	£6,000
Assets realised	15% of sum realised
Work done	Fee at an hourly rate.

Patent box

The patent box was introduced from 1 April 2013 to reduce the effective rate of corporation tax to 10% on profits from the exploitation of a patent.

This is done by making a deduction from corporation tax profits.

The deduction is: RP x FY x (MR-IPR)/MR

where RP is the relevant profit for patent box-related profits

FY is the relevant percentage for the financial year

MR is the main rate of corporation tax

IPR is the special patent box rate of corporation tax.

The relevant percentages are:

Financial year	*Percentage*
2013	60%
2014	70%
2015	80%
2016	90%
2017 and subsequently	100%

PAYE coding out limits

If an employee owes tax, this can be "coded out" up to a limit. This means that the tax code is adjusted so that the arrears are collected over the following tax year.

From 2012/13 to 2014/15, the maximum that could be coded out was £3,000.

From 2015/16, a higher figure may be coded out according to the taxpayer's income for the tax year in which the code is to be applied.

The amount of tax collected in any period is restricted to 50% of gross earnings.

Income	Maximum amount
to £30,000	£3,000
to £40,000	£5,000
to £50,000	£7,000
to £60,000	£9,000
to £70,000	£11,000
to £80,000	£13,000
to £90,000	£15,000
above £90,000	£17,000

Penalties

This is a summary of some of the main tax penalties

Late filed personal tax returns	**Penalty**
Filed up to three months late:	£100
more than three months late:	daily penalty of £10 a day up to £900
more than six months late:	greater of £300 and 5% of tax
12 months late:	greater of £300 and 5% of tax, more if taxpayer is deliberately withholding
12 months late and deliberate:	greater of £300 and 70% of tax
12 months late, deliberate and concealed:	greater of £300 and 100% of tax

Late paid tax

30 days late	5% of tax due
more than six months late:	another 5% of tax due
12 months late:	another 5% of tax due

In addition to penalties, interest is charged on late tax.

Penalties can be greater if there are offshore implications.

Incorrect return

Careless inaccuracy	30% of tax
Deliberate but not concealed	70% of tax
Deliberate and concealed	100% of tax

Late paid corporation tax

Up to three months late	£100
more than 3 months late	another £100
more than 6 months late	10% of estimated corporation tax
more than 12 months late	another 10% of estimated corporation tax

If tax returns are late three times in a row, the £100 penalties become £500.

Mitigation

A penalty may be set aside on grounds of reasonable excuse.

A penalty may be mitigated by up to these percentages:

- 30% for telling HMRC
- 40% for co-operating with HMRC
- 30% for giving access to record.

The interest charge cannot be set aside or mitigated.

Failure to notify HMRC of error

Unprompted disclosure	nil
Prompted disclosure	15% minimum

PAYE LATE FILING PENALTIES

Initial penalties

These are charged when a full payment submission is late, even if no tax is payable.

A penalty is not charged for the first late filing in a tax year.

Number of employees	*Monthly penalty*
1 to 9	£100
10 to 49	£200
50 to 249	£300
250 or more	£400

Additional penalties for being more than three months late

5% of tax and national insurance contributions on late payment

Late monthly or quarterly payments

No penalty is imposed for just one late PAYE payment unless it is more than six months late.

Number of defaults in tax year	*Penalty percentage*
1 – 3	1%
4 – 6	2%
7 – 9	3%
10 or more	4%

Additional penalties for late payment

6 months late	5%
12 months late	another 5%

Interest is also charged on late paid PAYE.

There are also penalties for other taxes, and for other offences.

Pensions contributions

A taxpayer may contribute as much as he or she wishes into a pension fund without limit. There are limits on how much of such contributions qualify for income tax relief.

Pension contributions do not qualify for national insurance relief.

No income tax relief is given for contributions made by a taxpayer who is 75 or older

Annual contributions limit

An individual may contribute in a tax year the greater of:

- 100% of earnings up to the annual allowance (see below), and
- £3,600 regardless of earnings.

Limits	**2020/21**	**2019/20**	**2018/19**	**2017/18**
Lifetime allowance	£1,073,100	£1,055,000	£1,030,000	£1,000,000
Annual allowance	£40,000	£40,000	£40,000	£40,000
Restricted annual limit	£4,000	£10,000	£10,000	£10,000
Adjusted income (incl conts)	£240,000	£150,000	£150,000	£150,000
Adjusted income (excl conts)	£200,000	£110,000	£110,000	£110,000

From 2016/17, the annual allowance reduces by £1 for every £2 that the taxpayer's adjusted income exceeds the figure for adjusted income including pension contributions, provided the income excluding contributions is also above the figure. The reduction applies until the restricted annual limit is reached.

Tax rates (special circumstances)

Rate	*Applies to*
55%	excess pension pot above the lifetime limit taken as lump sum (s215)
25%	excess pension pot above the lifetime limit taken as a pension (s215)
40%	unauthorised payment charge (s208)
15%	unauthorised payment surcharge (s209)
20%	short service refund lump sum on first £20,000 (s205; SI 2010 No 536)
50%	short service refund lump sum above (s205; SI 2010 No 536)

55%	serious ill-health lump sum charge (s205A)
55%	special lump sum death benefits charge (s206)
35%	authorised surplus payments charge (35%)
5%-40%	scheme sanction charge (s240)
40%	deregistration charge (s242)

Withdrawal rights

- For a **normal pension** in payment, there is generally an entitlement to 25% of the fund as a tax-free lump sum. The balance of 75% or more is used to provide a pension which is taxed as income at the normal rates. The entitlement may be exercised between the ages of 55 and 74.
- From 6 April 2015, a member of a **defined contribution scheme** who is at least 55 may draw up to 100% of the fund as a lump sum. 25% of the fund is tax-free; the balance is added to taxable income subject to income tax in the year of withdrawal.
- Where a taxpayer has guaranteed pension **income of up to £12,000** (from 27 March 2014), the taxpayer may take all their fund in cash. 25% of this is tax-free; the balance is added to the taxable income subject to income tax in the year of withdrawal.
- As an alternative to a pension, a taxpayer may take a **drawdown** of up to 150% of the amount of an annuity that the fund could have bought (from 27 March 2014).
- Where an individual who is at least 60 has total pension rights of less than £30,000, this is called a **trivial pension.** From 27 March 2014, this may be taken in cash. 25% of this is tax-free; the balance is added to the taxable income subject to income tax in the year of withdrawal.
- From 27 March 2014, up to **three pension pots** with a total value below £10,000 may be taken as a lump sum.

Retirement age

The normal age range for exercising pension rights is 55 to 74.

On 3 September 2020, the government said that the lower age is to rise to 57 from 2028.

Certain occupations, mainly in sport, have a lower age below 55 if the person was engaged in that occupation on 5 April 2006.

Pension advice

From 6 April 2017, an employer may pay for pensions advice for an employee, former employee or prospective employee of up to £500 per person per year without that being taxed as a benefit in kind.

Pension levy

The pension levy is imposed to cover the cost of running The Pensions Regulator (TPR), the Pensions Ombudsman Service and the Pensions Advisory Service. It is due on 1 April each year.

n/a means not applicable.

The Pension Protection Fund is also collected by TPR for the separately administered fund.

Levy on occupational pension schemes for 2020

Band	*Number of members*	*General levy per member*	*Minimum payment per scheme*
1	2-11	n/a	£29

2	12-99	£2.88	n/a
3	100-999	£2.08	£290
4	1,000-4,999	£1.62	£2,080
5	5,000-9,999	£1.23	£8,100
6	10,000-499,999	£0.86	£12,300
7	500,000 plus	£0.65	£430,000

Levy on personal, stakeholder or group personal pension schemes for 2020

Band	*Number of members*	*General levy per member*	*Minimum payment per scheme*
1	2-11	n/a	£12
2	12-99	£1.15	n/a
3	100-999	£0.81	£120
4	1,000-4,999	£0.69	£810
5	5,000-9,999	£0.46	£3,450
6	10,000-499,999	£0.35	£4,600
7	500,000 plus	£0.26	£175,000

Pension Protection Fund

Band	*Number of members*	*Amount per member*	*Minimum amount of levy*
1	2-11	n/a	£49
2	12-99	£4.88	n/a
3	100-999	£3.52	£490
4	1,000-4,999	£2.74	£3,520
5	5,000-9,999	£2.07	£13,700
6	10,000 plus	£1.45	£20,700

Fraud compensation levy

This is charged at 25p per member.

On 16 December 2020, the government launched a consultation on changing the structure of the levy and increasing the amounts.

Plastic packaging tax

The government plans to introduce a plastic packaging tax in April 2022. The rate is £200 per tonne of packaging that contains less than 30% recycled plastic. There will be an exemption for producers of small quantities of packaging.

Postal order fees

A postal order may be bought from a Post Office for an amount of between 50p and £250. It is subject to a fee (or poundage):

Amount of order	**Fee**
50p to £4.99	50p
£5 to £9.99	£1
£10 to £99.99	12.5% of face value
£100 to £250	£12.50

Prescription charges

	2020/21	2019/20
Prescription charge:	£9.15	£9.00
Prepayment certificate for 3 months:	£29.65	£29.10
Prepayment certificate for 12 months:	£105.90	£104.00

Exemptions from prescription charges apply to

- those receiving income-based benefits, universal credit, tax credits or pension credit
- women who are pregnant or who have given birth in the last 12 months
- those aged 60 and over
- those who are either under 16, or who are aged 16 to 18 and in full-time education
- those who receive payments from a war pension scheme or armed forces compensation scheme
- those who have any of these medical conditions:
- a permanent fistula (for example, caecostomy, colostomy, laryngostomy or ileostomy) which needs continuous surgical dressing or an appliance
- a form of hypoadrenalism (for example, Addison's Disease) for which specific substitution therapy is essential
- diabetes insipidus and other forms of hypopituitarism
- diabetes mellitus, except where treatment is by diet alone
- hypoparathyroidism
- myasthenia gravis
- myxoedema (that is, hypothyroidism which needs thyroid hormone replacement)
- epilepsy which needs continuous anticonvulsive therapy
- a continuing physical disability which means you cannot go out without the help of another person
- cancer and are undergoing treatment for either, cancer, the effects of cancer or the effects of cancer treatment.

Other charges from April 2020

Abdominal or spinal support:	£45.35
Full bespoke human hair wig:	£287.20
Partial human wig:	£196.40
Stock modcacrylic wig	£74.15
Surgical brassiere:	£30.05

Probate fees

(in England and Wales from May 2020)

Circumstances	Fee
Net estate exceeds £5.000. Citizen's charge	£215
Net estate exceeds £5,000. Professional practitioner charge	£155
Net estate is below £5,000	nil
Application for a second grant of an estate	£20
Additional copy of grant of representation	£1.50

In Scotland and Northern Ireland, a flat fee of £200 is charged.

Solicitors' fees will usually be additional.

Prospective changes

These changes were announced by 31 December 2020.
However, the dates are subject to change.

2021	• petrol must contain 10% biofuel
	• loose coal and wet wood to be banned for stoves
1 January 2021	• introduction of new points system for immigration
	• sanitary products become zero-rated for VAT
February 2021	• introduction of Scottish child payments
28 February 2021	• new deadline for building under Help to Buy scheme
1 March 2021	• introduction of VAT reverse charge for construction work
3 March 2021	• Budget
31 March 2021	• end of temporary increase in stamp duty land tax threshold
	• end of 5% VAT hospitality rate
1 April 2021	• additional 2% stamp duty land tax imposed on non-resident purchases of residential property
	• large business must notify HMRC if it takes a contrary view on tax law
6 April 2021	• zero emission vans will have a zero tax charge for employees
	• IR 35 provisions to be introduced in private sector
	• digital link rules for Making Tax Digital to be introduced
	• HMRC gains a new right to recover a PAYE debt from a third party
April 2021	• carrier bag charge in England doubles to 10p and applies to all shops regardless of size
30 April 2021:	• end of Coronavirus Job Retention Scheme (postponed twice)
summer 2021	• HMRC given new power to issue a financial institution notice
September 2021	• EU students must pay for university education in Scotland
2022	• UK students may study overseas under the new Turing scheme which replaces the EU's Erasmus scheme
March 2022	• revised end date for Scottish help to buy scheme
April 2022	• Making Tax Digital extended to all VAT-registered businesses
	• climate change levy rates for electricity will be frozen, and those for gas increased
	• advertisements for fatty foods will be banned
1 April 2022	• introduction of plastic packaging tax
	• scope of red diesel exemptions is restricted
September 2022	• new Institute for Teaching to be launched
2023	• eight British overseas territories will introduce laws to allow public access to company ownership records
	• implementation of Basel III on banks' capital adequacy
1 January 2023	• change to accounting standard IAS 1 on defining current liabilities
March 2023	• deferred end date for affordable homes scheme
April 2023	• Making Tax Digital extended to all income tax self-assessment
2024	• national living wage will be two-thirds of median earnings
September 2024	• latest date to complete migration of claimants to universal credit

1 January 2025	• European Union introduces procedures for simplifying VAT
2025	• government plans to sell remaining stake in Royal Bank of Scotland
31 January 2025	• date to which EU extended state aid permission for film relief
2030	• Microsoft says it will be carbon neutral
2035	• target that 65% of municipal waste must be recycled
2050	• UK will be carbon-neutral

Quantitative easing

Date	Amount	Cumulative total
November 2009	£200 billion	£200 billion
July 2012	£175 billion	£375 billion
August 2016	£70 billion	£445 billion
March 2020	£200 billion	£645 billion
June 2020	£100 billion	£745 billion
November 2020	£150 billion	£895 billion

Quarter days

These are the days when rent is traditionally paid, though the dates have been used for other purposes.

England, Wales and Northern Ireland

25 March	Lady Day
24 June	Midsummer Day
29 September	Michaelmas
25 December	Christmas

Scotland (from 1991)

28 February
28 May
28 August
28 November

Recent events (2018 to 2020)

2018

1 January	• research and development tax credit rises from 11% to 12%
4 January	• employment appeal tribunal says an employer may need to consider "bumping" in redundancies. This is when an employee is given a second employee's job and the second employee is made redundant
9 January	• European Court rules that secret surveillance of employees is unlawful
	• first tier tribunal rules that a payment cannot be retrospectively classed as remuneration when this is not supported by evidence
10 January	• upper tier tribunal rules that the hope value of a maisonette should be reflected in its probate value
12 January	• HMRC produces guidance on serial tax avoidance regulations

13 January	• introduction of Open Banking where banks must share information when authorised by the customer
17 January	• HMRC publishes its last set of indexation factors for chargeable gains • new regulations aim to simplify claiming group relief
19 January	• first tier tribunal confirms that white goods are not VAT zero-rated when installed in a new dwelling
26 January	• tax tribunal rules that waiver of a director's loan account is taxable as remuneration
31 January	• unexplained wealth orders may be issued
6 February	• first tier tribunal rules that a penalty notice must be made by a "flesh and blood" officer of HMRC, not a computer. This rule changes in 2020 • Supreme Court rules that a UK-registered doctor must report disciplinary proceedings against her in another country
8 February	• first prosecution of an employer for failure to provide workplace pension
14 February	• upper tier tribunal rules that chocolate Nesquik milk shake powder is zero-rated for VAT, but the banana and strawberry flavours are standard-rated
20 February	• Nicola Shaw is given a suspended sentence for tax fraud by wrongly claiming to be a single mother. She worked for HMRC in the department checking claims for benefits
21 February	• it is confirmed that Scottish pension schemes will continue to deduct income tax at 20% despite different Scottish rates • Supreme Court rules that the police can be liable to individuals for operational failures in dealing with crime
23 February	• upper tier tribunal refuses to allow an appeal for fresh evidence • Court of Appeal rules that an employee's rights do not depend on the employee knowing them • HMRC revises code of practice COP8 on civil procedure and fraud
28 February	• Supreme Court rules that there is no limitation period against a director who made non-fraudulent but unlawful distributions
2 March	• Court of Appeal rules that a bank had no duty of care to a third party to explain the risks in dealing with interest rate swaps
7 March	• Supreme Court rules that a specialist air handling system is trade plant and therefore does not affect the property's rateable value
8 March	• first tax tribunal case to hear evidence by video link
9 March	• HMRC revises forms for companies and partnerships to claim UK residence • High Court rules that the police need not discuss the content of an anti-harassment letter with its recipient, though this is usually good practice
14 March	• Supreme Court rules that a local authority was justified in sacking a head teacher who hid her relationship with a convicted sex offender
15 March	• online platforms become jointly and severally liable for unpaid VAT • HMRC publishes list of software suppliers for Making Tax Digital

16 March	• employment appeal tribunal rules that misconduct must be serious but not gross to justify dismissal
20 March	• the upper tier tribunal decides that a document in a tax case may be provided to a third party for good reason
21 March	• Supreme Court rules that an employee may bring proceedings for personal injury even though it did not lead to immediate symptoms
	• Supreme Court rules that a defendant on legal aid has no right to choose his barrister
	• Federal Reserve increases US base rates by a quarter of one percent
	• MPs say that the Financial Reporting Council is "toothless and useless"
	• former French president Nicolas Sarkozy is charged with corruption
22 March	• VAT restrictions are imposed on cost-sharing groups
23 March	• new regulations on transfer pricing reflect OECD changes
25 March	• barristers become subject to police checks before being called to the bar
26 March	• employment appeal tribunal rules that a zero-hours worker may bring a claim for unfair treatment of a part-time worker
27 March	• new restrictions are imposed on spread betting and contracts for difference
29 March	• Countingup Bank, which includes accounting services, starts trading
1 April	• Welsh Assembly takes responsibility for landfill tax and land transaction tax (equivalent to stamp duty land tax) in Wales
4 April	• deadline for first pay gap reporting
6 April	• charging an electric car at the workplace ceases to be a taxable benefit
	• company car supplement for diesel engines increases from 3% to 4%
	• PAYE settlement agreements last indefinitely and do not need renewal
	• introduction of soft drinks industry levy
	• dividend allowance is reduced from £5,000 to £2,000
9 April	• enforcement action starts against employers who have not published gender pay gap details
11 April	• former MP Andrew Tyrie is appointed chairman of Competition and Markets Authority
12 April	• new rules give consumers greater protection for holiday bookings
	• new guidance is issued on the legal requirements of a joint venture
	• the job of lion tamer becomes extinct when last tamer is refused a licence
13 April	• employment tribunal rules that a dismissal policy must allow for an appeal
	• High Court rules that the duties of a shadow director depends on the facts of each case. It gave guidance
17 April	• immigration solicitor Tiki Emezie was declared bankrupt when he ran up legal costs contesting a parking ticket

18 April	• Supreme Court rules that "negotiating damages" could be awarded for a breach of contract where the loss could be measured as an asset
19 April	• Court of Appeal rules that whether an employee who continues working after a pay cut can be held to have accepted the cut depends on the circumstances
20 April	• High Court rules that the two-child limit was perverse with regard to children in care
	• Court of Appeal rules that part of a settlement for discrimination may be regarded as compensation for injury to feelings and thus not taxable
21 April	• *The Times* reports that China has an unfair trading advantage as it can post goods to the UK for as little as half a penny
23 April	• Court of Appeal rules that neither members nor trustees had authority to make a non-party application to set aside a judgment
24 April	• Colin Rodgers is first tax agent to be prosecuted for dishonesty
25 April	• Supreme Court rules that a redundancy notice period starts from when the employee had a chance to read the notice
26 April	• Court of Appeal holds that a tour operator was not liable to pay damages to a customer who was raped by a hotel employee
	• Court of Appeal holds that a "persistent offender" can include someone convicted of seven offences in 2013
	• a director or company secretary may ask for their personal address not to appear on documents filed at Companies House
27 April	• a further exception to the two-child rule for universal credit applies for children who would otherwise be taken into care
29 April	• first ride on a self-driving motorcycle
	• Amber Rudd MP resigns as home secretary when she wrongly tells a parliamentary committee that there were no targets for deportations
30 April	• MPs are told that Brexit has increased HMRC's work load by 15%
1 May	• it becomes possible to file for divorce online
	• alcohol sales in Scotland are subject to unit pricing
2 May	• first occasion that police seize bitcoins in a raid
4 May	• Court of Appeal rules that a witness to a will does not have to sign it
8 May	• tax tribunal rules that a stripper could claim tax relief for school uniforms and nurse costumes worn in her act
10 May	• Laser Misuse (Vehicles) Act receives Royal Assent
	• commissioners are appointed to run Northamptonshire County Council
14 May	• upper tier tribunal rules that ignorance of the law can be reasonable excuse for obscure points of tax law
15 May	• High Court rules that a coroner was wrong not to expedite Jewish and Muslim hearings to allow funerals within the time limits of their religion
16 May	• Supreme Court rules that a contract clause is valid when it allows the contract to be amended only by signed written agreement of both parties

	• motorists may allow driverless cars to park themselves
18 May	• Court of Appeal rules that a claim for refund of VAT must identify the period
20 May	• Shadow Chancellor John McDonnell says he wanted to overthrow capitalism
	• there are significant changes to the MOT test
23 May	• Supreme Court rules that losses from a transferred trade may not be offset against profits of the acquiring company
	• Sanctions and Anti-Money Laundering Act receives Royal Assent
24 May	• Financial Conduct Authority says it will ensure that businesses are accountable for sexual harassment at work
25 May	• Data Protection Act receives Royal Assent, implementing GDPR
	• a couple watch £9,000 disappear from their account while waiting for TSB to answer the telephone to report the fraud
31 May	• BBC broadcasts *Killed By Debt* about 21-year old Jerome Rogers who committed suicide when a traffic penalty escalated to over £1,000
1 June	• the sanction rules for accountants are extensively revised
	• Italy forms a populist government as a coalition between opposite extremes
	• Spain removes its prime minister Mariano Rajoy because of political scandal including tax evasion
	• Northern Ireland introduces provisions to collect fines from wages
6 June	• Court of Appeal rules that the government may tell local authority pension funds not to invest so as to contravene foreign or defence policy
	• Aston Villa football club is ordered to pay £4.2 million tax within 7 days
7 June	• first prison sentence passed in relation to workplace pensions. The company improperly logged into NEST to opt out their employees
	• European Council agrees new rules to deal with money laundering
11 June	• a first tier tribunal cancels a tax penalty of £0
12 June	• Court of Appeal holds that an unlawful curfew is false imprisonment
13 June	• Supreme Court rules that the Project Blue scheme was successful in avoiding stamp duty land tax
	• Supreme Court rules that owners of trade marks who get injunctions banning websites from selling fake goods must pay the Internet supplier's costs of complying with the injunction
	• Federal Reserve raises US base rate by a quarter percentage point
	• King of Spain's brother-in-law is sent to jail for 5 years 10 months for tax evasion and fraud
	• Supreme Court rules that HMRC may withdraw gross payment status from a company under the construction industry scheme without having to consider the consequences for the company
	• Supreme Court rules that a plumber working for Pimlico Plumbing is entitled to workers' rights

14 June • Court of Appeal rules that a trade union official should not be dismissed because he received illegally obtained documents

18 June • HMRC says that VAT must be charged on goods supplied on approval

19 June • High Court rules that the scope of property for seizure includes copies of property

• Court of Appeal rules that the time limit for tax assessment runs from when HMRC has had a chance to read and digest documents, not from when it has those documents in its possession

• Financial Reporting Council gives first advice on blockchain

• ban on selling products containing plastic microbeads

22 June • EU adopts a directive making 15% the lowest standard rate of VAT for all member states

• High Court refuses an application for a gender-neutral passport

25 June • government amends rules on outsourcing

• government abandons plans for Swansea lagoon energy scheme

26 June • Institute of Chartered Accountants in England and Wales must approve all beneficial owners, officers and managers of firms which the Institute supervises under money-laundering laws

• European court rules that UK pensions discriminate against transgender women

• Parliament passes EU Withdrawal Act to leave the EU

29 June • Court of Appeal rules that the Land Tribunal may award costs in exceptional cases

• Court of Appeal rules that right to claim VAT input can (not must) depend on having an invoice showing the VAT

30 June • the Scottish government introduces a relief from land and buildings transaction tax for first time buyers

• former Treasury secretary Jonathan Aitken is ordained in Church of England

1 July • cash machine operators receive a lower fee from banks

• public lending rights payments are extended to e-books

2 July • a new employer who takes over an employee under TUPE is liable for any shortfall in national minimum wage before the transfer

• works and pensions secretary Esther McVey MP inadvertently misleads Parliament about roll-out of universal credit

3 July • Royal Mint changes design for Britannia gold bullion coins

4 July • employment appeal tribunal rules that an employee may not include a period of notice in determining whether she had worked for two years and could therefore bring a claim for unfair dismissal

• Chartered Institute of Taxation says HMRC does not follow its own procedures on mediation

• it is disclosed that in 1976 prime minister Harold Wilson gave a peerage to Joseph Kagan despite being told he was part of a major tax investigation

5 July	• Court of Appeal rules that a company may claim against a former director who arranged to be paid more than he was entitled to • ticket touting is effectively banned
6 July	• Parliamentary speeches from 1803 become available online • Theresa May gets Cabinet approval for the Chequers agreement on leaving the EU. Several ministers resign in the following week
9 July	• Scotland varies the rates at which student loans are repaid
10 July	• European Court finds that Jehovah's Witnesses did not comply with data protection laws when engaged in door-to-door visiting • upper tribunal rules that irrecoverable loans to a trading company are capital expenditure and cannot be deducted from taxable income • Amazons' Alexa device can provide answers to tax queries
11 July	• Supreme Court rules that a group company could not claim a repayment of VAT in respect of a former group company • Supreme Court rules that a reasonable assumption is sufficient to hold that funds are used for terrorism
12 July	• it is disclosed that 30,000 taxpayers who used the failed loan scheme owe more than £1 billion in tax • Public Health England produces guide to help employers when an employee is a victim of domestic abuse
13 July	• Court of Appeal rules that sleep-in shifts are not working hours for which the national minimum wage must be paid • HMRC gives guidance on Making Tax Digital, some of which has the force of law
15 July	• UK government decides it will not collect VAT for other EU countries after Brexit
16 July	• in last eight days, ten government ministers resign from government in protest at the Chequers agreement on a post-Brexit deal
17 July	• HMRC says that dealer deposit contributions in the motor trade are accounted for VAT as a discount on the selling price
18 July	• Court of Appeal rules that a Customs officer has no duty to give reasons for stopping a traveller and searching their baggage • Supreme Court rules that a husband is not liable when his ex-wife was given enough to buy a mortgage-free house but lost the funds in unwise decisions • European Union imposes a record €4.3 billion fine on Google for breaching competition law • Department of Work and Pensions agrees to making backdated claims to some disabled claimants • government agrees to compensate military personnel for higher taxes in Scotland
20 July	• Court of Appeal reduces tax penalty on barrister Romie Tager QC from £1.2 million to £220,000 in first known challenge to rules in Finance Act 2008

23 July	• government decides not to make caste discrimination a separate offence
	• papers released from national archives show that the cost of Black Wednesday in 1992, when UK left the EU exchange rate mechanism, was deliberately understated
25 July	• Supreme Court rules that interest on refunded tax is calculated as simple interest and not compound interest
	• Supreme Court rules that election expenditure for a constituency includes central party expenditure on that constituency
	• former GP and churchwarden David Crichton is cleared of attempted murder to kill a financial consultant over a £300,000 tax penalty but is fined for sending malicious communications
	• European Court rules that the design of Kit-Kat bars is not a trade mark
26 July	• Supreme Court holds that the general requirement to pay VAT before appealing against it does not infringe the principle of equivalence
27 July	• Form IHT 407 is revised to disclose personal goods for inheritance tax
30 July	• Supreme Court rules that there is no need for a court order to withdraw nutrition and hydration from a patient if conditions are met
31 July	• tax revenue for a year exceeds £600 billion for first time
	• freemasons rule that a man who becomes a woman may remain a member
1 August	• Court of Appeal said that summary action for contempt of court should be used sparingly
	• range of offences is widened for automatic disqualification of charity trustee
2 August	• Bank of England increases base rate from 0.5% to 0.75%
	• Psychic Sally goes into liquidation for an unforeseen tax liability
9 August	• Russian currency loses 4% of value from US sanctions
	• new scheme proposed to allow lawyers to enter court without being searched
10 August	• House of Fraser goes into administration and is bought by Sports Direct
14 August	• HMRC releases first software for new Customs Declaration Service
15 August	• first successful prosecution for making a false declaration in connection with pension enrolment
16 August	• former Inland Revenue employee Mike Hughes is sentenced for conspiracy to cheat the Revenue
17 August	• Support the Heroes military charity is to be wound up over concerns about fund raising
18 August	• former cricketer Imran Khan becomes prime minister of Pakistan
20 August	• Venezuela changes its currency at the rate 1 bolivar soberano = 100,000 bolivar fuerte
	• High Court rejects claim that Access To Work fails deaf people
21 August	• new regulations require larger companies to report on their pay gap

	• interest rate on late tax rises from 3% to 3.25%
29 August	• death of Prof Sir James Mirrlees who worked out how to calculate optimal tax rates
30 August	• Supreme Court rules that the widowed parent's allowance is discriminatory
	• pay day lender Wonga goes into administration
31 August	• *Sunday Times* discloses that tax avoiders have been denied honours
1 September	• employers are allowed to reimburse employees 4p a mile tax-free for private use of their electric car
	• sale of halogen light bulbs starts to be phased out
4 September	• European Court rules that a vehicle capable of being driven but is kept off road still requires insurance against civil liability
	• footballer José Marino accepts a prison sentence and €2 million fine for tax evasion in Spain
5 September	• government confirms it will proceed with pensions dashboard
6 September	• Court of Appeal rules that a judgment debtor who disobeyed a court order to attend could be imprisoned for contempt of court under rule 71.2
	• government abandons plans to scrap class 2 national insurance
8 September	• fine for unsolicited calls for personal injury claims increases to £500,000
9 September	• government announces plans for green number plates for environmentally friendly cars
10 September	• government offers grants to farmers to plant woodlands
11 September	• Jersey allows investors to set up a limited liability company
12 September	• government launches its Help to Buy scheme for benefit claimants
13 September	• Taxation (Cross-border) Trade Act receives Royal Assent. It deals with post-Brexit arrangements
17 September	• President Trump imposes large increases in tariffs on Chinese goods
21 September	• HMRC launches Check if You Can Claim service so employees can check claims for tax-deductible expenses
22 September	• HMRC tells Ronald Pomeroy that they will investigate his claim that he is not dead, as they had previously stated in a letter to him
23 September	• Labour party proposes that 10% of shares in all large companies must be held in an Inclusive Ownership Fund
26 September	• US Federal Reserve cuts base rates by a quarter of one percent
28 September	• new governance code is issued for companies listed on Alternative Investment Market
1 October	• Financial Reporting Council revises the taxonomy for filing accounts to reflect changes in international accounting standards
	• package of changes in business law ensuring tips are passed to staff, payments are made promptly, and other changes
2 October	• government creates a new specialist unit to freeze bank accounts of those involved in organised crime
3 October	• High Court upholds the first unexplained wealth order

	• International Standard on Auditing ISA 540 is amended requiring a statement on inherent risk when an estimate is used in accounts
	• borrowing restrictions are lifted on local authorities to allow them to build more houses
4 October	• the tax free childcare voucher scheme is closed to new participants
5 October	• government admits that half of lone parents and two-thirds of couples with children will lose £200 a month when migrated to universal credit
	• Court of Appeal rules that a dividend paid to a subsidiary and then passed to the parent company is taxed on the parent. This is the first known case when a court has overruled accounts prepared in accordance with standards
6 October	• Shell starts providing electric charging points at its service stations
8 October	• first smart road studs installed at junction of M57, M58 and three A-roads. These switch on when traffic lights change
9 October	• government says it will create a new counter fraud profession
11 October	• first penalty notice to pension fund trustees for late investment of funds
	• Court of Appeal holds an employer is vicariously liable when an employee punched a colleague in the head after a company event
	• HMRC chief executive Jon Thompson reveals he has received death threats
12 October	• finance director of Patisserie Valerie is arrested for accounting irregularities
13 October	• Treasury confirms that it is keeping the £50 note
15 October	• Treasury issues official statement that Gladstone, its cat, is funded by voluntary donations at no cost to the taxpayer
	• Frank Field MP says that universal credit is driving women into prostitution
16 October	• government opens new office hub in Canary Wharf for 6,000 civil servants, including 2,000 HMRC staff
	• Court of Appeal rules that a clause in a contract saying it is governed by English law is persuasive but nor decisive
	• Court of Appeal rules that a person retains money paid into court to fortify a cross-undertaking or to provide security for another person's costs
	• pilot scheme is launched for Making Tax Digital
18 October	• France allows a €1500 tax deduction for taking in a refugee
22 October	• police end their lost property service except for cash, bank cards and personal documents
23 October	• European Union takes unprecedented step of ordering Italy to cancel its budget proposals
24 October	• BBC is criticised for its policy of requiring presenters to provide their services through a personal service company to avoid payroll taxes
	• Sir Mark Sedwill is announced as new head of civil service

29 October	• voluntary tax returns are put on the same footing as compulsory returns for such matters as enquiry and penalties • entrepreneur's relief is amended so that the taxpayer must be entitled to 5% of a distribution and 5% of assets on winding up, in addition to owning 5% of shares and having 5% of the votes
1 November	• Court of Appeal rules that a part-time worker received less favourable treatment when paid 50% of wages for working 53.5% of hours
2 November	• plans are submitted to build a new HMRC centre in Nottingham in two buildings of 10 and 13 storeys, and housing 4,000 staff
5 November	• government says it will introduce statutory parental bereavement leave • new probate fees limit charges to 0.5% of the estate's value
6 November	• European Court rules that an heir is entitled to payment for unpaid annual leave due to a deceased employee
7 November	• Supreme Court rules that a pension scheme may not change its choice of index for measuring inflation • government announces plans to stop council tax being avoided on second homes by declaring them as holiday lettings
8 November	• KPMG stops doing non-audit work for audit clients
9 November	• French authorities seize a Ryanair aeroplane in dispute about subsidies
10 November	• BBC reveals that most hybrid cars in fleets never run on electricity
12 November	• NEST pension fund launches sidecar savings trial • subsidy for electric cars reduced from £4,500 to £3.500, and scrapped for hybrid cars
14 November	• Court of Appeal rules that the right of timeshare apartment owners to use sports and recreational facilities is an easement that applies to future owners
23 November	• introduction of new code of practice on parking tickets
25 November	• prime minister Theresa May concludes Withdrawal Agreement with other 27 EU states. It is repeatedly rejected by Parliament
26 November	• Disclosure and Barring Service amends advice on changes of personal details • new laws introduced making householders liable for fly tipping
28 November	• Court of Appeal rules that a dividend payment may only be treated as such on basis of when paid. A director cannot retrospectively reclassify payments as dividends
30 November	• Charity Commission says charities should stop collecting used stamps, as they are used for fraud
4 December	• House of Lords economic affairs committee criticises HMRC for unfairly targeting freelance workers, particularly with accelerated payment notices

	• government loses three Brexit votes in House of Commons. It found the government guilty of contempt of Parliament, and gave the Commons control of its agenda
	• European Court rules that UK government may cancel Brexit
10 December	• Financial Reporting Council issues Wates principles on corporate governance
11 December	• Financial Reporting Council withdraws Practice Notes 25 and 27
13 December	• HMRC issues factsheets on accounting standard FRS 102
18 December	• plans are announced to name and shame employers who do not pay awards of at least £200 given by an employment tribunal
	• Court of Appeal rules that there was no abuse of power when HMRC issued an accelerated payment notice when it had agreed to postpone the tax
19 December	• Court of Appeal rules that Uber drivers should be treated as employees
	• government sets out its post-Brexit immigration policy
29 December	• UK reaches agreement with Iceland, Liechtenstein and Norway on residence rights
2019	
1 January	• accounting standard IFRS 16 on leases comes into effect
	• Irish Republic introduces real-time reporting of PAYE
	• it becomes illegal for a customer to require a supplier not to factor invoices
	• VAT rules on vouchers change
7 January	• British overseas territories are allowed to mint a 12-sided £1 coin
9 January	• cold calling people about pensions becomes illegal
10 January	• start of trial in Berlin for stealing the world's biggest and most valuable coin. It was 53 cm in diameter, made of gold and valued at £3.4 million
11 January	• universal credit two-child limit for universal credit is scrapped for children born from April 2017
15 January	• House of Commons rejects EU Withdrawal Bill by 432 votes to 202
16 January	• House of Lords criticises Office of National Statistics for refusing to correct an error that overstates inflation by 0.8% in retail prices index
17 January	• Disclosure and Barring Service offers basic checks to everyone
18 January	• HMRC admits it wrongly issued fines for missing a filing deadline before the deadline had even been reached
21 January	• government scraps the fee for someone to get settled status in UK
22 January	• Court of Appeal rules that an applicant could be given extra time for filing documents as the 10 megabyte limit on email attachments was given insufficient prominence in guidance notes
	• footballer Cristiano Ronaldo says he has paid more than £16 million to settle a tax dispute in Spain
30 January	• Supreme Court says disclosure of convictions of young offenders is unfair

	• Supreme Court rules that the presumption of innocence only applies in criminal cases and does not stop a civil claim for compensation
31 January	• Court of Appeal rules against Asda saying that female shopworkers are entitled to the same pay as male warehouse workers
1 February	• an additional sum is payable under pension credit in respect of the oldest dependant child
3 February	• a brothel owner avoids a prison sentence because, among other reasons, the court was told she paid tax on her business
4 February	• offices of Moore Stephens merged with BDO to make the fifth largest accounting firm
5 February	• government widens scope of investments for defined contribution pension
6 February	• Eileen Jolly wins an age discrimination case at the age of 88
12 February	• Court of Appeal rules that solicitors negotiating a baggage handling claim with an airline are not engaged in litigation and therefore have no lien on the airline's payment
13 February	• Supreme Court rules that a term could be implied in an agreement to make it a legally binding contract when that was the clear intention
20 February	• Supreme Court rules that a claim could not be brought against an unknown person who could not be identified
21 February	• Court of Appeal rules that an upper tier tribunal may correct clerical mistakes and reasons for its decisions
1 March	• VAT law is clarified so tax is charged on goods and services which a customer has ordered but not collected or used
	• time limit for paying stamp duty land tax reduces from 30 to 14 days
6 March	• start of pilot scheme for new system of seasonal workers
7 March	• amendments to immigration rules to make it easier to set up a business in the UK
8 March	• Court of Appeal rules that there is no breach of privacy when the government collects information people have voluntarily posted online
11 March	• government announces that Financial Reporting Council is to be replaced by the tougher Audit, Reporting and Governance Authority
	• death of Ken Dodd, comedian, who was acquitted of tax evasion in 1989. He said he thought he owed nothing to Inland Revenue as he lived by the sea
12 March	• House of Commons rejects EU withdrawal agreement for second time
13 March	• Spring statement by Chancellor of the Exchequer Philip Hammond
15 March	• first known case of an unqualified legal aide, or McKenzie friend, being sued for negligence
19 March	• Court of Appeal rules that an expert witness who deliberately or recklessly makes a false statement should be imprisoned
20 March	• Supreme Court rules that a body providing services to a university can come within the scope of VAT exemption for education

	• Supreme Court rules that a court judgment obtained by fraud can be set aside, regardless of whether the party seeking such order did due diligence
25 March	• increase in postal rates
27 March	• Supreme Court rules that a stationary car is not "in use" when being repaired by its owner. Accordingly the car insurer was not liable when the car caught fire • the EU names seven member states as tax havens
29 March	• on the day the UK was due to leave the EU, the withdrawal agreement is rejected by the House of Commons for a third time
1 April	• the scope of quarterly interest payments of corporation tax is widened • two Barclays traders are jailed for rigging the EUROBOR rate • maximum stake on a fixed odds betting terminal is reduced from £100 to £2 • local authorities are allowed to increase council tax on empty properties
6 April	• company diesel cars avoid the 4% addition to taxable value if they comply with Euro 6d standard • introduction of the loan charge to defeat a common tax avoidance scheme • ownership period for entrepreneur's relief extended from one year to two • non-employee workers have the right to receive a payslip • Making Tax Digital becomes compulsory for VAT-registered businesses with a turnover above £85,000 • Wales gets the right to vary the rate of income tax, but does not • rates change for Scottish arrestment orders
8 April	• ultra low emission zone starts in London
11 April	• European Commission postpones Brexit date to 31 October
12 April	• second date that UK was supposed to leave EU
15 April	• TSB becomes first bank to promise to refund fraud victims
16 April	• Court of Appeal rules that Home Office acted improperly when it decided that differences between a migrant's stated income and that on their tax returns must be due to dishonesty
17 April	• Court of Appeal rules that a claim for equal pay ranks as preferential arrears of pay when the employer becomes insolvent
22 April	• new provisions allow a stamp for stamp duty to be produced by computer
24 April	• it is disclosed that intelligence service GCHQ assists banks with credit card fraud
25 April	• proposed merger of Sainsbury's and Asda is blocked
1 May	• Gavin Williamson is sacked as defence secretary on suspicion of leaking security details, which he denied • Emperor Naruhito becomes new Emperor of Japan

2 May	• European court rules that it is legal to give a discount to customers who pay their electricity bills electronically • Court of Appeal rules that overpayments for car parking are part of the parking charge and so subject to VAT • Treasury decides not to scrap 1p and 2p coins
4 May	• government says it will accept payment from Apple Pay and Google Pay
6 May	• end of first five-day period when Britain used no coal to produce electricity since power stations began in 1882
14 May	• Court of Appeal rules that costs will not be awarded against HMRC for judicial review when the taxpayer had not first exhausted other appeals
15 May	• Supreme Court rules that the benefits cap does not discriminate against lone parents
20 May	• death of John Moore, secretary of state for social security 1987-89
21 May	• Tesco stops offering mortgages
23 May	• European election is won by Brexit party formed earlier in the year
24 May	• Theresa May announces she is resigning as prime minister
28 May	• new €100 and €200 notes go into circulation in European Union
1 June	• Tenant Fees Act 2019 comes into effect. It protects tenants from unfair fee and caps deposits at five weeks' rent
3 June	• investors are banned from withdrawing funds from £4 billion fund run by Neil Woodford. He continues to charge fees
12 June	• the Supreme Court rules that a person's living expenses must be considered when deciding whether someone is intentionally homeless • Supreme Court rules that costs of recovery and repair must be considered when deciding whether a ship is lost • government sets target of being carbon neutral by 2050
13 June	• "same roof" rule is abolished, whereby someone could not claim compensation for abuse before 1979 if they lived under the same roof as the abuser
18 June	• prime minister candidate Boris Johnson abandons promise to raise threshold for higher rate income tax from £50,000 to £80,000
21 June	• Bank of Scotland is fined £45 million for failure to alert authorities to a major fraud
25 June	• Southern Water is fined a record £126 million for pollution
27 June	• government says it will ban new sales of leasehold houses
1 July	• £500 government grant available for smart electric car chargers • tobacco for heating becomes subject to tobacco products duty
3 July	• the employment appeal tribunal rules that an employer's counterclaim against an employee may continue even when the employee has withdrawn the claim
10 July	• European court rules that passengers cannot claim against an airline for cancelled air tickets when the tour organiser cannot make a refund

15 July	• it is announced that computer scientist Alan Turing will feature on the new £50 note to be issued in 2021
16 July	• Ursula von der Leyen is chosen as new president of European Commission
17 July	• Bulgarian tax office is hacked and details of taxpayers posted online
18 July	• Sir Jonathan Thompson, chief executive of HMRC, is announced as the chief executive of the Financial Reporting Council
22 July	• Jo Swinson is elected as leader of the Liberal Democrat party
23 July	• the government pays for the costs of a funeral for a child under 18
24 July	• Boris Johnson replaces Theresa May as prime minister
	• Sajid Javid MP is appointed Chancellor of the Exchequer
29 July	• Credit Suisse loses case that the bank tax of 2009/10 was unlawful
31 July	• an employee could bring a claim under her contract of employment even though her leave to remain had expired, of which she was unaware
	• Federal Reserve cuts US base rate by a quarter of one percent to 2% to 2.25%
	• new law allows a guardian to be appointed when a person has gone missing for 90 days
1 August	• VAT exemption for higher education is extended in scope
9 August	• Court of Appeal rules than an employment tribunal has no power to prohibit publication of its decision other than on grounds of national security
15 August	• *The Times* reports that Action Fraud which deals with fraud cases is ineffective and incompetent
21 August	• government introduces automatic enrolment of economic operator registration for post-Brexit exports
29 August	• deadline for making claims for missold personal protection insurance (PPI)
30 August	• Blue Badge scheme is extended in scope to sufferers of dementia, anxiety disorders and reduced mobility
3 September	• former Chancellors Kenneth Clarke and Philip Hammond lose the Conservative whip for voting against a government EU withdrawal Bill
4 September	• record £7.8 million fine is imposed for money-laundering on Touma Foreign Exchange
10 September	• Parliament is prorogued for five weeks
18 September	• Federal Reserve cuts US interest rates by a quarter of one percent
24 September	• Supreme Court rules that prorogation of Parliament is unlawful
25 September	• European Court rules that the "right to be forgotten" only applies within the EU
	• European Court rules that data protection laws apply to search engines
1 October	• European Court rules that a person has not consented to computer cookies just by being able to untick a box
	• Companies House tightens rules on penalties for late filing

	• VAT on solar panels and wind turbines increases from 5% to 20%
2 October	• Court of Appeal rules that legal advice privilege between a company and its solicitors continues after the company has been dissolved
24 October	• European Court of Human Rights rules that the bedroom tax is unfair on victims of domestic violence who need a panic room
30 October	• Supreme Court rules that a bank is liable when it has reasonable grounds for believing there was a fraud perpetrated by a director
2 November	• government withdraws support for fracking, in effect banning it
4 November	• Court of Appeal rules that main residence relief ownership starts from completion and not purchase
19 November	• government announces grants for businesses and individuals affected by flooding
12 December	• general election is won by Conservative party with an overall majority of 80
15 December	• auditing standard ISA 540 is revised
17 December	• accounting standard FRS 102 is amended in respect of benchmark reform for when LIBOR is abolished
18 December	• government announces £5,000 bursaries for student nurses
30 December	• two people of opposite sex may enter a civil partnership in England
31 December	• insurance company Equity Life ceases to exit. It was formed in 1762
	• China informs World Health Organisation of coronavirus
2020	
10 January	• changes in money-laundering laws, including bringing tax advisers within its scope
11 January	• devolved government in Northern Ireland is restored after three years
21 January	• High Court rules that a director's fiduciary duties continue after the company has entered administration or voluntary liquidation
	• employment tribunal rules that ethical veganism is a protected belief
29 January	• European Court rules that a worker accrues holiday entitlement between dismissal and reinstatement
	• Time To Play claims may be made online
31 January	• UK leaves European Union
6 February	• statutory legacy for surviving spouse increases from £250,000 to £270,000
	• government gives details of Breathing Space to help people in debt
7 February support	• High Court rules that restrictions on higher rate of bereavement payment are unlawful
	• Kate Forbes becomes Scottish Finance Minister and delivers Budget
	• First Homes scheme launched with locked-in price reductions of up to one third for key workers
8 February	• General election in Irish Republic leads to a hung parliament
11 February	• World Health Organisation names new coronavirus as COVID-19
13 February	• Rishi Sunak MP becomes Chancellor of the Exchequer in Cabinet reshuffle

14 February	• Court of Appeal rules that failure to submit tax returns does not automatically justify deportation
18 February	• package of measures introduced to help victims of flooding
19 February	• details given of new points-based post Brexit immigration scheme
20 February	• new polymer £20 note issued
24 February	• new scheme established to compensate those permanently disabled by Northern Ireland troubles between 1966 and 2010
29 February	• Luxembourg becomes first country to make all public transport free
3 March	• Federal Reserve cuts US interest rates by half of one percent
9 March	• Dow Jones index falls by a new record of more than 2,000 points
	• oil prices fall by about 30%, biggest one-day fall since 1991
11 March	• bank rate reduces from 0.75% to 0.25%
	• entrepreneur's relief lifetime limit reduced from £10m to £1m
	• Budget details infrastructure spending and coronavirus support
	• World Health Organisation declares coronavirus is a pandemic
12 March	• stock markets around the world fall in reaction to coronavirus
13 March	• start of new statutory sick pay scheme for coronavirus
16 March	• Andrew Bailey replaces Mark Carney as governor of the Bank of England
	• Dow Jones index falls by 12.9%, bigger than Black Monday in 1929
17 March	• further support provisions for coronavirus announced
18 March	• bank rate is reduced to new record low of 0.1%
19 March	• Bank of England provides £200 billion of quantitative easing
	• date from which a person must be employed for Coronavirus Job Retention Scheme
23 March	• start of coronavirus lockdown
	• Coronavirus Business Interruption Loan Scheme starts
	• COVID-19 Corporate Financing Facility is introduced
	• London congestion charge and other road user charges are temporarily suspended
	• postal rates increased
25 March	• Coronavirus Act 2020 becomes law
26 March	• European Court rules that TUPE applies when a person's job is transferred to more than one employer
27 March	• Customs duty and import VAT suspended on some personal protective equipment
28 March	• company law amended to suspend wrongful trading and to allow a company in difficulties to continue buying supplies
30 March	• oil price war between Russia and Saudi Arabia sees price of oil fall to $23 a barrel
31 March	• larger companies required to comply with Streamlined Energy and Carbon Reporting
	• all banks asked to suspend dividends and share buybacks for seven months
1 April	• introduction of digital services tax

	• corporate non-resident landlords pay corporation tax rather than income tax
	• statutory parental bereavement leave and statutory parental bereavement pay introduced
	• DWP stops deductions from pay under Direct Earnings Attachments
	• restrictions introduced on bringing forward capital losses
	• generous rates relief given to many small businesses
	• contactless limit on debit cards increased from £30 to £45
	• Supreme Court gives two decisions which restrict vicarious liability
	• Government Gateway scheme ceases to work on Windows XP and other old operating systems
4 April	• Sir Keir Starmer becomes leader of the Labour party
5 April	• Anneliese Dodds becomes Shadow Chancellor
6 April	• employment allowance rises from £3,000 to £4,000 but is restricted
	• capital gains tax on residential property must be reported within 30 days
	• new basis for taxing benefit of a hybrid company car
	• landlords restricted to 20% tax relief on property loan interest
	• maximum assets for unsecured creditors increases from £600,000 to £800,000
	• new form of class 1A national insurance introduced for termination payments and sporting testimonials
	• final absence relief for main residence relief is generally reduced from 18 months to 9 months
	• class 1 national insurance employees annual threshold increased to £9,500
	• holiday reference period is extended from 12 weeks to 52 weeks
8 April	• funeral expense claims increased from £700 to £1,000 for benefit claimants
9 April	• Russia refuses to reach agreement with OPEC on falling oil prices
14 April	• ban on using credit cards to place bets
16 April	• HMRC suspends tax enquiries
	• Companies House suspends striking off companies
20 April	• some oil prices become negative
21 April	• introduction of coronavirus support scheme for larger businesses
1 May	• e-publications are zero-rated for VAT
20 May	• HMRC makes clear that expenses to allow employees to work from home are not a taxable benefit in kind
21 May	• High Court rules that "no recourse to public funds" rule is illegal if it leads to destitution
28 May	• employees obliged to self-isolate may claim statutory sick pay
3 June	• UK offers pathway to citizenship for Hong Kong citizens
18 June	• Bank of England provides a further £100 billion of quantitative easing
22 June	• Court of Appeal rules that universal credit payment periods are irrational and illegal

24 June	• merger law changed so government may consider implications for national emergencies
25 June	• German payment processor Wirecard files for insolvency
27 June	• Companies House extends filing deadlines
	• Micheál Martin becomes Taoiseach in the Irish Republic
29 June	• Leicester becomes first place to have a local lockdown
	• restrictions are imposed on enforcing commercial leases
30 June	• government announces New Deal of public spending
	• banks introduce confirmation of payee system to protect bank customers from fraud and error
1 July	• European directive DAC 6 on tax co-operation comes into effect
	• furloughed workers are allowed to work part-time
6 July	• first travel corridors are introduced to avoid quarantine
	• Financial Reporting Council announces plans for accounting firms to separate their audit functions
8 July	• Chancellor gives summer statement with more help regarding coronavirus
9 July	• HMRC confirms that personal protective equipment for employees is not a taxable benefit in kind
	• Ministry of Defence makes permanent arrangements to compensate armed forces in Scotland for higher Scottish tax rates
	• tax gap falls to 4.7%
10 July	• Bulgaria and Croatia are accepted by EU into ERM II as a precursor to adopting the euro
13 July	• announced that an audit report does not require a wet ink signature
15 July	• introduction of 5% hospitality rate of VAT
	• Supreme Court rules that "no reflective loss" rule remains for shareholders but not necessarily for creditors
	• increase in threshold for stamp duty land tax on residential properties
	• scope of disregards for some social security benefits is widened
21 July	• EU agrees a €750 billion recovery fund to rebuild coronavirus-blighted economies
22 July	• Finance Act 2020 receives Royal Assent
	• Business and Planning Act 2020 receives Royal Assent
25 July	• wills may legally be witnessed online
27 July	• Land Registry accepts witnessed electronic signatures
	• change in law announced that means customers will have title to goods they paid for when a supplier becomes insolvent
28 July	• Scotland passes law allowing civil partnerships between people of opposite sexes
29 July	• announced that video links will be tested at tax tribunals
	• Supreme Court rules that a court may order a member of a charity company to vote in favour of a financial settlement
30 July	• limits increased for society lotteries

	• Privy Council rules that a shareholder who hides his identity is bound by ostensible authority of his agent
31 July	• income tax due on this day may be deferred to 2021
1 August	• people over 75 must pay for television licence unless receiving pension credit
3 August	• start of Eat Out to Help Out Scheme
4 August	• non-contentious probate fees are reduced
5 August	• statutory sick pay extended for ten days of self-isolation
6 August	• foreign currency company Travelex goes into administration
9 August	• another seven gilts are exempted from capital gains tax
12 August	• UK is declared in recession for first time in 11 years
13 August	• maximum penalty for not wearing a mask doubles to £3,200
	• Israel and United Arab Emirates reach a peace agreement
	• police given new powers to detain individuals in relation to espionage and foreign interference
17 August	• applications may be made for second self-employment income support scheme
19 August	• Apple becomes first US company to be valued at $2 trillion
	• Supreme Court changes the law on restrictive covenants
21 August	• national debt reaches £2 trillion
26 August	• Amazon CEO Jeff Bezos is first person to be worth $200 billion
27 August	• Sir Ed Davey becomes leader of Liberal Democrat party
29 August	• new laws introduced to restrict evictions from commercial property
1 September	• Department for International Aid becomes part of Foreign Office
	• first children become eligible to access child trust funds
	• schools and colleges reopen after coronavirus lockdown
	• new scheme allowing some claimants to claim £13 a day while self-isolating
	• changes are made to use classes in planning law
	• new apprenticeship scheme is launched with government financial support
2 September	• Kickstart scheme is launched
3 September	• government announces that the minimum age at which a pension may be taken will increase from 55 to 57 in 2028
4 September	• construction work starts on HS2 railway line
	• High Court sanctions first restructuring plan under Corporate Insolvency and Governance Act 2020
7 September	• a will may be witnessed by video link
10 September	• Companies House resumes striking off companies
14 September	• government introduces rule of six, restricting most gatherings
	• first major post-Brexit trade agreement, with Japan
15 September	• first prosecution for not wearing a face mask when required
	• Court of Appeal rules that increases in state pension age for women born in 1950s and 1960s are legal

16 September	• government announces proposals to reduce rehabilitation periods for those who have criminal convictions
17 September	• package of measures announced to deal with backlog of employment tribunal cases
18 September	• Companies House requires identity verification of new directors
	• Financial Conduct Authority consults on whether to list cannabis-related companies
20 September	• government says coronavirus restrictions could last another six months
24 September	• government gives winter economy plan with another package of coronavirus measures, including a new job support scheme
	• venues required to display NHS track-and-trace poster with QR code
	• it is compulsory to wear a face covering on public transport in England
28 September	• New York Times says President Trump only paid $750 in tax in 2016, which he denied
30 September	• launch of new online service for duplicate log books for vehicles
1 October	• general ban on sale of plastic straws, stirrers and cotton buds
	• overseas health and care workers are allowed to reclaim immigration health surcharge
	• British seafarers are entitled to the national minimum wage
5 October	• interest regime for disguised remuneration comes into force
6 October	• cohabiting partner may now claim under Fatal Accidents Act 1975
	• government announces plans to "build back greener"
7 October	• government gives details of new scheme for freeports
9 October	• new package of government measures to help hospitality sector
12 October	• Supreme Court rules that a court may consider commercial disputes when deciding whether a two-man company should be wound up
14 October	• interest rates are given for digital services tax
19 October	• provision enacted to ensure all flu and coronavirus vaccines are free
21 October	• compensation under Human Rights Act 1998 is extended to when a person is wrongly detained
22 October	• Sentencing Act 2020 becomes law, introducing a new Sentencing Code
3 November	• US presidential election won by Joe Biden
4 November	• exit payments to someone who worked in public sector is capped at £95,000
	• USA formally leaves the Paris Agreement on climate change
5 November	• start of second coronavirus lockdown in England
	• second Coronavirus Job Retention Scheme announced and coronavirus job retention bonus is scrapped
	• BHS buyer Dominic Chappell sentenced to six years imprisonment for tax offences
	• Coronavirus Job Retention Scheme extended to 31 March 2021
8 November	• government announces Covid Winter Grant Scheme

9 November	• Pfizer announces a coronavirus vaccine that is 90% effective • firearms legislation extended to antique firearms • government announces first Sovereign Green Bond to be issued in 2021 • Joe Biden is declared the winner in US presidential election • Companies House stops sending paper reminders to companies
10 November	• consultation starts on banning television advertisements for junk foods • government announces reductions in tariffs for goods from 47 developing countries
11 November	• government announces a new Office for Investments • Agriculture Act receives Royal Assent. It changes the basis of farming subsidies • Immigration Act receives Royal Assent. It sets out rights of movement from 2021 • official COVID deaths in UK reach 50,000
12 November	• prisoners given temporary release because of coronavirus may claim means-tested benefits
14 November	• government commissions research into space-based solar power
15 November	• Regional Comprehensive Economic Partnership is signed by 15 Asia-Pacific countries, covering one third of the world's population
16 November	• amendments are made to universal credit periods to deal with problems when pay dates vary from month to month
23 November	• law is changed to amend basis for revising social security rates for 2021/22 year • Fisheries Act 2020 becomes law, regulating fishing from 2021
25 November	• disclosed that UK economy is scheduled to shrink by 11.3% in 2020, the biggest decline in more than 300 years
30 November	• Arcadia retail group goes into administration
1 December	• changes to the definition of a skilled worker in relation to immigration skills charge • applications are open for foreign skilled workers to come to UK • Crossrail is allowed to borrow another £825 million
2 December	• UK approves Pfizer/BioNTech coronavirus vaccine, the first coronavirus vaccine approved anywhere in the world • end of second coronavirus lockdown in England
4 December	• Liverpool mayor Joe Anderson is arrested on corruption charges which he denies
5 December	• Russia starts coronavirus vaccination programme with its Sputnik vaccine
7 December	• same sex civil partnership in Northern Ireland may convert to a marriage, and opposite sex marriage may convert to civil partnership
8 December	• EU and UK agree arrangements for Northern Ireland from 2021 • government says it will raise age for buying lottery tickets from 16 to 18 from October 2021

	• main suppliers of hydrogen fuel form Green Hydrogen Catapult to find ways to reduce production costs
	• reforms announced regarding verification of directors by Companies House
11 December	• European Union agrees to reduce greenhouse gases by 55% over the next decade
14 December	• variant of coronavirus is detected, said to be 70% more transmissible
16 December	• USA accuses Switzerland and Vietnam of currency manipulation
	• Supreme Court allows Heathrow Airport to build a third runway
17 December	• Trade (Disclosure) Act becomes law, requiring HMRC to analyse import and export figures
	• Internal Market Act becomes law guaranteeing that goods may circulate freely in all parts of the UK
19 December	• new Tier 4 coronavirus lockdown category is introduced
20 December	• more than 40 countries ban travel from UK because of coronavirus variant
23 December	• more areas are moved into coronavirus Tier 4
24 December	• UK concludes trade deal with European Union
31 December	• end of transitional period between EU and UK
	• local authorities may use a new clean air zones central service to administer congestion charges

See **Prospective Changes** for changes announced for dates from 2021.

Redundancy pay

An employee is entitled to statutory redundancy pay if he or she is made redundant after more than two years of employment.

The pay is a week's wages to a maximum multiplied by a number representing the employee's age and years of employment.

The maximum is reviewed each year in April. The maximum is £538 a week for 2020/21; £525 for 2019/20.

The employee is entitled to half a week's wages for each full year of employment under the age of 22.

The employee is entitled to one week's wages for each full year of employment between the ages of 22 and 40.

The employee is entitled to one and a half weeks' wages for each full year of employment from the age of 41.

The maximum number of years for which redundancy pay be claimed is 20 years.

So the maximum amount that may be claimed (by someone made redundant from the age of 61) is 30 years: 20 years at 1½ times.

Using 2020/21 rates, this gives a maximum payment of 30 x £538 = £16,140.

Statutory redundancy pay is tax-free but counts towards the £30,000 limit for termination payments.

Rent-a-room

Rent-a-room is an income tax relief from letting a room in one's house, such as to a lodger.

From	Annual	Monthly	Weekly
6 April 2016	£7,500	£625.00	£144.23
6 April 1997	£4,250	£354.17	£81.73
6 April 1992	£3,250	£270.83	£62.50

Research and development

For expenditure on research and development (as defined), additional tax relief may be claimed. For example, where 130% additional relief is claimable, the taxpayer may claim 230% of the expenditure.

A small or medium-sized enterprise that does not pay tax may claim a payable tax credit. A small or medium-sized enterprise is one that has fewer than 500 staff, and either turnover below €100 million or a balance sheet value under €86 million.

From	Add R&D relief	SME tax credit
1 April 2020	130%	13%
1 January 2018	130%	12%
1 April 2015	130%	14.5%
1 April 2014	125%	14.5%
1 April 2013	125%	11%
1 April 2011	100%	12.5%

Retail prices index (RPI)

This index has been replaced by the consumer prices index for the general measure of UK inflation. RPI is retained for certain purposes, including indexation of chargeable gains between 1982 and 2017 subject to corporation tax.

The index was set at January 1987 = 100.

Year	JAN	FEB	MAR	APR	MAY	JUN	JUL	AUG	SEP	OCT	NOV	DEC
1915	4.1	4.2	4.2	4.2	4.3	4.5	4.5	4.5	4.5	4.7	4.8	4.9
1916	4.9	4.9	5.0	5.0	5.1	5.2	5.3	5.3	5.4	5.5	5.8	6.0
1917	6.0	6.0	6.1	6.2	6.3	6.4	6.5	6.5	6.6	6.4	6.7	6.7
1918	6.8	6.9	6.9	7.0	7.1	7.2	7.3	7.6	7.6	7.9	8.0	7.9
1919	7.9	7.9	7.8	7.6	7.4	7.4	7.5	7.8	7.8	7.9	8.1	8.1
1920	8.1	8.3	8.3	8.4	8.7	9.0	9.1	9.2	9.4	9.5	10.0	9.7
1921	9.6	9.1	8.7	8.4	8.2	7.9	7.9	8.0	7.9	7.6	7.3	7.2
1922	6.9	6.8	6.7	6.6	6.5	6.5	6.6	6.5	6.5	6.4	6.5	6.5
1923	6.4	6.4	6.4	6.3	6.1	6.1	6.1	6.2	6.2	6.3	6.3	6.4
1924	6.4	6.5	6.4	6.2	6.2	6.1	6.1	6.2	6.2	6.4	6.5	6.5
1925	6.5	6.5	6.5	6.3	6.2	6.2	6.2	6.2	6.3	6.4	6.4	6.4
1926	6.3	6.2	6.2	6.1	6.0	6.1	6.1	6.1	6.2	6.3	6.5	6.5
1927	6.3	6.2	6.2	6.0	5.9	5.9	6.0	5.9	6.0	6.0	6.1	6.1
1928	6.1	6.0	5.9	5.9	5.9	6.0	6.0	6.0	6.0	6.0	6.0	6.1
1929	6.0	6.0	6.0	5.9	5.8	5.8	5.8	5.9	5.9	6.0	6.0	6.0
1930	6.0	5.9	5.8	5.7	5.6	5.6	5.6	5.7	5.7	5.6	5.7	5.6

1931	5.5	5.5	5.4	5.3	5.3	5.2	5.3	5.2	5.2	5.2	5.3	5.3
1932	5.3	5.3	5.3	5.2	5.2	5.1	5.2	5.1	5.1	5.2	5.2	5.2
1933	5.1	5.1	5.0	4.9	4.9	4.9	5.0	5.0	5.1	5.1	5.2	5.2
1934	5.1	5.1	5.1	5.0	4.9	5.0	5.1	5.1	5.2	5.2	5.2	5.2
1935	5.2	5.1	5.1	5.0	5.0	5.1	5.2	5.2	5.2	5.2	5.3	5.3
1936	5.3	5.3	5.3	5.2	5.2	5.2	5.3	5.3	5.3	5.3	5.5	5.5
1937	5.5	5.5	5.5	5.5	5.5	5.5	5.6	5.6	5.6	5.7	5.8	5.8
1938	5.7	5.7	5.6	5.6	5.6	5.6	5.7	5.6	5.6	5.6	5.6	5.6
1939	5.6	5.6	5.5	5.5	5.5	5.5	5.6	5.6	5.6	6.0	6.1	6.2
1940	6.3	6.4	6.5	6.4	6.5	6.5	6.8	6.7	6.8	6.8	6.9	7.0
1941	7.1	7.1	7.1	7.2	7.2	7.2	7.2	7.2	7.2	7.2	7.2	7.3
1942	7.2	7.2	7.2	7.2	7.2	7.2	7.2	7.3	7.2	7.2	7.2	7.2
1943	7.2	7.2	7.2	7.2	7.2	7.2	7.2	7.2	7.2	7.2	7.2	7.2
1944	7.2	7.2	7.2	7.2	7.2	7.2	7.3	7.3	7.3	7.3	7.3	7.3
1945	7.3	7.3	7.3	7.3	7.3	7.4	7.5	7.4	7.3	7.3	7.3	7.3
1946	7.3	7.3	7.3	7.3	7.4	7.3	7.4	7.4	7.3	7.3	7.3	7.4
1947	7.4	7.3	7.4	7.3	7.3	7.3	7.4	7.3	7.4	7.4	7.6	7.6
1948	7.6	7.8	7.8	7.9	7.9	8.0	7.9	7.9	7.9	7.9	8.0	8.0
1949	8.0	8.0	8.0	8.0	8.1	8.1	8.2	8.2	8.2	8.2	8.2	8.3
1950	8.3	8.3	8.3	8.3	8.4	8.3	8.3	8.3	8.3	8.4	8.5	8.5
1951	8.6	8.7	8.7	8.9	9.1	9.1	9.3	9.3	9.4	9.4	9.5	9.5
1952	9.7	9.7	9.8	9.9	9.9	10.1	10.1	10.0	10.0	10.1	10.1	10.2
1953	10.1	10.2	10.2	10.3	10.3	10.4	10.4	10.3	10.3	10.3	10.3	10.3
1954	10.3	10.3	10.4	10.4	10.4	10.4	10.6	10.5	10.5	10.6	10.6	10.7
1955	10.7	10.7	10.7	10.8	10.7	11.0	11.0	10.9	11.0	11.1	11.3	11.3
1956	11.2	11.2	11.4	11.6	11.5	11.5	11.5	11.5	11.5	11.6	11.6	11.6
1957	11.7	11.7	11.7	11.8	11.8	11.9	12.0	12.0	11.9	12.0	12.1	12.2
1958	12.2	12.1	12.2	12.3	12.3	12.4	12.2	12.2	12.2	12.3	12.4	12.4
1959	12.4	12.4	12.4	12.3	12.3	12.3	12.3	12.3	12.2	12.3	12.4	12.4
1960	12.36	12.36	12.34	12.41	12.41	12.47	12.50	12.42	12.43	12.53	12.59	12.62
1961	12.63	12.63	12.68	12.74	12.78	12.89	12.89	13.01	12.99	13.01	13.15	13.17
1962	13.22	13.23	13.28	13.47	13.51	13.60	13.55	13.43	13.41	13.40	13.45	13.52
1963	13.57	13.69	13.71	13.74	13.73	13.73	13.65	13.61	13.65	13.71	13.74	13.77
1964	13.84	13.85	13.90	14.02	14.14	14.19	14.19	14.25	14.25	14.26	14.38	14.43
1965	14.47	14.47	14.52	14.80	14.85	14.89	14.89	14.92	14.93	14.95	15.01	15.08
1966	15.11	15.12	15.15	15.33	15.44	15.48	15.41	15.50	15.48	15.52	15.61	15.63
1967	15.66	15.67	15.67	15.79	15.78	15.85	15.75	15.71	15.70	15.82	15.91	16.02
1968	16.07	16.15	16.20	16.49	16.51	16.57	16.59	16.61	16.63	16.71	16.74	16.97
1969	17.06	17.15	17.22	17.41	17.38	17.46	17.46	17.42	17.47	17.60	17.64	17.76
1970	17.91	18.00	18.11	18.38	18.44	18.49	18.62	18.61	18.70	18.90	19.03	19.16
1971	19.43	19.53	19.69	20.11	20.25	20.39	20.51	20.52	20.55	20.67	20.79	20.89
1972	21.01	21.12	21.19	21.38	21.49	21.63	21.70	21.87	21.99	22.30	22.37	22.49
1973	22.64	22.78	22.92	23.35	23.52	23.64	23.75	23.82	24.03	24.50	24.69	24.87
1974	25.35	25.78	26.01	26.89	27.27	27.55	27.81	27.83	28.14	28.69	29.20	29.63
1975	30.39	30.90	31.51	32.72	34.09	34.75	35.11	35.31	35.61	36.12	36.55	37.01

1976	37.49	37.97	38.17	38.91	39.34	39.54	39.62	40.18	40.71	41.44	42.03	42.59
1977	43.70	44.13	44.56	45.70	46.06	46.54	46.59	46.82	47.07	47.27	47.50	47.76
1978	48.04	48.31	48.62	49.33	49.61	49.99	50.22	50.54	50.75	50.98	51.33	51.76
1979	52.52	52.95	53.38	54.30	54.73	55.67	58.07	58.53	59.11	59.72	60.25	60.68
1980	62.18	63.07	63.93	66.11	66.72	67.35	67.91	68.06	68.49	68.92	69.48	69.86
1981	70.29	70.93	71.99	74.07	74.55	74.98	75.31	75.87	76.30	76.98	77.79	78.28
1982	78.73	78.76	79.44	81.04	81.62	81.85	81.88	81.90	81.85	82.26	82.66	82.51
1983	82.61	82.97	83.12	84.28	84.64	84.84	85.30	85.68	86.06	86.36	86.67	86.89
1984	86.84	87.20	87.48	88.64	88.97	89.20	89.10	89.94	90.11	90.67	90.95	90.87
1985	91.20	91.94	92.80	94.78	95.21	95.41	95.23	95.49	95.44	95.59	95.92	96.05
1986	96.25	96.60	96.73	97.67	97.85	97.79	97.52	97.82	98.30	98.45	99.29	99.62
1987	100.0	100.4	100.6	101.8	101.9	101.9	101.8	102.1	102.4	102.9	103.4	103.3
1988	103.3	103.7	104.1	105.8	106.2	106.6	106.7	107.9	108.4	109.5	110.0	110.3
1989	111.0	111.8	112.3	114.3	115.0	115.4	115.5	115.8	116.6	117.5	118.5	118.8
1990	119.5	120.2	121.4	125.1	126.2	126.7	126.8	128.1	129.3	130.3	130.0	129.9
1991	130.2	130.9	131.4	133.1	133.5	134.1	133.8	134.1	134.6	135.1	135.6	135.7
1992	135.6	136.3	136.7	138.8	139.3	139.3	138.8	138.9	139.4	139.9	139.7	139.2
1993	137.9	138.8	139.3	140.6	141.1	141.0	140.7	141.3	141.9	141.8	141.6	141.9
1994	141.3	142.1	142.5	144.2	144.7	144.7	144.0	144.7	145.0	145.2	145.3	146.0
1995	146.0	146.9	147.5	149.0	149.6	149.8	149.1	149.9	150.6	149.8	149.8	150.7
1996	150.2	150.9	151.5	152.6	152.9	153.0	152.4	153.1	153.8	153.8	153.9	154.4
1997	154.4	155.0	155.4	156.3	156.9	157.5	157.5	158.5	159.3	159.5	159.6	160.0
1998	159.5	160.3	160.8	162.6	163.5	163.4	163.0	163.7	164.4	164.5	164.4	164.4
1999	163.4	163.7	164.1	165.2	165.6	165.6	165.1	165.5	166.2	166.5	166.7	167.3
2000	166.6	167.5	168.4	170.1	170.7	171.1	170.5	170.5	171.7	171.6	172.1	172.2
2001	171.1	172.0	172.2	173.1	174.2	174.4	173.3	174.0	174.6	174.3	173.6	173.4
2002	173.3	173.8	174.5	175.7	176.2	176.2	175.9	176.4	177.6	177.9	178.2	178.5
2003	178.4	179.3	179.9	181.2	181.5	181.3	181.3	181.6	182.5	182.6	182.7	183.5
2004	183.1	183.8	184.6	185.7	186.5	186.8	186.8	187.4	188.1	188.6	189.0	189.9
2005	188.9	189.6	190.5	191.6	192.0	192.2	192.2	192.6	193.1	193.3	193.6	194.1
2006	193.4	194.2	195.0	196.5	197.7	198.5	198.5	199.2	200.1	200.4	201.1	202.7
2007	201.6	203.1	204.4	205.4	206.2	207.3	206.1	207.3	208.0	208.9	209.7	210.9
2008	209.8	211.4	212.1	214.0	215.1	216.8	216.5	217.2	218.4	217.7	216.0	212.9
2009	210.1	211.4	211.3	211.5	212.8	213.4	213.4	214.4	215.3	216.0	216.6	218.0
2010	217.9	219.2	220.7	222.8	223.6	224.1	223.6	224.5	225.3	225.8	226.8	228.4
2011	229.0	231.3	232.5	234.4	235.2	235.2	234.7	236.1	237.9	238.0	238.5	239.4
2012	238.0	239.9	240.8	242.5	242.4	241.8	242.1	243.0	244.2	245.6	245.6	246.8
2013	245.8	247.6	248.7	249.5	250.0	249.7	249.7	251.0	251.9	251.9	252.1	253.4
2014	252.6	254.2	254.8	255.7	255.9	256.3	256.0	257.0	257.6	257.7	257.1	257.5
2015	255.4	256.7	257.1	258.0	258.5	258.9	258.6	259.8	259.6	259.5	259.8	260.6
2016	258.8	260.0	261.1	261.4	262.1	263.1	263.4	264.4	264.9	264.8	265.5	267.1
2017	265.5	268.4	269.3	270.6	271.7	272.3	272.9	274.7	275.1	275.3	275.8	278.1
2018	276.0	278.1	278.3	279.7	280.7	281.5	281.7	284.2	284.1	284.5	284.6	285.6
2019	283.0	285.0	285.1	288.2	289.2	289.6	289.5	291.7	291.0	290.4	291.0	291.9
2020	290.6	292.0	292.6	292.6	292.2	292.7	294.2	293.3	294.3	294.3	293.5	295.4

Rollover relief classes

These are the qualifying classes of assets for which proceeds of a disposal may be rolled over into the acquisition of a new asset.

Class Description
1A Land and buildings for a trade
1B Fixed plant and machinery
2 Ships, aircraft and hovercraft
3 Satellites, space stations and spacecraft
4 Goodwill
5 Milk and potato quotas (both now abolished)
6 Ewe and suckler cow premium quotas
7 Fish quotas
7A Payment entitlements under Single Payment for farmers
7B Payment entitlements under Basic Payment Scheme for farmer
8A Lloyd's underwriters' syndicate capacity
8B Lloyd's members' agent pooling arrangements

Savings depletion table

This table says for how many whole months a capital sum of £100,000 will last if the saver withdraws a regular sum each month, and the balance earns monthly interest at the annual rate stated.

For example, if someone's withdraws £100 each month and the balance earns 1/12 of 1% annual interest each month (i.e. 0.083%), the savings are exhausted after 2,152 months.

The tables will remain correct if both the capital sum and monthly withdrawal are multiplied by the same amount. So a monthly withdrawal of £300 from a capital sum of £300,000 will last for 2,152 months. Otherwise, multiplication will not give the correct answer.

A dash means that the interest earned is greater than the monthly withdrawal, so the savings will never be depleted to zero.

Monthly withdrawal	0%	1%	2%	3%	4%	5%
100	1000	2151	-	-	-	-
200	500	647	1075	-	-	-
300	333	390	486	717	-	-
400	250	280	323	392	539	-
500	200	218	243	277	331	430
600	166	179	195	215	244	285
700	148	152	163	176	195	217
800	125	132	140	150	161	176
900	111	116	122	130	139	149
1000	100	104	109	115	121	129
1500	66	68	70	73	75	78
2000	50	51	52	53	54	56
2500	40	40	41	42	43	43

Monthly withdrawal	0%	1%	2%	3%	4%	5%
3000	33	33	33	34	35	35
4000	25	25	25	25	26	26
5000	20	20	20	20	20	20

Scholarship income

Employees on full-time or sandwich courses at a university or college may receive tax-free pay up to an annual limit.

From	Amount
1 September 2007	£15,480
1 September 2005	£15,000
6 April 1992	£7,000

Simplified income tax for small businesses

From 2013/14, a small business may use a simplified income tax system instead of the normal basis of assessment. The two main differences are:

- the assessment is based on the cash basis, that is when invoices are paid not when they are issued or received; and
- many expenses are replaced by fixed amounts.

From 6 April 2017, the maximum income limit for using this system is £150,000 a year, though some income is disregarded for this purpose.

The expense deductions are given below.

House expenses

A monthly amount may be deducted for use of a home which has both business and personal and business use. This depends on the number of people who treat the premises as their home.

Number of occupants	Deduction
1	£350
2	£500
3 or more	£650

Mileage rate for business travel

The same as for an employee, namely 45p a mile for car; 25p for a motorcycle; 20p for a bicycle.

Working hours

A monthly deduction may be claimed for hours worked instead of claiming the house expenses above.

Hours worked	Deduction
up to 25	nil
26 to 50	£10.00
51 to 100	£18.00
more than 100	£26.00

The business may also deduct normal business expenditure such as stock, advertising, staff and similar.

Small and medium-sized companies

Small and medium-sized companies have specific provisions for company law. These are based on EU regulations where amounts are expressed in euros.

They are also used for some tax purposes and in relation to state aid.

The scope generally requires the company to meet two out three criteria for the current financial year and the previous year.

Small company

From	*Max turnover*	*Max assets*	*Maximum employees*
1 January 2016	£10.2 million	£5.1 million	50
6 April 2008	£6.5 million	£3.26 million	50
30 January 2004	£5.6 million	£2.8 million	50
16 November 1992	£2.8 million	£1.4 million	50

Medium-sized company

From	*Max turnover*	*Max assets*	*Maximum employees*
1 January 2016	£36 million	£18 million	250
6 April 2008	£25.9 million	£12.9 million	250
30 January 2004	£22.8 million	£11.2 million	250
16 November 1992	£11.4 million	£5.6 million	250

Micro-entity#

From	*Max turnover*	*Max assets*	*Maximum employees*
1 January 2016	£632,000	£316,000	10

Small gifts allowance

A trader may claim tax relief for small gifts, such as diaries and pens, provided the gift contains a conspicuous advertisement; does not comprise food, tobacco or alcohol; and its value does not the limit below.

From	Amount
1 April 2001	£50
6 April 1985	£10
6 April 1971	£2
6 April 1965	£1

Social security rates

Rates are weekly amounts unless otherwise stated.
This list gives main rates and so is not complete or comprehensive.
There are many exceptions, special provisions and rules.

	2020/21	2019/20
Attendance allowance		
lower rate	£59.70	£58.70
higher rate	£89.15	£87.65
Bereavement support payment		
higher rate one-off lump sum	£3,500	£3,500
higher rate monthly amount	£350	£350
lower rate one-off lump sum	£2,500	£2,500
lower rate monthly amount	£100	£100

Carer's allowance		
carer's allowance	£67.25	£66.15
supplement in Scotland	£230.10	£226.20
Child benefit		
eldest child	£21.05	£20.70
other children	£13.95	£13.70
Child tax credit (rates per year)		
family element	£545	£545
child element	£2,830	£2,780
disabled child element	£3,415	£3,355
severely disabled child	£1,385	£1.360
Disability living allowance care component		
highest rate	£89.15	£87.65
middle rate	£59.70	£58.70
lowest rate	£23.60	£23.20
Disability living allowance mobility component		
higher rate	£62.25	£61.20
lower rate	£23.60	£23.20
Employment and support allowance assessment phase		
under 25	£58.90	£57.90
25 or over	£74.35	£73.10
Employment and support allowance main phase		
16 or over	£74.35	£73.10
work-related activity component	£29.55	£29.05
support component	£39.20	£38.55
Guardian's allowance	£17.90	£17.20
Housing benefit allowances		
being phased out		
Incapacity benefit short-term		
higher rate	£114.15	£112.25
lower rate	£109.50	£107.65
adult dependant	£63.80	£62.75
Incapacity benefit long-term	£114.15	£112.25
age addition under 35	£12.10	£11.90
age addition 35-44	£6.70	£6.60
adult dependant	£66.30	£65.20
Income support personal allowances		
single person under 25	£58.90	£57.90
single person 25 or older	£74.35	£73.10
lone parent under 18	£58.90	£57.90
lone parent 18 or older	£74.35	£73.10
couple both under 18	£58.90	£57.90
both under 18 special cases	£89.00	£87.50
one under 18, other 18-24	£58.90	£57.90
one under 18, other 25+	£74.35	£73.10

one under 18, special cases	£116.80	£114.85
both 18 or older	£116.80	£114.85
Income support premiums		
single carer	£37.50	£36.85
disability single	£34.95	£34.35
disability couple	£49.80	£48.95
enhanced disability single	£17.10	£16.80
enhanced disability couple	£24.50	£24.10
severe disability for one	£66.95	£65.85
severe disability for two	£133.90	£131.70
pensioner couple	£148.40	£140.40
Income support children addition		
under 20 personal allowance	£68.27	£66.90
family premium	£17.60	£17.45
disabled child premium	£65.52	£64.19
enhanced disability	£26.60	£26.04
Industrial injuries disablement benefit		
20% disability (minimum)	£36.40	£35.80
100% disability	£182.00	£179.00
Jobseeker's allowance		
under 25	£58.90	£57.90
25 or over	£74.35	£73.10
Maternity allowance	£151.20	£148.68
Pension credit		
guarantee credit single	£173.75	£167.25
guarantee credit couple	£265.20	£255.25
severe disability addition	£66.95	£65.85
severe disability for both	£133.90	£131.70
carer addition	£37.50	£53.34
child addition standard	£54.32	£53.34
child addition for eldest	£64.82	£63.84
savings credit single	£150.47	£144.38
savings credit couple	£239.17	£229.67
maximum single	£13.97	£13.72
maximum couple	£15.62	£15.35
Personal independence payment		
daily living component standard	£59.70	£58.70
daily living component enhanced	£89.15	£87.65
mobility component standard	£23.60	£23.20
mobility component enhanced	£62.25	£61.20
Retirement pension		
category A	£175.20	£168.60
category B	£134.25	£129.20
category D	£80.45	£77.45
Severe disablement allowance	£80.85	£79.50

age addition under 40	£12.10	£11.90
age addition 40-49	£6.70	£6.60
age addition 50-59	£6.70	£6.60
adult dependant	£39.75	£39.10
Universal credit allowances (per month)		
single allowance under 25	£342.72	£251.77
single allowance 25 or older	£409.89	£317.82
couple both under 25	£488.59	£395.20
couple one is 25 or older	£594.04	£498.89
Universal credit elements (per month)		
first child born before 6.4.17	£281.25	£277.08
first child born after 5.4.17	£235.83	-
each subsequent child	£235.83	£231.67
disabled child lower rate	£128.25	£126.11
disabled child higher rate	£400.29	£392.08
limited capacity for work	£128.25	£126.11
limited work-related ability	£341.92	£336.20
carer	£162.92	£160.20
childcare: one child max	£646.35	£646.35
childcare: two or more max	£1,108.04	£1,108.04
percentage covered	85%	85%
Universal credit capital limits		
lower	£6,000	£6,000
upper	£16,000	£16,000
tariff income per £250	£4.35	£4.35
Working tax credit (per year)		
basic element	£3,040	£1,960
couple element	£2,045	£2,010
lone parent element	£2,045	£2,010
30-hour element	£825	£810
disabled worker element	£3,220	£3,165
childcare element	£1,390	£1,365

Claimants also receive £10 Christmas bonus, and an extra 25p a week pension at the age of 80, both unchanged since 1971.

BENEFIT CAP

Benefit cap restricts the total amount of benefit that may be claimed from these benefits:

- bereavement allowance
- child benefit
- child tax credit
- employment and support allowance
- housing benefit
- incapacity benefit
- income support
- jobseeker's allowance
- maternity allowance

- severe disablement allowance
- universal credit
- widowed parent's allowance.

There are exceptions for people over state pension age or receiving some benefits. This includes anyone receiving working tax credit, or universal credit because of a disability or health condition.

The amount of annual benefit cap (from 7 November 2016) is:

Status of claimant	in Greater London	outside Greater London
Couple or single parent	£23,000	£20,000
Single adult	£15,410	£13,400

The cap was introduced in April 2013 at higher rates of £26,000 for a couple or single parent, and £18,200 for a single adult, regardless of whether they lived in London.

UNDER-OCCUPANCY CHARGE (commonly known as bedroom tax)

This charge was introduced from 1 April 2013

This restricts benefits when a claimant has more bedrooms than allowed. One bedroom is allowed for:

- an adult couple
- each other person aged 16 or over
- two children of the same sex under 16
- two children of opposite sexes under 10
- a child whose disability prevents bedroom sharing
- a non-resident carer for a person who requires overnight care.

There are some exemptions, such as temporary accommodation, houseboats and mobile homes. It does not apply to claimants of pension age.

The reduction in benefit is 14% for one room, and 25% for two or more. This is taken from housing benefit or the housing element of universal credit.

If a spare bedroom is created because of a death, there is no reduction for one year.

UNIVERSAL CREDIT

Universal credit is a means-tested social security benefit that replaces these legacy benefits:

- child tax credit
- housing benefit
- income-based employment and support allowance
- income-based jobseeker's allowance
- income support
- working tax credit.

It was introduced in April 2013 for new claimants, with those receiving legacy benefits being progressively migrated to universal credit. This migration programme was due to be completed by 2017 but has been subject to repeated delays.

Spotlights

A Spotlight is information from HMRC about tax avoidance schemes that HMRC believes do not work.

No.	*Date*	*Summary of scheme*

1	5 August 2010	Goodwill: companies acquiring businesses carried on before 1 April 2002 by a related party
2	5 August 2010	VAT and artificial leasing
3	5 August 2010	Artificial surplus in a pension scheme
4	5 August 2010	Contrived employment liabilities and losses
5	5 August 2010	PAYE and national insurance: using trusts and similar entities to reward employees
6	5 August 2010	Employer-finance retirement benefits scheme
7	5 August 2010	Avoidance using Gift Aid
8	5 August 2010	Investments to obtain sideways loss relief
9	5 August 2010	Gift Aid with no real gift
10	5 August 2010	Stamp duty land tax avoidance
11	23 August 2011	Avoiding income tax on pay
12	6 November 2012	Taxing the rewards for work done for a UK based employer
13	26 November 2012	Property business loss relief schemes
14	11 January 2013	Stamp duty land tax avoidance
15	11 January 2013	Share loss relief schemes
16	14 February 2013	Plan Green car benefit scheme
17	17 April 2013	Employment benefit schemes using fettered payments
18	12 June 2013	Stripped bond tax avoidance scheme
19	12 June 2013	Stamp duty land tax avoidance: update
20	20 July 2013	Gift Aid with no real gift
21	4 November 2013	Business premises renovation allowance schemes
22	5 November 2013	VAT contrived schemes to obtain exemptions for sporting or educational/training supplies
23	27 December 2013	Employee bonuses: using restricted securities
24	29 June 2015	Employment allowance: contrived arrangements
25	20 August 2015	Stamp duty land tax avoidance: no human rights breach
26		*withdrawn and replaced by Spotlight 33*
27	23 October 2015	Interest relief avoidance schemes
28	3 February 2016	Employee bonus schemes: growth securities ownership plan
29	5 February 2016	Misleading claims from tax avoidance scheme promoters
30	6 May 2016	Gold bullion schemes
31	31 August 2016	Transitional relief on investment growth: change of withdrawal date
32	25 February 2020	Managed service company legislation
33	7 July 2016	Contractor tax: loan schemes can cost you more
34	14 September 2016	Capital gains tax: entrepreneur's relief schemes
35	14 February 2017	Disguised remuneration: using annuities
36	2 December 2017	Disguised remuneration: claiming to avoid the loan charge
37	17 March 2017	Disguised remuneration: job board avoidance schemes
38	26 June 2017	VAT: supply splitting tax avoidance schemes
39	10 August 2017	Disguised remuneration: re-describing loans
40	25 October 2017	Disguised remuneration trust schemes: misleading advertising

41	29 September 2017	Disguised remuneration: Supreme Court decision
42	14 February 2018	Contractor loan scheme: misleading advertising
43	21 March 2018	Stamp duty land tax: misleading advertising
44	31 May 2019	Disguised remuneration: schemes affected by loan charge
45	12 September 2018	Umbrella companies offering to increase your take home pay
46	16 January 2019	Rewarding employees and contractors using contrived loan arrangements
47	4 February 2019	Attempts to avoid an income tax charge when a company is wound up
48	14 February 2019	Disguised remuneration: contract loans settlements and obtaining a deed of release
49	8 March 2019	Disguised remuneration: schemes claiming to avoid the loan charge
50	26 March 2019	Disguised remuneration: asset transfer arrangements set up to avoid the loan charge
51	10 May 2019	Remuneration trust: tax avoidance using loans or fiduciary receipts
52	15 May 2019	Disclosure of tax avoidance schemes: tax avoidance using offshore trusts
53	22 July 2019	Disguised remuneration: tax avoidance using capital advances, joint and mutual share ownership
54	9 April 2020	Tax avoidance promoters targeting returning NHS workers
55	27 April 2020	Comparison and broker websites marketing umbrella companies are not always what they seem
56	1 September 2020	Disguised remuneration: tax avoidance by owner managed companies using remuneration trusts.

Stamp duty

Stamp duty is now largely restricted to stock transfers such as when shares are sold.

Although "stamp duty" is often referred to in property transactions, that tax is actually stamp duty land tax.

Historically stamp duty was applied to a wide range of documents at either a fixed duty or as an ad valorem duty.

The only fixed duty remaining is a £5 charge for certain instruments affecting land (FA 2008 Sch 32 para 22).

Otherwise stamp duty is charged on an ad valorem basis:

Description of transfer	*Rate of stamp duty*
share transfers up to £1,000	nil
stocks, or shares for more than £1,000	1.0%
depositary receipts	1.5%
bearer instruments	1.5%

Stamp duty land tax

Stamp duty land tax (SDLT)is charged on property transactions.

This tax is now charged only in England and Northern Ireland.

The equivalent for Scotland is land and buildings transaction tax from 1 April 2015.

The equivalent for Wales is land transaction tax from 1 April 2018.

SDLT is charged at different rates for residential property and non-residential property.

The rates were temporarily reduced during the coronavirus outbreak.

It is now charged at the appropriate rate for each slice of value.

Rates for residential property were temporarily reduced between 8 July 2020 and 31 March 2021.

Residential property bought before 8 July 2020 or from 1 April 2021

Slice of property value	*Main rate*	*Higher rate*
up to £125,000	0%	3%
£125,001 to £250,000	2%	5%
£250,001 to £925,000	5%	8%
£925,001 to £1.5 million	10%	13%
over £1.5 million	12%	15%

A higher rate generally applies for second homes completed from 1 April 2016 unless contracts had been agreed by 26 November 2015. Otherwise these rates apply from 4 December 2014.

The higher rate also applies when a company acquires a freehold for £40,000 or more, or a leasehold with more than 21 years to run.

A first-time buyer in these periods, pays no SDLT up to £300,000; and 5% on the slice from £300,001 to £500,000. Above £500,000, there is no discount for a first-time buyer.

Residential property bought between 8 July 2020 and 31 March 2021

Slice of property value	*Rate*
up to £500,000	0%
£500,001 to £925,000	5%
£925,001 to £1.5 million	10%
over £1.5 million	12%

The discount for a first-time buyer does not apply for this period.

Residential property leased

NPV of rents	*Rate*
up to £125,000	0%
over £125,000	1%

SDLT is charged on the net present value (NPV) of rent.

These rates apply from 1 January 2010.

Commercial property bought

Property value	*Rate*
up to £150,000	0%
£150,001 to £250,000	2%
over £250,000	5%

These rates apply from 17 March 2016.

Commercial property leased

NPV of rents	*Rate*

up to £150,000	0%
£150,001 to £5 million	1%
over £5 million	2%

These rates apply from 17 March 2016.
Previously, from 1 January 2010, there was no 2% rate.

Stamp duty reserve tax

Stamp duty reserve tax (SDRT) is paid on transfers of securities which do not involve a paper contract, and so avoid stamp duty.
It is paid at a standard rate and higher rate. The latter is paid for transfers into depositary receipt schemes and clearance services.

Charge	*Rate*
Standard rate	0.5%
Higher rate	1.5%

State pension

The state pension is payable as a fixed weekly amount plus any additional pension to those who reached state pension age on or before 6 April 2016.
The single tier pension is payable from 6 April 2016 at the single tier rate or, if more, the standard pension plus additional pension.
The rates of these pensions are given earlier in this section under Social Security Rates
The state pension age is given below.
Entitlement to state pension depends on having a full national insurance contributions record (of classes 1, 2 or 3 contributions) for:

From	**Contribution requirement**
6 April 2016	35 years
6 April 2010	30 years
1948	9 years out of every 10 working life

For fewer years, a portion of the pension may be paid, provided at least 10 years of contributions were paid. Any missing or incomplete years may be topped up by paying class 3 contributions for the current tax year and up to the six previous tax years.
A married woman who elected to pay reduced contributions before May 1977 may receive a pension of about two-thirds the full amount on the basis of her husband's contributions.
At the age of 80, someone with no contributions or insufficient contributions receives a non-contributory Category D pension of about two-thirds the full pension.
All state pensions increase by 25p a week (unchanged since 1971) from the age of 80. Spend it wisely.
Details on all state pension entitlement already earned can be found by emailing www.gov.uk/get-state-pension or telephoning 0800 731 7898.

Additional pension

The additional pension was one or more of the following for employment in the stated years.

Period	*Additional pension*
1961 to 1975	graduated pension
1978 to 2002	state earnings-related pension scheme (SERPS)

2002 to 2016 state second pension (S2P)

Someone with insufficient pension may be eligible for pension credit.

Graduated pension

The graduated pension applied to employees from 1961 to 1975.

Men bought units for every £7.50, and women for every £9.00

The number of units was reduced if the employee was in a contracted-out pension scheme.

The maximum number of units that could be bought is:

Man (not contracted-out)	86
Man (contracted-out)	72
Woman (not contracted-out)	48
Woman (contracted-out)	40

These numbers were adjusted in 2010 so that women have the same number of units as a man would have received.

Year	Payment per unit
2020/21	14.40p
2019/20	14.16p
2018/19	13.83p
2017/18	13.43p
2016/17	13.30p
2015/16	13.30p
2014/15	13.14p

Year	Payment per unit
2013/14	12.79p
2012/13	12.51p
2011/12	11.89p
2010/11	11.53p
2009/10	11.53p
2008/09	10.98p
2007/08	10.57p

Year	Payment per unit
2006/07	9.93p
2005/06	9.93p
2004/05	9.63p
2003/04	9.37p
2002/03	9.21p
2001/02	9.06p
2000/01	8.77p

State earnings-related pension scheme (SERPS)

SERPS applies to earnings between 1978 and 2002.

It is calculated as the total of percentages of the qualifying earnings factor (QEF) for each year.

The QEF is band earnings between the lower earnings limit and upper accruals point (or upper earnings limit for years with no upper accruals point) for class 1 national insurance.

The percentage was 25% up to 1999/2000, and then reduces by half of one per cent for each subsequent year down to 20% by 2009/2010.

These calculations are done by the government.

State second pension (S2P)

State second pension was introduced from 6 April 2002 and continues many of the provisions of SERPS.

The two main changes are:

- the eligibility criteria are widened to include non-employees such as those who are carers, who were looking after a child under 10 (from 2010), or were disabled but in work for at least one tenth of their working life
- the QEFs are re-stratified so that, instead of accruing entitlement at 20% of all band earnings, they are divided into three strata. QEFs accrue 40% on the lowest stratum, then 10%, then 20%. Someone with maximum band earnings accrues 20% as before. Anyone with lower earnings accrues between 20% and 40%.

If a spouse or civil partner dies, the surviving partner may inherit between 50% and 100% of the deceased's state second pension depending on their date of birth:

% inherited	Man's date of birth	Woman's date of birth
100	before 6 October 1937	before 6 October 1942
90	before 6 October 1939	before 6 October 1944
80	before 6 October 1941	before 6 October 1946
70	before 6 October 1943	before 6 October 1948
60	before 6 October 1945	before 6 October 1950
50	from 6 October 1945	from 6 October 1950

State pension age (SPA)

This is the age at which a person is entitled to receive their state pension.
It is also the age at which the person ceases to be liable to pay national insurance.
"Pension paid from" dates from 2020 are subject to change.
For a man born before 6 April 1959, the SPA is 65 years
For a woman born before 6 April 1950, the SPA is 60 years
A woman born from 6 November 1953 has the same SPA as a man.
In the tables below "62.3" means 62 years and 3 months, and similar.

State pension age for women born between 6 April 1950 and 6 November 1953

Born from	*SPA*	*Pension paid from*
6 April 1950	60.1	6 May 2010
6 May 1950	60.2	6 July 2010
6 June 1950	60.3	6 September 2010
6 July 1950	60.4	6 November 2010
6 August 1950	60.5	6 January 2011
6 September 1950	60.6	6 March 2011
6 October 1950	60.7	6 May 2011
6 November 1950	60.8	6 July 2011
6 December 1950	60.9	6 September 2011
6 January 1951	60.10	6 November 2011
6 February 1951	60.11	6 January 2012
6 March 1951	61	6 March 2012
6 April 1951	61.1	6 May 2012
6 May 1951	61.2	6 July 2012
6 June 1951	61.3	6 September 2012
6 July 1951	61.4	6 November 2012
6 August 1951	61.5	6 January 2013
6 September 1951	61.6	6 March 2013
6 October 1951	61.7	6 May 2013
6 November 1951	61.8	6 July 2013
6 December 1951	61.9	6 September 2013
6 January 1952	61.10	6 November 2013
6 February 1952	61.11	6 January 2014
6 March 1952	62	6 March 2014
6 April 1952	62.1	6 May 2014

6 May 1952	62.2	6 July 2014
6 June 1952	62.3	6 September 2014
6 July 1952	62.4	6 November 2014
6 August 1952	62.5	6 January 2015
6 September 1952	62.6	6 March 2015
6 October 1952	62.7	6 May 2015
6 November 1952	62.8	6 July 2015
6 December 1952	62.9	6 September 2015
6 January 1953	62.10	6 November 2015
6 February 1953	62.11	6 January 2016
6 March 1953	63	6 March 2016
6 April 1953	63.3	6 July 2016
6 May 1953	63.6	6 November 2016
6 June 1953	63.9	6 March 2017
6 July 1953	64	6 July 2017
6 August 1953	64.3	6 November 2017
6 September 1953	64.6	6 March 2018
6 October 1953	64.9	6 July 2018
6 November 1953	65	6 November 2018 or 65th birthday

Thereafter men and women have the same state pension age:

Born from	**SPA**	**Pension paid from**
6 November 1953	65	6 November 2018
6 December 1953	65.3	6 March 2019
6 January 1954	65.4	6 May 2019
6 February 1954	65.5	6 July 2019
6 March 1954	65.6	6 September 2019
6 April 1954	65.7	6 November 2019
6 May 1954	65.8	6 January 2020
6 June 1954	65.9	6 March 2020
6 July 1954	65.10	6 May 2020
6 August 1954	65.11	6 July 2020
6 September 1954	66	6 September 2020 or 66th birthday
6 April 1960	66.1	6 May 2026
6 May 1960	66.2	6 July 2026
6 June 1960	66.3	6 September 2026
6 July 1960	66.4	6 November 2026
6 August 1960	66.5	6 January 2027
6 September 1960	66.6	6 March 2027
6 October 1960	66.7	6 May 2027
6 November 1960	66.8	6 July 2027
6 December 1960	66.9	6 September 2027
6 January 1961	66.10	6 November 2027
6 February 1961	66.11	6 January 2028
6 March 1961	67	6 March 2028 or 67th birthday
6 April 1977	67.1	6 May 2044

6 May 1977	67.2	6 July 2044
6 June 1977	67.3	6 September 2044
6 July 1977	67.4	6 November 2044
6 August 1977	67.5	6 January 2045
6 September 1977	67.6	6 March 2045
6 October 1977	67.7	6 May 2045
6 November 1977	67.8	6 July 2045
6 January 1978	67.9	6 September 2045
6 February 1978	67.10	6 November 2045
6 March 1978	67.11	6 January 2046
6 April 1978	68	6 March 2046 or 68th birthday

These ages are given statutory effect as follows:

From 6 April 1950:	Pensions Act 1995
From 6 April 1953:	Pensions Act 2011
From 6 April 1960:	Pensions Act 2014
From 6 April 1977:	Pensions Act 2007

Statutory set rates

	2020/21	**2019/20**	**2018/19**	**2017/18**
Statutory maternity/paternity pay and similar per week	£151.20	£148.68	£145.18	£140.98
Maternity allowance	£145.18	£140.98	£139.58	£139.58
Statutory sick pay per week	£95.85	£94.25	£92.05	£89.35

Statutory maternity pay (SMP) is paid at 90% of weekly wages for the first six weeks, or at the set rate given above if lower, and then at the set rate for up to 33 weeks. She is then entitled to a further 13 weeks (bringing the total to 52 weeks) of unpaid leave. She may transfer between 2 and 26 weeks to her partner.

The employer may recover a percentage of SMP from the state by deduction from PAYE payments. The rate is more than 100% for "small employers", this provides part compensation for employer's national insurance. For this purpose, a small employer is one whose total national insurance in the previous tax year did not exceed £45,000.

The recovery rates are:

Tax years	**Small employer NI limit**	**Recovery rate**	**Other employers**
2011/12-2020/21	£45,000	103%	92%
2004/05-2010/11	£45,000	104.5%	92%
2002/03-2003/04	£40,000	104.5%	92%
1999/00-2000/01	£20,000	105%	92%

Historic flat rates

Year	*SMP*	*SSP*
2016/17	£139.58	£88.45
2015/16	£139.58	£88.45
2014/15	£138.18	£87.55
2013/14	£136.78	£86.70

2012/13	£135.45	£85.85
2011/12	£128.73	£81.60
2010/11	£124.88	£79.15
2009/10	£123.06	£79.15
2008/09	£117.18	£75.40
2007/08	£112.75	£72.55
2006/07	£108.85	£70.05
2005/06	£106.00	£68.20
2004/05	£102.80	£66.15
2003/04	£100.00	£64.35
2002/03	£75.00	£63.25
2001/02	£62.20	£62.20
2000/01	£60.20	£60.20

Statutory residence test

From 6 April 2013, UK residence is determined by the statutory residence test.

It is a three-part test which is followed until one set of conditions is met for one of the tests.

If an individual is resident in the UK for fewer than 16 days, they are non-resident

If an individual is resident in the UK for more than 183 days, they are resident.

For other circumstances, the tests must be followed in the following order.

Automatic overseas tests (compliance means taxpayer is non-resident)

1 • was resident in UK for one or more of three previous tax years
  • spends fewer than 16 days in the UK in current year

2 • was resident in UK for none of three previous years
  • spends fewer than 46 days in the UK

3 • works full-time overseas without any significant breaks from overseas work
  • spends fewer than 91 days in the UK
  • works for more than 3 hours a day in UK for no more than 31 days of the tax year

(No 3 is varied for those who work in international transport.)

Automatic UK tests (compliance means taxpayer is UK-resident)

1 • spends 183 days in UK in current tax year

2 • has a home in the UK for any part of the tax year
  • spends at least 91 days in the UK, at least 30 of which fall in the tax year
  • has no overseas home, or spends a short amount of time in overseas home

3 • works full-time in UK for whole of tax year
  • more than 75% of total number of days in UK when they do more than three hours of work are days in UK
  • there is at least one day in the tax year where they do more than three hours of work in the UK

If none of these sets of conditions are met, it is next necessary to determine whether the taxpayer was UK resident for at least one of the previous three years.

Sufficient ties tests when taxpayer has been non-resident for three previous years

There are four ties, or connection factors, that need to be considered:

- a UK-resident family

- substantive employment or self-employment in the UK
- accessible accommodation in UK (not necessarily owned by taxpayer)
- spent 90 days or more in UK in either of two previous tax years.

A taxpayer is UK-resident if he or she meets sufficient ties for the days spent in the UK as shown in this table:

Days in UK	Number of ties
fewer than 46	always non-resident
46 to 90	4
91 to 120	3
121 to 182	2
183 or more	always resident

Sufficient ties tests when taxpayer has been UK resident in at least one of the three previous years

There are five ties, or connection factors, that need to be considered:

- a UK-resident family
- substantive employment or self-employment in the UK
- accessible accommodation in UK (not necessarily owned by taxpayer)
- spent 90 days or more in UK in either of two previous tax years.
- spends more days in UK in tax year than in any other country.

A taxpayer is UK-resident if he or she meets sufficient ties for days spent in the UK as shown in this table:

Days in UK	Number of ties
fewer than 16	always non-resident
17 to 45	4
46 to 90	3
91 to 120	2
121 to 182	1
183 or more	always resident

A day counter is provided in this section of the dictionary.

Student loan repayments

	2020/21	2019/20	2018/19	2017/18
Plan 1 annual threshold	£19,390	£18,935	£18,330	£17,775
Rate of repayment	9%	9%	9%	9%
Plan 2 annual threshold	£26,575	£25,725	£25,000	£21,000
Rate of repayment	9%	9%	9%	9%
Postgraduate annual threshold	£21,000	£21,000	-	-
Rate of repayment	6%	6%	-	-

Plan 1 refers to loans granted for courses that started from 1 September 1998 to August 2012.

Plan 2 refers to loans granted for courses that started from 1 September 2012.

Postgraduate loans apply for courses that started from 1 August 2016, with the first repayment from 6 April 2019.

From 6 April 2021, the Scottish government is introducing Plan 4 loans for Scottish borrowers.

This replaces Plan 1 loans. The repayment is 9% of income above £25,000.

Tax codes

- BR — all earnings are taxed at 20%
- C — prefix to a tax code indicating that the taxpayer is liable to pay Welsh rates
- D0 — all earnings are taxed at 40%
- D1 — all earnings are taxed at 45%
- K — prefix where taxpayer's pay is more than gross pay (usually because of unpaid tax from previous year or the employee receives a high value of benefits in kind). The addition is 10 times the number so code K100 means that the employee pays tax on £1,000 more than his or her gross pay
- L — suffix indicating that the employee receives the basic personal allowance. The number before the prefix indicates one tenth of the employee's tax-free amount, so a code of 1250L means the employee pays tax on earnings above £12,500 a year
- M — suffix indicating that the employee receives the basic personal allowance plus one tenth of their spouse's or civil partner's. So if the personal allowance is £12,500, their code will probably be 1375M, meaning the employee pays tax on earnings above £13,750
- N — rare suffix indicating that the employee has passed one tenth of his or her personal allowance to their spouse or civil partner. If the personal allowance is £12,500, their tax code will probably be 1125N
- NT — no tax is deducted. This may apply when another arrangement has been agreed to collect tax or when the employee is not liable to pay tax, such as by working for certain international organisations
- 0T — this is actually a T code where the number is zero. It means that the taxpayer pays tax on all earnings with no free pay, and only HMRC may alter their code
- S — prefix indicating that the employee is subject to Scottish rates of tax
- SD0 — Scottish taxpayer who pays 21% tax on all earnings
- SD1 — Scottish taxpayer who pays 41% tax on all earnings
- SD2 — Scottish taxpayer who pays 46% tax on all earnings
- SK — Scottish taxpayer subject to provisions of a K code
- T — suffix indicating that only HMRC may alter the tax code. This often arises when the taxpayer has an unusual element. The code is operated on the same basis as an L code.

The suffixes L, M and N are used for automatic adjustment of tax codes when the personal allowance changes. So if the personal allowance increased by £1,000, all L codes would be increased by 100 points; M codes by 110 points; and N codes by 90 points.

Historically other suffixes have been used.

Taxes charged in UK

This list is not exhaustive

Tax	Years charged
Aggregates levy	2002 – present
Air passenger duty	1994 – present
Alcoholic liquor duty	1660 – present
Annual tax on enveloped dwellings	2013 - present
Bank levy	2011 - 2021
Betting and gaming duties	various – present
Capital gains tax	1965 – present
Capital transfer tax	1974 – 1986 (replaced by inheritance tax)
Climate change levy	2001 – present
Community charge	1990 (1989 in Scotland) – 1993 (replaced by council tax)
Council tax	1993 – present (never introduced in Northern Ireland)
Customs duties	1055 – present
Death duties	1694 – 1949 (when only estate duty remained)
Development gains tax	1973 – 1976
Development land tax	1976 – 1985
Digital services tax	2020 – present
Diverted profits tax	2015 - present
Dog licence	1867 – 1987 (still charged in Northern Ireland)
Estate duty	1894 – 1975
Excess profits duty	1915 – 1921
Excess profits tax	1946 – 1954
Excise licences	unknown – 1986 (except for betting and gaming)
HGV road user levy	2014 – present
Hydrocarbon oil duty	1909 – present
Income tax	1842 – present (introduced for periods from 1799)
Inheritance tax	1986 – present
Insurance premium tax	1994 – present
Land tax	1693 - 1963
Landfill tax	1996 – present
Machine games duty	2013 – present
National defence contribution	1937 - 1946
National insurance	1912 – present (strictly not a tax)
National insurance surcharge	1977 - 1985
Petroleum revenue tax	1974 – present
Profits tax	1946 – 1966
Purchase tax	1940 – 1973
Radio licence	1904 – 1971
Selective employment tax	1965 – 1973
Special contribution	1947 - 1948
Stamp duty	1694 – present

Stamp duty land tax	2003 – present
Stamp duty reserve tax	1986 – present
Supertax	1908 – 1920
Supplementary petrol duty	1981 – 198
Surtax	1909 – 1973
Television advertisement duty	1961 - 1963
Television licence	1946 – present
Tobacco duty	1660 – present
Unified business rates	1990 - present
Value added tax	1973 – present
Vehicle excise duty	1921 – present (replacing older duties)
Windfall tax	1997

Tax revenue

UK tax collected in 2019/20

Tax	*£m*	%
Income tax	193,243	28.9
National insurance	142,871	21.4
Value added tax	129,885	19.4
Corporation tax	61.106	9.1
Hydrocarbon oil duty	27,573	4.1
Stamp duty land tax	11,601	1.7
Capital gains tax	9,826	1.5
Tobacco products duty	8,804	1.3
Insurance premium tax	6,415	1.0
Inheritance tax	5,122	0.8
Wine duty	4,296	0.6
Spirits duty	3,825	0.6
Air passenger duty	3,641	0.5
Stamp duty	3,619	0.5
Beer duty	3,446	0.5
Customs duties	3,287	0.5
Betting and gaming duties	3,019	0.5
Apprenticeship levy	2,798	0.4
Bank levy	2,472	0.4
Climate change levy	2,004	0.3
Bank surcharge to CT	1,978	0.3
Landfill tax	641	0.1
Penalties	641	0.1
Aggregates levy	397	0.1
Cider duty	270	0.0
Annual tax on enveloped dwellings	128	0.0
Diverted profits tax	5	0.0
Petroleum revenue tax	-408	-0.1
Total collected by HMRC	632,842	

SECTION 3: TAX RATES AND OTHER DATA

Analysis of taxes in recent years

This table shows the total amount of tax collected in recent tax years, with percentages of how much groups of taxes raised:

IT means income tax, capital gains tax and national insurance

VAT means value added tax

CT means corporation tax

Other means other taxes, including excise duties, inheritance tax and environmental taxes.

Year	**Total £bn**	**IT %**	**VAT %**	**CT**	**%**
	Other				
2019/20	634.641	55	21	10	14
2018/19	620.329	55	21	9	15
2017/81	592.224	54	21	10	14
2016/17	567,800	55	21	9	15
2015/16	532.884	54	22	9	15
2014/15	514.057	54	22	9	15
2013/14	492.802	54	21	9	16
2012/13	473.626	54	21	9	16
2011/12	472.035	54	21	10	15
2010/11	453.957	56	18	10	16
2009/10	414.920	59	17	9	15
2008/09	445.531	58	18	10	14
2007/08	456.121	56	18	11	15
2006/07	428.629	56	18	11	15
2005/06	402.874	55	18	11	16
2004/05	375.801	55	19	9	17
2003/04	347.946	55	20	9	16
2002/03	324.725	54	20	9	17
2001/02	321.741	54	19	10	17
2000/01	315.638	54	19	11	16

Television licence

	2020/21	**2019/20**	**2018/19**	**2017/18**
The television licence is legally a tax				
Colour licence	£157.50	£154.50	£150.50	£147.00
Black and white licence	£53.00	£52.00	£50.50	£49.50

Tobacco Products Duty

This is an excise duty charged on tobacco products and other smoking material.

These are also subject to VAT.

The rates changed at 6pm on the dates shown.

Tobacco for heating became separately excised from 1 July 2019.

Product	**From 11 March 2020**	**From 29 Oct 2018**	**From 22 Nov 2017**
Cigarettes	£237.34 per 1000	£228.29 per 1000	£217.23 per 1000
	plus 16.5% of retail price for all dates		

Cigars	£296.04/kg	£284.76/kg	£270.96/kg
Hand-rolling	£253.33/kg	£234.65/kg	£221.18/kg
Other smoking	£130.16/kg	£125.20/kg	£119.13/kg
For heating	£243.95/kg	£234.65/kg	-

Tonnage tax

The tonnage tax may be used by merchant shipping companies as an alternative to corporation tax on their profits from shipping. Tax is charged on the tonnage of the ships in its fleet.

The **daily profit** is calculated for each ship according to its tonnage. These rates are unchanged from 2000. They are an amount for each complete 100 tons:

- to 1,000 tons: 60p
- 1,001 to 10,000 tons: 45p
- 10,001 to 25,000 tons: 30p
- over 25,000 tons: 15p.

A company using tonnage tax is required to provide training, or make a payment in lieu of training (PILOT). If a company delivers less than 50% of its training requirement, it must pay a surcharge which increases for a second and third year.

From	**PILOT**	**Surcharge**
1 October 2019	£1,309	£1,218
1 October 2018	£1,284	£1,195
1 October 2017	£1,259	£1,172
1 October 2016	£1,236	£1,151
1 October 2015	£1,218	£1,134
1 October 2014	£1,202	£1,119
1 October 2013	£1,092	£1,020
1 October 2012	£798	£726
1 October 2011	£798	£726
1 October 2010	£743	£676
1 October 2009	£685	£623
1 October 2008	£671	£610
1 October 2007	£652	£593
1 October 2006	£634	£577
1 October 2005	£621	£565
1 October 2004	£608	£553
1 October 2003	£591	£538
1 October 2002	£573	£522
1 February 2002	£562	£512
1 January 2000	£550	£550

Travel and subsistence allowances

An employer may pay up to these allowances to an employee tax-free when the employee is away on business. The employee must have incurred the expenses.

An employer may reimburse a higher figure of actual costs tax-free if supported by evidence.

Subsistence rates (from 2019/20)

Duration of travel	*Amount*
5 hours or more	£5
10 hours or more	£10
supplement if travelling after 8pm	£10
15 hours or more and ongoing at 8pm	£25
Incidental overnight expenses (from 1995)	***Average amount per day***
In UK	£5
Overseas	£10
Lorry drivers subsistence rates (from 2013)	
Lorry has a sleeper cab	£26.20
Lorry has no sleeper cab	£34.90

Value added tax

The standard rate has been 20% since 4 January 2011. The VAT fraction is 1/6

The reduced rate has been 5% since its introduction. The VAT fraction is 1/21.

Registration and deregistration thresholds

From	**Registration**	**Deregistration**
1 April 2017	£85,000	£83,000
1 April 2016	£83,000	£81,000
1 April 2015	£82,000	£80,000
1 April 2014	£81,000	£79,000

From 1 January 1993, a business must also register if its supplies from other EU states exceeds £70,000.

Schemes

From 1 April 2006, a business may use annual accounting if its taxable supplies in the next year are not expected to exceed £1,350,000. It may remain in the scheme until its supplies exceed £1,600,000.

From 1 April 2007, a business may use cash accounting if its taxable supplies in the next year are not expected to exceed £1,350,000. It may remain in the scheme until its supplies exceed £1,600,000.

The flat rate scheme may be used by a business who expects its supplies in the next 12 months not to exceed £150,000. Once using the scheme, a business may remain in it until either its turnover exceeds £230,000 or its income in the following year is expected not to exceed £191,500.

Flat rate scheme for small traders

Category of business	*Flat rate*
Accountancy or bookkeeping	14.5%
Advertising	11%
Agricultural services	11%
Any other activity not otherwise listed	12%
Architect, civil or structural engineer, or surveyor	14.5%
Boarding or care of animals	12%

Business services not listed elsewhere	12%
Catering services, including restaurants and takeaways	12.5% (up to 14 July 2020)
	4.5% (15 Jul 2020 to 31 Mar 2021)
Computer and IT consultancy or data processing	14.5%
Computer repair service	10.5%
Entertainment or journalism	12.5%
Estate agency of property management services	12%
Farming or agriculture not listed elsewhere	6.5%
Film, radio, television or video production	13%
Financial services	13.5%
Forestry or fishing	10.5%
General building or construction services (see below)	9.5%
Hairdressing or other beauty treatment	13%
Hiring or renting goods	9.5%
Hotel or accommodation	10.5% (up to 14 July 2020)
	0% (15 Jul 2020 to 31 Mar 2021)
Investigation or security	12%
Labour-only building or construction (see below)	14.5%
Laundry or dry cleaning	12%
Library, archive, museum or cultural activity	9.5%
Management consultancy	14%
Manufacturing fabricated metal products	10.5%
Manufacturing food	9%
Manufacturing not listed elsewhere	9.5%
Manufacturing of yarn, textiles or clothing	9%
Membership organisation	8%
Mining or quarrying	10%
Packaging	9%
Photography	11%
Post offices	5%
Printing	8.5%
Pubs	6.5% (up to 14 July 2020)
	1% (15 Jul 2020 to 31 Mar 2021)
Real estate activity not listed elsewhere	14%
Repairing personal or household goods	10%
Repairing vehicles	.5%
Retailing food, confectionery, tobacco, newspapers or children's clothing	4%
Retailing pharmaceuticals, medical goods, cosmetics or toiletries	8%
Retailing not listed elsewhere	7.5%

Secretarial services	13%
Sport or recreation	8.5%
Transport, storage, couriers, freight, removals and taxis	10%
Travel agency	10.5%
Veterinary medicine	11%
Wholesaling agricultural products	8%
Wholesaling food	7.5%
Wholesaling not listed elsewhere	8.5%

These rates apply from 4 January 2011 unless otherwise stated.

In the first year of the scheme, a business may use a rate 1 percentage point lower.

General building and labour-only building rates apply where the value of materials is less than 10% of turnover.

From 1 April 2017, a limited cost trader of any occupation has the rate of 16.5%. That is a trader whose VAT-inclusive expenditure is less than either 2% of turnover or £1,000.

Where a business category is not listed above, the business should either use the nearest category or one of the "not listed elsewhere" categories.

Partial exemption

A trader may wholly exempt supplies if the input tax does not exceed £625 a month or 50% of total input tax for the period. These figures are unchanged from 1 December 1994.

EUROPEAN UNION PROVISIONS

These provisions are likely to change in 2021.

From 1 January 1993, a taxable person in another EU state must register if making supplies to non-registered UK customers of more than £70,000 a year.

From 1 January 2019, a supplier of cross-border digital services must charge VAT at the rate of the customer's state if more than £8,818 a year. These are given below as VAT cross-border sales rates.

The threshold for acquisitions from other EU states is the same as the registration threshold.

Van benefit

Year	**Emissions**	**No emissions**
2020/21	£3,490	£2,792
2019/20	£3,430	£2,058
2018/19	£3,350	£1,340
2017/18	£3,230	£646
2016/17	£3,170	£634
2015/16	£3,150	£630
2014/15	£3,090	nil

The "emissions" rate apply unless the van emits no carbon dioxide when driven.

For 2015/16 to 2017/18, the "no emissions" rate is 20% of the full rate.

This rose to 40% in 2018/19; 60% in 2019/20; and 80% in 2020/21.

It is proposal that the percentage rises to 90% in 2021/22 and 100% in 2022/23.

Van fuel benefit

Year	**Benefit**
2020/21	£666
2019/20	£655
2018/19	£633
2017/1	£610
2016/17	£598
2015/16	£594
2014/15	£581

VAT MOSS exchange rates

These are HMRC's exchange rates for VAT MOSS businesses registered in the UK for 2020.

EXCHANGE RATES ENDING DECEMBER 2020

Currency exchange rates outside the EU

Country	*Country code*	*Currency*	*Currency code*	*£1 =*
Australia	AU	Dollar	AUD	1.7681
Canada	CA	Dollar	CAD	1.7389
China	CN	Yuan renminbi	CNY	8.9235
Hong Kong	HK	Dollar	HKD	10.5827
India	IN	Rupee	INR	99.7303
Israel	IL	Israeli shekel	ILS	4,3877
Japan	JP	Yen	JPY	140.6961
New Zealand	NZ	New Zealand dollar	NZD	1.8891
Norway	NO	Norwegian krone	NOK	11.6462
Russia	RU	Rouble	RUB	101.7398
Singapore	SG	Dollar	SGD	1.8039
Switzerland	CH	Franc	CHF	1.2015
United States	US	Dollar	USD	1.3649

Currency exchange rates inside the EU

Country	*Country code*	*Currency*	*Currency code*	*£1 =*
European Community	EC	Euro	EUR	1.1123
Bulgaria	BG	Bulgarian lev	BGN	2.1755
Croatia	HR	Croatian kuna	HRK	8.4001
Czech Republic	CZ	Czech koruna	CZK	29.1892
Denmark	DK	Danish krone	DKK	8.2766
Hungary	HG	Hungarian forint	HUF	404.7585
Poland	PL	Polish zloty	PLN	5.0718
Romania	RO	Romanian leu	RON	5.4151
Sweden	SE	Swedish krona	SEK	11.1613

EXCHANGE RATES ENDING SEPTEMBER 2020

Currency exchange rates outside the EU

Country	*Country code*	*Currency*	*Currency code*	*£1 =*
Australia	AU	Dollar	AUD	1.8017
Canada	CA	Dollar	CAD	1.7182
China	CN	Yuan renminbi	CNY	8.7379
Hong Kong	HK	Dollar	HKD	9.9460
India	IN	Rupee	INR	94.5898
Israel	IL	Israeli shekel	ILS	4.4146
Japan	JP	Yen	JPY	135.6497
New Zealand	NZ	New Zealand dollar	NZD	1.9509
Norway	NO	Norwegian krone	NOK	12.1673
Russia	RU	Rouble	RUB	100.5933
Singapore	SG	Dollar	SGD	1.7575
Switzerland	CH	Franc	CHF	1.1842
United States	US	Dollar	USD	1.2833

Currency exchange rates inside the EU

Country	*Country code*	*Currency*	*Currency code*	*£1 =*
European Community	EC	Euro	EUR	1.0961
Bulgaria	BG	Bulgarian lev	BGN	2.1437
Croatia	HR	Croatian kuna	HRK	8.2825
Czech Republic	CZ	Czech koruna	CZK	29.8493
Denmark	DK	Danish krone	DKK	8.1616
Hungary	HG	Hungarian forint	HUF	400.6467
Poland	PL	Polish zloty	PLN	4.9830
Romania	RO	Romanian leu	RON	5.3406
Sweden	SE	Swedish krona	SEK	11.5869

EXCHANGE RATES ENDING JUNE 2020

Currency exchange rates outside the EU

Country	*Country code*	*Currency*	*Currency code*	*£1 =*
Australia	AU	Dollar	AUD	1.7913
Canada	CA	Dollar	CAD	1.6795
China	CN	Yuan renminbi	CNY	8.6822
Hong Kong	HK	Dollar	HKD	9.5117
India	IN	Rupee	INR	92.7452
Israel	IL	Israeli shekel	ILS	4.2547
Japan	JP	Yen	JPY	132.2403
New Zealand	NZ	New Zealand dollar	NZD	1.9158
Norway	NO	Norwegian krone	NOK	11.9593
Russia	RU	Rouble	RUB	87.2724
Singapore	SG	Dollar	SGD	1.7150

Switzerland	CH	Franc	CHF	1.1673
United States	US	Dollar	USD	1.2273

Currency exchange rates inside the EU

Country	*Country code*	*Currency*	*Currency code*	*£1 =*
European Community	EC	Euro	EUR	1.0960
Bulgaria	BG	Bulgarian lev	BGN	2.1435
Croatia	HR	Croatian kuna	HRK	8.2974
Czech Republic	CZ	Czech koruna	CZK	29.3064
Denmark	DK	Danish krone	DKK	8.1679
Hungary	HG	Hungarian forint	HUF	390.8026
Poland	PL	Polish zloty	PLN	4.8837
Romania	RO	Romanian leu	RON	5.3042
Sweden	SE	Swedish krona	SEK	11.5020

EXCHANGE RATES ENDING MARCH 2020

Currency exchange rates outside the EU

Country	*Country code*	*Currency*	*Currency code*	*£1 =*
Australia	AU	Dollar	AUD	2.0269
Canada	CA	Dollar	CAD	1.7618
China	CN	Yuan renminbi	CNY	8.7750
Hong Kong	HK	Dollar	HKD	9.5828
India	IN	Rupee	INR	93.5195
Israel	IL	Israeli shekel	ILS	44017.0121
Japan	JP	Yen	JPY	134.1335
New Zealand	NZ	New Zealand dollar	NZD	2.0777
Norway	NO	Norwegian krone	NOK	12.9847
Russia	RU	Rouble	RUB	96.9604
Singapore	SG	Dollar	SGD	1.7636
Switzerland	CH	Franc	CHF	1.1941
United States	US	Dollar	USD	1.2360

Currency exchange rates inside the EU

Country	*Country code*	*Currency*	*Currency code*	*1 GBP =*
European Community	EC	Euro	EUR	1.1281
Bulgaria	BG	Bulgarian lev	BGN	2.2064
Croatia	HR	Croatian kuna	HRK	8.6025
Czech Republic	CZ	Czech koruna	CZK	30.8112
Denmark	DK	Danish krone	DKK	8.4241
Hungary	HG	Hungarian forint	HUF	406.1460
Poland	PL	Polish zloty	PLN	5.1336
Romania	RO	Romanian leu	RON	5.4469
Sweden	SE	Swedish krona	SEK	12.4785

VAT private fuel scale charges

If a business pays for any fuel used for private motoring by a director or employee with a company car, it must pay VAT on a VAT-inclusive figure taken from the table below.
The VAT element is one sixth of the figure.
The figure depends on the carbon dioxide emission of the vehicle in grams per kilometre, and whether the VAT return is for a year, a quarter or a month.
Where the emission figure is not shown in the table, the next lowest figure should be used.
Note that these are *not* the same tables as used for income tax company car benefit.

Fuel scale charge from 1 May 2020 to 30 April 2021

CO2 emission figure	*12 months*	*3 months*	*1 month*
120 or less	£581	£144	£48
125	£870	£218	£72
130	£930	£231	£76
135	£986	£246	£81
140	£1,047	£261	£87
145	£1,103	£275	£91
150	£1,163	£290	£96
155	£1,219	£305	£101
160	£1,279	£319	£106
165	£1,335	£334	£111
170	£1,396	£348	£115
175	£1,452	£362	£120
180	£1,512	£377	£125
185	£1,568	£392	£130
190	£1,628	£406	£135
195	£1,684	£421	£140
200	£1,745	£436	£144
205	£1,801	£450	£149
210	£1,861	£464	£154
215	£1,917	£479	£159
220	£1,977	£493	£164
225 and above	£2,033	£508	£168

VAT rates for cross-border sales

These are the rates of VAT that must be charged for cross-border sales to a EU state where the rate must be that of the customer's state.
These only apply when a business makes sales above a limit to non-registered customers in another EU state. This is known as B2C (business to consumer).
To avoid having to register in many EU states, HMRC offers a Mini One Stop Service (MOSS) that allows rates to be charged, sometimes at a rate below the country's standard rate, for supplies.
These rates change frequently and should be checked on the website
https://www.gov.uk/guidance/changes-to-the-vat-moss-rate-for-other-countries .
The position is not clear for what will happen in 2021 after the end of the Brexit transition period.

EU rates as at 1 January 2020

	EU country rate	*Standard rate*	*MOSS Reduced rates*
Austria	20%	10%	13%, 0%
Belgium	21%	6%	12%, 0%
Bulgaria	20%	20%	9%, 0%
Croatia	25%	5%	13%, 0%
Cyprus	19%	5%	9%, 0%
Czech Republic	21%	10%	15%, 0%
Denmark	25%	25%	0%
Estonia	20%	20%	9%, 0%
Finland	24%	10%	14%, 0%
France	20%	5.5%	10%, 2.1%, 0%
Germany	19%	7%	0%
Greece	24%	24%	13%, 6%, 0%
Hungary	27%	27%, 5%	18%, 0%
Ireland	23%	9%	13.5%, 4.8%. 0%
Italy	22%	4%	10%, 5%, 0%
Latvia	21%	21%	12%, 5%, 0%
Lithuania	21%	21%	9%, 5%, 0%
Luxembourg	17%	3%	14%, 8%, 0%
Malta	18%	5%	7%, 0%
Netherlands	21%	9%	0%
Poland	23%	5%	8%, 0%
Portugal	23%	6%	13%, 0%
Romania	19%	19%	9%, 5%, 0%
Slovakia	20%	20%	10%, 0%
Slovenia	22%	5%	9.5%, 0%
Spain	21%	21%	10%, 4%, 0%
Sweden	25%	6%	12%, 0%
UK	20%	20%	5%, 0%

Changes during 2020

Austria: From 1 July 2020 to 31 December 2020, reduced rate on books to 5%

Bulgaria: From 1 July 2020 to 31 December 2021, reduced rate on books to 9%

Czech Republic: From 1 May 2020, introduced 10% rate for books

Estonia: From 1 May 2020, introduced 9% rate on books etc

Germany: From 1 July 2020 to 31 December 2020, reduced the standard rate from 19% to 16%, and the reduced rate from 7% to 5%

Ireland: Reduced standard-rated from 23% to 21% from 1 September 2020 to 28 February 2021

Netherlands: From 1 January 2020, introduced new 9% rate for books

Slovenia: From 1 January 2020, introduced new 5% rate for books

Spain: From 23 April 2020, introduced new 4% rate for books

Reductions for books usually apply also to newspapers and other printed material.

VAT Schedules

These list the main headings for the VAT schedules of items not subject to the standard rate.

It must be appreciated that the scope of items is not fully reflected in the heading.

Schedule 8: zero-rated supplies

Group	*Heading*	*Notes*
1	Food	Hot takeaway food is standard-rated from 1.10.12
2	Sewerage and water	
3	Books etc	E-books are zero-rated from 1 May 2020
4	Talking books for blind	Also includes wireless sets for the blind
5	Construction	
6	Protected buildings	
7	International services	
8	Transport	
9	Caravans, houseboats	From 6.4.13, zero-rating depends on size of caravan
10	Gold	
11	Bank notes	
12	Drugs etc for handicapped	
13	Imports, exports	
15	Charities	
16	Children's clothing	
18	Goods to European Research Infrastructure Consortium	

Schedule 7A: reduced-rate supplies

1	Domestic fuel and power	
2	Energy-saving materials	
3	Grant-funded installation of hearing or security goods	
4	Sanitary products	These become zero-rated from 1.1.21
5	Children's car seats	Includes base units from 1.7.09
6	Residential conversions	
7	Residential renovations and alterations	
8	Contraceptives	From 1.7.06
9	Welfare advice	From 1.7.06
10	Mobility aids for elderly	From 1.7.07
11	Smoking cessation	From 1.7.08
12	Caravans	From 1.4.13
13	Cable car rides	From 1.4.13
14	Catering	From 15.7.20 to 31.3.21
15	Holiday accommodation	From 15.7.20 to 31.3.21
16	Shows and attractions	From 15.7.20 to 31.3.21

Schedule 9: exempt supplies

1	Land	Subject to many exceptions
2	Insurance	
3	Postal services	From 31.1.11 only universal service provider services
4	Betting, gaming, lotteries	
5	Finance	

6	Education	
7	Health and welfare	
8	Burial and cremation	
9	Subscriptions to professional bodies, trade unions and others	
10	Sports, competitions and physical education	
11	Works of art etc	
12	Fund raising events by charities and other bodies	
13	Cultural services	From 1.6.96
14	Where input tax cannot be recovered	From 1.3.00
15	Investment gold	From 1.1.00
16	Cost sharing supplies	

Vehicle excise duty (road tax)

For cars registered from 1 April 2017

For cars registered from 1 April 2017, there is a higher charge for the first year

From 1 April 2018, there is a higher rate for diesel cars unless they meet the Euro 6d standard.

Standard rates

From	**Amount**
1 April 2019	£145
1 April 2017	£140

First year rates

CO_2	2020/21		2019/20		2018/19		2017/18
gm/km	Diesel	Other	Diesel	Other	Diesel	Other	Other
0	£0	£0	£0	£0	£0	£0	£0
1-50	£25	£10	£25	£10	£25	£10	£10
51-75	£110	£25	£110	£25	£105	£25	£25
76-90	£135	£110	£130	£110	£125	£105	£100
91-100	£155	£135	£150	£130	£145	£125	£120
101-110	£175	£155	£170	£150	£165	£145	£140
111-130	£215	£175	£210	£170	£205	£165	£160
131-150	£540	£215	£530	£210	£515	£205	£200
151-170	£870	£540	£855	£530	£830	£515	£500
171-190	£1,305	£870	£1,280	£855	£1,240	£830	£800
191-225	£1,850	£1,305	£1,815	£1,280	£1,760	£1,240	£1,200
226-255	£2,175	£1,850	£2,135	£1,815	£2,070	£1,760	£1,700
over 255	£2,175	£2,175	£2,135	£2,135	£2,070	£2,070	£2,000

These rates are reduced by £10 for an alternative fuel

If the vehicle cost more than £40,000 and is not a zero-emission vehicle, an additional sum is payable for five years of

From	**Sum**
1 April 2020	£325
1 April 2019	£320
Previously	£310

For cars registered before 1 April 2017

Band	CO2	2019/20	2018/17	2017/18
A	to 100 gm/km	£0	£0	£0
B	101-110 gm/km	£20	£20	£20
C	111-120 gm/km	£30	£30	£30
D	121-130 gm/km	£125	£120	£115
E	131-140 gm/km	£145	£140	£135
F	141-150 gm/km	£160	£155	£150
G	151-165 gm/km	£200	£195	£190
H	166-175 gm/km	£235	£230	£220
I	176-185 gm/km	£260	£250	£240
J	186-200 gm/km	£300	£290	£280
K	201-225 gm/km	£325	£315	£305
L	226-255 gm/km	£555	£540	£520
M	over 255 gm/km	£570	£555	£535

Website addresses

- This is a list of selected free websites that may be useful to tax practitioners and those involved in related disciplines. There are many other useful websites available for a fee.
- **accounting:** Financial Reporting Council: accounting standards for UK and Republic of Ireland, and supporting guidance: https://www.frc.org.uk/accountants/accounting-and-reporting-policy/uk-accounting-standards
- **banking:** BACS rules, guidance and other information on bank transfers: www.bacs.co.uk
- employment: Advisory Conciliation and Arbitration Service (ACAS) provides services to improve workplace relationships, such as resolving disputes. It seeks to help both employers and employees. It also produces publications providing guidance on hot topics in employment: https://www.acas.org.uk/
- **first tier tax tribunal decisions:** This gives details of first tier tax tribunal decisions since their formation in 2009. It also gives details of VAT tribunals, Special Commissioners decisions and other predecessor bodies from 2003. http://www.tribunals.gov.uk/Tax
- **government information:** comprehensive, easily searchable and well-written information on government services and provisions. This includes information on law and regulations: https://www.gov.uk/
- **government news:** daily press releases and announcements from the government:
- https://www.gov.uk/search/news-and-communications
- **HMRC**: latest news on tax and other matters dealt with by HMRC https://www.gov.uk/government/latest?departments%5B%5D=hm-revenue-customs
- **law reports:** summaries of law cases from UK and some other countries on 102 databases (as at August 2019): www.bailli.org.uk
- **legislation:** extant Acts from 1267 and all legislation from 1988, including repealed laws. It includes laws from devolved legislatures, and statutory instruments. Tax laws

are included as originally passed, but are not always kept up to date. https://www.gov.uk/government/latest?departments%5B%5D=hm-revenue-customs

- **news:** most news media provide some comment free on their websites. This includes BBC: https://www.bbc.co.uk/news; ITV https://www.itv.com/news; Sky https://news.sky.com/uk .
- **Parliament:** developments in Parliament, including reports of proceedings in the House of Commons, and the House of Lords. This includes speeches, questions and other proceedings. The website aims to report speeches within three hours. It provided current content from 2010, and has added historic content for the previous 200 years: hansard.parliament.uk/
- **passport office:** to get a passport or deal with passport queries: https://www.gov.uk/government/organisations/hm-passport-office/contact/hm-passport-office-webchat
- **Samaritans:** the 24-hour helpline for people who are suicidal or distressed can be contacted by email at jo@samaritans.org
- **social security:** details of social security and pensions provisions provided by the Department of Work and Pensions: http://www.dwp.gov.uk
- statistics: the Office of National Statistics provides statistics on gross domestic product, employment, inflation, population, earnings, spending patterns and similar: https://www.ons.gov.uk/
- **tax manuals:** HMRC Manuals. These are guidance prepared for HMRC staff and made public under Freedom of Information Act 2000. Some parts are redacted, such as when they relate to a confidential information or identity a specific taxpayer outside litigation. HMRC explains that these manuals are not comprehensive and are not always up to date:
  https://www.gov.uk/government/collections/hmrc-manuals
- **tax news:** news on tax and related subjects produced by Tax Training Ltd, the company owned by the compiler of this dictionary: www.taxtrainingltd.co. The company Ross Martin provides a free news update service, and a more comprehensive service on subscription: https://www.rossmartin.co.uk
- **tax policy:** independent comment on tax and economic news from the Institute of Fiscal Studies: http://www.ifs.org.uk
- tax returns: tax returns, and claims for tax credits and child benefit, may be filed online. Payments of tax may also be paid. A taxpayer must first be registered with HMRC. Some taxes may now only be filed online.
  https://www.gov.uk/government/organisations/hm-revenue-customs
- **Treasury:** the website of HM Treasury includes Budget documents, pre-Budget reports and details on economic policy. www.hm-treasury.gov.uk
- upper tier tax tribunal decisions; decisions from the upper tier tribunal for tax, financial services, pensions, charity and land regulation:
- https://www.gov.uk/tax-and-chancery-tribunal-decisions
- visas and immigration: government advice on visas and immigration, including application forms:
  https://www.gov.uk/government/organisations/uk-visas-and-immigration

Working Time Directive

This EU directive was adopted by the UK in 1988.

In 2001, it was extended to all workers, not just those who had a contract for 13 weeks or more.

In 2003, it was extended to all workers (not necessarily employees) over school age.

The directive imposes these general restrictions on working a maximum 48-hour week over a 17-week period unless the worker opts out by written agreement

- a minimum 11 consecutive hours rest per day
- a break of at least 20 minutes for each period of work of 6 hours
- night workers must have an average 8 hours rest in 24 hours averaged over 17 weeks
- a minimum of 4 week's paid annual leave (3 weeks until 1998)
- a minimum rest period of 1 day a week, or 2 days for those aged 15 to 18.

UK law has increased the scope of some of these provisions.

Many of these provisions are subject to conditions. There are some exceptions.

Workplace pensions

All employees are automatically enrolled in a workplace pension unless they are either in another occupational pension scheme which is at least as good, or the employee has opted out.

Where the employer operates the minimum scheme, the minimum contributions are:

From	Employer	Employee	Tax relief	Total
before 6 April 2018	1%	0.8%	0.2%	2%
6 April 2018	2%	2.4%	0.6%	5%
6 April 2019	3%	4%	1%	8%

The employer must contribute if the employee's earnings are at least £520 a month or £120 a week.

Contributions are based on total earnings between the lower earnings limit and upper earnings limit for class 1 national insurance. For 2020/21, these figures are £6,240 and £50,000 before tax.

www.ingramcontent.com/pod-product-compliance
Lightning Source LLC
LaVergne TN
LVHW081957200926
848481LV00010B/2753